P9-CSH-019

Fodor's

ITALY
2009

Fodor's Travel Publications   New York, Toronto, London, Sydney, Auckland
www.fodors.com

Be a Fodor's Correspondent

Your opinion matters. It matters to us. It matters to your fellow Fodor's travelers, too. And we'd like to hear it. In fact, we need to hear it.

When you share your experiences and opinions, you become an active member of the Fodor's community. That means we'll not only use your feedback to make our books better, but we'll publish your names and comments whenever possible. Throughout our guides, look for "Word of Mouth," excerpts of your unvarnished feedback.

Here's how you can help improve Fodor's for all of us.

Tell us when we're right. We rely on local writers to give you an insider's perspective. But our writers and staff editors—who are the best in the business—depend on you. Your positive feedback is a vote to renew our recommendations for the next edition.

Tell us when we're wrong. We're proud that we update most of our guides every year. But we're not perfect. Things change. Hotels cut services. Museums change hours. Charming cafés lose charm. If our writer didn't quite capture the essence of a place, tell us how you'd do it differently. If any of our descriptions are inaccurate or inadequate, we'll incorporate your changes in the next edition and will correct factual errors at fodors.com immediately.

Tell us what to include. You probably have had fantastic travel experiences that aren't yet in Fodor's. Why not share them with a community of like-minded travelers? Maybe you chanced upon a beach or bistro or B&B that you don't want to keep to yourself. Tell us why we should include it. And share your discoveries and experiences with everyone directly at fodors.com. Your input may lead us to add a new listing or highlight a place we cover with a "Highly Recommended" star or with our highest rating, "Fodor's Choice."

Give us your opinion instantly at our feedback center at www.fodors.com/feedback. You may also e-mail editors@fodors.com with the subject line "Italy Editor." Or send your nominations, comments, and complaints by mail to Italy Editor, Fodor's, 1745 Broadway, New York, NY 10019.

You and travelers like you are the heart of the Fodor's community. Make our community richer by sharing your experiences. Be a Fodor's correspondent.

Buon Viaggio! (Or simply: Happy traveling!)

Tim Jarrell, Publisher

FODOR'S ITALY 2009
Editor: Matthew Lombardi

Editorial Production: Astrid deRidder
Editorial Contributors: Linda Cabasin, Joanna Cantor, Erica Duecy, Robert Fisher, Cate Wells, Mark Sullivan, Lynda Albertson, Robert Andrews, Nicole Arriaga, Martin Wilmot Bennett, Peter Blackman, Ruth Edenbaum, Shannon Essa, Erica Firpo, Madeleine Johnson, Fergal Kavanagh, Dana Klitzberg, Jen Laskey, Bruce Leimsidor, Nan McElroy, Eric J. Lyman, Megan McCaffrey-Guerrara, Ann Reavis, Patricia Rucidlo, Pamela Santini, Margaret Stenhouse, Mark Walters, Jonathan Willcocks, Megan K. Williams
Maps & Illustrations: Henry Colomb and Mark Stroud, Moon Street Cartography, David Lindroth, *cartographers*; William Wu; Bob Blake and Rebecca Baer, *map editors*
Design: Fabrizio LaRocca, *creative director*; Guido Caroti, Siobhan O'Hare, *art directors*; Tina Malaney, Chie Ushio, Ann McBride, *designers*; Melanie Marin, *senior picture editor;* Moon Sun Kim, *cover designer*
Cover Photo (Milan): SIME s.a.s./eStock Photo
Production/Manufacturing: Steve Slawsky

COPYRIGHT

ISBN 978–1–4000–1950–2

ISSN 0361–977X

SPECIAL SALES

This book is available at special discounts for bulk purchases for sales promotions or premiums. Special editions, including personalized covers, excerpts of existing books, and corporate imprints, can be created in large quantities for special needs. For more information, write to Special Markets/Premium Sales, 1745 Broadway, MD 6-2, New York, New York 10019, or e-mail specialmarkets@randomhouse.com.

AN IMPORTANT TIP & AN INVITATION

Although all prices, opening times, and other details in this book are based on information supplied to us at press time, changes occur all the time in the travel world, and Fodor's cannot accept responsibility for facts that become outdated or for inadvertent errors or omissions. So **always confirm information when it matters,** especially if you're making a detour to visit a specific place. Your experiences—positive and negative—matter to us. If we have missed or misstated something, **please write to us.** We follow up on all suggestions. Contact the Italy editor at editors@fodors.com or c/o Fodor's at 1745 Broadway, New York, NY 10019.

PRINTED IN SINGAPORE
10 9 8 7 6 5 4 3 2

CONTENTS

ITALY IN FOCUS

CONTENTS

CONTENTS

ABOUT THIS BOOK

Our Ratings

Sometimes you find terrific travel experiences and sometimes they just find you. But usually the burden is on you to select the right combination of experiences. That's where our ratings come in.

As travelers we've all discovered a place so wonderful that its worthiness is obvious. And sometimes that place is so experiential that superlatives don't do it justice: you just have to be there to know. These sights, properties, and experiences get our highest rating, **Fodor's Choice,** indicated by orange stars throughout this book.

Black stars highlight sights and properties we deem **Highly Recommended,** places that our writers, editors, and readers praise again and again for consistency and excellence.

By default, there's another category: any place we include in this book is by definition worth your time, unless we say otherwise. And we will.

Disagree with any of our choices? Care to nominate a place or suggest that we rate one more highly? Visit our feedback center at www.fodors.com/feedback.

Budget Well

Hotel and restaurant price categories from ¢ to $$$$ are defined in the opening pages of each chapter. For attractions, we always give standard adult admission fees; reductions are usually available for children, students, and senior citizens. Want to pay with plastic? **AE, DC, MC, V** following restaurant and hotel listings indicate if American Express, Diners Club, MasterCard, and Visa are accepted.

Restaurants

Unless we state otherwise, restaurants are open for lunch and dinner daily. We mention dress only when there's a specific requirement and reservations only when they're essential or not accepted—it's always best to book ahead.

Hotels

Hotels have private bath, phone, TV, and air-conditioning. We indicate whether they operate on the European Plan (a.k.a. EP, meaning without meals), Breakfast Plan (BP, with a full breakfast), Modified American Plan (MAP, with breakfast and dinner) or American Plan (AP, including all meals). We always list facilities but not whether you'll be charged an extra fee to use them, so when pricing accommodations, find out what's included.

Many Listings
★ Fodor's Choice
★ Highly recommended
⊠ Physical address
⊹ Directions
🏚 Mailing address
☎ Telephone
🖷 Fax
⊕ On the Web
✎ E-mail
🖃 Admission fee
☉ Open/closed times
Ⓜ Metro stations
▱ Credit cards

Hotels & Restaurants
🏨 Hotel
🛏 Number of rooms
♤ Facilities
†⊙† Meal plans
✕ Restaurant
⟰ Reservations
↘ Smoking
🄱🄵 BYOB
✕🏨 Hotel with restaurant that warrants a visit

Outdoors
🏌 Golf
⛺ Camping

Other
☾ Family-friendly
⇨ See also
⊠ Branch address
☞ Take note

Experience
Italy

WHAT'S NEW

Change comes slowly in the Bel Paese. There's a certain romance to the idea that the historical centers of Rome or Florence would be easily recognizable to residents from Leonardo daVinci's time. Tiny cars and whining scooters in Italian cities and towns maneuver narrow cobblestone streets designed for horses and carriages; many restaurants rely on well-practiced classic dishes that haven't changed for centuries; and some of the world's most magnificent classical architecture demands to be contemplated and studied rather than admired from the window of a passing vehicle.

But that timelessness quality is matched by other aspects of Italian culture that are thoroughly modern. A proud G-8 nation and a leading member of the European Union, Italy is active on the international stage and modernizing its economy in an increasingly global marketplace. Life is becoming faster paced and increasingly cosmopolitan. In numerous ways the country is indeed changing—perhaps faster than many Italians realize.

Food & Wine
The old joke says that three-quarters of the food and wine served in Italy is good…and the rest is amazing. If that's true, the "good" 75% is getting even better.

Italy is home of one of the world's greatest cuisines, so it may seem disingenuous to claim that it's improving—but it clearly is. Ingredients that in the past were available only to the very wealthy can now be found even in the remotest parts of the country at reasonable prices. Dishes originally conceived to make the most of inferior cuts of meat or the least flavorful part of vegetables are now made with the best.

The same is true of Italian wine. A generation ago, the omnipresent straw-basket Chianti was a mainstay of pizzerias around the world, but the wine inside was often watery and insipid. Today, through investment and experimentation, Italy's winemakers are figuring out how to get the most from their gorgeous vineyards. It's fair to say that Italy now produces more types of high-quality wine from more different grape varieties than any other country in the world.

Italian restaurateurs are keeping up with the changes. Though the quaint family-run trattoria with traditional dishes and informal atmosphere is still very common, nearly every town has a newer eatery with matching flatware, a proper wine list, and an innovative menu.

August
Italy used to be the best example of Europe's famous August exodus—where city dwellers would spend most of the month at the seaside or in the mountains, leaving the cities nearly deserted. Today, the phenomenon is much less prevalent, as economic pressures have forced companies to keep operating through August. As a result, vacations are more staggered and vacationers' plans are often more modest.

The loss of shared vacation time for Italian workers can be an advantage for visitors, both because in August there is more room at the seaside and in the mountains, and because cities have taken to promoting local events designed to appeal to residents who are staying put. These days, summers in Italy boast a plethora of outdoor concerts and plays; longer restaurant and museum hours; and food, wine, and culture fairs.

Religion

Rome is still the spiritual home of the world's 1.1 billion Catholics, but church attendance in Italy has been eroding since the 1950s, and today only about a fourth of Italians attend church regularly. But religion still maintains a powerful hold on Italian culture, with the Church regularly weighing in on political and social issues. Churches themselves remain a centerpiece of almost every Italian town, with the church on the main square the de facto meeting place for locals.

While church attendance slips, religion remains a hot topic in Italy as citizens react to increasing immigration from North Africa, Eastern Europe, Asia, the Middle East, and elsewhere. Today, there are more different religions in Italy than at any point since Roman times—with Muslims, Protestants, Buddhists, Christian Orthodox, Jews, Scientologists, and Mormons all present in significant numbers. All told, a little over one in seven Italian residents is non-Catholic.

Ara Pacis

Well before its opening in 2006, the museum housing Rome's ancient Ara Pacis monument was the topic of emotional debate. The first significant civic building project in Rome since just after World War II, the glass-and-metal structure from Pritzker Prize–winning architect Richard Meier is an unexpected flourish of modernity set among several major structures from Rome's past. Within several yards are the pre-Christian Mausoleum of Augustus and the massive Fascist-era Piazza Augusto Imperatore, all fit between the august Tiber River and the Renaissance buildings of the Campo Marzio.

Within the museum is the Ara Pacis itself, a large and well-preserved altar from 9 BC meant to symbolize peace (the name is Latin for "Altar of Peace") but actually celebrating a period of rapid Roman military conquest. The longstanding irony of the name, however, garners much less interest than the question of whether the modern Meier structure is appropriate for Rome's historic center.

Slow Italy

The Slow Food movement was initiated in the 1980s to oppose the opening of a McDonald's restaurant in Rome's historic Piazza di Spagna area. Though it failed to prevent the opening—today the McDonald's is one of the busiest in Europe—the movement sparked a flourishing "Slow" phenomenon, with the central goal of preserving tradition and pushing back against the forces of mass-production and cultural homogenization.

Today, the organization Slow Food, based in the northern region of Piedmont, has more than 80,000 members scattered around the world and an increasingly famous logo that includes the stylized image of a snail. It has also sparked a minor mania for all things "slow"; in your travels you may well encounter Slow Cities, Slow Design, and Slow Companies, not to mention Slow Travel. One member of the movement has even founded the World Institute of Slowness.

—Eric J. Lyman

WHAT'S WHERE

1 Rome. Italy's capital is one of the great cities of Europe. It's a large, busy metropolis that lives in the here and now, yet there's no other place on earth where you'll encounter such powerful evocations of a long and spectacular past, from the Colosseum to the dome of St. Peter's.

2 Northern Italy. The prosperous north has Italy's most sophisticated culture and its most diverse landscape. **Venice** is a rare jewel of a city, while **Milan** and **Turin** are centers of commerce and style. Along the country's northern border, the mountain peaks of the **Dolomites** and **Valle d'Aosta** attract skiers in winter and hikers in summer, while the **Lake District** and the coastline of the **Riviera** are classic summertime playgrounds. Food here is also exceptional, from the French-influenced cuisine of **Piedmont** to Italian classics prepared with unrivaled skill in **Emilia-Romagna.**

3 Central Italy. No place better epitomizes the greatness of the Renaissance than **Florence**, where there's a

masterpiece around every corner, from Michelangelo's David to Botticelli's Venus. Elsewhere, the central regions of **Tuscany** and **Umbria** are characterized by midsize cities and small hilltop towns, each with its own rich history and art treasures. Highlights include the walled city of **Lucca**; **Pisa** and its Leaning Tower; **Siena**, home of the Palio; and **Assisi**, the city of St. Francis. In between, the gorgeous countryside produces some of Italy's finest wine.

4 Southern Italy. The region of **Campania** is a popular place both to unwind—on the pint-size island of **Capri** or the resort towns of the **Amalfi Coast**—and to explore the past—at the archaeological ruins of **Pompeii, Herculaneum,** and **Paestum.** In the middle of everything is the vibrant, chaotic city of **Naples.** Farther south, in the off-the-beaten-path regions of **Puglia, Basilicata,** and **Calabria,** you'll find attractive beaches, mysterious ancient dwellings, and the charming town of **Lecce.** Across a narrow strait from Calabria is **Sicily.** Baroque church-hopping could be a sport on the cacophonous streets of **Palermo** and **Siracusa**, while amid the almond groves of **Agrigento** there stands one of the world's best-preserved Greek ruins.

ITALY PLANNER

Getting Here

The major gateways to Italy are Rome's Aeroporto Leonardo da Vinci (FCO), better known as Fiumicino, and Milan's Aeroporto Malpensa (MIL). There are some direct flights to Venice and Pisa, but to fly into most other Italian cities you need to make connections at Fiumicino and Malpensa or another European airport. You can also take the FS airport train to Rome's Termini station or a bus to Milan's central train station (Centrale) and catch a train to any other location in Italy. It will take about one hour to get from either Fiumicino or Malpensa to the appropriate train station.

Italy's major airports are not known for being new, fun, or efficient. Airports in Italy have been ramping up security measures, which include random baggage inspection and bomb-detection dogs. All of the airports have restaurants and snack bars, and there is Internet access. Each airport has at least one nearby hotel. In the case of Florence and Pisa, the city centers are only a 15-minute taxi ride away—so if you encounter a long delay, spend it in town.

For further information about getting where you want to go, see "Getting Here" at the beginning of each part section of this book.

What to Pack

In summer, stick with light clothing, as things can get steamy in June, July, and August, but throw in a sweater in case of cool evenings, especially if you're headed for the mountains and/or islands. Sunglasses, a hat, and sunblock are essential. Brief summer afternoon thunderstorms are common in inland cities, so an umbrella will come in handy. In winter, bring a coat, gloves, hats, scarves, and boots. In winter, weather is generally milder than in the northern and central United States, but central heating may not be up to your standards, and interiors can be cold and damp; take wools or flannel rather than sheer fabrics. Bring sturdy shoes for winter and comfortable walking shoes in any season.

As a rule, Italians dress exceptionally well. They do not usually wear shorts. Men aren't required to wear ties or jackets anywhere, except in some of the grander hotel dining rooms and top-level restaurants, but are expected to look reasonably sharp—and they do. Formal wear is the exception rather than the rule at the opera nowadays, though people in expensive seats usually do get dressed up.

A certain modesty of dress (no bare shoulders or knees) is expected in churches, and strictly enforced in many.

For sightseeing, **pack a pair of binoculars**; they will help you get a good look at painted ceilings and domes. If you stay in budget hotels, **take your own soap.** Many such hotels do not provide it or give guests only one tiny bar per room. Washcloths, also, are rarely provided even in three- and four-star hotels.

Restaurants: The Basics

A meal in Italy has traditionally consisted of five courses, and every menu you encounter will still be organized along this five-course plan:

First up is the antipasto (appetizer), often consisting of cured meats or marinated vegetables. Next to appear is the primo, usually pasta or soup, and after that the secondo, a meat or fish course with, perhaps, a contorno (vegetable dish) on the side. A simple dolce (dessert) rounds out the meal.

This, you've probably noticed, is a lot of food. Italians have noticed as well—a full, five-course meal is an indulgence usually reserved for special occasions. Instead, restaurant meals are a mix-and-match affair: you might order a primo and a secondo, or an antipasto and a primo, or a secondo and a contorno.

The crucial rule of restaurant dining is that you should order at least two courses. It's a common mistake for tourists to order only a secondo, thinking they're getting a "main course" complete with side dishes. What they wind up with is one lonely piece of meat.

Hotels: The Basics

Hotels in Italy are usually well maintained (especially if they've earned our recommendation in this book), but in some respects they won't match what you find at comparably priced U.S. lodgings. Keep the following points in mind as you set your expectations, and you're likely to have a good experience:

■ First and foremost, rooms are usually smaller, particularly in cities. If you're truly cramped, ask for another room, but don't expect things to be spacious.

■ A "double bed" is commonly two singles pushed together.

■ In the bathroom, tubs are not a given—request one if it's essential. In budget places, showers sometimes use a drain in the middle of the bathroom floor. And washcloths are a rarity.

■ Most hotels have satellite TV, but there are fewer channels than in the United States, and only one or two will be in English.

■ Don't expect wall-to-wall carpeting. Particularly outside the cities, tile floors are the norm.

Speaking the Language

In most cities and many towns, you won't have a hard time finding locals who speak at least rudimentary English. Odds are if the person you want to talk with doesn't know English, there will be someone within earshot who can help translate. The farther south you travel, the fewer English speakers you'll encounter, but if nothing else someone at your hotel will know a few words. No matter where in Italy you're going, if you learn some common phrases in Italian, your effort will be appreciated.

Italy from Behind the Wheel

Americans tend to be well schooled in defensive-driving techniques. Many Italians are not. When you hit the road, don't be surprised to encounter tailgating and high-risk passing. Your best response is to take the same safety-first approach you use at home. On the upside, Italy's roads are very well maintained. Note that wearing a seat belt and having your lights on at all times are required by law. Bear in mind that a vehicle in Italian cities is almost always a liability, but outside of the cities it's often crucial. An effective strategy is to start and end your Italian itinerary in major cities, car-free, and to pick up wheels for countryside touring in between.

ITALY TODAY

Soccer

Soccer stands without rival as the national sport of Italy, but recent years have seen some changes to the beautiful game. On the positive side, Italy won its fourth World Cup in 2006, giving the country more world titles than any other this side of Brazil. But since then, soccer lovers have digested a series of unwelcome developments involving alleged match fixing, backroom deals for television contracts, drug scandals among players, and a rising level of violence between rival fans.

Italian professional soccer leagues are trying to put those issues behind them and focus on on-the-field play, where the Italian leagues rank with England and Spain as the best in Europe. One emerging positive trend is geographic parity. After several years of the top Serie A league being dominated by northern teams, along with a small handful from the central part of the country, success recently has been spread more evenly around the country, much to the joy of soccer-mad fans from the south.

The Beloved Lira

Italy was among a dozen European Union countries that switched to the euro currency at the start of 2002. For many Italians, the change was not a welcome one.

In day-to-day conversations, the euro is blamed for higher prices and for the handing over of more control of the Italian economy to bureaucrats in Brussels, the seat of the European government. The most common complaint is that many vendors simply took the old prices in lire and erased three zeros, meaning something that used to cost 1,000 lire (around 0.52 euro) now costs one euro.

Many Italians still value purchases in their beloved lira. Years after the switch, it is still common to hear someone in the midst of a negotiation argue the price in the now-dead currency, "Eight euros? But that's 16,000 lire!"

Politics

The political landscape in Italy is less stable than in any other industrialized nation. The country has endured a new government an average of about once a year since the end of World War II, and hopes are slim that the situation will change much in the near future.

This virtual turnstile outside the prime minister's office takes a toll on Italy in any number of ways: economic growth is slow in part because businesses are continually adapting to new sets of government policies, and polls show that rank-and-file Italians are increasingly cynical about their political institutions. As a result, they're much less likely to trust in or depend upon the government than neighbors elsewhere in Europe do.

National Parks

Italy boasts 22 national parks covering a total of around 1.5 million hectares (58,000 square mi), or about 5% of the entire surface area of the country—more than twice as much as 25 years ago. And a new park is added or an existing park is expanded every few months. (In 2008, three new parks were in line to join the existing 22.)

Part of the reason for the expansion has been a growing environmental movement in Italy, which has lobbied the government to annex undeveloped land for parks, thus protecting against development. But the trend is a boon for visitors

and nature lovers, who can enjoy huge expanses of unspoiled territory.

Old Italy

Italy is the oldest country in Europe (worldwide, only Japan is older)—the result of its low birth rate, relatively strict immigration standards, and one of the highest life expectancy rates in the world. As of 2008, the average Italian was 42.5 years old, and the number keeps rising.

The result is a remarkably stable population: the total number of Italian residents rises just 0.1% per year. But the situation is putting a strain on the country's pension system and on families, since elderly family members are likely to live with their children or grandchildren in a country where nursing homes are rare.

The trend also has an impact on other areas, including politics (where older politicians are eager to promote policies aimed at older voters) and the popular culture (where everything from fashion to television programming takes older consumers into consideration).

The Black Market

Nobody knows how big Italy's black-market economy is, though experts all agree it's massive. Estimates place it at anywhere from a fourth to a half of the official, legal economy. Put another way, if the highest estimates are correct, Italy's black-market economy is about as large as the entire economy of Mexico or India, and if the black-market figures were added to Italy's official GDP the country would leapfrog France, the U.K., and China to become the world's fourth-largest economy.

The presence of the black market isn't obvious to the casual observer, but whenever a customer is not given a printed receipt in a store or restaurant, tobacco without a tax seal is bought from a street seller, or a product or service is exchanged for another product or service, that means the transaction goes unrecorded, unreported, and untaxed.

Television

For most of the last generation, the two biggest players in the Italian television business have been Mediaset and RAI. Together, they control six of the seven television networks and about 90% of viewer hours.

Mediaset is owned by media-tycoon-turned-politician Silvio Berlusconi, Italy's richest citizen, while the Italian government controls RAI. For years, these two giants dominated the airwaves in Italy. But, now, competition is slowly developing a presence on the scene.

The most obvious newcomer is satellite broadcaster Sky Italia, owned by News Corp., the world's largest media conglomerate. And rules requiring television broadcasters to switch to digital television technologies by the end of 2009 are partially aimed at freeing up frequencies for new broadcasters itching to get a place in the Italian market. Stay tuned.

—Eric J. Lyman

TOP ITALY ATTRACTIONS

The Vatican

(D) The home of the Catholic Church, a tiny independent state tucked within central Rome, holds some of the city's most spectacular sights, including St. Peter's Basilica, the Vatican Museums, and Michelangelo's Sistine ceiling. (⇨ Chapter 1.)

Ancient Rome

(A) The Colosseum and the Roman Forum are remarkable ruins from Rome's ancient past. Sitting above it all is the Campidoglio, with a piazza designed by Michelangelo and museums containing Rome's finest collection of ancient art. (⇨ Chapter 1.)

Venice's Grand Canal

A trip down Venice's "Main Street," whether by water bus or gondola, is a signature Italian experience. (⇨ Chapter 3.)

Palladio's Villas and Palazzi

The 16th-century genius Andrea Palladio is one of the most influential figures in the history of architecture. You can visit his creations in his hometown of Vicenza, in and around Venice, and outside Treviso. (⇨ Chapter 4.)

Galleria degli Uffizi, Florence

The Uffizi—Renaissance art's hall of fame—contains masterpieces by Leonardo, Michelangelo, Raphael, Botticelli, Caravaggio, and dozens of other luminaries. (⇨ Chapter 10.)

Duomo, Florence

(B) The massive dome of Florence's Cathedral of Santa Maria del Fiore (aka the Duomo) is one of the world's great feats of engineering. (⇨ Chapter 10.)

Piazza del Campo, Siena
(C) Siena is Tuscany's classic medieval hill town, and its heart is the Piazza del Campo, the beautiful, one-of-a-kind town square. (⇨ Chapter 11.)

Basilica di San Francesco, Assisi
(G) The giant basilica—made up of two churches, one built on top of the other—honors St. Francis with its remarkable fresco cycles. (⇨ Chapter 12.)

Palazzo Ducale, Urbino
No other building better exemplifies the principles and ideals of the Renaissance than this palace in the Marches region, east of Umbria. (⇨ Chapter 12.)

The Ruins of Pompeii
(F) When Vesuvius erupted in AD 79, its fallout froze the town of Pompeii in time. Walking its streets brings antiquity to life. (⇨ Chapter 13.)

Ravello, on the Amalfi Coast
(H) Nowhere else better captures the essence of the gorgeous Amalfi Coast than Ravello, perched high above the Tyrrhenian Sea. It's the place to go for your blissful la dolce vita moment. (⇨ Chapter 13.)

Lecce, Puglia
With it's lavish baroque architecture and engaging street life, Lecce takes the prize for the most appealing town in Italy's deep south. (⇨ Chapter 14.)

Valle dei Templi, Sicily
(E) The Greek influence in Sicily dates to ancient days, as born out by these well-preserved temple ruins. (⇨ Chapter 15.)

TOP EXPERIENCES

Church Going

Few images are more identifiable with Italy than the country's great churches, amazing works of architecture that often took centuries to build. The name Duomo (derived from the Latin for "house," domus, and the root of the English "dome") is used to refer to the principal church of a town or city. Generally speaking, the bigger the city, the more splendid its duomo. Still, some impressive churches inhabit some unlikely places—in the Umbrian hill towns of **Assisi** and **Orvieto,** for example (⇨ Chapter 12).

In Venice, the Byzantine-influenced **Basilica di San Marco** (⇨ Chapter 3) is a testament to the city's East-meets-West character. **Milan's Duomo** (⇨ Chapter 6) is the largest, most imposing Gothic cathedral in Italy. The spectacular dome of **Florence's Duomo** (⇨ Chapter 10) is a work of engineering genius. The **Basilica di San Pietro** in Rome (⇨ Chapter 1) has all the grandeur you'd expect from the seat of the Catholic Church. And Italy's classical past is on display at **Siracusa's Duomo** (⇨ Chapter 15), which incorporates the columns of a 6th-century BC Greek temple.

Driving the Back Roads

If you associate Italian roads with unruly motorists and endless traffic snarls, you're only partly right. Along the rural back roads, things are more relaxed. You might stop on a lark to take a picture of a crumbling farmhouse, have a coffee in a time-frozen hill town, or enjoy an epic lunch at a rustic *agriturismo* inaccessible to public transportation. Driving, in short, is the best way to see Italy.

Among the countless beautiful drives, these are three of the most memorable: the legendary mountain ascent on **SS48,** the **Grande Strada delle Dolomiti** (⇨ Chapter 5), takes you through the Heart of the Dolomites, the famous Passo di Sella, and into the Val Gardena, passing unforgettable, craggy-peaked views. Every time the A1 autostrada tunnels through the mountains, this smaller **SS1, Via Aurelia** (⇨ Chapter 8), stays out on the jagged coastline of the Italian Riviera, passing terraced vineyards, cliff-hanging villages, and shimmering seas. **SS222, the Strada Chiantigiana** (⇨ Chapter 11), between Florence and Siena meanders through classic Tuscan landscapes.

Hiking the Hills

Even if you don't fancy yourself a disciple of Reinhold Messner (the favorite son of the Dolomites and the first man to reach the peak of Everest without oxygen), you'll find great summer hiking aplenty all over Italy. The **Vie Ferrate (Iron Paths)** are reinforced trails through the mountains of Trentino–Alto Adige (⇨ Chapter 5), once forged by the Italian and Austro-Hungarian armies; they're a great way to get off the beaten path in the Dolomites.

The **Cinque Terre**—five cliff-clinging villages along the Italian Riviera (⇨ Chapter 8)—are spectacular, and they're all connected by hiking trails with memorable views of the towns, the rocks, and the Ligurian Sea. In Umbria (⇨ Chapter 12), you hike the **Paths of St. Francis:** outside Assisi, an easy half-hour walk takes you from the town of Cannara to Pian d'Arca, site of St. Francis's sermon to the birds; with a bit more effort you can make the walk from Assisi to the Eremo delle Carceri and from here to the summit of Monte Subasio, which has views for miles in every direction.

Tasting the Wine

When it comes to wine making, the Italian Renaissance is happening right now: from tip to toe, vintners are challenging themselves to produce wines of ever-higher quality. You can taste the fruits of their labor at wine bars and restaurants throughout the country, and in many areas you can visit the vineyards as well.

For touring guidance in the northeastern region of the Veneto, see **Traveling the Wine Roads** (⇨ Chapter 4). For the lowdown on Italy's "King of Wines," see **On the Trail of Barolo** (⇨ Chapter 7). And for a full primer on the wines of Tuscany, see **Grape Escapes** (⇨ Chapter 11).

Picking up Some Italian Style

"Made in Italy" is synonymous with style, quality, and craftsmanship, whether it refers to high fashion or Maserati automobiles. Every region has its specialties: Venice is known for glassware, lace, and velvet; Milan and Como for silk; and the Dolomites and the mountains of Calabria and Sicily for hand-carved wooden objects. Bologna and Parma are the places for cheeses and hams; Modena for balsamic vinegar; Florence for straw goods, gold jewelry, leather, and paper products (including beautiful handmade notebooks); Assisi for embroidery; and Deruta, Gubbio, Vietri, and many towns in Puglia and Sicily for ceramics.

In Milan, Italy's fashion capital, the streets of the **Quadrilatero** district (⇨ Chapter 6) are where to go for serious shopping—or just for taking in the chic scene. Rome's **Piazza di Spagna** (⇨ Chapter 1) is another mecca for high-fashion shopping, and a few steps away is the Via del Corso, with more than a mile of stores of all varieties. To be overwhelmed by the aromas of Emilia-Romagna's legendary food, head to **Tamburini** in Bologna (⇨ Chapter 9), where you can get delicacies vacuum-packed to take home with you.

Il Dolce Far Niente

"The sweetness of doing nothing" has long been an art form in Italy. This is a country in which life's pleasures are warmly celebrated, not guiltily indulged.

Of course, doing "nothing" doesn't really mean nothing. It means doing things differently: lingering over a glass of wine for the better part of an evening just to watch the sun slowly set; savoring a slow and flirtatious evening passeggiata along the main street of a little town; and making a commitment—however temporary—to thinking that there is nowhere that you have to be next, that there is no other time than the magical present.

In the quiet, stunningly positioned hilltop village **Ravello** above the Amalfi Coast (⇨ Chapter 13), it's easy to achieve such a state of mind. The same holds true for **Bellagio,** on Lake Como (⇨ Chapter 6), where you can meander through stately gardens, dance on the wharf, or just watch the boats float by in the shadow of the Alps. And there's still nothing more romantic than a **gondola ride** along Venice's canals (⇨ Chapter 3), your escorted trip to nowhere, watched over by Gothic palaces with delicately arched eyebrows.

QUINTESSENTIAL ITALY

Il Caffè (Coffee)

The Italian day begins and ends with coffee, and more cups of coffee punctuate the time in between. To live like the Italians do, drink as they drink, standing at the counter or sitting at an outdoor table of the corner bar. (In Italy, a "bar" is a coffee bar.) A primer: *caffè* means coffee, and Italian standard issue is what Americans call espresso—short, strong, and usually taken very sweet. *Cappuccino* is a foamy half-and-half of espresso and steamed milk; cocoa powder *(cacao)* on top is acceptable, cinnamon is not. If you're thinking of having a cappuccino for dessert, think again—Italians drink only caffè or caffè *macchiato* (with a spot of steamed milk) after lunchtime. Confused? Homesick? Order caffè *americano* for a reasonable facsimile of good-old filtered joe.

Il Calcio (Soccer)

Imagine the most rabid American football fans—the ones who paint their faces on game day and sleep in pajamas emblazoned with the logo of their favorite team. Throw in a dose of melodrama along the lines of a tear-jerking soap opera. Ratchet up the intensity by a factor of 10, and you'll start to get a sense of how Italians feel about their national game, soccer—known in the mother tongue as *calcio*. On Sunday afternoons throughout the long September-to-May season, stadiums are packed throughout Italy. Those who don't get to games in person tend to congregate around television sets in restaurants and bars, rooting for the home team with a passion that feels like a last vestige of the days when the country was a series of warring medieval city-states. How calcio mania affects your stay in Italy depends on how eager you are to get involved. At the very least, you may notice

If you want to get a sense of contemporary Italian culture and indulge in some of its pleasures, start by familiarizing yourself with the rituals of daily life. These are a few highlights—things you can take part in with relative ease.

an eerie Sunday-afternoon silence on the city streets, or erratic restaurant service around the same time, accompanied by cheers and groans from a neighboring room. If you want a memorable, truly Italian experience, attend a game yourself. Availability of tickets may depend on the current fortunes of the local team, but they often can be acquired with help from your hotel concierge.

Il Gelato (Ice Cream)

During warmer months, *gelato*—the Italian equivalent of ice cream—is a national obsession. It's considered a snack rather than a dessert, bought at stands and shops in piazzas and on street corners, and consumed on foot, usually at a leisurely stroll *(see La Passeggiata, below)*. Gelato is softer, less creamy, and more intensely flavored than its American counterpart. It comes in simple flavors that capture the essence of the main ingredient. (You

won't find Chunky Monkey or Cookies 'n' Cream.) Standard choices include pistachio, *nocciola* (hazelnut), caffè, and numerous fresh-fruit varieties. Quality varies; the surest sign that you've hit on a good spot is a line at the counter.

La Passeggiata (Strolling)

A favorite Italian pastime is the *passeggiata* (literally, the promenade). In the late afternoon and early evening, especially on weekends, couples, families, and packs of teenagers stroll the main streets and piazzas of Italy's towns. It's a ritual of exchanged news and gossip, window-shopping, flirting, and gelato-eating that adds up to a uniquely Italian experience. To join in, simply hit the streets for a bit of wandering. You may feel more like an observer than a participant, until you realize that observing is what la passeggiata is all about.

BEATING THE EURO

Below are suggestions for ways to save money on your trip, courtesy of the Travel Talk Forums at Fodors.com.

Transportation

"I take regional trains instead of the Eurostar trains. For example, Florence to Rome on Eurostar is 32.50 euro; the regional train is 15.80 euro. That's half the price; so what if it takes 15 minutes longer…big deal." —JoanneH

"Instead of taking the Leonardo Express from Fiumicino to Termini in Rome, take the FR1 to whichever station is most convenient for you. The FR1 departs every 15 minutes (instead of every 30 minutes for the Express), costs only €5 (instead of €9.50 for the Express), and avoids the hullabaloo of Termini." —Therese

Food & Drink

"Buy snacks and bottled water in bulk at a neighborhood supermarket at the beginning of your stay and keep them cool in your apartment or hotel fridge. Grab a bottle each when leaving in the AM and that way avoid buying expensive water or snacks near tourist attractions, where prices are much higher. Save your euros for espresso or gelato." —cruisinred

"Bars always have two different prices: If you have your coffee at the counter it's cheaper than when a waiter serves it at a table (servizio al tavolo)." —quokka

"Visit wine fill-up shops in Italy; get table wine from the cask for 2-3 euros a liter. In Rome we would get them filled at the Testaccio market…I will usually ask at the local bar where I go for my coffee." —susanna

"If you aren't hungry, skip to secondo—the "second course." Rarely do Italians eat a primo e secondo when they go out." —glittergirl

Sights

"The small cities can be less expensive but still fabulous. We were just in Assisi—all the sites were free, a delicious dinner for two with wine was 22 euros, and our hotel was reasonable at 65 euros per night." —rosetravels

"For the art lover on a budget: Most of the art I saw in Rome is free. Where else can you see countless Caravaggios, two Michelangelos, and even more Berninis for the cost of the wear and tear on the soles of your shoes?" —amyb

"One way to save on the expense of guided tours is to register online at Sound Guides (http://www.sound-guides.com/) and download the various free self-guided tours to your Ipod or MP3 player." —monicapileggi

Lodging

"Go off-season—March or November have better air prices and also accommodations, particularly if you stay in apartments, which you can rent for much less off-season (and plan some meals in-house—make the noon meal your biggest of the day, then have a small dinner in the apartment)." —bobthenavigator

"Everyone talks about going in the off season and mentions November or March. But in Florence at least, July is a shoulder season. I got a hotel room for half to a third the cost of the same room during the high season." – isabel

"We try to book apartments whenever we can…and in Tuscany we rent farm houses. Especially if you are traveling with more than 2 persons these are usually much more reasonable." – caroltis

A GREAT ITINERARY

ROME, FLORENCE, VENICE & HIGHLIGHTS IN BETWEEN

This itinerary is designed for maximum impact—it will keep you moving. Think of it as rough draft for you to revise according to your own interests and time constraints.

Day 1: Venice

Arrive in Venice's Marco Polo Airport (there are some direct flights from the United States), take the boat across the lagoon to Venice, check into your hotel, then get out, and get lost in the back canals for a couple of hours before dinner. If you can get a reservation, Osteria da Fiore would make a memorable first meal in Italy; it's an unforgettable place for sweet, delicate Adriatic seafood.

Logistics: At the airport, follow signs for water transport and look for Alilaguna, which operates the soothing one-hour boat trip into Venice. The boats stop at the Lido and finally leave you near Piazza San Marco; from there you can get to your hotel on foot or by vaporetto. The water taxis are much more expensive and aren't really worth the cost, although they'll take you directly to your hotel.

Day 2: Venice

Begin by skipping the coffee at your hotel and have a real Italian coffee at a real Italian coffee shop. Spend the day at Venice's top few sights, including the Basilica di San Marco, Palazzo Ducale, and Galleria dell'Accademia. Stop for lunch, perhaps sampling Venice's traditional specialty, *sarde in saor* (grilled sardines in a mouthwatering sweet-and-sour preparation that includes onions and raisins), and be sure to check out the ancient fish market, Rialto Bridge, and sunset at the Zattere before dinner. Later, stop at one of the pubs around the Campo San Luca or Campo Santa Margarita, where you can toast to freedom from automobiles.

Logistics: Venice is best seen by wandering. The day's activities can be done on foot, with the occasional vaporetto ride.

Day 3: Ferrara/Bologna

Get an early start and head out of Venice on a Bologna-bound train. The ride to Ferrara—your first stop in Emilia-Romagna—is about an hour and a half. Visit the Castello Estense and Duomo before lunch; a panino and a beer at one of Ferrara's prim and proper cafés should fit the bill. Wander Ferrara's cobblestone streets before hopping on the train to Bologna (a ride of less than an hour). In Bologna, check into your hotel and take a walk around Piazza Maggiore before dinner. At night, you can check out some of northern Italy's best nightlife.

Logistics: In Ferrara, the train station lies a bit outside the city center, so you'll want to take a taxi into town (check your luggage at the station). Going out, there's a taxi stand near the back of the castle, toward Corso Ercole I d'Este. In Bologna the walk into town from the station is more manageable, particularly if you're staying along Via dell'Indipendenza.

Day 4: Bologna/Florence

After breakfast, spend the morning checking out some of Bologna's churches and piazzas, including a climb up the leaning Torre degli Asinelli for a red rooftop–studded panorama. After lunch, head back to the train station, and take the short ride to Florence. You'll arrive in Florence in time for an afternoon siesta and an evening passeggiata.

A GREAT ITINERARY

Logistics: Florence's Santa Maria Novella train station is within easy access to some hotels, farther from others. Florence's traffic is legendary, but taxis at the station are plentiful; make sure you get into a licensed, clearly marked car that's outside in line.

Day 5: Florence
This is your day to see the sights of Florence. Start with the Uffizi Gallery (reserve your tickets in advance), where you'll see Botticelli's *Primavera* and *Birth of Venus*. Next, walk to the Piazza del Duomo, the site of Brunelleschi's spectacular dome, which you can climb for an equally spectacular view. By the time you get down, you'll be more than ready for a simple lunch at a laid-back café. Depending on your preferences, either devote the afternoon to art (Michelangelo's *David* at the Galleria dell'Accademia, the magnificent Medici Chapels, and perhaps the church of Santa Croce) or hike up to Piazzale Michelangelo, overlooking the city. Either way, finish the evening in style with a traditional *bistecca alla fiorentina* (grilled T-bone steak with olive oil).

Day 6: Lucca/Pisa
After breakfast, board a train for Lucca. It's an easy 1½-hour trip on the way to Pisa to see this walled medieval city. Don't miss the Romanesque Duomo, or a walk in the park that lines the city's ramparts. Have lunch at a local trattoria before continuing on to Pisa, where you'll spend an afternoon seeing—what else—the Leaning Tower, along with the equally impressive Duomo and Battistero. Walk down to the banks of the Arno River, contemplate the majestic views at sunset, and have dinner at one of the many inexpensive local restaurants in the real city center—a bit away from the most touristy spots.

Logistics: Lucca's train station lies just outside the walled city, so hardier travelers may want to leave the station on foot; otherwise, take a taxi. Check your luggage at the station. Pisa's train station isn't far from the city center, although it's on the other side of town from the Campo dei Miracoli (site of the Leaning Tower).

Day 7: Orvieto/Rome
Three hours south of Pisa is Orvieto, one of the prettiest and most characteristic towns of the Umbria region, conveniently situated right on the Florence–Rome train line. Check out the memorable cathedral before a light lunch accompanied by one of Orvieto's famous white wines. Get back on a train bound for Rome, and in a little more than an hour you'll arrive in the Eternal City in time to make your way to your hotel and relax for a bit before you head out for the evening. When you do, check out Piazza Navona, Campo de' Fiori, and the Trevi Fountain—it's best in the evening—and take a stand-up *aperitivo* (Campari and soda is the classic) at an unpretentious local bar before dinner. It's finally pizza time; you can't go wrong at any of Rome's popular local pizzerias.

Logistics: To get from Pisa to Orvieto, you'll first catch a train to Florence and then get on a Rome-bound train from here. Be careful at Rome's Termini train station, which is a breeding ground for scam artists. Keep your possessions close at hand, and only get into a licensed taxi at the taxi stand.

Day 8: Rome
Rome took millennia to build, but unfortunately on this whirlwind trip you'll

only have a day and a half to see it. In the morning, head to the Vatican Museums to see Michelangelo's glorious *Adam* at the Sistine Chapel. See St. Peter's Basilica and Square before heading back into Rome proper for lunch around the Pantheon, followed by a coffee from one of Rome's famous coffee shops. Next, visit ancient Rome—first see the magnificent Pantheon, and then head across to the Colosseum, stopping along the way along Via dei Fori Imperiali to check out the Roman Forum from above. From the Colosseum, take a taxi to Piazza di Spagna, a good place to see the sunset and shop at stylish boutiques. Take another taxi to Piazza Trilussa at the entrance of Trastevere, a beautiful old working-class neighborhood where you'll have a relaxing dinner.

Day 9: Rome/Departure
Head by taxi to Termini station and catch the train ride to the Fiumicino airport. Savor your last cup of the world's richest coffee at one of the coffee bars in the airport before boarding.

Logistics: The train from Termini station to the airport is fast, inexpensive, and easy—for most people, it's preferable to an exorbitantly priced taxi ride that, in bad traffic, can take twice as long.

TIPS

1 The itinerary can also be completed by car on the modern autostrade, although you'll run into dicey traffic in Florence and Rome. For obvious reasons, you're best off waiting to pick up your car on Day 3, when you leave Venice.

2 Among trains, aim for the reservations-only Eurostar Italia—it's more comfortable and faster.

3 The sights along this route are highly touristed; you'll have a better time if you make the trip outside the busy months of June, July, and August.

Part I: Rome & Environs

WHAT'S WHERE

1 **Ancient Rome.** Backstopped by the most stupendous monument of ancient Rome—the Colosseum—the Roman Forum and Palatine Hill were once the hub of western civilization.

2 **The Vatican.** The Vatican draws hundreds of thousands of pilgrims and art-lovers to St. Peter's Basilica, the Vatican Museums, and the Sistine Chapel.

3 **Navona & Campo.** The *cuore*—heart—of the centro storico (historic quarter), these districts revolve around the ancient Pantheon, Campo de' Fiori, and spectacular Piazza Navona.

4 **Corso.** Rome's "Broadway" begins at Piazza Venezia and neatly divides the city center in two—an area graced by historic landmarks like the 17th-century Palazzo Doria-Pamphilj (famed for its Old Master collection).

5 **Spagna.** Travel back to the days of the Grand Tour in this glamorous area. After some people-watching on Piazza de Spagna, shop like a true VIP along Via dei Condotti, then be sure to throw a coin in the Trevi Fountain.

6 **Repubblica & Quirinale.** A largely 19th-century district, Repubblica lets art lovers go for baroque with a bevy of Bernini works, including his St. Theresa in Ecstasy at Santa Maria della Vittoria. To the south looms the Quirinale hill, crowned by Italy's presidential palace.

7 **Villa Borghese & Piazza del Popolo.** Rome's largest park is home to playful fountains, sculptured gardens, and the art treasures of the Galleria Borghese. Piazza del Popolo—a beautiful place to watch the world go by—lies west.

8 **Trastevere.** Rome's "Greenwich Village" has kept its authentic roots thanks to mom-and-pop trattorie, medieval alleyways, and Santa Maria in Trastevere, stunningly spotlighted at night (when hot new clubs take center stage in this quarter).

9 **The Ghetto & Isola Tiberina.** Once a Jewish quarter, the newly gentrified Ghetto still preserves the flavor of Old Rome. Alongside is moored Tiber Island, so picturesque it will click your camera for you.

10 **The Catacombs & Appian Way.** Follow in the footsteps of St. Peter to this district, home to the spirit-warm Catacombs and Tomb of Cecilia Metella.

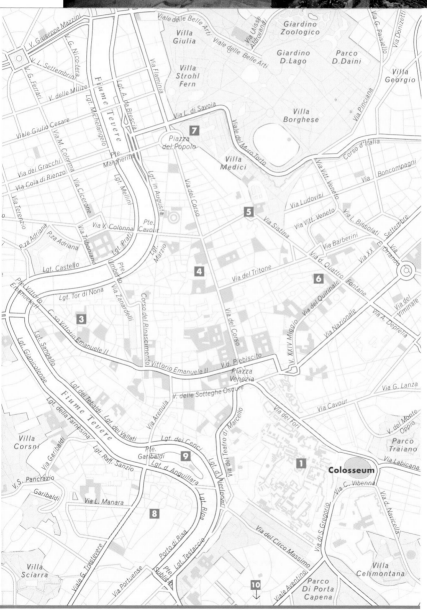

Villa
Giulia

Villa
Strohl
Fern

Giardino
Zoologico

Giardino
D.Lago

Parco
D.Daini

Villa
Georgio

7

Piazza
del Popolo

Villa
Medici

Villa
Borghese

Corso d'Italia

5

Via Ludovisi

Via Barberini

6

4

Via del Tritone

3

Vittorio Emanuele II

V.d. Plebiscito

Piazza
Venezia

V. delle Sotteghe Oscure

Via G. Lanza

Via Cavour

Villa
Corsni

9

Parco
Traiano

1

Colosseum

Villa
Sciarra

8

Via del Circo Massimo

10

Parco
Di Porta
Capena

Villa
Celimontana

ROME & ENVIRONS PLANNER

Don't Miss the Metro

Fortunately for tourists, many of Rome's main attractions are concentrated in the centro storico (historic center) and can be covered on foot.

Some sights that lie nearer the border of this quarter can be reached via the Metro Line A, nicknamed the linea turistica (tourist line) and include: the Spanish Steps (Spagna stop), the Trevi Fountain (Barberini stop), St. Peter's Square (Ottaviano stop), and the Vatican Museums (Cipro-Musei Vaticani stop), to name a few.

Tickets for the bus and metro can be purchased for €1 at any tabacchi (tobacco shop) and at most newsstands.

These tickets are good for approximately 75 minutes on buses, or a single metro ride. Day passes can be purchased for €4, and weekly passes, which allow unlimited use of both buses and the metro, for €16.

For a better explanation of the metro routes, pick up a free map from one of the tourist information booths scattered around the city: Tech-savvy tourists can navigate their way around Rome by accessing the web site of Rome's public transportation system, the ATAC (⊕ www.atac.roma.it).

Making the Most of Your Time

Roma, non basta una vita ("Rome, a lifetime is not enough"): this famous saying should be stamped on the passport of every first-time visitor to the Eternal City. On the other hand, it's a warning: Rome is so packed with sights that it is impossible to take them all in; it's easy to run yourself ragged trying to check off the items on your "Santa Claus" list.

At the same time, the saying is a celebration of the city's abundance. There's so much here, you're bound to make discoveries you hadn't anticipated. To conquer Rome, strike a balance between visits to major sights and leisurely neighborhood strolls.

In the first category, the Vatican and the remains of ancient Rome loom the largest. Both require at least half a day; a good strategy is to devote your first morning to one and your second to the other.

Leave the afternoons for exploring the neighborhoods that comprise "Baroque Rome" and the shopping district around the Spanish Steps and Via Condotti. If you have more days at your disposal, continue with the same approach.

Among the sights, Galleria Borghese and the multilayered church of San Clemente are particularly worthwhile, and the neighborhoods of Trastevere and the Ghetto make for great roaming.

Since there's a lot of ground to cover in Rome, it's wise to plan your busy sightseeing schedule with possible savings in mind, and purchasing the Roma Pass (⊕ www.romapass.it) allows you to do just that. The 3-day pass costs €20 and is good for unlimited use of buses, trams and the metro.

It includes free admission to two of over 40 participating museums or archaeological sites, including the Colosseum (and bumps you to the head of the long line there, to boot!), the Ara Pacis museum, the Musei Capitolini, and Galleria Borghese, plus discounted tickets to many other museums. The Roma Pass can be purchased at tourist information booths across the city, at Termini Station, or at Terminal C of the International Arrivals section of Fiumicino Airport.

How's the Weather?

Not surprisingly, spring and fall are the best times to visit, with mild temperatures and many sunny days; the famous Roman sunsets are also at their best. Summers are often sweltering. In July and August, come if you like, but learn to do as the Romans do—get up and out early, seek refuge from the afternoon heat, resume activities in early evening, and stay up late to enjoy the nighttime breeze. Come August, many shops and restaurants close as locals head out for vacation. Remember that air-conditioning is still a relatively rare phenomenon in this city. Roman winters are relatively mild, with persistent rainy spells.

Hop-On, Hop-Off

Rome has its own "hop-on, hop-off" sightseeing buses. The Trambus Open Roma 110 bus leaves with 10-minute frequencies from Piazza dei Cinquecento (at the main Termini railway station), with a two-hour loop including the Quirinale, the Colosseum, Piazza Navona, St. Peter's, the Trevi Fountain, and Via Veneto. Tickets are €16 (kids 6–12, €7). A variant is the Archeobus, which departs every 20 minutes from the Piazza dei Cinquecento and heads on out to the Via Appia Antica, including stops at the Colosseum, Baths of Caracalla, and the Catacombs. Tickets are €13 (kids 6–12, €6). The Web site for both is ⊕ www.trambusopen.com.

Roman Hours

Virtually the entire city shuts down on Sundays, although museums, pastry shops, and most restaurants are closed Mondays. However, most stores in the centro storico area, the part of town that caters to tourists, remain open. Shop hours generally run from 10 AM to 1 PM, then reopen around 4 PM until 7:30 or 8 PM. Unless advertised as having *orario continuato* (open all day), most businesses close from 1 to 4 PM for lunch, or *riposo*. On Mondays, shops don't open until around 3 or 4 PM. Pharmacies have the same hours of operation as stores unless they advertise *orario notturno* (night hours); two can be found at Piazza Barberini and Piazza Risorgimento (near St. Peter's Square). As for churches, most open at 8 or 9 in the morning, close from noon to 3 or 4, then reopen until 6:30 or 7. St. Peter's, however, is open 7 AM to 7 PM (6 in the fall and winter).

Information, Please

Rome's main APT (Azienda Per Turismo) Tourist Information Office is at Via Parigi 5–11 (☎ 06/488991 ⊕ www.romaturismo.it), near the main Termini rail station.

In addition, green APT information kiosks with multilingual personnel are situated near the most important sights and squares, as well as at Termini Station and Leonardo da Vinci Airport. These kiosks, called Tourist Information Sites (Punti Informativi Turistici, or PIT) can be found at:

PIT Castel S. Angelo, Lungotevere Vaticano; open 9:30–7 PM

PIT Cinque Lune, Piazza delle Cinque Lune (Piazza Navona); open 9:30–7 PM

PIT Fiumicino, Aeroporto Leonardo Da Vinci–Arrivi Internazionali Terminal C; open 9–7:30 PM

PIT Minghetti, Via Marco Minghetti (corner of Via del Corso); open 9:30–7 PM

PIT Nazionale, Via Nazionale (Palazzo delle Esposizioni); open 9:30–7 PM

PIT Santa Maria Maggiore, at Via dell'Olmata; open 9:30–7 PM

PIT Termini, Stazione Termini, at Via Giovanni Giolitti 34; open 8–8 PM

PIT Trastevere, on Piazza Sidney Sonnino; open 9:30–7 PM

TOP ROME ATTRACTIONS

The Pantheon

Constructed to honor all pagan gods, this best preserved temple of ancient Rome was rebuilt in the 2nd century AD by Emperor Hadrian, and to him much of the credit is due for the perfect dimensions: 141 feet high by 141 feet wide, with a vast dome that was the largest ever designed until the 20th century.

The Vatican

Though its population numbers only in the few hundreds, the Vatican—home base for the Catholic Church and the pope—makes up for them with the millions who visit each year. Embraced by the arms of the colonnades of St. Peter's Square, they attend Papal Mass, marvel at St. Peter's Basilica, and savor Michelangelo's Sistine Ceiling.

The Colosseum

(B) Legend has it that as long as the Colosseum stands, Rome will stand; and when Rome falls, so will the world. One of the seven wonders of the world, the mammoth amphitheater was begun by Emperor Vespasian and inaugurated by Titus in the year 80. For "the grandeur that was Rome," this yardstick of eternity can't be topped.

Piazza Navona

(D) You couldn't concoct a more Roman street scene: caffès and crowded tables at street level, coral- and rust-colored houses above, most lined with wrought-iron balconies, and, at the center of this urban "living room," Bernini's spectacular Fountain of the Four Rivers and Borromini's super-theatrical Sant'Agnese.

Roman Forum

(A) Set between the Capitoline and Palatine hills, this fabled labyrinth of ruins variously served as a political playground, a commerce mart, and a place where justice was dispensed during the days of

the emperors (500 BC to 400 AD). Once adorned with stately buildings, triumphal arches, and impressive temples, the Forum today is a silent ruin—*sic transit gloria mundi* ("so passes away the glory of the world").

The Campidoglio
(C) Catch an emperor's-eye view of the Roman Forum from Michelangelo's piazza, situated atop one of the highest spots in Rome, the Capitoline Hill. Here you'll find the Capitoline Museums and beloved Santa Maria in Aracoeli.

Trevi Fountain
(E) One of the few fountains in Rome that's actually more absorbing than the people crowding around it, the Fontana di Trevi was designed by Nicola Salvi in 1732. Immortalized in *Three Coins in a Fountain* and *La Dolce Vita*, this fountain may be your ticket back to Rome—that is, if you throw a coin into it.

The Spanish Steps
(F) Byron, Shelley, and Keats all drew inspiration from this magnificent "Scalinata," constructed in 1723. Connecting the shops at the bottom with the hotels at the top, this is the place for prime people-watching. The steps face beautiful sunsets.

Galleria Borghese
(G) Only the best could only satisfy the aesthetic taste of Cardinal Scipione Borghese, and that means famed Bernini sculptures, great paintings by Titian and Raphael, and the most spectacular 17th-century palace in Rome.

Trastevere
Located just across the Tiber River, this charming neighborhood is a maze of jumbled alleyways, cobblestone streets, and medieval houses. The area also boasts the oldest church of Rome—Santa Maria in Trastevere.

TOP ROME EXPERIENCES

Don't Just Read *Angels & Demons*, Walk It!

What Dan Brown did for Paris in *The Da Vinci Code*, he does for Rome—big-time—in *Angels & Demons*, the 2000 "prequel." This time Brown's Robert Langdon does battle with the Illuminati, a secret society trying to unleash scientific terrorists against the Catholic church. To find out if they succeed in incinerating the Vatican with an antimatter bomb during a papal enclave you'll have to read the book or see the Ron Howard movie (starring Tom Hanks and opening May 2009). But crowds are already flocking to "Angels & Demons" walking tours in Rome, tracking down the "Path of Illumination" to such scenic stunners as Raphael's Chigi Chapel and Bernini's *Ecstasy of St. Theresa*, plus many other famous (and not-so-famous) Roman sights. Just a few of the tour companies offering this walk: ⊕ www.darkrome.com; ⊕ www.angelsanddemonstours.com; ⊕ www.througheternity.com; ⊕ www.viator.com.

Say "Cheese," Spartacus

Taking a photo with one of those ersatz gladiators in front of the Colosseum will win some smiles—but maybe some frowns, too. Many of these costumed gladiators pounce on tourists who simply aim a camera at them and then proceed to shake them down for a "photo fee." Others have a craftier approach: before you know it, one may envelop your eight-year-old in his red cape and say *"Formaggio."* Indeed, this may turn out to be the greatest souvenir back home in fourth-grade class, so if interested, step right up, shake hands, and exchange some euros. But pick your Spartacus very carefully: some sloppy guys wear a helmet and cloak but have sweatsuits or sneakers on. Rumor has it that Rome's government is going to crack down on these "gladiators," but so far it is caveat emptor.

Roma di Notte

A great way to lift the curtain on a night of romance is a serenaded dinner cruise along the Tiber, where dessert includes views of some of Rome's jewels by night: Castel Sant'Angelo, St. Peter's, and the Janiculum (Gianicolo) hill. See ⊕ www.battellidiroma.it for more details.

Life is a Piazza

For Italians young and old, la piazza serves as a *punto d'incontro*—a meeting place—for dinner plans, drinks, people-watching, catching up with friends and, as Romans would say, exchanging *due chiacchiere* (two words). One of the most popular piazzas is Campo de' Fiori, right in the heart of the beautiful historic center. By day, the piazza is famous for its fresh food and flower market—no rival to Piazza Navona for picturesqueness, the market is nevertheless a favorite photo-op, due to the *ombrelloni* (canvas umbrella) food stands. By night, the piazza turns into a popular hangout for Romans and foreigners lured by its pubs and street caffès, so much so that it has been dubbed "the American college campus of Rome." As dinner approaches at 9, the big question is: Are you "in" or "out" (inside or outside table)? No matter: the people-watching is unrivaled anywhere you sit.

Truth or Dare

Long before the advent of lie-detector machines, and even before there were bibles to swear on, there was the Bocca della Verità—the Mouth of Truth, the famous gaping mouth that so successfully terrified Audrey Hepburn in *Roman*

Holiday. Long-ago legends have it that people suspected of telling lies would be marched up to the Bocca and have their hand put inside the mouth of this massive stone relief (originally an ancient street drain cover). If the suspect told the truth, nothing to fear. But if lies were told, the grim unsmiling stone mouth would take its revenge.

This is a great spot for kids to get the truth out of their brother or sister, so have your camera—and your probling questions!—ready. Don't forget to take in the adjacent Santa Maria in Cosmedin church, one of Rome's most evocative and spooky churches.

White Nights

The Eternal City becomes magical during its annual *La Notte Bianca*—"The White Night"—(usually the first week of September) when museums, archaeological sites, and shops stay open into the wee hours of the night. You can also catch a variety of free concerts and theatrical performances in some of Rome's finest piazzas. Check out ⊕ www.lanottebianca.it for details.

Two Coins in the Fountain

Rome has always been in love with *amore*. But romance is certainly nowhere more contagious than around its famous fountains. If a besotted couple can spare the time, a trip up to Tivoli's Villa D'Este (an hour outside Rome via bus) is nirvana. Its seductive garden and endless array of fountains (about 500 of them) is the perfect setting to put anyone in the mood for love—it won't be long before you hear Frank Sinatra warble "Three Coins in the Fountain" in your head.

That's your cue to return to Rome and make a bee-line for the luminous Trevi Fountain, even more enchanting at night than in the daytime. Make sure you and that special someone throw your coins into the fountain, for good luck. Legend has it that those who do so are guaranteed a return trip back to Rome.

L'Aperitivo

Borrowed from *i Milanesi*, the trend of *l'aperitivo* has become moda in Rome. Similar to the concept of happy hour sans the two-for-one drinks, l'aperitivo is a time to meet up with friends and colleagues after work or on weekends—definitely an event to see and be seen. Aperitivo hours are usually from 7—9 PM, with Sunday being the most popular day.

Depending on where you go, the price of a drink often includes an all-you-can-eat appetizer buffet of finger foods, sandwiches, and pasta salads. Some aperitivo hotspots on the trendissimo list are Crudo (Via degli Specchi); Societè Lutece (Piazza Monte Vecchio) and Salotto 42 (Piazza di Pietra) in the centro storico; and Friends Cafè (Piazza Trilussa) and Freni and Frizioni (Via del Politeama) in the Trastevere area.

Trawling for Treasure

There are plenty of street markets scattered about Rome which specialize in clothing, fashion accessories, and every imaginable knickknack. The two largest are the one on Via Sannio in the San Giovanni district (Mon.–Sat.), which deals mostly in new and used clothing and accessories, and the Porta Portese market in Trastevere (Sunday only), offering everything from antiques and bric-a-brac to clothing and souvenirs. Make sure to ask for a *piccolo sconto*—or a small discount.

GETTING HERE & AROUND

Getting Here by Car

The main access routes from the north are A1 (Autostrada del Sole) from Milan and Florence and the A12-E80 highway from Genoa. The principal route to or from points south, including Naples, is the A2. All highways connect with the Grande Raccordo Anulare Ring Road (GRA), which channels traffic into the city center. For driving directions, check out ⊕ www.tuttocitta.it. Note: Parking in Rome can be a nightmare—private cars are not allowed access to the entire historic center during the day (weekdays 8–6; Saturday 2 pm–6 pm), except for residents.

Getting Here by Bus

Bus lines cover all of Rome's surrounding Lazio region and are operated by the Consorzio Trasporti Lazio, or COTRAL (☎ 800/150008 ⊕ www.cotralspa.it). These bus routes terminate either near Tiburtina Station or at outlying Metro stops, such as Rebibbia and Ponte Mammolo (Line B) and Anagnina (Line A). COTRAL and buses run by SENA (☎ 800/930960 ⊕ www.sena.it) are good options for taking short day trips from Rome, such as those that leave daily from Rome's Ponte Mammolo (Line B) metro station for the town of Tivoli, where Hadrian's Villa and Villa D'Este are located.

Getting Here by Air

Rome's principal airport is Leonardo da Vinci Airport/Fiumicino (☎ 06/65951 ⊕ www.adr.it) commonly known by the name of its location, Fiumicino (FCO). It's 30 km (19 mi) southwest of the city but has a direct train link with downtown Rome. Rome's other airport, with no direct train link, is Ciampino (☎ 06/794941 ⊕ www.adr.it) or CIA, 15 km (9 mi) south of downtown and used mostly by low-cost airlines. Two trains link downtown Rome with Fiumicino. Inquire at the APT tourist information counter in the International Arrivals hall (Terminal B) or train information counter near the tracks to determine which takes you closest to your destination in Rome. The 30-minute nonstop Airport-Termini express (called the Leonardo Express) goes directly to Track 25 at Termini Station, Rome's main train station; tickets cost €11. The FM1 train stops in Trastevere. Always stamp your tickets in the little machines near the track before you board. As for Ciampino, COTRAL buses connects to trains that go to the city.

Getting Here by Train

State-owned Trenitalia (☎ 892/2021 within Italy, 06/68475475 from abroad ⊕ www.trenitalia.it) trains also serve some destinations on side trips outside Rome. The main Trenitalia stations in Rome are Termini, Tiburtina, Ostiense, and Trastevere. On long-distance routes (to Florence and Venice, for instance), you can either travel by the cheap, but slow, diretto trains, or the fast, but more expensive Intercity, or the Eurostar. The state railways' site at ⊕ www.trenitalia.it is user-friendly.

Getting Around by Public Transportation

Rome's integrated transportation system is ATAC (☎ 06/46952027 or 800/431784 ⊕ www.atac.roma.it), which includes the Metropolitana subway, city buses, and municipal trams. A ticket (BIT) valid for 75 minutes on any combination of buses and trams and one entrance to the Metro costs €1. Day passes can be purchased for €4, and weekly passes for €16. Tickets (singly or in quantity—it's a good idea to have a few tickets handy so you don't have to hunt for a vendor when you

need one) are sold at tobacconists, newsstands, some coffee bars, automatic ticket machines in Metro stations, some bus stops, and ATAC and COTRAL ticket booths. Time-stamp tickets at Metro turnstiles and in little yellow machines on buses and trams when boarding the first vehicle and stamp it again when boarding for the last time within 75 minutes.

Getting Around by Bus & Tram

ATAC city buses and trams are orange, gray-and-red, or blue-and-orange. Remember to board at the rear and to exit at the middle; you must buy your ticket before boarding, and stamp it in a machine as soon as you enter. The ticket is good for a transfer within the next 75 minutes.

Buses and trams run from 5:30 am to midnight, plus there's an extensive network of night (*notturno*) buses. ATAC has a Web site (www.atac.roma.it) that will help you calculate the number of stops and bus routes needed. To navigate the site, look for *"Muoversi a Roma"* and then click on *"Calcola il percorso"* to get to another page that changes the site into English.

Be aware that *festivi* buses are ones that only run on Sundays and holidays; regular buses will either say *feriali*, which means "daily," or won't have any special distinction. Pick up a free Metro Routes map from a tourist info booth scattered through the city.

Getting Around by Metropolitana

The Metropolitana (or Metro) is the easiest and fastest way to get around Rome. The Metro A line—known as the linea turistica (tourist line) will take you to a chunk of the main attractions in Rome: Piazza di Spagna (Spagna stop), Piazza del Popolo (Flaminio), St. Peter's Square

and the Vatican Museums (Cipro-Musei Vaticani), and the Trevi Fountain (Barberini). The B line will take you to the Coliseum (Colosseo stop), Circus Maximus, the Pyramid (Ostiense Station and trains for Ostia Antica), Basilica di San Paolo Fuori le Mura, and also lead you to the heart of Testaccio, Rome's nightlife district. The two lines intersect at Rome's main station, Termini.

Street entrances are marked with red "M" signs. At press time, due to reconstruction, the Metro A line underground services end at 9 pm, at which time they are substituted by buses (MA1 and MA2) at the terminals that run until 11:30 pm. The Metro runs from 5:30 am to 11:30 pm (Saturday: 12:30 am).

Getting Around by Taxi

Taxis in Rome do not cruise, but if free they will stop if you flag them down. They wait at stands but can also be called by phone (06/6645, 06/3570, 06/4994, 06/5551, or 06/4157).

Always ask for a receipt (*ricevuta*) to make sure the driver charges you the correct amount. Use only licensed cabs with a plaque next to the license plate reading "Servizio Pubblico."

Getting Around by Moped & Melex

As bikes are to Beijing, so mopeds are to Rome; that means they are everywhere. Riders are required to wear helmets.

Yours truly, can also hire an electric MELEX four-seater, golf-cart-style car, with battery power lasting up to eight hours. To rent one, you need a valid driver's license. Cost: €18 per hour.

ROME TODAY

...is not the Roma your mother knew
Home to nearly 3 million residents and a gazillion tourists, Rome is virtually busting at the seams. For decades, the city was all about its *centro storico*, where a chunk of the city's most fabled museums, monuments, and cultural relics have stood for centuries. Replete with postcard landmarks, Baroque palaces, and hyper-luxury hotels, the "Disneyfication" of the historic center is well under way.

As there was no room to grow upward, Rome has had to stretch outward. To relieve pressure in the city center, city officials have focused on building a "new" Rome beyond the historic quarter. In the process, old, economically weaker, satellite districts have been revitalized. Former working-class neighborhoods—San Lorenzo to the north, Ostiense and Testaccio to the south—have become trendy. This "other" Rome is now studded with buildings designed by superstar architects and neighborhoods that are shabby-chic, alternative, and full of flair.

...is creating new "It" neighborhoods
The leader among Rome's "It" nabes is San Lorenzo, set just a stone's throw away from the Termini train station. Just beyond the city walls near Via Tiburtina, Rome's new "Left Bank" district is filled with students and a young bohemian crowd thanks to its close proximity to the La Sapienza University.

The area has an *alternativa* feel to it, thanks to the plethora of starving artists and hippy musicians. In fact, if you don't know what you're looking for, you could easily get lost in this maze of dark narrow streets, many now lined with underground caffès, bars, hip restaurants, and locales with live-music venues.

The leading scene-arenas include Formula 1 (Via degli Equi 13), for top pizzas; Da Franco ar Vicoletto (Via dei Falisci 1/b), just around the corner, for fish lovers; and Arancia Blu (Via dei Latini 55), which drawns the green crowds thanks to its vegetarian menus. Everything get amped up at night. The likes of bands such as The Cure, U2, and Pearl Jam have been known to play at I Giardini di Adone (Via dei Reti 38/a)—after midnight, the house music gets turned up.

...is going multi-culti

Want to know what the face of Italy will look like in 10 years? Spend a day

...IS GOING HOLLYWOOD

A physicist with a secret symbol branded on his dead body. An antimatter bomb meant to incinerate the Vatican. A 400-year-old secret society unleashing scientific terrorists against the Catholic church. Take these elements, then add in Gian Lorenzo Bernini's great-est sculptures, Rome's historic settings, and a climax that features everything but the *Starship Enterprise*, and you have *Angels & Demons*, the page turner that is Dan Brown's prequel to his smash, *The Da Vinci Code*. Hollywood arrived in Rome June 2008 to film. Director Ron Howard probably called out for "Lights...camera...and *lots* of violent action!" For when four cardinals (candidates to be the new pope) wind up missing and murdered at a papal enclave, it is up to Tom Hanks and Naomi Watts to track down

in Rome's Esquilino neighborhood and you'll see just how multicultural the Eternal City is becoming. Once famous for its ethnic food and spice market at Piazza Vittorio, the area neighborhood has fast become a multiethnic stomping ground. In fact, finding a true Roman restaurant or a local shopkeeper is hard to come by in this area, now that Chinese, Indian African, and Middle Eastern restaurants have moved in (a typical example: the Syrian restaurant, Zenobia, perched on Piazza Dante, just a few blocks away from Piazza Vittorio, even includes a weekend belly-dancing show).

Homegrown and locally produced, the Orchestra di Piazza Vittorio is a perfect picture of the neighborhood's growing ethnic population. Made up of 16 musicians from Brasil, Senegal, Tunisia, Cuba, Argentina, Hungary, Ecuador, and Italy, the troupe was founded in 2002 and got its start in the ramshackle district just steps away from Rome's Termini train station.

...is breaking new ground

Eternal Rome is in the middle of a building boom, one kick-started by the Vatican's 2000 Jubilee celebrations. Voguish new landmarks, like the Parco della Musica,

a set of three armadillo-like music halls designed by modernist Renzo Piano, garned magazine covers; the slaughter-house-turned-contemporary art museum of MACRO al Mattatoio earned head-lines; and minimalist masterpieces like Richard Meier's Jubilee Church may yet prove to be as enduring and image-defin-ing as were Michelangelo's Palazzo Sena-torio or Bernini's St. Peter's Square.

When it comes to transforming an old working-class district into a scene-arena, "starchitects" and their new iconic build-ings often lead the way. New case in point: Rem Koolhaas recently won the competition to revamp Ostiense's Mercati Generali food market. Before long this moldering landmark will be transformed into Rome's "Convent Garden."

Magliana is now the site of a new model residential complex rising up near Rome's airport and designed by Richard Rogers, architect of Paris's Beaubourg Centre and New York City's Hearst Tower. Among the latest projects is the Casa della Ballo (House of Dance), which now joins the newly opened Casa del Cinema and Casa del Jazz.

the trail of the Illuminati, the secret society founded by Galileo, Bernini, and others to bolster science against the 17th-century Inquisition. The "Path of Illumination" that they follow through Rome leads to four Altars of Science: Raphael's Chigi Chapel in Santa Maria del Popolo (Earth); the "West Ponente" disk in St.

Peter's Square (Air); Bernini's *Ecstasy of St. Theresa* in Santa Maria della Vittoria (Fire); and Bernini's Piazza Navona fountain (Water). Along the way, they decipher mysterious ambigrams, fight off assassins, uncover corpses in St. Peter's, and unlock the Illuminati's lair (in Castel Sant'Angelo, no less).

Many of the sights in the book and film are now included on "Angels & Demons" walking tours. No matter that critics have faulted Brown for factual errors and James Bond–like shenanigans—any project that can bring Bernini's greatest masterpieces to the world's movie multiplexes gets our vote.

EATING & DRINKING WELL IN ROME

In Rome, traditional cuisine reigns supreme. Most chefs follow the mantra of freshness over fuss, simplicity of flavor and preparation over complex cooking methods.

So when Romans continue ordering the standbys, it's easy to understand why. And we're talking about very old standbys: some restaurants re-create dishes that come from ancient recipes of Apicius, probably the first celebrity chef (to Emperor Tiberius) and cookbook author of the Western world. Today, Rome's cooks excel at what has taken hundreds, or thousands, of years to perfect.

Still, if you're hunting for newer-than-now developments, things are slowly changing. Talented young chefs are exploring new culinary frontiers, with results that tingle the taste buds: potato gnocchi with sea urchin sauce, artichoke strudel, and oysters with red-onion foam are just a few recent examples. Of course, there's grumbling about the number of chefs who, in a clumsy effort to be nuovo, end up with collision rather than fusion. That noted, Rome is the capital city, and the influx of residents from other regions of the country allows for many variations on the Italian theme.

FOODIE FINDS

Via Cola di Rienzo is home to two of Rome's best specialty shops: **Castroni** (⊠Via Cola di Rienzo 200, Prati ☎06/6874651), pictured above, a gastroshop that sells high-quality cured meats, Italian cheeses, wines, pastas, and fresh truffles. Next door, **Franchi** (⊠Via Cola di Rienzo 196, Prati ☎06/68743382) is well known among expats for its imported foreign foods from the United States, Great Britain, Japan, India, and Mexico, as well as its impressive selection of candies, preserves, olive oils, and balsamic vinegars. Franchi is a great place to stop in for caffè and a cornetto (an Italian croissant).

ARTICHOKES

If there's one vegetable Rome is known for, it's the artichoke, or *carciofo*. The classic Roman preparation, *carciofo alla romana*, is a large, globe-shaped artichoke stuffed with wild mint and garlic, then braised. It's available at restaurants throughout the city in spring, when artichokes are in season. For the excellent Roman-Jewish version, *carciofo alla giudia*—a younger artichoke that is deep-fried until crisp and leathery brown in color—head to any restaurant in the Ghetto.

BUCATINI ALLA MATRICIANA

What may appear to the naked eye as spaghetti with red sauce is actually *bucatini alla matriciana*—a spicy, rich, and complex dish that owes its flavor to an important ingredient: *guanciale,* or cured pig's cheek. The simple sauce features crushed tomatoes and red pepper flakes. It is served over bucatini, a hollow, spaghetti-like pasta, and topped with grated pecorino romano cheese.

CODA ALLA VACCINARA

Rome's largest slaughterhouse in the 1800s was housed in the Testaccio neighborhood. That's where you'll find dishes like *coda alla vaccinara,* or "oxtail in the style of the slaughterhouse." This sweet-and-sour dish is made from oxtails stewed with tomatoes and wine, and seasoned with gar-

lic, cinnamon, pancetta, and myriad other flavorings. The stew cooks for a day or two, then is finished with the sweet-and-sour element—often raisins or bittersweet chocolate. It often is served over polenta or pasta.

GELATO

For many travelers, the first taste of *gelato*—Italian ice cream—is one of the most memorable moments of their Italian trip. Almost a cross between regular American ice cream and soft serve, gelato's texture is dense but softer than hard ice cream because of the process by which it's whipped when freezing. A few common flavors are *stracciatella* (chocolate chip), *caffè* (coffee), *nocciola* (hazelnut), *fragola* (strawberry), and *cioccolato* (chocolate).

PIZZA

Roman pizza comes in two types: *pizza rustica* and *pizza al taglio* (by the slice), which have a thicker focaccia-like crust and is cut into squares. These slices are sold by weight and are available all day. The other type, *pizza tonda* (whole rounds), has a very thin crust. *Pizza tonda* is cooked in wood-burning ovens that reach extremely high temperatures. Since they're so hot, the ovens are usually fired up only in the evenings, which is why Roman pizzerias are only open for dinner.

A GREAT ITINERARY

Rome wasn't built in a day and even locals themselves will tell you that it takes a lifetime to discover all the treasures that the Eternal City has to offer. Jam packed with monuments, museums, fountains, galleries, and picturesque neighborhoods, Mamma Roma makes it hard for visitors to decide which to tackle first during their adventurous Roman Holiday. As Romans like to say, this one-day itinerary *basta e avanza* ("is more than enough") to get you started!

Rome 101

So you want to taste Rome, gaze at its beauty, and inhale its special flair, all in one breathtaking (literally) day? Think Rome 101, and get ready for a spectacular sunrise-to-sunset span. Begin at 9 by exploring Rome's most beautiful neighborhood—"Vecchia Roma" (the area around Piazza Navona) by starting out on the Corso (the big avenue which runs into Piazza Venezia, the traffic hub of the historic center).

A block away from each other are two opulently over-the-top monuments that show off Rome at its Baroque best: the church of Sant'Ignazio and the princely Palazzo Doria-Pamphilj, aglitter with great Old Master paintings. By 10:30, head west a few blocks to find the granddaddy of monuments, the fabled Pantheon, still looking like Emperor Hadrian might arrive. A few blocks north is San Luigi dei Francesi, home to the greatest Caravaggio paintings in the world. At 11:30 saunter a block or so westward into beyond-beautiful Piazza Navona, studded with Bernini fountains. Then take Via Cucagna (at the piazza's south end) and continue several blocks toward Campo de' Fiori's open-air food market for some lunch-on-the-run fixings. Two

more blocks toward the Tiber brings you to fashionable Via Giulia, laid out by Pope Julius II in the early 16th century. Walk past 10 blocks of Renaissance palaces and antique shops to take a bus (from the stop near the Tiber) over to the Vatican. Arrive around 1:00 to gape at St. Peter's Basilica, then hit the treasure-filled Vatican Museums (Sistine Chapel) around 1:45—during lunch, the crowds empty out! After two hours at the Vatican, head for the Ottaviano stop near the museum and Metro your way to the Colosseo stop.

Around 4, climb up into the Colosseum and picture it full of screaming toga-clad citizens enjoying the spectacle of gladiators in mortal combat. Striding past the massive Arch of Constantine, enter the back-entrance of the Roman Forum around 4:45. Photograph yourself giving a "Friends, Romans, Countrymen" oration (complete with upraised hand) on one of the marble fragments.

At sunset, the Forum closes but the floodlights come on. March down the forum's Via Sacra and out into Via dei Fori Imperiali where you will head around "the wedding cake"—the looming Vittorio Emanuele Monument (Il Vittoriano)—over to the Campidoglio. Here, on the Capitoline Hill, tour the great ancient Roman art treasures of the Musei Capitolini (which is open most nights until 8), and snap the view from the terrace over the spotlit Forum. After dinner, hail a cab—or take a long passeggiata walk down Dolce Vita memory lane—to the Trevi Fountain, a gorgeously lit sight at night. Needless to say, toss that coin in to insure your return trip back to the Mother of Us All.

Rome

WORD OF MOUTH

"There's something very powerful to being surrounded by all that history (and I'm not a history buff). It's not a place where you walk up, snap a picture, and say, 'All right I've seen it.' It's an imposing experience (in a good way). The effect is very strong. There are other beautiful scenic places in the world, but there's only one Rome."

—flatfeet

Updated by
Megan K.
Williams,
Dana
Klitzberg,
Jen Laskey,
Erica Firpo
& Lynda
Albertson

COMING OFF THE AUTOSTRADA at Roma Nord or Roma Sud, you know by the convergence of heavily trafficked routes that you are entering a grand nexus: All roads lead to Rome. And then the interminable suburbs, the railroad crossings, the intersections—no wonder they call it the Eternal City. As you enter the city proper, features that match your expectations begin to take shape: a bridge with heroic statues along its parapets; a towering cake of frothy marble decorated with allegorical figures in extravagant poses; a piazza and an obelisk under an umbrella of pine trees. Then you spot what looks like a multistory parking lot; with a gasp, you realize it's the Colosseum.

You have arrived. You're in the city's heart. You step down from your excursion bus onto the broad girdle of tarmac that encircles the great stone arena of the Roman emperors, and scurry out of the way of the passing Fiats—the motorists behind the wheels seem to display the panache of so many Ben-Hurs. The excitement of arriving here jolts the senses and sharpens expectations.

The timeless city to which all roads lead, Mamma Roma enthralls visitors today as she has since time immemorial. More than Florence, more than Venice, this is Italy's treasure storehouse. Here, the ancient Romans made us heirs-in-law to what we call Western Civilization; where centuries later Michelangelo painted in the Sistine Chapel; where Gian Lorenzo Bernini's baroque nymphs and naiads still dance in their marble fountains; and where, at Cinecittà Studios, Fellini filmed *La Dolce Vita* and *8½*. Today, the city remains a veritable Grand Canyon of culture: Ancient Rome rubs shoulders with the medieval, the modern runs into the Renaissance, and the result is like nothing so much as an open-air museum.

Little wonder Rome's enduring popularity feeds a gluttonous tourism industry that can feel more like *National Lampoon's European Vacation* than *Roman Holiday*. As tour buses belch black smoke and the line at the Vatican Museums stretches on into eternity, even the steeliest of sightseers have been known to wonder, why am I here? The answer, with apologies to Dorothy, is: There's no place like Rome. Yesterday's Grand Tourists thronged the city for the same reason today's Expedians do. Majestic, complicated, enthralling, romantic, chaotic, monumental Rome is one of the world's great cities—past, present, and, probably, future.

But always remember: *Bisogna vivere a Roma coi costumi di Roma* ("When you are in Rome, do as Rome does"). Don't feel intimidated by the press of art and culture. Instead, contemplate the grandeur from a table at a sun-drenched caffè on Piazza Navona; let Rome's colorful life flow around you without feeling guilty because you haven't seen everything. It can't be done, anyway. There's just so much here that you will have to come back again, so be sure to throw a coin in the Trevi Fountain. It works.

Rome Metro & Suburban Railway

EXPLORING ROME

Updated by Megan K. Williams

Most everyone begins by discovering the grandeur that was Rome: the Colosseum, the Forum, and the Pantheon. Then many move on to the Vatican, the closest thing to heaven on earth for some.

The historical pageant continues with the 1,001 splendors of the baroque era: glittering palaces, jewel-studded churches, and Caravaggio masterpieces. Arrive refreshed—thanks to an espresso at Antico Caffè Greco—at the foot of the Spanish Steps, where the picturesque world of the classic Grand Tour (peopled by such spirits as John Keats and Tosca) awaits you.

Thankfully, Rome provides delightful ways to catch your historic breath along the way: a walk through the cobblestone valleys of Trastevere or an hour stolen alongside a splashing Bernini fountain. Keep in mind that an uncharted ramble through the heart of the old city can be just as satisfying as the contemplation of a chapel or a trek through marbled museum corridors. No matter which aspect of Rome you end up enjoying the most, a visit to the Eternal City will live up to its name in memory.

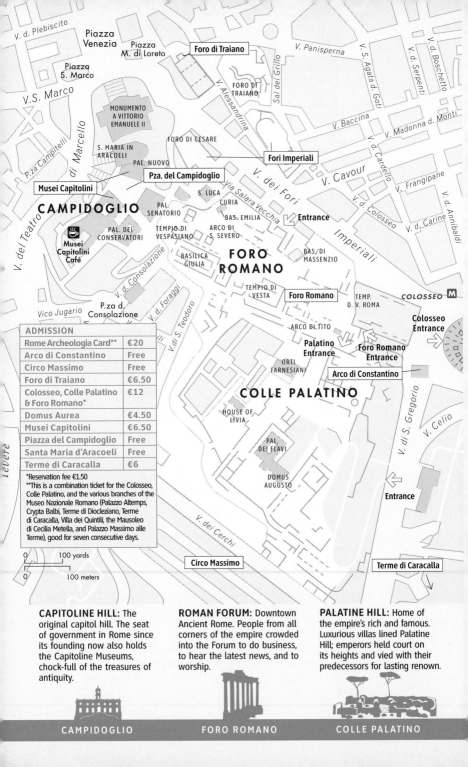

Foro di Traiano

V. d. Plebiscito

Piazza Venezia

Piazza M. di Loreto

Piazza S. Marco

V. S. Marco

V. Panisperna

V. S. Agata d. Goti

V. d. Serpenti

V. d. Boschetto

FORO DI TRAIANO

Sal. del Grillo

MONUMENTO A VITTORIO EMANUELE II

V. Baccina

V. Madonna d. Monti

P.za Campitelli

di Marcello

FORO DI CESARE

S. MARIA IN ARACOELI

PAL. NUOVO

Fori Imperiali

V. dei Fori

V. Cavour

V. d. Cardello

V. Frangipane

Pza. del Campidoglio

Musei Capitolini

CAMPIDOGLIO

PAL. SENATORIO

S. LUCA

Via Salara Vecchia

CURIA

BAS. EMILIA

Entrance

V. d. Colosseo

V. d. Carine

V. d. Annibaldi

V. del Teatro

Musei Capitolini Café

PAL. DEI CONSERVATORI

TEMPIO DI VESPASIANO

ARCO DI S. SEVERO

BASILICA GIULIA

FORO ROMANO

BAS. DI MASSENZIO

Imperiali

V. d. Consolazione

TEMPIO DI VESTA

Foro Romano

TEMP. D. V. ROMA

COLOSSEO Ⓜ

Vico Jugario

P.za d. Consolazione

V. d. Foraggi

V. d. S. Teodoro

ARCO DI TITO

Palatino **Entrance**

Foro Romano Entrance

Colosseo Entrance

ORTI FARNESIANI

Arco di Constantino

COLLE PALATINO

HOUSE OF LIVIA

Tevere

PAL. DEI FLAVI

V. di S. Gregorio

V. Celio

DOMUS AUGUSTO

Entrance

V. dei Cerchi

Circo Massimo

Terme di Caracalla

ADMISSION	
Rome Archeologia Card**	€20
Arco di Constantino	Free
Circo Massimo	Free
Foro di Traiano	€6.50
Colosseo, Colle Palatino & Foro Romano*	€12
Domus Aurea	€4.50
Musei Capitolini	€6.50
Piazza del Campidoglio	Free
Santa Maria d'Aracoeli	Free
Terme di Caracalla	€6

*Reservation fee €1.50
**This is a combination ticket for the Colosseo, Colle Palatino, and the various branches of the Museo Nazionale Romano (Palazzo Altemps, Crypta Balbi, Terme di Diocleziano, Terme di Caracalla, Villa dei Quintili, the Mausoleo di Cecilia Metella, and Palazzo Massimo alle Terme), good for seven consecutive days.

0   100 yards
0   100 meters

CAPITOLINE HILL: The original capitol hill. The seat of government in Rome since its founding now also holds the Capitoline Museums, chock-full of the treasures of antiquity.

ROMAN FORUM: Downtown Ancient Rome. People from all corners of the empire crowded into the Forum to do business, to hear the latest news, and to worship.

PALATINE HILL: Home of the empire's rich and famous. Luxurious villas lined Palatine Hill; emperors held court on its heights and vied with their predecessors for lasting renown.

CAMPIDOGLIO   FORO ROMANO   COLLE PALATINO

ANCIENT ROME
GLORIES OF
THE CAESARS

Time has reduced ancient Rome to fields of silent ruins, but the powerful impact of what happened here, of the genius and power that made Rome the center of the Western world, echoes across the millennia.

In this one compact area of the city, you can step back into the Rome of Cicero, Julius Caesar, and Virgil. Walk along the streets they knew, cool off in the shade of the Colosseum that loomed over the city, and see the sculptures poised above their piazzas. At the end of a day of exploring, climb one of the famous seven hills and watch the sun set over what was once the heart of the civilized world.

Today, this part of Rome, more than any other, is a perfect example of that layering of historic eras, the overlapping of ages, of religions, of a past that is very much a part of the present. Christian churches rise from the foundations of ancient pagan temples. An immense marble monument to a 19th-century king shares a square with a medieval palace built by a pope. Still, the history and memory of ancient Rome dominate the area. It's fitting that in the aftermath of centuries of such pageantry Percy Bysshe Shelley and Edward Gibbon reflected here on the meaning of *sic transit gloria mundi* (so passes away the glory of the world).

KEY

☕ Cafe / Restaurant

COLOSSEUM: Gladiators fought for the chance to live another day on the floor of the Colosseum, iconic symbol of ancient Rome.

CAMPIDOGLIO

The Capitoline Museums are closed on Monday. Late evening is an option for this area. Though the Santa Maria d'Aracoeli church is closed, the museums are open until 9 PM, and the views of the city lights and the illuminated Victor Emmanuel II monument and the Foro Romano are striking.

CLIMB MICHELANGELO'S DRAMATIC RAMP TO THE SUMMIT of one of Rome's seven hills, the Campidoglio (also known as Capitoline Hill), for views across the rooftops of modern Rome in one direction and across the ruins of ancient Rome in the other. Check out the stellar Musei Capitolini, crammed with a collection of masterpieces rivaled only by the Vatican museums.

★ **Piazza del Campidoglio.** In Michelangelo's piazza at the top of the Campidoglio stands a bronze equestrian statue of Marcus Aurelius (AD 121–180). A legend foretells that some day the statue's original gold surface will return, heralding the end of the world. Pending the arrival of that day, the original 2nd century statue was moved inside the Musei Capitolini; a copy sits on the piazza. Stand with your back to it to survey central Rome.

The Campidoglio, the site of the Roman Empire's first and holiest temples, had fallen into ruin by the Middle Ages and was called *Monte Caprino* (Goat Hill). In 1536 Pope Paul III (1468–1549) decided to restore its grandeur for the triumphal entry into the city of Charles V (1500–1558), the Holy Roman Emperor. He called upon Michelangelo to create the staircase ramp, the buildings and facades

on the square, the pavement decoration, and the pedestal for the bronze statue.

The two buildings that make up the **Musei Capitolini** are on the piazza, flanking the **Palazzo Senatorio**. The Campidoglio has always been the seat of Rome's government; its Latin name is the root for the word capitol. Today, Rome's city hall occupies the Palazzo Senatorio. Head to the vantage points in the belvederes on the sides of the palazzo for great views of the ruins of ancient Rome.

★ **Musei Capitolini** (Capitoline Museums). Housed in the twin Palazzi del Museo Capitolino and Palazzo dei Conservatori buildings, this is a greatest hits collection of Roman art through the ages, from the ancients to the baroque.

The **Palazzi del Museo Capitolino** contains hundreds of Roman busts of phi-

AN EMPEROR CHEAT SHEET

OCTAVIAN/AUGUSTUS (27 BC–AD 14)

After the death of Julius Caesar, Octavian gained control of Rome after a series of battles that culminated with the defeat of Antony and Cleopatra at Actium. Later known as Caesar Augustus, he was Rome's first emperor. His rule began a 200-year period of peace known as the Pax Romana.

Colle Palatino

CALIGULA (AD 37–41)

Caligula was tremendously popular when he came to power at the age of 25, but he very soon became infamous for his excessive cruelty, immorality, and erratic behavior. His contemporaries universally considered him to be insane. He was murdered by his own guard within four years.

losophers and emperors—a fascinating Who's Who of the ancient world. Forty-eight Roman emperors are represented. Unlike the Greeks, whose portraits are idealized, the Romans preferred the warts-and-all school of representation. Other notable sculptures include the poignant *Dying Gaul* and the regal *Capitoline Venus*. In the Capitolino courtyard is a gigantic, reclining sculpture of Oceanus, found in the Roman Forum and later dubbed *Marforio*. This was one of Rome's "talking statues" to which citizens from the 1500s to the 1900s affixed anonymous satirical verses and notes of political protest. Opened in 2007, the Esedra di Marco Aurelio displays the famous bronze equestrian statue of emperor Marcus Aurelius (180 AD).

Lining the courtyard of the **Palazzo dei Conservatori** are the colossal fragments of a head, leg, foot, and hand—all that remains of the famous statue of the emperor Constantine the Great, who believed that Rome's future lay with Christianity. These immense effigies were much in vogue in the later days of the Roman Empire. The renowned symbol of Rome, the *Capitoline Wolf*, a 6th-century BC Etruscan bronze, holds a place of honor in the museum; the suckling twins were added during the Renaissance to adapt the statue to the legend of Romulus and Remus. The Palazzo also contains some of baroque painting's great masterpieces, including Caravaggio's *La Buona Ventura* (1595) and *San Giovanni Battista* (1602), Peter Paul Rubens's *Romulus and Remus* (1614), and Pietro da Cortona's sumptuous portrait of Pope Urban VIII (1627). When museum fatigue sets in, enjoy the view and refreshments on a large open terrace in the Palazzo dei Conservatoria. ☎ 06/39967800 *or* 06/82059127 ⊕ *www.pierreci.it* ☽ *Tues.–Sun. 9–8.*

Santa Maria d'Aracoeli. Seemingly endless, steep stairs climb from Piazza Venezia to the Santa Maria. There are 15th-century frescoes by Pinturicchio (1454–1513) in the first chapel on the right. ⊠ *Via del Teatro di Marcello* ☽ *Oct.–May, daily 7–noon and 4–6; June–Sept., daily 7–noon and 4–6:30.*

NERO (AD 54–68)

Nero is infamous as a violent persecutor of Christians. He also murdered his wife, his mother, and countless others. Although it's not certain whether he actually fiddled as Rome burned in AD 64, he was well known as a singer and a composer of music.

Domus Aurea

DOMITIAN (AD 81–96)

The first emperor to declare himself "Dominus et Deus" (Lord and God), he stripped away power from the Senate. After his death, the Senate retaliated by declaring him "Damnatio Memoriae" (his name and image were erased from all public records).

Colle Palatino

FORO ROMANO

⏱ TIMING TIPS

It takes about an hour to explore the Roman Forum. There are entrances on the Via dei Fori Imperiali and near the Colosseum. Another hour's walk will cover the Imperial Fora. You can reserve tickets online or by phone—operators speak English. If you are buying tickets in person, remember there are shorter lines here than at the Colosseum and the ticket is good for both sights.

EXPERIENCE THE ENDURING ROMANCE OF THE FORUM. Wander among its lonely columns and great, broken fragments of sculpted marble and stone— once temples, palaces, and shops crowded with people from all corners of the known world. This was the heart of ancient Rome and a symbol of the values that inspired Rome's conquest of an empire.

★ **Foro Romano** (Roman Forum). Built in a marshy valley between the Capitoline and Palatine hills, the Forum was the civic core of Republican Rome, the austere era that preceded the hedonism of the emperors. The Forum was the political, commercial, and religious center of Roman life. Hundreds of years of plunder and the tendency of later Romans to carry off what was left of the better building materials reduced it to the series of ruins you see today. Archaeological digs continue to uncover more about the sight; bear in mind that what you see are the ruins not of one period but of almost 900 years, from about 500 BC to AD 400.

The **Basilica Giulia**, which owes its name to Julius Caesar who had it built, was where the Centumviri, the hundred-or-so judges forming the civil court, met to hear cases. The open space before it was the core of the forum proper and prototype of Italy's famous piazzas. Let your imagination dwell on Mark Antony (circa 81 BC–30 BC), who delivered the funeral address in Julius Caesar's honor from the rostrum left of the **Arco di Settimio Severo**. This arch, one of the grandest of all antiquity, was built several hundred years later in AD 203 to celebrate the victory of the emperor Severus (AD 146–211) over the Parthians, and was topped by a bronze equestrian statuary group with six horses. You can explore the reconstruction of the large brick senate hall, the **Curia**; three Corinthian columns (a favorite of 19th-century poets) are all that remains of the **Tempio di Vespasiano**. In the **Tempio di Vesta**, six highly privileged vestal virgins kept the sacred fire, a tradition that dated back to the very earliest days of Rome, when guarding the community's precious fire was essential to its well-being. The cleaned and restored **Arco di Tito**, which stands in a slightly

AN EMPEROR CHEAT SHEET

TRAJAN (AD 98–117)

Trajan, from Southern Spain, was the first Roman emperor not born in Italy. He enlarged the empire's boundaries to include modern-day Romania, Armenia, and Upper Mesopotamia.

Colonna di Traiano

HADRIAN (AD 117–138)

He expanded the empire in Asia and the Middle East. He's best known for designing and rebuilding the Pantheon, constructing a majestic villa at Tivoli, and initiating myriad other constructions across the empire, including the famed wall across Britain.

Pantheon, in Baroque Rome

elevated position on a spur of the Palatine Hill, was erected in AD 81 to celebrate the sack of Jerusalem 10 years earlier, after the great Jewish revolt. A famous relief shows the captured contents of Herod's Temple—including its huge seven-branched menorah—being carried in triumph down Rome's Via Sacra. Making sense of the ruins isn't always easy; consider renting an audio guide (€4) or buying a booklet that superimposes an image of the Forum in its heyday over a picture of it today. Guided tours in English usually begin at 10:30 AM. In summer the Forum is sometimes open for midnight (guided) tours—look for signs at the entrance or ask at your hotel. ☎ *06/39967700* ⊕ *www. pierreci.it* ⊗ *Daily, May–Oct. 8:30–7:30, Nov.–April 8:30–4:30.*

THE OTHER FORA

Fori Imperiali (Imperial Fora). These five grandly conceived squares flanked with columnades and temples were built by the emperors Caesar, Augustus, Vespasian, Nerva, and Trajan. The original Roman Forum, built up over 500 years of Republican Rome, had grown crowded, and Julius Caesar was the first to attempt to rival it. He built the **Foro di Cesare** (Forum of Caesar), including a temple dedicated to himself and the goddess Minerva. Four later emperors followed his lead, creating their own fora. The grandest was the **Foro di Traiano** (Forum of Trajan) a veritable city unto itself built by Trajan (AD 53–117). The adjoining Mercati Traianei (Trajan's Markets), a huge multilevel brick complex of shops, walkways, and terraces, was one of the marvels of the ancient world. In the 20th century, Benito Mussolini built the Via dei Fori Imperiali directly through the Imperial Fora area. Marble and bronze maps on the wall along the avenue portray the extent of the Roman Empire and Republic, and many of the remains of the Imperial Fora lay buried beneath its surface.

Colonna di Traiano (Trajan's Column). The ashes of Trajan were buried inside the base of this column (the ashes have since been removed). Remarkable reliefs spiral up its sides, celebrating his military campaigns in Dacia (Romania). The column has stood in what was once the Forum of Trajan since AD 113. ☎ *06/69780532* ⊗ *Tues.–Sun. 9–6.*

MARCUS AURELIUS (AD 161–180)

Remembered as a humanitarian emperor, Marcus Aurelius was a Stoic philosopher and his *Meditations* are still read today. Nonetheless, he was an aggressive leader devoted to expanding the empire.

Piazza del Campidoglio

CONSTANTINE I (AD 306–337)

Constantine changed the course of history by legalizing Christianity. He legitimized the once-banned religion and paved the way for the papacy in Rome. Constantine also founded Constantinople, an Imperial capital in the East.

Arco di Constantino

COLLE PALATINO

A stroll on the Palatino, with a visit to the Museo Palatino, takes about two hours. The Lupercal shrine dedicated to Romulus and Remus, newly unearthed in 2007, is scheduled to open to the public by 2010. The Colle Palatino entrances are in the Roman Forum and on Via S. Gregorio.

IT ALL BEGAN HERE. ACCORDING TO LEGEND, ROMULUS, THE FOUNDER OF ROME, lived on the Colle Palatino (Palatine Hill). It was an exclusive address in ancient Rome, where emperors built palaces upon the slopes. Tour the Palatine's hidden corners and shady lanes, take a welcome break from the heat in its peaceful gardens, and enjoy a view of the Circo Massimo fit for an emperor.

★ **Colle Palatino** (Palatine Hill). A lane known as the Clivus Palatinus, paved with worn stones that were once trod by emperors and their slaves, climbs from the Forum area to a site that historians identify with Rome's earliest settlement. The legend goes that the infant twins Romulus and Remus were nursed by a she-wolf on the banks of the Tiber and adopted by a shepherd. Encouraged by the gods to build a city, the twins chose this site in 735 BC, fortifying it with a wall that archaeologist Rudolfo Lanciani identified in the late 19th century when digging on Palatine Hill.

During the Republican era the hill was an important religious center, housing the Temple of Cybele and the Temple of Victory, as well as an exclusive residential area. Cicero, Catiline, Crassus, and Agrippa all had homes here. Augustus was born on the hill, and as he rose in power, he built libraries, halls, and temples here; the **House of Livia,** reserved for his wife, is best preserved. Emperor Tiberius was the first to build a palace here; others followed. The structures most visible today date back to the late 1st century AD, when the Palatine experienced an extensive remodeling under Emperor Domitian. His architects put up two separate palaces, the **Domus Augustana** and the **Domus Livia.** During the Renaissance, the powerful Farnese family built gardens atop the ruins overlooking the Forum. Known as the **Orti Farnesiani,** they were Europe's first botanical gardens. The **Museo Palatino** charts the history of the hill. Splendid sculptures, frescoes, and mosaic intarsia from various imperial buildings are on display. ☎ *06/39967700* ⊕ *www.pierreci.it* ⏱ *Tues.–Sun. 9–1 hr before sunset.*

THE RISE AND FALL OF ANCIENT ROME

ca. 800 BC	Rise of Etruscan city-states.
510	Foundation of the Roman republic; expulsion of Etruscans from Roman territory.
343	Roman conquest of Greek colonies in Campania.
264–241	First Punic War (with Carthage): increased naval power helps Rome gain control of southern Italy and then Sicily.
218–200	Second Punic War: Hannibal's attempted conquest of Italy, using elephants, is eventually crushed.

218 BC

NEAR THE COLLE PALATINO

Circo Massimo (Circus Maximus). Ancient Rome's oldest and largest racetrack lies in the natural hollow between Palatine and Aventine hills. From the imperial box in the palace on Palatine Hill, emperors could look out over the oval course. Stretching about 650 yards from end to end, the Circus Maximus could hold more than 300,000 spectators. On certain occasions there were as many as 24 chariot races a day, and competitions could last for 15 days. The central ridge was the sight of two Egyptian obelisks (now in the Piazza del Popolo and Piazza San Giovanni in Laterano). Check out the panoramic views of the Circus Maximus from the Palatine Hill's Belvedere. You can also see the green slopes of the Aventine and Celian hills, as well as the bell tower of Santa Maria in Cosmedin.

Terme di Caracalla (Baths of Caracalla). For the Romans, public baths were much more than places to wash. The baths also had recital halls, art galleries, libraries, massage rooms, sports grounds, and gardens. Even the smallest public baths had at least some of these amenities, and in the capital of the Roman Empire, they were provided on a lavish scale. Ancient Rome's most beautiful and luxurious public baths were opened by the emperor Caracalla in AD 217 and were used until the 6th century.

Taking a bath was a long and complex process, and a social activity first and foremost. Remember, too, that for all their sophistication, the Romans didn't have soap. You began by sweating in the *sudatoria*, small rooms resembling saunas. From these you moved on to the *calidarium* for the actual business of washing, using a *strigil*, or scraper, to get the dirt off. Next was the *tepidarium*, where you gradually cooled down. Finally, you splashed around in the *frigidarium*, the only actual "bath" in the place, in essence a cold water swimming pool. There was a nominal admission fee, often waived by officials and emperors wishing to curry favor with the plebeians. The baths' functioning depended on the slaves who cared for the clients and stoked the fires that heated the water. ☎*06/39967700* ⊕ *www.pierreci.it* ☉ *Tues.–Sun. 9 AM–1 hr hour before sunset, Mon. 9–2.*

150 BC	Roman Forum begins to take shape as the principal civic center in Italy.
146	Third Punic War: Rome razes city of Carthage and emerges as the dominant Mediterranean force.
133	Rome rules entire Mediterranean Basin except Egypt.
49	Julius Caesar conquers Gaul.
44	Julius Caesar is assassinated.
27	Rome's Imperial Age begins; Octavian (now named Augustus) becomes the first emperor and is later deified. The Augustan Age is celebrated in the works of Virgil (70 BC–AD 19), Ovid (43 BC–AD 17), Livy (59 BC–AD 17), and Horace (65–8 BC).

44 BC

COLOSSEO

You can give the Colosseum a cursory look in about 30 minutes, but it deserves at least an hour. Make reservations by phone (there are English-speaking operators) or online at least a day in advance to avoid long lines. Or buy your ticket for the Colosseum at the Roman Forum, where the lines are usually shorter.

LEGEND HAS IT THAT AS LONG AS THE COLOSSEUM STANDS, ROME WILL STAND; and when Rome falls, so will the world. No visit to Rome is complete without a trip to the obstinate oval that has been the iconic symbol of the city for centuries.

★**Colosseo.** A program of games and shows lasting 100 days celebrated the opening of the massive and majestic Colosseum in AD 80. On the opening day alone, 5,000 wild beasts perished. More than 70,000 spectators could sit within the arena's 573-yard circumference, which had marble facing, hundreds of statues for decoration, and a *velarium*—an ingenious system of sail-like awnings rigged on ropes manned by imperial sailors—to protect the audience from the sun and rain. Before the imperial box, gladiators would salute the emperor and cry, "*Ave, imperator, morituri te salutant*" ("Hail, emperor, men soon to die salute you"); it is said that when one day they heard the emperor Claudius respond, "Or maybe not," they were so offended that they called a strike.

Originally known as the Flavian Amphitheater, it took the name Colosseum after a truly colossal gilt bronze statue of Nero that stood nearby. Gladiator combat and staged animal hunts ended by the 6th century. The arena later served as a quarry from which materials were looted to build Renaissance churches and palaces. Finally, it was declared sacred by the Vatican in memory of the many Christians believed martyred here. (Scholars now maintain that Christians met their death elsewhere.) During the 19th century, romantic poets lauded the glories of the ruins when viewed by moonlight. Now its arches glow at night with mellow golden spotlights—less romantic, perhaps, but still impressive.

Expect long lines at the entrance and actors dressed as gladiators who charge a hefty fee to pose for pictures. Once inside you can walk around much of the outer ring of the structure and look down into the exposed passages under what was once the arena floor, now represented by a thin gangway and a small stage at one end. Climb the steep stairs for panoramic views in the

THE RISE AND FALL OF ANCIENT ROME

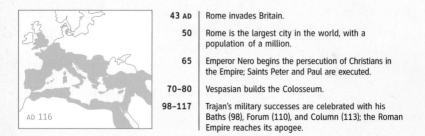

AD 116

43 AD	Rome invades Britain.
50	Rome is the largest city in the world, with a population of a million.
65	Emperor Nero begins the persecution of Christians in the Empire; Saints Peter and Paul are executed.
70–80	Vespasian builds the Colosseum.
98–117	Trajan's military successes are celebrated with his Baths (98), Forum (110), and Column (113); the Roman Empire reaches its apogee.

Colosseum and out to the Forum and Arch of Constantine. A museum space on the upper floor holds temporary archaeological exhibits. ☎ 06/7005469, 06/39967700 *reservations* ⊕ *www.pierreci.it* ☽ *Daily. 8:30–1 hr before sunset.*

Arco di Costantino. The largest (69 feet high, 85 feet long, 23 feet wide) and the best preserved of Rome's triumphal arches was erected in AD 315 to celebrate the victory of the emperor Constantine (280–337) over Maxentius (died 312). It was just before this battle that Constantine, the emperor who converted Rome to Christianity, had a vision of a cross in the heavens and heard the words "In this sign, thou shalt conquer."

NEAR THE COLOSSEO
Domus Aurea. Nero's "Golden House," after further restoration has now reopened—admission is by guided tour only. The site gives a good sense of the excesses of Imperial Rome. After fire destroyed much of the city in AD 64, Nero took advantage of the resulting open space to construct a lavish palace so large that it spread over four of Rome's seven hills. It

had a facade of pure gold, seawater piped into the baths, decorations of mother-of-pearl, and vast gardens. Not much has survived of all this; a good portion of the building and grounds was buried under the public works with which subsequent emperors sought to make reparation to the Roman people for Nero's phenomenal greed. As a result, the site of the Domus Aurea itself remained unknown for many centuries. A few of Nero's original halls were discovered underground at the end of the 15th century. Raphael (1483–1520) was one of the artists who had themselves lowered into the rubble-filled rooms, which resembled grottoes. The artists copied the original painted Roman decorations, barely visible by torchlight, and scratched their names on the ceilings. Raphael later used these models—known as *grotesques* because they were found in the so-called grottoes—in his decorative motifs for the Vatican Loggia.

The palace remains impressive in scale, even if a lot of imagination is required to envision the original. ✉ *Via della Domus Aurea* ☎ *06/39967700* ⊕ *www. ticketclic.it* 🎟 *€4.50* ☽ *Tues.–Fri. 10–4.*

AD 450

238 AD	The first wave of Germanic invasions penetrates Italy.
293	Diocletian reorganizes the Empire into West and East.
330	Constantine founds a new Imperial capital (Constantinople) in the East.
410	Rome is sacked by Visigoths.
476	The last Roman emperor, Romulus Augustus, is deposed. The Roman Empire falls.

NAVONA & CAMPO: BAROQUE ROME

Long called Vecchia Roma ("Old Rome"), this time-burnished district is the city's most beautiful neighborhood. Set between the Corso and the Tiber bend, it is filled with narrow streets bearing curious names, airy piazzas, and half-hidden courtyards. Some of Rome's most coveted residential addresses are nestled here. So, too, are the ancient Pantheon and the medieval square of Campo de' Fiori, but the spectacular, over-the-top baroque monuments of the 16th and 17th centuries predominate.

The hub of the district is the queen of squares, Piazza Navona—a cityscape adorned with the most eyeknocking fountain by Gian Lorenzo Bernini, father of the baroque. Streets running off the square lead to many historic must-sees, including noble churches by Borromini and Caravaggio's greatest paintings at San Luigi dei Francesi. This district has been an integral part of the city since ancient times, and its position between the Vatican and Lateran palaces, both seats of papal rule, put it in the mainstream of Rome's development from the Middle Ages onward. Craftsmen, shopkeepers, and famed artists toiled in the shadow of the huge palaces built to consolidate the power of leading figures in the papal court. Artisans and artists still live here, but their numbers are diminishing as the district becomes increasingly posh and—so critics say—"Disneyfied." But three of the liveliest piazzas in Rome, Piazza Navona, Piazza del Pantheon, and the Campo de' Fiori, are lodestars in a constellation of some of Rome's most authentic cafés, stores, and wine bars.

GETTING HERE   To bus it from Termini rail station or the Vatican, take the No. 40 Express or the No. 64 and get off at Largo Torre Argentina, a 10-minute stroll to either Campo dei Fiori or Piazza Navona or take little electric No. 116 from Via Veneto past the Spanish Steps to Campo de' Fiori.

THE MAIN ATTRACTIONS

★ ⑩ **Campo de' Fiori.** Home to Rome's oldest (since 1490) daily outdoor produce market, this bustling square was originally used for public executions, making its name—"Field of Flowers"—a bit sardonic. In fact, the central statue commemorates the philosopher Giordano Bruno, who was burned at the stake here in 1600 by the Inquisition. Today, he frowns down upon food vendors galore, who, by early afternoon, are all gone, giving way to the square's caffès and bars which attract throngs of Rome's hip, young professionals as the hours wend their way into evening.

▌ **NEED A BREAK?**   Some of Rome's best pizza comes out of the ovens of Il Forno di Campo de' Fiori (⌖*Campo de' Fiori* ☎*06/68806662*). Choose pizza *bianca*, topped with olive oil, or *rossa*, with tomato sauce. Move to the annex next door to have your warm pizza filled with prosciutto and figs, or other mouthwatering combinations.

⑥ **Palazzo Altemps.** Containing some of the finest ancient Roman statues in the world, this collection formerly formed the core of the Museo

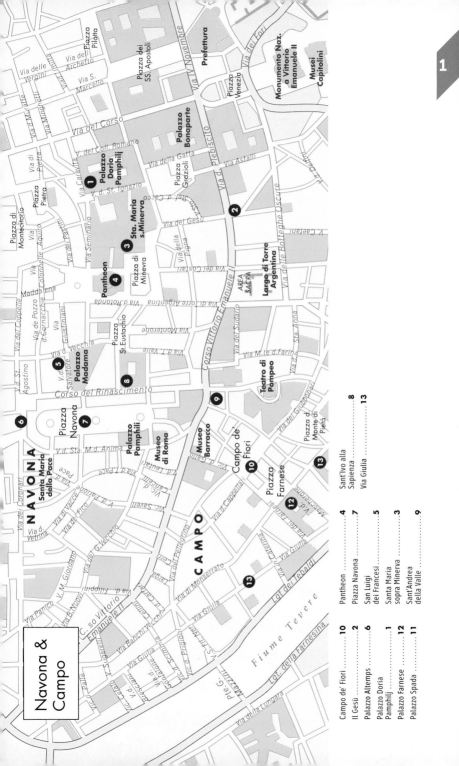

Navona & Campo

Nazionale Romano. As of 1995, it was moved to these new, suitably grander digs. The palace's sober exterior belies a magnificence that appears as soon as you walk into the majestic courtyard. Set within some gorgeously frescoed, 16th-century rooms are an array of noted antiquities. Look for two works in the famed Ludovisi collection: the large, intricately carved Ludovisi Sarcophagus and *Galata,* a poignant work portraying a barbarian

warrior who chooses death for himself and his wife rather than humiliation by the enemy. ⊠*Piazza Sant'Apollinare 46, near Piazza Navona* ☎*06/39967700* ⬚*€6.50* ⊙*Tues.–Sun. 9–7:45.*

⑫ **Palazzo Farnese.** The most beautiful Renaissance palace in Rome, the Palazzo Farnese is noted for the grandeur of its rooms, notably the Galleria Carracci, whose ceiling is to the baroque age what the Sistine ceiling is to the Renaissance. The Farnese family rose to great power and wealth during the Renaissance, in part because of the favor Pope Alexander VI and Pope Paul III paid to the family. The uppermost frieze decorations and main window overlooking the piazza are the work of Michelangelo, who also designed part of the courtyard, as well as the graceful arch over Via Giulia at the back. The showpiece of the palace is the Galleria Carracci vault painted by Annibale Carracci between 1597 and 1604, depicting the loves of the pagan gods in a swirling style that announced the birth of the baroque style. Also eye-popping is the Salon of Hercules, with its massive replica of the ancient Farnese Hercules. Now housing the French Embassy, the historic salons can be seen on free tours (in French and Italian only) four times a week. You'll need to send a letter or e-mail to reserve tickets, one to four months in advance (depending on peak season visit or not), specifying the number in your party, when you wish to visit, and a local phone number, for confirmation a few days before the visit. ⊠*French Embassy, Servizio Culturale, Piazza Farnese 67, near Piazza Navona* ☎*06/686011* ✐*visitefarnese@france-italien.it* ⬚*Free* ⊙*By appointment only.*

⑪ **Palazzo Spada.** An impressive stuccoed facade on Piazza Capo di Ferro, west of Piazza Farnese, fronts an equally magnificent inner courtyard. On the southeast side of the inner courtyard, the gallery designed by Borromini creates an elaborate optical illusion, appearing to be much longer than it really is. On the first floor there are paintings and sculptures that belonged to Cardinale Bernardino Spada, an art connoisseur who collected works by Italian and Flemish masters. Note that the palazzo occasionally closes in the afternoon because of staff shortages. ⊠*Piazza Capo di Ferro 13, near Campo de' Fiori, Campo* ☎*06/6832409* ⬚*www.galleriaborghese.it* ⬚*€5* ⊙*Tues.–Sun. 8:30–7:30.*

④ Pantheon. One of Rome's most impressive and best-preserved ancient
Fodor's Choice monuments, the Pantheon is particularly close to the hearts of Romans.
★ The emperor Hadrian designed it around ad 120 and had it built on
the site of an earlier temple that had been damaged by fire. Although
the sheer size of the Pantheon is impressive (until 1960 the dome was
the largest ever built), what's most striking is its tangible sense of harmony. In large part this feeling is the result of the building's symmetrical
design: the height of the dome is equal to the diameter of the circular
interior. The oculus, or opening in the dome, is meant to symbolize the
all-seeing "Eye of Heaven"; in practice, it illuminates the building and
lightens the heavy stone ceiling. The original bronze doors have survived more than 1,800 years, centuries longer than the interior's rich
gold ornamentation, which was plundered by popes and emperors. Art
lovers can pay homage to the tomb of Raphael, who is buried in an
ancient sarcophagus under the altar of Madonna del Sasso. ⊠*Piazza
della Rotonda, Navona* ☎*06/68300230* 🕾*Free* ⊗*Mon.–Sat. 8:30–
7:30, Sun. 9–5:30.*

★ ⓒ **⑦ Piazza Navona.** With its carefree air of the days when it was the scene
of Roman circus games, medieval jousts, and 17th-century carnivals,
the beautiful Piazza Navona today often attracts fashion photogra-
phers on shoots and Romans out for their *passeggiata* (evening stroll).
Bernini's splashing **Fontana dei Quattro Fiumi** (Fountain of the Four
Rivers), with an enormous rock squared off by statues representing the
four corners of the world, makes a fitting centerpiece. Behind the fountain is the church of **Sant'Agnese in Agone,** an outstanding example
of baroque architecture built by the Pamphilj Pope Innocent X. The
facade—a wonderfully rich mélange of bell towers, concave spaces, and
dovetailed stone and marble—is by Borromini, a contemporary and
rival of Bernini, and by Carlo Rainaldi (1611–91). One story has it that
the Bernini statue nearest the church, which represents the River Plate,
has its hand up before its eye because it can't bear the sight of the Borromini facade. Though often repeated, the story is fiction: the facade
was built after the fountain. From early December through January 6
a Christmas market fills the square with games, Nativity scenes (some
well crafted, many not), and multiple versions of the Befana, the ugly
but good witch who brings candy and toys to Italian children on Epiphany. (Her name is a corruption of the Italian word for "epiphany,"
Epifania.) ⊠*Junction of Via della Cuccagna, Corsia Agonale, Via di
Sant'Agnese, and Via Agonale, Navona*

★ **⑤ San Luigi dei Francesi.** A pilgrimage spot for art lovers everywhere, San
Luigi is home to the Cerasi Chapel, adorned with three stunningly dramatic works by Caravaggio (1571–1610), the baroque master of the
heightened approach to light and dark. Set in the Chapel of St. Matthew (at the altar end of the left nave), they were commissioned for
San Luigi, the official church of Rome's French colony. The inevitable
coin machine will light up his *Calling of St. Matthew, Matthew and the
Angel,* and *Matthew's Martyrdom,* seen from left to right, and Caravaggio's mastery of light takes it from there. When painted, they caused
considerable consternation to the clergy of San Luigi, who thought the

CLOSE UP

Going Baroque

Flagrantly emotional, heavily expressive, and visually sensuous, the 17th-century artistic movement known as the baroque was born in Rome. It was the creation of three geniuses: the sculptor and architect Gianlorenzo Bernini (1598–1680), the painter and architect Pietro da Cortona (1596–1669), and the architect and sculptor Francesco Borromini (1599–1667). From the drama found in the artists' paintings to the jewel-laden, gold-on-gold detail of 17th-century Roman palaces, baroque style was intended

both to shock and delight by upsetting the placid, "correct" rules of proportion and scale in the Renaissance. If a building looks theatrical—like a stage or a theater, especially with curtains being drawn back—it is usually baroque. Look for over-the-top, curvaceous marble work, trompe l'oeil, allusions to other art, and high drama to identify the style. Baroque's appeal to the emotions made it a powerful weapon in the hands of the Counter-Reformation.

artist's dramatically realistic approach was scandalously disrespectful. But these paintings did to 17th-century art what Picasso's *Demoiselles d'Avignon* did to the 20th century. ⊠*Piazza San Luigi dei Francesi, Navona* ☎*06/688271* ◷*Fri.–Wed. 7–12:30 and 3:30–7.*

❸ Santa Maria sopra Minerva. Michelangelo's *Risen Christ* and the tomb of the gentle 15th-century artist Fra Angelico are two noted sights in the only Gothic-style church in Rome. Have some coins handy to light up the Cappella Carafa in the right transept, where exquisite 15th-century frescoes by Filippino Lippi (circa 1457–1504) are well worth the small investment. (Lippi's most famous student was Botticelli.) In front of the church, Bernini's charming elephant bearing an Egyptian obelisk has an inscription on the base stating that it takes a strong mind to sustain solid wisdom. ⊠*Piazza della Minerva, Navona* ☎*06/6793926* ◷*Daily 7–noon and 4–7.*

★ **⓭ Via Giulia.** Named after Pope Julius II and serving for more than four centuries as the "salon of Rome," this street—running between Piazza Farnese and the Tiber—is still the address of choice for Roman aristocrats and rich foreigners. Built with funds garnered by taxing prostitutes, the street is lined with elegant palaces, including the Palazzo Falconieri, old churches (one, San Eligio, reputedly designed by Raphael himself), and, in springtime, glorious hanging wisteria. The area around Via Giulia is a wonderful place to wander in to get the feeling of daily life as carried on in a centuries-old setting—an experience enhanced by the dozens of antiques shops in the neighborhood. ⊠*One block east of the Tiber river, Navona*

ALSO WORTH SEEING

❷ Il Gesù. Grandmother of all baroque churches, this huge structure was designed by the architect Vignola (1507–73) to be the tangible symbol of the Jesuits, a major force in the Counter-Reformation in Europe. It remained unadorned for about 100 years, but when it finally was decorated, no expense was spared: the interior drips with lapis lazuli, precious marbles, gold, and more gold. A fantastically painted ceiling by Baciccia (1639–1709) seems to merge with the painted stucco figures at its base. St. Ignatius's apartments, reached from the side entrance of the church, are also worth a visit (afternoons only) for the trompe l'oeil frescoes and relics of the saint. ☒ *Piazza del Gesù, near Piazza Venezia, Corso* ☎ *06/3613717* ☾ *Daily 8:30–12:30 and 4–7:30.*

❾ Sant'Andrea della Valle. Topped by the second tallest dome in Rome, this huge 17th-century church looms mightily over a busy intersection. Puccini set the first act of his opera *Tosca* here; fans have been known to hire a horse-drawn carriage at night to trace the course of the opera from Sant'Andrea up Via Giulia to Palazzo Farnese—Scarpia's headquarters—to the locale of the opera's climax, Castel Sant'Angelo. Inside, above the apse, are striking frescoes depicting scenes from St. Andrew's life by the Bolognese painter Domenichino (1581–1641). ☒ *Corso Vittorio Emanuele II, Navona* ☎ *06/6861339* ☾ *Daily 7:30– noon and 4:30–7:30.*

❽ Sant'Ivo alla Sapienza. Borromini's eccentric 17th-century church has what must surely be Rome's most unusual dome—topped by a golden spiral said to have been inspired by a bee's stinger. ☒ *Corso Rinascimento 40, Navona* ☾ *Sun. 10–noon.*

CORSO & SPAGNA: PIAZZA VENEZIA TO THE SPANISH STEPS

In spirit, and in fact, this section of the city is its most grandiose. The overblown Vittoriano monument, the labyrinthine treasure-chest palaces of Rome's surviving aristocracy, even the diamond-draped denizens of Via Condotti's shops—all embody the exuberant ego of a city at the center of its own universe. Here's where you'll see ladies in furs, gobbling pastries at caffè tables, and walk through a thousand snapshots as you climb the famous Spanish Steps, admired by generations from Byron to Versace. Cultural treasures abound around here: gilded 17th-century churches, glittering palaces, and the greatest example of portraiture in Rome: Velázquez's incomparable *Innocent X* at the Galleria Doria Pamphilj. Have your camera ready—along with a coin or two— for that most beloved of Rome's landmarks, the Trevi Fountain.

GETTING HERE   One of Rome's handiest subway stations, the Spagna metro station is tucked just to the left of the Spanish Steps. Buses No. 117 (from Via Veneto area) and No. 119 (from Piazza del Popolo) hum through the neighborhood.

THE MAIN ATTRACTIONS

★ **❻ Fontana di Trevi** *(Trevi Fountain).* The huge fountain designed by Nicola Salvi (1697–1751) is a whimsical rendition of mythical sea creatures amid cascades of splashing water. The fountain is the world's most spectacular wishing well: legend has it that you can ensure your return to Rome by tossing a coin into the fountain. It was featured in the 1954 film *Three Coins in the Fountain* and was the scene of Anita Ekberg's aquatic frolic in Fellini's *La Dolce Vita*. By day this is one of the most crowded sites in town; at night the spotlighted piazza feels especially festive. ⊠*Piazza di Trevi, off Via del Tritone, Corso.*

❶ Monumento a Vittorio Emanuele II. Known as the Vittoriano, this vast marble monument was erected in the late 19th century to honor Italy's first king, Vittorio Emanuele II (1820–78), and the unification of Italy. Aesthetically minded Romans have derided the oversize structure, visible from many parts of the city, calling it "the typewriter," "the wedding cake," and "the eighth hill of Rome." Whatever you think of its design, the views from the top are memorable. Here also is the **Tomb of the Unknown Soldier** with its eternal flame. A side entrance in the monument leads to the rather somber **Museo del Risorgimento,** which charts Italy's struggle for nationhood. For those not interested or able to climb the many stairs, there's now an elevator to the top (located to the right as you face the monument). Before you head up, stop at the museum entrances (to the left and right of the structure) to get a pamphlet identifying the sculpture groups on the monument itself and the landmarks you will be able to see once at the top. ⊠*Entrance at Piazza Ara Coeli, near Piazza Venezia, Corso* ☎ *06/6991718* ⊕*www. ambienterm.arti.beniculturali.it/vittoriano/index.html* ⊠ *Monument free, museum free, elevator €7* ⊙ *Tues.–Sun. 10–4.*

❾ Palazzetto Zuccaro. The real treasure at the top of the Spanish Steps is Fodor'sChoice not the somewhat dull church of Trinità dei Monti, but to the right ★ on Via Gregoriana, the street that leads off to the right of the obelisk. Shaped to form a monster's face, this Mannerist-era house was designed in 1591 by noted painter Federico Zuccaro (1540–1609). Typical of the outré style of the period, the eyes are the house's windows; the entrance portal is through the monster's mouth (this is one of the best photo-ops in Rome—have someone photograph you standing in front of the door with your own mouth gaping wide). Via Gregoriana is a real charmer and has long been one of Rome's most elegant addresses, with residents ranging from French 19th-century painters Ingres and David to famed couturier Valentino. ⊠ *Via Gregoriana 30, Spagna.*

❸ Palazzo Colonna. Inside the fabulous, private Palazzo Colonna, the 17th-century **Sala Grande**—more than 300 feet long, with bedazzling chandeliers, colored marble, and enormous paintings—is best known as the site where Audrey Hepburn met the press in *Roman Holiday.* The entrance to the picture gallery, the **Galleria Colonna,** hides behind a plain, inconspicuous door. The private palace is open to the public Saturday only; reserve ahead to get a free guided tour in English. ⊠ *Via della Pilotta 17, Corso, near Piazza di Trevi* ☎ *06/6784350* ⊕ *www. galleriacolonna.it* ⊠ *€7* ⊙ *Sept.–July, Sat. 9–1.*

★ ❹ Palazzo Doria Pamphilj. This bona fide patrician palace is still home to a princely family, which rents out many of its 1,000 rooms. You can visit the remarkably well-preserved **Galleria Doria Pamphilj** (pronounced pam-*fee*-lee), a picture-and-sculpture gallery that gives you a sense of the sumptuous living quarters. Numbered paintings (the bookshop's museum catalog comes in handy) are packed onto every available inch

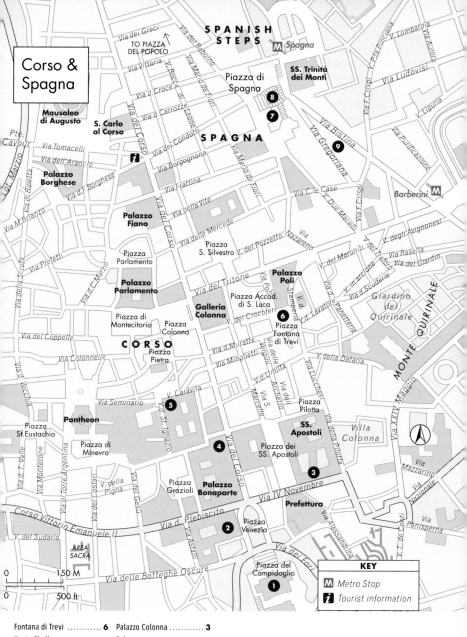

Corso & Spagna

SPANISH STEPS

M **Spagna**

Via dei Greci

TO PIAZZA DEL POPOLO

Via del Babuino

Via Vittoria

Bocca di Leone

Via Mario de' Fiori

Via d. Croce

SS. Trinità dei Monti

Piazza di Spagna

8

7

Via d. Carrozze

Via d. Carrozze

Mausoleo di Augusto

S. Carlo al Corso

SPAGNA

9

Via Bisina

Via Gregoriana

Pte. Cavour

Via Tomacelli

Via dell'Aranco

Via del Corso

Via del Condotti

Via Borgognona

Via Frattina

Via della Vite

Palazzo Borghese

Via di Ripetta

Via M. Brianzo

Via d. Borghese

i

Via C.le Case

V. Due Macelli

Barberini

M

Via F. Crispi

Via Purificazione

V. Lombardia

V. Aurora

V. Ludovisi

V Liguria

V. Pta Pinciana

Via del Corso

Palazzo Fiano

Via delle Mercede

Piazza S. Silvestro

V. del Pozzetto

Nazareno

Via del Tritone

V. degli Avignonesi

V. del Maroniti

V. del Tritone

Via Rasella

Via del Giardin

Via M.Brianzo

Via Prefetti

Via d. C.Marzo

Piazza Parlamento

Palazzo Parlamento

Piazza di Montecitorio

Piazza Colonna

Galleria Colonna

Piazza Accad. di S. Luca

V. del Crocoferi

Palazzo Poli

Stamperia

6

Piazza Fontana di Trevi

V. in arcione

V. d.Scuderie

V.d. Lavatore

Panetteria

Giardino del Quirinale

Via della Scrofa

Via della Vecchia

Via del Coppelle

Via Colonnelle

CORSO

Piazza Pietra

V.d.Muratte

Via Minghetti

Vergini

Via delle

V.d.Umilta

Via S. Marcello

Via dell'Archeto

Piazza Pilotta

V. della Dataria

V. Lucchesi

MONTE QUIRINALE

Via XXIV Maggio

Piazza St.Eustachio

Pantheon

Via Seminario

V. Caravita

St. Ignazio

5

Piazza di Minevra

Piazza di Pigna

4

Via del Corso

Piazza di SS. Apostoli

SS. Apostoli

3

Villa Colonna

Via Mazzarino

Via Nazionale

V. d. Pilotta

Piazza St.Eustachio

V. di T. Valle

Via Monterone

V. di Torre Argentina

V. di Costari

Piazza Grazioli

Palazzo Bonaparte

Via d. Gesù

Via Astalli

Via IV Novembre

Prefettura

Via Panisperna

Via di Conti

V. T. de Conti

Via Alessandrina

Corso Vittorio Emanuele II

V. del Sudario

2

Piazza Venezia

Via d. Plebiscito

Piazza del Campidoglio

1

AREA SACRA

Via delle Botteghe Oscure

Via dei Fori

0 ——— 150 M

0 ——— 500 ft

KEY

M *Metro Stop*

i *Tourist information*

of wall space. The first large salon is nearly wallpapered with paintings, and not just any paintings: on one wall, you'll find no less than three pictures by Caravaggio, including his *Magdalen* and his breathtaking early *Rest on the Flight to Egypt.* Off the gilded **Galleria degli Specchi** (Gallery of Mirrors)—reminiscent of Versailles—are the famous Velázquez portrait and the Bernini bust of the Pamphjii pope Innocent X. The audio guide by Jonathan Doria Pamphilj, the current heir, provides an intimate family history well worth listening to. ⊠ *Piazza del Collegio Romano 2, near Piazza Venezia, Corso* ☎ *06/6797323* ⊕ *www.doriapamphilj.it* ✉ *€8* ⊙ *Fri.–Wed. 10–5.*

★ ❺ **Sant'Ignazio.** Rome's largest Jesuit church, this 17th-century landmark harbors some of the most magnificent illusions typical of the baroque style. Capping the 17th-century nave is a trompe l'oeil oddity: the cupola is painted as, well, a cupola—but open at the top, and full of flying angels, saints, and heavenly dignitaries who float about in what appears to be a rosy sky above. To get the full effect of the illusionistic ceiling painted by Andrea del Pozzo (1642–1709), stand on the small disk set into the floor of the nave. The church also contains some of Rome's most splendid, jewel-encrusted altars. If you're lucky, you might catch an evening concert performed here (check the posters). Step outside the church to look at it from Filippo Raguzzini's 18th-century piazza, where the buildings, as in much baroque art, are arranged resembling a stage set. ⊠ *Piazza Sant'Ignazio, Corso* ☎ *06/6794406* ⊙ *Daily 7:30–12:15 and 3–7:15.*

★ ❽ **Spanish Steps.** That icon of postcard Rome, the Spanish Steps—called the Scalinatella di Spagna in Italian—and the Piazza di Spagna from which they ascend both get their names from the Spanish Embassy to the Vatican on the piazza, opposite the American Express office—in spite of the fact that the staircase was built with French funds in 1723. In an allusion to the church of Trinità dei Monti at the top of the hill, the staircase is divided by three landings (beautifully banked with azaleas from mid-April to mid-May). For centuries, the Scalinatella ("staircase," as natives refer to the Spanish Steps) has always welcomed tourists: 18th-century dukes and duchesses on their Grand Tour, 19th-century artists and writers in search of inspiration—among them Stendhal, Honoré de Balzac, William Makepeace Thackeray, and Byron—and today's enthusiastic hordes. The **Fontana della Barcaccia** (Fountain of the Old Boat) at the base of the steps is by Pietro Bernini, father of the famous Gianlorenzo. ⊠ *Piazza di Spagna, at head of Via Condotti Spagna*

ALSO WORTH SEEING

❼ **Keats-Shelley Memorial House.** English Romantic poet John Keats (1795–1821), famed for "Ode to a Nightingale" and "She Walks in Beauty," once lived in what is now a (very small) museum dedicated to him and his great contemporary and friend Percy Bysshe Shelley (1792–1822). You can visit his tiny rooms, at the foot of the Spanish Steps, preserved as they were when he died here. Just across the steps is Babington's Tea Shops, a relic from the 19th-century Grand Tour era and still a favorite for Rome's grande dames. ⊠ *Piazza di Spagna 26, Spagna*

☎*06/6784235* ⊕*www.keats-shelley-house.org* ▣*€3.50* ⊙ *Weekdays 9–1 and 3–6, Sat. 11–2 and 3–6.*

❷ Palazzo Venezia. A Roman landmark on the city's busiest square, this palace is best known for the balcony over the main portal, from which Mussolini gave public addresses to crowds in Piazza Venezia during the dark days of Fascism. Today it's home to a haphazard collection of mostly early-Renaissance weapons, ivories, and paintings in its grand salons; the palace also hosts touring art exhibits. ⊠*Piazza San Marco 49, near Piazza Venezia, Corso* ☎*06/32810* ⊕*www.ticketeria.it/palazzovenezia-eng.asp* ▣*€4* ⊙*Tues.–Sun. 9–7.*

PIAZZA DELLA REPUBBLICA TO QUIRINALE

This sector of Rome stretches down from the 19th-century district built up around the Piazza della Repubblica—originally laid out to serve as a monumental foyer between the Termini rail station and the rest of the city—and on to Il Quirinale. The highest of Rome's seven hills, it is crowned by the massive Palazzo Quirinale, once home to the popes and now Italy's presidential palace. Along the way, you can see ancient Roman sculptures, Early Christian churches, and highlights from the 16th and 17th centuries, when Rome was conquered by the baroque—and by Bernini. While Bernini's work feels omnipresent in much of the city center, the Renaissance-man range of his work is particularly notable here. The artist as architect considered the church of Sant'Andrea al Quirinale one of his best; Bernini the urban designer and waterworker is responsible for the muscle-bound sea gods who wrestle so provocatively in the fountain at the center of whirling Piazza Barberini. And Bernini the master gives religious passion a joltingly corporeal treatment in what is perhaps his greatest work, the *Ecstasy of St. Theresa,* in the church of Santa Maria della Vittoria.

GETTING HERE   Bus No. 40 will get you from Termini station to the Quirinale in two stops; from the Vatican take bus No. 64. The very busy and convenient Repubblica Metro stop is on the piazza of the same name. The Metro also stops at Piazza Barberini, near the Quirinale.

THE MAIN ATTRACTIONS

❶ Palazzo Massimo alle Terme. This 19th-century palace in neobaroque style holds part of the collections of antiquities belonging to the Museo Nazionale Romano (also exhibited in the Palazzo Altemps). Here you can see extraordinary examples of the fine mosaics and masterful paintings that decorated ancient Rome's palaces and villas. Don't miss the fresco—depicting a lush garden in bloom—that came from the villa that Livia, wife of Emperor Augustus, owned outside Rome. ⊠*Largo Villa Peretti 1, Repubblica* ☎ *06/480201* ⊕*www.pierreci.it* ▣*€8* ⊙ *Tues.–Sun. 9–7:30.*

❾ Il Quirinale. The highest of ancient Rome's seven hills, this is where ancient Romans, and later popes, built their residences in order to escape the deadly miasmas and malaria of the low-lying area around the Forum. Framing the hilltop vista, the fountain in the square has

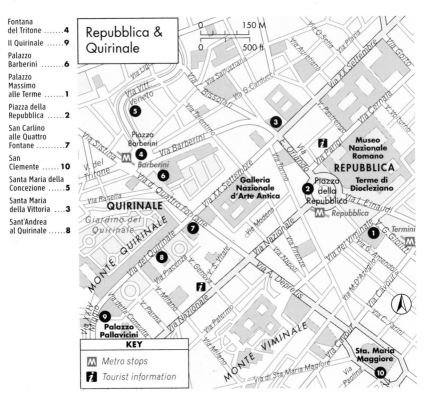

gigantic ancient statues of Castor and Pollux reining in their unruly steeds. The **Palazzo del Quirinale** passed from the popes to Italy's kings in the 19th century; it's now the official residence of the nation's president. Every day at 4 PM the ceremony of the changing of the guard at the portal includes a miniparade complete with band. ⊠*Piazza del Quirinale, near Piazza di Trevi* ☎ *06/46991* ☜*€5* ⊙ *Sept.–June, Sun. 8:30–noon.*

Directly opposite the main entrance of the Palazzo del Quirinale sits the **Scuderie Papale al Quirinale**, *the former papal stables.* Designed by Alessandro Specchi (1668–1729) in 1722, it was among the major achievements of baroque Rome. Now remodeled by eminent architect Gae Aulenti, they serve as a venue for touring art exhibits. ⊠*Piazza del Quirinale, Quirinale* ☎ *06/39967500 or 06/696271* ⊕ *www.scuderiequirinale.it* ☜ *€10* ⊙*Mon.–Thurs. 10–7, Fri. and Sat. 10–9:30.*

❻ Palazzo Barberini. Along with architect Carlo Maderno (1556–1629), Borromini helped make the splendid 17th-century Palazzo Barberini a residence worthy of Rome's leading art patron, Pope Urban VIII, who began the palace for his family in 1625. Inside, the **Galleria Nazionale d'Arte Antica** has some fine works by Caravaggio and Raphael, including the latter's portrait of his lover, *La Fornarina.* Rome's biggest ballroom is here; its ceiling, painted by Pietro da Cortona, depicts

Immortality bestowing a crown upon Divine Providence escorted by a "bomber squadron"—to quote Sir Michael Levey—of mutant bees. The museum expanded its exhibition space in late 2006, opening eight newly refurbished rooms. ⊠ *Via Barberini 18, Quirinale* ☎06/32810 ⊕*www.galleriaborghese.it* ☜€6 ⊘*Tues.–Sun. 9–6:30.*

★ ⑩ **San Clemente.** Worth the long detour, this extraordinary church-cum-archaeological site lies a good 15 blocks southeast of Piazza della Repubblica, nestled at the bottom of the Esqueline Hill and just a few blocks east of the Colosseum. This ancient reference point is apropos because San Clemente is a 12th-century church built over a 4th-century church, which in turn was constructed over a 2nd-century pagan temple to the god Mithras. The upper church holds a beautiful early-12th-century mosaic showing a cross on a gold background, surrounded by swirling green acanthus leaves teeming with little scenes of everyday life. The marble choir screens, salvaged from the 4th-century church, are decorated with Early Christian symbols: doves, vines, and fish. Off the left aisle is the **Cappella Castiglioni,** with frescoes painted around 1400 by Masolino da Panicale and note for their early use of perspective. Before you leave the upper church, take a look at the pretty cloister—evening concerts are held here in summer. From the right aisle, stairs lead down to the remains of the **4th-century church**—the vestibule is decorated with marble fragments found during the excavations and in the nave are colorful 11th-century frescoes of the life of St. Clement. Another level down is the famous **Mythraeum,** a shrine dedicated to the god Mithras, whose cult spread from Persia and gained a hold in Rome during the 2nd and 3rd centuries. Farther up the Esqueline Hill are two other churches fabled for their Early Christian mosaics, Santa Prassede (Via di Santa Prassede 9/a) and Santa Pudenziana (Via Urbana 160). ⊠ *Via San Giovanni in Laterano 108, Esquelino* ☎06/70451018 ☜€3 ⊘*Mon.–Sat. 9–noon and 3–6, Sun. 10–12:30 and 3–6.*

☾ ❺ **Santa Maria della Concezione.** In the crypt under the main Capuchin church, the bones of some 4,000 dead Capuchin monks are arranged in peculiar decorative designs around the skeletons of their kinsmen, a macabre reminder of the impermanence of earthly life. Signs declare WHAT YOU ARE, WE ONCE WERE; WHAT WE ARE, YOU SOMEDAY WILL BE. Although not for the easily spooked, the crypt is oddly beautiful. ⊠ *Via Veneto 27, Quirinale* ☎06/4871185 ☜*Donation expected* ⊘*Fri.–Wed. 9–noon and 3–6.*

❸ **Santa Maria della Vittoria.** The most famous feature here is Bernini's triumph of baroque decoration of the **Cappella Cornaro,** an exceptional fusion of architecture, painting, and sculpture. *The Ecstasy of St. Theresa,* an example of Counter-Reformation art at its most alluring, is the focal point. Bernini's audacious conceit was to model the chapel after a theater: members of the Cornaro family—sculpted in white marble—watch from theater boxes as, center stage, St. Theresa, in the throes of mystical rapture, is pierced by an angel's gilded arrow. To quote one 18th-century observer, President de Brosses: "If this is divine love, I know

Fodor's Choice
★

it well." ✉ *Via XX Settembre 17, Repubblica* ☎ *06/42740571* ⊘ *Mon.–Sat. 9–noon and 3–6, Sun. 3–6.*

ALSO WORTH SEEING

❹ **Fontana del Tritone** *(Triton Fountain).* The centerpiece of busy Piazza Barberini is Bernini's graceful fountain designed in 1637 for the sculptor's patron, Pope Urban VIII. The pope's Barberini family coat of arms, featuring bees, is at the base of the large shell. Close by is the **Fontana delle Api** (Fountain of the Bees), the last fountain designed by Bernini. ✉ *Piazza Barberini, Repubblica.*

❷ **Piazza della Repubblica.** Smog-blackened porticoes, a subway station, and a McDonald's can make this grand piazza feel a bit derelict. The racy **Fontana delle Naiadi** (Fountain of the Naiads), however, is anything but. An 1870 addition to the square, the fountain depicts voluptuous bronze ladies wrestling happily with marine monsters. In ancient times, the Piazza della Repubblica served as the entrance to the immense **Terme di Diocleziano** *(Baths of Diocletian),* an archaeological site today. Built in the 4th century AD, these were the largest and most impressive of the baths of ancient Rome, with vast halls, pools, and gardens that could accommodate 3,000 people at a time. The *aula ottagonale* (octagonal hall) now holds a sampling of the ancient sculptures unearthed here, including two beautiful bronzes. ✉ *Via Romita 8, near Termini* ☎ *06/4870690* ▣ *Free* ⊘ *Tues.–Sat. 9–2, Sun. 9–1.*

The curving ancient Roman brick facade on one side of the Piazza della Repubblica marks the church of **Santa Maria degli Angeli,** adapted by Michelangelo from the vast central chamber of the colossal baths. Look for the sundial carved on the floor. ✉ *Via Cernaia 9, Repubblica* ☎ *064880812* ⊕ *www.santamariadegliangeliroma.it* ⊘ *Mon.–Sat. 7– 6:30, Sun. 7* AM*–7:30* PM.

❼ **San Carlino alle Quattro Fontane.** In a church no larger than the base of one of the piers of St. Peter's, Borromini attained geometric architectural perfection. Characteristically, he chose a subdued white stucco for the interior decoration, so as not to distract from the form. Don't miss the cloister, which you reach through the door to the right of the altar. The exterior of the church is Borromini at his bizarre best, all curves and rippling movement. (Keep an eye out for cars whipping around the corner as you're looking.) Outside the *quattro fontane* (four fountains) frame views in four directions. ✉ *Via del Quirinale 23, Quirinale* ☎ *06/4883261* ⊘ *Weekdays 10–noon and 1–3, Sat. 10–1, Sun. noon–1.*

❽ **Sant'Andrea al Quirinale.** This small but imposing baroque church was designed and decorated by Bernini, Borromini's rival, who considered it one of his finest works. ✉ *Via del Quirinale, Piazza di Trevi* ☎ *06/4740807* ⊘ *Mon.–Sat. 8–noon and 3:30–7, Sun. 9–noon and 4–7.*

VILLA BORGHESE & PIAZZA DEL POPOLO

Touring Rome's artistic masterpieces while staying clear of its hustle and bustle can be, quite literally, a walk in the park. Some of the city's finest sights are tucked away in or next to green lawns and pedestrian piazzas, offering a breath of fresh air for sightseers, especially in the Villa Borghese park, home to the Galleria Borghese. This park—one of Rome's largest—can alleviate gallery gout by offering an oasis in which to cool off under the umbrella pine trees. If you feel like a picnic, have an *alimentare* (food shop) make you some *panini* (sandwiches) before you go; food carts within the park are overpriced. For dessert, head to a caffè on the Piazza del Popolo, one of Rome's best people-watching spots.

GETTING HERE   Electric bus No. 119 does a loop that connects Piazza del Popolo to Piazza Venezia. The No. 116, starting at the Villa Borghese museum, motors through the park. Piazza del Popolo has a metro stop of the same name.

THE MAIN ATTRACTIONS

★ ❹ **Ara Pacis Augustae** *(Altar of Augustan Peace).* This magnificent classical monument, with an exquisitely detailed frieze, was erected in 13 BC to celebrate Emperor Augustus's triumphant return from military conflicts in Gaul and Spain. It's housed in one of Rome's newest landmarks, a glass-and-travertine structure designed by American architect Richard Meier. The building was opened in 2006 after 10 years of delays and heated controversy concerning the altar's relocation. Overlooking the Tiber on one side and the ruins of the marble-clad Mausoleo di Augusto (Mausoleum of Augustus) on the other, the result is a luminous oasis in the center of Rome. ⊠*Lungotevere in Augusta, near Piazza di Popolo* ☎*06/82059127* ⊕*www.arapacis.it* ☐*€6.50* ☉*Tues.–Sun. 9–6.*

❸ **Galleria Borghese.** It's a real toss-up which is more magnificent—the villa built for Cardinal Scipione Borghese in 1615 or the collection of 17th- and 18th-century art that lies within. The luxury-loving cardinal built Rome's most splendiferous palace as a showcase for his fabulous antiquities collection. The interiors are a monument to 18th-century Roman interior decoration at its most luxurious, dripping with porphyry and alabaster and they are a fitting showcase for the statues of various deities, including one officially known as *Venus Victrix*. There has never been any doubt, however, as to the statue's real subject: Pauline Bonaparte, Napoléon's sister, who married Prince Camillo Borghese in one of the storied matches of the 19th century. Sculpted by Canova (1757–1822), the princess reclines on a chaise, bare-breasted, her hips swathed in classical drapery, the very model of haughty detachment and sly come-hither. Pauline is known to have been shocked that her husband took pleasure in showing off the work to his guests. This coyness seems curious given the reply she is supposed to have made to a lady who asked her how she could have

Fodor's Choice
★

WORD OF MOUTH

"The Borghese Gallery is one of the most precious places I have ever had the good fortune to visit—twice. The Bernini Statues bring tears to my eyes. The building is gorgeous. Just a little jewel box of a museum." –bugswife1

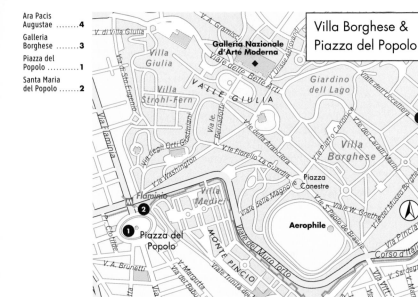

posed for the work: "Oh, but the studio was heated." Other rooms hold important sculptures by Bernini, including *David* and the breathtaking *Apollo and Daphne*. The picture collection has splendid works by Titian, Caravaggio, and Raphael, among others. Entrance is every two hours, and reservations are required. Make sure to book online or by phone at least a few days in advance. ⊠*Piazza Scipione Borghese 5, off Via Pinciana, Villa Borghese* ☎*06/8413979 information, 06/32810 reservations* ⊕*www.galleriaborghese.it* 🎫*€10.50 (including €2 reservation fee); audio guide or English tour €5* ⊙*Tues.–Sun. 9–7, with sessions on the hour every two hours*

❶ **Piazza del Popolo.** Designed by neoclassical architect Giuseppe Valadier (1762–1839) in the early 1800s, this piazza is one of the largest in Rome, and it has a 3,000-year-old obelisk in the middle. A favorite spot for café-sitting and people-watching, the pedestrian-only piazza is landmarked by its two bookend baroque churches, **Santa Maria dei Miracoli** and **Santa Maria in Montesanto**. On the piazza's eastern side, stairs lead uphill to Villa Borghese's **Pincio**, a formal garden that highly fashionable in 19th-century Rome. Here you'll find the magnificent park pavilion restaurant known as the Casino Valadier (⊠Piazza Bucarest, Pincio Gardens ☎06/69922090). First designed in 1814, it has always attracted celebrities like King Farouk of Egypt, Richard Strauss, Gandhi, and Mussolini, all who came to see the lavish Empire-style salons and, of course, be seen. At the north end of the piazza is the 400-year-old **Porta del Popolo,** Rome's northern city gate, and next to it the church of Santa Maria del Popolo. The city gate was designed by Bernini to welcome the Catholic convert Queen Christina of Sweden to Rome in 1605. ⊠ *At head of the Corso, near Villa Borghese.*

★ ❷ **Santa Maria del Popolo.** This church next to the Porta del Popolo goes almost unnoticed, but it has one of the richest art collections of any church in Rome. Here is Raphael's High Renaissance masterpiece the **Cappella Chigi** (which has found new fame as one of the "Altars of Science" in Dan Brown's *Angels & Demons* novel and 2009 Tom Hanks film), as well as two stunning Caravaggios in the **Cappella Cerasi.** Each December an exhibit of Christmas Nativity scenes is held in the adjacent building. ⊠ *Piazza del Popolo, near Villa Borghese* ☎ *06/3610836* ☉ *Mon.–Sat. 7–noon and 4–7, Sun. 7:30–1:30 and 4:30–7:30.*

THE VATICAN: ROME OF THE POPES

Capital of the Catholic Church, this tiny walled city-state is a place where some people go to find a work of art—Michelangelo's frescoes, rare ancient Roman marbles, or Bernini's statues. Others go to find their soul. Whatever the reason, thanks to being the seat of world Catholicism and also address to the most overwhelming architectural achievement of the Renaissance—St. Peter's Basilica—the Vatican attracts millions of travelers every year. In addition, the Vatican Museums are famed for magnificent rooms decorated by Raphael, sculptures such as the *Apollo Belvedere* and the *Laocoön,* frescoes by Fra Angelico, paintings by Giotto and Leonardo, and the celebrated ceiling of the Sistine Chapel. The Church power that emerged as the Rome of the emperors declined gave impetus to a profusion of artistic expression and shaped the destiny of the city for a thousand years. Allow yourself an hour to see the St. Peter's Basilica, two hours for the museums, an hour for Castel Sant'Angelo, and an hour to climb to the top of the dome. Note that ushers at the entrance of St. Peter's Basilica and the Vatican Museums bar entry to people with "inappropriate" clothing—which means no bare knees or shoulders.

GETTING HERE From Termini station, hop on the No. 40 Express or the No. 64 to deliver you to Piazza San Pietro. Metro stops Cipro or Musei Vaticani will get you within about a 10-minute walk of the entrance to the Vatican Museums.

THE MAIN ATTRACTIONS

★ ❷ **Basilica di San Pietro.** The largest church of Christendom, St. Peter's Basilica covers about 18,100 square yards, extends 212 yards in length, and carries a dome that rises 435 feet and measures 138 feet across its base. Its history is equally impressive: No less than five of Italy's greatest artists—Bramante, Raphale, Peruzzi, Antonio Sangallo the

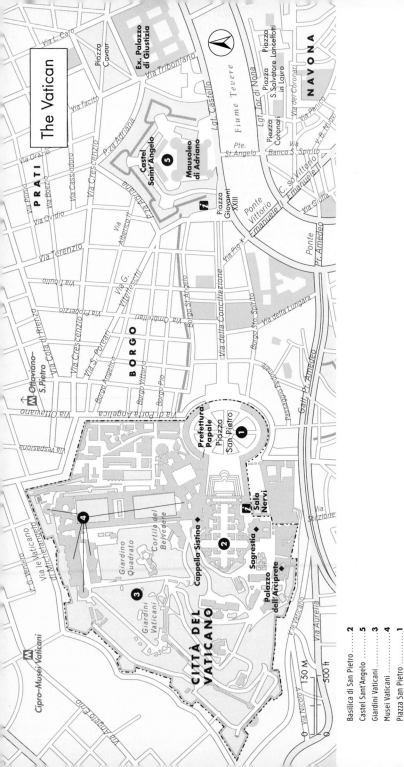

The Vatican

Younger, and Michelangelo—died while striving to erect this "new" St. Peter's. In fact, the church's history dates back to the year AD 319, when the emperor Constantine built a basilica over the site of the tomb of St. Peter (died AD 64). This early church stood for more than 1,000 years, undergoing a number of restorations, until it was on the verge of collapse.

In 1506 Pope Julius II (1443–1513) commissioned the architect Bramante to build a new and greater basilica, but construction would take more than 170 years. In 1546 Michelangelo was persuaded to take over the job, but the magnificent cupola was finally completed by Giacomo della Porta (circa 1537–1602) and Domenico Fontana (1543–1607). The new church wasn't dedicated until 1626; by that time Renaissance had given way to baroque, and many of the plan's original elements had gone the way of their designers. At the entrance, the 15th-century bronze doors by Filarete (circa 1400–69) fill the central portal. Off the entry portico, architect and sculptor Gianlorenzo Bernini's famous *Scala Regia,* the ceremonial entry to the Vatican Palace, is one of the most magnificent staircases in the world and is graced with Bernini's dramatic statue of Constantine the Great.

Entering the sanctuary, take a moment to adjust to the enormity of the space stretching in front of you. The cherubs over the holy-water fonts have feet as long as the distance from your fingertips to your elbow. It is because the proportions are in such perfect harmony that the vastness may escape you at first. The megascale was inspired by the size of the ancient Roman ruins.

Over an altar in a side chapel near the entrance is Michelangelo's *Pietà,* a sculpture of Mary holding her son Jesus's body after crucifixion—the star attraction here other than the basilica itself. Legend has it that the artist, only 22 at the time the work was completed, overheard passersby expressing skepticism that such a young man could have executed such a sophisticated and moving piece. It's said that his offense at the implication was why he crept back that night and signed the piece—in big letters, on a ribbon falling from the Virgin's left shoulder across her breast.

Inlaid in the gorgeous marble pavement of the nave's central aisles are the names of the world's great cathedrals organized by church size—the message is clear, St. Peter's has them all beaten. At the crossing of the aisles four massive piers support the dome, and the mighty Bernini **baldacchino** (canopy) rises high above the papal altar, where the pope celebrates Mass. "What the barbarians didn't do, the Barberini did," 17th-century wags quipped when Barberini Pope Urban VIII had the bronze stripped from the Pantheon's portico and melted down to make the baldacchino (using what was left over for cannonballs). The bronze throne behind the main altar in the apse, the *Cathedra Petri* (Chair of St. Peter), is Bernini's work (1656), and it covers a wooden-and-ivory chair that St. Peter himself is said to have used. However, scholars contend that this throne probably dates only from the Middle Ages. See how the adoration of a million kisses has completely worn down the bronze on the right foot of the statue of St. Peter in front of the near-right pillar in the transept. Free one-hour English-language tours of the basilica depart Monday–Saturday at 10 and 3, Sunday at 2:30 (sign up at the little desk under the portico). St. Peter's is closed during ceremonies in the piazza. ⊠*Piazza di San Pietro, Vatican* ⊙*Apr.–Sept., daily 7–7; Oct.–Mar., daily 7–6.*

The **Grotte Vaticane** *(Vatican Grottoes)* in the basilica contain the tombs of many popes, including John Paul II, and the Tomb of St. Peter. The entrance is opposite the baldacchino, near a pillar where the dome begins. The only exit leads outside the church, so don't go down until you're finished elsewhere. ⊡*Free* ⊙*Apr.–Sept., daily 7–6; Oct.–Mar., daily 7–5.*

The **roof** of St. Peter's Basilica, reached by elevator or stairs, provides a view among a landscape of domes and towers. An interior staircase (170 steps) leads to the base of the dome for a dove's-eye look at the interior of St. Peter's. Only if you are stout of heart and sound of lung should you attempt the taxing and claustrophobic climb up the remaining 330 steps to the balcony of the lantern, where the view embraces the Vatican Gardens and all of Rome. The up and down staircases are one way; once you commit to climbing, there's no turning back. ☎*06/69883462* ⊡*Elevator €7, stairs €4* ⊙*Daily 8–5 (11:30–5 on Wed. if pope has audience in Piazza San Pietro).*

☾ ➎ **Castel Sant'Angelo.** For hundreds of years this fortress guarded the Vatican, to which it is linked by the **Passetto,** an arcaded passageway (the secret "lair of the Illuminati," according to Dan Brown's *Angels & Demons,* the Rome-based prequel to *The Da Vinci Code*). According to legend, Castel Sant'Angelo got its name during the plague of 590, when Pope Gregory the Great (circa 540–604), passing by in a religious procession, had a vision of an angel sheathing its sword atop the stone ramparts. Though it may look like a stronghold, Castel Sant'Angelo was in fact built as a tomb for the emperor Hadrian (76–138) in AD 135. By the 6th century it had been transformed into a fortress, and it remained a refuge for the popes for almost 1,000 years. It has dungeons, battlements, cannon and cannonballs, and a collection of antique weaponry and armor. The lower levels formed the base of Hadrian's mausoleum; ancient ramps and narrow staircases climb through the castle's core to courtyards and frescoed halls, where temporary exhibits are held. Off the loggia is a café.

The upper terrace, with the massive angel statue commemorating Gregory's vision, evokes memories of Tosca, Puccini's poignant heroine in the opera of the same name, who threw herself off these ramparts with the cry, *"Scarpia, avanti a Dio!"* ("Scarpia, we meet before God!") On summer evenings a book fair with musical events and food stalls surrounds the castle. One of Rome's most beautiful pedestrian bridges, **Ponte Sant'Angelo** spans the Tiber in front of the fortress and is studded with graceful angels designed by Bernini. ⊠*Lungotevere Castello 50, near Vatican* ☎*06/39967600* ⊕*www.pierreci.it* ⊡*€5* ⊙*Tues.– Sun. 9–7:30.*

CLOSE UP

A Morning with the Pope

1

The pope holds audiences in a large, modern hall (or in St. Peter's Square in summer) on Wednesday morning at 10. To attend, you must get tickets; apply in writing at least 10 days in advance to the **Papal Prefecture** (*Prefettura della Casa Pontificia*) ✆ *00120 Vatican City* ☎ *06/69883273* 🖷 *06/69885863*), indicating the date you prefer, your language, and your hotel. Or go to the prefecture, through the Porta di Bronzo, the bronze door at the end of the colonnade on the right side of the piazza; the office is open Monday–Saturday 9–1, and last-minute tickets may be available.

You can also arrange to pick up free tickets on Tuesday from 5 to 6:45 at the **Santa Susanna American Church** (✉ *Via XX Settembre 15, near Termini* ☎ *06/42014554*); call first. For a fee, travel agencies make arrangements that include transportation. Arrive early, as security is tight and the best places fill up fast.

❹ **Musei Vaticani** (*Vatican Museums*). The building on your left as you exit St. Peter's Basilica is the Vatican Palace, the papal residence since 1377, with an estimated 1,400 rooms, chapels, and galleries. Other than the pope and his court, the occupant is the Musei Vaticani (Vatican Museums), containing some of art's greatest masterpieces. The Sistine Chapel is the headliner here, but in your haste to get there, don't overlook the Museo Egizio, with its fine Egyptian collection; the famed classical sculptures of the Chiaramonti and the Museo Pio Clementino; and the Stanze di Raffaello (Raphael Rooms), a suite of halls covered floor-to-ceiling in some of the master's greatest works.

Fodor's Choice ★

On a first visit to the Vatican Museums, you may just want to see the highlights—even that will take several hours and a good, long walk. In peak tourist season, be prepared for at least an hour's wait to get into the museums and large crowds once inside. The best time to avoid lines and crowds is not first thing in the morning but during lunch hour and the Wednesday papal audiences. The collection is divided among different galleries, halls, and wings connected end to end. Pick up a leaflet at the main entrance to the museums to see the overall layout. The Sistine Chapel is at the far end of the complex, and the leaflet charts two abbreviated itineraries through other collections to reach it. An audio guide (€5.50, about 90 minutes) for the Sistine Chapel, the Stanze di Raffaello, and 350 other works and locations is worth the added expense. Phone or e-mail at least a week in advance (a month for peak season) to book a guided tour (€21.50) through the Guided Visit to Vatican Museums. The main entrance to the museums, on Viale Vaticano, is a long walk from Piazza San Pietro along a busy thoroughfare. Some city buses stop near the main entrance: Bus 49 from Piazza Cavour stops right in front; buses 81 and 492 and Tram 19 stop at Piazza Risorgimento, halfway between St. Peter's and the museums. The Ottaviano–S. Pietro and the Cipro–Musei Vaticani stops on Metro A also are in the vicinity. Entry is free the first Sunday of the month, and the museum is closed on Catholic holidays, of which there are many. Last admission is an hour before closing.

Continued on page 88

AGONY AND ECSTASY:
THE SISTINE CEILING

Forming lines that are probably longer than those waiting to pass through the Pearly Gates, hordes of visitors arrive at the Sistine Chapel daily to view what may be the world's most sublime example of artistry:

Michelangelo: *The Creation of Adam*, Sistine Chapel, The Vatican, circa 1511.

Michelangelo's Sistine Ceiling. To paint this 12,000-square-foot barrel vault, it took four years, 343 frescoed figures, and a titanic battle of wits between the artist and Pope Julius II. While in its typical fashion, Hollywood focused on the element of agony, not ecstasy, involved in the saga of creation, a recently completed restoration of the ceiling has revolutionized our appreciation of the masterpiece of masterpieces.

By Martin Wilmot Bennett

View of the Cappella Sistina

MICHELANGELO'S
MISSION IMPOSSIBLE

Designed to match the proportions of Solomon's Temple described in the Old Testament, the Sistine Chapel is named after Pope Sixtus VI, who commissioned it as a place of worship for himself and as the venue where new popes could be elected. Before Michelangelo, the barrel-vaulted ceiling was an expanse of azure fretted with golden stars. Then, in 1504, an ugly crack appeared. Bramante, the architect, managed do some patchwork using iron rods, but when signs of a fissure remained, the new Pope Julius II summoned Michelangelo to cover it with a fresco 135 feet long and 44 feet wide.

Taking in the entire span of the ceiling, the theme connecting the various participants in this painted universe could be said to be mankind's anguished waiting. The majestic panel depicting the Creation of Adam leads, through the stages of the Fall and the expulsion from Eden, to the tragedy of Noah found naked and mocked by his own sons; throughout all runs the underlying need for man's redemption. Witnessing all from the side and end walls, a chorus of ancient Prophets and Sibyls peer anxiously forward, awaiting the Redeemer who will come to save both the Jews and the Gentiles.

APOCALYPSE NOW

The sweetness and pathos of his Pietà, carved by Michelangelo only ten years earlier, have been left behind. The new work foretells an apocalypse, its congregation of doomed sinners facing the wrath of heaven through hanging, beheading, crucifixion, flood, and plague. Michelangelo, by nature a misanthrope, was already filled with visions of doom thanks to the fiery orations of Savonarola, whose thunderous preachments he had heard before leaving his hometown of Florence. Vasari, the 16th-century art historian, coined the word "terribilità" to describe Michelangelo's tension-ridden style, a rare case of a single word being worth a thousand pictures.

Michelangelo wound up using a *Reader's Digest* condensed version of the stories from Genesis, with the dramatis personae overseen by a punitive and terrifying God. In real life, poor Michelangelo answered to a flesh-and-blood taskmaster who was almost as vengeful: Pope Julius II. Less vicar of Christ than latter-day Caesar, he was intent on uniting Italy under the power of the Vatican, and was eager to do so by any means, including riding into pitched battle. Yet this "warrior pope" considered his most formidable adversary to be Michelangelo. Applying a form of blackmail, Julius threatened to wage war on Michelangelo's Florence, to which the artist had fled after Julius canceled a commission for a grand papal tomb unless Michelangelo agreed to return to Rome and take up the task of painting the Sistine Chapel ceiling.

MICHELANGELO, SCULPTOR

A sculptor first and foremost, however, Michelangelo considered painting an inferior genre— "for rascals and sissies" as he put it. Second, there was the sheer scope of the task, leading Michelangelo to suspect he'd been set up by a rival, Bramante, chief architect of the new St. Peter's Basilica. As Michelangelo was also a master architect, he regarded this fresco commission as a Renaissance mission-impossible. Pope Julius's powerful will prevailed—and six years later the work of the Sistine Ceiling was complete. Irving Stone's famous novel *The Agony and the Ecstasy*—and the granitic 1965 film that followed—chart this epic battle between artist and pope.

THINGS ARE LOOKING UP

To enhance your viewing of the ceiling, bring along opera-glasses, binoculars, or just a mirror (to prevent your neck from becoming bent like Michelangelo's). Note that no photos are permitted. Insiders know the only time to get the chapel to yourself is during the papal blessings and public audiences held in St. Peter's Square. Failing that, get there during lunch hour. Admission and entry to the Sistine Chapel is only through the Musei Vaticani (Vatican Museums).

SCHEMATIC OF THE SISTINE CEILING

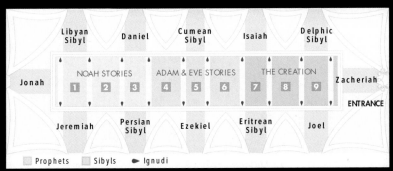

HEAVEN'S ABOVE

The ceiling's biblical symbols were ideated by three Vatican theologians, Cardinal Alidosi, Egidio da Viterbo, and Giovanni Rafanelli, along with Michelangelo. As for the ceiling's painted "framework," this *quadratura* alludes to Roman triumphal arches because Pope Julius II was fond of mounting "triumphal entries" into his conquered cities (in imitation of Christ's procession into Jerusalem on Palm Sunday).

THE CENTER PANELS

Prophet turned art-critic or, perhaps doubling as ourselves, the ideal viewer, Jonah the prophet (painted at the altar end) gazes up at the

Creation, or Michelangelo's version of it.

1 The first of three scenes taken from the Book of Genesis: God separates Light from Darkness.

2 God creates the sun and a craterless pre-Galilean moon

while the panel's other half offers an unprecedented rear view of the Almighty creating the vegetable world.

3 In the panel showing God separating the Waters from the Heavens, the Creator

tumbles towards us as in a self-made whirlwind.

4 Pausing for breath, next admire probably Western Art's most famous image—God giving life to Adam.

5 The Creation of Eve from Adam's rib leads to the sixth panel.

6 In a sort of diptych divided by the trunk of the Tree of Knowledge of Good and Evil, Michelangelo retells the Temptation and the Fall.

7 Illustrating Man's fallen nature, the last three panels narrate, in un-chronological order, the Flood. In the first Noah offers a pre-Flood sacrifice of thanks.

8 Damaged by an explosion in 1794, next comes

Michelangelo's version of Flood itself.

9 Finally, above the monumental Jonah, you can just make out the small, wretched figure of Noah, lying drunk—in pose, the shrunken anti-type of the majestic Adam five panels down the wall.

THE CREATION OF ADAM

Michelangelo's Adam was partly inspired by the Creation scenes Michelangelo had studied in the sculpted doors of Jacopo della Quercia in Bologna and Lorenzo Ghiberti's Doors of Paradise in Florence. Yet in Michelangelo's version Adam's hand hangs limp, waiting God's touch to impart the spark of life. Facing his Creation, the Creator—looking a bit like the pagan god Jupiter—is for the first time ever depicted as horizontal, mirroring the Biblical "in his own likeness." Decades after its completion, a crack began to appear, amputating Adam's fingertips. Believe it or not, the most famous fingers in Western art are the handiwork, at least in part, of one Domenico Carnevale.

Besides the galleries mentioned here, there are many other wings along your way—full of maps, tapestries, classical sculpture, Egyptian mummies, Etruscan statues, and even Aztec treasures. From the main entrance of the Vatican Museums take the escalator up to the **Pinacoteca** (Picture Gallery) on your right. This is a self-contained section, and it's worth visiting first for works by such artists as Leonardo (1452–1520), Giotto (circa 1266–1337), Fra Angelico (1387–1455), and Filippo Lippi (circa 1406–69),

and the exceptional *Transfiguration, Coronation,* and *Foligno Madonna* by Raphael (1483–1564).

The **Cortile Ottagano** (Octagonal Courtyard) of the Vatican Museums displays some of sculpture's most famous works, including the 4th century BC *Apollo Belvedere* (and Canova's 1801 *Perseus,* heavily influenced by it) and the 2nd-century *Laocoön.*

The **Stanze di Raffaello** (Raphael Rooms) are second only to the Sistine Chapel in artistic interest—and draw crowds comparable. In 1508 Pope Julius II employed Raphael, on the recommendation of Bramante, to decorate the rooms with biblical scenes. The result is a Renaissance tour de force. Of the four rooms, the second and third were decorated mainly by Raphael. The others were decorated by Giulio Romano (circa 1499–1546) and other assistants of Raphael; the first room is known as the Stanza dell'Incendio, with frescoes by Romano of the *incendio* (fire) in the Borgo neighborhood.

The frescoed **Stanza della Segnatura** (Room of the Signature), where papal bulls were signed, is one of Raphael's finest works; indeed, they are thought by many to be some of the finest paintings in the history of Western art. This was Julius's private library, and the room's use is reflected in the frescoes' themes, philosophy and enlightenment. A paradigm of High Renaissance painting, the works demonstrate the revolutionary ideals of naturalism (Raphael's figures lack the awkwardness of those painted only a few years earlier); humanism (the idea that human beings are the noblest and most admirable of God's creations); and a profound interest in the ancient world, the result of the 15th-century rediscovery of classical antiquity. The *School of Athens* glorifies some of philosophy's greats, including Plato (pointing to Heaven) and Aristotle (pointing to Earth) at the fresco's center. The pensive figure on the stairs is thought to be modeled after Michelangelo, who was painting the Sistine ceiling at the same time Raphael was working here.

In 1508, just before Raphael started work on his rooms, the redoubtable Pope Julius II commissioned Michelangelo to paint single-handedly the more-than-10,000-square-foot ceiling of the **Cappella Sistina**

(Sistine Chapel). The task cost the artist four years of mental and physical anguish. It's said that for years afterward Michelangelo couldn't read anything without holding it up over his head. The result, however, was the masterpiece that you now see, its colors cool and brilliant after restoration. Bring a pair of binoculars to get a better look at this incredible work (unfortunately, you're not allowed to lie down on the floor to study the frescoes above, the viewing position of choice in decades past). Tourists in the 19th century used pocket mirrors so as not to strain their necks. For an in-depth look at Michelangelo's masterpiece, see our photo feature, "Agony & Ecstasy: The Sistine Ceiling." ⊠ *Main museum entrance, Viale Vaticano; guided visit office, Piazza San Pietro* ☎*06/69883332* ⊕*www.vatican.va* ☞€ *14* ◷*Mon.–Sat. 8:30–6 (last entrance at 4); closed Sun., except for last Sun. of month (when admission is free)* ☞*Note: ushers at entrance of St. Peter's and Vatican Museums will bar entry to people with bare knees or bare shoulders* Ⓜ *Cipro-Musei Vaticani.*

NEED A BREAK?

You don't have to snack at the touristy joints outside the Vatican Museums; a short walk away are neighborhood restaurants catering to locals. Among them is Il Mozzicone (⊠*Borgo Pio 180, near San Pietro*), where you can fill up on solid Roman fare at moderate prices. La Caravella (⊠*Via degli Scipioni 32, at Via Vespasiano, off Piazza Risorgimento, near San Pietro*) serves pizza at lunch every day but Thursday, when it's closed.

❶ Piazza San Pietro. As you enter St. Peter's Square you are officially entering Vatican territory. The piazza is one of Bernini's most spectacular masterpieces. It was completed in 1667 after 11 years' work, a relatively short time, considering the vastness of the task. The piazza can hold 400,000 people—as it did in the days following the death of Pope John Paul II.

The piazza is surrounded by a curving pair of quadruple colonnades, topped by a balustrade and statues of 140 saints. Look for the two disks set into the pavement on either side of the obelisk at the center of the piazza. When you stand on either disk, a trick of perspective makes the colonnades seem to consist of a single row of columns. Bernini had an even grander visual effect in mind when he designed the square: the surprise of stepping into an immense, airy space after approaching it through a neighborhood of narrow, shadowy streets. The contrast was intended to evoke the metaphor of moving from darkness to light. But in the 1930s Mussolini spoiled the effect. To celebrate the "conciliation" between the Vatican and the Italian government under the Lateran Pact of 1929, he conceived of the Via della Conciliazione, the broad avenue that now forms the main approach to St. Peter's.

Remember to look for the Swiss Guards in their colorful uniforms; they've been standing at the Vatican entrances for the past 500 years. ⊠ *At head of Via delle Conciliazione*

③ Giardini Vaticani *(Vatican Gardens)*. Generations of popes have strolled in these beautifully manicured gardens, originally laid out in the 16th century. A two-hour guided tour, half by bus and half on foot, takes you through a haven of shady walkways, elaborate fountains, and exotic plants. Make reservations two or three days in advance and pick up your tickets in the Guided Visit to Vatican Museums Office at the museum entrance. If you have a reservation, you can skip the line (go in through the "Exit" door); the office window is inside the atrium. ✉ *Viale Vaticano* ☎ *06/69884466 reservations* ⊕ *www.vatican.va* 💶 *€10* 🕙 *Tours: Mon.–Sat. 10* AM. *Office: Mon.–Sat. 8:30–7.*

THE GHETTO, TIBERINA ISLAND & TRASTEVERE

Each staunchly resisting the tides of change, these three areas are hard to beat for the authentic atmosphere of Old Rome. You begin in the old Ghetto, a warren of twisting, narrow streets, where Rome's Jewish community was once confined, then deported, and now, barely, persists. Ancient bridges, the Ponte Fabricio and Ponte Cestio, link the Ghetto to Tiberina Island, the tiny island that is one of Rome's most picturesque sights. On the opposite side of the Tiber lies Trastevere—"across the Tiber"—long cherished as Rome's Greenwich Village and now subject to rampant gentrification. In spite of this, Trastevere remains about the most tightly knit community in the city, the Trasteverini proudly proclaiming their descent from the ancient Romans. This area is Rome's enchanting, medieval heart.

GETTING HERE | From Termini station, nab the No. 40 Express or the No. 64 bus to Largo Torre Argentina, where you can get off to visit the Ghetto area. Switch to Tram 8 to get to Trastevere. The No. 41 bus ascends the Janiculum Hill.

THE MAIN ATTRACTIONS

⑥ Fontana delle Tartarughe. The 16th-century Fountain of the Turtles in Piazza Mattei is one of Rome's loveliest. Designed by Giacomo della Porta (1539–1602) in 1581 and sculpted by Taddeo Landini (1550–96), the piece revolves around four bronze boys, each clutching a dolphin that jets water into marble shells. Several bronze tortoises, thought to have been added by Bernini, are held in each of the boys' hands and drink from the fountain's upper basin. The piazza is lined by a few interesting cafés and shops. It was named for the Mattei family, who built the **Palazzo Mattei** on Via Caetani, famed for its sculpture-rich, bust-adorned 17th-century courtyard—one of Rome's most photogenic. ✉ *Piazza Mattei, Ghetto.*

★ **⑦ Isola Tiberina.** Tiber Island is where a city hospital stands on a site that has been dedicated to healing ever since a temple to Aesculapius was erected here in 291 BC. Back then, the ancient Romans sheathed the entire island in travertine, sculpting it into a "boat" complete with obelisk "mast." Be sure to walk down the wide river embankment to the southern tip to see one of the most astonishing remnants of ancient

Rome: the island's sculpted marble "prow" carved with a figure of Aesculapius. Every July, the city's Estate Romana hosts an open-air cinema on the island's paved shores. ⊠*Ponte Fabricio and Ponte Cestio, near Ghetto.*

Jewish Ghetto. Rome has had a Jewish community since the 1st century BC, and from that time until the present its living conditions have varied widely according to its relations with the city's rulers. In 1555 Pope Paul II established Rome's Ghetto Ebraico in the neighborhood marked off by the Portico d'Ottavia, the Tiber, and Via Arenula. The area quickly became Rome's most densely populated. The laws were rescinded around the time of the Italian unifications in the 1870s but German troops tragically occupied Rome during World War II and in 1943 wrought havoc here. Today, there are a few Judaica shops and kosher groceries, bakeries, and restaurants (especially on Via di Portico d'Ottavia) but the neighborhood mansions are now being renovated and much coveted by the rich and stylish. **Tours of the Ghetto** (€8, about two hours) that explore Rome's Jewish history can be booked through the SIDIC historical society. ⊠*SIDIC Office, Via Garibaldi 28, Ghetto* ☎*06/67015555* ⊕*www.sidic.org.*

❺ Portico d'Ottavia. Along Via del Portico d'Ottavia in the heart of the Jewish Ghetto are buildings where medieval inscriptions, ancient friezes, and half-buried classical monuments attest to the venerable history of the neighborhood. The old **Chiesa di Sant'Angelo in Pescheria** was built right into the ruins of the ancient Roman Portico d'Ottavia, which was a monumental area enclosing a temple, library, and other buildings within colonnaded porticoes. ⊠*Via del Portico d'Ottavia, Ghetto.*

Fodor'sChoice **Santa Maria in Trastevere.** Shimmering at night thanks to its medieval
★ facade mosaics, this is one of Rome's most magnificent and oldest
❿ churches, first built in the 4th century and then greatly enlarged in the 12th century. Inside, the nave framed by a grand processional of two rows of columns taken from ancient Roman temples often produced involuntary gasps from unsuspecting visitors—this is probably as close as we can get to the imperial splendor of an ancient Roman basilica. A shining burst of Byzantine color and light is added by the celebrated 12th-century mosaics in the apse; also note the Cosmati work, a mosaic style from the 12th and 13th centuries in which tiny squares and triangles were laid with larger stones to form geometric patterns, in the church floors. Outside, the **Piazza di Santa Maria in Trastevere** is a very popular spot for afternoon coffee and evening cocktails at its outdoor cafés. The 13th-century mosaics on Santa Maria's facade—which add light and color to the piazza, especially at night when they are in spotlight—are believed to represent the Wise and Foolish Virgins. In August, processions honoring the Virgin Mary gather at the church as part of Trastevere's famous traditional feast, called *Festa de Noantri* (Our Own Feast). ⊠*Piazza di Santa Maria, Trastevere* ☎*06/5814802* ☉*Daily 7:30–1 and 4–7.*

❹ Teatro di Marcello. The Teatro, hardly recognizable as a theater today, was originally designed to hold 20,000 spectators. It was begun by Julius

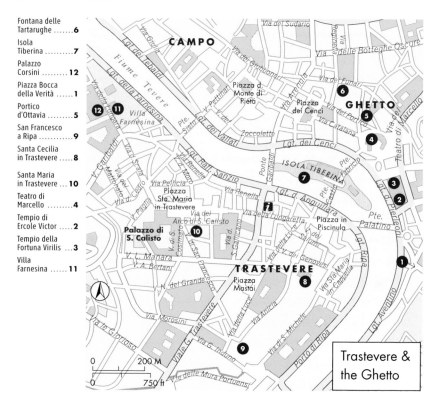

Trastevere &
the Ghetto

Caesar; today, the 16th-century apartment building that sprouted out of its remains has become one of Rome's most prestigious residential addresses. The area south of the theater makes a grand stage for chamber music concerts in summer. ⊠ *Via del Teatro di Marcello, Ghetto* ☎*06/87131590 concert information* ⊕*www.tempietto.it* ⊙ *Open during concerts only.*

Trastevere. This area consists of a maze of narrow streets that is still, despite evident gentrification, one of the city's most authentically Roman neighborhoods. Literally translated, its name means "across the Tiber," and indeed the Trasteverini—the neighborhood's natives— are a breed apart. The area is hardly undiscovered, but among its self-consciously picturesque trattorias and trendy tearooms you can also find old shops and dusty artisans' workshops in alleys festooned with laundry hung out to dry. Stroll along Via dell'Arco dei Tolomei and Via dei Salumi, shadowy streets showing the patina of the ages. One of the least affected parts of Trastevere is a block in from the Tiber: on Piazza in Piscinula, north of Via dei Salumi and south of the Ponte Cestio Fabricio, the smallest medieval church in the city, San Benedetto, stands opposite the restored medieval Casa dei Mattei. ⊠*Just east of the Tiber river, accessed by Ponte Sisto, Ponte Garibaldi, Ponte Fabricio, Ponte Palatino, and Ponte Principe Amedeo, Trastevere*

★ ⑪ **Villa Farnesina.** Money was no object to extravagant patron Agostino Chigi, a Sienese banker who financed many a papal project. His munificence is evident in his elegant villa, built about 1511. When Raphael could steal some precious time from his work on the Vatican Stanze and wooing Fornarina, he executed some of the frescoes, notably a luminous *Galatea.* Chigi

delighted in impressing guests by having his servants cast precious dinnerware into the Tiber when it was time to clear the table. The guests didn't know of the nets he had stretched under the waterline to catch everything. His extravagant ways meant that his villa had to be eventually sold to the grand Farnese family. ⊠ *Via della Lungara 230, Trastevere* ☎ *06/68027268* ⊕ *www.lincei.it/informazioni/villafarnesina/index.php* 🎫 *€5* ⊗ *Mon.–Sat. and 1st Sun. of month 9–1.*

ALSO WORTH SEEING

⑫ **Palazzo Corsini.** This elegant palace holds the 16th- and 17th-century painting collection of the **Galleria Nazionale d'Arte Antica;** even if you're not interested in the paintings, stop in to climb the extraordinary 17th-century stone staircase, itself a drama of architectural shadows and sculptural voids. The adjacent Corsini gardens, now Rome's **Giardino Botanico,** offer delightful tranquillity, with native and exotic plants and a marvelous view at the top. ⊠ *Via della Lungara 10, Trastevere* ☎ *06/68802323* ⊕ *www.galleriaborghese.it* 🎫 *€4* ⊗ *Tues.–Sun., entrance at 9:30, 11, and 12:30.*

❶ **Piazza Bocca della Verità.** On the site of the Forum Boarium, ancient Rome's cattle market, this square was later used for public executions. Its name is derived from the marble **Bocca della Verità** (Mouth of Truth), a huge medieval drain cover in the form of an open-mouth face that is now set into the entry portico of the magically medieval 12th-century church of **Santa Maria in Cosmedin.** In the Middle Ages, legend had it that any person who told a lie with his hand in the mouth would have it chomped off. Today tour groups line up in this noisy, traffic-jammed piazza to give this ancient lie detector (which starred with Audrey Hepburn and Gregory Peck in *Roman Holiday*) a go. *By Tiber river, along Lungotevere dei Pierleoni,* ⊠ *near Ghetto.*

❾ **San Francesco a Ripa.** Ask the sacristan to show you the cell where St. Francis slept when he came to seek the pope's approval for his new order. Also in this church is one of Bernini's most dramatic sculptures, the figure of the *Blessed Ludovica Albertoni,* ecstatic at the prospect of entering heaven. ⊠ *Piazza San Francesco d'Assisi, Trastevere* ☎ *06/5819020* ⊗ *Daily 7–noon and 4–7:30.*

☾ ❽ **Santa Cecilia in Trastevere.** Mothers and children love to dally in the delightful little garden in front of this church. Duck inside for a look at the 9th-century mosaics and the languid statue of St. Cecilia under

WALKING TOURS OF ROME

All About Rome, American Express, Context: Rome, Enjoy Rome, Through Eternity, and Walks of Rome offer walking tours of the city and its sites.

Fascinating tours are offered: Renaissance Rome and "Angels & Demons" tours are just two of the main theme walks scheduled.

Here are their contact points:

All About Rome (☎ 06/7100823 ⊕ www.allaboutromewalks.

netfirms.com). **American Express** (☎ 06/67641).

Context: Rome (✉ Via Baccina 40, near Termini ☎ 06/4820911 or 888/4671986 ⊕ www.contextrome. com). **Enjoy Rome** (✉ Via Marghera 8A, near Termini ☎ 06/4451843 ⊕ www.enjoyrome.com).

Through Eternity (☎ 06/7009336 ⊕ www.througheternity.com). **Walks of Rome** (☎ 347/7955175).

the altar. Fragments of a *Last Judgment* fresco cycle by Pietro Cavallini (circa 1250–1330), dating from the late 13th century, remain one of his most important works. Though the Byzantine-influenced fragments are obscured by the structure, what's left reveals a rich luminosity in the seated apostles' drapery and a remarkable depth in their expressions. A pretty cloister and remains of Roman houses are visible under the church. To see them, ask at the booth to the left of the main nave. ✉ *Piazza Santa Cecilia, Trastevere* ☎ 06/5899289 ☜ *Church free, frescoes €2.50* ⊙ *Daily 9:30–12:30 and 4–6:30. Frescoes Mon.–Sat. 10:15–12:15, Sun. 11:15–noon.*

❸ **Tempio della Fortuna Virilis.** This rectangular temple devoted to "manly fortune" dates from the 2nd century BC and is built in the Greek style, as was the norm in the early years of Rome. For its age, its remains are remarkably well preserved, in part due to its subsequent consecration as a Christian church. ✉ *Piazza Bocca della Verità, near Ghetto.*

❷ **Tempio di Ercole Victor.** All but 1 of the 20 original Corinthian columns in Rome's most evocative small ruin remain intact. It was built in the 2nd century BC. Long considered a shrine to Vesta, it is now believed the temple was devoted to Hercules by a successful olive merchant. ✉ *Piazza Bocca della Verità, near Ghetto.*

THE CATACOMBS & VIA APPIA ANTICA

The Early Christian sites on the ancient Appian Way are some of the religion's oldest. Catacombs, where both ancient pagan Romans and early Christians buried their dead, and where Christians gathered to worship in secret, lie below the very road where tradition says Christ appeared to St. Peter. The Via Appia Antica, built 400 years before, is a quiet, green place to walk and ponder the ancient world. The Rome APT office provides an informative free pamphlet for this itinerary.

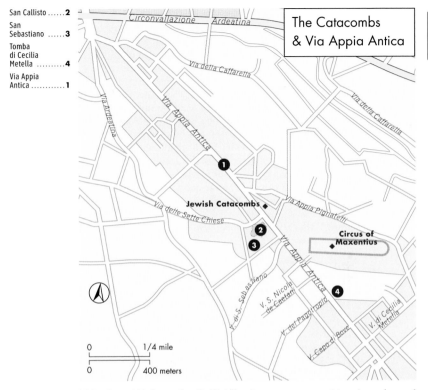

The Catacombs
& Via Appia Antica

GETTING HERE Take Bus 660 from the Colli Albani metro stop on Line A to the end of the line, at Via Appia Antica, or opt for the Archeobus OpenTram bus from Piazza Venezia.

THE MAIN ATTRACTIONS

❸ San Sebastiano. The 4th-century catacomb, named for the saint who was buried here, burrows underground on four levels. The only one of the catacombs to remain accessible during the Middle Ages, it's the origin of the term "catacomb," for it was in a spot where the road dips into a hollow, a place the Romans called *catacumbas* ("near the hollow"). Eventually the Christian cemetery that had existed here since the 2nd century came to be known by the same name, which was applied to all underground cemeteries discovered in Rome in later centuries. ⊠ *Via Appia Antica 136* ☎ *06/7850350* 🖭 *€5* ⊙ *Mid-Nov.–mid-Oct., Mon.–Sat. 9–noon and 2–5.*

❹ Tomba di Cecilia Metella. The circular mausoleum of a Roman noble-woman, who lived at the time of Julius Caesar, was transformed into a fortress in the 14th century. The tomb houses a tiny museum with sculptures from the Via Appia Antica and an interesting reconstruction of the area's geological and historical past. ⊠ *Via Appia Antica 161* ☎ *06/78021465 or 06/39967700* ⊕ *www.pierreci.it* 🖭 *€6* ⊙ *Mon.– Sat. 9 AM–1 hr before sunset.*

★ ☾ ❶ **Via Appia Antica.** This Queen of Roads, "Regina Viarium," was the most important of the extensive network of roads that traversed the Roman Empire, a masterful feat of engineering that made possible Roman control of a vast area by allowing for the efficient transport of armies and commercial goods. Completed in 312 BC by Appius Claudius, the road was ancient Europe's first highway, connecting Rome with Brindisi, 584 km (365 mi) away on the Adriatic coast. Part of the route exists as Via Appia (SS7), but it is a paved, modern highway. The stretch indicated here is closed to traffic; the ancient roadway passes through grassy fields and shady groves and by the villas of movie stars (Marcello Mastroianni and Gina Lollobrigida had homes here) and other VIPs. This part is still paved with the ancient *basoli* (basalt stones) over which the Romans drove their carriages—look for the wheel ruts. Pick a sunny day for your visit, wear comfortable shoes, and bring a bottle of water. You can take Bus 660 from the Colli Albani metro station (Line A) for Via Cecilia Metella at Via Appia Antica. ⊠ *Exit Via Cristoforo Colombo at Circonvallazione Ardeatina, follow signs to Appia Antica parking lot.*

ALSO WORTH SEEING

❷ **San Callisto.** A friar will guide you through the crypts and galleries of the well-preserved San Callisto catacombs. ⊠ *Via Appia Antica 110* ☏ *06/4465610* ⌑ *€5* ⊗ *Mar.–Jan., Thurs.–Tues. 8:30–12:30 and 2:30–5.*

WHERE TO EAT

Updated by Dana Klitzberg and Jen Laskey

Rome has been known since ancient times for its great feasts and banquets, and though the days of the triclinium and the Saturnalia are long past, dining out is still the Romans' favorite pastime. The city is distinguished more by its good attitude toward eating out than by a multitude of world-class restaurants; simple, traditional cuisine reigns, although things are slowly changing as talented young chefs explore new culinary frontiers. Many of the city's restaurants cater to a clientele of regulars, and atmosphere and attitude are usually friendly and informal. The flip side is that in Rome the customer is not always right—the chef and waiters are in charge, and no one will beg forgiveness if you wanted *skim* milk in that cappuccino. Be flexible and you're sure to *mangiar bene* (eat well). Lunch is served from approximately 12:30 to 2:30 and dinner from 7:30 or 8 until about 11, though some restaurants stay open later, especially in summer, when patrons linger at sidewalk tables to enjoy the parade of people and the *ponentino* (evening breeze).

WHAT IT COSTS IN EUROS				
	¢	$	$$	$$$	$$$$
AT DINNER	under €15	€15–€25	€25–€35	€35–€45	over €45

Prices are for a first course (*primo*), second course (*secondo*), and dessert (*dolce*).

PANTHEON, NAVONA, TREVI & QUIRINALE

$$$$ ✕**Il Convivio.** In a tiny, nondescript vicolo north of Piazza Navona, the
MODERN three Troiani brothers—Angelo in the kitchen, and brothers Giuseppe
ITALIAN and Massimo presiding over the dining room and wine cellar—have
Fodor's Choice quietly been redefining the experience of Italian eclectic *alta cucina* for
★ many years. Antipasti include a "roast beef" of tuna fillet lacquered
with chestnut honey, rosemary, red peppercorns, and ginger served
with a green apple salad, while a squid ink risotto with baby cuttlefish, sea asparagus, lemongrass, and basil sates the appetites of those
with dreams of *fantasia*. Main courses include a fabulous version of a
cold-weather pigeon dish for which Il Convivio is famous. Service is
attentive without being overbearing, and the wine list is exceptional. A
splurge spot. ⊠*Vicolo dei Soldati 31, Navona* ☎*06/6869432* ⚐*Reservations essential* ⊟*AE, DC, MC, V* ⊙*Closed Sun., 1 wk in Jan., and
2 wks in Aug. No lunch.*

$$$ ✕ **Etabli.** On a narrow vicolo off beloved Piazza del Fico, this multidi-
MEDI- mensional locale opened last year, serving as caffè by day, and becom-
TERRANEAN ing a hot spot by aperitivo hour. Beautifully finished with vaulted wood
Fodor's Choice beam ceilings, wrought iron touches, plush leather sofas, and chande-
★ liers, it's all modern Italian farmhouse chic. In the restaurant section
(the place is sprawling), it's minimalist Provençal hip (*etablí* is French
for the regionally typical tables within). And the food is clean and
Mediterranean, with touches of Asia in the raw fish appetizers. Pas-
tas are more traditional Italian, and the secondi run the gamut from
land to sea. Arrive early as the place fills up by dinnertime and it's a
popular post-dining spot for sipping and posing. ⊠*Vicolo delle Vacche
9/a, Navona* ☎*06/6871499* ⊕*www.etabli.it* ⚐*Reservations recom-
mended* ⊟*MC, V* ⊙*Closed Sun. in summer, Mon. in winter.*

$$ ✕**Maccheroni.** This boisterous, convivial trattoria north of the Pan-
ITALIAN theon makes for a fun evening out. The decor is basic: white walls
with wooden shelves lined with wine bottles, blocky wooden tables
covered in white butcher paper—but there's an "open" kitchen (with
even the dishwashers in plain view of the diners) and an airy feel that
attracts a young clientele as well as visiting celebrities. The menu sticks
to Roman basics such as simple pasta with fresh tomatoes and basil
or rigatoni *alla gricia* (with bacon, sheep's-milk cheese, and black pepper). The specialty pasta, *trofie* (short pasta twists) with a black truffle
sauce, inspires you to lick your plate. Probably the best choice on the
menu is the *tagliata con rughetta*, a juicy, two-inch-thick steak sliced
thinly and served on arugula. ⊠*Piazza delle Coppelle 44, Pantheon*
☎*06/68307895* ⊟*AE, MC, V.*

$$ ✕**Ōbikā.** If you've ever wanted to take in a "mozzarella bar," here's
ITALIAN your chance. Mozzarella is featured here much like sushi bars show-
case fresh fish—even the decor is modern Japanese minimalism–meets–
ancient Roman grandeur. The cheese, in all its varieties, is the focus of
the dishes: there's the familiar cow's milk, the delectable water buffalo
milk varieties from the Campagnia region, and the sinfully rich *burrata*
from Puglia (a fresh cow's milk mozzarella encasing a creamy center
of unspun mozzarella curds and fresh cream). They're all served with
various accompanying cured meats, vegetables, sauces, and breads. An

outdoor deck is a great plus for dining alfresco. ✉ *Piazza di Firenze 26, Navona* ☎ *06/6832630* ⊟ *AE, DC, MC, V*

$ ✕ **Cul de Sac.** This popular wine bar near Piazza Navona is among the
WINE BAR city's oldest enoteche and offers a book-length selection of wines from
Fodor'sChoice Italy, France, the Americas, and elsewhere. Food is eclectic, ranging
★ from a huge assortment of Italian meats and cheeses (try the delicious *lonza*, cured pork loin, or *speck*, a northern Italian smoked prosciutto) to various Mediterranean dishes, including delicious baba ghanoush, a tasty Greek salad, and a spectacular wild boar pâté. Outside tables get crowded fast, so arrive early, or come late, as they serve until about 1 AM. ✉ *Piazza Pasquino 73, 00186, Navona* ☎ *06/68801094* ⊟ *AE, MC, V* ⊘ *Closed 2 wks in Aug.*

$ ✕ **Da Baffetto.** Down a cobblestone street not far from Piazza Navona,
PIZZA this is Rome's most popular pizzeria and a summer favorite for street-
Fodor'sChoice side dining. The plain interior is mostly given over to the ovens, but
★ there's another room with more paper-covered tables. Outdoor tables (enclosed and heated in winter) provide much-needed additional seating. Turnover is fast and lingering is not encouraged. ✉ *Via del Governo Vecchio 114, Navona* ☎ *06/6861617* ⊟ *No credit cards* ⊘ *Closed Aug. No lunch.*

CAMPO DE' FIORI & GHETTO

$$$ ✕ **Ditirambo.** Don't let the country-kitchen ambience fool you. At this
MODERN little spot off Campo de' Fiori, the constantly changing selection of
ITALIAN offbeat takes on Italian classics is a step beyond ordinary Roman fare. The place is usually packed with diners who appreciate the adventuresome kitchen, though you may overhear complaints about the brusque service. Antipasti can be delicious and unexpected, like Gorgonzola-pear soufflé drizzled with aged balsamic vinegar, or a mille-feuille of eggplant, wild fennel, and anchovies. But people really love this place for rustic dishes like osso buco, Calabrian eggplant "meatballs," and hearty pasta with rabbit ragù. Vegetarians will adore the cheesy potato gratin with truffle shavings. ✉ *Piazza della Cancelleria 74, Campo de' Fiori* ☎ *06/6871626* ⊟ *AE, MC, V* ⊘ *Closed Aug. No lunch Mon.*

$$$ ✕ **Evangelista.** This restaurant seems to be so tucked away, even the
ITALIAN locals have difficulty stumbling upon it. Everybody, however, seems
Fodor'sChoice to know and love its *carciofi al mattone* (roasted artichokes pressed
★ flat between two hot bricks); this fame is well deserved, as the artichoke comes out crispy and delicious, looking almost like a perfectly seared vegetable carpaccio. Pastas are excellent, including the home-made potato gnocchi, light and fluffy and unadorned in a vegetable ragoût with a touch of saffron. Then feast on roast pork loin with juniper berries in winter, swordfish with Marsala, mint, and pistachio in summer. The arched white ceilings and decorating details lend an air of comfortable elegance. ✉ *Via delle Zoccolette 11/a, Campo de' Fiori* ☎ *06/6875810* ⊟ *AE, MC, V* ⊘ *Closed Sun. and Aug. No lunch.*

$$$ ✕ **Roscioli.** This food shop and wine bar is dark and decadent, more
WINE BAR like a Caravaggio painting than a place of business. The shop in front beckons with top-quality comestibles: whole prosciuttos, wild Alaskan

smoked salmon, more than 300 cheeses, and a dizzying array of wines. Venture further inside to be seated in a wine cave-like room where you'll be served artisanal cheeses and salamis, and the same oil, vinegar, and bread that you can purchase out front. Beyond display case items, the menu features creative dishes like homemade pasta with duck prosciutto, or potato gnocchi with a sea urchin sauce, both original uses of fairly esoteric (but steadfastly Italian) ingredients. Tip: book ahead to reserve a table in the cozy wine cellar beneath the dining room. ⊠ *Via dei Giubbonari 21/22, Campo de' Fiori* ☎*06/6875287* ▭*AE, DC, MC, V* ⊘*Closed Sun.*

$$–$$$ ✕**La Taverna Degli Amici.** This restaurant, on an idyllic ivy-draped piazza
ROMAN tucked away in the Jewish Ghetto, has what is considered one of the most delightful outdoor dining settings in Rome. Generally the menu features high-quality versions of Roman and Roman-Jewish classics. The *amatriciana* and *cacio e pepe* pastas are delicious, and the secondi courses continue the friendly feast with well-executed beef fillets with rosemary, roasted sea bream with potatoes, and a veal chop, pounded extra-thin, breaded and fried and topped with chopped cherry tomatoes and arugula. A selection from the unusual dessert list is a special treat here; try the cinnamon mousse. The wine list is edited and the markup substantial, but hey, what's a few extra euros among *amici?* ⊠*Piazza Margana 36, Ghetto* ☎*06/69920637* ▭*AE, DC, MC, V* ⊘*Closed Sun. and Mon. and 2 wks in Aug.*

$$ ✕**Da Sergio.** Every neighborhood has at least one "old-school" Roman
ROMAN trattoria and, for the Campo de' Fiori area, Da Sergio is it. Once you're seated (there's usually a wait), the red-and-white-check paper tablecovering, bright lights, '50s kitsch, and the stuffed boar's head on the wall remind you that you're smack in the middle of the genuine article. Go for the delicious version of pasta *all'amatriciana,* or the generous helping of gnocchi with a tomato sauce and lots of Parmesan cheese, served, as tradition dictates, on Thursday. ⊠*Vicolo delle Grotte 27, Campo de' Fiori* ☎*06/6864293* ▭*DC, MC, V* ⊘*Closed Sun. and 2 wks in Aug.*

$ ✕**Brasia.** This spacious trattoria on a back street off of the Campo de'
ITALIAN Fiori is a welcome, inexpensive addition to an area filled with tourist-riddled pizzerias and overpriced restaurants. The place itself is a huge space, but remains cozy because of brick walls and arched ceilings (the space actually harks back to the 17th century, and the name of the street it's on means "street of caves"). There's a wood-burning oven for homemade pizzas, and grilled meats are the other house specialty, here less expensive than in most spots. All typical Roman menu staples are found here as well: bruschette, mixed salumi and antipasti, and a variety of pasta standards. ⊠ *Vicolo delle Grotte 17, Campo de' Fiori* ☎*06/97277119.*

¢ ✕**Filetti di Baccalà.** For years, Filetti di Baccalà has been serving just
ITALIAN that—battered, deep-fried fillets of salt cod—and not much else. You'll find no-frills starters such as *bruschette al pomodoro* (garlic-rubbed toast topped with fresh tomatoes and olive oil), sautéed zucchini, and, in winter months, the cod is served alongside *puntarelle,* chicory stems topped with a delicious anchovy-garlic-lemon vinaigrette. The loca-

BEST BETS FOR ROME DINING

With hundreds of restaurants to choose from, how will you decide where to eat? Fodor's writers and editors have selected their favorite restaurants by price, cuisine, and experience in the Best Bets lists below. In the first column, Fodor's Choice properties represent the "best of the best" in every price category.

FODOR'S CHOICE ★

Agata e Romeo, $$$$ p. 104
Alle Fratte di Trastevere, $$ p. 107
Il Convivio, $$$$ p. 97
Cul de Sac, $ p. 98
Da Baffetto, $ p. 98
Etablì, $$$ p. 97
Evangelista, $$$ p. 98
Il Gelato di San Crispino, p. 109
La Pergola, $$$$ p. 105
Taverna Angelica, $$$ p. 106
Tazza d'Oro, ¢ p. 109
Tram Tram, $$ p. 105
Trattoria Monti, $$ p. 105
Uno e Bino, $$$ p. 104

Best by Price

¢

Caffe Sant'Eustachio p. 108
Filetti di Baccalà p. 99
Il Gelato di San Crispino p. 109
Tazza d'Oro p. 109

$

Brasia p. 99
Cul de Sac p. 98
Da Baffetto p. 98
Dar Poeta p. 107
Remo p. 108

$$

Alle Fratte di Trastevere p. 107
Da Sergio p. 99
Ōbikā p. 97
Tram Tram p. 105
Trattoria Monti p. 105

$$$

Ditirambo p. 98
Etablì p. 97
Evangelista p. 98
Taverna Angelica p. 106
Uno e Bino p. 104

$$$$

Agata e Romeo p. 104
Il Convivio p. 97
La Pergola p. 105

Best by Cuisine

CAFFÈ

GiNa p. 104

Caffe Sant'Eustachio p. 108
Tazza d'Oro p. 109

CENTRAL ITALIAN

Dal Bolognese p. 101
Trattoria Monti p. 105

MODERN ITALIAN

Agata e Romeo p. 104
Ditirambo p. 98
Il Convivio p. 97
Il Palazzetto p. 101
La Pergola p. 105
Taverna Angelica p. 106
Uno e Bino p. 104

OLD-SCHOOL ROMAN

Ai Tre Scalini p. 108
Checchino dal 1887 p. 107
Da Sergio p. 99

OSTERIA/TRATTORIA

Alle Fratte di Trastevere p. 107
Etablì p. 97
Maccheroni p. 97
Trattoria Monti p. 105

SOUTHERN ITALIAN

Siciliainbocca p. 106
Tram Tram p. 105

WINE BAR

Cul de Sac p. 98
Del Frate p. 106
Enoteca Trastevere p. 107
L'Enoteca Antica di Via della Croce p. 104

Best by Experience

CHILD-FRIENDLY

Alle Fratte di Trastevere p. 107
'Gusto p. 101

GOOD FOR GROUPS

Alle Fratte di Trastevere p. 107
Dar Poeta p. 107
'Gusto p. 101
Maccheroni p. 97

GORGEOUS SETTING

Agata e Romeo p. 104
Il Convivio p. 97
La Pergola p. 105

OUTDOOR DINING

Alle Fratte di Trastevere p. 107
Dal Bolognese p. 101
Maccheroni p. 97
Taverna degli Amici p. 99

MOST ROMANTIC

Il Convivio p. 97
La Pergola p. 105

tion, down the street from Campo de' Fiori in a little piazza in front of the beautiful Santa Barbara church, begs you to eat at one of the outdoor tables, weather-permitting. Long operating hours allow those still on U.S. time to eat as early (how gauche!) as 6 PM. ⊠*Largo dei Librari 88, Campo de' Fiori* ☎*06/6864018* ▭*No credit cards* ⊗*Closed Sun. and Aug. No lunch.*

> ### WORD OF MOUTH
>
> "If I were a vegetarian, I'd head to the Ghetto area and order artichokes prepared a variety of ways. Those things are almost enough to turn this committed meat eater into a vegetarian!!"—NeoPatrick

VENETO, BORGHESE & SPAGNA

$$$$
ITALIAN
✕**Dal Bolognese.** The darling of the media, film, and fashion communities, this classic restaurant on Piazza del Popolo is not only an "in-crowd" dinner destination but makes a convenient shopping-spree lunch spot. As the name promises, the cooking adheres to the hearty tradition of Bologna. Start with a plate of sweet *San Daniele* prosciutto with melon, then move on to the traditional egg pastas of Emilia-Romagna. Second plates include the famous Bolognese *bollito misto,* a steaming tray of an assortment of boiled meats (some recognizable, some indecipherable) served with a tangy, herby green sauce. ⊠*Piazza del Popolo 1, Spagna* ☎*06/3611426* ▭*AE, DC, MC, V* ⊗*Closed Mon. and 3 wks in Aug.*

$$$–$$$$
MEDI-
TERRANEAN
✕**'Gusto.** There's an urban-loft feel to this trendy two-story space, a bit like Pottery Barn exploded in Piazza Agusto Imperatore (the name of the restaurant is a play on this location and the Italian word for taste/flavor). The ground floor contains a buzzing pizzeria-trattoria, while upstairs is the more upscale restaurant, where a Mediterranean-meets-Asia menu results in some real misses. We prefer the casual-but-hopping vibe of the ground-floor wine bar in the back, where a rotating selection of wines by the glass and bottle are served up alongside a vast array of cheeses, salami, and bread products. And for the kitchen enthusiast, the 'Gusto "complex" includes a store, selling everything from cookware to cookwear. ⊠*Piazza Augusto Imperatore 9, Spagna* ☎*06/3226273* ▭*AE, DC, MC, V.*

$$–$$$
MODERN
ITALIAN
✕**Il Palazzetto.** This small restaurant by the Piazza di Spagna is part of the International Wine Academy of Rome. Chef Antonio Martucci creates seasonal menus using traditional Roman ingredients, which he gives a unique "twist" to in preparation and flavor pairings. Stuffed calamari on an eggplant puree with sautéed baby peppers is a study in contrasting flavor and texture; homemade ricotta-filled gnocchi with sausage and asparagus hits all the right notes. It's wise to call in advance, both for reservations and to find out about regular prix-fixe dinners, sometimes with guest chefs, focusing on wine-food pairings. ⊠*Vicolo del Bottino 8, Spagna* ☎*06/6990878* ▭*AE, DC, MC, V.*

$$
ITALIAN
✕**Margutta Vegetariano.** Parallel to posh Via del Babuino, Via Margutta has long been known as *the* street where artists have their studios in Rome. How fitting, then, that the rare Italian vegetarian restaurant,

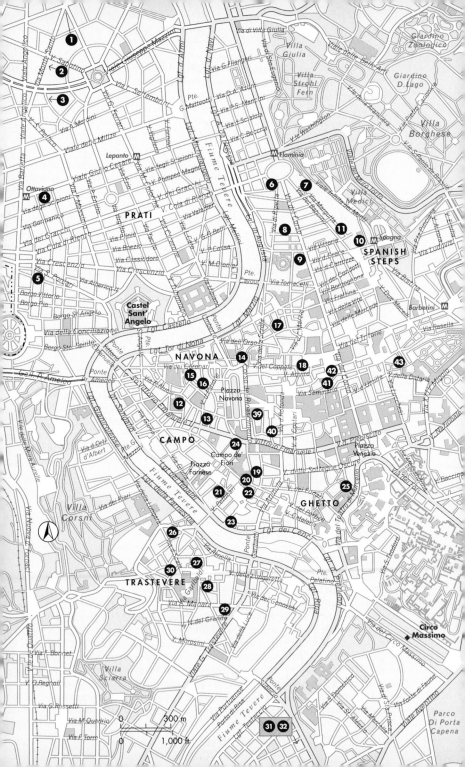

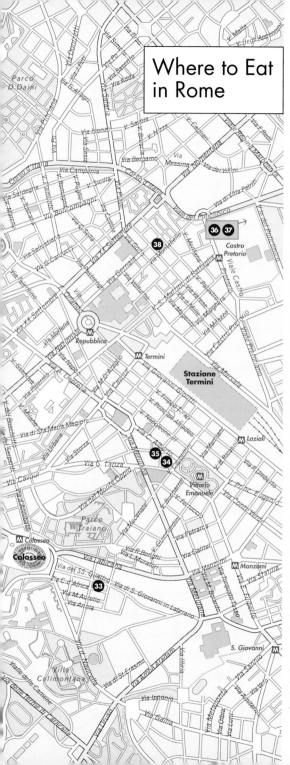

Where to Eat in Rome

1

with changing displays of modern art, sits on the far end of this gallery-lined street closest to Piazza del Popolo. Here it takes on a chic and cosmopolitan air, where you'll find meat-free versions of classic Mediterranean dishes as well as more daring tofu concoctions. Lunch is essentially a pasta/salad bar to which you help yourself, while dinner offers alla carte and prix fixe options. ⊠ *Via Margutta 118, Spagna* ☎*06/32650577* ⊟*AE, DC, MC, V.*

$ ✕**GiNa.** "Homey minimalism" isn't a contradiction at this white-
ITALIAN washed caffè with a modern edge. The block seats and sleek booths, the single flowers in Mason jars, white chandeliers, and multiplicity of mirrors, make this small but multilevel space a tiny gem tucked away on the street leading from Piazza di Spagna up to Villa Borghese. With a menu ranging from various bruschette to interesting mixed salads, sandwiches, and pastas, this is the perfect spot for a light lunch, an aperitivo, or a light dinner that won't break the bank in this high-end neighborhood. Also available are fully stocked gourmet picnic baskets, complete with checked tablecloth, to pick up on the way to the Villa Borghese. ⊠ *Via San Sebastianello 7A, Spagna* ☎*06/6780251* ⊟*AE, MC, V* ⊘ *Closed Sun. and Aug.; open only for lunch and aperitivi (until 8 pm) in summer.*

$ ✕**L'Enoteca Antica di Via della Croce.** This wine bar is always crowded,
WINE BAR and for good reason. It's long on personality: colorful ceramic-tile tables are always filled with locals and foreigners, as is the half-moon-shape bar where you can order from the large selection of salumi and cheeses on offer. Peruse the chalkboard highlighting the special wines by-the-glass for that day to accompany your nibbles. There's waiter service at the tables in back and out front on the bustling Via della Croce, where people-watching is in high gear. ⊠ *Via della Croce 76/b, Spagna* ☎*06/6790896* ⊟*AE, DC, MC, V* ⊘ *Closed 2 wks in Aug.*

MONTI, ESQUILINO, REPUBBLICA & SAN LORENZO

$$$$ ✕**Agata e Romeo.** For the perfect marriage of fine dining, creative cui-
MODERN sine, and rustic Roman tradition, the husband-and-wife team of Agata
ITALIAN Parisella and Romeo Caraccio is the top. Romeo presides over the din-
Fodor's Choice ing room and delights in the selection of wine-food pairings. And Chef
★ Agata was perhaps the first in the capital city to put a gourmet spin on Roman ingredients and preparations, elevating dishes of the common folk to new levels, wherein familiar staples like *coda alla vaccinara* are transformed into a rich oxtail ragoût with celery root, both as a puree and as shoestring fries. From antipasti to desserts, many dishes are the best versions of classics you can get. The prices here are steep, but for those who appreciate extremely high-quality ingredients, an incredible wine cellar, and warm service, dining here is a real treat. ⊠ *Via Carlo Alberto 45, Termini* ☎*06/4466115* ⊟*AE, DC, MC, V* ⊘ *Closed weekends, 2 wks in July, and 2 wks in Aug.*

$$$ ✕**Uno e Bino.** The setting is simple: wooden tables and chairs on a stone
ITALIAN floor with little more than a few shelves of wine bottles lining the walls
Fodor's Choice for decor. Giampaolo Gravina's restaurant in this artsy corner of the
★ San Lorenzo neighborhood is popular with foodies and locals alike, as

the kitchen turns out inventive cuisine inspired by the family's Umbrian and Sicilian roots. Dishes like octopus salad with asparagus and carrots, and spaghetti with swordfish, tomatoes, and capers are specialties. The parmesan soufflé is a study in lightness and silky-salty. Desserts are delicious and upscale-simple as well, making this small establishment one of the top dining deals—and pleasurable meals—in Rome. ⊠ *Via degli Equi 58, San Lorenzo* ☏*06/4460702* ▭*MC, V* ☉*Closed Mon. and Aug. No lunch.*

$$
ITALIAN
Fodor'sChoice
★
✕**Tram Tram.** This bustling trattoria is usually snugly packed with hungry Romans. The name refers to its proximity to the tram tracks, but could also describe its size, as it's narrow-narrow and often stuffed to the rafters-rafters. In warmer weather, there's a "side car" of tables enclosed along the sidewalk. The focus of the food is the cook's hometown region of Puglia. You'll find an emphasis on seafood and vegetables—maybe prawns with saffron-kissed sautéed vegetables—as well as pastas of very particular shapes. Fish is a good bet here; try the homemade *orecchiette,* ear-shaped pasta, made here with clams and broccoli. ⊠ *Via dei Reti 44/46, San Lorenzo* ☏*06/490416* ▭*AE, DC, MC, V* ☉*Closed Mon. and 1 wk in mid-Aug.*

$$
ITALIAN
Fodor'sChoice
★
✕**Trattoria Monti.** Not far from Santa Maria Maggiore and one of the most dependable, moderately priced trattorias in the city, Monti favors the cuisine of the Marches, an area to the northeast of Rome. There are surprisingly few places specializing in this humble fare considering there are more *marchegiani* in Rome than in the whole region of Le Marche. The fare served up by the Camerucci family is hearty and simple, represented by various roasted meats and game and a selection of generally vegetarian timbales and soufflés that change seasonally. The region's rabbit dishes are much loved, and here the *timballo di coniglio con patate* (rabbit casserole with potatoes) is no exception. ⊠ *Via di San Vito 13, Monti* ☏*06/4466573* ▭*AE, DC, MC, V* ☉*Closed Aug., 2 wks at Easter, and 10 days at Christmas.*

$$
WINE BAR
✕**Trimani Il Winebar.** This is a handy address for diners in a town where most restaurants don't open before 8 PM. Trimani operates nonstop from 11 AM to 12:30 AM and serves hot food at lunch and dinner. Decor is minimalist, and the second floor provides a subdued, candlelit space to sip wine. There's always a choice of a soup and pasta plates, as well as second courses and *torte salate* (savory tarts). Around the corner is a wineshop, one of the oldest in Rome, of the same name. Call about wine tastings and classes (in Italian). ⊠ *Via Cernaia 37/b, Repubblica* ☏*06/4469630* ▭*AE, DC, MC, V* ☉*Closed Sun. and 2 wks in Aug.*

VATICAN, BORGO & PRATI

$$$$
MODERN
ITALIAN
Fodor'sChoice
★
✕**La Pergola.** La Pergola's rooftop location offers a commanding view of the city, and as you're seated in your plush chair, you know you're in for a three–Michelin star experience. First, your waiter will present you with menus—food, wine, and water (you read correctly). Then you must choose between the German Wunder-chef Heinz Beck's *alta cucina* specialties, though most everything will prove to be the best version of the dish you've ever tasted. Lobster is oh-so-lightly poached,

and melt-in-your-mouth lamb in a veggie-accented jus is deceptively simple but earthy and perfect. Each course comes with a flourish of sauces or extra touches that makes it an event in its own right, while the cheese cart is well-explained by knowledgeable servers. And the dessert course is extravagant, including tiny petits fours and treats tucked away in small drawers that make up the serving "cabinet." The wine list is as thrilling as one might expect with the financial backing of the Hilton and their investment in one of the top wine cellars in Italy. ⊠ *Cavalieri Hilton, Via Cadlolo 101, Monte Mario, Northwest Rome* ☎*06/3509221* ⌂ *Reservations essential. Jacket and tie* ▤ *AE, DC, MC, V* ⊘ *Closed Sun. and Mon., and 2 wks in Dec. No lunch.*

WORD OF MOUTH

"No matter where you go, be bold and order from the list of daily specialties—usually handwritten in Italian on a chalkboard near the front door…it's what looked good at the market that day."
—Thomarob

$$$–$$$$
SOUTHERN
ITALIAN

✕ **Siciliainbocca.** The owners, both natives of the southernmost Italian island, decided to open up Siciliainbocca after years of frustration at not finding decent renditions of the food for which their home region is so renowned. As a result, the pasta *alla norma*—with eggplant, tomato sauce, and aged ricotta cheese—here is one of the best versions in Rome. Try specialties like *caponata*, a sweet-and-sour eggplant ratatouille, or *risotto ai profumi di Sicilia* with lemon, orange, mozzarella, and zucchini. Be sure to try the delicious grilled swordfish, shrimp, and squid. Even in the dead of winter, Siciliainbocca's yellow walls and brightly colored ceramic plates make you feel as if you're in sunny Sicily. ⊠ *Via E. Faà di Bruno 26, Prati* ☎*06/37358400* ▤ *AE, DC, MC, V* ⊘ *Closed Sun.*

$$$
MODERN
ITALIAN
Fodor'sChoice
★

✕ **Taverna Angelica.** The area surrounding St. Peter's Basilica isn't known for culinary excellence, but Taverna Angelica is an exception. Its tiny size allows the chef to concentrate on each individual dish, and the menu is creative without being pretentious. Dishes such as warm octopus salad on a bed of warm mashed potatoes with a basil-parsley pesto drizzle are more about taste than presentation. The lentil soup with pigeon breast brought hunter's cuisine to a new level. And the breast of duck in balsamic vinegar was exquisitely executed. It may be difficult to find, on a section of the street that's set back and almost subterranean, but it's worth searching out. ⊠ *Piazza A. Capponi 6, Borgo* ☎*06/6874514* ⌂ *Reservations essential* ▤ *AE, V.*

$$
WINE BAR

✕ **Del Frate.** This impressive wine bar, adjacent to one of Rome's noted wineshops, matches sleek and modern decor with creative cuisine and three dozen wines available by the glass. The house specialty is marinated meat and fish, and you can also get cheeses, smoked meats, and composed salads. For dessert, dip into the chocolate fondue. ⊠ *Via degli Scipioni 118, Prati* ☎*06/3236437* ▤ *AE, MC, V* ⊘ *Closed 3 wks in Aug.*

TRASTEVERE

$$$
TUSCAN

✕ **Il Ciak.** This Tuscan staple in Trastevere is a carnivore's delight. Specializing in the Tuscan *chianina* beef as well as the many game and pork dishes of the region (wild boar sausage, anyone? Or perhaps pasta with wild hare sauce?), Il Ciak prepares reliably tasty fare. It's probably best appreciated during the autumn and winter months, when hunter's dishes get accompaniments like porcini mushrooms and truffles with polenta that even vegetarians will appreciate. Be prepared to share the pleasure of your oversized fiorentina steak—prepared *al sangue* (rare), of course. ⊠ *Vicolo del Cinque, Trastevere* ☎ *06/5890774* ☰ *MC, V* ⊗ *Closed Sun.*

$$
ROMAN
Fodor'sChoice
★

✕ **Alle Fratte di Trastevere.** Here you can find staple Roman trattoria fare as well as dishes with a southern slant. This means that *spaghetti alla carbonara* (with pancetta, eggs, and cheese) shares the menu with the likes of penne *alla Sorrentina* (with tomato, basil, and fresh mozarella). For starters, the bruschette here are exemplary, as is the pressed octopus carpaccio on a bed of arugula. As for secondi, you can again look south and to the sea for a mixed seafood pasta or a grilled sea bass with oven-roasted potatoes, or go for the meat with a fillet *al pepe verde* (green peppercorns in a brandy cream sauce). Service is always with a smile, as the owners and their trusted waitstaff make you feel at home. ⊠ *Via delle Fratte di Trastevere 49/5000153* ☎ *06/5835775* ☰ *AE, DC, MC, V* ⊗ *Closed Wed. and 2 wks in Aug.*

$
PIZZA

✕ **Dar Poeta.** Romans drive across town for great pizza from this neighborhood institution on a small street in Trastevere. Maybe it's the dough—it's made from a secret blend of flours that's reputed to be easier to digest than the competition. They offer both thin-crust pizza and a thick-crust ("*alta*") Neapolitan-style pizza with any of the given toppings. For dessert, there's a ridiculously good calzone with Nutella chocolate-hazelnut spread and ricotta cheese, so save some room. Service from the owners and friendly waitstaff is smile-inducing. ⊠ *Vicolo del Bologna 45, Trastevere* ☎ *06/5880516* ☰ *AE, MC, V.*

$
WINE BAR

✕ **Enoteca Trastevere.** Most wine bars in Rome seem to share the same interior decorator and this one is no exception, with its dark-wood tables, chairs, and shelves lined with bottles of Italian wines. Rome's enoteca menu consultant is a busy person as well; the usual crostini, cheeses, cured meats, and salads are all here. But what sets this wine bar apart from others is its central location with a large outdoor seating space and big, white umbrellas. Its large selection of organic wine is another selling point, as well as its rich selection of grappas, distilled liquors, and *amari* (Italian bitter herbal digestives). The reasonable prices and friendly service round out the pleasant experience. ⊠ *Via della Lungaretta 86, Trastevere* ☎ *06/5885659* ☰ *AE, MC, V* ⊗ *Closed 3 wks in Jan.*

COLOSSEO, AVENTINO & TESTACCIO

$$$$
ROMAN
Testaccio

✕ **Checchino dal 1887.** Literally carved out of a hill of ancient shards of amphorae, Checchino remains an example of a classic, family-run Roman restaurant, with one of the best wine cellars in the region.

Though the slaughterhouses of this quarter, Testaccio, are long gone, an echo of their past existence lives on in the restaurant's soul food—mostly offal and other less-traditionally appealing cuts like *trippa* (tripe), *pajata* (intestine with the mother's milk still inside), and *coratella* (sweetbreads and heart of beef) are all still on the menu for die-hard Roman purists. For the less adventuresome, house specialties include braised milk-fed lamb with seasonal vegetables. Head here for a taste of old Rome, but note that Checchino is really beginning to show its age. ⊠ *Via di Monte Testaccio 30* ☎*06/5746318* ▭*AE, DC, MC, V* ☉*Closed Sun., Mon., Aug, and 1 wk at Christmas.*

$$$
ROMAN
Colosseo

✕**Ai Tre Scalini.** A traditional restaurant by the Colosseum, Ai Tre Scalini is old-school Roman with touches of the Sicilian. Some dishes don't appear as described on the menu: eggplant "flan" arrived as parmigiana, and newborn-fish fritters were dry, baked, briny balls. But seating outside in warm weather is pleasant, and some dishes highlight the chef's playfulness, like the unusual radicchio and cheese-stuffed *zagnolotti* (small ravioli) in a lobster sauce. A wide variety of second courses, from gilthead bream topped with paper-thin potato rounds, to simple beef with rosemary, are indeed what they seem, served by waiters who have clearly been around for quite some time. ⊠ *Via SS. Quattro 30, Colosseo* ☎*06/7096309* ▭*AE, DC, MC, V* ☉*Closed Mon. and 10 days in Sept.*

$
PIZZA
Testaccio

✕**Remo.** Expect a wait at this perennial favorite in Testaccio frequented by students and neighborhood locals. You won't find tablecloths or other nonessentials, just classic Roman pizza and boisterous conversation. ⊠*Piazza Santa Maria Liberatrice 44, Testaccio* ☎*06/5746270* ▭*No credit cards* ☉*Closed Sun., Aug., and Christmas wk. No lunch.*

CAFFÉS

Caffé-sitting is a popular leisure-time activity in Rome, practiced by all and involving nothing more strenuous than gesturing to catch the waiter's eye. Part of the pleasure is resting your tired feet; you won't be rushed, even when the cafés are most crowded, just before lunch and dinner. (Be aware, though, that you pay for your seat—prices are higher at tables than at the counter.) Nearly every corner in Rome holds a faster-paced coffee bar, where locals stop for a quick caffeine hit at the counter. You can get coffee drinks, fruit juices, pastries, sandwiches, liquor, and beer there, too.

Caffè Sant'Eustachio (⊠*P. Sant'Eustachio 82, Pantheon* ☎*06/68802048*), traditionally frequented by Rome's literati, has what is generally considered Rome's best cup of coffee. Just walking into the blue-and-yellow spot, the smell of freshly ground beans wafts over you, letting you know that this is *the* place. Servers purposely hidden behind a huge espresso machine vigorously mix the sugar and coffee for you to protect their "secret method" for the perfectly prepared cup. (If you want your *caffè* without sugar here, ask for it *amaro*.) Don't miss the *gran caffè*, a secret concoction unlike anything else in the city.

1

Fodors Choice **Tazza d'Oro** (⊠ *Via degli Orfani, Pantheon* ☎*06/6789792*) has many
★ admirers who contend it serves the city's best cup of coffee. The hot
chocolate in winter, all thick and gooey goodness, is a treat. And in
warm weather, the coffee granita is the perfect cooling alternative to
a regular espresso.

With its sidewalk tables taking in Santa Maria della Pace's adorable piazza,
Caffè della Pace (⊠ *Via della Pace 3, Navona* ☎*06/6861216*) has long been
the haunt of Rome's *beau monde*. Set on a quiet street near Piazza Navona,
it also has two rooms filled with old-world personality.

GELATO

For many travelers, the first taste of *gelato*—Italian ice cream—is one
of the most memorable moments of their Italian trip. Almost a cross
between regular American ice cream and soft serve, gelato's texture is
lighter and fluffier than hard ice cream because of the process by which
it's whipped when freezing.

Along with the listings here, you can find a number of gelaterias in Via
di Tor Millina, a street off the west side of Piazza Navona.

Fodors Choice **Il Gelato di San Crispino** (⊠ *Via della Panetteria 54, Piazza di Trevi*
★ ☎*06/6793924* ⊘ *Closed Tues.*) makes perhaps the most celebrated
gelato in all of Italy, without artificial colors or flavors. It's worth crossing town for—nobody else creates flavors this pure. To preserve the
"integrity" of the flavor, the ice cream is only served in paper cups.

For years **Giolitti** (⊠ *Via degli Uffici del Vicario 40, Pantheon*
☎*06/6991243*) was considered the best gelateria in Rome, and it's
still worth a stop if you're near the Pantheon.

Immediately beside the Pantheon is **Cremeria Monteforte** (⊠ *Via della
Rotonda 22, Pantheon* ☎*06/6867720*), which has won several awards
for its flavors. Also worth trying is its chocolate sorbetto—it's an icier
version of the gelato without the dairy (instead ask for whipped cream
on top).

Gelateria alla Scala (⊠ *Via della Scala 51, Trastevere* ☎*06/5813174*
⊘ *Closed Dec. and Jan.*) is a tiny place, but don't let the size fool
you. It does a good business offering artisanal gelato prepared in small
batches, so when one flavor runs out on any given day, its finished.

Al Settimo Gelo (⊠ *Via Vodice 21/a, Prati* ☎*06/3725567*), in Prati, has
been getting rave reviews for both classic flavors and newfangled inven-
tions. Inventive flavors, such as cardamom and chestnut, wow locals
and gelato fans from all over Rome.

WHERE TO STAY

Updated by
Jen Laskey

When planning your Roman Holiday, you may be surprised to learn that you really will have to *do* as the Romans do, meaning that unless you're coveting a luxury suite at the Eden, you'll probably find yourself in a tiny room. The air-conditioning may be weak and the customer service will likely be indifferent. Naturally, there are exceptions, but the Eternal City simply doesn't offer the cushy standards that most Americans are accustomed to, though standards in general are improving.

There are more luxury lodgings, bed-and-breakfasts, and designer "boutique" hotels in Rome than ever before, but if you prefer more modest accommodations (because really, who comes to Rome to hang out in the hotel room?), you still have plenty of options. There are many mid-range and budget hotels and *pensioni* (small, family-run lodgings) available. You may also consider staying at a monastery or convent, a hostel, or an apartment.

If you're looking for luxury, you're most likely to find it around Via Veneto and the Spanish Steps area. On the contrary, many of the city's cheapest accommodations are located near Stazione Termini. But for the most authentic Roman experience, stay in or near the *centro storico* (the historic center).

WHAT IT COSTS IN EUROS					
	¢	$	$$	$$$	$$$$
FOR TWO PEOPLE	under €75	€75–€150	€151–€225	€226–€300	over €300

Prices are for a standard double room in high season.

PANTHEON, NAVONA, TREVI & QUIRINALE

$$$ **Pantheon.** The Pantheon is a superb place to stay right next door to the grand monument of the same name. The lobby is the very epitome of a Roman hotel lobby—a warm, cozy, yet opulent setting that comes replete with Stil Liberty stained glass, sumptuous wood paneling, a Renaissance beamed ceiling, and a massive and glorious chandelier. A print of one of Rome's obelisks on the door welcomes you to your room, where you'll find antique walnut furniture, fresh flowers, and more wood-beam ceilings. **Pros:** proximity to the Pantheon; big, clean bathrooms; friendly staff. **Cons:** rooms are in need of some upgrading; the lighting is low and the carpets are worn; the breakfast lacks variety. ⊠ *Via dei Pastini 131, Pantheon, 00186* ☎*06/6787746* ☎*06/6787755* ⊕*www.hotelpantheon.com* ⇱*13 rooms, 1 suite* ⌂*In-room: safe, refrigerator, Wi-Fi. In-hotel: bar, room service, laundry service, public Wi-Fi, no-smoking rooms* ⊟*AE, DC, MC, V* ⦿*CP.*

$$ **Albergo Santa Chiara.** With its white shutters and pretty canteloupe-hue stone, this hotel is comprised of three historic buildings set behind the Pantheon. It's been in the same family for 200 years, and the personal attention shows in meticulously decorated and maintained lounges and

Fodor's Choice
★

rooms. The lobby is *alla Romana*—an all white affair; it's elegantly accented with a Venetian chandelier, a stucco statue, a gilded baroque mirror, and a walnut concierge desk. Upstairs, the pricier rooms are most fetching, with stylish yet comfortable furniture. Each room has built-in oak headboards, a marble-top desk, and a travertine bath. Double-glaze windows make a difference in those rooms that look out over the Piazza della Minerva. There are also three apartments, for two to five people, with full kitchens. **Pros:** great location in the historical center behind the Pantheon; most of the rooms are spacious; the staff is both polite and helpful. **Cons:** layout is maze-like (you must take two elevators to some of the rooms); rooms don't get a lot of light; no Internet access at the hotel. ⊠ *Via Santa Chiara 21, Pantheon, 00186* ☎*06/6872979* 🖷*06/6873144* ⊕*www.albergosantachiara.com* ⇋*96 rooms, 3 suites, 3 apartments* ⌂*In-room: safe, kitchen (some), refrigerator. In-hotel: room service, bar, laundry service, concierge, airport shuttle (fee)* ⊟*AE, DC, MC, V* ⓘⓄⅠ*CP.*

$$ **Hotel Trevi.** Location, location, location: this delightful place is tucked away down one of Old Rome's quaintest alleys near the Trevi Fountain. The smallish rooms are bright and clean, and a few of the larger ones have antique furniture and wooden ceilings with massive beams. There's also an arborlike roof-garden restaurant where you can eat marvelous pasta as you peer out at the city below. **Pros:** pass the Trevi Fountain each day as you come and go; comfortable rooms; roof-garden restaurant. **Cons:** breakfast room is cramped; staff is brusque; no Internet connection in the rooms or in the public spaces. ⊠ *Vicolo del Babbuccio 20/21, Piazza di Trevi, 00187* ☎*06/6789563* 🖷*06/69941407* ⊕*www.gruppotrevi.it* ⇋*29 rooms* ⌂*In-room: safe, refrigerator. In-hotel: restaurant, room service, laundry service, airport shuttle (fee), parking (fee), no-smoking rooms* ⊟*AE, DC, MC, V* ⓘⓄⅠ*CP.*

$–$$ **Genio.** Just at the ancient entrance to Piazza Navona, this medium-size hotel offers top-floor rooms with terraces and citywide views. There's also a roof terrace for all, where you can eat your breakfast. Modeled along classic Roman lines, the lobby and public areas are cozy. Rooms are decorated in warm colors and have parquet floors and a harmonious mix of modern and antique reproduction furnishings. **Pros:** you can sip wine on the rooftop and take in the view; rooms are a decent size for a Roman hotel; the bathrooms have been designed especially well. **Cons:** Genio is on a busy street so there is often traffic noise; you might hear your neighbors through the walls; both the decor and the carpet have seen better days. ⊠ *Via G. Zanardelli 28, Navona, 00186* ☎*06/6832191* 🖷*06/68307246* ⊕*www.leonardihotels.com/Genio/index.jsp* ⇋*60 rooms* ⌂*In-room: refrigerator. In-hotel: room service, bar, laundry services, public Internet, parking (fee)* ⊟*AE, DC, MC, V* ⓘⓄⅠ*CP.*

CAMPO DE' FIORI AND GHETTO

$$$$ **Hotel Ponte Sisto.** With one of the prettiest patio-courtyards in Rome, this hotel offers its own blissful definition of *Pax Romana*. Peace, indeed, will be yours sitting in this enchanting spot, shadowed by palm trees, set with tables, and adorned with pink and white flowers, all surrounded by the ochre walls of the hotel. Inside, the sleek decors, replete with cherry wood accents, recessed lighting, and luminous marble floors also give a calming effect. Guest rooms are refined—suites come with Jacuzzis and furnished balconies or terraces, bathrooms can be lavishly modern, and there's also a bar and restaurant. The location is an award-winner—just off the Ponte Sisto, the pedestrian bridge that connects the Campo de' Fiori area with Trastevere (whose trattorias and bars are thus just a quick jaunt away), and a second from Via Giulia, Rome's prettiest street. **Pros:** some rooms with views; luxury bathrooms; beautiful courtyard garden. **Cons:** street-side rooms can be a bit noisy; some rooms are on the small side; restaurant doesn't serve lunch or dinner. ☒ *Via dei Pettinari 64, Campo de' Fiori, 00186* ☎ *06/686310* 🖷 *06/68301712* ⊕ *www.hotelpontesisto.it* 📞 *103 rooms, 4 suites* ♿ *In-room: safe, refrigerator, dial-up. In-hotel: restaurant, room service, bar, laundry service, public Internet, airport shuttle (fee), parking (fee), some pets allowed, no-smoking rooms* ▤ *AE, DC, MC, V* ⴲ *BP.*

\$\$ Hotel Campo de' Fiori. Frescoes, exposed brickwork, and picturesque effects throughout this little hotel could well be the work of a set designer, but a recent renovation attributes the charming ambience to interior designer Dario di Blasi. Each room is entirely unique in its colors, furniture, and refined feel. The hotel underwent a complete renovation in 2006, retaining its old-world charm, but modernizing with soundproofing, air-conditioning, flat-screen TVs, pay-per-view movies, DSL, and Wi-Fi in all the rooms. There is also a marvelous view from the roof terrace. If you desire more extensive accommodations, Hotel Campo de' Fiori offers an additional selection of 15 different apartments in the area that can accommodate two to five guests. **Pros:** newly reonovated; superb location; modern amenities that many Roman hotels haven't caught up with yet; rooftop terrace. **Cons:** some of the rooms are very small; breakfast works on a voucher system with a nearby caffè; the staff doesn't necessarily go out of their way to help you settle in. ☒ *Via del Biscione 6, Campo de' Fiori, 00186* ☎ *06/68806865* 🖷 *06/6876003* ⊕ *www.hotelcampodefiori.it* 📞 *28 rooms* ♿ *In-room: safe, refrigerator, high-speed Internet, Wi-Fi. In-hotel: no-smoking rooms* ▤ *MC, V* ⴲ *CP.*

\$\$ Teatro di Pompeo. Where else can you breakfast under the ancient stone vaults of Pompey's Theater, historic site of Julius Caesar's assassination? At this intimate and refined little hotel in the heart of Old Rome you are part of that history. At night, you sleep under restored beamed ceilings that date from the days of Michelangelo. Rooms are simple but tasteful, with terra-cotta floors, comfortable old-fashioned beds, and attractive antique furniture. The staff is also sincere and helpful. Hotel Teatro di Pompeo is the kind of place that really makes you feel like you're living among the true Romans. Do yourself a favor, and book well in advance. **Pros:** location is central to the Campo but not right on the market square; helpful staff; affordable with an old-school Roman feel. **Cons:** it can be noisy on both the street side and the interior courtyard; rooms are small; no Wi-Fi. ☒ *Largo del Pallaro*

1

8, Campo de' Fiori, 00186 ☎*06/68300170* 🖷*06/68805531* ⊕*www. hotelteatrodipompeo.it* 🛏*13 rooms* ♿*In-room: safe, refrigerator. In-hotel: room service, bar, laundry service, public Internet* ▤*AE, DC, MC, V* ꙮ*CP.*

$ **Arenula.** Standing on an age-worn byway off central Via Arenula, this hotel is a superb bargain by Rome standards. With an imposingly elegant stone exterior, this hotel welcomes you with a luminous and cheerful all-white interior. Guest rooms are simple in decor but have pale-wood furnishings and gleaming bathrooms, as well as double-glaze windows and air-conditioning (in summer only; ask when you reserve). Two of the rooms accommodate four beds. Of course, you can't have everything, so that the graceful oval staircase of white marble and wrought iron in the lobby cues you that there is no elevator. Those guests with rooms on the fourth floor had better be in good shape! **Pros:** it's a real bargain; conveniently located in the Ghetto (close to Campo de' Fiori and Trastevere), and it's spotless. **Cons:** totally no-frills accommodations; four floors and no elevator; traffic and tram noise can be heard throughout the night despite the double-glazing. ⊠ *Via Santa Maria dei Calderari 47, off Via Arenula, Ghetto, 00186* ☎*06/6879454* 🖷*06/6896188* ⊕*www.hotelarenula.com* 🛏*50 rooms* ♿*In-room: no a/c (some). In-hotel: no elevator* ▤*AE, DC, MC, V* ꙮ*CP.*

VENETO, BORGHESE & SPAGNA

$$$$ **Eden.** Once the preferred haunt of Hemingway, Bergman, and Fellini,
Fodor'sChoice this superlative hotel combines dashing elegance and stunning vistas
★ of Rome with the warmth of Italian hospitality. Set atop a hill near the Villa Borghese (and a bit out of the historic center for serious sightseers), this hotel was opened in the late 19th century and quickly became famous for its balcony views and Roman splendor. You'll now dive deep here into the whoosh of luxury, with antiques, sumptuous Italian fabrics, linen sheets, and marble baths competing for your attention. Banquette window seats, rich mahogany furniture, soaring ceilings, Napoléon-Trois sofas are just some of the allurements here. **Pros:** gorgeous panoramic view from roof terrace; you could be rubbing elbows with the stars; 24-hour room service. **Cons:** expensive (unless money is no object for you); no Wi-Fi in the rooms; some say the staff can be hit-or-miss. ⊠ *Via Ludovisi 49, Veneto, 00187* ☎*06/478121* 🖷*06/4821584* ⊕*www.lemeridien.com/eden* 🛏*121 rooms, 13 suites* ♿*In-room: safe, refrigerator, DVD (some), high-speed Internet. In-hotel: restaurant, room service, 2 bars, gym, concierge, laundry service, public Internet, Wi-Fi, airport shuttle (fee), parking (fee), no-smoking rooms, some pets allowed* ▤*AE, DC, MC, V* ꙮ*EP.*

$$$$ **Hassler.** Here, in villas atop the Pincian Hill, Poussin, Piranesi, Ingres,
Fodor'sChoice and Berlioz once enjoyed having all of Rome at their feet. Today, movie
★ stars and millionaires do the same by staying at this hotel, which sits just to the right of the church atop the Spanish Steps. The guest rooms here are among the world's most beautiful and opulent. If you're not willing to pay V.I.P prices, you'll get more standard-issue rooms at the rear of the hotel, but many are soigné and some come with views of the

BEST BETS FOR ROME LODGING

Fodor's offers a selective listing of quality lodging experiences at every price range, from the city's best budget motel to its most sophisticated luxury hotel. Here, we've compiled our top recommendations by price and experience. The very best properties—in other words, those that provide a particularly remarkable experience in their price range—are designated in the listings with the Fodor's Choice logo.

FODOR'S CHOICE ★

Albergo Santa Chiara, $$ p. 101
The Beehive, $ p. 121
Daphne Veneto, $$ p. 118
Eden, $$$$ p. 113
Hassler, $$$$ p. 113
Hotel San Pietrino, ¢ p. 124
Relais Le Clarisse, $$ p. 124
Scalinata di Spagna, $$$ p. 115
Yes Hotel, $ p. 121

Best by Price

¢

Hotel San Pietrino p. 124
Italia p. 121
Arenula p. 113
The Beehive p. 121
Hotel Trastevere p. 125
Yes Hotel p. 121

$$

Albergo Santa Chiara p. 110
Alimandi p. 123
Daphne Veneto p. 118
Hotel Campo de' Fiori p. 112
Hotel Santa Maria p. 124
Relais Le Clarisse p. 124
San Carlo p. 118

$$$

Pantheon p. 110
Scalinata di Spagna p. 115

$$$$

Capo d'Africa p. 126
Eden p. 113
Hassler p. 113

Best by Experience

BEST B&BS

Daphne Veneto p. 118
Relais Le Clarisse p. 124

BEST FOR BUSINESS TRAVEL

Cavalieri Hilton p. 123
Exedra p. 119

BEST CONCIERGE

The Beehive p. 121
Daphne Veneto p. 118
Hotel Lancelot p. 126
Scalinata di Spagna p. 115

BEST DESIGN

Capo d'Africa p. 126
Exedra p. 119

BEST POOLS

Cavalieri Hilton p. 123
Exedra p. 119

BEST SPAS

Cavalieri Hilton p. 123
Exedra p. 119

CHILD-FRIENDLY

Cavalieri Hilton p. 123
Hassler p. 113
Hotel Lancelot p. 126
Hotel Ponte Sisto p. 111

GREAT VIEWS

Cavalieri Hilton p. 123
Eden p. 113
Genio p. 111
Hassler p. 113
Hotel Campo de' Fiori p. 112
San Carlo p. 118

HIDDEN OASIS

Capo d'Africa p. 126
Domus Aventina p. 125
Hotel Lancelot p. 126
Hotel San Anselmo p. 125
Hotel Santa Maria p. 124
Relais Le Clarisse p. 124

MOST ROMANTIC

Daphne Veneto p. 118
Hotel Ponte Sisto p. 111
Relais Le Clarisse p. 124

NEIGHBORHOOD FEEL

Domus Aventina p. 125
Giuliana p. 120
Hotel Santa Maria p. 124
Hotel Trastevere p. 125
Relais Le Clarisse p. 124
Sant' Anna p. 124
Teatro di Pompeo p. 112

Villa Medici park. Better, the hotel has several elegant bars, restaurants, and retreats. The Rooftop Restaurant is world-famous for its view if not for its food; the Hassler Bar was where Princess Diana savored one of the hotel's "Veruschkas" (pomegranate juice, vodka, and champagne); and the Palm Court Garden, which becomes the hotel bar in summer, is overflowing with flowers. **Pros:** charming old-world feel; prime location and panoramic views at the top of the Spanish Steps; just "steps" away from some of the best shopping in the world. **Cons:** V.I.P. prices; many think the staff are too standoffish; some say the cuisine at the rooftop restaurant isn't worth the gourmet price tag. ⊠*Piazza Trinità dei Monti 6, Spagna, 00187* ☎*06/699340* 🖷*06/6789991* ⊕*www.lhw. com* ⟿*85 rooms, 13 suites* ⟳*In-room: safe, refrigerator, high-speed Internet. In-hotel: restaurant, room service, bar, gym, spa, concierge, laundry service, public Wi-Fi, parking (fee), no-smoking rooms* ⊟*AE, DC, MC, V* ⦿|*EP.*

$$$
Fodor's Choice
★

Scalinata di Spagna. An old-fashioned pensione that has hosted generations of romantics, this tiny hotel is booked solid for months ahead. Its location at the very top of the Spanish Steps, inconspicuous little entrance, and quiet, sunny charm add up to the feeling of your own pied-à-terre in the city's most glamorous neighborhood. Guest rooms are chic, with high-style floral fabrics and Empire-style sofas. The rooms most in demand are those overlooking the Spanish Steps, but even if you don't land one of those few, you can repair to the hotel's exquisite roof garden, where you can have breakfast with Rome unfolding before you. Amenities, such as in-room Internet access and breakfast service until noon are a nice touch. **Pros:** friendly and helpful concierge; fresh fruit in the rooms; free Wi-Fi throughout the Scalinata. **Cons:** it's a hike up the hill to the hotel; no porter and no elevator; service can be hit-or-miss. ⊠*Piazza Trinità dei Monti 17, Spagna, 00187* ☎*06/6793006* 🖷*06/69940598* ⊕*www.hotelscalinata.com* ⟿*16 rooms* ⟳*In-room: safe, refrigerator, Wi-Fi. In-hotel: room service, no elevator, laundry service, concierge, public Internet, public Wi-Fi, parking (fee), no-smoking rooms* ⊟*AE, D, MC, V* ⦿|*BP*

$$-$$$
Hotel Homs. At this midsize hotel, on a quiet street in the heart of the historic center, two rooftop terraces provide fine views of the whole area; the larger terrace is suitable for breakfast year-round. Although room furnishings are a bit plain overall, beautiful antiques accent strategic spots for an air that's a cut above average. Rome's most complete English-language bookshop, the Anglo-American, is directly across the street. **Pros:** walking distance to Piazza di Spagna; recently renovated; helpful staff. **Cons:** no breakfast included in the room rate; small rooms; fee for the Wi-Fi. ⊠*Via della Vite 71–72, Spagna, 00187* ☎*06/6792976* 🖷*06/6780482* ⟿*53 rooms, 5 suites, 1 apartment* ⟳*In-room: safe, refrigerator, high-speed Internet. In-hotel: room service, bar, laundry service, public Wi-Fi, airport shuttle (fee), parking (fee), some pets allowed, no-smoking rooms* ⊟*AE, DC, MC, V* ⦿|*EP.*

$$-$$$
Locarno. The sort of place that inspired a movie (Bernard Weber's 1978 *Hotel Locarno*, to be exact), this has been a longtime choice for art aficionados and people in cinema. But everyone will appreciate this

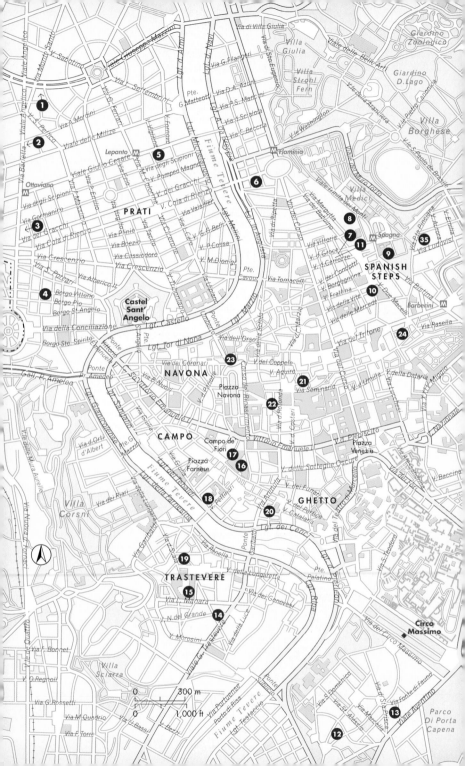

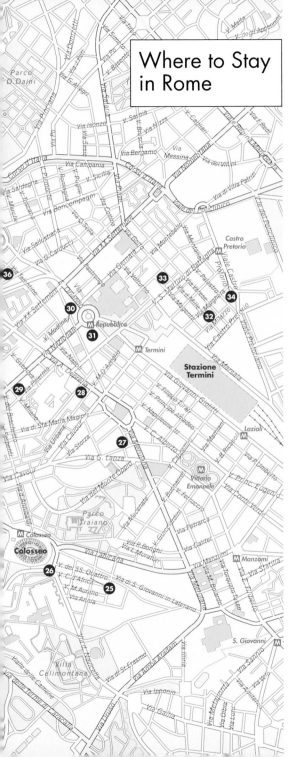

Where to Stay in Rome

hotel's fin de siècle charm, intimate feel, and central location off Piazza del Popolo. Exquisite wallpaper and fabric prints are coordinated in the rooms, and some rooms are decorated with antiques. Everything is lovingly supervised by the owners, a mother-daughter duo. The buffet breakfast is ample, there's bar service on the panoramic roof garden, and complimentary bicycles are available if you feel like braving the traffic. A newly renovated annex is done in Art Deco style. **Pros:** luxurious feel (it may even seem like you're in a movie); spacious rooms (even by American standards); free bicycles for exploring Rome. **Cons:** some of the rooms are dark; the annex doesn't compare to the main hotel; the regular staff probably won't go out of their way to help you. ✉ *Via della Penna 22, Spagna, 00186* ☎*06/3610841* 🖷*06/3215249* ⊕*www. hotellocarno.com* ↩*64 rooms, 2 suites* ☌*In-room: safe, refrigerator, Wi-Fi. In-hotel: restaurant, bar, bicycles, laundry service, public Internet, public Wi-Fi, airport shuttle (fee), no-smoking rooms* ▭*AE, DC, MC, V* ⦿|*BP.*

$$ **Daphne Veneto.** Inspired by baroque artist Gianlorenzo Bernini's exqui-
Fodor's Choice   site Apollo and Daphne sculpture at the Borghese Gallery, the Daphne
★   Inn at Via Veneto is an "urban B&B" run by people who love Rome and who will do their best to make sure you love it too. This boutique hotel offers an intimate lodging experience, elegantly designed rooms, comfortable beds, a cell phone to use during your stay, fresh fruit and pastries with your coffee each morning, and a small staff of people who promise to give you the opportunity to see Rome "like an insider." They will help you map out your destinations, schedule itineraries, plan day trips, and book tours. **Pros:** you get a priceless introduction to Rome by lovers of Rome; the beds have plush mattresses and fluffy comforters. **Cons:** no TVs; Daphne only accepts Visa or Mastercard to hold bookings (though you can actually pay with an AmEx); there are only seven rooms at the Daphne Veneto (and five at Daphne Trevi), and they're usually booked ahead. ✉ *Via di San Basilio 55, Veneto, 00187* ☎*06/87450087* 🖷*06/233240967* ⊕*www.daphne-rome.com* ↩*7 rooms, 2 suites* ☌*In-room: safe, refrigerator, no TV, high-speed Internet. In-hotel: bicycles, laundry service, concierge, public Internet, public Wi-Fi, airport shuttle (fee), parking (fee), no-smoking rooms* ▭*AE, MC, V* ⦿|*CP.*

$$ **San Carlo.** Marble accents are everywhere at this renovated 17th-century mansion, and there's an overall effect that's refined and decidedly classical. Rooms are bright and comfortable; some have their own terraces with rooftop views. A top-floor terrace is ideal for having breakfast or taking in the sun throughout the day. The rooms also feature flat-screen TVs and free Wi-Fi. **Pros:** rooms with terraces and views of historic Rome; rooftop garden; attentive staff. **Cons:** there are a lot of stairs and no elevator; breakfast is basic Italian fare (great coffee but otherwise just cornetti, cereal, and yogurt); the rooms can be noisy. ✉ *Via delle Carrozze 92–93, Spagna, 00187* ☎*06/6784548* 🖷*06/69941197* ⊕*www.hotelsancarloroma.com* ↩*50 rooms, 2 suites* ☌*In-room: refrigerator, Wi-Fi. In-hotel: bar, no elevator, laundry service, public Wi-Fi, no-smoking rooms* ▭*AE, DC, MC, V* ⦿|*CP.*

$ **Panda.** One of the best deals in Rome, the Panda is particularly remarkable given that the neighborhood is Via della Croce, one of Piazza di Spagna's chic shopping streets. Guest rooms are outfitted in terra-cotta and wrought iron; they're smallish, but quiet, thanks to double-glaze windows, and spotlessly clean. Pay even less by sharing a bath—in low season, you may have it to yourself anyway. **Pros:** discount if you pay cash; free Wi-Fi; located on a quiet street, but still close to the Spanish Steps. **Cons:** some say the Wi-Fi signal is weak; not all rooms have private bathrooms; Panda doesn't have an elevator; no TVs in the rooms. ⊠ *Via della Croce 35, Spagna, 00187* ☎*06/6780179* 🖷*06/69942151* ⊕*www.hotelpanda.it* ↩*20 rooms, 14 with bath* ⌂*In-room: no a/c (some), no TV, Wi-Fi. In-hotel: no elevator, laundry service, public Wi-Fi, airport shuttle (fee)* ▭*MC, V* ⦿❘*CP.*

MONTI, ESQUILINO, REPUBBLICA & SAN LORENZO

$$$$ **Exedra.** If Rome's semi-stodgy hotel scene has an It-Girl, it's the Exedra. Hardly a travel column unfolds without a mention of it, celebs vie for face time, and it's the hostess of the moment for out-of-town high rollers and Roman big spenders alike. The Exedra is a model of neoclassical respectability, all gilt-framed mirrors and fresh flowers, but there's a glint of cutting edge in the paparazzi-inspired (and inspiring) Tazio brasserie. Rooms are luscious in an uptown way, with silky linens and handsome nouveau-colonial bedsteads, and many face the spectacular fountain in the piazza outside. Why stay here, rather than at the umpteen other expensively elegant hotels in central Rome? You can think about it while you lounge by the rooftop swimming pool. **Pros:** spacious and attractive rooms; great spa and pool; terrace with cocktail service. **Cons:** pricey food and beverages; hotel seems overstaffed at times; beyond the immediate vicinity; parts of the neighborhood seem unsavory. ⊠*Piazza della Repubblica 47, Repubblica, 00185* ☎*06/489381* 🖷*06/48938000* ⊕*www.boscolohotels.com* ↩*240 rooms, 18 suites* ⌂*In-room: safe, refrigerator, high-speed Internet. In-hotel: 3 restaurants, room service, 2 bars, pool, gym, spa, laundry service, concierge, public Internet, public Wi-Fi, parking (fee), some pets allowed, no-smoking rooms* ▭*AE, DC, MC, V* ⦿❘*CP.*

$$ **D'Este.** The decor in this distinguished 19th-century hotel tries to evoke turn-of-the-20th-century comfort, with brass bedsteads and lamps as well as dark-wood period furniture. Rooms are quiet, light, and spacious; many can accommodate families. The attentive owner-manager likes to have fresh flowers in the halls and sees that everything works. He encourages inquiries about special rates, particularly during the slack summer months. The location is within hailing distance of Santa Maria Maggiore and close to Termini Station. (You can arrange to be picked up there, free of charge, by the hotel car.) **Pros:** good value for budget travelers; the cleaning staff is especially friendly; hotel car picks you up at Santa Maria Maggiore. **Cons:** the walls are thin; breakfast is the standard Continental fare; some of the beds are squeaky. ⊠*Via Carlo Alberto 6, Monti, 00185* ☎*06/4465607* 🖷*06/4465601* ⊕*www. hotel-deste.com* ↩*37 rooms* ⌂*In-room: safe, refrigerator, Wi-Fi. In-*

hotel: room service, bar, concierge, public Wi-Fi, airport shuttle (fee), parking (fee), no-smoking rooms ▤*AE, DC, MC, V* ⦿|*CP.*

$–$$ **Des Artistes.** The three personable Riccioni brothers have transformed their hotel into the best in the neighborhood in its price range. It's bedecked with paintings and handsome furnishings in mahogany, and rooms are decorated in attractive fabrics. Marble baths are smallish but luxurious for this price, and they're stocked with hair dryers and towel warmers. Des Artistes hasn't forgotten its roots, though: there's also a "hostel" floor with 11 simpler rooms for travelers on a budget. Book well ahead. As for location, this is somewhat on the fringe, being several blocks (in the wrong direction) from Stazione Termini. **Pros:** good value; decent-sized rooms; relaxing roof garden. **Cons:** breakfast area is overcrowded; no Internet access in the building; reception is on the fifth floor. ✉ *Via Villafranca 20, San Lorenzo, 00185* ☎*06/4454365* 🖷*06/4462368* ⊕*www.hoteldesartistes.com* ⇆*40 rooms, 27 with bath* ☐*In-room: no a/c (some), safe, refrigerator. In-hotel: bar, concierge, parking (fee), no-smoking rooms* ▤*AE, DC, MC, V* ⦿|*BP.*

WORD OF MOUTH

"I've stayed both in the area of the Spanish Steps and also close to Piazza Navona. The latter is more centrally located, and I think better for someone who is coming to Rome for the first time. From my hotel just north of Piazza Navona, I was able to walk quite easily to the Vatican, the Pantheon, Campo de' Fiori, Trastevere, and to the Spanish Steps."—wanderful

$–$$ **Giuliana.** A friendly family operates this small, cozy residence with pride. The decor is unprepossessing, with 1960s modern furniture but guest rooms are large (if sparely furnished) and the tiled baths are shiny clean. Make sure to specify bath or shower when you make your reservation; it's one or the other. If you need to check your e-mail while you're on vacation, there is wireless Internet access in the rooms and in the lobby, though it's limited to daytime hours. The hotel doesn't provide laundry service, but you can drop your clothes at the laundry service right next door (and there are several coin-operated laundries in the neighborhood if you need them). **Pros:** spacious, clean rooms; staff is warm and welcoming; with only 11 rooms, it's an intimate experience. **Cons:** you may hear noise from the local market; air-conditioning is an extra €10 charge; bathroom has either a shower or a tub. ✉ *Via Agostino Depretis 70, Esquilino, 00184* ☎*06/4880795* 🖷*06/4824287* ⊕*www.hotelgiuliana.com* ⇆*11 rooms* ☐*In-room: no a/c (some), safe, refrigerator. In-hotel: room service, bar, concierge, parking (fee), no-smoking rooms* ▤*AE, MC, V* ⦿|*CP.*

$ **Adler.** This tiny pensione run by the same family for more than three decades provides a comfortable stay on a quiet street near the main station for a very good price. Ideal for families, Adler has six spacious rooms that sleep three, four, or five, as well as a single and a double. Rooms are basic, but impeccably clean. Worn but cozy chairs line the lobby, and in summer, breakfast can be taken on the leafy courtyard balcony. **Pros:** breakfast on the terrace; free Internet point in the lobby; strong a/c. **Cons:** some rooms are dark; showers are tiny; no safes in the rooms. ⊠ *Via Modena 5, Esquilino, 00184* ☎*06/484466* 🖷*06/4880940* ⊕*www.hoteladler-roma.com* 🛏*8 rooms* ◊*In-room: refrigerator. In-hotel: room service, bar, public Internet, airport shuttle (fee), parking (fee)* ☰*AE, DC, MC, V* ⁞⊚⁞*CP.*

$
Fodor'sChoice
★
The Beehive. Rome meets the best of Southern California at The Beehive. Started by a Los Angeles couple following their dream, The Beehive might be the most unique budget hotel in Rome—although, it's not just a hotel; it's more of an ecologically minded little empire that also offers hostel accommodations, a vegetarian cafe, a yoga space and an art gallery with a garden, a reading lounge, and a few off-site apartments. It offers a respite from Rome's chaos, but is conveniently located only a few blocks from Termini. The design is contemporary and hip and the vibe is mellow. All of the rooms come with shared bathrooms. There is a lovely garden with fruit trees, herbs, and flowers. The Beehive offers free Wi-Fi, but no TVs or air-conditioning (rooms do have ceiling fans). If you would prefer your own self-catering apartment (and private bathroom) for your group or family, or if you'd just like an individual room in an apartment, The Beehive also has three apartments in the neighborhood that can be rented. **Pros:** yoga, massage, and other therapies offered on-site; free Wi-Fi and Beehive's own guidebook. **Cons:** no TV, a/c, baggage storage, or private bathroom; breakfast is not included in the room rate. ⊠ *Via Marghera 8, Repubblica, 00185* ☎*06/44704553* ⊕*www.the-beehive.com* 🛏*8 rooms, 1 dormitory, 3 apartments* ◊*In-room: no a/c, kitchen (some), no TV, Wi-Fi. In-hotel: no elevator, public Wi-Fi, no-smoking rooms* ☰*MC, V* ⁞⊚⁞*EP.*

$
Fodor'sChoice
★
Yes Hotel. A newcomer to the Rome budget hotel scene, Yes was opened in April of 2007 by the same folks who own Hotel Des Artistes. It's centrally located near Stazione Termini, and thus close to many restaurants and transportation options. One of the nicest things about Yes is that, even though it's a budget hotel, the rooms have a flair for style with a contemporary feel. Yes also offers the kind of amenities that are usually found in more expensive hotels, like flat-screen TVs and air-conditioning. Unfortunately, there is no Internet access at the hotel, but they do have a special deal with a nearby Internet Point shop that allows guests free access for 15 minutes a day. **Pros:** it doesn't feel like a budget hotel, but it is; discount if you pay cash; great value. **Cons:** rooms are small; no individual climate control or refrigerators in the rooms; no Internet in the hotel. ⊠ *Via Magenta 15, San Lorenzo, 00185* ☎*06/44363836* 🖷*06/44363829* ⊕*www.yeshotelrome.com* 🛏*29 rooms, 1 suite* ◊*In-room: safe. In-hotel: parking (fee), no-smoking rooms* ☰*MC, V* ⁞⊚⁞*CP.*

¢
Italia. It looks and feels like a classic pensione: low-budget with a lot of heart. A block off the very trafficky Via Nazionale, this friendly, family-run hotel offers inexpensive rooms with big windows, desks, parquet floors, and baths with faux-marble tiles, but the rooms aren't really the point. The price is, and it's made all the more tempting by a generous buffet breakfast and thoughtful touches like an ice machine and free wireless Internet access. Ask for even lower midsummer rates.

CLOSE UP

Renting an Apartment in Rome

For parties of more than two, Roman hotel rooms can be a little too cozy for comfort (and too cramped to keep more than one suitcase open at a time). If you're traveling in a group or with your family, the best solution may be a short-term apartment rental that offers more space, privacy, and bang for your buck.

As a renter, you can find an apartment through an agency, a hotel, or a private owner. There is usually a minimum of a three-night stay. Prices will vary, but expect them to be higher in the historic city center, the Vaticano/Borgo, the Campo de' Fiori, and Trastevere areas.

Start your research online. Rome's official Web site, ⊕ *www.romaturismo.it*, offers a search function for a number of different housing options.

The Bed & Breakfast Association of Rome is an agency that offers an online apartment rental database in addition to its B&B search, at ⊕ www.b-b.rm.it. They inspect all properties advertised on their site.

Hotels with Apartments

There are a number of Roman hotels that—in addition to rooms and suites—offer a selection of local apartments to their prospective guests. Albergo Santa Chiara, 3 apartments (⊠ *Via Santa Chiara 21, Pantheon, 00186* ☎ *06/6872979* 🖨 *06/6873144* ⊕ *www.albergosantachiara.com*). Campo de' Fiori, 15 apartments (⊠ *Via del Biscione 6, Campo de' Fiori, 00186* ☎ *06/68806865* 🖨 *06/6876003* ⊕ *www.hotelcampodefiori.it*). Italia, 1 apartment (⊠ *Via Venezia 18, Termini, 00184* ☎ *06/4828355* 🖨 *06/4745550* ⊕ *www.hotelitaliaroma.com*). Julia, 3 apartments (⊠ *Via Rasella 29, Via Veneto, 00187* ☎ *06/4881637* 🖨 *06/4817044* ⊕ *www.hoteljulia.it*). Mecenate Palace Hotel, 2 apartments (⊠ *Via Carlo Alberto 3, Termini, 00185* ☎ *06/44702024* 🖨 *06/4461354* ⊕ *www.mecenatepalace.com*).

Residence Hotels

Residence hotels also specialize in short-let vacation rentals. They usually have fully equipped kitchens and offer linens, laundry, and cleaning services. Most are available for weekly or monthly rentals. Cost for an apartment for two ranges from about €1,300 for a week to €2,600 per month. Residence Aldrovandi (⊠ *Via Ulisse Aldrovandi 11, Parioli, 00197* ☎ *06/3221430* 🖨 *06/3222181* ⊕ *www.aldrovandiresidence.it*.) Residence Ripetta (⊠ *Via di Ripetta 231, Piazza di Spagna, 00186* ☎ *06/3231144* 🖨 *06/3203959* ⊕ *www.ripetta.it*).

Pros: free Wi-Fi and Internet access in the lobby; great price; individual attention and personal care. **Cons:** no Internet access in the rooms; it's sometimes noisy; a/c is an extra €10. ⊠ *Via Venezia 18, Monti, 00184* ☎ *06/4828355* 🖨 *06/4745550* ⊕ *www.hotelitaliaroma.com* 📞 *31 rooms, 1 apartment* ♿ *In-room: no a/c (some), safe. In-hotel: bar, concierge, public Internet, public Wi-Fi, airport shuttle (fee), parking (fee), no-smoking rooms* ⊟ *AE, MC, V* ⊺⊙⊺ *CP.*

VATICAN, BORGO & PRATI

$$$$ **Cavalieri Hilton.** Though the Cavalieri is outside the city center, slightly northwest of the Vatican, distance has its advantages. One of them is this property's magnificent view over Rome. Occupying a vast area atop modern Rome's highest hill, the Cavalieri Hilton is an oasis of good taste that feels more like a resort than a city hotel. Central to its appeal, particularly in summer, is a terraced garden that spreads out from an Olympic-size pool and smart poolside restaurant; legions of white-clothed cushioned lounge chairs are scattered throughout the greenery, so there's always a place to sun yourself. Inside, spacious rooms, often with large balconies, are done up in striped damask, puffy armchairs, and such Hiltonesque amenities as a "pillow menu." If you can tear yourself away, the city center is just a 15-minute complimentary shuttle bus ride away. The strawberry on top: La Pergola restaurant *(see the Where to Eat section)* is renowned as one of Rome's very best. **Pros:** beautiful bird's-eye view of Rome; shuttle to the city center; three-Michelin-star dining. **Cons:** you definitely pay for the luxury of staying here—everything is expensive; outside the city center; not all rooms have the view. ⊠ *Via Cadlolo 101, Monte Mario, Northwest Rome 00136* ☎*06/35091* 🖷*06/35092241* ⊕*www.cavalieri-hilton.com* 📞*357 rooms, 17 suites* ☝*In-room: safe, refrigerator, DVD (some), high-speed Internet. In-hotel: 2 restaurants, 3 bars, tennis court, pools, gym, spa, laundry service, concierge, public Internet, airport shuttle (fee), no smoking rooms* ⊟*AE, DC, MC, V* ⦿*CP.*

$$–$$$ **Farnese.** Polished walnut antiques, linen sheets, and the occasional painted ceiling—it's all in the details here. An early-20th-century mansion, the Farnese is carefully authentic, preserving a polished Belle Epoque elegance that sits well with its well-traveled clientele. Add to this a comfortable sitting room you'll actually want to use and a roof garden with a view. It's also near the Metro and within walking distance of St. Peter's. **Pros:** comfy linen sheets; free Internet; quick walk to the Vatican. **Cons:** small rooms; small shower stalls; small and slow elevator. ⊠ *Via Alessandro Farnese 30, Prati, 00192* ☎*06/3212553* 🖷*06/3215129* 📞*23 rooms* ☝*In-room: safe, refrigerator, Wi-Fi. In-hotel: room service, bar, laundry service, concierge, public Internet, public Wi-Fi, parking (no fee), no smoking rooms* ⊟*AE, DC, MC, V* ⦿*BP.*

$$ **Alimandi.** On a side street a block from the Vatican Museums, this family-operated hotel offers excellent value in a neighborhood with moderately priced shops and restaurants. A spiffy lobby, spacious lounges, a tavern, terraces, and roof gardens are some of the perks, as is an exercise room equipped with step machines and a treadmill. Rooms are spacious and well-furnished; many can accommodate extra beds. Needless to say the location here is quite far away from Rome's historic center. **Pros:** nice family-owned hotel with a friendly staff, a terrace, a tavern, and a gym. **Cons:** breakfast is a good spread but it goes quickly; rooms are small; not close to much of interest other than the Vatican. ⊠ *Via Tunisi 8, Vatican, 00192* ☎*06/39723948* 🖷*06/39723943* ⊕*www.alimandi.it* 📞*35 rooms* ☝*In-room: safe, refrigerator (some), Wi-Fi. In-hotel: bar, gym, public Internet, airport shuttle (fee), parking (no fee), no-smoking rooms* ⊟*AE, DC, MC, V* ⦿*BP.*

$–$$ **Sant'Anna.** In the picturesque old Borgo neighborhood in the shadow of St. Peter's, this fashionable small hotel has exceedingly stylish ample bedrooms with new wood-beam ceilings, designer fabrics, and comfy beds. The frescoes in the vaulted breakfast room and fountain in the courtyard add an individual touch. The marvelously decorated and spacious attic rooms also have tiny terraces. **Pros:** Borgo Pio is a pedestrian-only zone during the day; beds are comfy; staff is eager-to-please. **Cons:** street-side rooms are noisy; not many amenities; no bar or restaurant in the hotel. ✉ *Borgo Pio 133, Borgo, 00193* ☎ *06/68801602* 🖷 *06/68308717* ⊕ *www.hotelsantanna.com* ⇌ *20 rooms* ♿ *In-room: safe, refrigerator. In-hotel: parking (fee)* ☰ *AE, DC, MC, V* ⦿ *BP.*

¢ **Hotel San Pietrino.** It may seem like a miracle, but the San Pietrino is a

Fodor's Choice well-appointed, stylish hotel with bargain prices near the Vatican. It's

★ located on the third floor of a 19th-century palazzo that's only a five-minute walk to St. Peter's Square. In addition to clean, simple rooms, San Pietrino offers air-conditioning, TVs with DVD players, and high-speed Internet to guests. There is no breakfast included and no bar in the hotel, but not to worry—with all the local caffès and bars, you won't have any trouble finding yourself a *cornetto* and cappuccino in the morning or a prosecco for aperitivo in the evening. **Pros:** heavenly prices near the Vatican; TVs with DVD players; high-speed Internet. **Cons:** a couple of metro stops away from the center of Rome; no breakfast; no bar. ✉ *Via Giovanni Bettolo 43, Prati, 00195* ☎ *06/3700132* 🖷 *06/3701809* ⊕ *www.sanpietrino.it* ⇌ *12* ♿ *In-room: DVD (some), high-speed Internet, Wi-Fi. In-hotel: public Internet, public Wi-Fi, airport shuttle (fee)* ☰ *MC, V* ⦿ *EP.*

TRASTEVERE

$$ **Hotel Santa Maria.** A Trastevere treasure, this hotel has a pedigree going back four centuries. This ivy-covered, mansard-roofed, rosy-brick-red, erstwhile Renaissance-era convent has been transformed by Paolo and Valentina Vetere into a true charmer. Surrounded by towering tenements, the complex is centered around a monastic porticoed courtyard, lined with orange trees—a lovely place for breakfast. The guest rooms are sweet and simple: a mix of brick walls, "cotto" tile floors, modern oak furniture, and stylishly floral bedspreads and curtains. Best of all, the location is *buonissimo*—just a few blocks from the Tiber and its *isola.* **Pros:** a quaint and pretty oasis in a chaotic city; relaxing courtyard; stocked wine bar. **Cons:** it might be tricky to find; some of the showers drain slowly; it's not always easy finding a cab in Trastevere. ✉ *Vicolo del Piede 2, Trastevere, 00153* ☎ *06/5894626* 🖷 *06/5894815* ⊕ *www.htlsantamaria.com* ⇌ *18 rooms, 2 suites* ♿ *In-room: safe, refrigerator. In-hotel: bar, bicycles, laundry service, concierge, public Internet, airport shuttle (fee), no-smoking rooms* ☰ *AE, DC, MC, V* ⦿ *BP.*

$$ **Relais Le Clarisse.** In one of Rome's most popular neighborhoods, this

Fodor's Choice charming little oasis features five simple, but classically styled accom-

★ modations (two doubles and three suites) with terra-cotta-tiled floors, wrought-iron bed frames, and oak furnishings. Each room opens up onto a bright courtyard surrounded by a Mediterranean garden of grapevines and olive and lemon trees. Rooms are equipped with the most modern technologies, including individual climate control, flat-screen TVs, and Wi-Fi. It feels more like staying in a villa than a former cloister, and with only five rooms, you have a very personal experience with the staff. **Pros:** spacious rooms with comfy beds; high-tech showers/tubs with good water pressure; staff is multilingual, friendly, and at your service. **Cons:** this part of Trastevere can be noisy at night; the rooms here fill up quickly; they only serve American coffee. ⊠ *Via Cardinale Merry del Val 20, Trastevere, 00153* 🕾 *06/58334437* 🖷 *06/58334437* ⊕ *www.leclarisse.com* ⇆ *5 rooms, 3 suites* ⚐ *In-room: safe, refrigerator, high-speed Internet. In-hotel: room service, laundry service, public Internet, public Wi-Fi, airport shuttle (fee), parking (fee), no-smoking rooms* ⊟ *AE, MC, V* ⦾ *CP.*

$ **Hotel Trastevere.** This tiny hotel captures the village-like charm of the Trastevere district. The entrance hall features a mural of the famous Piazza di Santa Maria, a block away, and hand-painted Art Nouveau wall designs add a touch of graciousness throughout. Open medieval brickwork and a few antiques here and there complete the mood. Most rooms face Piazza San Cosimato, where there's an outdoor food market every morning except Sunday. **Pros:** cheap with a good location; convenient to transportation; friendly staff. **Cons:** no frills; few amenities; no Internet access. ⊠ *Via Luciano Manara 24–25, Trastevere, 00153* 🕾 *06/5814713* 🖷 *06/5881016* ⊕ *www.hoteltrastevere.net* ⇆ *19 rooms, 3 apartments* ⚐ *In-room: safe (some), refrigerator (some), kitchen (some). In-hotel: no-smoking rooms* ⊟ *AE, DC, MC, V* ⦾ *CP.*

AVENTINO, TESTACCIO & PALATINO

$$ **Domus Aventina.** Set between a municipal rose garden and Rome's famous Orange Garden, this friendly little hotel is right in the heart of the historic Aventine. It's also not far from the Temple to Mithras and the House of Aquila and Priscilla (where St. Peter touched down). The 17th-century facade has been so restored it almost looks modern—ditto for the inside, where guest rooms have standard modern decors. Half of them also have balconies, and set around an ancient cloister, they all make for islands of tranquillity. **Pros:** quiet location; walking distance to tourist attractions; complimentary Wi-Fi in rooms and public spaces. **Cons:** no elevator in the hotel; small showers; no tubs. ⊠ *Via di Santa Prisca 11/b, Aventino, 00153* 🕾 *06/5746135* 🖷 *06/57300044* ⊕ *www. domus-aventina.com* ⇆ *26 rooms* ⚐ *In room: safe, refrigerator, Wi-Fi. In-hotel: bar, no elevator, laundry service, public Wi-Fi, airport shuttle (fee), parking (fee)* ⊟ *AE, DC, MC, V* ⦾ *CP.*

$$ **Hotel San Anselmo.** Birdsongs emanating from the tree-lined avenues tell you the San Anselmo is as much a retreat as a hotel. It's far from the bustle of the city center, perched on top of the Aventine Hill in a residential neighborhood. This 19th-century villa glows in archetypal Roman cantaloupe-hue stone. Inside, the lobby and adjacent "tea room" are stuffed with a quirky mix of gilded mirrors, plate-glass win-

dows, and a riot of Italianate Rococo chairs and sofas. Others will find the best features here are the verdant garden and terrace bar. Guest rooms are period in flavor, complete with huge armoires, old-fashioned painted headboards, and Empire-style drapes and chandeliers. Two of them have been specially designed with facilities for disabled guests. **Pros:** historic building with artful decor; great showers with jets; a garden where you can enjoy your breakfast. **Cons:** some consider it a bit of a hike to sights; limited public transportation; the wireless is pricey. ⊠*Piazza San Anselmo 2, Aventino, 00153* 📠*06/570057* 📠*06/5783604* ⊕*www.aventinohotels.com* 🛏*45 rooms* ⚐*In-room: safe, refrigerator, high-speed Internet. In-hotel: room service, bar, laundry service, public Wi-Fi (fee), parking (no fee), no-smoking rooms* ⊟*AE, DC, MC, V* ⦿*BP.*

COLOSSEO AREA

$$$$ **Capo d'Africa.** Many find the modern look and feel of Capo d'Africa—not to mention its plush beds and deep bathtubs—refreshing after a long day's journey through ancient Rome. Each room is decorated in warm, muted color tones with sleek furniture, stylish accents, and contemporary art. The hotel features a nonsmoking floor, fitness center, and solarium. There is also access for disabled guests. It sits on a quiet street near the Colosseum, Palatine, and Forum, and it's not far from the metro. A delicious breakfast is served on the rooftop terrace, where you can also enjoy an *aperitivo* overlooking Rome at the end of your day. **Pros:** luxury digs near the ancient digs; quiet, comfortable rooms; fitness center. **Cons:** despite proximity to Colosseum, there isn't a great view of it from the hotel; far from the other Roman sites and the rest of the city scene; not a lot of restaurants in the immediate neighborhood. ⊠*Via Capo d'Africa 54, Colosseo, 00184* 📠*06/772801* 📠*06/77280801* ⊕*www.hotelcapodafrica.com* 🛏*65* ⚐*In-room: safe, refrigerator, DVD (some), high-speed Internet. In-hotel: gym, room service, bar, concierge, airport shuttle (fee), parking (fee), no-smoking rooms* ⊟*AE, MC, V, DC* ⦿*CP.*

$$ **Hotel Lancelot.** Originally a guesthouse that started hosting visitors in the 1950s, Hotel Lancelot has been run by the same family since 1970, and is well-known for its wonderfully attentive staff and the personal care they give to those who stay here. Located in a quiet residential area near the Colosseum, rooms at Hotel Lancelot tend to have big windows, so they're bright and airy, and some have terraces or balconies as well. Rooms have air-conditioning, bathrooms, TVs, and Wi-Fi. In the restaurant, where hearty breakfasts and dinners are served, guests sit at Lancelot's "round tables"—a play on the knight's tale and an effort to encourage communal dining among guests from around the world. They seem to be a big hit, as Hotel Lancelot boasts that most of their guests are return visitors or new guests recommended by others who've spent vacations here. **Pros:** their motto is "hospitality" and they have the staff to prove it; secluded and quiet; very family-friendly. **Cons:** some of the bathrooms are on the small side; no refrigerators in the rooms; the location may be a little too quiet for some travelers. ⊠*Via*

Capo d'Africa 47, Colosseo, 00184 ☎*06/70450615* 📠*06/70450640* ⊕*www.lancelothotel.com* ⇆*60* ♿*In-room: safe, Wi-Fi. In-hotel: restaurant, room service, bar, laundry service, concierge, public Internet, public Wi-Fi, airport shuttle (fee), parking (fee), no-smoking rooms* ▤*AE, MC, V, DC* ⟲*CP.*

NIGHTLIFE & THE ARTS

THE ARTS

Updated by Erica Firpo

Cultural events are publicized well in advance through the city's Web site ⊕*www.comune.roma.it.* Weekly events listings can be found in the Cronaca and Cultura sections of Italian newspapers, as well in *Metro* (the free newspaper). The most comprehensive listings are in the weekly *roma c'è* booklet, which comes out every Wednesday. It has a brief yet very detailed English-language section at the back. On the Web, check out www.inromenow.com, an events site written exclusively for the English-speaking community and updated monthly, as well as the site for *Time Out Roma* (⊕*www.timeout.com/travel/rome*). Two monthly English-language periodicals (with accompanying Web sites), *Wanted in Rome* (⊕*www.wantedinrome.com*), and *The American* (⊕*www. theamericanmag.com*), available at many newsstands, have good coverage of arts events. Events and concert listings can also be found in both English and Italian at www.musicguide.it.

VENUES

★ Rome used to be a performing arts backwater until 2002, when it opened its state-of-the-art **Auditorium-Parco della Musica** (✉*Via de Coubertin 15, Flaminio* ☎*06/80241, 06/6880144 information and tickets* ⊕*www.musicaperroma.it*), located a 10-minute tram ride from Piazza del Popolo. Three futuristic concert halls designed by famed architect Renzo Piano have excellent acoustics and a large courtyard used for concerts and other events—everything from chamber music to jazz to big-name pop, even film screenings, art exhibits, fashion shows, and "philosophy festivals." **Teatro Argentina** (✉*Largo Argentina 52, near Campo de' Fiori* ☎*06/68400345* ⊕*www.teatrodiroma. net*), built in 1732 by the architect Theoldi, has been the home of the Teatro Sabile theater company since 1994. The theater is a beautiful, ornate structure, with velvet seats and chandeliers, and plays host to many plays, classical music performances, operas, and dance performances. Both the city's ballet and opera companies, as well as visiting international performers, appear at the **Teatro dell'Opera** (✉*Piazza Beniamino Gigli 8, near Termini* ☎*06/481601, 06/48160255 tickets* ⊕*www.operaroma.it*). **Teatro Olimpico** (✉*Piazza Gentile da Fabriano 17, Flaminio* ☎*06/3265991*) hosts both concerts and dance performances. **Teatro Valle** (✉*Via del Teatro Valle 23A, near Piazza Navona* ☎*06/68803794*) hosts dramatic performances of the same caliber as its neighbor, Teatro Argentina, but often with a more-experimental bent, particularly in fall. Dance and classical music are also presented here. The ancient **Terme di Caracalla** (✉*Via delle Terme di Caracalla*

52, Aventino ☎*No phone* ⊕*www.operaroma.it*) has one of the most spectacular and enchanting outdoor stages in the world, often hosting performances presented by Rome's opera company ranging from *Aida* (with elephants) to avant-garde.

TICKETS

Tickets for major events can be bought online at **Ticket One** (⊕*www. ticketone.it*). Tickets for larger musical performances as well as many cultural events can usually be found at **Hello Ticket** (⊕*www.helloticket. it*), which lists all cultural events and the many *punta di vendita*, ticket sellers, in Rome. Or go in person to **Orbis** (✉*Piazza Esquilino 37, Repubblica* ☎*06/4744776*) or to **Mondadori** (✉ *Via del Corso 472, Spagna* ☎*06/684401*), a huge and central store that sells music, DVDs, books, and concert tickets.

CONCERTS

Christmastime is an especially busy classical concert season in Rome. Many small classical concert groups perform in cultural centers and churches year-round; all performances in Catholic churches are religious music and are free. Look for posters outside the churches. Pop, jazz, and world music concerts are frequent, especially in summer, although they may not be well advertised. Many of the bigger-name acts perform outside the center, so it's worth asking about transportation *before* you buy your tickets (about €10–€40).

CLASSICAL

A year-round classical concert series, often showcasing the famed Orchestra dell'Accademia di Santa Cecilia, is organized by the **Accademia di Santa Cecilia** (*Concert hall and box office* ✉*Via Pietro de Coubertin 34, Flaminio* ☎*06/8082058* ⊕*www.santacecilia.it*). The **Accademia Filarmonica Romana** (✉*Via Flaminia 118, near Flaminio* ☎*06/3201752, 06/3265991 tickets*) has concerts at the Teatro Olimpico. **Il Tempietto** (☎*06/87131590* ⊕*www.tempietto.it*) organizes classical music concerts indoors in winter and in the atmospheric settings of Teatro di Marcello and Villa Torlonia in summer. The internationally respected **Oratorio del Gonfalone series** (✉*Via del Gonfalone 32/a, Campo de' Fiori* ☎*06/6875952* ⊕*www.oratoriogonfalone.it*) focuses on baroque music. The church of **Sant'Ignazio** (✉*Piazza Sant'Ignazio, near Corso* ☎*06/6794560*) often hosts classical concerts in its spectacularly frescoed setting. The Renaissance-era **Chiostro del Bramante** (✉*Vicolo della Pace 2,near Piazza Navona* ☎*06/68809098*) has a summer concert series. The **Orto Botanico** (✉*Largo Cristina di Svezia 23/a, Trastevere* ☎*06/6868441*), off Via della Lungara in Trastevere, has a summer concert series with a beautiful, verdant backdrop.

DANCE

Modern dance and classical ballet companies from Russia, the United States, and Europe sporadically visit Rome; performances are at the Teatro dell'Opera, Teatro Olimpico, or one of the open-air venues in summer. Small dance companies from Italy and abroad perform in numerous venues.

Entertainment Alfresco

Roman nightlife moves outdoors in summertime, and that goes not only for pubs and discos but for higher culture as well. Open-air opera in particular is a venerable Italian tradition; competing companies commandeer church courtyards, ancient villas, and soccer stadiums for performances that range from student-run mom-and-poperas to full-scale extravaganzas. The same goes for dance and for concerts covering the spectrum of pop, classical, and jazz. Look for performances at the Baths of Caracalla, site of the famous televised "Three Tenors" concert; regardless of the production quality, it's a breathtaking setting. In general, though, you can count on performances being quite good, even if small productions often resort to school-play scenery and folding chairs to cut costs. Tickets run about €15–€50. The more-sophisticated productions may be listed in newspapers and magazines such as *roma c'è,* but your best sources for information are old-fashioned posters plastered all over the city, advertising classics such as *Tosca* and *La Traviata.*

The **Rome Opera Ballet** (☎*06/481601, 06/48160255 tickets* ⊕*www. operaroma.it*) performs at the Teatro dell'Opera, often with international guest stars.

FILM

Movie tickets range in price from €4.50 for matinees and some weeknights up to €10 for reserved seats on weekend evenings. Check listings in *roma c'è* or www.inromenow.com for reviews of all English-language films currently playing or visit www.mymovies.it for a list of current features. The **Metropolitan** (⊠*Via del Corso 7, near Piazza di Popolo* ☎*06/32600500*) has four screens, one dedicated to English-language films September–June. The five-screen **Warner Village Moderno** (⊠*Piazza della Repubblica 45–46, Repubblica* ☎*06/47779202*), close to the train station, usually has one theater with an English-language film.

OPERA

The season for the **Opera Theater of Rome** (☎*06/481601, 06/48160255 tickets* ⊕*www.operaroma.it*) runs from November or December to May. Main performances are staged at the Teatro dell'Opera, on Piazza Beniamino Gigli, in cooler weather and at outdoor locations, such as Piazza del Popolo and the spectacular Terme di Caracalla (Baths of Caracalla) in summer.

THEATER

Theater performances are staged throughout the year in Italian, English, and several other languages, depending on who is sponsoring the performance.

For a bit of comedy with a Monty Python slant, check out the **Miracle Players** (⊕*www.miracleplayers.org*), a group of English-speaking actors who write and produce free public performances every summer in the Roman Forum, presenting a perfectly balanced mix of the historical and the hilarious.

NIGHTLIFE

Rome's nightlife is decidedly more happening for locals and insiders who know whose palms to grease and when to go where. The "flavor of the month" factor is at work here, and many places fade into oblivion after their 15 minutes of fame. Smoking has been banned in all public areas in Italy (that's right, it actually happened); Roman aversion to clean air has meant a decrease in crowds at bars and clubs. The best sources for an up-to-date list of nightspots are the *roma c'è* and *Time Out Roma* magazines. Trastevere and the area around Piazza Navona are both filled with bars, restaurants, and, after dark, people. In summer, discos and many bars close to beat the heat (although some simply relocate to the beach, where many Romans spend their summer nights). The city-sponsored Estate Romana (Rome Summer) festival takes over, lighting up hot city nights with open-air concerts, bars, and discos. Pick up the event guide at newsstands.

CAFFÈS, ENOTECHE & WINE BARS

First and foremost among the bar scene is the wine bar, found (often with outdoor seating) in almost every piazza and on side streets throughout the city. These *enoteche* are mostly small in size, offering a smattering of antipasti to accompany a variety of wines. In addition, the following selections, caffès included, are among the best in the city.

Ai Tre Scalini (⊠ *Via Panisperna 251, Monti* ☎06/48907495) is a rustic local hangout with a wooden bar in the new boho section of Rome. It serves delicious antipasti and light entrées.

★ The wood-paneled walls of **L'Angolo Divino** (⊠ *Via dei Balestrari 12, Campo* ☎06/6864413) are racked with over 700 of bottles of wine. A quiet enoteca in a back alley behind Campo, L'Angolo Divino allows you to sidestep the crowds while enjoying homemade pastas with a vintage bottle.

Celebrities and literati hang out at the coveted outdoor tables of **Antico Caffè della Pace** (⊠ *Via della Pace 5, near Piazza Navona* ☎06/6861216), set on the enchanting *piazzatina* (tiny piazza) of Santa Maria della Pace. The only drawbacks: overpriced table service and distracted waiters.

L'Enoteca Antica di Via della Croce (⊠ *Via della Croce 76/b, near Piazza di Spagna* ☎06/6790896) is Piazza di Spagna's most celebrated wine bar, occupying a prime people-watching corner just below the piazza. In addition to a vast selection of wine (also available for take away), Enoteca Antica has delectable antipasti, perfect for a snack or a light lunch. **Fluid** (⊠ *Via del Governo Vecchio 46/47, near Piazza Navona* ☎06/6832361), with its slick design and zen waterfall, is all about the scene, especially with its looking-glass front window where pretty young things primp on ice cube–shaped chairs. For the cocktail crowd, Fluid's many variations on the traditional martini are quite laudable. **Freni e Frizioni** (⊠ *Via de Politeama 4–6, Trastevere* ☎06/58334210) is one of Rome's latest artsy hangouts—it spills out onto its Trastevere piazza and down the stairs, filling the area around Piazza Trilussa with an attractive crowd of local mojito-sippers. **Stardust** (⊠ *Via Santa Maria dell'Anima 52, near Piazza Navona* ☎06/6868986) has cocktails and music that keep a loyal and eclectic clientele (a mix of locals, expats, and entertainment types) happy. There's occasional live music, from jazz to opera.

ROOFTOP TERRACES AND UPSCALE BARS

Crudo (⊠ *Via Degli Specchi 6, Campo* ☎06/6838989), is a spacious, modern, New York–style lounge serving well-made cocktails and *crudo* (raw) nibbles such as sushi and carpaccio. With a large lounge decked out in mod design and hued in gray, white, and red, Crudo also doubles as art space.

★ For a dip into La Dolce Vita, the **Jardin de Hotel de Russie** (⊠ *Via del Babuino 9, near Piazza del Popolo* ☎06/328881 ⊕*www.hotelderussie. it*) is the location for every Hollywood VIP, as well as up-and-coming starlets. Mixed drinks are well above par, as are the prices.

Fodor'sChoice **Rosé Terrazzo at the St. George Hotel** (⊠ *Via Giulia 62, near Piazza* ★ *Navona* ☎06/686611 ⊕*www.stgeorgehotel.it*) is the latest front-run-ner in Rome's ever-growing list of rooftop sweet spots. With a delicious oyster selection headlining its seafood-only menu, the Rosé Terrazzo's dizzying drink selection includes cocktails, beer, and many rosés—from pink champagnes to Italian *rosati*.

Sitting in front of a 2nd-century temple, **Salotto 42** (⊠ *Piazza di Pietra 42, near Piazza Navona* ☎06/6785804) holds court from morning until late in the evening. The cozy-sleek room (high-backed velvet chairs, zebra-print rugs, chandeliers) is a smorgasbord of the own-ers' Roman–New York–Swedish pedigree. The den, complete with art books, local sophisticates, and models moonlighting as waitresses, is the fashionista's favorite choice for late-night drinks.

★ **Tazio** (⊠ *Hotel Exedra, Piazza della Repubblica 47, Repubblica* ☎06/489381), named after the original Italian *paparazzo* (celebrity photographer), is an Adam Tihany-designed champagne bar. The red, black, and white lacquered interior, with crystal chandeliers, has a distinct '80s feel (think Robert Palmer, *Addicted to Love*), while the outside seating area is simple and modern. The favorite pastime here is sipping champagne while watching the people parade through the colonnade. In summer, the hotel's rooftop bar **Sensus** is the place to be, with its infinity pool and terrace view overlooking downtown.

Terrace Bar of the Hotel Raphael (⊠ *Largo Febo 2, near Piazza Navona* ☎06/682831) is noted for its bird's-eye view of the campaniles and palazzi of the Piazza Navona. High up in the moonlit sky, the Terrace Bar tends to be the choice place for a romantic evening.

NIGHTCLUBS & DISCOS

Most dance clubs open about 10:30 PM and charge an entrance fee of about €20, which may include the first drink (subsequent drinks cost about €10). Clubs are usually closed Monday, and all those listed here close in summer, some opening instead at the beaches of Ostia or Fregene. The liveliest areas for clubs with a younger clientele are the grittier working-class districts of Testaccio and Ostiense. Any of the clubs lining Via Galvani, leading up to Monte Testaccio, are fair game for a trendy, crowded dance-floor experience—names and ownership of clubs change frequently, but the overall scene has shown some staying power.

Behind the Vatican Museums, **Alexanderplatz** (⊠ *Via Ostia 9, near Vaticano* ☎*06/39742171*), Rome's most famous jazz and blues club, has a bar and a restaurant. Local and internationally known musicians play nightly. In trendy Testaccio, **Caffè Latino** (⊠ *Via Monte Testaccio 96, Aventino* ☎*06/57288556*) is a vibrant Roman locale that has live music (mainly Latin) almost every night, followed by recorded soul, funk, and '70s and '80s revival; it's closed Monday. **Gilda** (⊠ *Via Mario de' Fiori 97, near Piazza di Spagna* ☎*06/6784838*) used to be the place to spot famous Italian actors and politicians. Now it is host to B-actors and leftover politniks. This nightspot near the Spanish Steps has a piano bar as well as a restaurant and dance floors with live and disco music. Jackets are required. **Hulala** (⊠ *Via dei Conciatori 7, Aventino* ☎*06/57300429*) is home to Rome's fashionistas. Mod films are projected on the walls, and champagne is drunk through straws.

★ Housed in a medieval palazzo is **La Cabala** (⊠ *Via dei Soldati 23, near Piazza Navona* ☎*06/68301192*), Rome's version of a supper club. This three-level space has a piano bar, restaurant, and club, and often has very dressy crowd vying to get past the velvet rope.

★ Lounge fever is all over Rome, with **La Maison** (⊠ *Vicolo dei Granari 4, near Piazza Navona* ☎*06/6833312*) as one of the best. Bedecked in purple velvet and crystal chandeliers, the club has two distinct spaces, a VIP area and a dance floor, with a DJ dishing up the latest dance tunes. Head straight to the back room and grab a couch. **Qube** (⊠ *Via di Portonaccio 212, San Lorenzo* ☎*06/4385445*), open only Thursday through Saturday, is Rome's biggest underground disco, where bodies mix and mingle like a rugby game. Friday night hosts the **Muccassassina** (⊕*www.muccassassina.it*), Rome's most popular gay event. It has paid a price for its fame, and is now more straight than gay.

SHOPPING

Updated by
Lynda
Albertson

They say when in Rome to do as the Romans do—and the Romans love to shop. Stores are generally open from 9 or 9:30 to 1 and from 3:30 or 4 to 7 or 7:30. There's a tendency for shops in central districts to stay open all day, and hours are becoming more flexible throughout the city. Many places close Sunday, though this is changing, too, especially in the city center. With the exception of food stores, many stores also close Monday morning from September to mid-June and Saturday afternoon from mid-June through August. Stores selling food are usually closed Thursday afternoon.

You can stretch your euros by taking advantage of the Tax-Free for Tourists V.A.T. tax refunds, available at most large stores for purchases over €155. Or hit Rome in January and early February or in late July, when stores clean house with the justly famous biannual sales. There are so many hole-in-the-wall boutiques selling top-quality merchandise in Rome's center that even just wandering you're sure to find something that catches your eye.

SHOPPING DISTRICTS

The city's most famous shopping district, **Piazza di Spagna,** is conveniently compact, fanning out at the foot of the Spanish Steps in a galaxy of boutiques selling gorgeous wares with glamorous labels. Here you can ricochet from Gucci to Prada to Valentino to Versace with less effort than it takes to pull out your credit card. If your budget is designed for lower altitudes, you also can find great clothes and accessories at less-extravagant prices. But here, buying is not necessarily the point—window displays can be works of art, and dreaming may be satisfaction enough. Via Condotti is the neighborhood's central axis, but there are shops on every street in the area bordered by Piazza di Spagna on the east, Via del Corso on the west, between Piazza San Silvestro and Via della Croce, and extending along Via del Babuino to Piazza del Popolo. Shops along **Via Campo Marzio,** and adjoining Piazza San Lorenzo in Lucina, stock eclectic, high-quality clothes and accessories—both big names (Bottega Veneta, Louis Vuitton) and unknowns—at slightly lower prices. Running from Piazza Venezia to Piazza del Popolo lies **Via del Corso,** a main shopping avenue that has more than a mile of clothing, shoes, leather goods, and home furnishings from classic to cutting-edge. Running west from Piazza Navona, **Via del Governo Vecchio** has numerous women's boutiques and second-hand-clothing stores. **Via Cola di Rienzo,** across the Tiber from Piazza del Popolo, is block after block of boutiques, shoe stores, department stores, and mid-level chain shops, as well as street stalls and upscale food shops. **Via dei Coronari,** across the Tiber from Castel Sant'Angelo, has quirky antiques and home furnishings. Via Giulia and other surrounding streets are good bets for decorative arts. Should your gift list include religious souvenirs, look for everything from rosaries to Vatican golf balls at the shops between Piazza San Pietro and **Borgo Pio.** Liturgical vestments and statues of saints make for good window-shopping on **Via dei Cestari,** near the Pantheon. **Via Nazionale** is a good bet for affordable stores of the Benetton ilk, and for shoes, bags, and gloves. The **Termini** train station has become a good one-stop place for many shopping needs. Its 60-plus shops are open until 10 PM and include a Nike store, the Body Shop, Sephora, Mango (women's clothes), a UPIM department store, and a grocery store.

MARKETS

Outdoor markets are open Monday–Saturday from early morning to about 1 PM (a bit later on Saturday), but get there early for the best selection. Remember to keep an eye on your wallet—the money changing hands draws Rome's most skillful pickpockets. And don't go if you can't stand crowds. Downtown Rome's most colorful outdoor food market is at **Campo de' Fiori,** south of Piazza Navona. The **Trionfale market** (⊠ *Via Andrea Doria, near Vatican*) is big and bustling; it's about a five-minute walk north of the entrance to the Vatican Museums. There's room for bargaining at the Sunday-morning flea market at **Porta Portese** (⊠ *Via Ippolito Nievo, Trastevere*). Seemingly endless rows of merchandise include new and secondhand clothing, bootleg CDs, old furniture, car stereos of suspicious origin, and all manner of old junk and hidden treasures.

SPECIALTY STORES

DESIGNER CLOTHING

All of Italy's top fashion houses and many international designers have stores near Piazza di Spagna. Buying clothes can be a bit tricky for American women, as sizes tend to be cut for a petite Italian frame. A size 12 (European 46) is not always easy to find, but the more-expensive stores should carry it. Target less-expensive stores for accessories if this is an issue.

D & G (⊠ *Piazza di Spagna 82, Spagna* 🖀 *06/69924999*), a spin-off of the top-of-the-line Dolce & Gabbana, shows trendy casual wear and accessories for men and women. The flagship store for **Fendi** (⊠ *Largo Carlo Goldoni 419–421, near Piazza di Spagna* 🖀 *06/696661*) is in the former Palazzo Boncompagni, renamed "Palazzo Fendi." It overlooks the intersection of famed Via Condotti and Via del Corso, and it's the quintessential Roman fashion house, presided over by the Fendi sisters. Their signature baguette bags, furs, accessories, and sexy separates are all found here. The **Giorgio Armani** (⊠ *Via Condotti 77, near Piazza di Spagna* 🖀 *06/6991460*) shop is as understated and elegant as its designs. **Gucci** (⊠ *Via Condotti 8, near Piazza di Spagna* 🖀 *06/6790405*) often has lines out the door of its two-story shop, testament to the continuing popularity of its colorful bags, wallets, and shoes in rich leathers. Edgy clothes designs are also available. Sleek, vaguely futuristic **Prada** (⊠ *Via Condotti 92, near Piazza di Spagna* 🖀 *06/6790897*) has two entrances: the one for the men's boutique is to the left of the women's. Rome's leading local couturier, **Valentino** (*Valentino Donna* ⊠ *Via Condotti 13, near Piazza di Spagna* 🖀 *06/6795862 Valentino Uomo* ⊠ *Via Bocca di Leone 15, near Piazza di Spagna* 🖀 *06/6783656*), is recognized the world over by the "V" logo. The designer has shops for the *donna* (woman) and the *uomo* (man) not far from his headquarters in Piazza Mignanelli beside the Spanish Steps. In 2008, the grand master announced his retirement and fashionistas await the anointment of a successor to continue the hyper-glamorous brand. **Versace** (*Versace Uomo* ⊠ *Via Borgognona 24–25, near Piazza di Spagna* 🖀 *06/6795037 Versace Donna* ⊠ *Via Bocca di Leone 26–27, near Piazza di Spagna* 🖀 *06/6780521*) sells the rock-star styles that made the house's name.

MEN'S CLOTHING

Ermenegildo Zegna (⊠ *Via Borgognona 7/e, near Piazza di Spagna* 🖀 *06/6789143*) has the finest in men's elegant styles and accessories.

Brioni (✉ *Via Condotti 21, near Piazza di Spagna* ☎*06/485855* ✉ *Via Barberini 79, near Piazza di Trevi* ☎*06/484517*) has a well-deserved reputation as one of Italy's top tailors. There are ready-to-wear garments in addition to impeccable custom-made apparel. **Davide Cenci** (✉ *Via Campo Marzio 1–7, near Piazza Navona* ☎*06/6990681*) is famed for conservative clothing of exquisite craftsmanship. **Il Portone** (✉ *Via delle Carrozze 71, near Piazza di Spagna* ☎*06/6793355*) embodies a tradition in custom shirt making.

WOMEN'S CLOTHING

Arsenale (✉ *Via del Governo Vecchio 64, near Piazza Navona* ☎*06/6861380*) has a sleek layout and a low-key elegance that stands out, even in Rome. Whether you are looking for a wedding dress or a seductive bustier, you are bound to find something unconventional here. Designer and owner Patriza Pieroni creates many of the pieces on display, all cleverly cut and decidedly captivating.**Galassia** (✉ *Via Frattina 21, near Piazza di Spagna* ☎*06/6797896*) has expensive, extreme, and extravagant women's styles by Gaultier, Westwood, and Yamamoto—this is the place for feather boas and hats with ostrich plumes.

FodorśChoice **L'Anatra all'Arancia** (✉ *Via Tiburtina 105 , San Lorenzo* ☎*06/4456293*)
★ has the locals in this bustling working class district agog at its window displays of flowing innovative designer clothes, teeny-weeny bikinis, and zany underwear. Owner Donatella Baroni believes in fashion being fun. The men's shop is across the road at No. 130, where style-conscious hipsters can find pure linen shirts and trousers in unusual colors. The clientele includes Italian TV and stage personalities who live in the trendy area.

★ **Maga Morgana** (✉ *Via del Governo Vecchio 27, near Piazza Navona* ☎*06/6879995* ✉ *Via del Governo Vecchio 98, Navona* ☎*06/6878085*) is a family-run business where everyone's nimble fingers contribute to producing the highly original clothes and accessories. From hippie chic to bridal chic, designer Luciana Iannace creates lavishly ornate clothes that are as inventive as they are distinguishing. **Victory** (✉ *Via S. Francesco a Ripa 19, Trastevere* ☎*06/5812437*) spotlights youthful, lighthearted styles created by lesser known stylists, such as Rose D, Nina, Alessandrini, and Marithé et François Girbaud. Victory's clothing is made for flaunting. A menswear version of the store is located at Piazza San Calisto 10 in Trastevere.

EMBROIDERY & LINENS

Frette (✉*Piazza di Spagna 11, Spagna* ☎*06/6790673*) is a Roman institution for luxurious linens. **Venier Colombo** (✉ *Via Frattina 79, near Piazza di Spagna* ☎*06/6787705*) is one of Rome's most historic shops. For the coquette that favors retro classicism, and has a penchant for all things Victorian, the shop offers a breathtaking selection of lace-trimmed lingerie and linens, as well as exquisite christening robes for babies and hand-embroidered lavender bags.

JEWELRY

Fodor's Choice

★ **Gioielli in Movimento** (✉ *Via della Stelletta 22/b, near Piazza Navona* ☎*06/6867431*) draws customers like Andie McDowell, hooked on Carlo Cardena's ingenious designs. Carlo's "Twice as Nice" earrings, which can be transformed from fan-shaped clips into elegant drops, were Uno Erre's best selling earrings between 1990 and 1998 and his "Up and Down" pendant, which can be worn two different ways, is set to become another hit. **Quattrocolo** (✉ *Via della Scrofa 54, near Piazza Navona* ☎*06/68801367*) has been specializing in antique micromosaic jewelry and baubles from centuries past since 1938.

SHOES & LEATHER ACCESSORIES

For gloves as pretty as Holly Golightly's, shop at **Sermoneta** (✉*Piazza di Spagna 61, Spagna* ☎*06/6791960*). Any color or style one might desire, from elbow-length black leather to scallop-edged lace-cut lilac suede, is available at this glove institution. **Furla** (✉*Piazza di Spagna 22, Spagna* ☎*06/69200363*) has 14 franchises in Rome alone. Its flagship store, to the left of the Spanish Steps, has been entirely refurbished in 2005 to make it even more inviting. Be prepared to fight your way through crowds of passionate handbag lovers, all anxious to possess one of the delectable bags, wallets, or watch straps in ice-cream colors. **Salvatore Ferragamo** (✉ *Via Condotti 64, near Piazza di Spagna* ☎*06/6781130* ✉ *Via Condotti 73/74, Piazza di Spagna* ☎*06/6791565*) is one of the top-ten most-wanted men's footwear brands in the world and for years has been providing Hollywood glitterati and discerning clients with unique handmade designs. The Florentine design house also specializes in handbags, small leather goods, men's and women's ready-to-wear, and scarves and ties. Men's styles are found at Via Condotti 64, women's at 73/74. **Di Cori** (✉*Piazza di Spagna 53, Spagna* ☎*06/6784439*) has gloves in every color of the spectrum. **Bruno Magli** (✉*Via Condotti 6, near Piazza di Spagna* ☎*06/69292121*) has classy shoes with simple, elegant lines for men and women that have character without compromising comfort.

Fodor's Choice

★ **Tod's** (✉ *Via Fontanella di Borghese 56a/c, near Piazza di Spagna* ☎*06/68210066*) has become hyperfashionable again due in large part to owner Diego Della Valle's ownership of Florence's soccer team. The brand is known for its sporty flats and comfortable, casual styling. Tod's occupies the ground floor in the celebrated 16th-century Palazzo Ruspoli. **Fausto Santini** (✉ *Via Frattina 120, near Piazza di Spagna* ☎*06/6784114*) gives a hint of extravagance in minimally decorated, all-white show windows displaying surprising shoes that fashion mavens love. Santini's footwear for men and women is bright, colorful, and trendy, sporting unusual forms, especially in heels. Coordinated bags and wallets add to the fun.

Side Trips from Rome

WORD OF MOUTH

"Villa d'Este's gardens lived up to everything they were supposed to be, though the villa itself was nothing special and unfurnished. The fountains were spectacular, and I can only imagine how they must have been new."

—Vickitty

WELCOME TO LAZIO

TOP REASONS TO GO

★ **Ostia Antica:** Perhaps even more than Pompeii, the excavated port city of ancient Rome conveys a picture of everyday life in the days of the Empire.

★ **Tivoli's Villa d'Este:** Hundreds of fountains cascading and shooting skyward (one even imitating bird songs) will delight you at this spectacular garden.

★ **Castelli Romani:** Be a Roman for a day and enjoy the pleasures of the ancient hilltop wine towns on the city's doorstep.

★ **Get "Middle-Aged" in Viterbo:** This town may be modern but it has a Gothic papal palace, a Romanesque cathedral, and the magical medieval quarter of San Pellegrino.

★ **Gardens Bizarre & Beautiful:** Just a few miles from each other, the 16th century proto-Disneyland Parco dei Mostri (Monster Park) is famed for its fantastic sculptures while the Villa Lante remains the stateliest Renaissance garden of them all.

TUSCANY

Lago di Bolsena

Montefiascone

Bomarzo

2   Bagnaia   204

Viterbo

Tuscania   Vetralla   Caprarola

Civita Castellana

Tarquinia   495   1

Lago di Bracciano

3

Civitavecchia   Bracciano

Santa Marinella   Cerveteri   2

Ladispoli   1

ROME

0 ——— 20 mi
0 ——— 20 km

Mare Tirreno

Fiumicino   2 **Ostia Antica**
Lido di Ostia

A12

A91

296

148

601

1 Tuscia. The San Pellegrino district of **Viterbo** is a 13th-century time capsule, while at the gardens and palaces of nearby **Bagnaia**, **Caprarola**, and **Bomarzo** you can time-travel back to the Renaissance.

2 Ostia Antica. This ancient Roman port is now a parklike archaeological site.

3 East of Rome. Rising above the heat of Rome is cool, green **Tivoli**, a fitting setting for the regal Villa Adriana and Villa d'Este. A few miles to the south, **Palestrina's** majestic hillside once protected a great Roman temple and now shelters the Palazzo Barberini museum.

4 **Castelli Romani.** Clustered amidst the Alban hills, these towns are history-rich and relentlessly picturesque: **Frascati** is address to the majestic Villa Aldobrandini; **Castelgandolfo** is the pope's summer retreat; **Aricia** has its grand Palazzo Chigi; while **Nemi** enjoys an eagle's-nest perch.

GETTING ORIENTED

All roads may indeed lead to Rome, but for thousands of years emperors, popes, and princes have been heading *fuori porta* (beyond the gates) for a change of pace from city life. To the west lies ancient Ostia Antica; as you work your way north you encounter lava-rich Tuscia, with its Renaissance gardens. East of Rome is Tivoli, famed for retreats ranging from the noble—the Villa d'Este—to the imperial—Villa Adriana (Hadrian's Villa). South lie the enchanting towns of the Castelli Romani.

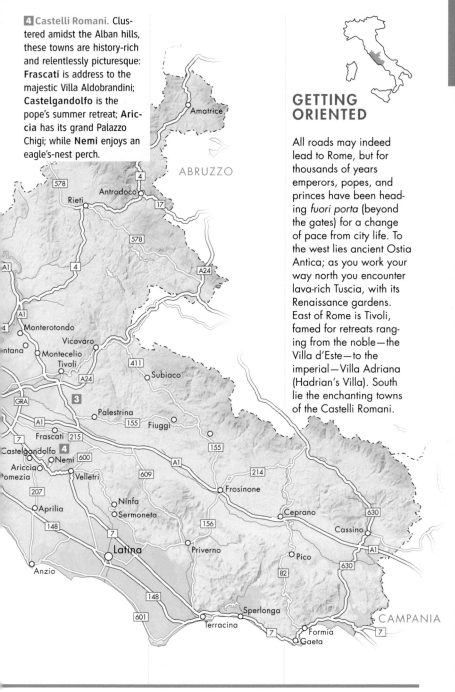

ROME SIDE TRIPS PLANNER

Making the Most of Your Time

Ostia Antica is in many ways an ideal day trip from Rome: it's a fascinating sight, not far from the city, reachable by public transit, and takes about half a day to "do." Villa d'Este and Villa Adriana in Tivoli also make for a manageable, though fuller, day trip. You can use up a flash-card just on these two sights alone but leave room to photograph Tivoli's picturesque gorge strikingly crowned by an ancient Roman temple to Vesta (now part of the famed Sibilla restaurant). Other destinations in Lazio can be visited in a day, but you'll get more out of them if you stay the night. A classic five-day itinerary would have you first visiting Ostia Antica, the excavated port town of ancient Rome. Then head north to explore Viterbo's medieval borgo on Day 2. On Day 3, take in the hot springs or the gardens of Bomarzo, Bagnaia, and Caprarola. For Day 4, head to Tivoli's delights. Then on Day 5 take a relaxing trip to the Castelli Romani, where Frascati wine is produced. Admire the monumental gardens of the aristocrats of yore and explore the narrow streets of these small hill towns. Grand villas, ancient ruins, pretty villages—what more could any vacationer want?

Getting Around

There's reliable public transit from Rome to Ostia Antica, Tivoli, and Viterbo. For other destinations in the region, a car is a big advantage—going by train or bus can add hours to your trip, and routes and schedules are often puzzling. For train information, check with **Ferrovie dello Stato** (☎892021 ⊕www.trenitalia.com),the national rail service. Buses in the region are handled by **COTRAL** (☎06/57031 ⊕www.cotralspa.it).

Tourist Information

Tourist information kiosks in Rome can give you information about the Castelli Romani, Ostia Antica, and Tivoli. For information about Viterbo, Bomarzo, Bagnaia, and Caprarola, contact either the local tourist offices or the central **APT Provincia di Roma tourist office** (⊠ Via XX Settembre 26 ☎06/421381 ⊕www.aptprovroma.it) in Viterbo.

Finding a Place to Stay

With relatively few exceptions (spas, beaches, and hill resorts such as Viterbo), accommodations in Lazio cater more to commercial travelers than to tourists. Rooms can tend to be short on character, but they'll do the trick for an overnight.

DINING & LODGING PRICE CATEGORIES (IN EUROS)				
¢	$	$$	$$$	$$$$
Restaurants				
under €15	€15–€25	€25–€35	€35–€45	over €45
Hotels				
under €70	€70–€110	€110–€160	€160–€220	over €220

Restaurant prices are for a first course (primo), second course (secondo), and dessert (dolce). Hotel prices are for two people in a standard double room in high season, including tax and service.

Updated by
Margaret
Stenhouse

A TRIP OUT OF ROME introduces you to a different kind of Italy: people are friendlier (but speak less English), schedules are looser, and it feels as though you've stepped a few years back in time. You'll find fewer lines, lower prices, and a more-relaxed style of tourism. The monastery of San Benedetto at Subiaco is a good example of small-town charm: the monks and nuns here will take you in as a pilgrim, just as they've done for centuries.

Ostia Antica, Ancient Rome's seaport, is one of the region's top attractions—it rivals Pompeii in the quality of its preservation, and for evocativeness and natural beauty, it easily outshines the Roman forum. The pre-Roman inhabitants of the area were wiped out in the city, but their remains—and some say, their bloodlines—persist in the rolling hills of Tuscia and the Etruscan seaboard north and northeast of Rome. So if the screeching traffic and long lines at the Colosseo start to wear on you, do as the Romans do—get out of town. There's plenty to see and do.

OSTIA ANTICA

GETTING HERE

The best way to get to Ostia Antica is by train. The Ostia Lido train leaves every half hour from the station adjacent to Rome's Piramide Metro B subway station, stopping off at Ostia Antica en route. The trip takes 35 minutes. By car, take the Via del Mare that leads off from Rome's EUR district. Be prepared for heavy traffic, especially at peak hours, on weekends, and in summer.

EXPLORING

Founded around the 4th century BC, Ostia served as Rome's port city for several centuries until the Tiber changed course, leaving the town high and dry. What has been excavated here is a remarkably intact Roman town in a pretty, parklike setting. Fair weather and good walking shoes are essential. On hot days, be here when the gates open or go late in the afternoon. A visit to the excavations takes two to three hours, including 20 minutes for the museum. Inside the site, there's a snack bar and a bookshop. Ostia Antica is 30 km (19 mi) southwest of Rome.

Before exploring Ostia Antica's ruins, it's worthwhile to take a tour through the medieval *borgo* (town). The distinctive **Castello della Rovere,** easily spotted as you come off the footbridge from the train station, was built by Pope Julius II when he was the cardinal bishop of Ostia in 1483. Its triangular form is unusual for military architecture. Inside are (badly faded) frescoes by Baldassare Peruzzi. ⊠ *Piazza della Rocca* 🕿 *06/56358024* ✉ *Free* ⏱ *Tues.–Sun. tours at 10 and noon; Tues. and Thurs. additional tour at 3.*

Fodor'sChoice
★
Tidal mud and windblown sand covered the ancient port town, which lay buried until the beginning of the 20th century when it was extensively excavated. The **Scavi di Ostia Antica** *(Ostia Antica excavations)* continue to be well maintained today. A cosmopolitan population of rich businessmen, wily merchants, sailors, slaves, and their respective

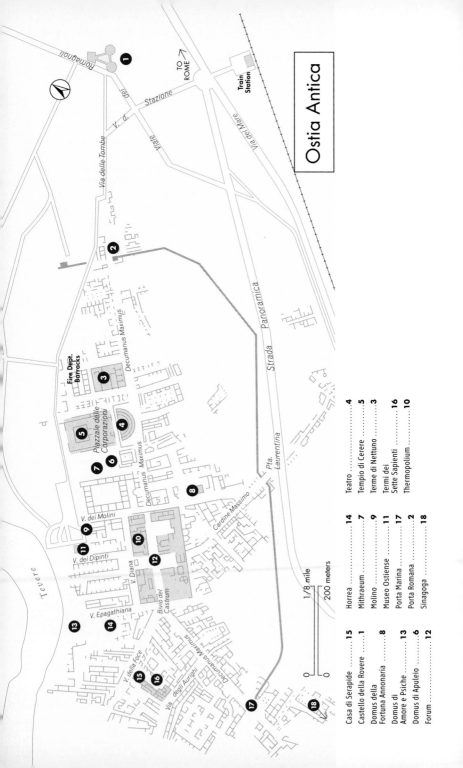

Ostia Antica

TO ROME

Train Station

Via del Mare

Fire Dept. Barracks

Piazzale delle Corporazioni

Decumanus Maximus

Strada Panoramica

Pta. Laurentina

Cardine Massimo

V. dei Molini

V. dei Dipinti

V. Diana

Bivio del Castrum

V. Epagathiana

V. della Foce

Via degli Aurighi

Decumanus Maximus

Tevere

Romagnoli

Via delle Tombe

Stazione

0   1/8 mile
0   200 meters

A GOOD WALK: OSTIA ANTICA

The **Porta Romana**, one of the city's three gates, is where you enter the Ostia Antica excavations. It opens onto the Decumanus Maximus, the main thoroughfare crossing the city from end to end. To your right, a staircase leads to a platform—the remains of the upper floor of the **Terme di Nettuno** (*Baths of Neptune*)—from which you get a good view of the mosaic pavements representing a marine scene with Neptune and the sea goddess Amphitrite. Directly behind the baths are the barracks of the fire department. On the north side of the Decumanus Maximus is the beautiful **Teatro** (*Theater*), built by Agrippa, remodeled by Septimius Severus in the 2nd century AD, and restored by the Rome City Council in the 20th century. In the vast Piazzale delle Corporazioni, where trade organizations had their offices, is the **Tempio di Cerere** (*Temple of Ceres*)—only appropriate for a town dealing in grain imports, Ceres being the goddess of agriculture. From there you can visit the **Domus di Apuleio** (*House of Apuleius*), built in Pompeian style, lower to the ground and with fewer windows than was characteristic of Ostia. Next door, the **Mithraeum** has balconies and a hall decorated with symbols of the cult of Mithras, a male-only religion imported from Persia.

On Via Semita dei Cippi, just off Via dei Molini, the **Domus della Fortuna Annonaria** (*House of Fortuna Annonaria*) is the richly decorated residence of a wealthy Ostian; one of the rooms opens onto a secluded garden. On Via dei Molini you can see a **molino** (*mill*), where grain was ground with stones that are still here. Along Via di Diana you come upon a **thermopolium** (*bar*) with a marble counter and a fresco depicting the foods sold here. At the end of Via dei Dipinti is the **Museo Ostiense** (*Ostia Museum*), which displays sarcophagi, massive marble columns, and statuary too large to be shown anywhere else. (The last entry to the museum is a half hour before the Scavi closes.) The **Forum**, on the south side of Decumanus Maximus, holds the monumental remains of the city's most important temple, dedicated to Jupiter, Juno, and Minerva. It's also the site of other ruins of baths, a basilica (which in Roman times was a hall of justice), and smaller temples. Via Epagathiana leads toward the Tiber, where there are large **horrea** (*warehouses*) erected during the 2nd century AD for the enormous amounts of grain imported into Rome during the height of the Empire. West of Via Epagathiana, the **Domus di Amore e Psiche** (*House of Cupid and Psyche*), a residence, was named for a statue found here (now on display in the museum); the house's enclosed garden is decorated with marble and mosaic motifs and has the remains of a large pool. The **Casa di Serapide** (*House of Serapis*) on Via della Foce is a 2nd-century multilevel dwelling; another apartment building stands a street over on Via degli Aurighi. Nearby, the **Termi dei Sette Sapienti** (*Baths of the Seven Wise Men*) are named for a group of bawdy frescoes. The **Porta Marina** leads to what used to be the seashore. About 1,000 feet to the southeast are the ruins of the **sinagoga**, one of the oldest in the Western world (from the 4th century AD).

families once populated the city. The great warehouses were built in the 2nd century AD to handle huge shipments of grain from Africa; the *insulae* (forerunners of the modern apartment building) provided housing for the city's growing population. Under the combined assaults of the barbarians and the malaria-carrying mosquito, and after the Tiber changed course, the port was eventually abandoned. ⊠ *Viale dei Romagnoli 717* ☎ *06/56358099* ⊕ *www.itnw.roma.it/ostia/scavi* 🎟 *€4–€6.50 includes Museo Ostiense, €2.50 rental of audio guide in English* ☉ *Tues. –Sun. 8:30–1 hr before sunset.*

WHERE TO EAT

$$ ✕ **Cipriani.** In the little medieval borgo near the excavations is an elegant trattoria serving Roman specialties and seafood. A business-like mood at lunchtime contrasts with an upgrade in menu, style, and price in the evening. A comprehensive wine list is available. ⊠ *Via del Forno 11* ☎ *06/56359560* ▤ *AE, DC, MC, V* ☉ *Closed Wed. No dinner Sun.*

TUSCIA

The region of Tuscia (the modern name for the Etruscan domain of Etruria) is a landscape of dramatic beauty punctuated by deep, rocky gorges and thickly forested hills, with dappled light falling on wooded paths. This has long been a preferred locale for the retreats of wealthy Romans, a place where they could build grand villas and indulge their sometimes eccentric gardening tastes. The provincial capital, Viterbo, which overshadowed Rome as a center of papal power for a time during the Middle Ages, lies in the heart of Tuscia. The farmland east of Viterbo conceals small quarries of the dark, volcanic peperino stone, which shows up in the walls of many buildings here. Lake Bolsena is an extinct volcano, and the sulfur springs still bubbling up in Viterbo's spas were used by the ancient Romans. Bagnaia and Caprarola are home to palaces and gardens; the garden statuary at Bomarzo is in a league of its own—somewhere between the beautiful and the bizarre.

The ideal way to explore this region is by car. By train from Rome you can reach Viterbo and then get to Bagnaia by local bus. If you're traveling by train or bus, check schedules carefully; you may have to allow for an overnight if you want to see all four locations.

VITERBO

25 km (16 mi) east of Tuscania, 104 km (64 mi) northwest of Rome.

GETTING HERE

Viterbo is well served by public transport from Rome. A direct train service takes an hour and 40 minutes. Try to avoid peak hours, as many commuters live in towns along the line. By road, take the A1 toll highway to Attigliano. The trip can take a couple of hours, depending on traffic.

Side Trips
from Rome

VISITOR INFORMATION
Viterbo tourism office (⊠ *Piazza San Carluccio 5* ☎ *0761/304795* ⊕ *www. comune.viterbo.it*).

EXPLORING

Viterbo's moment of glory was in the 13th century, when it became the seat of the papal court. The medieval core of the city still sits within 12th-century walls. Its old buildings, with windows bright with geraniums, are made of dark peperino, the local stone that colors the medieval part of Viterbo a dark gray, contrasted here and there with the golden tufa rock of walls and towers. Peperino is also used in the characteristic and typically medieval exterior staircases that you see throughout the old town. More recently, Viterbo has blossomed into a regional commercial center, and much of the modern city is loud and industrial. However, Viterbo's San Pellegrino district is a place to get the feel of the Middle Ages, seeing how daily life is carried on in a setting that has remained practically unchanged over the centuries. The Palazzo Papale and the cathedral enhance the effect. The city has also remained a renowned spa center for its natural hot springs just outside town, frequented by popes—and the laity—since medieval times.

The Gothic **Palazzo Papale** *(Papal Palace)* was built in the 13th century as a residence for popes looking to get away from the city. At that time Rome was a notoriously unhealthful place, ridden with malaria and plague and rampaging factions of rival barons. In 1271 the palace was the scene of a novel type of rebellion. A conclave held here to elect a new pope had dragged on for months, apparently making no progress. The people of Viterbo were exasperated by the delay, especially as custom decreed that they had to provide for the cardinals' board and lodging for the duration of the conclave. So they tore the roof off the great hall where the cardinals were meeting, and put them on bread and water. Sure enough, a new pope—Gregory X—was elected in short order. ⊠ *Piazza San Lorenzo* ☎ *338/1336529* ⊠ *€5 includes Museo del Colle del Duomo* ⊗ *Tues.–Sun., arrange for visit at Museo del Colle del Duomo.*

Viterbo's Romanesque Duomo, **Chiesa di San Lorenzo,** was built over the ruins of the ancient Roman Temple of Hercules. During World War II, the roof and the vault of the central nave were destroyed by a bomb. Subsequently, the church was rebuilt to its original medieval design. Three popes are buried here, including Pope Alexander IV (1254–61), whose body was hidden so well by the canons, who feared it would be desecrated by heretics, that it has never since been found. The small adjoining **Museo del Colle del Duomo** has a collection of 18th-century reliquaries, Etruscan sarcophagi, and a crucifixion painting attributed to Michelangelo. ⊠ *Piazza San Lorenzo* ☎ *338/1336529* ⊠ *Church free, museum €5 (includes Palazzo Papale)* ⊗ *Church: daily 8–12:30 and 3:30–7. Museum: Tues.–Sun. 10–1 and 3–6.*

The medieval district of **San Pellegrino** is one of the best preserved of such neighborhoods in Italy. It has charming vistas of arches, vaults, towers, exterior staircases, worn wooden doors on great iron hinges, and tiny hanging gardens. You pass many antiques shops and craft workshops as you explore the little squares and byways. The **Fontana Grande** in the piazza of the same name is the largest and most extravagant of Viterbo's authentic Gothic fountains. ⊠ *Via San Pellegrino.*

Viterbo has been a spa town for centuries, and the **Terme dei Papi** continues the tradition. This excellent spa has the usual rundown of health and beauty treatments with an Etruscan twist: try a facial with local volcanic mud, or a steam bath in an ancient cave, where scalding hot mineral water direct from the Bullicam spring splashes down a waterfall to a pool under your feet. The Terme dei Papi's main draw, however, is the *terme* (baths) themselves: a 21,000-square-foot outdoor limestone pool into the shallow end of which Viterbo's famous hot water pours at 59°C (138°F)—and intoxicates with its sulfurous odor. Floats and deck chairs are for rent, but bring your own bathrobe and towel unless you're staying at the hotel. ⊠ *Strada Bagni 12* ⊹ *5 km (3 mi) west of town center* ☎ *0761/3501* ⊕ *www.termedeipapi.it* ⊠ *Weekdays €12, Sat. €15, Sun. €18* ⊗ *Pool: Wed.–Mon. 9–7. Spa: daily 9–7.*

WHERE TO STAY & EAT

$$$ ✕ **Enoteca La Torre.** One of the best wine cellars in Italy takes center stage at the elegant Enoteca La Torre. It's also a temple to good eating: in addition to an ever-changing menu there are lists for cheeses, mineral waters, oils, and vinegars. Chestnut fritters and rabbit stew are unusual delicacies, but whatever you choose will be local, traditional, and of the highest quality. ⊠ *Via della Torre 5* ☎ *0761/226467* ▭ *AE, DC, MC, V* ⊗ *Closed Tues. No lunch Wed.*

★ **$$–$$$** ✕ **Tre Re.** Viterbo's oldest restaurant—and one of the most ancient in Italy—has been operating in the *centro storico* (historic center) since 1622. The kitchen focuses on traditional local dishes, such as *acquacotta viterbese* (literally, "cooked water"), a hearty vegetable-and-hot-pepper soup. The wine list offers the best of Italian wines. The small, wood-paneled dining room was a favorite haunt of movie director Federico Fellini and, before that, of Anglo-American soldiers during World War II. Local diners make a point of touching the old inn sign of the "Three Kings," hanging on the wall inside, as this is supposed to bring good luck. ⊠ *Via Macel Gattesco 3* ☎ *0761/304619* ▭ *AE, MC, V* ⊗ *Closed Thurs.*

★ **$** ✕ **Cantina Palazzo dei Mercanti.** Enjoy impeccably executed classics for pocket change at the casual Cantina, which shares a kitchen with the elegant Enoteca La Torre—it's the best lunch value in town. Try whatever is listed as the daily rotating special, such as pappardelle (fresh, wide-cut pasta) with a tomato-and-meat sauce. You can select a glass or bottle from the Enoteca's epic wine list, which includes a complex matrix of ratings from Italy's foremost wine reviewers. ⊠ *Via della Torre 1* ☎ *0761/226467* ▭ *AE, DC, MC, V* ⊗ *Closed Tues. No lunch Wed.*

$$$$ ⊡ **Hotel Niccolò V.** This upscale hotel is connected to Viterbo's mineral baths and spa at Terme dei Papi. With its air of relaxed, country-house elegance, the hotel provides a sharp contrast to the brisk and clinical atmosphere of the spa complex, bustling with doctors, bathers in bathrobes, and uniformed staff. The guest rooms are comfortable spots to relax after your treatment. Breakfast, a sumptuous buffet, is taken in a wood-beam gallery overlooking a small garden. Hotel guests have free access to the pool, as well as a 15% discount on all spa treatments. **Pros:** Friendly, helpful staff; comfortable rooms to relax in. **Cons:** Spa atmosphere with people lounging in the lobby in bathrobes may feel a bit like a hospital, some miles out of town so not convenient for sightseeing unless you have a car. ⊠ *Strada Bagni 12* ✚ *5 km (3 mi) west of center01100* 🖀 *0761/350555* ⊕ *www.termedeipapi.it/soggiornare/hotel.html* ➪ *20 rooms, 3 suites* ☐ *In-room: safe. In-hotel: restaurant, bar, pool, spa* ▭ *AE, DC, MC, V* ‖◎| *BP.*

BAGNAIA

5 km (3 mi) east of Viterbo.

GETTING HERE

Bagnaia is just outside Viterbo and can be reached by local city bus. By local train, it is ten minutes beyond the Viterbo stop—if your train actually stops here (very few local trains actually do, so be sure to check).

EXPLORING

The village of Bagnaia is the site of 16th-century cardinal Alessandro Montalto's summer retreat. The hillside garden and park that surround the two small, identical residences are the real draw, designed by virtuoso architect Giacomo Barozzi (circa 1507–73), known as Vignola, who later worked with Michelangelo on St. Peter's.

Villa Lante is a terraced extravaganza. On the lowest terrace a delightful Italian garden has a centerpiece fountain fed by water channeled down the hillside. On another terrace, a stream of water runs through a groove carved in a long stone table where the cardinal entertained his friends alfresco, chilling wine in the running water. That's only one of the most evident of the whimsical water games that were devised for the cardinal. The symmetry of the formal gardens contrasts with the wild, untamed park adjacent to it, reflecting the paradoxes of nature and artifice that are the theme of this pleasure garden. ⊠ *Via G. Baroni 71* 🖀 *0761/288008* ➪ *€2* ⊘ *Park and gardens: Tues.–Sun. 8:30–1 hr before sunset. Buildings closed to public.*

CAPRAROLA

21 km (16 mi) southeast of Bagnaia, 19 km (12 mi) southeast of Viterbo.

GETTING HERE

Caprarola is served by COTRAL bus, leaving from the Saxa Rubra station on the Roma Nord line.

EXPLORING

The wealthy and powerful Farnese family took over this sleepy village in the 1500s and had the architect Vignola design a huge palace and gardens to rival the great residences of Rome. He also rearranged the little town of Caprarola, to enhance the palazzo's setting.

The huge and splendid 400-year-old **Palazzo Farnese,** built on an unusual pentagonal plan, has an ingenious system of ramps and terraces that leads right up to the main portal. This nicety allowed carriages and mounts to arrive directly in front of the door. Though the salons are unfurnished, the palace's grandeur is still evident. An artificial grotto decorates one wall, the ceilings are covered with frescoes glorifying the Farnese family, and an entire room is frescoed with maps of the world as it was known to 16th-century cartographers. The palace is surrounded by a magnificent formal garden. ✉*Piazza Farnese* ☎*0761/646052* 💶*€2* 🕙*Palazzo: Tues.–Sun. 8:30–1 hr before sunset; garden: daily 8:30–1 hr before sunset.*

BOMARZO

15 km (9 mi) northeast of Viterbo.

GETTING HERE

Bomarzo is 6 km (3½ mi) from the A1 autostrada Attigliano exit, so if you are coming to Viterbo by car, it's easy to stop off on the way. Alternatively, you can get a public bus from Viterbo.

EXPLORING

☘ The eerie 16th-century **Parco dei Mostri** *(Monster Park)* was originally known as the Village of Marvels, or the Sacred Wood. Created in 1552 by Prince Vicino Orsini, it's a kind of Disneyland forerunner, populated with weird and fantastic sculptures of mythical creatures, intended to astonish illustrious guests. The sculptures, carved in outcroppings of mossy stone in shady groves and woodland, include giant tortoises and griffins and an ogre's head with an enormous gaping mouth. Children love it, and there are photo ops galore. The park has a self-service café and a souvenir shop. ✛*1½ km (1 mi) west of Bomarzo* ☎*0761/924029* 💶*€9* 🕙*Daily 8:30–sunset.*

TIVOLI & PALESTRINA

Tivoli is a five-star draw, its attractions being its two villas——an ancient one in which Hadrian reproduced the most beautiful monuments in the then-known world, and a Renaissance one, in which cardinal Ippolito d'Este put a river to work for his delight. Unfortunately, the road from Rome to Tivoli passes through miles of uninspiring industrial areas with chaotic traffic. Grit your teeth and persevere. It'll be worth it. In the heart of this gritty shell lie two pearls that are rightly world famous. You'll know you're close to Tivoli when you see vast quarries of travertine marble and smell the sulfurous vapors of the little spa, Bagni di Tivoli. Both sites in Tivoli are outdoors and entail walking. With a car, you can continue your loop through the mountains east of Rome, taking the ancient pagan sanctuary at Palestrina, spectacularly set on the slopes of Mount Ginestro.

TIVOLI

36 km (22 mi) northeast of Rome.

GETTING HERE

Unless you have nerves of steel, it's best not to drive to Tivoli. Hundreds of industries line the Via Tiburtina from Rome and bottleneck traffic is nearly constant. You can avoid some, but not all, of the congestion by taking the Roma–L'Aquila toll road. Luckily, there is abundant public transport. Buses leave every 15 minutes from the Ponte Mammolo stop on the Metro A line. The ride takes an hour. Regional Trenitalia trains connect from both Termini and Tiburtina stations and will have you there in under an hour. Villa d'Este is in the town center and a frequent bus service from Tivoli main square goes to Hadrian's Villa.

VISITOR INFORMATION

Tivoli tourism office (⊠ *Largo Garibaldi* ☎ *0774/334522* ⊕ *www.tivoli.it/turismo.htm*).

EXPLORING

In ancient times, just about anybody who was anybody had a villa in Tivoli, including Crassius, Trajan, Hadrian, Horace, and Catullus. Tivoli fell into obscurity in the medieval era until the Renaissance, when popes and cardinals came back to the town and built villas showy enough to rival those of their extravagant predecessors. Nowadays Tivoli is small but vibrant, with winding streets and views over the surrounding countryside, including the deep Aniene river gorge, which runs right through the center of town, and comes replete with a romantically sited bridge, cascading waterfalls, and two jewels of ancient Roman architecture that crown its cliffs——the round Temple of Vesta and the ruins of the rectangular Sanctuary of the Sibyl, probably built earlier. These can be picturesquely viewed across the gorge from the park of the Villa Gregoriana park, named for Pope Gregory XVI, who saved Tivoli from chronic river damage by diverting the river through a tunnel, weakening its flow. An unexpected (but not unappreciated) side effect was the creation of the Grande Cascata (Grand Cascade), which shoots a huge jet of water into the valley below. The Villa Gregoriana is at Largo Sant'Angelo (from the Largo Garibaldi bus stop, follow V. Pacifici——it changes name six times——and veer left on V. Roma to the Largo). There's a small admission charge to the park, which affords a sweaty, steep hike down to the river, so you may prefer to repair to the Antico Ristorante Sibilla, set right by the Temple of Vesta. From its dining terrace, you can drink in one of the most memorably romantic landscape views in Italy, one especially prized by 19th-century painters.

★ The astonishingly grand 2nd-century **Villa Adriana** *(Hadrian's Villa)*, 6 km (4 mi) south of Tivoli, was an emperor's theme park, an exclusive

2

retreat below the ancient settlement of Tibur where the marvels of the classical world were reproduced for a ruler's pleasure. Hadrian, who succeeded Trajan as emperor in AD 117, was a man of genius and intellectual curiosity, fascinated by the accomplishments of the Hellenistic world. From AD 125 to 134, architects, laborers, and artists worked on the villa, periodically spurred on by the emperor himself when he returned from another voyage full of ideas for even more daring constructions (he also gets credit for Rome's Pantheon). After his death in AD 138 the fortunes of his villa declined. It was sacked by barbarians and Romans alike; many of his statues and decorations ended up in the Vatican Museums, but the expansive ruins are nonetheless compelling. It's not the single elements but the delightful effect of the whole that makes Hadrian's Villa a treat. Oleanders, pines, and cypresses growing among the ruins heighten the visual impact. To help you get your bearings, maps are issued free with the audio guides (€4). A visit here takes about two hours, more if you like to savor antiquity slowly. In summer visit early to take advantage of cool mornings. ⊠ *Bivio di Villa Adriana off Via Tiburtina* ✛ *6 km (4 mi) southwest of Tivoli* ☎ *0774/382733 reservations* 🖾 *€6.50* ⊙ *Daily 9–1 hr before sunset.*

★ Right in the center of Tivoli, **Villa d'Este**, created by Cardinal Ippolito d'Este in the 16th century, was the most amazing pleasure garden of its day and still stuns visitors with its beauty. Inspired by the recent excavation of Villa Adriana and a devotee of the Renaissance celebration of human ingenuity over nature, Este (1509—72) paid architect Pirro Ligorrio an astronomical sum to create a mythical garden with water as its artistic centerpiece. To console himself for his seesawing fortunes in the political intrigues of his time (he happened to be cousin to Pope Alexander VI), he had his builders tear down part of a Franciscan monastery to clear the site, then divert the Aniene River to water the garden and feed the fountains——and what fountains: big, small, noisy, quiet, rushing, running, and combining to create a late-Renaissance, proto Busby Berkeley masterpiece in which sunlight, shade, water, gardens, and carved stone create an unforgettable experience. There are fountains of all shapes and sizes, from the tiny cascades that line the stone staircases leading down to the fish ponds at the bottom of the garden to the massive organ fountain. To this day, several hundred fountains cascade, shoot skyward, imitate bird songs, and simulate rain. The musical **Fontana dell'Organo** and the animated **Fontana della Civetta** have been restored to working order: the organ plays a watery tune every two hours 10:30–6:30 (until 4:30 in winter), and the mechanical *civetta* (owl) chases warbling sparrow figures out of the bath every two hours 10–6 (until 4 in winter). Romantics will love the night tour of the gardens and floodlit fountains, available on Friday and Saturday from June through September (for annual dates, see the Web site). Allow at least an hour for the visit, and bear in mind that there are a lot of stairs to climb. There's also a caféé on the upper terrace leading from the palace entrance, where you can sit and admire the view. ⊠ *Piazza Trento 1* ☎ *0774/312070* ⊕ *www.villadestetivoli.info* 🖾 *€6.50, €9.50 for Villa d'Este by Night tour* ⊙ *Tues.–Sun. 8:30–1 hr before sunset.*

WHERE TO STAY & EAT

★ $$$–$$$$ ✕ **Antico Ristorante Sibilla.** This famed restaurant should be included among the most beautiful sights of Tivoli. Built in 1730 beside the circular Roman Temple of Vesta and the Sanctuary of the Sibyl, the terrace garden has a spectacular view over the deep gorge of the Aniene river, with the thundering waters of the great waterfall in the background. The guest list reads like a visitor's book at Buckingham Palace. Marble plaques on the walls list the famous and the royals who have come here to dine over two and a half centuries. In decades gone by, the tour buses arrived and the food suffered. Today, however, food, wine, and service standards are high, as befits the sublime setting. ⊠ *Via della Sibilla 50* ☎*0774/335281* ▤*AE, DC, MC, V* ⊘*Closed Mon.*

$$ ✕▨ **Adriano.** At the entrance to Hadrian's Villa, this small restaurant-inn is a handy place to have lunch either before or after your trip round the ruins. The restaurant ($$) offers delicacies such as risotto *ai fiori di zucchine* (with zucchini flowers) or grilled porcini mushrooms in season. There is a garden for outdoor dining in summer. **Pros:** Wonderfully situated at the Villa gates, peaceful garden to relax in, attentive service. **Cons:** Busloads of tourists disembark under the windows, restaurant can be crowded. ⊠ *Via di Villa Adriana 194, 00010* ☎*0774/382235* ⊕*www.hoteladriano.it* ➳*10 rooms* ⬧*In-room: safe, refrigerator. In-hotel: restaurant, bar, tennis court* ▤*AE, DC, MC, V* ⊘*No dinner Sun. Nov.–Mar.* ⦿*BP.*

PALESTRINA

27 km (17 mi) southeast of Tivoli, 37 km (23 mi) east of Rome.

GETTING HERE

COTRAL buses leave from the Anagnina terminal on Rome's Metro A line and from the Tiburtina railway station. Alternatively, you can take a train to Zagarolo, where a COTRAL bus takes you on to Palestrina. The total trip takes 40 minutes. By car, take the A2 Autostrada del Sole to the San Cesario exit and follow the signs to Palestrina. Expect to take about an hour.

VISITOR INFORMATION

Palestrina tourism office (⊠ *Piazza della Cortina 1* ☎*06/9538100* ⊕*www.comune.palestrina.rm.it*).

EXPLORING

Except to students of ancient history and music lovers, Palestrina is surprisingly little known outside Italy. Its most famous native son, Giovanni Pierluigi da Palestrina, born here in 1525, is considered the master of counterpoint and polyphony. He composed 105 masses, as well as madrigals, magnificats, and motets. But the town was celebrated long before the composer's lifetime.

Ancient Praeneste (modern Palestrina) flourished much earlier than Rome. It was the site of the Temple of Fortuna Primigenia, which dates from the 2nd century BC. This was one of the largest, richest, most

2

frequented temple complexes in all antiquity—people came from far and wide to consult its famous oracle. In modern times no one had any idea of the extent of the complex until World War II bombings exposed ancient foundations occupying huge artificial terraces stretching from the upper part of the town as far downhill as its central Duomo.

Large arches and terraces scale the hillside up to the imposing **Palazzo Barberini,** which crowns a flight of steep, stone stairs. The palace was built in the 17th century along the semicircular lines of the original temple. It now contains the **Museo Nazionale Archeologico di Palestrina,** with material found on the site that dates from throughout the classical period. This well-labeled collection of Etruscan bronzes, pottery, and terra-cotta statuary as well as Roman artifacts takes second place to the chief attraction, a 1st-century BC mosaic representing the Nile in flood. This delightful work—a large-scale composition in which form, color, and innumerable details captivate the eye—is alone worth the trip to Palestrina. But there's more: a model of the temple as it was in ancient times helps you appreciate the immensity of the original construction. ⊠ *Piazza della Cortina 1* ☎ *06/9538100* 🖾 *€3, €2.50 rental of audio guide in English* ⊗ *Museum: daily 9–7. Archaeological temple zone: daily 9–1 hr before sunset.*

WHERE TO STAY & EAT

$$–$$$ ✕ **Il Piscarello.** Tucked away at the bottom of a steep side road, this elegant restaurant comes as a bit of a surprise. The yellow damask table linen and the deep gold curtains give the spacious dining room a warm and sunny look. There's a trim patio overlooking the garden for alfresco dining in good weather. Specialties on the menu include seafood and dishes anointed with black and white truffles. ⊠ *Via del Piscarello 2* ☎ *06/9574326* ▤ *AE, DC, MC, V* ⊗ *Closed Mon.*

$ ✕▥ **Hotel Stella.** Expect a cordial welcome at the restaurant ($) of the central Hotel Stella in Palestrina's public garden. The menu lists local dishes such as light and freshly made fettuccine served with a choice of sauces, as well as unusual combinations such as pasta *e fagioli con frutti di mare* (pasta and bean soup with shellfish). Decor tends toward the bright and fanciful. The guest rooms are frilly and a bit worn, but clean and comfortable. **Pros:** Old-fashioned and homely appeal for those who don't like grand hotel atmosphere. **Cons:** Basic accommodations; hotel is a long, uphill walk from the temple ruins and the archaeological museum. ⊠ *Piazzale Liberazione 3, 00036* ☎ *06/9538172* ⊕ *www. hotelstella.it* 🛏 *30 rooms* ⚘ *In-room: no a/c (some). In-hotel: restaurant, bar* ▤ *AE, DC, MC, V* ⊗ *BP.*

THE CASTELLI ROMANI

The "castelli" aren't really castles, as their name would seem to imply. They're little towns that are scattered on the slopes of the Alban Hills near Rome. And the Alban Hills aren't really hills, but extinct volcanoes. There were castles here in the Middle Ages, however, when each of these towns, fiefs of rival Roman lords, had its own fortress to defend it. Some centuries later, the area became given over to villas and retreats, notably the pope's summer residence at Castelgandolfo, and the 17th- and 18th-century villas that transformed Frascati into the Beverly Hills of Rome. Arrayed around the rim of an extinct volcano that encloses two crater lakes, the string of picturesque towns of the Castelli Romani are today surrounded by vineyards, olive groves, and chestnut woods—no wonder overheated Romans have always loved to escape here.

Ever since Roman times, the Castelli towns have been renowned for their wine. In the narrow, medieval alleyways of the oldest parts, you can still find old-fashioned hostelries where the locals sit on wooden benches, quaffing the golden nectar straight from the barrel. Following the mapped-out **Castelli Wine Route** (⊕*www.stradadeivinideicastelliromani.it*) around the numerous vineyards and wine cellars is a more sophisticated alternative. Exclusive local gastronomic specialties include the bread of Genzano, baked in traditional wood-fire ovens, the *porchetta* (roast suckling pig) of Ariccia, and the *pupi* biscuits of Frascati, shaped like women or mermaids with three or more breasts (an allusion to ancient fertility goddesses). Each town has its own feasts and saints' days, celebrated with costumed processions and colorful events. Some are quite spectacular, like Marino's annual Wine Festival in October, where the town's fountains flow with wine, or the Flower Festival of Genzano in June, when an entire street is carpeted with millions of flower petals, arranged in elaborate patterns.

FRASCATI

21 km (13 mi) southwest of Subiaco, 20 km (12 mi) south of Rome.

GETTING HERE
An hourly train service along a single-track line through vineyards and olive groves takes you to Frascati from Termini station. The trip takes 45 minutes. By car, take the Via Tuscolano, which branches off the Appia Nuova road just after St. John Lateran in Rome, and drive straight up.

VISITOR INFORMATION
Frascati tourism office (⊠*Piazza G. Marconi 1* ☎*06/942033* ⊕*www.frascati2000.it*).

EXPLORING
Frascati was the chosen sylvan retreat of prelates and princes, who built magnificent villas on the sun-drenched slopes overlooking the Roman plain. The most spectacular of these is **Villa Aldobrandini** (⊠*Via Cardinale Massaia* ☎*06/9420331 tourist office* ⊠*Free* ☉*Weekdays 9–1 and 3–6*), which dominates Frascati's main square from the top of its steeply sloped park. Built in the late 16th century and adorned with frescoes by the Zuccari brothers and the Cavalier d'Arpino, the hulking villa is still privately owned by the Princes Aldobrandini. However, its park is a marvel of baroque fountains and majestic box-shaded avenues and you can go and see the magnificent Water Theater that Cardinal Pietro Aldobrandini, Pope Clement VIII's favorite nephew, built to

impress his guests, thinking nothing of diverting the water supply that served the entire area in order to make his fountains play. The gigantic central figure of Atlas holding up the world is believed to represent the pope. You can also see another Water Theater in the grounds of nearby Villa Torlonia, which is now a public park. Visitors to the Villa Aldobrandini must apply for a permit from local Azienda Turismo Frascati first, located at Piazza Marconi 1.

Villa Aldobrandini looks across Piazza Marconi to the Belvedere terrace, a sort of outdoor parlor for the town. This is a favorite gathering place for young and old alike, especially on summer evenings when the lights of Rome can be seen twinkling in the distance. It's worth taking a stroll through Frascati's lively old center. Via Battisti, leading from the Belvedere, takes you into Piazza San Pietro with the imposing gray-and-white **Cathedral.** Inside is the cenotaph of Prince Charles Edward, last of the Scottish Stuart dynasty, who tried unsuccessfully to regain the British Crown, and died an exile in Rome in 1788. A little arcade beside the monumental fountain at the back of the piazza leads into Market Square, where the smell of fresh baking will entice you into the Purificato family bakery to see the traditional *pupi* biscuits, modeled on old pagan fertility symbols.

Take your pick from the cafés and trattorias fronting the central Piazzale Marconi, or do as the locals do—buy fruit from the market gallery at Piazza del Mercato, then get a huge slice of *porchetta* (roast suckling pig) from one of the stalls, a hunk of *casareccio* bread, and a few *ciambelline frascatane* (ring-shaped cookies made with wine), and take your picnic to any one of the numerous local *cantine* (homey wine bars), and settle in for some sips of tasty, inexpensive vino. ✉ *Via Cardinale Massaia* ☎*06/9420331 tourist office* ✉*Free* ☉ *Weekdays 9–1 and 3–6.*

WHERE TO STAY & EAT

$$$–$$$$ ✕ **Al Fico Vecchio.** This is a historic coaching inn, dating to the 16th cen-
★ tury, situated on an old Roman road a couple of miles outside Frascati. Don't confuse it with the Nuovo Fico just up the road. It has a charming garden, shaded by the branches of the old fig tree that gave it its name. The dining room has been tastefully renovated, preserving many of the characteristic antique features. The menu offers a wide choice of local dishes. ✉ *Via Anagnini 257* ☎*06/9459261* ✉*AE, DC, MC, V.*

$$$$ ▦ **Park Hotel Villa Grazioli.** One of Frascati's famous noble residences,
★ this elegant patrician villa, halfway between Frascati and Grottaferrata, is now converted into a first-class hotel. Built in 1580 and modeled after Rome's Villa Farnesina, the house was owned over the centuries by the regal Borghese and Odelscalchi families, and was nearly destroyed by bombs in World War II. Happily, the vast reception rooms on the *piano nobile (main floor)*—covered with frescoes of landscapes, mythological figures, and garden scenes by eminent 17th-century painters—survived mostly unscathed. The showpiece remains the South Gallery, frescoed by Giovanni Paolo Pannini in a swirl of trompe-l'oeil scenes, a masterpiece of baroque decorative art. The drama ends when you get to the guest rooms, which are standard-issue, white-wall salons with traditional furniture; rooms found in the adjacent rustic-style Limonaia

lodge have lovely wood-beam ceilings. The hotel is surrounded by a vast park, with swimming pool, hanging gardens, and a panoramic terrace. The cherry on top is the luxurious Acquaviva restaurant, where you can enjoy half- or full-board plans. **Pros:** Wonderful views of Roman countryside, unique atmosphere and surroundings, very helpful and professional staff. **Cons:** Entrance is at the end of a 1/3-mi narrow, rutted track and is poorly indicated from main road; only 13 rooms are in main building. ⊠ *Via Umberto Pavoni 19, 00046 Grottaferrata* ☎ *06/9454001* ⊕ *www.villagrazioli.com* ☎ *56 rooms, 2 suites* ☝ *In-room: safe. In-hotel: restaurants, pool, minibar* ⊟ *AE, DC, MC, V* ⧆ *BP*

CASTELGANDOLFO

8 km (12 mi) southwest of Frascati, 25 km (15 mi) south of Rome.

GETTING HERE

There is an hourly train service for Castelgandolfo from Termini station (Rome–Albano line). Otherwise, buses leave frequently from the Anagnina terminal of the Metro A subway. The trip takes about 30 minutes. By car, take the Appian Way from San Giovanni in Rome and follow it straight to Albano, where you branch off for Castelgandolfo (about an hour, depending on traffic).

EXPLORING

This little town is well known as the pope's summer retreat. It was the Barberini pope Urban VIII who first headed here, eager to escape the malarial miasmas that afflicted summertime Rome; before long, the city's princely families also set up country estates around here. The 17th-century **Villa Pontificia** has a superb position overlooking Lake Albano and is set in one of the most gorgeous gardens in Italy; unfortunately, neither the house nor the park are open to the public (although crowds are admitted into the inner courtyard for papal audiences). On the little square in front of the palace there's a fountain by Bernini, who also designed the nearby Church of San Tommaso da Villanova, which has works by Pietro da Cortona. The village has a number of interesting craft workshops and food purveyors, in addition to the souvenir shops on the square. On the horizon, the silver astronomical dome belonging to the Specola Vaticana observatory—one of the first in Europe—where the scientific Pope Gregory XIII indulged his interest in stargazing, is visible for miles around.

To the right of the papal palace, a walled road leads down to the lakeside, 300 feet below.

The **lakeside lido** is lined with restaurants, ice-cream parlors, and cafés and is a favorite spot with Roman families. No motorized craft are allowed on the lake, but you can rent paddleboats and kayaks. The waters are full of seafowl, such as swans and herons, and nature trails are mapped out along both ends of the shore. All along the central part there are bathing establishments where you can rent deck chairs, or stop to eat a plate of freshly prepared pasta or a gigantic Roman sandwich at one of the little snack bars under the oaks and alder trees. There's also a small, permanent fairground for children.

WHERE TO EAT

$$$–$$$$ ✕**Antico Ristorante Pagnanelli.** One of most refined restaurants in the
★ Castelli Romani, this has been in the same family since 1882—the present generation, Aurelio Pagnanelli and Jane, his Australian wife, with the help of their four sons, have lovingly restored this old railway inn perched high above Lake Albano. The dining room windows open onto a breathtaking view across the lake to the conical peak of Monte Cavo. In winter a log fire blazes in a corner; in summer dine out on the flower-filled terrace. Many of the dishes are prepared with produce from the family's own farm. The wine cellar, carved out of the living tufa rock, boasts more than 3,000 labels. ⊠ *Via Gramsci 4* ☎*06/9360004* ▭*AE, DC, MC, V* ⊘*Closed Tues.*

ARICCIA

8 km (13 mi) southwest of Castelgandolfo, 26 km (17 mi) south of Rome.

GETTING HERE

For Ariccia, take the COTRAL bus from the Anagnina terminal (☎*06/7222153*) of the Metro A underground line. All buses on the Albano–Genzano–Velletri line go through Ariccia. If you take a train to Albano, you can proceed by bus to Ariccia or go on foot (it's just under two miles). If you are driving, follow the Appian road to Albano and carry on to Ariccia.

EXPLORING

Ariccia is a gem of baroque town planning. When millionaire banker Agostino Chigi became Pope Alexander VII, he commissioned Gian Lorenzo Bernini to redesign his country estate to make it worthy of his new station. Bernini consequently restructured not only the existing 16th-century palace, but also the town gates, the main square with its loggias and graceful twin fountains, and the round church of **Santa Maria dell'Assunzione** (the dome is said to be modeled on the Pantheon). The rest of the village coiled around the apse of the church down into the valley below. Strangely, Ariccia's splendid heritage has been largely forgotten in the 20th century, and yet it was once one of the highlights of every artist's and writer's Grand Tour. Corot, Ibsen, Turner, Longfellow, and Hans Christian Andersen all came to stay at the Martorelli Inn on the main square (next to the pharmacy, but only open for rare temporary exhibitions; inside are some lovely 19th-century frescoed rooms).

★ **Palazzo Chigi** is a rare example of a baroque residence whose original furniture, paintings, drapes, and decorations are still mostly intact. The Italian film director Lucchino Visconti shot most of the internal scenes of the film *The Leopard* inside the villa. The rooms contain intricately carved pieces of 17th-century furniture, like the Pharmacy designed by Carlo Fontana and Bernini's splendid consoles, as well as textiles and costumes from the 16th to the 20th century. See the Room of Beauties, lined with paintings of the loveliest ladies of the day, and the Nuns' Room, with portraits of 10 Chigi sisters, all of whom took the veil. The park stretching behind the palace is a wild wood, the last remnant of the ancient Latium forest, where herds of deer still graze under the trees. ⊠*Piazza di Corte 14* ☎*06/9330053* ⊕*www.palaz-zochigiariccia.it/* ⛁*€7* ⊘*Guided tours only: Tues.–Fri. at 11, 4, and 5:30; weekends every hr 10:30–7.*

WHERE TO EAT

A visit to Ariccia is not complete without tasting the local gastronomic specialty: *porchetta,* the delicious roast whole pig stuffed with herbs. The shops on the Piazza di Corte will make up a sandwich for you, or you can do what the Romans do: take a seat at one of the *fraschette* wine cellars that serve cheese, cold cuts, pickles, olives, and sometimes a plate of pasta. Conditions are rather rough and ready—you sit on a wooden bench at a trestle table covered with simple white paper—but there's no better place to make friends and maybe join in a sing-along.

$ ✕**La Locanda del Brigante Gasparone.** The first of the string of *fraschette* (informal hostelries) you find clustered under the Galloro bridge, on the right-hand side of Palazzo Chigi, this locanda (inn) has seats either inside or outside under an awning—a fine place to enjoy simple, robust pasta dishes, washed down with a carafe of local Castelli wine. ⊠*Via Borgo San Rocco 7* ☎*06/9333100* ▤No credit cards ⊘Closed Wed.

NEMI

8 km (5 mi) west of Ariccia, 34 km (21 mi) south of Rome.

GETTING HERE

Nemi is a bit difficult to get to unless you come by car. Buses from the Anagnina Metro A station go to the town of Genzano, where a local bus travels to Nemi every two hours. If the times don't fit, you can take a taxi or walk the 5 km (3 mi) around Lake Nemi to get to the village. By car, take the panoramic route known as the Via dei Laghi (Road of the Lakes). Follow the Appia Nuova from St. John Lateran and branch off after Ciampino airport (the route is well signposted). Follow the Via dei Laghi (direction Velletri) until you come to the signs for Nemi.

EXPLORING

Nemi is the smallest and prettiest village of the Castelli Romani. Perched on a spur of rock 600 feet above the small crater lake of the same name, it has an eagle's-nest view over the rolling Roman countryside as far as the coast some 18 km (29 mi) away. The one main street, Corso Vittorio Emanuele, takes you to the (now privately owned) baronial Castello Ruspoli, with its 11th-century watchtower, and the quaint little Piazza Umberto 1, lined with outdoor cafés serving the tiny wood-strawberries harvested from the crater bowl. If you continue on through the arch that joins the castle to the former stables, you come to the entrance of the dramatically landscaped public gardens, which curve steeply down to the panoramic **Belvedere** terrace. If you enjoy walking, you can follow the road past the garden entrance and go all the way down to the bottom of the crater.

2

Nemi may be small in size, but it has a long and fascinating history. In Roman times there was an important sanctuary to the moon goddess Diana on the lakeside, which drew thousands of pilgrims from all over the Roman Empire. In the 1930s, the Italian government drained the lake in order to recover two magnificent ceremonial ships, loaded with sculptures, bronzes, and art treasures, that had lain submerged for 2,000 years. Unfortunately, the ships were burned during World War II. The state-of-the-art **Museo delle Navi Romani** *(Roman Ship Museum)* on the lakeshore, which was built to house them, has scale models and photographs of the complex recovery operation, as well as some finds from the sanctuary. ⊠ *Via del Tempio di Diana 9* 🕾 *06/9398040* 💶 *€2* 🕙 *Daily 9–6:30.*

WHERE TO EAT

$$ ✕ **Specchio di Diana.** Situated halfway down the main street is Nemi's most historic inn—Byron reputedly stayed here when visiting the area. A wine bar and café are on street level while the restaurant proper on the second floor offers marvelous views, especially at sunset. Pizzas are popular, but don't neglect Nemi's regional specialties: *fettucine al sugo di lepre* (fettucine with hare sauce), roast *porcini* mushrooms, and the little wood-strawberries with whipped cream. ⊠ *Corso Vittorio Emanuele 13* 🕾 *06/9368805* ⊟ *AE, DC, MC, V.*

Part II: Northern Italy

WHAT'S WHERE

1 Venice. One of the world's most novel cities, Venice has canals where the streets should be and an atmosphere of faded splendor that practically defines the word decadent.

2 The Venetian Arc. The green plains stretching west of Venice hold three of northern Italy's most appealing midsize cities: Padua, Vicenza, and Verona. Farther north, Alpine foothills are dotted with small, welcoming towns and some of Italy's most distinguished vineyards.

3 The Dolomites. Along Italy's northeast border, the Dolomites are the country's finest mountain playground, with gorgeous cliffs, curiously shaped peaks, lush meadows, and crystal-clear lakes. The skiing, hiking, and mountain drives are comparable to what you find in the Austrian Alps to the north, at better prices and with an Italian sensibility.

4 Milan, Lombardy & the Lakes. The deep-blue lakes of the Lombardy region—Como, Garda, and Maggiore—have been attracting pleasure-seekers since the days of ancient Rome. At the center of Lombardy is Milan, Italy's second largest city and its business capital. It holds some sophisticated pleasures of its own, including Italy's most renowned opera house and its most stylish shopping district.

AUSTRIA

TRENTINO-
ALTO ADIGE

Bolzano

Cortina
d'Ampezzo

FRIULI-VENEZIA
GIULIA

Trento

Belluno

Udine

Lake
Garda

VENETO

Treviso

Trieste

escia

Vicenza

Verona

Padua

Venice

Gulf of
Venice

antua

Adige

Po

Ferrara

EMILIA-ROMAGNA 7

Modena

Bologna

Ravenna

Adriatic Sea

Rimini

SAN MARINO

Pistoia

SAN MARINO

Arno

Florence

Ancona

TUSCANY

Arezzo

THE
MARCHES

Siena

Macerata

Assisi

Perugia

UMBRIA

Grosseto

Orvieto

5 Piedmont & Valle d'Aosta. A step off the usual tourist circuit, these regions in Italy's northwest corner have attractions that rival those of their neighbors. You'll find here geat Alpine peaks along the French and Swiss borders, a highly esteemed food-and-wine culture, and an elegant regional capital in Turin.

6 The Italian Riviera. Northern Italy's most attractive coastline runs along the Italian Riviera in the region of Liguria. Though there are some fine beaches, the main appeal is the beauty of the seaside cliffs and coves, and the towns interspersed among them. In the middle of it all is Genoa, Italy's busiest port city.

7 Emilia-Romagna. Many of Italy's signature foods come from here—including Parmigiano-Reggiano cheese, procsciutto di Parma, and balsamic vinegar—and the pasta is considered Italy's finest. But there's more than food to draw you here. Attractive cities dot the map: Bologna is the principal cultural center; the mosaics of Ravenna are glittering Byzantine treasures; and Ferrara, Parma, and Modena all reward your attention.

NORTHERN ITALY PLANNER

Speaking the Language

English is widely spoken in northern Italy, especially in the cities. Odds are if the person you want to talk with doesn't know English, there will be someone within ear-shot who understands enough to translate. Nonetheless, if you pick up a few common phrases in Italian, your effort will be appreciated.

The north has Italy's only land border with the rest of Europe, and you can sense the influence of the neighboring countries in the language. The region of Alto Adige actually has two official languages: Italian and German. Street signs, menus, city names, and street chatter are completely bilingual. Piedmont and Valle d'Aosta were once under Napoleon's rule, and a few French words continue to find there way into the local vocabulary.

In remote locales, you can discover some interesting linguistic anomalies. The Ladin language, an offshoot of Latin, is still spoken in the Val Gardena and Val di Fassa of the Dolomites. And in the valleys of western Piedmont, many locals speak Occitan, a language they share with residents of France's Languedoc region.

Getting Here

Aeroporto Malpensa, 50 km (31 mi) northwest of Milan, is the major northern Italian hub for intercontinental flights and also sees substantial European and domestic traffic. Venice's **Aeroporto Marco Polo** also serves international destination, mainly from other European cities, though there are direct flights from New York's JFK.

There are regional airports in Turin, Genoa, Bologna, Verona, Trieste, Treviso, Bolzano, and Parma, and Milan has a secondary airport, Linate. You can reach all of these connecting flights from within Italy and from other European cities. If you fly into Malpensa, but Milan isn't your final destination, you can also get where you're going by train, using the Italian national rail system, **Ferrovie dello Stato** (☎ 892021 *toll-free within Italy* ⊕ *www.trenitalia.com*). Shuttle buses run three times an hour between Malpensa and Milan's main train station, Stazione Centrale; the trip takes about 75 minutes, depending on traffic. Note that the Malpensa Express Train, which takes 40 minutes, delivers you to Cadorna station, from which you have to take the metro or a taxi across town to reach Stazione Centrale.

Typical Travel Times

	Hours by Car	Hours by Train
Milan–Venice	3:30	3:00
Milan–Turin	2:00	1:45
Milan–Genoa	2:00	1:45
Milan–Bologna	2:30	2:00
Venice–Bologna	2:15	2:00
Venice–Turin	5:00	5:00
Venice–Genoa	4:45	5:00
Bologna–Genoa	3:15	4:00
Bologna–Turin	3:30	4:00
Genoa–Turin	2:00	2:00

How's the Weather?

Winter: In the Dolomites, most ski resorts are open from mid-December through April, but snowfall in early winter is unreliable, and the best conditions often aren't seen until late February. Likewise, in Piedmont and Valle d'Aosta, snow conditions vary drastically year to year—some years there's good snow beginning in November, while others don't see much more than a flake or two until February.

With the exception of the skiing destinations, winter is the off season. In Venice, winters are relatively mild and tourist-free, but there are frequent rainy spells, and at the beginning and end of the season there's the threat of *acqua alta*, when tides roll in and flood low-lying parts of the city, including Piazza San Marco. The larger cities are active year round, but the resort towns of the Lake District and the Riviera are all but shut down. Frequent fog and below-freezing temperatures make winter a time to avoid the Veneto and Emilia-Romagna.

Spring: Late April, May, and early June are ideal times to tour northern Italy: the weather is mild, and the volume of tourists isn't as large as in summer. By May, the coastal towns of Liguria are beginning to come to life. Meanwhile, in the mountains hiking trails can remain icy well into June.

Summer: Anywhere away from the mountains or the water, summers are warm and humid. Summer temperatures in Venice have soured many a traveler on the magnificent city. If you're an opera buff, though, it's worth tolerating the heat in order to see a performance at the arena in Verona (where the season runs from July through September). Summer is prime hiking season in the Alps, and the lakes and the Riviera are in full swing (meaning lodging reservations are a must).

Fall: Much like spring, autumn, with its mild weather, is an ideal time for touring most of the region. In September the tourist season is winding down at the coastal resorts, and by October many properties are closed for the year. In the mountains, temperatures drop sharply in September. Many of the mountain tourist facilities close down entirely until the ski season kicks in.

On the Calendar

Taking part in seasonal events can give your trip an added dose of local culture. Here are a few of the north's best:

From December through June, **stagione operistica** (opera season) is in full swing, most notably in Milan, Turin, Parma, and Genoa. The **Festa di Sant'Ambrogio** officially launches the season at Milan's La Scala.

Venice's **Carnevale**, during the 10 days preceding Lent (usually falling in February), includes concerts, plays, masked balls, fireworks, and indoor and outdoor happenings of every sort. It is probably Italy's most famous festival, attracting hundreds of thousands. The **Carnevale d'Ivrea,** near Turin, includes three days of street festivals, culminating in the raucous Battle of the Oranges.

The town of Camogli comes alive on the second Sunday of May with the **Sagra del Pesce** (Feast of the Fish), a high-spirited community fish fry.

L'Arena di Verona Stagione Lirica (Arena of Verona Outdoor Opera Season), from early July to late August, is known for its grand productions, performed in Verona's 22,000-seat Roman amphitheater.

The **Festa del Redentore** (Feast of the Redeemer) in Venice on July 16 is a procession of boats commemorating the end of the plague of 1575. The fireworks over the lagoon are spectacular.

NORTHERN ITALY TOP ATTRACTIONS

Venice's Piazza San Marco

(A) Perhaps nowhere else in the world gathers together so many of man's noblest artistic creations. The centerpiece of the piazza is the Basilica di San Marco, arguably the most beautiful Byzantine church in the West, with not only its shimmering Byzantine Romanesque facade, but also it's jewel-like mosaic-encrusted interior. Right next door is the Venetian Gothic Palazzo Ducale, which was so beloved by the Venetians that when it burnt down in the 16th century, they rejected projects by the greatest architects of the Renaissance and had their palace rebuilt come era, dove era—exactly how and where it was.(⇨ Chapter 3.)

Venice's Grand Canal

(B) No one ever forgets a first trip down the Grand Canal. The sight of its magnificent palaces, with the light reflected from the canal's waters shimmering across their facades, is one of Italy's great experiences. (⇨ Chapter 3.)

Ravenna's Mosaics

(C) This small, out of the way city houses perhaps the world's greatest treasure trove of early Christian art. After the decline of Rome, Ravenna was the capital of the Western Roman Empire and, a bit later, the seat of the Byzantine Empire in the West. The exquisite and surprisingly moving 5th and 6th century mosaics decorating several churches and other religious buildings still retain their startling brilliance. (⇨ Chapter 9.)

Palladio's Villas and Palazzi

(D) The great 16th-century architect Palladio created harmoniously beautiful buildings that were influential in spreading the neoclassical style to northern Europe, England, and, later, America. He did most of his work in and around his native city of Vicenza. If a visit to Vicenza simply whets

your appetite for Palladio, you can see another wonderful Palladian villa outside Venice (La Malcontenta) and his famous collaboration with Veronese outside Treviso (Villa Barbaro). (⇨ Chapter 4.)

Lake Como

(E) Just a short drive or train ride north of Milan, Lake Como combines spectacular mountain scenery with the elegance of baroque villas and gardens and the charm of picturesque villages. It's great any time of year, but best in the spring, when the azaleas are in bloom in the gardens of Villa Carlotta. (⇨ Chapter 6.)

Giotto's Frescoes in the Scrovegni Chapel, Padua

(F) Dante's contemporary Giotto decorated this chapel with an eloquent and beautiful fresco cycle. Its convincing human dimension helped to change the course of western art. (⇨ Chapter 4.)

Mantua

(G) This charming town, slightly off the beaten track in Lombardy, contains a highpoint of 15th-century painting: Mantegna's frescoes in the wedding chamber of the Palazzo Ducale, a masterpiece of spatial illusion. On the outskirts of town, Giulio Romano's Palazzo Te is an elegant pleasure palace, frescoed with illusionistic painting carrying the tradition established by Mantegna several steps further. (⇨ Chapter 6.)

Leonardo's Last Supper

(H) On the refectory wall of Santa Maria della Grazia in Milan, one of the world's most famous paintings still evokes wonder, not at all trivialized by millions of reproductions or dulled by its poor state of conservation. (⇨ Chapter 6.)

NORTHERN ITALY TOP EXPERIENCES

Discovering the Cinque Terre

Along the Italian Riviera east of Genoa are five tiny, remote fishing villages known collectively as the Cinque Terre. Tourism here was once limited to backpackers, but the beauty of the landscape—with steep, vine-covered hills pushing smack-dab against an azure sea—and the charm of the villages have turned the area into one of Italy's top destinations. The number-one activity is hiking the trails that run between the villages—the views are once-in-a-lifetime gorgeous—but if hiking isn't your thing, you can still have fun lounging about in cafés, admiring the water, and perhaps sticking a toe in it.

Taking Part in Venice's Festivals

Few people love a good party as much as the Venetians, and they're happy when visitors join in. The biggest is, of course, Carnevale, culminating on Fat Tuesday, the day before Lent, but with revelry beginning about 10 days earlier. Visitors from the world over join the Venetians in a period of institutionalized fantasy, dressing in sometimes exquisitely elaborate costumes. The program changes each year and includes public, mostly free cultural events in all the districts of the city.

The Redentore, on the third weekend in July, is a festival essentially for Venetians, but guests are always welcome. The Venetians pack a picnic dinner and eat in boats decorated with paper lanterns in the Bacino di San Marco. Just before midnight, there's a magnificent fireworks display. The next day (Sunday), everyone crosses a temporary bridge spanning the Canale della Giudecca to Palladio's Redentore church to light a candle.

Venice Biennale is a cutting edge international art exposition held in odd numbered years from June to November in special exhibition halls in the Venice Public Gardens (Giardini) and in the XIV century industrial complex (Le corderie) in the Arsenale. It's the most important exhibition of contemporary art in Italy and one of the three most important in Europe.

Eating in Bologna

Italians recognize Emilia as the star of its culinary culture and Bologna as its epicenter. Many dishes native to Bologna, such as the slow-cooked meat-and-tomato sauce sugo alla Bolognese, have become so famous that they are widely available in all regions of Italy and abroad. But you owe it to yourself to try them in the city where they were born and are a subject of local pride. Take note, however: in Bologna a sugo is never served with spaghetti, but rather with an egg pasta in the form of tagliatelle, lasagne, or tortellini.

Fashion and Style in Milan

Italian clothing and furniture design are world famous, and the center of the Italian design industry is Milan. The best way to see what's happening in the world of fashion is to browse the designer showrooms and boutiques of the fabled quadrilatero della moda, along and around Via Montenapoleone. The central event in the world of furniture design is Milan's annual Salone Internazionale del Mobile, held at the Milan fairgrounds for a week in April. Admission is generally restricted to the trade, but the Salone is open to the general public for one day, generally on a Sunday, during the week of the show.

NORTHERN ITALY TODAY

The People

The population of northern Italy, especially the western regions, has undergone a substantial transformation because of immigration. Beginning during the economic boom of the 1960s and continuing to the 1980s, Italians from the south moved to the great industrial centers of Turin and Milan, changing the face of those cities.

The southerners, or at least their children, adopted most northern customs and attitudes—few now go home for lunch and then sleep a couple of hours before returning to work—but their presence has had an unmistakable influence upon the culture of the north. Especially in the cities, the local northern dialects died out, and at the dinner table, the traditional northern polenta and risotto now share the scene with spaghetti and other forms of pasta, and southern dishes appear frequently on menus.

Prosperity came much later to the regions of the northeast. Venetians still laugh heartily at the 18th century dialect comedies of Goldoni, and it's not uncommon to hear dialect spoken by the elegantly dressed opera fans at Venice's La Fenice. Emilia-Romagna, an essentially agricultural region that attracted few Italian immigrants, has kept most of its great local culinary culture intact.

Northern Italy, like the rest of the country, has recently experienced an influx of foreign immigrants. Their welcome has varied widely from city to city: Venice, proud of its cosmopolitan tradition, is fairly open to the newcomers, while other cities, where city hall is controlled by the overtly xenophobic Northern League, have made their integration difficult. But despite fears stemming from cultural and religious differences, northern Italians tend to accept new arrivals.

The Economy

Some regions of northern Italy are among the most prosperous areas in Europe. But recently, even these economic powerhouses have run into trouble. Their industrial base consists mainly of small and midsize businesses, many of which have had either to close or to outsource to Eastern Europe or even Central Asia because of a lack of unskilled and semi skilled labor at home. And many of those businesses, such as those in the textile sector, have had difficulty dealing with competition from China.

Religion and Politics

Despite Italy's being officially a secular state, most Italians, whether pious or pagan, would agree that it is impossible to separate Italian politics from the Roman Catholic Church. No matter whether a region has a liberal or a conservative tradition, the Church is an active force in public life. The Veneto has been the stronghold of the socially conservative, Church-oriented Christian Democratic Party and its successors. Emilia-Romagna, on the other hand, has had a strong socialist, and even communist tradition, but the Church still is a powerful force in society. The dichotomy has been raised to the level of a folk legend by the novels and popular film series featuring the disputes between Don Camillo and Peppone, a priest and the communist mayor of Brescello, a town in Emilia.

A GREAT ITINERARY

Day 1: Genoa

Fly into Genoa's pint-size Aeroporto Internazionale Cristoforo Colombo, pick up your rental car, and drive to your hotel (try to get a place near Piazza de Ferrari, the gateway to the *centro storico*). Leave your car there for the rest of the day. Spend the afternoon wandering the old city's ancient streets—*vicoli*—some of which are so narrow that lovers on upper floors would leap across to each other's rooms. Don't miss the Porta Soprana, the fortified portal to Europe's largest medieval city; the black-and-white-striped San Lorenzo cathedral; Via Garibaldi, lined with some of northern Italy's most impressive palazzi; and a ramble around the old port, site of Europe's largest aquarium. Do some window-shopping during the evening passeggiata along Via XX Settembre, then sample the city's culinary delights—the fresh fish with a water view at Antica Osteria del Bai, for example (you'll want to take a taxi there), or *trofie al pesto* (stubby, dense pasta twists with pesto, potatoes, and green beans) anywhere in town. Genoa is the birthplace of pesto—and focaccia, too.

Logistics: International flights to Genoa connect through Milan, Rome, or, if you're on a European carrier, other European cities including Zürich, Paris, London, and Munich. Try to get in as early in the morning as possible. Genoa is a vertical city, implausibly sandwiched between the mountains and the sea. Maps have a hard time conveying this third dimension, so be sure to ask your hotel for detailed driving and parking directions.

Day 2: Riviera di Levante/Cinque Terre

Heading out of Genoa, cross your fingers for good weather, and spend the morning driving one of Italy's most scenic roads, the Via Aurelia, in the direction of La Spezia (along the Riviera di Levante, or the "Riviera of the Rising Sun"). This road hugs the coast for hours. Stop for a brief wander around one or two of the many idyllic villages you pass; good candidates include Camogli and Santa Margherita Ligure, less than an hour outside Genoa. Portofino is on a promontory framed by those two towns; it's a bit more of a detour, but its allure is unmistakable. When you arrive in the Cinque Terre, check into a hotel in Riomaggiore or Vernazza; the latter is perhaps the most beautiful of these fishing ports that cling implausibly to the cliffs. From there, hike some of the impressive paths that connect the towns, including the Via dell'Amore between Manarola and Riomaggiore. Eat in whichever town you end up in at dinnertime, then take the train back to your hotel.

Logistics: The Via Aurelia (SS1) first heads out of town past the Genoese neighborhoods of Quarto, Quinto, and then Nervi. If you're not in view of the water, you're probably on the wrong road. From there it's a slow but beautiful drive to the Cinque Terre. If you're running short on time, switch over to the parallel A10 autostrada.

Day 3: Parma

Your next stop will be the stately food capital of Parma. When you arrive, check out the city's harmonious piazzas and medieval architecture. Shop for Parmigiano-Reggiano cheese and prosciutto di Parma (Parma ham)—where better?—or simply acquaint yourself with the *dolce far niente* (sweetness of doing nothing), perhaps browsing the city's stately boutiques with breaks for coffee (order simply "caffè"), gelato, or an aperitivo.

When night comes, seize the occasion to welcome yourself to Italy with an elaborate meal. There are many fine restaurants in this food town, but perhaps none finer than La Greppia.

Logistics: From the Cinque Terre, take the Via Aurelia to La Spezia, where you'll head north on the A15—it's no more than an hour up to Parma on this fast highway.

Day 4: Verona

After breakfast, depart from Parma for Verona, which might be the most quintessentially Italian city on this itinerary. Standing along the side of the fast-flowing River Adige, gazing at the rows of old palazzi along its banks and the rolling hills of cypress beyond, you'll find it hard not to fall in love with this city of Romeo and Juliet. Spend your morning wandering the city's medieval piazzas. Skip the touristy so-called House of Juliet, but don't miss Verona's stunning Roman Arena, the Castelvecchio (old castle), and San Zeno Maggiore, possibly Italy's finest Romanesque church. Accompany your dinner with a bottle of the Amarone wine for which the region is known. If it's summer and you plan things right, you might even time your day in Verona to coincide with an opera performance in the Arena.

Logistics: Take the A1 autostrada and then turn onto the A22 after about 50 km (31 mi), before you hit Modena. The A22 heads straight north past Mantua to Verona. Once there, park your car and go it on foot; Verona is definitely a walking city.

Day 5: Trento/Bolzano

Head north on the highway after breakfast, stopping for lunch and a walk around Trento's castle and Piazza del Duomo with its beautifully crenellated Palazzo Pretorio. After lunch, it's back on the road north. If you're not familiar with the region, you may be surprised, upon reaching beautiful Bolzano, to discover that everybody is speaking German. This is Alto Adige, also known as Südtirol, a semiautonomous region of Italy in which Italian is only one of the two official languages. The feel of the town, with its dim beer halls and elegant Piazza Walther, is positively Germanic. Not to be missed in town is the archaeological museum and a face-to-5,300-year-old-face visit with its amazingly preserved Iceman. Have a casual dinner of grilled meats and microbrewed beer at the young and laid-back Hopfen & Co, or gorge yourself with rich Tirolean mountain food at the more formal Zür Kaiserkron.

A GREAT ITINERARY

Logistics: Trento is due north of Verona on the A22 autostrada. It shouldn't take more than an hour and a half to get there. Continue north on the A22 to reach Bolzano—it's only another 50 km (31 mi).

Day 6: Padua/Venice

Leave bright and early and head back to the Veneto, where you'll be stopping in Padua, a wondrous university town full of bicycles and beautiful medieval architecture. The drive should take about two hours. Stop to see Giotto's unbelievable fresco cycle in the Cappella degli Scrovegni before continuing into the centro storico, parking wherever you can, and wandering through the streets of the old town (watch out for those bikes!). After lunch, drive straight to Venice (less than an hour), return your rental car, check into your hotel, and if all goes well, you'll still have time for some afternoon sightseeing. Get lost in the city's back canals for a couple of hours before finding your way to a seafood dinner. Afterward, consider having a nightcap around the Campo San Luca or Campo Santa Margarita.

Logistics: This day really requires an early start. Head south on the A22—back through Verona—and then east on the A4. Padua is on the way to Venice on the A4. When you arrive in Venice, return your car at Piazzale Roma, where most major companies have a garage. Then at the Piazzale Roma vaporetto stop, buy 72-hour vaporetto "travel cards," and take the vaporetto to your hotel. If you're not in the mood for such a hectic day, then skip Padua.

Day 7: Venice

Begin with a morning vaporetto cruise along the Grand Canal. Proceed with a visit to Piazza San Marco, the Byzantine

TIPS

1 The itinerary can also be done by train. All these stops are well connected by Italy's rail network, and none of the trips will take more than a couple of hours. In most cases you'll want to take a taxi from the train station to your hotel. The only tricky parts will be on Days 5 and 6, when you'll be stopping for lunch in Trento and Padua, respectively. You can check your luggage at the train station.

2 Winter is not the time for this trip. Northern Italy can get very cold in December, January, and especially February.

splendor of the Basilica di San Marco, and the imposing Palazzo Ducale. Stop for lunch, perhaps at a traditional Venetian *bacaro* (wine bar). Next, take the Accademia footbridge across the Grand Canal, and see the Gallerie dell'Accademia, Venice's most important art gallery. Wander through the Dorsoduro neighborhood, finishing up with a romantic sunset walk around the Zattere before proceeding to dinner.

Day 8: Venice/Departure

Have breakfast at your hotel and head by vaporetto to San Marco, where you'll transfer to the airport boat. Savor your last cup of the world's richest coffee at the airport's coffee bar before boarding.

Logistics: Alilaguna operates the one-hour, €10 boat trip from Venice to the airport. Water taxis are much more expensive but they pick you up at your hotel.

Venice

WORD OF MOUTH

"There's no way to adequately describe the uniqueness, the beauty, and the charm that is Venice. It's like the Grand Canyon. It doesn't matter how many pictures you've seen, until you've come face to face with her, you can't begin to imagine her splendor."

—dcd

WELCOME TO VENICE

TOP REASONS TO GO

★ **Basilica di San Marco:** Whether its opulence seduces you or overwhelms you, it's a sight to be seen.

★ **Gallerie dell'Accademia:** It only makes sense that you find the world's best collection of Venetian paintings here.

★ **Santa Maria Gloriosa dei Frari:** Of Venice's many gorgeous churches, this one competes with San Marco for top billing.

★ **Cruising the Grand Canal:** Whether seen by gondola or by water bus, Venice's Main Street is something from another world.

★ **Snacking at a bacaro:** The best way to sample genuine Venetian cuisine is to head for one of the city's classic wine bars.

1 The Grand Canal. Venice's major thoroughfare is lined with grand palazzos that once housed the city's richest families.

2 San Marco. In the city's center, this sestiere is one of Italy's most expensive neighborhoods. Its streets are lined with fashion boutiques, art galleries, and grand hotels. Piazza San Marco, called by Napoléon "the world's most beautiful drawing room," is the heart of Venice and the location of its two most distinctive sights, the **Basilica di San Marco** and the **Palazzo Ducale.**

3 Dorsoduro. This elegant residential area is home to the **Gallerie dell'Accademia** and the **Peggy Guggenheim Collection.** The Zattere promenade is one of the best spots to stroll with a gelato or linger at an outdoor café.

4 Santa Croce and San Polo. These neighboring sestieri are largely commercial districts, with many shops, several major sights, and the Rialto fish and produce markets.

Piazza San Marco

Bridge to Mainland

Stazione Ferrovia Santa Lucá

Canal Della Giudecca

5 Cannaregio. Short on architectural splendor, this sestiere provides some of the prettiest canal-side walks in town. **The Fondamenta della Misericordia** is a nightlife center, and the **Jewish Ghetto** has a fascinating history and tradition all its own.

6 Castello. Along with Cannaregio, this area is home to most of the locals. It's the sestiere that's least influenced by Venice's tourist culture—except when the Biennale art festival is on.

GETTING ORIENTED

Seen from the window of an airplane, central Venice looks like a fish laid out on a blue platter. The train station at the western end is the fish's eye, and the Castello *sestiere* (neighborhood) is the tail. In all, the "fish" consists of six sestieri—Cannaregio, Santa Croce, San Polo, Dorsoduro, San Marco, and Castello. More sedate outer islands swim around them—San Giorgio Maggiore and the Giudecca just to the south, beyond them the Lido, and to the east Murano, Burano, and Torcello.

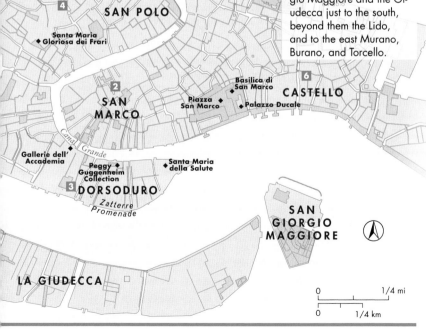

VENICE PLANNER

Festivals to Build a Trip Around

Venice's most famous festival is **Carnevale**, drawing revelers from all over the world. For 10 days leading up to Ash Wednesday, it takes over the city—think Mardi Gras meets Casanova.

The prestigious **Biennale** is a century-old international art festival held in late summer and early fall of odd-number years. It's spawned several other festivals, including the **Biennale Danza, Biennale Musica,** and, most famously, **Biennale Cinema,** also known as the Venice Film Festival, held every year at the end of August.

The **Festa Redentore** (Feast of the Redeemer), on the third Sunday in July, is the biggest celebration of the year among locals, who float out in boats on Bacino San Marco and watch midnight fireworks displays.

There are three noteworthy annual contests of Venetian-style rowing: the **Regata delle Bafane,** on January 6; **Vogalonga** (long row), on a Sunday in May; and **Regata Storica,** on the first Sunday in September.

Making the Most of Your Time

A great introduction to Venice is a ride on *vaporetto* (water bus) Line 1 from the train station all the way down the Grand Canal. If you've just arrived and have luggage in tow, you'll need to weigh the merits of taking this trip right away versus getting settled at your hotel first. (Crucial factors: your mood, the bulk of your bags, and your hotel's location.)

Seeing Piazza San Marco and the sights bordering it can fill a day, but if you're going to be around awhile, consider holding off on your visit here—the crowds can be overwhelming, especially when you're fresh off the boat. Instead, spend your first morning at Santa Maria Gloriosa dei Frari and the Scuola Grande di San Rocco, then wander through the Dorsoduro sestiere, choosing between visits to Ca' Rezzonico, the Gallerie dell'Accademia, the Peggy Guggenheim Collection, and Santa Maria della Salute—all A-list attractions. End the afternoon with a gelato-fueled stroll along the Zattere boardwalk. Then tackle San Marco on Day 2.

If you have more time, make these sights your priorities: the Rialto fish and produce markets; Ca' d'Oro and the Jewish Ghetto in Cannaregio; Santa Maria dei Miracoli and Santi Giovanni e Paolo in Castello; and, across the water from Piazza San Marco, San Giorgio Maggiore. (In Venice, there's a spectacular church for every day of the week, and then some.) A day on the outer islands of Murano, Burano, and Torcello is good for a change of pace.

Tourist Offices

The multilingual staff of the **Venice tourism office** (☎041/ 5298711 ⊕ www.turismovenezia.it) can help you out with directions and up-to-the-minute information about events in the city and sight closures. There are office branches at Marco Polo Airport; the train station; Procurate Nuove, near Museo Correr on Piazza San Marco; Garage Comunale, on Piazzale Roma; the Venice Pavilion, near Ghardini Reali in San Marco; and Santa Maria Elisabetta 6/a, on the Lido. The train-station branch is open daily 8–6:30; other branches generally open at 9:30.

Sight Passes & Discount Cards

Sixteen of Venice's most significant churches (noted throughout this chapter) are part of an umbrella group known as the **Chorus Foundation** (☎041/2750462 ⊕ www. chorusvenezia.org), which coordinates their administration, including hours and admission fees. Churches in the group are open to visitors all day except Sunday morning, and usually someone there can provide information and a free leaflet in English. Single church entry costs €3, or you can visit them all with a €9 Chorus pass. Note that the Baslica di San Marco is not part of the Chorus group.

Eleven museums make up Venice's **Musei Civici** (☎041/ 2715911 ⊕ www.museicivicivenezinai.it). A museum pass costing €18 and valid for six months lets you make one visit to each museum. A Museum Card, good only at the Piazza San Marco museums—Palazzo Ducale, Museo Correr, Museo Archeologico, and Biblioteca Nazionale Marciana—costs €12.

The **VENICEcard** (☎041/2424 ⊕ www.venicecard.it) offers discounts on a variety of services throughout the city. It is available in two versions—blue or orange. The first includes reductions on public transport fares and discounts at some shops, restaurants, and hotels. In addition to these discounts, the orange card provides free entrance to museums and the Chorus churches. The passes are valid for durations of 12 hours, 48 hours, or 7 days, with blue costing €18.50, €34, or €55, and orange €30, €55, or €81. Cards can be purchased online, at the welcome desks of VeneziaSi at the airport, Tronchetto parking garage, the train station, and at the ACTV/Vela ticket office at Piazzale Roma. Although the cards are convenient, you'll have to do some calculating to see if they're really a money saver for you.

Venetian Vocabulary

Venetians use their own terms to describe their unique city. In fact, they have their own dialect; if you have an ear for Italian, you'll notice a distinct difference in the language. Here are some key words to know:

Sestiere: A neighborhood in central Venice. (There are six of them.)

Rio: A small canal.

Riva: A street running along a canal.

Fondamenta: Another name for a riva.

Calle: A street not running along a canal.

Campo: A square—what elsewhere in Italy would be called a piazza. (The only piazza in Venice is Piazza San Marco.)

Bacaro: A wine bar.

Ombra: A glass of wine served at a bacaro.

Cicchetto (pronounced "chick-ay-toh"): A snack served at a bacaro—roughly the Venetian equivalent of tapas.

GETTING HERE & AROUND

Getting Here by Car

Venice is on the east–west A4 autostrada, which connects with Padua, Verona, Brescia, Milan, and Turin. If you bring a car to Venice, you will have to pay for a garage or parking space.

A warning about parking: don't be waylaid by illegal touts, often wearing fake uniforms, who may try to flag you down and offer to arrange parking and hotels; drive on to one of the parking garages. Parking at **Autorimessa Comunale** (☎041/2727211 ⊕ www. asmvenezia.it) costs €21 for 24 hours. The private **Garage San Marco** (☎041/5232213 ⊕ www.garagesanmarco.it) costs €20 for up to 12 hours and €26 for 12–24 hours. You can reserve a space in advance at either of these garages; you'll come upon both immediately after crossing the bridge from the mainland. Another alternative is **Tronchetto** (☎041/5207555) parking (€20 for 1–24 hours); watch for signs for it coming over the bridge—you'll have to turn right before you get to Piazzale Roma. Many hotels have negotiated guest discounts with San Marco or Tronchetto garages; get a voucher when you check in at your hotel and present it when you pay the garage.

Getting Here by Air

Venice's **Aeroporto Marco Polo** (☎041/2609260 ⊕ www. veniceairport.it) is 10 km (6 mi) north of the city on the mainland. It's served by domestic and international flights, including connections from 21 European cities, plus direct flights from New York's JFK.

From Marco Polo terminal it's a €10 taxi ride or a 10-minute walk to the dock where public and private boats depart for Venice's historic center. **Alilaguna** (☎041/2401701 ⊕ www.alilaguna.it) has regular ferry service from predawn until nearly midnight. The charge is €12 per person, including bags, and it takes about an hour to reach the landing near Piazza San Marco, with a stop at the Lido on the way. A *motoscafo* (water taxi) carries up to four people and four bags to the city center in a sleek, modern powerboat. The base cost is €90, and the trip takes about 25 minutes. Each additional person, bag, and stop costs extra, so it's essential to agree on a fare before boarding.

Blue buses run by **ATVO** (☎0421/383672 ⊕ www.atvo. it) make a less scenic but quicker (20-minute) and cheaper (€3) nonstop trip from the airport to Piazzale Roma, from where you can get a vaporetto to the landing nearest your hotel. Tickets are sold at the airport ticket booth (open daily 9 to 7:30), and on the bus when the booth is closed. A land taxi to Piazzale Roma costs about €40.

Getting Here by Train

Venice has rail connections with every major city in Italy and Europe. Note that Venice's station is **Stazione Ferroviaria Santa Lucia,** not to be confused with Stazione Ferroviaria Venezia-Mestre, which is located on the mainland 12 km (7 mi) outside of town. Some Continental trains stop only at the Mestre station; in such cases you can catch the next Venice-bound train. Be aware that if you change from a regional train to an Intercity or Eurostar, you'll need to upgrade with a *supplemento* (extra charge) or be liable for a hefty fine. You're also subject to a fine if before boarding you don't validate your ticket in one of the yellow machines found on or near platforms.

Getting Around by Vaporetto

Venice's primary means of public transportation is by vaporetto (water bus). **ACTV** (☎ 041/2424 ⊕ www.hello-venezia.it) operates vaporetti on several routes through and around the city. Beginning at 11 PM there is limited service through the night. Landing stages are clearly marked with name and line number, but check before boarding to make sure the boat is going in your direction. Line 1 is the Grand Canal local, calling at every stop and continuing via San Marco to the Lido. The trip takes about 35 minutes from Ferrovia to Vallaresso, San Marco.

A vaporetto ticket for all lines costs €6 one-way (children under four ride free). Another option is a Travel Card: €15 buys 24 hours and €30 buys 72 hours of unlimited travel. For travelers between ages 14 and 29, the 72-hour pass is €18 with the Rolling Venice card. Ask for the card (€4) before buying your tickets. A shuttle ticket allows you to cross a canal, one stop only, for €2.

Line information is posted at each landing, and complete timetables for all lines are available for €.60 at ACTV/Vela ticket booths, located at most major stops. Buy your ticket before getting on the boat and validate it in the yellow time-stamp machine. Tickets are also sold on the boat; you must ask to buy one immediately upon boarding, which can be a hassle. When inspectors come aboard, ticketless riders are fined, as are those who haven't validated their tickets. The fine is €35, and pleading ignorance will not spare you. The law says you must also buy tickets for bags more than 28 inches long (there's no charge for your bag if you have a Travel Card), but this is generally enforced only for very bulky bags.

Getting Around by Water Taxi

A *motoscafo* (water taxi) isn't cheap; you'll spend about €60 for a short trip in town, €75 to the Lido, and €90 per hour to visit the outer islands. The fare system is convoluted, with luggage handling, waiting time, early or late hours, and even ordering a taxi from your hotel adding expense. Always agree on the price before departing.

Getting Around by Gondola

As your gondola glides away from the fondamenta, a transformation takes place. To some it feels like a Disney ride, but if you insist that your gondolier take you through the tiny side canals, you'll get an intimate glimpse of the city that can't be experienced any other way.

San Marco is loaded with gondola stations, but to get off the circuit, try the San Tomà or Santa Sofia (near Ca' d'Oro) stations. The price of a 40-minute ride is supposed to be fixed at €80 for up to six passengers, rising to €100 between 7:30 PM and 8 AM, but these are minimums and you may have difficulty finding a gondolier who will work for that unless the city is empty. Come to terms on cost and duration before you start, and make it clear that you want to see more than just the Grand Canal.

Getting Around by Traghetto

Many tourists are unaware of the two-man gondola ferries that cross the Grand Canal at numerous strategic points. At €.50, they're the cheapest and shortest gondola ride in Venice, and they can save a lot of walking. Look for TRAGHETTO signs and hand your fare to the gondolier when you board.

EATING & DRINKING WELL IN VENICE

The catchword in Venice, at both fancy restaurants and holes-in-the-wall, is fish, often at its tastiest when it looks like nothing you've seen before. How do you learn firsthand about the catch of the day? An early-morning visit to the Rialto's *pescheria* (fish market) is more instructive than any book.

Dining options in Venice range from the ultra-high end, where jackets and ties are required, to the supercasual, where the clientele (almost all of them tourists) won't notice if you're wearing shorts. Some of Venice's swankiest restaurants—the ones that usually have only male waiters wearing white jackets and bow ties—trade on long-standing reputations and might seem a little stuffy and faded. The food at such places tends toward interpretations of international cuisine and, though often expertly prepared, can seem as old-fashioned as the waiters who serve it. On the other hand, mid-range restaurants are often more willing to break from tradition, incorporating ingredients such as ginger and wasabi in their creations.

GOING BACARO

You can sample wines of the region in *bacari* (wine bars), which are a great Venetian tradition. For centuries, locals have gathered at these neighborhood spots to chat and have a glass of wine (known as an *ombra* in Venetian dialect) accompanied by *cicchetti* (snacks), often substantial enough for a light meal. *Crostini,* toast topped with a fish, meat, or vegetable spread, is a popular cicheti, as are small sandwiches, crescents of melon wrapped with prosciutto, marinated seafood salads, and toothpick-speared items like roasted peppers, marinated artichokes, deep-fried mozzarella balls, and meatballs.

SEAFOOD

Venetian cuisine is based on seafood—*granseola* (crab), *moeche* (soft-shell crab), and *seppie* or *seppioline* (cuttlefish) are all prominently featured—and trademark dishes include *sarde in saor* (fried sardines with olive oil, onions, pine nuts, and raisins), photo right, and *baccalà mantecato* (cod creamed with milk and olive oil).

When served whole, fish is usually priced by the *etto* (100 grams, about ¼ pound) and can be quite expensive.

RISOTTO, PASTA, POLENTA

As a first course, Venetians favor risotto, the creamy rice dish, prepared with vegetables or shellfish. Pasta, too, is paired with seafood sauces: *pasticcio di pesce* is pasta baked with fish, usually baccalà, and *bigoli* is a strictly local pasta shaped like short, thick spaghetti, usually served with *nero di seppia* (squid-ink sauce).

A classic first course is pasta e fagioli (thick bean soup with pasta). Polenta (creamy cornmeal) is another pillar of regional cooking; it's often served with *fegato alla veneziana* (calves' liver and onions).

VEGETABLES

The salty soil of the larger islands of the lagoon is legendary for the fine vegetables that grow from it. Now just a few stalls at the Rialto Market sell locally grown crops, but produce from the surrounding regions is of high quality. Spring treats are the fat white asparagus from Bassano and artichokes, usually sautéed with olive oil, parsley, and garlic. From December to March, red radicchio from Treviso is grilled or used as a base for risotto. Fall brings small, brown wild mushrooms called chiodini and zucca barucca, a bumpy squash often baked, used in soups, or stuffed into ravioli.

TIRAMISU

Tiramisu, pictured below, is the most popular dessert in town, but no matter how many times you try it, it's always a bit different, as each restaurant follows its own tiramisu creed. Just to mention a few of the possible variations: sweet liqueur can be added to the coffee, whipped cream or crème anglaise can be stirred into the basic mascarpone and egg-yolk filling, or bits of bitter chocolate can be scattered on top instead of cocoa.

WINES

Local wines are the dry white tocai and pinot grigio from the Friuli region and the bubbly white prosecco, a naturally fermented sparkling wine that is a shade less dry. Popular red wines include merlot, cabernet, raboso, and refosco.

Updated by
Pamela Santini

IT'S CALLED LA SERENISSIMA, "THE most serene," a reference to the majesty, wisdom, and monstrous power of this city that was for centuries the unrivaled mistress of trade between Europe and the Orient and the bulwark of Christendom against the tides of Turkish expansion. "Most serene" could also describe the way lovers of this miraculous city feel when they see it, imperturbably floating on its calm blue lagoon.

Built entirely on water by men who defied the sea, Venice is unlike any other town. No matter how many times you've seen it in movies or on TV, the real thing is more dreamlike than you could ever imagine. Its landmarks, the Basilica di San Marco and the Palazzo Ducale, seem hardly Italian: delightfully idiosyncratic, they are exotic mixes of Byzantine, Gothic, and Renaissance styles. Shimmering sunlight and silvery mist soften every perspective here, and you understand how the city became renowned in the Renaissance for its artists' rendering of color. It's full of secrets, inexpressibly romantic, and at times given over entirely to pleasure.

You'll see Venetians going about their daily affairs in *vaporetti* (water buses), aboard the *traghetti* (traditional gondola ferries) that carry them across the Grand Canal, in the *campi* (squares), and along the *calli* (narrow streets). They are nothing if not skilled—and remarkably tolerant—in dealing with the veritable armies of tourists from all over the world who fill the city's streets for most of the year.

PIAZZA SAN MARCO

One of the world's most evocative squares, Piazza San Marco (St. Mark's Square) is the heart of Venice, a vast open space bordered by an orderly procession of arcades marching toward the fairy-tale cupolas and marble lacework of the Basilica di San Marco. Perpetually packed by day with people and fluttering pigeons, it can be magical at night, especially in winter, when mists swirl around the lampposts and the Campanile.

If you face the basilica from in front of the Correr Museum, you'll notice that rather than being a strict rectangle, this square opens wider at the basilica end, creating the illusion that it's even larger than it is. On your left, the long, arcaded building is the Procuratie Vecchie, built in the early 16th century as offices and residences for the powerful procurators (magistrates) of San Marco.

On your right is the Procuratie Nuove, built half a century later in a more-grandiose classical style. It was originally planned by Venice's great Renaissance architect, Jacopo Sansovino (1486–1570), to carry on the look of his Libreria Sansoviniana (Sansovinian Library), but he died before construction on the Nuove had begun. Vincenzo Scamozzi (circa 1552–1616), a neoclassicist pupil of Andrea Palladio (1508–80), completed the design and construction. Still later, the Procuratie Nuove was modified by architect Baldassare Longhena (1598–1682), one of Venice's baroque masters.

Continued on page 190

CRUISING THE GRAND CANAL

THE BEST INTRODUCTION TO VENICE IS A TRIP DOWN MAIN STREET

Venice's Grand Canal is one of the world's great thoroughfares. It winds its way in the shape of a backward "S" from Ferrovia (the train station) to Piazza San Marco, passing 200 palazzos born of a culture obsessed with opulence and fantasy. There's a theatrical quality to a boat ride on the canal: it's as if each pink- or gold-tinted facade is trying to steal your attention from its rival across the way.

The palaces were built from the 12th to 18th centuries by the city's richest families. A handful are still private residences, but many have been converted to other uses, including museums, hotels, government offices, university buildings, a post office, a casino, and even a television station.

It's romantic to see the canal from a gondola, but the next best thing, at a fraction of the cost, is to take the Line 1 *vaporetto* (water bus) from Ferrovia to San Marco. The ride costs €6 and takes about 35 minutes. Invest in a Travel Card (€15 buys 24 hours of unlimited passage) and you can spend the better part of a day hopping on and off at the vaporetto's 16 stops, visiting the sights along the banks.

Either way, keep your eyes open for the highlights listed here; the major sites also have fuller descriptions later in this chapter.

FROM FERROVIA TO RIALTO

Palazzo Labia

On September 3, 1951, during the Venice Film Festival, the Palazzo Labia hosted what's been dubbed "the party of the century." The Aga Khan, Winston Churchill, Orson Welles, and Salvador Dali were among those who donned 18th-century costume and danced in the Tiepolo-frescoed ballroom.

Santa Maria di Nazareth

Ponte di Scalzi

R. Di BIASIO

FERROVIA

Stazione Ferrovia Santa Lucia

S A N T A C R O C E

As you head out from Ferrovia, the baroque church immediately to your left is **Santa Maria di Nazareth**. Its shoeless friars earned it the nickname Chiesa degli Scalzi (Church of the Barefoot).

One of the four bridges over the Grand Canal is the **Ponte di Scalzi**. The original version was built of iron in 1858; the existing stone bridge dates from 1934.

After passing beneath the Ponte di Scalzi, ahead to the left you'll spy **Palazzo Labia**, one of the most imposing buildings in Venice, looming over the bell tower of the church of San Geremia.

A hundred yards or so further along on the left bank, the uncompleted façade of the church of **San Marcuola** gives you an idea of what's behind the marble decorations of similar 18th-century churches in Venice.

Across the canal, flanked by two *torricelle* (side wings in the shape of small towers) and a triangular *merlatura* (crenellation), is the **Fondaco dei Turchi,** one of the oldest Byzantine palaces in Venice; it's now a natural history museum. Next comes the plain brick **Depositi del Megio**, a 15th-century granary—note the lion marking it as Serenissima property—and beyond it the obelisk-topped **Ca' Belloni-Battagia**. Both are upstaged by the **Palazzo Vendramin-Calergi** on the opposite bank: this Renaissance gem was built in the 1480s, at a time when late-Gothic was still the prevailing style. A gilded banner identifies the palazzo as site of Venice's casino.

CANNAREGGIO

Palazzo Vendramin-Calergi
The German composer Richard Wagner died in Palazzo Vendramin-Calergi in 1883, soon after the success of his opera Parsifal. His room has been preserved—you can visit it on Saturday mornings by appointment.

Church of San Marcuola

GHETTO

S. MARCUOLA

Ca' Belloni-Battagia

Ca' d'Oro
Ca' d'Oro means "house of gold," but the gold is long gone—the gilding that once accentuated the marble carvings of the facade has worn away over time.

S. STAE

Ca' Pesaro

Fondaco dei Turchi

Depositi del Megio

San Stae Church

CA' D'ORO

SAN POLO

Ca' Corner della Regina

Pescheria
The pescheria has been in operation for over 1,000 years. Stop by in the morning to see the exotic fish for sale—one of which may wind up on your dinner plate. Produce stalls fill the adjacent fondamenta, and butchers and cheesemongers occupy the surrounding shops.

Fondaco dei Tedeschi

Ca' dei Camerlenghi

 RIALTO

SAN MARCO

The white, whimsically baroque church of **San Stae** on the right bank is distinguished by a host of marble saints on its facade. Further along the bank is another baroque showpiece, **Ca' Pesaro**, followed by the tall, balconied **Ca' Corner della Regina**. Next up on the left is the flamboyant pink-and-white **Ca' d'Oro**, arguably the finest example of Venetian Gothic design.

Across from Ca' d'Oro is the loggia-like, neo-Gothic **pescheria**, Venice's fish market, where boats dock in the morning to deliver their catch.

The canal narrows as you approach the impressive Rialto Bridge. To the left, just before the bridge, is the **Fondaco dei Tedeschi**. This was once the busiest trading center of the republic—German, Austrian, and Hungarian merchants kept warehouses and offices here; today it's the city's main post office. Across the canal stands

the curiously angled **Ca' dei Camerlenghi**. Built in 1525 to accommodate the State Treasury, it had a jail for tax evaders on the ground floor.

FROM RIALTO TO THE PONTE DELL' ACCADEMIA

SAN POLO

Ponte di Rialto

▲ **RIALTO**

Ca' Foscari
Positioned at one of the busiest junctures along the Grand Canal, Ca' Foscari was recently restored after suffering severe foundation damage as a result of the relentless wake from passing boats.

Palazzo Barzizza

Ca' Loredan

S. SILVESTRO ▲

Ca' Farsetti

Palazzo Pisani Moretta

Ca' Grimani

▲ **S. ANGELO**

TOMA ▲

Ca' Corner-Spinelli
If Ca' Corner-Spinelli has a familiar look, that's because it became a prototype for later Grand Canal buildings—and because its architect, Mauro Codussi, himself copied the windows from Palazzo Vendramin-Calergi.

Ca' Garzoni

Palazzo Grassi

Ca' Rezzonico

Palazzo Falier
Palazzo Falier is said to have been the home of Doge Martin Fallier, who was beheaded for treason in 1355.

SAN MARCO

REZZONICO ▲

ACCADEMIA ▲

Gallerie dell'Accademia

DORSODURO

Until the 19th century, the shop-lined **Ponte di Rialto** was the only bridge across the Grand Canal.

Rialto is the only point along the Grand Canal where buildings don't have their primary entrances directly on the water, a consequence of the two spacious *rive* (waterside paths) once used for unloading two Venetian staples: coal and wine. On your left along Riva del Carbon stand **Ca' Loredan** and **Ca' Farsetti**, 13th-century Byzantine palaces that today make up Venice's city hall. Just past the San Silvestro vaporetto landing on Riva del Vin is the 12th- and 13th-century facade of **Palazzo Barzizza**, an elegant example of Veneto-Byzantine architecture that managed to survive a complete renovation in the 17th century. Across the water, the sternly Renaissance **Ca' Grimani** has an intimidating presence that seems appropriate for today's Court of Appeals. At the Sant'Angelo landing, the vaporetto passes close to another massive Renaissance palazzo, **Ca' Corner-Spinelli**.

Back on the right bank, in a salmon color that seems to vary with the time of day, is elegant **Palazzo Pisani Moretta**, with twin water entrances. To your left, four-storied **Ca' Garzoni**, part of the Universita di Venezia Ca' Foscari, stands beside the San Toma *traghetto* (gondola ferry), which has operated since 1354. The boat makes a sharp turn and, on the right, passes one of the city's tallest Gothic palaces, **Ca' Foscari**.

The vaporetto passes baroque **Ca' Rezzonico** so closely that you get to look inside one of the most fabulous entrances along the canal. Opposite stands the Grand Canal's youngest palace, **Palazzo Grassi**, commissioned in 1749. Just beyond Grassi and Campo San Samuele, the first house past the garden was once Titian's studio. It's followed by **Palazzo Falier**, identifiable by its twin loggias (windowed porches).

Approaching the canal's fourth and final bridge, the vaporetto stops at a former church and monastery complex that houses the world-renowned **Gallerie dell'Accademia**.

The wooden pilings on which Venice was built (you can see them at the bases of the buildings along the Grand Canal) have gradually hardened into mineral form.

ARCHITECTURAL STYLES ALONG THE GRAND CANAL

BYZANTINE: 12th and 13th centuries. **Distinguishing characteristics:** high, rounded arches, relief panels, multicolored marble. **Examples:** Fondaco dei Turchi, Ca' Loredan, Ca' Farsetti, Palazzo Barzizza (and, off the canal, Basilica di San Marco).

GOTHIC: 14th and 15th centuries. **Distinguishing characteristics:** Pointed arches, high ceilings, and many windows. **Examples:** Ca' d'Oro, Ca' Foscari, Ca' Franchetti, Palazzo Falier (and, off the canal, Palazzo Ducale).

RENAISSANCE: 16th century. **Distinguishing characteristics:** classically influenced emphasis on order, achieved through symmetry and balanced proportions. **Examples:** Palazzo Vendramin-Calergi, Ca' Grimani, Ca' Corner-Spinelli, Ca' dei Camerlenghi (and, off the canal, Libreria Sansoviniana on Piazza San Marco and the church of San Giorgio Maggiore).

BAROQUE: 17th century. **Distinguishing characteristics:** Renaissance order wedded with a more dynamic style, achieved through curving lines and complex decoration. **Examples:** churches of Santa Maria di Nazareth and San Stae, Ca' Pesaro, Ca' Rezzonico (and, off the canal, the church of Santa Maria della Salute).

FROM THE PONTE DELL'ACCADEMIA TO SAN ZACCARIA

Ca' Franchetti
Until the late 19th century, Ca' Franchetti was a *squero* (gondola workshop). A few active *squeri* remain, though none are on the Grand Canal. The most easily spotted is Squero di San Trovaso, in Dorsoduro on a small canal near the Zattere boat landing.

Ca' Barbaro
Monet, Henry James, and Cole Porter are among the guests who have stayed at Ca' Barbaro. Porter later lived aboard a boat in Giudecca Canal.

SAN MARCO

Ponte dell' Accademia

Casetta Rossa

Ca' Pisani-Gritti

ACCADEMIA

S. M. DEL GIGLIO

DORSODURO

Ca' Barbarigo

SALUTE

Palazzo Venier dei Leoni
When she was in residence at Palazzo Venier dei Leoni, Peggy Guggenheim kept her private gondola parked at the door and left her dogs standing guard (in place of Venetian lions).

Palazzo Salviati

S. Maria della Salute

Ca' Dario
However tilted Dario might be, it has outlasted its many owners, who seem plagued by misfortune. They include the Italian industrialist Raul Gardini, whose 1992 suicide followed charges of corruption and an unsuccessful bid to win the America's Cup.

The wooden **Ponte dell' Accademia**, like the Eiffel Tower (with which it shares a certain structural grace), wasn't intended to be permanent. Erected in 1933 as a quick replacement for a rusting iron bridge built by the Austrian military in 1854, it was so well liked by Venetians that they kept it. (A perfect replica, with steel bracing, was installed 1986.)

You're only three stops from the end of the Grand Canal, but this last stretch is packed with sights. The lovely **Ca' Franchetti**, with a central balcony made in the style of Palazzo Ducale's loggia, dates from the late Gothic period, but its gardens are no older than the cedar tree standing at their center.

Ca' Barbaro, next door to Ca' Franchetti, was the residence of the illustrious family who rebuilt the church of Santa Maria del Giglio.

Farther along on the left bank, a garden, vibrant with flowers in summer, surrounds **Casetta Rossa** (small red house) as if it were the centerpiece of its bouquet. Across the canal, bright 19th-century mosaics on

Ca' Barbarigo give you some idea how the frescoed facades of many Venetian palaces must have looked in their heyday. A few doors down are the lush gardens within the walls of the unfinished **Palazzo Venier dei Leoni**, which holds the **Peggy Guggenheim Collection** of contemporary art.

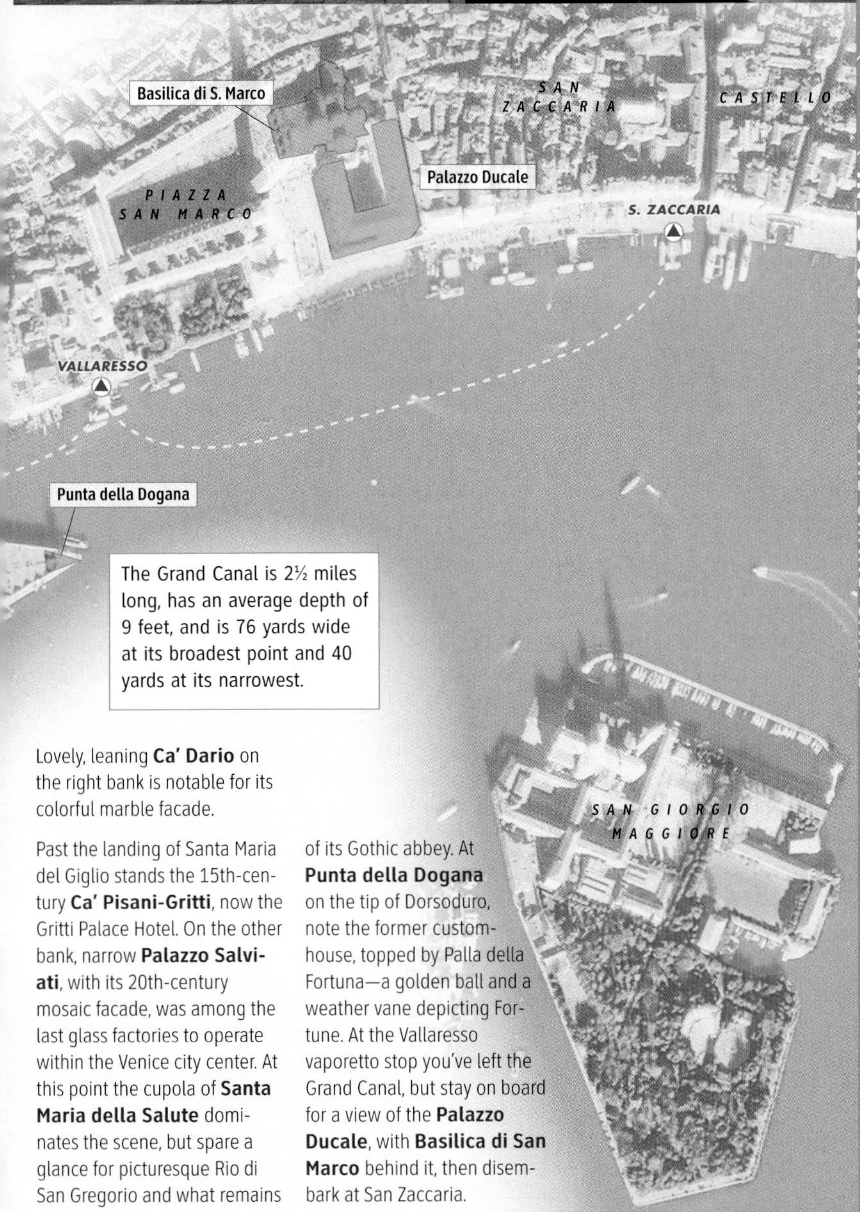

Basilica di S. Marco

SAN ZACCARIA

CASTELLO

Palazzo Ducale

PIAZZA SAN MARCO

S. ZACCARIA

VALLARESSO

Punta della Dogana

The Grand Canal is 2½ miles long, has an average depth of 9 feet, and is 76 yards wide at its broadest point and 40 yards at its narrowest.

SAN GIORGIO MAGGIORE

Lovely, leaning **Ca' Dario** on the right bank is notable for its colorful marble facade.

Past the landing of Santa Maria del Giglio stands the 15th-century **Ca' Pisani-Gritti**, now the Gritti Palace Hotel. On the other bank, narrow **Palazzo Salviati**, with its 20th-century mosaic facade, was among the last glass factories to operate within the Venice city center. At this point the cupola of **Santa Maria della Salute** dominates the scene, but spare a glance for picturesque Rio di San Gregorio and what remains of its Gothic abbey. At **Punta della Dogana** on the tip of Dorsoduro, note the former customhouse, topped by Palla della Fortuna—a golden ball and a weather vane depicting Fortune. At the Vallaresso vaporetto stop you've left the Grand Canal, but stay on board for a view of the **Palazzo Ducale**, with **Basilica di San Marco** behind it, then disembark at San Zaccaria.

When Napoléon (1769–1821) entered Venice with his troops in 1797, he called Piazza San Marco "the world's most beautiful drawing room"—and promptly gave orders to redecorate it. His architects demolished a 16th-century church with a Sansovino facade in order to build the Ala Napoleonica (Napoleonic Wing), or Fabbrica Nuova (New Building), which linked the two 16th-century procuratie and effectively enclosed the piazza.

Piazzetta San Marco, the "little square" leading from Piazza San Marco to the waters of Bacino San Marco (St. Mark's Basin), is a *molo* (landing) that was once the grand entryway to the republic. It's distinguished by two columns towering above the waterfront. One is topped by the winged lion, a traditional emblem of St. Mark that became the symbol of Venice itself; the other supports St. Theodore, the city's first patron, along with his dragon. Between these columns the republic traditionally executed convicts.

TIMING

It takes a full day to take in everything on the piazza thoroughly; so if time is limited you'll have to prioritize. Plan on 1½ hours for the basilica and its Pala d'Oro, Galleria, and Museo di San Marco. You'll want at least two hours to appreciate the Palazzo Ducale. Do take time to enjoy the piazza itself from a café table, or on a clear day, from atop the Campanile.

THE MAIN ATTRACTIONS

❶ Basilica di San Marco. An opulent synthesis of Byzantine and Romanesque styles, Venice's gem is laid out in a Greek-cross floor plan and topped with five plump domes. It didn't become the cathedral of Venice until 1807, but its role as the Chiesa Ducale (doge's private chapel) gave it immense power and wealth. The original church was built in 828 to house the body of St. Mark the Evangelist. His remains, filched from Alexandria by the doge's agents, were supposedly hidden in a barrel under layers of pickled pork to sneak them past Muslim guards. The escapade is depicted in the 13th-century mosaic above the door farthest left of the front entrance, one of the earliest mosaics on the heavily decorated facade; look closely to see the church as it appeared at that time.

Fodor's Choice
★

A 976 fire destroyed most of the original church. It was rebuilt and reopened in 1094, and for centuries it would serve as a symbol of Venetian wealth and power, endowed with all the riches admirals and merchants could carry off from the Orient, to the point where it earned the nickname Chiesa d'Oro (Golden Church). The four bronze horses that prance and snort over the doorway are copies of sculptures that victorious Venetians took from Constantinople in 1204 after the fourth crusade (the originals are in the Museo di San Marco). The rich, colorful exterior decorations, including the numerous different marble columns, all came from the same source. Look for a medallion of red porphyry in the floor of the porch inside the main door. It marks the spot where, in 1177, Doge Sebastiano Ziani orchestrated the reconciliation between

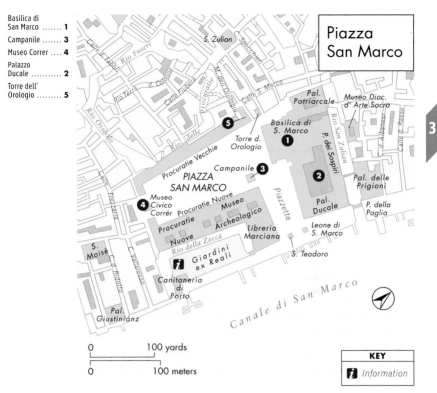

Piazza San Marco

0 — 100 yards
0 — 100 meters

KEY
🛈 *Information*

Barbarossa—the Holy Roman emperor—and Pope Alexander III. Dim lighting, galleries high above the naves—they served as the *matroneum* (women's gallery)—the *iconostasis* (altar screen), and the single massive Byzantine chandelier all seem to wed Christianity with the Orient, giving San Marco its exotic blend of majesty and mystery.

The basilica is famous for its 43,055 square feet of mosaics, which run from floor to ceiling thanks to an innovative roof of brick vaulting. Many of the original windows were filled in to make room for even more artwork. At midday, when the interior is fully illuminated, the mosaics truly come alive, the shimmer of their tiny gold tiles becoming nothing short of magical. The earliest mosaics are from the 11th and 12th centuries, and the last were added in the early 1700s. One of the most recent is the *Last Judgment,* believed to have been designed by Tintoretto (1518–94), on the arch between the porch and the nave. Inside the main entrance, turn right on the porch to see the Book of Genesis depicted on the ceiling. Ahead through a glass door, 13th-century mosaics depict St. Mark's life in the **Cappella Zen** (Zen Chapel). The **Cappella della Madonna di Nicopeia,** in the left transept, holds the altar icon that many consider Venice's most powerful protector. In nearby **Cappella della Madonna dei Mascoli,** the life of the Virgin Mary is depicted in fine 15th-century mosaics, believed to be based on drawings by Jacopo Bellini (1400–71) and Andrea Mantegna (1431–1506).

In the **Santuario** (Sanctuary), the main altar is built over the tomb of St. Mark, its green marble canopy lifted high on carved alabaster columns. Perhaps even more impressive is the **Pala d'Oro,** a dazzling gilt silver screen encrusted with 1,927 precious gems and 255 enameled panels. Originally commissioned in Constantinople by Doge Orseolo I (976–978), it was enlarged and embellished over four centuries by master craftsmen and wealthy merchants. The bronze door leading from the sanctuary into the sacristy is by Jacopo Sansovino. In the top left corner the artist included a self-portrait, and above that, he pictured friend and fellow artist Titian (1485–1576). The **Tesoro** (Treasury), entered from the right transept, contains many treasures carried home from conquests abroad.

Climb the steep stairway to the **Galleria** and the **Museo di San Marco** for the best overview of the basilica's interior. From here you can step outdoors for a sweeping panorama of Piazza San Marco and out over the lagoon to San Giorgio. The displays focus mainly on the types of mosaic and how they have been restored over the years. But the highlight is a close-up view of the original gilt bronze horses that were once on the outer gallery. The four were most probably cast in Rome and taken to Constantinople, where the Venetians pillaged them after sacking that city. When Napoléon sacked Venice in 1797, he took them to Paris. They were returned after the fall of the French Empire, but came home "blind"—their big ruby eyes had been sold.

Be aware that guards at the basilica door turn away anyone with bare shoulders or knees; no shorts, short skirts, or tank tops are allowed. If you want a free guided tour in English during summer months (less certain in winter, as the guides are volunteers), look for groups forming on the porch inside the main door. You may also arrange tours by appointment. ⊠ *Piazza San Marco* ☎ *041/2708311 basilica, 041/2702421 for free tours Apr.–Oct. (call weekday mornings)* ⊠ *Basilica free, Tesoro €2, Santuario and Pala d'Oro €1.50, Galleria and Museo di San Marco €3* ☉ *May–Sept., Mon.–Sat. 9:45–5:30, Sun. 2–4; Oct.–Apr., Mon.– Sat. 9:45–4:30, Sun. 2–4. Last entry ½ hr before closing* Ⓥ *Vallaresso/ San Zaccaria.*

★ ❷ **Palazzo Ducale** *(Doge's Palace).* Rising above the Piazzetta San Marco, this Gothic-Renaissance fantasia of pink-and-white marble is a majestic expression of the prosperity and power attained during Venice's most glorious period. Some architectural purists find the building topheavy—its hulking upper floors rest upon a graceful ground-floor colonnade—but the design is what gives the palace its distinctive identity; it's hard to imagine it any other way. Always much more than a residence, the palace was Venice's White House, Senate, torture chamber, and prison rolled into one.

Though a fortress for the doge stood on this spot in the early 9th century, the building you see today was begun in the 12th century, and, like the basilica next door, was continually remodeled over the centuries.

Near the basilica you'll see the ornately Gothic **Porta della Carta** (Gate of the Paper), where official decrees were traditionally posted, but visitors enter under the portico facing the water. You'll find yourself in an immense courtyard with the **Scala dei Giganti** (Stairway of the Giants) directly ahead, guarded by Sansovino's huge statues of Mars and Neptune. Though ordinary mortals must use the central interior staircase, its upper flight is the lavishly gilded **Scala d'Oro** (Golden Staircase), also by Sansovino. It may seem odd that you have to climb so many steps to reach the government's main council rooms and reception halls, but imagine how this extraordinary climb must have impressed, and perhaps intimidated, foreign emissaries.

The palace's sumptuous chambers have walls and ceilings covered with works by Venice's greatest artists. Visit the **Anticollegio,** a waiting room outside the Collegio's chamber, where you'll see the *Rape of Europa* by Veronese (1528–88) and Tintoretto's *Bacchus and Ariadne Crowned by Venus.* Veronese also painted the ceiling of the adjacent **Sala del Collegio.** The ceiling of the **Sala del Senato** (Senate Chamber), featuring *The Triumph of Venice* by Tintoretto, is magnificent, but it's dwarfed by his masterpiece *Paradise* in the **Sala del Maggiore Consiglio** (Great Council Hall). A vast work commissioned for a vast hall, this dark, dynamic piece is the world's largest oil painting (23 by 75 feet). The room's carved, gilt ceiling is breathtaking, especially with Veronese's majestic *Apotheosis of Venice* filling one of the center panels. Around the upper walls, study the portraits of the first 76 doges, and you'll notice one picture is missing near the left corner of the wall opposite *Paradise.* A black painted curtain, rather than a portrait, marks Doge Marin Falier's fall from grace; he was beheaded for treason in 1355, which the Latin inscription bluntly explains.

A narrow canal separates the palace's east side from the cramped cell blocks of the **Prigioni Nuove** (New Prisons). High above the water arches the enclosed marble **Ponte dei Sospiri** (Bridge of Sighs), which earned its name from the sighs of those being led to their fate. Look out its windows to see the last earthly view these prisoners beheld.

The palazzo's "Secret Itinerary" tour takes you to the doge's private apartments, through hidden passageways to the interrogation (torture) chambers, and into the rooftop *piombi* (lead) prison, named for its lead roofing. Venetian-born writer and libertine Giacomo Casanova (1725–98), along with an accomplice, managed to escape from the piombi in 1756, the only men ever to do so. ⊠*Piazzetta San Marco* ☎*041/2715911, 041/5209070 "Secret Itinerary" tour* ✆*Piazza San Marco museum card €12, Musei Civici museum pass €18, "Secret Itinerary" tour €16* ☉*Apr.–Oct., daily 9–7; Nov.–Mar., daily 9–5. Last tickets sold 1 hr before closing. English "Secret Itinerary" tours in morning; reservations advisable* Ⓥ *Vallaresso/San Zaccaria.*

NEED A BREAK? Caffè Florian (☎*041/5205641*), located in the Procuratie Nuove, has served coffee to the likes of Casanova, Charles Dickens, and Marcel Proust. It's Venice's oldest café, continuously in business since 1720 (though you'll find it closed Wednesday in winter). Counter seating is less expensive than taking a table, especially when there's live music. In the Procuratie Vecchie, Caffè Quadri (🕾 *041/5289299*) exudes almost as much history as Florian across the way, and is similarly pricey. It was shunned by 19th-century Venetians when the occupying Austrians made it their gathering place. In winter it closes Monday.

ALSO WORTH SEEING

🐚 ❸ **Campanile.** Venice's famous brick bell tower (325 feet tall, plus the angel) had been standing nearly 1,000 years when in 1902, practically without warning, it collapsed, taking with it Jacopo Sansovino's 16th-century marble loggia at the base. The crushed loggia was promptly restored, and the new tower, rebuilt to the old plan, reopened in 1912. In the 15th century, clerics found guilty of immoral behavior were suspended in wooden cages from the tower. Some were forced to subsist on bread and water for as long as a year, and others were left to starve. The stunning view from the tower on a clear day includes the Lido, the lagoon, and the mainland as far as the Alps, but, strangely enough, none of the myriad canals that snake through the city. ⊠ *Piazza San Marco* 🕾 *041/5224064* 🎫 *€6* 🕙 *Apr.–June, daily 9:30–5; July–Sept., daily 9:45–8; Oct.–Mar., daily 9:45–4. Last entry ½ hr before closing* Ⓥ *Vallaresso/San Zaccaria.*

❹ **Museo Correr.** Exhibits in this museum of Venetian art and history range from the absurdly high-soled shoes worn by 16th-century Venetian ladies (who walked with the aid of a servant) to the huge *Grande Pianta Prospettica* by Jacopo de' Barbari (circa 1440–1515), which details in carved wood every nook and cranny of 16th-century Venice. The city's proud naval history is evoked in several rooms through highly descriptive paintings and numerous maritime objects, including ships' cannons and some surprisingly large iron mast-top navigation lights. The Correr has a room devoted entirely to antique games, and its second-floor **Quadreria** (Picture Gallery) has works by Venetian, Greek, and Flemish painters. The Correr exhibition rooms lead directly into the **Museo Archeologico** and the **Stanza del Sansovino**, the only part of the **Biblioteca Nazionale Marciana** open to visitors. ⊠ *Piazza San Marco, Ala Napoleonica* 🕾 *041/2405211* 🎫 *Piazza San Marco museum card €12, Musei Civici museum pass €18* 🕙 *Apr.–Oct., daily 9–7; Nov.–Mar., daily 9–5. Last tickets sold 1 hr before closing* Ⓥ *Vallaresso/San Zaccaria.*

NEED A BREAK? If you'd like to attend happy hour with the ghosts of Ernest Hemingway, Aristotle Onassis, and Orson Welles, head to Harry's Bar (🕾 *041/5285777*). Walk out Piazza San Marco near the Correr Museum and turn left at Calle Vallaresso; you'll find the legendary hangout right at the vaporetto landing. Harry's still boasts Venice's driest martinis and freshest Bellinis (white peach juice and sparkling *prosecco* wine).

❺ **Torre dell'Orologio.** Five hundred years ago, when this enameled clock was built, twin Moor figures would strike the hour, and three wise men

VENICE THROUGH THE AGES

Up from the Muck. Venice was founded in the 5th century when the Veneti, inhabitants of the mainland region roughly corresponding to today's Veneto, fled their homes to escape invading Lombards. The unlikely city, built atop wooden posts driven into the marshes, would evolve into a great maritime republic. Its fortunes grew as a result of its active role in the Crusades, beginning in 1095 and culminating in the Venetian-led sacking of Constantinople in 1204. The defeat of rival Genoa in the Battle of Chioggia (1380) established Venice as the dominant sea power in Europe.

Early Democracy. As early as the 7th century, Venice was governed by a participatory democracy, with a ruler, the doge, elected to a lifetime term. Beginning in the 12th century, the doge's power was increasingly subsumed by a growing number of councils, commissions, and magistrates. In 1268 a complicated procedure for the doge's election was established to prevent nepotism, but by that point power rested foremost with the Great Council, which at times numbered as many as 2,000 members.

Laws were passed by the Senate, a group of 200 elected from the Great Council, and executive powers belonged to the College, a committee of 25. In 1310 the Council of Ten was formed to protect state security. When circumstances dictated, the doge could expedite decision making by consulting only the Council of Ten. To avoid too great a concentration of power, these 10 served only one year and belonged to different families.

A Long Decline. Venice reached its height of power in the 15th and 16th centuries, during which time its domain included all of the Veneto region and part of Lombardy. But beginning in the 16th century, the tide turned. The Ottoman Empire blocked Venice's Mediterranean trade routes, and newly emerging sea powers such as Britain and the Netherlands ended Venice's monopoly by opening oceanic trading routes. The republic underwent a slow decline. When Napoléon arrived in 1797, he took the city without a fight, eventually delivering it to the Austrians, who ruled until 1848. In that tumultuous year throughout Europe, the Venetians rebelled, an act that would ultimately lead to their joining the Italian Republic in 1866.

Art Stars. In the 13th through 15th centuries the influence of Gothic architecture resulted in palaces in the florid Gothic style, for which the city is famous. Renaissance sensibilities arrived comparatively late. Early Venetian Renaissance artists—Carpaccio, Giorgione, and the Bellini brothers, Giovanni and Gentile—were active in the late 15th and early 16th centuries. Along with the stars of the next generation—Veronese, Titian, and Tintoretto—they played a key role in the development of Western art, and their best work remains in the city.

Like its dwindling fortunes, Venice's art and culture underwent a prolonged decline, leaving only the splendid monuments to recall a fabled past. The 18th-century paintings of Canaletto and Tiepolo were a glorious swan song.

3

with an angel would walk out and bow to the Virgin Mary on Epiphany (January 6) and during Ascension Week (40 days after Easter). An inscription on the tower reads HORAS NON NUMERO NISI SERENAS ("I only count happy hours"). After years of painstaking work, the clock tower has been reassembled and returned to its former glory. Visits in English are offered daily and must be booked in advance. ⊠*North side of Piazza San Marco* ☎*041/5209070* ⊕*www.museicivicivenezziani.it* 🎫*€12* ⊙*Tours in English Mon.–Wed. at 10 and 11; Thurs.–Sun. at 1, 2, and 3* Ⓥ*Vallaresso/San Zaccaria.*

DORSODURO

The sestiere Dorsoduro (named for its "hard back" solid clay foundation) is across the Grand Canal to the south of San Marco. It is a place of monumental churches, meandering canals, the city's finest art museums, and a boardwalk called the Zattere, where on sunny days you'll swear half the city is out for a *passeggiata*, or stroll. The eastern point of the peninsula, Punta della Dogana, has one of the best views in town. The Stazione Marittima, where in summer cruise ships line the dock, lies at the western end. Midway between these two points, just off the Zattere, is the Squero di San Trovaso, where gondolas have been built and repaired for centuries.

Dorsoduro is also home to the Gallerie dell'Accademia, which has an unparalleled collection of Venetian painting, and Ca' Rezzonico, which houses the Museo del Settecento Veneziano. Another of its landmark sites, the Peggy Guggenheim Collection, has a fine selection of 20th-century art.

TIMING
The Gallerie dell'Accademia demands a few hours, but if time is short an audio guide can help you cover the highlights in about an hour. Give yourself at least 1½ hours for the Guggenheim Collection. Ca' Rezzonico deserves a couple of hours.

THE MAIN ATTRACTIONS

★ ❸ **Ca' Rezzonico.** Designed by Baldassare Longhena in the 17th century, this palace was completed nearly 100 years later by Giorgio Massari and became the last home of English poet Robert Browning (1812–89). Elizabeth Taylor and Richard Burton danced in the baroque ballroom in the 1960s. Today Ca' Rezzonico is the home of the **Museo del Settecento** (Museum of Venice in the 1700s). Its main floor is packed with period furniture and tapestries in gilded salons (note the four Tiepolo ceiling frescoes) and successfully retains the feel of an old Venetian palazzo. Upper floors contain hundreds of paintings, most from Venetian schools of artists. There's even a restored apothecary, complete with powders and potions. ⊠*Fondamenta Rezzonico, Dorsoduro 3136* ☎*041/2410100* 🎫*€6.50, Musei Civici museum pass €18* ⊙*Apr.–Oct., daily 10–6; Nov.–Mar., daily 10–5. Last entry 1 hr before closing* Ⓥ*Ca' Rezzonico.*

CLOSE UP

Wading Through the Acqua Alta

You have to walk almost everywhere in Venice, and where you can't walk, you go by water. Occasionally you walk *in* water, when normally higher fall and spring tides are exacerbated by falling barometers and south-easterly winds. The result is *acqua alta*—flooding in the lowest parts of town, especially Piazza San Marco, which lasts a few hours, until the tide recedes.

Venetians handle the high waters with aplomb, donning waders and erect-ing temporary walkways, but they're well aware of the damage caused by the flooding and the threat it poses to their city. Work has begun on the Moses Project, a plan that would close off the lagoon when high tides threaten, but it's a much-debated response to an emotionally charged problem. Protecting Venice and its lagoon from high tides—as well as high use and the damaging wave action caused by powerboats—is among the city's most contentious issues.

★ ❼ **Gallerie dell'Accademia.** Napoléon founded these galleries in 1807 on the site of a religious complex he'd suppressed, and what he initiated now amounts to the world's most extraordinary collection of Venetian art. Jacopo Bellini is considered the father of the Venetian Renaissance, and in Room 2 you can compare his *Madonna and Child with Saints* with such later works as *Madonna of the Orange Tree* by Cima da Conegliano (circa 1459–1517) and *Ten Thousand Martyrs of Mt. Ararat* by Vittore Carpaccio (circa 1455–1525). Jacopo's son Giovanni (circa 1430–1516) draws your eye not with his subjects but with his rich color. Rooms 4 and 5 are full of his Madonnas; note the contrast between the young Madonna and child and the neighboring older Madonna after the crucifixion—you'll see the colors of dawn and dusk in Venice. Room 5 contains *Tempest* by Giorgione (1477–1510), a work that was revolutionary in its time and has continued to intrigue viewers and critics over the centuries. It depicts a storm approaching as a nude woman nurses her child and a soldier looks on. The overall atmosphere that Giorgione creates is as important as any of his figures.

In Room 10, *Feast in the House of Levi*, commissioned as a Last Supper, got Veronese dragged before the Inquisition over its depiction of dogs, jesters, and German (therefore Protestant) soldiers. The artist saved his neck by simply changing the title, so that the painting represented a different biblical feast. Titian's *Presentation of the Virgin* (Room 24) is the collection's only work originally created for the building in which it hangs. Don't miss Rooms 20 and 21, with views of 15th- and 16th-century Venice by Carpaccio and Gentile Bellini (1429–1507), Giovanni's brother—you'll see how little the city has changed.

Booking tickets in advance isn't essential but helps during busy seasons and costs only an additional €1. Booking is necessary to see the **Quadreria**, where additional works cover every inch of a wide hallway. A free map names art and artists, and the bookshop sells a more-informative English-language booklet. In the main galleries a

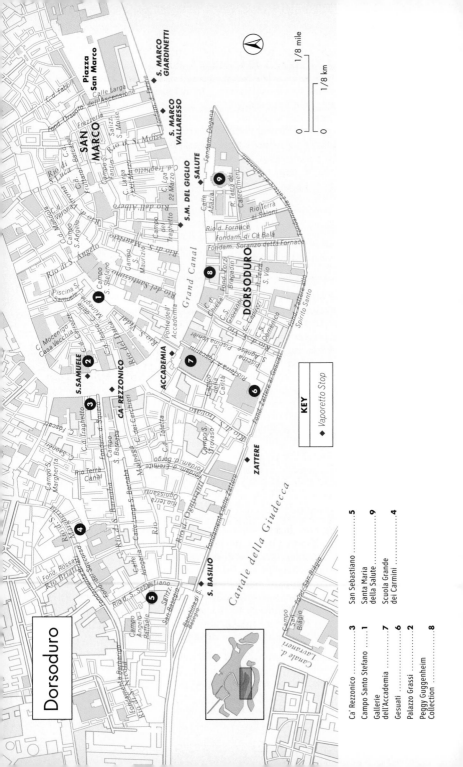

Dorsoduro

KEY

◆ Vaporetto Stop

0 1/8 mile

0 1/8 km

€4 audio guide saves reading but adds little to each room's excellent annotation. ⊠*Campo della Carità, Dorsoduro 1050* ☏*041/5222247, 041/5200345 reservations* ⊕*www.gallerieaccademia.org* ☑*€6.50, €11 includes Ca' d'Oro and Museo Orientale* ⊙*Tues.–Sun. 8:15–7:15, Mon. 8:15–2* Ⓥ*Accademia.*

NEED A BREAK?

There's no sunnier spot in Venice than Fondamenta delle Zattere, along the southern edge of Dorsoduro. It's the city's gigantic public terrace, with bustling bars and gelato shops; come here to stroll, read in the open air, and play hooky from sightseeing. The Zattere's most decadent treat is found at Gelateria Nico (⊠*Dorsoduro 922* ☏*041/5225293*)—order their famous *gianduiotto*, a nutty slab of chocolate ice cream floating on a cloud of whipped cream, and relax on the big, welcoming deck.

🖐 ❽ **Peggy Guggenheim Collection.** A small but choice selection of 20th-century painting and sculpture is on display at this gallery in the heiress Guggenheim's former Grand Canal home. Through wealth and social connections, Guggenheim (1898–1979) became a serious art patron, and her collection here in Palazzo Venier dei Leoni includes works by Picasso, Kandinsky, Pollock, Motherwell, and Ernst (at one time her husband). The museum serves beverages, snacks, and light meals in its refreshingly shady, artistically sophisticated garden. On Sunday at 3 PM the museum offers a free tour and art workshop for children 12 and under. ⊠*Fondamenta Venier dei Leoni, Dorsoduro 701* ☏*041/5209083* ⊕*www.guggenheim-venice.it* ☑*€10* ⊙*Wed.–Mon. 10–6* Ⓥ*Accademia.*

❾ **Santa Maria della Salute.** The view of La Salute (as this church is commonly called) from the Riva degli Schiavoni at sunset or from the Accademia bridge by moonlight is unforgettable. Baldassare Longhena was 32 years old when he won a competition to design a shrine honoring the Virgin Mary for saving Venice from a plague that killed 47,000 residents. Outside, this simple white octagon is adorned with a colossal cupola lined with snail-like buttresses and a Palladian-style facade; inside are a polychrome marble floor and six chapels. The Byzantine icon above the main altar has been venerated as the Madonna della Salute (of health) since 1670, when Francesco Morosini brought it here from Crete. Above it is a sculpture showing Venice (left) on her knees while the plague (right) is driven from the city. The **Sacrestia Maggiore** contains a dozen works by Titian, including his *San Marco Enthroned with Saints* altarpiece. You'll also see Tintoretto's *The Wedding at Canaan,* and on special occasions the altar displays a 15th-century tapestry depicting the Pentecost. For the Festa della Salute, held November 21, Venetians make a pilgrimage here and light candles in thanksgiving for another year's health. ⊠*Punta della Dogana, Dorsoduro* ☏*041/2743928* ☑*Church free, sacristy €1.50* ⊙*Apr.–Sept., daily 9–noon and 3–6:30; Oct.–Mar., daily 9–noon and 3–5:30* Ⓥ*Salute.*

NEED A BREAK?

Filled with cafés and restaurants, Campo Santa Margarita also has produce vendors, pizza by the slice, and benches where you can sit and eat.

For more than a portable munch, bask in the sunshine at popular Il Caffé (☎ *041/5287998*), commonly called Caffé Rossa for its bright red exterior. It's open past midnight, serving drinks and light refreshment every day except Sunday.

ALSO WORTH SEEING

❶ **Campo Santo Stefano.** In Venice's most prestigious residential neighborhood, you'll find one of the city's busiest crossroads just over the Accademia bridge; it's hard to believe this square once hosted bullfights, with bulls (or oxen) tied to a stake and baited by dogs. For centuries the campo was grass except for a stone avenue called the *liston*. It was so popular for strolling that in Venetian dialect *"andare al liston"* still means "to go for a walk." A sunny meeting spot popular with Venetians and visitors alike, the campo also hosts outdoor fairs during Christmas and Carnevale seasons. Check out the 14th-century **Chiesa di Santo Stefano** and its ship's-keel roof, created by shipbuilders. You'll see works by Tintoretto and the tipsiest bell tower in town—best appreciated from nearby Campo San Angelo. ⊠ *Campo Santo Stefano, San Marco* ☎ *041/2750462 Chorus* ✆ *€3, Chorus pass €9* ☉ *Mon.–Sat. 10–5, Sun. 1–5* Ⓥ *Accademia.*

❻ **Gesuati.** When the Dominicans took over the church of Santa Maria della Visitazione from the suppressed order of Gesuati laymen in 1668, Giorgio Massari was commissioned to build this structure. It has a score of works by Giambattista Tiepolo (1696–1770), Giambattista Piazzetta (1683–1754), and Sebastiano Ricci (1659–1734). ⊠ *Zattere, Dorsoduro* ☎ *041/2750462 Chorus* ✆ *€3, Chorus pass €9* ☉ *Mon.– Sat. 10–5, Sun. 1–5* Ⓥ *Zattere.*

❷ **Palazzo Grassi.** This 18th-century palazzo, which was once owned by auto magnate Giovanni Agnelli, was bought by the French businessman François Pinaut in 2005 to house his collection of modern and contemporary art. Japanese architect Tadao Ando was brought in for the latest restoration of the interior. Check the Web site for a schedule of temporary exhibitions. ⊠ *Campo San Samuele, San Marco* ☎ *041/5231680* ⊕ *www.palazzograssi.it* ✆ *€10* ☉ *Daily 9–6* Ⓥ *San Samuele.*

❺ **San Sebastiano.** Paolo Veronese (1528–88) established his reputation while still in his twenties with the frescoes at this, his parish church, and for decades he continued to embellish them with amazing trompe-l'oeil scenes. Don't miss his altarpiece *Madonna in Glory with Saints*. Veronese is buried beneath his bust near the organ. ⊠ *Campo San Sebastiano, Dorsoduro* ☎ *041/2750462 Chorus* ✆ *€3, Chorus pass €9* ☉ *Mon.–Sat. 10–5, Sun. 1–5* Ⓥ *San Basilio.*

❹ **Scuola Grande dei Carmini.** When the order of Santa Maria del Carmelo commissioned Baldassare Longhena to build Scuola Grande dei Carmini in the late 1600s, their brotherhood of 75,000 members was the largest in Venice and one of the wealthiest. Little expense was spared in the decorating of stuccoed ceilings and carved ebony paneling, and the artwork was choice, even before 1739, when Tiepolo painted the

CLOSE UP

Touring Venice

If you want some expert guidance around Venice, you have several options to choose from. **Cooperativa Guide Turistiche Autorizzate** (✉ *San Marco 750, near San Zulian* ☎ *041/5209038* ⊕ *www.guidevenezia.it*) has a list of more than 100 licensed guides. Tours lasting about two hours with an English-speaking guide start at €125 for up to 30 people. Agree on a total price before you begin, as there can be some hidden extras. Guides are of variable quality.

More than a dozen major travel agents offer a two-hour walking tour of the San Marco area (€30), which ends with a glassblowing demonstration daily (no Sunday tour in winter). From April to October there's also an afternoon walking tour that ends with a gondola ride (€40). **Venicescapes** (✉ *Campo San Provolo, Castello 4954* ☎ *041/5206361* ⊕ *www.venices-*

capes.org), an Italo-American cultural association, offers several themed itineraries focusing on history and culture as well as tourist sights. Their three-to seven-hour tours are in small groups (generally six to eight people). Reservations are recommended during busy seasons, and prices start at €240 for two people. **Walks Inside Venice** (☎ *041/5202434* ⊕ *www.walksinsidevenice.com*) also does several themed tours for small groups starting at €70 per hour and lasting up to three hours.

Serenaded gondola trips, with or without dinner (€73, €35), can be purchased at local travel agencies or at **American Express** (✉ *Salizzada San Moisè, San Marco 1471* ☎ *041/5200844* 🖷 *041/5229937*). Nightly tours leave at 7:30 and 8:30 April–September, at 7:30 only in October, and at 3:30 November–March.

Sala Capitolare. In what many consider his best work, Tiepolo's nine great canvases vividly transform some rather unpromising religious themes into flamboyant displays of color and movement. ✉ *Campo dei Carmini, Dorsoduro 2617* ☎ *041/5289420* 🖷 *€5* ⊙ *Daily 10–5* Ⓥ *Ca' Rezzonico.*

SAN POLO & SANTA CROCE

The two smallest of Venice's six sestieri, San Polo and Santa Croce were named after their main churches, though the Chiesa di Santa Croce was demolished in 1810. The city's most famous bridge, the Ponte di Rialto, unites sestiere San Marco (east) with San Polo (west). The Rialto Bridge takes its name from Rivoaltus, the high ground on which it was built. San Polo has two other major sites, Santa Maria Gloriosa dei Frari and the Scuola Grande di San Rocco, as well as some worthwhile but lesser-known churches.

Shops abound in the area surrounding the Rialto Bridge. On the San Marco side you'll find fashions, on the San Polo side food. Chiesa di San Giacometto, where you see the first fruit vendors as you come off the bridge on the San Polo side, was probably built in the 11th and 12th centuries, about the time the surrounding market came into being.

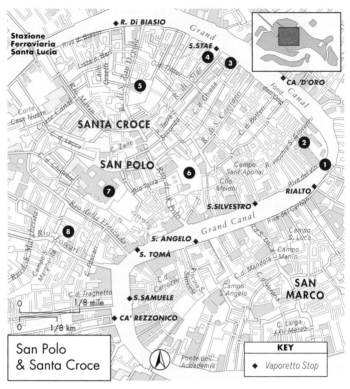

San Polo
& Santa Croce

KEY

◆ *Vaporetto Stop*

Public announcements were traditionally read in the church's campo; its 24-hour clock, though lovely, has rarely worked.

TIMING

To do the area justice requires at least half a day. If you want to take part in the food shopping, come early to beat the crowds. Bear in mind that a *metà kilo* is about a pound and an *etto* is a few ounces. The campo of San Giacomo dell'Orio, west of the main thoroughfare that takes you from the Ponte di Rialto to Santa Maria Gloriosa dei Frari, is a peaceful place for a drink and a rest. The museums of Ca' Pesaro are a time commitment—you'll want at least two hours to see them both.

THE MAIN ATTRACTIONS

★ ❶ **Ponte di Rialto** *(Rialto Bridge).* The competition to design a stone bridge across the Grand Canal (replacing earlier wooden versions) attracted the late-16th-century's best architects, including Michelangelo, Palladio, and Sansovino, but the job went to the less-famous but appropriately named Antonio da Ponte. His pragmatic design featured shop space and was high enough for galleys to pass beneath; it kept decoration and cost to a minimum at a time when the republic's coffers were low due to continual wars against the Turks and the opening of oceanic trade routes. Along the railing you'll enjoy one of the city's most famous views: the Grand Canal vibrant with boat traffic. Ⓥ *Rialto.*

❼ Santa Maria Gloriosa dei Frari. This immense Gothic church of russet-color brick, completed in the 1400s after more than a century of work, is deliberately austere, befitting the Franciscan brothers' insistence on spirituality and poverty. However, *I Frari* (as it's known locally) contains some of the most brilliant paintings in any Venetian church. Visit the sacristy first, to see Giovanni Bellini's 1488 triptych *Madonna and Child with Saints* in all its mellow luminosity, painted for precisely this spot. The Corner Chapel on the other side of the chancel is graced by Bartolomeo Vivarini's (1415–84) 1474 altarpiece *St. Mark Enthroned and Saints John the Baptist, Jerome, Peter, and Nicholas,* of similar exquisite detail and color. There is also a fine sculpture of St. John the Baptist here by Jacopo Sansovino. You can see the rapid development of Venetian Renaissance painting by contrasting Bellini and Vivarini with the heroic energy of Titian's *Assumption,* over the main altar, painted only 30 years later. Unveiled in 1518, this work was not initially accepted by the church, precisely because of the innovative style and bright colors, especially Titian's trademark red, which would make it famous.

Titian's beautiful *Madonna di Ca' Pesaro,* in the left aisle, was modeled after his wife, who died in childbirth. The painting took almost 10 years to complete, and in it Titian totally disregarded the conventions of his time by moving the Virgin out of center frame and making the saints active participants. On the same side of the church look at the spooky, pyramid-shaped monument to the sculptor Antonio Canova (1757–1822). Across the nave is a neoclassical 19th-century monument to Titian, executed by two of Canova's pupils. ✉ *Campo dei Frari, San Polo* ☎ *041/2728618, 041/2750462 Chorus* 🎫 *€3, Chorus pass €9* ⏰ *Mon.–Sat. 9–6, Sun. 1–6* Ⓥ *San Tomà.*

NEED A BREAK?

On a narrow passage between the Frari and San Rocco, Gelateria Millevoglie (*Thousand Desires* ☎ *041/5244667*) has pizza slices, calzones, and gelato so popular it backs up traffic. It's closed December and January, but it's open seven days a week—10 AM to midnight in summer and until 9 PM October–March. Just off Campo San Tomà is the decadent Vizio Virtù (☎ *041/2750149* ⊕ *www.viziovirtu.com*). If it's too cold for a gelato, have a hot chocolate to go or choose from a selection of gourmet chocolate creations.

❽ Scuola Grande di San Rocco. St. Rocco's popularity stemmed from his miraculous recovery from the plague and his care for fellow sufferers. Throughout the plague-filled Middle Ages, followers and donations abounded, and this elegant example of Venetian Renaissance architecture was the result. Although it is bold and dramatic outside, its contents are even more

WORD OF MOUTH

"Scuola Grande di San Rocco is absolutely mind-boggling. It is near Santa Maria Gloriosa dei Frari—also well worth a visit. The bonus is that in the small street between these two places is Millevoglie, a sandwich/pizza shop with *the best* gelato." –Rosemary

stunning—a series of more than 60 paintings by Tintoretto. In 1564 Tintoretto edged out competition for a commission to decorate a ceiling by submitting not a sketch, but a finished work, which he moreover offered free of charge. *Moses Striking Water from the Rock, The Brazen Serpent,* and *The Fall of Manna* represent three afflictions—thirst, disease, and hunger—that San Rocco and later his brotherhood sought to relieve. ⊠*Campo San Rocco, San Polo 3052* ☎*041/5234864* ⊕*www. scuolagrandesanrocco.it* 🎫*€7* ⊘*Apr.–Oct., daily 9–5:30; Nov.–Mar., daily 10–5. Last entry ½ hr before closing* Ⓥ*San Tomà.*

NEED A BREAK?

Just over the bridge in front of the Frari church is Caffè dei Frari (⊠*Fondamenta dei Frari, San Polo* ☎*041/5241877*), where you'll find a delightful assortment of sandwiches and snacks. Established in 1870, it's one of the last Venetian tearooms with its original decor. Pasticceria Tonolo (⊠*Calle Crosera, Dorsoduro 3764* ☎*041/5237209*) has been fattening up Venetians since 1886. During Carnevale it's still the best place in town for *fritelle*, fried doughnuts (traditional raisin or cream-filled); during *acqua alta* flooding, the staff dons rubber boots and keeps working. The place is closed Monday, and there's no seating anytime.

ALSO WORTH SEEING

❻ Campo San Polo. Only Piazza San Marco is larger than this square, where not even the pigeons manage to look cozy, and the echo of children's voices bouncing off the surrounding palaces makes the space seem even more cavernous. Not long ago Campo San Polo hosted bull races, fairs, military parades, and packed markets, but now it only really comes alive on summer nights, when it hosts the city's outdoor cinema. The **Chiesa di San Polo** has been restored so many times that little remains of the original 9th-century church, and sadly, 19th-century alterations were so costly that the friars sold off many great paintings to pay bills. Though Giambattista Tiepolo is represented here, his work is outdone by 16 paintings by his son Giandomenico (1727–1804), including the *Stations of the Cross* in the oratory to the left of the entrance. The younger Tiepolo also created a series of expressive and theatrical renderings of the saints. Look for altarpieces by Tintoretto and Veronese that managed to escape auction. San Polo's bell tower remained unchanged through the centuries—don't miss the two lions guarding it, playing with a disembodied human head and a serpent. ⊠*Campo San Polo* ☎*041/2750462 Chorus* 🎫*€3, Chorus pass €9* ⊘*Mon.–Sat. 10–5, Sun. 1–5* Ⓥ*San Tomà.*

❸ Ca' Pesaro. Baldassare Longhena's grand baroque palace is the beautifully restored home of two impressive collections. The **Galleria Internazionale d'Arte Moderna** has works by 19th- and 20th-century artists such as Klimt, Kandinsky, Matisse, and Miró. It also has a collection of representative works from Venice's Biennale art show that amounts to a panorama of 20th-century art. The **Museo Orientale** has a small but striking collection of Oriental porcelains, musical instruments, arms, and armor. ⊠*San Stae, Santa Croce 2076* ☎*041/721127 Gal-*

Venice's Scuola Days

An institution you'll inevitably encounter from Venice's glory days is the *scuola* (plural *scuole*). These weren't schools, as the word today translates, but an important network of institutions established by different social groups—enclaves of foreigners, tradesmen, followers of a particular saint, and parishioners.

For the most part secular despite their devotional activities, the scuole concentrated on charitable work, either helping their own membership or assisting the city's neediest citizens.

The tradesmen's and servants' scuole formed social security nets for elderly and disabled members. Wealthier scuole assisted orphans or provided dowries so poor girls could marry. By 1500 there were more than 200 major and minor scuole in Venice, some of which contributed substantially to arts and crafts guilds. The republic encouraged their existence—the scuole kept strict records of the names and professions of contributors to the brotherhood, which helped when it came time to collect taxes.

---

leria, 041/5241173 Museo Orientale ⌦*€5.50 includes both museums* ☉*Apr.–Oct., daily 10–6; Nov.–Mar., daily 10–5* Ⓥ*San Stae.*

❺ **San Giacomo dell'Orio.** It was named after a laurel tree *(orio)*, and today trees give character to this square. Add benches and a fountain (with a drinking bowl for dogs), and the pleasant, oddly shaped campo becomes a welcoming place for friendly conversation, picnics, and neighborhood kids at play. Legend has it the **Chiesa di San Giacomo dell'Orio** was founded in the 9th century on an island still populated by wolves. The current church dates from 1225; its short unmatched Byzantine columns survived renovation during the Renaissance, and the church never lost the feel of an ancient temple sheltering beneath its 15th-century ship's-keel roof. In the sanctuary, large marble crosses are surrounded by a bevy of small medieval Madonnas. The altarpiece is *Madonna with Child and Saints* (1546) by Lorenzo Lotto (1480–1556), and the sacristies contain works by Palma il Giovane (circa 1544–1628). ⌧*Campo San Giacomo dell'Orio, Santa Croce* ☎*041/2750462 Chorus* ⌦*€3, Chorus pass €9* ☉*Mon.–Sat. 10–5, Sun. 1–5* Ⓥ*San Stae.*

❷ **San Giovanni Elemosinario.** Storefronts make up the facade, and the altars were built by market guilds—poulterers, messengers, and fodder merchants—at this church intimately bound to the Rialto Market. It's as rich inside as it is simple outside. During San Giovanni Elemosinario's restoration, workers stumbled upon a frescoed cupola by Pordenone (1484–1539) that had been painted over centuries earlier. Don't miss Titian's *St. John the Almsgiver* and Pordenone's *Sts. Catherine, Sebastian, and Roch,* which in 2002 were returned after 30 years by the Gallerie dell'Accademia, a rare move for an Italian museum. ⌧*Rialto Ruga Vecchia San Giovanni, Santa Croce* ☎*041/2750462 Chorus* ⌦*€3, Chorus pass €9* ☉*Mon.–Sat. 10–5, Sun. 1–5* Ⓥ*San Silvestro/Rialto.*

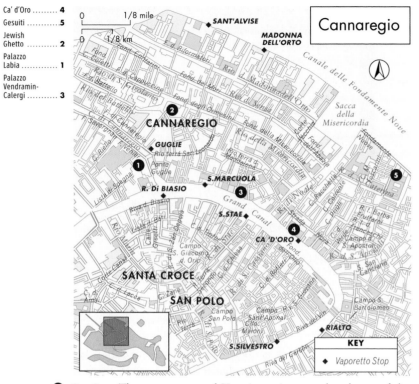

Cannaregio

4 **San Stae.** The most renowned Venetian painters and sculptors of the early 18th century—known as the Moderns—decorated this church with the legacy left by Doge Alvise Mocenigo II, who's buried in the center aisle. A broad sampling of these masters includes works by Tiepolo, Ricci, Piazzetta, and Lazzarini. ⊠*Campo San Stae, Santa Croce* ☎*041/2750462 Chorus* ✆*€3, Chorus pass €9* ☉*Mon.–Sat. 9–5, Sun. 1–5* Ⓥ*San Stae.*

CASTELLO & CANNAREGIO

Twice the size of tiny San Polo and Santa Croce, Castello and Cannaregio combined spread east to west from one end of Venice to the other. From working-class shipbuilding neighborhoods to the world's first ghetto, here you see a cross section of city life that's always existed beyond the palace walls. There are churches that could make a Renaissance pope jealous and one of the Grand Canal's prettiest palaces, Ca' d'Oro, as well as detour options for leaving the crowds behind.

TIMING

Visiting both sestieri involves a couple of hours of walking, even if you never enter a building, and there are few chances to hop a boat and save your legs. Some sights have restricted hours, making it virtually impossible to see everything even in a full day. Your best bet is to choose a few sights as priorities, time your tour around their open hours, and then drop in at whatever others happen to be open as you're passing by. If you're touring on Friday, keep in mind that synagogues close at sunset.

THE MAIN ATTRACTIONS

⑪ **Arsenale.** The Venetian Republic never could have thrived without the Arsenale shipyard. Today it belongs to the Italian Navy and isn't regularly open to the public, but it opens for the Biennale and for Venice's festival of traditional boats, held every May. If you're here during those times, don't miss the chance for a look inside. At other times, it's still worthwhile to walk by and observe the place from the outside.

The Arsenale is said to have been founded in 1104 on twin islands. The immense facility that evolved was given the old Venetian dialect name *arzanà,* borrowed from the Arabic *darsina'a,* meaning "workshop." At times it employed as many as 16,000 *arsenalotti,* workers who were among the most respected shipbuilders in the world. (Dante immortalized these sweating men armed with pitch and boiling tar in his *Inferno.*) Their diligence was confirmed time and again—whether building 100 ships in 60 days to battle the Turks in Cyprus (1597) or completing one perfectly armed warship—start to finish—while King Henry III of France attended a banquet.

The Arsenale's impressive Renaissance **gateway** (1460) is guarded by four lions, war booty of Francesco Morosini, who took the Peloponnese from the Turks in 1687. The 10-foot-tall lion on the left stood sentinel more than 2,000 years ago near Athens, and experts say its mysterious inscription is runic "graffiti" left by Viking mercenaries hired to suppress 11th-century revolts in Piraeus. If you look at the winged lion above the doorway, you'll notice that the Gospel at his paws is open but lacks the customary *Pax* inscription; praying for peace perhaps seemed inappropriate above a factory that manufactured weapons. ⊠ *Campo dell'Arsenale, Castello* Ⓥ *Arsenale.*

★ ❹ **Ca' d'Oro.** This exquisite Venetian Gothic palace was once literally a "Golden House," when its marble traceries and ornaments were embellished with pure gold. Created in 1434 by the enamored patrician Marino Contarini for his wife, Ca' d'Oro became a love offering a second time when a 19th-century Russian prince gave it to Maria Taglioni, a celebrated classical dancer who collected palaces along the Grand Canal. The last proprietor, perhaps more taken with Venice than with any of his lovers, left Ca' d'Oro to the city, after having had it carefully restored and filled with antiquities, sculptures, and paintings that today make up the **Galleria Franchetti.** Besides Andrea Mantegna's celebrated *St. Sebastian* and other first-rate Venetian works, the Galleria Franchetti contains the type of fresco that once adorned the exteriors of Venetian buildings (commissioned by those who could not afford a marble facade). One such detached fresco displayed here was made by a young Titian for the (now grayish-white) facade of the

Fondaco dei Tedeschi, now the main post office. ⊠*Calle Ca' d'Oro, Cannaregio 3933* ☎*041/5222349* ⊕*www.cadoro.org* 🎫*€6 includes Museo Orientale, €11 includes Gallerie dell'Accademia and Museo Orientale* ⊙*Tues.–Sun. 8:15–7, Mon. 8:15–2; last entry ½ hr before closing* Ⓥ*Ca' d'Oro.*

❷ **Jewish Ghetto.** The neighborhood that gave the world the word *ghetto* is today a quiet warren of backstreets that is still home to five Jewish institutions, a kosher restaurant, a rabbinical school, and five synagogues. Though Jews may have arrived earlier, the first synagogues weren't built and a cemetery wasn't founded until the Askenazim, or Eastern European Jews, came in the late 1300s. Dwindling coffers may have prompted the republic to sell temporary visas to Jews, but over the centuries they were alternately tolerated and expelled. The Rialto commercial district, as vividly recounted in Shakespeare's *The Merchant of Venice,* depended on Jewish merchants and moneylenders for trade, and to help cover ever-increasing war expenses.

In 1516 relentless local opposition forced the Senate to confine Jews to an island in Cannaregio, named for its *geto* (foundry), which produced cannons. Gates at the entrance were locked at night, and boats patrolled the surrounding canals. The German accents of early residents changed the soft g sound of "geto" (pronounced zheto) into the hard g in "ghetto." Jews were allowed only to lend money at low interest, operate pawnshops controlled by the government, trade in textiles, or practice medicine. Jewish doctors were highly respected and could leave the ghetto at any hour when on duty. Though ostracized, Jews were nonetheless safe in Venice, and in the 16th century the community grew considerably, with refugees from the Near East, southern and central Italy, Spain, and Portugal. The ghetto was allowed to expand twice, but it still had the city's densest population and consequently ended up with the city's tallest buildings (nine stories); notice the slanting apartment blocks on Campo del Ghetto Nuovo. Although the gates were pulled down after Napoléon's 1797 arrival, the Jews realized full freedom only in the late 19th century with the founding of the Italian state. On the eve of World War II there were about 1,500 Jews left in the ghetto: 247 were deported by the Nazis; 8 returned.

The area has Europe's highest density of Renaissance-era synagogues, and visiting them is a unique cross-cultural experience. Though each is marked by the tastes of its individual builders, Venetian influence is evident throughout. Women's galleries resemble those of theaters from the same era, and some synagogues were decorated by artisans who were simultaneously active in local churches.

The small but well-arranged **Museo Ebraico** highlights centuries of Jewish culture with splendid silver Hanukkah lamps and Torahs, and handwritten, beautifully decorated wedding contracts in Hebrew. Tours of the ghetto in Italian and English leave hourly from the museum. ⊠*Campo del Ghetto Nuovo, Cannaregio 2902/b* ☎*041/715359* ⊕*www.museoebraico.it* 🎫*Museum €3, museum and synagogues €8.50* ⊙*June–Sept.,*

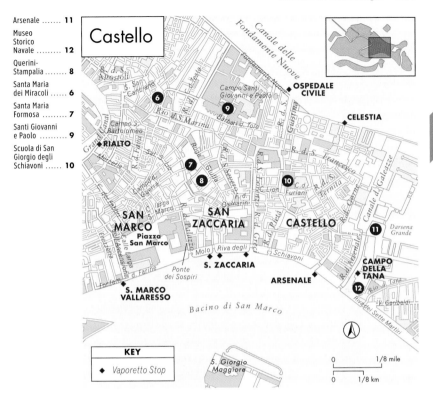

Sun.–Fri. 10–7, last tour 5:30; Oct.–May, Sun.–Fri. 10–6, last tour 3:30 Ⓥ*San Marcuola/Guglie.*

You might complete your circuit of Jewish Venice with a visit to the **Antico Cimitero Ebraico** *(Ancient Jewish Cemetery)* on the Lido, full of fascinating old tombstones half hidden by ivy and grass. The earliest grave dates from 1389; the cemetery remained in use until the late 18th century. ✉*Via Cipro, Lido* ☎*041/715359* 💶*€8.50* ⊘*Tours Apr.– Oct., Sun. at 2:30; call for arrangements* Ⓥ*Lido/S. Maria Elisabetta.*

★ ❻ **Santa Maria dei Miracoli.** Tiny yet perfectly proportioned, this early-Renaissance gem is sheathed in marble and decorated inside with exquisite marble reliefs. Architect Pietro Lombardo (circa 1435–1515) miraculously compressed the building into its confined space, then created the illusion of greater size by varying the color of the exterior, adding extra pilasters on the building's canal side, and offsetting the arcade windows to make the arches appear deeper. The church was built in the 1480s to house *I Miracoli,* an image of the Virgin Mary that is said to perform miracles—look for it on the high altar. ✉*Campo Santa Maria Nova, Cannaregio* ☎*041/2750462 Chorus* 💶*€3, Chorus pass €9* ⊘*Mon.–Sat. 10–5, Sun. 1–5* Ⓥ*Rialto.*

★ **❾** **Santi Giovanni e Paolo.** This massive Dominican church, commonly called San Zanipolo, contains a wealth of art. The 15th-century stained-glass window near the side entrance is breathtaking for its brilliant colors and beautiful figures, made from drawings by Bartolomeo Vivarini and Gerolamo Mocetto. The second official church of the republic after San Marco, San Zanipolo is the Venetian equivalent of London's Westminster Abbey, with a great number of important people, including 25 doges, buried here. Artistic highlights include an outstanding polyptych by Giovanni Bellini (right aisle, second altar); Alvise Vivarini's *Christ Carrying the Cross* (sacrestia); and Lorenzo Lotto's *Charity of St. Antonino* (right transept). Don't miss the *Cappella del Rosario* (Rosary Chapel), off the left transept, built in the 16th century to commemorate the 1571 victory of Lepanto, in western Greece, when Venice led a combined European fleet to defeat the Turkish Navy. The chapel was devastated by a fire in 1867 and restored in the early years of the 20th century with works from other churches, among them the sumptuous Veronese ceiling paintings. However quick your visit, don't miss the Pietro Mocenigo tomb to the right of the main entrance, a monument built by the ubiquitous Pietro Lombardo and his sons. ⊠ *Campo dei Santi Giovanni e Paolo, Castello* ☎ *041/5235913* ☞ *€2.50* ⊙ *Mon.– Sat. 9:30–6:30, Sun. noon–5:30* Ⓥ *Fondamente Nuove/Rialto.*

NEED A BREAK? To satisfy your sweet tooth, head for Campo Santa Marina and the family-owned and -operated Didovich Pastry Shop (☎ *041/5230017*). It's a local favorite, especially for Carnevale-time *fritelle* (fried doughnuts). There is limited seating inside, but in the warmer months you can sit outside. Bar ai Miracoli (☎ *041/5231515*) in Campo Santa Maria Nova is a good place to grab a quick bite and gaze across the canal at Santa Maria dei Miracoli, Lombardo's miracle in marble.

ALSO WORTH SEEING

❺ **Gesuiti.** Extravagantly baroque, this 18th-century church completely abandons classical Renaissance straight lines in favor of flowing, twisting forms. Its interior walls resemble brocade drapery, and only touching them will convince skeptics that rather than paint, the green-and-white walls are inlaid marble. Over the first altar on the left, the *Martyrdom of St. Lawrence* is a dramatic example of Titian's feeling for light and movement. ⊠ *Campo dei Gesuiti, Cannaregio* ☎ *041/5286579* ⊙ *Daily 10–noon and 4–6* Ⓥ *Fondamente Nuove.*

🐾 **⓬** **Museo Storico Navale** *(Museum of Naval History).* The boat collection here includes scale models such as the doges' ceremonial *Bucintoro*, and full-size boats such as Peggy Guggenheim's private gondola complete with romantic *felze* (cabin). There's a range of old galley and military pieces, and also a large collection of seashells. ⊠ *Campo San Biagio, Castello 2148* ☎ *041/2441399* ⊕ *www.marina.difesa.it/venezial* ☞ *€1.55* ⊙ *Weekdays 8:45–1:30, Sat. 8:45–1* Ⓥ *Arsenale.*

❶ **Palazzo Labia.** Once the home of 18th-century Venice's showiest family, this palace is now the Venetian headquarters of the Italian media giant

Let's Get Lost

Getting around Venice presents some unusual problems: the city's layout has few straight lines; house numbering seems nonsensical; and the *sestieri* (six districts) of San Marco, Cannaregio, Castello, Dorsoduro, Santa Croce, and San Polo all duplicate each other's street names. The numerous vaporetto lines can be bewildering, and often the only option for getting where you want to go is to walk. Yellow signs, posted on many busy corners, point toward the major landmarks—San Marco, Rialto, Accademia, etc.—but don't count on finding such markers once you're deep into residential neighborhoods. Even buying a good map at a newsstand—the kind showing all street names and vaporetto routes—won't necessarily keep you from getting lost.

Fortunately, as long as you maintain your patience, getting lost in Venice can be a pleasure. For one thing, being lost is a sign that you've escaped the tourist throngs. And although you might not find the Titian masterpiece you'd set out to see, instead you could wind up coming across an ageless bacaro or a quirky shop that turns out to be the highlight of your afternoon. Opportunities for such serendipity abound. Keep in mind that the city is nothing if not self-contained: sooner or later, perhaps with the help of a patient native, you can rest assured you'll regain your bearings.

RAI—modern broadcasting goes baroque. In the **Tiepolo Room,** the Labia's gorgeous ballroom, the final flowering of Venetian painting is seen in Giambattista Tiepolo's playful frescoes of Antony and Cleopatra among dwarfs and Barbary pirates. You have to call ahead to arrange a visit here. ⊠ *Campo San Geremia, Cannaregio 275* ☎ *041/781277* ☒ *Free* ⊙ *Wed.–Fri. 3–4, by appointment* Ⓥ *Ferrovia.*

❸ Palazzo Vendramin-Calergi. This Renaissance classic with an imposing carved frieze is the work of Mauro Codussi (1440–1504). You can see some of its interior by dropping into the **Casinò di Venezia.** Fans of Richard Wagner (1813–83) might enjoy visiting the **Sala di Wagner,** the room (separate from the casino) in which the composer died. Though rather plain, it's loaded with music memorabilia. ⊠ *Cannaregio 2040* ☎ *041/5297111 Casino, 041/2760407 by Fri.* AM *to reserve Wagner Room tours* ☒ *Casino €10, tour €5 suggested donation* ⊙ *Slots: daily 2:45* PM*–2:30* AM*; tables: daily 3:30* PM*–2:30* AM*; Wagner Room: Tues., Thurs., Sat.* AM *by appointment* Ⓥ *San Marcuola.*

❽ Querini-Stampalia. The art collection at this Renaissance palace includes Giovanni Bellini's *Presentation in the Temple* and Sebastiano Ricci's triptych *Dawn, Afternoon, and Evening.* Portraits of newlyweds Francesco Querini and Paola Priuli were left unfinished on the death of Giacomo Palma il Vecchio (1480–1528); note the groom's hand and the bride's dress. Original 18th-century furniture and stuccowork are a fitting background for Pietro Longhi's portraits. Nearly 70 works by Gabriele Bella (1730–99) capture scenes of Venetian street life. Admission Friday and Saturday includes concerts with antique instruments at 5 and 8:30. ⊠ *Campo Santa Maria Formosa, Castello 5252*

☎041/2711411 ⊕*www.querinis-
tampalia.it* 🖃€8 ⊘*Tues.–Thurs.
and Sun. 10–6, Fri. and Sat. 10–
10* ⊽*San Zaccaria.*

❼ **Santa Maria Formosa.** Guided by his
vision of a beautiful Madonna, 7th-
century St. Magno is said to have
followed a small white cloud and
built a church where it settled. Gracefully white, the marble building
you see today dates from 1492, built by Mauro Codussi on an older
foundation. The interior is a blend of Renaissance decoration, a Byzantine cupola, barrel vaults, and narrow-columned screens. Of interest
are two fine paintings: *Our Lady of Mercy* by Bartolomeo Vivarini and
Santa Barbara by Palma il Vecchio. The surrounding square bustles with
sidewalk cafés and a produce market on weekday mornings. ⊠*Campo
Santa Maria Formosa, Castello* ☎041/5234645, 041/2750462 *Chorus*
🖃€3, *Chorus pass €9* ⊘*Mon.–Sat. 10–5, Sun. 1–5* ⊽*Rialto.*

❿ **Scuola di San Giorgio degli Schiavoni.** Founded in 1451 by the Dalmatian
community, this small scuola was, and still is, a social and cultural
center for migrants from what is now Croatia. It's dominated by one
of Italy's most beautiful rooms, lavishly yet harmoniously decorated
with the *teleri* (large canvases) of Vittore Carpaccio. A lifelong Venice resident, Carpaccio painted legendary and religious figures against
backgrounds of Venetian architecture. Here he focused on saints especially venerated in Dalmatia: St. George, St. Tryphone, and St. Jerome.
He combined observation with fantasy, a sense of warm color with a
sense of humor (don't miss the priests fleeing St. Jerome's lion, or the
body parts in the dragon's lair). ⊠*Calle dei Furlani, Castello 3259/a*
☎041/5228828 🖃€3 ⊘*Tues.–Sat. 9:15–1 and 2:45–6, Sun. 9:15–1;
last entry ½ hr before closing* ⊽*Arsenale/San Zaccaria.*

SAN GIORGIO MAGGIORE & THE GIUDECCA

Beckoning travelers across St. Mark's Basin, sparkling white through
the mist, is the island of San Giorgio Maggiore, separated by a small
channel from the Giudecca. A tall brick campanile on that distant bank
perfectly complements the Campanile of San Marco. Beneath it looms
the stately dome of one of Venice's greatest churches, San Giorgio Maggiore, the creation of Andrea Palladio.

You can reach San Giorgio Maggiore via vaporetto Line 82 from San
Zaccaria. The next three stops on the line take you to the Giudecca.
The island's past may be shrouded in mystery, but today it's about as
down to earth as you can get and one of the city's few remaining neighborhoods that feels truly Venetian.

TIMING

A half day should be plenty of time to visit the area. Allow about a half
hour to see each of the churches, and an hour or two to look around
the Giudecca.

THE MAIN ATTRACTIONS

Giudecca. The island's name is something of a mystery. It may come from a possible 14th-century Jewish settlement, or because 9th-century nobles condemned to *giudicato* (exile) were sent here. It became a pleasure garden for wealthy Venetians during the republic's long and luxurious decline, but today, like Cannaregio, it's largely working class. The Giudecca provides spectacular views of Venice and is becoming increasingly gentrified. While here, visit the **Santissimo Redentore** church, designed by Palladio and built to commemorate a plague. The third weekend in July it's the site of the Venetians' favorite festival, Redentore, featuring boats, fireworks, and outdoor feasting. Thanks to several bridges, you can walk the entire length of the Giudecca's promenade, relaxing at one of several restaurants or just taking in the lively atmosphere. Accommodations run the gamut from youth hostels to the city's most exclusive hotel, Cipriani. ⊠ *Fondamenta San Giacomo, Giudecca* ☎ *041/5231415, 041/2750462 Chorus* ⊠ *€3, Chorus pass €9* ◷ *Mon.–Sat. 10–5, Sun. 1–5* Ⓥ *Redentore.*

San Giorgio Maggiore. There's been a church on this island since the 8th century, with a Benedictine monastery added in the 10th century (closed to the public). Today's refreshingly airy and simply decorated church of brick and white marble was begun in 1566 by Palladio and displays his architectural hallmarks of mathematical harmony and classical influence. *The Last Supper* and the *Gathering of Manna*, two of Tintoretto's later works, line the chancel. To the right of the entrance hangs *The Adoration of the Shepherds* by Jacopo Bassano (1517–92); his affection for his foothills home, Bassano del Grappa, is evident in the bucolic subjects and terra-firma colors he chooses. The monks are happy to show Carpaccio's *St. George and the Dragon,* hanging in a private room, if they have time. The campanile is so tall that it was struck by lightning in 1993. Take the elevator to the top for some of the finest views in town. ⊠ *Isola di San Giorgio Maggiore* ☎ *041/5227827* ⊠ *Church free, campanile €3* ◷ *Daily 9–12:30 and 2:30–6* Ⓥ *San Giorgio.*

ISLANDS OF THE LAGOON

The perfect vacation from your Venetian vacation is an escape to Murano, Burano, and sleepy Torcello, the islands of the northern lagoon. Torcello offers greenery, breathing space, and picnic opportunities (remember to pack lunch). Burano is a toy town of houses painted in a riot of colors—blue, yellow, pink, ocher, and dark red. Visitors still love to shop here for "Venetian" lace, even though the vast majority of it is machine-made in Taiwan. Murano is renowned for its glass, but also notorious for the high-pressure sales on its factory tours, even those organized by top hotels. Vaporetto connections to Murano aren't difficult, and for the price of a boat ticket you'll buy your freedom and more time to explore. The Murano "guides" herding new arrivals follow a rotation so that factories take turns giving tours, but you can avoid the hustle by just walking away.

TIMING

Hitting all the sights on all the islands takes a full day. If you limit yourself to Murano and San Michele, a half day will suffice. In summer San Zaccaria is connected to Murano by express vaporetto Line 5; the trip takes 25 minutes. In winter the local Line 41 takes about 45 minutes. The boat leaves San Zaccaria (in front of the Savoia e Jolanda hotel) every 20 minutes, circling the east end of Venice and stopping at Fondamente Nuove before making the five-minute hop to the San Michele island cemetery and then heading on to Murano. To see glassblowing, get off at Colonna; the Museo stop will put you near the Museo Vetrario.

> **WORD OF MOUTH**
>
> "A ferry ride (cheap) to Burano is a great way to see how the average person outside the city lives and works. Yes, lace is very expensive, but you can always just look, and you can even watch a woman making it by hand in a store window. Pretty, colorful homes, more canals. Have lunch on a canal. It's laid back and just darn nice."
> –Carole

Line LN goes from Fondamente Nuove direct to Murano, Burano, and Torcello every 30 minutes, and the full trip takes 45 minutes each way. To get to Burano and Torcello from Murano, pick up Line LN at the Faro stop (Murano's lighthouse), which runs to Burano before continuing on to Torcello, only five minutes away.

THE MAIN ATTRACTIONS

★ ❸ **Burano.** Cheerfully painted houses line the canals of this quiet village where lace making rescued a faltering fishing-based economy centuries ago. As you walk the 100 yards from the dock to Piazza Galuppi, the main square, you pass stall after stall of lace vendors. These good-natured ladies won't press you with a hard sell, but don't expect precise product information or great bargains—real handmade Burano lace costs $1,000 to $2,000 for a 10-inch doily.

The **Museo del Merletto** *(Lace Museum)* lets you marvel at the intricacies of Burano's lace making. It's also a skills center—more sewing circle than school—where on weekdays you'll usually find women carrying on the tradition. They sometimes have authentic pieces for sale privately. ⊠ *Piazza Galuppi 187* ☏ *041/730034* €4, *Musei Civici pass* €18 ⊗ *Apr.–Oct., daily 10–5; Nov.–Mar., daily 10–4* Ⓥ *Burano.*

⟳ ❷ **Murano.** As in Venice, bridges here link a number of small islands, which are dotted with houses that once were workmen's cottages. In the 13th century the republic, concerned about fire hazard, moved its glassworks to Murano, and today you can visit the factories and watch glass being made. Many of them line the Fondamenta dei Vetrai, the canal-side walkway leading from the Colonna vaporetto landing.

Before you reach Murano's Grand Canal (a little more than 800 feet from the landing) you'll pass **Chiesa di San Pietro Martire**. Reconstructed in the 16th century, it houses Giovanni Bellini's *Madonna and Child*

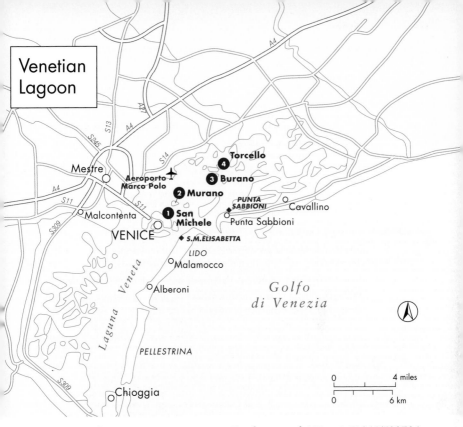

and Veronese's *St. Jerome.* ⊠*Fondamenta dei Vetrai* ☎*041/739704* ⊙ *Weekdays 9–6, Sat. 2–6, Sun. 11:30–5* Ⓥ*Colonna.*

The collection at the **Museo Vetrario** *(Glass Museum)* ranges from priceless antiques to only slightly less-expensive modern pieces. You'll see authentic Venetian styles and patterns, including the famous Barovier wedding cup (1470–80). ⊠*Fondamenta Giustinian 8* ☎*041/739586* ⊠*€5.50, Musei Civici museum pass €18* ⊙ *Apr.–Oct., daily 10–6; Nov.–Mar., daily 10–5. Last tickets sold ½ hr before closing* Ⓥ*Museo.*

The **Basilica dei Santi Maria e Donato,** just past the glass museum, is among the first churches founded by the lagoon's original inhabitants. The elaborate mosaic pavement includes the date 1140; its ship's-keel roof and Veneto-Byzantine columns add to the semblance of an ancient temple. ⊠*Fondamenta Giustinian* ☎*041/739056* ⊠*Free* ⊙ *Mon.–Sat. 8–6, Sun. 2–6* Ⓥ*Museo.*

★ ❹ **Torcello.** In their flight from barbarians 1,500 years ago, the first Venetians landed here, prospering even after many left to found the city of Venice. As malaria took its toll and the island's wool manufacturing was priced out of the market, Torcello became a ghost town. In the 16th century there were 10 churches and 20,000 inhabitants; today you'll be lucky to see one of the island's 16 permanent residents.

Santa Maria Assunta was built in the 11th century, and Torcello's wealth at the time is evident in the church's high-quality Byzantine mosaics. The massive *Last Judgment* shows sinners writhing in pain, while opposite, above the altar, the Madonna looks calmly down from her field of gold. Ask to see the inscription dated 639 and a sample of mosaic pavement from the original church. The adjacent **Santa Fosca** church, added when the body of the saint arrived in 1011, is still used for religious services. It's worth making the climb up the adjacent **campanile** for an incomparable view of the lagoon wetlands. ✉*Torcello* 🕿*041/730119* 📧*Santa Maria Assunta €4, campanile €4* ⊙*Basilica: Mar.–Oct., daily 10:30–6; Nov.–Feb., daily 10–5. Campanile: Mar.–Oct., daily 10:30–5:30; Nov.–Feb., daily 10–4:30. Last entry ½ hr before closing* Ⓥ*Torcello*.

NEED A BREAK?

Locanda Cipriani (🕿*041/730150*), closed Tuesday and January, is famous for good food and its connection to Ernest Hemingway, who often came to Torcello seeking solitude. Today the restaurant (not to be confused with the Giudecca's Cipriani hotel) is busy, with well-heeled customers speeding in for lunch (dinner also on weekends). Dining is pricey, but you can relax in the garden with just a glass of prosecco.

ALSO WORTH SEEING

❶ **San Michele.** This cypress-lined island is home to the pretty Renaissance church of **San Michele in Isola**—and to some of Venice's most illustrious deceased. The church was designed by Codussi; the graves include those of poet Ezra Pound (1885–1972), impresario and art critic Sergey Diaghilev (1872–1929), and composer Igor Stravinsky (1882–1971). Surrounded by the living sounds of Venice's lagoon, this would seem the perfect final resting place. However, these days newcomers are exhumed after 10 years and transferred to a less-grandiose location. 🕿*041/7292811* 📧*Free* ⊙*Apr.–Sept., daily 7:30–6; Oct.–Mar., daily 7:30–4* Ⓥ*San Michele*.

WHERE TO EAT

Updated by
Shannon
Essa &
Ruth
Edenbaum

The catchword in Venice, at both fancy restaurants and holes-in-the-wall, is fish, often at its tastiest when it looks like nothing you've seen before. How do you learn firsthand about the catch of the day? An early-morning visit to the Rialto's *pescheria* (fish market) is more instructive than any book.

There's no getting around the fact that Venice has more than its share of overpriced, mediocre eateries that prey on tourists. Avoid places with cajoling waiters standing outside, and beware of restaurants that don't display their prices. At the other end of the spectrum, showy *menu turistico* (tourist menu) boards make offerings clear in a dozen languages, but for the same 15–20 euros you'd spend at such places you could do better at a *bacaro* (the local version of a wine bar) making a meal of *cicchetti* (savory snacks).

Dining options in Venice range from the ultrahigh end, where jackets and ties are required, to the supercasual, where the clientele (almost all of them tourists) won't notice if you're wearing shorts. Some of Venice's swankiest restaurants—the ones that usually have only male waiters wearing white jackets and bow ties—trade on long-standing reputations and might seem a little stuffy and faded. The food at such places tends toward interpretations of international cuisine and, though often expertly prepared, can seem as old-fashioned as the waiters who serve it. On the other hand, mid-range restaurants are often more willing to break from tradition, incorporating ingredients such as ginger and wasabi in their creations.

Budget-conscious travelers, and those simply looking for a good meal in unpretentious surroundings, might want to stick to trattorias and bacari. Trattorias often serve less-highfalutin versions of classic Venetian dishes at substantially reduced prices; bacari offer lighter fare, usually eaten at the bar (though sometimes tables are available), and wine lists that offer lots of choices by the glass.

WHAT IT COSTS IN EUROS				
	¢	$	$$	$$$	$$$$
AT DINNER	under €15	€15–€25	€25–€35	€35–€45	over €45

Prices are for a first course (primo), second course (secondo), and dessert (dolce).

CANNAREGIO

$$$ ✕ Al Fontego dei Pescaori. Having had a stall at the Rialto fish market for over 25 years, Lolo, the proprietor, really knows fish, and diners fill two cheerful dining rooms to savor what might just be the freshest fish in Venice. There are several spectacular offerings of pesce crudo (raw fish) among the antipasti. Pastas are excellent and the fish entrées are prepared simply but with a twist. Branzino (sea bass) may be topped with its own crispy skin and a frizzle of zucchini or wrapped around itself with the succulent skin becoming the stuffing. Meat dishes are available, but the wine list is built around local wines that go best with fish. ⊠Sottoportego del Tagiapier, *Cannaregio 3711* ☎*041/5200538* ☰*MC, V* ☺*Closed Mon., 3 wks in Jan., 2 wks in Aug.* Ⓥ*Ca' d'Oro.*

★ $$–$$$ ✕ Vini da Gigio. This family-run trattoria on the San Felice Canal is deservedly popular with Venetians and visitors. Homemade pastas, such as rigatoni with duck sauce and arugula-stuffed ravioli nestled in a rich cheese sauce, are excellent. Fish is well represented on the menu, but the meat dishes steal the show: the Burano-style duck is a flavorful fricassee, the steak with red-pepper sauce and the lamb with a heavenly crusty coating are both superb, and the *fegato alla Veneziana* (Venetian style liver with onions) is among the best in Venice. Desserts are worth every luscious calorie. The wine list of over one thousand bottles is a major attraction; an oenophile will be in ecstasy here. ⊠*Fondamenta de la Chiesa, Cannaregio 3628/a* ☎*041/5285140* ☰*DC, MC, V* ☺*Closed Mon. and Tues., 2 wks in Jan., and 3 wks in Aug.* Ⓥ*Ca' d'Oro.*

BEST BETS FOR VENICE DINING

With hundreds of restaurants to choose from, how will you decide where to eat? Fodor's writers and editors have selected their favorite restaurants by price and experience in the Best Bets lists below. In the first column, Fodor's Choice properties represent the "best of the best."

Fodor'sChoice ★

Al Paradiso, $$$–$$$$, San Polo

Cantinone Gia Schiavi, ¢, Dorsoduro

La Zucca, $$, Santa Croce

Ristorante Riviera, $$$$, Dorsoduro

Best by Price

BEST ¢

Cantinone Gia Schiavi, Dorsoduro

Enoteca al Volto, San Marco

BEST $

Al Prosecco, Santa Croce

Antica Birreria La Corte, San Polo

Ostaria al Garanghelo, San Polo

BEST $$

Bancogiro, San Polo

Anice Stellato, Cannaregio

La Zucca, Santa Croce

BEST $$$

Al Fontego dei Pescaori, Cannaregio

Antiche Carampane, San Polo

Vecio Fritolin, Santa Croce

Vini da Gigio, Cannaregio

BEST $$$$

Alle Testiere, Castello

Al Paradiso, San Polo

Osteria da Fiore, San Polo

Ristorante Riviera, Dorsoduro

Best Experiences

OUTDOOR DINING

Algiubagiò, $–$$$, Cannaregio

Bancogiro, $–$$$, San Polo

Ristorante Riviera, $$$$, Dorsoduro

ROMANTIC

Al Paradiso, $$$–$$$$, San Polo

Osteria da Fiore, $$$$, San Polo

Ristorante Riviera, $$$$, Dorsoduro

GOOD FOR KIDS

Antica Birraria La Corte, $–$$, San Polo

Ostaria al Garanghelo, $–$$, San Polo

IF YOU DON'T WANT FISH

Antica Birraria La Corte, $–$$, San Polo

La Bitta, $$, Dorsoduro

La Zucca, $$, Santa Croce

Vini da Gigio, $$–$$$, Cannaregio

GREAT VIEWS

Algiubagiò, $–$$$, Cannaregio

Bancogiro, $–$$$, San Polo

Ristorante Riviera, $$$$, Dorsoduro

EXCEPTIONAL WINE LIST

Antiche Carampane, $$$–$$$$, San Polo

Osteria da Fiore, $$$$, San Polo

Vini da Gigio, $$–$$$, Cannaregio

GOOD FOR LUNCH

Alla Vedova, $, Cannaregio

Antica Birraria La Corte, $–$$, San Polo

La Zucca, $$, Santa Croce

Vecio Fritolin, $$$, Santa Croce

ALTA CUCINA (SOPHISTICATED CUISINE)

Alle Testiere, $$$$, Castello

Osteria da Fiore, $$$$, San Polo

CASALINGA (HOME COOKING)

La Bitta, $$, Dorosduro

Ostaria al Garanghelo, $–$$, San Polo

$-$$$ ✕ **Algiubagiò.** A waterfront table is still relatively affordable here on Venice's northern Fondamente Nuove, where you can gaze out toward San Michele and Murano—on a clear day, you can even see the Dolomites. Algiubagiò has a dual personality: pizzas and big, creative salads at lunch; elegant secondi such as Angus fillets and duck with prunes and rosemary at dinner. (There's no fish on the dinner menu.) The young, friendly staff also serves ice cream, drinks, and sandwiches all day. A table here is worth the walk. ⊠ *Fondamente Nuove, Cannaregio 5039* ☎ *041/5236084* ▤ *MC, V* Ⓥ *Fondamente Nuove.*

$$ ✕ **Anice Stellato.** Hidden away on one of the most romantic *fondamente* (canal-side streets) of Cannaregio, this family-run *bacaro*-trattoria is the place to stop for fairly priced, great-tasting food, though service can feel indifferent. The space has plenty of character: narrow columns rise from the colorful tile floor, dividing the room into cozy sections. Traditional Venetian fare is enriched with such offerings as *carpacci di pesce* (thin slices of raw tuna, swordfish, or salmon dressed with olive oil and fragrant herbs), tagliatelle with king prawns and zucchini flowers, and several tasty fish stews. Meat dishes are also served, including a tender beef fillet stewed in Barolo wine with potatoes. ⊠ *Fondamenta de la Sensa, Cannaregio 3272* ☎ *041/720744* ▤ *MC, V* ⊗ *Closed Mon. and Tues., 1 wk in Feb., and 3 wks in Aug.* Ⓥ *S. Alvise.*

★ $ ✕ **Alla Vedova.** This warm trattoria not far from the Ca' d'Oro (it's also known as Trattoria Ca' d'Oro) was opened as a *bacaro* by the owner's great-grandparents. A Venetian terrazzo floor, old marble counter, and rustic furnishings lend a pleasant authenticity that's matched by the food and service. Cicchetti include tender *seppie roste* (grilled cuttlefish), *polpette* (meatballs), and *baccalà mantecato* (cod creamed with milk and olive oil). The house winter pasta is the *pastisso de radicio rosso* (lasagna with sausage, radicchio, and béchamel sauce). In spring the chef switches to pastisso *de asparagi* (with asparagus). ⊠ *Calle del Pistor, Cannaregio 3912* ☎ *041/5285324* ▤ *No credit cards* ⊗ *Closed Thurs. No lunch Sun.* Ⓥ *Ca' d'Oro.*

CASTELLO

★ $$$$ ✕ **Alle Testiere.** A strong local following can make it tough to get one of the 22 seats at this tiny trattoria near Campo Santa Maria Formosa. With its decidedly unglamorous ceiling fans, the place feels as informal as a bistro (or a saloon); the food, however, is much more sophisticated. Chef Bruno Gavagnin's dishes stand out for lightness and balance: try the *gnocchetti con moscardini* (little gnocchi with baby octopus) or the linguine with *coda di rospo* (monkfish), or inquire about the carpaccio of the day. The wine list is particularly strong on local whites. ⊠ *Calle del Mondo Novo, Castello 5801* ☎ *041/5227220* ⬧ *Reservations essential* ▤ *MC, V* ⊗ *Closed Sun. and Mon., 3 wks Jan.–Feb., and 4 wks July–Aug.* Ⓥ *Rialto/San Zaccaria.*

$$$$ ✕ **Do Leoni.** The Two Lions, in the Hotel Londra Palace, is a sumptuous candlelit setting in which to sample modern and traditional Venetian and other Italian cuisine. The kitchen turns out creative dishes like tagliatelle with chicory, Gorgonzola, and peanuts. The summer terrace occupies a good portion of the Riva. ⊠ *Riva degli Schiavoni, Castello*

4171 ☎041/5200533 ⌖*Reservations essential* ═*AE, DC, MC, V*
Ⓥ*San Zaccaria.*

★ **$$–$$$** ✗ **Corte Sconta.** You're close to seafood heaven at this firm favorite on the Venetian dining scene. Simple wooden tables are arranged around an open courtyard with outdoor seating in summer. You could make a meal of the seafood antipasti alone, but you'd miss out on such delights as spaghetti *neri con scampi e spinaci* (cuttlefish-ink pasta with scampi and spinach) and *vongole veraci spadellate allo zenzero* (clams sautéed in ginger). The house dessert is a warm zabaglione with Venetian cookies, and the house pour is a smooth, still prosecco, backed up by a good range of bottled wines. ✉*Calle del Pestrin, Castello 3886* ☎*041/5227024* ⌖*Reservations essential* ═*MC, V* ⊗*Closed Sun. and Mon., 3 wks in Jan., and 4 wks in July and Aug.* Ⓥ*Arsenale.*

DORSODURO

★ **$$$$** ✗**Ristorante Riviera.** Two lovely dining rooms and a canal-side terrace with an exquisite view, combined with truly inspired cuisine, make a visit to Riviera one to remember. Chef Monica Scarpa brings her creative touch to both traditional and contemporary dishes. Fish lovers will enjoy the tuna tartare, seafood risotto, or a mixed fish platter, while carnivores can dig into prosciutto with figs and pecorino cheese followed by a plate of succulent lamb chops with blueberry sauce. Host Luca excels at selecting the perfect wine for any combination of foods. Desserts include a plate of homemade cookies served with vin santo (sweet wine). A simple but appealing children's menu is offered. ✉*Zattere, Dorsoduro 1473* ☎*041/5227621* ⌖*Reservations essential* ═*MC, V* ⊗*Closed Mon., 4 weeks in Jan. and Feb.* Ⓥ*San Basilio.*

★ **$$$–$$$$** ✗ **Avogaria.** In terms of both food and architecture, ultrafashionable Avogaria lends modern flavor to the Venice restaurant scene. The clean, elegant design of the dining room and garden leaves no doubt that here, you're in the Venice of the present, not the past. The cuisine is Pugliese (from the region in the heel of Italy's boot); highlights among the primi include *orecchiette* (small, round pasta) with turnip tops, and zucchini *involtini* (roll-ups) made with fresh stracciatella cheese. Pugliese cooking, like Venetian, reveres fresh seafood, and you can taste this sensibility in the slow-cooked, sesame-encrusted tuna steak. ✉*Calle Avogaria, Dorsoduro 1629* ☎*041/2960491* ═*AE, DC, MC, V* ⊗*Closed Tues.* Ⓥ*S. Basilio.*

★ **$$** ✗ **La Bitta.** The decor is more discreet, the dining hours longer, and the service friendlier and more efficient here than in many small restaurants in Venice—and the creative non-fish menu is a temptation at every course. You can start with a light salad of Treviso radicchio and crispy bacon, followed by smoked-beef carpaccio or *gnocchetti ubriachi al Montasio* (small marinated gnocchi with Montasio cheese). Then choose from secondi such as lamb chops with thyme, *anatra in pevarada* (duck in a pepper sauce), or Irish Angus fillet steak. Secondi are served with vegetables, which helps bring down the price. The restaurant is open only for dinner, but serves much later than most, continuously from 6:30 to 11. ✉*Calle Lunga San Barnaba, Dorsoduro*

2753/a ☎*041/5230531* ▭*No credit cards* ⊙*Closed Sun. and July. No lunch* ⓥ*Ca' Rezzonico.*

$ ✕ **Ai 4 Feri.** The paper tablecloths and cozy, laid-back ambience are part of this small restaurant's charm. The menu varies according to what's fresh that day; imaginative combinations of ingredients in the primi—herring and sweet peppers, salmon and radicchio, giant shrimp and broccoli (with pumpkin gnocchi)—are the norm. A meal here followed by after-dinner drinks at Campo Santa Margherita, a five-minute walk away, makes for a lovely evening. The kitchen is open until 10:30 PM. ⊠*Calle Lunga San Barnaba, Dorsoduro 2754/a* ☎*041/5206978* ▭*No credit cards* ⊙*Closed Sun. and 2 wks in June* ⓥ*Ca' Rezzonico.*

¢ ✕ **Cantinone Già Schiavi.** This beautiful 19th-century *bacaro* opposite the *squero* (gondola repair shop) of San Trovaso has original furnishings and one of the best wine selections in town—the walls are covered floor to ceiling by bottles for purchase. Cicchetti here are some of the most inventive in Venice: try the crostini-style layers of bread, smoked swordfish, and slivers of raw zucchini, or pungent slices of parmeggiano, fig, and toast. They also have a creamy version of baccalà mantecato spiced with herbs. There are nearly a dozen open bottles of wine for experimenting at the bar. ⊠*Fondamenta* Maravegie*, Dorsoduro 992* ☎*041/5230034* ▭*No credit cards* ⊙*Closed 2 wks in Aug.* ⓥ*Zattere.*

SAN MARCO

¢–$ ✕ **Enoteca al Volto.** A short walk from the Rialto Bridge, this bar has been around since 1936; the fine cicchetti and primi have a lot to do with its staying power. Two small, dark rooms with wooden tables and chairs are the backdrop for the enjoyment of simple fare. The place prides itself on its considerable wine list of both Italian and foreign vintages; if you stick to the *panini* (sandwiches) and a cicchetto or two, you'll eat well for relatively little. If you opt for one of the primi of the day, the price category goes up a notch. ⊠*Calle Cavalli, San Marco 4081* ☎*041/5228945* ▭*No credit cards* ⊙*Closed Sun.* ⓥ*Rialto.*

SAN POLO

★ $$$$ ✕ **Osteria da Fiore.** Tucked away on a little calle near Campo San Polo, da Fiore is a favorite among high-end diners for its superbly prepared Venetian cuisine and refined yet relaxed atmosphere. The Martin family are hands-on owners, with Mara in the kitchen and Maurizio running every aspect of the dining room. A superlative seafood lunch or dinner here might include delicate hors d'oeuvres of soft-shell crab, scallops, and tiny octopus, followed by a succulent risotto or pasta *con scampi e radicchio* (with shrimp and radicchio), and a perfectly cooked main course of *rombo* (turbot) or *tagliata di tonno* (tuna steak). The formerly all-fish menu has been expanded to include dishes such as a sublime risotto made with butternut squash and balsamic vinegar and a buffalo burger. A jacket is not required, but is highly recommended. ⊠*Calle del Scaleter, San Polo 2202* ☎*041/721308* ✍*Reservations*

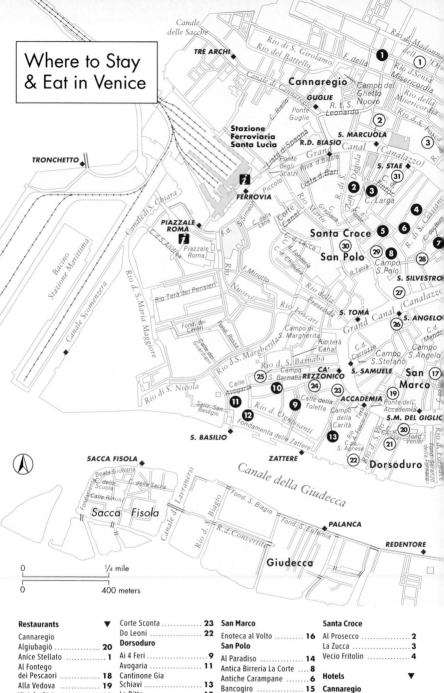

Where to Stay & Eat in Venice

TRE ARCHI

Canale delle Sacche

Rio di S. Girolamo

Rio del Battello

Cannaregio

GUGLIE

Stazione Ferroviaria Santa Lucia

TRONCHETTO

FERROVIA

PIAZZALE ROMA

Piazzale Roma

Bacino Stazione Marittima

Canale Scomenzera

Canale di S. Maria Maggiore

Rio di S. Nicola

S. BASILIO

SACCA FISOLA

Sacca Fisola

Rio di S. Girolamo

Rio di Cannaregio

R.D. BIASIO

S. MARCUOLA

Canal
Grand *(Canalazzo)*

Santa Croce

San Polo

S. STAE

Campo S. Polo

S. SILVESTRO

S. TOMÀ

Grand Canal (Canalazzo)

S. ANGELO

CA' REZZONICO

ACCADEMIA

S. SAMUELE

San Marco

Campo S. Angelo

Campo S. Stefano

Ponte dell' Accademia

S.M. DEL GIGLIO

Dorsoduro

ZATTERE

Canale della Giudecca

PALANCA

Giudecca

REDENTORE

0 — ¼ mile
0 — 400 meters

Restaurants ▼

Cannaregio
Algiubagiò **20**
Anice Stellato **1**
Al Fontego
dei Pescaori **18**
Alla Vedova **19**
Vini da Gigio **17**

Castello
Alle Testiere **21**

Corte Sconta **23**
Do Leoni **22**

Dorsoduro
Ai 4 Feri **9**
Avogaria **11**
Cantinone Gia
Schiavi **13**
La Bitta **10**
Ristorante Riviera **12**

San Marco
Enoteca al Volto **16**

San Polo
Al Paradiso **14**
Antica Birreria La Corte **8**
Antiche Carampane **6**
Bancogiro **15**
Ostaria al Garanghelo **7**
Osteria da Fiore **5**

Santa Croce
Al Prosecco **2**
La Zucca **3**
Vecio Fritolin **4**

Hotels ▼

Cannaregio
Ca' Gottardi **3**
Ca' San Marcuola **2**

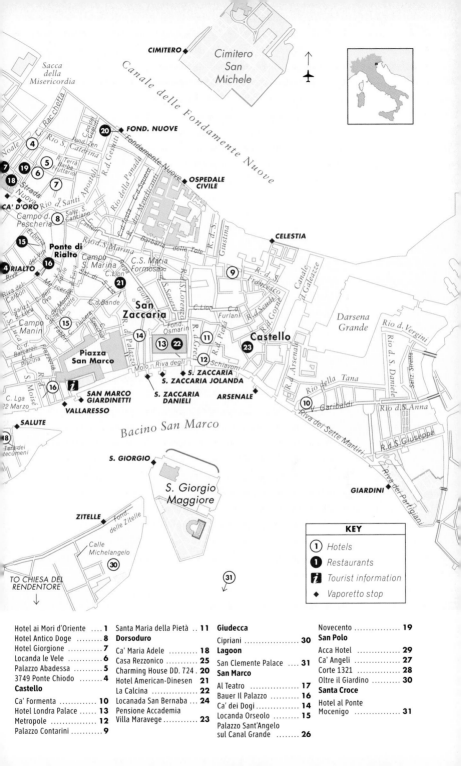

KEY

- ① Hotels
- ① Restaurants
- 🛈 Tourist information
- ◆ Vaporetto stop

essential ⊟*AE, DC, MC, V* ⊘*Closed Sun. and Mon., Aug., and Dec. 24–Jan. 15* ⒱*San Silvestro/San Stae.*

$$$-$$$$ ✕**Al Paradiso.** In a small dining room made warm and cozy by its pleasing and unpretentious decor, proprietor Giordano makes all diners feel like honored guests. Pappardelle "al Paradiso" takes pasta with seafood sauce to new heights while risotto with shrimp, champagne, and grapefruit puts a delectable twist on a traditional dish. The inspired and original array of entrées includes meat and fish selections such as a salmon with honey and balsamic vinegar in a stunning presentation. Desserts include a perfect panna cotta. There's an inspired wine list, but the house wines are infinitely better than those in other restaurants. ⊠*Calle dei Paradiso, San Polo 767* ☎*041/5234910* ⚲*Reservations essential* ⊟*AE, MC, V* ⊘*Closed Mon. and 3 wks in Jan. and Feb.* ⒱*San Silvestro.*

$$$-$$$$ ✕**Antiche Carampane.** Since its appearance in the first of Donna Leon's Inspector Brunetti mysteries, Piera Bortoluzzi Librai's trattoria has lost none of its charm but gained considerably in elegance. You'll find all the classic Venetian fish dishes ranging from a mixed seafood antipasto to fish soups, pasta, and perfectly grilled fish. Updated plates such as seafood and fruit salads for starters and entrées like turbot with citrus sauce also delight diners. Chocolate mousse, panna cotta, and sweet wine with biscotti make delectable desserts. Francesco, the son of Franco and Piera, whose family recipes elevate many of the classics, is responsible for some of the new presentations. ⊠*Rio Terà della Carampane, San Polo 1911* ☎*041/5240165* ⚲*Reservations essential for dinner* ⊟*AE, MC, V* ⊘*Closed Sun. and Mon., 10 days in Jan., 3 wks in July and Aug.* ⒱*San Silvestro.*

★ $-$$$ ✕ **Bancogiro.** Come to this casual spot in the heart of the Rialto Market in a 15th-century loggia for a change from standard Venetian food. Yes, fish is on the menu, and some of the dishes are Venice classics; but highlights such as mousse *di gamberoni con salsa di avocado* (shrimp mousse with an avocado sauce) and Sicilian-style *sarde incinte* (stuffed, or "pregnant," sardines) are far from typical fare, though portions can be small. The wine list and cheese plate are both divine. There are tables upstairs in a carefully restored room with a partial view of the Grand Canal; when it's warm you can sit outdoors and get the full canal view. ⊠*Campo San Giacometto, San Polo, 122 under the porch* ☎*041/5232061* ⊟*No credit cards* ⊘*Closed Mon.* ⒱*Rialto.*

$-$$ ✕**Antica Birreria La Corte.** Locals, students, and tourists flock here daily not only for the dazzling list of pizzas (including one topped with porcini mushrooms and wild-boar salami) but also for starters such as a salad of arugula and pecorino with a drizzle of chestnut honey. Gnocchi with white meat sauce or a rich creamy risotto can be followed with one of several excellent meat and fish entrées. Two kitchens—one for pizza and one for everything else—can result in courses arriving haphazardly. Beer's a better bet than wine here, thanks to the large selection on tap. ⊠*Campo San Polo, San Polo 2168* ☎*041/2750570* ⊟*MC, V* ⒱*San Silvestro/San Tomà.*

★ $-$$ ✕ **Ostaria al Garanghelo.** Superior quality, competitive prices, and great ambience means this place is often packed with Venetians, especially for lunch and an after-work *ombra* (small glass of wine) and cicchetti. Chef Renato takes full advantage of the fresh ingredients from the Rialto Market, located a few steps away, bakes his own bread daily, and prefers cooking many dishes *al vapore* (steamed). The spicy *fagioli al uciletto* (literally beans, bird-style) has an unusual name and Tuscan origins; it's a perfect companion to a plate of fresh pasta. Don't confuse this centrally located restaurant with one of the same name in Via Garibaldi. ⊠ *Calle dei Boteri, San Polo 1570* ☎ *041/721721* ▤ *MC, V* ⊘ *Closed Sun.* Ⓥ *Rialto.*

SANTA CROCE

$$$ ✕ **Vecio Fritolin.** At this tidy *bacaro con cucina* (with kitchen) you can have a traditional meal featuring such dishes as *bigoli in salsa* (thick spaghetti with anchovy sauce), baked fish with herbs, and ravioli with scampi and chicory. The name, which translates as "Old Fry Shop," refers to a bygone Venetian tradition of shops selling fried fish "to go," like in London, except paired with polenta rather than chips. For €8, you can still get a paper cone of *fritto* here. ⊠ *Calle della Regina, Santa Croce 2262* ☎ *041/5222881* ▤ *AE, DC, MC, V* ⊘ *Closed Mon.* Ⓥ *San Stae.*

$$ ✕ **La Zucca.** The simple place settings, lattice-wood walls, canal window, and mélange of languages make this place feel as much like a typical vegetarian restaurant as you could expect to find in Venice. Though the menu does have superb meat dishes such as the *piccata di pollo ai caperi e limone con riso* (sliced chicken with capers and lemon served with rice), more attention is paid to dishes from the garden: try the radicchio *di Treviso con funghi e scaglie di Montasio* (with mushrooms and shavings of Montasio cheese) or the *finocchi piccanti con olive* (fennel in a spicy tomato-olive sauce). ⊠ *Calle del Tintor, Santa Croce 1762* ☎ *041/5241570* ⌦ *Reservations essential* ▤ *AE, DC, MC, V* ⊘ *Closed Sun. and 1 wk in Dec.* Ⓥ *San Stae.*

$–$$ ✕ **Al Prosecco.** Locals stream into this friendly wine bar, down a "Spritz" (a combination of white wine, Campari or Aperol, and seltzer water), and continue on their way. Or they linger over a glass of one of the numerous wines on offer, perhaps also tucking into a tasty panino, such as the *porchetta romane verdure* (roasted pig, Roman style, with greens). Proprietors Davide and Stefano preside over a young and friendly staff who reel off the day's specials with ease. There are a few tables in the back room, and when the weather's warm you can eat outside on the lively campo. ⊠ *Campo San Giacomo dell'Orio, Santa Croce 1503* ☎ *041/5240222* ▤ *No credit cards* ⊘ *Closed Sun.* Ⓥ *San Stae.*

WHERE TO STAY

Updated by
Nan McElroy

Most of Venice's hotels are in renovated palaces, but space is at a premium—and comes for a price—and even relatively ample rooms may seem cramped by American standards. The most exclusive hotels are indeed palatial, although they may well have some small, dowdy rooms, so it's best to verify ahead of time that yours isn't one of them.

Also, not all hotels have lounge areas, and because of preservation laws, some hotels are not permitted to install elevators, so if these features are essential, ask ahead of time. Although the city has no cars, it does have boats plying the canals and pedestrians chattering in the streets sometimes late into the night (most likely along principal thoroughfares, in San Marco and near the Rialto), so ask for a quiet room if noise bothers you.

In temperate weather, be careful about leaving room lights on and your window wide open: mosquitoes can descend en masse. If you find that these creatures are a problem, ask for a Vape, a plug-in anti-mosquito device (or head for the nearest hardware store and pick one up yourself).

From April through November, and during holiday periods, well-reputed hotels fill up well in advance, particularly over weekends, so book as far ahead as you can.

Many travelers assume a hotel near Piazza San Marco will give them the most convenient location, but keep in mind that Venice is scaled to humans (on foot) rather than automobiles; it's difficult to find a location that's *not* convenient to most of the city. Areas away from San Marco may also offer the benefit of being less overrun by day-trippers whose primary destination is the Piazza.

It is essential to have detailed directions to your hotel when you arrive. Arm yourself with not only a detailed map and postal address (Dorsoduro 825), but the actual street name (Fondamenta San Trovaso). Transfer options range from the luxurious, private water taxi to the more economical water bus combined with on-foot navigation, which can be accompanied by the more than occasional occurrence of déjà vu if you don't know exactly where you are going.

Many hotels accept reservations from their personal Web site and will guarantee the lowest prices there. Book ahead using any of the numerous Web booking portals; ⊕*www.venezia.net* is unusual in that it furnishes hotels' official Web site links. **Venezia Sì** (☎*39/041/5222264 from abroad, 199/173309 from Italy* ⊗ *Mon.–Sat. 9* AM*–11* PM ⊕*www.veneziasi.it*) can also help for last-minute reservations, as their Web site lists most hotels in town (with some photographs), and they offer a free reservation service over the phone. It's the public relations arm of **AVA** *(Venetian Hoteliers Association)* and has booths where you can make same-day reservations at **Piazzale Roma** (☎*041/5231397* ⊗*Daily 9* AM*–10* PM), **Santa Lucia train station** (☎*041/715288 or 041/715016* ⊗*Daily 8* AM*–9* PM), and **Marco Polo Airport** (☎*041/5415133* ⊗*Daily 9* AM*–10* PM).

PRICES

Venetian hotels cater to all tastes and come in a variety of price ranges. Rates are about 20% higher than in Rome and Milan, but can be reduced by as much as half off-season, from November–March (excluding Christmas, New Year's, and Carnevale), and likely in August as well.

WHAT IT COSTS IN EUROS					
	¢	$	$$	$$$	$$$$
HOTELS	under €80	€80–€140	€140–€210	€210–€290	over €290

Prices are for a standard double room in high season.

CANNAREGIO

$$$$

Fodor'sChoice

★

🏠 **Palazzo Abadessa.** At this elegant late-16th-century palazzo, you'll experience gracious hospitality and a luxurious atmosphere in keeping with Venice's patrician heritage. You'll feel like nobility yourself as you ascend the majestic staircase and enter the expansive piano nobile which overlooks a side canal. Unusually spacious rooms are well-appointed with antique furniture, frescoed ceilings, and fine silk fabrics. The location is remote enough to escape the San Marco throngs while still within striking distance of all of major sights, and there's a private dock for taxi arrival. In summer, breakfast is served in a walled garden complete with sculptures and marble benches. **Pros:** A unique, historic lodging; spacious rooms and garden; superb guest service. **Con:** Not the best choice for families with young children, who may have difficulty dodging the antique accessories sprinkled throughout. ⊠*Calle Priuli off Strada Nova, Cannaregio 4011, 30131* ☎*041/2413784* ⊕*www. abadessa.com* ⌐*5 palazzo rooms, 3 palazzo deluxe, 4 suites, 1 presidential suite* ⌂*In-room: safe, refrigerator, Wi-Fi. In-hotel: room service, bar, no elevator, concierge, laundry service, public Internet, public Wi-Fi, some pets allowed* ⊟*AE, DC, MC, V* ⦿*BP* Ⓥ*Ca' d'Oro.*

$$$–$$$$

🏠 **Hotel Antico Doge.** Once the home of Doge Marino Falier, this palazzo has been modernized in an elegant Venetian style, with a wealth of textiles and some fine original furnishings. Some rooms have *baldacchini* (canopied beds) and views; all have fabric walls and hardwood floors. The location, on the main thoroughfare from the station to San Marco, is handy but can stay quite lively well into the night, especially during festivals. An ample buffet breakfast is served in a room with a frescoed ceiling and a Murano chandelier. **Pro:** Convenient to the Rialto. **Cons:** On a busy street, no outdoor garden or terrace. ⊠*Campo SS. Apostoli, Cannaregio 5643, 30131* ☎*041/2411570* ⊕*www.anticodoge.com* ⌐*8 standard, 2 superior, 9 junior suites, 1 suite* ⌂*In-room: safe, dial-up, Wi-Fi. In-hotel: room service, bar, no elevator, concierge, laundry service, public Internet, public Wi-Fi* ⊟*MC, V* ⦿*BP* Ⓥ*Ca' d'Oro/Rialto.*

$$–$$$$

🏠 **Ca' Gottardi.** Ca' Gottardi is part of a new generation of small hotels that refresh traditional Venetian style with contemporary design. The clean white-marble entrance leading up to the luminous piano nobile (main floor) of the 15th-century palace gracefully contrasts the opulent Murano chandeliers and rich wall brocades in the guest rooms. Some rooms have canal views, bathrooms are large and modern, and a rich breakfast is served in a bright salon that overlooks a wide canal. Location, just off the Grand Canal near the Ca' d'Oro and a variety of good eateries, is another plus. Do confirm the type of room (suite or standard, with or without a view) and its location (in the annex or the main hotel) when booking. **Pros:** Location, mix of old and new styles, canal views. **Con:** No outdoor garden or terrace. ⊠*Strada Nova, Cannaregio 2283, 30121* ☎*041/2759333* ⊕*www.cagottardi.com* ⚲*14 rooms, 2 junior suites, 3 suites, 9 annex rooms* ⌂*In-room: safe, refrigerator, dial-up. In-hotel: bar, no elevator, concierge, public Wi-Fi* ⊟*DC, MC, V* ⌾*BP* ▼*Ca' d'Oro.*

$$$ ⬚ **Hotel ai Mori d'Oriente.** The theme here, reflected in the decor, is Venice's connection with the exotic East. Some rooms and suites overlook the expansive canal along the Fondamenta della Sensa, one of the bright, broad byways typical of the upper Cannaregio district. In good weather, you can also take breakfast or a Venetian Spritz cocktail at a sunny table along the canal. Though the atmosphere hearkens back to Venice's past, facilities and amenities are everything you'd expect from a 21st-century establishment, and the staff is accommodating. Ask about the type and location of room you're reserving when booking. **Pros:** Modern construction, nice for families, large number of rooms makes it a good last-minute option. **Con:** Some might consider the hotel remote from the Piazza. ⊠*Fondamenta della Sensa, Cannaregio 3319, 30131* ☎*041/711001* ⊕*www.morihotel.com* ⚲*58 rooms, 2 suites* ⌂*In-room: safe, refrigerator, DVD, dial-up. In-hotel: room service, bar, concierge, laundry facilities, laundry service, public Internet, some pets allowed* ⊟*AE, DC, MC, V* ⌾*BP* ▼*San Marcuola/Madonna dell'Orto.*

$$$ ⬚ **Hotel Giorgione.** Family owned and operated, this quietly elegant hotel charms guests with its original terrazzo flooring, gracious courtyard and marble fountain, and billiard salon. The staff is professional and helpful, and the location is convenient for exploring in any direction. Rooms are decorated with traditional Venetian fabric and furniture, are comfortably appointed, and have either rooftop or courtyard views. Room sizes vary considerably, so book early and ask about the size and view if this is important. Seasonal refreshments are offered each afternoon. **Pros:** Family run, unique ambience, elegant garden. **Con:** No canal views. ⊠*Off Campo Santi Apostoli, Cannaregio 4587, 30131* ☎*041/5225810* ⊕*www.hotelgiorgione.com* ⚲*76 rooms* ⌂*In-room: safe, refrigerator, dial-up. In-hotel: bar, concierge, laundry service, public Internet* ⊟*AE, DC, MC, V* ⌾*BP* ▼*Ca' d'Oro/Fondamente Nuove.*

$-$$$ ⬚ **Locanda le Vele.** Gracious yet understated Venetian decor, original open-beam ceilings, spotless marble baths, and friendly, attentive service are the hallmarks of this intimate, family-owned locanda. The rooms overlooking the canals are the best in terms of size as well as view. A tasty breakfast is served in your room. The location is tranquil, but still handy to the Ca' d'Oro stop, the traghetto across to the Rialto Market, and the San Marco area. Spring for the airy suite if it's available. **Pros:** Standout service, canal views from some rooms. **Con:** Not for modern-decor lovers. ⊠*Calle delle Vele, Cannaregio 3969, 30126* ☎*041/2413960* ⊕*www.locandalevele.com* ⚲*6 rooms, 1 junior suite, 1 suite, 1 apartment* ⌂*In-room: safe, refrigerator, ethernet, dial-up,*

Wi-Fi. *In-hotel: no elevator, laundry facilities, public Wi-Fi* ⊟AE, DC, MC, V ⍟⏀BP V *Ca' d'Oro.*

★ $$ 3749 Ponte Chiodo. This cheery, homey bed-and-breakfast takes its name from the bridge leading to its entrance (one of the only two left in the lagoon without hand railings). Attentively appointed rooms with geranium-filled window boxes overlook either the bridge and expansive canals below or the spacious enclosed garden. It's a family-owned operation, and service is accommodating and friendly; you'll get lots of suggestions for dining and sightseeing. The private garden and patio are perfect for a relaxing breakfast or scribbling postcards or e-mails to the folks back home. Some bathrooms are smallish, but overall it's an excellent value. The location is also handy to the Ca' d'Oro vaporetto. **Pros:** Highly attentive service; warm, relaxed atmosphere; canal views. **Con:** No elevator will be a problem for some. ⊠ *Calle Racchetta, Cannaregio 3749, 30121* ☎ *041/2413935* ⊕ *www.pontechiodo.it* ⇆ *6 rooms* ⌂ *In-room: no phone, safe, refrigerator, Wi-Fi. In-hotel: room service, bar, private kitchen for guest use, no elevator, public Internet, public Wi-Fi* ⊟MC, V ⍟⏀BP V *Ca' d'Oro.*

$ Ca' San Marcuola. Tucked in a busy area of shops, trattorias, and wine bars frequented by Venetians and tourists alike, this family-owned hotel stands out for its relaxed and familiar atmosphere. The comfortable rooms are furnished in delicate pastel colors and full of light; spacious bathrooms are a plus. An elevator that provides access to all floors and a convenient location close to a water-bus stop on the Grand Canal make this a good choice if you have limited mobility. ⊠ *Campo San Marcuola, Cannaregio 1763, 30121* ☎ *041/716048* 🖷 *041/2759217* ⊕ *www.casanmarcuola.com* ⇆ *12 rooms* ⌂ *In-room: safe, refrigerator, dial-up. In-hotel: bar, concierge, room service, public Internet* ⊟AE, MC, V ⊗ *Closed 4 wks in Dec.–Jan.* ⍟⏀BP V *San Marcuola.*

CASTELLO

$$$$ Hotel Londra Palace. A wall of windows makes this the hotel of choice for soaking up extraordinary, sweeping views of the lagoon and the island of San Giorgio. The downstairs restaurant is all glass, light, and water views, and the superior rooms and junior suites offer the same spectacle. The vista must have been pleasing to Tchaikovsky, who wrote his 4th Symphony here in 1877. Neoclassical public rooms, with splashes of blue-and-green glass suggesting the sea, play nicely off guest rooms, which have fine fabric, damask drapes, Biedermeier furniture, and Venetian glass. The staff is top-notch, as are the restaurant and the bar. **Pros:** Superlative views, professional service. **Con:** The Riva's liveliness extends late into the evening. ⊠ *Riva degli Schiavoni, Castello 4171, 30122* ☎ *041/5200533* ⊕ *www.hotelondra.it* ⇆ *36 standard and deluxe rooms, 17 suites* ⌂ *In-room: safe, refrigerator, dial-up, Wi-Fi. In-hotel: restaurant, room service, bars, concierge, laundry service, public Internet, public Wi-Fi* ⊟AE, DC, MC, V ⍟⏀BP V *San Zaccaria.*

★ $$$$ Metropole. Eccentrics, eclectics, and fans of Antonio Vivaldi (who taught music here) love the Metropole, a labyrinth of intimate, opulent spaces featuring exotic Eastern influences and jammed with cabinets displaying collections of ivory-adorned cigarette cases, antique corkscrews, beaded bags, and more. The owner, a lifelong collector of odd objects, fills common areas and the sumptuously appointed guest rooms with endless antiques. The best rooms are up on the roof, where there are also two spacious rooftop terraces. Only six of the standard double rooms offer lagoon views. Suites feature sparkling mosaic sunken baths, Fortuny fabrics, and other notable architectural details that commingle to create a unique atmosphere highlighting colorful aspects of Venice's exotic past. **Pro:** Owner has exquisite taste and collections. **Con:** The Riva is one of the most densely touristy spots in the city. ⊠ *Riva degli Schiavoni, Castello 4149, 30122* ☏*041/5205044* ⊕*www.hotelmetropole.com* ⤳*67 rooms, 13 junior suites, 5 suites, 4 exclusive suites* ⚭*In-room: safe, refrigerator, dial-up. In-hotel: restaurant, room service, bar, concierge, laundry service, public Wi-Fi, some pets allowed* ⊟*AE, DC, MC, V* ⏐⊙⏐*BP* Ⓥ*San Zaccaria.*

$$$$ 🏨 **Palazzo Contarini della Porta di Ferro.** Formerly the residence of the Contarini family, one of Venice's most powerful families, this late-14th-century palace has been a hotel since 2001. The building's aristocratic past shows in the elegant inner courtyard with a majestic marble staircase. All uniquely furnished, the spacious, light-filled rooms have high wood-beam ceilings and Venetian terrazzo or wood flooring; apartments have kitchens, dining rooms, and open mezzanines. The large Torcello Suite also has a wooden roof terrace from which you can take in a spectacular view of the city. In sunny weather breakfast is served in the small garden. Private dinners, meetings, and small conferences are sometimes held in a large, well-appointed hall overlooking the garden. **Pros:** Spacious, residential neighborhood, good for longer stays. **Con:** May be a bit remote for some. ⊠ *Salizzada San Giustina, Castello 2926, 30122* ☏*041/2770991* ⊕*www.palazzocontarini.com* ⤳*6 rooms, 11 apartments* ⚭*In-room: safe, kitchen (some), refrigerator, dial-up. In-hotel: room service, concierge, laundry service, some pets allowed* ⊟*AE, MC, V* ⏐⊙⏐*BP* Ⓥ*Celestia/San Zaccaria.*

$$$–$$$$ 🏨 **Ca' Formenta.** This simple 15th-century building underwent a complete makeover before opening as a hotel in 2003. Located in residential rather than tourist Venice, Ca' Formenta offers high-quality services and a canal-side entrance for guests arriving by water taxi; front rooms have a wonderful view of the lagoon. The 15-minute stroll along the waterfront between Piazzo San Marco and this friendly gem of a hotel is through a genuinely "local" part of the city, with plenty of cafés and restaurants. One of the rear rooms has direct access to a pleasant rooftop terrace with tables. **Pros:** Castello area still feels like authentic Venice; convenient to the Piazza, the Lido, and the north Lagoon islands. **Con:** Not as convenient to San Polo or upper Dorsoduro. ⊠ *Via Garibaldi, Castello 1650, 30122* ☏*041/5285494* ⊕*www.hotelcaformenta.it* ⤳*12 rooms, 2 junior suites* ⚭*In-room: safe, refrigerator, dial-up. In-hotel: room service, bar, concierge, laundry service, public Wi-Fi, some pets allowed* ⊟*AE, DC, MC, V* ⏐⊙⏐*BP* Ⓥ*Arsenale/Giardini.*

$$ 🏨 **Santa Maria della Pietà.** Though this *casa per ferie* (vacation house) is more spartan than sumptuous, there's more light and space here than in many of Venice's four-star hotels. The hotel, which occupies the upper floors of two historic palaces, opened 10 years ago; it has big windows, restored Venetian terrazzo floors, and a huge rooftop terrace with a coffee shop, bar, and unobstructed lagoon views. On top of these advantages, it's well situated—just 100 yards from the main waterfront and about a 10-minute walk from St. Mark's—which means you'll have to book early to stay here. The shared bathrooms are plentiful, spacious, and scrupulously clean. Some rooms have been remodeled to include en-suite baths, and family rooms with up to six beds are available. **Pro:** Space, light, and views at a bargain price. **Con:** Not luxurious. ✉ *Calle della Pietà, Castello 3701, 30122* 📠 *041/2443639* ⊕ *www.pietavenezia.org/casaferie.htm* 🛏 *15 rooms* ☐ *In-room: no phone, no TV. In-hotel: bar* ☐ *No credit cards* ⑩ *BP* Ⓥ *Arsenale/San Zaccaria.*

DORSODURO

★ $$$$ 🏨 **Ca' Maria Adele.** Venice's most elegant small hotel is an updated mix of classic style—terrazzo floors, dramatic Murano chandeliers, antique furnishings—and touches of the contemporary, found in the African-wood reception area and breakfast room. Five dramatic "concept rooms" take on themes from Venetian history; the Doge's Room is draped in deep red brocades, while the Oriental Room is inspired by the travels of Marco Polo. Ca' Maria Adele's location is a tranquil yet convenient spot near the church of Santa Maria della Salute. **Pros:** Quiet and romantic; imaginative, contemporary furnishings and decor. **Con:** More formal atmosphere may not be ideal for those with young children. ✉ *Campo Santa Maria della Salute, Dorsoduro 111, 30123* 📠 *041/5203078* ⊕ *www.camariaadele.it* 🛏 *12 rooms, 4 suites* ☐ *In-room: safe, refrigerator, Wi-Fi. In-hotel: room service, bar, concierge, laundry service, some pets allowed* ☐ *AE, DC, MC, V* ⑩ *BP* Ⓥ *Salute.*

★ $$$$ 🏨 **Charming House DD 724.** This ultramodern boutique hotel abandons all things traditionally Venetian, opting instead to create the air of a stylish residence. With impeccable, minimalist decor, Charming House has a contemporary, warmly romantic, and occasionally even dramatic atmosphere. Some rooms overlook small canals and side calli; apartment options with kitchenettes are available for families or small groups. The location is convenient to the Guggenheim, Accademia, Zattere, and San Marco. There are also art exhibits borrowed from neighboring museums on display in common areas. See their Web site for additional locations and apartments with similar ambience located in Castello. **Pros:** Unique decor, variety of lodging options. **Con:** Not for those who prefer more traditional Venetian style. ✉ *Ramo da Mula off Campo San Vio, Dorsoduro 724, 30163* 📠 *041/2770262* ⊕ *www.thecharminghouse.com* 🛏 *5 rooms, 2 junior suites, 2 suites* ☐ *In-room: safe, refrigerator (some), Wi-Fi. In-hotel: room service, concierge, laundry service, public Internet, public Wi-Fi, some pets allowed* ☐ *AE, DC, MC, V* ⑩ *BP* Ⓥ *Accademia.*

$$$$ 🏨 **Hotel American–Dinesen.** This quiet, family-run hotel has a yellow
FodorśChoice stucco facade typical of Venetian houses. A hall decorated with repro-
★ duction antiques and Oriental rugs leads to a breakfast room reminis-

cent of a theater foyer, with red velvet chairs and gilt wall lamps. Guest rooms are spacious and tastefully furnished in sage-green and delicate pink fabrics with lacquered Venetian-style furniture throughout. Some front rooms have terraces with canal views. A water taxi can deposit you directly in front of the hotel on arrival, and although the four-story building has no elevator, you'll have assistance with your luggage if needed. The exceptional service will help you feel at home at the hotel and in Venice. **Pros:** High degree of personal service; located on a quiet, exceptionally picturesque canal. **Con:** Lack of elevator will be a problem for some. ⊠*San Vio, Dorsoduro 628, 30123* ☎*041/5204733* ⊕*www.hotelamerican.com* ◁*28 rooms, 2 suites* ⌂*In-room: safe, refrigerator, Wi-Fi. In-hotel: room service, bar, no elevator, concierge, laundry service, public Wi-Fi, some pets allowed* ▭*AE, MC, V* ⧖*BP* Ⓥ*Accademia/Salute.*

★ **$$–$$$$**   ▦ **La Calcina.** In 1877, Stones of Venice author John Ruskin lodged at the eclectic La Calcina, which sits in an enviable position along the sunny Zattere, and has front rooms offering heady vistas across the expansive Giudecca Canal. You can sunbathe on the *altana* (wooden roof terrace) or enjoy an afternoon tea in one of the lounge's reading corners with flickering candlelight and barely perceptible classical music. A stone staircase leads to the rooms upstairs, which have parquet floors, original art deco furniture, and firm beds. Besides full meals at lunch and dinner, the Piscina bar and restaurant offers drinks and fresh snacks all day in the elegant dining room or on the waterside terrace. A variety of apartments are also available. One single room does not have a private bath. **Pros:** A historic and perennial favorite, rare rooftop altana, panoramic views from some rooms. **Cons:** Not for travelers who want for contemporary surroundings, no elevator. ⊠*Zattere, Dorsoduro 780, 30123* ☎*041/5206466* ⊕*www.lacalcina.com* ◁*27 rooms, 5 suites* ⌂*In-room: safe, refrigerator, dial-up, Wi-Fi. In-hotel: restaurant, room service, bar, no elevator, concierge, laundry service, public Wi-Fi* ▭*AE, DC, MC, V* ⧖*BP* Ⓥ*Zattere.*

$$–$$$$ ▦ **Pensione Accademia Villa Maravege.** Aptly nicknamed "Villa of the
Fodor's Choice   Wonders," this patrician retreat once served as the Russian embassy
★   and was the fictional residence of Katharine Hepburn's character in the film *Summertime*. Outside, a secret garden awaits just beyond an iron gate, complete with a mini Palladian-style villa, flower beds, stone cupids, and verdant trees—all rarities in Venice. The hotel is located on a peaceful promontory where two side canals converge with the Grand Canal. The conservative rooms are outfitted with Venetian-style antiques and fine tapestry. Book well in advance. **Pro:** A historic, classic Venetian property. **Con:** Formal surroundings with lots of antiques are not well suited to families with young children. ⊠*Fondamenta Bollani, Dorsoduro 1058, 30123* ☎*041/5210188* ⊕*www.pensioneaccademia.it* ◁*27 rooms, 2 suites* ⌂*In-room: safe, dial-up. In-hotel: bar, no elevator, concierge, laundry service* ▭*AE, DC, MC, V* ⧖*BP* Ⓥ*Accademia.*

★ **$$$**   ▦ **Locanda San Barnaba.** In contrast to the recent onslaught of international chain hotels, the Locanda San Barnaba, housed in a 16th-century palazzo, is a welcome, family-run find. It's handy, too, just off the Ca'

Rezzonico vaporetto stop, and you'll cross no bridges to reach it. The arches in the garden walls peek through to the side canal and there's a rooftop terrace for soaking up Venetian sunsets. There's no elevator, but there are some ground floor rooms available and the staff will happily assist with your luggage. The two superior rooms have original 18th-century frescoes, and one of the junior suites has two small balconies and is exceptionally luminous, but all the rooms are spacious and attractive. There's a water entrance for taxi arrival. **Pros:** Outdoor space, a variety of room options, excellent value. **Con:** Lack of elevator will be a drawback for some. ⊠ *Calle del Traghetto Dorsoduro 2785–2786 30125* ☎ *041/2411233* ⊕ *www.locanda-sanbarnaba.com* ⇆ *1 single, 8 double, 2 superior, 2 junior suites* ₫ *In-room: safe, dial-up. In-hotel: room service, bar, no elevator, concierge* ⊟ *AE, DC, MC, V* ⦿ *BP* Ⓥ *Ca' Rezzonico.*

$$ 🖼 **Casa Rezzonico.** Rooms here are the rarest site in Venice: good value. A bright canal graces the hotel entrance, and a private garden (where breakfast is served in temperate weather) makes the inner courtyard particularly inviting. Rooms vary in size but are pleasant and comfortable, and overlook either the garden or the canal. Young owners Matteo and Mattia are attentive and helpful, and the location is convenient for exploring the sights from the Rialto to the Salute, hopping the vaporetto at Ca' Rezzonico for any San Marco location. The hotel is easily reachable on foot from Piazzale Roma as well, for coming and going by car. **Pros:** A garden for relaxing, canal views at a reasonable rate, convenient to many locations, great for families. **Con:** The six rooms fill up early, especially on weekends. ⊠ *Fondamenta Gherardini, Dorsoduro 2813, 30123* ☎ *041/2770653* ⊕ *www.casarezzonico.it* ⇆ *6 rooms, from single to quad* ₫ *In-room: safe, dial-up. In-hotel: room service, no elevator* ⊟ *AE, MC, V, cash preferred* ⦿ *BP* Ⓥ *Ca' Rezzonico.*

GIUDECCA

$$$$ 🖼 **Cipriani.** It's impossible to feel stressed in this oasis of stunning rooms and suites, some with garden patios. The hotel launch whisks you to Giudecca from San Marco and back at any hour; those opting for a cocktail at the patio bar before dinner can use it as well. Rooms of extraordinary luxury are available both in the main building and in the adjoining 16th-century-style annexes, Palazzo Vendramin and Palazzetto, which offer views across to Piazza San Marco. Prices are high even by Venetian standards, but this is the only place in town with such extensive facilities and services, from an Olympic-size pool and tennis courts to cooking courses, a beauty-and-wellness center, fitness programs, and even a vineyard. **Pros:** Many amenities, private getaway feeling. **Con:** Even with the hotel taxi, coming and going can be somewhat inconvenient. ⊠ *Giudecca 10, 30133* ☎ *041/5207744* ⊕ *www.hotelcipriani.it* ⇆ *46 rooms, 58 suites* ₫ *In-room: safe, refrigerator, Wi-Fi. In-hotel: 4 restaurants, room service, bar, tennis courts, pool, gym, spa, concierge, laundry service, public Wi-Fi* ⊟ *AE, DC, MC, V* ⊗ *Main hotel closed Nov.–Mar.; Palazzo Vendramin and Palazzetto closed 4 wks in Jan. and Feb.* ⦿ *BP* Ⓥ *Zitelle.*

LAGOON

$$$$ ⌂ **San Clemente Palace.** If you prefer wide-open spaces to the intimacy of Venice, this is your hotel. This massive complex occupies an entire island, about 15 minutes from Piazza San Marco by (free) shuttle launch, with acres of parkland, a swimming pool, tennis courts, a wellness center, and four restaurants. The 19th-century buildings are on the site of a 12th-century monastery, of which only the chapel remains. They form a large quadrangle and contain spacious, modern rooms. The view back to Venice with the Dolomites behind on a clear day is stunning. This hotel, open since 2003, offers all the five-star comforts: it even has three holes of golf. **Pro:** True five-star service and amenities. **Con:** Quite remote. ⊠ *Isola di San Clemente 1, 30124* ☏ *041/2445001* ⊕ *www.sanclemente.thi.it* ⇆ *107 rooms, 96 suites* ⌂ *In-room: safe, refrigerator, ethernet, dial-up. In-hotel: 4 restaurants, bar, golf course, tennis courts, pool, gym, spa, laundry service, public Wi-Fi, some pets allowed* ☰ *AE, DC, MC, V* ⍩ *BP.*

SAN MARCO

★ $$$$ ⌂ **Bauer Il Palazzo.** Il Palazzo, under the same management as the larger Bauer Hotel, is the ultimate word in luxury. Tufted Bevilacqua and Rubelli fabrics cover the walls, and no two rooms are decorated the same. What they have in common, however, are high ceilings, Murano glass, marble bathrooms, and damask drapes. Many have sweeping views. Breakfast is served on Venice's highest rooftop terrace, appropriately named Il Settimo Cielo (Seventh Heaven). The outdoor hot tub, also on the seventh floor, offers views of La Serenissima that will leave you breathless, and personable, professional staff will accommodate your every whim. **Pro:** Il Palazzo will pamper you while making you feel right at home. **Con:** Located in one of the busiest areas of the city. ⊠ *Campo San Moisè, San Marco 1413/d, 30124* ☏ *041/5207022* ⊕ *www.ilpalazzovenezia.com* ⇆ *44 rooms, 38 suites* ⌂ *In-room: safe, refrigerator, DVD, Wi-Fi. In-hotel: restaurant, room service, bars, gym, concierge, laundry service, public Internet, public Wi-Fi, some pets allowed* ☰ *AE, DC, MC, V* ⍩ *EP* ▼ *San Marco/Vallaresso.*

★ $$$$ ⌂ **Locanda Orseolo.** This cozy, elegant hotel offers a welcome respite from the throngs churning around Piazza San Marco. Family owned, it has an attentive staff and comfortable, well-appointed rooms. Classic Venetian designs are given a Carnevale theme, with each room's decor dedicated to one of the traditional masks. The relaxed atmosphere pervades at breakfast, where it's common to get engrossed in conversation with the other guests. **Pros:** Intimate and romantic, extraordinarily friendly staff. **Con:** Located in the one of the busiest and most commercial areas of the city. ⊠ *Corte Zorzi off Campo San Gallo, San Marco 1083, 30124* ☏ *041/5204827* ⊕ *www.locandaorseolo.com* ⇆ *12 rooms* ⌂ *In-room: safe, refrigerator, Wi-Fi. In-hotel: room service, concierge, laundry facilities, laundry service, public Internet, public Wi-Fi* ☰ *AE, DC, MC, V* ⊗ *Closed Jan.* ⍩ *BP* ▼ *Rialto/Vallaresso.*

$$$$ ⌂ **Novecento.** This small, family-run hotel is nestled away on a quiet street just a 10-minute walk from the Piazza San Marco. Inspired by the style of Mariano Fortuny, the early-1900s Spanish artist and fashion designer who made Venice his home, the intimate rooms are a surprisingly elegant mélange of multiethnic and exotic furnishings. The Mediterranean, Indian, and Venetian fabrics, silverware, chandeliers, and furniture create a sensual turn-of-the-20th-century atmosphere. In fine weather, breakfast is served in the inner courtyard. **Pro:** Intimate atmosphere and unusual decor make this a particularly romantic nest. **Con:** A bit of a walk from the Piazza. ⊠*Calle del Dose, Campo San Maurizio, San Marco 2683/84, 30124* ☎*041/2413765* ⊕*www.novecento.biz* ⤙*9 rooms* ♿*In-room: safe, refrigerator, dial-up, Wi-Fi. In-hotel: bar, laundry service, public Internet, public Wi-Fi, some pets allowed* ▤*AE, DC, MC, V* �‖*BP* ▼*Santa Maria del Giglio.*

★ **$$$$** 🏨 **Palazzo Sant'Angelo sul Canal Grande.** There's a distinguished yet comfortable feel to this elegant palazzo, which is large enough to deliver expected facilities and services, but small enough to pamper its guests. Rooms have tapestry-adorned walls and Carrara and Alpine marble in the bath; those facing the Grand Canal have balconies that practically bring the Canal to you. Common areas include an entrance hall with original Palladian flooring, a bright front lounge, and an intimate bar that puts the Canal almost at arm's length. Ask ahead for a room with a view if it's important. **Pro:** Nearby Sant'Angelo vaporetto stop is convenient for visiting the city. **Con:** Some rooms have no particular view. ⊠*Campo Sant'Angelo, San Marco 3488, 30124* ☎*041/2411452* ⊕*www.palazzosantangelo.com* ⤙*14 rooms* ♿*In-room: safe, refrigerator, ethernet. In-hotel: room service (limited), bar, concierge, laundry service, some pets allowed* ▤*AE, DC, MC, V* �‖*EP* ▼*Sant'Angelo.*

$$$ 🏨 **Al Teatro.** Nestled behind the Fenice Theater, just off the Maria Callas bridge, this small B&B is the renovated home of owners Fabio and Eleonora—in fact, it's where Eleonora was born. There are three spacious, comfortable, and conscientiously-appointed rooms with private baths, each overlooking a gondola-filled canal; the largest room has a broad balcony. An ample breakfast (served at a common table) and exceptional service make Al Teatro an excellent value and a relaxing choice in the sometimes-frenetic San Marco atmosphere. Book well in advance, especially for weekend stays. **Pros:** Airy rooms, convenient San Marco location, nice for families. **Con:** The intimacy of a three-room B&B is not for everyone. ⊠*Fondamenta della Fenice, San Marco 2554, 30124* ☎*041/5204271* ⊕*www.bedandbreakfastalteatro.com* ⤙*3 rooms* ♿*In-room: safe, refrigerator, Wi-Fi. In-hotel: room service, no elevator, public Internet, public Wi-Fi* ▤*AE, MC, V* �‖*BP* ▼*Santa Maria del Giglio.*

$$ 🏨 **Ca' dei Dogi.** In the crush of hotels in and around Piazza San Marco, there are many undesirables, since the location alone attracts lodgers. This delightful gem, eked out of a 15th-century palace and located in a quiet courtyard secluded from the melee, is one notable exception. The thoughtful, personal touches added by owners Stefano and Susanna are evident everywhere, from the six individually decorated rooms (some with private terraces), to the carefully chosen contemporary furniture, to classic Venetian elements such as wall tapestries and mosaic tiles. There's highly personal service; guests are often welcomed by one of the owners. There's a courtyard where you can enjoy breakfast or an evening interlude, and one attic apartment is available. **Pro:** Terraces, with views of the Doge's Palace, are a definite plus. **Con:** Rooms are not expansive. ⊠ *Corte Santa Scolastica, Castello 4242, 30122* ☎ *041/2413751* ⊕ *www.cadeidogi.it* ↩ *6 rooms* ⌂ *In-room: safe, dial-up. In-hotel: room service, no elevator, public Internet, public Wi-Fi, some pets allowed* ▤ *AE, DC, MC, V* ¶◎∣ *BP* ▼ *San Zaccaria.*

SAN POLO

★ $$$–$$$$ 🏠 **Oltre il Giardino—Casaifrari.** It's easy to overlook (and can be a challenge to find) this secluded palazzo, sheltered behind a brick wall not far from the Frari church. Especially in high season, the six-room hotel with a pleasant, expansive garden is an oasis of peace. The prevalent white-and-pastel color scheme and elegant, understated decor contribute to the relaxed environment. The house was once the residence of Alma Mahler, widow of composer Gustav Mahler and a fascinating woman in her own right; it still conveys her style and charm today. Service and professional attention is as conscientious as the renovation. **Pro:** A peaceful, gracious setting. **Con:** No Grand Canal views. ⊠ *San Polo 2542, 30125* ☎ *041/2750015* ⊕ *www.oltreilgiardino-venezia.com* ↩ *4 rooms, 2 suites* ⌂ *In-room: safe, refrigerator, dial-up, Wi-Fi. In-hotel: room service, bar, no elevator, public Internet, some pets allowed* ▤ *AE, DC, MC, V* ¶◎∣ *BP* ▼ *San Tomà.*

$$–$$$$ 🏠 **Ca' Angeli.** The heirs of a Venetian architect have transformed his former residence, located on the third and top floors of a palace along the Grand Canal, into an elegant B&B. It retains the classic style of its former owner—most of the furniture was his, including an 18th-century briarwood bureau, an original icon, as well as 18th- and 19th-century art. The five rooms and two suites have views of either the Grand Canal or a side canal—or in the case of the smallish Room 6, rooftops from a terrace twice the size of the room. A rich breakfast, including select cheeses and meats from local producers, is served in a salon overlooking the Grand Canal. There's also an attic apartment option for groups or small families. **Pros:** Historic residence with Grand Canal views, helpful staff. **Con:** A bit of a walk from the vaporetto stop to the hotel. ⊠ *Calle del Traghetto della Madoneta, San Polo 1434, 30125* ☎ *041/5232480* ⊕ *www.caangeli.it* ↩ *5 rooms, 1 junior suite, 1 suite* ⌂ *In-room: safe, refrigerator, Wi-Fi. In-hotel: public Wi-Fi* ▤ *No credit cards* ¶◎∣ *BP* ▼ *San Silvestro.*

$$$ 🏠 **Corte 1321.** If you're looking for something more up-to-date than the 18th-century-style decor that predominates in Venetian hotels, try Corte 1321, which is nestled away off the main drag. It has friendly, personal service; spacious, carefully-renovated rooms with sparkling baths and "ethnic-chic" decor; and an intimate garden. Unwind here after a long day of exploring, perhaps sharing discoveries of the day with other guests or using the public Wi-Fi to catch up on e-mails. Corte 1321's owner is an American of Italian decent. **Pro:** Lively, eclectic atmosphere great for meeting other guests. **Con:** No canal views. ⊠ *Campiello Ca' Bernardi, San Polo 1321, 30125* ☎ *041/5224923* ⊕ *www.corte1321.com* ↩ *4 rooms, 1 mini-flat* ⌂ *In-room: safe, eth-*

ernet, Wi-Fi. In-hotel: bar, no elevator, laundry service, public Internet, public Wi-Fi ▭*MC, V* ✆*Closed Jan.* ⟋○⟍*BP* Ⅴ*San Silvestro.*

$$ ▦ **Acca Hotel.** This small hotel is one of Venice's better moderately priced options, with bright, well-appointed rooms and simple but attentive service. There's no staff on hand in the evening, but you get your own key. The location is good, and breakfast is served in the courtyard, weather permitting. **Pros:** Lots of amenities, new construction, an excellent value. **Cons:** No canal views, no night porter. ✉*Calle Pezzana, San Polo 2160, 30124* ☎*041/2440126* ⊕*www. accahotel.com* ⟿*8 rooms, 1 suite* ♿*In-room: safe, refrigerator, Wi-Fi. In-hotel: no elevator, laundry service, public Internet, public Wi-Fi* ▭*MC, V* ⟋○⟍*BP* Ⅴ*San Silvestro.*

SANTA CROCE

★ $$$ ▦ **Hotel al Ponte Mocenigo.** A columned courtyard welcomes you to this elegant, charming palazzo, former home of the Santa Croce branch of the Mocenigo family (the same for which the nearby Museo is named, not to mention a few dogi). The meticulously renovated interior has an updated 18th-century Venetian feel, incorporating a number of distinctive architectural elements such as open-beam ceilings, fireplaces transformed into writing nooks, and Murano chandeliers. The courtyard offers an ideal ambience both for breakfast or to enjoy an aperitivo, and there's even a Turkish sauna that guests may take advantage of after a day of intensive sightseeing. The hotel is located on a side-canal and the delightful surrounding area is convenient to any number of popular sights, eateries, and shopping. **Pros:** Enchanting courtyard, water access, personable staff. **Con:** Rooms do not overlook a canal. ✉*Fondamento de Rimpeto a Ca' Mocenigo, Santa Croce 2063, 30135* ☎*041/5244797* ⊕*www.alpontemocenigo.com* ⟿*10 rooms, 1 junior suite* ♿*In-room: safe, refrigerator, Wi-Fi. In-hotel: room service, bar, public Internet, public Wi-Fi* ▭*AE, DC, MC, V* ⟋○⟍ Ⅴ*San Stae.*

NIGHTLIFE & THE ARTS

THE ARTS

A Guest in Venice, a monthly bilingual booklet free at most hotels, is your most accessible, up-to-date guide to Venice happenings. It also includes information about pharmacies, vaporetto and bus lines, and the main trains and flights. You can visit their Web site, ⊕*www.aguestinvenice.com,* for a preview of musical, artistic, and sporting events. *Venezia News,* available at newsstands, has similar information but also includes in-depth articles about noteworthy events. The tourist office publishes *Leo* and *Bussola,* bimonthly brochures in Italian and English listing events and updated museum hours. *Venezia da Vivere* is a seasonal guide listing nightspots and live music. Several Venice Web sites allow you to scan the cultural horizon before you arrive; try ⊕*www. ombra.net* (which has a fantastic map function to find any address in Venice), ⊕*www.veniceonline.it,* and ⊕*www.venicebanana.com.* Last but not least, don't ignore the posters you see everywhere in the streets. They're often the most up-to-date information you can find.

CARNEVALE

The first historical evidence of Carnevale (Carnival) in Venice dates from 1097, and for centuries the city marked the days preceding *quaresima* (Lent, the 40 days of abstinence leading up to Palm Sunday) with abundant feasting and wild celebrations. The word *carnivale* is derived from the words for meat (*carne*) and to remove (*levare*), as eating meat was prohibited during Lent. Venice earned its international reputation as the "city of Carnevale" in the 18th century, when partying would begin right after Epiphany (January 6) and the city seemed to be one continuous decadent masquerade. With the republic's fall in 1797, the city lost a great deal of its vitality, and the tradition of Carnevale celebrations was abandoned.

Carnevale was revived in the 1970s when residents began taking to the calli and campi in their own impromptu celebrations. It didn't take long for the tourist industry to embrace the revival as a means to stimulate business during low season. The efforts were successful. Each year over the 10- to 12-day Carnevale period (ending on the Tuesday before Ash Wednesday) more than a half million people attend concerts, theater and street performances, masquerade balls, historical processions, fashion shows, and contests. *A Guest in Venice* (⊕*www.aguestinvenice. com*) gives free advertising to public and private event festivities and is therefore one of the most complete Carnevale guides. For general Carnevale information, contact **Consorzio Comitato per il Carnevale di Venezia** (⊠*Santa Croce 1714, 30135* ☏*041/717065, 041/2510811 during Carnevale* 🖥*041/5200410* ⊕*www.carnevale.venezia.it*). The **Tourist Office** (☏*041/5298711*) has detailed information about daily events. If you're not planning on joining in the revelry, you'd be wise to choose another time to visit Venice. Enormous crowds clog the streets (which become one-way, with police directing foot traffic), bridges are designated "no-stopping" zones to avoid gridlock, and prices absolutely skyrocket.

FESTIVALS

The **Biennale** (⊕*www.labiennale.org*) cultural institution organizes events year-round, including the Venice Film Festival, which begins the last week of August. The Biennale international exhibition of contemporary art is held in odd-numbered years, usually from mid-June to early November, at the Giardini della Biennale, and in the impressive Arsenale. On the third weekend of July, the **Festa del Redentore** *(Feast of the Redeemer)* commemorates the end of a 16th-century plague that killed about 47,000 city residents. Just as doges have done annually for centuries, you, too, can make a pilgrimage across the temporary bridge connecting the Zattere to the Giudecca. Venetians take to the water to watch fireworks at midnight, but if you can't find a boat, the Giudecca is the best place to be. Young people traditionally greet sunrise on the Lido beach while their elders attend church.

MUSIC

Although there are occasional jazz and Italian pop concerts in clubs around town, the vast majority of music you'll hear is classical, with Venice's famed composer, Vivaldi, frequently featured. A number of churches and palazzi regularly host concerts, as do the Ca' Rezzonico and Querini-Stampalia museums. You'll find these events listed in publications such as *A Guest in Venice*; also try asking the tourist information office or your concierge. The **Vela Call Center** (☎*041/2424* ☉*Daily 8–8*) has information about musical events, and you can buy tickets at Vela sales offices in Piazzale Roma, Ferrovia, and Calle dei Fuseri (a 10-minute walk from San Marco). (When busy, the Vela Call Center number doesn't give a signal, but instead is silent.)

The travel agency **Kele & Teo** (✉*Ponte dei Bareteri, San Marco 4930* ☎*041/5208722*) has tickets for a number of venues and is conveniently located midway between Rialto and San Marco.

OPERA

Teatro La Fenice (✉*Campo San Fantin, San Marco* ☎*041/786511* ⊕*www.teatrolafenice.it*), one of Italy's oldest opera houses, has witnessed many memorable premieres, including the 1853 first-night flop of Verdi's *La Traviata*. It's also had its share of disasters, the most recent being a terrible fire, deliberately set in January 1996. It was completely and luxuriously restored, and reopened to great fanfare in 2004. Visit the Fenice Web site for a schedule of performances and to buy tickets.

NIGHTLIFE

Piazza San Marco is a popular meeting place in nice weather, when the cafés stay open late and all seem to be competing to offer the best live music. The younger crowd, Venetians and visitors alike, tends to gravitate toward the area around Rialto Bridge, with Campi San Bartolomeo and San Luca on one side and Campo Rialto Nuovo on the other. Especially popular with university students are the bars along Cannaregio's Fondamenta della Misericordia and around Campo Santa Margarita and San Pantalon. Pick up a booklet of *2Night* or visit their Web site ⊕*www.2night.it* for nightlife listings and reviews.

BARS

Bácaro Jazz (✉*Across from Rialto post office* ☎*041/5285249*) has music (not usually live) and meals until 2 AM, and its gregarious staff is unlikely to let you feel lonely. Nothing special by day, **Bar Torino** (✉*Campo San Lucaz* ☎*041/5223914*) is one of Venice's liveliest nightspots, open late and spilling out onto the campo in summer. **L'Olandese Volante** (✉*Campo San Lio near Rialto* ☎*041/5289349*) is a popular hangout for many young Venetians. The **Martini Scala Club** (✉*Campo San Fantin, San Marco 1983* ☎*041/5224121*), the Antico Martini restaurant's elegant bar, has live music from 10 PM to 3:30 AM. Full meals are served until 2 AM. One of the hippest bars for the late-night chill-out crowd, **Centrale** (✉*Piscina Frezzeria, San Marco 1659/B* ☎*041/2960664*) is in a former movie theater—and the crowd does look more Hollywood than Venice. Excellent mojitos and other mixed drinks, black-leather couches, and dim lighting strike a loungey note, and the DJ keeps the beats cool. Hidden in plain sight behind the plate-glass windows of a Mondadori bookstore, the simply named **Bacaro** (⊠ *Piscina Frezzeria, San Marco 1345* ☎ *041/2960687*) adds a much-needed dash of modern to the antiquities surrounding Piazza San Marco. The circular bar is more crowded and lively than the restaurant upstairs, and serves strong cocktails until 2 AM.

Campo Santa Margarita is a student hangout all day and late into the night. Try **Orange** (⊠ *Campo Santa Margarita, Dorsoduro 3054/a* ☎ *041/5234740*) for *piadine* sandwiches, drinks, and soccer games on a massive screen. Bohemian **Il Caffè** (⊠ *Campo Santa Margarita, Dorsoduro 2963* ☎ *041/5287998*), also known as Caffè Rosso for its red exterior, is especially popular in nice weather.

CASINOS

The city-run casino in the splendid **Palazzo Vendramin-Calergi** is a classic scene of well-dressed high-rollers playing French roulette, Caribbean poker, chemin de fer, 30–40, and slots. You must be 18 to enter, and men must wear jackets; no sneakers allowed. ⊠ *Cannaregio 2040* ☎ *041/5297111* 💳 *€10 entry includes €10 in chips* ⊙ *Slots: daily 2:45 PM–2:30 AM, tables: daily 3:30 PM–2:30 AM* Ⓥ *San Marcuola*.

Mestre's **Ca' Noghera** casino, near the airport, has slots, blackjack, craps, poker, and roulette. Minimum age is 18. A free shuttle bus runs from Piazzale Roma from 4:05 PM until closing. ⊠ *Via Triestina 222, Tessera Mestre* ☎ *041/5297111* 💳 *€10 entry includes €10 in chips* ⊙ *Slots: daily 11 AM–3:30 AM, tables: daily 3:30 PM–3:30 AM*.

SHOPPING

Updated by
Pamela Santini

Alluring shops abound in Venice. You'll find countless vendors of trademark Venetian wares such as glass and lace; the authenticity of some goods can be suspect, but they're often pleasing to the eye regardless of their place of origin. For more-sophisticated tastes (and deeper pockets), there are jewelers, antiques dealers, and high-fashion boutiques on a par with those in Italy's larger cities but often maintaining a uniquely Venetian flair. There are also some interesting craft and art studios, where you can find high-quality, one-of-a-kind articles, from handmade shoes to decorative lamps and mirrors.

It's always a good idea to mark on your map the location of a shop that interests you; otherwise you may not be able to find it again in the maze of tiny streets. Regular store hours are usually 9–12:30 and 3:30 or 4–7:30; some stores are closed Saturday afternoon or Monday morning. Food shops are open 8–1 and 5–7:30, and are closed Wednesday afternoon and all day Sunday. Many tourist-oriented shops are open all day, every day. Some shops close for both a summer and a winter vacation.

FOOD MARKETS

The morning open-air fruit-and-vegetable market at **Rialto** offers animated local color and commerce. On Tuesday through Saturday mornings the **fish market** (adjacent to the Rialto produce market) provides an impressive lesson in ichthyology, with species you've probably never seen before. In the Castello district you'll find a lively food market weekday mornings on **Via Garibaldi.**

SHOPPING DISTRICTS

The **San Marco** area is full of shops and couture boutiques such as Armani, Missoni, Valentino, Fendi, and Versace. **Le Mercerie,** along with the Frezzeria and Calle dei Fabbri, leading from Piazza San Marco, are some of Venice's busiest shopping streets. Other good shopping areas surround Calle del Teatro and Campi San Salvador, Manin, San Fantin, and San Bartolomeo. Less-expensive shops are between the Rialto Bridge and San Polo.

SPECIALTY STORES

GLASSWARE
Glass, most of it made in Murano, is Venice's number one product, and you'll be confronted by mind-boggling displays of traditional and contemporary glassware, much of it kitsch. Take your time and be selective. You will probably find that prices in Venice's shops and the showrooms of Murano's factories are pretty much the same. However, because of competition, shops in Venice with wares from various glassworks may charge slightly less.

Domus (⊠ *Fondamenta dei Vetrai, Murano 82* ☎ *041/739215*) has a selection of smaller objects and jewelry from the best glassworks.

For chic, contemporary glassware, Carlo Moretti is a good choice; his designs are on display at **L'Isola** (⊠ *Campo San Moisè, San Marco 1468* ☎ *041/5231973* ⊕ *www.carlomoretti.com*). **Marina Barovier** (⊠ *Calle delle Botteghe off Campo Santo Stefano, San Marco 3216* ☎ *041/5236748* ⊕ *www.barovier.it*) has an excellent selection of contemporary collectors' glass. Go to Michel Paciello's **Paropàmiso** (⊠ *Frezzeria, San Marco 1701* ☎ *041/5227120*) for stunning Venetian glass beads and traditional jewelry from all over the world. **Pauly** (⊠ *Piazza San Marco 73, 77, and 316; Ponte dei Consorzi* ☎ *041/5209899* ⊕ *www.paulyglassfactory.com*) has four centrally located shops with an impressive selection of glassware at better prices than for Murano. **Venini** (⊠ *Piazzetta dei Leoncini 314, San Marco* ☎ *041/5224045*

⊕*www.venini.com*) has been an institution since the 1930s, attracting some of the foremost names in glass design.

LACE & FABRICS

Much of the lace and embroidered linen sold in Venice and on Burano is really made in China or Taiwan. However, at **Il Merletto** (⊠*Sotoportego del Cavalletto under the Procuratie Vecchie, Piazza San Marco 95* ☎*041/5208406*), you can ask for the authentic, handmade lace kept in the drawers behind the counter. This is the only place in Venice connected with the students of the Scuola del Merletto in Burano, who, officially, do not sell to the public. Hours of operation are daily 10 to 5. A top address for linen is **Jesurum** (⊠*Cannaregio 3219, Fondamenta della Sensa* ☎*041/5242540* ⊕*www.jesurum.it*). Go to **Lorenzo Rubelli** (⊠*Palazzo Corner Spinelli, San Marco 3877* ☎*041/5236110* ⊕*www. rubelli.it*) for the same brocades, damasks, and cut velvets used by the world's most prestigious decorators. **Venetia Studium** (⊠*Calle Larga XXII Marzo, San Marco 2403* ☎*041/5229281* ⊠*Calle Larga XXII Marzo, San Marco 723* ☎*041/5229859* ⊕*www.venetiastudium.com*) sells silk scarves, bags, and cushion covers, as well as the famous Fortuny lamps.

MASKS

Guerrino Lovato, proprietor of **Mondonovo** (⊠*Rio Terà Canal, Dorsoduro 3063* ☎*041/5287344* ⊕*www.mondonovomaschere.it*) is one of the most respected mask makers in town. He was called on to oversee reconstruction of reliefs and sculptures in Teatro La Fenice after it burned to the ground in 1996.

The Venetian Arc

WORD OF MOUTH

"Verona and Vicenza are both stunningly beautiful cities that we liked very much. Vicenza is smaller and seems to have more green space. It's also less touristy. Verona gives you the 'Romeo and Juliet' thing. Although I personally did not find any one attraction in Verona that impressive, the city as a whole stole my heart."

–Jocelyn P

WELCOME TO THE VENETIAN ARC

Villa Barbaro, Maser

TOP REASONS TO GO

★ **Giotto's frescoes in the Capella degli Scrovegni:** In this Padua chapel, Giotto's expressive and innovative frescos foreshadowed the painting techniques of the Renaissance.

★ **Villa Barbaro in Maser:** Master architect Palladio's graceful creation meets Veronese's splendid paintings in a one-time-only collaboration.

★ **Opera in Verona's ancient arena:** The performances may not be top-notch, but even serious opera fans can't resist the almost campy spectacle of these shows.

★ **The scenery of Asolo:** Few places in Italy more perfectly exemplify the hillside country town than Asolo, once the stomping grounds of Robert Browning and Eleonora Duse.

★ **The wine roads north of Treviso:** A series of routes takes you through beautiful hillsides to some of Italy's finest wines.

Juliet's House, Verona

1 Padua. A city of both high-rises and history, Padua is most noted for Giotto's frescoes in the Capella degli Scrovegni, where Dante's contemporary painted with a human focus that foreshadowed the Renaissance.

2 Verona. Shakespeare placed Romeo, Juliet, and a couple of gentlemen in Verona, one of the oldest, best preserved, and most beautiful cities in Italy. Try to catch *Aida* at the gigantic Roman arena.

Arena, Verona

3 **Vicenza.** This elegant art city, nestled on the green plain reaching inland from Venice's lagoon, bears the signature of the great 16th-century architect Andrea Palladio, including several private palazzi and other important buildings.

4 **Treviso & the Hillside Towns.** Home to the mighty tiramisu, known to dessert lovers everywhere, Treviso is a busy town with a touch of Venetian style. Asolo (the City of a Hundred Horizons) is the most prominent in a series of charming towns that dot the wine-producing hills north of Treviso.

GETTING ORIENTED

The Venetian Arc is the sweep of land curving north and east from the Adige River to the Slovenian border. It's made up of two Italian regions—the Veneto and Friuli–Venezia Giulia— that were once controlled by Venice, and the culture is a mix of Venetian, Alpine, and central European sensibilities.

AUSTRIA

Tarvisio

Tolmezzo

52

A23 Gemona
O del Friuli

CARNIA

5

FRIULI-VENEZIA
GIULIA

Belluno

Udine

Cormóns

A27

Vittorio
Veneto

Pordenone

13

Gorizia

Conegliano

A28

A4

SLOVENIA

13

53

A4

14

Monfalcone

354

Treviso **4**

Lignano
Sabbiadoro

Grado

Trieste

Caorle

Lido di Jesolo

Mare Adriatico

Mestre
Marghera

Venice

0   20 mi

0   20 km

CROATIA

Laguna Veneta

Chioggia

Adria   Contarina

309

5 **Friuli–Venezia Giulia.** Set between the Adriatic Sea and Slovenia in the eastern corner of Italy, this is a region where menus run the gamut from gnocchi to goulash. The port city of Trieste has a mixed Venetian-Austrian heritage. It's filled with belle-epoque cafés and palaces built for Habsburg royalty.

Treviso

THE VENETIAN ARC PLANNER

Planning Ahead

Three of the top sights in the region demand advance planning:

Reservations are required to see the Giotto frescoes in Padua's Cappella degli Scrovegni—though if there's space, you can "reserve" on the spot.

On the outskirts of Vicenza, Villa La Rotonda, one of star architect Palladio's masterpieces, is open to the public only on Wednesday from mid-March through October. (Hours for visiting the grounds are less restrictive.)

Another important Palladian villa, Villa Barbaro near Maser, is open from March through October on Tuesday, Saturday, and Sunday afternoons. For the rest of the year, it's open only on weekends.

For details about Cappela degli Scrovegni, look in this chapter under "The Main Attractions" in Padua. For the villas, see "The Main Attractions" in Vicenza and Palladio Country.

Making the Most of Your Time

Lined up in a row west of Venice are Padua, Vicenza, and Verona—three prosperous small cities, each worth at least a day on a northern Italy itinerary. Verona has the greatest charm, and it's probably the best choice for a base in the area (though this is no secret—Verona also draws the most tourists). Treviso is worth a stop, but you're more likely to fall for the smaller towns of Asolo and Bassano del Grappa.

East of the Veneto, the region of Friuli–Venezia Giulia is off the main tourist circuit. You probably won't go here on a first trip to Italy, but by your second or third visit you may be drawn by its caves and castles, its battle-worn hills, and its mix of Italian and central European culture. The port city of Trieste, famous for its elegant cafés, has quiet character that some people find dull and others find intriguing. (Famed travel writer Jan Morris's book in praise of the city is tellingly titled *Trieste and the Meaning of Nowhere*.)

Finding a Place to Stay

There's a full range of accommodations throughout the region. Ask about weekend discounts, which are often available at hotels catering to business clients. Rates tend to be higher in Padua and Verona than in the rest of the region; in Verona especially, seasonal rates vary widely and soar during commercial fairs. *Agriturismo* (farm stay) information is available at local tourist information offices and sometimes on the offices' Web sites.

DINING & LODGING PRICE CATEGORIES (IN EUROS)				
¢	$	$$	$$$	$$$$
Restaurants				
under €15	€15–€25	€25–€35	€35–€45	over €45
Hotels				
under €70	€70–€110	€110–€160	€160–€220	over €220

Restaurant prices are for a first course (primo), second course (secondo), and dessert (dolce). Hotel prices are for two people in a standard double room in high season, including tax and service.

GETTING AROUND

By Car

Padua, Vicenza, and Verona are on the highway and train line between Venice and Milan. Seeing them without a car isn't a problem, and having a car can complicate matters. The cities sometimes limit access, permitting only cars with plates ending in an even number on even days, odd on odd, or prohibiting cars altogether on weekends. There's no central source for information about these sporadic traffic restrictions; the best strategy is to check with your hotel before arrival for an update. On the other hand, you'll need a car to get the most out of the hill country that makes up much of the Venetian Arc.

The two main access roads to the Venetian Arc from southern Italy are both linked to the A1 (Autostrada del Sole), which connects Bologna, Florence, and Rome. They are the A13, which culminates in Padua, and the A22, which passes through Verona running north–south. Linking the region from east to west is the A4, the primary route from Milan to Trieste, skirting Verona, Padua, and Venice along the way. The distance from Verona to Trieste via A4 is 263 km (163 mi), with one break in the autostrada near Venice/Mestre. Branches link the A4 with Treviso (A27), Pordenone (A28), and Udine (A23).

By Bus

There are interurban and interregional connections throughout the Veneto and Friuli, handled by nearly a dozen private bus lines. To figure out which line will get you where you want to you're your best strategy is to get assistance from local tourist offices (listed throughout this chapter).

By Train

Trains on the main routes from the south stop almost hourly in Verona, Padua, and Venice. From northern Italy and the rest of Europe, trains usually enter via Milan or through Porta Nuova station in Verona. Treviso and Udine both lie on the main line from Venice to Tarvisio, from which Eurocity trains continue to Vienna and Prague.

To the west of Venice, the main line running across the north of Italy stops at Padua (30 minutes from Venice), Vicenza (1 hour), and Verona (1½ hours); to the east is Trieste (2 hours). Local trains link Venice to Bassano del Grappa (1 hour), Padua to Bassano del Grappa (1 hour), Vicenza to Treviso (1 hour), and Udine to Trieste (1 hour).

Be sure to take express trains—a local "milk run" that stops in every village along the way can take considerably longer. The fastest trains are the Eurostars, but reservations are obligatory and fares are much higher than on regular express trains. You can check schedules at the Web site of the Italian national railway, **FS** (☎ *892021* ⊕ *www.trenitalia.com*).

EATING & DRINKING WELL IN VENETIAN ARC

THE BEST IN BEANS

Pasta e fagioli, a thick bean soup with pasta, served slightly warm or at room temperature, is made all over Italy, but folks in Veneto are justly proud of their version, featuring beans from around the village of Lamon, near Belluno. Even in the Veneto, the beans from Lamon cost over double the next most expensive variety, but their rich and delicate taste is worth it. You never knew bean soup could taste so good.

With the decisive seasonal changes of the Venetian Arc, it's little wonder that many restaurants shun printed menus. Elements from field and forest define much of the region's cuisine, including white asparagus, wild herbs, chestnuts, radicchio, and mushrooms.

Restaurants of the Venetian Arc tend to cling to tradition, not only in the food they serve but how they serve it. This means that from three in the afternoon until eight in the evening most places are closed tight (though you can pick up a snack at a bar during these hours), and on Sunday afternoon restaurants are packed with Italian families and friends indulging in a weekly ritual of lunching out.

One of the prime pleasures of this mellow region is buying provisions at an open-air market or *salumeria* (deli) and relaxing over a picnic. In the countryside, good picnicking spots abound. In the cities, two good spots are the Ponte Scaligero footbridge in Verona, and Padua's Basilica di Sant'Antonio—one of the rare churches in Italy that welcomes picnickers.

4

PASTA, RISOTTO, POLENTA

For *primi* (first courses), the Veneto dines on *bigoli* (thick whole-wheat pasta) generally served with an anchovy-onion sauce, and risotto—saturated with red wine in Verona and prosecco in Conegliano. Polenta is everywhere, varying from a stiff porridge topped with Gorgonzola or stew, to a patty grilled alongside meat or fis, as in the photo below.

FISH

The catch of the day is always a good bet, whether sweet and succulent Adriatic shellfish, sea bream, bass, or John Dory, or freshwater fish from Lake Garda near Verona. But be sure to note whether the fish is wild or farmed—the taste, texture, and price difference is considerable. A staple in the Veneto is *baccalà*, dried salt cod, soaked in water or milk, and then prepared in a different way in each city. In Vicenza, *baccalà alla vicentina,* pictured at left, is cooked with onions, milk, and cheese, and is generally served with polenta. Locals consider it as central to their city's identity as Palladio.

MEAT

Inland, meat prevails: pork and veal are standards, while goose, duck, and guinea fowl are common poultry options. Lamb is best in the spring, when it's young and delicate. In Friuli–

Venezia Giulia, menus show the influences of Austria-Hungary: you may find deer and hare on the menu, as well as Eastern European–style goulash. Throughout the Veneto an unusual treat is *nervetti*—cubes of gelatin from a cow's knee with onions, parsley, oil, and lemon.

RADICCHIO DI TREVISO

In fall and winter be sure to try the radicchio di Treviso, pictured above, a red endive grown near that town but popular all over the region. It's best in a stew with chicken or veal, in a risotto, or just grilled or baked with a drizzle of olive oil and perhaps a bit of taleggio cheese from neighboring Lombardy.

WINE

Wine is excellent here: the Veneto produces more D.O.C. (Denominazione di Origine Controllata) wines than any other region in Italy. Amarone, the region's crowning achievement, is a robust and powerful red with an alcohol content as high as 16%. Valpolicella and Bardolino are other notable appellations. The best of the whites are Soave; sweet, sparkling prosecco; and pinot bianco (pinot blanc). In Friuli–Venezia Giulia, the local wine par excellence is Tocai Friulano, a dry, lively white made from Tocai grapes that has attained international stature.

Updated
by Bruce
Leimsidor

THE ARC AROUND VENICE—stretching from Verona to Trieste, encompassing the Veneto and Friuli–Venezia Giulia regions—has, in recent centuries fallen under the cultural influence of its namesake city. Whether coastal or inland, the emblem of Venice, St. Mark's winged lion, is emblazoned on palazzi or poised on pedestals, and the art, architecture, and way of life all reflect, since the 16th century, the splendor of La Serenissima. But in the Middle Ages Padua and Verona were independent cities that developed substantial cultural traditions of their own, leaving behind many artistic treasures. And 16th-century Vicenza, even while under Venetian political domination, contributed more to the cultural heritage of La Serenissima than it took from her.

The area is primarily flat green farmland. As you move inland, though, you encounter low hills, which swell and rise in a succession of plateaus and high meadows, culminating in the snowcapped Dolomite Alps. Much of the pleasure of exploring here comes from discovering the variations on the Venetian theme that give a unique character to each of the towns. Some, such as Verona, Treviso, and Udine, have a solid medieval look; Asolo, dubbed "the town of a hundred horizons," has an idyllic setting; Bassano del Grappa combines a bit of both of these qualities. Padua, with its narrow arcaded streets, is romantic. Vicenza, ennobled by the architecture of Palladio, is elegant. In Friuli–Venezia Giulia, Udine is a genteel, intricately sculpted city that's home to the first important frescoes by Giambattista Tiepolo. In Trieste, its past as a port of the Austro-Hungarian Empire is still alive in its Viennese-inspired coffeehouses.

PADUA

A romantic warren of arcaded streets, Padua has long been one of the major cultural centers of northern Italy. It's home to Italy's second-oldest university, founded in 1222, which attracted such cultural icons as Dante (1265–1321), Petrarch (1304–74), and Galileo Galilei (1564–1642), thus earning the city the sobriquet *La Dotta* (The Learned). Padua's Basilica di Sant'Antonio, begun around 1238, is dedicated to St. Anthony, and it attracts droves of pilgrims, especially on his feast day, June 13. Three great artists—Giotto (1266–1337), Donatello (circa 1386–1466), and Mantegna (1431–1506)—left significant works here, with Giotto's Scrovegni Chapel one of the best-known, and most meticulously preserved, works of art in the country. Today, a cycle-happy student body—some 50,000 strong—flavors every aspect of local culture. Don't be surprised if you spot a *laurea* (graduation) ceremony marked by laurel leaves, mocking lullabies, and X-rated caricatures.

GETTING HERE
Many people visit Padua from Venice: the train trip between the cities is short and regular bus service originates from Venice's Piazzale Roma. By car from Milan or Venice, Padua is on the Autostrada Torino Trieste A4/E70. Take the San Carlo exit and follow Via Guido Reni to Via Tiziano Aspetti into town. From the south, take the Autostrada Bologna

Padova A13 to its Padua terminus at Via Ballaglia. Regular bus service connects Venice's Marco Polo airport with downtown Padua.

Padua is a pedestrian's city. If you arrive by car, leave your vehicle in one of the parking lots on the outskirts, or at your hotel. Unlimited bus service is included with the Padova Card (€14, valid for 48 hours), which allows entry to all the city's principal sights. It is available at tourist information offices and some museums.

VISITOR INFORMATION

Padua tourism office (⊠ *Padova Railway Station, 35100* ☎ *049/8752077* ⊠ *Galleria Pedrocchi, 35100* ☎ *049/8767927* ⊕ *www.turismopadova.it*).

EXPLORING PADUA

THE MAIN ATTRACTIONS

★ ❻ **Basilica di Sant'Antonio** *(Basilica del Santo).* Thousands of faithful make the pilgrimage here each year to pray at the tomb of St. Anthony. The huge church was probably begun around 1238, seven years after the death of the Portuguese-born saint, and completed in 1310, with structural modifications added from the end of the 14th century into the mid-15th century; it combines elements of Byzantine, Romanesque, and Gothic styles. The imposing interior contains works by the 15th-century Florentine master Donatello. He sculpted the series of bronze reliefs illustrating the miracles of St. Anthony, as well as the bronze statues of the Madonna and saints, on the high altar. But because of the site's popularity with pilgrims, masses are held in the basilica almost constantly, which makes it difficult to see these works. The more accessible **Cappella del Santo** housing the tomb of the saint dates from the 16th century. Its walls are covered with impressive reliefs by various important Renaissance sculptors, including Jacopo Sansovino (1486–1570), the architect of the library in Venice's Piazza San Marco, and Tullio Lombardo (1455–1532), the greatest in a family of sculptors who decorated many churches in the area, among them Venice's Santa Maria dei Miracoli. In front of the church is an undisputed masterpiece of Italian Renaissance sculpture, Donatello's equestrian statue (1453) of the *condottiere* (mercenary general) Erasmo da Narni, known as Gattamelata. Inspired by the ancient statue of Marcus Aurelius in Rome's Campidoglio, it is the first in a series of Italian Renaissance monumental equestrian statues. ⊠ *Piazza del Santo* ☎ *049/8789722* ⊕ *www.santantonio.org* ☉ *Sept.–May, daily 6:30 AM–7 PM; June–Aug., daily 6:30 AM–8 PM.*

❶ **Cappella degli Scrovegni** *(The Arena Chapel).* This world-famous chapel and its frescoes were commissioned by Enrico Scrovegno to atone for the sins of his deceased father, Reginaldo, the usurer encountered by Dante in the Seventh Circle of the Inferno in his Divine Comedy. Giotto and his assistants decorated the interior from 1303 to 1305 with a universally acclaimed fresco cycle illustrating the lives of Mary and Jesus. The 38 panels are arranged in tiers and are to be read from left to right. The spatial depth, emotional intensity, and naturalism of

Fodor'sChoice
★

THE VENETIAN ARC, PAST & PRESENT

Long before Venetians made their presence felt on the mainland in the 15th century, Ezzelino III da Romano (1194–1259), a larger-than-life scourge who was excommunicated by Pope Innocent IV, laid claim to Verona, Padua, and the surrounding lands and towns. After he was ousted, powerful families such as Padua's Carrara and Verona's della Scala (Scaligeri) vied throughout the 14th century to dominate these territories. With the rise of Venetian rule came a time of relative peace, when noble families from the lagoon and the mainland commissioned Palladio and other accomplished architects to design their palazzi and villas. This rich legacy, superimposed upon medieval castles and fortifications, is central to the identities of present-day Padua, Vicenza, and Verona. The region remained under Venetian control until the Napoleonic invasion and the fall of the Venetian Republic in 1797. The Council of Vienna ceded it, along with Lombardy, to Austria in 1815. The region revolted against Austrian rule and joined the Italian Republic in 1866.

Friuli–Venezia Giulia has a diverse cultural history that's reflected in its architecture, language, and cuisine. It's been marched through, fought over, hymned by patriots, and romanticized by James Joyce, Rainer Maria Rilke, and Jan Morris. Trieste was also vividly depicted in the novels of the towering figure of early-20th-century Italian letters, Italo Svevo. The region has seen Fascists and Communists, Romans, Habsburgs, and Huns. It survived by forging sheltering alliances—Udine beneath the wings of San Marco (1420), Trieste choosing Duke Leopold of Austria (1382) over Venetian domination.

Some of World War I's fiercest fighting took place in Friuli–Venezia Giulia, where memorials and cemeteries commemorate hundreds of thousands who died before the arrival of Italian troops in 1918 finally liberated Trieste from Austrian rule. Trieste, along with the whole of Venezia Giulia was annexed to Italy in 1920. During World War II, the Germans occupied the area and placed Trieste in an administrative zone along with parts of Slovenia. One of Italy's two concentration camps, still visitable, was near Trieste. After the war, during a period of Cold War dispute, Trieste was governed by an allied military administration; it was officially reannexed to Italy in 1954, when Italy ceded the Istrian peninsula to the south to Yugoslavia. These arrangements, long de facto in effect, were ratified by Italy and Yugoslavia in 1975.

these frescoes—note the use of blue sky instead of the conventional, depth-destroying gold background of medieval painting—broke new ground in Western art. Opposite the altar is a *Last Judgment,* most likely designed and painted by Giotto's assistants, where Enrico offers his chapel to the Virgin, celebrating her role in human salvation—particularly appropriate, given the penitential purpose of the chapel.

Mandatory reservations, which should be made at least two days ahead online or by phone, are for a specific time and are nonrefundable. Reservations are necessary even if you have a Padova Card. In order to preserve the artwork, doors are opened only every 15 minutes. A

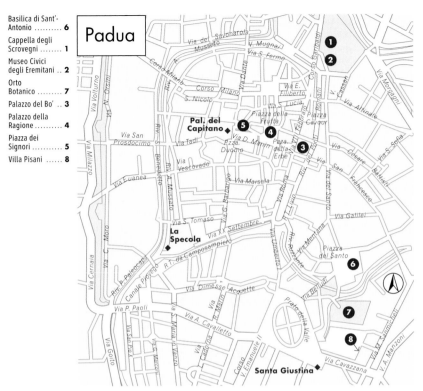

Padua

maximum of 25 visitors at a time must spend 15 minutes in an acclimatization room before making a 15-minute (20-minute in winter) chapel visit. Punctuality is essential; it's best to arrive at the chapel before your reservation time. If you don't have a reservation, it's sometimes possible to buy your chapel admission on the spot—but you might have to wait a while until there's a group with an opening. You can see fresco details as part of a virtual tour at Musei Civici degli Eremitani. A good place to get some background before visiting the chapel is the multimedia room, which offers films and interactive computer presentations. ✉*Piazza Eremitani 8* ☎*049/2010020 for reservations* ⊕*www.cappelladegliscrovegni.it* 🎟*€12 includes Musei Civici, or €1 with Padova Card* ⊙*Daily 9* AM*–7* PM*, entry by appointment only.*

★ ❹ **Palazzo della Ragione.** Also known as Il Salone, this spectacular arcaded reception hall, which divides the Piazza delle Frutta from the Piazza delle Erbe, was built between 1303 and 1309, with later 15th century additions. Giotto painted the original frescoes, which were destroyed in a fire in 1420. In the Middle Ages, as its name implies, the building housed Padua's law courts; today, its street-level arcades shelter shops and cafés. Art shows are often held upstairs in the frescoed **Salone,** at 85 feet high one of the largest and most architecturally pleasing halls in Italy. In the Salone there's an enormous wooden horse, crafted for a 15th-century public tournament, with a head and tail later remodeled to replicate the steed from Donatello's *Gattamelata*. In the piazza surrounding the building are Padua's colorful open-air fruit and vegetable markets. ✉*Piazza della Ragione* ☎*049/8205006* ✆*Salone €4 or Padova Card* ⊙*Feb.–Oct., Tues.–Sun. 9–7; Nov.–Jan., Tues.–Sun. 9–6.*

❺ Piazza dei Signori. Some fine examples of 15th- and 16th-century buildings line this square. On the west side, the **Palazzo del Capitanio** (facade constructed 1598–1605) has an impressive **Torre dell'Orologio**, with an astronomical clock dating from 1344 and a portal made by Falconetto in 1532 in the form of a Roman triumphal arch. The **Battistero del Duomo (12th century, with frescoes by** Giusto de Menabuoi, 1374–78) is just a few steps away.

☉ **❽ Villa Pisani.** Extensive grounds with rare trees, ornamental fountains, and garden follies surround this extraordinary palace built in 1721 for the Venetian doge Alvise Pisani in Stra, 13 km (8 mi) southeast of Padua. Recalling Versailles more than it does a Veneto villa, it was one of the last and grandest of many stately residences constructed along the Brenta River from the 16th to 18th centuries by wealthy Venetians for their *villeggiatura*—vacation and escape from the midsummer humidity. Tiepolo's (1696–1770) spectacular frescoes on the ballroom ceiling alone are worth the visit. If you have youngsters in tow surfeited with old masters, explore the gorgeous **park** and **maze.** To get here from Venice, you can take the Brenta River bus that leaves from Piazzale Roma. ✉*Via Doge Pisani 7, Stra* ☎*049/502074* ✆*Villa, maze, and park €5; maze and park only €2.50* ⊙*Apr.–Sept., Tues.–Sun. 9–7; villa and park only: Oct.–Mar., Tues.–Sun. 9–4. Last entry 1 hr before closing.*

ALSO WORTH SEEING

❷ Musei Civici degli Eremitani *(Civic Museum).* What was once a monastery now houses works of Venetian masters, as well as fine collections of archaeological pieces and ancient coins. Notable are the Giotto Crucifix, which was once in the Scrovegni Chapel, and the *Portrait of a Young Senator* by Giovanni Bellini (1430–1516). ✉*Piazza Eremitani 10* ☎*049/8204551* ✆*€10, €12 with Scrovegni Chapel, or free with Padova Card* ⊙*Tues.–Sun. 9–7.*

❼ Orto Botanico *(Botanical Garden).* The Venetian Republic ordered the creation of Padua's botanical garden in 1545 to supply the university with medicinal plants. You can stroll the arboretum and wander through hothouses and beds of plants that were first introduced to Italy in this Renaissance garden, which still maintains its original layout. A St. Peter's palm, planted in 1585, stands protected in its own private greenhouse. ✉*Via Orto Botanico 15* ☎*049/8272119* ⊕*www.ortobo-*

tanico.unipd.it ✉€4 *or free with Padova Card* ☉*Apr.–Oct., daily 9–1 and 3–7; Nov.–Mar., Mon.–Sat. 9–1.*

 Palazzo del Bo'. The University of Padua, founded in 1222, centers around this 16th-century palazzo with an 18th-century facade. It's named after the Osteria del Bo' (*bo'* means "ox"), an inn that once stood on the site. It's worth a visit to see the exquisite and perfectly proportioned anatomy theater (1594), the beautiful "Old Courtyard," and a hall with a lectern used by Galileo. You can enter only as part of a guided tour. Most guides speak English, but it is worth checking ahead by phone. ⊠ *Via VIII Febbraio* ☎*049/8273044* ⊕*www.unipd.it* ✉€5 ☉*Nov.–Feb., Mon., Wed., and Fri. at 3:15 and 4:15; Tues., Thurs., and Sat. at 10:15 and 11:15; Mar.–Oct., Mon., Wed., and Fri. at 3:15, 4:15, and 5:15; Tues., Thurs., and Sat. at 9:15, 10:15, and 11:15.*

Chiesa degli Eremitani houses substantial fragments of Andrea Mantegna's frescoes (1448–50), damaged by allied bombing in World War II. Despite their fragmentary condition, Mantegna's still beautiful and historically important frescoes depicting the martyrdom of St. James and St. Christofer show the very young artist's mastery of extremely complex problems of perspective. ⊠*Piazza degli Eremitani* ☎*049/8756410* ☉*Daily 8–noon and 4–7.*

WHERE TO EAT

$$$$ ✕ **Le Calandre.** Make reservations well in advance. Le Calandre is in the village of Sarmeola di Rubano, a few kilometers west of Padua and easily reached by taxi. ⊠ *Via Liguria 1, Sarmeola di Rubano* ☎*049/630303* ⊕*www.calandre.com* ▭*MC, V* ☉*Closed Sun. and Mon. and mid-Aug.–early Sept.*

$$–$$$$ ✕ **Antico Brolo.** One of Padua's top restaurants lets you choose between pampered elegance in an historic 16th-century formal dining room, or more casual dining in the cantina or on the terrace. The seasonal menu changes daily. The traditional Veneto combination of radicchio di Treviso and taleggio cheese is transformed into a delicate taleggio-stuffed homemade ravioli topped with the sautéed radicchio. Or you can try a tour de force presentation of four different variations on baccalà, the Veneto's famous dried cod. This very distinguished restaurant also serves pizza in the evening (amazingly at regular pizzeria prices) and stays open late to accommodate the post-theater crowd (it's across from Padua's main theater). Whether you have a pizza on the terrace or a full meal in the formal dining room, you'll receive the same attentive friendly service. The cantina, stocked with more than 600 labels, is a more than adequate complement to the exceptional food. ⊠*Corso Milano 22* ☎*049/664555* ⊕*www.anticobrolo.it* ▭*AE, MC, V* ☉*No lunch Mon.*

★ $$–$$$ ✕ **Osteria Dal Capo.** A friendly trattoria in the heart of what used to be Padua's Jewish ghetto, Osteria Dal Capo serves almost exclusively traditional Veneto dishes and does so with refinement and care. The Venetian liver and onions is extraordinarily tender. Even the accompanying polenta is grilled to perfection—slightly crisp on the outside

Cocktail Hour on Padua's Piazzas

One of Padua's greatest traditions is the outdoor en-masse consumption, most nights in decent weather, of **aperitifs**: *spritz* (a mix of Aperol or Campari, soda water, and wine), *prosecco* (sparkling wine), or wine.

It all happens in the Piazza delle Erbe and Piazza delle Frutta. Several bars there provide drinks in plastic cups, so you can take them outside and drink while mingling among the crowds.

The ritual, practiced religiously by students most of all, begins at 6 PM or so, at which hour you can also pick up a snack from one of the outdoor seafood vendors. On weekends, the open-air revelry continues into the wee hours, transitioning from a cocktail hour to a bash.

and moist on the inside. And the desserts are nothing to scoff at, either. Word is out among locals about this hidden gem, and the tiny place fills up quickly, so reservations are necessary. ⊠ *Via degli Oblizzi 2* ☎ *049/663105* ⊟ *AE, DC, MC, V* ⊗ *No lunch Sun. and Mon. Closed 3 wks in Aug.*

$–$$ ✕ **Gigi Bar.** Simple and unpretentious: yellow walls and tablecloths brighten this inexpensive restaurant where high ceilings open up to a second-floor seating area. The central kitchen is behind a counter low enough for the convivial owner-chef Ferruccio to see and supervise the equally friendly dining-room staff. The terrific and popular fish soup is one of the affordable seafood dishes that keep locals queuing up. There are also tasty steaks, salads, vegetable plates, and pizzas with a surprisingly light crust. ⊠ *Via Verdi 18/20* ☎ *049/8760028* ⊟ *DC, MC, V* ⊗ *Closed Tues. and 2 wks in July.*

★ $–$$ ✕ **L'Anfora.** This mix between a traditional Veneto bacaro (wine bar) and an *osteria* (tavernlike restaurant) is a local institution. Stand at the bar shoulder to shoulder with a cross section of Padovano society, from construction workers to professors, and let the friendly and knowledgeable proprietors help you choose a wine. The reasonably priced menu offers simple *casalinga* (home-cooked dishes), plus salads and a selection of cheeses. Portions are ample, and no one will look askance if you don't order the full meal. The place is packed with loyal regulars at lunchtime, so come early or expect a wait; if you come alone, you'll probably end up with a table of friends before you leave. ⊠ *Via Soncin 13* ☎ *049/656629* ⊟ *AE, V* ⊗ *Closed Sun. (except in Dec.), 1 wk in Jan., and 1 wk in Aug.*

WHERE TO STAY

★ $$$ ⛭ **Majestic Toscanelli.** The charming entrance, with potted evergreens flanking the steps, sets the tone in this pleasant, central hotel close to the Piazza delle Erbe (it's easily the best-located hotel in the city). The cozy bedrooms are furnished in different styles from 19th-century mahogany and brass to French Empire. Your very welcoming hosts offer discounts to seniors, AAA members, and those carrying Fodor's guidebooks. **Pros:** Excellent location, attentive staff, pleasant and warm atmosphere. **Cons:** Rooms, while ample, are not large; little natural light and few views (hotel is on a narrow street); some street noise at night, especially on weekends; hefty parking fee (€19 per night). ✉ *Via dell'Arco 2, near Piazza delle Erbe, 35122* ☎ *049/663244* 🖶 *049/8760025* 🌐 *www.toscanelli.com* 🛏 *26 rooms, 6 suites* ♿ *In-room: safe (some), refrigerator, dial-up, Wi-Fi. In-hotel: restaurant, bar, public Internet, parking (fee), some pets allowed (fee), no-smoking rooms* ⊟ *AE, DC, MC, V* ¶❙*BP.*

★ **$$$** ⚄ **Methis.** The strikingly modern Methis takes its name from the Greek word for style and spirit. Four floors of sleekly designed guest rooms reflect the elements: gentle earth tones, fiery red, watery cool blue, and airy white (in the top-floor suites). Rooms have Japanese-style tubs, and four are equipped for guests with disabilities. The lobby has one lounge and a quieter reading room. There's a pleasant view from the front rooms, which face the canal. **Pros:** Rooms are very attractive, staff is helpful and attentive, pleasant little extras like umbrellas are provided free of charge, views from some rooms. **Cons:** Although in historic center, hotel is far (15-minute walk) from major sights and restaurants; rooms are beautiful, but public spaces are cold and uninviting. ✉ *Riviera Paleocapa 70, 35141* ☎ *049/8725555* 🖶 *049/8725135* 🌐 *www. methishotel.com* 🛏 *52 rooms, 7 suites* ♿ *In-room: safe, refrigerator, Wi-Fi. In-hotel: bar, gym, public Internet, parking (no fee)* ⊟ *AE, DC, MC, V* ¶❙*BP.*

$ ⚄ **Al Fagiano.** This delightfully funky budget hotel, near Basilica di Sant'Antonio, has spruced up its existing rooms and added new ones by acquiring an adjacent structure. Artistic decoration includes sponge-painted walls, paintings by the owner, brush-painted chandeliers, and an elevator where self-proclaimed artists can add graffiti to their heart's content. An amiable staff and relatively central location make Al Fagiano pleasant and convenient, and some rooms have views of the basilica's spires and cupolas. Breakfast is available for €7. **Pros:** Large rooms for budget property; youthful, relaxed atmosphere; fairly convenient location. **Cons:** No parking facilities, room service, or help with baggage; some may find the eclectic decor to be a bit much. ✉ *Via Locatelli 45, 35100* ☎ *049/8750073* 🖶 *049/8753396* 🌐 *www. alfagiano.com* 🛏 *40 rooms* ♿ *In-room: dial-up. In-hotel: bar, some pets allowed* ⊟ *AE, DC, MC, V* ¶❙*EP.*

CAFÉS & WINE BARS

No visit to Padua is complete without a trip to **Caffè Pedrocchi** (✉ *Piazzetta Pedrocchi* ☎ *049/8781231*). The café has long been central to the city's social life, and you can still sit here, as the French writer Stendahl did shortly after the café was established in 1831, and observe a good slice of Veneto life, especially, as he noted, the elegant Veneto ladies sipping their coffee. The massive café, built in a style reflecting the fashion set by Napoléon's expeditions in Egypt, has long been central to the city's social life. It also serves lunch and dinner, and is proud of its innovative menu. Open 9 AM to midnight daily from mid-June to mid-September; hours for the rest of the year are Sunday to Wednesday 9 to 9, Thursday to Saturday 9 AM to midnight.

Frequented by a blend of students and an older neighborhood crowd, **Hostaria Ai Do Archi** (✉ *Via Nazario Sauro 23* ☎ *049/652335*) is nothing more—or less—than a Padovan version of the *bacari* that are so typical of the Veneto: wine bars where people sit and stand all day long, sipping wine, tasting local snacks, and talking politics. It's a true experience.

VICENZA

Vicenza bears the distinctive signature of the 16th-century architect Andrea Palladio, whose name has been given to the "Palladian" style of architecture. He effectively emphasized the principles of order and harmony in the classical style of architecture established by Renaissance architects such as Brunelleschi, Alberti, and Sansovino. He used these principles and classical motifs not only for public buildings but also for private dwellings. His elegant villas and palaces were influential in propagating classical architecture in Europe, especially Britain, and later in America—most notably at Thomas Jefferson's Monticello.

In the mid-16th century Palladio was commissioned to rebuild much of Vicenza, which had been greatly damaged during wars waged against Venice by the League of Cambrai, an alliance of the papacy, France, the Holy Roman Empire, and several neighboring city-states. He made his name with the basilica, begun in 1549 in the heart of Vicenza, and then embarked on a series of lordly buildings, all of which adhere to the same classicism and principles of harmony.

GETTING HERE
Vicenza is midway between Padua and Verona, and several trains leave from both cities every hour. By car, take the Autostrada Brescia–Padova/Torino–Trieste A4/E70 to SP247 North directly into Vicenza.

VISITOR INFORMATION
Vicenza tourism office (✉ *Piazza Giacomo Matteotti 12, 36100* ☎ *0444/320854* ✉ *Piazza dei Signori 8* ☎ *0444/544122* ⊕ *www.vicenzae.org*).

EXPLORING VICENZA

Many of Palladio's works are near the Venetian gothic and baroque palaces that line Corso Palladio, an elegant shopping thoroughfare where Vicenza's status as one of Italy's wealthiest cities is evident. Part of this wealth stems from Vicenza's being a world center for gold jewelry.

THE MAIN ATTRACTIONS
❷ **Teatro Olimpico.** Palladio's last, and perhaps most spectacular work, was completed after his death by Vincenzo Scamozzi (1552–1616). Based closely on the model of ancient Roman theaters, it represents an important development in theater and stage design and is noteworthy for its

Fodor's Choice
★

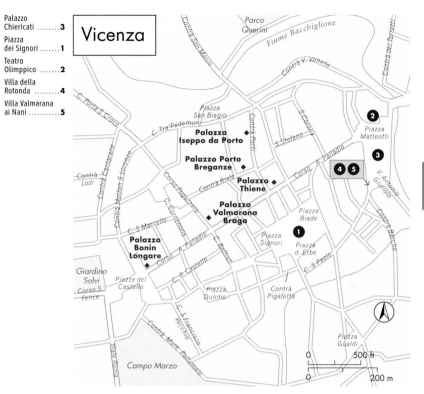

Vicenza

acoustics and the cunning use of perspective in Scamozzi's permanent backdrop. The anterooms are frescoed with images of important figures in Venetian history. ⊠*Piazza Matteotti* ☎*0444/222800* ⊞*€8 includes admission to Palazzo Chiericati* ☉*Sept.–June, Tues.–Sun. 9–5; July and Aug., Tues.–Sun. 9–7.*

❹ **Villa della Rotonda (Villa Almerico Capra).** This very beautiful Palladian villa, commissioned in 1556 as a suburban residence for Paolo Almerico, is undoubtedly the purest expression of Palladio's architectural theory and aesthetic. Although it seems more of a pavilion showplace, it was in fact commissioned as a residence, and as such demonstrates the priority Palladio gave to architectural symbolism of celestial harmony over practical considerations. It's more a villa-temple than a house to live in, and in this respect, it goes beyond the rational utilitarianism of Renaissance architecture. Although a visit to the interior of the building may be difficult to schedule (it's still privately owned), it is well worth the effort in order to get an idea of how the people who commissioned the residence actually lived. Viewing the exterior and the grounds is a must for any visit to Vicenza. The villa is a 20-minute walk from town or a short ride on the No. 8 bus from Piazza Roma. ⊠*Via della Rotonda* ☎*0444/321793* ⊞*€10 grounds and interior, €5 grounds only* ☉*Grounds: Tues.–Sun. 10–noon and*

2:30–6 (5 PM closing mid-Nov.–mid-Mar.); interior: Mar.–Nov., Wed. 10–noon and 2:30–6.

⑤ Villa Valmarana ai Nani. Inside this 17th- to 18th-century country house, named for the statues of dwarfs adorning the garden, is a series of frescoes executed in 1757 by Gianbattista Tiepolo depicting scenes from *The Illiad*, Tasso's *Gerusalemme Liberata*, and Ariosto's *Orlando Furioso*. They include his *Sacrifice of Iphigenia, unanimously acclaimed by critics as a major masterpiece of 18th-century painting.* The neighboring *foresteria* (farmworkers' dormitory) is also part of the museum; it contains frescoes showing 18th-century Veneto life at its most charming, and scenes of *chinoiserie* popular in the 18th century, by Tiepolo's son Giandomenico (1727–1804). The garden dwarves are probably taken from designs by Giandomenico. You can reach the villa on foot by following the same path that leads to Palladio's Villa della Rotonda. ⊠ *Via dei Nani 2/8* ☎ *0444/321803* 🖾 *€8* ⊗ *Mid-Mar.–Oct., Tues.–Sun. 10–noon and 3–6; Nov.–mid-Mar., weekends 10–noon and 2–4:30.*

ALSO WORTH SEEING

③ Palazzo Chiericati. This imposing Palladian palazzo (1550) would be worthy of a visit even if it didn't house Vicenza's **Museo Civico.** Because of the ample space surrounding the building site, Palladio combined here elements of an urban palazzo with those he used in his country villas. The museum's important Venetian collection includes significant paintings by Cima, Tiepolo, Piazzetta, and Tintoretto, but its main attraction is an extensive collection of highly interesting and rarely found painters from the Vicenza area, such as Jacopo Bassano (1515–92) and the eccentric and innovative Francesco Maffei (1605–60), whose work foreshadowed important currents of Venetian painting of subsequent generations. ⊠ *Piazza Matteotti* ☎ *0444/321348* 🖾 *€8 includes admission to Teatro Olimpico* ⊗ *Sept.–June, Tues.–Sun. 9–5; July and Aug., Tues.–Sun. 9–6.*

① Piazza dei Signori. At the heart of Vicenza sits this square, which contains the **Palazzo della Ragione (1549),** commonly known as Palladio's basilica, a courthouse and public meeting hall (the original Roman meaning of the term "basilica"). The previously almost-unknown Palladio made his name by successfully modernizing the medieval building, grafting a graceful two-story exterior loggia onto the existing Gothic structure. Take a look also at the **Loggia del Capitaniato,** opposite, which Palladio designed but never completed. The palazzo and the loggia are open to the public only when there's an exhibition; ask at the tourist office.

WHERE TO EAT

$$ ✕ **Antico Ristorante agli Schioppi.** When they want to eat well, Vicenza's natives generally travel to the adjoining countryside—agli Schioppi is one of the few restaurants in the city frequented by Vicentino families and businessmen. Veneto country-style decor, with enormous murals, matches simple, well-prepared regional cuisine at this family-run res-

Continued on page 266

PALLADIO COUNTRY

Wealthy 16th-century patrons commissioned Andrea Palladio to design villas that would reflect their sense of cultivation and status. Using a classical vocabulary of columns, arches, and domes, he gave them a series of masterpieces in the towns and hills of the Veneto that exemplify the neo-Platonic ideals of harmony and proportion. Palladio's creations are the perfect expression of how a learned 16th century man saw himself and his world, and as you stroll through them today, their serene beauty is as powerful as ever. Listen closely and you might even hear that celestial harmony, the music of the spheres, that so moved Palladio and his patrons.

TOWN & COUNTRY

Although the villa, or "country residence," was still a relatively new phenomenon in the 16th century, it quickly became all the rage once the great lords of Venice turned their eyes from the sea toward the fertile plains of the Veneto. They were forced to do this once their trade routes had faltered when Ottoman Turks conquered Constantinople in 1456 and Columbus opened a path to the riches of America in 1492. In no time, canals were built, farms were laid out, and the fashion for *villeggiatura*—the attraction of idyllic country retreats for the nobility—became a favored lifestyle.

As a means of escaping an overheated Rome, villas had been the original brainchild of the ancient emperors and it was no accident that the Venetian lords wished to emulate this palatial style of country residence. Palladio's method of evaluating the standards, and standbys, of ancient Roman life through the eye of the Italian Renaissance, combined with Palladio's innate sense of proportion and symmetry, became the lasting foundation of his art. In turn, Palladio threw out the jambalaya of styles prevalent in Venetian architecture—Oriental, Gothic, and Renaissance—for the pure, noble lines found in the buildings of the Caesars.

PALLADIO, STAR ARCHITECT

Andrea Palladio (1508–1580)

"Face dark, eyes fiery. Dress rich. His appearance that of a genius." So was Palladio described by his wealthy mentor, Count Trissino. Trissino encouraged the young student to trade in his birth name, Andrea di Pietro della Gondola, for the elegant Palladio. He did, and it proved a wise move indeed. Born in Padua in 1508, Andrea moved to nearby Vicenza in 1524 and was quickly taken up by the city's power elite. He experienced a profound revelation on his first

THE OLD BECOMES NEW

La Malcontenta

Studying ancient Rome with the eyes of an explorer, Palladio employed a style that linked old with new—but often did so in unexpected ways. Just take a look at Villa Foscari, nicknamed **"La Malcontenta"** (Mira, 041/5470012, www.lamalcontenta.com €8. Open May–Oct., Tues. and Sat. 9–noon; from Venice, take an ACTV bus from Piazzale Roma to Mira or opt for a boat ride up on the Burchiello). Shaded by weeping willows and mirrored by the Brenta Canal, "The Sad Lady" was built for Nicolò and Alvise Foscari and is the quintessence of Palladian poetry. Inspired by the grandeur of Roman public buildings, Palladio applied the ancient motif of a temple facade to a domestic dwelling, topped off by a pediment, a construct most associated with religious structures. Inside, he used the technique of vaulting seen in ancient Roman baths, with giant windows and immense white walls ready-made for the colorful frescoes painted by Zelotti. No one knows for certain the origin of the villa's nickname—some say it came from a Venetian owner's wife who was exiled there due to her scandalous behavior. Regardless of the name, it's hard today to associate such a beautiful, graceful villa with anything but harmony and contentment.

trip, in 1541, to Rome, where he sensed the harmony of the ancient ruins and saw the elements of classicism that were working their way into contemporary architecture. This experience led to his spectacular conversion of the Vicenza's Palazzo della Ragione (1545) into a basilica recalling the great meeting halls of antiquity. In years to come, after relocating to Venice, he created some memorable churches, such as S. Giorgio Maggiore (1564). Despite these varied projects, Palladio's unassailable position as one of the world's greatest architects is tied to the countryside villas, which he spread across the Veneto plains like a firmament of stars. Nothing else in the Veneto illuminates more clearly the idyllic beauty of the region than these elegant residences, their stonework now nicely mellowed and suntanned after five centuries.

VICENZA, CITY OF PALLADIO

Palazzo della Ragione

La Rotonda

To see Palladio's pageant of palaces, head for Vicenza. His **Palazzo della Ragione**, or "Basilica," marks the city's heart, the Piazza dei Signori. This building rocketed young Palladio from an unknown to an architectural star. Across the way is his redbrick **Loggia dei Capitaniato**.

One block past the Loggia is Vicenza's main street, appropriately named Corso Andrea Palladio. Just off this street is the Contrà Porti, where you'll find the **Palazzo Barbaran da Porto** (1570) at No. 11, with its fabulously rich facade erupting with Ionic and Corinthian pillars. Today, this is the Centro Internazionale di Studi di Architettura Andrea Palladio (0444/323014, www.cisapalladio. org), a study center which mounts impressive temporary exhibitions. A few steps away, on the Contrà San Gaetano Thiene, is the Palazzo Thiene (1542-58), designed by Giulio Romano and completed by Palladio.

Doubling back to Contrà Porti 21, you find the **Palazzo Iseppo da Porto** (1544), the first palazzo where you can see the neoclassical effects of young Palladio's trip to Rome. Following the Contrà Reale, you come to Corso Fogazzaro 16 and the **Palazzo Valmarana Braga** (1565). Its gigantic pilasters were a first for domestic architecture.

Returning to the Corso Palladio, head left to the opposite end of the Corso, about five blocks, to the Piazza Matteoti and **Palazzo Chiericati** (1550). This was practically a suburban area in the 16th century, and for the palazzo Palladio combined elements of urban and rural design. The pedestal raising the building and the steps leading to the entrance—unknown in urban palaces— were to protect from floods and to keep cows from wandering in the front door. (For opening times and details, see the main text).

Across the Corso Palladio is Palladio's last and one of his most spectacular works, the **Teatro Olimpico** (1580). By careful study of ancient ruins and architectural texts, he reconstructed a Roman theater with archaeological precision. Palladio died before it was completed, but he left clear plans for the project. (For opening times and details, see the main text.)

Although it's on the outskirts of town, the **Villa Almerico Capra**, better known as **La Rotonda** (1566), is an indispensable part of any visit to Vicenza. It's the iconic Palladian building, the purest expression of his aesthetic. (For opening times, details, and a discussion of the villa, see the main text.)

A MAGNIFICENT COLLABORATION

Villa Barbaro

At the **Villa Barbaro** (1554) near the town of Maser in the province of Treviso, 48 km (30 miles) northeast of Vicenza, you can see the results of a one-time collaboration between two of the greatest artists of their age.

Palladio was the architect, and Paolo Veronese decorated the interior with an amazing cycle of trompe l'oeil frescoes—walls dissolve into landscapes, and illusions of courtiers and servants enter rooms and smile down from balustrades.

Legend has it a feud developed between Palladio and Veronese, with Palladio feeling the illusionistic frescoes detracted from his architecture; but there is practically nothing to support the idea of such a rift.

It's also noteworthy that Palladio for the first time connected the two lateral granaries to the main villa. This was a working farm, and Palladio thus created an architectural unity by connecting with graceful arcades the working parts of the estate to the living quarters, bringing together the Renaissance dichotomy of the active and the contemplative life. *Via Cornuda 7, Maser, 0432/923004 www. villadimaser.it , €5 Open April- October Tues. and weekends 3-6; Nov.- March, weekends 2:30- 5, or by reservation; Closed 24 Dec.- 6 Jan.*

ALONG THE BRENTA CANAL

During the 16th century the Brenta was transformed into a landlocked version of Venice's Grand Canal with the building of nearly 50 waterside villas. Back then, boating parties viewed them in *"burchielli"*—beautiful boats. Today, the Burchiello excursion boat (Via Orlandini 3, Padua, 049/8206910, www.ilburchiello. it) makes full- and half-day tours along the Brenta, from March to November, departing from Padua on Wednesday, Friday, and Sunday and from Venice on Tuesday, Thursday, and Saturday; tickets are €40–€71 and can also be bought at American Express at Salizzada San Moisè in Venice. You visit three houses, including the Villas Pisani and Foscari, with a lunchtime break in Oriago. Another canal excursion is run by the Battelli del Brenta (www.battellidel brenta.it). Note that most houses are on the left side coming from Venice, or the right from Padua.

taurant. The risotto, flavored heartily with Savoy cabbage and fresh cheese, is creamy and—a rarity in restaurant risottos—beautifully textured. This is also an excellent place to try *baccalà* (dried cod), a Vicenza specialty. ⊠ *Contrà Piazza del Castello 26* ☎ *0444/543701* ⊕ *www.ristoranteaglischioppi.com* ⊟ *AE, DC, MC, V* ✆ *Closed Sun., last wk of July–mid-Aug., and Jan. 1–6. No dinner Sat.*

★ **$-$$** ✕ **Ponte delle Bele.** Vicenza lies at the foot of the Alps, and many residents spend at least a part of the summer in the mountains to escape the heat. So, Alpine cuisine has been incorporated into the local culture and can be enjoyed at this popular and friendly Veneto trattoria. Your homemade pasta may resemble dumplings or spaetzle and your prosciutto might be made from deer or boar. Try Alpine preparations of game, such as venison in blueberry sauce or guinea fowl roasted with white grapes. The rather kitsch Alpine decor doesn't detract from the good, hearty food. ⊠ *Contrà Ponte delle Bele 5* ☎ *0444/320647* ⊕ *www.pontedellebele.it* ⊟ *AE, DC, MC, V* ✆ *Closed Sun. and 2 wks in mid-Aug.*

$ ✕ **Dai Nodari.** A good cross section of Vicenza society, from students to businessmen frequents this popular wine bar, which is also a creative yet economical restaurant. At lunch, there's a choice of fixed-priced menus ranging from €7 to €9. At dinner, appetizers include interesting cheeses, such as bastardo del Grappa (aged 60 days). Move on to fish or steak, or try rabbit roasted with juniper berries. There are also several pasta and salad choices. But don't wait until mealtime: from 5:30 until midnight you can stop in to have a glass of wine and sample some of the excellent bar snacks. ⊠ *Contrà Do Rode 20* ☎ *0444/544085* ⊟ *AE, DC, MC, V* ✆ *Closed Mon.*

¢-$ ✕ **Righetti.** Stake out your seats, then line up at the self-service food counters here. There's a daily pasta, a risotto, and a hearty soup such as *orzo e fagioli* (barley and bean) on the menu. Vegetables, salads, and baccalà are standards; at dinner, meats are grilled to order. Once you have your meal on your tray, help yourself to bread, wine, and water. After you've finished, tell the cashier what you had and he'll total your (very reasonable) bill. Low prices and simple, enjoyable food has generated a loyal following. ⊠ *Piazza Duomo 3* ☎ *0444/543135* ⊟ *No credit cards* ✆ *Closed weekends, 1st wk in Jan., and Aug.*

WHERE TO STAY

During annual gold fairs in January, May, and September, it may be quite difficult to find lodging. Be sure to reserve well in advance and expect to pay higher rates.

$$ ⊡ **Campo Marzio.** A five-minute walk from the railway station, this comfortable hotel is right in front of the city walls. You can borrow a bicycle to tool around town. Rooms are ample and furnished in a pleasant modernized-traditional style, but don't expect anything spectacular or romantic. This is the only full-service hotel in Vicenza, so it fills up quickly during the gold fairs—when rates nearly double. **Pros:** Central location; more amenities than most hotels in the city; set back from the street, so it's quiet and gets natural light. **Cons:** Room decor and public spaces are uninspiring, incredibly expensive during gold fairs. ✉ *Viale Roma 21, 36100* 🕿🕿*0444/5457000* ⊕*www.hotelcampomarzio.com* ⇴*36 rooms* ⌂*In-room: safe, refrigerator, ethernet, Wi-Fi. In-hotel: bar, parking (no fee), some pets allowed* ▤*AE, DC, MC, V* ⊗. ⦿|*BP.*

$ 🏠 **Due Mori.** Authentic turn-of-the-century antiques fill the rooms at
★ this 1883 hotel Due Mori, one of the oldest in the city. Loyal regulars favor the place, because it's light and airy (with tall ceilings and pale walls), yet cozy. Breakfast is available for €5. This comfortable hotel is a true bargain—rates stay the same throughout the year, with no high-season or gold-fair price hikes. **Pros:** Large rooms, very tastefully furnished; friendly staff; central location off the Piazza dei Signori. **Cons:** No TV or air-conditioning in rooms (although thick walls and ceiling fans minimize the need for a/c), no one to help with baggage. ✉*Contrà Do Rode 24, 36100* 🕿*0444/321886* ⊕*www.hotelduemori. com* ⇴*30 rooms* ⌂*In-room: no a/c, no TV. In-hotel: bar, parking (no fee), some pets allowed* ▤*MC, V* ⊗*Closed 1st 2 wks of Aug. and 2 wks in late Dec.* ⦿|*EP.*

NIGHTLIFE & THE ARTS

Vicenza hosts a jazz festival in May and classical concerts in June, with performances throughout the city. Any event you can catch at **Teatro Olimpico** (✉*Piazza Matteotti* 🕿*0444/222800* ⊕*www.comune. vicenza.it*) is especially worth attending. The teatro also hosts classical drama performances in September; even if your Italian is dismal, it can be thrilling to see a performance in Palladio's magnificent theater.

VERONA

On the banks of the fast-flowing River Adige, 60 km (37 mi) west of Vicenza, enchanting Verona has timeless monuments, a picturesque town center, and a romantic reputation as the setting of Shakespeare's *Romeo and Juliet*. With its lively Venetian air and proximity to Lake Garda, it attracts hordes of tourists, especially Germans and Austrians. Tourism peaks during summer's renowned season of open-air opera in the Arena and during spring's Vinitaly (✉*Fiera di Verona, Viale del Lavoro 8* 🕿*045/8298170* ⊕*www.vinitaly.com*), one of the world's most important wine expos. For five days you can sample the wines of more than 3,000 wineries from dozens of countries.

Verona grew to power and prosperity within the Roman Empire as a result of its key commercial and military position in northern Italy. With its Roman arena, theater, and city gates, it has the most significant monuments of Italian antiquity north of Rome. After the fall of the Empire, the city continued to flourish under the guidance of barbarian kings such as Theodoric, Alboin, Pepin, and Berenger I, reaching its cultural and artistic peak in the 13th and 14th centuries under the della Scala (Scaligero) dynasty. (Look for the *scala,* or ladder, emblem all over town.) In 1404 Verona traded its independence for security and placed itself under the control of Venice. (The other recurring architectural motif is the lion of St. Mark, a symbol of Venetian rule.)

GETTING HERE

Verona is midway between Venice and Milan. It is served by a small airport, Aeroporto Valerio Catullo, which accommodates domestic and European flights; however, many travelers still prefer to fly into Venice or Milan and drive or take the train to Verona. Several trains per hour depart from any point on the Milan–Venice line. By car, from the east or west, take the Autostrada Trieste–Torino A4/E70 to the SS12 and follow it north into town. From the north or south, take the Autostrada del Brennero A22/E45 to the SR11 East (initially, called the Strada Bresciana) directly into town.

VISITOR INFORMATION

Verona tourism office (⊠ *Piazza Brà, 37121* ☎ *045/8068680* ⊠ *Porta Nuova railway station* ☎ *045/8000861* ⊕ *www.tourism.verona.it*).

EXPLORING VERONA

If you're going to visit more than one or two sights, it's worthwhile to purchase a VeronaCard, available at museums, churches, and tobacconists for €8 (one day) or €12 (three days). It buys a single admission to most of the city's significant museums and churches, plus you can ride free on city buses. A €5 Chiese Vive Card is sold at Verona's major churches and gains you entry to the Duomo, San Fermo Maggiore, San Zeno Maggiore, Sant'Anastasia, and San Lorenzo. Do note that Verona's churches strictly enforce their dress code: no sleeveless shirts, shorts, or short skirts.

THE MAIN ATTRACTIONS

❸ Arena di Verona. Only Rome's Colosseum and Capua's arena surpass this amphitheater in size. Though four arches are all that remain of the arena's outer arcade, the main structure is complete. It dates from the early Imperial age, and was used for gymnastic competitions, choreographed sacrificial rites, and games involving hunts, fights, battles, and wild animals. Unlike at Rome's Colosseum, there is no evidence that Christians were ever put to death here. Today you can visit the arena year-round; in summer, you can join up to 16,000 people packing the stands for one of Verona's spectacular opera productions. Even those who aren't crazy about opera can sit in the stands and enjoy Italians enjoying themselves—including, at times, singing along with their favorite hits. ⊠ *Arena di Verona, Piazza Brà 5* ☎ *045/8003204* ⊕ *www.arena.it* ⊠ *€5 or VeronaCard, €1 1st Sun. of month* ☉ *Mon. 1:30–7:15, Tues.–Sun. 8:30–7:15, 8–3:30 on performance days; last entry 45 mins before closing.*

Fodor's Choice ★

❷ Castelvecchio *(Old Castle)*. This crenellated, russet brick building with massive walls, towers, turrets, and a vast courtyard was built for Cangrande II della Scala in 1354. It presides over a street lined with attractive old buildings and palaces of the nobility. Only by going inside the **Museo di Castelvecchio** can you really appreciate this massive castle

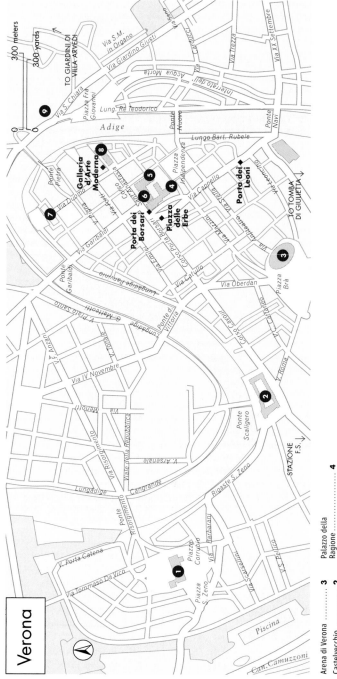

Verona

complex with its vaulted halls. You also get a look at a significant collection of Venetian art, medieval weapons, and jewelry. The interior of the castle was restored and redesigned as a museum between 1958 and 1975 by one of the most important architects of the 20th century, Carlo Scarpa. Behind the castle is the Ponte Scaligero (1355), which spans the River Adige. ⊠ *Corso Castelvecchio 2* 🕾 *045/8062611* 🎫 *€4 or VeronaCard, free 1st Sun. of month* ⊗ *Mon. 1:30–7:30, Tues.–Sun. 8:30–7:30; last entry 6:45.*

❼ Duomo. The present church was begun in the 12th century in the Romanesque style; its later additions are mostly Gothic. On pilasters guarding the main entrance, are 12th-century carvings thought to represent Oliver and Roland, two of Charlemagne's knights and heroes of several medieval epic poems. Inside, Titian's *Assumption* (1532) graces the first chapel on the left. ⊠ *Via Duomo* 🕾 *045/592813* ⊕ *www.chieseverona.it* 🎫 *€2.50, €5 for combined churches ticket, or VeronaCard* ⊗ *Nov.–Feb., Tues.–Sat. 10–4, Sun. 10–5; Mar.–Oct., Mon.–Sat. 10–5:30, Sun. 1:30–5:30.*

❻ Loggia del Consiglio. This graceful structure on the north flank of the Piazza dei Signori was finished in 1492 and built to house city council meetings. Although the city was already under Venetian rule, Verona still had a certain degree of autonomy, which was expressed by the splendor of the loggia. Very strangely for a Renaissance building of this quality, its architect remains unknown, but it is undoubtedly the finest surviving example of such architecture in Verona. ⊠ *Piazza dei Signori* ⊗ *Closed to the public.*

❺ Palazzo degli Scaligeri (Palazzo di Cangrande). The della Scalas ruled Verona from this stronghold built at the end of the 13th century by Cangrande I. At that time Verona controlled the mainland Veneto as far as Treviso and Lombardy to Mantua and Brescia. The portal facing the Piazza dei Signori was added in 1533 by the accomplished Renaissance architect Michele Sanmicheli.

❹ Palazzo della Ragione. An elegant pink marble staircase leads up from the *mercato vecchio* (old market) courtyard to the magistrates' chambers in the 12th-century palace, built at the intersection of the main streets of the ancient Roman city. Following massive restoration, the building reopened in March 2007 and is now used for art exhibitions. It is also available as a conference center. You can get the highest view in town from atop the attached 270-foot-tall **Torre dei Lamberti,** which attained its present height through a modification in 1452. ⊠ *Piazza dei Signori* 🕾 *045/8032726* 🎫 *€2, €3 with elevator* ⊗ *Mon. 1:30–7:30, Tues.–Sun. 8:30–7:30; last entry 6:45.*

Arche Scaligere. On a little piazza adjacent to the Piazza dei Signori are the fantastically sculpted gothic tombs of the della Scalas, who ruled Verona during the late Middle Ages. The 19th-century English traveler and critic, John Ruskin, described the tombs as graceful places where people who have fallen asleep live. The tomb of Cangrande I, hangs over the portal of the adjacent church and is the work of the Maestro di Sant'Anastasia. The tomb of Mastino II, begun in 1345, has an elaborate baldachino, originally painted and gilded, and is surrounded by an iron grillwork fence and topped by an equestrian statue. The latest and most elaborate tomb is that of Cansignorio (1375), the work principally of Bonino di Campione. The major tombs are all visible from the street.

Piazza delle Erbe. Frescoed buildings surround this medieval square, located on a site where a Roman forum once bustled. During the week it's still bustling, as vendors hawk produce and trinkets. Relax at one of the cafés and take in the chaos.

★ ⑪ **San Zeno Maggiore.** San Zeno is one of Italy's finest Romanesque churches. The rose window by the 13th-century sculptor Brioloto represents a wheel of fortune, with six of the spokes formed by statues depicting the rising and falling fortunes of mankind. The 12th-century porch is the work of Maestro Niccolò. Eighteen 12th-century marble reliefs flanking the porch by Niccolò and Maestro Guglielmo depict scenes from the Old and New Testaments and profane scenes from the legend of Theodoric. The bronze doors are from the 11th and 12th centuries; some were probably imported from Saxony and some are from Veronese workshops. They combine allegorical representations with scenes from the lives of saints. Inside, look for the 12th-century statue of *San Zeno* to the left of the main altar. In modern times it has been dubbed the "laughing San Zeno" because of a misinterpretation of its conventional Romanesque grin. A justly famous *Madonna and Saints* triptych by Andrea Mantegna (1431–1506) hangs over the main altar, and a peaceful cloister (1120–38) lies to the north (left) of the nave. The detached bell tower was begun in 1045, before the construction of much of the present church, and finished in 1173. ⊠ *Piazza San Zeno* ☎ *045/592813* ⊕ *www.chieseverona.it* ⛁ *€2.50, €5 for combined churches ticket, or VeronaCard* ⊗ *Nov.–Feb., Tues.–Sat. 10–4, Sun. 1–5; Mar.–Oct., Mon.–Sat. 8:30–6, Sun. 1–6.*

❽ **Sant'Anastasia.** Verona's largest church, begun in 1290 but consecrated only in 1471, is a fine example of Gothic brickwork and has a grand doorway with elaborately carved biblical scenes. The main reason for visiting this church, however, is *St. George and the Princess* (1434, but perhaps earlier) by Pisanello (1377–1455) above the Pellegrini Chapel right off the main altar. As you come in, look also for the *gobbi* (hunchbacks) supporting holy-water stoups. ⊠ *Vicolo Sotto Riva 4* ☎ *045/592813* ⊕ *www.chieseverona.it* ⛁ *€2.50, €5 for combined churches ticket, or VeronaCard* ⊗ *Nov.–Feb., Tues.–Sat. 10–4, Sun. 1–5; Mar.–Oct., Mon.–Sat. 9–6, Sun. 1–6.*

ALSO WORTH SEEING

🕙 **Ancient City Gates/Triumphal Arch.** In addition to its famous arena and Roman theater, two of ancient Verona's city gates and a very beautiful triumphal arch have survived from antiquity. These graceful and elegant portals give us an idea of the high aesthetic standards of ancient Verona. The oldest, the Porta dei Leoni (on Via Leoni, just a few steps from Piazza delle Erbe), dates from the 1st century BC, but its original earth-and-brick structure was sheathed in local marble during early

Imperial times. The Porta dei Borsari (at the beginning of Corso Porta Borsari, just a few steps from the opposite side of Piazza della Erbe), as its elegant decoration suggests, was the main entrance to ancient Verona, and, in its present state, dates from the 1st century AD. Continuing down Corso Cavour, which starts on the other (front) side of Porta dei Borsari, you'll find the very beautiful Arco dei Gavi, which is simpler and less imposing, but certainly more graceful, than the triumphal arches in Rome. It was built in the 1st century AD by the architect Lucius Vitruvius Cerdo to celebrate the accomplishments of the patrician Gavia family. It was highly esteemed by several renaissance architects, including Palladio.

❾ Museo Archeologico and Teatro Romano. Housed in what was a 15th-century monastery, the museum's collections were formed largely out of the donated collections of Veronese citizens proud of their city's classical past. Though there are few blockbusters here, there are some very noteworthy pieces (especially among the bronzes), and it is interesting to see what cultured Veronese from the 17th to 19th centuries collected. The museum sits high above the Teatro Romano, ancient Verona's theater, dating from the 1st century AD. ⊠*Rigaste del Redentore 2* ☎*045/8000360* 🎫*€3, free 1st Sun. of month, or VeronaCard* ⊗*Mon. 1:30–7:30, Tues.–Sun. 8:30–7:30; last entry 6:45.*

WHERE TO EAT

Book hotels months in advance for spring's Vinitaly, usually the second week in April, and for opera season. Verona hotels are also very busy during the January, May, and September gold fairs in neighboring Vicenza. Hotels jack up prices considerably during trade fairs and the opera season.

★ $$$$ ✗ **Arquade.** An 8-km (5-mi) trip northwest of the city brings you to one of the region's most esteemed high-end restaurants. Chef Bruno Barbieri has earned commendations for a creative menu that might include foie gras ravioli, *tegame tiepido* (pan-steamed seafood), or a soft-cooked egg, ingeniously poached and then fried, nestled in a bed of spinach. Tasting menus are a great way to sample a variety of Barbieri's creations. The wine list has more than 1,000 labels, including more than 100 of the best local wines. You can choose between dining in a converted chapel or on the beautiful terrace surrounding the 16th-century Villa del Quar, the small hotel where Arquade is located. Driving out for lunch or a pre-opera dinner is a great break from summer in the city. ⊠*Via Quar 12, 37020 Pedemonte di San Pietro in Cariano* ☎*045/6800681* ⌂*Reservations essential* ▭*AE, DC, MC, V* ⊗*Closed Mon. and Jan.–mid-Mar. No lunch Tues.*

$$$$ ✕ **Dodici Apostoli.** A Veronese institution, in a city where many high-end restaurants tend toward nouvelle cuisine, this highly esteemed restaurant is an exceptional place to enjoy classic regional dishes made with elegant variations on traditional recipes. Near Piazza delle Erbe, it stands on the foundations of a Roman temple. Specialties include gnocchi *di zucca e ricotta* (with squash and ricotta cheese) and *vitello alla Lessinia* (veal with mushrooms, cheese, and truffles). ⊠ *Vicolo Corticella San Marco 3* ☎ *045/596999* ⊕ *www.12apostoli.it* ⊟ *AE, DC, MC, V* ⊗ *Closed Mon., Jan. 1–10, and June 15–30. No dinner Sun.*

$$$$ ✕ **Il Desco.** *Cucina dell'anima* (food of the soul) is how Chef Elia Rizzo describes his cuisine, which, true to the Italian culinary tradition, preserves natural flavors through quick cooking and limits the number of ingredients per dish. But there is little tradition in the inventive and even daring way in which he combines those few ingredients in dishes such as duck breast with grappa, grapes, and eggplant puree, or beef cheeks with goose liver and caramelized pears. For a gastronomic adventure, order the tasting menu (€125, without wine), which includes appetizers, two first courses, two second courses, and dessert. Decor is elegant, if overdone, with tapestries, paintings, and an impressive 16th-century lacunar ceiling. ⊠ *Via Dietro San Sebastiano 7* ☎ *045/595358* ⚐ *Reservations essential* ⊟ *AE, DC, MC, V* ⊗ *Closed Sun. and Mon., Dec. 25–Jan. 8, and June 6–25. Dinner served Sun. in July, Aug., and Dec.*

★ **$** ✕ **Antica Osteria al Duomo.** This friendly side-street eatery lined with old wooden walls and ceilings, and decked out with musical instruments, serves Veronese food to a Veronese crowd; they come to quaff the local wine (€1–€3 per glass) and to savor excellent versions of local dishes like *bigoli con sugo di asino* (thick whole-wheat spaghetti with sauce made from donkey meat) and *pastisada con polenta* (horse-meat stew with polenta). Don't be put off by the dishes featuring unconventional meats; they're tender and delicious and this is probably the best place in town to sample them. First-rate Veronese home cooking comes at very reasonable prices here and is served by helpful, efficient staff. This is a very popular place, so reservations are recommended. ⊠ *Via Duomo 7/a* ☎ *045/8004505* ⊟ *AE, MC, V* ⊗ *Closed Sun. (except in Dec. and during wine fair).*

$ ✕ **Ristorante Redentore.** Across the Ponte Pietra pedestrian bridge from the heart of historic Verona, Redentore gives you a break from the busy city without quite having to leave it. Tall windows, pale walls, and bright paintings may make the interior inviting, but don't pass up the chance to dine alfresco beside the River Adige. Pizzas are the house special at €4.50–€7, but you can also choose among several homemade pastas or opt for a plate of local salamis and cheeses. ⊠ *Via Redentore 15/17* ☎ *045/8005932* ⊟ *MC, V* ⊗ *Closed Jan. 8–23. No lunch Mon.*

WHERE TO STAY

Book hotels months in advance for spring's Vinitaly, usually the second week in April, and for opera season. Verona hotels are also very busy during the January, May, and September gold fairs in neighboring Vicenza. Hotels jack up prices considerably during trade fairs and the opera season.

★ **$$$$** ⊡ **Villa del Quar.** Leopoldo and Evelina Montresor spared no expense when converting part of their 16th-century villa into a luxurious hotel oasis. It's surrounded by gardens and vineyards, yet only a 10-minute drive from Verona's city center. It's richly appointed with tapestries, antiques, and marble bathrooms, and the lounge is reminiscent of a castle's great hall. Quar's youthful staff provides attentive but relaxed service whether at the poolside bar or in the acclaimed Arquade restaurant (see review, above). **Pros:** Beautiful grounds, one of Italy's best restaurants is on-site. **Cons:** Outside the city center, very pricey, some rooms are starting to show wear. ⊠ *Via Quar 12, 37020 Pedemonte di San Pietro in Cariano* ✛ *8 km (5 mi) northwest of Verona* ☎ *045/6800681* 🖷 *045/6800604* ⊕ *www.hotelvilladelquar.it* ➥ *18 rooms, 10 suites* ♿ *In-room: safe, refrigerator, dial-up, Wi-Fi (some). In-hotel: restaurant, bars, pool, gym, public Internet, public Wi-Fi, parking (no fee), some pets allowed* ▭ *AE, DC, MC, V* ☉ *Closed Jan.–mid-Mar.* ⵙ *BP.*

$$$ ⊡ **Hotel Victoria.** Busy business executives and tourists demanding comfort and quiet luxury frequent this full-service hotel centrally located near the Piazza delle Erbe. The Victoria offers a modern, sleek entryway and traditionally decorated, comfortable rooms. As is the case with many Verona hotels, lower rates are available depending on the season. Standard rooms are attractive and well proportioned, but the "superior" rooms (€290) are really quite lavish (some have hydro-massage showers). **Pros:** Quiet and tasteful rooms, very central location, billiards room. **Cons:** No views, not all standard rooms have Internet, contemporary decor in lobby may not be to everyone's taste. ⊠ *Via Adua 8, 37121* ☎ *045/5905664* ⊕ *www.hotelvictoria.it* ➥ *66 rooms* ♿ *In-room: safe, refrigerator, ethernet (some). In-hotel: bar, gym, laundry service, public Internet, public Wi-Fi, parking (€35)* ▭ *AE, DC, MC, V* ⵙ *BP.*

$ ⊡ **Torcolo.** At this budget hotel you can count on: a warm welcome from the owners and courteous, helpful service from the staff; pleasant rooms, decorated tastefully with late-19th-century furniture; and a central location close to Piazza Brà and the Arena. Breakfast (optional except for July and August), which costs an extra €7.50–€15, is quite generous and is served outside on the front terrace in summer. Note that during opera season and during the wine fair, the price for a double jumps to €140 (though breakfast is included). **Pros:** Despite the central location, the hotel is very quiet; rooms are decorated very tastefully; staff gives reliable advice on visiting Verona. **Cons:** No Internet, no views, no room service or help with baggage (but there is an elevator). ⊠ *Vicolo Listone 3, 37121* ☎ *045/8007512* 🖷 *045/8004058* ⊕ *www. hoteltorcolo.it* ➥ *19 rooms* ♿ *In-room: safe, refrigerator. In-hotel: bar,* *parking (fee), some pets allowed* ⊟*AE, DC, MC, V* ⊙*Closed Dec. 21–27 and 2 wks in Feb.* ⊺⊙*EP.*

OPERA

Fodor's Choice ★ Milan's La Scala, Venice's La Fenice, and Parma's Teatro Regio offer performances more likely to satisfy serious opera fans, but none offers a greater spectacle than the **Arena di Verona** (*Box office* ✉ *Via Dietro Anfiteatro 6/b* ☎*045/8005151* ⊕*www.arena.it* ✍*Tickets start at €22* ⊙*Box office Sept.–June 20, weekdays 9–noon and 3:15–5:45, Sat. 9–noon; June 21–Aug., daily noon–9*). During its summer season (July–September) audiences of as many as 16,000 sit on the original stone terraces or in modern cushioned stalls. The best operas are the big, splashy ones, like *Aïda,* that demand huge choruses, lots of color and movement, and, if possible, camels, horses, or elephants. Order tickets by phone or online: if you book a spot on the cheaper terraces, be sure to take or rent a cushion—four hours on a 2,000-year-old stone bench can be an ordeal. Sometimes you can even hear the opera from Piazza Brà cafés.

SHOPPING

FOOD & WINE
Salumeria Albertini (✉*Corso S. Anastasia 41* ☎*045/8031074*) is Verona's oldest delicatessen: look for the prosciutto and salami hanging outside. **De Rossi** (✉*Corso Porta Borsari 3* ☎*045/8002489*) sells baked bread and cakes, pastries, and biscotti that are lusciously caloric.

MARKETS
On the third Saturday of every month an antiques and arts-and-crafts market fills **Piazza San Zeno.** The city's main general market takes place at the **Stadio** on Saturday 8:30 AM–1 PM.

TREVISO & THE HILLSIDE TOWNS

North of Venice, the Dolomites spawn rivers and streams that flow through market towns dotting the foothills. Villa Barbaro, one of Palladio's most graceful country villas, is here, as are the arcaded streets and romantic canals of undiscovered Treviso and the graceful Venetian Gothic structures of smaller hill towns.

MAROSTICA

26 km (16 mi) northeast of Vicenza, 93 km (58 mi) northwest of Venice.

GETTING HERE
There is no train station in Marostica. The closest rail connection is Bassano del Grappa, about 8 km (5 mi) away. There are regular bus connections from Vicenza's main station on FTV's No. 5; the trip takes

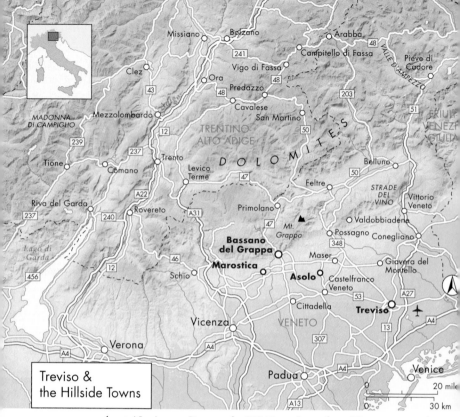

Treviso & the Hillside Towns

about 45 minutes. By car, take SP248 northeast from Vicenza, or south-west from Bassano.

VISITOR INFORMATION

Marostica tourism office (✉ *Piazza Castello 1, 36063* ☎ *0424/72127* 🌐 *www.marosticaeventi.it*). Fact checked JAN 2008

EXPLORING

From the 14th-century Castello Inferiore, where the town council still meets, an ancient stone wall snakes up the hill to enclose the Castello Superiore, with its commanding views. Marostica's most celebrated feature is the checkerboard-like square made with colored stone, Piazza Castello.

☙ A game of human-scale chess known as **Partita a Scacchi** is acted out in Piazza Castello by players in medieval costume on the second weekend in September in even-number years. The game dates from 1454 and originated as a peaceful way of settling a love dispute for the hand of the daughter of the Lord of Marostica Castle. The orders are still given in Venetian dialect. There's a game presented Friday–Sunday evenings and there's a Sunday-afternoon show. Tickets (€10–€60) go on sale in April; the tourist office can help with bookings.

WHERE TO STAY

★ $$ **Due Mori.** Recessed lighting adds to the modern, minimalist design at this historic inn, which has been this medieval town's only refuge for travelers since the 18th century. Warm wooden floors and soft-beige marble bathrooms are all made of local materials. Some windows look out onto the city walls or olive tree–filled terraces, but rooms 7, 8, 11, and 12 have picture-perfect views of the upper castle. There's a comfortably chic restaurant downstairs. **Pros:** Central location, pickup from Bassano train station on request, great views of castle from some rooms. **Cons:** Parking fee (unheard of for hotel in rural location). ✉*Corso Mazzini 7336063* ☎*0424/471777* 📠*0424/476920* 🌐*www.duemori.com* *10 rooms* *In-room: refrigerator, Wi-Fi. In-hotel: restaurant, public Internet, parking (fee), some pets allowed* 💳*AE, DC, MC, V* ⏲*Closed 1st wk in Jan. and 1 wk in mid-Aug.* *BP.*

BASSANO DEL GRAPPA

7 km (4½ mi) east of Marostica, 37 km (23 mi) north of Venice by local roads, 85 km (53 mi) by highway.

GETTING HERE

Several trains leave every hour from Venice's Santa Lucia station. The trip takes a little over an hour. By car, take the A13 from Venice, via Padua, to Bassano (1 hour, 20 minutes).

VISITOR INFORMATION

Bassano del Grappa tourism office (✉*Largo Corona d'Italia 35, 36061* ☎*0424/524351* 🌐*www.vicenzae.org*).

EXPLORING

Nestled at the base of the Mt. Grappa massif (5,880 feet), with the mountain-fresh Brenta River sluicing through, this town seems to be higher in the mountains than it actually is. Bassano has old streets lined with low-slung buildings adorned with wooden balconies and pretty flowerpots. Bright ceramic wares produced in the area are displayed in shops along byways that curve uphill toward a centuries-old square and, even higher, to a belvedere with a good view of Mt. Grappa and the beginning of the Val Sugana.

★ Bassano's most famous landmark is the **Ponte degli Alpini,** a covered bridge named for Italy's Alpine soldiers. There's been a bridge spanning the Brenta here since 1209, but floods and wars have necessitated repeated rebuilding. Following World War II, Alpine soldiers constructed the present version using Andrea Palladio's 16th-century design, which astutely calls for easily replaceable wood as the building material.

Almost as famous as Bassano's bridge is the adjacent **Grapperia Nardini** (✉*Ponte Vecchio 2* ☎*0424/527741* ⏲*Closed Mon. Jan.–Mar.*). The site of this family's first grappa distillery and its original 220-year-old still is open to the public. There are also a bar and liquor store in Bassano's Piazzale Giardino (open daily except Wednesday) that are very popular with locals for prelunch or after-work *aperitifs,* such as the Nardine *mezza-mezza* (a half-and-half blend of *aperitivo rosso* and rhubarb liquor). Visitors can schedule visits to the current distillery, 2 km (1 mi) out of town, where *Le Bolle,* striking architectural "Bubbles" (futuristic constructions housing a research center and reception halls designed by Massimilliano Fuksas), have become nearly as popular as the grappa itself.

Grappa was once considered by alchemists to have supernatural qualities, and its distillation techniques, you might say, were half science, half black magic. A few steps uphill from Ponte degli Alpini, grappa producer Poli has set up the **Poli Grappa Museum** (⊠ *Ponte Vecchio* ☎ *0424/524426* ⊒ *Free* ⊙ *Daily 9* AM–*9:30* PM). Most interesting are the old grappa stills, their glass tubes twisting into improbably shaped coils. You can taste almost all of Poli's numerous grappas (for free) and take home a bottle or two (not for free).

WHERE TO STAY & EAT

★ $$ ✕ **Al Sole da Tiziano.** With the personable Franco Chiurato in the dining room, you can't help but leave here satisfied. Within these walls, decorated with hefty, ornamental ceramic whistles (of the sort once used to warn of enemy approaches), Bassano home cooking flirts with the international: duck ends up in pomegranate, pheasant in cognac, and cauliflower and cheese hand-stuffed into luscious pasta pillows. ⊠ *Via Vittorelli 41/43* ☎ *0424/523206* ⊒ *AE, DC, MC, V* ⊙ *Closed Mon. and 3 wks late July–mid-Aug.*

$–$$ ✕ **Ristorante Birreria Ottone.** Proprietor Otto Wipflinger's Austrian ancestors might not recognize the beer hall they opened a century ago—the ceiling frescoes, starched tablecloths, and innovative dropdown lighting now give it the feel of a comfortable restaurant. The menu mixes old family recipes—such as goulash with cumin—with such innovations as veal in creamy balsamic sauce, and chocolate torte served with coffee syrup and whipped cream. ⊠ *Via Matteotti 48/50* ☎ *0424/522206* ⊒ *AE, DC, MC, V* ⊙ *Closed Tues. and June 15–July 15. No dinner Mon.*

$$$ ✕ ⊡ **Ca' Sette.** The main building is in an 18th-century villa with original frescoed ceilings in the rooms; there are also rooms available in the former granary, which dates from the 16th century and has rustic beamed ceilings. The furnishings of the rooms are modern, but do not intrude upon the historic atmosphere. **Ca' 7** restaurant ($$$) is among the best in the area. Chef Alex Lorenzon's seasonal selection always includes a wide variety of salt- and freshwater fish, as well as meat and game. The €65 tasting menu is a worthwhile indulgence. **Pros:** Very atmospheric, great restaurant, well-informed and helpful staff. **Cons:** Rooms that face the busy road are noisy, slightly outside city's historic center. ⊠ *Via Cunizza da Romano 4, 36061* ☎ *0424/383350* 🖶 *0424/393287* ⊕ *www.ca-sette.it* ⮒ *17 rooms, 2 suites* ⚏ *In-room: safe, refrigerator, ethernet. In-hotel: restaurant, bicycles, public Wi-Fi, parking (no fee), some pets allowed* ⊒ *AE, DC, MC, V* ⊙ *Restaurant closed Mon., 1st wk in Jan., and 2 wks in mid-Aug. No dinner Sun.* ⍾ *BP.*

$-$$ 🏠 **Villa Palma.** This gracefully refurbished 18th-century country villa only a short drive from Asolo (10 km [6 mi]) and Bassano (5 km [3 mi]) combines modern comforts and conveniences with rural calm and old-fashioned style and charm—wooden beams, vaulted brick ceilings, and tasteful furnishings. Four rooms have whirlpool baths, one a Turkish bath. In summer, meals are served on the terrace overlooking the splendid garden. ⊠ *Via Chemin Palma 30, Mussolente36065* ☎*0424/577407* 🖷*0424/87687* ⊕*www.villapalma.it* 📲*20 rooms, 1 suite* ♿*In-hotel: restaurant, bar* 🚬*AE, DC, MC, V.*

$ 🏠 **Al Castello.** In a restored town house at the foot of the medieval Torre Civica, the Cattapan family's Castello is a reasonably priced, attractive choice. The simply furnished rooms all differ in shape and size, some have wood-beam ceilings. Request a room at the front for a small balcony with a view of the charming square below. **Pros:** Central location, some rooms have views of square. **Cons:** Not a good deal in high season, additional €6 for breakfast. ⊠*Piazza Terraglio 19, 36061* ☎🖷*0424/228665* ⊕*www.hotelalcastello.it* 📲*11 rooms* ♿*In-room: dial-up. In-hotel: bar, no elevator, parking (no fee), some pets allowed* 🚬*AE, MC, V* 🍴*EP.*

ASOLO

Fodor's Choice ★ *11 km (7 mi) east of Bassano del Grappa, 33 km (20½ mi) northwest of Treviso.*

GETTING HERE
There is no train station in Asolo; the closest one is in Montebelluna. Bus service is available from Treviso (1 hour), Bassano del Grappa (20 minutes), or Castelfranco (20 minutes). Check the bus schedules, since connections are infrequent at certain times of day. There is also service to and from Maser.

By car from Treviso take Via Feltrina and continue onto Via Padre Agostino Gemelli (SR348). Follow SR348 about 16 km (10 mi), then turn left on SP667, which you follow for 3.7 km (2.5 mi). At the roundabout, take the first exit, Via Monte Grappa (SP284) and follow it for 6.5 km (4 mi) to Via Loredan, where you turn right and then left onto Via Bordo Vecchio. Asolo is less than 7 km (4.3 mi) away from the Palladian Villa Barbaro at Maser.

VISITOR INFORMATION
Asolo tourism office (⊠*Piazza Garibaldi, 31011* ☎*0423/529046* ⊕*www.asolo.it*).

EXPLORING
The romantic, charming hillside hamlet of Asolo was the consolation prize of an exiled queen. At the end of the 15th century, Venetian-born Caterina Cornaro was sent here by Venice's doge to keep her from interfering with Venetian administration of her former kingdom of Cyprus, which she had inherited from her husband. To soothe the pain of exile she established a lively and brilliant court in Asolo. It was in this court that the Renaissance poet-essayist, Pietro Bembo, set his

famous "Gli asolani" (1505), dedicated to Lucrezia Borgia, in which six Venetian courtiers discuss the pros and cons of love. Through the centuries, Venetian aristocrats continued to build gracious villas on the hillside, and in the 19th century Asolo once again became the idyllic haunt of musicians, poets, and painters. And it's no wonder why—this aerie is one of Italy's most strikingly situated villages, combining views across miles of mountainous countryside with a slow-paced, fortified–hill town feel. Here, you can stroll past villas once inhabited by Robert Browning and actress Eleonora Duse. Be warned that the town's charm vaporizes on holiday weekends when the crowds pour in. Asolo hosts a two-day antiques market on the second Sunday of every month except July and August.

Renaissance palaces and antique cafés grace **Piazza Maggiore,** Asolo's town center. In the piazza, the frescoed 15th-century Loggia del Capitano contains the **Museo Civico,** which displays memorabilia—Eleonora Duse's correspondence, Robert Browning's spinet, and portraits of Caterina Cornaro. ⊠*Piazza Maggiore* ☎*0423/952313* 🏷*€4* ☉*Weekends 10–noon and 3–7 and by reservation.*

<table>
<tr><td>

NEED A BREAK?

</td><td>

While away some idle moments at Caffè Centrale (⊠ *Via Roma 72* ☎*0423/952141* ⊕*www.caffecentrale.com* ☉*Closed Tues.*), which has overlooked the fountain in Piazza Maggiore and the Duomo since about 1700. It's open until 1 AM.

</td></tr>
</table>

Asolo's **Duomo** was erected on a site where Roman baths and a succession of cathedrals, the earliest dating to 590, have stood. This version, rather small to bear the title "Duomo," was built in 1747 and contains a baptismal font formerly belonging to Queen Caterina Cornaro. Jacopo Bassano (circa 1510–92) and Lorenzo Lotto (1480–1556) painted *Assumption* altarpieces. ⊠*Piazzetta San Pio X 192* ☎*0423/952376* ☉*Daily 8–noon and 3:30–6:15.*

Walking along Via Browning takes you past smart shops, Browning's house at No. 153, and the *enoteca* (wine bar) **Alle Ore** (⊠*Via Browning 183* ☎*0423/951022*), where you can sample the local wine and grappa. It's closed Monday.

Heading uphill from Piazza Maggiore, you'll pass Caterina Cornaro's ruined **Castello** (⊠*Piazzetta E. Duse*), whose theater was transported to Florida in 1930. The castle is closed to the public.

Above the Castello stands the imposing **Villa Pasini** (closed to the public), its ground floor still occupied by the signora Pasini.

One of the major monuments of contemporary Italian architecture, the **Brion family tomb** (⊠ SP6, Via Castellan, ✛About 7 km [4 mi] south of Asolo, near the village of San Vito ☎ *No phone* 🏷*Free* ☉*Apr.–Sept. daily 8–7, Oct.–Mar. daily 9–3:30*) was designed and built by the highly celebrated architect Carlo Scarpa (1906–78) between 1970 and 1972. Combining Western rationalism with Eastern spirituality, Scarpa avoids the gloom and bombast of conventional commemorative monuments, creating, in his words, a secluded Eden.

WHERE TO STAY & EAT

$$$–$$$$ ✕ **Ca' Derton.** Just behind the main square you can choose between the formality of Ca' Derton's white-lace tablecloths or the rustic tables and outdoor terrace (and lower prices) of its adjacent enoteca, named Nino and Antonietta. Masters of traditional cuisine, they take pride in their homemade pasta, bread, and desserts, all of which you can order in either eatery. The exquisite *sopa coada* (pigeon-and-bread soup) takes two days to prepare from a centuries-old recipe. Follow that with such dishes as venison with pomegranate, pasta with partridge and radicchio, and vanilla ice cream with pure Modena balsamic vinegar. ✉ *Piazza Gabriele d'Annunzio 11* ☎ *0423/529648* ⊕ *www.caderton.com* ☐ *AE, DC, MC, V* ⊗ *Closed Sun. and 2 wks in late Feb. No lunch Mon.*

$ ✕ **Al Bacaro.** Since 1892 this osteria has been a second home to Asolani laborers and craftsmen. Whether you eat downstairs in the bar with hanging copper kettles or upstairs in the dining room beneath lacy lamps, you get affordable wines and pastas and home-style food. Take the leap and try a dish with stewed game, tripe, or snails. Less-adventurous diners can go for goulash, polenta with cheese and mushrooms, or one of Bacaro's open-face sandwiches generously topped with fresh salami, speck, or other cold cuts. ✉ *Via Browning 165* ☎ *0423/55150* ☐ *AE, DC, MC, V* ⊗ *Closed Wed. and 2 wks in July.*

★ $$$$ ⌂ **Villa Cipriani.** A romantic garden surrounded by gracious country homes is the setting for this 16th-century villa, now part of the Starwood chain. From 19th-century antiques to a 21st-century spa facility, the experience is opulent from start to finish. Superior-class rooms have views; the two suites with private terraces are significantly more expensive but absolutely stunning. The restaurant ($$$$)has its own terrace overlooking the garden and hills, a perfect place to sip an aperitif. Substantial discounts are available on the Web site (make sure the rate quoted is for the entire stay not one night). **Pros:** Lovely grounds, spa services. **Cons:** Small bathrooms; standard rooms in annex are very small, with limited views; some readers complain about indifferent service. ✉ *Via Canova 298, 31011* ☎ *0423/523411* 🖶 *0423/952095* ⊕ *www.starwood.com/italy* 🛏 *31 rooms* ⌂ *In-room: safe, refrigerator, Wi-Fi. In-hotel: restaurant, bar, spa, parking (fee), some pets allowed* ☐ *AE, DC, MC, V* ⊚|*BP.*

★ $$$ ⌂ **Al Sole.** The smell of the polished wood floor greets you as you enter this 1920s pink-washed hotel overlooking the main square. This was once actress Eleonora Duse's preferred haunt, and her favorite room has been preserved. All the rooms are large and furnished in antique style. The more-expensive superior rooms enjoy great views over the town, while the back rooms have leafy, rural views. Decoratively tiled, the bathrooms come equipped with hydro-massage showers, which might come in handy for legs that have climbed up the hill for a view. Less-demanding vistas are available from the hotel's pleasant terrace, where you can gaze upon picturesque Asolo as you have a sunset drink or dinner (summer only). **Pros:** Central location, beautiful views, attentive service. **Cons:** Restaurant closed in off-season. ✉ *Via Collegio 33, 31011* ☎ *0423/951332* 🖷 *0423/951007* ⊕ *www.albergoalsole.com* 🛏 *22 rooms, 1 suite* ♿ *In-room: safe, refrigerator, dial-up. In-hotel: restaurant (Apr.–Oct.), bar, gym, public Internet, public Wi-Fi, parking (no fee), some pets allowed (fee)* ▤ *AE, MC, V* 🍽 *BP.*

WORD OF MOUTH

"If you do stay in Treviso, make sure you have a cappuccino in Piazza dei Signori—the best place to people watch and enjoy the ambience!" –Paulareg

$$ 🏨 **Duse.** A spiral staircase winds its way up this narrow, centrally located building to rooms with a view of the town square. The scene gets lively on antiques fair weekends, but if the sights don't make up for the sounds, ask for the larger and quieter attic room—skylights instead of windows mean your only view is the stars. Some rooms are smallish, but for Asolo, the price is a real deal. **Pros:** Simple but tastefully decorated rooms, central location. **Cons:** No Internet, most rooms get some street noise, not as much of a bargain when you add the parking fee. ✉ *Via Browning 190, 31011* ☎ *0423/55241* 🖷 *0423/950404* ⊕ *www.hotelduse.com* 🛏 *14 rooms* ♿ *In-room: refrigerator. In-hotel: bar, parking (fee)* ▤ *AE, MC, V* 🕘 *Closed 3 wks in Jan. and Feb.* 🍽 *EP.*

TREVISO

35 km (22 mi) southeast of Maser, 30 km (19 mi) north of Venice.

GETTING HERE

Treviso is only 30 minutes by express train from Venice; there are frequent daily departures. By car from Venice, pick up the SS13 in Mestre (Via Terraglio) and follow it all the way to Treviso; the trip takes about 45 minutes.

VISITOR INFORMATION

Treviso tourism office (✉ *Piazza Monte di Pietà 8, 31100* ☎ *0422/547632* ⊕ *http://turismo.provincia.treviso.it*).

EXPLORING

Treviso has been dubbed "Little Venice" because of its meandering, moss-banked canals. They can't really compare with Venice's spectacular waterways, but on the whole Treviso's historic center, with its medieval arcaded streets, has its own unique charm.

A more apt description is "the painted city," for frescoed exteriors abound—a creative response to the area's lack of stone suitable for use as facades. There are fashionable shops and boutiques at every turn in the busy city center, which was a commercial hub as early as the 8th century and a hive of literary and artistic activity by the 13th century. Though a World War II Allied bombing on Good Friday 1944 destroyed half the city, Treviso meticulously preserved what remained of its old town's narrow streets while simultaneously introducing modernity far more gently than many other parts of Italy.

CLOSE UP

Traveling the Wine Roads

You'd be hard-pressed to find a more-stimulating and varied wine region than northeastern Italy. From the Valpolicella, Bardolino, and Soave produced near Verona to the superlative whites of the Collio region, wines from the Veneto and Friuli–Venezia Giulia earn more Denominazione di Origine Controllata (DOC) seals for uniqueness and quality than those of any other area of Italy.

You can travel on foot, by car, or by bicycle over hillsides covered with vineyards, each field nurturing subtly different grape varieties. On a casual trip through the countryside you're likely to come across wineries that will welcome you for a visit; for a more-organized tour, check at local tourist information offices, which have maps of roads, wineries, and vendors. (If you find yourself in Bassano del Grappa, stop by Nardini distillery to pick up some grappa, the potent liquor made from grape husks.) Be advised that Italy has become more stringent about its driving regulations; seat belts and designated drivers can save fines, embarrassment, or worse.

One of the most hospitable areas in the Veneto for wine enthusiasts is the stretch of country north of Treviso, where you can follow designated wine roads—tours that blend a beautiful rural setting with the delights of the grape. Authorized wine shops where you can stop and sample are marked with a sign showing a triangular arrangement of red and yellow grapes. There are three routes to choose from, and they're manageable enough that you can do them all comfortably over the course of a day or two.

MONTELLO & ASOLO HILLS

This route provides a good balance of vineyards and non-wine sights. It winds from Nervesa della Battaglia, 18 km (10 mi) north of Treviso, past two prime destinations in the area, the lovely village of Asolo and the Villa Barbaro at Maser. Asolo produces good prosecco, whereas Montello favors merlot and cabernet. Both areas also yield pinot and chardonnay.

PIAVE RIVER

The circular route follows the Piave River and runs through orchards, woods, and hills. Among the area's gems are the DOC Torchiato di Fregona and Refrontolo Passito, both made according to traditional methods. Raboso del Piave, renowned since Roman times, ages well and complements local dishes such as beans and pasta or goose stuffed with chestnuts. Other reds are cabernet, merlot, and cabernet sauvignon. As an accompaniment to fish, try a Verduzzo del Piave or, for an aperitif, the warm-yellow Pinot Grigio del Piave.

PROSECCO

This route runs for 47 km (29 mi) between Valdobbiadene and Conegliano, home of Italy's first wine institute, winding between knobby hills covered in grapevines. These hang in festoons on row after row of pergolas to create a thick mantle of green. Turn off the main route to explore the narrower country lanes, most of which eventually join up. They meander through tiny hamlets and past numerous family wineries where you can taste and purchase the wines. Spring is an excellent time to visit, with no fewer than 15 local wine festivals held between March and early June.

4

The **Piazza dei Signori** is the center of medieval Treviso and still the town's social hub, with outdoor cafés and some impressive public buildings. One of these, the Palazzo dei Trecento, has a small alley behind it that leads to the *pescheria* (fish market), on an island in one of the small canals that flow through town.

While strolling the city, take in the restored **Quartiere Latino,** an area between Riviera Garibaldi and Piazza Santa Maria Battuti. It's the site of university buildings, upscale apartments, and a number of new restaurants and shops. If you walk along the northern part of the historic city wall, you'll look down on the island home of a number of ducks, geese, and goats. Their little farm occupies some of the city's prettiest real estate.

The most important church in Treviso is **San Nicolò,** an impressive Gothic structure with an ornate vaulted ceiling and frescoes of the saints by Tommaso da Modena (circa 1325–79); the depiction of *St. Agnes* on the north side is particularly charming. More remarkable are Tommaso's astoundingly realistic portraits of 40 Dominican friars in the seminary next door. They include one of the earliest-known paintings of a subject wearing glasses. ⊠ *Seminario Vescovile, Via San Nicolò* ☏ *0422/3247* ☉ *Daily 8–noon and 3:30–6:30.*

Inside Treviso's seven-domed **Duomo,** the Malchiostro Chapel contains an *Annunciation* by Titian and frescoes by Pordenone (1484–1539), including an *Adoration of the Magi.* The crypt has 12th-century columns. Bring a handful of 10- and 20-cent coins for the lights to illuminate the artwork. ⊠ *Piazza del Duomo* ☉ *Mon.–Sat. 7:15–noon and 3:30–7; Sun. 8–1 and 3:30–8.*

■ OFF THE
BEATEN
PATH

Conegliano. The town of Conegliano, 23 km (14 mi) north of Treviso, is in wine-producing country. The town itself is attractive, with Venetian-style villas, frescoed houses, and an elegant 14th-century Duomo, but the real draw is the wine, particularly the effervescent prosecco, sold in local wine bars and shops.

WHERE TO STAY & EAT

$$$ ✕ **Beccherie.** The name means butcher shop, and in fact this area behind Treviso's Palazzo Trecento was where centuries of people bought and sold meat. Only fitting that Beccherie should offer carnivores one of the most entertaining and sociable ways to feast. With *filetto alla pietra,* a preheated stone arrives at your table complete with a variety of condiments and one raw fillet—like a fondue minus the oil. Locals have been keeping this family-owned restaurant busy since 1939; reservations are recommended for dinner. ⊠ *Piazza Ancilotto 10* ☏ *0422/540871* ▭ *AE, DC, MC, V* ☉ *Closed Mon. and last 2 wks in July. No dinner Sun.*

★ $$ ✕ **Vineria.** You won't be the first to step extra carefully onto Vineria's transparent dining room floor—while watching a canal rush beneath your feet. One of the first tenants in Treviso's restored Quartiere Latino, this restaurant incorporated into its design a canal that had been covered for years. Visit here to experience Italian cuisine from other regions, such as Tuscan steak or Piemontese La Granda beef, grilled or tartar, or fried mozzarella. And though the food is good, the wine list is even better, with more than 1,200 labels in the cantina. ⊠ *Quartiere Latino* ☎ *0422/419787* ▤ *AE, DC, MC, V* ☉ *Closed Sun.*

★ $–$$ ✕ **Osteria Ponte Dante.** What could be more romantic than dining alfresco, at the junction of two quiet canals, in a spot once described by Dante? You can do it here, and, incredibly, the food lives up to the setting. The kitchen turns out great, simple local dishes like ravioli *ai porcini e ricotta affumicata* (with porcini mushrooms and smoked mozzarella) and a classic *fritto misto di pesce* (mixed fried fish), all at reasonable prices. ⊠ *Piazza Garibaldi 6* ☎ *0422/582924* ▤ *No credit cards* ☉ *Closed Sun.*

$–$$ ✕ **Toni del Spin.** Wood paneled and styled with 1930s decor, this friendly, bustling place oozes old-fashioned character. The reasonably priced, wholesome menu, chalked on a hanging wooden board, sometimes changes twice a day. In autumn and winter, don't miss trying Treviso's hallmark product: radicchio, in risotto or pasta. They also do a great job with *coniglio all casereccia* (stewed rabbit) and *faraona* (guinea fowl). Don't leave without quaffing a glass or two of prosecco. ⊠ *Via Inferiore 7* ☎ *0422/543829* ⊕ *www.ristorantetonidelspin.com* ♨ *Reservations essential* ▤ *AE, MC, V* ☉ *Closed Sun. and 3 wks in June and July. No lunch Mon.*

★ $ ⌂ **Il Focolare.** Spitting distance from the back of the Palazzo dei Trecento, in the very heart of Treviso's *centro storico* (historic city center), Il Focolare has a location that's the envy of most Treviso hotels. It's also a pleasant enough place to stay, with some of the decently furnished, if smallish, rooms with canal views. Management also lets eight additional rooms in a nearby building. **Pros:** Pleasant rooms, canal views, central location. **Cons:** Not for light sleepers—rooms get noise from a nearby bar that's open until late. ⊠ *Piazza Ancilotto 4, 31100* ☎ *0422/56601* 🖨 *0422/56601* ⊕ *www.albergoilfocolare.net* ⇥ *14 rooms* ♿ *In-room: refrigerator. In-hotel: bar, no elevator* ▤ *AE, DC, MC, V* ⑩ *BP.*

FRIULI–VENEZIA GIULIA

The peripheral location of the Friuli–Venezia Giulia region in Italy's northeastern corner makes it easy to overlook, but with its ethnic mix of Italian, Slavic, and central European cultures, along with a legendary wine tradition, it's a fascinating area to explore. Venetian culture crept northward until it merged with northern European into the Veneto-Byzantine style evident in places like the medieval city of Udine. The Cividale del Friuli and the Collio wine regions are a short hop away from Udine, and the old Austrian port of Trieste was once an important symbol of Italian nationalism.

UDINE

94 km (58 mi) northeast of Treviso, 127 km (79 mi) northeast of Venice.

GETTING HERE

There is frequent train service from both Venice and Trieste; the trip takes about 1½ hours on the fastest express train from Venice, and a little over an hour from Trieste. By car from Venice, take the SR11 to the E55 and head east. Take the E55 (it eventually becomes the Autostrada Alpe Adria) to SS13 (Viale Venezia) east into Udine. Driving from Trieste, take the SS202 to the E70, which becomes the A4. Turn off onto the E55 north, which is the same road you would take coming from Venice. Driving times are 1½ hours from Venice and one hour from Trieste.

VISITOR INFORMATION

Udine tourism office (✉ *Piazza I Maggio 7, 33100* ☎ *0432/295972* ⊕ *www.turismo.fvg.it*).

EXPLORING

Udine, the largest city on the Friuli side of the region, has a more-provincial, genteel atmosphere than Venezia Giulia's sprawling Trieste. Give the old center a day of your strolling time, and you'll find unevenly spaced streets bursting with fun little wine bars, open-air cafés, and gobs of Friulian character. The city sometimes seems completely unaffected by tourism or even modernity. Commanding a view from the Alpine foothills to the Adriatic Sea, Udine stands on a mound that, according to legend, was erected so Attila the Hun could watch the burning of Aquileia, an important Roman center to the south. In the Middle Ages Udine flourished, thanks to its favorable trade location and the right granted by the local patriarch to hold regular markets.

★ There is a distinctly Venetian architectural feel to the medieval city, noticeable in the large main square, the **Piazza della Libertà**. The Palazzo del Comune, a typical 15th-century Venetian palace, built in imitation of the Palazzo Ducale in Venice, dominates the square. Opposite stands the Renaissance Porticato di San Giovanni and the Torre dell'Orologio, a clock tower complete with naked *mori* (the Moors who strike the

hours) on the top, inspired by the Torre d'Orologio in Venice's Piazza San Marco.

The **Palazzo Arcivescovile** (also known as Palazzo Patriarcale) contains several rooms of frescoes by the young Gianbattista Tiepolo, painted from 1726 to 1732. They comprise the most important collection of early works by Italy's most brilliant 18th-century painter. The Galleria del Tiepolo (1727) contains superlative Tiepolo frescoes depicting the stories of Abraham, Isaac, and Jacob. The *Judgment of Solomon* (1729) graces the Pink Room. There are also beautiful and important Tiepolo frescoes in the staircase, throne room, and the palatine chapel of this palazzo. In the same building, the Museo Diocesano features a collection of sculptures from Friuli churches from the 13th through the 18th century. ⊠*Piazza Patriarcato 1* ☎*0432/25003* ⊕*www. museiprovinciaud.it* ⊠*€5, includes Museo Diocesano* ⊗ *Wed.–Sun. 10–noon and 3:30–6:30.*

From the hilltop **Castello** panoramic views extend to Monte Nero (7,360 feet) in neighboring Slovenia. Here Udine's civic museums of art and archaeology are centralized under one roof. Particularly worth seeing is the national and regional art collection in the **Galleria d'Arte Antica**, which has canvases by Venetians Vittore Carpaccio (circa 1460–1525) and Giambattista Tiepolo. ⊠*Castello di Udine*

☎0432/271591 🌐www.comune.udine.it 🎫€3, €1 Sun. ⏲Tues.–Sat. 9:30–12:30 and 3–6, Sun. 9:30–12:30.

One of the legends of the grappa world, **Nonino** has operated in the little town of Percoto, 13 km (8 mi) south of Udine, since 1897. The grappa giant's distillery is open for tours and tasting during the autumn manufacturing season. Take Viale Palmanova (SS56) south from Udine and bear left onto SP2; after passing Pavia di Udine, continue until you see Nonino. *✉Via Aquileia 104 ☎0432/676331 🌐www.nonino.it 🎫Free ⏲Sept.–Nov. by appointment only.*

WHERE TO STAY & EAT

$–$$ ✕ **Hostaria alla Tavernetta.** One of Udine's most trusted food addresses since 1954, this restaurant has rustic fireside dining downstairs, and smaller, more-elegantly decorated rooms upstairs, where there's even a small terrace. Steps from the Piazza Duomo, it serves specialties such as guinea fowl with rosemary and *musetto,* a local sausage cooked with pickled turnips. There's a different *orzotto* (barley prepared like risotto) daily. After your meal, enjoy your coffee with shaved chocolate and *cantucci,* cookies most Americans know as biscotti. *✉Via di Prampero 2 ☎0432/501066 ▭AE, MC, V ⏲Closed Sun. and Mon., 2 wks in June, and 2nd wk in Jan.*

★ $ ✕ **Osteria Al Vecchio Stallo.** Down a narrow, winding street, this former stable bursts with trinkets and character, its beautiful courtyard shaded by grape arbors. The menu includes a bevy of traditional Friuli *casalinga* (home-cooked specialties) with spellings tough to wrap your mouth around, such as *cjalzòns* (ravioli stuffed with spinach, apple, pear, or cheese, and topped with butter and cinnamon). Adventurous eaters should try the *nervetti* (gelatinous cubes of veal's knee), which you probably won't find anywhere west of here. There's a great selection of wines by the glass, and the gregarious chef-owner is a gracious host. *✉Via Viola 7 ☎0432/21296 ▭No credit cards ⏲Closed Wed. Aug.–Jun., Mon. in Jul., 3 weeks in Aug., and Dec. 25–Jan. 6.*

$$ 🏨 **Hostaria Hotel Allegria.** In this 1400s building, where the owner was born and raised, what started out as a humble osteria has grown into a stylish, comfortable hotel. Design includes plenty of wood, polished into finely crafted furnishings and wall treatments. Lighting is done to dramatic effect, and soft jazz plays in the common areas. The attractive cantina hosts private dinner parties. **Pros:** Recently refurbished, great staff, discounted weekend rates. **Cons:** Rooms may be too minimalist and modern for some tastes, fee for parking. *✉Via Grazzano 18, 33100 ☎0432/201116 🌐www.hotelallegria.it 🛏20 rooms 🛎In-room: safe, refrigerator, dial-up. In-hotel: bar, restaurant, public Wi-Fi, parking (fee) ▭AE, MC, V 🍽BP.*

★ $–$$ 🏨 **Hotel Clocchiatti.** You have two choices here: stay in the restored 19th-century villa, where large double doors open onto canopy beds and Alpine-style wood ceilings and paneling; or opt for the rich colors and spare furnishings of the starkly angular rooms in the ultramodern (and pricier) "Next" wing. Some suites have sunken Japanese baths and gardens. Centuries-old trees shade the terrace, and high-design chaises surround the pool that's entirely painted black. **Pros:** Lovely, individually decorated rooms; quiet; swimming pool. **Cons:** Ten-minute drive from town center, small bathrooms. ✉ *Via Cividale 29, 33100* ☎☎*0432/505047* ⊕*www.hotelclocchiatti.it* ➯*27 rooms* ⌂*In-room: safe, refrigerator, Wi-Fi. In-hotel: bar, pool, bicycles, no elevator, laundry service, parking (no fee), some pets allowed* ▭*AE, DC, MC, V* ⊙*BP.*

CIVIDALE DEL FRIULI

17 km (11 mi) east of Udine, 144 km (89 mi) northeast of Venice.

GETTING HERE

There is regular bus and train service from Udine (the buses leave from the train station). By car from Udine, take Via Cividale, which turns into SS54; follow SS54 into Cividale.

VISITOR INFORMATION

Cividale del Friuli tourism office (✉*Corso Poalino d'Aquileria 10, 33051* ☎*0432/731398*).

EXPLORING

Cividale was founded in AD 53 by Julius Caesar, then commander of Roman legions in the area. Locals say their Ponte del Diavolo, bridging the Natisone River, is supported by rocks the devil tossed down during a tantrum. Here you can find Celtic and Roman ruins alongside Venetian Gothic buildings, including the Palazzo Comunale.

Cividale's Renaissance **Duomo** contains a magnificent 12th-century silver gilt altarpiece. ✉*Piazza Duomo* ☎*0432/731144* ⊙*Apr.–Oct., Mon.–Sat. 9:30–noon and 3–7, Sun. 3–7; Nov.–Mar., Mon.–Sat. 9:30– noon and 3–6, Sun. 3–6.*

The **Tempietto Longobardo,** perched above the meandering river, is a little gem of a Lombard church from the 8th or 9th century. It has an archway with a vine motif, guarded by an 8th-century procession of female figures. The fine carved wooden stalls date from the 14th century. ✉*Via Monastero Maggiore* ☎*0432/700867* ⊕*www.museiprovinciaud.it* ▭*€2* ⊙*Apr.–Sept., Mon.–Sat. 9:30–12:30 and 3–6:30, Sun. 9:30–1 and 3–7:30; Oct.–Mar., Mon.–Sat. 9:30–12:30 and 3–5, Sun. 9:30–12:30 and 2:30–6.*

WHERE TO STAY & EAT

$–$$ ✕ **Ai Tre Re.** Here, legend says, three kings once divided up the countryside, and since the 1500s the Three Kings has refreshed travelers within its stone-wall garden or beside its 6-foot-square woodstove. Beneath the beamed ceiling everything is homemade, including the bread of wheat and *maize* (corn). Try pumpkin gnocchi with smoked ricotta, followed by sausage in cream sauce or cheese grilled with wild herbs. ✉*Via Stretta San Valentino 31* ☎*0432/700416* ▭*MC, V* ⊙*Closed Tues., 3 wks in June, and 1 wk in Oct.*

$–$$ ✕ **Trattoria Dominissini.** The rustic wood furnishings and simple decor here are perfectly in keeping with Cividale's old-world charm. The menu is built around old recipes from Friuli. Try the wonderful *frico con patate*, a mixture of potato and local Montasio cheese cooked in the pan like an omelet; meat dishes might include stewed wild game with polenta. There's also a healthy selection of vegetables, along with mixed salads, tempting desserts, and excellent Friulian wines. ⊠ *Via Jacopo Stellini 18* ☎ *0432/733763* ▤ *AE, DC, MC, V* ⊘ *Closed Mon., last 2 wks in June, and 2 wks in mid-Nov.*

$$ ▥ **Locanda Al Castello.** Set on a peaceful hillside a few minutes' drive out of town, this creeper-covered, crenellated hotel was once a monastery. Rooms are spacious and furnished in varying styles, some antique, some modern, but all with large bathrooms. Locals gather here for Sunday lunch outdoors on the terrace, or indoors beside the large Friulian open fireplace. The most popular special is *maltagliata alla lungobarda*, thinly sliced beef, marinated and char-grilled. **Pros:** Quiet area; discounts possible, depending on availability. **Con:** Outside of town (not viable without a car). ⊠ *Via del Castello 12, 33043* ☎ *0432/733242* ⊕ *www.alcastello.net* ⇆ *25 rooms, 2 suites* ⚙ *In-room: no a/c (some), safe, refrigerator, Wi-Fi. In-hotel: restaurant, bar, tennis courts, spa, parking (no fee), some pets allowed* ▤ *AE, DC, MC, V* ▥*BP.*

AQUILEIA

77 km (48 mi) west of Trieste, 163 km (101 mi) east of Venice.

GETTING HERE
There is frequent train service from Venice and Trieste to Cervignano di Friuli, which is 8 km (5 mi) away; from here, you can reach Aquileia by bus or taxi. There is also direct bus service from Trieste's airport. By car from Venice or Trieste, take Autostrada A4 (Venezia–Trieste) to the Palmanova exit and continue 17 km (11 mi) to Aquileia. From Udine, take Autostrada A23 to the Palmanova exit.

VISITOR INFORMATION
Aquileia tourism office (⊠ *Piazza Capitolo* ☎ *0431/919491*).

EXPLORING
This sleepy little town was, in the time of Emperor Augustus, Italy's fourth most important city (after Rome, Milan, and Capua). It was the principal Adriatic port of Italy and the beginning of Roman routes north. Its prominence endured into the Christian era. The patriarchate (bishopric) of Aquileia was founded here around 314, just after the Edict of Milan halted the persecution of Christians and about the time that the Emperor Constantine officially declared his Christianity. After several centuries of decline and frequent pillaging, including a sacking by Attila the Hun in 452, the town regained its stature in the 11th century, which it held onto until the end of the 14th century. Aquileia's magnificent Roman and early Christian remains offer an image of the transition from pagan to Christian Rome. Beautifully preserved right in the middle of the serene village, they are refreshingly free of the mass tourism that you might expect at such a culturally historic place.

Aquileia's **Basilica** was founded by Theodore, its first patriarch, and later extended. It was rebuilt between 1021 and 1031, and later accumulated different elements including the Romanesque portico and the

Gothic bell tower. But the highlight of this monument is the staggering 4th-century mosaic covering the entire floor, one of the finest relics of the early Christian period in Italy. Before the Edict of Milan, Christians had adopted images of pagan symbolism to express their faith, some of which can be seen here. The winged figure of Victory with her laurel wreath and palm frond equates with triumph over death; the tortoise symbolizes darkness; and the cockerel, which crows at dawn, is light. Fish, of course, represent Christ, and birds such as peacocks represent immortality. Down a flight of steps, the Cripta degli Affreschi contains soft-hue frescoes, among them St. Peter sending St. Mark to Aquileia and the beheading of Saints Hermagoras and Fortunatus, to whom the basilica is dedicated. The Cripta degli Scavi contains another huge area of mosaic paving surrounding the base to the campanile and allows you to see how the successive layers of building took place from the 4th century on. ⊠*Piazza Capitolo<* ☎*0431/91067* ✉*Basilica free, both crypts €2.60, campanile €1* ☾*Apr.–Oct., Mon.–Sat. 8:30–6, Sun. 8:30–6:30; Nov.–Mar., daily 8:30–12:30 and 2:30–5:30. Visits suspended during Sun. and Mon. Mass (10:30–11:15).*

Beyond the basilica and across the road, the **archaeological site** among the cypresses reveals Roman remains of the forum, houses, cemetery, and port. The little stream was once a navigable and important waterway extending to Grado. The area is well signposted. ⊕*www.museo-archeo-aquileia.it* ✉*Free* ☾*Daily 8:15–1 hr before sunset.*

The **Museo Archeologico** is very rewarding, containing a wealth of material from the Roman era. Notable are the portrait busts from Republican times, semiprecious gems, amber- and gold-work—including preserved flies—a fine glass collection in iridescent hues, and miniature priapic bronzes. ⊠*Via Roma 1* ☎*0431/91096* ⊕*www.museoarcheo-aquileia.it* ✉*€4* ☾ *Tues.–Sun. 8:30–7:30, Mon. 8:30–2.*

The **Museo Paleocristiano** houses more mosaics and traces the development of art from Roman to Christian times. ⊠*Località Monastero* ☎*0431/91035* ⊕*www.museoarcheo-aquileia.it* ✉*Free* ☾*Daily 8:30–1:45.*

TRIESTE

77 km (48 mi) east of Aquileia, 163 km (101 mi) east of Venice.

GETTING HERE
Trains to Trieste depart regularly from Venice, Udine, and other major Italian cities. By car, it is the eastern terminus of the Autostrada Torino–Trieste (E70). Trieste is served by Ronchi dei Ligioneri Airport, which receives flights from major Italian airports and some European cities. The airport is 33 km (20.5 mi) from the city; transportation into Trieste is by taxi or bus No. 51.

VISITOR INFORMATION
Trieste tourism office (⊠*Piazza dell'Unità d'Italia 4/b, 34100* ☎*040/3478312* ⊕*www.triesteturismo.com*).

EXPLORING

Trieste is built along a mere fringe of coastline where the rugged Karst Plateau tumbles abruptly into the beautiful Adriatic. Once the chief port of the Austro-Hungarian Empire, its quays now serve as parking lots, and the container port has moved to the south side of Trieste. In recent years, the city has been undergoing rejuvenation and has become something of a center for science and the computer industry. Having absorbed new waves of Slavic and Eastern European immigrants, Trieste now balances the tattered romance of wars past with the idiosyncrasies of a modern frontier town.

Italian revolutionaries of the early 1800s rallied their battle cry around Trieste, because of what they believed was foreign occupation of their rightful motherland. After World War II, the sliver of land including Trieste and a small part of Istria became an independent, neutral state that was officially recognized in a 1947 peace treaty. Although it was actually occupied by British and American troops for its nine years of existence, the Free Territory of Trieste issued its own currency and stamps. In 1954 a Memorandum of Understanding was signed in London, giving civil administration of Trieste to Italy and the rest of the former Free Territory to Yugoslavia, but it was not until the 1975 Treaty of Osimo that the territory was finally formally divided.

Like Vienna's coffeehouses, Trieste's belle epoque cafés are social and cultural centers and much-beloved refuges from winter's bitter *bora* (wind from the north). Though often clogged with traffic, the spacious streets hold a lively mix of monumental, neoclassical, and art nouveau–style architecture, granting an air of stateliness to the city.

★ The sidewalk cafés on the vast seaside **Piazza dell'Unità d'Italia** are popular meeting places in the summer months. The memorably imposing square, ringed by grandiose facades, is similar to Piazza San Marco in Venice; both are focal points of architectural interest and command fine views of the water. On the inland side of the piazza is the majestic Viennese **Palazzo Comunale** (Town Hall). Steps behind it lead uphill, tracing Trieste's upward expansion from its roots as a Roman fishing port.

A statue of Habsburg emperor Leopold I looks out over **Piazza della Borsa,** which contains Trieste's original stock exchange, the **Borsa Vecchia,** a neoclassical building now serving as the chamber of commerce.

The 1st century AD amphitheater, **Teatro Romano,** ruins, opposite the city's *questura* (police station), were discovered during 1938 demolition work. Its statues are now displayed at the Museo Civico and the space that once held 6,000 spectators is filled with grass and flowers. ⊠ *Via del Teatro Romano.*

The 14th-century **Cattedrale di San Giusto** contains remnants of two previous churches built on the same ground, the earliest dating from the 5th century. The exterior includes fragments of Roman tombs and temples, adding to the jumble of styles: the pillars of the main doorway are the most conspicuous Roman element. Inside, don't miss the 12th-

Trieste's Caffè Culture

Trieste is justly famous for its coffee. The elegant civility of Trieste plays out beautifully in a *caffè* culture rivaling that of Vienna. In Trieste, as elsewhere in Italy, ask for a *caffè* and you'll get a thimbleful of high-octane espresso. Your cappuccino here will also come in an espresso cup, with only half as much frothy milk as you'll find elsewhere and, in the Viennese fashion, a dollop of whipped cream. Many cafés are part of a *torrefazione* (roasting shop), so you can sample a cup and then buy beans to take with you.

Few cafés in Italy—or in the world—can rival **Antico Caffè San Marco** (⊠ *Via Battisti 18* ☎ *040/363538* ⊗ *Closed Wed.*) for its art deco style and bohemian atmosphere. After being destroyed in World War I, it was rebuilt in the 1920s and became a meeting place for local intellectuals. For a great view of the great piazza,

you couldn't do better than **Caffè Degli Specchi** (⊠ *Piazza dell'Unità d'Italia 7* ☎ *040/365777*), where the many mirrors heighten the opportunities for people-watching It's open daily until midnight. Founded in 1830, classic **Caffè Tommaseo** (⊠ *Piazza Tommaseo 4/c* ☎ *040/362666*) is a comfortable place to linger, especially on weekend evenings and Sunday morning (11–1:30), when there's live music. It's open daily until 12:30 AM. **Cremcaffè** (⊠ *Piazza Carlo Goldoni 10* ☎ *040/636555* ⊗ *Closed Sun.*) isn't the ideal place to sit and read the paper, but its downtown location and selection of 20 coffee blends make it one of the busiest cafés in town. The atmosphere is more modern than old-world at **I Paesi del Caffè** (⊠ *Via Einaudi 1* ☎ *040/633897* ⊗ *Closed Sun.*), which brews and sells beans of top international varieties, including Jamaica Blue Mountain.

century gold mosaic behind the main altar. ⊠ *Piazza della Cattedrale 2* ☎ *040/309666* ⊗ *Apr.–Oct., Mon.–Sat. 7:30–6:30, Sun. until 7:30; Nov.–Mar., Mon.–Sat. 7:30–noon and 2:30–6:30, Sun. until 7:30.*

The hilltop **Castello di San Giusto** was built on the ruins of the Roman town of Tergeste. Given the excellent view, it's no surprise that 15th-century Venetians turned the castle into a shipping observation point; the structure was further enlarged by Trieste's subsequent rulers, the Habsburgs. At this writing, the castle and museum were set to reopen in April 2008 after major renovations; call to confirm open hours. ⊠ *Piazza della Cattedrale 3* ☎ *040/309372* €3.50

On the hill near the Castello is the **Civico Museo di Storia ed Arte,** an eclectic history and art museum with statues from the Roman theater and artifacts from Egypt, Greece, and Rome. There's also an assortment of glass and manuscripts. The **Orto Lapidario** (Lapidary Garden) has classical statuary, pottery, and a small Corinthian temple. ⊠ *Via Cattedrale 15* ☎ *040/310500* €2 ⊗ *Tues.–Sun. 9–1.*

The **Civico Museo Revoltella e Galleria d'Arte Moderna** was founded in 1872, when the city inherited the palazzo, library, and art collection of shipping magnate Baron Pasquale Revoltella, vice president of the consortium that built the Suez Canal. The gallery holds one of the country's most important collections of 19th- and 20th-century art, with Italian artists particularly well represented. Call for hours during special exhibits. The museum's rooftop café, where the view rivals the artwork, is open some evenings in summer. ⊠ *Via Armando Diaz 27* ☎*040/6754350* 💶*€5* ☉*Mon. and Wed.–Sun. 10–7.*

At Trieste's **Museo del Mare** *(Museum of the Sea)* you can learn how Venetian galley rowers managed to sit three abreast and not smash one another with their oars. Displays include lots of boat models and a diorama with *casoni* (fishermen's grass huts) and submerged *seragi* (fishnet traps). Outside is a park with giant anchors and shady benches. ⊠ *Via di Campo Marzio 5* ☎*040/304987* 💶*€3.50* ☉*Tues.–Sun. 8:30–1:30. Extended hours during special exhibits.*

WHERE TO STAY & EAT

★ $$–$$$ ✕ **Al Ritrovo Marittimo.** Beneath a lofty ceiling of a former warehouse, Giulio and Valentina Cusma have built a loyal clientele by serving fresh, innovative, affordable seafood dishes in an unpretentious setting. Unusual dishes like *tonna prosciutto* (salt-cured tuna) and sea bream tartar are well executed, while the classic *fritto misto* (mixed fried fish) benefits from the fresh oil used to prepare each serving. The indecisive can start with mixed-seafood antipasto to sample a number of options you might not think of ordering individually; you can end with the assorted dessert plate and relish the privilege of having a taste of everything. ⊠ *Via Lazzaretto Vecchio 3* ☎*040/301377* ▭*AE, MC, V* ☉*Closed Sun. and Mon., and 2 wks in July.*

$$ ✕ **Suban.** Head for the hills—to the landmark trattoria operated by members of the hospitable Suban family since 1865. Sit by the dining room fire or relax on a huge terrace and watch the sunset. This is fish-free Italian food with a Slovene, Hungarian, and Austrian accent. Start with *jota carsolina* (a rich soup of cabbage, potatoes, and beans), and then you might order a steak grilled and sliced at your table. Lighter fare includes *insalatine tiepide* (warm salads with smoked pork or duck) and a locally smoked beef that is truly special. To get here you can take Bus No. 35 from Piazza Oberdan. ⊠ *Via Comici 2* ☎*040/54368* ▭*AE, DC, MC, V* ☉*Closed Tues., 1st 3 wks in Aug., and 1 wk in early Jan. No lunch weekdays.*

★ $ ✕ **Antipastoteca di Mare.** Hidden halfway up the hill to the Castello di San Giusto, nautical kitsch provides homey charm to this little eatery that serves seafood accompanied by salad, potatoes, polenta, and house wine. A specialty is hot and cold seafood combinations, from calamari and barley salad, to scallops, mussels, and *sardoni in savor* (big sardines with raisins, pine nuts, and caramelized onions). The extraordinary fish soup of sardines, mackerel, and tuna, sprinkled with lightly fried, diced garlic bread and polenta, won owner-chef Roberto Surian his first in a series of awards at Trieste's prestigious Sarde Day competition. ⊠ *Via della Fornace 1* ☎*040/309606* ▭*No credit cards* ☉*Closed Mon. No dinner Sun. Call to confirm summer hrs.*

¢–$ ✕ **Trattoria da Giovanni.** Hit this place during lunch rush and you'll experience Trieste's version of fast food. Familiar, tiny, and spilling onto a street filled with tables when the weather allows, Giovanni's menu is full of simple, home-style pastas, meats, and vegetables.

Try prosciutto sliced from the bone, fried seafood, or a simple side dish of chicory; don't forget to drizzle it with local oil. ⊠ *Via San Lazzaro 14* ☎*040/639396* ▭*No credit cards* ☽*Closed Sun. and 3 weeks in Aug.*

★ $$$$ 🖫 **Riviera & Maximilian's.** Seven kilometers (4½ mi) north of Trieste, this lovely hotel commands views across the Golfo di Trieste, including nearby Castello di Miramare; dining areas, the bar, and all guest rooms enjoy this stunning panorama. There's no sand on this stretch of coast, but an elevator leads to the hotel's own private bathing quay below, as well as to a children's area. Some rooms have balconies and kitchenettes. The restaurant ($$–$$$$) has indoor trompe l'oeil decor and an outdoor terrace. **Pros:** Great views, gorgeous grounds. **Cons:** Far from town, some rooms are cramped, some rooms need updating. ⊠*Strada Costiera 22, 34010* ☎*040/224551* 🖷*040/224300* ⊕*www.hotelrivieraemaximilian.com* ⤴*56 rooms, 2 suites, 9 apartments* ⚄*In-room: safe, refrigerator, Wi-Fi. In-hotel: restaurant, bar, pool, beachfront, public Internet, parking (no fee), some pets allowed* ▭*AE, DC, MC, V* ⦿*BP.*

★ $$ 🖫 **L'Albero Nascosto Hotel Residence.** Though hardly noticeable on this busy, narrow street, this hotel residence is one of the best values in Trieste. Freshly renovated and furnished with antiques, each room is decorated with paintings by a local artist. The lobby boasts an old Roman column, recycled when the 18th-century building was constructed, and the outdoor smokers' lounge is enclosed by Trieste's 15th-century city walls. All rooms have kitchenettes, and though they lack phones, the kindly owners offer loaner cell phones. **Pros:** Very central location, clean and spacious rooms. **Cons:** No staff on-site after 8 PM, rooms get street noise. ⊠ *Via Felice Venezian 18, 34124* ☎*040/300188* ⊕*www. alberonascosto.it* ⤴*10 rooms* ⚄*In-room: no phone, kitchenette, Wi-Fi. In-hotel: bar, no elevator, parking (fee), some pets allowed* ▭*AE, MC, V* ⦿*BP.*

$ 🖫 **Filoxenia.** The location on the city waterfront, and the reasonable prices, make this small hotel a choice accommodation. Members of Trieste's Greek community run the Filoxenia, and there's a good Greek restaurant on-site. The staff makes up in friendliness for what it might lack in professionalism. Rooms are simple and fresh, with white walls and two single beds covered in Mediterranean blue–stripe spreads; family rooms sleep four (€135). **Pros:** Central location, good value, friendly staff. **Cons:** Some rooms are very small, soundproofing isn't great, rooms are very basic for the price. ⊠*Via Mazzini 3, 34121* ☎*040/3481644* 🖷*040/661371* ⊕*www.filoxenia.it* ⤴*20 rooms* ⚄*In-room: dial-up. In-hotel: restaurant, bar, public Internet, parking (fee), some pets allowed* ▭*DC, MC, V* ⦿*BP.*

CASTELLO DI MIRAMARE

★ ☝   *7 km (4½ mi) northwest of Trieste.*

GETTING HERE
Bus No. 36 from Piazza Oberdan in Trieste runs here every half hour.

EXPLORING

Archduke Maximilian of Habsburg, brother of Emperor Franz Josef and retired commander of the Austrian Navy, built this seafront extravaganza in the 19th century. It has ship's-keel wooden ceilings, marine-blue furnishings, and windows onto the wide, open Adriatic. His peaceful retirement was interrupted in 1864 when he reluctantly became emperor of Mexico; he was killed three years later by a Mexican firing squad. The castle was later owned by Duke Amadeo of Aosta, who renovated in the rationalist style and installed modern plumbing in his art deco bathroom. Guided tours in English are available by reservation.

Surrounding the castle is a 54-acre **Tropical Park,** partly wooded, and partly sculpted into magnificent gardens. Within the park, you can stroll through a greenhouse where free-flying birds and, in summer, butterflies will swoop by your head. Park guides are proud to introduce you to some of the world's rarest hummingbirds, which they've managed to breed in captivity. ⊠ *Viale Miramare off SS14, Miramare* ☎ *040/224143* ⊕ *www.castello-miramare.it* ⊡ *Castle €4, guided tour €3.50, park free, greenhouse €6.50* ☉ *Castle: daily 9–7, last entry ½ hr before closing. Park: daily Apr.–Sept., 8–7; Nov.–Feb., 8–5; Mar. and Oct., 8–6. Greenhouse: daily Apr.–Oct., 9–6; Nov.–Mar., 10–5.*

☾ Beyond the shoreline lies the **Natural Marine Reserve of Miramare,** a World Wildlife Fund Oasis. Their visitor center within the park's *Casteletto* (small castle) has ecological learning displays. From June to September, they organize snorkel and scuba outings, which offer a chance to swim within the reserve, which without a guide is forbidden.

At the western Grignano Marina entrance to the park you'll find the **Science Center Immaginario Scientifico,** a hands-on place to discover science while having fun. Their five-screen theater shows films of scientific material so brilliantly photographed that learning becomes entertainment and language is not a problem. ⊠ *Riva Massimiliano e Carlotta 15, <city>Grignano</city>* ☎ *040/224424* ⊕ *www.immaginarioscientifico.it* ⊡ *Films free, museum €6, planetarium €3* ☉ *Oct.–May, Sun. 10–8; June–Sept., weekends 3–8.*

The Dolomites: Trentino–Alto Adige

WORD OF MOUTH

"There are so many beautiful valleys and mountains, it's hard to choose. My favorite drive is through the Val Gardena from north of Bolzano to Cortina. The area around Cortina, especially to the west, is full of great little villages."

—Wayne

WELCOME TO THE DOLOMITES

TOP REASONS TO GO

★ **Museo Archeologico dell'Alto Adige, Bolzano:** The impossibly well-preserved body of the iceman Ötzi, the star attraction here, provokes countless questions about the meaning of life 5,000 years ago.

★ **Hiking:** No matter your fitness level, there's a memorable walk in store for you here.

★ **Trento:** A graceful fusion of Austrian and Italian styles, this breezy, frescoed town is famed for its imposing castle.

★ **Grande Strada delle Dolomiti (Great Dolomites Road):** Your rental Fiat will think it's a Ferrari as it wends its way along this gorgeous drive through the Heart of the Dolomites.

Trentino

1 Trentino. This butterfly-shaped province is Italy with a German accent. Its principal city, history-rich **Trento**, is situated at the center. To the northwest are **Madonna di Campiglio**, Italy's most fashionable ski resort, and **Bormio**, another notable skiing destination that doubles as a gateway to the Parco Nazionale dello Stelvio.

2 Bolzano. Alto Adige's capital is the Dolomites' most lively city. Look for high-gabled houses, wrought-iron signs, and centuries-old wine cellars.

3 Alto Adige & Cortina. This region was a part of Austria until the end of World War I, and Austrian sensibilities still predominate over Italian. At the spa town of **Merano** you can soak in hot springs, take the "grape cure," and stroll along lovely walkways. **Cortina d'Ampezzo**, a former hangout of the ultrahip, has aged gracefully into the Grand Dame of Italian ski resorts.

Merano

AUSTRIA

A L P

40

Glorenza
Spondigna

41

38

SWITZERLAND   38

Parco Nazionale
dello Stelvio

ORTLES-ORTLERGRUPPE

Bormio

38   PIEMONTE

VAL DI SOLE

42   Madonna di
Campiglio

Pinzolo

TRENTINO

239

Tione

237

Arco

240

1

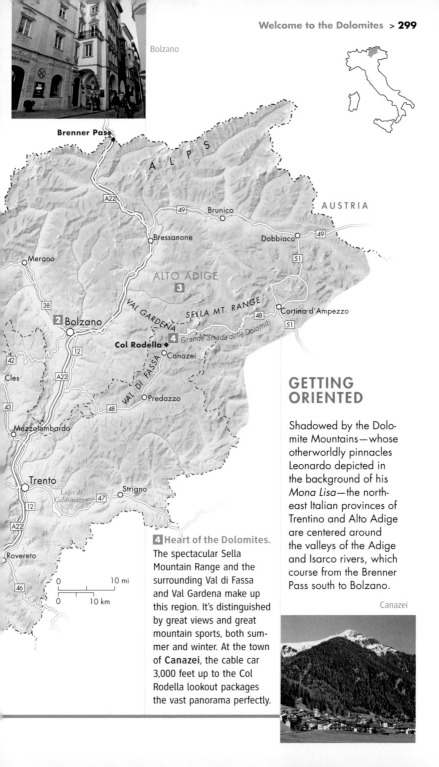

Bolzano

Brenner Pass

A L P S

AUSTRIA

A22

49   Brunico

Bressanone

Dobbiaco

Merano

51

ALTO ADIGE

3

38

VAL GARDENA

SELLA MT. RANGE

48   Cortina d'Ampezzo

2 Bolzano

51

12

Col Rodella ◆

4 Grande Strada delle Dolomiti

42

Canazei

Cles

VAL DI FASSA

A22

48

Predazzo

Mezzolombardo

43

Trento

Lago di
Caldonazzo

Strigno

12

47

A22

Rovereto

46

0   10 mi

0   10 km

GETTING ORIENTED

Shadowed by the Dolomite Mountains—whose otherworldly pinnacles Leonardo depicted in the background of his *Mona Lisa*—the northeast Italian provinces of Trentino and Alto Adige are centered around the valleys of the Adige and Isarco rivers, which course from the Brenner Pass south to Bolzano.

Canazei

4 **Heart of the Dolomites.**
The spectacular Sella Mountain Range and the surrounding Val di Fassa and Val Gardena make up this region. It's distinguished by great views and great mountain sports, both summer and winter. At the town of **Canazei**, the cable car 3,000 feet up to the Col Rodella lookout packages the vast panorama perfectly.

THE DOLOMITES PLANNER

Making the Most of Your Time

For a general pleasure tour (as opposed to a skiing- or hiking-intensive vacation), your best choice for a base is vibrant Bolzano, where you'll get a sense of the region's contrasts—Italian and German, medieval and ultramodern. The Archaeological Museum shouldn't be missed. After a day or two in town, venture out to history-laden Trento or the lovely spa town of Merano; both are viable day trips from Bolzano and good places to spend the night as well.

If you have more time in the region, you're going to want to get higher into the mountains. The trip on the Grande Strada delle Dolomiti (Great Dolomites Road) through the Heart of the Dolomites to Cortina d'Ampezzo is one of Italy's most spectacular mountain drives. You can either spend a full day on the road and return to Bolzano, splurge on a night in Cortina, or bed down in one of the homier towns along the way.

Hitting the Slopes

The Dolomites have some of the most spectacular downhill skiing in Europe, with the facilities to match. The most comprehensive centers are the upscale resorts of Cortina d'Ampezzo and Madonna di Campiglio, which draw an international clientele with impressive terrain, expansive lift systems, and lively après-ski. For traditional Tirolean *Gemütlichkeit* (congeniality), try one of the more rustic resorts: in the Val di Fassa or Val Gardena your liftmate is more likely to be from a neighboring town than from Milan (or Tokyo). Both major resorts and out-of-the-way villages have well-marked trails for *sci di fondo* (cross-country skiing). With the exception of the main bargain period known as *settimane bianche* (white weeks) in January and February, the slopes are seldom overcrowded.

Finding a Place to Stay

Classic Dolomite lodging options range from restored castles to chalets to stately 19th-century hotels. Small villages often have scores of places to stay, many of them inexpensive. Hotel information offices at train stations and tourist offices can help if you've arrived without reservations. The Bolzano train station has a 24-hour hotel service, and tourist offices will give you a list of all the hotels in the area, arranged by location and price. Hotels at ski resorts cater to longer stays at full or half board: you should book ski vacations as packages in advance. Most rural accommodations close from early November to mid- or late December, as well as for a month or two after Easter.

DINING & LODGING PRICE CATEGORIES (IN EUROS)				
¢	$	$$	$$$	$$$$
Restaurants				
under €15	€15–€25	€25–€35	€35–€45	over €45
Hotels				
under €70	€70–€110	€110–€160	€160–€220	over €220

Restaurant prices are for a first course (primo), second course (secondo), and dessert (dolce). Hotel prices are for two people in a standard double room in high season, including tax and service.

GETTING AROUND

By Car

Driving is easily the most convenient way to travel in the Dolomites; it can be difficult to reach the ski areas (or any town outside of Rovereto, Trento, Bolzano, and Merano) without a car. Driving is also the most exhilarating way to get around, as you rise from broad valleys into mountains with narrow, winding roads straight out of a sports car ad. Caution is essential, especially in winter, when roads are often covered in snow and buffeted by high winds. Sudden closures are common, especially on high mountain passes, and can occur as early as November and as late as May. Even under the best conditions, expect to negotiate mountain roads at speeds no greater than 50 kph (30 mph).

The most important route in the region is the A22, the main north–south highway linking Italy with central Europe by way of the Brenner Pass. It connects Innsbruck with Bressanone, Bolzano, Trento, and Rovereto, and near Verona joins autostrada A4 (which runs east–west across northern Italy, from Trieste to Turin). By car, Trento is 3 hours from Milan and 2½ hours from Venice. Bolzano is another hour's drive to the north, with Munich 4 hours farther on.

If you're planning a driving tour of the Dolomites, consider flying into Munich. Car rentals are less expensive in Germany, and it's far easier to get automatic transmission.

By Train

The rail line following the course of the Isarco and Adige valleys—from Munich and Innsbruck, through the Brenner Pass, and southward past Bressanone, Bolzano, Trento, and Rovereto en route to Verona—is well trafficked, making trains a viable option for travel between these towns. Eurocity trains on the Dortmund–Venice and Munich–Innsbruck–Rome routes stop at these stations, and you can connect with other Italian lines at Verona. Although branch lines from Trento and Bolzano do extend into some of the smaller valleys (including hourly service between Bolzano and Merano), most of the mountain attractions are beyond the reach of trains. Contact **Trenitalia** (☎ *892021* ⊕ *www. trenitalia.com*) for more information.

By Bus

Regular bus service connects larger cities to the south (Verona, Venice, and Milan) with valley towns in Trentino–Alto Adige (Rovereto, Trento, Bolzano, and Merano). You'll need to change to less-frequent local buses to reach resorts in the mountains beyond.

Although it's certainly possible to visit even the remotest villages without a car (if you're equipped with schedules and lots of time), most towns are designed for automobiles. For information, contact **Trentino Trasporti** (☎ *0461/983627* ⊕ *www.ttspa.it*) or Alto Adige's **SIT** (*Servizio Integrato di Trasporto* ☎ *0471/415480* ⊕ *www. sii.bz.it*).

A convenient bus service between Cortina d'Ampezzo and the Venice airport (€20 round-trip, complimentary at some hotels) is available on weekends from mid-December to March; bookings must be made through your hotel. **DolomitiBus** (☎ *0437/217111* ⊕ *www.dolomitibus.it*) covers the Eastern Dolomites and provides winter weekend service between Cortina and the Venice train station.

EATING & DRINKING WELL IN THE DOLOMITES

Everything in Alto Adige (and, to a lesser extent, Trentino as well) has more than a tinge of the Teutonic—and the food is no exception. The rich and creamy food here, including fondues, polentas, and barley soups, reflects the Alpine climate and Austrian and Swiss influence.

The quintessential restaurant here is the wood-panel Tirolean *Stube* (pub) serving hearty meat-and-dumpling fare, and there's also a profusion of pastry shops and lively beer halls.

Although the early dining schedule you'll find in Germany or Austria is somewhat tempered here, your options for late-night meals are more limited than in southern Italy, where *la dolce vita* has a firmer grip.

Thankfully, the coffee is every bit as good as in parts south—just expect to hear "*danke, grazie*" when paying for your cappuccino.

BEST OF THE WURST

Not to be missed are the outdoor wurst carts, even (or perhaps especially) in colder weather. After placing your order you'll get a sheet of wax paper, followed by a dollop of mustard, a Kaiser roll, and your chosen sausage. You can sometimes make your selection by pointing to whatever picture is most appealing; if not, pass on the familiar-sounding *Frankfurter* and try the local *Meraner*. Carts can reliably be found in Bolzano (try Piazza delle Erbe, or in front of the archaeological museum) and Merano (Piazza del Grano, or along the river).

POLENTA & DUMPLINGS

Polenta is a staple in the region, in both its creamy and firm varieties, often topped with cheese or mushrooms (or both). Dumplings also appear on many menus; the most distinctive to the region are *canederli* (also known as *Knoedel*), pictured at right, made from seasoned bread in many variations, and served either in broth or with a sauce.

Other dumplings to look for are the dense *strangola preti* (literally "priest-chokers") and *gnocchi di ricotta alla zucca* (ricotta and pumpkin dumplings).

CHEESE

Cheese from the Alpine dairy cows of Trentino–Alto Adige is a specialty, with each isolated mountain valley seeming to make its own variety, to be found nowhere else—it's often simply called *nostrano* (ours).

The best known of the cheeses are the mild Asiago and *fontal* and the more-pungent *puzzone di Moena* (literally, "stinkpot"). If your doctor permits it, try the *schiz*: fresh cheese that is sliced and fried in butter, sometimes with cream added.

PASTRIES & BAKED GOODS

Bakeries turn out a wide selection of crusty dark rolls and caraway-studded rye breads—maybe not typical Italian bread, but full of flavor.

Pastries are reminiscent of what you'd expect to find in Vienna. Apple strudel, pictured below, is everywhere, and for good reason: the best apples in Italy are grown here. There's other exceptional fruit as well, including pears, plums, and grapes, that make its way into baked goods.

ALIMENTARI

If you're planning a picnic or getting provisions for a hike, you'll be well served by the fine *alimentari* (food shops) of Trentino and Alto Adige. They stock a bounty of regional specialties, including cheeses, pickles, salami, and smoked meats. They're a good place to pick up a sample of *speck tirolese*, ham that's usually cut in paper-thin slices, like *prosciutto*. Don't discard the fat of the speck—it's considered the best part.

WINE

Though Trentino and Alto Adige aren't as esteemed for their wines as many other Italian regions, they produce a wide variety of crisp, dry whites—not surprisingly, more like what you'd expect from German vineyards than Italian. Among the reds, look for Teroldego, made in the valley north of Trento.

5

Updated
by Peter
Blackman

THE VAST, MOUNTAINOUS DOMAIN of northeastern Italy, unlike other celebrated Alpine regions, has remained relatively undeveloped. Strange, rocky pinnacles jut straight up like chimneys, looming over scattered, pristine mountain lakes. Below, rivers meander through valleys dotted with peaceful villages and protected by picture-book castles. In the most secluded Dolomite vales, unique cultures have flourished: the Ladin language, an offshoot of Latin still spoken in the Val Gardena and Val di Fassa, owes its unlikely survival to centuries of topographic isolation.

The more-accessible parts of Trentino–Alto Adige, on the other hand, have a history of near-constant intermingling of cultures. The region's Adige and Isarco valleys make up the main access route between Italy and central Europe, and as a result the language, cuisine, and architecture are a blend of north and south. Whereas the province of Trentino is largely Italian-speaking, Alto Adige is predominantly Germanic: until World War I, the area was Austria's South Tirol. As you move north toward the famed Brenner Pass—through the prosperous valley towns of Rovereto, Trento, and Bolzano—the Teutonic influence is increasingly dominant; by the time you reach Bressanone, it's hard to believe you're in Italy at all.

TRENTINO

Until the end of World War I, Trentino was Italy's frontier with the Austro-Hungarian Empire, and although this province remains unmistakably Italian, Germanic influences are tangible in all aspects of life here, including architecture, cuisine, culture, and language. Visitors are drawn by historical sights reflecting a strategic position at the intersection of southern and central Europe: Trento was the headquarters of the Catholic Counter-Reformation; Rovereto the site of an emblematically bloody battle during the Great War. Numerous year-round mountain resorts, including fashionable Madonna di Campiglio, are nestled in the wings of the butterfly-shaped region.

TRENTO

51 km (32 mi) south of Bolzano, 24 km (15 mi) north of Rovereto.

VISITOR INFORMATION
Trento tourism office (✉ *Via Manci 2* ☏ *0461/216000* ⊕ *www.apt. trento.it*).

EXPLORING
Trento is a prosperous, cosmopolitan university town that retains an architectural charm befitting its historical importance. It was here, from 1545 to 1563, that the structure of the Catholic Church was redefined at the Council of Trent. This was the starting point of the Counter-Reformation, which brought half of Europe back to Catholicism. The word *consiglio* (council) appears everywhere in Trento—in hotel, restaurant, and street names, and even on wine labels.

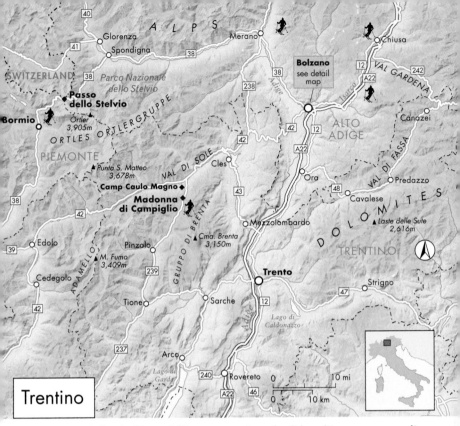

Trentino

Today the Piazza del Duomo remains splendid, and its enormous medieval palazzo dominates the city landscape in virtually its original form. The 24-hour Trento Card (€10) grants admission to all major town sights and can be purchased at the tourist office or any museum. A 48-hour card (€15) is also available, and includes entrance to the modern art museum in Rovereto. Both cards provide a number of other perks, including free public transportation, wine tastings, and the cable car ride to Belvedere di Sardagna.

Guided tours of Trento depart Saturday from the **Trento tourist office.** You can meet at 10 AM for a visit to the Castello del Buonconsiglio (€6, including admission to the castle), or at 3 PM for a tour of the city center (€3). Reservations are not required. ⊠ *Via Manci 2* ☎*0461/216000* ⊕*www.apt.trento.it.*

The massive Romanesque **Duomo,** also known as the Cathedral of San Vigilio, forms the southern edge of the Piazza del Duomo. Locals refer to this square as the city's *salotto* (sitting room), as in fine weather it's always filled with students and residents drinking coffee, sipping an aperitif, or reading the newspaper. The baroque **Fontana del Nettuno** presides over it all. When skies are clear, pause here to savor the view of the mountaintops enveloping the city.

Within the Duomo, unusual arcaded stone stairways border the austere nave. Ahead is the *baldacchino* (altar canopy), a copy of Bernini's masterpiece in St. Peter's in Rome. To the left of the altar is a mournful 16th-century crucifixion, flanked by the Virgin Mary and John the Apostle. This crucifix, by German artist Sisto Frey, was a focal point of the Council of Trent: each decree agreed on during the two decades of deliberations was solemnly read out in front of it. Outside, walk around to the back of the cathedral to see an exquisite display of 14th-century stonemason's art, from the small porch to the intriguing knotted columns on the graceful apse. ⊠ *Piazza del Duomo* ☎ *0461/980132* ⊘ *Daily 6:30–noon and 2–6.*

★   The crenellated **Palazzo Pretorio,** situated so as to seem like a wing of the Duomo, was built in the 13th century as the fortified residence of the prince-bishops, who enjoyed considerable power and autonomy within the medieval hierarchy. The remarkable palazzo has lost none of its original splendor. The crenellations are not merely decorative: the square pattern represents ancient allegiance to the Guelphs (the triangular crenellations seen elsewhere in town represent Ghibelline loyalty). The Palazzo now houses the **Museo Diocesano Tridentino,** where you can see paintings showing the seating plan of the prelates during the Council of Trent; early-16th-century tapestries by Pieter van Aelst (1502–56), the Belgian artist who carried out Raphael's 15th-century designs for the Vatican tapestries; carved wood altars and statues; and an 11th-century sacramentary, or book of services. These and other precious objects all come from the cathedral's treasury. Accessible through the museum, a subterranean **archaeological area** reveals ancient ruins of a 6th-century Christian basilica and a gate dating from the 9th century. ⊠ *Piazza del Duomo 18* ☎ *0461/234419* ⊠ *€4 includes archaeological area* ⊘ *June–Sept., Wed.–Mon. 9:30–12:30 and 2:30–6; Oct.–May, Wed.–Mon. 9:30–12:30 and 2–5:30.*

NEED A BREAK?   Scrigno del Duomo (⊠ *Piazza del Duomo 30* ☎ *0461/220030*) serves more than 30 wines by the glass, with an excellent selection of local cheeses to match, in a building with some of the oldest frescoes in town. Salads and regional specialties are also available; the *canederli* (seasoned bread balls in broth) are especially flavorful here. If you walk downstairs to the wine-shop, you can see excavated Roman-era walls—this was the level of the ancient square that became Piazza del Duomo.

Many sessions of the Council of Trent met at the Renaissance church **Santa Maria Maggiore.** Limited light enters through the simple rose window over the main door, so you have to strain to see the magnificent ceiling, an intricate combination of stucco and frescoes. The church is off the northwest side of the Piazza del Duomo, about 200 yards down Via Cavour. ⊠ *Vicolo Orsoline 1* ☎ *0461/230037* ⊘ *Daily 8–noon and 2:30–6.*

Locals refer to **Via Belenzani** as Trento's outdoor gallery because of the frescoed facades of the hallmark Renaissance palazzi. It's an easy 50-yard walk up the lane behind the church of Santa Maria Maggiore.

The **Torre Vanga** is a 13th-century tower near the Adige River and one of the bridges that crosses it, the Ponte San Lorenzo.

You can take a cable car up to the **Belvedere di Sardagna,** a lookout point 1,200 feet above medieval Trento. The trip is free if you have a Trento Card. *Cable car* ✉*Ponte San Lorenzo* ☎*0461/983627* 💶*€2 round-trip* ☉*Daily 7–5.*

★ The **Castello del Buonconsiglio** *(Castle of Good Counsel)* was once the stronghold of the prince-bishops; its position and size made it easier to defend than the Palazzo Pretorio. Look for the evolution of architectural styles: the medieval fortifications of the Castelvecchio section (on the far left) were built in the 13th century; the fancier Renaissance Magno Palazzo section (on the far right) wasn't completed until 300 years later. Part of the Castello now houses the **Museo Provinciale d'Arte,** where permanent and visiting exhibits of art and archaeology hang in frescoed medieval halls or under Renaissance coffered ceilings. The 13th-century **Torre dell'Aquila** (Eagle's Tower) is home to the castle's artistic highlight, a 15th-century *ciclo dei mesi* (cycle of the months). The four-wall fresco is full of charming and detailed scenes of medieval life in both court and countryside. To visit the tower, check for scheduled tour times at the ticket office. ✉*Via Bernardo Clesio 5* ☎*0461/233770* ⊕*www.buonconsiglio.it* 💶*Museo €6, Torre dell'Aquila €1 extra* ☉*June–Oct., Tues.–Sun. 10–6; Nov.–May, Tues.–Sun. 9:30–5.*

The **Torre Verde** *(Green Tower)* is part of Trento's 13th-century fortifications, standing alongside other fragments of the city walls. You can't go inside, but the exterior is worth a look. ✉*Piazza Raffaello Sanzio near the castle.*

The **Museo d'Arte Moderna e Contemporanea di Trento** is installed in the Palazzo delle Albere, a Renaissance villa on the Adige River. Works in the permanent collection date from the 19th and 20th centuries, but the real focus here is the rotating exhibitions of contemporary artists. ✉*Palazzo delle Albere, Via Roberto da Sanseverino 45* ☎*0461/234860* ⊕*www.mart.tn.it* 💶*€10* ☉*Tues.–Thurs. and weekends 10–6, Fri. 10–9.*

About 20 km (12 mi) southeast of Trento in the Val Sugana, **Levico Terme** is a medieval spa town with thermal waters. This valley enclave was inhabited by the Celts and then conquered by the Romans; the Latin-derived Ladin dialect is still spoken today. Two weeks' advance booking is recommended for the spa services at **Palazzo delle Terme.** ✉*Viale Vittorio Emanuele 1, 38056 Levico Terme* ☎*0461/706481* 🖨*0461/707722* ⊕*www.termedilevico.it* ☉*May–Oct., Mon.–Sat. 7–12:30.*

WHERE TO STAY & EAT

★ $$$$ ✕ **Le Due Spade.** This Tirolean tavern has been around the corner from the Duomo since the Council of Trent. Able servers bring superb local dishes to you amid the coziness created by the wood paneling and an antique stove. You can sample traditional *gnocchetti di ricotta* (miniature ricotta cheese dumplings) and such savory second courses as *tagliata di angus alla griglia* (grilled slivers of beef) served with an aromatic herb sauce. Given the restaurant's deserved popularity with locals and the limited seating, reservations are a must. ⊠ *Via Rizzi 11* ☎ *0461/234343* ⌕ *Reservations essential* ☰ *AE, DC, MC, V* ⊘ *Closed Sun. No lunch Mon.*

$$ ✗**Chiesa.** Near the castle, a 15th-century building conceals a bright, modern restaurant that attracts romancing couples and power lunchers alike. Ubiquitous apple imagery and excellent risotto *alle mele* (with apples) celebrate the local produce—there's even a set meal featuring apples in every course. Otherwise, the food is traditional: specialties are *maccheroncini con salsiccia e verze* (short, narrow pasta tubes with sausage and cabbage) and *tonco de Pontesel* (a stew of mixed meat made according to a 15th-century recipe). ⊠ *Via San Marco 64* ☎ *0461/238766* ☰ *AE, DC, MC, V* ⊘ *Closed Sun.*

$ ✗ **Al Vò.** Trento's oldest trattoria (it's the descendant of a 14th-century tavern) remains one of its most popular lunch spots. Locals crowd into a simple, modern dining room to enjoy rich pastas like *gnocchi di ricotta alla zucca* (sugared ricotta and pumpkin dumplings) and grilled meats served in copper skillets, such as the reliable *filetto di maialino* (pork fillet). An impressive (and inexpensive) selection of local wines is available; try the food-friendly red Teroldego, made in the valley north of Trento. ⊠ *Vicolo del Vò 11* ☎ *0461/985374* ☰ *MC, V* ⊘ *Closed Sun. No dinner Sat.–Wed.*

$ ✗ **Pizzeria Laste.** Owner Guido Rizzi is a national pizza-making champion; he invented pizza Calabrese, a white pizza with garlic, mozzarella, and red-pepper flakes. Each of his 35 pies—especially the *sedano* (mozzarella, celery root, aged Parmesan cheese, oregano)—is delectable. Save room for desserts like the pizza *dolce* (sweet), which is made with bananas, strawberries, kiwi, and caramel. In a pleasant hilltop villa above the city center, the pizzeria is a bit hard to reach, but worth it. ⊠ *Via alle Laste 39* ☎ *0461/231570* ☰ *MC, V* ⊘ *Closed Tues.*

★ $$$ ⌂ **Accademia.** This friendly hotel occupies an ancient, character-filled house in the historic center of Trento, close to Piazza del Duomo. Enter through a beautiful arched passage; the public rooms also retain the original vaulting. Bedrooms have comfortable beds and handsome lithographs of the town. In warm weather, you can enjoy a meal or a drink in the courtyard garden. **Pros:** Central location, charming outdoor restaurant. **Cons:** Rooms are small, not much decor, basic breakfast. ⊠ *Vicolo Colico 4, 38100* ☎ *0461/233600* ⊕ *www.accademiahotel.it* ⇄ *41 rooms, 2 suites* ⌂ *In-room: safe, refrigerator. In-hotel: restaurant, bar, public Wi-Fi, some pets allowed* ☰ *AE, DC, MC, V* ⊘ *Closed late Dec.–early Jan.* ⦿ *BP.*

$$$ ⌂ **Aquila d'Oro.** A prime location near Piazza del Duomo is the main selling point for the Aquila d'Oro. The friendly owner gives good suggestions about what to see, do, and eat in the area. **Pros:** Excellent location, friendly service. **Cons:** Nondescript decor. ⊠ *Via Belenzani 76, 38100* ☎ *0461/986282* ⊕ *www.aquiladoro.it* ⇄ *19 rooms* ⌂ *In-room: refrigerator, Wi-Fi. In-hotel: bar, public Wi-Fi* ☰ *AE, DC, MC, V* ⊘ *Closed late Dec.–mid-Feb.* ⦿ *BP.*

$$$ ▨ **Imperial Grand Hotel Terme.** If you're in the mood for some pampering, choose the graciously restored, golden yellow palace in the nearby spa town of Levico Terme. It's not hard to imagine yourself as Austrian nobility (for whom this was once home) while you idle in the beautiful swimming pool set in a restful garden, or dine at one of the elegant restaurants. Your room may even have a frescoed ceiling. In summer a poolside bar and grill is open. **Pros:** Beautiful park setting, pleasant indoor pool. **Cons:** Standard rooms are small, use of thermal pools not included in rates. ⊠ *Via Silva Domini 1, Levico Terme 38056* ✛ *20 km (12 mi) east of Trento* ☏ *0461/706104* ⊕ *www.imperialhotel.it* ⤙ *69 rooms, 12 suites* ♿ *In-room: safe, refrigerator. In-hotel: 4 restaurants, bars, pools, gym, spa, bicycles, laundry service, public Wi-Fi, parking (fee), some pets allowed (fee)* ⊟ *AE, DC, MC, V* ⊗ *Closed Nov.–Mar.* †⦿❙ *BP.*

$$ ▨ **Boscolo Grand Hotel Trento.** Its contemporary rounded facade amid ancient palaces makes this hotel on Piazza Dante an anomaly. Inside you'll find a handsome marble lobby, rich draperies in the restaurant, and ample rooms with clubby wood-trim furniture. Business travelers, drawn by the hotel's conveniences and efficient service, are most of the guests. **Pros:** Modern rooms, professional service. **Cons:** Lacks charm, busy neighborhood ⊠ *Via Alfieri 1, 38100* ☏ *0461/271000* ⊕ *www. grandtrento.boscolohotels.com* ⤙ *126 rooms, 10 suites* ♿ *In-room: safe, refrigerator. In-hotel: restaurant, bar, spa, laundry service, public Internet, parking (fee), no-smoking rooms* ⊟ *AE, DC, MC, V* †⦿❙ *EP.*

$–$$ ▨ **Castel Pergine.** A 13th-century castle, appropriated by Trento's prince-bishops in the 16th century, is now skillfully managed by Theo Schneider, an Austrian architect, and his charming Swiss wife, Verena Neff (a former translator). Amid the labyrinth of stone and brick chambers, prisons, and chapels are sparse, rustic rooms with carved-wood trim, lace curtains, and heavy wooden beds, some canopied. The grounds host a different modern-art installation each year. The popular candlelit restaurant serves ages-old seasonal recipes from Trento in lighter guises: risotto with lemon and rosemary, for example. **Pros:** Romantic setting, great restaurant. **Cons:** Simple accommodations, need a car to get around. ⊠ *Via al Castello 10, Pergine Val Sugana 38057* ✛ *12 km (7½ mi) east of Trento* ☏ *0461/531158* ⊕ *www. castelpergine.it* ⤙ *21 rooms, 14 with bath* ♿ *In-room: no a/c, no TV. In-hotel: restaurant, bar, no elevator, parking (free)* ⊟ *AE, MC, V* ⊗ *Closed Nov.–Mar. No lunch Mon.* †⦿❙ *MAP.*

SHOPPING

You can pick up meats, cheeses, produce, local truffles, and porcini mushrooms at the small morning market in **Piazza Alessandro Vittoria. Enoteca di Corso** (⊠ *Corso 3 Novembre 54* ☏ *0461/916424*), a bit outside the town center, is a delightful shop laden with local products, including cheese, wine, and candies. A picnic can be handily assembled with local salamis and cheeses from **La Salumeria Mattei** (⊠ *Via Mazzini 46* ☏ *0461/238053*). Fresh bread and pastries can be purchased at fragrant **Panificio Pulin** (⊠ *Via Cavour 23* ☏ *0461/234544*).

MADONNA DI CAMPIGLIO

130 km (80 mi) northwest of Trento, 88 km (55 mi) southwest of Bolzano.

VISITOR INFORMATION

Madonna di Campiglio tourism office (⊠ *Via Pradalago 4* ☎*0465/447501* 📠*0465/440404* ⊕*www.campiglio.to*).

EXPLORING

The chichi winter resort of Madonna di Campiglio has surpassed Cortina d'Ampezzo as the most fashionable place for young Italians to ski and be seen in the Dolomites. Madonna's popularity is well deserved, with more than 130 km (80 mi) of well-groomed ski runs served by 39 lifts. The resort itself is a modest 5,000 feet above sea level, but the downhill runs, summer hiking paths, and mountain-biking trails venture high up into the surrounding peaks (including Pietra Grande at 9,700 feet). Madonna's cachet is evident in its well-organized lodging, skiing, and trekking facilities.

The stunning pass at **Campo Carlo Magno** (5,500 feet) is 3 km (2 mi) north of Madonna di Campiglio. This is where Charlemagne is said to have stopped in AD 800 on his way to Rome to be crowned emperor. Stop here to glance over the whole of northern Italy. If you continue north, take the descent with caution—in the space of a mile or so, hairpin turns and switchbacks deliver you down more than 2,000 feet.

WHERE TO STAY & EAT

★ $$ ✕ **Cascina Zeledria.** This remote, rustic mountain restaurant near Campo Carlo Magno is not accessible by car; in winter, you'll be collected on a motorized Sno-Cat and ferried up the slopes. After the 10-minute ride, sit down to grill your own meats and vegetables over stone griddles; the kitchen-prepared mushrooms and polenta are house specialties. Although the majority of meals in Madonna are taken in resort hotels, Italians consider an on-mountain dinner to be an indispensable part of a proper ski week. Call in advance to reserve a table—and arrange for transportation. ⊠*Località Zeledria* ☎*0465/440303* ⚞*Reservations essential* ▭*No credit cards* ⊙*Closed May, June, Oct., and Nov.*

$$$$ 🏨 **Golf Hotel.** You need to make your way north to the Campo Carlo Magno Pass to reach this grand hotel, the former summer residence of Habsburg emperor Franz Josef. A modern wing has been added, but there's still tons of old-world charm. Rooms 114 and 214 retain the lavish imperial style, and the rest of the resort is replete with verandas, Persian rugs, and bay windows. In summer the golf course attracts a tony crowd. **Pros:** Attractive indoor pool, elegant rooms. **Cons:** Long walk into town, often filled with business groups. ⊠*Via Cima Tosa 3, 38084* ☎*0465/441003* ⊕*www.golfhotelcampiglio.it* ⚞*104 rooms, 8 suites* ⚙*In-room: no a/c, refrigerator. In-hotel: restaurant, room service, bar, golf course, pool, gym, spa, laundry service, public Wi-Fi, parking (no fee)* ▭*AE, DC, MC, V* ⊙*Closed mid-Apr.–June and Sept.–Nov.* ⦿*MAP.*

$$$$ 🏨 **Grifone.** A comfortable lodge sits catching the sun with a distinctive wood facade and flower-bedecked balconies. Contemporary singles,

doubles, and triples have views of the forested slopes. The restaurant serves home cooking as well as international dishes. The hotel is a bit out of town, but the Spinale cable car is nearby. **Pros:** Convenient location, charming decor. **Cons:** Half board is mandatory, lacks air-conditioning. ✉ *Via Vallesinella 7, 38084* ☎*0465/442002* ⊕*www. hotelgrifone.it* ↩*38 rooms, 2 suites* ⌂*In-room: no a/c, safe. In-hotel: restaurant, bar, spa, public Internet, parking (no fee)* ▤*AE, DC, MC, V* ⊘*Closed mid-Apr.–June and Sept.–Nov.* ⊙*MAP.*

SPORTS & THE OUTDOORS

HIKING & CLIMBING

The Madonna di Campiglio tourism office has maps of a dozen trails leading to waterfalls, lakes, and stupefying views. The cable car to 6,900-foot **Punta Spinale** *Spinale Peak* ✉*Off Via Monte Spinale* ☎*0465/447744* ✆*Cable car €8 round-trip*) offers skiers magnificent views of the Brenta Dolomites in winter. It also runs during peak summer season.

SKIING

Miles of interconnecting ski runs—some of the best in the Dolomites—are linked by the cable cars and lifts of **Funivie Madonna di Campiglio** (✉*Via Presanella 12* ☎*0465/447744* ⊕*www.funiviecampiglio.it*). Advanced skiers will delight in the extremely difficult terrain found on certain mountain faces, but there are also many intermediate and beginner runs, all accessible from town. There are also plenty of off-piste opportunities. Ski passes (€36 per day) can be purchased at the main *funivia* (cable car) in town.

**EN
ROUTE**

The route between Madonna di Campiglio and Bormio (2½ hours) takes you through a series of high mountain passes. After Campo Carlo Magno, turn left at Dimaro and continue 37 km (23 mi) west through Passo del Tonale (6,200 feet). At Ponte di Legno, turn north on SS300. You pass the *Lago Nero* (Black Lake) on your left just before the summit. Continue on to Bormio through the Passo di Gavia (8,600 feet).

BORMIO

97 km (60 mi) northwest of Madonna di Campiglio, 100 km (62 mi) southwest of Merano.

VISITOR INFORMATION

Bormio tourism office (✉ *Via Roma 131/b* ☎*0342/903300* 🖷*0342/904696* ⊕*www.valtellinaonline.com*).

EXPLORING

At the foot of Stelvio Pass, Bormio is the most famous ski resort on the western side of the Dolomites, with 38 km (24 mi) of long pistes and a 5,000-plus-foot vertical drop. In summer its cool temperatures and clean air entice Italians away from cities in the humid Lombard plain. This dual-season popularity supports the plentiful shops, restaurants,

BUS TOURS IN THE DOLOMITES

Bus tours from Bolzano or Trento let you see the Dolomites without having to navigate the mountain roads. However, tours are offered only in the snow-free summer months.

In July and August, the bus company **SAD** (⊠ *Via Conciapelli 60* ☎ *0471/450111* ⊕ *www.sii.bz.it*) conducts full-day mountain tours, including a "Great Dolomites Tour" from Bolzano to Cortina and a tour of the Val Venosta that climbs over the Stelvio Pass into Switzerland. A tour of the Val Gardena and the

Siusi Alps is available from April to October.

From June through September the travel agency **Calderari e Moggioli** (⊠ *Corso Tre Novembre* ☎ *0461/380800* ⊕ *www.trento. lemarmotte.it*) offers a full-day guided bus tour of the Brenta Dolomites and its own "Great Dolomites Tour," a full-day drive over the Pordoi and Falzarego passes to Cortina d'Ampezzo and Lake Misurina.

The Trentino tourist office also organizes guided tours and excursions by train to castles in the region.

and hotels in town. Bormio has been known for the therapeutic qualities of its waters since the Roman era, and there are numerous spas.

Ancient Roman baths predate the wonderland of thermal springs, caves, and waterfalls now known as the **Bagni Vecchi** *(Old Baths)*; Leonardo da Vinci soaked here in 1493. ⊠ *Strada Statale Stelvio* ☎ *0342/910131* ⊕ *www.bagnidibormio.it* ⊠ *Weekdays €35, weekends €38* ⊙ *Daily 10–8.*

Modern facilities and comprehensive spa treatments are available at **Bormio Terme.** ⊠ *Via Stelvio 14* ☎ *0342/901325* ⊕ *www.bormioterme. com* ⊠ *Day pass €15* ⊙ *Jan.–Apr. and July–Sept., daily 9–9; May, June, and Oct.–Dec., Wed.–Mon. 9–9.*

Bormio makes a good base for exploring the Alps' biggest national park, the **Parco Nazionale dello Stelvio** (⊕ *www.parks.it/parco.nazionale. stelvio)* spread over 1,350 square km (520 square mi) and four provinces. Opened in 1935 to preserve flora and protect fauna, today it has more than 1,200 types of plants, 600 different mushrooms, and more than 160 species of animals, including the chamois, ibex, and roe deer. There are many entrances to the park, and a dozen visitor centers; the closest entrance to Bormio is the year-round gateway at Torre Alberti. ⊠ *Via Roma 26* ☎ *0342/910100* ⊠ *Free.*

WHERE TO STAY & EAT

$$ ✕ **Kuerc.** This building was for centuries where justice was publicly served to accused witches, among others. These days, things at the restaurant are rather more refined: enjoy local specialties like *brasaola* (salted, air-dried beef) with lemon and olive oil, or *pizzoccheri* (buckwheat pasta) with garlic and winter vegetables. ⊠ *Piazza Cavour 7* ☎ *0342/904738* ⊟ *MC, V* ⊙ *Closed Tues.*

$$$ ⊞ **Nazionale.** Bordering Stelvio National Park, the Nazionale caters to both the winter and summer crowds. Behind the Alpine exterior, rooms

are small but have solid wood furniture, refrigerators, and balconies on all floors except the top one. The hotel operates a shuttle bus to the cable cars. **Pros:** Great location, winter and summer activities, family-friendly environment. **Cons:** No air-conditioning, rooms are small. ⊠ *Via al Forte 28, 23032* ☎*0342/903361* ⊕*www.hotelnazionale.info* ⤴*48 rooms* ♨*In-room: no a/c, safe, refrigerator. In-hotel: 2 restaurants, bar, pool, public Wi-Fi, parking (no fee)* ▭*AE, DC, MC, V* ⊙*Closed mid-Apr.–May and mid-Sept.–Dec.* ⦿|*BP.*

$$$ ▦ **Posta.** The Ostelli della Posta stagecoach inns are a time-honored tradition in northern Italy. The warm reception at this town-center hotel helps to temper the winter cold, as does the rustic decoration, with its warm wood detail in the low-vault areas. Rooms are cozy and comfortable, with heavy drapery and bed linens. Perks include a small health club with a pool, sauna, gym, and Turkish bath—and a shuttle bus to the slopes. **Pros:** Central location, historic setting. **Cons:** Low ceilings, mismatched furnishings. ⊠ *Via Roma 66, 23032* ☎*0342/904753* ⊕*www.hotelposta.bormio.it* ⤴*50 rooms* ♨*In-room: no a/c, safe. In-hotel: restaurant, bar, pool, gym, public Internet, parking (no fee)* ▭*AE, DC, MC, V* ⊙*Closed May, June, and Sept.–Nov.* ⦿|*BP.*

SKIING

You can buy a ski pass (€32 per day) and pick up a trail map at the base **funivia** (*cable car* ⊠ *Via Battaglion Morbegno 25* ☎*0342/902770* ⊕*www.skipassaltavaltellina.it*) in the center of town to connect to the Bormio 2000 station (6,600 feet) on Vallecetta, the main resort mountain. From there, you can ski down intermediate trails (which comprise the majority of Bormio's runs), use the extensive lift network to explore secondary ski areas, or get another funivia up to the Bormio 3000 station at Cima Bianca (9,800 feet) for more-challenging terrain. The cable car also runs July to mid-September, when it is used by mountain bikers to reach long trails through breathtaking Alpine terrain; less-ambitious visitors can wander around and then ride the cable car back down.

PASSO DELLO STELVIO

★ *20 km (12 mi) north of Bormio, 80 km (48 mi) west of Merano.*

At more than 9,000 feet, the Passo dello Stelvio is the second-highest pass in Europe, connecting the Valtellina in Lombardy with the Val Venosta in Alto Adige. The view from the top is well worth the drive; looking north you can see Switzerland. The pass is open from May or June to October, depending on weather conditions. Stelvio itself is a year-round skiing center, with many of its runs open in summer.

EN ROUTE Between the Stelvio Pass and the town of Spondigna, 30 km (19 mi) of road wind down 48 hair-raising hairpin turns. The views are spectacular, but this descent is not for the faint of heart. In Spondigna keep to the right for the road to Naturno.

BOLZANO (BOZEN)

32 km (19 mi) south of Merano, 50 km (31 mi) north of Trento.

Bolzano (Bozen), capital of the autonomous province of Alto Adige, is tucked among craggy peaks in a Dolomite valley just 77 km (48 mi) from the Brenner Pass and Austria. Tirolean culture dominates Bolzano's language, food, architecture, and people. It may be hard to remember that you're in Italy when walking the city's colorful cobblestone streets and visiting its lantern-lighted cafés, where you may enjoy sauerkraut and a beer among a lively crowd of blue-eyed German speakers. However, fine Italian espresso, fashionable boutiques, and reasonable prices will help remind you where you are. With castles and steeples topping the landscape, this quiet city at the confluence of the Isarco (Eisack) and Talvera rivers has retained a provincial appeal. Proximity to fabulous skiing and mountain climbing—not to mention the world's oldest preserved mummy—make it a worthwhile, and still undiscovered, tourist destination. And its streets are immaculate: with the highest per capita earnings of any city in Italy, Bolzano's residents enjoy a standard of living that is second to none.

VISITOR INFORMATION

Bolzano tourism office (⊠*Piazza Walther 8* ☎*0471/307000* 🖷*0471/980128* ⊕*www.bolzano-bozen.it*).

EXPLORING BOLZANO

THE MAIN ATTRACTIONS

❸ **Chiesa dei Domenicani.** The 13th-century Dominican Church is renowned as Bolzano's main repository for paintings, especially frescoes. In the adjoining **Cappella di San Giovanni** you can see works from the Giotto school that show the birth of a pre-Renaissance sense of depth and individuality. The chapel is closed Sunday. ⊠*Piazza Domenicani* ☎*0471/973133* ⊗*Mon.–Sat. 9:30–5, Sun. noon–5.*

❷ **Duomo.** A lacy spire looks down on the mosaic-like roof tiles of the city's Gothic cathedral, built between the 12th and 14th centuries. Inside are 14th- and 15th-century frescoes and an intricately carved stone pulpit dating from 1514. Outside, don't miss the **Porta del Vino** (Wine Gate) on the northeast side; decorative carvings of grapes and harvest workers attest to the long-standing importance of wine to this region. ⊠*Piazza Walther* ☎*0471/978676* ⊗*Weekdays 10–noon and 2–5, Sat. 10–noon, Sun. 1–5.*

❻ **Museo Archeologico dell'Alto Adige.** This museum has gained international fame for Ötzi, its 5,300-year-old iceman, discovered in 1991 and the world's oldest naturally preserved body. In 1998 Italy acquired it from Austria after it was determined that the body lay 100 yards inside Italy. The iceman's leathery remains are displayed in a freezer, preserved along with his longbow, ax, and clothing. The rest of the museum relies on models and artifacts from nearby archaeological sites (an eloquent English audio guide is €2) to lead you not only through Ötzi's Cop-

Fodor'sChoice
★

per Age, but also into the preceding Paleolithic and Neolithic eras, and the Bronze and Iron ages that followed. ⊠ *Via Museo 43, 39100* ☎*0471/320100* ⊕*www.iceman.it* ☞*€8* ⊗*Jan.–June and Sept.–Nov., Tues.–Sun. 10–5:30; July, Aug., and Dec., daily 10–5:30.*

❹ **Piazza delle Erbe.** A bronze statue of Neptune, which dates to 1745, presides over a bountiful fruit-and-vegetable market in this square. The stalls spill over with colorful displays of local produce; bakeries and grocery stores showcase hot breads, pastries, cheeses, and delicatessen meats—a complete picnic. Try the *speck tirolese* (a thinly sliced smoked ham) and the apple strudel.

❶ **Piazza Walther.** This pedestrians-only square is Bolzano's heart; in warmer weather it serves as an open-air living room where locals and tourists alike can be found at all hours sipping a drink (such as a glass of chilled Riesling). In the center stands Heinrich Natter's white-marble, neo-Romanesque **Monument to Walther,** built in 1889. The piazza's namesake was the 12th-century German wandering minstrel Walther von der Vogelweide, whose songs lampooned the papacy and praised the Holy Roman Emperor.

ALSO WORTH SEEING

Castel Roncolo *(Schloss Runkelstein).* The green hills and farmhouses north of town surround the meticulously kept castle with a red roof. It was built in 1237, destroyed half a century later, and then rebuilt soon thereafter. There's a beautifully preserved cycle of medieval frescoes inside. A **tavern** in the courtyard serves excellent local food and wines. ⊠ *Via San Antonio 1, Number 12 bus from Piazza Walther, or 20-min walk from Piazza delle Erbe* ✥ *Head north along Via Francescani, continue through Piazza Madonna, connecting to Via Castel Roncolo* ☎ *0471/329808 castle, 0471/324073 tavern* ⊕ *www.comune.bolzano.it/roncolo* ⊠ *€8* ☉ *Tues.–Sun. 10–6.*

Messner Mountain Museum Firmian. The Tibetan tradition of *kora*, a circular pilgrimage around a sacred site, is an inspiration for this museum perched on a peak overlooking Bolzano. Circumambulating the crumbling tower of the walled 10th-century Castle Sigmundskron, visitors contemplate the relationship between man and mountain, guided by images and objects collected during the adventures of the world's most celebrated alpinist, Reinhold Messner. Guided tours begin every half hour. The museum is located 3 km (2 mi) southwest of Bolzano, just off the Appiano exit on the highway to Merano. ⊠ *Via Castel Firmiano 53* ☎ *0471/631264* ⊕ *www.messner-mountain-museum.it* ⊠ *€8* ☉ *Mar.–Dec., Tues.–Sun. 10–6.*

❺ Museo Civico. Bolzano's municipal museum has a rich collection of traditional costumes, wood carvings, and archaeological exhibits. At the time of going to press, the museum was closed for extensive renovations. No definite date has been set for reopening. ⊠ *Via Cassa di Risparmio 14* ☎ *0471/974625.*

Passeggiata del Guncina. An 8-km (5-mi) botanical promenade dating from 1892 ends with a panoramic view of Bolzano. ⊠ *Entrance near Vecchia Parrocchiale, in Gries, across river and up Corso Libertà.*

Vecchia Parrocchiale *(Old Parish Church).* Visit this church, said to have been built in 1141, to see its two medieval treasures: an 11th-century Romanesque crucifix and an elaborately carved 15th-century wooden altar by Michael Pacher—a true masterpiece of the Gothic style. ⊠ *Via Martin Knoller, in Gries, across river and up Corso Libertà* ☎ *0471/283089* ☉ *Apr.–Oct., weekdays 10:30–noon and 2:30–4.*

WHERE TO STAY & EAT

★ **$$$–$$$$** ✕ **Zür Kaiserkron.** Traditional Tirolean opulence and attentive service set the stage for some of the best food in town. Appetizers might include potato blini with salmon caviar, and marinated artichokes with butter (not to be missed if available). Main dishes, such as veal with black truffle–and–spinach canederli make use of ingredients from the local valleys. This place is popular with dignified local businesspeople. ⊠*Piazzetta Mostra* ☎*0471/303233* ▭*AE, DC, MC, V* ⊘*Closed Sun. No dinner Sat.*

$$ ✕ **Alexander.** Typical Tirolean dishes are served at this convivial city-center restaurant. The venison ham and the lamb cutlets *al timo con salsa all'aglio* (with thyme and garlic sauce) are particularly good, but make sure to leave room for the rich chocolate cake. ⊠*Via Aosta 37* ☎*0471/918608* ▭*MC, V* ⊘*Closed Sat.*

★ $–$$ ✕ **Batzenhausl.** Locals hold animated conversations over glasses of regional wine in a modern take on the traditional Weinstube (wine tavern, often abbreviated to "stube"). Tasty South Tirolean specialties include speck tirolese and *mezzelune casarecce ripiene* (house-made stuffed half-moons of pasta). If you're seeking a quiet meal, ask for a table on the second floor, near the handsome stained-glass windows of this medieval building. ⊠*Via Andreas Hofer 30* ☎*0471/050950* ▭*MC, V.*

$ ✕ **Cavallino Bianco.** Ask a local for a restaurant recommendation in Bolzano, and you're likely to be pointed toward this dependable favorite near Via dei Portici. A wide selection of Italian and German dishes is served in a spacious, comfortable dining room, where there are usually many extended families enjoying their meals together. ⊠*Via Bottai 6* ☎*0471/973267* ▭*No credit cards* ⊘*Closed Sun. No dinner Sat.*

$ ✕ **Hopfen & Co.** Fried white *Würstel* (sausage), sauerkraut, and grilled ribs complement the excellent home-brewed Austrian-style pilsner and wheat beer at this lively pub-restaurant. There's live music on Thursday night, attracting Bolzano's students and young professionals. ⊠*Piazza delle Erbe 17* ☎*0471/300788* ▭*MC, V.*

★ $$$–$$$$ ⬚ **Park Hotel Laurin.** An exercise in art nouveau opulence, Park Hotel Laurin is considered the finest lodging in all of Alto Adige, with art-filled modern guest rooms and handsome public spaces (the frescoes in the bar tell the legend of the dwarf King Laurin). The hotel presides over a large park in the middle of town. Its history is speckled with visits from Europe's grand nobility, including Archduke Franz Ferdinand (whose murder in Sarajevo sparked World War I). Restaurant Laurin is superb, using only local ingredients, and bringing a lighter sensibility to rustic regional dishes. **Pros:** Convenient location, excellent restaurant. **Cons:** Rooms facing park can be noisy, packed with business groups. ⊠*Via Laurin 4, 39100* ☎*0471/311000* ⊕*www.laurin.it* ⬗*88 rooms, 8 suites* ♿*In-room: safe, refrigerator, ethernet. In-hotel: restaurant, bar, pool, laundry service, parking (fee), no-smoking rooms* ▭*AE, DC, MC, V* ⍟*BP.*

$$$ ⬚ **Hotel Greif.** Even in a hospitable region, the Greif is a rare gem. This small central hotel has been a Bolzano landmark for centuries, and a beautiful renovation has set a standard for modernity in Alto Adige. In-room computers with high-speed Internet connections and private whirlpool baths are just a few of the perks. Public spaces are airy and immaculate; each guest room was designed by a different local artist—contemporary installations are thoughtfully paired with 19th-cen-

Fodor's Choice ★

tury paintings and sketches. The clean-line modern furnishings contrast with views of the Gothic cathedral across the square. **Pros:** Elegant decor, helpful staff. **Cons:** Rooms vary in size, sometimes filled with tour groups. ⊠*Piazza Walther 1, 39100* ☎*0471/318000* ⊕*www. greif.it* ↩*33 rooms* ⌂*In-room: safe, refrigerator, ethernet. In-hotel: laundry service, parking (fee)* ☰*AE, DC, MC, V* ⦿*BP.*

★ **$$–$$$** ⊞ **Schloss Korb.** This romantic 13th-century castle with crenellations and a massive tower is perched in a park amid vine-covered hills. Much of the ancient character is preserved, and the public rooms are filled with antiques, elaborately carved wood, paintings, and attractive plants. The guest rooms have solid, rustic, pine beds with pillow-top mattresses; some in the tower have striking Romanesque arched windows. It's well worth the 5-km (3-mi) drive west from Bolzano to get here. **Pros:** Romantic setting, charming traditional furnishings. **Cons:** Not all rooms are in the castle, need a car to get around. ⊠*Via Castel d'Appiano 5, 39050 Missiano* ☎*0471/636000* ⊕*www.schlosskorb. com* ↩*57 rooms, 5 suites* ⌂*In-room: no a/c. In-hotel: restaurant, bar, tennis courts, pools, gym, no elevator, laundry service, public Internet, parking (fee), no-smoking rooms* ☰*No credit cards* ⊘*Closed Nov.– Mar.* ⦿*MAP.*

$$ ⊞ **Luna-Mondschein.** This central yet secluded hotel in a tranquil garden dates from 1798. The comfortable rooms have wood paneling throughout; those overlooking the garden have balconies, others have good views of the mountains. First-rate dining is available in the art nouveau Ristorante Van Gogh, among the city's best in blending German traditions with Italian methods; the eclectic menu changes frequently. A convivial, traditional 17th-century Tirolean stube serves more-rustic fare. In summer the courtyard is filled with the scent of barbecue from the outdoor garden restaurant. **Pros:** Central location, great buffet breakfast. **Cons:** Rooms vary in size, noisy garage. ⊠*Via Piave 15, 39100* ☎*0471/975642* ⊕*www.hotel-luna.it* ↩*85 rooms* ⌂*In-room: no a/c. In-hotel: 3 restaurants, room service, bar, laundry service, public Wi-Fi, parking (fee), some pets allowed* ☰*AE, DC, MC, V* ⦿*BP.*

ALTO ADIGE & CORTINA

Prosperous valley towns (such as the famed spa center Merano) and mountain resorts (including the archetypal Cortina d'Ampezzo) entice those seeking both relaxation and adventure. Alto Adige (Südtirol) was for centuries part of the Austro-Hungarian Empire, only ceded to Italy at the end of World War I. Ethnic differences led to inevitable tensions in the 1960s and again in the '80s, though a large measure of provincial autonomy has, for the most part, kept the lid on nationalist ambitions. Today Germanic and Italian balance harmoniously, as do medieval and modern influences, with ancient castles regularly playing host to contemporary art exhibitions.

NATURNO (NATURNS)

44 km (27 mi) northwest of Bolzano, 61 km (38 mi) east of Passo dello Stelvio.

VISITOR INFORMATION

Naturno tourism office (⊠*Piazza Municipio 1* ☎*0473/666077* 📠*0473/666369* ⊕*www.naturns.it*).

EXPLORING

Colorful houses covered with murals line the streets of Naturno (Naturns), a sunny horticultural center.

Art lovers will appreciate the church of **San Procolo** *(Prokolus).* The frescoes inside are some of the oldest in the German-speaking world, dating from the 8th century. A small, modern museum offers multimedia installations (in Italian or German only) presenting four epochs in the region's history: ancient, medieval, Gothic, and the era of the Great Plague of 1636 (which claimed a quarter of Naturno's population, some of whom are buried in the church's cemetery). ⊠*Via San Procolo* ☎*0473/667312* ⊕*www.procolo.org* 🎫*€5* ☉*Apr.–Nov., Tues.–Sun. 9:30–noon and 2:30–5:30.*

A five-minute drive west of Naturno, in the hills above the hamlet of Stava, is the 13th-century **Castel Juval**, since 1983 the home of the South Tirolese climber and polar adventurer Reinhold Messner—the first man to conquer Everest solo and the first to reach its summit without oxygen. Part of the castle has been turned into a museum, showing Messner's collection of Tibetan art and masks from around the world. ⊠*Viale Europa 2* ☎*0473/221852* 🎫*€7* ☉*Apr.–June, Sept., and Oct., Thurs.–Tues. 10–4.*

WHERE TO EAT

$$ ✕ **Schlosswirt Juval.** Below Castel Juval, Reinhold Messner's restored farmhouse is home to an old-style restaurant serving Mediterranean standards and traditional local dishes. Not to be missed are the smoked hams and flavorful cheeses provisioned from the farm outside; they are well paired with the estate's Castel Juval wine. Dinner is often accompanied by live jazz. ⊠*Via Municipio 1* ☎*0473/668238* ▤*No credit cards* ☉*Closed Wed., Nov.–Mar.*

MERANO (MERAN)

★ 16 km (10 mi) east of Naturno, 24 km (15 mi) north of Bolzano.

VISITOR INFORMATION

Merano tourism office (⊠*Corso Libertà 45* ☎*0473/272000* 📠*0473/235524* ⊕*www.meraninfo.it*).

EXPLORING

The second-largest town in Alto Adige, Merano (Meran) was once the capital of the Austrian region of Tirol. When the town and surrounding area were ceded to Italy as part of the 1919 Treaty of Versailles, Innsbruck became the capital. Merano, however, continued to be known

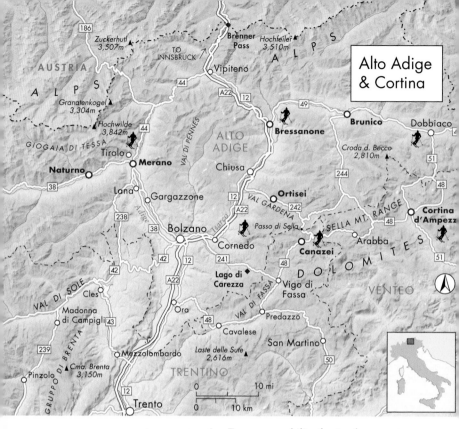

as a spa town, attracting European nobility for its therapeutic waters and its grape cure, which consists simply of eating the grapes grown on the surrounding hillsides. Sheltered by mountains, Merano has an unusually mild climate, with summer temperatures rarely exceeding 80°F (27°C) and winters that usually stay above freezing, despite the skiing that is within easy reach. Along the narrow streets of Merano's old town, houses have little towers and huge wooden doors, and the pointed arches of the Gothic cathedral sit next to neoclassical and art nouveau buildings. Merano serves as a good respite from mountain adventures, or from the bustle of nearby Trento and Bolzano.

The 14th-century Gothic **Duomo,** with a crenellated facade and an ornate campanile, sits in the heart of the old town. The Capella di Santa Barbara, just behind the cathedral, is an octagonal church containing a 15th-century pietà. ⊠*Piazza del Duomo* ☉*Easter–Sept., daily 8–noon and 2:30–8; Oct.–Easter, daily 8–noon and 2:30–7.*

★ ℭ The **Terme di Merano** is a sprawling spa complex with 25 pools (including a brine pool with underwater music) and eight saunas (with an indoor "snow room" available for cooling down). Along with the family-friendly options for bathing, personalized services for grown-ups include traditional cures using local products, such as grape-based applications and whey baths. An admission charge of €9.50 gets you two hours in thermal baths; €22 is for a full day's use of all baths and saunas. ⊠ *Piazza Terme 9* ☎ *0473/252000* ⊕ *www.termemerano.it* ⊙ *Daily 9* AM–*10* PM.

Castel Trauttmansdorff, a Gothic castle 2 km (1 mi) southeast of town, was restored in the 19th century, and now serves as a museum, celebrating 200 years of tourism in South Tirol. Outside, a sprawling garden has an extensive display of exotic flora organized by country of origin. An English-language audio guide is available for €2.50. ⊠ *Via Valentino 51a* ☎ *0473/235730* ⊕ *www.trauttmansdorff.it* ⊠ *€10* ⊙ *Apr.–mid-May and mid-Sept.–mid-Nov., daily 9–6; mid-May–mid-Sept., daily 9–9.*

Overlooking the town atop Mt. Tappeinerweg is a castle that was the home of poet Ezra Pound from 1958 to 1964. Still in the Pound family, the castle now houses the **Museo Agricolo di Brunnenburg**, devoted to Tirolean country life. Among its exhibits are a blacksmith's shop and, not surprisingly, a room with Pound memorabilia. To get here, take Bus 3, which departs every hour on the hour, from Merano to Dorf Tirol (20 minutes). ⊠ *Via Castello 17, Brunnenburg* ☎ *0473/923533* ⊠ *€3* ⊙ *Apr.–Oct., Wed.–Mon. 10–5.*

Fodor's Choice ★ A stroll along one of Merano's well-marked, impossibly pleasant **promenades** may yield even better relaxation than a spa treatment. **Passeggiata Tappeiner** (Tappeiner's Promenade) is a 3-km (2-mi) path with panoramic views from the hills north of the Duomo and diverse botanical pleasures along the way. **Passeggiata d'Estate** (Summer Promenade) runs along the shaded south bank of the Passirio River, and the **Passeggiata d'Inverno** (Winter Promenade), on the exposed north bank, provides more warmth and the Wandelhalle—a sunny area decorated with idyllic paintings of surrounding villages. The popular Austrian empress Sissi (Elisabeth of Wittelsbach, 1837–98) put Merano on the map as a spa destination; a trail named in her honor, the **Sentiero di Sissi** (Sissi's Walk), follows a path from Castel Trauttmansdorff to the heart of Merano.

NEED A BREAK? Cafe Saxifraga (⊠ *Passeggiata Tappeiner* ☎ *0473/237249*) occupies an enviable position overlooking Merano and the peaks enveloping the town; an extensive selection of teas and other beverages can be enjoyed on the patio, which has panoramic views. You can enjoy a rich hot chocolate or a cold beer above a gurgling waterfall at Cafe Glif (⊠ *Passeggiata Glif 51* ☎ *0473/234701*), at the northeast edge of the Passeggiata d'Inverno.

WHERE TO STAY & EAT

★ **$$$** ✕ **Sissi.** In this relaxed, light-filled restaurant just off Via dei Portici, rustic regional dishes are prepared with the precision of haute Italian cooking. Menu choices may include risotto *alle erbe* (with herbs) and *filetto di vitello con salsa di alloro* (veal fillet with bay-leaf sauce); a set menu (about €60) provides a complete five-course dinner. ⊠ *Via Gali-*

lei 44 ☎*0473/231062* ⚄*Reservations essential* ⊟*MC, V* ⊘*Closed Mon. and Jan. and Feb.*

$$ ✕ **Haisrainer.** Among the rustic wine taverns lining Via dei Portici, this one is most popular with locals and tourists alike; a menu in English is available for the latter. Warm wooden walls provide a comfortable setting for Tirolean and Italian standards: try the *zuppa al vino bianco* (stew with white wine) or the seasonal risottos (with asparagus in spring, or Barolo wine in chillier months). ⊠*Via dei Portici 100* ☎*0473/237944* ⊟*MC, V* ⊘*Closed Sun.*

$$ ✕ **Sieben.** Young Meraners crowd the hip bar on the ground floor of this modern bistro, in the town's central arcade. Upstairs, a more-mature crowd enjoys the contemporary cooking and attentive service in the jazz-theme dining room. Don't miss the Blues Brothers, poised over the staircase. ⊠*Via dei Portici 232* ☎*0473/210636* ⊟*MC, V* ⊘*Closed Wed.*

$ ✕ **Vinoteca-Pizzeria Relax.** If you have difficulty choosing from the long list of appetizing pizzas here, ask the friendly English-speaking staff for help with the menu. You're unlikely to find a better selection of wine, or a more-pleasant environment for sampling. You can also buy bottles of the locally produced vintage to take home. ⊠*Via Cavour 31, opposite Grand Hotel Palace* ☎*0473/236735* ⊟*AE, MC, V* ⊘*Closed Sun. and 2 wks in late Feb.*

★ $$$$ 🏨 **Palace Merano.** Merano's finest hotel is an old-world institution in an extensive garden. The art nouveau touches in the public spaces—Tiffany glass, marble pillars, and high ceilings—spill over into the spacious guest rooms. The renowned Espace Henri Chenot spa has baths, massages, mud treatments, and other cures that attract fatigued soccer stars and others in search of renewal. Rooftop suites have balconies with stunning views of Merano's steeples and the surrounding mountains. **Pros:** Great location, atmospheric building. **Cons:** Impersonal service, expensive rates. ⊠*Via Cavour 2, 39012* ☎*0473/271000* ⊕*www.palace.it* ⮌*125 rooms, 12 suites* ⚄*In-room: safe, refrigerator, ethernet. In-hotel: 2 restaurants, room service, bar, pool, spa, laundry service, public Internet, airport shuttle, parking (no fee)* ⊟*AE, DC, MC, V* ⦿*BP.*

$$$–$$$$ 🏨 **Castello Labers.** The red-tile gables, towers, and turrets give this castle its unmistakably Tirolean style, as it sits on a hilltop amid forested slopes. Ceiling beams, painted fresco decorations, and crossed halberds on the walls complete the look inside. The hospitable Stapf-Neubert family owns the hotel and takes an active part in its management. The hotel is 3 km (2 mi) northeast of Merano's center. **Pros:** Romantic setting, spectacular views. **Cons:** Long walk into town, some bathrooms are small. ⊠*Via Labers 25, 39012* ☎*0473/234484* ⊕*www.labers. it* ⮌*32 rooms, 1 suite* ⚄*In-room: no a/c, safe. In-hotel: restaurant, tennis court, pool, public Internet* ⊟*AE, DC, MC, V* ⊘*Closed mid-Nov.–Mar.* ⦿*BP.*

$ 🏨 **Conte di Merano.** If you don't feel like paying for one of Merano's resorts, this simple central hotel is a good alternative. Steps away from Via dei Portici and open year-round, it's an efficient base for exploring the town. Rooms have spartan furnishings, but are clean and comfortable. **Pros:** Excellent base for exploring Merano, reasonable rates. **Cons:** Basic decor, some street noise. ⊠ *Via delle Corse 78, 39012* ☎*0473/490260* ⊕*www.grafvonmeran.com* ⟲*23 rooms* ⚙*In-room: safe. In-hotel: restaurant, bar* ▤*AE, DC, MC, V* ⦿*BP.*

BRESSANONE (BRIXEN)

14 km (9 mi) north of Chiusa, 40 km (25 mi) northeast of Bolzano.

VISITOR INFORMATION

Bressanone tourism office (⊠ *Via Stazione 9* ☎*0472/836401* ⊕*www. brixen.org*).

EXPLORING

Bressanone (Brixen) is an important artistic center and was the seat of prince-bishops for centuries. Like their counterparts in Trento, these medieval administrators had the delicate task of serving two masters—the pope (the ultimate spiritual authority) and the Holy Roman Emperor (the civil and military power), who were virtually at war throughout the Middle Ages. Bressanone's prince-bishops became experts at tact and diplomacy.

The imposing **Duomo** was built in the 13th century but acquired a baroque facade 500 years later; its 14th-century cloister is decorated with medieval frescoes. Free guided tours (in German or Italian) are available April–October, Monday–Saturday at 10:30 and 3. ⊠*Piazza Duomo* ⊗*Daily 6–noon and 3–6.*

The Bishop's Palace houses the **Museo Diocesano** *(Diocesan Museum)* and its abundance of local medieval art, particularly Gothic wood carvings. The wooden statues and liturgical objects were all collected from the cathedral treasury. During the Christmas season, curators arrange the museum's large collection of antique Nativity scenes; look for the shepherds wearing Tirolean hats. ⊠*Palazzo Vescovile 2* ☎*0472/830505* ⊕*www.dioezesanmuseum.bz.it* ▣*€6* ⊗*Museum: mid-Mar.–Oct., Tues.–Sun. 10–5.*

At **Abbazia di Novacella,** an Augustinian abbey founded in 1142, they've been making wine for at least nine centuries. In the tasting room you can sample varietals produced in the Isarco Valley; Novacella is most famous for the delicate stone-fruit character of its dry white Sylvaner. You can also wander the delightful grounds; note the progression of Romanesque, Gothic, and baroque building styles. Guided tours of the abbey (in Italian and German) depart daily at 10, 11, 2, 3, and 4, as well as at noon and 1 in summer. ⊠*Località Novacella 1, 39040 Varna* ⊹*3 km (2 mi) north of Bressanone* ☎*0472/836189* ▣*Grounds and tasting room free, guided tours €5* ⊗*Grounds: Mon.–Sat. 10–7. Tasting room: Mon.–Sat. 9:15–noon and 2–6.*

WHERE TO STAY & EAT

$$–$$$ ✕ **Fink.** The rustic wood-paneled dining room is upstairs in this restaurant under the arcades of the pedestrians-only town center. Try the *carré di maiale gratinato* (pork chops roasted with cheese and served

with cabbage and potatoes) or the *castrato alla paesana*, a substantial lamb stew. In addition to hearty Tirolean specialties, there's an affordable daily set menu, as well as international dishes. ⊠ *Via Portici Minori 4* ☎ *0472/834883* ▬ *AE, DC, MC, V* ⊘ *Closed Wed. and Feb. No dinner Tues.*

★ $$$ 🍴 **Elephant.** This cozy inn, one of the region's best, takes its name from the 1551 visit of King John III of Portugal, who stopped here while leading an elephant (a present for Austria's Emperor Ferdinand) over the Alps. Each room is unique, many filled with antiques and paintings. Housed on the park property is the separate Villa Marzari, with 14 rooms. A rustic three-room stube serves tasty fare. **Pros:** Central location, good restaurant. **Cons:** Rooms vary in size, often filled with groups. ⊠ *Via Rio Bianco 4, 39042* ☎ *0472/832750* ⊕ *www.hotelelephant.com* 🛏 *44 rooms* △ *In-room: refrigerator, ethernet. In-hotel: restaurant, bar, tennis courts, pool, gym, parking (fee)* ▬ *DC, MC, V* ⊘ *Closed mid-Jan.–mid-Feb. and Nov.* ⬤ *BP.*

BRUNICO (BRUNECK)

★   *33 km (20 mi) east of Bressanone, 65 km (40 mi) northwest of Cortina d'Ampezzo.*

VISITOR INFORMATION
Brunico tourism office (⊠ *Piazza Municipio 7* ☎ *0474/555722* ⊕ *www. bruneck.com*).

EXPLORING
With its medieval quarter nestling below the 13th-century bishop's castle, Brunico (Bruneck) is in the heart of the Val Pusteria. This quiet and quaint town is divided by the Rienza River, with the old quarter on one side and the modern town on the other.

The **Museo Etnografico dell'Alto Adige** (*Alto Adige Ethnographic Museum*) re-creates a Middle Ages farming village, built around a 300-year-old mansion. The wood-carving displays are most interesting. The museum is in the district of Teodone, northeast of the center. ⊠ *Via Duca Diet 27* ☎ *0474/552087* ⊕ *www.provincia.bz.it/volkskundemuseen* 🎫 *€5* ⊘ *Mid-Apr.–Oct., Tues.–Sat. 9:30–5:30, Sun. 2–6.*

WHERE TO STAY
$$$ 🏨 **Post.** The Von Grebmer family runs a homey hotel in a building dating from the 1880s. The efficient service is the hotel's trademark. This is the most central, appealing lodging choice in town, especially if you've got a sweet tooth: the attached pastry shop is as popular with locals as with international guests. The hotel has its own parking, an unusual perk in the pedestrians-only center. **Pros:** Family-run friendliness, central location. **Cons:** No air-conditioning, deposit required to confirm reservations. ⊠ *Via Bastioni 9, 39031* ☎ *0474/555127* ⊕ *www.hotelpost-bruneck.com* 🛏 *54 rooms, 45 with bath* △ *In-room: no a/c, safe, refrigerator, ethernet. In-hotel: restaurant, spa, laundry service, parking (no fee), some pets allowed* ▬ *AE, MC, V* ⬤ *BP.*

SKIING

The **Alta Badia** (☎0471/836176 ⊕www.altabadia.org) ski area can be reached by heading 30 km (19 mi) south on SS244 from Brunico. It's less expensive—and more Austrian in character—than other, more-famous ski destinations in this region.

CORTINA D'AMPEZZO

Fodor'sChoice ★
30 km (19 mi) south of Dobbiaco.

VISITOR INFORMATION

Cortina d'Ampezzo tourism office (✉Piazzetta San Francesco 8 ☎0436/3231 ⊕www.cortina.dolomiti.com).

EXPLORING

Cortina d'Ampezzo has been the Dolomites' mountain resort of choice for more than 100 years; half a century before Turin, the Winter Olympics were held here in 1956. Although its glamorous appeal to younger Italians may have been eclipsed by steeper, sleeker Madonna di Campiglio, Cortina remains, for many, Italy's most idyllic incarnation of an Alpine ski town.

Surrounded by mountains and dense forests, the "Pearl of the Dolomites" is in a lush meadow 4,000 feet above sea level. The town hugs the slopes beside a fast-moving stream, and a public park extends along one bank. Higher in the valley, luxury hotels and the villas of the rich are identifiable by their attempts to hide behind stands of firs and spruces. The bustling center of Cortina d'Ampezzo has little nostalgia, despite its Alpine appearance. The tone is set by smart shops and cafés as chic as their well-dressed patrons, whose corduroy knickerbockers may well have been tailored by Armani. Unlike neighboring resorts that have a strong Germanic flavor, Cortina d'Ampezzo is unapologetically Italian and distinctly fashionable.

On Via Cantore, a winding road heading up out of town to the northeast (becoming SS48), you can stop and see the **Pista Olimpica di Bob** *(Olympic Bobsled Course)* used in the 1956 Winter Games. It remains in use, and regularly hosts the Bobsleigh World Cup.

WHERE TO STAY & EAT

$$$–$$$$ ✕ **Tavernetta.** Near the Olympic ice-skating rink, this popular restaurant has Tirolean-style wood-paneled dining rooms. Join the local clientele in sampling Cortina specialties such as *zuppa di porcini* (porcini mushroom soup), ravioli *di cervo* (stuffed with venison), and wild game. ✉*Via Castello 53* ☎*0436/868102* ▤*AE, DC, MC, V* ⊗*Closed May, June, Nov., and Wed. No lunch Thurs.*

$$$$ ▥ **Corona.** Noted ski instructor Luciano Rimoldi, who has coached such luminaries as Alberto Tomba, runs a cozy Alpine lodge. Modern art adorns small but comfortable pine-paneled rooms; the convivial bar is a pleasant place to relax. The hotel is a 10-minute walk—across the river—from the center of town, and a 10-minute ride from the lifts (a ski shuttle stops out front). **Pros:** Cozy atmosphere, friendly staff, quiet location. **Cons:** Small rooms, outside the town center. ✉*Via Val di*

Sotto 12, 32040 ☎*0436/3251* ⊕*www.cortina.dolomiti.com/alberghi/corona* ⤳*44 rooms* &*In-room: no a/c. In-hotel: restaurant, bar, public Internet, parking (no fee)* ▭*AE, DC, MC, V* ⊗*Closed Apr.–June and Sept.–Nov.* †◯†*MAP.*

$$$$
Fodor's Choice
★

▦ **De la Poste.** Loyal skiers return year after year to this lively hotel; its main terrace bar is one of Cortina's social centers. De la Poste has been under the careful management of the Manaìgo family since 1936. Each unique room has antiques in characteristic Dolomite style; almost all have wooden balconies. A refined main dining room—with high ceilings and large chandeliers—serves nouvelle cuisine and superb soufflés; there's also a more-informal grill room with wood paneling and the family's pewter collection. **Pros:** Professional service, romantic atmosphere. **Cons:** Half board compulsory in high season, in a busy neighborhood. ⊠*Piazza Roma 14, 32043* ☎*0436/4271* ⊕*www.delaposte.it* ⤳*83 rooms* &*In-room: no a/c, safe, refrigerator. In-hotel: 2 restaurants, bar, public Internet, parking (no fee)* ▭*AE, DC, MC, V* ⊗*Closed Apr.–mid-June and Oct.–mid-Dec.* †◯†*MAP.*

$$$$

▦ **Miramonti Majestic.** This imposing and luxe hotel, more than a century old, has a magnificent mountain-valley position about 1 km (½ mi) south of town. A touch of formality comes through in the imperial Austrian design. There's always a roaring fire in the splendid bar, and the hotel's recreation rooms are lined with windows overlooking mountain vistas. The history of Cortina is intricately tied to the Miramonti, and you can feel a part of it all here. **Pros:** Magnificent location, old-world charm, splendid views. **Cons:** Outside town center, minimum stay in high season. ⊠*Località Peziè 103, 32043* ☎*0436/4201* ⊕*www.cortina.dolomiti.org/hmiramonti* ⤳*105 rooms* &*In-room: no a/c, refrigerator. In-hotel: restaurant, bar, golf course, tennis courts, pool, gym, laundry service, public Internet, parking (no fee)* ▭*AE, DC, MC, V* ⊗*Closed Apr.–June and Sept.–mid-Dec.* †◯†*MAP.*

SPORTS

BOBSLEDDING

Cortina Adrenalin Center's **Taxi-Bob** (⊠*Località Ronco* ☎*0436/860808* ⊕*www.adrenalincenter.it* ⤳*€90 per person)* offers visitors the chance to don bodysuits and hurtle down a 4,000-foot Olympic bobsled course at more than 70 mph; two paying passengers wedge between a professional pilot and brakeman.

HIKING & CLIMBING

Hiking information is available at the excellent local **tourism office** (⊠*Piazzetta San Francesco 8* ☎*0436/3231* ⊕*www.cortina.dolomiti.com*). Cortina's **Scuola di Alpinismo** (*Mountaineering School* ⊠*Corso Italia 69* ☎*0436/868505* ⊕*www.guidecortina.com*) organizes climbing trips and trekking adventures.

SKIING

Cortina's long and picturesque ski runs will delight intermediates, but advanced skiers might lust for steeper terrain, which can be found only off-piste. Efficient ski bus service connects the town with the high-speed chairlifts and gondolas that ascend in all directions from the valley.

The **Dolomiti Superski pass** (✉ *Via Marconi 15* ☎*0471/795397* ⊕*www. dolomitisuperski.com*) provides access to the surrounding Dolomites (€40 per day)—with 450 lifts and gondolas serving 1,200 km (750 mi) of trails. Buy one at the ticket office next to the bus station. The **Faloria gondola** (✉ *Via Ria de Zeta 8* ☎*0436/2517*) runs from the center of town. From its top you can get up to most of the central mountains. Some of the most impressive views (and steepest slopes) are on **Monte Cristallo,** based at Misurina, 15 km (9 mi) northeast of Cortina by car or bus. The topography of the **Passo Falzarego** ski area, 16 km (10 mi) east of town, is quite dramatic.

HEART OF THE DOLOMITES

The area between Bolzano and the mountain resort Cortina d'Ampezzo is dominated by two major valleys, Val di Fassa and Val Gardena. Both share the spectacular panorama of the Sella mountain range, known as the Heart of the Dolomites. Val di Fassa cradles the beginning of the Grande Strada delle Dolomiti (Great Dolomites Road—SS48 and SS241), which runs from Bolzano as far as Cortina. This route, opened in 1909, comprises 110 km (68 mi) of relatively easy grades and smooth driving between the two towns—a slower, more-scenic alternative to traveling by way of Brunico and Dobbiaco along SS49.

In both Val di Fassa and Val Gardena, recreational options are less expensive, though less comprehensive, than in better-known resorts like Cortina. The culture here is firmly Germanic. Val Gardena is freckled with well-equipped, photo-friendly towns with great views overlooked by the oblong *Sasso Lungo* (Long Rock), which is more than 10,000 feet above sea level. It's also home to the Ladins, descendants of soldiers sent by the Roman emperor Tiberius to conquer the Celtic population of the area in the 1st century AD. Forgotten in the narrow cul-de-sacs of isolated mountain valleys, the Ladins have developed their own folk traditions and speak an ancient dialect that is derived from Latin and similar to the Romansch spoken in some high valleys in Switzerland.

CANAZEI

60 km (37 mi) west of Cortina d'Ampezzo, 52 km (32 mi) east of Bolzano.

VISITOR INFORMATION
Canazei tourism office (✉*Piazza Marconi 5* ☎*0462/601113* ⊕*www. fassa.com*).

EXPLORING
Of the year-round resort towns in the Val di Fassa, Canazei is the most popular. The mountains around this small town are threaded with hiking trails and ski slopes, surrounded by large clutches of conifers.

About 4 km (2½ mi) west of Canazei, an excursion from Campitello di Fassa to the vantage point at **Col Rodella** is a must. A cable car rises some

CLOSE UP

Hiking the Dolomites

For many overseas visitors, the Dolomites conjure images of downhill skiing at Cortina d'Ampezzo and Madonna di Campiglio. But summer, not winter, is high season here; Italians, German-speaking Europeans, and in-the-know travelers from farther afield come here for clear mountain air and world-class hiking. Nature has done most of the work—impressive terrain, inspiring vistas, an impossibly pleasant climate—but the man-made facilities for enjoying the mountains are also exceptional.

PICKING A TRAIL

The Dolomites boast a well-maintained network of trails for hiking and rock climbing. As long as you're in reasonably good shape, the number of appealing hiking options can be overwhelming. Trails are well marked and designated by grades of difficulty: T for tourist path, H for hiking path, EE for expert hikers, and EEA for equipped expert hikers. On any of these paths you're likely to see carpets of mountain flowers between clutches of dense evergreens, with chamois and roe deer mulling about. If you're just out for a day in the mountains, you can leave the particulars of your walk open until you're actually on the spot; local tourist offices (especially those in Cortina, Madonna, and the Heart of the Dolomites) can help you choose the right route based on trail conditions, weather, and desired exertion level. **Club Alpino Italiano** (⊕ *www.cai.it*), the world's oldest organization of its kind, is an excellent resource for more ambitious adventures. It has offices in Bolzano (⊠ *Piazza delle Erbe 46* ☎ *0471/981391*), Merano (⊠ Corso della Libertà 188 ☎ *0473/448944*),

and Trento (⊠ Via Manci 57 ☎ *0461/981871*).

TRAVELING THE VIE FERRATE

If you're looking for an adventure somewhere between hiking and climbing, consider a guided trip along the Vie Ferrate (Iron Paths). These routes offer fixed climbing aids (steps, ladders, bridges, safety cables) left by Alpine divisions of the Italian and Austro-Hungarian armies and later converted for recreational use. Previous experience is generally not required, but vertigo-inducing heights do demand a strong stomach. Detailed information about Vie Ferrate in the eastern Dolomites can be found at ⊕ *www.dolomiti. org*. Capable tour organizers include **Scuola di Alpinismo** (Mountaineering School) in Madonna di Campiglio (☎ *0465/442634* ⊕ *www.guidealpinecampiglio.it*) and Cortina d'Ampezzo (☎ *0436/868505* ⊕ *www.guide cortina.com*).

BEDDING DOWN

One of the pleasures of an overnight adventure in the Dolomites is staying at a *rifugio,* one of the refuges that dot the mountainsides. There are hundreds of them, often in remote locations and ranging from spartan shelters to posh retreats. Most fall somewhere in between—they're cozy mountain lodges with dormitory-style accommodations. Pillows and blankets are provided (so there's no need to carry a sleeping bag), but you have to supply your own sheet. Bathrooms are usually shared, as is the experience of a cold shower in the morning.

The majority of rifugi are operated by the Club Alpino Italiano (⊕ *www. cai.it*). Contact information for both CAI-run and private rifugi is available from local tourist offices; most useful are those in Madonna di Campiglio (⊕ www.campiglio.to), Cortina d'Ampezzo (⊕ www.dolomiti.org), Val di Fassa (⊕ www.fassa.com), and Val Gardena (⊕ www.val-gardena.net). Reservations are a must, especially in August, although Italian law requires rifugi to accept travelers for the night if there is insufficient time to reach other accommodations before dark.

EATING WELL

Food is as much a draw at rifugi as location. Although the dishes served are the sort of the rustic cuisine you might expect (salami, dumplings, hearty stews), the quality is uniformly excellent—an impressive feat, made all the more remarkable when you consider that supplies often have to arrive by helicopter. Your dinner may cost as much as your bed for the night—about €20 per person—and it's difficult to determine which is the better bargain.

Snacks and packed lunches are available for purchase, but many opt to sit down for the midday meal. Serving as both holiday hiking destination and base camp for difficult ascents, the rifugi welcome walkers and climbers of all stripes from intersecting trails and nearby faces. Multilingual stories are swapped, food and wine shared, and new adventures launched.

STUMBLING ON ÖTZI

It was at the Similaun rifugio in September 1991 that a German couple arrived talking of a dead body they'd discovered near a "curious pickax." This was to be the world's introduction to Ötzi, the oldest mummy ever found (now on display in Bolzano's Museo Archeologico dell'Alto Adige).

The couple, underestimating the age of the corpse by about 5,300 years, thought it was a matter for the police. World-famous mountaineers Reinhold Messner and Hans Kammerlander happened to be passing through the same rifugio during a climbing tour, and a few days later they were on scene, freeing the iceman from the ice. Ötzi's remarkable story was under way. You can see him on display, along with his longbow, ax, and clothes, at Bolzano's archaeological museum, where he continues to be preserved at freezing temperatures.

5

3,000 feet to a full-circle vista of the Heart of the Dolomites, including the Sasso Lungo and the rest of the Sella range.

WHERE TO STAY

$$–$$$ 🏨 **Alla Rosa.** The view of the imposing Dolomites is the real attraction at this central hotel, so ask for a room with a balcony. The reception area is spacious and welcoming, and guest rooms pleasantly blend rustic and modern elements. There's a modest restaurant serving local and international cuisine, and a cozy bar. **Pros:** In the center of town, great views. **Cons:** Half board mandatory in high season, busy neighborhood. ⊠ *Via del Faure 18, 38032* ☎ *0462/601107* ⊕ *www.hotelallarosa.com* 📞 *49 rooms* ⚘ *In-room: no a/c, refrigerator. In-hotel: restaurant, bar, gym, public Internet, parking (fee)* ☰ *MC, V* ❏ *MAP.*

EN ROUTE   The **Passo di Sella** *(Sella Pass)* can be approached from SS48, affording some of the most spectacular mountain vistas in Europe before it descends into the Val Gardena. The road continues to Ortisei, passing the smaller resorts of Selva Gardena and Santa Cristina.

ORTISEI (ST. ULRICH)

28 km (17 mi) north of Canazei, 35 km (22 mi) northeast of Bolzano.

VISITOR INFORMATION

Ortisei (⊠ *Via Rezia 1* ☎ *0471/777600* ⊕ *www.val-gardena.net*).

EXPLORING

Ortisei (St. Ulrich), the jewel in the crown of Val Gardena's resorts, is a hub of activity in both summer and winter; there are hundreds of miles of hiking trails and accessible ski slopes. Hotels and facilities are abundant—swimming pools, ice rinks, health spas, tennis courts, and bowling alleys. Most impressive of all is the location, a valley surrounded by formidable views in all directions.

For centuries Ortisei has also been famous for the expertise of its wood carvers, and there are still numerous workshops. Apart from making religious sculptures—particularly the wayside calvaries you come upon everywhere in the Dolomites—Ortisei's carvers were long known for producing wooden dolls, horses, and other toys. As itinerant peddlers they traveled every spring on foot with their loaded packs as far as Paris, London, and St. Petersburg. Shops in town still sell woodcrafts.

Fine historic and contemporary examples of local woodworking can be seen at the **Museo della Val Gardena.** ⊠ *Via Rezia 83* ☎ *0471/797554* 💶 *€3* 🕐 *Feb.–Mar., Tues., Thurs., and Fri. 2–6; June and Sept.–mid-Oct., Tues., Wed., and Fri. 2–6, Thurs. 10–noon and 2–6; July and Aug., weekdays 10–noon and 2–6, Sun. 2–6.*

WHERE TO STAY

★ $$$$ 🏨 **Adler.** This hotel, the best in the valley, has been under the same family management since 1810. The original building has been enlarged several times, yielding spacious guest rooms and an expansive spa complex but retaining much of the old turreted-castle appeal. Most guests stay for a full week, picking up the busy schedule of activities (such as guided ski tours and snowshoe walks) when they arrive on Saturday evening. The same activities, at a slower pace, are available for children. **Pros:** Breathtaking views, superb staff, lots of family activities. **Cons:** Standard rooms need redecorating, long walk to town center. ⊠ *Via Rezia 7, 39046* ☎*0471/775000* ⊕*www.hotel-adler.com* ↘*123 rooms* ♿*In-room: safe, refrigerator, ethernet. In-hotel: restaurant, bar, pool, gym, spa, children's programs (ages 4–12), parking (no fee)* ▭*MC, V* ☾*Closed mid-Apr.–mid-May* ❙◎❙*MAP.*

$$$$ ▦ **Cavallino Bianco.** The pink Cavallino Bianco looks like a gigantic dollhouse, with delicate wooden balconies and an eye-catching wooden gable. Beyond this facade lies a sprawling, all-inclusive modern resort, but the cozy bar—with its large, handcrafted fireplace—retains some of the charm it had as the old postal hotel. Guest rooms have upholstered furniture with cheery, large-scale plaids and honey-tone wood accents. The hotel is only a five-minute walk from the main ski facilities; ski guides are available. **Pros:** Family-friendly atmosphere, cheerful rooms. **Cons:** In the busy town center, a bit impersonal. ⊠ *Via Rezia 22, 39046* ☎*0471/783333* ⊕*www.cavallino-bianco.com* ↘*184 rooms* ♿*In-room: safe, refrigerator, ethernet. In-hotel: 2 restaurants, bar, pool, spa, bicycles, children's programs (ages 2–12), parking (fee)* ▭*AE, DC, MC, V* ❙◎❙*FAP.*

SKIING

With almost 600 km (370 mi) of accessible downhill slopes and more than 90 km (56 mi) of cross-country skiing trails, Ortisei is one of the most popular ski resorts in the Dolomites. Prices are good, and facilities are among the most modern in the region. In warmer weather, the slopes surrounding Ortisei are a popular hiking destination, as well as a playground for vehicular mountain adventures: biking, rafting, even paragliding.

An immensely popular ski route, the **Sella Ronda** relies on well-placed chairlifts to connect 26 km (16 mi) of downhill skiing around the colossal Sella massif, passing through several towns along the way. You can ski the loop, which requires intermediate ability and a full day's effort, either clockwise or counterclockwise. Going with a guide is recommended. Chairlifts here, as elsewhere in the Dolomites, are covered by the €40 **Dolomiti Superski pass** (⊕*www.dolomitisuperski.com*). The **Val Gardena tourism office** (⊠ *Via Dursan 81, Santa Cristina* ☎*0471/777777* ⊕*www.valgardena.it*) can provide detailed information about sport-equipment rental outfits and guided-tour operators. **Gardena Mountain Adventures** (☎*335/6849031* ⊕*www.val-gardena.com/gma*) outfits a particularly large choice of year-round mountain sport activities.

LAGO DI CAREZZA

22 km (14 mi) west of Canazei, 29 km (18 mi) east of Bolzano.

Glacial Lake Carezza is some 5,000 feet above sea level. The azure blue of the waters can at times change to magical greens and purples, reflections of the dense surrounding forest and rosy peaks of the Dolomites.

You can hike down to this most quintessential of mountain lakes from the nearby village of the same name; there's a fountain with two marmots in the center of town.

CALDARO (KALTERN)

45 km (28 mi) southwest of Lago di Carezza, 15 km (9 mi) south of Bolzano.

VISITOR INFORMATION

Caldaro tourism office (⊠*Piazza Mercato 8* 🕾*0471/963169* ⊕*www. suedtirol-it.com/caldaro*).

A vineyard village with clear views of castles high up on the surrounding mountains represents the centuries of division that forged the unique character of the area. Caldaro architecture is famous for the way it blends Italian Renaissance elements of balance and harmony with the soaring windows and peaked arches of the Germanic Gothic tradition. The church of Santa Caterina, on the main square, is a good example.

Close to Caldaro's main square is the **Museo Provinciale del Vino,** with exhibits on how local wine has historically been made, stored, served, and worshipped. You can call ahead to reserve a wine tasting (€5) in the museum's cellar. ⊠*Via dell'Oro 1* 🕾*0471/963168* ⊕*www.provinz. bz.it/volkskundemuseen* 🖃*€3* ⊙*Apr.–mid-Nov., Tues.–Sat. 9:30–noon and 2–6, Sun. 10–noon.*

Milan, Lombardy & the Lakes

WORD OF MOUTH

"Italy's Lake Maggiore is one of Europe's top vacation meccas for good reason. It's a long sliver of water ringed by Alpine scenery freckled with villas and resorts."

—PalQ

WELCOME TO MILAN, LOMBARDY & THE LAKES

Piazza del Duomo, Milan

TOP REASONS TO GO

★ **Lake Como:** Ferries crisscross the waters, taking you from stately villas to tiny towns.

★ **Leonardo Da Vinci's** *The Last Supper:* Behold one of the world's most famous works of art.

★ **Bergamo Alta:** A funicular ride takes you up to the magnificent medieval city.

★ **Window shopping in Milan:** Italians' refined fashion sense is on full display in the famed *quadrilatero* shopping district.

★ **La Scala:** There's no better place to spend a night at the opera.

1 Milan. Italy lives in the present tense here. The country's leading city of commerce is also one of the world's fashion capitals, and there are cultural treasures here that rival those of Florence and Rome.

2 Pavia, Cremona & Mantua. South of Milan are the walled cities where Renaissance dukes built towering palaces and intricate churches. They sit on the Po Plain, one of Italy's wealthiest regions.

3 Lake Garda. Italy's largest lake measures 11 mi across at its widest point and 33 mi from end to end. There are more tourists here than at the other lakes, but that means you'll also find more opportunities for outdoor activities.

4 Lake Como. This relatively narrow lake is probably the country's best-known body of water. You can almost always see across to the other side, which lends a great sense of intimacy. Lake Lecco, to the southeast, is actually a branch of Lake Como.

5 Lake Maggiore. It may be smaller than Lake Garda and less famous than Lake Como, but Lake Maggiore is impressively picturesque with the Alps as a backdrop. One of the greatest pleasures here is exploring the lake's islands.

Lake Como

Mantua

SWITZERLAND

Chiavenna

36

A L P S

Sondrio

Edolo

38

Morbegno

4

Lago
Como

llagio

42

Darfo-Boario

TRENTINO-
ALTO ADIGE

Lecco

LOMBARDY

342

Bergamo

Lago
d'Iseo

42

Gargnano

A4

A4

510

Gardone Riviera

11

Brescia

3

Lago
Garda

11

235

Sirmione

415

11

elegnano

Crema

Oglio

A21

VENETO

Lodi

River

236

9

River

Mantua

10

ne Po

Cremona

2

River

EMILIA-
ROMAGNA

0   20 mi

0   20 km

GETTING ORIENTED

In Lombardy, jagged mountains and deep glacial lakes stretch from the Swiss border down to Milan's outskirts, where they meet the flat, fertile plain that extends from the banks of the River Po. Lake Como is north of Milan, while Lake Maggiore is to the northwest and Lake Garda is to the east. Scattered across the plains to the south are the Renaissance city-states of Pavia, Cremona, and Mantua.

MILAN, LOMBARDY & THE LAKES PLANNER

Supper Reservations

Reservations are required to see Leonardo da Vinci's *The Last Supper*, housed in the refectory of Milan's Santa Maria delle Grazie church. You should call as far in advance as possible to make them, particularly if you're planning to go on a weekend. For details, see the Santa Maria delle Grazie listing in this chapter.

A Night at the Opera

Attending a performance at the world's most venerated opera house, La Scala, is an unforgettable experience, regardless of whether you're an opera buff. Tickets go on sale two months in advance, and they sell out quickly. Your best bet is to order online at ⊕ *www.teatroallascala.org* (phone orders aren't accepted). Once you're in Milan, you can check on ticket availability at the Scala box office, located in the Duomo metro station and open daily from noon to 6 PM. About 100 tickets for seats in the second gallery go on sale three hours before a performance—they're available at the ticket office of the theater itself.

Making the Most of Your Time

Italy's capital of commerce isn't a top priority for most leisure travelers, but the city has a sophisticated urban appeal: its fashionable shops rival New York and Paris, its soccer teams are Italy's answer to the Yankees and the Mets, its opera performances set the standard for the world, and its art treasures are considerable.

The biggest draw in the region, though, is the lake district. Lakes Como, Garda, Maggiore, and Orta all have long histories as travel destinations, and each has its own distinct character. If you have limited time, visit the lake you think best suits your style, but if you have more time, make the rounds to two or three to get a sense of their contrasts.

Finding a Place to Stay

The hotels in Italy's wealthiest region generally cater to a clientele willing to pay for extra comfort. Outside Milan, many are converted villas with well-landscaped grounds. Most of the famous lake resorts are expensive; more reasonable rates can be found in the smaller towns. Local tourism offices can be an excellent source of information about affordable lodging. In Milan, reservations are recommended year-round.

DINING & LODGING PRICE CATEGORIES (IN EUROS)				
¢	$	$$	$$$	$$$$
Restaurants				
under €15	€15–€25	€25–€35	€35–€45	over €45
Hotels				
under €70	€70–€110	€110–€160	€160–€220	over €220

Restaurant prices are for a first course (primo), second course (secondo), and dessert (dolce). Hotel prices are for two people in a standard double room in high season, including tax and service.

GETTING AROUND

Lake Como

By Train

Milan's central station (Stazione Centrale), 3 km (2 mi) northwest of the Duomo, is one of Italy's major passenger-train hubs, with frequent direct service within the region to Como, Bergamo, Brescia, Sirmione, Pavia, Cremona, and Mantua. Currently being renovated, the entrances move around, so allow for some extra time here. For general information on trains and schedules, as well as online ticket purchase, visit the Web site of the Italian national railway, **FS** (☎ *892021* ⊕ *www.trenitalia.com*). The automated telephone line requires that you speak Italian, but the Web site has an English version.

Electronically-purchased tickets should be printed out at machines in the station and then stamped by one of the machines at the track's head.

By Bus

Bus service isn't a good option for travel between cities here—it's neither faster, cheaper, nor more convenient than the train. For those determined to travel by bus, Autostradale (☎ *02/637901*) goes to Turin, Bergamo, and Brescia from its hub at Autostazione Garibaldi, north of Milan's city center. Reservations are required.

By Car

Outside of Milan, driving is the best way to see the region. Getting almost anywhere is a snap, as several major highways intersect at Milan, all connected by the *tangenziale*, the road that rings the city. The A4 runs west to Turin and east to Venice; A1 leads south to Bologna, Florence, and Rome; A7 angles southwest down to Genoa. A8 goes northwest toward Lake Maggiore, and A9 north runs past Lake Como and over the St. Gotthard Pass into Switzerland.

Your car-rental company should be your first resource if you have a problem while driving in Italy, but it's also good to know that the **ACI** (☎ *803/116*), the Italian auto club, offers 24-hour roadside assistance (free for members, for a fee for non-members). Regularly spaced roadside service phones are available on the autostrade.

La Scala, Milan

EATING & DRINKING WELL IN LOMBARDY

Lombardy may well offer Italy's most varied cuisine. Local cooking is influenced by the neighboring regions of the north; foreign conquerors have left their mark; and today well-traveled Milanese, business visitors, and industrious immigrants all appreciate exotic flavors not so eagerly embraced elsewhere in Italy.

Milan runs counter to many of the established Italian dining customs. A "real" traditional Milanese meal is a rarity; instead, Milan offers something for every taste, budget, and time of day, from expense-account elegance in fancy restaurants to all-day nibbles in wine bars. The city's cosmopolitan nature means trends arrive here first, and things move fast. Meals are not the drawn-out pastime they tend to be elsewhere in Italy. But food is still consistently good—competition between restaurants is fierce and the local clientele is demanding, which means you can be reasonably certain that if a place looks promising, it won't disappoint.

THE COTOLETTA QUESTION

Everyone has an opinion on *cotoletta*, photo upper right, the breaded veal cutlet known across Italy as *una Milanese*. It's clearly related to Austria's Wiener schnitzel, but did the Austrians introduce it when they dominated Milan or take it home when they left? Should it be thick or thin? With bone or without? Some think it best with fresh tomato and arugula on top; others find this sacrilege. Two things unite all camps: the meat must be well beaten until it is thin, and it must never leave a grease spot after it is fried.

REGIONAL SPECIALTIES

Ask an Italian what Lombards eat, and you're likely to hear *cotoletta, càsoeûla,* and *risotto giallo*—all dishes that reinforce Lombardy's status as the crossroads of Italy. *Cotoletta alla Milanese* has likely Austrian influences. *Càsoeûla* is a cabbage and pork stew that resembles French cassoulet, though some say it has Spanish origins. *Risotto giallo* (also known as *Milanese*) pictured at left, is colored and perfumed with exotic saffron. With no tomatoes, olive oil, or pasta, these dishes hardly sound Italian.

BUTTER & CHEESE

Agricultural traditions and geography mean that animal products are more common here than in southern Italy—and that means butter and cream take olive oil's place. A rare point of agreement about cotoletta is that it's cooked in butter. The first and last steps of risotto making—toasting the rice and letting it "repose" before serving—use ample amounts of butter. And the second-most famous name in Italian cheese (after Parmesan) is likely Gorgonzola, named for a town near Milan. The best now comes from Novara.

RISOTTO

Novara is the center of Italian (and European) rice production. Introduced from the Orient and grown here since the 15th century, rice is Lombardy's answer to pasta. From Milan's risotto giallo with its costly saffron tint to Mantua's risotto with pumpkin or sausage, there's no end to the variety of rice dishes. Canonic risotto should be *all'onda,* or flow off the spoon like a wave. Keeping with the Italian tradition of nothing wasted, yesterday's risotto is flattened in a pan and fried in butter to produce *riso al salto,* which at its best has a crispy crust and a tender middle.

PANETTONE

Panettone, a sweet yeast bread with raisins and citron, pictured below left, is a national Christmastime treat invented in Milan. It's now so ubiquitous that its price is used as an economic indicator: is it up or down, compared to last year? Consumption begins on December 7, Milan's patron saint's day, and goes until supplies run out at January's end.

WINE

Lombardy is not one of Italy's better-known wine regions, though local producers are doing their best to change that. Production is scattered throughout the province, from the temperate shores of Lake Garda to the Alpine slopes to the north. Look for Oltrepò Pavese reds from the far side of the Po. The Valtellina area to the northeast of Milan produces the notable DOCG red Sforzato di Valtellina. And the Franciacorta region around Brescia makes highly regarded *méthode champenoise* bubblies.

IT'S TEMPTING TO DESCRIBE LOMBARDY as a region that offers something for everyone. Milan is the country's business capital and the center for everything that's up-to-the-minute. The great Renaissance cities of the Po Plain—Pavia, Cremona, and Mantua—are stately and serene, embracing their past with nostalgia while ever keeping an eye on the present. Topping any list of the region's attractions are the lakes—glacial waters stretching out below the Alps—which have been praised as the closest thing to paradise by writers throughout the ages, from Virgil to Hemingway.

Millions of travelers have concurred: for sheer beauty, the lakes of northern Italy—Como, Maggiore, Garda, and Orta—have few equals. Along their shores are 18th- and 19th-century villas, exotic formal gardens, sleepy villages, and dozens of resorts that were once Europe's most fashionable, and still retain a powerful allure.

Milan can be disappointingly modern—a little too much like the place you've come to Italy to escape—but its historic buildings and art collections in many ways rival those of Florence and Rome. And if you love to shop, Milan is a mecca. It truly offers a fashion experience for every taste, from Corso Buenos Aires, which has a higher ratio of stores per square foot than anywhere else in Europe, to upscale but affordable Corso Vercelli and elegant Via Montenapoleone, where there is no limit on what you can spend. Milan is home to global fashion giants such as Armani, Prada, and Trussardi; behind these famous names stands a host of smaller, less-renowned designers who help fill all those fabulous shops.

MILAN

Updated by
Madeleine
Johnson

Milan is Italy's business hub and crucible of chic. Between the Po's rich farms and the industrious mountain valleys, it has long been the country's capital of commerce, finance, fashion, and media. Rome may be bigger and have the political power, but Milan and the affluent north is what really makes the country go. It's also Italy's transport hub, with the biggest international airport, the most rail connections, and the best subway system. Leonardo da Vinci's *The Last Supper* and other great works of art are here, as well as a spectacular Gothic Duomo, the finest of its kind. Milan even reigns supreme where it really counts (in the minds of many Italians), routinely trouncing the rest of the nation with its two premier soccer teams.

And yet, Milan hasn't won the battle for hearts and minds. Most tourists prefer Tuscany's hills and Venice's canals to Milan's hectic efficiency and wealthy indifference, and it's no surprise that in a country of medieval hilltop villages and skilled artisans, a city of grand boulevards and global corporations leaves visitors asking the real Italy to please stand up. They're right, of course. Milan is more European than Italian, a new buckle on an old boot, and although its old city can stand cobblestone for cobblestone against the best of them, seekers of Roman ruins and fairy-tale towns may pass. But Milan's secrets reveal themselves

LOMBARDY THROUGH THE AGES

Lombardy has had a tumultuous history. Control by outsiders dates back more than 3,000 years, to when the Etruscans of central Italy first wandered north of the River Po. They dominated the region for centuries, to be followed by the Cenomani Gauls, then the Romans in the later days of the Republic. The region was known as Cisalpine Gaul ("Gaul this side of the Alps"), and under the rule of Augustus became a Roman province.

The decline of the Roman Empire was followed by invasion by Attila of the Huns and Theodoric of the Goths. These conquerors gave way to the Lombards, who then ceded to Charlemagne their iron crown, which became the emblem of his vast, unstable empire. Even before the bonds of the empire had begun to snap, the cities of Lombardy were erecting walls in defense against the Hungarians, and against each other.

These city-states formed the Lombard League, which in the 12th century finally defeated the German ruler Frederick Barbarossa. With the northern invaders gone, new and even bloodier strife began. In each city the Guelphs (bourgeois supporters of the popes) and the Ghibellines (noblemen loyal to the Holy Roman Empire) clashed. The city-states declined, falling under the yoke of a few powerful regional rulers. The Republic of Venice dominated Brescia and Bergamo. Mantua was ruled by the Gonzaga family, and the Visconti and Sforza families took over Como, Cremona, Milan, and Pavia.

The Battle of Pavia in 1525, in which the generals of Holy Roman Emperor Charles V defeated the French, brought on 200 years of occupation by the Spanish—who proved generally less cruel than the local tyrants. The War of the Spanish Succession in the early years of the 18th century brought in the Austrians.

Napoléon and his generals defeated the Austrians at the turn of the 19th century. The Treaty of Campoformio resulted in the proclamation of the Cisalpine Republic, which soon became the Republic of Italy and then the Kingdom of Italy—which lasted only until Napoléon's defeat brought back the Austrians. In March of 1848, demonstrations in Milan took on surprising force: the Austrians were driven out of the city, and a provisional government of Milan soon became a provisional government of Lombardy. In June of the same year, Lombardy united with Sardinia—the first step toward Italian unification in 1870.

The spirit of 1848 was rekindled in 1943. Discontent with Fascism provoked workers to strike in Turin and Milan, marking the beginning of the end of Fascist dominance. The Lombardy-based partisan insurrection against Mussolini and the German regime was better organized and more successful than in many other parts of the country. Indeed, Milan was liberated from the Germans by its own partisan organization before the Allied troops entered the city.

Dissatisfaction with the federal government is practically a given among Lombardy residents, and the prevailing attitude has been to ignore Rome and get on with business. It's an approach that's proven successful: Lombardy accounts for one-fifth of Italy's economy.

6

slowly to those who look. A side street conceals a garden complete with flamingoes (Via dei Cappuccini, just off Corso Venezia), and a renowned 20th-century art collection hides modestly behind an unspectacular facade a block from Corso Buenos Aires (the Museo Boschi-di Stefano). Visitors lured by the world-class shopping will appreciate Milan's European sophistication while discovering unexpected facets of a country they may have thought they knew.

Virtually every invader in European history—Gaul, Roman, Goth, Longobard, and Frank—as well as a long series of rulers from France, Spain, and Austria, took a turn at ruling the city. After being completely sacked by the Goths in AD 539 and by the Holy Roman Empire under Frederick Barbarossa in 1157, Milan became one of the first independent city-states of the Renaissance. Its heyday of self-rule proved comparatively brief. From 1277 until 1500 it was ruled by the Visconti and subsequently the Sforza dynasties. These families were known, justly or not, for a peculiarly aristocratic mixture of refinement, classical learning, and cruelty, and much of the surviving grandeur of Gothic and Renaissance art and architecture is their doing. Be on the lookout in your wanderings for the Visconti family emblem—a viper, its jaws straining wide, devouring a child.

VISITOR INFORMATION

The **tourism office** (⊠ *Piazza Duomo 19/A, Piazza Duomo* ☎ *02/74043431* ⊕ *www.visitamilano.it* ☉ *Mon.–Sat. 8:45–1 and 2–6, Sun. 9–1 and 2–5*) Piazza Duomo is an excellent place to begin your visit. It is now accessible by a stairway under the arches on the north side of Piazza Duomo. You can also enter from the Galleria in front of the Hyatt hotel. The Autostradale bus operator, sightseeing companies, and a few theaters have desks here that sell tickets. There are also free maps on a variety of themes and a selection of brochures about smaller museums and cultural initiatives. Pick up a copy of the English-language *Hello Milano* (ask, if it is not on display). This monthly magazine includes a day-to-day schedule of events of interest to visitors and a comprehensive map.

THE DUOMO & POINTS NORTH

Milan's main streets radiate out from the massive Duomo, a late-Gothic cathedral that was started in 1386. Leading north is the handsome Galleria Vittorio Emanuele, an enclosed walkway that takes you to the world-famous opera house known as La Scala. Beyond are the winding streets of the elegant Brera neighborhood, once the city's bohemian quarter. Here you'll find many art galleries, as well as the academy of fine arts. Heading northeast from La Scala is Via Manzoni, which leads to the *Quadrilatero della moda,* or fashion district. Its streets are lined with elegant window displays from the world's most celebrated designers—the Italians taking the lead, of course.

Leading northeast from the Duomo is Corso Vittorio Emanuele. Locals and visitors stroll along this pedestrians-only street, looking at the shop windows, buying ice cream, or stopping for a coffee at one of the sidewalk cafés. Northwest of the Duomo is Via Dante, at the top of which is the imposing outline of the Castello Sforzesco.

MAIN ATTRACTIONS

★ ❽ **Castello Sforzesco.** For the serious student of Renaissance military engineering, the Castello must be something of a travesty, so often has it been remodeled or rebuilt since it was begun in 1450 by the *condottiere* (hired mercenary) who founded the city's second dynastic family, Francesco Sforza, fourth duke of Milan. Though today the word "mercenary" has a pejorative ring, during the Renaissance all Italy's great soldier-heroes were professionals hired by the cities and principalities that they served. Of them—and there were thousands—Francesco Sforza (1401–66) is considered one of the greatest, most honest, and most organized. It is said he could remember the names not only of all his men but of their horses as well. His rule signaled the enlightened age of the Renaissance that preceded the next foreign rule by a scant 50 years. The castle's secret crypts and battlements, including a tunnel that emerges well into the Parco Sempione behind, can be visited with privately reserved guides from **Ad Artem** (☎02/6596937 ✉*info@adartem.it*) or **Opera d'Arte** (☎02/45487400 ✉*info@peradartemilano.it*).

6

Since the turn of the 20th century, the Castello has been the depository of several city-owned collections of Egyptian and other antiquities, musical instruments, arms and armor, decorative arts and textiles, prints and photographs (on consultation), paintings, and sculpture. Highlights include the **Sala delle Asse,** a frescoed room still sometimes attributed to Leonardo da Vinci (1452–1519). Michelangelo's unfinished *Rondanini Pietà* is believed to be his last work—an astounding achievement for a man nearly 90, and a moving coda to his life. The *pinacoteca* (picture gallery) features paintings from medieval times to the 18th century, including 230 works by Antonello da Messina, Canaletto, Andrea Mantegna, and Bernardo Bellotto. The Museo dei Mobili (furniture museum), which illustrates the development of Italian furniture from the Middle Ages to current design, includes a delightful collection of Renaissance treasure chests of exotic woods with tiny drawers and miniature architectural details. A single ticket purchased in the office in an inner courtyard admits visitors to these separate installations, which are dispersed around the castle's two immense courtyards. ✉*Piazza Castello, Brera* ☎02/88463700 ⊕*www.milanocastello.it* 💶€3, free Fri. 2–5 ⊙*Castle: daily 7–6; museums: Tues.– Sun. 9–5:30* Ⓜ*Cairoli; Tram 1, 3, 4, 7, 12, 14, 27.*

★ ❶ **Duomo.** This intricate Gothic structure has been fascinating and exasperating visitors and conquerors alike since it was begun by Galeazzo Visconti III (1351–1402), first duke of Milan, in 1386. Consecrated in the 15th or 16th century, it was not completed until just before the coronation of Napoléon as king of Italy in 1809. Whether or not you concur with travel writer H. V. Morton's 1964 assessment that the cathedral is "one of the mightiest Gothic buildings ever created," there is no denying that for sheer size and complexity it is unrivaled. It is the second-largest church in the world—the largest being St. Peter's in Rome. The capacity is reckoned to be 40,000. Usually it is empty,

Milan

TO MALPENSA

Parco Sempione

TO STAZIONE CENTRALE

Pta. Nuova
Bast. di Pta. Nuova

V. Melzi d'Eril
V. Bertani
V. Bramante
V. Niccolini
V. Legnano

V. Crispi

Moscova M

V. Moscova

Pza. d. Repubblica

Republica M

Via Vittor Pisani
V. S. Gregorio
V. Tonale

Vle. Montello
Vle. Tunisia

Vle. Vittorio Veneto
Bastioni di Pta. Venezia

Giardini Pubblici

Turati
V. Palestro

Monte Napoleon

Palestro M

Stazione Cadorna

Lanza M
Cadorna M

Cairoli M

Pza. della Scala

Duomo

Pza. del Duomo

San Babila M

TO MILANO LINATE

San Ambrogio M

San Vittore

Missori M

San Augustino M

Corso Italia

Navigli

TO MILANO LINATE

1/4 mile
400 meters

Pta. Genova
Pta. Ticinese

Vle. Galeazzo
Vle. Col di Lana
Vle. Beatrice d'Este

KEY

Ⓜ Metro stops

ℹ Tourist information

Basilica di Sant'Ambrogio **15**	Museo Civico Archeologico **13**
Battistero Paleocristiano **2**	Museo Nazionale della Scienza e Tecnica **16**
Castello Sforzesco **8**	Museo Poldi–Pezzoli **5**
Duomo **1**	Navigli district **18**
Galleria Vittorio Emanuele **3**	Parco Sempione **9**

Pinacoteca Ambrosiana **12**	Teatro alla Scala **4**
Pinacoteca di Brera **7**	Triennale Design Museum **10**
San Lorenzo Maggiore **17**	Villa Belgioioso Bonaparte **6**
San Satiro **11**	
Santa Maria delle Grazie **14**	

a sanctuary from the frenetic pace of life outside and the perfect place for solitary contemplation.

The building is adorned with 135 marble spires and 2,245 marble statues. The oldest part is the **apse.** Its three colossal bays of curving and counter-curved tracery, especially the bay adorning the exterior of the stained-glass windows, should not be missed. At the end of the southern transept down the right aisle lies the **tomb of Gian Giacomo Medici.** The tomb owes

some of its design to Michelangelo but was executed by Leone Leoni (1509–90) and is generally considered to be his masterpiece; it dates from the 1560s. Directly ahead is the Duomo's most famous sculpture, the gruesome but anatomically instructive figure of **San Bartolomeo** (St. Bartholomew), whose glorious martyrdom consisted of being flayed alive. It is usually said the saint stands "holding" his skin, but this is not quite accurate. It would appear more that he is luxuriating in it, much as a 1950s matron might have shown off a new fur stole.

As you enter the apse to admire those splendid windows, glance at the **sacristy doors** to the right and left of the altar. The lunette on the right dates from 1393 and was decorated by Hans von Fernach. The one on the left also dates from the 14th century and is ascribed jointly to Giacomo da Campione and Giovanni dei Grassi. Don't miss the view from the Duomo's **roof**; walk out the left (north) transept to the stairs and elevator. Sadly, air pollution drastically reduces the view on all but the rarest days. As you stand among the forest of marble pinnacles, remember that virtually every inch of this gargantuan edifice, including the roof itself, is decorated with precious white marble dragged from quarries near Lake Maggiore by Duke Visconti's team along road laid fresh for the purpose and through the newly dredged canals.

At this writing, the facade facing the piazza is shrouded in scaffolding for restoration work. ⊠*Piazza del Duomo* ☎*02/86463456* ⛵*Stairs to roof €3.50, elevator €5* ⊙*Mid-Feb.–mid-Nov., daily 9–5:45; mid-Nov.–mid-Feb., daily 9–4:15* Ⓜ*Duomo.*

Exhibits at the **Museo del Duomo** shed light on the cathedral's history and include some of the treasures removed from the exterior for preservation purposes. ⊠*Piazza del Duomo 14* ☎*02/860358* ⛵*€6, €7 including ticket for elevator to Duomo roof* ⊙*Daily 10–1:15 and 3–6.*

★ ❸ **Galleria Vittorio Emanuele.** This spectacular, late-19th-century glass-top, barrel-vaulted tunnel is essentially one of the planet's earliest and most select shopping malls. Like its suburban American cousins, the Galleria Vittorio Emanuele fulfills numerous social functions. This is the city's heart, midway between the Duomo and La Scala. It teems with life, inviting people-watching from the tables that spill from the bars and

GETTING AROUND MILAN

The city center is compact and walkable, while the efficient Metropolitana (subway), as well as buses and trams, provides access to locations farther afield. Driving the streets of Milan is difficult at best, and parking can be downright miserable, so leave the car behind. In addition, as of January 2008, drivers entering the second ring of streets (the so-called *bastioni*) will have to pay a €2 charge between 7:30 and 7:30, weekdays (⊕ *www.comune.milano.it/ ecopass*). To park on the street (only in blue areas; yellow is for residents), purchase scratch-off cards from tobacconists or parking attendants who are often near busy areas.

BY PUBLIC TRANSIT

Tickets valid for one trip on the subway or 75 minutes on buses and trams must be purchased before you board and then stamped in machines at station entrances or on poles inside trolleys and buses. Standard tickets cost €1 and can be purchased from news vendors, tobacconists, and—at larger stops—machines (some of which require exact change). Buying an all-inclusive subway, bus, and tram pass will save you the hassle of purchasing individual tickets. They cost €3 for 24 hours or €5.50 for 48 hours and are available at Duomo Metro and Stazione Centrale Metro stations. Another option is a ticket for 10 tram or subway rides, called a *carnet*, which can be purchased at a discount. These new electronic tickets are delicate and will not function if bent or demagnetized. For problems, contact station managers, who can usually issue new ones. Trains run from 6 AM to 12:30 AM. For more information, check the Web site of **ATM (Azienda Trasporti Milanesi)** (⊕ *www.atm-*

mi.it), which has an English-language version, or visit the information office at the Duomo stop.

BY TAXI

Taxi fares in Milan are high compared to those in American cities. A short downtown ride will come to about €15. Taxis wait at stands, or you can call one of the city's taxi companies—**Amicotaxi** (☎ *02/4000*), **Autoradiotaxi** (☎ *02/8585*), **Radiotaxi** (☎ *02/6969*), **Taxiblu** (☎ *02/4040*). Dispatchers may speak some English; they'll ask for the phone number you're calling from, and they'll tell you the number of your taxi and how many minutes your wait will be. If you're in a restaurant or bar, ask the staff to call a cab for you. It's not customary to flag taxis down in the street, but drivers do sometimes stop if you hail them.

For car service, contact **Autonoleggio Pini** (☎ *02/29400555* 🖷 *02/2047843* ⊕ *www.pini.it*). English-speaking drivers are available.

TOURS

A refurbished 1920s tramcar operates a hop-on-hop-off tour of the city. Tickets (€20) are valid all day and can be purchased on board. Departures are at 11 and 1 (also at 3, April–October) from Piazza Castello. The organization **A Friend in Milan** (⊕ *www.friendinmilan. co.uk*) conducts walking tours of the city, including a visit to *The Last Supper*, day trips to the lakes, and shopping tours.

restaurants, where you can enjoy an overpriced coffee. Books, records, clothing, food, pens, and jewelry are all for sale. Known as Milan's "parlor," the Galleria is often viewed as a barometer of the city's well-being. By the 1990s, the quality of the stores (with the exception of the Prada flagship) and restaurants was uninspired. The city government, which owns the Galleria, and merchants' groups evicted some longtime tenants who had enjoyed anomalously low rents, in favor of Gucci, Tod's, and Louis Vuitton. After the restoration, historic Savini restaurant reopened in 2008, ready to host the beautiful and powerful of the city. Like the cathedral, the Galleria is cruciform in shape. Even in poor weather the great glass dome above the octagonal center is a splendid sight. And the floor mosaics are a vastly underrated source of pleasure, even if they are not to be taken too seriously. They represent Europe, Asia, Africa, and the United States; those at the entrance arch are devoted to science, industry, art, and agriculture. Be sure to follow tradition and spin your heels once or twice on the more "delicate" parts of the bull beneath your feet in the northern apse; the Milanese believe it brings good luck. ⊠ *Piazza del Duomo* Ⓜ *Duomo.*

NEED A BREAK?

One thing has stayed constant in the Galleria: the Caffè Zucca, known by the Milanese as Camparino. Its inlaid counter, mosaics, and wrought-iron fixtures have been welcoming tired shoppers since 1867. Enjoy a Campari or Zucca *aperitivo* (aperitif) as well as the entire range of Italian coffees, served either in the Galleria or in an elegant upstairs room.

❺ Museo Poldi-Pezzoli. This exceptional museum, opened in 1881, was once a private residence and collection, and contains not only pedigreed paintings but also porcelain, textiles, and a cabinet with scenes from Dante's life. The gem is undoubtedly the *Portrait of a Lady* by Antonio Pollaiuolo (1431–98), one of the city's most prized treasures and the source of the museum's logo. The collection also includes masterpieces by Botticelli (1445–1510), Andrea Mantegna (1431–1506), Giovanni Bellini (1430–1516), and Fra Filippo Lippi (1406–69). ⊠ *Via Manzoni 12, Brera* ☎ *02/794889* ⊕ *www.museopoldipezzoli.it* ☒ *€8* ⏰ *Tues.–Sun. 10–6* Ⓜ *Montenapoleone.*

❿ Triennale Design Museum. After decades of false starts and controversy, Milan finally opened a real museum in 2007 that honors its design talent. Originally the home of triennial decorative arts shows, a spectacular bridge entrance leads to a permanent collection, an exhibition space, and a stylish café (whose seating is an encyclopedia of design icons). The Triennale also manages the museum-studio of designer Achille Castiglione in nearby Piazza Castello. ⊠ *Via Alemagna 6* ☎ *02/724341* ⊕ *www.triennaledesignmuseum.com/* ☒ *Variable, according to exhibition* ⏰ *Tues.–Sun. 10:30–8:30*

❾ Parco Sempione. Originally the gardens and parade ground of the Castello Sforzesco, this park was reorganized during the Napoleonic era, when the arena on its northeast side was constructed, and then it was turned into a park during Milan's building boom at the end of the 19th century. The park is still the lungs of the city's fashionable western neighborhoods, and the **Aquarium** (✉ *Viale Gadio 2* 🕾 *02/878459* 📠 *Free* ⊙ *Tues.–Sun. 9:30–5:30*) still attracts Milan's school children. The park became a bit of a design showcase in 1933 with the construction of the Triennale (*see above*). The Fiat café offers outdoor dining in summer along with a view of De Chirico's sculpture-filled fountain *Bagni Misteriosi (Mysterious Baths)*, which is currently dry.

Even if a walk in the park is not appealing, it is worth visiting to see the **Torre Branca** (✉ *Parco Sempione* 🕾 *02/3324120* 📠 *€3* ⊙ *Winter: Wed. 10:30–12:30 and 4–6:30; Sat. 10:30–1, 3–6:30, and 8:30–10:30; Sun. 10:30–2 and 2:30–7:30. Summer: Tues. 9:30 PM–1 AM; Wed. 10:30–12:30, 4–6:30, and 9:30–1 AM; Thurs. 9:30 PM–1 AM; Fri. 2:30–6 and 9:30 PM–1 AM; Sat. 10:30–2, 2:30–7:30, and 9:30 PM–1 AM; Sun. 10:30–2, 2:30–7:30, and 9:30 PM–1 AM*). Designed by architect Gio Ponti, who was behind so many of the projects that made Milan the design capital that it is, this steel tower rises 330 feet over the Triennale. Take the elevator up to get a view of the city from a height that offers a sometimes intimate view into the city's topography and hidden spaces and monuments. Then have a drink at the glitzy Just Cavalli Café (Monday–Saturday 8 PM–2 AM) at its base. *Parco Sempione:* ✉ *Piazza Castello, Brera* ⊙ *Nov.–Feb., daily 6:30–8; Mar. and Apr., daily 6:30–9; May, daily 6:30–10; June–Sept., daily 6:30–9; Oct., daily 6:30–9* Ⓜ *Cadorna; Bus 61.*

★ ❼ **Pinacoteca di Brera** *(Brera Gallery)*. The collection here is star-studded even by Italian standards. The entrance hall (Room I) displays 20th-century sculpture and painting, including Carlo Carrà's (1881–1966) confident, stylish response to the schools of cubism and surrealism. The museum has nearly 40 other rooms, arranged in chronological order—pace yourself.

The somber, moving *Cristo Morto (Dead Christ)* by Mantegna dominates Room VI, with its sparse palette of umber and its foreshortened perspective. Mantegna's shocking, almost surgical precision—in the rendering of Christ's wounds, the face propped up on a pillow, the day's growth of beard—tells of an all-too-human agony. It is one of Renaissance painting's most quietly wondrous achievements, finding an unsuspected middle ground between the excesses of conventional gore and beauty in representing the Passion's saddest moment.

Room XXIV offers two additional highlights of the gallery. Raphael's (1483–1520) *Sposalizio della Vergine,* with its mathematical composition and precise, alternating colors, portrays the betrothal of Mary and Joseph (who, though older than the other men gathered, wins her hand when the rod he is holding miraculously blossoms). *La Vergine con il Bambino e Santi (Madonna with Child and Saints)*, by Piero della Francesca (1420–92), is an altarpiece commissioned by Federico da Montefeltro (shown kneeling, in full armor, before the Virgin); it was intended for a church to house the duke's tomb. The ostrich egg hanging from the apse, depending on whom you ask, either commemorates the miracle of his fertility—Federico's wife died months after giving birth to a long-awaited male heir—or alludes to his appeal for posthumous mercy, the egg symbolizing the saving power of grace. ⊠ *Via Brera 28* ☎ *02/722631* ⊕ *www.brera.beniculturali.it* ⊠ *€5* ⊙ *Tues.–Sun. 8:30–7:15; last admission 45 mins before closing* Ⓜ *Montenapoleone.*

❹ **Teatro alla Scala.** You need know nothing of opera to sense that, like Carnegie Hall, La Scala is closer to a cathedral than an auditorium. Here Verdi established his reputation and Maria Callas sang her way into opera lore. It looms as a symbol—both for the performer who dreams of singing here and for the opera buff who knows every note of *Rigoletto* by heart. Audiences are notoriously demanding and are apt to jeer performers who do not measure up. The opera house was closed after destruction by Allied bombs in 1943, and reopened at a performance led by Arturo Toscanini in 1946.

If you are lucky enough to be here during the opera season, which runs for approximately six months, do whatever is necessary to attend. Tickets go on sale two months before the first performance and are usually sold out the same day. Hearing opera sung in the magical acoustic of La Scala is an unparalleled experience. ⊠ *Piazza della Scala* ☎ *02/72003744* ⊕ *www.teatroallascala.org* Ⓜ *Duomo.*

At **Museo Teatrale alla Scala** you can admire librettos, posters, costumes, instruments, design sketches for the theater, curtains, and viewing-box decorations, along with an explanation of the reconstruction project and several interactive exhibits. Exhibition themes reflect current productions. A highlight is the collection of antique gramophones and phonographs. ⊠ *Piazza della Scala* ☎ *02/43353521* ⊠ *€5* ⊙ *Daily 9–noon and 1:30–5.*

ALSO WORTH SEEING

❷ **Battistero Paleocristiano.** Beneath the Duomo's piazza lies this baptistery ruin dating from the 4th century. Although opinion remains divided, it is widely believed to be where Ambrose, Milan's first bishop and patron saint, baptized Augustine. Tickets are available at the kiosk inside the cathedral. ⊠ *Piazza del Duomo, enter through Duomo* ☎ *02/86463456* ⊠ *€1.50* ⊙ *Daily 9:30–5:15* Ⓜ *Duomo.*

★ ❻ **Villa Belgioioso Bonaparte—Museo dell'Ottocento.** Formerly known as the Galleria di Arte Moderna, this museum is one of the city's most beautiful buildings. An outstanding example of neoclassical architecture, it was built between 1790 and 1796 as a residence for a member of the Belgioioso family. It later became known as the Villa Reale (royal) when it was donated to Napoléon, who lived here briefly with Empress Josephine. Its origins as residence are reflected in the elegance of its proportions and its private garden behind.

Likewise, the collection of paintings is domestic rather than monumental. There are many portraits, as well as collections of miniatures on porcelain. Unusual for an Italian museum, this collection derives from private donations from Milan's hereditary and commercial aristocracies. On display are the collection left by prominent painter and sculptor Marino Marini and the immense *Quarto Stato* (*Fourth Estate*), which is at the top of the grand staircase. Completed in 1901 by

Pellizza da Volpedo, this painting of striking workers is an icon of 20th-century Italian art and labor history, and as such it has been satirized almost as much as the *Mona Lisa*. This museum is a unique glimpse of the splendors hiding behind Milan's discreet and often stern facades. ✉ *Via Palestro 16* ☎ *02/76340809* ⊕ *www.villabelgiojosobonaparte.it* ⊙ *Tues.–Sun. 9–1 and 2–5:30* Ⓜ *Palestro.*

The **Giardini Pubblici** (Public Gardens), across Via Palestro from the Villa Reale, were laid out by Giuseppe Piermarini, architect of La Scala, in 1770. They were designed as public pleasure gardens, and today they still are popular with families who live in the city center. Generations of Milanese have taken pony rides and gone on the miniature train and merry-go-round. The park also contains a small planetarium and the **Museo Civico di Storia Naturale** (Municipal Natural History Museum). One of the unenclosed grassy areas near the fountain on the Via Manin side is set aside for dogs to run free.

Parents may want to visit the garden of the Villa Belgioioso-Bonaparte, on Via Palestro, which is entered from a gate to the building's left. Access to the garden, which has statuary and a water course designed in 1790 (the first English-style garden in Milan), is restricted to children accompanied by an adult. Adults without children wanting to see the garden are tolerated, as long as they do not linger in this protected area.

NEED A BREAK?

If your energy is flagging after shopping or chasing children around the park, try some of Milan's best cappuccino and pastry at Dolce In (✉ *Via Turati 2/3* ⊙ *Closed Mon.*), which is equally close to Via della Spiga and the Giardini Pubblici. It's famous for its pastry and also serves sandwiches and cold plates at lunch. On Sunday mornings, classic-car enthusiasts meet informally here, parking their handsome machines out front while they have coffee.

SOUTH & WEST OF THE DUOMO

If the part of the city to the north of the Duomo is dominated by its shops, the section to the south is famous for its works of art. The most famous is *Il Cenacolo*—known in English as *The Last Supper*. If you have time for nothing else, make sure you see this masterwork, which has now been definitively restored, after many, many years of work. Reservations will be needed to see this fresco, housed in the refectory of Santa Maria delle Grazie. Make these at least three weeks before you depart for Italy, so you can plan the rest of your time in Milan.

There are other gems as well. Via Torino, the ancient road for Turin, leads to a half-hidden treasure: Bramante's Renaissance masterpiece, the church of San Satiro. At the intersection of Via San Vittore and Via Carducci is the medieval Basilica di Sant'Ambrogio, named for Milan's patron saint. Another lovely church southeast of Sant'Ambrogio along Via de Amicis is San Lorenzo Maggiore. It's also known as San Lorenzo alle Colonne because of the 16 columns running across the facade.

MAIN ATTRACTIONS

⓯ **Basilica di Sant'Ambrogio** *(Basilica of St. Ambrose)*. Noted for its medieval architecture, the church was consecrated by Milan's bishop, St. Ambrose, in AD 387 (one of the original Doctors of the Catholic Church), and he is buried here. St. Ambroeus, as he is known in Milanese dialect, is the city's patron saint. Until the construction of the more imposing Duomo, this was Milan's most important church. Much restored and reworked over the centuries (the gold and gem encrusted altar dates from the 9th century), Sant'Ambrogio still preserves its Romanesque characteristics. The church is often closed for weddings on Saturday. ✉ *Piazza Sant'Ambrogio 15* 📞 *02/86450895* 🕐 *Mon.–Sat. 7–noon and 2:30–7, Sun. 3–8* Ⓜ *Sant'Ambrogio.*

NEED A BREAK?

A bit overcrowded at night, when teenagers virtually block the sidewalk and traffic, the Bar Magenta (✉ *Via Carducci 13, at Corso Magenta, Sant'Ambrogio* 📞 *02/8053808* Ⓜ *Sant'Ambrogio*) can be a good stop en route during the day. Beyond coffee at all hours, lunch, and beer, the real attraction is its mix of old and new, trendy and aristocratic—a quintessentially Milanese ambience. It celebrated its 100th birthday in 2007 and is open until 2 AM.

⓬ **Pinacoteca Ambrosiana.** Cardinal Federico Borromeo, one of Milan's native saints, founded this picture gallery in 1618 with the addition of his personal art collection to a bequest of books to Italy's first public library. Recent renovations have reunited the core works of the collection, including such treasures as Caravaggio's *Basket of Fruit* and Raphael's monumental preparatory drawing (known as a "cartoon") for *The School of Athens,* which hangs in the Vatican. Heavy on Lombard artists, there are also paintings by Leonardo, Botticelli, Luini, Titian, and (Jan) Brueghel. Previous renovations done in the 1930s with their mosaics and stained-glass windows are worth a look, as are other odd items, including 18th-century scientific instruments and gloves worn by Napoléon at Waterloo. Access to the library, the Biblioteca Ambrosiana, is limited to researchers who can apply for entrance tickets. ✉ *Piazza Pio XI 2, near Duomo* 📞 *02/806921* 🌐 *www.ambrosiana.it* 💶 *€80* 🕐 *Tues.–Sun. 10–5:30* Ⓜ *Duomo.*

⓱ **San Lorenzo Maggiore.** Sixteen ancient Roman columns line the front of this sanctuary; 4th-century paleo-Christian mosaics survive in the Cappella di Sant'Aquilino (Chapel of St. Aquilinus). ✉ *Corso di Porta Ticinese 39* 📞 *02/89404129* 💶 *Mosaics €2* 🕐 *Daily 8:30–12:30 and 2:30–6:30.*

★ ⓫ **San Satiro.** First built in 876, this architectural gem was later perfected by Bramante (1444–1514), demonstrating his command of proportion and perspective, keynotes of Renaissance architecture. Bramante tricks the eye with a famous optical illusion that makes a small interior seem extraordinarily spacious and airy, while accommodating a beloved 13th-century fresco. ✉ *Via Torino 9, near Duomo* 🕐 *Weekdays 7:30–11:30 and 3:30–6:30, weekends 9–noon and 3:30–7* Ⓜ *Duomo.*

6

★ ⑭ **Santa Maria delle Grazie.** Leonardo da Vinci's *The Last Supper,* housed in the church and former Dominican monastery of Santa Maria delle Grazie, has had an almost unbelievable history of bad luck and neglect—its near destruction in an American bombing raid in August 1943 was only the latest chapter in a series of misadventures, including, if one 19th-century source is to be believed, being whitewashed over by monks. Well-meant but disastrous attempts at restoration have done little to rectify the problem of the work's placement: it was executed on a wall unusually vulnerable to climatic dampness. Yet Leonardo chose to work slowly and patiently in oil pigments—which demand dry plaster—instead of proceeding hastily on wet plaster according to the conventional fresco technique. Novelist Aldous Huxley (1894–1963) called it "the saddest work of art in the world." After years of restorers' patiently shifting from one square centimeter to another, Leonardo's masterpiece is free of the shroud of scaffolding—and centuries of retouching, grime, and dust. Astonishing clarity and luminosity have been regained.

Despite Leonardo's carefully preserved preparatory sketches in which the apostles are clearly labeled by name, there still remains some small debate about a few identities in the final arrangement. But there can be no mistaking Judas, small and dark, his hand calmly reaching forward to the bread, isolated from the terrible confusion that has taken the hearts of the others. One critic, Frederick Hartt, offers an elegantly terse explanation for why the composition works: it combines "dramatic confusion" with "mathematical order." Certainly, the amazingly skillful and unobtrusive repetition of threes—in the windows, in the grouping of the figures, and in their placement—adds a mystical aspect to what at first seems simply the perfect observation of spontaneous human gesture.

Reservations are required to view the work. Viewings are in 15-minute, timed slots, and visitors must arrive 15 minutes before their assigned time if they are not to lose their slot. Reservations can be made via phone (☎02/89421146) or online (⊕*www.cenacolovinciano.it*); it is best to call because more tickets are set aside for phone reservations. Call about three weeks ahead to be sure of getting the Saturday slot you want; two weeks before for a weekday slot. The telephone reservation office is open 9 AM–6 PM weekdays and 9 AM–2 PM on Saturday. Operators do speak English, though not fluently, and to reach one, you must wait for the Italian introduction to finish and then press "2." However, you can sometimes get tickets from one day to the next. Some city bus tours include a visit in their regular circuit, which may be a good option.

The painting was executed in what was the order's refectory, which is now referred to as the **Cenacolo Vinciano.** Take a moment to visit Santa Maria delle Grazie itself. It's a handsome church, with a fine dome, which Bramante added along with a cloister about the time that Leonardo was commissioned to paint *The Last Supper.* If you're wondering how two such giants came to be employed decorating and remodeling the refectory and church of a comparatively modest religious order, and not, say, the Duomo, the answer lies in the ambitious but largely unrealized plan to turn Santa Maria delle Grazie into a magnificent Sforza family mausoleum. Though Ludovico il Moro Sforza (1452–1508), seventh duke of Milan, was but one generation away from the founding of the Sforza dynasty, he was its last ruler. Two years after Leonardo finished *The Last Supper*, Ludovico was defeated by Louis XII and spent the remaining eight years of his life in a French dungeon. ⊠ *Piazza Santa Maria delle Grazie 2, off Corso Magenta, Sant'Ambrogio* ☎ *02/89421146* ⊕ *www.cenacolovinciano.org* 🖃 *€6.50 plus €1.50 reservation fee* ⊗ *Weekdays 9–6, Sat. 9–2* Ⓜ *Cadorna.*

ALSO WORTH SEEING

Museo Boschi-di Stefano *(Boschi-di Stefano Museum).* To most of us Italian art means Renaissance art. But the 20th century in Italy was a productive—if less-well-known—era. Just a block behind the Corso Buenos Aires shopping area, the Museo Boschi-di Stefano is a tribute to the enlightened private collectors who replaced popes and nobles as Italian patrons. An apartment on the second floor of a stunning art deco building designed by Milan architect Portaluppi houses this private collection, which was donated to the city of Milan in 2003. Its walls burst with masterpieces by postwar greats, such as Fontana, De Chirico, and Morandi, collected by the Boschi-di Stefano couple. The works mingle with distinctive postwar furniture and stunning Murano glass chandeliers. ⊠ *Via Jan 15, Corso Buenos Aires* ☎ *02/20240568* 🖃 *Free* ⊗ *Wed.–Sun. 2–6; last entry at 5:30.*

⑬ Museo Civico Archeologico *(Municipal Archaeological Museum).* Appropriately situated in the heart of Roman Milan, this museum's garden encloses the polygonal Ansperto tower, which was once part of the Roman walls. Housed in a former monastery, this museum has some everyday utensils, jewelry, an important silver plate from the last days of paganism, and several fine examples of mosaic pavement. ⊠ *Corso Magenta 15, Sant'Ambrogio* ☎ *02/86450011* 🖃 *€2, free Fri. 2–5* ⊗ *Tues.–Sun. 9–1 and 2–5:30* Ⓜ *Cadorna.*

☾ ⑯ Museo Nazionale della Scienza e Tecnica *(National Museum of Science and Technology).* This converted cloister is best known for the collection of models based on Leonardo da Vinci's sketches (although these are not captioned in English, the labeling in many other exhibits is bilingual). On the ground level—in the hallway between the courtyards—is a room featuring interactive, moving models of the famous *vita aerea* (aerial screw) and *ala battente* (beating wing), thought to be forerunners of the modern helicopter and airplane, respectively. The museum also houses a varied collection of industrial artifacts including trains, a celebrated Italian-built submarine, and several reconstructed workshops including a watchmaker's, a lute maker's, and an antique pharmacy. Displays also illustrate papermaking and metal founding, which were fundamental to Milan's—and the world's—economic growth. There's a bookshop and a bar. ⊠ *Via San Vittore 21, Sant'Ambrogio* ☎ *02/48555200* ⊕ *www.museoscienza.org* 🖃 *€8* ⊗ *Tues.–Fri. 9:30–5, weekends 9:30–6:30* Ⓜ *Sant'Ambrogio; Bus 50, 58, 94.*

6

18 **Navigli district.** In medieval times, a network of *navigli,* or canals, criss-crossed the city. Almost all have been covered over, but two—Naviglio Grande and Naviglio Pavese—are still navigable. Once a down-at-the-heels neighborhood, the Navigli district has been gentrified over the last 20 years. Humble workshops have been replaced by boutiques, art galleries, cafés, bars, and restaurants. The Navigli at night is about as close as you will get to more-southern-style Italian street life in Milan. On weekend nights, it is difficult to walk (and impossible to park) among the youthful crowds thronging the narrow streets along the canals. Check out the antiques fair on the last Sunday of the month. ⊠*South of Corso Porta Ticinese, Porta Genova* Ⓜ*Porta Genova; Tram 3, 9, 15, 29, 30.*

WHERE TO EAT

★ **$$$$**   ✕**Antica Osteria del Ponte.** Rich, imaginative seasonal cuisine composed according to the inspired whims of chef Ezio Santin is reason enough to make your way 20 km (12 mi) southwest of Milan to one of Italy's finest restaurants. The setting is a traditional country inn, where a wood fire warms the rustic interior in winter. The menu changes regularly; in fall, wild porcini mushrooms are among the favored ingredients. Various fixed menus (at €110 and €150) offer broad samplings of antipasti, primi, and meat or fish; some include appropriate wine selections, too. ⊠*Piazza G. Negri 9 Cassinetta di Lugagnano* ✛*3 km (2 mi) north of Abbiategrasso* ☎*02/9420034* ⚜*Reservations essential* ▭*AE, DC, MC, V* ⊘*Closed Sun. and Mon., Dec. 25–1st wk of Jan., and Aug.*

★ **$$$$**   ✕**Cracco.** Although renowned local chef Carlo Cracco has ended his collaboration with the city's top gourmet food store (Peck, around the corner in Via Spadari), the Milan culinary establishment has not begrudged the two Michelin stars that Cracco still receives. (Though they sniff a bit at the underground premises.) The dining room is done in an elegant style that favors cool earth tones. Specialties include Milanese classics revisited—Cracco's take on saffron risotto and breaded veal cutlet should not be missed. Be sure to save room for the light, steam-cooked tiramisu. If you can't decide, opt for one of the tasting menus. ⊠*Via Victor Hugo 4, near Duomo* ☎*02/876774* ⚜*Reservations essential* ▭*AE, DC, MC, V* ⊘*Closed Sun., 10 days in Jan., and 2 wks in Aug. No lunch Sat. No dinner Sat. in July and Aug.* Ⓜ*Duomo.*

★ **$$$$**   ✕**Don Carlos.** One of the few restaurants open after La Scala lets out, Don Carlos, in the Grand Hotel et de Milan, is nothing like its indecisive operatic namesake (whose betrothed was stolen by his father). Flavors are bold, their presentation precise and full of flair: broiled red mullet floats on a lacy layer of crispy leeks. Walls are blanketed with sketches of the theater, and the opera recordings are every bit as well chosen as the wine list, setting the perfect stage for discreet business negotiation or, better yet, refined romance. A gourmet menu costs €75 for six courses (two-person minimum), excluding wine. ⊠*Grand Hotel et de Milan, Via Manzoni 29, Duomo* ☎*02/723141* ⚜*Reservations essential* ▭*AE, DC, MC, V* ⊘*Closed Aug. No lunch* Ⓜ*Montenapoleone; Tram 1, 2.*

$$$$ ✗**Joia.** At this haute-cuisine vegetarian restaurant near Piazza della Repubblica, delicious dishes are artistically prepared by chef Pietro Leemann. Vegetarians, who often get short shrift in Italy, will marvel at the variety of culinary traditions—Asian and European—and artistry offered here. The ever-changing menu offers dishes in unusual formats: tiny glasses of creamed cabbage with ginger, spheres of crunchy vegetables that roll across the plate. Fish also makes an appearance. Joia's restful dining room has been refurbished, another room added, and its kitchen enlarged. The fixed-price lunch "box" is a good value, but be sure to reserve ahead. Multicourse menus range from €60 to €100, excluding wine. ⊠ *Via Panfilo Castaldi 18, Porta Venezia* ☎*02/29522124* ☐*AE, DC, MC, V* ⊘*Closed Sun., 3 wks in Aug., and Dec. 24–Jan. 7. No lunch Sat.* Ⓜ*Repubblica; Tram 1, 5, 11, 29, 30.*

$$–$$$$ ✗**Da Giacomo.** The fashion and publishing crowd, as well as international bankers and businessmen, favor this Tuscan/Ligurian restaurant. The emphasis is on fish; even the warm slice of pizza served while you study the menu has seafood in it. The specialty, *gnocchi Da Giacomo*, has a savory seafood-and-tomato sauce. Service is friendly and efficient; the wine list broad; and the dessert cart, with tarte tatin and Sicilian cassata (a concoction of sponge cake, ricotta, and candied fruit), rich and varied. With its tile floor and bank of fresh seafood, it has a refined neighborhood bistro style. Don't even think of trying for same-day reservations during fashion or furniture weeks. ⊠ *Via P. Sottocorno 6, entrance in Via Cellini, Cinque Giornate* ☎*02/76023313* ⊰*Reservations essential* ☐*AE, DC, MC, V* ⊘*Closed Mon., Christmas wk, and last 3 wks of Aug. No lunch Tues.* Ⓜ*Tram 9, 29, 30.*

$$–$$$ ✗**La Libera.** Although this establishment in the heart of Brera calls itself a *birreria con cucina* (beer cellar with kitchen), locals come here for excellent evening meals in relaxed surroundings. A soft current of jazz and sylvan decor soothe the ripple of conversation. The creative cooking varies with the season, but could include linguine *al pescato* (with a fish sauce); *fritto di gamberi, zucchine e totanetti* (fried shrimp, zucchini, and baby squid); or *rognone alla senape* (veal kidneys cooked in mustard). ⊠ *Via Palermo 21, Brera* ☎*02/8053603 or 02/86462773* ☐*AE, DC, MC, V* ⊘*No lunch* Ⓜ*Moscova.*

$$–$$$ ✗**Paper Moon.** Hidden behind Via Montenapoleone and thus handy to the restaurant-scarce Quadrilatero, Paper Moon is a cross between neighborhood restaurant and celebrity hangout. Clients include families from this wealthy area, professionals, football players, and television stars. What the menu lacks in originality it makes up for in consistency—reliable pizza and cotoletta. Like any Italian restaurant, it's not child friendly in an American sense—no high chairs or children's menu—but children will find food they like. Open until 12:30 AM. ⊠ *Via Bagutta 1, Quadrilatero* ☎*02/76022297* ☐*AE, MC, V* ⊘*Closed Sun., 2 wks in Aug., and Dec. 25–Jan 7* Ⓜ*San Babila.*

$$–$$$ ✗**Trattoria Montina.** Twin brothers Maurizio and Roberto Montina have
Fodor's Choice turned this restaurant into a local favorite. Don't be fooled by the "trat-
★ toria" name. The sage-green paneling makes it airy and cozy on a gray Milan day. Chef Roberto creates exquisite modern Italian dishes such as warmed risotto with merlot and taleggio cheese, while Maurizio

chats with guests, regulars, and local families. Milan's famous cotoletta is light and tasty. Try fish or the *frittura impazzita,* a wild-and-crazy mix of delicately fried seafood. Unlike many Italian menus, there's a fine selection on the hard-to-choose dessert cart. ⊠ *Via Procaccini 54, Procaccini* ☎ *02/3490498* ⊟ *AE, DC, MC, V* ⊗ *Closed Sun., Aug., and Dec. 25–Jan. 7. No lunch Mon.* Ⓜ *Tram 1, 19, 29, 33.*

$–$$ ✕ **Al Rifugio Pugliese.** Just outside the center of town, this is a fun place to sample specialties from the Puglia region of southern Italy. These include homemade *orecchiette* (a small, ear-shaped pasta) with a variety of sauces. There is a choice of 60 first courses, as well as plenty of vegetable and fish dishes. The lunch buffet is a good deal as are the fixed-price menus of €29 and €39 that can include wine, coffee, and after-dinner drinks. ⊠ *Via Costanza 2, corner of Via Boni 16, Fiera* ☎ *02/48000917* ⊟ *AE, DC, MC, V* ⊗ *Closed Sun., Aug. 5–25, and Dec. 25–Jan. 7* Ⓜ *Wagner.*

★ $–$$ ✕ **Da Abele.** If you love risotto, then make a beeline for this neighborhood trattoria. The superb risotto dishes change with the season, and there may be just two or three on the menu at any time. It is tempting to try them all. The setting is relaxed, the service informal, the prices strikingly reasonable. Outside the touristy center of town but quite convenient by subway, this trattoria is invariably packed with locals. ⊠ *Via Temperanza 5, Loreto* ☎ *02/2613855* ⊟ *AE, DC, MC, V* ⊗ *Closed Mon., Aug., and Dec. 22–Jan. 7. No lunch* Ⓜ *Pasteur.*

$–$$ ✕ **La Bruschetta.** This tiny, bustling first-class pizzeria near the Duomo serves specialties from Tuscany and other parts of Italy. The wood oven is in full view, so you can see your pizza cooking in front of you. Aside from the pizza, the menu is essentially Tuscan. Try the seasonal specialities: in summer, the *panzanella,* a salad with toasted bread; and in winter, the *ribollita,* a dense soup of vegetables, cabbage, and bread. The *tagliata,* thin slices of grilled Tuscan beef garnished with rosemary and peppercorns or arugula, is another specialty. Reservations are essential on weekends, when two sittings of diners are squeezed in between the cinema showtimes. ⊠ *Piazza Beccaria 12, Duomo* ☎ *02/8692494* ⊟ *AE, MC, V* ⊗ *Closed Mon., 3 wks in Aug., and late Dec.–early Jan.* Ⓜ *Duomo.*

¢–$$ ✕ **Joia Leggero.** In the Porta Ticinese area, and near the Navigli district, Joia Leggero (light) is a lower-price, more-informal initiative of innovative chef Pietro Leemann, the man behind Joia. With a pleasant view of the church of St. Eustorgio and a few tables outside, this airy restaurant serves haute-vegetarian food. "Leggero" does not necessarily refer to the calorie content; the offerings—especially the excellent desserts—are often satisfyingly rich. This is not typical sprouts-and-grains health food. Try the well-priced set meals (vegetarian lunch is €11, €14 with fish), which are attractively presented on Japanese-inspired trays. ⊠ *Corso di Porta Ticinese 106* ☎ *02/89404134* ⊟ *AE, MC, V* ⊗ *Closed Sun. and 3 wks in Aug. No lunch Mon.*

¢–$ ✕ **Pizza Ok.** Pizza is almost the only item on the menu at this popular spot near Corso Buenos Aires in the Porta Venezia area. The pizza is extra thin and very good, and possibilities for toppings seem endless. A good choice for families, this dining experience will be easy on your pocketbook. Pizza Ok has added locations in other areas. ✉ *Via Lambro 15, Porta Venezia* ☎*02/29401272* ▭*No credit cards* ⊘*Closed Aug. and Dec. 24–Jan. 7. No lunch Sun.* Ⓜ*Porta Venezia* ✉ *Via San Siro 9, Corso Vercelli* ☎*02/48017132* ⊘*Closed Aug. and Dec. 24–Jan. 7. No lunch Mon. and Sun.* Ⓜ*Buonarotti* ✉ *Via Cenisio 19, Cimitero Monumentale* ☎*02/33614582* ⊘*Closed Aug. and Dec. 24–Jan. 7. No lunch Sun. and Mon.* Ⓜ*Tram 12, 14.*

¢ ✕**Bar Tempio.** This wine bar, not far from Giardini Pubblici and the shops of the Quadrilatero, was once so unprepossessing that it didn't have a name—but it turned out some of Milan's best panini. It's been renovated and given a name, but the same artist is still making the sandwiches. This is a lunch-only establishment, and you might have to wait your turn, as panini are made to order from a list (not in English, so bring your phrase book). They feature cured ham, *cipolle* (onions), and various cheeses (including easily recognizable Brie). ✉*Piazza Cavour Senter from Via Turati, near Quadrilatero* ☎*02/6551946* ▭*No credit cards* ⊘*Closed Sun. No dinner* Ⓜ*Turati; Tram 1, 2.*

¢ ✕**Taverna Morigi.** This dusky, wood-panel wine bar near the stock exchange is the perfect spot to enjoy a glass of wine with cheese and cold cuts. At lunch, pasta dishes and select entrées are available; pasta is the only hot dish served in the evening. Platters of cheese and cold cuts are always available; if you're coming for a meal, a reservation is a good idea. ✉*Via Morigi 8, Sant'Ambrogio* ☎*02/86450880* ▭*AE, DC, MC, V* ⊘*Closed Sun. and Aug. No lunch Sat.* Ⓜ*Cairoli.*

WHERE TO STAY

$$$$ 🏨**Four Seasons.** The Four Seasons has been cited more than once by the Italian press as the country's best city hotel—perhaps because once you're inside, the feeling is anything but urban. Built in the 15th century as a convent, the hotel surrounds a colonnaded cloister, and some rooms have balconies looking on to a glassed-in courtyard. Everything about the place is standard Four Seasons (high) style. The Theater restaurant has some of Milan's best hotel dining. **Pro:** Beautiful setting that feels like Tuscany rather than central Milan. **Con:** Fodors.com readers find the rooms a little on the sad side. ✉ *Via Gesù 6–8, Quadrilatero, 20121* ☎*02/7708167* 🖶*02/77085000* ⊕*www.fourseasons. com* ➫*77 rooms, 41 suites* ⌂*In-room: ethernet, Wi-Fi. In-hotel: 2 restaurants, room service, bar, gym, laundry service, parking (fee)* ▭*AE, DC, MC, V* ⑪*EP* Ⓜ*Montenapoleone.*

$$$$ 🏨**Grand Hotel et de Milan.** Only blocks from La Scala, this hotel, which opened in 1863, is sometimes called the Hotel Verdi, because the composer lived here for 27 years. His apartment, complete with his desk, is now the Presidential Suite. It's everything you hope for in a traditional European hotel; dignified but not stuffy, elegant but not ostentatious. Moss-green and persimmon velvet enliven the 19th-century look without sacrificing dignity and luxury. The Don Carlos restaurant is one of Milan's best. **Pros:** Traditional and elegant, great location. **Con:** Fitness center has natural light, but is not well appointed. ✉ *Via Manzoni 29, Scala, 20121* ☎*02/723141* 🖶*02/86460861* ⊕*www.grandhotelet-*

demilan.it ↻*87 rooms, 8 suites* ◌*In-room: Wi-Fi. In-hotel: restaurant, room service, bar, gym, laundry service, parking (fee)* ▤*AE, DC, MC, V* ⦿*EP* Ⓜ*Montenapoleone.*

$$$$ 🏨**Hotel Spadari al Duomo.** That this hotel is owned by an architect's family shows in the details, including architect-designed furniture and a fine collection of contemporary art. The owner's idea of creating a hotel/gallery extends to the guest rooms, where paintings by young Milanese artists are on rotating display. For all the artistic accents, this is still a comfortable, homey hotel, with an inviting frescoed breakfast room and many rooms with private terraces. Personal touches, such as a collection of short stories on the turned-down beds, abound. **Pros:** Feedback on Fodor's.com: "excellent breakfast, perfect location, and, above all, staff that seems to care about your having a wonderful experience." **Con:** Rooms and hallways may seem small to some. ✉ *Via Spadari 11, near Duomo, 20123* ☎*02/72002371* 🖷*02/861184* ⊕*www.spadarihotel.com* ↻*40 rooms, 3 suites* ◌*In-room: ethernet, Wi-Fi. In-hotel: bar, no-smoking rooms* ▤*AE, DC, MC, V* ⦿*BP* Ⓜ*Duomo.*

★ $$$$ 🏨**Principe di Savoia.** Milan's grande dame has all the trappings of an exquisite traditional hotel: lavish mirrors, drapes, and carpets, and Milan's largest guest rooms, outfitted with eclectic fin de siècle furnishings. Forty-eight Deluxe Mosaic rooms (named for the glass mosaic panels in their ample bathrooms) are even larger, and the three-bedroom Presidential Suite features its own marble pool. The Winter Garden is an elegant aperitivo spot, and the Acanto restaurant has garden seating. Lighter food is served in the Lobby Lounge. **Pro:** Probably the most serious spa/health club (considered very chic by Milanese) in town. **Cons:** Overblown luxury in a not-very-central or attractive neighborhood; close enough to the train station to attract pickpockets. ✉*Piazza della Repubblica 17, Porta Nuova, 20124* ☎*02/62301* 🖷*02/653799* ⊕*www.hotelprincipedisavoia.com* ↻*269 rooms, 132 suites* ◌*In-room: Wi-Fi. In-hotel: 2 restaurants, room service, bar, pool, gym, spa, laundry service* ▤*AE, DC, MC, V* ⦿*EP* Ⓜ*Repubblica.*

$$$–$$$$ 🏨**Ariston.** This hotel claims it is designed around "bio-architectural" principles. Breakfast offers a selection of organic foods. There's Internet access for free in the lobby (and for a fee in the rooms), and bicycles are available in summer. The location is close to the lively Porta Ticinese shops and restaurants and the young people's fashion mecca, Via Torino. Although a longish walk from the nearest subway stop, the Duomo, it is well served by tram. **Pro:** Although for a fee, it has its own parking. **Con:** Rooms are characterless. ✉*Largo Carrobbio 2, Duomo, 20123* ☎*02/72000556* 🖷*02/72000914* ⊕*www.aristonhotel.com* ↻*52 rooms* ◌*In-room: Wi-Fi. In-hotel: bar, bicycles, laundry service, public Wi-Fi, parking (fee)* ▤*AE, DC, MC, V* ⦿*BP* Ⓜ*Duomo; Tram 2, 14.*

$$$ 🏨**Hotel Gran Duca di York.** This small hotel has spare but classically elegant and efficient rooms—four with private terraces. Built around a courtyard, the 1890s building was originally a seminary and still belongs to a religious institution. With an ideal location a few steps west of the Duomo, it offers exceptional value for Milan and is managed by the same family that owns the Spadari. **Pros:** Central, airy, a good value. **Con:** Rooms are simple. ✉*Via Moneta 1/a, Duomo,*

20123 ☎02/874863 📠02/8690344 ⊕*www.ducadiyork.com* ⤶33 *rooms* ⚿*In-hotel: bar, laundry service, parking (fee)* ⊟*AE, MC, V* ⊘*Closed Aug.* ⍾*EP* Ⓜ*Cordusio.*

$$–$$$ 🏨**Alle Meraviglie.** This deluxe bed-and-breakfast shares a reception and breakfast area with the Antica Locanda dei Mercanti around the corner. But its rooms are bigger—in fact they are big by Milan standards in general. Families should ask for Suite 4, with two rooms connected by a single entrance. Each room is tastefully furnished with individual color schemes and an appealing mix of modern and antique furniture. Although several features make this technically a hotel, it is more like staying in a Milan apartment. Though breakfast is served in the room at street level, the reasonable price (€5) and homey feel make room service the almost universal choice. **Pro:** In a great neighborhood. **Con:** Some visitors may find it old-fashioned. ⊠*Via San Tomaso 8, Duomo, 20121* ☎*02/8051023* ⤶*10 rooms* ⚿*In-room: Wi-Fi. In-hotel: bar, public Internet* ⊟*MC, V* ⍾*EP* Ⓜ*Cordusio; Tram 1, 12, 20, 27.*

★ $$–$$$ 🏨**Antica Locanda dei Mercanti.** On a quiet side street off Via Dante, this 14-room hotel is minutes—and light-years—away from Milan's bustling downtown. Rooms are on the second and third floors (four have private terraces), but you check in at ground-floor reception and take breakfast in the dining room at number 8. Reserve early for the terrace rooms. **Pros:** Central and cozy. **Con:** Rooms are scattered around floors. ⊠*Via San Tomaso 6, Duomo, 20121* ☎*02/8054080* 📠*02/8054090* ⊕*www.lalocanda.it* ⤶*14 rooms* ⚿*In-room: Wi-Fi. In-hotel: bar* ⊟*MC, V* ⍾*EP* Ⓜ*Cordusio; Tram 1, 12, 20, 27.*

$$–$$$ 🏨**Antica Locanda Leonardo.** Only a block from the church which houses *The Last Supper* and in one of Milan's most desired and historic neighborhoods with elegant shops and bars, it has been family-run for 100 years. Half the rooms face a courtyard and the others a back garden. Many have balconies and one ground-floor room has a private garden with table and chairs. The hotel has a relaxed feel and the owners who live in the building are helpful. They have a special relationship with a car service that offers moderate-price airport pickups and tours to nearby factory outlets. **Pros:** Very quiet and homey, breakfast is ample. **Con:** More like a bed-and-breakfast than a hotel. ⊠*Corso Magenta 78, Sant'Ambrogio, 20123* ☎*02/463317* 📠*02/48019012* ⊕*www. anticalocandaleonardo.com* ⤶*20 rooms* ⚿*In-room: Wi-Fi. In-hotel: bar, laundry service* ⊟*AE, DC, MC, V* ⊘*Closed Dec. 31–Jan. 7 and 3 wks in Aug.* ⍾*BP* Ⓜ*Sant'Ambrogio.*

$$ 🏨**Hotel Vittoria.** You'll forgive this hotel its baroque decor when you see how it reflects the owners' eager-to-please hospitality. Although out of the central tourist area (on a quiet residential street), the Vittoria is on the bus line from Linate Airport and on other major tram lines. It's about a 20-minute walk from the Duomo, and there's a good selection of restaurants nearby. English-speaking staff (not a given in smaller hotels) and spotless, comfortable rooms make this an attractive haven after a day out. **Pros:** Good value, friendly staff. **Cons:** Out of the city center, rooms can seem overly decorated. ⊠*Via Pietro Calvi 32, East Central Milan, 20129* ☎*02/5456520* 📠*02/55190246* ⊕*www.*

hotelvittoriamilano.it ↻40 *rooms* ⚭*In-room: safe, ethernet. In-hotel: parking (fee)* ⊟*AE, DC, MC, V* ⊙|*EP* Ⓜ*Tram 29, 30.*

$–$$ 🖼 **Hotel Casa Mia Milan.** Easy to reach from the central train station (a few blocks away) and easy on the budget, this tiny hotel, up a flight of stairs, is family-run. Rooms are simple and clean with individual (small) baths. Although not in the center of things, it is two blocks from transport center Piazza Repubblica (tram and metro lines), which also hosts the doyenne of Milan's palace hotels, the Principe di Savoia. **Pros:** Clean, good value. **Con:** Neighborhood is not the nicest in Milan. ⊠*Viale Vittorio Veneto 30, Piazza Repubblica, 20124* ☎*02/6575249* ⊕*www.casamiahotel.it* ↻*15 rooms* ⚭*In-hotel: no elevator* ⊟*MC, V* ⊙|*BP* Ⓜ*Republica.*

NIGHTLIFE & THE ARTS

THE ARTS

For events likely to be of interest to non-Italian speakers, see *Hello Milano* (⊕*www.hellomilano.it*), a monthly magazine available at the tourist office in Piazza Duomo, or *The American* (⊕*www.theamericanmag.com*), which is available at international bookstores and newsstands, and which has a thorough cultural calendar. The tourist office publishes the monthly *Milano Mese,* which also includes some listings in English.

MUSIC

The two halls belonging to the **Conservatorio** (⊠*Via del Conservatorio 12, Duomo* ☎*02/7621101* ⊕*www.consmilano.it* Ⓜ*San Babila*) host some of the leading names in classical music. Series are organized by several organizations, including the venerable chamber music society, the **Società del Quartetto** (⊕*www.quartettomilano.it*). The modern **Auditorium di Milano** (⊠*Largo Gustav Mahler [Corso San Gottardo, at Via Torricelli], Conchetta* ☎*02/83389201 up to 03* ⊕*www.laverdi. org*), known for its excellent acoustics, is home to the **Orchestra Verdi,** founded by Milan-born conductor Richard Chailly. The season, which runs from September to June, includes many top international performers and rotating guest conductors. The **Teatro Dal Verme** (⊠*Via San Giovanni sul Muro 2, Castello* ☎*02/87905201* ⊕*www. dalverme.org* Ⓜ*Cairoli*) stages frequent classical music concerts from October to May.

OPERA

Milan's hallowed **Teatro alla Scala** (⊠*Piazza della Scala* ☎*02/72003744* ⊕*www.teatroallascala.org* Ⓜ*Duomo*) has undergone a complete renovation, with everything refreshed, refurbished, or replaced except the building's exterior walls. Special attention was paid to the acoustics, which have always been excellent. The season runs from December 7, the feast day of Milan patron St. Ambrose, through June. Plan well in advance, as tickets sell out quickly. For tickets, visit the **Biglietteria Centrale** (⊠*Galleria del Sagrato, Piazza Del Duomo* ☉*Daily noon–6* Ⓜ*Duomo*), which is in the Duomo subway station. To pick up tickets for performances from two hours prior until 15 minutes after the start

CLOSE UP

'Appy Hour

The *aperitivo*, or prelunch or predinner drink, is part of life everywhere in Italy, and each town has its own rites and favorite drinks. Milan bar owners came up with something to fit their city's fast pace and work-oriented culture. They enriched the nibbles from olives, nuts, and chips into full finger (and often fork) buffets serving cubes of pizza and cheese, fried vegetables, rice salad, sushi, and even pasta, and they baptized it 'Appy Hour—with the first "h" dropped and the second one pronounced. For a fixed fee per drink (around €8), you can fill yourself up—don't be rude; remember Italian standards are moderate—on hors d'oeuvres and make a meal of it.

There are 'Appy Hours and *aperitivi* for all tastes and in all neighborhoods. Changes happen fast, but these are reliable: The elegant **Hotel Sheraton Diana Majestic** (⊠ *Viale Piave 42* ☎ *02/20582081*) attracts a young professional crowd in good weather to

its beautiful garden, which gets yearly thematic transformations. **Arthé** (⊠ *Via Pisacane 57* ☎ *02/29528353*) is a chic enoteca with fresh and fried vegetables and pasta. **G Lounge** (⊠ *Via Larga 8* ☎ *02/8053042*) has rotating DJ's and quality music. The **Capo Verde** (⊠ *Via Leoncavallo 16* ☎ *02/26820430*) is in a greenhouse/nursery and is especially popular for after-dinner drinks. In the Brera neighborhood, the highly rated enoteca **'N Ombra de Vin** (⊠ *Via S. Marco 2* ☎ *02/6599650*) serves wine by the glass and, in addition to the plates of sausage and cheese nibbles, has light food and not-so-light desserts. Check out the impressive vaulted basement where the bottled wine and spirits are sold. **Peck** (⊠ *Via Cesare Cantù 3* ☎ *02/8693017*), the Milan gastronomical shrine near the Duomo, also has a bar that serves up traditional—and excellent—pizza pieces, olives, and toasted nuts in a refined setting.

6

of a performance, go to the box office at the theater, which is around the corner in Via Filodrammatici 2. Although you might not get seats for the more-popular operas with big stars, it is worth trying; ballets are easier. The theater is closed from the end of July through August and on national and local holidays.

NIGHTLIFE

BARS

Milan has a bar somewhere to suit any style; those in the better hotels are respectably chic and popular meeting places for Milanese as well as tourists. The bar of the **Sheraton Diana Majestic** (⊠ *Viale Piave 42* ☎ *02/20581*), which has a splendid garden, is a prime meeting place for young professionals and the fashion people from the showrooms of the Porta Venezia neighborhood. **Brellin Caffé** (⊠ *Vicolo Lavandai at Alzaia Naviglio Grande* ☎ *02/58101351*) in the arty Navigli district has live music and serves late-night snacks. In Brera, check out the **Giamaica** (⊠ *Via Brera 32* ☎ *02/876723*), a traditional hangout for students from the nearby Brera art school. On summer nights this neighborhood pulses with life; street vendors and fortune-tellers jostle for space alongside the outdoor tables. For a break from the traditional, check out ultratrendy

SHU (✉ *Via Molino delle Armi, Ticinese* ☎ *02/58315720*), whose gleaming interior looks like a cross between *Star Trek* and Cocteau's *Beauty and the Beast*. The **Trussardi Bar** (✉ *Piazza della Scala 5, Duomo* ☎ *02/80688295*) has an enormous plasma screen that keeps hip barflies entertained with video art. Open throughout the day, it's a great place for coffee. **Blue Note** (✉ *Via Borsieri 37, Garibaldi* ☎ *02/69016888* ⊕ *www.bluenotemilano.com*), the first European branch of the famous New York nightclub, features regular performances by some of the most famous names in jazz, as well as blues and rock concerts. There's a popular jazz brunch on Sunday.

> ## "LET'S GO TO THE COLUMNS"
>
> *Andiamo al Le Colonne* in Milanese youthspeak means to meet up at the sober Roman columns in front of the Basilica San Lorenzo Maggiore. Attracted by the bars and shops along Corso di Porta Ticinese, the young spill out on the street to chat and drink. Neighbors may complain about the noise and confusion, but students and night hawks find it indispensable for socializing at all hours. It's a street—no closing time.

Monday evenings are reserved for Italian musicians. For an evening of live music—predominantly rock to jazz—head to perennial favorite **Le Scimmie** (✉ *Via Ascanio Sforza 49, Navigli* ☎ *02/89402874* ⊕ *www.scimmie.it*). It features international stars, some of whom jet in to play here, while others, including Ronnie Jones, are longtime residents in Milan.

NIGHTCLUBS

La Banque (✉ *Via Bassano Porrone 6, Scala* ☎ *02/86996565* ⊕ *www.labanque.it*) is an exclusive and expensive bar, restaurant, and dance club in a converted early-20th-century bank. Enjoy anything from an aperitivo to a night on the town among its marble columns. There's a €15–€20 cover. The hip **Café l'Atlantique** (✉ *Viale Umbria 42, Porta Romana* ☎ *02/55193906* ⊕ *www.cafeatlantique.com*) is a popular place for dancing the night away and enjoying a generous buffet brunch on Sunday afternoon. The €20 cost of admission varies by the evening and the show. To its regular discotheque fare, **Tocqueville** (✉ *Via Alexis de Tocqueville, Corso Como* ☎ *02/29002973* ⊗ *Closed Mon.*) has added two nights per week of live music, featuring young and emerging talent. The cover at this ever-popular Milan club is €10–€13.

For nightclubs, note that the cover charges can change depending on the day of the week. **Hollywood** (✉ *Corso Como 15/c, Centro Direzionale* ☎ *02/6598996* ⊕ *www.discotecahollywood.com*) continues to be one of the most popular places for the sunglasses set. The €16–€20 cover includes a drink. **Magazzini Generali** (✉ *Via Pietrasanta 14, Porta Vigentina* ☎ *02/55211313* ⊕ *www.magazzinigenerali.it*), in what was an abandoned warehouse, is a fun, futuristic venue for dancing and concerts. The €20 cover charge includes a drink. Its venerable age notwithstanding, **Plastic** (✉ *Viale Umbria 120* ☎ *02/733996*), closed Monday throughWednesday and some Thursdays, is still considered Milan's most transgressive, avant-garde, and fun club, complete with

CLOSE UP

Calcio Crazy

For the vast majority of Italians, *il calcio* (soccer) is much more than a national sport—it's a way of life. The general level of passion for the game exceeds that expressed by all but the most die-hard sports fans in the United States. In a country that's fine-tuned to nuance and inclined to see conspiracy around every corner, controversial referee calls can spark arguments that last weeks. In 2006, a game-fixing scandal that involved Turin's Juventus team convulsed Italy. For weeks on the eve of Italy's victory in the 2006 World Cup, the scandal, known as Moggi-gate in honor of a key fixer whose intercepted telephone calls opened it up, obsessed Italy's people and press.

Nowhere is the passion for the game more feverish than in big soccer cities, of which Milan is the prime example. It's home to two of the country's dominant teams: AC Milan (pronounced with the accent on the "MI") and F.C. Internazionale (aka, Inter). With Turin's Juventus ("la Juve"), they form Italy's ruling football triumvirate. At the stadium, even the most innocuous games are events where chants, insults, and creative banners make crowd-watching an appealing sideshow—especially the banners, whose legendary inside jokes are collected in anthologies.

drag-queen shows. The action starts late, even by Italian standards—don't bother going before midnight. Cover is €15–€20. **Rolling Stone** (⌧*Corso XXII Marzo 32, Porta Vittoria* ☎*02/733172* ⊕*www.rollingstone.it* ⊙*Closed Mon.–Wed.*) has been Milan's temple of rock since 1982, hosting the best of foreign and local talent. It reopened with a new sound system and renewed commitment to rock and roll in 2007. Check the Web site for the concert schedule. The €14 cover includes a drink.

SPORTS

SOCCER

AC Milan and Inter Milan, two of the oldest and most successful teams in Europe, vie for the heart of soccer-mad Lombardy. For residents, the city is *Milano* but the teams are *Milan,* a vestige of their common founding as the Milan Cricket and Football Club in 1899. When an Italian-led faction broke off in 1908, the new club was dubbed F.C. Internazionale (or "Inter") to distinguish it from the bastion of English exclusivity that would become AC Milan (or simply "Milan"). Since then, the picture has become more clouded: although Milan prides itself as the true team of the city and of its working class, Inter can more persuasively claim Pan-Italian support.

AC Milan and Inter Milan share the use of **San Siro Stadium (Stadio Meazza)** (⌧*Via Piccolomini*) during their August through May season. With more than 60,000 of the 85,000 seats appropriated by season-ticket holders and another couple thousand allocated to visiting fans, tickets to Sunday games can be difficult to come by. You can purchase advance AC Milan tickets at Cariplo bank branches, including one at

Continued on page 368

THE FASHIONISTA'S MILAN

Opera buffs and lovers of Leonardo's *Last Supper,* skip ahead to the next section. No one else should be dismayed to learn that clothing is Milan's greatest cultural achievement. The city is one of the fashion capitals of the world and home base for practically every top Italian designer. The same way art aficionados walk the streets of Florence in a state of bliss, the style-conscious come here to be enraptured.

It all happens in the *quadrilatero della moda,* Milan's toniest shopping district, located just north of the Duomo. Along the cobblestone streets, Armani, Prada, and their fellow *stilisti* sell the latest designs from flagship stores that are as much museums of chic as retail establishments. Any purchase here qualifies as a splurge, but you can have fun without spending a euro—just browse, window-

FLORENCE HAS THE *DAVID.*

ROME HAS THE PANTHEON.

MILAN HAS THE CLOTHES.

shop, and people-watch. Not into fashion? Think of the experience as art, design, and theater all rolled into one. If you wouldn't visit Florence without seeing the Uffizi, you shouldn't visit Milan without seeing the quadrilatero.

On these pages we give a selective, street-by-street list of stores in the area. Hours are from around 10 in the morning until 7 at night, Monday through Saturday.

VIA DELLA SPIGA
(east to west)

Dolce & Gabbana
(No. 2)
☎ 02/795747
www.dolcegabbana.it
women's accessories

Gio Moretti (No. 4)
☎ 02/76003186
women's and men's
clothes: many labels,
as well as books,
CDs, flowers, and an
art gallery

Bulgari Italia (No. 6)
☎ 02/777001
www.bulgari.com
jewelry, fragrances,
accessories

Malo (No. 7)
☎ 02/76016109
www.malo.it
everything cashmere

cross Via Sant'Andrea

Sergio Rossi (No. 15)
☎ 02/76002663
www.sergiorossi.com
women's shoes

Fay (No. 15)
☎ 02/76017597
www.fay.it
women's and men's
clothes, accessories: a
flagship store, designed
by Philip Johnson

Prada (No. 18)
☎ 02/76394336
www.prada.com
accessories

Giorgio Armani (No. 19)
☎ 02/783511
www.giorgioarmani.com
accessories

Tod's (No. 22)
☎ 02/76002423
www.tods.com
shoes and handbags:
the Tod's flagship store

Dolce & Gabbana (No. 26)
☎ 02 76001155
www.dolcegabbana.it
women's clothes, in a
baroque setting

✔ **Just Cavalli** (No. 30)
☎ 02/76390893
www.robertocavalli.net
women's and men's
clothes, plus a café
serving big salads
and carpaccio. It's
the offspring of the
Just Cavalli Café
in Parco Sempione,
one of the hottest
places in town for

drinks (with or without
dinner).

Moschino (No. 30)
☎ 02/76004320
www.moschino.it
women's, men's, and
children's clothes: Chic
and Cheap, so they say

Roberto Cavalli
(No. 42)
☎ 02/76020900
www.robertocavalli.net
women's and men's
clothes, accessories:
3,200 square feet of
Roberto Cavalli

I Pinco Pallino (No.
42) ☎ 02/781931
www.ipincopallino.it
extravagant children's
clothing

Marni (No. 50)
☎ 02/76317327
www.marni.com
women's clothes

VIA MONTENAPOLEONE
(east to west)

Fratelli Rossetti
(No. 1)
☎ 02/76021650
www.rossetti.it
shoes

Louis Vuitton (No. 2)
☎ 02/7771711
www.vuitton.com
leather goods, accessories, women's clothes

Armani Collezioni
(No. 2)
☎ 02/76390068
www.giorgioarmani.com
women's and men's clothes: the "white label"

Etro (No. 5)
☎ 02/76005049
www.etro.it
women's and men's clothes, leather goods, accessories

Agnona (No. 21)
☎ 02/76316530
www.agnona.com
women's clothes: Ermenegildo excellence for women

Bottega Veneta (No. 5)
☎ 02/76024495
www.bottegaveneta.com
leather goods: signature woven-leather bags

Gucci (No. 5/7)
☎ 02/771271
www.gucci.com
women's and men's clothes

Prada (No. 6)
☎ 02/76020273
www.prada.com
men's clothes

Prada (No. 8)
☎ 02/7771771
www.prada.com
women's clothes and accessories

Ermenegildo Zegna
(No. 27A)
☎ 02/76006437
www.zegna.com.
men's clothes, in the finest fabrics

cross Via Sant'Andrea

Armani Junior (in galleria) (No. 10)
☎ 02/783196
www.giorgioarmani.com
children's clothes: for the under-14 fashionista

Versace in
Via Montenapoleone

Versace (No. 11)
☎ 02/76008528
www.versace.com
everything Versace, except Versus and children's clothes

FASHION SHOPPING, ACCESSORIZED

Milan's most ambitious shops don't just want to clothe you— they want to trim your hair, clean your pores, and put a cocktail in your hand. Some "stores with more" in and around the quadrilatero are indicated by a ✔.

Corneliani (No. 12)
☎ 02/777361
www.corneliani.com
men's clothes: bespoke tailoring excellence

Aspesi (No. 13)
☎ 02/76022478
www.aspesi.it
low-key local design genius

Lorenzi (No. 9)
☎ 02/76003390
unique Milan—cutlery, razors, gifts

Map labels

Pal. di Brera
V. Borgonuovo
V. F.lli Gabba
V. d. Giardin
Via Manzoni
Via della Spiga
Via Senato
Just Cavalli Café
Bulgari ◆ Hotel
Armani Café Nobu
V. Monte di Pietà
M MONTENAPOLEONE
Via Montenapoleone
Via Gesù
Via Sant'Andrea
B R E R A
Via Manzoni
Via Bigli
Museo Poldi-Pezzoli
Teatro alla Scala
Via Verri
Via S.
Cova
Cso. Venezia
Martini Bar
Sant' Ambroeus
Pza. della Scala
Pza. Liberty
Cso. Matteotti
M SAN BABILA
Via Marino
Via Agnello
Via S. Paolo
P. all'Orto
Gucci Café
Galleria Vittorio Emanuele
Cso. Vittorio Emanuele II
0   100 yards
0   100 meters
M DUOMO
Pza. Duomo
Duomo
Pza. Fontana
Palazzo Reale

REFUELING

If you want refreshments and aren't charmed by the quadrilatero's in-store cafés, try **Cova** (Via Montenapoleone 8, ☎ 02/76000578) or **Sant'Ambroeus** (Corso Matteotti 7, ☎ 02/76000540). Both serve coffee, tea, aperitifs, sandwiches, and snacks in an ambience of starched tablecloths and chandeliers.

Cova's courtyard café

When the hurly-burly's done, head for the **Bulgari Hotel** (Via Fratelli Gabba 7b, ☎ 02/8058051), west of Via Manzoni, for a quiet (if pricey) drink. In summer, the bar extends into a beautiful, mature garden over an acre in size.

Valentino
corner Via Santo Spirito
☎ 02/76020285
www.valentino.it
women's clothes:
elegant designs for
special occasions

Loro Piana (No. 27c)
☎ 02/7772901
www.loropiana.it
women's and men's
clothes, accessories:
cashmere everything

VIA SAN PIETRO ALL'ORTO
(east to west)

Pomellato (No. 17)
☎ 02/76006086
www.pomellato.it
classic Milan—style
jewelry

Belfe-Postcard
(No. 7)
☎ 02/781023
www.belfe.it
chic sport and skiwear

Jimmy Choo (No. 17)
☎ 02/45481770
www.jimmychoo.com
women's and men's
shoes

CORSO VENEZIA
(south to north)

Prada Linea Rossa
(No. 3)
☎ 02/76001426
www.prada.com
Prada's sports line for
men and women

D&G (No. 7)
☎ 02/76004095
www.dolcegabbana.it
swimwear, underwear,
accessories: Dolce &
Gabbana's younger line

✔ **Dolce & Gabbana**
(No. 15)
☎ 02/76028485
www.dolcegabbana.it
Men's clothes, sold
in a four-story, early
19th-century patrician
home. Added features
are a barbershop (☎
02/ 76408881), a
beauty parlor (☎ 02/
76408888), and the
Martini Bar, which also
serves light lunches.

VIA VERRI
(south to north)

cross Via Bigli

Etro Profumi
corner Via Bigli
☎ 02/76005450
www.etro.it
fragrances

D&G in Via della Spiga

VIA SANT'ANDREA
(south to north)

✔ **Trussardi** (No. 5)
☎ 02/76020380
www.trussardi.com
Women's and men's
clothes. The nearby
flagship store (Piazza
della Scala 5) includes
the Trussardi Marino
alla Scala Café (☎
02/80688242), a
fashion-forward bar
done in stone, steel,
slate, and glass. For
a more substantial
lunch, and views of
Teatro alla Scala, head
upstairs to the Marino
alla Scala Ristorante
(☎ 02/80688201),
which serves creative
Mediterranean cuisine.

Banner (No. 8/A)
☎ 02/76004609
women's and men's
clothes: a multibrand
boutique

Giorgio Armani
(No. 9)
☎ 02/76003234
www.giorgioarmani.
com
women's and men's
clothes: the "black
label"

Moschino (No. 12)
☎ 02/76000832
www.moschino.it
women's clothes:
world-renowned
window displays

BARGAIN-HUNTING AT THE OUTLETS

Milan may be Italy's richest city, but that doesn't mean all its well-dressed residents can afford to shop at the boutiques of the quadrilatero. Many pick up their designer clothes at outlet stores, where prices can be reduced by 50 percent or more.

Salvagente (Via Bronzetti 16, ☎ 02/76110328, www.salvagentemilano.it) is the top outlet for designer apparel and accessories from both large are small houses. There's a small men's department. To get there, take the 60 bus, which runs from the Duomo to the Stazione Centrale, to the intersection of Bronzetti and Archimede. Look for the green iron gate with the bronze sign, between the hairdressers and an apartment building. No credit cards.

DMagazine Outlet (Via Montenapoleone 26, ☎ 02/76006027, www.dmagazine.it) has bargains in the

✔ **Gianfranco Ferré**
(No. 15)
☎ 02/794864
www.gianfrancoferre.com
Everything Ferré, plus a spa providing facials, Jacuzzis, steam baths, and mud treatments. Reservations are essential (☎ 02/76017526), preferably a week in advance.

Miu Miu (No. 21)
☎ 02/76001426
www.prada.com
Prada's younger line

VIA MANZONI
(south to north)

Valextra (No. 3)
☎ 02/99786000
www.valextra.it
glamorous bags and luggage

Armani in Via Manzoni

✔ **Armani Megastore**
(No. 31)
☎ 02/72318600
www.giorgioarmani.com
The quadrilatero's most conspicuous shopping complex. Along with many Armani fashions, you'll find a florist, a bookstore, a chocolate shop (offering Armani pralines), the Armani Caffè, and Nobu (of the upscale Japanese restaurant chain). The Armani Casa furniture collection is next door at number 37.

CORSO COMO
✔ **10 Corso Como**
☎ 02/29000727
www.10corsocomo.com
Outside the quadrilatero, but it's a must see for fashion addicts. The bazaar-like 13,000-square-foot complex includes women's and men's boutiques, a bar and restaurant, a bookstore, a record shop, and an art gallery specializing in photography. You can even spend the night (if you can manage to get a reservation) at Milan's most exclusive B&B, Three Rooms (P 02/626163). The furnishings are a modern design-lover's dream.

Prada store in the Galleria

GALLERIA VITTORIO EMANUELE
(not technically part of the quadrilatero, but nearby)

✔ **Gucci**
☎ 02/8597991
www.gucci.com

Gucci accessories, plus the world's first Gucci café. Sit outside behind the elegant boxwood hedge and watch the world go by.

Prada (No. 63-65)
☎ 02/876979
www.prada.com
the original store:

look for the murals downstairs.

Louis Vuitton
☎ 02/72147011
www.vuitton.com
accessories, women's and men's shoes, watches

Tod's
☎ 02/877997
www.tods.com
women's and men's shoes, leather goods, accessories

Borsalino (No. 92
☎ 02/804337
www.borsalino.com
hats

Galleria Vittorio Emanuele

midst of the quadrilatero. Names on sale include Armani, Cavalli, Gucci, and Prada.

DT-Intrend (Galleria San Carlo 6, ☎ 02/76000829) sells last year's Max Mara, Max & Co, Sportmax, Marella, Penny Black, and Marina Rinaldi. It's just 300 meters from the Max Mara store located on Corso Vittorio Emanuele at the corner of Galleria de Cristoforis.

At the **10 CorsoComo** outlet (Via Tazzoli 3, ☎ 02/29015130, www.10corsocomo.com) you can find clothes, shoes, bags, and accessories.

Fans of **Marni** who have a little time on their hands will want to check out the outlet (Via Tajani 1, ☎ 02/70009735 or 02/71040332, www.marni.com). Take the 61 bus to the terminus at Largo Murani, from which it's about 200 meters on foot.

Giorgio Armani has an outlet, but it's way out of town—off the A3, most of the way to Como. The address is Strada Provinciale per Bregnano 13, in the town of Vertemate (☎ 031 887373, www.giorgioarmani.com).

Via Verdi 8, or at the club's **Web site** (⊕*www.acmilan.com*). Inter tickets are available at Banca Popolare di Milano branches, including one at Piazza Meda 4, or at the club's **Web site** (⊕*www.inter.it*). To reach San Siro, take subway Line 1 (red) toward Molino Dorino, exit at the Lotto station, and board a bus for the stadium.

If you're a soccer fan but can't get in to see a game, you might settle for a **stadium tour** (☎*02/4042432* ⊕*www.sansirotour.com*), which includes a visit to the Milan-Inter museum. Tours are available every half hour from Gate 21 from 10 AM to 5 PM, except on game Sundays; they cost €12.50. Call for reservations a few days before your visit.

SHOPPING

The heart of Milan's shopping reputation is the **Quadrilatero della moda** district north of the Duomo. Here the world's leading designers compete for shoppers' attention, showing off their ultrastylish clothes in stores that are works of high style themselves. You won't find any bargains, but regardless of whether you're making a purchase, the area is a great place for window-shopping and people-watching. But fashion is not limited to one neighborhood, and there is a huge and exciting selection of clothing that is affordable, well made, and often more interesting than what is offered by the international luxury brands with shops in the Quadrilatero.

Wander around the **Brera** to find smaller shops with some appealing offerings from lesser-known names that cater to the well-schooled taste of this upscale neighborhood. The densest concentration is along Via Brera, Via Solferino, and Corso Garibaldi. For inexpensive and trendy clothes—for the under-25 set—stroll **Via Torino,** which begins in Piazza Duomo. Stay away on Saturday afternoon if you don't like crowds. Milan has several shopping streets that serve nearby residential concentrations. In the Porta Venezia area, visit **Corso Buenos Aires,** which runs northeast from the Giardini Pubblici. The wide and busy street is lined with affordable shops. It has the highest concentration of clothing stores in Europe, so be prepared to give up halfway. Avoid Saturday after 3 PM, when it seems the entire city is here looking for bargains. Near the Corso Magenta area, walk a few blocks beyond *The Last Supper* to **Corso Vercelli,** where you will find everything from a branch of the Coin department store to the quintessentially Milanese **Gemelli** (⊠*Corso Vercelli 16* ☎*02/48004689* ⊕*www.gemelli.it*).

NEED A BREAK?

Pasticceria Biffi (⊠*Corso Magenta 87* ☎*02/48006702*) is a Milan institution and the official pastry shop of this traditionally wealthy neighborhood. Have a coffee or a rich hot chocolate in its paneled room before facing the crowds in Corso Vercelli.

MARKETS

Weekly open markets selling fruits and vegetables—and a great deal more—are still a regular sight in Milan. Many also sell clothing and shoes. Bargains in designer apparel can be found at the huge **Mercato Papiniano** (⊠*Porta Genova*) on Saturday and Tuesday from about 9 to 1. The stalls to look for are at the Piazza Sant'Agostino end of the market. It's very crowded and demanding—watch out for pickpockets. Monday- and Thursday-morning markets in **Mercato di Via S. Marco** (⊠ *Brera*) cater to the wealthy residents of this central neighborhood. In addition to food stands where you can get cheese, roast chicken, and dried beans and fruits, there are several clothing and shoe stalls that are important stops for some of Milan's most elegant women. Check out the knitwear at Valentino, about midway down on the street side. Muscle in on the students from the prestigious high school nearby who rush here for the french fries and potato croquettes at the chicken stand at the Via Montebello end.

PAVIA, CREMONA & MANTUA

Once proud medieval fortress towns rivaling Milan in power, these centers of industry and commerce on the Po Plain still play a key role in Italy's wealthiest, most populous region. Pavia is celebrated for its extraordinarily detailed Carthusian monastery, Cremona for its incomparable violin-making tradition. Mantua—the most picturesque of the three—was the home of the fantastically wealthy Gonzaga dynasty for almost 300 years.

6

PAVIA

41 km (25 mi) south of Milan.

GETTING HERE
By car from Milan, start out on the A7 autostrada and exit onto A53 as you near Pavia; the drive is 40 km (25 mi) and takes about 45 minutes. Pavia is about 30 minutes by train from Milan and 1½ hours (by slower regional service) from Cremona.

VISITOR INFORMATION
Pavia tourism office (⊠ *Via Fabio Filzi 2* ☎ *0382/22156* 🖷 *0382/32221* ⊕ *www.apt.pavia.it*).

EXPLORING
Pavia was once Milan's chief regional rival. The city dates from at least the Roman era and was the capital of the Lombard kings for two centuries (572–774). It was at one time known as "the city of a hundred towers," but only a handful have survived the passing of time. Its prestigious university was founded in 1361 on the site of a 10th-century law school, but has roots that can be traced to antiquity.

The 14th-century **Castello Visconteo** now houses the local **Museo Civico** (Municipal Museum), with an archaeological collection and a picture gallery featuring works by Correggio, Giovanni Bellini, Giambattista Tiepolo, and Vincenzo La Foppa, among others. ⊠ *Viale 11 Febbraio, near Piazza Castello* ☎ *0382/33853* 🎟 *€6.50* 🕐 *Feb.–June and Sept.– Nov., Tues.–Sun. 10–5:45; last entry 5:15. Dec., Jan., July and Aug., Tues.–Sun. 9–1; last entry 12:30.*

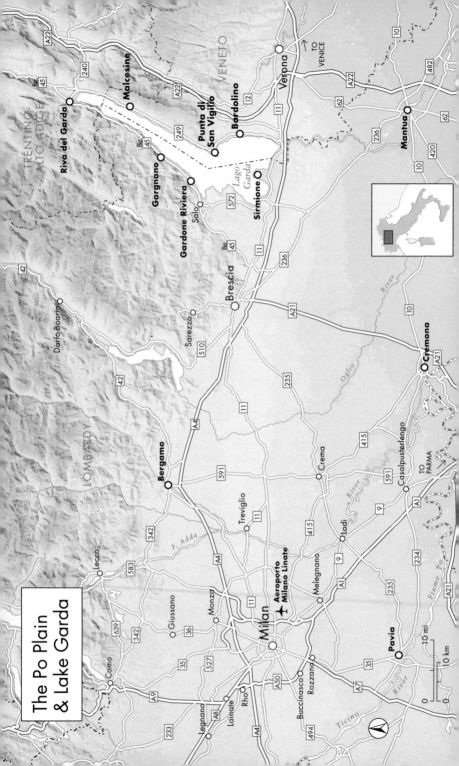

The Po Plain & Lake Garda

In the Romanesque church of **San Pietro in Ciel d'Oro** you can visit the tomb of Christianity's most celebrated convert, St. Augustine, housed in a Gothic marble ark on the high altar. ✉ *Via Matteotti* ☎*0382/303040* ☉*Daily 7–noon and 3–7. Mass: Mon.–Sat. 9 and 6:30, Sun. 9, 11, and 6:30.*

The main draw in Pavia is the **Certosa** *(Carthusian monastery)*, 9 km (5½ mi) north of the city center. Its elaborate facade shows the same relish for ornamentation as the Duomo in Milan. The Certosa's extravagant grandeur was due in part to the plan to have it house the tombs of the family of the first duke of Milan, Galeazzo Visconti III (who died during a plague, at age 49, in 1402). The very best marble was used, taken undoubtedly by barge from the quarries of Carrara, roughly 240 km (150 mi) away. Though the floor plan may be Gothic—a cross shape divided into a series of squares—the gorgeous fabric that rises above it is triumphantly Renaissance. On the facade, in the lower frieze, are medallions of Roman emperors and Eastern monarchs; above them are low reliefs of scenes from the life of Christ and from the career of Galeazzo Visconti III.

The first duke was the only Visconti to be interred here, and not until some 75 years after his death, in a tomb designed by Gian Cristoforo Romano. Look for it in the right transept. In the left transept is a more-appealing tomb—that of a rather stern middle-age man and a beautiful young woman. The man is Ludovico il Moro Sforza (1452–1508), seventh duke of Milan, who commissioned Leonardo to paint *The Last Supper*. The woman is Ludovico's wife, Beatrice d'Este (1475–97), one of the most celebrated women of her day, the embodiment of brains, culture, birth, and beauty. Married when he was 40 and she was 16, they had enjoyed six years together when she died while delivering a stillborn child. Ludovico commissioned the sculptor Cristoforo Solari to design a joint tomb for the high altar of Santa Maria delle Grazie in Milan. Originally much larger, the tomb for some years occupied the honored place as planned. Then, for reasons that are still mysterious, the Dominican monks, who seemed to care no more for their former patron than they did for their faded Leonardo fresco, sold the tomb to their Carthusian brothers to the south. Sadly, part of the tomb and its remains were lost. ✉*Certosa,* ✛*9 km (5½ mi) north of Pavia* ☎*0382/925613* ⊕*www.comune.pv.it/certosadipavia* ✉*Free* ☉*Tues.–Sun. 9–11:30 and 2:30–5.*

WHERE TO EAT

$$$$ ✕ **Locanda Vecchia Pavia al Mulino.** At this sophisticated art nouveau restaurant 150 yards from the Certosa you'll find creative versions of traditional regional cuisine, including *risotto alla certosina* (with sturgeon eggs, frogs' legs, and river shrimp). *Casoncelli* (stuffed pasta), *petto d'anatra* (duck breast), and veal cutlet *alla milanese* are done with style, as are the imaginative seafood dishes. For dessert, consider the hot chocolate soufflé with white-chocolate sauce, but be sure to order it ahead of time. ✉*Via al Monumento 5, Certosa* ☎*0382/925894* ⏲*Reservations essential* ▭*AE, DC, MC, V* ☉*Closed Mon., 3 wks in Aug., and 3 wks in early Jan. No lunch Wed.*

CREMONA

104 km (65 mi) east of Pavia, 106 km (66 mi) southeast of Milan.

GETTING HERE

By car from Milan, start out on the A1 autostrada and switch to A21 at Piacenza; the drive is 100 km (62 mi) and lasts about 1½ hours. From Pavia, take SS617 to A21; the trip is 70 km (44 mi) and lasts about 1¼ hours. By train, Cremona is about an hour from Milan and 1½ hours from Desenzano, near Sirmione on Lake Garda.

VISITOR INFORMATION

Cremona tourism office (✉*Piazza del Comune 5* ☎*0372/23233* ☒*0372/534080* ⊕*www.aptcremona.it*).

EXPLORING

Cremona is where the world's best violins are made. Andrea Amati (1510–80) invented the modern instrument here in the 16th century. Though cognoscenti continue to revere the Amati name, it was an apprentice of Amati's nephew for whom the fates had reserved wide and lasting fame. In a career that spanned an incredible 68 years, Antonio Stradivari (1644–1737) made more than 1,200 instruments—including violas, cellos, harps, guitars, and mandolins, in addition to his fabled violins. Labeled simply with a small printed slip reading ANTONIUS STRADIVARIUS CREMONENSIS. FACIEBAT ANNO ...—the date inserted in a neat italic hand—they remain the most coveted, most expensive stringed instruments in the world.

Strolling about this quiet, medium-size city, you cannot help noting that the violin making continues to flourish. There are, in fact, more than 50 *liutai,* many of them graduates of the Scuola Internazionale di Liuteria (International School of Violin Making). You are usually welcome to these ateliers, where traditional craftsmanship reigns supreme, especially if you are contemplating the acquisition of your own instrument; the tourist office can provide addresses.

Cremona's other claim to fame is *torrone* (nougat), which is said to have been created here in honor of the marriage of Bianca Maria Visconti and Francesco Sforza, which took place in October 1441. The new confection, originally prepared by heating almonds, egg whites, and honey over low heat and shaped and named after the city's tower, was created in symbolic celebration. The annual Festa del Torrone is held in the main piazza on the third Sunday in October.

The **Piazza del Comune,** surrounded by the Duomo, tower, baptistery, and city hall, is distinctive and harmonious: the combination of old brick, rose- and cream-color marble, terra-cotta, and old copper roofs brings Romanesque, Gothic, and Renaissance together with unusual success.

Dominating Piazza del Comune is the **Torrazzo** *(Big Tower),* the city's symbol and perhaps the tallest campanile in Italy, visible for a considerable distance across the Po Plain. It's open to visitors, but in winter, hours fluctuate depending on the weather. The tower's astronomical clock is the 1583 original. ✉*Piazza del Comune* ☒€6.50 ☉*Daily 9–6.*

Cremona's Romanesque **Duomo** was consecrated in 1190. Here you'll find the beautiful *Story of the Virgin Mary and the Passion of Christ,* the central fresco of an extraordinary cycle commissioned in 1514 and featuring the work of local artists, including Boccacio Boccancino, Giovan Francesco Bembo, and Altobello Melone. ⊠*Piazza del Comune* ⊘*Daily 7:30–noon and 3:30–7.*

Legendary violin maker Antonio Stradivari lived, worked, and died near the verdant square at **No. 1 Piazza Roma.** According to local lore, Stradivari kept each instrument in his bedroom for a month before varnishing it, imparting part of his soul before sealing and sending it out into the world. In the center of the park is **Stradivari's grave,** marked by a simple tombstone.

The **Museo Stradivariano** *(Stradivarius Museum)* in Palazzo Affaitati houses the city's collection of stringed treasures: a viola and five violins, including the golden-orange "Il Cremonese 1715" Stradivarius. Informative exhibits display Stradivari's paper patterns, wooden models, and various tools. ⊠*Via Ugolani Dati 4* ☎*0372/407770* ⊠*€7* ⊘*Tues.–Sat. 9–6, Sun. 10–6.*

WHERE TO STAY & EAT

$–$$ ✕ **La Sosta.** This traditional Cremonese restaurant looks to the 16th century for culinary inspiration, following a time-tested recipe for a favored first course, gnocchi *Vecchia Cremona.* The homemade salami is also excellent. To finish off the evening, try the *semifreddo al torroncino* (chilled almond cake) and a dessert wine. ⊠*Via Sicardo 9* ☎*0372/456656* ⊟*AE, DC, MC, V* ⊘*Closed Mon. and 3 wks in Aug. No dinner Sun.*

★ $ ✕ **Centrale.** Close to the cathedral, this old-style trattoria is a favorite among locals for traditional Cremonese fare, such as succulent *cotechino* (pork sausage) and *tortelli di zucca* (a small pasta with pumpkin filling), at moderate prices. ⊠*Vicolo Pertusio 4* ☎*0372/28701* ⊟*V* ⊘*Closed Thurs. and July.*

$$–$$$ ⊡ **Delle Arti Design Hotel.** The name fits at this central hotel with elegant modern interiors and eclectic designer furniture. The contemporary feel provides a nice contrast to the surrounding historic center. ⊠*Via Bonomelli 8, 26100* ☎*0372/23131* ⊟*0372/21654* ⊕*www.dellearti. com* ⟿*33 rooms* ⊘*In-room: refrigerator. In-hotel: bar, gym, parking (fee)* ⊟*AE, DC, MC, V* ⊘*Closed Aug. 5–29* ⊚*BP.*

$–$$ ⊡ **Hotel Continental.** This comfortable modern hotel is well equipped to satisfy its international business clientele. At the end of the road to the autostrada, on the periphery of the historic center, the Continental makes a convenient base for those wisely disinclined to navigate old Cremona by car. ⊠*Piazza Libertà 26, 26100* ☎*0372/434141* ⊟*0372/454873* ⊕*www.hotelcontinentalcremona.it* ⟿*62 rooms In-hotel: restaurant, bar, public Internet, parking (fee)* ⊟*AE, DC, MC, V* ⊚*BP.*

SHOPPING

For Cremona's specialty nougat, visit famed **Sperlari** (⊠*Via Solferino 25* ☎*0372/22346* ⊕*www.fieschi1867.com*). In addition to nougat, Cremona's best *mostarda* (a condiment made from preserved fruit served with meat and cheese) has been sold from this handsome shop since 1836; Sperlari and parent company Fieschi have grown into a confectionery empire. Look for the historical product display in the back.

MANTUA

192 km (119 mi) southeast of Milan.

GETTING HERE

Mantua is 5 km (3 mi) west of the A22 autostrada. The drive from Milan, following A4 to A22, takes a little over two hours. The drive from Cremona, along SS10, is 1¼ hours. By train, Mantua is two to three hours from Milan, depending on the type of service, and about 1½ hours from Desenzano, near Sirmione on Lake Garda, via Verona.

VISITOR INFORMATION

Mantua tourism office (⊠*Piazza A. Mantegna 6* ☎*0376/328253* 🖷*0376/363292* ⊕*www.turismo.mantova.it*).

EXPLORING

Mantua stands tallest among the ancient walled cities of the Po Plain. Its fortifications are circled on three sides by the passing Mincio River, which long provided Mantua with protection, fish, and a steady stream of river tolls as it meandered from Lake Garda to join the Po. It may not be flashy or dramatic, but Mantua's beauty is subtle and deep, hiding a rich trove of artistic, architectural, and cultural gems beneath its slightly somber facade.

Although Mantua first came to prominence in Roman times as the home of Virgil, its grand monuments date from the glory years of the Gonzaga dynasty. From 1328 until the Austrian Habsburgs sacked the city in 1708, the dukes and marquesses of the Gonzaga clan reigned over a wealthy independent *commune,* and the arts thrived in the relative peace of that period. Raphael's star pupil Andrea Mantegna, who served as court painter for 50 years, was the best known of a succession of artists and architects who served Mantua through the years, and some of his finest work, including his only surviving fresco cycle, can be seen here. Giulio Romano (circa 1499–1546), Mantegna's apprentice, built his masterpiece, Palazzo Te, on an island in the river. Leon Battista Alberti (1404–72), who designed two impressive churches in Mantua, was widely emulated later in the Renaissance.

★ The 500-room **Palazzo Ducale,** the palace that dominates the skyline, was built for the Gonzaga family. Unfortunately, as the Gonzaga dynasty waned in power and prestige, much of the art within the castle was sold or stolen. The highlight is the Camera Degli Sposi—literally, the "Chamber of the Wedded Couple"—where Duke Ludovico and his wife held court. Mantegna painted it over a nine-year period at the height of his power, finishing at age 44. He made a startling advance in painting by organizing the picture plane in a way that systematically mimics the experience of human vision. Even now, more than five centuries later, you can sense the excitement of a mature artist, fully aware of the great importance of his painting, expressing his vision with a masterly, joyous confidence. The circular tromp l'oeil around the vaulted ceiling is famous for the many details that attest to Mantegna's greatness: the three-dimensional quality of the seven Caesars (the Gonzagas saw themselves as successors to the Roman emperors

and paid homage to classical culture throughout the palazzo); the self-portrait of Mantegna (in purple, on the right side of the western fresco); and the dwarf peering out from behind the dress of Ludovico's wife (on the northern fresco). Only 20 people at a time are allowed in the Camera Degli Sposi, and only for 10 minutes at a time. Read about the room before you enter so that you can spend your time looking up.

Walk-up visitors to Mantua's Palazzo Ducale may take a fast-paced guided tour conducted in Italian; signs in each room provide explanations in English. Alternatively, call the **tourism office** (☎0376/328253) to arrange for English-language tours. ⊠ *Piazza Sordello* ☎0376/224832 ☑€6.50 ☉ *Tues.–Sun. 8:45–7:15; last entry 6:30.*

Serious Mantegna aficionados will want to visit the **Casa di Andrea Mantegna,** designed by the artist himself and built around an intriguing circular courtyard, which is usually open to view. The interior can be seen only by appointment or during occasional art exhibitions. ⊠ *Via Acerbi 47* ☎0376/360506 ☑€3 ☉ *Tues.–Sun. 10–12:30 by appointment; also 3–6 during exhibitions.*

Mantegna's tomb is in the first chapel to the left in the basilica of **Sant'Andrea,** most of which was built in 1472. The current structure, a masterwork by the architect Alberti, is the third built on this spot to house the relic of the Precious Blood. The crypt holds two reliquaries containing earth believed to be soaked in the blood of Christ, brought to Mantua by Longinus, the soldier who pierced his side. They are displayed only on Good Friday. ⊠ *Piazza delle Erbe* ☉ *Daily 8–12:30 and 3–6.*

★ **Palazzo Te** is one of the greatest of all Renaissance palaces, built between 1525 and 1535 by Federigo II Gonzaga. It is the mannerist masterpiece of artist-architect Giulio Romano, who created a pavilion where the strict rules of courtly behavior could be relaxed for libertine pastimes. Romano's purposeful breaks with classical tradition are lighthearted and unprecedented. For example, note the "slipping" triglyphs along the upper edge of the inside courtyard. Two highlights are the Camera di Amore e Psiche (Room of Cupid and Psyche) that depicts a wedding set among lounging nymphs, frolicking satyrs, and even a camel and an elephant; and the gasp-producing Camera dei Giganti (Room of the Giants) that shows Jupiter expelling the Titans from Mount Olympus. The scale of the work is overwhelming; the floor-to-ceiling work completely envelops the viewer. The room's rounded corners, and the river rock covering the original floor, were meant to give it a cavelike feeling. It is a "whisper chamber" in which words softly uttered in one corner can be heard in the opposite one. For fun, note the graffiti from as far back as the 17th century. ⊠ *Viale Te* ☎ *0376/323266* ⊕ *www. centropalazzote.it* 🔊 *€8* 🕙 *Mon. 1–6, Tues.–Sun. 9–5:30.*

WHERE TO STAY & EAT

★ **$$$$** ✕ **Al Bersagliere.** One of Lombardy's best restaurants is this rustic four-room tavern in the tiny riverside hamlet of Goito, 16 km (10 mi) north of Mantua on Route 236. It has been run by a single family for more than 150 years. The fish in particular is excellent, as is a Mantuan classic, frog soup. ⊠ *Via Goitese 260, Goito* ☎ *0376/60007* ♟ *Reservations essential* 🟰 *AE, DC, MC, V* 🕙 *Closed Mon. and Tues., and 3 wks in Aug.*

★ **$$$$** ✕ **Ambasciata.** Heralded by food critics the world over as one of Italy's finest restaurants, Ambasciata (Italian for "embassy") takes elegance and service to new levels. Chef Romano Tamani makes frequent appearances abroad but is at home in tiny Quistello, 20 km (12 mi) southeast of Mantua, where he offers to those willing to make the trek (and pay the bill) an ever-changing array of superlative creations such as *timballo di lasagne verdi con petto di piccione sauté alla crème de Cassis* (green lasagne with breast of pigeon and red currant). ⊠ *Via Martiri di Belfiore 33, Quistello* ☎ *0376/619169* ♟ *Reservations essential* 🟰 *AE, DC, MC, V* 🕙 *Closed Mon., Jan. 1–20, and Aug. 5–25. No dinner Sun.*

¢–$ ✕ **Ristorante Pavesi.** Locals have been coming to this central restaurant for delicious food at reasonable prices since 1918. The menu changes every other month; homemade pasta is always a good bet. In warmer months you can dine on Mantua's handsome main square. ⊠ *Piazza delle Erbe 13* ☎ *0376/323627* 🟰 *AE, DC, MC, V.*

$$$ 🛏 **San Lorenzo.** As if spacious, comfortable rooms, authentic early-19th-century furnishings, and a prime location weren't enough, many rooms here have wonderful views overlooking Piazza Concordia, and some have private terraces. In summer, breakfast is served on the roof. ⊠ *Piazza Concordia 14, 46100* ☎ *0376/220500* 🖷 *0376/327194* ⊕ *www.hotelsanlorenzo.it* 🛏 *32 rooms* ♿ *In-hotel: bar, parking (no fee)* 🟰 *AE, DC, MC, V* ⦿ *BP.*

$–$$ 🛏 **Hotel Broletto.** Here you'll get comfortable, clean digs in a perfect location. The furniture was new in the '60s and has stuck around long enough to come back in style. ⊠ *Via Accademia 1, 46100* ☎ *0376/223678* 🖷 *0376/221297* 🛏 *16 rooms* 🟰 *AE, DC, MC, V* 🕙 *Closed part of July and late Dec.* ⦿ *BP.*

LAKE GARDA

Lake Garda has had a perennial attraction for travelers and writers alike; even essayist Michel de Montaigne (1533–92), whose 15 months of travel journals contain not a single other reference to nature, paused to admire the view down the lake from Torbole, which he called "boundless."

Lake Garda is 50 km (31 mi) long, ranges roughly 1 km–16 km (½ mi–10 mi) wide, and is as much as 1,135 feet deep. The terrain is flat at the lake's southern base and mountainous at its northern tip. As a consequence, its character varies from stormy inland sea to crystalline Nordic-style fjord. It's the biggest lake in the region and by most accounts the cleanest. Drivers should take care on the hazardous hairpin turns on the lake road.

GETTING HERE

The town of Sirmione, at the south end of the lake, is 10 km (6 mi) from Desenzano, which has regular train service; it's about an hour and 20 minutes by train from Milan and 25 minutes from Verona. The A4 autostrada passes to the south of the lake, and A22 runs north–south about 10 km (6 mi) from the eastern shore.

BERGAMO

52 km (32 mi) east of Milan.

GETTING HERE

Bergamo is located along the A4 autostrada. By car from Milan, take A51 out of the city to pick up A4; the drive is 52 km (32 mi) and takes about 45 minutes. By train, Bergamo is about one hour from Milan and 1½ hours from Sirmione.

VISITOR INFORMATION

Bergamo tourism office (⊠ *Vicolo Aquila Nera at Piazza Vecchia, Bergamo Alta* ☎ *035/242226* 🖷 *035/232730* ⊠ *Viale Vittorio Emanuele 20, Bergamo Bassa* ☎ *035/210204* 🖷 *035/230184* ⊕ *www.provincia. bergamo.it/turismo).*

EXPLORING

If you're driving from Milan to Lake Garda, the perfect deviation from your autostrada journey is the lovely medieval town of Bergamo. Bergamo is also a wonderful side trip by train from Milan. In less than an hour, you will be whisked from the restless pace of city life, to the medieval grandeur of Bergamo Alta where the pace is a tranquil remnant of the past.

From behind a set of battered Venetian walls high on an Alpine hilltop, Bergamo majestically surveys the countryside. Behind are the snow-capped Bergamese Alps, and two funiculars connect the modern **Bergamo Bassa** (Lower Bergamo) to the ancient **Bergamo Alta** (Upper Bergamo). Bergamo Bassa's long arteries and ornate piazze speak to its centuries of prosperity, but it's nonetheless overshadowed by Bergamo Alta's magnificence.

The massive **Torre Civica** offers a great view of the two cities. ⊠ *Piazza Vecchia* ☎ *035/247116* 💶 *€3* 🕙 *Apr.–Oct., Sun.–Tues. 9:30–7, Sat. 9:30–9:30; Nov.–Mar., Sat. 9:30–4:30, Tues.–Fri. by appointment only.*

6

Bergamo's **Duomo** and **Battistero** are the most substantial buildings in Piazza Duomo. But the most impressive structure is the **Cappella Colleoni,** with stunning marble decoration. ⊠*Piazza Duomo* 🖮*Free* ☉*Daily 10–12:30 and 2:30–5:30.*

In the **Accademia Carrara** you will find an art collection that is surprisingly rewarding given its size and remote location. Many of the Venetian masters are represented—Mantegna, Bellini, Carpaccio (circa 1460–1525/26), Tiepolo (1727–1804), Francesco Guardi (1712–93), Canaletto (1697–1768)—as well as Botticelli (1445–1510). ⊠*Bergamo Bassa, Piazza Carrara 82* 🖮*035/247149* ⊕*www.accademiacarrara.bergamo.it* 🖮*€2.60* ☉*Daily 10–1:30 and 2:30–5:30.*

WHERE TO STAY & EAT

★ **$$–$$$$** ✕ **Taverna Colleoni dell'Angelo.** Angelo Cornaro is the name behind the Taverna Colleoni, on the Piazza Vecchia right behind the Duomo. He serves imaginative fish and meat dishes, both regional and international, all expertly prepared. ⊠*Piazza Vecchia 7* 🖮*035/232596* 🖮*AE, DC, MC, V* ☉*Closed Mon. and 1 wk in Aug.*

$$ ✕ **Da Ornella.** The vaulted ceilings of this popular trattoria on the main street in the upper town are marked with ancient graffiti, created by (patiently) holding candles to the stone overhead. Ornella herself is in the kitchen, turning out *casoncelli* (stuffed pasta) in butter and sage and platters of assorted roast meats. Ask her to suggest the perfect wine pairing for your meal. Three prix-fixe menus are available during the week, two on the weekend. Reservations are recommended. ⊠*Via Gombito 15* 🖮*035/232736* 🖮*AE, DC, MC, V* ☉*Closed Thurs.*

$$ ✕ **La Trattoria del Teatro.** Traditional regional food tops the bill at this good-value restaurant in the upper town. The polenta is a silky delight, and game is recommended in season. Fettuccine *con funghi* (with mushrooms) is deceptively simple but a rich and memorable specialty. ⊠*Piazza Mascheroni 3* 🖮*035/238862* 🖮*No credit cards* ☉*Closed Mon. and 2 wks mid-July.*

$$ ✕ **Vineria Cozzi.** The wine list at this romantic but informal *vineria* (wine bar) is exceptional, whether you order by the glass or the bottle. There's also an array of flavorful foods, from snacks to sumptuous full-course meals typical of the region. The atmosphere is warm and charming, harkening back to 150 years ago, when the age of the vineria reached its height. ⊠*Via B. Colleoni, 22a Bergamo Alta* 🖮*035/238836* 🖮*No credit cards* ☉*Closed Wed.*

$–$$ ✕**Agnello d'Oro.** A 17th-century tavern on the main street in Upper Bergamo, with wooden booths and walls hung with copper utensils and ceramic plates, Agnello d'Oro is a good place to imbibe the atmosphere as well as the good local wine. Specialties are typical Bergamese risotto and varieties of polenta served with game and mushrooms. The same establishment has 20 modestly priced ($) rooms. ⊠*Via Gombito 22*

☎035/249883 🖷035/235612 ⤦20 rooms ♿In-room: no a/c. In-hotel: restaurant ▤AE, MC, V ☺Restaurant closed Mon. and Jan. 7–Feb. 5. No dinner Sun. ⏳EP.

$–$$
Fodor's Choice
★
✕ **Al Donizetti.** Find a table in the back of this central, cheerful *enoteca* (wine bar) before choosing local hams and cheeses to accompany your wine (more than 800 bottles are available, many by the glass). Heartier meals are also available, such as eggplant stuffed with cheese and salami, but save room for the desserts, which are well paired with dessert wines. ✉*Via Gombito 17/a* ☎035/242661 ▤AE, MC, V.

$$–$$$$
🏨 **Excelsior San Marco.** The most comfortable hotel in Lower Bergamo, the Excelsior San Marco is only a short walk from the walls of the upper town. The rooms are surprisingly quiet considering the central location. You can breakfast on the rooftop terrace. ✉*Piazza della Repubblica 6, 24122* ☎035/366111 🖷035/223201 ⊕*www.hotelsanmarco. com* ⤦*155 rooms* ♿In-room: safe. In-hotel: restaurant, bar, laundry service, public Internet parking (fee) ▤AE, DC, MC, V ⏳BP.

SIRMIONE

★ *138 km (86 mi) east of Milan.*

6

VISITOR INFORMATION
Sirmione tourism office (✉*Viale Marconi 2* ☎*030/916114* 🖷*030/916222*).

EXPLORING

Dramatically rising out of Lake Garda is the enchanting town of Sirmione. *"Paene insularum, Sirmio, insularumque ocelle,"* sang Catullus in a homecoming poem: "It is the jewel of peninsulas and islands, both." The forbidding Castello Scaligero stands guard behind the small bridge connecting Sirmione to the mainland; beyond, cobbled streets wind their way through medieval arches past lush gardens, stunning lake views, and gawking crowds. Originally a Roman resort town, Sirmione served under the dukes of Verona and later Venice as Garda's main point of defense. It has now reclaimed its original function, bustling with visitors in summer. Cars aren't allowed into town; parking is available by the tourist office at the entrance.

Locals will almost certainly tell you that the so-called **Grotte di Catullo** *(Grottoes of Catullus)* was once the site of the villa of Catullus (87–54 BC), one of the greatest pleasure-seeking poets of all time. Present archaeological wisdom, however, does not concur, and there is some consensus that this was the site of two villas of slightly different periods, dating from about the 1st century AD. But never mind—the view through the cypresses and olive trees is lovely, and even if Catullus didn't have a villa here, he is closely associated with the area and undoubtedly did have a villa nearby. The ruins are at the top of the isthmus and are poorly signposted: walk through the historic center and past the various villas to the top of the spit; the entrance is on the right. A small museum offers a brief overview of the ruins (on the far wall); for guided group tours in English, call 02/20421469. ✉*Via*

GETTING AROUND THE LAKES

Frequent daily ferry and hydrofoil services link the lakeside towns and villages. Residents take them to get to work and school, while visitors use them for exploring the area. There are also special round-trip excursions, some with (optional) dining service on board. Schedules and ticket price are available on the Web site of **Navigazione Laghi** (⊠ *Via Ariosto 21, Milan* ☎ *02/4676101* ⊕ *www.navigazionelaghi.it*) and are posted at the landing docks.

To get around the lakes by car, you have to follow secondary roads—often of great beauty. S572 follows the southern and western shores of Lake Garda, SS45b edges the northernmost section of the western shore, and S249 runs along the east-ern shore. Around Lake Como, follow S340 along the western shore, S36 on the eastern shore, and S583 on the lower arms. S33 and S34 trace the western shore of Lake Maggiore. Although the roads around the lake can be beautiful, they're full of harrowing twists and turns, making for a slow, challenging drive.

There's regular bus service between the small towns on the lakes. It's less convenient than going by boat or by car, and it's used primarily by locals (particularly schoolchildren), but sightseers can use it as well. The bus service around Lake Garda serves mostly towns on the western shore. Call the bus operator **SIA** (☎ *030/3774237*) for information.

Catullo Sirmione, Sirmione ☎ *030/916157* 🎫 *€4* ⊙ *Mar.–mid-Oct., Tues.–Sun. 8:30–7; mid-Oct.–Feb., Tues.–Sun. 8:30–5.*

The **Castello Scaligero** was built, along with almost all the other castles on the lake, by the Della Scala family. As hereditary rulers of Verona for more than a century before control of the city was seized by the Visconti in 1402, they counted Garda among their possessions. You can go inside to take in the nice view of the lake from the tower, or you can swim at the nearby beach. ⊠ *Piazza Castello, Sirmione* ☎ *030/916468* 🎫 *€4* ⊙ *Tues.–Sun. 8:30–7.*

WHERE TO STAY & EAT

$$$–$$$$ ✕ **La Rucola.** Next to Sirmione's castle, this elegant, intimate restaurant has a creative menu, with seafood and meat dishes accompanied by a good choice of wines. Three fixed-price menus are available. ⊠ *Via Strentelle 3* ☎ *030/916326* ▭ *AE, DC, MC, V* ⊙ *Closed Thurs. and Jan.–mid-Feb. No lunch Fri.*

$–$$ ✕ **Ristorante Al Pescatore.** Lake fish is the specialty at this simple, popular restaurant in Sirmione's historical center. Try grilled trout with a bottle of local white wine and settle your meal with a walk in the nearby public park. ⊠ *Via Piana 20* ☎ *030/916216* ▭ *AE, DC, MC, V.*

★ $$$$ 🏠 **Villa Cortine.** This former private villa in a secluded park risks being just plain ostentatious, but it's saved by the sheer luxury of its setting and the extraordinary professionalism of its staff. The hotel dominates a low hill, and the grounds—a colorful mixture of lawns, trees, statues, and fountains—go down to the lake. The villa itself dates from the early part of the 19th century, although a wing was added in 1952:

the trade-off is between the more-charming decor in the older rooms and the better lake views from the newer ones. In summer a three-night minimum stay and half board are required. ✉ *Via Grotte 6, 25010* ☎*030/9905890* 🖷*030/916390* ⊕*www.palacehotelvillacortine.com* 🛏*40 rooms* ◇*In-hotel: restaurant, bar, tennis court, pool, beachfront, parking (no fee)* ▭*AE, DC, MC, V* ⊙*Closed late Oct.–mid-Apr.* ¶◎*MAP.*

$$$–$$$$ 🛏 **Hotel Sirmione.** Just inside the city walls, near the Castello, this hotel and spa sits amid lakeside gardens and terraces. Rooms are furnished with comfortable Scandinavian slat beds, matching floral draperies and wall coverings, and built-in white furniture. Many guests have been returning for years, due largely to the homey feel and the attentiveness of the staff. ✉*Piazza Castello 19, 25019* ☎*030/916192* 🖷*030/916558* ⊕*www.termedisirmione.com* 🛏*101 rooms* ◇*In-hotel: restaurant, bars, pool, spa, parking (fee)* ▭*AE, DC, MC, V* ¶◎*BP.*

TOWNS ALONG LAKE GARDA'S EASTERN SHORE

VISITOR INFORMATION
Malcesine tourism office (✉ *Via Capitanato 6/8* ☎*045/7400044* 🖷*045/7401633* ⊕*www.aptgardaveneto.com*).

Bardolino, famous for its red wine, hosts the Cura dell'Uva *(Grape Cure Festival)* in late September–early October. It's a great excuse to indulge in the local vino, which is light, dry, and often slightly sparkling. (Bring aspirin, just in case the cure turns out to be worse than the disease.) Bardolino is one of the most popular summer resorts on the lake. It stands on the eastern shore at the wider end of the lake. Here there are two handsome Romanesque churches: **San Severo,** from the 11th century, and **San Zeno,** from the 9th. Both are in the center of the small town.

Just about everyone agrees that **Punta San Vigilio** is the prettiest spot on Garda's eastern shore. The highlight is the cypress-filled gardens of the 15th-century **Villa Guarienti di Brenzone** (✉*Frazione Punta San Vigilio 1*). You can visit the gardens, but the villa itself is closed to the public.

Malcesine, about 30 km (20 mi) north of Punta San Vigilio, is one of the loveliest areas along the upper eastern shore of Lake Garda. It's principally known as a summer resort, with sailing and windsurfing schools. It tends to be crowded in season, but there are nice walks from the town toward the mountains. Six ski lifts and more than 11 km (7 mi) of runs of varying degrees of difficulty serve skiers. Dominating the town is the 12th-century **Castello Scaligero,** built by Verona's dynastic Della Scala family.

The futuristic *funivia* (cable car) zipping visitors to the top of **Monte Baldo** (5,791 feet) is unique because it rotates. After a 10-minute ride you're high in the Veneto, where you can stroll while enjoying spectacular views of the lake. You can ride the cable car down or bring along a mountain bike (or hang glider) for the descent. ✉ *Via Navene Vecchia*

12 ☎045/7400206 🌐www.funiviamalcesine.com 🎟€13 round-trip ⏲Daily 8–4.

RIVA DEL GARDA

18 km (11 mi) north of Malcesine, 180 km (112 mi) east of Milan.

VISITOR INFORMATION

Riva del Garda tourism office (*✉Giardini di Porta Orientale 8 ☎0464/554444 📠0464/520308 🌐www.gardatrentino.it*).

EXPLORING

Set on the northern tip of Lake Garda against a dramatic backdrop of jagged cliffs and miles of beaches, Riva del Garda is the lake's quintessential resort town. The old city, set around a pretty harbor, was built up during the 15th century, when it was a strategic outpost of the Venetian Republic.

The heart of Riva del Garda, the lakeside **Piazza 3 Novembre** is surrounded by medieval palazzi. Standing in the piazza and looking out onto the lake you can understand why Riva del Garda has become a windsurfing mecca: air currents ensure good breezes on even the most sultry midsummer days.

The **Torre Apponale,** predating the Venetian period by three centuries, looms above the medieval residences of the main square; its crenellations recall its defensive purpose.

WHERE TO STAY & EAT

$$$ ✕ **Castel Toblino.** A lovely stop for a lakeside drink or a romantic dinner, this castle is right on a lake in Sarche, about 20 km (12 mi) north of Riva toward Trento. The compound is said to have been a prehistoric, then Roman, village, and was later associated with the Church of Trento. Bernardo Clesio had it rebuilt in the 16th century in the Renaissance style. It's now a sanctuary of fine food, serving such local specialties as lake fish and guinea fowl. *✉Via Caffaro 1, Sarche ☎0461/864036 💳MC, V ⏲Closed Tues. and mid-Nov.–Feb.*

$$$–$$$$ 🏨 **Hotel du Lac et du Parc.** Riva's most splendid hotel has elegance befitting its cosmopolitan name, with personalized service rarely found on Lake Garda since its aristocratic heyday. The airy public spaces include a dining room, bar, and beautifully manicured private garden leading to the public beach. The rooms are well appointed and comfortable; be sure to ask for air-conditioning. The outdoor pool has separate areas for adults and children. *✉Viale Rovereto 44, 38066 ☎0464/566600 📠0464/566566 🌐www.dulacetduparc.com 🛏164 rooms, 5 suites In-hotel: 2 restaurants, bar, tennis courts, pools, gym, beachfront, parking (no fee) 💳DC, MC, V ⏲Closed Nov.–Mar. 🍽BP.*

$$$ 🏨 **Hotel Sole.** Within a lakeside 15th-century palazzo in the center of town, this lovely, understated hotel offers comfortable, affordable rooms. The terraced front rooms open to breathtaking views of the lake, and a secluded rooftop terrace is a perfect retreat from crowded beaches in summer. *✉Piazza 3 Novembre 35, 38066 ☎0464/552686 📠0464/552811 🌐www.hotelsole.net 🛏52 rooms In-room: safe,* *refrigerator. In-hotel: restaurant, room service, bar, bicycles, parking (fee)* ☰*AE, DC, MC, V* ⭘|*BP.*

\$\$–\$\$\$ ⬚ **Luise.** This cozy, reasonably priced hotel has great amenities, including a big garden and a large swimming pool. The restaurant, La Limonaia, is recommended for its Trentino specialties. ✉*Viale Rovereto 9, 38066* ☎*0464/550858* 🖷*0464/554250* ⊕*www.feelinghotelluise.com* ➘*68 rooms* ♿*In-hotel: restaurant, tennis court, pool, laundry facilities* ☰*AE, DC, MC, V* ⭘|*BP.*

EN ROUTE After passing the town of Limone—where it is said the first lemon trees in Europe were planted—take the fork to the right about 5 km (3 mi) north of Gargnano and head to Tignale. The view from the Madonna di Monte Castello church, some 2,000 feet above the lake, is spectacular. Adventurous travelers will want to follow this pretty inland mountain road to Tremosine; be warned that the road winds its way up the mountain through hairpin turns and blind corners that can test even the most experienced drivers.

GARGNANO

6

30 km (19 mi) south of Riva del Garda, 144 km (89 mi) east of Milan.

EXPLORING

This small port town was an important Franciscan center in the 13th century, and now comes alive in the summer months when German tourists, many of whom have villas here, crowd the small pebble beach. An Austrian flotilla bombarded the town in 1866, and some of the houses still bear marks of cannon fire. Mussolini owned two houses in Gargnano: one is now a language school and the other, Villa Feltrinelli, has been restored and reopened as a luxury hotel.

WHERE TO STAY & EAT

\$\$\$\$ ✕ **La Tortuga.** This rustic trattoria is more sophisticated than it first appears, with an extensive wine cellar and nouvelle-style twists on local dishes. Specialties include *agnello con rosmarino e timo* (lamb with rosemary and thyme), *persico con rosmarino* (perch with rosemary), and *carpaccio d'anatra all'aceto balsamico* (duck carpaccio with balsamic vinegar). ✉*Via XXIV Maggio at small harbor* ☎*0365/71251* 🖷*0365/71938* ☰*DC, MC, V* ⊗*Closed Tues. No lunch Dec.–Mar.*

\$\$\$\$ ⬚ **Villa Feltrinelli.** This 1892 art nouveau villa hotel, named for the Italian publishing family that used to vacation here, is immersed in private gardens and faces the lake. Meticulously restored, it has frescoed ceilings, wood paneling, and original tile floors. The rooms are spacious and equipped with every luxury (as befits the final bill). If you can afford it, take the tower room. There's an extensive library open to guests. ✉*Via Rimembranza 38/40, 25084* ☎*0365/798000* 🖷*0365/798001* ⊕*www.villafeltrinelli.com* ➘*21 rooms* ♿*In-hotel: restaurant, room service, bar, pool, laundry service* ☰*AE, DC, MC, V* ⊗*Closed late Oct.–Easter* ⭘|*BP.*

¢ ⬚ **Hotel Bartabel.** This cozy hotel on the main street offers comfortable accommodations at a rock-bottom price. The restaurant has an elegant terrace overlooking the lake. ✉ *Via Roma 39, 25084* ☎*0365/713300* 🖷*0365/790009* ⇆*10 rooms* ☍*In-room: no a/c. In-hotel: restaurant* ▤*AE, DC, MC, V* ♥*Closed mid- to late Nov.–late Dec. Restaurant closed Mon.* ❢*EP.*

SPORTS & THE OUTDOORS

The **Upper Brescian Garda Park** stretches over nine municipalities on the western side of the lake, from Salò to Limone, covering 380 square km (147 square mi). Call the **Limone Hotel Owners Association** (✉ *Via Quattro Novembre 2/c* ☎*0365/954720*) for trail and bicycle-rental information. They're also the people to contact if you'd like to take part in one of the free treks led by the Gruppo Alpini Limone every Sunday from June to September.

GARDONE RIVIERA

12 km (7 mi) south of Gargnano, 139 km (86 mi) east of Milan.

Gardone Riviera, a once-fashionable 19th-century resort now delightfully faded, is the former home of the flamboyant Gabriele d'Annunzio (1863–1938), one of Italy's greatest modern poets. D'Annunzio's estate, **Il Vittoriale,** perched on the hills above the town, is an elaborate memorial to himself, filled with the trappings of conquests in art, love, and war (of which the largest is a ship's prow in the garden), and complete with an imposing mausoleum. ✉*Gardone Riviera* ☎*0365/296511* ⊕*www. vittoriale.it* 🖘*€11 for house or museum, €16 for both* ♥*Grounds: Apr.–Sept., daily 8:30–8; Oct.–Mar., daily 9–5. House and museum: Apr.–Sept., Tues.–Sun. 9:30–7; Oct.–Mar., Tues.–Sun. 9–1 and 2–5.*

More than 2,000 Alpine, subtropical, and Mediterranean species thrive at the **Giardino Botanico Hruska.** ✉*Via Roma* ☎*0365/20347* 🖘*€7* ♥*Mar. 15–Oct. 15, daily 9:30–6:30.*

OFF THE
BEATEN
PATH

Salò Market. Four kilometers (2½ mi) south of Gardone Riviera is the enchanting lakeside town of Salò, which history buffs may recognize as the capital of the ill-fated Social Republic set up in 1943 by the Germans after they liberated Mussolini from the Gran Sasso. Every Saturday morning an enormous market is held in the Piazza dei Martiri della Libertà, with great bargains on everything from household goods to clothing to foodstuffs. In August or September a lone vendor often sells locally unearthed *tartufi neri* (black truffles) at affordable prices.

WHERE TO STAY & EAT

★ $$$–$$$$ ✕🖬 **Villa Fiordaliso.** The pink-and-white lakeside Villa Fiordaliso—once home to Claretta Petacci, given to her by Benito Mussolini—is a high-quality restaurant, but it also has seven tastefully furnished rooms, some overlooking the lake. The Claretta Suite is where Mussolini and Petacci were said to have carried on an affair. The art nouveau restaurant ($$$–$$$$) features seasonal ingredients such as zucchini flowers and porcini mushrooms, paramount in salads and soups. ✉*Corso Zanardelli 15025083* ☎*0365/20158* 🖷*0365/290011* ⊕*www.villafiordaliso.it* ⇆*6 rooms, 1 suite* ☍*In-hotel: restaurant, no elevator,* *parking (no fee)* ☐ *AE, DC, MC, V* ☺ *Closed mid-Nov.–mid-Feb. Restaurant closed Mon. No lunch Tues.* ¶◎|*BP.*

★ $$$–$$$$ ⚄ **Villa del Sogno.** A narrow winding road takes you from town to this imposing villa, which surveys the valley and the lake below it. The large hotel terrace and the quiet surrounding grounds create a sense of escape. You may think twice about a busy sightseeing itinerary once you've settled into position in the sun, cool drink in hand. ☒ *Corso Zanardelli 107, 52083* ☎ *0365/290181* ☐ *0365/290230* ⊕ *www.villadelsogno.it* ⟿ *26 rooms, 5 suites* ⚲ *In-hotel: restaurant, tennis court, pool* ☐ *AE, DC, MC, V* ☺ *Closed late Oct.–late Mar.* ¶◎|*BP.*

$$–$$$$ ⚄ **Grand Hotel Fasano.** A former 19th-century hunting lodge between Gardone and Maderno, the Fasano has matured into a seasonal hotel of a high standard. To one side you face the deep waters of Lake Garda; on the others you're surrounded by a 31,080-square-km (12,000-square-mi) private park where the original Austrian owners no doubt spent their days chasing game. Besides myriad activities on the water, there are two golf courses in the vicinity. All the rooms have a lake view. There are older rooms filled with antiques, but these lack air-conditioning. ☒ *Corso Zanardelli 190, 25083* ☎ *0365/290220* ☐ *0365/290221* ⊕ *www.ghf.it* ⟿ *68 rooms* ⚲ *In-room: no a/c (some). In-hotel: restaurant, tennis court, pool, beachfront, parking (no fee)* ☐ *No credit cards* ☺ *Closed mid-Oct.–mid-May* ¶◎|*BP.*

★ $$–$$$ ⚄ **Gran Hotel Gardone.** Directly facing the lake, this majestic 1800s palace is surrounded by an attractive landscaped garden. Nearly all the rooms look out over the water, and all bathrooms have been renovated in marble. The ground-floor Winnie's Bar, named after Winston Churchill, a frequent guest, envelopes you in charming art nouveau furniture and decorations. ☒ *Via Zanardelli 84, 25083* ☎ *0365/20261* ☐ *0365/22695* ⊕ *www.grangardone.it* ⟿ *143 rooms, 25 suites* ⚲ *In-hotel: pool, laundry service, parking (fee)* ☐ *AE, DC, MC, V* ☺ *Closed mid-Oct.–Mar.* ¶◎|*BP.*

¢ ⚄ **Villa Maria Elisabetta.** Many of the rooms in this charming hotel run by a group of hospitable nuns have views of Lago di Garda. You can sit in the hotel's garden or take one of the ground's trails down for a dip in the lake or a bask in the sun. ☒ *Corso Zanardelli 180, 25083* ☎ *0365/20206* ☐ *0365/2020818* ⟿ *42 rooms* ⚲ *In-room: no a/c, no TV. In-hotel: restaurant, bar* ☐ *No credit cards* ☺ *Closed Oct. 18–Dec. 18* ¶◎|*BP.*

LAKE COMO

If your idea of nirvana is palatial villas, rose-laden belvederes, hanging wisteria and bougainvillea, lanterns casting a glow over lake-shore restaurants, and majestic Alpine vistas, heaven is Lake Como. In his *Charterhouse of Parma*, Stendhal described it as an "enchanting spot, unequaled on earth in its loveliness." Virgil called it simply "our greatest" lake. Though summer crowds threaten to diminish the lake's dreamy mystery and slightly faded old-money gentility, the allure of this spectacular place endures. Como remains a consummate pairing of natural and man-made beauty. The villa gardens, like so many in Italy, are a union of two landscape traditions: that of Renaissance Italy, which values order, and that of Victorian England, which strives to create the illusion of natural wildness. Such gardens are often framed by vast areas of picturesque farmland—fruit trees, olive groves, and vineyards.

Lake Como is some 47 km (30 mi) long north to south and is Europe's deepest lake (almost 1,350 feet). Como itself is a leading textile center famous for its silks. Many travelers hasten to the vaporetti waiting to take them to Bellagio and the *centro di lago,* the center region of the lake's three branches, and its most beautiful section. The 2,000-year-old walled city of Como should not be missed, however. Car ferries traverse the lake in season, making it easy to get to the other main towns, Cernobbio, Tremezzo, and Varenna. Remember that Como is extremely seasonal: if you go to Bellagio, for example, from November through February, you will find nothing open—not a bar, restaurant, or shop.

GETTING HERE

Trains run regularly from Milan to the town of Como; the trip takes from half an hour to an hour, depending on the type of train. There's also service to the tiny town of Varenna, just across the lake from Bellagio; the trip from Milan takes 1¼ hours. Como is off the A9 autostrada. To get to the town from Milan, take A8 to A9; the drive takes about an hour.

BELLAGIO

Fodor'sChoice
★   *30 km (19 mi) northeast of Como, 56 km (35 mi) northwest of Bergamo.*

VISITOR INFORMATION

Bellagio tourism office (⊠ *Piazza Mazzini [Pontile Imbarcadero]* 🕾🕾 *031/950204* ⊕ *www.bellagiolakecomo.com*).

EXPLORING

Sometimes called the prettiest town in Europe, Bellagio always seems to be flag-bedecked, with geraniums ablaze in every window and bougainvillea veiling the staircases, or *montées,* that thread through the town. At dusk Bellagio's nightspots—including the wharf, where an orchestra serenades dancers under the stars—beckon you to come and make merry. It's an impossibly enchanting location, one that inspired French composer Gabriel Fauré to call Bellagio "a diamond contrasting brilliantly with the sapphires of the three lakes in which it is set."

Boats ply the lake to Tremezzo, where Napoléon's worst Italian enemy, Count Sommariva, resided at Villa Carlotta; and a bit farther south of Tremezzo, to Villa Balbianello. Check with the **Bellagio tourist office** (⊠ *Piazza Mazzini [Pontile Imbarcadero]* 🕾 *031/950204* ⊕ *www.bellagiolakecomo.com*) for the hours of the launch to Tremezzo.

★   **Villa Serbelloni,** a property of the Rockefeller Foundation, has celebrated gardens on the site of Pliny the Elder's villa overlooking Bellagio. There

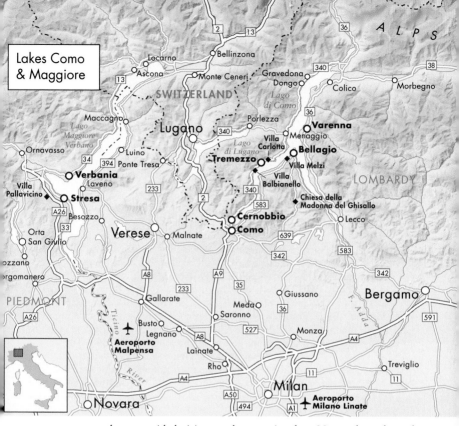

Lakes Como & Maggiore

are only two guided visits per day, restricted to 30 people each, and in May these tend to be commandeered by group bookings. ✉ *Near Palazza della Chiesa* ☎ *031/950204* ✉ *€5* ⊙ *Guided visits Apr.–Oct., Tues.–Sun. at 11 and 4; tours gather 15 mins before start.*

The famous gardens of the **Villa Melzi** were once a favorite picnic spot for Franz Lizst, who advised author Louis de Ronchaud in 1837: "When you write the story of two happy lovers, place them on the shores of Lake Como. I do not know of any land so conspicuously blessed by heaven." The gardens are open to the public, and though you can't get into the 19th-century villa, don't miss the lavish Empire-style family chapel. The Melzi were Napoléon's greatest allies in Italy (the family has passed down the name "Josephine" to the present day). ✉ *Via Lungolago Marconi* ☎ *031/951281* ✉ *€5* ⊙ *Apr.–Oct., daily 9–6.*

By ferry from Bellagio it's a quick trip across the lake to Varenna. The principal sight here is the spellbinding garden of the **Villa Monastero**, which, as its name suggests, was originally a monastery. Now it's an international science and convention center. ✉ *Varenna* ☎ *0341/295450* ✉ *€2* ⊙ *Apr.–Oct., daily 9–7.*

WHERE TO STAY & EAT

$$ ✕⌂ **La Pergola.** Try to reserve a table on the terrace at this popular lakeside restaurant about 1 km (½ mi) from Bellagio, on the other side of the peninsula. The best dining option is the freshly caught fish. You can also stay in one of the inn's 11 rooms, all of which have baths. ⊠ *Piazza del PorteP-escallo, 22021* ☎*031/950263* 🖷*031/950253* ⊕*www.lapergolabellagio.it* 🛏*11 rooms* ⌂*In-hotel: restaurant* ▤*AE, MC, V* ⊙*Restaurant closed Tues.* ⦿*BP.*

$ ✕⌂ **Silvio.** At the edge of town, this family-owned trattoria with a lakeshore terrace specializes in fresh fish. Served cooked or marinated, with risotto or as a ravioli stuffing, the fish is caught by Silvio's family—it's local cooking at its best. Many of the modestly priced guest rooms have balconies and lake views. ⊠*Lòppia di Bellagio, Via Carcano 10, 22021* ☎*031/950322* ⊕*www.bellagiosilvio.com* 🛏*21 rooms, 9 apartments* ⌂*In-hotel: restaurant* ▤*MC, V* ⊙*Closed Jan. and Feb.* ⦿*BP.*

★ $$$$ ⌂ **Grand Hotel Villa Serbelloni.** Designed to cradle nobility in high style, this hotel is a refined haven for the discreetly wealthy, set within a pretty park down the road from the Punta di Bellagio. The sense of 19th-century luxury has not so much faded as mellowed: the rooms are immaculate and plush; public areas are gilt and marble with thick, colorful carpets. The staff is unobtrusive and very knowledgeable about lake transportation. Churchill's and John Kennedy's former rooms face the Tremezzina, a group of towns across the lake. ⊠*Via Roma 1, 22021* ☎*031/950216* 🖷*031/951529* ⊕*www.villaserbelloni.it* 🛏*81 rooms* ⌂*In-hotel: 2 restaurants, room service, tennis court, pools, gym, laundry service, public Internet, parking (no fee)* ▤*AE, DC, MC, V* ⊙*Closed mid-Nov.–early Apr.* ⦿*BP.*

$$$ ⌂ **Du Lac.** In the center of Bellagio, by the landing dock, this comfortable, medium-size hotel owned by an Anglo-Italian family has a relaxed and congenial feel. Most rooms have views of the lake and mountains, and there's a rooftop terrace garden for drinks or dozing. ⊠*Piazza Mazzini 32, 22021* ☎*031/950320* 🖷*031/951624* 🛏*48 rooms* ⌂*In-hotel: 2 restaurants, bar, parking (no fee)* ▤*MC, V* ⊙*Closed Nov.–Mar.* ⦿*BP.*

$$–$$$ ⌂ **Hotel Florence.** This villa dating from the 1880s has an impressive lobby with vaulted ceiling and an imposing Florentine fireplace. Most of the rooms, furnished with interesting antiques, are large and comfortable and have splendid views of the lake. The restaurant and bar draw locals and visitors who appreciate the friendly and helpful staff. The hotel is across from the ferry stop. ⊠*Piazza Mazzini 46, 22021* ☎*031/950342* 🖷*031/951722* ⊕*www.hotelflorencebellagio.it* 🛏*30 rooms* ⌂*In-room: no a/c. In-hotel: restaurant, bar, spa* ▤*AE, MC, V* ⊙*Closed Nov.–Mar.* ⦿*MAP.*

★ $–$$$ ⌂ **Hotel Belvedere.** In Italian, belvedere means "beautiful view," and it's an apt name for this enchanting spot. The hotel has been in the Martinelli-Manoni family since 1880, and the unbroken tradition of service makes it one of the best places to stay in town. Antique chairs and eye-catching rugs complement the modern rooms, many of which have balconies and views of the lake. The marble bathrooms are designed for comfort. Outstanding terraced gardens have replaced the vineyards that once surrounded the house. The restaurant is very good. ⊠ *Via Valassina 31, 22021* ☎*031/950410* 🖷*031/950102* ⊕*www.belvedere-bellagio.com* ⇦*62 rooms* ⌂*In-room: no a/c. In-hotel: restaurant, bar, pool, parking (no fee)* ☰*AE, DC, MC, V* ⊗*Closed Nov.–Mar.* ⦿*BP.*

TREMEZZO

34 km (21 mi) north of Cernobbio, 78 km (48 mi) north of Milan.

VISITOR INFORMATION

Tremezzo tourism office (⊠*Piazzale Trieste* ☎*0344/40493* ⊕*www.tremezzina.com*).

EXPLORING

If you're lucky enough to visit the small lakeside town of Tremezzo in late spring or early summer, you will find the magnificent **Villa Carlotta** a riot of color, with more than 14 acres of azaleas and dozens of varieties of rhododendrons in full bloom. The height of the blossoms is late April to early May. The villa was built between 1690 and 1743 for the luxury-loving marquis Giorgio Clerici. The garden's collection is remarkable, particularly considering the difficulties of transporting delicate plants before the age of aircraft. Palms, banana trees, cacti, eucalyptus, a sequoia, orchids, and camellias are counted among the more than 500 species.

The villa's interior is worth a visit, particularly if you have a taste for the romantic sculptures of Antonio Canova (1757–1822). The best known is his *Cupid and Psyche,* which depicts the lovers locked in an odd but graceful embrace, with the young god above and behind, his wings extended, while Psyche awaits a kiss that will never come. The villa can be reached by boats from Bellagio. ☎*0344/40405* ⊕*www. villacarlotta.it* 🖾*€7* ⊗*Apr.–Sept., daily 9–6; Mar. and Oct., daily 9–11:30 and 2–4:30.*

Villa Balbianello may be the most magical house in all of Italy. It sits on its own little promontory, Il Dosso d'Avedo—separating the bays of Venus and Diana—around the bend from the tiny fishing village of Ossuccio. Relentlessly picturesque, the villa is composed of loggias, terraces, and *palazzini* (tiny palaces), all spilling down verdant slopes to the lakeshore, where you'll find an old Franciscan church, a magnificent stone staircase, and a statue of San Carlo Borromeo blessing the waters. The villa is most frequently reached by launch from Como and Bellagio. Check with the **Como tourism office** (☎*031/269712*) for hours. Visits are usually restricted to the gardens, but if you plan in advance it's also possible to tour the villa itself. You pay €30 for a guide—regardless of how many are in your party—and an additional €5 entrance fee. ⊠*Il Dosso d'Avedo* ☎*0344/56110* 🖾*Gardens €5* ⊗*Apr.–Oct., daily 10–6. Pedestrian entrance open Tues. and weekends, otherwise by boat only.*

WHERE TO STAY

$$$$ 🏨 **Grand Hotel Tremezzo.** One hundred windows of this turn-of-the-20th-century building face the lake. The hotel, in the middle of a private park stretching over 12½ acres, has many creature comforts, from three heated swimming pools (one of them actually floats on pontoons on the lake) and private landing on the lake to a hillside bursting with flowers. The 18-hole Menaggio & Cadenabbia golf course is about five minutes away by car. ⊠ *Via Regina 8, 22019* ☎*0344/42491* 📠*0344/40201* ⊕*www.grandhoteltremezzo.com* 🛏*98 rooms, 2 suites* ⚐ *In-hotel: 2 restaurants, room service, bars, tennis court, pools, gym, parking (no fee)* ⊟*AE, DC, MC, V* ☉*Closed mid-Nov.–Feb.* 🍴*BP.*

$ 🏨 **Rusall.** On the hillside above Tremezzo in the midst of a large garden, this small and reasonably priced hotel offers quiet and privacy. You can lie out on the terrace and enjoy a nice view. Rooms are simple and comfortable. ⊠ *Via San Martino 2, 22019* ☎*0344/40408* 📠*0344/40447* ⊕*www.rusallhotel.com* 🛏*23 rooms* ⚐*In-room: no a/c (some). In-hotel: restaurant, bar, tennis court, no elevator* ⊟*AE, DC, MC, V* 🍴*EP.*

CERNOBBIO

5 km (3 mi) north of Como, 53 km (34 mi) north of Milan.

VISITOR INFORMATION

Cernobbio tourism office (⊠ *Via Regina* ☎📠*031/510198*).

EXPLORING

The legendary resort of Villa d'Este is reason enough to visit this jewel on the lake, but the town itself is worth a stroll. Despite the fact that George Clooney lunches here regularly, the place still has a neighborhood feel to it, especially on summer evenings and weekends when the piazza is full of families and couples taking their *passeggiata* (stroll).

Built over the course of roughly 45 years for fisherman-turned-cardinal Tolomeo Gallio, the **Villa d'Este** has had a colorful and somewhat checkered history since its completion in 1615, swinging wildly between extremes of grandeur and dereliction. Its tenants have included the Jesuits, two generals, a ballerina, Caroline of Brunswick—the disgraced and estranged wife of the future king of England, George IV—a family of ordinary Italian nobles, and, finally, a czarina of Russia. Its life as a private summer residence ended in 1873, when it was turned into the fashionable hotel it has remained ever since.

WHERE TO STAY & EAT

$$ ✕ **Il Gatto Nero.** This restaurant in the hills above Cernobbio has a splendid view of the lake. Specialties include *filetto con aceto balsamico* (filet mignon with balsamic vinegar), *pappardelle al ragù di selvaggini* (pasta with wild game sauce), and lake fish. Save room for the warm chocolate torte with its delicious liquid chocolate center. Reservations are encouraged as this is a regular haunt of Italian soccer stars as well as the jet set. ⊠ *Via Monte Santo 69, Rovenna* ☎*031/512042* ⊟*AE, DC, V* ☉*Closed Mon. No lunch Tues.*

¢–$ ✕ **Pizzeria L'Ancora.** For the best pies in Como, and perhaps in the region, you won't want to miss this local haunt, run by a Neapolitan family that has been making pizza for three generations. Even Italians from out of town rave about the pizza here. Three sisters— Barbara, Grazie, and Linda—dish out hospitality as fine as the food. ⊠ *Via Conciliazione 12, Tavernola* ☎ *031/340769* ▭ *No credit cards* ⊘ *Closed Wed.*

$$$$ 🏨 **Villa d'Este.** One of the grandest hotels in Italy, the 17th-century

Fodor's Choice   Villa d'Este has long welcomed Europe's rich and famous, from

★   Napoléon to the Duchess of Windsor. The chandeliers in the vast lobby illuminate marble staircases leading to guest rooms furnished in the Empire style: walnut paneling, sofas in striped silk, and gorgeous antiques. A broad veranda sweeps out to the lakefront, where a swimming pool extends above the water. The fanciful pavilions, temples, miniature forts, and mock ruins make for an afternoon's walk of quietly whimsical surprises. ⊠ *Via Regina 40, 22012* ☎ *031/3481* 🖷 *031/348844* ⊕ *www.villadeste.it* ⟿ *152 rooms, 8 suites* ⚒ *In-room: ethernet. In-hotel: 3 restaurants, room service, bar, tennis courts, pools, spa, laundry service, parking (no fee)* ▭ *AE, MC, V* ⊘ *Closed mid-Nov.–Feb.* ⦿ *FAP.*

COMO

5 km (3 mi) south of Cernobbio, 30 km (19 mi) southwest of Bellagio, 49 km (30 mi) north of Milan.

VISITOR INFORMATION

Como tourism office (⊠ *Piazza Cavour 17* ☎ *031/269712* 🖷 *031/240111* ⊕ *www.lakecomo.org*).

EXPLORING

Como, on the south shore of the lake, is only part elegant resort, where cobbled pedestrian streets wind their way past parks and bustling cafés. The other part is an industrial town renowned for its fine silks. If you're traveling by car, leave it at the edge of the town center in the clean, well-lighted underground parking facility right on the lake.

The splendid 15th-century Renaissance-Gothic **Duomo** was begun in 1396. The facade was added in 1455, and the transepts were completed in the mid-18th century. The dome was designed by Filippo Juvara (1678–1736), chief architect of many of the sumptuous palaces of the royal house of Savoy. The facade has statues of two of Como's most famous sons, Pliny the Elder and Pliny the Younger, whose writings are among the most important documents from antiquity. Inside, the works of art include Luini's *Holy Conversation,* a fresco cycle by Morazzone, and the *Marriage of the Virgin Mary* by Ferrari. ⊠ *Piazza del Duomo* ⊘ *Daily 7–noon and 3–7.*

At the heart of Como's medieval quarter, the city's first cathedral, **San Fedele,** is worth a peek, if only because it is one of the oldest churches in the region. ⊠ *Piazza San Fedele* ⊘ *Daily 7–noon and 3–7.*

6

If you brave Como's industrial quarter, you will find the beautiful church of **Sant'Abbondio,** a gem of Romanesque architecture begun by Benedictine monks in 1013 and consecrated by Pope Urban II in 1095. Inside, the five aisles of the church converge on a presbytery with a semicircular apse decorated with a cycle of 14th-century frescoes—now restored to their original magnificence—by Lombard artists heavily influenced by the Sienese school. In the nave the cubical capitals are the earliest example of this style in Italy. ⊠ *Via Sant'Abbondio* ⊘ *Daily 7–6.*

Exhibiting the path of production from silkworm litters to *moiré*-finishing machinery, the **Museo Didattico della Seta** *(Silk Museum)* is small but complete. The museum preserves the history of a manufacturing region that continues to supply almost three-fourths of Europe's silk. The friendly staffers will give you an overview of the museum; they are also happy to provide brochures and information about local retail shops. The museum's location isn't well marked: follow the textile school's driveway around to the low-rise concrete building on the left, and follow the shallow ramp down to the entrance. ⊠ *Via Velleggio 3* ☎ *031/303180* ⊕ *www.museosetacomo.com* ⊠€8 ⊘ *Tues.–Fri. 9–noon and 3–6. Tours in English available by reservation.*

WHERE TO STAY & EAT

$$–$$$ ✕ **Raimondi.** This elegant restaurant in the Hotel Villa Flori (2 km [1 mi] toward Cernobbio) offers good value and a superb location, with a large terrace poised over the lake. The local freshwater fish is your best option, but a wide range of Italian dishes is capably prepared. The restaurant's season is longer than most, owing to its popularity with local residents. ⊠ *Via Cernobbio 12* ☎ *031/338233* ▤ *AE, DC, MC, V* ⊘ *Closed Mon. and Dec.–Feb. 14. No lunch Sat.*

★ $$–$$$ ✕▥ **Terminus.** Commanding a panoramic view over Lake Como, this early-20th-century art nouveau building is the city's finest hotel. The marbled public spaces have an understated elegance, and the guest rooms are done in floral patterns and furnished with large walnut wardrobes and silk-covered sofas. In summer the garden terrace is perfect for relaxing over a drink. Bar delle Terme (¢–$), the candelit restaurant, is worth a trip. The cranberry-hue space, filled with plush velvet sofas, resembles a large living room. The food and service are as fine as the decor. Reservations are strongly advised, as there are only a few tables. It is closed Tuesday. ⊠ *Lungolario Trieste 14, 22100* ☎ *031/329111* ▤ *031/302550* ⊕ *www.albergoterminus.com* ⤶ *40 rooms* ⊘ *In-room: safe, dial-up. In-hotel: restaurant, parking (no fee)* ▤ *AE, DC, MC, V* ▥ *EP.*

$$–$$$ ▥ **Villa Flori.** Italian patriot Garibaldi spent his wedding night here, in a suite that now bears his name. The hotel enjoys a panoramic view of Lake Como and attracts locals with its highly acclaimed restaurant, Raimondi. ⊠ *Via Cernobbio 12, 22100* ☎ *031/33820* ▤ *031/570379* ⊕ *www.hotelvillaflori.com* ⤶ *45 rooms* ⊘ *In-hotel: restaurant* ▤ *AE, DC, MC, V* ▥ *EP.*

$ ▥ **Tre Re.** This clean, spacious, welcoming hotel is a few steps west of the cathedral and convenient to the lake. Although the exterior gives away the age of this 16th-century former convent, the rooms are airy, comfortable, and modern. The moderately priced restaurant shares an ample terrace with the hotel. ⊠ *Via Boldoni 20, 22100* ☎ *031/265374* ▤ *031/241349*

⊕*www.hoteltrere.com* ⟵*41 rooms* ♨ *In-hotel: restaurant, bar, parking (no fee)* ▤*MC, V* ⊗*Closed mid-Dec.–mid-Jan.* ℹ❙*BP.*

SPORTS & THE OUTDOORS

The lake has many opportunities for sports enthusiasts, from windsurfing at the lake's northern end, to boating, sailing, and jet skiing at Como and Cernobbio. The lake is also quite swimmable in the summer months. For hikers there are lovely paths all around the lake. For an easy trek, take the funicular up to Brunate, and walk along the mountain to the lighthouse for a stunning view of the lake. For more information, contact the **tourism office** (⊠*Piazza Cavour 17* ☎*031/269712*). Varese, ideally nestled in the soft hills of the lake district and known as la Città Verde (the Green City), will host a prestigious world championship bicycling event, the Ciclismo Mondiale, in September 2008. It is a spectacular event to witness, especially when combined with the beauty of the lakes. For more information, see ⊕*www.varese2008.org.*

LAKE MAGGIORE

Magnificently scenic, Lake Maggiore has a unique geographical position: its mountainous western shore is in Piedmont, its lower eastern shore is in Lombardy, and its northern tip is in Switzerland. The lake stretches nearly 50 km (30 mi) and is up to 5 km (3 mi) wide. The better-known resorts are on the western shore.

GETTING HERE

Trains run regularly from Milan to the town of Stresa on Lake Maggiore; the trip takes from an hour to an hour and a half, depending on the type of train. By car from Milan to Stresa, take the A8 autostrada to A8dir, and from A8dir take A26; the drive is about 1¼ hours.

STRESA & THE ISOLE BORROMEE

16 km (10 mi) east of Orta San Giulio, 80 km (50 mi) northwest of Milan.

VISITOR INFORMATION

Stresa tourism office (⊠*Piazza Marconi 16* ☎*0323/30150* ⊟*0323/32561* ⊕*www.distrettolaghi.it*).

One of the better-known resorts on the western shore, Stresa is a tourist town that provided one of the settings for Hemingway's *A Farewell to Arms.* It has capitalized on its central lakeside position and has to some extent become a victim of its own success. The luxurious elegance that distinguished its heyday has faded; the grand hotels are still grand, but traffic now encroaches upon their parks and gardens. Even the undeniable loveliness of the lakeshore drive has been threatened by the roar of diesel trucks and BMW traffic. The best way to escape is to head for the Isole Borromee (Borromean Islands) in Lake Maggiore.

As you wander around the palms and semitropical shrubs of **Villa Pallavicino,** don't be surprised if you're followed by a peacock or even an ostrich: they're part of the zoological garden and are allowed to roam almost at will. From the top of the hill on which the villa stands you can see the gentle hills of the Lombardy shore of Lake Maggiore and, nearer and to the left, the jewel-like Borromean Islands. In addition to a bar and restaurant, the grounds also have picnic spots. ⊠ *Via Sempione 8* ☎*0323/31533* ⊕*www.parcozoopallavicino.it* ⊠*€6.70* ۞*Early Mar.–Oct., daily 9–6.*

Boats to the **Isole Borromee** (⊕*www.borromeoturismo.it*) depart every 15–30 minutes from the dock at Stresa's Piazza Marconi. There is also a boat from Verbania; check locally for the seasonal schedule. Although you can hire a private boatman, it's cheaper and just as convenient to use the regular service. Make sure you buy a ticket allowing you to visit all the islands—Bella, Dei Pescatori, and Madre. The islands take their name from the Borromeo family, which has owned them since the 12th century.

Isola Bella *(Beautiful Island)* is the most famous of the three, and the first that you'll visit. It is named after Isabella, whose husband, Carlo III Borromeo (1538–84), built the palace and terraced gardens for her as a wedding present. Before Count Carlo began his project, the island was rocky and almost devoid of vegetation; the soil for the garden had to be transported from the mainland. Wander up the 10 terraces of the gardens, where peacocks roam among the scented shrubs, statues, and fountains, for a splendid view of the lake. Visit the palazzo to see the rooms where famous guests—including Napoléon and Mussolini—stayed in 18th-century splendor. ☎*0323/30556* ⊠*Garden and palazzo €10* ۞*Late Mar.–Oct., daily 9–5:30.*

Stop for a while at the tiny **Isola dei Pescatori** *(Island of the Fishermen)*, less than 100 yards wide and only about ½ km (¼ mi) long. It's the perfect place for a seafood lunch before, after, or in between your visit to the other two islands. Of the 10 or so restaurants on this tiny island, the three worth visiting are Ristorante Unione (☎*0323/933798*), Ristorante Verbano (☎*0323/30408*), and Ristorante Belvedere (☎*323/32292*). The island's little lanes strung with fishing nets and dotted with shrines to the Madonna are the definition of picturesque; little wonder that in high season the village is crowded with postcard stands.

Isola Madre *(Mother Island)* is nicknamed the "Botanical Island." The entire island is a botanical garden, whose season stretches from late March to late October due to the climatic protection of the mighty Alps and the tepid waters of Lago Maggiore. The vision of cacti and palm trees on Isola Madre, its position so far north and so near the border of Switzerland, is a beautiful and unexpected surprise. Take time to see the profusion of exotic trees and shrubs running down to the shore in every direction. Two special times to visit are April (for the camellias) and May (for azaleas and rhododendrons). Also on the island is a 16th-century palazzo, where an antique puppet theater is on display, complete with string puppets, prompt books, and elaborate scenery designed by Alessandro Sanquirico, who was a scenographer at La Scala in Milan. ☎*0323/31261* ⊠*€9* ۞*Late Mar.–Oct., daily 9–5:30.*

For more information about the islands, contact the **Stresa tourism office** (✉*Piazza Marconi 16* ☎*0323/30150*) or ask at the docks (look for Navigazione Lago Maggiore signs).

WHERE TO STAY

$$$$ Grand Hotel des Iles Borromées. This palatial establishment has catered to a demanding European clientele since 1863. And though it still has the spacious salons and lavish furnishings of the turn of the 20th century, it has been discreetly modernized. The bathrooms are luxurious. ✉*Corso Umberto I 67, 28838* ☎*0323/938938* ☎*0323/32405* ⊕*www.borromees.it* ↗*161 rooms, 11 suites* &In-room: ethernet. In-hotel: restaurant, room service, bar, tennis court, pool, spa, laundry service, public Wi-Fi, parking (no fee)* ☐*AE, DC, MC, V* ⫶*BP.*

$ Primavera. A few blocks up from the lake, Primavera has compact, simply furnished rooms in a 1950s building hung with flower boxes. Most rooms have balconies overlooking the streets of Stresa's old center. ✉*Via Cavour 39, 28838* ☎*0323/31286* ☎*0323/33458* ↗*34 rooms* &In-room: no a/c. In-hotel: bar, public Internet, parking (fee)* ☐*AE, DC, V* ⊙*Closed mid-Nov.–mid-Mar.* ⫶*BP.*

VERBANIA

6

16 km (10 mi) north of Stresa, 95 km (59 mi) northwest of Milan.

Quaint Verbania is across the Gulf of Pallanza from its touristy neighbor Stresa. It is known for the **Villa Taranto,** which has magnificent botanical gardens. The villa was acquired in 1931 by Scottish captain Neil McEachern, who expanded the gardens considerably, adding terraces, waterfalls, more than 3,000 plant species from all over the world, and broad meadows sloping gently to the lake. In 1938 McEachern donated the entire complex to the Italian people. ✉*Via Vittorio Veneto 111* ☎*0323/404555* ⊕*www.villataranto.it* ⫶*€8.50* ⊙*Late Mar.–Oct., daily 8:30–7; last admission 1 hr before closing.*

OFF THE BEATEN PATH

Santa Caterina del Sasso Ballaro. Near the town of Laveno, this beautiful lakeside hermitage was constructed in the 12th century by a local merchant to express his gratitude for having been saved from the wrath of a storm. It's particularly striking as you approach it by boat or ferry. About 20 km (12 mi) farther north on the eastern side of the lake, you will find comfortable and charming Liberty-style lodgings at the family-run **Camin Hotel Luino** ($$). ✉*Via Dante 35, 21016Luino* ☎*0332/530118* ☎*0332/537226* ⊕*www. caminhotelluino.com* ☐*AE, DC, MC, V.* ⫶*MAP.*

WHERE TO STAY & EAT

$–$$ Da Cesare. Off Piazza Cadorna and close to the embarcadero, this restaurant serves tasty risotto *con filetti di persico* (with perch fillets) and typical Piedmontese meat dishes, such as beef braised in Barolo wine. ✉*Via Mazzini 14* ☎*0323/31386* ☐*AE, DC, MC, V.*

$$$ Il Sole di Ranco. The same family has run this lakeside inn for Fodor's Choice more than 150 years. The latest addition is a stunning new pool with ★ views of the lake. The present chefs, Davide Brovelli and his father,

Carlo, do the family proud. Lake trout and perch find their way onto the menu, as do artichoke dishes in spring and eggplant in summer. Guest rooms are in two late-19th-century villas surrounded by a garden and overlooking the lake. Restaurant ($$–$$$) reservations are essential. ⊠*Piazza Venezia 5, Ranconear Angera* ☎*0331/976507* ⊟*0331/976620* ⊕*www.ilsolediranco.it* ⇨*14 rooms* ⌂*In-hotel: restaurant, pool* ⊟*AE, DC, MC, V* ⊗*Closed Dec. and Jan. Restaurant closed Tues. No lunch Mon.* ⦿|*BP.*

$ ⛉ **Il Chiostro.** Originally a 17th-century convent, this hotel expanded into the adjoining 19th-century textile factory, adding some conference facilities. Rooms are clean and functional. ⊠*Via Fratelli Cervi 14, 28900* ☎*0323/404077* ⊟*0323/401231* ⊕*www.chiostrovb.it* ⇨*100 rooms* ⌂*In-hotel: restaurant* ⊟*AE, DC, MC, V* ⦿|*BP.*

Piedmont &
Valle d'Aosta

WORD OF MOUTH

"Piedmont is way off the tourist track and as pretty as Tuscany...
Lots of wineries and wonderful undiscovered small towns."

—Barolo

WELCOME TO PIEDMONT & VALLE D'AOSTA

Landscape, Langhe

TOP REASONS TO GO

★ **Sacra di San Michele:** Explore one of the country's most spectacularly situated religious buildings.

★ **Castello Fénis:** This castle transports you back in time to the Middle Ages.

★ **Monte Bianco:** The cable car ride over the snowcapped mountain will take your breath away.

★ **Turin's Museo Egizio:** A surprising treasure—one of the word's richest collections of Egyptian art outside Cairo.

★ **Regal wines:** Some of Italy's most revered reds—led by Barolo, dubbed "the king wines"—come from the hills of southern Piedmont.

1 Turin. The region's main city isn't just the car capital of Italy and home to the Holy Shroud. Neoclassical piazzas, shops filled with chocolates and chic fashions, and elegant baroque palazzos have been restored in grand style.

2 The Colline. Gracing the "little hills" west of Turin are some opulent monuments of the 17th-century Piedmontese style, including the palace at **Stupinigi**, designed by Juvarra for the Savoy kings. Less worldly is the mesmerizingly medieval hilltop monastery of Sacra di San Michele.

3 Monferrato and the Langhe. These hills are famous among food and wine connoisseurs. **Asti** gave the world Asti Spumante, **Alba** is known for its truffles and mushrooms, and the Langhe hills produce some of Italy's finest wines.

4 Valle d'Aosta. The mountains and valleys of this region fairly cry out to be strolled, climbed, and skied. Here, the highest Alpine peaks—including Monte Bianco (aka Mont Blanc) and the Matterhorn—shelter resorts such as Breuil-Cervinia and Courmayeur and the great nature preserve known as the Gran Paradiso.

Castello Fénis

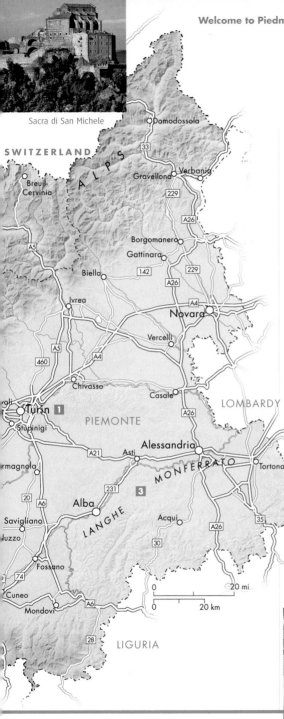

Sacra di San Michele

SWITZERLAND

ALPS

Domodossola

33

Breuil-
Cervinia

Gravellona

Verbania

229

A26

Borgomanero

Gattinara

Biella

142

229

A5

A26

Ivrea

A4

Novara

Vercelli

A5

A4

460

Chivasso

Casale

LOMBARDY

Turin **1**

PIEMONTE

A26

Stupinigi

Asti

Alessandria

rmagnola

A21

MONFERRATO

Tortona

20

A6

231

3

Alba

Acqui

35

Savigliano

LANGHE

A26

luzzo

30

74

Fossano

Cuneo

A6

Mondovi

28

LIGURIA

0 ——— 20 mi

0 ——— 20 km

GETTING ORIENTED

Piedmont (Piemonte in Italian) means "foot of the mountains," and the name fits: Turin, the region's major city, sits on the eastern end of the Po Plain, with the Maritime Alps due south and the hills of the Monferrato and Langhe districts to the southeast. To the north is mountainous Valle d'Aosta, where imposing castles sit in the shadow of Europe's most impressive peaks.

PIEDMONT & VALLE D'AOSTA PLANNER

Making the Most of Your Time

The region was the site for the 2006 Winter Olympics, which is a good reason to pay a visit—even now that the games are history. Lots of work, and many euros, went into development and renovation, the effects of which linger well after the handing out of the last medal.

Turin is an underrated travel destination. If you like the idea of an Italian city with touches of Parisian sophistication, Turin is likely to strike your fancy.

Turin's residents will tell you how much it lifts their spirits when, on clear days, they have views of the surrounding mountains. In them you'll find exceptional hiking and climbing. Along the Piedmont–Valle d'Aosta border, the Gran Paradiso National Park has beautiful, well-marked trails. Farther north is Monte Bianco, which should be a priority; you can ascend it by cable car, or, if you're an experienced climber, make a go of it with professional guides. If food and wine is your thing, also schedule a day or two on the less lofty slopes of the Langhe, south of Turin.

The French Connection

Napoléon's regime controlled Piedmont and Valle d'Aosta in the 19th century, and French influence remains evident in everything from traditional recipes redolent of mountain cheeses, truffles, and cream to Versailles-style gardens and wide, tree-lined boulevards. Well-dressed women in the cafés of Turin are addressed more often as *madama* than *signora,* and French is often spoken in the more remote mountain hamlets.

Finding a Place to Stay

High standards and opulence are characteristic of Turin's better hotels, and the same is true, translated into the Alpine idiom, at the top mountain resort hotels. The less-expensive hotels in cities and towns are generally geared to business travelers; make sure to ask if lower weekend rates are available.

Summer vacationers and winter skiers keep occupancy rates and prices high at the resorts during peak seasons. Many mountain hotels accept half- or full-board guests only and require that you stay for several nights; some have off-season rates that can reduce the cost by a full price category. If you're a skier, ask about package deals that give you a discount on lift tickets.

DINING & LODGING PRICE CATEGORIES (IN EUROS)				
¢	$	$$	$$$	$$$$
Restaurants				
under €15	€15–€25	€25–€35	€35–€45	over €45
Hotels				
under €70	€70–€110	€110–€160	€160–€220	over €220
Restaurant prices are for a first course (primo), second course (secondo), and dessert (dolce). Hotel prices are for two people in a standard double room in high season, including tax and service.				

GETTING AROUND

By Car

Like any rugged, mountainous region, the Italian Alps can be tricky to navigate by car. Roads that look like super-highways on the map can be narrow and twisting, with steep slopes and cliff-side drops. Generally, roads are well maintained, but the sheer distance covered by all of those curves tends to take longer than you might expect, so it's best to figure in extra time for getting around. This is especially true in winter, when weather conditions can cause slow traffic and road closings. Check with local tourist offices, or in a pinch with the police, to make sure roads are passable and safe, and to find out whether you may need tire chains for snowy and icy roads.

For travel across the French, Swiss, and Italian borders in Piedmont and Valle d'Aosta, only a few routes are usable year-round: the 12-km (7-mi) Mont Blanc tunnel connecting Chamonix with Courmayeur; the Colle del Gran San Bernardo/Col du Grand St. Bernard (connecting Martigny with Aosta on Swiss highway E27 and Italian highway SS27, with 6 km [4 mi] of tunnel); and the Traforo del Fréjus (between Modane and Susa, with 13 km [8 mi] of tunnel). There are other passes, but they become increasingly unreliable between November and April.

By Bus

Turin's main bus station is on the corner of Corso Inghilterra and Corso Vittorio Emanuele. Urban buses, trams, and the subway are operated by the agency **GTT** (☎ *800/019152* ⊕ *www.comune.torino.it/gtt*). Turin-based bus lines **SADEM** (☎ *800/801600* ⊕ *www.sadem. it*) and **SAPAV** (☎ *800/801901* ⊕ *www.sapav.it*) both have service throughout Piedmont and Valle d'Aosta. Aosta-based **SAVDA** (☎ *0165/262027* ⊕ *www.savda.it*) specializes in mountain service, providing frequent links between Aosta, Turin, and Courmayeur as well as Milan. There's also a major bus station at Aosta, across the street from the train station.

By Train

Turin is on the main Paris–Rome TGV express line and is also connected with Milan, only 90 minutes away on the fast train. The fastest (Eurostar) trains cover the 667-km (414-mi) trip to Rome in about six hours; other trains take between seven and 10 hours.

Services to the larger cities east of Turin are part of the extensive and reliable train network of the Lombard Plain. West of the region's capital, however, the train services soon peter out in the mountains. Continuing connections by bus serve these valleys; information about train-bus mountain services can be obtained from train stations and tourist information offices, or by contacting **FS–Trenitalia** (☎ *892021* ⊕ *www.trenitalia. com*), the Italian national train service.

Turin

EATING & DRINKING WELL IN PIEDMONT & VALLE D'AOSTA

In Piedmont and Valle d'Aosta you will find rustic specialties from farmhouse hearths, fine cuisine with a French accent, and everything in between. The Piedmontese take their food and wine very seriously.

Although you will find a similar range of eating establishments here as in other regions of Italy, the number of formal restaurants, with elaborate service and extraordinary wine lists, exceeds the national average. This holds true both in cities and in the country, where even simply named trattorias may offer a *menu di degustazione* (a multicourse tasting menu) accompanied by wines appropriate to each dish.

In Turin the ritual of the *aperitivo* has been finely tuned, and most cafés from the early evening onward provide lavish buffets that are included in the price of a cocktail—a respectable substitute for dinner if you are traveling on a limited budget. As a result, restaurants in Turin tend to fill only after 9 PM.

GREAT GRISSINI

Throughout the region, though especially in Turin, you will find that most meals are accompanied by *grissini* (bread sticks), pictured above. Invented in Turin in the 17th century to ease the digestive problems of little Prince Vittorio Amedeo II (1675–1730), these, when freshly made and hand-rolled, are a far cry from the thin and dry, plastic-wrapped versions available elsewhere. Napoléon called them *petits batons* and was, according to legend, addicted to them.

TRUFFLES

The truffle (*tartufo* in Italian) is a peculiar delicacy—a gnarly clump of fungus that grows wild in forests a few inches underground. It's hunted down using truffle-sniffing dogs (or sometimes pigs) and can sell for a small fortune. The payoff is a powerful, perfumy flavor that makes gourmets swoon. Though truffles are more abundant farther south in Umbria, the most coveted ones are the *tartufi bianchi* (white truffles), pictured at right, from Alba in Piedmont. A thin shaving of truffle often tops pasta dishes; they're also used to flavor soups and other dishes.

POLENTA & PASTA

The area's best-known dish is probably polenta, creamy cornmeal served with *carbonada* (a meat stew), melted cheese, or wild mushrooms. *Agnolotti*—crescent-shaped pasta stuffed with meat filling, pictured below—is another specialty, often served with the pan juices of roast veal. *Agnolotti del Plin* is a smaller version topped with melted butter and shaved truffles.

CHEESE

In keeping with their northern character, a regional specialty in both Piedmont and Valle d'Aosta is *fonduta,* a version of fondue made with melted cheese, eggs, and sometimes grated truffles. Fontina and ham also often deck out the ubiquitous French-style *crepes alla valdostana,* served casserole style.

MEAT

The locally raised beef of Piedmont is some of Italy's most highly prized; it's often braised or stewed with the region's hearty red wine. In winter, *bollito misto* (various meats, boiled and served with a rich sauce) shows up on many menus, and *fritto misto,* a combination of fried meats and vegetables, is another specialty.

DESSERTS & SWEETS

Though desserts here are less sweet than in some other Italian regions, treats like *panna cotta* (a cooked milk custard), *torta di nocciole* (hazelnut torte), and *bonet* (a pudding made with hazelnuts, cocoa, milk, and macaroons) are delights. Turin is renowned for its delicate pastries and fine chocolates, especially for *gianduiotti,* made with hazelnuts.

WINE

Piedmont is one of Italy's most important wine regions, producing full-bodied reds, such as Barolo, Barbaresco, Freisa, Barbera, and the lighter Dolcetto. Asti Spumante, a sweet sparkling wine, comes from the region, while Valle d'Aosta is famous for schnappslike brandies made from fruits or herbs.

7

Updated
by Peter
Blackman

A PAIR OF CONTRASTING CHARACTERISTICS define the appeal of northwest Italy's Piedmont and Valle d'Aosta regions: mountain splendor and bourgeois refinement. Two of Europe's most famous peaks—Monte Bianco (aka Mont Blanc) and Monte Cervino (the Matterhorn)—straddle Valle d'Aosta's borders with France and Switzerland, and the entire region is a magnet for skiers and hikers. To the south, the mist-shrouded lowlands skirting the Po River are home to Turin, a city that may not have the artistic treasures of Rome or the cutting-edge style of Milan, but has developed a sense of urban sophistication that makes it a pleasure to visit. You also taste a mountain/city contrast in the cuisine: the hearty peasant cooking served in tiny stone villages and the French-accented delicacies found in the plain are both eminently satisfying. Meals are accompanied by Piedmontese wines commonly held to be Italy's finest.

TURIN

Turin—Torino, in Italian—is roughly in the center of Piedmont/Valle d'Aosta and 128 km (80 mi) west of Milan; it's on the Po River, on the edge of the Po Plain, which stretches eastward all the way to the Adriatic. Turin's flatness and wide, angular, tree-lined boulevards are a far cry from Italian *metropoli* to the south; the region's decidedly northern European bent is quite evident in its nerve center. Apart from its role as northwest Italy's major industrial, cultural, intellectual, and administrative hub, Turin also has a reputation as Italy's capital of black magic and the supernatural. This distinction is enhanced by the presence of Turin's most famous, and controversial, relic, the Sacra Sindone (Holy Shroud), still believed by many Catholics to be the cloth in which Christ's body was wrapped when he was taken down from the cross.

GETTING HERE
Turin is well served by the Italian highway system and can be reached easily by car from all directions: from Milan on the A4 highway (2 hours); from Bologna (4 hours) and Florence (5 hours) on the A1 and A21 highways; from Genoa on the A6 highway (2 hours).

Bus service to and from other major Italian cities is also plentiful, and Turin can be reached by fast train service from Paris in under six hours. Fast train service also connects the city with Milan, Genova, Bologna, Florence, and Rome.

VISITOR INFORMATION
Turin's group and personally guided tours are organized by the city's tourist office. Here you can also get information about the Touristibus, a two-hour guided bus trip that leaves from Piazza Castello, at the corner of Via Po, every day but Tuesday at 2:30. Touristibus goes through the historic center of Turin, including Via Roma and Porta Nuova, and then out to view such locations as the Palazzina di Caccia in Stupinigi and the Parco del Valentino.

Turin tourism office (✉*Atrium Torino, Piazza Solferino, 10121* ☎*011/535181* ⊕*www.turismotorino.org*).

DOWNTOWN TURIN

Many of Turin's major sights are clustered around Piazza Castello, and others are on or just off the portico-lined Via Roma, one of the city's main thoroughfares, which leads 1 km (½ mi) from Piazza Castello south to Piazza Carlo Felice, a landscaped park in front of the train station. First opened in 1615, Via Roma was largely rebuilt in the 1930s, during the Mussolini era.

THE MAIN ATTRACTIONS

❶ Duomo di San Giovanni. The most impressive part of Turin's 15th-century cathedral is the shadowy, black marble–wall **Cappella della Sacra Sindone** (Chapel of the Holy Shroud), where the famous relic was housed before a fire in 1997. The chapel was designed by the priest and architect Guarino Guarini (1604–83), a genius of the baroque style who was official engineer and mathematician to the court of Duke Carlo Emanuele II of Savoy. The fire caused severe structural damage, and the chapel is closed indefinitely while restoration work proceeds.

The Sacra Sindone is a 4-yard-long sheet of linen, thought by millions to be the burial shroud of Christ, bearing the light imprint of his crucified body. The shroud first made an appearance around the middle of the 15th century, when it was presented to Ludovico of Savoy in Chambéry. In 1578 it was brought to Turin by another member of the Savoy royal family, Duke Emanuele Filiberto. It was only in the 1990s that the Catholic Church began allowing rigorous scientific study of the shroud. Not surprisingly, results have bolstered both sides of the argument. On the one hand, three separate university teams—in Switzerland, Britain, and the United States—have concluded, as a result of carbon 14 dating, that the cloth is a forgery dating from between 1260 and 1390. On the other hand, they are unable to explain how medieval forgers could have created the shroud's image, which resembles a photographic negative, and how they could have had the knowledge or means to incorporate traces of Roman coins covering the eyelids and endemic Middle Eastern pollen woven into the cloth. Either way, the shroud continues to be revered as a holy relic, exhibited to the public on very rare occasions—the next official display is planned for 2025. In lieu of the real thing, a photocopy is on permanent display near the altar of the Duomo. ✉*Piazza San Giovanni, Centro* ☎*011/4361540* ☉*Mon.–Sat. 6:30–noon and 3–7, Sun. 8–noon and 3–7.*

❼ Galleria Sabauda. Some of the most important paintings from the vast collections of the house of Savoy are displayed here. The collection is particularly rich in 16th- and 17th-century Dutch and Flemish paintings: note the *Stigmate di San Francesco* (*St. Francis receiving Stigmata*) by Jan Van Eyck (1395–1441), in which the saint receives the marks of Christ's wounds while a companion cringes beside him. Other Dutch masterpieces include paintings by Anthony Van Dyck (1599–1641) and Rembrandt (1606–69). *L'arcangelo Raffaele e Tobiolo (Tobias and the*

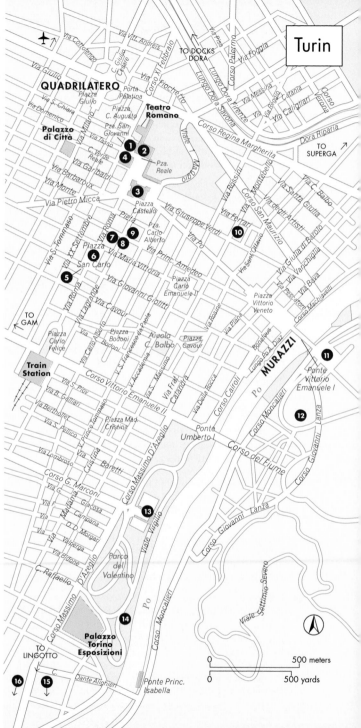

Turin

PIEDMONT & VALLE D'AOSTA, PAST & PRESENT

Ancient History. Piedmont and Valle d'Aosta were originally inhabited by Celtic tribes, who over time were absorbed by the conquering Romans. As allies of Rome, the Celts held off Hannibal when he came down through the Alpine passes with his elephants, but they were eventually defeated, and their capital—Taurasia, the present Turin—was destroyed. The Romans rebuilt the city, giving its streets the grid pattern that survives today. (Roman ruins can be found throughout both regions and are particularly conspicuous in the town of Aosta.)

The Middle Ages and the Savoy. With the fall of the Roman Empire, the region suffered the fate of the rest of Italy and was successively occupied and ravaged by barbarians from the east and the north. In the 11th century, the feudal French Savoy family ruled Turin briefly; toward the end of the 13th century it returned to the area, where it would remain, almost continuously, for 500 years. In 1798 the French republi-

can armies invaded Italy, but when Napoléon's empire fell, the house of Savoy returned to power.

Risorgimento. Beginning in 1848, Piedmont was one of the principal centers of the Risorgimento, the movement for Italian unity. In 1861 the Chamber of Deputies of Turin declared Italy a united kingdom. Rome became the capital in 1870, effectively marking the end of Piedmont's prominence in national politics.

Industry and Affluence. Piedmont became one of the first industrialized regions in Italy, and the automotive giant FIAT—the Fabbrica Italiana Automobili Torino—was established here in 1899. Today the region is the center of Italy's automobile, metal-working, chemical, and candy industries, having attracted thousands of workers from Italy's south. The FIAT company, led by the Agnelli family—roughly Italy's equivalent of the Kennedys—has been arguably the most important factor in the region's rise to affluence.

Angel) by Piero del Pollaiuolo (circa 1443–96) is showcased, and other featured Italian artists include Fra Angelico (circa 1400–55), Andrea Mantegna (1431–1506), and Paolo Veronese (1528–88). Along with the Egyptian Museum, the gallery is housed in the **Palazzo dell'Accademia delle Scienze,** a baroque tour de force designed by priest-architect Guarino Guarini. ⊠ *Via Accademia delle Scienze 6, Centro* ☎ *011/547440* ⊕ *www.museitorino.it* ✉ *€4, €8 includes admission to Museo Egizio* ⊗ *Fri.–Sun. and Tues. 8:30–2, Wed. and Thurs. 2–7:30.*

★ ♺ ❿ **Mole Antonelliana.** You can't miss the unusual square dome and thin, elaborate spire of this Turin landmark above the city's rooftops. This odd structure, built between 1863 and 1889, was originally intended to be a synagogue, but costs escalated and eventually it was bought by the city of Turin. In its time it was the tallest brick building in the world. You can take the crystal elevator to reach the terrace at the top of the dome for an excellent view of the city, the plain, and the Alps beyond. Also worth a visit is the Mole Antonelliana's **Museo Nazionale del Cin-**

ema (National Cinema Museum ⊕*www.museonazionaledelcinema.it*), which embraces more than 34,000 square feet and houses many items of film memorabilia as well as a film library with some 7,000 titles. ⊠ *Via Montebello 20, Centro* ☏*011/8125658 museum* ☏*Museum €6.50, elevator €4.50, combination ticket €8* ⊙ *Museum: Tues.–Fri. and Sun. 9–8, Sat. 9 AM–11 PM; ticket sales end 75 mins before closing. Elevator: Tues.–Fri. and Sun. 10–8, Sat. 10 AM–11 PM.*

❽ Museo Egizio. The Egyptian Museum's superb collection includes statues
Fodor'sChoice of pharaohs and mummies and entire frescoes taken from royal tombs—
★ all in all, it's one of the world's finest and largest museums of its kind. Look for the magnificent 13th-century BC statue of Ramses II and the fascinating Tomb of Kha. The latter was found intact with furniture, supplies of food and clothing, writing instruments, and a complete set of personal cosmetics and toiletries. Unfortunately, the museum's objects are not always displayed according to modern standards. Along with carefully constructed exhibits with detailed information in English and Italian you will also find rooms that resemble warehouses filled with objects, with little or no information identifying what they are. ⊠ *Via Accademia delle Scienze 6, Centro, 10123* ☏*011/5617776* ⊕*www. museoegizio.it* ☏*€7.50, €8 includes admission to Galleria Sabauda* ⊙ *Tues.–Sun. 8:30–7:30; ticket sales end 1 hr before closing.*

❸ Palazzo Madama. In the center of Piazza Castello, this castle was named for the Savoy queen Maria Cristina, who made it her home in the 17th century. The building incorporates the remains of a Roman gate with later-medieval and Renaissance additions. The castle's monumental baroque facade and grand entrance staircase were designed by Filippo Juvarra (1678–1736). The palace now houses the **Museo d'Arte Antica,** whose collections comprise more than 30,000 items dating from the Middle Ages to the baroque era. The paintings, sculptures, illuminated manuscripts, and various decorative objects on display illustrate almost 10 centuries of Italian and European artistic production. Works by Jan van Eyck (circa 1390–1441), Antonella da Messina (circa 1430–79), and Orazio Gentileschi (1563–1639) highlight the collection. ⊠*Piazza Castello, Centro* ☏*011/4433501* ⊕*www.palazzomadamatorino. it* ☏*Grand staircase and medieval courtyard free, museum €7.50* ⊙ *Grand staircase and medieval courtyard: Tues.–Fri. and Sun. 9–7, Sat. 9–8; museum: Tues.–Fri. 10–6, Sun. 10–8. Ticket sales end 1 hr before closing.*

❻ Piazza San Carlo. Surrounded by shops, arcades, fashionable cafés, and elegant baroque palaces, this is one of the most beautiful squares in Turin. In the center stands a statue of Duke Emanuele Filiberto of Savoy, victor at the battle of San Quintino in 1557. The melee heralded the peaceful resurgence of Turin under the Savoy after years of bloody dynastic fighting. The fine bronze statue erected in the 19th century is one of Turin's symbols.

NEED A BREAK? A chocolate lover's pilgrimage to Turin inevitably leads to Al Bicerin (⊠ *Piazza della Consolata 5, Centro* ☏ *011/4369325* ⊕ *www.bicerin.it* ⊙ *Closed Wed.*), which first opened its doors in 1763. Cavour, Nietzsche, Puccini, and

Dumas have all sipped here, and if you order the house specialty, the *bicerin* (a hot drink with layers of chocolate, coffee, and cream), you'll understand why. Don't be surprised if the friendly and energetic owner, Marité Costa, also tries to tempt you with one of her flavored *zabajoni* (warm eggnogs). Chocolate goodies, including choco-

WORD OF MOUTH

"The highlights of our stay in Turin were walking under the grand arcades that run alongside miles of the streets downtown, window-shopping, and stopping for coffee, pastries, or chocolate at one of the many elegant cafés." –Anne

late-flavor pasta, are on sale in the café store. The historic Caffè San Carlo (⊠ *Piazza San Carlo 156, Centro* ☎ *011/532586*) is usually lively with locals gathered at the marble-top tables under the huge crystal chandelier. Breakfast and lunch, afternoon snacks, and evening aperitifs are all served in this particularly elegant neoclassical setting.

❹ San Lorenzo. Architect Guarino Guarini was in his mid-sixties when he began this church in 1668. The masterful use of geometric forms and the theatrical control of light and shadow show him working at his mature and confident best. Stand in the center of the church and look up into the cupola to enjoy the full effect. ⊠ *Piazza Castello, Centro* ☎ *011/4361527* ☯ *Daily 8:30–noon and 4–7.*

NEED A BREAK? Baratti e Milano (⊠ *Piazza Castello 27, Centro* ☎ *011/5613060*), in the glass-roofed Galleria Subalpina near Via Po, is one of Turin's charming old cafés. It's famous for its exquisite chocolates—indulge your sweet tooth or buy some *gianduiotti* (hazelnut chocolates) or candied chestnuts to take home to friends. Light lunches are served at the tables to the rear of the café. The tiny café Mulassano (⊠ *Piazza Castello 15, Centro* ☎ *011/547990*), decorated with marble and finely carved wood panels, is famous for its *tramezzini* (small triangular sandwiches made with lightly toasted white bread), invented here in the 1920s. Popular with the pre- and post-theater crowd, the café also offers a unique roulette system for clients trying to decide on who pays the bill—ask the cashier for an explanation.

ALSO WORTH SEEING

❾ Palazzo Carignano. A baroque triumph by Guarino Guarini (the priest who designed several of Turin's most noteworthy structures), this red-brick palace was built between 1679 and 1685 and played an important role in the 19th-century unification of Italy. Vittorio Emanuele II of Savoy (1820–78), united Italy's first king, was born within these walls, and Italy's first parliament met here from 1860 to 1865. The palace now houses the **Museo del Risorgimento,** a museum honoring the 19th-century movement for Italian unity. At this writing, the palace is closed until late 2009 for restoration. ⊠ *Via Accademia delle Scienze 5, Centro* ☎ *011/5641711* ⊕ *www.regione.piemonte. it/cultura/risorgimento* ⊠ *€5* ☯ *Tues.–Sun. 9–7; ticket sales end 1 hr before closing.*

2 **Palazzo Reale.** This 17th-century palace, the former Savoy royal residence, is an imposing work of brick, stone, and marble that stands on the site of one of Turin's ancient Roman city gates. In contrast to its sober exterior, the palace's interior is swathed in luxurious, mostly rococo trappings, including tapestries, gilt ceilings, and sumptuous 17th- to 19th-century furniture. Behind the palace you can relax in the royal gardens. At this writing, the first floor of the palace was closed for restoration work that may last through 2008; the second floor will remain open. ⊠*Piazza Castello, Centro* ☎*011/4361455* ☜*Gardens free, palace €6.50* ⊙*Palace: Tues.–Sun. 8:30–7:30; guided visits depart every 40 mins. Gardens: daily 9* AM *to 1 hr before sunset.*

The **Armeria Reale** *(Royal Armory),* in a wing of the Royal Palace, holds one of Europe's most extensive collections of arms and armor. It's a must-see for connoisseurs. ⊠*Entrance at Piazza Castello 191, Centro* ☎*011/543889* ☜*€4* ⊙*Tues.–Fri. 9–2, weekends 1–7.*

5 **San Carlo.** The ornate baroque facade of this 17th-century church was enhanced in the latter part of the 19th century to harmonize with the facade of neighboring **Santa Cristina.** ⊠*Piazza San Carlo, south end of square, right corner, Centro* ☎*011/5620922* ⊙*Weekdays 8–noon and 4–6:30, Sat. 8–noon and 4–6, Sun. 9–12:45 and 4–6.*

OFF THE BEATEN PATH

Galleria Civica d'Arte Moderna e Contemporanea (GAM). In 1863 Turin was the first Italian city to begin a public collection devoted to contemporary art. Housed in a modern building on the edge of downtown, a permanent display of more than 600 paintings, sculptures, and installation pieces provides an exceptional glimpse of how Italian contemporary art has evolved since the late 1800s. The futurist, pop, neo-Dada, and arte povera movements are particularly well represented, and the gallery has a fine video and art film collection. ⊠ *Via Magenta 31, Centro* ☎*011/4429610* ⊕*www.gamtorino.it* ☜*€7.50* ⊙*Tues.–Sun. 10–6.*

ALONG THE PO

The Po River is narrow and unprepossessing here in Turin, only a hint of the broad waterway that it becomes as it flows eastward toward the Adriatic. It's flanked, however, by formidable edifices, a park, and a lovely pedestrian path.

THE MAIN ATTRACTIONS

☾ **14** **Borgo Medioevale.** Along the banks of the Po, this complex, built for a General Exhibition in 1884, is a faithful reproduction of a typical Piedmont village in the Middle Ages: crafts shops, houses, a church, and stores cluster the narrow lanes, and in the center of the village the **Rocca Medioevale,** a medieval castle, provides the town's main attraction. ⊠*Southern end of Parco del Valentino, San Salvario* ☎*011/4431701* ⊕*www.borgomedioevaletorino.it* ☜*Village free, Rocca Medioevale €5* ⊙*Village: Apr.–Oct., daily 9–8; Nov.–Mar., daily 9–7. Rocca Medioevale: Tues.–Sun. 9–7; groups of no more than 25 enter the castle every ½ hr. Ticket counter closes at 6:15.*

★ ⓯ **Museo dell'Automobile.** No visit to car-manufacturing Turin would be complete without a pilgrimage to see perfectly conserved Bugattis, Ferraris, and Isotta Fraschinis. Here you'll get an idea of the importance of FIAT—and automobiles in general—to Turin's economy. There's a collection of antique cars from as early as 1896, and displays show how the city has changed over the years as a result of its premier industry. For the true automobile fan, there's even a section devoted to the history of car tires. At this writing, several sections of the museum were closed for renovations through 2008. ⊠ *Corso Unità d'Italia 40, Millefonti* ☎*011/677666* ⊕ *www.museoauto.it* ᛫*€7* ⊗ *Tues.–Sun. 10–6:30.*

⓭ **Parco del Valentino.** This pleasant riverside park is a great place to stroll, bike, or jog. Originally the grounds of a relatively simple hunting lodge, the park owes its present arrangement to Madama Maria Cristina of France, who received the land and lodge as a wedding present after her marriage to Vittorio Amedeo I of Savoy. With memories of 16th-century French châteaus in mind, she began work in 1620 and converted the lodge into a magnificent palace, the **Castello del Valentino.** The building, now home to the University of Turin's Faculty of Architecture, is not open to the general public. Next to the palace are botanical gardens, established in 1729, where local and exotic flora can be seen in a hothouse, herbarium, and arboretum. ⊠ *Parco del Valentino, San Salvario* ☎*011/6707446 botanical gardens* ᛫*Gardens €3* ⊗ *Gardens: Apr.–Sept., weekends 9–1 and 3–7.*

⓰ **Pinacoteca Giovanni e Marella Agnelli.** This gallery was opened by Gianni Agnelli (1921–2003), the head of FIAT and patriarch of one of Italy's most powerful families, just four months before his death. The emphasis here is on quality rather than quantity: 25 works of art from the Agnelli private collection are on permanent display, along with temporary exhibitions. There are four magnificent scenes of Venice by Canaletto (1697–1768); two splendid views of Dresden by Canaletto's nephew, Bernardo Bellotto (1720–80); several works by Manet (1832–83), Renoir (1841–1919), Matisse (1869–1954), and Picasso (1881–1973); and fine examples of the work of Italian futurist painters Balla (1871–1958) and Severini (1883–1966). The gallery is located on the top floor of the **Lingotto,** a former FIAT factory that was completely transformed between 1982 and 2002 by architect Renzo Piano. The multilevel complex now contains two hotels, a shopping mall, several movie theaters, restaurants, and an auditorium. ⊠ *Via Nizza 230, Lingotto* ☎*011/0062008* ⊕ *www.pinacoteca-agnelli.it* ᛫*€7* ⊗ *Tues.–Sun. 10–7.*

ALSO WORTH SEEING

⓫ **Gran Madre di Dio.** On the east bank of the Po, this neoclassical church is modeled after the Pantheon in Rome. It was built between 1827 and 1831 to commemorate the return of the house of Savoy to Turin after the fall of Napoléon's empire. ⊠ *Piazza Gran Madre di Dio, Borgo Po* ☎*011/8193572* ⊗ *Mon.–Sat. 7:30–noon and 3:30–7, Sun. 7:30–1 and 3:30–7.*

⑫ Santa Maria del Monte. The church and convent standing on top of 150-foot Monte dei Cappuccini date from 1583. Don't be surprised if you find yourself in the middle of a wedding party, as couples often come here to be photographed. Next to the church is the tiny **Museo Nazionale della Montagna,** dedicated to mountains and to mountain climbing. ⊠ *Monte dei Cappuccini, above Corso Moncalieri, Borgo Po* ☎ *011/6604414 church, 011/6604104 museum* ⊕ *www.museomontagna.org* ⊠ *Church free, museum €6* ☉ *Church: daily 9–noon and 2:30–6, museum: Tues.–Sun. 9–7.*

OFF THE BEATEN PATH

Basilica di Superga. Since 1731, the Basilica di Superga has been the burial place of kings. Visible from miles around, the thoroughly baroque church was designed by Juvarra in the early 18th century, and no fewer than 58 members of the Savoy family are memorialized in the crypt. ⊠ *Strada della Basilica di Superga 73, Sassi* ☎ *011/8980083 basilica, 011/8997456 crypt* ⊠ *Basilica free, crypt €3* ☉ *Basilica: Apr.–Oct., daily 9–noon and 3–6; Nov.–Mar., daily 9–noon and 3–5. Crypt: Apr.–Oct., Mon.–Thurs. 9:30–1:30 and 2:30–6:30, weekends 9:30–7:30; Nov.–Mar., weekends 9:30–1:30 and 2:30–6:30.*

Sassi–Superga Cog Train. The 18-minute ride from Sassi up the Superga hill is an absolute treat on a clear day. The view of the Alps is magnificent at the hilltop **Parco Naturale Collina Torinese,** a tranquil retreat from the bustle of the city. If you feel like a little exercise, you can walk back down to Sassi (about 2 hours) on one of the well-marked wooded trails that start from the upper station. Other circular trails lead through the park and back to Superga, where mountain bikes are also available for rent. ⊠ *Piazza G. Modena, Sassi* ☎ *011/5764733 cog train, 011/8903667 bikes* ⊕ *www.comune.torino.it/gtt* ⊠ *Weekdays €2 one-way, weekends €3.50 one-way* ☉ *Hourly service Mon. and Wed.–Fri. 9–noon and 2–5, hourly service weekends 9–8; bus service replaces the train on Tues.*

WHERE TO EAT

$$$$
Fodor's Choice
★

✕ **Al Garamond.** The ocher-color walls and the ancient brick vaulting in this small, bright space set the stage for traditional meat and seafood dishes that have a bit of creative flair. Try the tantalizing *rombo in crosta di patate al barbera* (turbot wrapped in sliced potatoes and baked with Barbera wine). For dessert, the mousse *di liquirizia e salsa di cioccolato bianco* (licorice mousse with white-chocolate sauce) is a must, even if you don't usually like licorice. The level of service here is high, even by demanding Turin standards. ⊠ *Via G. Pomba 14, Centro, 10123* ☎ *011/8122781* ⊟ *AE, MC, V* ☉ *Closed Sun., Jan. 1–6, and 3 wks in Aug. No lunch Sat.*

$$$$
✕ **Del Cambio.** Set in a palace dating from 1757, this is one of Europe's most beautiful and historic restaurants, with decorative moldings, mirrors, and hanging lamps that look just as they did when Italian national hero Cavour dined here more than a century ago. The cuisine draws heavily on Piedmontese tradition and is paired with fine wines of the

region. Agnolotti pasta with *sugo d'arrosto* (roast veal sauce) is a recommended first course. ⊠ *Piazza Carignano 2, Centro* ☎ *011/546690* ⌔ *Reservations essential* ▤ *AE, DC, MC, V* ⊘ *Closed Sun., Jan. 1–6, and 3 wks in Aug.*

★ **$$$$** ✕ **Vintage 1997.** The first floor of an elegant town house in the center of Turin makes a fitting location for this sophisticated restaurant. You might try such specialties as *vitello tonnato alla nostra maniera* (roast veal with a light tuna sauce) or *code di scampi con costolette di coniglio su crema di scalogno* (shrimp and rabbit in a scallion sauce). For the especially hungry gourmet there's the *menu del Vintage,* a 13-course feast that covers the full range of the restaurant's cuisine. There's an excellent wine list, with regional, national, and international vintages well represented. ⊠ *Piazza Solferino 16/h, Centro* ☎ *011/535948* ▤ *AE, DC, MC, V* ⊘ *Closed Sun. and 3 wks in Aug. No lunch Sat.*

$$$ ✕ **L'Agrifoglio.** This intimate local favorite has just 10 tables. Specialties change with the seasons, but you might find such delicacies as risotto *al Barbaresco* (with Barbaresco wine) and agnolotti *dal plin al sugo d'arrosto* (crescent-shaped stuffed pasta with the pan juices of roast veal) on the menu. L'Agrifoglio stays open late for the after-theater and after-cinema crowd. ⊠ *Via Andrea Provana 7/e, Centro* ☎ *011/8136837* ▤ *MC, V* ⊘ *Closed Sun.*

★ ✕ **Savoia.** The enthusiasm of chef and owner Mario Ferrero permeates
$$–$$$ three small rooms decorated with a few choice pictures and antique furniture. His kitchen turns out creative takes on Piedmontese specialties that change with the seasons. The bread and pasta are homemade, and the wine cellar is tended with equal care. ⊠ *Via Corta d'Appello 13, Centro* ☎ *011/4362288* ▤ *AE, DC, MC, V* ⊘ *Closed Sun. No lunch Sat.*

$$ ✕ **Porto di Savona.** Look for this centuries-old tavern under the arcades of vast Piazza Vittorio Veneto, where it once served as a terminal for the Turin–Savona stagecoach line. The small street-level and upstairs dining rooms have a decidedly old-fashioned air; the marble stairs are well worn, and the walls are decked with photos of Old Turin. Customers sit at long wooden tables to eat home-style Piedmontese cooking, including gnocchi with Gorgonzola and *bollito misto* (mixed boiled meats, appropriately served only in winter). The Barbera house wine is good. ⊠ *Piazza Vittorio Veneto 2, Centro* ☎ *011/8173500* ▤ *MC, V.*

$ ✕ **Locanda da Betty.** At this small and homey trattoria, traditional Piedmont cuisine is served to a usually packed house. The inexpensive four-course *menu di degustazione* (tasting menu) is an especially good deal. ⊠ *Via Bogino 17/e, Centro* ☎ *011/8170583* ▤ *MC, V* ⊘ *Closed Sun.*

WHERE TO STAY

The **Turin Tourist Board** (⊠ *Via Bogino 8, Centro* ☎ *011/535181* 🖷 *011/530070* ⊕ *www.turismotorino.org*) provides a booking service for hotels and bed-and-breakfast–style accommodations in the city. In order to use the service, you must book hotels 48 hours in advance and B&Bs seven days in advance. The tourism agency **Montagnedoc** (⊠ *Via Bogino 8, Centro* ☎ *0121/8185011* 🖷 *0121/883426* ⊕ *www.*

montagnedoc.it) can help locate and book accommodations in the mountain valleys to the west of Turin.

★ $$$$ 🏨 **Grand Hotel Sitea.** One of the city's finest hotels, the Sitea is ideally located in the historic center. Decorated in a warmly classical style, the public areas and guest rooms are elegant and comfortable. Top-notch service is provided by a courteous and efficient staff. Week-end rates are slightly lower. **Pros:** Central location, well-appointed rooms, large bathrooms. **Cons:** Some find the a/c noisy, carpets are a little worn. ⊠ *Via Carlo Alberto 35, Centro, 10123* ☎ *011/5170171* 🖷 *011/548090* ⊕ *www.sitea.thi.it* 📞 *118 rooms, 4 suites* ⚒ *In-room: safe, refrigerator. In-hotel: restaurant, bar, spa, public Wi-Fi, parking (fee), some pets allowed* ☰ *AE, DC, MC, V* ⍡ *BP.*

$$$$ 🏨 **Le Meridien Turin Art+Tech.** Designed by architect Renzo Piano, this luxury hotel is part of the former Lingotto FIAT factory. The approach throughout is typically minimalist, with ultramodern fixtures and designer furniture decorating the rooms. The track on the roof, once used by FIAT to test its cars, is available to clients for jogging. **Pros:** Interesting design and location, very good ($$) weekend rates. **Cons:** Outside the city center, some signs of wear and tear, services are a little limited for the price. ⊠ *Via Nizza 230, Lingotto, 10126* ☎ *011/6642000* 🖷 *011/6642004* ⊕ *www.lemeridien.com* 📞 *141 rooms, 1 suite* ⚒ *In-room: safe, refrigerator. In-hotel: restaurant, bar, gym, public Internet, public Wi-Fi.* ☰ *AE, DC, MC, V* ⍡ *BP.*

$$$ 🏨 **Genio.** The Genio, like many hotels in Turin, underwent a complete transformation in preparation for the Winter Olympics in 2006. Though steps away from the main train station, spacious and tastefully decorated rooms provide a quiet haven from the bustle of the city. Best of all is the service, which resembles that of a friendly family-run inn rather than a big-city business hotel. **Pros:** Recently refurbished property, close to the central train station, very friendly service. **Cons:** 15-minute walk to the center of town, area around the hotel is a little seedy. ⊠ *Corso Vittorio Emanuele II 47, Centro, 10125* ☎ *011/6505771* 🖷 *011/6508264* ⊕ *www.hotelgenio.it* 📞 *125 rooms, 3 suites* ⚒ *In-room: refrigerator. In-hotel: public Wi-Fi, parking (fee)* ☰ *AE, DC, MC, V* ⍡ *BP.*

$$$ 🏨 **Victoria.** Rare style, attention to detail, and comfort are the hall-
FodorsChoice marks of this boutique hotel furnished and managed to create the feeling
★ of a refined English town house. The sitting room has deep-cushioned floral sofas, a library, a collection of bric-a-brac, and windows overlooking an enclosed garden. A newer wing has a grand marble staircase and individually decorated guest rooms in which fine prints and patterned fabrics abound. The same care is found in the refurbished rooms of the original wing, and the well-equipped spa area, an attractive addition. **Pros:** Tranquil location in the center of town, excellent spa facilities, wonderful breakfast. **Cons:** Entrance is a little run-down, hotel parking lot is a couple of blocks away and finding a spot on the street is difficult, no views from the rooms. ⊠ *Via Nino Costa 4, Centro, 10123* ☎ *011/5611909* 🖷 *011/5611806* ⊕ *www.hotelvictoria-torino.com* 📞 *97 rooms, 9 suites* ⚒ *In room: safe, refrigerator, Wi-Fi.*

In-hotel: bar, pool, spa, bicycles, public Wi-Fi, parking (fee) $\boxminus$ *AE, DC, MC, V* ⊘|*BP.*

$$ ⛱ **La Maddalena.** It may be difficult to book a stay at this small B&B (there are only three rooms), but it's worth a try. You'll be made to feel instantly at home by the proprietor, Maddalena Vitale, in this delightfully decorated and comfortably cluttered apartment not far from the main train station. One room has a double bed and en suite bathroom; the other two rooms have twin beds and private bathrooms across the hall. **Pros:** Homey atmosphere, wonderful hostess. **Cons:** Limited space makes snagging a room difficult, in a run-down section of Turin that is a 30-minute walk to the center of town, no a/c. ⊠ *Via San Secondo 31, Centro, 10128* ☎⧓*011/591267* ⊕*www.iam-maddalena.com* ⬱*3 rooms* ♿ *In-room: no a/c, dial-up* $\boxminus$ *No credit cards* ⊘|*BP.*

NIGHTLIFE & THE ARTS

THE ARTS

MUSIC

Classical music concerts are held in the famous **Conservatorio Giuseppe Verdi** (⊠ *Via Mazzini 11, Centro* ☎*011/8121268* ⊠*Piazza Bodoni, Centro* ☎*011/888470*) throughout the year but primarily in winter. The **Settembre Musica Festival** (☎*011/4424703*), held for three weeks in September, highlights classical works. Traditional sacred music and some modern religious pieces are performed in the **Duomo** (⊠ *Via Montebello 20, Centro* ☎*011/8154230*) on Sunday evening; performances are usually advertised in the vestibule or in the local edition of Turin's nationally distributed newspaper, *La Stampa*. The Thursday edition comes with a supplement on music and other entertainment possibilities.

OPERA

The **Teatro Regio** (⊠*Piazza Castello 215, Centro* ☎*011/8815557* ⊕*www.teatroregio.torino.it*), one of Italy's leading opera houses, has its season from October to June. You can buy tickets for most performances (premieres sell out well in advance) at the box office or on the Web site, where discounts are offered on the day of the show.

NIGHTLIFE

Two areas of Turin are enormously popular nightlife destinations: the Docks Dora, to the north of the city center, and the Murazzi embankment, near the Ponte Vittorio Emanuele I.

The **Docks Dora** (⊠*Via Valprato 68, Madonna di Campagna* ☎*011/280251* ⊘*Mon.–Sat. 9 PM–4 AM*) is a complex of old warehouses that have been converted into artists' studios, gallery spaces, bars, cafés, and theaters. Live music and performances keep the area hopping, and the disco **Café Blue** serves up dance music all night long. Take Bus 51 from the Porta Susa train station or catch it heading north past the Duomo. On the Murazzi, near the Ponte Vittorio Emanuele I, is **Jammin's** (⊠*Murazzi del Po 17, Centro* ☎*011/882869* ⊘*May–Sept., Mon.–Sat. 9 PM–4 AM*), a popular disco with a mixed crowd; there's live music on Friday. The center of town is also popular, especially earlier in

CLOSE UP

The Olympic Legacy in Turin

Turin played host to the 20th Winter Olympics in 2006, and although the international spotlight has moved on, you can still sense the impact of the games. With the Olympics as an impetus (and further spurred by crises in the auto industry), Turin has worked to transcend its image as a city of industry and identify itself as a dynamic cultural and recreational travel destination.

The Olympics have brought about nothing less than a fundamental reorientation of the city. The central train station, Porta Nuova, and the nearby historical center have long been the focal points of activity, but the Olympics spurred development both to the west and along the city's north–south axis. The Olympic Village and Olympic skating rink are near a former FIAT factory, known as the Lingotto, to the south of the city core. For the games,

the Lingotto train station, little used after the closure of the FIAT factory, was enlarged, and the industrial zone was largely transformed into a residential and commercial center, with new hotels and restaurants.

With the Olympics in mind, the city developed its first subway system; construction wrapped up on a section linking the Lingotto Olympic area with downtown Turin in late 2005. From the Porta Nuova station, the subway heads toward the now secondary Porta Susa station and then continues toward Turin's rapidly expanding western limits; the first stage of this plan was completed in late 2006. Eventually Porta Susa will become Turin's principal train station and the Porta Nuova station will close, perhaps to be turned into a museum, like the d'Orsay train station in Paris.

the evening. A trendy meeting place for an aperitif or a pre-disco drink in the piazza at the end of Via Po is the wine bar **Caffè Elena** (⊠ *Piazza Vittorio Veneto 5, Centro* ☎ *011/8123341*). South of the main train station is **Rockcity** (⊠ *Via Bertini 2, San Salvario* ☎ *011/3184737*), where you'll find a smart crowd in their mid-twenties to mid-thirties listening to rock, techno, and commercial music.

SPORTS

SOCCER

Turin's two professional soccer clubs, Juventus and Torino, play their games in the **Stadio delle Alpi** (✛ *6 km [4 mi] northwest of city, Venaria* ☎ *011/7395759*). Juventus is one of Italy's most successful and most popular teams. There is fierce rivalry between its supporters and those of visiting clubs, especially Inter Milan and AC Milan. Home matches are usually played on Sunday afternoon during the season, which runs from late August to mid-May. It's possible to purchase tickets for Juventus and Torino games in any *tabaccheria* (tobacco shop) with a sign bearing a capital "T."

SHOPPING

CHOCOLATE

The tradition of making chocolate began in Turin in the early 17th century. Chocolate at that time was an aristocratic drink, but in the 19th century a Piedmontese invention made it possible to further refine cocoa, which could then be used to create solid bars and candies.

★ The most famous of all Turin chocolates is the *gianduiotto* (with cocoa, sugar, and hazelnuts), first concocted in 1867. The tradition of making these delicious treats has been continued at the small, family-run **Peyrano** (⊠ *Corso Moncalieri 47, Centro* ☎ *011/6602202* ⊕ *www.peyrano.it*), where more than 80 types of chocolates are concocted. **Stratta** (⊠ *Piazza San Carlo 191, Centro* ☎ *011/547920*), one of Turin's most famous chocolate shops, has been in business since 1836 and sells confections of all kinds—not just the chocolates in the lavish window displays but also fancy cookies, rum-laced fudges, and magnificent cakes.

MARKETS

Go to the famous **Balon Flea Market** (⊠ *Piazza Repubblica, Centro*) on Saturday morning for excellent bargains on secondhand books and clothing and good browsing among stalls selling local specialties such as gianduiotti. (Be aware, however, that the market is also famous for its pickpockets.) The second Sunday of every month a special antiques market, appropriately called the **Gran Balon,** sets up shop in Piazza Repubblica.

SPECIALTY STORES

Most people know that Turin produces more than 75% of Italy's cars, but they are often unaware that it's also a hub for clothing manufacturing. Top-quality boutiques stocking local, national, and international lines are clustered along Via Roma and Via Garibaldi. Piazza San Carlo, Via Po, and Via Maria Vittoria are lined with antiques shops, some—but not all—specializing in 18th-century furniture and domestic items.

Specialty food stores and delicatessens abound in central Turin. For a truly spectacular array of cheeses and other delicacies, try Turin's famous **Borgiattino** (⊠ *Via Accademia Albertina 38/a, Centro* ☎ *011/8394686*). For hand-rolled *grissini* (bread sticks)—some as long as 4 feet—the bakery **Bersano** (⊠ *Via Barbaroux 5, Centro* ☎ *011/5627579*) is the best place in town. **Tabernalibraria** (⊠ *Via Bogino 5, Centro* ☎ *011/836515*) is a delightful combination of *enoteca* (wineshop), delicatessen, and bookstore.

THE COLLINE & SAVOY PALACES

As you head west from Turin into the Colline ("little hills"), castles and medieval fortifications begin to pepper the former dominion of the house of Savoy, and the Alps come into better and better view. In the region lie the storybook medieval town of Rivoli; 12th-century abbeys;

and, farther west in the mountains, the ski resort of Sestriere, one of the venues used during the 2006 Winter Olympics.

STUPINIGI

8 km (5 mi) southwest of Turin.

GETTING HERE
From the Porta Nuova train station in Turin, take the Number 4 tram and then Bus 41 to reach Stupinigi in approximately 45 minutes. A signed, and completely flat, bicycle path also passes the Porta Nuova train station and follows the same route as the tram and bus.

By car, follow Corso Turati and then Corso Unione Sovietica directly southwest from Turin's Porta Nuova train station.

EXPLORING
★ The **Palazzina di Caccia,** in the town of Stupinigi, was built by Juvarra in 1729 as a hunting lodge for the house of Savoy. More like a sumptuous royal villa, its many wings, landscaped gardens, and surrounding forests give a clear idea of the level of style to which the Savoy were accustomed. This regal aspect was not lost on Paolina Buonaparte, who briefly held court here during her brother Napoléon's reign over Italy. Today the Palazzina houses the **Museo d'Arte di Ammobiliamento** (Museum of Decorative Arts), a vast collection of paintings and furniture gathered from numerous Savoy palaces in the area. At this writing, the museum was closed for extensive renovations, but will reopen at the end of 2008. ⊠ *Via Principe Amedeo 7* ☎*011/3581220* 💳*€6.20* ⊙*Apr.–Oct., Tues.–Sun. 10–7:30; Nov.–Mar., Fri.–Sun. 10–11:30 and 1:30–3:15.*

RIVOLI

16 km (10 mi) northwest of Stupinigi, 13 km (8 mi) west of Turin.

GETTING HERE
GTT buses and trams regularly link central Turin with Rivoli. The journey takes just over one hour.

By car, follow Corso Francia from central Turin all the way to Rivoli. Unless there's a lot of traffic the trip should take a half hour.

EXPLORING
The Savoy court was based in Rivoli in the Middle Ages. The 14th-to 15th-century **Casa del Conte Verde** *(House of the Green Count)* sits right in the center of town, and the richness of its decorations hints at the wealth and importance of its owner, Amedeo VI of Savoy, during the period. Inside, a small gallery hosts temporary exhibitions. ⊠ *Via Fratelli Piol 8* ☎*011/9563020* 💳*Admission varies with exhibits* ⊙ *Varies with exhibits.*

Fodor'sChoice The castle of Rivoli now houses the **Museo d'Arte Contemporanea**
★ *(Museum of Contemporary Art).* The building was begun in the 17th

century and then redesigned but never finished by Juvarra in the 18th century; it was finally completed in the late 20th century by minimalist Turin architect Andrea Bruno. On display are changing international exhibitions and a permanent collection of 20th-century Italian art. To get to Rivoli from downtown Turin, take Tram 1 and then Bus 36. ⊠ *Piazzale Mafalda di Savoia* ☎ *011/9565222* ⊕ *www.castellodi-rivoli.org* ⬛ *€6.50* ⊙ *Tues.–Thurs. 10–5, Fri.–Sun. 10–9.*

SACRA DI SAN MICHELE

★ *20 km (13 mi) west of Abbazia di Sant'Antonio di Ranverso, 43 km (27 mi) west of Turin.*

GETTING HERE

Unless you want to do a 14-km (9-mi) hike from the town of Avigliana, a car is essential for an excursion to the Abbey of St. Michael—take the Avigliana Est exit from the Torino–Bardonecchia highway (A32).

Perhaps best known as inspiration for the setting of Umberto Eco's novel *The Name of the Rose,* San Michele was built on Monte Pirchiriano in the 11th century so it would stand out: it occupies the most prominent location for miles around, hanging over a 3,280-foot bluff. When monks came to enlarge the abbey they had to build part of the structure on supports more than 90 feet high—an engineering feat that was famous in medieval Europe and is still impressive today. By the 12th century this important abbey controlled 176 churches in Italy, France, and Spain; one of the abbeys under its influence was Mont-Saint-Michel in France. Because of its strategic position the Abbey of St. Michael came under frequent attacks over the next five centuries and was eventually abandoned in 1622. It was restored, somewhat heavy-handedly, in the late 19th and early 20th centuries.

From **Porta dello Zodiaco,** a splendid Romanesque doorway decorated with the signs of the zodiac, you climb 150 steps, past 12th-century sculptures, to reach the church. On the left side of the interior are 16th-century frescoes representing New Testament themes; on the right are depictions of the founding of the church. In the crypt are some of the oldest parts of the structure, three small 9th- to 12th-century chapels. Note that some sections of the abbey are only open on weekends and, when particularly crowded, visits may be limited to hour-long tours. ☎ *011/939130* ⊕ *www.sacradisanmichele.com* ⬛ *€4* ⊙ *Mid-Mar.–mid-Oct., Tues.–Sat. 9:30–12:30 and 3–6, Sun. 9:30–noon and 2:40–6; mid-Oct.–mid-Mar., Tues.–Sat. 9:30–12:30 and 3–5, Sun. 9:30–noon and 2:40–5.*

On the Slopes in Piedmont & Valle d'Aosta

Skiing is the major sport in both Piedmont and Valle d'Aosta. Excellent facilities abound at resort towns such as Courmayeur and Breuil-Cervinia. The so-called Via Lattea (Milky Way)—five skiing areas near Sestriere with 400 km (almost 250 mi) of linked runs and 90 ski lifts—provides practically unlimited skiing. Lift tickets, running around €35 for a day's pass, are significantly less expensive than at major U.S. resorts.

To Italian skiers, a weeklong holiday on the slopes is known as a *settimana* *bianca* (white week). Ski resort hotels in Piedmont and Valle d'Aosta encourage these getaways by offering six- and seven-day packages, and though they're designed with the domestic market in mind, you can get a bargain by taking advantage of the offers. The packages usually, though not always, include half- or full-board.

You should have your passport with you if you plan to day-trip into France or Switzerland—though odds are you won't be asked to show it.

SESTRIERE

32 km (20 mi) east of Briançon, 93 km (58 mi) west of Turin.

GETTING HERE
By car, follow the A32 west from Turin, exit at Oulx, and follow the SS24 to Sestriere. Train service is available from Turin as far as Oulx—regularly running SAPAV buses complete the journey to Sestriere.

VISITOR INFORMATION
Sestriere tourism office (⌂ *Via Louset 14, 10058* ☎*0122/755444* ⊕*www.comune.sestriere.to.it*).

EXPLORING
In the early 1930s, before skiing became a more egalitarian sport, the patriarch of the FIAT automobile dynasty had this resort built to cater to the elite. The resort has two distinctive tower hotels and ski facilities that have been developed into some of the best in the Alps. It lacks the charm of older Alpine centers, overdevelopment has added some eyesores, and the mountains don't have the striking beauty of those in Valle d'Aosta, but skiers have an excellent choice of trails, some of which cross the border into France.

WHERE TO STAY
$$–$$$$ ⛳ **Hotel Cristallo.** Half of the rooms at this hotel face the slopes of Sestriere, and the ski-lift station is just across the road. You'll find all the facilities you need for a stay in the mountains either in the hotel or just steps away from the lobby entrance. Rooms are elegantly and warmly furnished in the style of a modern ski lodge; ask for one with a terrace facing the view. **Pros:** Excellent location in the center of town, professional and helpful staff, good restaurant, very pleasant decor. **Cons:** Not all rooms have views and terraces, standard rooms are small. ⌂ *Via Pinerolo 5, 10058* ☎*0122/750707* ⊟*0122/755152* ⊕*www.*

newlinehotels.com ↩*46 rooms* ⌂*In-room: safe, refrigerator, dial-up. In-hotel: restaurant, bar, gym, public Wi-Fi, parking (fee)* ⊟*AE, DC, MC, V* ⦿|*BP.*

$$$ ⊡ **Principi di Piemonte.** Large and elegant, this luxurious hotel sits on the slopes above the town, near the lifts and the town's golf course. Its secluded location heightens the sense of exclusivity, and though it's showing signs of age, the hotel still attracts a stylish clientele. The restaurant and a cozy bar invite après-ski relaxation. A minimum stay of one week is required during high season. **Pros:** Secluded location, great service, outstanding views. **Cons:** Outside the town center, pool area and rooms are a little run-down. ⊠ *Via Sauze 3/b, 10058* ☎*0122/7941* 🖷*0122/755411* ⊕*www.gh-principipiemonte.it* ↩*96 rooms, 4 suites* ⌂*In-room: safe, refrigerator. In-hotel: restaurant, bar, pool, spa, public Wi-Fi, some pets allowed* ⊟*AE, DC, MC, V* ⊘*Closed early Apr.– June and Sept.–Nov.* ⦿|*BP.*

$ ⊡ **Miramonti.** Nearly every room has a terrace at this pleasant, central, modern chalet. The ample, comfortable rooms are done in traditional mountain style, with lots of exposed wood and coordinated floral-print fabrics. **Pros:** Central location close to ski lifts, rooms with terraces and views of the mountains. **Cons:** Lobby area is a little run-down. ⊠ *Via Cesana 3, 10058* ☎*0122/755333* 🖷*0122/755375* ⊕*miramontesestriere.it* ↩*30 rooms, 1 suite* ⌂*In room: refrigerator. In-hotel: restaurant, bar, some pets allowed* ⊟*AE, DC, MC, V* ⦿|*BP.*

SPORTS & THE OUTDOORS

SKIING

At 6,670 feet, the ski resort of **Sestriere** (☎*0122/799411 for conditions* ⊕*www.vialattea.it*) was built in the late 1920s under the auspices of Turin's Agnelli family. The slopes get good snow some years from November through May, other years from February through May. The **tourist office** (☎*0122/755444* ⊕*www.comune.sestriere.to.it*) in Sestriere provides complete information about lift tickets, ski runs, mountain guides, and equipment rentals, here and in neighboring towns such as Bardonecchia and Claviere. Its excellent Web site is also navigable in English. A quaint village with slate-roof houses, **Claviere** (⊹*17 km [11 mi] west of Sestriere*) is one of Italy's oldest ski resorts. Its slopes overlap with those of the French resort of Montgenèvre.

THE MONFERRATO & THE LANGHE

Southeast of Turin, in the hilly wooded area around Asti known as the Monferrato and farther south in a similar area around Alba known as the Langhe, the rolling landscape is a patchwork of vineyards and dark woods dotted with hill towns and castles. This is wine country, producing some of Italy's most famous reds and sparkling whites. And hidden away in the woods are the secret places where hunters and their dogs unearth the precious, aromatic truffles worth their weight in gold at Alba's truffle fair.

ASTI

60 km (37 mi) southeast of Turin.

GETTING HERE
Asti is just under an hour away from Turin by car on the A21.

GTT bus service connects the two towns, but is not direct. Train service to Asti, on the other hand, is frequent and fast.

VISITOR INFORMATION
Asti tourism office (⊠ *Piazza Alfieri 29, 14100* ☎*0141/530357* ⊕*www. atasti.it*).

EXPLORING
Asti is best known outside Italy for its wines—excellent reds as well as the famous sparkling white spumante—but its strategic position on trade routes between Turin, Milan, and Genoa has given it a broad economic base. In the 12th century Asti began to develop as a republic, at a time when other Italian cities were also flexing their economic and military muscles. It flourished in the following century, when the inhabitants began erecting lofty **towers** (⊠ *West end of Corso Vittorio Alfieri*) for its defense, giving rise to the medieval nickname "city of 100 towers." In the center of Asti some of these remain, among them the 13th-century **Torre Comentina** and the well-preserved **Torre Troyana,** a tall, slender tower attached to the **Palazzo Troya.** The 18th-century church of **Santa Caterina** has incorporated one of Asti's medieval towers, the **Torre Romana** (itself built on an ancient Roman base), as its bell tower. Corso Vittorio Alfieri is Asti's main thoroughfare, running west–east across the city. This road, known in medieval times as Contrada Maestra, was built by the Romans.

The **Duomo** is an object lesson in the evolution of Gothic architecture. Built in the early 14th century, it's decorated so as to emphasize geometry and verticality: pointed arches and narrow vaults contrast with the earlier, Romanesque attention to balance and symmetry. The porch on the south side of the cathedral facing the square was built in 1470 and represents Gothic at its most florid and excessive. ⊠ *Piazza Cattedrale* ☎*0141/592924* ⊗*Daily 8:30–noon and 3:30–5:30.*

The Gothic church of **San Secondo** is dedicated to Asti's patron saint, reputedly decapitated on the spot where the church now stands. Secondo is also the patron of the city's favorite folklore and sporting event, the annual Palio di Asti, the colorful medieval-style horse race (similar to Siena's) held each year on the third Sunday of September in the vast Campo del Palio to the south of the church. ⊠ *Piazza San Secondo, south of Corso Vittorio Alfieri* ☎*0141/530066* ⊗*Mon.–Sat. 10:45– noon and 3:30–5:30, Sun. 3:30–5:30.*

WHERE TO STAY & EAT

$$$$
Fodor's Choice
★

✕ **Gener Neuv.** One of Italy's best restaurants, the family-run Gener Neuv is known for its rustic elegance. The setting on the bank of the Tanaro River is splendid. The menu of regional specialties may include agnolotti *ai tre stufati* (with a filling of ground rabbit, veal, and pork), and to finish, *composta di prugne e uva* (prune and grape compote). Fixed-price menus are available with or without the wine included. As you might expect, the wine list is first-rate. ✉*Lungo Tanaro 4, 14100* ☎*0141/557270* ⊕*www.generneuv.it* ▭*AE, DC, MC, V* ⊘*Closed Aug. and Mon., and Sun. Jan.–July. No dinner Sun.*

$$$ ✕ **L'Angolo del Beato.** Regional specialties such as *bagna cauda* (literally "hot bath," a dip for vegetables made with anchovies, garlic, butter, and olive oil) and *tagliolini al ragu di anatra* (pasta with a duck sauce) are the main attractions at this central Asti restaurant, housed in a building that dates to the 12th century. There's also a good wine list. ✉*Via Guttuari 12* ☎*0141/531668* ▭*AE, DC, MC, V* ⊘*Closed Sun., last wk of Dec., 1st wk of Jan., and 3 wks in Aug.*

$$ ▦ **Reale.** This hotel in a 19th-century building is located on Asti's main square. The spacious rooms are somewhat eclectically decorated, with a mix of contemporary and period furniture. Though this is one of the oldest hotels in Asti, all the bathrooms have been modernized and are spotlessly maintained. **Pros:** Spacious rooms, very central location. **Cons:** Lobby area looking a little worn, rooms facing the main square can be noisy. ✉*Piazza Alfieri 6, 14100* ☎*0141/530240* 🖷*0141/34357* ⊕*www.hotelristorantereale.it* ↝*25 rooms, 2 suites* ⌂*In-room: refrigerator. In-hotel: parking (fee), some pets allowed* ▭*AE, DC, MC, V* †◉|*BP.*

$ ▦ **Rainero.** A modernized hotel near the train station, the Rainero has been run by the same family for three generations. It's fitted with cheerful contemporary furnishings and is popular with business travelers. **Pros:** Convenient location, good value. **Cons:** Caters mainly to a business clientele, in a busy area that has a lot of traffic. ✉*Via Cavour 85, 14100* ☎*0141/353866* 🖷*0141/594985* ⊕*www.hotelrainero.com* ↝*53 rooms, 2 suites* ⌂*In-room: refrigerator. In-hotel: bar, public Internet, parking (fee), some pets allowed* ▭*AE, V* ⊘*Closed Jan. 1–15* †◉|*BP.*

SHOPPING

The **Enoteca** on Piazza Alfieri, a square adjacent to Campo del Palio, is a wine center and shop, open Monday–Saturday 9–4:30, where you can try a range of Asti vintages, buy a bottle, and have a light snack. Be aware, though, that prices for spumante in Asti are not necessarily lower than those elsewhere.

ALBA

30 km (18 mi) southwest of Asti.

GETTING HERE

By car from Turin follow the A6 south to Marene and then take the A33 east. GTT offers frequent bus service between Alba and Turin—the journey takes approximately 1½ hours. There is no direct train service, but you can get to Alba from Turin by making one transfer in either Asti, Bra, or Cavallermaggiore; the entire trip takes about 1½ hours.

Continued on page 428

ON THE TRAIL OF BAROLO

Picture yourself in the background of a grand medieval mural, and you won't be far off from what you experience driving through the idyllic wooded landscape south of Turin, in Piedmont's Langhe district.

The crests of the graceful hills are dotted with villages, each lorded over by an ancient castle. The gentle slopes of the valleys below are lined with row upon row of Nebbiolo grapes, the choicest of which are used to make Barolo wine. Dubbed "the king of wines and wine of kings" in the 19th century after finding favor with King Carlo Alberto, Barolo still wears the crown, despite stiff competition from all corners of Italy.

Above, Serralunga's castle
Right, bottles of old vintage Barolo

The Langhe district is smaller and surprisingly less visited by food-and-wine enthusiasts than Chianti and the surrounding areas of Tuscany, but it yields similar rewards. The best way to tour the Barolo-producing region is on day trips from the delightful truffle town of Alba—getting around is easy, the country roads are gorgeous, and the wine is fit for a king.

ALL ABOUT BAROLO

The Nebbiolo grapes that go into this famous wine come not just from Barolo proper (the area surrounding the tiny town of Barolo), but also from a small zone that encompasses the hill towns of Novello, Monforte d'Alba, Serralunga d'Alba, Castiglione Falletto, La Morra, and Verduno. All are connected by small but easy-to-navigate roads.

When wine lovers talk about Barolo, they talk about tannins—the quality that makes red wine dry out your mouth. Tannins come from the grape skins; red wine—which gets its color from the skins—has them, white wine doesn't. Tannins can be balanced out by acidity (the quality that makes your mouth water), but they also soften over time. As a good red wine matures, flavors emerge more clearly, achieving a harmonious balance of taste and texture.

A bottle of Barolo is often born so overwhelmingly tannic that many aficionados won't touch the stuff until it has aged 10 or 15 years. But a good Barolo ages beautifully, eventually spawning complex, intermingled tastes of tobacco, roses, and earth. It's not uncommon to see bottles for sale from the 1960s, 1950s, or even the 1930s.

WHERE TO DRINK IT

The word *enoteca* in Italian can mean a wine store, or a wine bar, or both. The words "wine bar," on the other hand—which are becoming increasingly trendy—mean just that. Either way, these are great places to sample and buy the wines of the Langhe.

An excellent enoteca in Alba is **Vincafé** (Via V. Emanuele, 12, Alba, 0173/364603). It specializes in tastes of Langhe wines, accompanied by *salumi* (cured meats), cheeses, and other regional products. More than 350 wines, as well as grappas and liqueurs, grace Vincafé's distinguished list. It's open from noon to midnight, and there's food until 9 pm.

In the fortfied hill town of Barolo, visit the **Castello di Barolo** (Piazza Falletti, 0173/56277, www.baroloworld.it) which has a little wine bar and a museum dedicated to Barolo.

HOW MUCH DOES IT COST?

The most reasonably priced, but still enjoyable Barolos will cost you €20 to €30. A very good but not top-of-the-line bottle will cost €40 to €60. For a top-of-the-line bottle you may spend anywhere from €80 to €200.

LABELS TO LOOK FOR

Barolo is a strictly controlled denomination, but that doesn't mean all Barolos are equal. Legendary producers include Prunotto, Aldo Conterno, Giacomo Conterno, Bruno Giacosa, Famiglia Anselma, Mascarello, Pio Cesare, and Michele Chiarlo.

WINE ESTATES TO VISIT

Right in the town of Barolo, an easy, if touristy, option for a visit is **Marchesi di Barolo** (Via Alba 12, Barolo, 0173/564400, www.marchesibarolo. com). In the estate's user-friendly enoteca you can taste wine, buy thousands of different bottles from vintages going way back, and look at display bottles, including an 1859 Barolo. Marchesi di Barolo's *cantine* (wine cellars, Via Roma 1, Barolo) are open daily 10:30–5:30. The staff here is used to catering to visitors, so you won't have to worry too much about endearing yourself to them.

From there you might want to graduate to **Famiglia Anselma** (Loc. Castello della Volta, Barolo, 0173/787217, www.anselma.it). Winemaker Maurizio Anselma, in his mid-20s, is something of a prodigy in the Barolo world, and he's quite open to visitors. He is known for his steadfast commitment to produce only Barolo—nothing else—and for his policy of holding his wines for several years before release.

A good, accessible example of the new school of Barolo winemaking is **Podere Rocche dei Manzoni** (3, Loc. Manzini Soprano, Monforte d'Alba, 0173/78421, www.barolobig.com). The facade of the cantina is like a Roman temple of brick, complete with imposing columns. Rocche dei Manzoni's reds include four Barolos, one Dolcetto, one Langhe Rosso, two Langhe DOCs, and two Barbera d'Albas.

WINE TOUR TIPS

Keep in mind that visiting wineries in Italy is different from what you might have experienced in the Napa Valley or in France. Wherever you go, reservations are most definitely required, and you'll usually be the only person or group on the tour—so be sure to show up when you say you will, and keep in mind that it's impolite not to buy something in the end.

Wine buyers and wine professionals are the expected audience for tours. While this attitude is slowly changing and many winemakers are beginning to welcome interested outsiders, it's important to be humble and enthusiastic. You'll be treated best if you come in with an open mind, respect that the winemaker probably knows more about wine than you do, and make it clear that you aren't just looking to drink for free. It helps to speak Italian, but if you don't, the international language of effusive compliments can still go a long way.

BEYOND BAROLO

Neive, in the Barbaresco region

By no means do the fruits of the Langhe end with Barolo. The region boasts Italy's highest concentration of DOC (denominazione di origine controllata) and DOCG (denominazione di origine controllata e garantita) wines, the two most prestigious categories of appellation in Italy. The other DOCG in the Langhe is Barbaresco, which, like Barolo, is made from the Nebbiolo grape. Barbaresco is not quite as tannic as Barolo, however, and can be drunk younger.

VISITOR INFORMATION

Alba tourism office (✉ *Piazza Risorgimento 2, 12051* ☎ *0173/35833* ⊕ *www.langheroero.it*).

EXPLORING

This small town has a gracious atmosphere and a compact core studded with medieval towers and Gothic buildings. In addition to being a wine center of the region, Alba is known as the "City of the White Truffle" for the dirty little tubers that command a higher price per ounce than diamonds. For picking out your truffle and having a few wisps shaved on top of your food, expect to shell out an extra €16—which is well worth it. Visit in October for the Fiera del Tartufo (National Truffle Fair), Cento Torri Joust (a medieval jousting festival), and the Palio degli Asini (donkey races), held the first Sunday of the month.

WHERE TO STAY

$ 🏨 **La Meridiana.** If Alba strikes your fancy, consider a night at this reasonably priced belle epoque–style B&B, on a hill overlooking the historic center and surrounded by Dolcetto and Nebbiolo grapevines. **Pros:** Friendly, family atmosphere; in a secluded setting convenient for exploring the Langhe. **Cons:** Long walk to nearest restaurants, no a/c in some rooms. ✉ *Località Altavilla 948023* ☎📠 *0173/440112* ✎ *cascinareine@libero.it* 🛏 *9 rooms, 1 suite* ⚒ *In-room: no a/c (some), no phone. In-hotel: pool, gym, no elevator* ═ *No credit cards* ⫶○⫶ *BP.*

VALLE D'AOSTA

The unspoiled beauty of the highest peaks in the Alps, the Matterhorn and Monte Bianco, competes with the magnificent scenery of Italy's oldest national park in Valle d'Aosta, a semiautonomous, bilingual region tucked away at the border with France and Switzerland. Luckily, you don't have to choose—the region is small, so you can fit skiing, après-ski, and wild ibex into one memorable trip. The main Aosta Valley, largely on an east–west axis, is hemmed in by high mountains where glaciers have gouged out 14 tributary valleys, six to the north and eight to the south. A car is very helpful here, but take care: though distances are relatively short as the crow flies, steep slopes and winding roads add to your mileage and travel time.

Coming up from Turin, beyond Ivrea the road takes you through countryside that becomes hillier and hillier, passing through steep ravines guarded by brooding, romantic castles. Pont St. Martin, about 18 km (11 mi) north of Ivrea, is the beginning of bilingual (Italian and French) territory.

ST. VINCENT

93 km (58 mi) north of Turin.

Valle
d'Aosta

GETTING HERE

GETTING HERE

St. Vincent is just off the A5 highway that connects Aosta with Turin. SADEM buses operate between Turin and St. Vincent's casino, and regular local train service is available from Aosta.

VISITOR INFORMATION

St. Vincent tourism office (✉ *Via Roma 62, 11027* ☎ *0166/512239* ⊕ *www. saintvincentvda.it*).

EXPLORING

The town of St. Vincent has been a popular spa resort since the late 18th century. Its main draw these days is the **Casinò de la Vallée,** one of Europe's largest gambling casinos. You must present identification and be at least 18 years old to enter. Dress is elegant, with jacket and tie requested at the French gaming tables. ✉ *Via Italo Mus 1* ☎ *0166/5221* ⊕ *www.casinodelavallee.it* 💶 *€5* ⏱ *Sun.–Fri. 3* PM–*3:30* AM, *Sat. 3* PM–*4* AM.

WHERE TO STAY & EAT

★ **$$$$** ✕ **Nuovo Batezar—da Renato.** This tiny restaurant with only eight tables ranks among the best in all of Italy. The ambience is rustic yet elegant, with arches and beamed ceilings enhanced by local antiques and fine crystal. The menu, which changes with the seasons, is Valdostana and

Piedmontese, with creative variations. Mushrooms, fish, fresh game, and truffles often play prominent roles. As a starter, try the homemade pasta or the *pazzarella* (a small pizza with porcini mushrooms, mozzarella, and truffles). ⊠ *Via Marconi 1, near casino* ☎ *0166/513164* ⚞ *Reservations essential* ▤ *AE, DC, MC, V* ☾ *Closed Wed., 3 wks in June, and Nov. 15–30. No lunch weekdays.*

$$$$ ▥ **Billia.** A belle epoque hotel with faux-Gothic touches, the Billia is in a park in the middle of town and connects directly to the casino via a passageway. Half the rooms are done in modern and half in period decor, but all have high ceilings, finely upholstered furniture, and well-stocked bathrooms. **Pros:** Adjacent to the casino, surrounded by parkland, good for those who want old-world luxury. **Cons:** Lobby area and some rooms are showing signs of wear, long empty halls and cavernous public spaces give the place a somewhat forbidding air. ⊠ *Viale Piemonte 72, 11027* ☎ *0166/5231* 🖷 *0166/523799* ⊕ *www.grand-hotelbillia.com* ⋑ *233 rooms, 7 suites* ⚒ *In-room: dial-up. In-hotel: restaurant, bar, tennis court, pool, gym, public Internet* ▤ *AE, DC, MC, V* ⏧ *BP.*

$ ▥ **Elena.** A central location is the selling point of this hotel near the casino. The spacious rooms, some with balconies and king-size beds, are decorated in a comfortable modern style. **Pros:** Great location in the center of town, excellent value. **Cons:** No a/c, the area can be busy and noisy during peak season. ⊠ *Via Biavaz 2 Piazza Zerbion, 11027* ☎ *0166/512140* 🖷 *0166/537459* ⊕ *www.hotelelena.be* ⋑ *46 rooms, 2 suites* ⚒ *In-room: no a/c (some), refrigerator. In-hotel: restaurant, bar, gym, parking (fee), no-smoking rooms* ▤ *AE, DC, MC, V* ⏧ *BP.*

BREUIL-CERVINIA/THE MATTERHORN

30 km (18 mi) north of St. Vincent, 116 km (72 mi) north of Turin.

GETTING HERE

From Aosta take the A5 and then the SR46 (1 hour); from Turin take the A5 and then the SR46 (90 minutes). SADEM has regular bus service from Turin; SAVDA buses travel here from Milan. Breuil-Cervinia is not on a train line.

VISITOR INFORMATION

Breuil-Cervinia tourism office (⊠ *Via Guido Rey 17, 11021* ☎ *0166/949136* ⊕ *www.cervinia.it*).

EXPLORING

Breuil-Cervinia is a village at the base of the **Matterhorn** *(Monte Cervino in Italian; Mont Cervin in French).* Like the village, the famous peak straddles the border between Italy and Switzerland, and all sightseeing and skiing facilities are operated jointly. Splendid views of the peak can be seen from **Plateau Rosa** and the **Cresta del Furggen,** both of which can be reached by cable car from the center of Breuil-Cervinia. Although many locals complain that the tourist facilities and condominiums have changed the face of their beloved village, most would agree that the cable car has given them access to climbing and off-trail skiing in ridges that were once inaccessible.

WHERE TO STAY & EAT

★ $$$$ ✕⌂ **Les Neiges d'Antan.** In an evergreen forest at Perrères, just outside Cervinia, this family-run inn is quiet and cozy, with three big fireplaces and a nice view of the

Matterhorn. An excellent restaurant (¢–$$) serves French dishes and local specialties such as *zuppa Valpellinentze* (a hearty soup of bread, cabbage, and fontina cheese) and an opulent antipasto (local salami, country pâté, *tomino* cheese, and much more). **Pros:** Secluded and beautiful setting, excellent restaurant, well-designed spa facilities. **Cons:** 5 km (3 mi) outside Breuil-Cervinia (a car is essential), entrance and lobby areas are showing some wear. ✉*Località Perrères, 11021* ☎*0166/948775* 🖷*0166/948852* ⊕*www.lesneigesdantan.it* ➷*21 rooms, 3 suites* ♿*In-room: no a/c, safe, refrigerator, DVD, Wi-Fi. In-hotel: restaurant, bar, spa, public Wi-Fi* ▭*AE, MC, V* ⊗*Closed May and June* ⦿*BP.*

$$$ ✕⌂ **Cime Bianche.** This calm, quiet mountain lodge offers commanding views of the Matterhorn and surrounding peaks from the balconies of its guest rooms. Wood-paneled rooms are simply furnished with the trekker in mind. The restaurant (¢–$) is one of the few dining spots in town to offer regional Valdostana cuisine, serving *fonduta* (a local version of fondue, made with melted cheese, eggs, and sometimes grated truffles), polenta, and wild game in a rustic setting. The wood beams and tables are typical of a ski resort, but meals are produced with greater care than your average après-ski affairs. Reservations are highly recommended. **Pros:** Next to the ski slopes, great restaurant, lovely views. **Cons:** Lobby is showing wear, very busy during the ski season, location is far from everything but slopes. ✉*Località La Vieille 44, near the ski lift, 11021* ☎*0166/949046* 🖷*0166/948061* ⊕*www. hotelcimebianche.com* ➷*15 rooms* ♿*In-room: no a/c. In-hotel: restaurant, bar* ▭*MC, V* ⊗*Closed Mon., and May and June* ⦿*BP.*

$$$$ ⌂ **Hermitage.** The entryway's marble relief of St. Theodolus reminds you that this was the site of a hermitage, but asceticism has given way to comfort and elegance at what is now one of the most exclusive hotels in the region. It has the look of a relaxed but posh family chalet, with rustic antiques, petit-point upholstery, a fire always glowing in the enormous hearth, and a candlelit dining room. The bright bedrooms have balconies; suites have antique fireplaces and 18th-century furnishings. While here you can make use of Hermitage's extensive health and beauty facilities and play golf (for half price) at the Cervinia Golf Club. **Pros:** Superlative staff, refined atmosphere, frequent shuttle service into town and to ski lifts. **Cons:** Located 2 km (1 mi) from the town center, half board is mandatory during the winter season. ✉*Via Piolet 1, Località Chapellette, 11021* ☎*0166/948998* 🖷*0166/949032* ⊕*www. hotelhermitage.com* ➷*30 rooms, 6 suites* ♿*In-room: safe, refrigera-*

7

tor, Wi-Fi. In-hotel: restaurant, bar, pool, gym, public Wi-Fi ▣AE, DC, MC, V ✆Closed May, June, Sept., and Nov. ▯MAP.

SPORTS & THE OUTDOORS

CLIMBING

Serious climbers can make the ascent of the Matterhorn from Breuil-Cervinia after registering with the local mountaineering officials at the tourist office. This climb is for experienced climbers only. Before embarking on an excursion, contact the representative of the **Club Alpino Italiano** (✉*Piazza E. Chanoux 8, Aosta* ☎*0165/40194* ⊕*www. cai.it*) for information about hikes and the risks. Guides from the **Società delle Guide Alpine** (✉*Strada Villair 2, Courmayeur* ☎*0165/842064* ⊕*www.guidecourmayeur.com*) can accompany you on treks and also lead skiing, canyoning, and ice-climbing excursions. Less-demanding hikes follow the lower slopes of the valley of the River Marmore, to the south of town.

SKIING

Because its slopes border the Cervino glacier, this resort at the foot of the Matterhorn offers year-round skiing. Sixty lifts and a few hundred miles of ski runs ranging from beginner to expert make the area one of the best and most popular in Italy. Contact the tourist office for information.

CASTELLO FÉNIS

♺ *11 km (7 mi) west of St. Vincent, 104 km (65 mi) north of Turin.*

Fodor's Choice
★

GETTING HERE

To reach the castle by car, take the Nus exit from the main A5 highway. SAVDA buses provide infrequent service between Aosta and Fénis. The closest train station, in Nus, is a 5-km (3-mi) walk from the castle.

EXPLORING

The best-preserved medieval fortress in Valle d'Aosta, the many-turreted Castello Fénis was built in the mid-14th century by Aimone di Challant, a member of a prolific family related to the Savoys. The castle, which used a double ring of walls for its defense, is the sort imagined by schoolchildren, with pointed towers, portcullises, and spiral staircases. The 15th-century courtyard surrounded by wooden balconies is elegantly decorated with well-preserved frescoes. Inside you can see the kitchen, with an enormous fireplace that provided central heat in winter; the armory; and the spacious, well-lighted rooms used by the lord and lady of the manor. If you have time to visit only one castle in Valle d'Aosta, this should be it. ☎*0165/764263* ▣*€5* ✆*Mar.–June, daily 9–6:30; July and Aug., daily 9–7:30; Sept., daily 9–6:30; Oct.–Feb., Wed.–Mon. 10–5. Maximum of 25 people allowed to enter every ½ hr.*

**EN
ROUTE**

The highway continues climbing through Valle d'Aosta to the town of Aosta itself. The road at this point is heading almost due west, with rivulets from the wilderness reserve Parco Nazionale del Gran Paradiso streaming down from the left to join the Dora Baltea River, one of the major tributaries of the Po and an increasingly popular spot for rafting. Be careful driving here in late spring, when melting snow can turn some of these streams into torrents.

AOSTA

12 km (7 mi) west of Castello Fénis, 113 km (70 mi) north of Turin.

GETTING HERE
Aosta can easily be reached by car or bus from Milan and Turin. The town is off the main A5 highway. SAVDA buses regularly travel to and from Milan, Turin, and Chamonix in France. Direct train service (2 hours) is also available from Turin, but a change of trains is required if traveling here from Milan (3 hours).

VISITOR INFORMATION
Aosta tourism office (✉*Piazza E. Chanoux 2, 11100* ☎*0165/236627* ⊕*www.regione.vda.it/turismo*).

EXPLORING
Aosta stands at the junction of two of the important trade routes that connect France and Italy—the valleys of the Rhône and the Isère. Its significance as a trading post was recognized by the Romans, who built a garrison here in the 1st century BC. At the eastern entrance to town, in the Piazza Arco d'Augusto and commanding a fine view over Aosta and the mountains, is the **Arco di Augusto** *(Arch of Augustus)*, built in 25 BC to mark Rome's victory over the Celtic Salassi tribe. (The sloping roof was added in 1716 in an attempt to keep rain from seeping between the stones.) The present-day layout of streets in this small city tucked away in the Alps more than 644 km (400 mi) from Rome is the clearest example of Roman urban planning in Italy. Well-preserved Roman walls form a perfect rectangle around the center of Aosta, and the regular pattern of streets reflects its role as a military stronghold. St. Anselm, born in Aosta, later became archbishop of Canterbury in England.

The **Collegiata di Sant'Orso** is the sort of church that has layers of history in its architecture. Originally there was a 6th-century chapel on this site founded by the Archdeacon Orso, a local saint. Most of this structure was destroyed or hidden when an 11th-century church was erected over it. This church, in turn, was encrusted with Gothic, and later baroque, features, resulting in a jigsaw puzzle of styles, but, surprisingly, not a chaotic jumble. The 11th-century features are almost untouched in the crypt, and if you go up the stairs on the left from the main church you can see the 11th-century frescoes (ask the sacristan who let you in). These restored frescoes depict the life of Christ and the apostles: although only the tops are visible, you can see the expressions on the faces of the disciples. Take the outside doorway to the right of the main entrance to see the church's crowning glory, its 12th-century **cloister.** Next to the church, it's enclosed by some 40 stone columns with masterfully carved capitals depicting scenes from the Old and New Testaments and the life of St. Orso. The turrets and spires of Aosta peek out above. ⊠ *Via Sant'Orso* ☎ *0165/40614* ⏰ *Apr.–Sept., daily 9–5; Oct.–Mar., daily 10–5.*

The huge **Roman Porta Pretoria,** regally guarding the city, is a remarkable relic from the Roman era. The area between the massive inner and outer gates was used as a small parade ground for the changing of the guard. ⊠ *West end of Via Sant'Anselmo.*

The 72-foot-high ruin of the facade of the **Teatro Romano** guards the remains of the 1st-century BC amphitheater, which once held 20,000 spectators. Only a bit of the outside wall and seven of the amphitheater's original 60 arches remain. The latter, once incorporated into medieval buildings, are being brought to light by ongoing archaeological excavations. ⊠ *Via Anfiteatro 4.*

Aosta's **Duomo** dates from the 10th century, but all that remains from that period are the bell towers. The decoration inside is primarily Gothic, but the main attraction of the cathedral predates that era by 1,000 years: a carved ivory diptych portraying the Roman Emperor Honorius and dating from AD 406 is among the many ornate objects housed in the treasury. ⊠ *Via Monsignor de Sales* ☎ *0165/40251* ⏰ *Duomo: Easter–Sept. 7, Mon.–Sat. 6:30 PM–8 PM, Sun. 7 AM–8 PM; Sept. 8–Easter, Mon.–Sat. 6:30–noon and 3–7, Sun. 7–noon and 3–7. Treasury: Apr.–Sept., Tues.–Sun. 9–11:30 and 3–5:30; Oct.–Mar., Sun. 3–5:30.*

WHERE TO STAY & EAT

$$$$ ✕ **Vecchio Ristoro.** Housed in a converted mill, the intimate spaces of this elegant restaurant are furnished with antiques, and a traditional ceramic stove provides additional warmth in cool weather. The chef-proprietor takes pride in creative versions of regional recipes, including *cosciotto di maialino arrosto con composta di mele e salsa senape* (roast pork ribs with an apple and mustard sauce) and *quaglietto disossata farcita alle castagne fatta al forno* (roast quail with chestnut stuffing). ⊠ *Via Tourneuve 4* ☎ *0165/33238* ▭ *AE, DC, MC, V* ⏰ *Closed Sun., June, and 1 wk in Nov. No lunch Mon.*

$$ ✕ **La Brasserie du Commerce.** In the heart of Aosta, this small and lively eatery sits near the Piazza Emile Chanoux. On a sunny summer day try to snag a table in the restaurant's courtyard garden. Typical valley dishes such as fonduta are on the menu, as well as many vegetable dishes and salads. Pizza is also served, but only on the ground floor. ⊠ *Via de Tillier 10* ☎ *0165/35613* ▭ *AE, DC, MC, V* ⏰ *Closed Sun.*

$$ ✕ **Praetoria.** Just outside the Porta Pretoria, this simple and unpretentious restaurant serves hearty local dishes such as *crespelle alla valdostana* (crepes with cheese and ham). The pasta is made on the premises, and all of the menu offerings are prepared from traditional recipes. ⊠ *Via Sant'Anselmo 9* ☎ *0165/44356* ▭ *AE, DC, MC, V* ⏰ *Closed Thurs. No dinner Wed.*

$$ 🏠 **Milleluci.** This small and inviting family-run hotel sits in an enviable position overlooking Aosta, 1 km (½ mi) north of town. A huge brick hearth and rustic wooden beams highlight the lounge. Bedrooms, some with balconies, are bright and charmingly decorated; all with splendid views of the city and mountains. The same great views are available in

Fodor'sChoice ★

summer months from the pool. **Pros:** Panoramic views, great spa facilities, cozy and traditionally decorated rooms. **Cons:** Need a car to get around, no a/c. ⊠*Località Porossan Roppoz 15, 11100* ☎*0165/235278* ☐*0165/235284* ⊕*www.hotelmilleluci.com* ➷*26 rooms, 5 suites* ⊘*In-room: no a/c, safe, refrigerator, Wi-Fi. In-hotel: bar, pool, spa, public Wi-Fi, no-smoking rooms* ⊟*AE, DC, MC, V* ⦿*BP.*

$ 🏰 **Casa Ospitaliera del Gran San Bernardo.** Here's your chance to sleep in a 12th-century castle without emptying your wallet. In a monastery that Amedeo of Savoy gave to the Order of St. Bernard in 1137, this bargain-price lodging is still run by monks. Only 15 km (8 mi) north of Aosta, this simple pension is a good base for hikers and cross-country skiers. Hearty food is included in the full meal plan. **Pros:** Good base for budget-conscious skiers and hikers, secluded atmosphere. **Cons:** Isolated location (no towns or restaurants nearby), extremely simple accommodations. ⊠*Rue de Flassin 3, 11010Saint-Oyen* ☎*0165/78247* ☐*0165/789512* ➷*15 rooms* ⊘*In-room: no a/c, no phone, no TV. In-hotel: no elevator* ⊟*No credit cards* ⊗*Closed May* ⦿*FAP.*

COURMAYEUR/MONTE BIANCO

★ *35 km (21 mi) northwest of Aosta, 150 km (93 mi) northwest of Turin.*

GETTING HERE
Courmayeur is on the main A5 highway and can easily be reached by car from both Turin and Milan via Aosta. SAVDA buses run regularly from both Turin and Milan. Train service is not available.

VISITOR INFORMATION
Courmayeur tourism office (⊠*Piazzale Monte Bianco 13, 11013* ☎*0165/842060* ⊕*www.courmayeur.net*).

EXPLORING
The main attraction of Courmayeur is a knock-'em-dead view of Europe's tallest peak, **Monte Bianco** *(Mont Blanc).* Jet-set celebrities flock here, following a tradition that dates from the late 17th century, when Courmayeur's natural springs first began to draw visitors. The spectacle of the Alps gradually surpassed the springs as the biggest draw (the Alpine letters of the English poet Percy Bysshe Shelley were almost advertisements for the region), but the biggest change came in 1965 with the opening of the Mont Blanc tunnel. Since then, ever-increasing numbers of travelers have passed through the area.

Luckily, planners have managed to keep some restrictions on wholesale development within the town, and its angled rooftops and immaculate cobblestone streets maintain a cozy (if prepackaged) feeling.

From La Palud, a small town 4 km (2½ mi) north of Courmayeur, you can catch the cable car up to the top of Monte Bianco. In summer, if you get the inclination, you can then switch cable cars and descend into Chamonix, in France. In winter you can ski parts of the route off-piste. The Funivie La Palud whisks you up first to the Pavillon du

Mont Fréty—a starting point for many beautiful hikes—and then to the Rifugio di Torino, before arriving at the viewing platform at **Punta Helbronner** (more than 11,000 feet), which is also the border post with France. Monte Bianco's attraction is not so much its shape (much less distinctive than that of the Matterhorn) as its expanse and the vistas from the top.

The next stage up—only in summer—is on the **Télépherique de L'Aiguille du Midi,** as you pass into French territory. The trip is particularly impressive: you dangle over a huge glacial snowfield (more than 2,000 feet below) and make your way slowly to the viewing station above Chamonix. It's one of the most dramatic rides in Europe. From this point you're looking down into France, and if you change cable cars at the Aiguille du Midi station you can make your way down to Chamonix itself. The return trip covers the same route. Schedules are unpredictable, depending on weather conditions and demand; contact the **Courmayeur tourist office** (☎ *0165/842060* ⊕ *www.courmayeur.net*) for more information. ✉ *Frazione La Palud 22* ☎ *0165/89925 Italian side, 00/33450536210 French side* ⊕ *www. montebianco.com* ✆ *€13 round-trip to Pavillon du Mont Fréty, €32 round-trip to Helbronner, €48 round-trip to Aiguille du Midi, €75 round-trip to Chamonix* ☉ *Call for hrs. Closed mid-Oct.–mid-Dec., depending on demand and weather.*

WHERE TO STAY & EAT

★ **$$$$** ✕ **Maison de Filippo.** Here you'll find country-style home cooking in a mountain house with lots of atmosphere, furnished with antiques, farm tools, and bric-a-brac of all kinds. There's a set menu only, which includes an abundance of antipasti, a tempting choice of local soups and pasta dishes, and an equally impressive array of traditional second courses, including fonduta *valdostana* (cheese fondue), and an equally hearty *carbonada* (beef stew and polenta). Cheese, dessert, and fresh fruit complete the meal. Don't head here if you are looking for something light to eat, and make sure to reserve in advance—it's one of the most popular restaurants in Valle d'Aosta. ✉ *Entrèves* ☎ *0165/869797* ⌂ *Reservations essential* ▭ *MC, V* ☉ *Closed Tues., mid-May–June, Oct., and Nov.*

★ **$$$** ✕ **Cadran Solaire.** The Garin family made over the oldest tavern in Courmayeur to create a warm and inviting restaurant that has a 17th-century stone vault, old wooden floor, and huge stone fireplace. The menu offers seasonal specialties and innovative interpretations of regional dishes. The cozy bar is a popular place for a before-dinner drink. ✉ *Via Roma 122* ☎ *0165/844609* ⌂ *Reservations essential* ▭ *AE, MC, V* ☉ *Closed Tues., May, and Oct.*

$$$$ ✕🏨 **Royal e Golf.** A longtime landmark in the center of Courmayeur, the Royal rises high above the surrounding town. With wide terraces and wood paneling, it is the most elegant spot in town. The cheery rooms have plenty of amenities. The hotel's restaurant ($$$–$$$$) is renowned for its regional and national cuisine—the *scaloppina alla valdostana* (fillet of veal with cheese, wine, and nutmeg sauce) is excellent. Light lunches are served in the hotel bar. The heated outdoor pool, with its panoramic view, is a great place to relax after a day on the slopes. The hotel caters to longer stays with half- or full-board service. **Pros:** Central location on Courmayeur's main pedestrian street, panoramic views, heated outdoor pool. **Cons:** Standard rooms can be small, meal plan required, town center can be busy. ✉ *Via Roma 87, 11013* ☎*0165/831611* 📠*0165/842093* ⊕*www.hotelroyalegolf.com* 🛏*80 rooms, 6 suites* ♿*In-room: no a/c, safe, refrigerator, dial-up. In-hotel: restaurant, bar, pool, gym, some pets allowed, no-smoking rooms* ☰*AE, DC, MC, V* ⊘*Closed wk after Easter–mid-June and mid-Sept.–Nov.* 🍽*MAP.*

$$$$

Fodor'sChoice
★

🏠 **Villa Novecento.** Run with the friendly charm and efficiency of Franco Cavaliere and his son Stefano, the Novecento is a peaceful haven near Courmayeur's otherwise busy center. In keeping with the style of a comfortable mountain lodge, the lounge is warmed by a log fire in winter. Traditional fabrics, wooden furnishings, and early-19th-century prints lend a soothing quality to the rooms. The restaurant, with only a few extra tables for nonguests, serves creative adaptations of traditional cuisine; it's a good choice for a relaxed evening meal after an active day on the slopes. **Pros:** Charming and cozy accommodations, good restaurant, close to town center but away from the hubbub. **Cons:** Parking is limited, no a/c. ✉ *Viale Monte Bianco 64, 11013* ☎*0165/843000* 📠*0165/844030* ⊕*www.villanovecento. it* 🛏*24 rooms, 2 suites* ♿*In-room: no a/c, safe, refrigerator, Wi-Fi. In-hotel: restaurant, bar, gym, some pets allowed* ☰*AE, DC, MC, V* ⊘*Closed May and Nov.* 🍽*BP.*

$$$

🏠 **Auberge de la Maison.** This modern hotel's stone-and-wood construction, typical of this region, gives it the feeling of a country inn. Most of the cozy rooms have views of Monte Bianco. Alpine prints on the walls, plush fabrics, and wood-burning stoves make the accommodations very comfortable. A massage here can be the perfect ending to a day of hiking or skiing. **Pros:** Secluded location in the center of Entrèves, nice spa, charming decor. **Cons:** Isolated location (a car is essential), not all standard rooms have views of Monte Bianco. ✉ *Via Passerin d'Entrèves 16, 11013* ☎*0165/869811* 📠*0165/869759* ⊕*www.aubergemaison.it* 🛏*30 rooms, 3 suites* ♿*In-room: no a/c, safe, refrigerator, Wi-Fi. In-hotel: restaurant, spa, public Wi-Fi, parking (no fee)* ☰*AE, MC, V* ⊘*Closed May and 15 days in Nov.* 🍽*BP.*

$$

🏠 **Croux.** This bright, comfortable hotel is near the town center on the road leading to Monte Bianco. Half the rooms have balconies, the other half have great views of the mountains. The friendly staff goes out of its way to make you feel welcome. **Pros:** Central location, great views, B&B rates are available. **Cons:** Lobby area is a little run-down, located on a busy road in the town center. ✉ *Via Croux 8, 11013* ☎*0165/846735* 📠*0165/845180* ⊕*www.hotelcroux.it* 🛏*33 rooms* ♿*In-room: no a/c. In-hotel: bar, public Wi-Fi* ☰*AE, DC, MC, V* ⊘*Closed mid-Apr.–mid-June, Oct., and Nov.* 🍽*BP.*

SKIING

Courmayeur pales in comparison to its French neighbor, Chamonix, in both the number (it has only 24) and the quality of its trails. But with good natural snow cover, the trails and vistas are spectacular. A huge gondola leads from the center of Courmayeur to Plan Checrouit, where gondolas and lifts lead to the slopes. The skiing around Monte Bianco is particularly good, and the off-piste options are among the best in Europe. The off-piste routes from Cresta d'Arp (the local peak) to Dolonne, and from La Palud area into France, should be done with a guide. Contact the **Funivie Courmayeur/Mont Blanc** (☎*0165/89925*) for complete information about lift tickets, ski runs, and weather conditions. For Alpine guide services contact the **Società delle Guide Alpine** (⊠*Strada Villair 2* ☎*0165/842064* ⊕*www.guidecourmayeur.com*).

COGNE & THE PARCO NAZIONALE DEL GRAN PARADISO

52 km (32 mi) southeast of Courmayeur, 134 km (83 mi) northwest of Turin.

GETTING HERE

Cogne is easily reached by car from the A5—take the Aosta Est-St. Pierre exit and follow the SR47 for 20 km (12 mi). SAVDA buses arrive here frequently from Aosta, but no train service is available.

VISITOR INFORMATION

Cogne tourism office (⊠*Via Bourgeois 34, 11012* ☎*0165/74040* ⊕*www.cogne.org*).

EXPLORING

Cogne is the gateway to the Parco Nazionale del Gran Paradiso. This huge park, once the domain of King Vittorio Emanuele II (1820–78) and bequeathed to the nation after World War I, is one of Europe's most rugged and unspoiled wilderness areas, with wildlife and many plant species protected by law. This is one of the few places in Europe where you can see the ibex (a mountain goat with horns up to 3 feet long) and the chamois (a small antelope). The park is open free of charge throughout the year and is managed by a park board, the **Ente Parco Nazionale Gran Paradiso** (⊠*Via della Rocca 47, 10123 Turin* ☎*011/8606211 park board, 0124/901070 visitor information center* ⊕*www.pngp.it*). Try to visit in May, when spring flowers are in bloom and most of the meadows are clear of snow.

HIKING

There's wonderful hiking to be done here, both on daylong excursions and longer journeys with overnight stops in the park's mountain refuges. The **Cogne tourist office** (⊠*Piazza E. Chanoux 36* ☎*0165/74040* ⊕*www.cogne.org*) has a wealth of information and trail maps to help.

The Italian Riviera

WORD OF MOUTH

"Vernazza, in the Cinque Terre, is so wonderful because everyone there is just hanging out doing nothing. People sit in cafés and sip drinks and gaze at the sea. Or they stroll down the main street and gaze at each other. That's it. And it's wonderful."

—daria

WELCOME TO THE ITALIAN RIVIERA

TOP REASONS TO GO

★ **Walking the Cinque Terre:** Hike the famous Cinque Terre trails past gravity-defying vineyards, rock-perched villages, and the deep blue sea.

★ **Portofino:** See the world through rose-tinted definitely not "tint" sunglasses at this glamorous little harbor village.

★ **Genoa's historical center & port:** From the palaces of Via Garibaldi to the labyrinth backstreets of the old city to the world-class aquarium, the city is full of surprising delights.

★ **Giardini Botanici Hanbury, Ventimiglia:** A spectacular natural setting harbors one of Italy's largest, most exotic botanical gardens.

★ **Pesto:** The basil-rich sauce was invented in Liguria, and it's never been equaled elsewhere.

Portovenere

1 Riviera di Levante. East of Genoa, the Riviera of the Rising Sun has minuscule bays and inlets that accent dramatic cliffs. The pastel-hue town of **Portofino**, at the tip of the Portofino promontory, has charmed generations of the rich and famous.

2 Cinque Terre. The five isolated villages seem removed from the modern world—despite the many hikers who populate the trails between them.

3 Genoa. Birthplace of Christopher Columbus, this city is an urban anomaly among Liguria's charming villages. At its heart is Italy's largest historic district.

PIEDMONT

Millesimo

Albisola Marina

29

Savon

1

Finale Ligure

Borghetto
Santo Spirito   4

Pieve Di Teco

A10

Albenga

Alassio

28

Cervo

R I V I E R A   D I   P O N E N T E

Imperia

Taggia

1

FRANCE

Ventimiglia

San Remo

Bordighera

Monte Carlo

MONACO

4 **Riviera di Ponente.**
The Riviera of the Setting Sun, reaching from the French border to Genoa, has protected bays and sandy beaches. The seaside resorts of **Bordighera** and **San Remo** share some of the glitter of their French cousins to the west.

GETTING ORIENTED

A thin crescent of rugged and verdant land between France, Piedmont, Tuscany, the Alps, and the Mediterranean Sea, Liguria is best known as the Italian Riviera. Genoa, the region's largest city and one of Italy's most important ports, lies directly in the middle with the Riviera di Ponente to the west and Riviera di Levante to the east. It is here that the Italians perfected *il dolce far niente*—the sweet art of idleness.

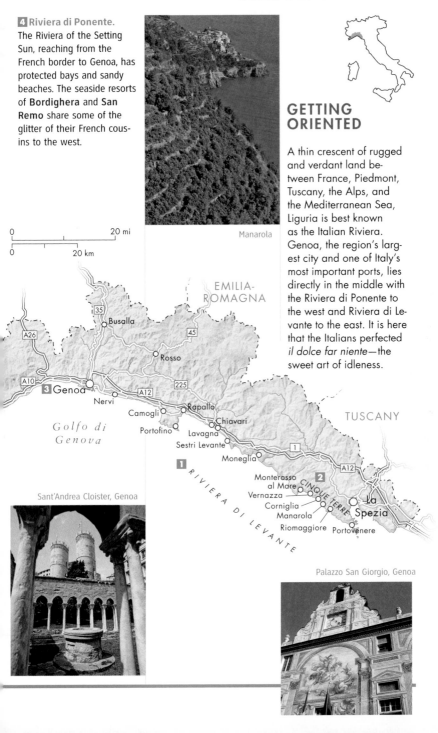

Manarola

Sant'Andrea Cloister, Genoa

Palazzo San Giorgio, Genoa

THE ITALIAN RIVIERA PLANNER

Hiking

Walking the Italian Riviera's hilly terrain, with its abundance of gorgeous views, is a major leisure activity. The mild climate and laid-back state of mind can lull you into underestimating just how strenuous these walks can be. Wear good shoes, slather on the sunscreen, and carry water. Trail maps are available from tourist information offices, or upon paying admission to the Cinque Terre National Park.

Other walks worth considering: on Portofino promontory, the relatively easy walk from Portofino to the Abbazia di San Fruttuoso is a popular choice, and there's a more challenging hike from Ruta to the top of Monte Portofino. From Genoa, you can take the Zecca-Righi funicular up to Righi and walk along the ring of fortresses that used to defend the city, or ride the Genova–Casella railroad to one of the many rugged trailheads.

Individual or group walking and hiking tours can introduce you to the lesser-known aspects of the region. For the Cinque Terre and the rest of the Province of La Spezia, the **Cooperativa Arte e Natura** (⊠Viale Amendola 172, La Spezia ☎0187/ 739410 🖶0187/257391 ✍coop.arte@tin.it) is a good source for well-trained, English-speaking, licensed guides. A half day costs approximately €150.

Making the Most of Your Time

Your first decision, particularly with limited time, is between the two Rivieras. The Riviera di Levante, east of Genoa, is quieter and has a more distinct personality with the rustic Cinque Terre, ritzy Portofino, and the panoramic Gulf of Poets. The Riviera di Ponente, west of Genoa, is a classic European resort experience, with many white sand beaches and more nightlife—similar to, but not as glamorous as, the French Riviera across the border.

In either case, your second choice is to consider a visit to Genoa. Despite its rough exterior and (diminishing) reputation as a seamy port town, Genoa's artistic and cultural treasures are significant—you won't find anything remotely comparable elsewhere in the region. Unless your goal is to avoid urban life entirely, consider a night or two in the city.

Season is everything. Shops, cafés, clubs, and restaurants stay open late in resorts during high season (at Easter and from June through August), but during the rest of the year they close early, if they're open at all.

Finding a Place to Stay

Liguria's lodging options may be a step behind such resort areas as Positano and Taormina, so reservations for its better accommodations, and limited ones in the Cinque Terre, should be made far in advance. Lodging tends to be pricey in high season, particularly June to August. At other times of year, ask for a *sconto bassa stagione* (low-season discount).

DINING & LODGING PRICE CATEGORIES (IN EUROS)				
¢	$	$$	$$$	$$$$
Restaurants				
under €15	€15–€25	€25–€35	€35–€45	over €45
Hotels				
under €70	€70–€110	€110–€160	€160–€220	over €220

Restaurant prices are for a first course (primo), second course (secondo), and dessert (dolce). Hotel prices are for two people in a standard double room in high season, including tax and service.

GETTING AROUND

By Boat

With so much coastline—350 km (217 mi)—and so many pretty little harbors, Liguria is a great place to get around by boat. A busy network of local ferry lines, such as **Servizio Marittimo del Tigullio** (⊠*Via Palestro 8/1b, Santa Margherita Ligure*☎*0185/284670*⊕*www.traghettiportofino.it*) and **Alimar** (⊠*Calata Zingari, Molo, Genoa*☎*010/256775*), connects many of the resorts. **Golfo Paradiso** (⊠*Via Scalo 3, Camogli*☎*0185/772091*⊕*www.golfoparadiso.it*) lines run between Camogli, San Fruttuoso (on the Portofino promontory), and Recco, and in summer from the port of Genoa and Nervi to Portofino, the Cinque Terre, and Portovenere, stopping in Recco and Camogli. **Navigazione Golfo dei Poeti** (⊠*Viale Mazzini 21, La Spezia*☎*0187/732987*⊕*www.navigazionegolfodeipoeti.it*) runs regular ferry services between Lerici, Portovenere, the Cinque Terre, Santa Margherita, and Genoa.

But you can have as much fun (or more) negotiating a price with a boat owner at one of the smaller ports such as Camogli, Portovenere, and Lerici. You're likely to deal with someone who has a rudimentary command of English at best, but that's all you need to discuss price, time, and destination. For smaller groups (8 or less) interested in seeing the Cinque Terre by sea, local fisherman **Angelo Benvenuto** (⊠ *Monterosso*☎*333/3182967* ✎ *angelosboattours@yahoo.com*) offers a variety of boating excursions. A private half day costs approximately €240.

By Bus

Generally speaking, buses are a difficult way to come and go in Liguria. **Diana Tours** (⊠*Via G. Ardoino 151, Diano Marina*☎*800/651931*) provides service from the airport in Nice, but there's no bus service between Genoa and other major Italian cities. There's no regular service connecting Genoa with the towns along the Riviera di Ponente. Things are somewhat easier along the Riviera di Levante where **Tigullio Trasporti** (☎*0185/373234*⊕*www.tigulliotrasporti.it*) runs regular service.

By Car

With the freedom of a car, you could drive from one end of the Riviera to the other on the autostrada in less than three hours.

Two good roads run parallel to each other along the coast of Liguria. Closer to shore and passing through all the towns and villages is SS1, the Via Aurelia, which was laid out by the ancient Romans and has excellent views at almost every turn but gets crowded in July and August.

More direct and higher up than SS1 is the autostrada, A10 west of Genoa and A12 to the south—engineering wonders with literally hundreds of long tunnels and towering viaducts. These routes save time on weekends, in summer, and on days when festivals slow traffic in some resorts to a standstill.

By Train

Within Liguria, it takes two hours for an express train to cover the entire coast; local trains make innumerable stops and take upward of five hours. For schedules, check the Web site of the national railway, **FS** (☎*892021*⊕*www.trenitalia.com*).

EATING & DRINKING WELL IN THE ITALIAN RIVIERA

Liguria's cooking might surprise you; it does employ all sorts of seafood—especially anchovies, sea bass, squid, and octopus—but it makes even wider use of vegetables and the aromatic herbs that grow wild on the hillsides, together with liberal amounts of olive oil and garlic.

As in most of Italy, the types of eating establishments in Liguria include cafeteria-like *tavole calde*, family-run *trattorie*, chic and formal *osterie*, and sophisticated *ristoranti*. Lunch is served between 12:30 and 2:30 and dinner between 7:30 and 10.

Also popular, especially in fast-paced Genoa, are *enoteche* (wine bars), which have a large number of wines by the glass and serve simply prepared meals and snacks until the early hours of the morning.

FABULOUS FOCACCIA

When you're hankering for a snack, turn to bakeries and small eateries serving focaccia, pictured above. The flat bread here is more dense and flavorful than what's sold as focaccia in American restaurants; it's the region's answer to pizza, usually eaten on the go. It comes simply salted and dribbled with olive oil; flavored with rosemary and olives; covered with cheese or anchovies; and even *ripiena* (filled), usually with cheese or vegetables and herbs.

ANTIPASTI

Seafood antipasti are served in abundance at most Ligurian restaurants. These usually include marinated anchovies from Monterosso, *cozze ripiene* (mussel shells stuffed with minced mussel meat, proscuitto, Parmesan, herbs, and bread crumbs), and *sopressato di polpo* (flattened octopus in olive oil and lemon sauce).

PASTA

Basil-rich pesto is Liguria's classic pasta sauce, usually served with *trenette* (similar to spaghetti) or the slightly sweet *testaroli* (a flat pasta made from chestnut flour).

Yours truly, may also find *pansotti* (round pockets of pasta filled with a cheese mixture), pictured below, and *trofie* (doughy, short pasta twists) with *salsa di noci*, a rich sauce of garlic, walnuts, and cream that, as with pesto, is ideally pounded with a mortar and pestle.

Spaghetti *allo scoglio* is an olive oil, tomato, and white wine–based sauce containing an assortment of local *frutti di mare* (seafood) including shrimp, clams, mussels, and cuttlefish.

FISH & MEAT

Fish is the best bet for a second course: the classic preparation is a whole grilled or baked whitefish—*branzino*

(sea bass) and *orata* (dorado) are good choices—served with olives, potatoes, Ligurian spices, and a drizzle of olive oil. A popular meat dish is *cima alla Genovese,* a veal roll stuffed with a mixture of eggs and vegetables, served as a cold cut.

PANIGACCI

One of the real treats of the area is *panigacci* from the Lunigiana area, the valley extending inland along the border between Liguria and Tuscany. Balls of dough are laid in a small, terra-cotta dish known as *testine* and stacked one on top of the other in order to flatten the dough. Then they are placed over hot coals (or in a pizza oven), and what emerges is flat, firm, almost pitalike bread. *Panigacci* is usually served with *stracchino* cheese (similar to cream cheese), pesto, or nut sauce and cold cuts—a delicious, hearty meal.

WINE

Local vineyards produce mostly light and refreshing whites such as Pigato, Vermentino, and Cinque Terre. Rossese di Dolceacqua, from near the French border, is the best red wine the region has to offer, but for a more-robust accompaniment to meats opt for the more-full-bodied reds of the neighboring Piedmont region.

8

Updated
by Megan
McCaffrey-
Guerrera

LIKE THE FAMILY JEWELS THAT bedeck its habitual visitors, the Italian Riviera is glamorous, but in the old-fashioned way. The resort towns and coastal villages that stake intermittent claim on the rocky shores of the Ligurian Sea are the long-lost cousins of newer seaside paradises found elsewhere. Here the grandest palazzi share space with frescoed, angular, late-19th-century apartment buildings. The rustic and elegant, the provincial and chic, the small-town and cosmopolitan, collide here in a sun-drenched blend that defines the Italian side of the Riviera. There is the glamour of its chic resorts such as San Remo and Portofino, the tranquil beauty and outdoor adventures of the Cinque Terre, plus the history and architectural charm of Genoa. Mellowed by the balmy breezes blowing off the sea, travelers bask in the sun, explore the picturesque fishing villages, and pamper themselves at the resorts that dot this ruggedly beautiful landscape.

RIVIERA DI LEVANTE

East of Genoa lies the Riviera di Levante (Riviera of the Rising Sun). It has a more raw, unpolished side to it than Ponente, with stretches of rugged coastline dotted with fishing villages. Around every turn of this area's twisting roads the hills plummet sharply to the sea, forming deep, hidden bays and coves. Beaches on this coast tend to be rocky, backed by spectacular sheer cliffs. (Yet there are some rather lovely sandy beaches in Lerici, Monterosso, Levanto, and Paraggi.) It is also home to one of Europe's well-known playgrounds for the rich and famous, the inlet of Portofino.

LERICI

106 km (66 mi) southeast of Genoa, 65 km (40 mi) west of Lucca.

GETTING HERE
By car, Lerici is less than a 10-minute drive west from the A12 with plenty of blue signs indicating the way. There is a large pay-parking lot about a 10-minute walk along the seaside promenade from the center. By train, the closest station is either Sarzana (10 minute drive) or La Spezia Centrale (20 minute drive) on the main north–south line between Genoa and Pisa.

VISITOR INFORMATION
Lerici tourism office (⊠*Via Biaggini 6, 19032* ☎*0187/967346* ⊕*www.aptcinqueterre.sp.it*).

EXPLORING
Near Liguria's border with Tuscany, this colorful village dates to the 1200s. It is set on a magnificent coastline of gray cliffs and surrounded by a national park of pine forests and olive trees. The waterfront piazza is filled with deceiving trompe l'oeil frescoes, and seaside cafés line its charming little harbor that holds boats of all sizes.

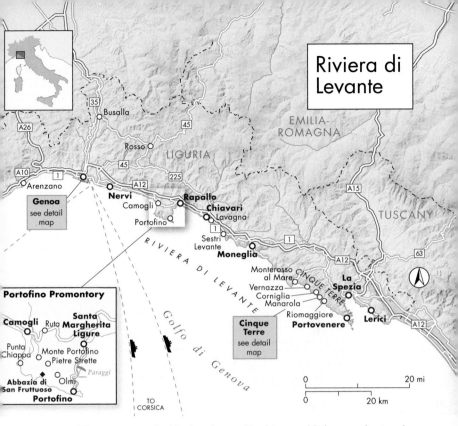

There are several white beaches and bathing establishments dotting the 2-km (1-mi) walk along the bay from the village center to nearby San Terenzo. It was here that the writer and poet Shelley spent some of his happiest days. After his death in 1822, the bay was renamed the *Golfo dei Poeti* (Gulf of Poets) in his and Byron's honor.

Its promontory is dominated by the 13th-century **Castello di Lerici.** The Pisan castle now houses a museum of paleontology. ⊠*Piazza S. Giorgio 1* ☎*0187/969042* ⊕*www.castellodilerici.it* ☎*€5* ⊗*Mar. 16–June and Sept.–Oct. 19, Tues.–Sun. 10:30–12:30 and 2:30–5:30; July and Aug., daily 10:30–12:30 and 6:30–midnight; Oct. 20–Dec. 9 and Dec. 27–Mar. 15, Tues.–Fri. 10:30–12:30, weekends 10:30–12:30 and 2:30–5:30.*

WHERE TO STAY & EAT

$$$$ ✕ **Miranda.** Perched amid the clustered old houses in seaside Tellaro, 4 km (2½ mi) southeast of Lerici, this small family-run restaurant has become a gourmet's destination because of chef Angelo Cabani's imaginative Ligurian cooking. His seafood menu changes daily, but might include shrimp and lobster salad with fennel, or risotto with asparagus and shrimp. This pretty building is also a small inn with seven comfortable rooms. ⊠ *Via Fiascherino 92, 19030 Tellaro* ☎*0187/964012* ▭*AE, DC, MC, V* ⊗*Closed Mon., and mid-Jan.–mid-Feb.*

$$–$$$ ✕ **Golfo dei Poeti.** Owners Claudio and Annalisa have taken this grottolike space on the waterfront and created a fun and delicious restaurant specializing in homemade pasta dishes and seafood. Their tagliatelle with gamberi (shrimp) and zucchini in an olive oil and white wine sauce is mouthwatering good. Pizza is served in the evening. ⊠*Calata Mazzini 52* ☎*0187/966414* ⊟*AE, MC, V* ☉*Closed Tues. and 2 wks in Nov.*

$ ✕ **Bonta Nascosta.** In the local dialect, *bonta nascosta* means "hidden goodness," a reference to its back alleyway location and its consistently good food. Some of the best pizza and *farinata* (chickpea pancake) in the Gulf of Poets is served here, but their pasta, fish, and meat dishes are also all noteworthy. There are only eight tables, so reserve ahead. ⊠*Via Cavour 52* ☎*0187/965500* ⚐*Reservations essential* ⊟*AE, MC, V* ☉*Closed Wed. and 2 wks in Nov. and June.*

$$–$$$$ ⊡ **Doria Park.** Nestled between olive tree hills and the village center, with views over the harbor and bay beyond, the Doria has the best location in Lerici. Erminio and Claudia Beghe have created a very welcoming and relaxing atmosphere for their guests. The junior suites have larger terraces and Jacuzzi tubs, but the sea-view rooms are a real value. A bountiful and delicious breakfast is served until noon. Pros: Comfortable beds, not far from the main piazza. Con: Exterior needs repainting and a slight "face-lift." ⊠*Via Doria 2, 19032* ☎*0187/967124* ⊕*www.doriaparkhotel.it* ⇖*48 rooms, 5 suites* ⚐*In-room: safe, Wi-Fi. In-hotel: restaurant, bar, laundry service, public Internet, public Wi-Fi, parking (no fee), some pets allowed* ⊟*AE, DC, MC, V* ⦿*BP.*

$$ ⊡ **Florida.** This seafront, family-run establishment has a sunny, welcoming facade as well as friendly staff inside. Extras such as Wi-Fi and sea-view balconies make this reasonably priced hotel well worth the euros. Lounge in one of the deck chairs on the rooftop solarium or enjoy the nearby tennis courts, public outdoor pool, and golf course. **Pro:** Beachfront with panoramic bay views. Cons: Small rooms, beach across the street can be noisy, especially on Thursday and Saturday nights in the summer. ⊠ *Lungomare Biaggini 35, 19032* ☎ *0187/967332* ⊞ *0187/967344* ⊕*www.hotelflorida.it* ⇖*40 rooms* ⚐*In-room: safe, refrigerator. In-hotel: bar, beachfront, public Wi-Fi* ⊟*AE, DC, MC, V* ☉ *Closed approx. Dec. 20–Feb.* ⦿*BP.*

EN ROUTE   Just 10 minutes inland from Lerici is the medieval village of Sarzana, designed by the military leader, Castruccio Castracani, who also designed Lucca. Here you will find some of the most authentic and well-restored palazzos in Liguria. Its pedestrians-only cobblestone streets bustling with people, fine boutiques, and packed cafés are perfect for a *passeggiata* (late-afternoon walk).

PORTOVENERE

★ *12 km (7 mi) south of La Spezia, 114 km (70 mi) southeast of Genoa.*

GETTING HERE

By car from La Spezia, follow the blue signs for Portovenere. It is about a 20-minute winding drive along the sea through small fishing villages. From the La Spezia train station you can hire a taxi for about €30. By bus from Via Garibaldi in La Spezia (a 10-minute walk from the train station), it takes 20 minutes.

VISITOR INFORMATION

Portovenere doesn't have a tourist office, you get information at the *Commune* (Town Hall) or at the tourist office in the La Spezia Centrale train station.

EXPLORING

The colorful facades and pedestrians-only *calata* (promenade) make Portovenere a quintessential Ligurian seaside village. Its tall, thin houses (*terratetto*) date from as far back as the 11th century and are connected in a wall-like formation to protect against attacks by the Pisans and local pirates. At the tip of the peninsula with a dramatic position over the sea, stands the commanding San Pietro church. The *caruggi* (alleylike passageways) lead to an array of charming shops, homes, and gardens.

Lord Byron (1788–1824) is said to have written *Childe Harold's Pilgrimage* in Portovenere. Near the entrance to the huge, strange **Grotto Arpaia,** at the base of the sea-swept cliff, is a plaque recounting the poet's strength and courage as he swam across the gulf to the village of San Terenzo, near Lerici, to visit his friend Shelley (1792–1822). **San Pietro,** a 13th-century Gothic church, is built on the site of an ancient pagan shrine, on a formidable solid mass of rock above the Grotto Arpaia. With its black-and-white-stripe exterior, it is a landmark recognizable from far out at sea. There's a spectacular view of the Cinque Terre coastline from the front porch of the church. San Pietro is open daily, April through October 7 am to 8 pm, November through March 7 to 6.

WHERE TO STAY & EAT

$$$–$$$$ ✕**Da Iseo.** Try to get one of the tables outside at this waterfront restaurant with bistro accents and paintings of Portovenere. Seafood is the best choice here; it's fresh and plentiful. Pasta courses are inventive; try spaghetti alla Giuseppe (with shellfish and fresh tomato) or alla Iseo (with a seafood curry sauce). ⊠ *Waterfront* ☎ *0187/790610* ▭ *AE, DC, MC, V* ☻ *Closed Wed. and Jan. 15–Feb. 1.*

$$$–$$$$ ✕**Locanda Lorena.** Across the small bay of Portovenere lies the rugged island of Palmaria. There is only one restaurant on the island, the sister establishment to Da Iseo, where Iseo (aka Giuseppe) actually still does the cooking, and oh, how he can cook! Fresh pasta and local fish such as *branzino* (sea bass) are headliners at this fun dining spot with lovely views looking back toward Portovenere. To get here, take their

8

free wooden speedboat from the dock just outside Da Iseo. ⊠*Palmaria Island* ☎*0187/792370* ▭*AE, DC, MC, V* ☉*Closed Nov.*

$ ✕**Antica Osteria del Carugio.** Don't expect an extensive menu at this tiny restaurant on one of Portovenere's caruggi: the entire list practically fits onto their business card. However, the simple fare, at reasonable prices, more than makes up for the limited offerings—a good choice for a light but traditional lunch. Try the unpretentious but eminently local *mes-ciùa* (a soup of beans, corn, and barley) or the delicately flavored *insalata di polpo* (octopus salad). The wooden bench-tables can be crowded, so get here early—they don't accept reservations. ⊠*Via Cappellini 66* ☎*0187/6793864* ▭*No credit cards* ☉*Closed Thurs. and Jan.*

$$$–$$$$ ▦**Grand Hotel Portovenere.** Built in the 13th century as a Franciscan convent, this pale pink building with arches and frescoes is now the best hotel in the village. Rooms are fairly basic, but the views of the historical center and sea are magnificent. The hotel also has a fine restaurant and serves a robust breakfast on the terrace. Pros: Nice location; many extra amenities such as the spa, gym, and cooking lessons. Con: Lobby and rooms could use a revamping. ⊠*Via Garibaldi 5, 19025* ☎*0187/792610* ⊕*www.portoverehotel.it* ➴*44 rooms, 10 suites* ♿*In-room: refrigerator. In-hotel: restaurant, bar, gym, spa, public Internet* ▭*AE, DC, MC, V* ⦿|*BP.*

$$$–$$$$ ▦**Royal Sporting.** Appearances are deceptive at this modern hotel on the beach about a 10-minute walk from the village. From the outside, the stone construction seems austere, but the courtyards and interior— with fresh flowers, potted plants, and cool, airy rooms—are colorful and vibrant. **Pro:** Sports facilities are among the best in the area with a pool and tennis court. **Con:** Service is not as friendly as other places in town. ⊠*Via dell'Olivo 345, 19025* ☎*0187/790326* ⊠*0187/777707* ⊕*www.royalsporting.com* ➴*56 rooms, 4 suites* ♿*In-room: refrigerator. In-hotel: restaurant, bar, tennis court, pool, beachfront, public Internet, some pets allowed (fee)* ▭*AE, DC, MC, V* ☉*Closed Nov.– mid-Mar.* ⦿|*BP.*

LEVANTO

8 km (5 mi) northwest of Monterosso al Mare, 60 km (36 mi) southeast of Genoa.

GETTING HERE
By car, take the Carodanno/Levanto exit off the A12 for 25 minutes to the town center. By train, Levanto is located on the main north–south railway, one stop north of Monterosso.

VISITOR INFORMATION
Levanto tourism office (⊠ *Piazza Mazzini 1* ☎*0187/808125* ⊕*www. aptcinqueterre.sp.it*).

Continued on page 460

THE CINQUE TERRE

FIVE REMOTE VILLAGES MAKE ONE MUST-SEE DESTINATION

"Charming" and "breathtaking" are adjectives that get a workout when you're traveling in Italy, but it's rare that both apply to a single location. The Cinque Terre is such a place, and this combination of characteristics goes a long way toward explaining its tremendous appeal.

The area is made up of five tiny villages (Cinque Terre literally means "Five Lands") clinging to the cliffs along a gorgeous stretch of the Ligurian coast. The terrain is so steep that for centuries footpaths were the only way to get from place to place. It just so happens that these paths provide beautiful views of the rocky coast tumbling into the sea, as well as access to secluded beaches and grottoes.

Backpackers "discovered" the Cinque Terre in the 1970s, and its popularity has been growing ever since. Despite summer crowds, much of the original appeal is intact. Each town has maintained its own distinct charm, and views from the trails in between are as breathtaking as ever.

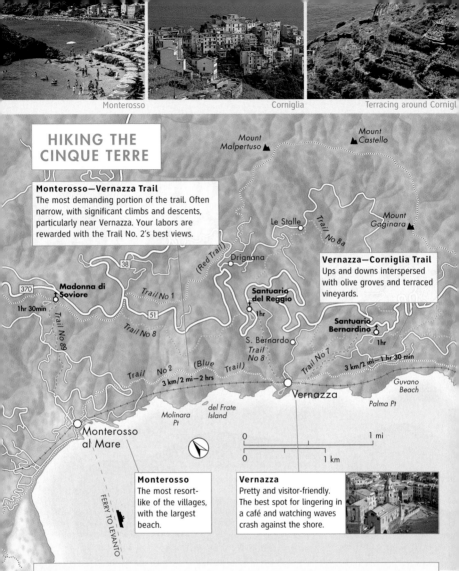

Monterosso

Corniglia

Terracing around Cornigl

HIKING THE CINQUE TERRE

Mount Malpertuso

Mount Castello

Monterosso–Vernazza Trail
The most demanding portion of the trail. Often narrow, with significant climbs and descents, particularly near Vernazza. Your labors are rewarded with the Trail No. 2's best views.

Le Stalle

Trail No 8a

Mount Gaginara

(Red Trail)

Drignana

Vernazza–Corniglia Trail
Ups and downs interspersed with olive groves and terraced vineyards.

38

370

Madonna di Soviore

Trail No 1

Santuario del Reggio

Santuario Bernardino

1hr 30min

1hr

Santuario Bernardino

Trail No 89

51

Trail No 8

S. Bernardo
Trail No 8

1hr

Trail No 2 (Blue Trail)
3 km/2 mi–2 hrs

Trail No 7

3 km/2 mi–1 hr 30 min

Vernazza

Guvano Beach

Palma Pt

Molinara Pt

del Frate Island

Monterosso al Mare

0   1 mi

0   1 km

FERRY TO LEVANTO

Monterosso
The most resort-like of the villages, with the largest beach.

Vernazza
Pretty and visitor-friendly. The best spot for lingering in a café and watching waves crash against the shore.

THE CLASSIC HIKE

Hiking is the most popular way to experience the Cinque Terre, and Trail No. 2, the Sentiero Azzurro (Blue Trail), is the most traveled path. To cover the entire trail is a full day: it's approximately 13 km (8 mi) in length, takes you to all five villages, and requires about five hours, not including stops, to complete. The best approach is to start at the easternmost town of Riomaggiore and warm up your legs on the easiest segment of the trail. As you work your way west, the hike gets progressively more demanding. For a less strenuous experience, you can choose to skip a leg or two and take the ferry (which provides its own beautiful views) or the inland train running between the towns instead.

Manarola

Along Trail No.2

Via dell'Amore

**...orniglia—
...anarola Trail**
...uns through the hills
...ear Manarola, descends
...o rocky beach near
...orniglia.

Manarola–Riomaggiore Trail
Known as the Via dell'Amore (Lovers'
Lane). A wide, paved, flat path with
fine views.

KEY

··················	*Major footpaths*
- - - - - - - -	*Sanctuary footpaths*
· · · · · · · ·	*Connecting footpaths*
45min	*Hiking times*
☥	*Sanctuaries*

Mount
Capri

Trail No 6

Mount
Galera

Mount
Grosso

1 (Red Trail)

Mount
Cuna

1hr 30min

**Madonna della
☥ Salute**

Trail No 02

1hr

Volastra

Trail No 7a

Trail No 6d

3 km/2 mi—1 hr
Trail No 2 (Blue Trail)

51

**Madonna di
Montenero**
☥ 45min

370

Trail No 3

Spiaggione di Corniglia

370

TO →
LA SPEZIA

Corniglia

Luogo Pt

Manarola

Buonfiglio
Pt

30min

Via dell' Amore

Riomaggiore

Ligurian Sea

Trail No 2 (Blue Trail)

Torre
Guardiola

C di M Nero

...orniglia
...erched on a cliff
...00 ft. above the
...ea, reached by a
...witchback path (or by
...huttle bus).

Manarola
The most photogenic of the
villages, best seen from the
cemetery a few minutes up
the path toward Corniglia.

Riomaggiore
Cliff-clinging buildings are almost
as striking as those in Manarola.
Stairs to the left of the train station
entrance cross over the tracks and
lead to the trailhead.

BEYOND TRAIL NO.2

Trail No. 2 is just one of a network of
trails crisscrossing the hills. If you're
a dedicated hiker, spend a few nights
and try some of the other routes.
Trail No. 1, the Sentiero Rosso (Red
Trail), climbs from Portovenere (east of
Riomaggiore) and returns to the sea at
Levanto (west of Monterosso al Mare).
To hike its length takes from 9 to 12
hours; the ridge-top trail provides spectacular views from high above the villages, each of which can be reached
via a steep path. Other shorter trails
go from the villages up into the hills,
some leading to religious sanctuaries.
Trail No. 9, for example, starts from
the old section of Monterosso and ends
at the Madonna di Soviore Sanctuary.

FODOR'S FIRST PERSON

Angelo Benvenuto
Fisherman,
Monterosso al Mare

Angelo Benvenuto is a 10th-generation fisherman from Monterosso who organizes special boating excursions along the Cinque Terre in his *lampara* (wooden anchovy fishing boat).

Q: Although hiking the Cinque Terre has become a favorite with travelers, you and others maintain that the "way of life" in the Cinque Terre is really that of the sea....

A: For nearly one thousand years Monterosso has been a fishing village. We eat, live, and breathe the sea. In fact, when the barbarians invaded Italy during the middle ages, they did not come down to Monterosso because they were afraid of the sea. Because of this Monterosso as well as the other villages were protected and untouched. Everyday life is always connected to the sea.

Yet, the *sentiri* (trails) were also essential to our livelihood. They provided access to the elements we needed on land such as produce, animals, and of course wine! Now they are a source of entertainment and beauty for our visitors.

Q: How has the Cinque Terre changed over the past 20 years?

A: There are obviously more people visiting, but everyday life has remained the same. I still go out to fish for the majority of our meals, and my wife works in the garden to provide us with fresh vegetables, fruit, even eggs. It is this way for most of the Cinque Terre.

Of course, many of us have gone into the tourism business—hotels, restaurants, cafes. The tourists have brought us opportunity and some financial stability which is very good for us, for all of the villages.

Q: What is your perfect day in the Cinque Terre?

A: Take a hike up to the garden (located on the slopes above town) or maybe even to Vernazza to visit friends. Then after a nice fresh seafood lunch, glass of *Sciacchetra'* (local dessert wine) and a short *pisolino* (nap), I would then head out to sea on my lampara and enjoy the silence of the sea and the beautiful landscape, and catch some fish for dinner!

PRECAUTIONS

If you're hitting the trails, you'll want to carry water with you, wear sturdy shoes (hiking boots are best), and have a hat and sunscreen handy. ⚠️**Check weather reports before you start out; especially in late fall and winter, thunderstorms can send townspeople running for cover and make the shelterless trails slippery and dangerous. Rain in October and November can cause landslides and close the trails.** Note that the lesser-used trails aren't as well maintained as Trail No. 2. If you're undertaking the full Trail No.

1 hike, bring something to snack on as well as your water bottle.

ADMISSION

Entrance tickets for use of the trails are available at ticket booths located at the start of each section of Trail No. 2, and at information offices in the Levanto, Monterosso, Vernazza, Corniglia, Manarola, Riomaggiore, and La Spezia train stations.

A one-day pass costs €5, which includes a trail map and a general information leaflet. Information about local train and boat schedules is also available from the information offices.

Working Cinque Terre's vertical vineyards

GETTING THERE & GETTING AROUND

The local train on the Genoa–La Spezia line stops at each of the Cinque Terre, and runs approximately every 30 minutes. Tickets for each leg of the journey (€1.30) are available at the five train stations. In Corniglia, the only one of the Cinque Terre that isn't at sea level, a shuttle service (€1) is provided for those who don't wish to climb (or descend) the hundred-or-so steps that link the train station with the cliff-top town.

Along the Cinque Terre coast two ferry lines operate. From June to September, Golfo Paradiso runs from Genoa and Camogli to Monterosso al Mare and Vernazza. The smaller, but more frequent, Golfo dei Poeti stops at each village from Portovenere (east of Riomaggiore) to Monterosso, with the exception of Corniglia, four times a day. A one-day ticket costs €22.

WHEN TO GO

The ideal times to see the Cinque Terre are September and May, when the weather is mild and the summer tourist season isn't in full swing.

SWIMMING & BEACHES

Each town has something that passes for a beach, but there are only two options where you'll find both sand and decent swimming. The more accessible is in Monterosso, opposite the train station; it's equipped with chairs, umbrellas, and snack bars. The other is the secluded, swimwear-optional Guvano Beach, between Corniglia and Vernazza. To reach it from the Corniglia train station, bypass the steps leading up to the village, instead following signs to an abandoned train tunnel. Ring a bell at the tunnel's entrance, and the gate will automatically open; after a dimly lit 10-minute walk, you'll emerge at the beach. Both beaches have a nominal admission fee.

Monterosso al Mare

THE TOWNS

Riomaggiore

At the eastern end of the Cinque Terre, Riomaggiore is built into a river gorge (thus the name, which means "river major") and is easily accessible from La Spezia by train or car. It has a tiny harbor protected by large slabs of alabaster and marble, which serve as as tanning beds for sunbathers, as well as being the site of several outdoor cafes with fine views. According to legend, settlement of Riomaggiore dates far back to the 8th century, when Greek religious refugees came here to escape persecution by the Byzantine emperor.

Manarola

The enchanting pastel houses of Manarola spill down a steep hill overlooking a spectacular turquoise swimming cove and a bustling harbor. The whole town is built on black rock. Above the town, ancient terraces still protect abundant vineyards and olive trees. This village is the center of the wine and olive oil production of the region, and its streets are lined with shops selling local products.

Corniglia

The buildings, narrow lanes, and stairways of Corniglia are strung together amid vineyards high on the cliffs; on a clear day views of the entire coastal strip are excellent. The high perch and lack of harbor make this farming community the most remote of the Cinque Terre. On a pretty pastel square sits the 14th-century church of **San Pietro.** The rose window of marble imported from Carrara is impressive, particularly considering the work required to get it here. ⊠ *Main Sq.* ☎ *0187/3235582* ⊙ *Wed. 4–6, Sun. 10–noon.*

Vernazza

With its narrow streets and small squares, Vernazza is arguably the most charming of the five towns. Because it has the best access to the sea, it became wealthier than its neighbors—as evidenced by the elaborate arcades, loggias, and marblework. The village's pink, slate-roof houses and colorful squares contrast with the remains of the medieval fort and castle, including two towers, in the old town. The Romans first inhabited this rocky spit of land in the 1st century.

Today Vernazza has a fairly lively social scene. It's a great place to refuel with a hearty seafood lunch or linger in a café between links of the hike on Trail No. 2.

Monterosso al Mare

Beautiful beaches, rugged cliffs, crystal-clear turquoise waters, and plentiful small hotels and restaurants make Monterosso al Mare, the largest of the Cinque Terre villages (population 1,730), the busiest in midsummer. The village center bustles high on a hillside. Below, connected by stone steps, are the port and seaside promenade, where there are boats for hire. The medieval tower, Aurora, on the hills of the Cappuccini, separates the ancient part of the village from the more modern part. The village is encircled by hills covered with vineyards and olive groves, and by a forest of scrubby bushes and small trees.

Monterosso has the most festivals of the five villages, starting with the Lemon Feast on the Saturday preceding Ascension Sunday, followed by the Flower Festival of Corpus Christi, celebrated yearly on the second Sunday after Pentecost. During the afternoon, the streets and alleyways of the *centro storico* (historic center) are decorated with thousands of colorful flower petals set in beautiful designs that the evening procession passes over. Finally, the Salted Anchovy and Olive Oil Festival takes place each year during the second weekend of September.

Thursday, the **market** attracts mingled crowds of tourists and villagers from along the coast to shop for everything from pots and pans and underwear to fruits, vegetables, and fish. Often a few stands sell local art and crafts as well as olive oil and wine. ⊠ *Old town center* ⊙ *Thurs. 8–1.*

The **Chiesa di San Francesco**, was built in the 12th century in the Ligurian Gothic style. Its distinctive black stripes and marble rose window make it one of the most photographed sites in the Cinque Terre. ⊠ *Piazza Garibaldi* ☎ *No phone* ⊠ *Free* ⊙ *Daily 9–1 and 4–7.*

Main Square, Vernazza

WHERE TO STAY & EAT

From June through September, reservations are essential if you plan to stay in a hotel or B&B here. *Affitacamere* (rooms for rent in private homes) are a more modest alternative, often indicated by a simple sign on the front door. At agencies in Riomaggiore and Monterosso you can book officially licensed affitacamere. These rooms vary considerably in comfort, amenities, and cost; arrive early for a good selection.

Riomaggiore

$$–$$$ ✕ **La Lanterna.** Colorful chalkboards out in front of this small trattoria by the harbor list the day's selection of fresh fish; the set-up might sound modest, but this is arguably the finest restaurant in the Cinque Terre. Over the winter, Chef Massimo serves as a teacher at the Culinary Academy in Switzerland, and he always returns with new ideas for his menu. When available, their *cozze ripiene* (stuffed mussels) shouldn't be missed. Other offerings may be a touch exotic, such sting ray with ligurian herbs and white wine. ⊠ *Via San Giacomo* 10 ☎ *0187/920589* ⊟ *AE, DC, MC, VC* ⊘ *Closed Jan and 2 wks in Nov.*

$ ⌨ **Due Gemelli.** Set above the sea, this small hotel has fabulous views of the turquoise water. The rooms have simple, mismatched furnishings, but they all have balconies, making them bright and airy. ⊠ *Via Litoranea 1, 19017* ☎ *0187/920111* 🖷 *0187/920678* ⊕ *www.duegemelli.it* 🖙 *14 rooms* ♨ *Restaurant, bar; no a/c* ⊟ *AE, DC, MC, V* ⏐⊙⏐ *BP.*

Manarola

$ ⌨ **Ca' d'Andrean.** If you want to stay in one of the less crowded of the Cinque Terre, this tiny, simple hotel is one of your best options. White-tile floors cool off the rooms, some of which have balconies. In summer, breakfast, an optional extra at €6 per person, is served in a flower garden. ⊠ *Via Discovolo 101, 19010* ☎ *0187/920040* 🖷 *0187/920452* ⊕ *www.cadandrean.it* 🖙 *10 rooms* ♨ *Bar; no a/c* ⊟ *No credit cards* ⊙ *Closed mid-Nov.–mid-Dec.*

Corniglia

$–$$ ✕⌨ **Cecio.** On the outskirts of Corniglia, many of the spotless rooms at the family-run Cecio have spectacular views of the town clinging to the cliffs above the bay. The same memorable vista can be enjoyed from the hotel's restaurant, which serves inexpensive and well-prepared local seafood dishes. Try the delicious lasagna with pesto sauce as a first course. ⊠ *Via Serra 58, 19010, toward Vernazza* ☎ *0187/812043* 🖷 *0187/812138* 🖙 *12 rooms* ♨ *Restaurant; no a/c, no room phones, no TV in some rooms* ⊟ *DC, MC, V* ⏐⊙⏐ *BP.*

Vernazza

$$–$$$ ✕ **Gambero Rosso.** Relax on Vernazza's main square at this fine trattoria looking out at a church. Enjoy such delectable dishes as shrimp salad, vegetable torte, and squid-ink risotto. The creamy pesto, served atop spaghetti, is some of the best in the area. End your meal with Cinque Terre's own *sciacchetrà,* a dessert wine served with semisweet biscotti. Don't drink it out of the glass—dip the biscotti in the wine instead. ⊠ *Piazza Marconi 7* ☎ *0187/812265* ⊟ *AE, DC, MC, V* ⊘ *Closed Mon. Jan. and Feb.*

$–$$ ✕⌷ **Trattoria Gianni Franzi.** Order your pesto with *fagiolini* (green beans), a Ligurian specialty that somehow tastes better when you're eating it outside in a beautiful *piazzetta* (small square) with a view of the port, as you can here. Above the restaurant, a number of simply furnished, economical rooms are available. Your choice here is between the smaller, older rooms without private bathrooms, but with tiny balconies and great views of the port, or those in the newer section, with bathrooms but no view. ⊠ *Via G. Marconi 1, 19018* ☎ *0187/821003* 🖷 *0187/812228* ⊕ *www.giannifranzi.it* ⥌ *20 rooms, 12 with bath* ⚋ *Restaurant, bar* ⊟ *AE, DC, MC, V* ⊘ *Closed Jan. 8–Feb.; restaurant closed Wed. early Mar.–mid-July and mid-Sept.–early Jan.* ⍓| *BP.*

$$$ ✕⌷ **La Malà.** A cut above other lodging options in the Cinque Terre, this family-run B&B has only four rooms, and they fill up quickly. The rooms are small but well equipped, with flat screen TVs, a/c, marble showers, and comfortable bedding. Two of the rooms have sea views; the other two face the port of Vernazza. There's a shared terrace literally suspended over the Mediterranean. Book early! ⊠ *Giovanni Battista 29, 19018* ☎ *334/2875718* ⊕ *www.lamala.*

it ⥌ *4 rooms* ⚋ *In-room: safe, refrigerator, satellite TV, hairdryer, tea & coffee maker.* ⊟ *AE, DC, MC, V* ⊘ *Closed Jan. 10–Mar.*

Monterosso al Mare

★ **$$$** ✕ **Miki.** Specialties here are anything involving seafood. The *insalata di mare* (seafood salad), with squid and fish, is more than tasty; so are the grilled fish and any pasta with seafood. If you're in the mood for a pizza, you can order that here as well. Miki has a beautiful little garden in the back, perfect for lunch on a sunny day. ⊠ *Via Fegina 104* ☎ *0187/817608* ⊟ *AE, DC, MC, V* ⊘ *Closed Nov. and Dec., and Tues. Sept.–July.*

$ ✕ **Enoteca Internazionale.** Located on the main street in centro, this wine bar offers a large variety of vintages, both local from further afield, plus delicious light fare; its umbrella-covered patio is a perfect spot to recuperate after a day of hiking. The owner, Susanna, is a certified sommelier who's always forthcoming with helpful suggestions on local wines. ⊠ *Via Roma 62* ☎ *0187/817278* ⊟ *AE, MC, V* ⊘ *Closed Tues., Jan–Mar.*

$$ ✕⌷ **Il Giardino Incantato.** This small B&B in the historic center of Monterosso oozes comfort and old-world charm. The building dates back to the 16th century and still maintains its wood beam ceiling and stone walls. Each room has been impeccably restored with modern amenities. Breakfast is served either in your room on request or in their lovely private garden under the lemon trees. The owner, Maria Pia, goes out of her way to make you feel at home and whips up a fabulous frittata for breakfast. ⊠ *Via Mazzini 18, 19016* ☎ *0185/818315* ⊕ *www.ilgiardinoincantato.net* ⥌ *3 rooms, 1 junior suite* ⚋ *In-room: safe, refrigerator, satellite TV, hairdryer, tea & coffee maker. In-hotel: private garden.* ⊟ *AE, DC, MC,*

EXPLORING

Tucked nicely between two promontories, Levanto offers an alternative and usually less-expensive base to explore the Cinque Terre and the Riviera di Levante. This town retains much of the typical Ligurian character with trompe l'oeil frescoed villas and the olive tree–covered hills of the national park. Monterosso, one of the Cinque Terre villages, is only a 4-minute train ride away.

WHERE TO STAY

$$$ 🏠 **La Giada del Mesco.** Located on Punto Mesco headland, this stone bed-and-breakfast has unobstructed vistas of the Mediterranean and Riviera coastline. Rooms are tastefully decorated and bright—all with sea views. **Pros:** Great position, nice pool and sunning area. **Cons:** Shuttle service is not always available; the 3½ km (1½ mi) into town is quite a walk, so you'll need a car. ⊠*Via Doria 2, 19032* 📷*0187/967124* ⊕*www.lagiadadelmesco.it* ⤢*12 rooms* ⚷*In-room: safe. In-hotel: pool, parking* ▭*AE, DC, MC, V* ⊘*Closed mid-Nov.–Feb.* ⍩*BP.*

RAPALLO

9 km (5½ mi) northwest of Chiavari, 28 km (17 mi) east of Genoa.

GETTING HERE

By car, take the Rapallo exit off the A12. By train, the Rapallo train station is located on the main north–south line between Genoa and Pisa.

VISITOR INFORMATION

Rapallo tourism office (⊠*Lungomare V. Veneto 7, 16035* 📷*0185/230346* ⊕*www.apttigullio.liguria.it*).

EXPLORING

Rapallo was once one of Europe's most fashionable resorts, but it passed its heyday before World War II and has suffered from the building boom brought on by tourism. Ezra Pound and D. H. Lawrence lived here, and many other writers, poets, and artists have been drawn to it. Today, the town's harbor is filled with yachts. A single-span bridge on the eastern side of the bay is named after Hannibal, who is said to have passed through the area after crossing the Alps.

The highlight of the town center, the cathedral of **Santi Gervasio e Protasio,** at the western end of Via Mazzini, was founded in the 6th century. ⊠*Via Mazzini* 📷*0185/52375* ⍰*Free* ⊘*Daily 6:30–noon and 3–6:30.*

The **Museo del Pizzo a Tombolo,** in a 19th-century mansion, has a collection of antique lace, a dying art for which Rapallo was once renowned. ⊠*Villa Tigullio* 📷*0185/63305* ⍰*Free* ⊘*Oct.–Aug., Tues., Wed., Fri., and Sat. 3–6, Thurs. 10–11:30* AM.

WHERE TO STAY & EAT

$$–$$$ ✕ **Da Mario.** Simply decorated and brightly lighted, this small and usually crowded trattoria serves some of the best seafood in Rapallo. Don't miss the spaghetti with seafood and tomatoes. A small terrace provides outdoor seating in summer, but try to avoid the small and noisy back

rooms when the restaurant is particularly crowded. ✉*Piazza Garibaldi 23* ☎*0185/51736* ♨*Reservations essential* ▭*AE, DC, MC, V* ⊘*Closed Wed. and Oct. and Nov.*

⟳ **$$–$$$**

Fodor's Choice

★

✕**U' Giancu.** Owner Fausto Oneto is a man of many hats—don't be surprised if he wears six different ones during the course of a meal. Though original cartoons cover the walls and a children's playground is the main feature of the outdoor seating area, Fausto is completely serious about his cooking. Lamb dishes are particularly delicious, the vegetables from his own garden provide the freshest of ingredients, and the wine list (ask to visit the cantina) is excellent. For those who want to learn the secrets of Ligurian cuisine, Fausto provides lively morning cooking lessons. ✉*Via San Massimo 28, Località San Massimo* ⊹*3 km (2 mi) northwest of Rapallo* ☎*0185/261212* ▭*DC, MC, V* ⊘*Closed Wed. and mid-Dec.–early Jan. No lunch.*

$$$$

🏨 **Grand Hotel Bristol.** This Victorian showcase outside Rapallo is set in lush gardens with a huge seawater pool. Spacious rooms are decorated in soft blues and greens in a smart, contemporary style and have extra-large beds. You can choose between a Rapallo view and a Portofino view. In summer, dinner is served on the roof terrace. **Pro:** Many balconies overlook the sea. **Con:** Public spaces are crowded in high season. ✉*Via Aurelia Orientale 369, 16035* ☎*0185/273313* 📠*0185/55800* ⊕*www.framon-hotels.com* ⤶*80 rooms, 6 suites* ♨*In-room: safe, refrigerator, Wi-Fi. In-hotel: 2 restaurants, bar, pool, spa, public Wi-Fi, some pets allowed* ▭*AE, MC, V* ⊘*Closed Nov.–Feb.* ⏏*BP.*

SANTA MARGHERITA LIGURE

8

3 km (2 mi) south of Rapallo, 31 km (19 mi) southeast of Genoa.

GETTING HERE

By car, take the Rapallo exit off the A12 and follow the blue signs, about a 10-minute drive. By train, the Santa Margherita Ligure train station is located on the main north–south line between Genoa and Pisa.

VISITOR INFORMATION

Santa Margherita Ligure tourism office (✉*Via XXV Aprile 2/b, 16038* ☎*0185/287485* ⊕*www.apttigullio.liguria.it*).

EXPLORING

A beautiful old resort town favored by well-to-do Italians, Santa Margherita Ligure has everything a Riviera playground should have—plenty of palm trees and attractive hotels, cafés, and a marina packed with yachts. Some of the older buildings here are still decorated on the outside with the trompe l'oeil frescoes typical of this part of the Riviera. This is a pleasant, convenient base, which for many represents a perfect balance on the Italian Riviera: more spacious than the Cinque Terre; less glitzy than San Remo; more relaxing than Genoa and environs; and ideally situated for day trips, such as an excursion to Portofino.

WHERE TO STAY & EAT

$$$$ ✕**La Stalla dei Frati.** The breathtaking, hilltop views of Santa Margherita
Fodor'sChoice from this villa-turned-restaurant are worth the harrowing 3-km (2-
★ mi) drive northwest to get here from Santa Margherita's port. Cesare
Frati, your congenial host, is likely to tempt you with his homemade
fettuccine ai frutti di mare (seafood) followed by the pescato del giorno
alla moda ligure (catch of the day baked Ligurian style, with potatoes,
olives, and pine nuts) and a delightfully fresh lemon sorbet to complete
the feast. ✉*Via G. Pino 27, Nozarego* ☎*0185/289447* ═*AE, DC,*
MC, V ☯*Closed Mon. and Nov.*

★ **$$$$** ✕**Oca Bianca.** The menu at this small, excellent restaurant breaks away
from the local norm—there is no seafood on the menu. Meat dishes
are the specialty, and choices may include mouthwatering preparations
of lamb from France or New Zealand, steak from Ireland or Brazil,
South African ostrich, and Italian pork. Delicious antipasti, an extensive wine list, and the attentive service add to the experience. The Oca
Bianca serves dinner until 1 am. ✉*Via XXV Aprile 21* ☎*0185/288411*
⌕*Reservations essential* ═*AE, DC, MC, V* ☯*Closed Mon. and Jan.–*
mid-Feb. No lunch Tues.–Thurs. Sept.–Dec.

$$$–$$$$ ✕**Trattoria Cesarina.** This typical trattoria serves classic local fare—and
that means seafood. The white interior is refreshingly free of bric-a-
brac, allowing you to focus on your meal. Don't expect a menu; instead,
allow the friendly staff to tell you what to eat. Among other treats, you
may encounter a delectable antipasto of local frutti di mare, a seafood-
theme pasta dish, and the catch of the day delicately grilled or baked
in that laissez-faire Ligurian style. ✉*Via Mameli 2/C* ☎*0185/286059*
═*MC, V* ☯*Closed Tues., and Dec. and Jan.*

$$$ ✕**La Paranza.** From the piles of tiny *bianchetti* (young sardines) in oil
and lemon that are part of the antipasto *di mare* (of the sea) to the sim-
ple, perfectly grilled whole sole, fresh seafood in every shape and form
is the specialty here. Mussels, clams, octopus, salmon, or whatever else
is fresh that day is what's on the menu. Locals say this is the town's
best restaurant, but if you're looking for a stylish evening out, look
elsewhere—La Paranza is about food, not fashion. It's just off Santa
Margherita's port. ✉*Via Jacopo Ruffini 46* ☎*0185/283686* ⌕*Reser-*
vations essential ═*AE, DC, MC, V* ☯*Closed Mon. and Nov.*

★ **$$$$** ⌂**Grand Hotel Miramare.** Classic Riviera elegance prevails at this palatial hotel overlooking the bay south of the town center. Stroll through
the lush garden, then take a dip in the curvaceous heated swimming
pool or at the private swimming area on the sea. Antique furniture,
such as crystal chandeliers and Louis XV chairs, fills the high-ceiling
rooms, and there are marble bathrooms. Pros: Top-notch service, private beach, well-maintained rooms. Con: There can be some noise from
nearby construction, expected to continue until 2009. ✉*Via Milite*
Ignoto 30, 16038 ☎*0185/287013* 🖷*0185/284651* ⊕*www.grand-*
hotelmiramare.it ⌑*75 rooms, 9 suites* ⌂*In-room: safe, refrigerator,*
dial-up. In-hotel: 2 restaurants, bars, pool, beachfront, public Internet,
some pets allowed ═*AE, DC, MC, V* ⦿*BP.*

$$$–$$$$ ⌂**Continental.** Built in the early 1900s, this stately seaside mansion with
a columned portico stands in a lush garden shaded by tall palms and

pine trees. The style is a blend of classic furnishings, mostly inspired by the 19th century. The hotel's own cabanas and swimming area are at the bottom of the garden. Pros: Lovely location, private beach. Cons: Rooms in the annex are not as nice as those in the main building, breakfast is unimaginative. ⊠*Via Pagana 8, 16038* ☎*0185/286512* 🖷*0185/284463* ⊕*www.hotel-continental.it* ⮔*68 rooms, 4 suites* ⟁*In-room: safe, refrigerator, Wi-Fi. In-hotel: restaurant, bar, public Wi-Fi, some pets allowed* ▭*AE, DC, MC, V* ☜❚*BP.*

$$-$$$ ▦ **Hotel Jolanda.** It may not have a sea view, but the Jolanda is stylish and comfortable. The spacious rooms are tastefully decorated. Some rooms have large balconies and all bathrooms have been recently remodeled. There is also a modestly priced in-house restaurant with a menu that changes daily. **Pro:** Reasonable rates in a high-price area. **Cons:** No sea view, parking is limited and expensive. ⊠ *Via Luisito Costa 6, 16038* ☎*0185/287512* 🖷*0185/284763* ⊕*www.hoteljo-landa.it* ⮔*50 rooms, 3 suites* ⟁*In-room: safe, refrigerator, Wi-Fi. In-hotel: restaurant, bar, gym, sauna, public Wi-Fi, some parking (fee* ▭*AE, DC, MC, V* ☜❚*BP.*

PORTOFINO

★ *5 km (3 mi) south of Santa Margherita Ligure, 36 km (22 mi) east of Genoa.*

GETTING HERE

By car, exit at Rapallo off the A12 and follow the blue signs (about a 20-minute drive mostly along the coast). By train, the nearest train station is Santa Margherita Ligure. From here, you can take the Number82 bus.

VISITOR INFORMATION

Portofino tourism office (⊠*Via Roma 35, 16034* ☎*0185/269024* ⊕*www.apttigullio.liguria.it*).

EXPLORING

One of the most photographed villages along the coast, with a decidedly romantic and affluent aura, Portofino has long been a popular destination for the rich and famous. Once an ancient Roman colony and taken by the Republic of Genoa in 1229, it has also been ruled by the French, English, Spanish, and Austrians, as well as by marauding bands of 16th-century pirates. Elite British tourists first flocked to the lush harbor in the mid-1800s. Some of Europe's wealthiest lay anchor in Portofino in summer, but they stay out of sight by day, appearing in the evening after buses and boats have carried off the day-trippers.

There's not actually much to *do* in Portofino other than stroll around the wee harbor, see the castle, walk to Punta del Capo, browse at the pricey boutiques, and sip a coffee while people-watching. However, weaving through picture-perfect cliff-side gardens and gazing at yachts framed by the turquoise Ligurian Sea and the cliffs of Santa Margherita can make for quite a relaxing afternoon. There are also several tame, photo-friendly hikes into the hills to nearby villages.

8

Unless you're traveling on a deluxe budget, you may want to stay in Rapallo or Santa Margherita Ligure rather than at one of Portofino's few very expensive hotels. Restaurants and cafés are good but also pricey (don't expect to have a beer here for much under €10). Trying to reach Portofino by bus or car on the single narrow road can be a nightmare in summer and on holiday weekends. No trains go directly to Portofino: you must stop at Santa Margherita and take the public bus from there (€1). An alternative is to take a boat from Santa Margherita, though even this can be a harrowing experience, as cruise ships also anchor here to disgorge their passengers for outings.

From the harbor, follow the signs for the climb to the **Castello di San Giorgio,** the most worthwhile sight in Portofino, with its medieval relics, impeccable gardens, and sweeping views. The castle was founded in the Middle Ages but restored in the 16th through 18th century. In true Portofino form, it was owned by Genoa's English consul from 1870 until its opening to the public in 1961. ⊠ *Above harbor* ☎ *0185/269046* ⊠ *€3* ⊘ *Apr.–Sept., Wed.–Mon. 10–6; Oct.–Mar., Wed.–Mon. 10–5.*

The small church **San Giorgio,** sitting on a ridge, was rebuilt four times during World War II. It is said to contain the relics of its namesake, brought back from the Holy Land by the Crusaders. Portofino enthusiastically celebrates St. George's Day every April 23. ⊠ *Above harbor* ☎ *0185/269337* ⊘ *Daily 7–6.*

Pristine views can be had from the deteriorating *faro* (lighthouse) at **Punta Portofino,** a 15-minute walk along the point that begins at the southern end of the port. Along the seaside path you can see numerous impressive, sprawling private residences behind high iron gates. The only sand beach near Portofino is at **Paraggi,** a cove on the road between Santa Margherita and Portofino. The bus will stop here on request.

On the sea at the foot of Monte Portofino, the medieval **Abbazia di San Fruttuoso** *(Abbey of San Fruttuoso,* built by the Benedictines of Monte Cassino) protects a minuscule fishing village that can be reached only on foot or by water—a 20-minute boat ride from Portofino and also reachable from Camogli, Santa Margherita Ligure, and Rapallo. The restored abbey is now the property of a national conservation fund (FAI) and occasionally hosts temporary exhibitions. The church contains the tombs of some illustrious members of the Doria family. The old abbey and its grounds is a delightful place to spend a few hours, perhaps lunching at one of the modest beachfront trattorias nearby (open only in summer). Boatloads of visitors can make it very crowded very fast; you might appreciate it most off-season. ⊠ *15-min boat ride or 2-hr walk northwest of Portofino* ☎ *0185/772703* ⊠ *€4, €6 during exhibitions* ⊘ *Mar., Apr., and Oct., Tues.–Sun. 10–4; May–Sept., daily 10–6; Dec.–Feb., weekends 10–4. Last entrance is 30 mins before closing time.*

WHERE TO STAY & EAT

$$$–$$$$ ✕ **Il Pitosforo.** A chic clientele, many from the luxury yachts in the harbor, gives this waterfront restaurant a high glamour quotient, which is augmented by outlandish prices. Spaghetti ai frutti di mare is rec-

ommended; adventurous diners might try *lo stocco accomodou* (dried cod in a sauce of tomatoes, raisins, and pine nuts). ✉*Molo Umberto I 9* ☎*0185/269020 or 0335/5615833* ✍*Reservations essential* ▤*AE, DC, MC, V* ✆*Closed Mon. and Tues., and Jan.–mid-Feb. No lunch.*

$$$ ✕ **Ristorante Puny.** A table at this tiny restaurant is difficult to come by in summer, as the manager caters mostly to friends and regulars. If you are lucky enough to get in, however, the food will not disappoint you, nor will the cozy but elegant yellow interior. The unforgettable *pappardelle* (large, flat noodles) *al portofino* delicately blends two of Liguria's tastes, tomato and pesto. Ligurian seafood specialties include baked fish with bay leaves, potatoes, and olives as well as the inventive *moscardini al forno* (baked mini octopus with lemon and rosemary in tomato sauce). ✉*P. Martiri dell'Olivetta 4–5, on the harbor* ☎*0185/269037* ✍*Reservations essential* ▤*AE, DC, MC, V* ✆*Closed Thurs., and Jan. and Feb.*

¢ ✕ **Canale.** If the staggering prices of virtually all of Portofino's restaurants put you off, the long line outside this family-run bakery indicates that you're not alone and that something special is in store. Here all the focaccia is baked on the spot and served fresh from the oven, along with all kinds of sandwiches, pastries, and other refreshments. The only problem is there's nowhere to sit—time for a picnic! ✉*Via Roma 30* ☎*0185/269248* ▤*No credit cards* ✆*Closed Nov. and Dec. No lunch Jan.–Apr. and Oct.*

$$$$ ▦ **San Giorgio.** If you decide to stay in Portofino, this is perhaps your best choice. Tucked away on a quiet backstreet with no views of the harbor, the San Giorgio offers rooms that are immaculate, comfortable, and soothingly designed with canopy beds, pastel walls, and ultramodern bathrooms. Two small 19th-century town houses were joined to form the hotel, making the hallways seem like a labyrinth, but the level of service is high. Pros: In the middle of the village, secluded garden at the back. Con: Some of the rooms do not receive much light. ✉*Via Del Fondaco 11, 16034* ☎*0185/26991* 🖷*0185/267139* ⊕*www.portofinohsg.it* ⬎*17 rooms, 1 suite* ⚲*In-room: safe, refrigerator, ethernet. In-hotel: bar, public Internet, some pets allowed* ▤*AE, DC, MC, V* ✆*Closed Dec.–Feb.* ☉*BP.*

$$$$ ▦ **Splendido.** Arriving at this 1920s luxury hotel is so much like entering a Jazz Age film set that you'd almost expect to see a Bugatti or Daimler roll up the winding drive from the seaside below. There's a particular attention to color, from the coordinated floral linens in corals and gold to the fresh flowers in the reception rooms and on the large terrace. Even grander than the hotel are its prices (more than €600). A half-board plan is mandatory during high season. The Mare location has non-sea-view rooms. **Pros:** Gorgeous rooms, caring staff, lovely views. **Con:** Not worth the king's ransom you pay to stay here. ✉*Salita Baratta 16, 16034* ☎*0185/267801* 🖷*0185/267806* ⊕*www. hotelsplendido.com* ⬎*31 rooms, 34 suites* ⚲*In-room: safe, refrigerator, Wi-Fi. In-hotel: restaurant, bars, tennis court, pool, gym, some pets allowed* ▤*AE, DC, MC, V* ✆*Closed mid-Nov.–late Mar.* ☉*MAP.*

8

CAMOGLI

★ *15 km (9 mi) northwest of Porto-fino, 20 km (12 mi) east of Genoa.*

GETTING HERE
By car, exit the A12 at Recco and follow the blue signs. There are several pay-parking lots near the village center. By train, Camogli is located on the main north–south line between Genoa and La Spezia.

VISITOR INFORMATION
Camogli tourism office (⊠*Via XX Settembre 33/r, 16032* ☎*0185/771066* ⊕*www.camogli.it*).

EXPLORING
Camogli, at the edge of the large promontory and nature reserve known as the Portofino Peninsula, has always been a town of sailors. By the 19th century it was leasing its ships throughout the continent. Today, multicolor houses, remarkably deceptive trompe l'oeil frescoes, and a massive 17th-century seawall mark this appealing harbor community, perhaps as beautiful as Portofino but without the glamour. When exploring on foot, don't miss the boat-filled second harbor, which is reached by ducking under a narrow archway at the northern end of the first one.

The Castello Dragone, built onto the sheer rock face near the harbor, is home to the **Acquario** *(Aquarium)*, which has tanks filled with local marine life built into the ramparts. ⊠*Via Isola* ☎*0185/773375* ☎*€3* ⏲*May–Sept., daily 10–noon and 3–7; Oct.–Apr., Fri.–Sun. 10–noon and 2:30–6, Tues.–Thurs. 10–noon.*

WHERE TO STAY & EAT
$$–$$$ ✕ **Vento Ariel.** This small, friendly restaurant serves some of the best seafood in town. Dine on the shaded terrace in summer months and watch the bustling activity in the nearby port. Only the freshest of seafood is served; try the spaghetti *alle vongole* (with clams) or the mixed grilled fish. ⊠*Calata Porto* ☎*0185/771080* ▭*AE, DC, MC, V* ⏲*Closed Wed. and Jan. 2–15.*

★ $$$–$$$$ 🏨**Cenobio dei Dogi.** Perched majestically a step above Camogli, overlooking harbor, peninsula, and sea, this is indisputably the best address in town. Genoa's doges once summered here. Ask for one of the rooms with expansive balconies and commanding vistas of Camogli's cozy port. You can relax in the well-kept park or enjoy a game of tennis. Pros: Location and setting are wonderful. Cons: Crowds make it seem overbooked in summer; decor is a bit old-fashioned. ⊠*Via Cuneo 34, 16032* ☎*0185/7241* 🖷*0185/772796* ⊕*www.cenobio.it* 🛏*102 rooms, 4 suites* ♿*In-room: safe, refrigerator, Wi-Fi. In-hotel: restaurant, bar, tennis court, pool, gym, beachfront, public Wi-Fi* ▭*AE, DC, MC, V* ⏲❙*BP.*

$$ ▥**Hotel Augusta.** This friendly, family-run hotel is an economical choice in the center of Camogli. Though you won't have a view of the sea, it's just a short walk away. Quiet guest rooms all have parquet floors and modern amenities. **Pro:** You can't beat the price, especially in high season. **Cons:** Some rooms face other buildings and are a little dark. ⊠*Via Schiaffino 100, 16032* ☎*0185/770592* 📠*0185/770593* ⊕*www.htlaugusta.com* 🛏*15 rooms* ⚫*In-room: safe. In-hotel: restaurant, bar, no elevator* ▤*AE, DC, MC, V* 🍴|*BP.*

NIGHTLIFE & THE ARTS

★ **Sagra del Pesce,** the highlight of the festival of San Fortunato, is held on the second Sunday of May each year. It's a crowded, festive, and free-to-the-public feast of freshly caught fish, cooked outside at the port in a frying pan 12 feet wide.

GENOA

GETTING HERE

By car, take the Genoa Ovest exit and take the upper bridge (sopralevata) to the second exit, Genova centro-Piazza Corvetto. By train, there are two main stations, Genova Principe on the north side of the center and Brignole to the south.

VISITOR INFORMATION

Genoa tourism offices (⊠*Stazione Principe, San Teodoro* ☎*010/2462633* ⊕*www.apt.genova.it* ⊠*Aeroporto Internazionale Cristoforo Colombo, Sestri Ponente* ☎*010/6015247* ⊠*Via Roma 11* ☎*010/576791* ⊠*Terminale Crociere, Ponte dei Mille* ☎*No phone* ☉*Closed Oct.–Apr.*).

8

EXPLORING

Genoa (Genova, in Italian) was the birthplace of Christopher Columbus, but the city's proud history predates that explorer by several hundred years. Genoa was already an important trading station by the third century bc, when the Romans conquered Liguria. The Middle Ages and the Renaissance saw it rise into a jumping-off place for the Crusaders, a commercial center of tremendous wealth and prestige, and a strategic bone of international contention. A network of fortresses defending the city connected by a wall second only in length to the Great Wall of China was constructed in the hills above, and Genoa's bankers, merchants, and princes adorned the city with palaces, churches, and impressive art collections.

Known as *La Superba* (The Proud), Genoa was a great maritime power in the 13th century, rivaling Venice and Pisa in strength and splendor. But its luster eventually diminished, and the city was outshined by these and other formidable cities. By the 17th century it was no longer a great sea power. It has, however, continued to be a profitable port. Modern container ships now unload at docks that centuries ago served galleons and vessels bound for the spice routes. Genoa is now a busy, sprawling, and cosmopolitan city, apt to break the spell of the coastal

GETTING AROUND GENOA

Be forewarned: driving in Genoa is harrowing and is best avoided whenever possible—if you want to see the city on a day trip, go by train; if you're staying in the city, park in a garage or by valet and go by foot and by taxi throughout your stay.

The main bus station in Genoa is at Piazza Principe. Local buses, operated by the municipal transport company AMT (⊠ *Piazza Acquaverde, Genoa* ☎ *010/5582414* ⊕ *www.amt. genova.it*), serve the steep valleys that run to some of the towns along the western coast. Tickets may be bought at local bus stations or at newsstands. (You must have a ticket before you board.) AMT also operates the funicular railways and the elevators that service the steeper sections of the city.

Regular train service operates from Genoa's two stations: departures from Stazione Principe (⊠ *Piazza del Principe, San Teodoro, Genoa*) travel to points west and from Stazione Brignole (⊠ *Piazza Giuseppe Verdi, Foce, Genoa* ☎ *892021*) to points east and south. All the coastal resorts are on this line.

towns in a hurry. Crammed into a thin crescent of land between sea and mountains, Genoa expanded up rather than out, taking on the form of a multilayer wedding cake, with churches, streets, and entire residential neighborhoods built on others' rooftops. Public elevators and funiculars are as common as buses and trains.

But with more than two millennia of history under its belt, magnificent palaces and museums, the largest medieval city center in Europe, and an elaborate network of ancient hilltop fortresses, Genoa may be just the dose of culture you are looking for. Europe's biggest boat show, the annual Salone Nautico Internazionale, is held here. Fine restaurants are abundant, and classical dance and music are richly represented; the Teatro Carlo Felice is the local opera venue, and where the internationally renowned annual Niccolò Paganini Violin Contest takes place.

With the occasional assistance of public transportation, the only way to visit Genoa is on foot. Many of the more-interesting districts are either entirely closed to traffic, have roads so narrow that no car could fit, or are, even at the best of times, blocked by gridlock. Although it might seem a daunting task, exploring the city is made simple by its geography. The historical center of Genoa occupies a relatively narrow strip of land running between the mountains and the sea. You can easily visit the most important monuments in one or two days.

THE MEDIEVAL CORE & POINTS ABOVE

The medieval center of Genoa, threaded with tiny streets flanked by 11th-century portals, is roughly the area between the port and Piazza de Ferrari. This mazelike pedestrian zone is officially called the Caruggi District, but the Genovese, in their matter-of-fact way, simply refer to the area as the place of the *vicoli* (narrow alleys). In this warren of narrow, cobbled streets extending north from Piazza Caricamento, the city's oldest churches sit among tiny shops selling antique furniture, coffee, cheese, rifles, wine, gilt picture frames, camping gear, and even live fish. The 500-year-old apartment buildings lean so precariously that penthouse balconies nearly touch those across the street, blocking what little sunlight would have shone down onto the cobblestones. Wealthy Genovese built their homes in this quarter in the 16th century, and prosperous guilds, such as the goldsmiths for whom Vico degli Indoratori and Via degli Orefici were named, set up shop here.

THE MAIN ATTRACTIONS

★ **Cimitero Monumentale di Staglieno.** One of the most famous of Genovese
⑭ landmarks is this bizarrely beautiful cemetery; its fanciful marble and bronze sculptures sprawl haphazardly across a hillside on the outskirts of town. A **pantheon** holds indoor tombs and some remarkable works like an 1878 *Eve* by Villa. Don't miss Rovelli's 1896 **Tomba Raggio,** which shoots Gothic spires out of the hillside forest. The cemetery began operation in 1851 and has been lauded by such visitors as Mark Twain and Evelyn Waugh. It covers a good deal of ground; allow at least half a day to explore. It's difficult to locate; reach it via Bus 480 or 482 from the Stazione Genova Brignole, Bus 34 from Stazione Principe, or a taxi. ✉*Piazzale Resasco, Piazza Manin* ☎*010/870184* ⊕*www.cimiterodis-taglieno.it* ▣*Free* ☉*Daily 7:30–5; entrance closes at 4:30.*

❼ **Galleria Nazionale.** This gallery, housed in the richly adorned **Palazzo Spinola** north of Piazza Soziglia, contains masterpieces by Luca Giordano and Guido Reni. The *Ecce Homo,* by Antonello da Messina, is a hauntingly beautiful painting, of historical interest because it was the Sicilian da Messina who first brought Flemish oil paints and techniques to Italy from his sojourns in the Low Countries. ✉*Piazza Pellicceria 1, Maddalena* ☎*010/2705300* ⊕*www.palazzospinola.it* ▣*€4, €6.50 including Palazzo Reale* ☉*Tues.–Sat. 8:30–7:30, Sun. 1:30–7:30.*

❿ **Palazzo Bianco.** It's difficult to miss the splendid white facade of this town palace as you walk down Via Garibaldi, once one of Genoa's most important streets. The building houses a fine collection of 17th-century art, with the Spanish and Flemish schools well represented. ✉*Via Garibaldi 11, Maddalena* ☎*010/2759185* ⊕*www.museopala-zzobianco.it* ▣*€7, includes Palazzo Rosso and Palazzo Doria Tursi* ☉*Tues.–Fri. 9–7, weekends 10–7.*

❷ **Palazzo Reale.** Lavish rococo rooms provide sumptuous display space
Fodor's Choice
★ for paintings, sculptures, tapestries, and Asian ceramics. The 17th-century palace—also known as Palazzo Balbi Durazzo—was built by the Balbi family, enormously wealthy Genovese merchants. Its regal pretensions were not lost on the Savoy, who bought the palace and turned it into a royal residence in the early 19th century. The gallery of mirrors and the ballroom on the upper floor are particularly decadent. Look for works by Sir Anthony Van Dyck, who lived in Genoa for six years, beginning in 1621, and painted many portraits of the Genovese nobility. The formal gardens, which you can visit for €1, provide a welcome respite from the bustle of the city beyond the palace walls, as well as great views of the harbor. ✉*Via Balbi 10, Pré* ☎*010/27101* ⊕*www.*

8

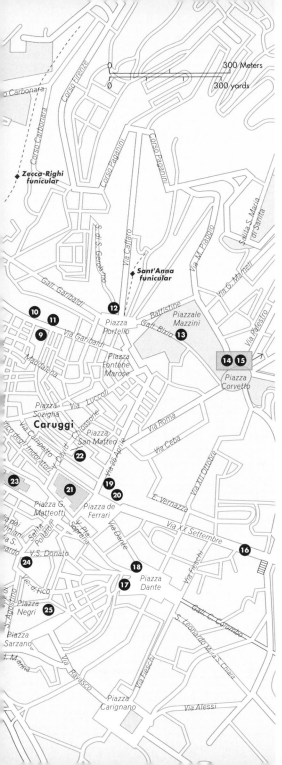

8

palazzorealegenova.it ▣*€4, €6 including Galleria Nazionale* ⊙*Tues. and Wed. 9–1:30, Thurs.–Sun. 9–7.*

❾ Palazzo Rosso. This 17th-century baroque palace was named for the red stone used in its construction. It now contains, apart from a number of lavishly frescoed suites, works by Titian, Veronese, Reni, and Van Dyck. ⊠*Via Garibaldi 18, Maddalena* ☎*010/2759185* ⊕*www. museopalazzorosso.it* ▣*€7, includes Palazzo Bianco and Palazzo Doria Tursi* ⊙*Tues.–Fri. 9–7, weekends 10–7.*

❺ Zecca-Righi funicular. This is a seven-stop commuter funicular beginning at Piazza della Nunziata and ending at a high lookout on the fortified gates in the 17th-century city walls. Ringed around the circumference of the city are a number of huge fortresses; this gate was part of the city's system of defenses. From Righi you can undertake scenic all-day hikes from one fortress to the next. ⊠*Piazza della Nunziata, Pré* ☎*010/5582414* ⊕*www.amt.genova.it* ▣*€1.20, free with bus ticket* ⊙*Daily 6 AM–11:45 PM.*

ALSO WORTH SEEING

⓬ Castelletto. One of Genoa's handy municipal elevators whisks you skyward from Piazza Portello, at the end of Galleria Garibaldi, for a good view of the old city. ⊠*Piazza Portello, Castelletto* ▣*€1* ⊙*Daily 6:40 AM–midnight.*

☺
⓯ Ferrovia Genova–Casella. In continuous operation since 1929, the Genova–Casella Railroad runs from Piazza Manin in Genoa (follow Via Montaldo from the center of town, or take Bus 33 or 34 to Piazza Manin) through the beautiful countryside above the city, finally arriving in the rural hill town of Casella. On the way, the tiny train traverses a series of precarious switchbacks that afford sweeping views of the forested Ligurian hills. In Casella Paese (the last stop) you can hike, eat lunch, or just check out the view and ride back. There are two restaurants and two pizzerias near the Casella station; try local cuisine at Trattoria Teresin in Località Avosso. **Canova** (two stops from the end of the line) is the start of two possible hikes through the hills: one a two-hour, one-way trek to a small sanctuary, **Santuario della Vittoria**, and the other a more-grueling four-hour hike to the hill town of **Creto**. Another worthwhile stop along the rail line is **Sant'Olcese Tullo**, where you can take a half-hour (one-way) walk along a river and through the **Sentiero Botanico di Ciaé,** a botanical garden and forest refuge with labeled specimens of Ligurian flora and a tiny medieval castle. For Canova and Sant'Olcese, inform your conductor that you want him to stop. The Genova–Casella railroad is a good way to get a sense of the rugged landscape around Genoa, and you may have it to yourself. The train runs about every hour. ⊠*Piazza Manin* ☎*010/837321* ⊕*www.ferroviagenovacasella.it* ▣*€4 round-trip Mon.–Sat., €6 Sun.* ⊙*Mon.–Sat. 7:30–7:30, Sun. 9–9.*

☺
❶ Granarolo funicular. Take a cog railway up the steeply rising terrain to another part of the city's fortified walls. It takes 15 minutes to hoist you from Stazione Principe, on Piazza Acquaverde, to **Porta Granarolo**, 1,000 feet above, where the sweeping view gives you a sense of Genoa's

size. The funicular departs about every half hour. ⊠*Piazza del Principe, San Teodoro* ☎*010/5582414* ⊕*www.amt.genova.it* 🎫*€1.20, free with bus ticket* ⊗*Daily 6 AM–10 PM, at 10:40 PM, and 11:20 PM.*

⑧ Loggia dei Mercanti. This merchants' row dating from the 16th century is lined with shops selling local foods and gifts as well as raincoats, rubber boots, and fishing line. ⊠*Piazza Banchi, Maddalena.*

⑬ Museo d'Arte Orientale Chiossone. In the Villetta di Negro park on the hillside above Piazza Portello, the Chiossone Oriental Art Museum has one of Europe's most noteworthy collections of Japanese, Chinese, and Thai objects. There's a fine view of the city from the museum's terrace. ⊠*Piazzale Mazzini 4, Maddalena* ☎*010/542285* ⊕*www.museochiossonegenova.it* 🎫*€4* ⊗*Tues.–Fri. 9–1, weekends 10–7.*

③ Palazzo dell'Università. Built in the 1630s as a Jesuit college, this has been Genoa's university since 1803. The exterior is unassuming, but climb the stairway flanked by lions to visit the handsome courtyard, with its portico of double Doric columns. ⊠*Via Balbi 5, Pré.* ⊕*www.unige.it*

⑪ Palazzo Doria Tursi. In the 16th century, wealthy resident Nicolò Grimaldi had a palace built of pink stone quarried in the region. It's been reincarnated as Genoa's Palazzo Municipale (Municipal Building), and so most of the goings-on inside are the stuff of local politics and quickie weddings. You can visit the richly decorated **Sala Paganini,** where the famous Guarnerius violin that belonged to Niccolò Paganini (1782–1840) is displayed, along with the gardens that connect the palace with the neighboring Palazzo Bianco. ⊠*Via Garibaldi 9, Maddalena* ☎*010/2759185* ⊕*www.stradanuova.it* 🎫*€7, includes Palazzo Bianco and Palazzo Rosso* ⊗*Tues.–Fri. 9–7, weekends 10–7.*

⑥ San Siro. Genoa's oldest church was the city's cathedral from the fourth to the ninth century. Rebuilt in the 16th and 17th centuries, it now feels a bit like a haunted house—imposing frescoes line dank hallways, and chandeliers hold crooked candles flickering in the darkness. ⊠*Via San Luca, Maddalena* ☎*010/22461468* ⊗*Daily 7:30–noon and 4–7.*

④ Santissima Annunziata. Exuberantly frescoed vaults decorate the 16th- to 17th-century church, which is an excellent example of Genovese baroque architecture. ⊠*Piazza della Nunziata, Pré* ☎*010/297662* ⊗*Daily 9–noon and 3–7.*

SOUTHERN DISTRICTS & THE AQUARIUM

Inhabited since the sixth century BC, the oldest section of Genoa lies on a hill to the southwest of the Caruggi District. Today, apart from a section of ninth-century wall near Porta Soprana, there is little to show that an imposing castle once stood here. Though the neighborhood is considerably run-down, some of Genoa's oldest churches make it a worthwhile excursion. No visit to Genoa is complete, however, without at least a stroll along the harbor front. Once a squalid and unsafe neighborhood, the port was given a complete overhaul during Genoa's preparations for the Columbus quincentennial celebrations of

1992, and additional restorations in 2003 and 2004 have done much to revitalize the waterfront. You can easily reach the port on foot by following Via San Lorenzo downhill from Genoa's cathedral, Via delle Fontane from Piazza della Nunziata, or any of the narrow vicoli that lead down from Via Balbi and Via Pré.

MAIN ATTRACTIONS

★ **Acquario di Genova.** Europe's biggest aquarium, second in the world only to Osaka's in Japan, is the third-most-visited museum in Italy and a must for children. Fifty tanks of marine species, including sea turtles, dolphins, seals, eels, penguins, and sharks, share space with educational displays and re-creations of marine ecosystems, including a tank of coral from the Red Sea. If arriving by car, take the Genova Ovest exit from the autostrada. Entrance is permitted every half hour and the ticket office closes 1½ hours before the aquarium. ⊠*Ponte Spinola, Porto Vecchio* ☎*0101/23451* ⊕*www.acquario.ge.it* ⊠*€14* ⊗*July and Aug., daily 9* AM*–11* PM*; Sept.–June, Mon.–Wed. and Fri. 9:30–7:30, Thurs. 9:30* AM*–10* PM*, weekends 9:30–8:30.*

㉙ **Galata Museo del Mare.** Devoted entirely to the city's seafaring history, this museum is probably the best way, at least on dry land, to get an idea of the changing shape of Genoa's busy port. Highlighting the displays is a full-size replica of a 17th-century Genovese galleon. ⊠*Calata de Mari 1, Ponte dei Mille* ☎*010/2345655* ⊕*www.galatamuseodelmare.it* ⊠*€10* ⊗*Mar.–Oct., daily 10–7:30; Nov.–Feb., Tues.–Fri. 10–6, weekends 10–7:30. Last entrance 1½ hrs before closing.*

㉚ **Harbor.** A boat tour gives you a good perspective on the layout of the harbor, which dates to Roman times. The Genoa inlet, the largest along the Italian Riviera, was also used by the Phoenicians and Greeks as a harbor and a staging area from which they could penetrate inland to form settlements and to trade. The port is guarded by the Diga Foranea, a striking wall 5 km (3 mi) long built into the ocean. The **Lanterna,** a lighthouse more than 360 feet high, was built in 1544; it's one of Italy's oldest lighthouses and a traditional emblem of Genoa. Boat tours of the harbor (€6), provided by the **Consorzio Liguria Viamare** (⊠ *Via Sottoripa 7/8, Porto Vecchio, Genoa* ☎*010/265712* ⊕*www. liguriaviamare.it*) launch from the aquarium pier and run about an hour. You can take a boat tour of Genoa harbor with Consorzio Liguria Viamare. The tour, which starts from the aquarium pier, costs €6, lasts about an hour, and includes a visit to the breakwater outside the harbor, the Bacino delle Grazie, and the Molo Vecchio (Old Port).

㉑ **Palazzo Ducale.** This palace was built in the 16th century over a medieval hall, and its facade was rebuilt in the late 18th century and later restored. It now houses temporary exhibitions and a restaurant-bar serving fusion cuisine. Reservations are necessary to visit the dungeons and tower. Guided tours of the palace and its exhibitions are sometimes available. ⊠*Piazza Matteotti 9, Portoria* ☎*010/5574004* ⊕*www. palazzoducale.genova.it* ⊠*Free* ⊗*Tues.–Sun. 9–9.*

㉓ **San Lorenzo.** Contrasting black slate and white marble, so common in Liguria, embellished the cathedral at the heart of medieval Genoa—

inside and out. Consecrated in 1118, the church honors St. Lawrence, who passed through the city on his way to Rome in the third century. For hundreds of years the building was used for religious and state purposes such as civic elections. Note the 13th-century Gothic portal, fascinating twisted barbershop columns, and the 15th- to 17th-century frescoes inside. The last campanile dates from the early 16th century. The **Museo del Tesoro di San Lorenzo** (San Lorenzo Treasury Museum) housed inside has some stunning pieces from medieval goldsmiths and silversmiths, for which medieval Genoa was renowned. ⊠*Piazza San Lorenzo, Molo* ☏*010/2471831* ⌦*Cathedral free, museum €5.50* ⊙*Cathedral: daily 8–11:45 and 3–6:45. Museum: Mon.–Sat. 9–11:30 and 3–5:30.*

㉕ Sant'Agostino. This 13th-century Gothic church was damaged during World War II, but it still has a fine campanile and two well-preserved cloisters that house an excellent museum displaying pieces of medieval architecture and fresco paintings. Highlighting the collection are the enigmatic fragments of a tomb sculpture by Giovanni Pisano (circa 1250–circa 1315). ⊠*Piazza Sarzano 35/r, Molo* ☏*010/2511263* ⊕*www.museosantagostino.it* ⌦*€4* ⊙*Tues.–Fri. 9–7, weekends 10–7.*

㉖ Santa Maria di Castello. One of Genoa's most significant religious buildings, an early Christian church, was rebuilt in the 12th century and finally completed in 1513. You can visit the adjacent cloisters and see the fine artwork contained in the museum. Museum hours vary during religious services. ⊠*Salita di Santa Maria di Castello 15, Molo* ☏*010/2549511* ⌦*Free* ⊙*Daily 9–noon and 3:30–6.*

ALSO WORTH SEEING

㉒ Accademia delle Belle Arti. Founded in 1751, the Academy of Fine Arts, as well as being a school, houses a collection of paintings from the 16th to the 19th century. Genovese artists of the baroque period are particularly well represented. ⊠ *Largo Pertini 4, Portoria* ☏*010/581957* ⊕*www.accademialigustica.it* ⌦*Free* ⊙*Mon.–Sat. 9–1.*

⑱ Childhood home of Christopher Columbus. The ivy-covered remains of this fabled medieval house stand in the gardens below the Porta Soprana. A small and rather disappointing collection of objects and reproductions relating to the life and travels of Columbus are on display inside. ⊠*Piazza Dante, Molo* ☏*010/2465346* ⌦*€4* ⊙*Tues.–Sun. 9–5.*

㉗ Il Bigo. The bizarre white structure erected in 1992 to celebrate the Columbus quincentennial looks like either a radioactive spider or an overgrown potato spore, depending on your point of view. Its most redeeming feature is the **Ascensore Panoramico Bigo** (Bigo Panoramic Elevator), from which you can take in the harbor, city, and sea. Next to the elevator, in an area covered by sail-like awnings, there's an ice-skating rink in winter. ⊠*Ponte Spinola, Porto Vecchio* ☏*010/23451, 347/4860524 ice-skating* ⌦*Elevator €3.30, skating rink €7.50* ⊙*Elevator: Feb. and Nov., weekends 10–5; June–Aug., Tues., Wed., and Sun. 10–8, Thurs.–Sat. 10 AM–11 PM; Mar.–May and Sept., Tues.–Sun. 10–6; Oct., Tues.–Sun. 10–5; Dec. 26–Jan. 6, daily 10–5. Skating rink:*

8

Nov. or Dec.–Mar., weekdays 8 AM–9:30 PM, Sat. 10 AM–2 AM, Sun. 10 AM–midnight.

16 **Mercato Orientale.** In the old cloister of a church along Via XX Settembre, this bustling produce, fish, and meat market is a wonderful sensory overload. Get a glimpse of colorful everyday Genovese life watching the merchants and buyers banter back and forth over the price. ⊠ *Via XX Settembre, Portoria* ◎ *Mon.–Fri. 7–1.*

17 **Porta Soprana.** A striking 12th-century twin-tower structure, this medieval gateway stands on the spot where a road from ancient Rome entered the city. It is just steps uphill from Columbus's boyhood home, and legend has it that the explorer's father was employed here as a gatekeeper. It's also known as Porta di Sant'Andrea (note the flags, with a red cross on a white background, flying atop the towers). ⊠ *Piazza Dante, Molo.*

24 **San Donato.** Although somewhat marred by 19th- and 20th-century restorations, the 12th-century San Donato—with its original portal and octagonal campanile—is a fine example of Genovese Romanesque architecture. Inside, an altarpiece by the Flemish artist Joos Van Cleve (circa 1485–1540) depicts the Adoration of the Magi. ⊠ *Piazza San Donato, Portoria* ☎ *010/2468869* ◎ *Mon.–Sat. 8–noon and 3–7, Sun. 9–12:30 and 3–7.*

22 **San Matteo.** This typically Genovese black-and-white-stripe church dates from the 12th century; its crypt contains the tomb of Andrea Doria (1466–1560), the Genovese admiral who maintained the independence of his native city. The well-preserved Piazza San Matteo was, for 500 years, the seat of the Doria family, which ruled Genoa and much of Liguria from the 16th to the 18th century. The square is bounded by 13th- to 15th-century houses decorated with portals and loggias. ⊠ *Piazza San Matteo, Maddalena* ☎ *010/2474361* ◎ *Mon.–Sat. 8–noon and 4–7, Sun. 9:30–10:30 and 4–5.*

19 **Teatro Carlo Felice.** The World War II–ravaged opera house in Genoa's modern center, Piazza de Ferrari, was rebuilt and reopened in 1991 to host the fine Genovese opera company; its massive tower has been the subject of much criticism. ⊠ *Passo Eugenio Montale 4, Piazza de Ferrari, Portoria* ☎ *010/53811* ⊕ *www.carlofelice.it.*

WHERE TO EAT

$$$$ ✗ **Antica Osteria del Bai.** Look out from a large dark-wood-paneled room over the Ligurian Sea from this romantic upscale restaurant perched high on a cliff. A seaside theme pervades the art and menu, which might include black gnocchi with lobster sauce or ravioli ai frutti di mare. The restaurant's traditional elegance is reflected in its white tablecloths, dress code, and prices. ⊠ *Via Quarto 16, Quarto* ☎ *010/387478* ⌒ *Jacket and tie required* ⊟ *AE, DC, MC, V* ◎ *Closed Mon., Jan. 10–20, and Aug. 1–20.*

$$$$ ✗ **Gran Gotto.** Innovative regional dishes are served in this posh, spacious restaurant brightened by contemporary paintings. Try *cappellacci*

The Art of the Pesto Pestle

You may have known Genoa primarily for its salami or its brash explorer, but the city's most direct effect on your life away from Italy may be through its cultivation of one of the world's best pasta sauces. The sublime blend of basil, extra-virgin olive oil, garlic, pine nuts, and grated pecorino and Parmigiano Reggiano cheeses that forms *pesto alla Genovese* is one of Italy's crowning culinary achievements, a concoction that Italian food guru Marcella Hazan has called "the most seductive of all sauces for pasta." Ligurian pesto is served only over spaghetti, gnocchi, lasagne, or—most authentically—*trenette* (a flat, spaghetti-like pasta) or *trofie*

(short, doughy pasta twists), and then typically mixed with boiled potatoes and green beans. Pesto is also occasionally used to flavor minestrone. The small-leaf basil grown in the region's sunny seaside hills is considered by many to be the best in the world, and pesto sauce was invented primarily as a showcase for that singular flavor. The simplicity and rawness of pesto is one of its virtues, as cooking (or even heating) basil ruins its delicate flavor. In fact, pesto aficionados refuse even to subject the basil leaves to an electric blender; Genovese (and other) foodies insist that true pesto can be made only with mortar and pestle.

di borragine con vellutata di pinoli (pasta with a pine-nut sauce) followed by *calamaretti brasati con porri e zucchine* (braised baby squid with leeks and zucchini), one of the many excellent second courses. Service is quick and helpful. ⊠*Viale Brigata Bisagno 69/r, Piazza della Vittoria, Foce* ☎*010/583644* ⚑*Reservations essential* ▭*AE, DC, MC, V* ⊗*Closed Sun. and Aug. 12–31. No lunch Sat.*

$$$$ ✕ **Zeffirino.** The five Belloni brothers share chef duties at a well-known restaurant full of odd combinations, including decor that has both rustic wood and modern metallic pieces. Try the *passutelli* (ravioli stuffed with ricotta cheese, herbs, and fruit) or any of the homemade pasta dishes. With a Zeffirino restaurant in Las Vegas and another in Hong Kong, the enterprising Bellonis have gone international. ⊠*Via XX Settembre 20, Portoria* ☎*010/591990* ⚑*Reservations essential. Jacket required* ▭*AE, DC, MC, V.*

$$–$$$ ✕ **Enoteca Sola.** Menus are chosen specifically to complement wines at Pino Sola's airy, casually elegant *enoteca* (wine bar) in the heart of the modern town. The short menu emphasizes seafood and varies daily but might include stuffed artichokes or baked stockfish. The real draw, though, is the wine list, which includes some of the winners of the *Tre Bicchieri* (Three Glasses) award denoting only the very best. ⊠*Via C. Barabino 120/r, Foce* ☎*010/594513* ▭*AE, DC, MC, V* ⊗*Closed Sun. and Aug.*

$$–$$$ ✕ **Maxela.** The cow is king at this upscale but casual trattoria. The building dates to a restaurant started in 1790. The owners have retained most of its original design including wood benches and slabs of marble for tables. Specials of the day hang from chalkboards throughout the eatery or you can just walk up to the butcher counter and pick your cut

8

of choice. ⊠Vico Inferiore del Ferro 9/r, Maddalena ☎010/2474209 ⊟AE, DC, MC, V ⊗Closed Sun.

$$ ✕ **Da Domenico.** Don't be dismayed by the labyrinth of rooms and wood passages that lead to your table at this restaurant in a quiet square near Piazza Dante—you've found one of those hidden corners that only the Genovese know. Traditional seafood and meat dishes make up most of the menu. ⊠*Piazza Leonardo 3, Molo* ☎*010/540289* ⚲*Reservations essential* ⊟*AE, DC, MC, V* ⊗*Closed Mon.*

$–$$ ✕ **Bakari.** Hip styling and ambient lighting hint at this eatery's creative, even daring, takes on Ligurian classics. Sure bets are the spinach-and-cheese gnocchi, any of several carpaccios, and the delicate beef dishes. Reserve ahead, requesting a table on the more-imaginative ground floor or just stop by for an aperitivo and people-watching. ⊠*Vico del Fieno 16/r, northwest of Piazza San Matteo, Maddalena* ☎*010/291936* ⊟*AE, MC, V* ⊗*Closed Sun. No dinner Wed. or Fri.*

¢ ✕ **Exultate.** When the weather permits, umbrella-shaded tables spread out from this tiny eatery into the nearby square. Its selection popular with locals, the restaurant's inexpensive daily menu is presented on a chalkboard for all to see, with elaborate salads and homemade desserts highlighting the list. ⊠*Piazza Lavagna 15/r, Maddalena* ☎*010/2512605* ⊟*MC, V* ⊗*Closed Sun.*

WHERE TO STAY

$$$$ ⊞ **The Bentley Hotel.** Glamour has returned to Genoa with this new luxury hotel on the wide, tree-lined road leading down to the port. The rooms are bright and sleekly decorated in muted tones with a wide variety of modern amenities such as plasma TVs and some with Jacuzzi tubs. Their in-house "Genovese gourmet" restaurant is frequented by local celebrities and soccer players. **Pro:** If you want top of the line, the Bentley, and nowhere else in Genoa, has it all. **Con:** It's a bit of a walk to the port and centro. ⊠ *Via Corsica 4, Carignano, 16128* ☎*010/5315111* ✉*010/5315800* ⊕*www.bentley.thi.it* ➷ *85 rooms, 14 suites* ⚙*In-room: safe, Wi-Fi. In-hotel: restaurant, bar, gym, spa, concierge, laundry service, public Internet, parking (fee)* ⊟*AE, DC, MC, V* ��❘*BP.*

$$$–$$$$ ⊞ **Bristol Palace.** The 19th-century grand hotel carefully guards its repu-
★ tation for courtesy and service. Spacious guest rooms all have high ceilings and elegant wood wardrobes or headboards. Public spaces, all connected to the hotel's central oval staircase, are comfortable, small, and pleasantly discreet with panel walls and soft lighting. Pro: In the heart of the shopping district. Con: Busy street outside can sometimes be noisy. ⊠*Via XX Settembre 35, Portoria, 16121* ☎*010/592541* ✉*010/561756* ⊕*www.hotelbristolpalace.com* ➷*128 rooms, 5 suites* ⚙*In-room: safe, refrigerator. In-hotel: restaurant, bar, gym, public Wi-Fi, parking (fee), some pets allowed* ⊟*AE, DC, MC, V* Ⲳ❘*BP.*

$$$ ⊞ **Best Western City.** In the heart of the city, near Via Roma, the grand shopping street, and one block from Piazza de Ferrari, which divides new Genoa from old Genoa, a bland apartment-building exterior gives way to a polished lobby and light, modern rooms. Suites, on the top floor, have spectacular views, as do many of the standard rooms on the upper floors. A choice of pillows—firm and low, or fluffy and soft—and coffeemakers in all the rooms are pleasant added touches. **Pro:** Location can't be beat. **Con:** Regular rooms are small. ⊠*Via San Sebastiano 6, Portoria, 16123* ☎*010/584707* 🖷*010/586301* ⊕*www.bwcityhotel-ge.it* 🛏*63 rooms, 3 suites* ⚒*In-room: safe, dial-up, Wi-Fi. In-hotel: restaurant, bar, public Wi-Fi, parking (fee)* ▭*AE, DC, MC, V* ⚏|*BP.*

$$ **Best Western Metropoli.** This welcoming hotel is on the border of the historic district and Via Garibaldi. Rooms and bathrooms both are bright and spacious with high ceilings. The staff is more than happy to offer you local advice, especially on dining options. Breakfast is abundant and the price is reasonable. **Pro:** Guest rooms and bathrooms are large. **Con:** Parking lot is a bit of a hike and can be confusing to find if you are driving. ⊠ *Via San Sebastiano 6, Portoria, 16123* ☎*010/584707* 🖷*010/586301* ⊕*www.bwcityhotel-ge.it* ⊕*www.bestwestern.it/BW/98125_hotel_Genova* 🛏*48 rooms* ⚒*In-room: refrigerator, dial-up. In-hotel: bar, laundry service, public Wi-Fi (fee), parking (fee), some pets allowed* ▭*AE, DC, MC, V* ⚏|*BP.*

$–$$ **Agnello d'Oro.** The friendly owner at Agnello d'Oro does double duty as a travel agent: he's happy to help you with plane reservations and travel plans. Only a few of the simple, modern rooms have balconies, but a surprisingly varied continental breakfast awaits you in the morning. **Pro:** Just 100 yards from Stazione Principe, near the Palazzo Reale. **Con:** Few amenities. ⊠*Vico delle Monachette 6, Pré, 16126* ☎*010/2462084* 🖷*010/2462327* ⊕*www.hotelagnellodoro.it* 🛏*25 rooms* ⚒*In-room: no a/c (some). In-hotel: restaurant, bar, parking (fee), some pets allowed* ▭*AE, DC, MC, V* ⚏|*BP.*

SIDE TRIPS FROM GENOA

NERVI

★ *11 km (7 mi) east of Genoa, 19 km (12 mi) west of Rapallo.*

GETTING HERE

By car, exit the A12 at Genova Nervi and follow the signs for "centro." By train, the Nervi train station is located on the main north–south line. You can also take the local commuter trains from Genova Principe and Brignole. By bus, it can be reached on the 15 from Genoa's Piazza Cavour.

EXPLORING

The identity of this stately late-19th-century resort, famous for its 1½-km-long (1-mi-long) seaside promenade, the **Passeggiata Anita Garibaldi**, its palm-lined roads, and its 300 acres of parks rich in orange trees, is given away only by the sign on the sleepy train station. Although Nervi is technically part of the city, its peace and quiet are as different from Genoa's hustle and bustle as its clear blue water is from Genoa's crowded port. From the centrally located train station, walk east along the seaside promenade to reach the beaches, a cliff-hanging restaurant, and the 2,000 varieties of roses in the public **Parco Villa Grimaldi,** all the while enjoying one of the most breathtaking views on the Riviera. Nervi—and the road along the way—is known for its nightlife in summer.

WHERE TO STAY & EAT

$–$$ ✕ **Marinella.** The impressive wrought-iron chandelier inside takes second billing to the great sea views from the dining room and the terrace. Try the *zuppa di pesce* (fish soup); main dishes change according to the day's catch. The restaurant, which perches on seaside shoals, has an inexpensive hotel, too. ⊠*Passeggiata Anita Garibaldi 18/r* ☎*010/3728343* ✽*MC, V* ⊘*Closed Mon. and Nov.*

$$$$ ⛩ **Romantik Hotel Villa Pagoda.** In a 19th-century merchant's man-

Fodor'sChoice sion modeled after a Chinese temple, this luxury hotel has a private

★ park, access to the famed cliff-top walk, and magnificent ocean views. Request a tower room for the best vantage point. Villa Pagoda is the best of both worlds, as you can enjoy peace and quiet or be in bustling Genoa in 15 minutes. **Pros:** Lovely guest and common rooms, everything has a touch of class. **Con:** Nearby train can be softly heard. ⊠*Via Capolungo 15, 16167* ☎*010/3726161* 🖷*010/321218* ⊕*www. villapagoda.it* ⤺*13 rooms, 4 suites* ♿*In-room: safe, refrigerator. In-hotel: restaurant, bar, tennis court, pool, some pets allowed* ✽*AE, DC, MC, V* ⨀*BP.*

RIVIERA DI PONENTE

The Riviera di Ponente (Riviera of the Setting Sun), covers the narrow strip of northwest Liguria from Genoa to the French border. The sapphire-color Mediterranean Sea to one side and the verdant foothills of the Alps on the other, allow for temperate weather and a long growing season—hence its nickname Riviera dei Fiori (Riviera of the Flowers). Once filled with charming seaside villages, elegant structures, and sophisticated visitors, this area now struggles to maintain a balance between its natural beauty and development. Highly populated resort areas are jammed into the thin stretch of white sand and pebble beaches. Yet, while its sister Riviera (di Levante) may retain more of its natural beauty, the Ponente remains a popular and well-organized retreat for visitors looking for sunshine, nightlife, and relaxation.

PEGLI

13 km (8 mi) west of Genoa.

GETTING HERE

By car, take the Genoa Pegli exit off the A10. It can also be reached by convenient commuter train from Stazione Principe in Genoa.

Once a popular summer home for many patrician Genovese families, Pegli has museums, parks, and some regal old homes with well-tended gardens. Two lovely villas—Villa Doria and Villa Durazzo Pallavicini—make Pegli worth an excursion. This suburb manages to maintain its dignity despite industrial development and the proximity of airport and port facilities.

Villa Doria, near the Pegli train station, has a large park. The villa itself, built in the 16th century by the Doria family, has been converted into a **naval museum.** ⊠*Piazza Bonavino 7* ☎*010/6969885* ⊕*www. museonavale.it* ⊠*€4* ⊘ *Villa: Tues.–Fri. 9–1, Sat. 10–1. Park: daily 9–noon and 2–6.*

Villa Durazzo Pallavicini, set in 19th-century gardens with temples and artificial lakes, contains an **archaeological museum.** ⊠*Via Pallavicini 11* ☎*010/6981048* ⊕*www.villapallavicini.net* ⊠*€3.5; €6.5 for villa and botanical gardens* ⊘*Apr.–Sept. 9–7, Oct.–Mar. 9–5.*

ALBISOLA MARINA

30 km (19 mi) southwest of Pegli, 43 km (26 mi) west of Genoa.

GETTING HERE

By car, take the Albisola exit off the A10 and follow the signs for the Albisola marina center. By train, Albisola is on the main line between Genoa and France.

EXPLORING

Albisola Marina has a centuries-old tradition of ceramic making. Numerous shops here sell the distinctive wares, and a whole sidewalk, **Lungomare degli Artisti,** has been transformed by the colorful ceramic works of well-known artists. It runs along the beachfront.

The 18th-century **Villa Faraggiana,** near the parish church, has exhibits on the history of pottery. ⊠*Via dell'Oratorio* ☎*019/480622* 🎫*Free* ⊙*Apr.–Sept., Wed.–Mon. 3–7.*

SHOPPING

Ceramiche San Giorgio (⊠*Corso Matteotti 5* ☎*019/482747*) has been producing ceramics since the 17th century, and is known for both classic and modern designs. **Ernan** (⊠*Corso Mazzini 77, Albisola Superiore* ☎*019/489916*) sells blue-and-white patterns typical of the 18th century. **Mazzotti** (⊠*Corso Matteotti 25* ☎*019/481626*) has an exclusive ceramics selection and a small museum.

FINALE LIGURE

24 km (15 mi) southwest of Savona, 72 km (44 mi) southwest of Genoa.

GETTING HERE

By car, take the Finale Ligure exit off the A10 and follow the signs for "centro." By train, Finale Ligure is on the main line between Genoa and France.

VISITOR INFORMATION

Finale Ligure tourism office (⊠ *Via San Pietro 13, 17024* ☎*019/681019* ⊕*www.inforiviera.it*)

EXPLORING

Finale Ligure is actually made up of three small villages: Finalmarina, Finalpia, and Finalborgo. The former two have fine sandy beaches and modern resort amenities. The most attractive of the villages is Finalborgo, less than 1 km (½ mi) inland. It's a hauntingly preserved medieval settlement, planned to a rigid blueprint, with 15th-century walls. The surrounding countryside is pierced by deep, narrow valleys and caves; the limestone outcroppings provide the warm pinkish stone found in many buildings in Genoa. Rare reptiles lurk among the exotic flora.

WHERE TO EAT

$$$$ ✕ **Ai Torchi.** You could easily become a homemade-pesto snob at this Finalborgo eatery. The high prices are justified by excellent inventive seafood and meat dishes and by the setting—a restored 5th-century olive-oil refinery. ⊠*Via dell'Annunziata 12* ☎*019/690531* ▤*AE, DC, MC, V* ⊙*Closed Jan. 7–Feb. 10, and Tues. Sept.–July.*

ALASSIO

100 km (60 mi) southwest of Genoa.

GETTING HERE

By car, take the Albenga exit off the A10 and follow the blue signs for Alassio. By train, Alassio is on the main line between Genoa and France.

VISITOR INFORMATION

Alassio tourism office (✉*Palazzo Commune, Piazza della Libertà* ☎*0182/6021* ⊕ *www.comune.alassio.sv.it*).

Although Alassio is no longer a sleepy fishing village, the centro still possesses some old-world charm, colorful buildings, a great beachfront promenade, and white sand beaches. Spend the day soaking up some sun, grab a seafood lunch or pizza along the boardwalk, and then finish off with a passeggiata and shopping on its caruggi.

SAN REMO

10 km (6 mi) west of Taggia, 146 km (90 mi) southwest of Genoa.

GETTING HERE

By car, take the San Remo exit off the A10 and follow the signs for "centro." By train, San Remo is on the main line between Genoa and France.

VISITOR INFORMATION

San Remo tourism office (✉*Palazzo Riviera, Largo Nuvoloni 1, 18038* ☎*0184/59059* ⊕*www.sanremonet.com*).

EXPLORING

Once the crown jewel of the Riviera di Ponente, San Remo is still the area's largest resort, lined with polished hotels, exotic gardens, and seaside promenades. Renowned for its VIPs, glittering casino, and romantic setting, San Remo maintains remnants of its glamorous past from the late 19th century to World War II, but it also suffers from the same epidemic of overbuilding that has changed so much of the western Riviera for the worse. Waterside palm fronds conceal a sizable old center that, unlike in other Ponente towns, is lively even in the off-season. Restaurants, wine bars, and boutiques are second in Liguria only to Genoa's, and San Remo's cafés bustle with activity at all hours.

The Mercato dei Fiori, Italy's most important wholesale flower market, is held here in a market hall between Piazza Colombo and Corso Garibaldi and open to dealers only. More than 20,000 tons of carnations, roses, mimosa flowers, and innumerable other cut flowers are dispatched from here each year. As the center of northern Italy's flower-growing industry, the town is surrounded by hills where verdant terraces are now blanketed with plastic to form immense greenhouses.

The city is home to a couple of famous festivals including the San Remo Music Festival in February and Parade of Flowers in January.

Explore the warren of alleyways in the old part of San Remo, **La Pigna** *(The Pinecone)*, which climbs upward to Piazza Castello and offers a splendid view of the town.

In addition to gaming, the art nouveau **San Remo Casinò** has a restaurant, a nightclub, and a theater that hosts concerts and the annual San Remo Music Festival. If you want to try your luck at the gaming tables, there's a €7.50 cover charge on weekends. Dress is elegant, with jacket and tie requested at the French gaming tables. ⊠*Corso Inglesi 18* ☎*0184/5951* ☺*Slot machines: Sun.–Fri. 10* AM*–2:30* AM*, Sat. 10* AM*–3:30* AM*. Tables: Sun.–Fri. 2:30* PM*–2:30* AM*, Sat. 2:30* PM*–3:30* AM.

The onion-dome Russian Orthodox church of **Cristo Salvatore, Santa Caterina d'Alessandria, e San Serafino di Sarov** testifies to a long Russian presence on the Italian Riviera. Russian empress Maria Alexandrovna, wife of Czar Alexander I, built a summerhouse here, and in winter San Remo was a popular destination for other royal Romanovs. The church was consecrated in 1913. ⊠*Via Nuvoloni 2* ☎*0184/531807* ✉*€1 donation* ☺*Daily 9:30–noon and 3–6.*

WHERE TO STAY & EAT

$ ✕ **Nuovo Piccolo Mondo.** Old wooden chairs dating from the 1920s,
Fodor'sChoice when the place opened, evoke the homey charm of this small, family-
★ run trattoria. The place has a faithful clientele, so get there early to grab a table and order Ligurian specialties such as *sciancui* (a roughly cut flat pasta with a mixture of beans, tomatoes, zucchini, and pesto) and *polpo e patate* (stewed octopus with potatoes). ⊠*Via Piave 7* ☎*0184/509012* ▭*No credit cards* ☺*Closed Mon. No dinner Sun.*

$$$$ ⊡**Royal.** This is arguably Liguria's second most luxurious resort after the Splendido in Portofino. Rooms here have a mixture of modern amenities and antique furnishings and most have views of the sea. The heated seawater swimming pool, open April through October, is in a large tropical garden. On the terrace, candlelight dining and music are offered each night in warm weather. Keep your eyes open for off-season discounts. The Royal is only a few paces from the casino. Pro: All the expected high-end amenities. Cons: Some of the property seems outdated, meals and beverages on the premises are expensive. ⊠*Corso Imperatrice 80, 18038* ☎*0184/5391* 🖷*0184/661445* ⊕*www.royal-hotelsanremo.com* ⇄*114 rooms, 13 suites* ⚒*In-room: safe, Wi-Fi. In-hotel: 3 restaurants, room service, bars, tennis court, pool, gym, beachfront, concierge, laundry service, public Wi-Fi* ▭*AE, DC, MC, V* ☺*Closed Oct. 2–Dec. 17* ☉*BP.*

$–$$ ⊡**Paradiso.** A quiet palm-fringed garden gives the Paradiso an air of seclusion in this sometimes hectic resort city. Rooms are well equipped and bright; all have nice size balconies. The hotel restaurant has a good fixed-price menu. This small central hotel is adjacent to a lush public park. **Pros:** Friendly service, comfortable accommodations. **Con:** A steep walk up some stairs and a hill from town. ✉*Via Roccasterone 12, 18038* ☎*0184/571211* 📠*0184/578176* ⊕*www.paradisohotel.it* ⤶*41 rooms* ♿*In-room: safe, refrigerator. In-hotel: restaurant, bar, pool, public Internet* ⊟*AE, DC, MC, V* ⦿*BP.*

BORDIGHERA

12 km (7 mi) west of San Remo, 155 km (96 mi) southwest of Genoa.

GETTING HERE
By car, take the Bordighera exit off the A10 and follow the signs for "centro," about a 10-minute drive. By train, Bordighera is on the main line between Genoa and France.

VISITOR INFORMATION
Bordighera tourism office (✉*Via Vittorio Emanuele II 172, 18012* ☎*0184/262322* ⊕*www.rivieradeifiori.org*).

EXPLORING
On a large, lush promontory, Bordighera wears its genteel past as a famous winter resort with unstudied ease. A large English colony, attracted by the mild climate, settled here in the second half of the 19th century and is still very much in evidence today; you regularly find people taking afternoon tea in the cafés, and streets named after Queen Victoria and Shakespeare. This garden spot was the first town in Europe to grow date palms, and its citizens still have the exclusive right to provide the Vatican with palm fronds for Easter celebrations.

Thanks partly to its many year-round English residents, Bordighera does not close down entirely in the off-season like some Riviera resorts but rather serves as a quiet winter haven for an older clientele. With plenty of hotels and restaurants, Bordighera makes a good base for exploring the region and is quieter and less commercial than San Remo.

Running parallel to the ocean, **Lungomare Argentina** is a pleasant promenade, 1½ km (1 mi) long, which begins at the western end of the town and provides good views westward to the French Côte d'Azur.

WHERE TO STAY & EAT
$$$$ ✕ **Le Chaudron.** A charming rustic interior, with ancient Roman arches, has the look of restaurants across the French border in Provence. Ligurian specialties are highlights on the predominantly seafood menu: try the cheese *pansoti con salsa di noci* (ravioli with walnut sauce) and the *branzino* (sea bass) with artichokes or mushrooms. ✉*Via Vittorio Emanuele 9* ☎*0184/263592* ☝*Reservations essential* ⊟*DC, MC, V* ⊘*Closed Mon., 1st 2 wks in Feb., and 1st 2 wks in July.*

$–$$ ✕**Bagni Sant'Ampeglio.** This combination beach club and restaurant has wonderful choices for both lunch and dinner. Try their house-speciality branzino in carciofi (sea bass with artichokes) and homemade des-

8

serts. ✉ *Lungomare Argentina 3* ☎ *0184/262106* ⊟ *AE, DC, MC, V* ⊘ *Closed Wed.*

$–$$ ✕ **Il Tempo Ritrovato.** A small wine bar and restaurant combine forces here on Bordighera's seaside promenade. Simple pasta dishes and a spectacular wine list make this a great choice. E*Bagni Amarea on Lungomare Argentin*P *0184/261207*c *AE, DC, MC, VC Closed Sun. and Mon.*

$$$ ⬚ **Hotel Piccolo Lido.** This quaint hotel along the promenade provides clean and simple rooms at reasonable prices year-round. Sea-view rooms have nice little balconies, perfect for enjoying the sunset and vistas of France. **Pro:** A good value. **Con:** Few amenities. ✉*Lungomare Argentina 2, 18012* ☎*0184/261297* ⊕*www.hotelpiccololido.it* ⤚*33 rooms* ⚭ *In-room: safe. In-hotel: restaurant, beachfront, parking* ⊟*AE, DC, MC, V* ⱺ*BP, MAP, FAP.*

GIARDINI BOTANICI HANBURY

Fodor'sChoice   *6 km (4 mi) west of Ventimiglia, 165 km (102 mi) southwest of Genoa.*
★

GETTING HERE
Take the S1 along the coast away from Ventimiglia centro and toward the French border. After passing through a tunnel, the gardens are about 1 km (½ mi) farther.

Mortola Inferiore, only 2 km (1 mi) from the French border, is the site of the world-famous Giardini Botanici Hanbury (Hanbury Botanical Gardens), one of the largest in Italy. Planned and planted in 1867 by a wealthy English merchant, Sir Thomas Hanbury, and his botanist brother Daniel, the terraced gardens contain species from five continents, including many palms and succulents. There are panoramic views of the sea from the gardens. The ticket office closes one hour before the garden. ✉*Località Mortola* ☎*0184/229507* ⤳*€7.50* ⊘*Mar.–June 15, daily 9:30–6; June 16–Sept. 15, daily 9:30–7; Sept. 16–last Sat. in Oct., daily 9:30–6; last Sun. in Oct.–Feb., Tues.–Sun. 10–5. Last entrance 1 hr before closing.*

Emilia–Romagna

WORD OF MOUTH

"Ah, Bologna…one of Italy's truly underrated gems. Sitting in an outdoor café in Piazza Maggiore is a true Italian experience."

–HowardR

WELCOME TO EMILIA–ROMAGNA

TOP REASONS TO GO

★ **The signature food of Emilia:** This region's food—*prosciutto crudo*, Parmigiano-Reggiano, balsamic vinegar, and above all, pasta—makes the trip to Italy worthwhile.

★ **Mosaics that take your breath away:** The intricate tiles in Ravenna's Mausoleo di Galla Placidia, in brilliantly well-preserved colors, depict vivid portraits and pastoral scenes.

★ **Europe's oldest wine bar:** Nicholas Copernicus tippled here while studying at Ferrara's university in the early 1500s; Osteria al Brindisi, in the *centro storico* (historic center), has been pouring wine since 1435.

★ **The nightlife of Bologna:** This red-roofed, leftist-leaning city has had a lively student culture since the university—Europe's oldest—was founded in the late 11th century.

★ **The medieval castles of San Marino:** The three castles are dramatically perched on a rock more than 3,000 feet above the flat landscape of Romagna.

1 Emilia. A landscape of medieval castles and crumbling farmhouses begins just east of Milan, in the western half of Emilia-Romagna. You'll find here the delicious delights of **Parma**, with its buttery prosciutto, famous cheese, and crenellated palaces. Next along the road, continuing east, comes **Reggio Emilia**, of Parmigiano-Reggiano cheese fame, then **Modena**, the city of balsamic vinegar.

2 Bologna. Emilia's principal cultural and intellectual center is famed for its arcaded sidewalks, grandiose medieval towers, and fabulous restaurants.

Ravenna

3 **Ferrara.** This prosperous, tidy city to the north of Bologna has a rich medieval past. The Ferraresi consider themselves part of Emilia.

4 **Romagna.** The eastern half of Emilia-Romagna begins east of Bologna, where spa towns span to the north and south of the Via Emilia and the A1 autostrada, and extends to the Adriatic, where **Rimini's** crowded beaches fill with throngs of tourists in August. **San Marino**, south of Rimini, is an anomaly in every way—it's its own tiny republic, hanging implausibly on a cliff above the Romagna plain.

Bologna

5 **Ravenna.** The main attractions of this well-preserved Romagna city are its memorable mosaics—glittering treasures left from Byzantine rule.

GETTING ORIENTED

Emilia-Romagna owes its beginnings to the Romans, who built the Via Emilia in 187 BC. Today the road bisects the flat, foggy region, paralleling the Autostrada del Sole (A1), making it easy to drive straight through. Bologna is in the middle of everything, with Piacenza, Parma, and Modena to the west, and Rimini to the east. Ferrara and Ravenna are the only detours—they're to the north of Via Emilia.

EMILIA–ROMAGNA PLANNER

Making the Most of Your Time

Plan on spending at least two days or nights in Bologna, the region's cultural and historical capital. You shouldn't miss Parma, with its stunning food and graceful public spaces. Also plan on visiting Ferrara, a misty, mysterious medieval city. If you have time, go to Ravenna for its memorable Byzantine mosaics and Modena for its harmonious architecture and famous balsamic vinegar.

If you only have a few days in the region, it's virtually impossible to do all five of those cities justice. If you're a dedicated foodie, move from Bologna west along the Via Emilia (SS9) to Modena and Parma. If you're more interested in architecture, art, and history, choose the eastern route, heading north on the A13 to Ferrara and then southeast on the SS16 to Ravenna.

If you have more time, you won't have to make such tough choices. You can start in Milan, go east, and finish on the Adriatic—or vice versa. Despite its hordes of summer tourists and so-so beaches, Rimini is worth a visit for its terrific cathedral and fine fish restaurants.

Seeing Through the Fog

Emilia-Romagna is famous for the low-lying fog that comes in from the Adriatic and blankets much of the region in fall and winter. In the cities, the mist can be ghostly and beautiful, but it can also be a driving hazard, with little visibility beyond about 10 yards. You should avoid driving at night in winter, but the problem can arise in the day, too.

If it gets too bad, pull off at an Autogrill or café and wait for the fog to lift, and if you're on the road, keep your headlights on (it's the law, anyway, in Italy) and don't exceed 60 kph. Road signs throughout the region indicate speed limits in fog (nebbia).

Finding a Place to Stay

Emilia-Romagna has a reputation for an efficiency uncommon in most of Italy. Even the smallest hotels are usually well run, with high standards of quality and service. Bologna is very much a businessperson's city, and many hotels here cater to the business traveler, but there are smaller, more intimate hotels as well. It's smart to book in advance—the region hosts many fairs and conventions that can fill up hotels even during low season.

Though prices are sometimes high, you can expect an experience delightfully free of the condescending attitude that sometimes mar Italy's tourist meccas. The one exception to the rule is Rimini, where numerous hotels have tourist-oriented full- and half-board packages. They overflow during July and August and close down for much of the off-season.

DINING & LODGING PRICE CATEGORIES (IN EUROS)

¢	$	$$	$$$	$$$$
Restaurants				
under €15	€15–€25	€25–€35	€35–€45	over €45
Hotels				
under €70	€70–€110	€110–€160	€160–€220	over €220

Restaurant prices are for a first course (primo), second course (secondo), and dessert (dolce). Hotel prices are for two people in a standard double room in high season, including tax and service.

GETTING AROUND

By Train

When it comes to public transportation in the region, trains are better than buses—they're fairly efficient and quite frequent, and most stations aren't too far from the center of town. The railway line follows the Via Emilia (SS9). In Emilia, it's generally 30 to 45 minutes from one major city to the next. To reach Ferrara or Ravenna, you'll usually have to change to a local train at the Bologna station. Trains run frequently, and connections are easy. Ferrara is a half hour north of Bologna on the train, and Ravenna is just over an hour.

Bologna is an important rail hub for northern Italy and has frequent, fast service to Milan, Florence, Rome, and Venice. The routes from Bologna to the south usually go through Florence, which is only an hour away. On the northeastern edge of the region, Venice is 1½ hours east of Ferrara by train. You can check the Web site of the state railway, the **Ferrovie dello Stato** (☎ *892021 toll-free within Italy* ⊕ *www.trenitalia.com*), for information, or stop in any travel agency, as many book and print train tickets and are likely to speak English.

By Car

Driving is the best way to get around Emilia-Romagna. Roads are wide, flat, and well marked; distances are short, and beautiful farmhouses and small villages make for easily accessible detours. A car is particularly useful for visiting the spa towns of Romagna, which aren't well connected by train. Many of the historic centers are off-limits to cars, but they're also easily walkable, so you may just want to park your car and get around by foot once you hit your hotel.

Entering Emilia-Romagna by car is as easy as it gets. Coming in from the west on the Autostrada del Sole (A1), Piacenza will be the first city you'll hit. It's a mere 45 minutes southeast of Milan. On the other side of the region, Venice is about an hour from Ferrara by car on the A13.

Bologna is on the autostrada network, so driving between cities is a breeze, though do take special care if you're coming from Florence, as the road is winding and drivers speed. The Via Emilia (SS9), one of the oldest roads in the world, runs through the heart of the region. It's a straight, low-lying modern road, the length of which can be traveled in a few hours. Although less scenic, the A1 toll highway, which runs parallel to the Via Emilia from Bologna, can get you where you're going about twice as fast. From Bologna, the A13 runs north to Ferrara, and the A14 takes you east to Ravenna and Rimini. Note that much of the historic center of Bologna is closed off to cars daily from 7 AM to 8 PM.

EATING & DRINKING WELL IN EMILIA-ROMAGNA

Italians rarely agree about anything, but most would say that the best food in the country is in Emilia-Romagna. Tortellini, fettucine, Parmesan cheese, and balsamic vinegar are just a few of the Italian delicacies born here.

One of the beauties of Emilia-Romagna is that its exceptional food can be had without breaking the bank. Many *trattorie* and *osterie* serve up classic dishes, mastered over the centuries, at reasonable prices. Cutting-edge restaurants and wine bars are often more expensive; their inventive menus are full of *fantasia*—reinterpretations of the classics. Bologna is a student-oriented town and has great places for those on shoestring budgets.

Between meals, you can sustain yourself with the region's famous sandwich, the *piadina*. It's made with pita-thin bread, usually filled with prosciutto or mortadella, cheese, and vegetables. It's put under the grill and served hot, with the cheese oozing at the sides. These addictive sandwiches can be had at sit-down places or ordered to go.

THE REAL RAGÙ

Emilia-Romagna's signature dish is *tagliatelle al ragù* (flat noodles with meat sauce), known as "spaghetti Bolognese" everywhere else. This primo is on every menu, and no two versions are the same. The sauce starts in a sauté pan with pancetta or guanciale, butter, and minced onions. Purists use nothing but beef, but some mix it with sausage, veal, or chicken. Regular ministrations of broth are added, and sometimes wine, milk, or cream. After a couple of hours of cooking, the ragù is ready to be joined with pasta and Parmesan and brought to the table.

PORK PRODUCTS

It's not just mortadella and cured pork products like prosciutto and *culatello* that Emilia-Romagnans go crazy for—they're wild about the whole hog.

You'll frequently find *cotechino* and *zampone,* both secondi, on menus; cotechino, photo below, is a savory, thick, fresh sausage served with lentils on New Year's Day (the combination is said to augur well for the new year) and with mashed potatoes year-round. *Zampone*, a stuffed pig's foot, is redolent of garlic, and is deliciously fatty.

BOLLITO MISTO

The name means "mixed boil," and they do it exceptionally well in this part of Italy. According to Emilia-Romagnans, it was invented here (its true origins are up for grabs, as other northern Italians, especially from Milan and the Piedmont, would argue this point). Chicken, beef, tongue, and zampone are tossed into a stockpot and boiled; they are then removed from the broth and served with a fragrant *salsa verde* (green sauce), made green by parsley and spiced with anchovies, garlic, and capers. This simple yet rich dish is usually served with mashed potatoes on the side, and savvy diners will mix some of the piquant *salsa verde* into the potatoes as well.

STUFFED PASTA

Among the many Emilian variations on stuffed pasta, *tortellini*, pictured at left, are the smallest. *Tortelli*, photo upper right, and *cappellacci* are larger pasta "pillows," about the size of a Brussels sprout, but with the same basic form as tortellini; they're often filled with pumpkin or spinach and cheese.

Tortelloni are, in theory, even bigger, although their sizes vary. Stuffed pastas are generally served simply, with melted butter, sage, and (what else?) Parmigiano-Reggiano cheese, or (in the case of tortellini) *in brodo* (in beef or chicken broth), which brings out the subtle richness of the filling.

WINES

Emilia-Romagna's wines accompany the region's fine food rather than vying with it for accolades. The best known is Lambrusco, a sparkling red produced on the Po Plain that has some admirers and many detractors. It's praised for its tartness and condemned for the same quality. The region's best wines include Sangiovese di Romagna, somewhat similar to Chianti, from the Romagnan hills, and Barbera, from the Colli Piacetini and Apennine foothills. Castelluccio, Bonzara, Zerbina, Leone Conti, and Tre Monti are among the region's top producers—keep an eye out for their bottles.

9

Updated
by Patricia
Rucidlo

GOURMETS THE WORLD OVER CLAIM that Emilia-Romagna's greatest contribution to humankind has been gastronomic. Birthplace of fettuccine, tortellini, lasagne, prosciutto, and Parmesan cheese, the region has a spectacular culinary tradition. But there are many reasons to come here aside from the desire to be well fed: Parma's Correggio paintings, Giuseppe Verdi's villa at Sant'Agata, the medieval splendor of Bologna's palaces and Ferrara's alleyways, the rolling hills of the Romagna countryside, and, perhaps foremost, the Byzantine beauty of mosaic-rich Ravenna—glittering as brightly today as it did 1,500 years ago.

As you travel through Emilia, the western half of the region, you'll encounter sprawling plants of the industrial food giants of Italy, such as Barilla and Fini, standing side by side with fading villas and farmhouses that have long punctuated the flat, fertile land of the Po Plain. Bologna, the principal city of Emilia, is a busy cultural and, increasingly, business center, less visited but in many ways just as engaging as Italy's more-famous tourist destinations—particularly given its acknowledged position as the leading city of Italian cuisine. The rest of the region follows suit: eating is an essential part of any Emilian experience.

You'll need to stay focused even just to make sure you try all the basics: Parma's famed prosciutto and Parmigiano-Reggiano cheese; Modena's balsamic vinegar; the *ragù*—slow-simmered meat sauce—whose poor imitations are known elsewhere in the world as *Bolognese*; and, of course, the best pasta in the world.

The historical border between Emilia to the west and Romagna to the east lies near the fortified town of Dozza. Emilia is flat; but just east of the Romagnan border, the landscape gets hillier and more-sparsely settled, in places covered with evergreen forests and steaming natural springs; finally, it flattens again into the low-lying marshland of the Po Delta, which meets the Adriatic Sea. Farther south, the down-market beach resort of Rimini draws hordes of Italian teenagers and German families every summer. Each fall, in both Romagna and Emilia, the trademark fog rolls in off the Adriatic to hang over the flatlands in winter, coloring the region with a spooky, gray glow.

EMILIA

The Via Emilia runs through Emilia's heart in a straight shot from medieval Piacenza, only 67 km (42 mi) southeast of Milan, through Bologna, and ultimately to Romagna and the Adriatic Coast. On the way you encounter many of Italy's cultural riches—from the culinary and artistic treasures of Parma to the birthplace and home of Giuseppe Verdi. Take time to detour into the countryside, with its ramshackle farmhouses and 800-year-old abbeys; to stop for a taste of prosciutto; and to detour north to the mist-shrouded tangle of streets that make up Ferrara's old Jewish ghetto.

EMILIA-ROMAGNA THROUGH THE AGES

Ancient History. Emilia-Romagna owes its beginnings to a road. In 187 BC the Romans built the Via Aemilia, a long road running northwest from the Adriatic port of Rimini to the central garrison town of Piacenza, and it was along this central spine that the primary towns of the region developed.

Despite the unifying factor of what came to be known as the Via Emilia, the region has had a fragmented history. Its eastern part, roughly the area from Faenza to the coast, known as Romagna, first looked to the Byzantine east and then to Rome for art, political power, and, some say, national character. The western part, Emilia, from Bologna to Piacenza, had a more-northern, rather dour sense of self-government and dissent.

Bologna was founded by the Etruscans and eventually came under the influence of the Roman Empire. The Romans established a garrison here, renaming the old Etruscan settlement Bononia. It was after the fall of Rome that the region began its fragmentation. Romagna, centered in Ravenna, was ruled from Constantinople. Ravenna eventually became the capital of the empire in the west in the fifth century, passing to papal control in the eighth century.

Even today, the city is still filled with reminders of two centuries of Byzantine rule.

Family Ties. The other cities of the region, from the Middle Ages on, became the fiefs of important noble families—the Este in Ferrara and Modena, the Pallavicini in Piacenza, the Bentivoglio in Bologna, and the Malatesta in Rimini. Today all these cities bear the marks of their noble patrons. When in the 16th century the papacy managed to exert its power over the entire region, some of these cities were divided among the papal families—hence the stamp of the Farnese family on Parma, Piacenza, and Ferrara.

A Leftward Tilt. Bologna and Emilia-Romagna have established a robust tradition of rebellion and dissent. The Italian socialist movement was born in the region, as was Benito Mussolini—in keeping with the political climate of his home state, he was a firebrand socialist during the early part of his career. Despite having Mussolini as a native son, Emilia-Romagna did not take to fascism: it was here that the antifascist resistance was born, and during World War II the region suffered terribly at the hands of the Fascists and the Nazis.

9

PIACENZA

67 km (42 mi) southeast of Milan, 150 km (93 mi) northwest of Bologna.

GETTING HERE

Regional trains run often from Milan to Piacenza and take a little over an hour; Eurostar service cuts the travel time in half. The Intercity from Bologna to Piacenza takes about 1½ hours and closer to two hours on regional trains. Both have frequent service. Piacenza is easily accessible by car via the A1, either from Milan or from Bologna. If you're coming from Milan, take the Piacenza Nord exit; from Bologna, the Piacenza Est exit.

VISITOR INFORMATION

PIACENZA TOURISM OFFICE (✉ *Piazza* Cavalli 7, 29100 ☎*0523/329324* ⊕*www.provincia.piacenza.it/turismo*).

EXPLORING

The city of Piacenza has always been associated with industry and commerce. Its position on the Po River has made it an important inland port since the earliest times; the Etruscans, and then the Romans, had thriving settlements here. As you approach the city today you could be forgiven for thinking that it holds little of interest. Piacenza is surrounded by ugly industrial suburbs (with particularly unlovely concrete factories and a power station), but forge ahead to discover a delightfully preserved medieval downtown and an unusually clean city. The prosperity is evidenced by the great shopping along Corso Vittorio Emanuele II.

The heart of the city is the **Piazza dei Cavalli** *(Square of the Horses)*. The flamboyant equestrian statues from which the piazza takes its name are depictions of Ranuccio Farnese (1569–1622) and, on the left, his father, Alessandro (1545–92). Alessandro was a beloved ruler, enlightened and fair; Ranuccio, his successor, was less admired. Both statues are the work of Francesco Mochi, a master baroque sculptor. Dominating the square is the massive 13th-century **Palazzo Pubblico,** also known as Il Gotico. This two-tone, marble-and-brick, turreted and crenellated building was the seat of town government before Piacenza fell under the iron fists of the ruling Pallavicini and Farnese families.

Attached like a sinister balcony to the bell tower of Piacenza's 12th-century **Duomo** is a *gabbia* (iron cage), where miscreants were incarcerated naked and subjected to the scorn (and projectiles) of the crowd in the marketplace below. Inside the cathedral, less-evocative but equally impressive medieval stonework decorates the pillars and the crypt, and there are extravagant frescoes in the dome of the cupola begun by Morazzone (1573–1626); Guercino (1591–1666) completed them upon Morazzone's death. The Duomo can be reached by following Via XX Settembre from Piazza dei Cavalli. ✉*Piazza Duomo* ☎*0523/335154* ⊗*Daily 7:30–noon and 4–7.*

The **Musei di Palazzo Farnese,** the city-owned museum of Piacenzan art and antiquities, is housed in the vast **Palazzo Farnese.** The ruling family had commissioned a monumental palace, but construction, begun in 1558, was never completed as planned. The highlight of the museum's rather eclectic collection is the second-century BC Etruscan *Fegato di Piacenza,* a bronze tablet in the shape of a *fegato* (liver), with the symbols of the gods of good and ill fortune marked on it. By comparing this master "liver" with one taken from the body of a freshly slaughtered sacrifice, priests could predict the future. The collection also contains Botticelli's *Madonna and Child with St. John the Baptist.* Reserve ahead for free 1½-hour guided tours. ✉*Piazza Cittadella 29* ☎*0523/492661* ⊕*www.musei.piacenza.it* ☑*€6* ⊗*Museum: Tues.–*

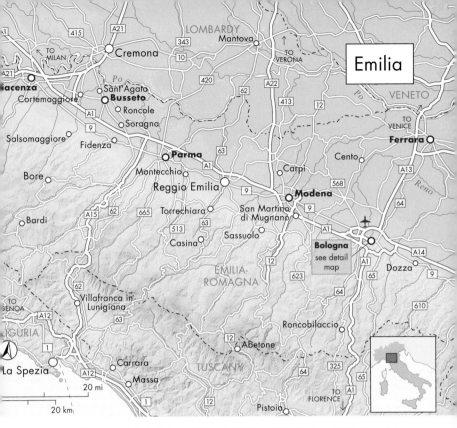

Thurs. 8:45–1, Fri. and Sat. 8:45–1 and 3–6, Sun. 9:30–1 and 3–6. Free tours: Tues.–Thurs. at 10, Fri. at 10 and 3:30, weekends at 9:30, 11, 3, and 4:30.

WHERE TO EAT

★ $$$$ ✕ **Antica Osteria del Teatro.** On a lovely little square in the center of town, this restaurant is one of the best in all Emilia-Romagna. The 15th-century palazzo, with coffered ceilings and sober furniture, effuses elegance. The pricey, French-influenced menu might be best described as haute Italian; some of the more nouveau flights of fancy might include, for example, a "panna cotta"of asparagus and black truffle served in a miniature jar. Service is excellent and the wine list impeccable. ✉ *Via Verdi 16* ☎ *0523/323777* ⊕ *www.anticaosteriadel-teatro.it* ✍ *Reservations essential* ▭ *MC, V* ✆ *Closed Sun. and Mon., Jan. 1–10, and Aug. 1–25.*

BUSSETO

30 km (19 mi) southeast of Piacenza, 25 km (16 mi) southeast of Cremona in Lombardy.

GETTING HERE

If you're coming by car from Parma, take the A1/E35, and follow signs for the A15 in the direction of Milan/La Spezia. Take the exit in the direction of Fidenza/Salsomaggiore Terme, following signs to the SP12, which connects to the SS9W. At Fidenza, take the SS588 heading north, which will take you in to Bussetto. If you are without a car, you'll have to take a bus, as there is no train service. Bus service runs from Parma to Bussetto.

VISITOR INFORMATION

Busseto tourism office (⊠*Comune, Piazza G. Verdi 10, 43011* ☎*0524/92487* ⊕*www.bussetolive.com*).

EXPLORING

Busseto's main claim to fame is its native son, master composer Giuseppe Verdi (1813–1901). The 15th-century **Villa Pallavicino** is where Verdi worked and lived with his mistress (and later wife) Giuseppina Strepponi. On display are the maestro's piano, scores, composition books, and walking sticks. However, the villa has been closed for renovations for seven years and, at this writing, the reopening date is not known. Call the local tourist information office for an update. ⊠*Via Provesi 36* ☎*0524/92487* ⊕*www.bussetolive.com*.

In the center of Busseto is the lovely **Teatro Verdi,** dedicated, as one might expect, to the works of the hamlet's famous son. Guided tours of the well-preserved, ornate 19th-century-style theater are offered every half hour. Check with the Busseto tourist office for the performance schedule. ⊠*Piazza G. Verdi 10* ☎*0524/92487* ⌨*Tours* €*4* ☉*Tours: by appointment Tues.–Sun. 9:30–12:30 and 3–6.*

For Verdi lovers, **Villa Sant'Agata** (also known as Villa Verdi) is a veritable shrine. It's the grand country home Verdi built for himself in 1849, the place where some of his greatest works were composed. Visits are by tour only, and you have to reserve a few days in advance by phone or on the Web. ⊠*Via Verdi 22, Sant'Agata Villanova sull'Arda* ⊹*4 km (2½ mi) north of Busseto on SS588, toward Cremona* ☎*0523/830000* ⊕*www.villaverdi.org* ⌨ *Tours* €*6* ☉*Tours: Tues.–Sun., by appointment only*

PARMA

40 km (25 mi) southeast of Busseto, 97 km (60 mi) northwest of Bologna.

GETTING HERE

Train service, via Eurostar, Intercity, and Regionale trains, runs frequently from Milan and Bologna. It takes a little over an hour from Milan, and just under an hour from Bologna. By car, Parma is just off the A1 autostrada, halfway between Bologna and Piacenza.

VISITOR INFORMATION

Parma tourism office (⊠*Via Melloni 1/a, 43100* ☎*0521/218889* ⊕*http://turismo.comune.parma.it*).

EXPLORING

Parma stands on the banks of a tributary of the Po River. Despite damage during World War II, much of the stately historic center seems untouched by modern times. Parma is a prosperous town, and it shows in its well-dressed residents, its clean streets, and immaculate piazzas.

Bursting with gustatory delights, Parma draws crowds for its sublime cured ham, prosciutto *crudo di Parma* (known locally simply as prosciutto *crudo*). The pale yellow Parmigiano-Reggiano cheese produced here and in nearby Reggio Emilia is the original—and best—of a class known around the world as Parmesan. Stuffed pastas such as spinach-and-cheese *tortelli* are another specialty here, perhaps the world's best.

Almost every major European power has had a hand in ruling Parma at one time or another. The Romans founded the city—then little more than a garrison on the Via Emilia—after which a succession of feudal lords held sway. In the 16th century came the ever-conniving Farnese family, which died out in 1731 upon the death of Antonio Farnese. It then went to the Spanish, and fell into French hands in 1796. In 1805, Marie-Louise (better known to the *parmigiani* as Maria Luigia), the wife of Napoléon, took command of the city. She was a much-beloved figure in her adopted town until her death in 1847.

★ **Piazza Garibaldi** is the heart of Parma. Here's where people gather to pass the time of day, start their *passeggiata* (evening stroll), or simply hang out. Strada Cavour, leading off the piazza, is Parma's prime shopping street. This square and nearby Piazza del Duomo make up one of the loveliest historic centers in Italy.

The delightful, 16th-century church of **Santa Maria della Steccata** has one of Parma's most recognizable domes, as well as a wonderful fresco cycle by Francesco Mazzola, better known as Parmigianino (1503–40). He took so long to complete it that his patrons briefly imprisoned him for breach of contract. ⊠ *Piazza Steccata 9, off Via Dante near Piazza Garibaldi* ☎ *0521/234937* ⊕ *www.santuari.it/steccata* ☒ *Free* ⊗ *Daily 9–noon and 3–6.*

The spacious **Piazza del Duomo** contains the cathedral and the Battistero, as well as the Palazzo del Vescovado (Bishop's Palace). Behind the Duomo is the baroque church of San Giovanni. The magnificent 12th-century **Duomo** has two vigilant stone lions standing guard beside the main door. The arch of the entrance is decorated with a delicate frieze of figures representing the months of the year, a motif repeated inside the baptistery. Some of the church's original artwork still survives, notably the simple yet evocative *Descent from the Cross,* a carving in the right transept by Benedetto Antelami (active from 1178–1230), a sculptor and architect whose masterwork is this cathedral's baptistery.

It's an odd juxtaposition to turn from this austere work to the exuberant fresco in the dome, the *Assumption of the Virgin* by Antonio Allegri, better known to us as Correggio (1494–1534). The fresco was not well received when it was unveiled in 1530. "A mess of frogs' legs," the bishop of Parma is said to have called it. Today Correggio is

9

acclaimed as one of the leading masters of mannerist painting. ⊠*Piazza del Duomo* ☎*0521/235886* ⊙*Daily 9–12:30 and 3–7.*

The impressive **Battistero** *(Baptistry)* has a simple pink-stone Romanesque exterior and an uplifting Gothic interior. The doors are richly decorated with figures, animals, and flowers, and the interior is adorned with figures carved by Antelami showing the months and seasons. ⊠*Piazza del Duomo* ☎*0521/235886* 💶*€4* ⊙*Daily 9–12:30 and 3–6:30.*

Once beyond the elaborate baroque facade of **San Giovanni Evangelista,** the Renaissance interior reveals several works by Correggio; his *St. John the Evangelist* (left transept) is considered the finest. Also in this church (in the second and fourth chapels on the left) are works by Parmigianino, a contemporary of Correggio's. Once seen, Parmigianino's long-necked Madonnas are never forgotten. ⊠*Piazzale San Giovanni 1, Piazza del Duomo* ☎*0521/235311* ⊙*Daily 8–noon and 3–7:45.*

Three museums outside of Parma showcase the city's and the region's most famous foods. The **Musei del Cibo** (Food Museums), as they are collectively known, offer tastings, a bit of history, and a tour through the process of making these specialties. None is more than a 20-minute drive or taxi ride from the city. The **Museo del Prosciutto di Parma,** the **Museo del Parmigiano Reggiano,** and the **Museo del Salame** honor world-famous prosciutto di Parma, Parmesan cheese, and cured meats, respectively. It's a good idea to call before making the trek, as opening hours are limited. ⊠*Museo del Prosciutto di Parma: Via Bocchialini, Langhirano; Museo del Parmigiano Reggiano: Soragna; Museo del Salame: Castello di Felino* ☎*0521/858347 Museo del Prosciutto di Parma, 0521/228152 Museo del Parmigiano Reggiano, 333/2362839 Museo del Salame* 💶*Museo del Prosciutto di Parma €3, plus €3 for tasting; Museo del Parmigiano Reggiano and Museo del Salame €5* ⊙*Museo del Prosciutto di Parma: weekends 10–6 by reservation only; Museo del Parmigiano Reggiano: Mar.–Oct., Fri.–Sun. 9–12:30 and 3–6, Tues.–Thurs. by reservation only; Museo del Salame: weekends 10–12:30 and 3–6, Wed.–Fri. by reservation only*

WHERE TO STAY & EAT

$$$$ ✗ **La Greppia.** The most elegant, most talked-about restaurant in the city is also one of the best. Taste well-known chef Paola Cavazzini's innovative treats like the *anelli con cavolo nero e mostarda della Paola* (small ring-shaped pasta with Tuscan kale and caramelized fruits) and the *faraona al tartufo nero di Fragno* (guinea hen with black truffle–and-chestnut puree). Service is personal and friendly, thanks to the place's tiny size, and the unpretentious surroundings keep the focus on the food. There's often a bargain set-price lunch for less than €30. ⊠*Via Garibaldi 39/a* ☎*0521/233686* ⊘*Reservations essential* 🚫*AE, DC, MC, V* ⊙*Closed Mon. and Tues., July, and Dec. 23–Jan. 5.*

$$$$ ✗ **Parizzi.** Named for its exciting young chef, Marco Parizzi, this restaurant rivals La Greppia for the title of Parma's finest. A stylish art-nouveau interior with Persian rugs complements traditional Parma classics like stuffed *tortelli* (large tortellini) and sublime risotto with

Parmigiano-Reggiano and shaved white truffles (in season). Try anti-pasti such as *culatello di Zibello* (the most highly touted of Parma prosciuttos, aged more than 11 months). The wine list is top-notch. ⊠*Strada Repubblica 71* ☎*0521/285952* ⌖*Reservations essential* ⊟*AE, DC, MC, V* ⊘*Closed Mon., Aug., and Jan. 8–15.*

$$ ⨯ **Parma Rotta.** In an old inn 2 km (1 mi) south of the center is an infor-
Fodor'sChoice mal neighborhood trattoria with a deep commitment to sourcing the
★ best local ingredients and to executing traditional recipes with nothing less than perfection. Parma Rotta serves absolutely spectacular grilled steaks, spit-roasted lamb, and other meats cooked on a wood-fire grill. The homemade pastas are quite simply among the best in Italy: among them, try *malfatti magri* (sheets of egg pasta) with artichoke in a *fonduta* (melted cheese sauce), or the classic tortelli stuffed with spinach and cheese. Dine outdoors under a pleasant trellis in warm weather. ⊠*Via Langhirano 158* ☎*0521/966738* ⊕*www.parmarotta. com* ⊟*AE, DC, MC, V* ⊘*Closed Sun. and Mon., Dec. 23–Jan. 10, and July 16–Aug. 7.*

¢ ⨯ **Enoteca Antica Osteria Fontana.** Gregarious locals flock to the bright
★ yellow, old-school *enoteca* (wine bar) that has a star-studded selection of wines at shockingly good prices. You have to queue up in anarchic fashion for a table—or eat at the bar—and service is sometimes brusque. The grilled *panini* (sandwiches), filled with Emilia's best *salumi* (cured meats), are delicious. Try the *coppa* (a full-flavor cured pork product) with artichokes, for example. The panini come quartered, so you can share. The place is also the best take-out wine store in town. ⊠*Strada Farini 24/a, near Piazza Garibaldi* ☎*0521/286037* ⌖*Reservations not accepted* ⊟*V* ⊘*Closed Sun. and Mon.*

$$$$ 🏨 **Hotel Palace Maria Luigia.** Top quality and convenient to the historic center of Parma and to the train station, this SINA hotel is popular with business travelers. Some of the traditional rooms, with heavy draper-ies and wood furniture, have lovely views; some suites have marble and ivory bathtubs. The bar is a perfect place to have an aperitif. **Pro:** High-quality business hotel. **Con:** Short on intimacy. ⊠*Viale Mentana 140, 43100* ☎*0521/281032* 🖷*0521/231126* ⊕*www.palacemarialu-igia.com* ⤳*90 rooms, 11 suites* ⚷ *In-room: safe, refrigerator, Wi-Fi. In-hotel: restaurant, bar, concierge, laundry service, public Wi-Fi, some pets allowed* ⊟*AE, DC, MC, V* ⊺◯⫠*EP*

$$$–$$$$ 🏨 **Palazzo dalla Rosa Prati.** The dalla Rosa Prati family has converted
★ seven rooms of their centuries-old palace into luxurious, self-catering accommodation just off Piazza del Duomo. This means that you can sleep like a king (or queen) and eat in, as each room comes fully fur-nished with small kitchenette and stove. Each room is different, but all have pastel-sponged walls, hardwood floors, large beds, and roomy bathrooms. You have an amazing view of the Baptistery just next door, and a few rooms connect, making it a good choice for families. **Pro:** Unbeatable location. **Con:** Staff leaves early in the evening. ⊠*Strada al Duomo 7, 43100* ☎*0521/386429* ⊕*www.palazzodallarosaprati.it* ⤳*7 rooms* ⚷*In-room: safe, kitchen, refrigerator, ethernet. In-hotel: some pets allowed* ⊟*AE, MC, V* ⊺◯⫠ *EP.*

9

MODENA

56 km (35 mi) southeast of Parma, 38 km (24 mi) northwest of Bologna.

GETTING HERE

Modena is easily accessible by train, as it's on the Bologna–Milan line. Trains run frequently, and it's an easy walk from the train station to the centro storico. There's an Intercity connection from Florence that takes about an hour and a half. By car, Modena is just off the A1 autostrada, between Bologna and Parma.

VISITOR INFORMATION

Modena tourism office (⊠ *Piazza Grande 14, 41100* ☎ *059/2032660* ⊕ *http://turismo.comune.modena.it*).

EXPLORING

Modena is famous for three local products: Maserati, Ferrari, and opera star Luciano Pavarotti, who was born near here and was buried in his family plot in Montale Rangone in September 2007. However, it's Modena's heavenly scented balsamic vinegar, aged up to 40 years, that is probably its greatest achievement. The town has become another Emilian food mecca, with terrific restaurants and *salumerie* (delicatessens) at every turn. Though extensive modern industrial sprawl surrounds the center, the small historic center is filled with narrow medieval streets, pleasant piazzas, and typical Emilian architecture.

The 11th-century **Duomo** is a fine example of Romanesque architecture. The exterior is decorated with medieval sculptures depicting scenes from Genesis, as well as a scene of the sacking of a city by barbarian hordes—a reminder to the faithful to be ever vigilant in defense of the church. The white-marble bell tower is known as **La Torre Ghirlandina** (the Little Garland Tower) because of its distinctive weather vane. The somber church interior is divided by an elaborate gallery carved with scenes of the Passion of Christ. The carvings were executed by Anselmo da Campione and his assistants circa 1160–80. The tomb of San Geminiano is in the crypt. At this writing, both the Duomo facade and the tower are undergoing a restoration. ⊠ *Piazza Grande* ☎ *059/216078* ⊕ *www.duomodimodena.it* ⊙ *Daily 7–12:30 and 3:30–7.*

Modena's principal museum is housed in the **Palazzo dei Musei,** a short walk from the Duomo. The collection was assembled in the mid-17th century by Francesco d'Este (1610–58), Duke of Modena, and the **Galleria Estense** is named in his honor. The gallery also houses the **Biblioteca Estense,** a huge collection of illuminated books, of which the best known is the beautifully illustrated *Bible of Borso d'Este (1455–61).* A map dated 1501 was one of the first in the world to show Columbus's discovery of America. To get here, follow Via Emilia, the old Roman road that runs through the heart of the town, to Via di Sant'Agostino. ⊠ *Piazza Sant'Agostino 337* ☎ *059/4395711* ☎ *€4* ⊙ *Museum: Mon.–Thurs. 8:30–7:15, Fri. 8:30–3:45, Sat. 8:30–1:45. Gallery: Tues.–Sun. 8:30–7:30, last entry at 7.*

Continued on page 508

EMILIA
ONE TASTE AT A TIME

4 towns, dozens of foods, and a mouthful of flavors you'll never forget

Imagine biting into the silkiest prosciutto in the world or the most delectable homemade tortellini you've ever tasted. In Emilia, Italy's most acclaimed food region, you'll discover simple tastes that exceed all expectations. Beginning in Parma and moving eastward to Bologna, you'll find the epicenters of such world-renowned culinary treats as *prosciutto crudo*, Parmigiano-Reggiano, *aceto balsamico*, and tortellini. The secret to this region is not the discovery of new and exotic delicacies, but rather the rediscovery of foods you thought you already knew—in much better versions than you've ever tasted before.

TASTE 1 | PROSCIUTTO CRUDO

From Piacenza to the Adriatic, ham is the king of meats in Emilia-Romagna, but nowhere is this truer than in **Parma**.

Parma is the world's capital of *prosciutto crudo*, raw cured ham (*crudo* for short). Ask for *crudo di Parma* to signal its local provenance; many other regions also make their own crudo.

CRUDO LANGUAGE

It's easy to get confused with the terminology. Crudo is the product that Americans simply call "prosciutto" or the Brits might call "Parma ham." *Prosciutto* in Italian, however, is a more general term that means any kind of ham, including *prosciutto cotto*, or simply *cotto*, which means "cooked ham." Cotto is an excellent product and frequent pizza topping that's closer to (but much better than) what Americans would put in a deli sandwich.

Crudo is traditionally eaten in one of three ways: in a dry sandwich (*panino*); by itself as an appetizer, often with shaved butter on top; or as part of an appetizer or snack platter of assorted *salumi* (cured meats).

WHAT TO LOOK FOR

For the best crudo di Parma, look for slices, always cut to order, that are razor thin and have a light, rosy red color (not dark red). Don't be shy about going into a simple *salumeria* (a purveyor of cured meats) and ordering crudo by the pound. You can enjoy it straight out of the package on a park bench—and why not?

BEST SPOT FOR A SAMPLE

You can't go wrong with any of Parma's famed salumerie, but **Salumeria Garibaldi** (Via Farini 9) is one of the town's oldest and most reliable. You'll find not only spectacular prosciutto crudo, but also delectable cheeses, wines, porcini mushrooms, and more.

LEARN MORE

For more information on crudo di Parma, contact the **Consorzio del Prosciutto di Parma** (Via Marco dell'Arpa 8/b, 0521/243987, www.prosciuttodiparma.com/eng).

Quality testing

Greasing the ham

Fire branding

Quality trademark

Prosciutto di Parma

TASTE 2 | PARMIGIANO-REGGIANO

From Parma, it's only a half-hour trip east to **Reggio Emilia**, the birthplace of the crumbly and renowned Parmigiano-Reggiano cheese. Reggio (not to be confused with Reggio di Calabria in the south) is a cute and characteristic little Emilian town that has been the center of production for this legendary cheese for more than 70 years.

Warming milk in copper cauldrons

SAY CHEESE
Grana is the generic Italian term for hard, aged, full-flavored cheese that can be grated. Certain varieties of Pecorino Romano, for example, or Grana Padano, also fall under this term, but Parmigiano-Reggiano, aged for as long as four years, is the foremost example.

Breaking up the curds

NOT JUST FOR GRATING
In Italy, Parmigiano-Reggiano is not only grated onto pasta, but also often served by itself in chunks, either as an appetizer—perhaps accompanied by local salumi (cured meats)—or even for dessert, when it might be drizzled with honey or Modena's balsamic vinegar.

MEET THE MAKERS
If you're a cheese enthusiast, you shouldn't miss the chance to take a free two-hour guided tour of a Parmigiano-Reggiano–producing farm. You'll witness the entire process and get to meet the cheesemakers. Tours can be arranged by contacting the **Consorzio del Formaggio Parmigiano-Reggiano** in Reggio Emilia (0522/506160, sezionere@parmigiano-reggiano.it, www.parmigiano-reggiano.it) at least 20 days in advance. (Ask specifically for an English-language tour if that's what you want.)

Placing cheese in molds

BEST SPOT FOR A SAMPLE
The production of Parmigiano-Reggiano is heavily controlled by the Consorzio del Formaggio, so you can buy the cheese at any store or supermarket in the region and be virtually guaranteed equal quality and price. For a more distinctive shopping experience, however, try buying Parmigiano-Reggiano at the street market on Reggio's central square. The market takes place on Tuesday and Friday from 8 AM to 1 PM year-round.

Aging cheese wheels

Parmigiano-Reggiano

IN FOCUS EMILIA: ONE TASTE AT A TIME

9

TASTE 3 | ACETO BALSAMICO DI MODENA

Tasting tradizionale vinegar

Modena is home to *Aceto Balsamico Tradizionale di Modena*, a species of balsamic vinegar unparalleled anywhere else on Earth. The balsamic vinegar you've probably tried—even the pricier versions sold at specialty stores—may be good on salads, but it bears only a fleeting resemblance to the real thing.

HOW IS IT MADE?

The *tradizionale* vinegar that passes strict government standards is made with Trebbiano grape must, which is cooked over an open fire, reduced, and fermented from 12 to 25 or more years in a series of specially made wooden casks. As the vinegar becomes more concentrated, so much liquid evaporates that it takes more than 6 gallons of must to produce one quart of vinegar 12 years later. The result is an intense and syrupy concoction best enjoyed sparingly on grilled meats, strawberries, or Parmigiano-Reggiano cheese. The vinegar has such a complexity of flavor that some even drink it as an after-dinner liqueur.

Wooden casks for fermenting

BEST SPOT FOR A SAMPLE

The **Consorzio Produttori Aceto Balsamico Tradizionale di Modena** (Corso Cavour 60, 059/236981, www. balsamico.it) offers tours and tastings by reservation only. The main objective of the consortium is to monitor the quality of the authentic balsamic vinegar, made by only a few licensed restaurants and small producers.

The consortium also limits production, keeping prices sky high. Expect to pay €60 for a 100-ml (3.4 oz) bottle of tradizionale, which is generally aged 12 to 15 years, or €90 and up for the older tradizionale extra vecchio variety, which is aged 25 years.

WHERE TO EAT

In Modena, it's hard to find a bad meal. Local trattorie do great versions of tortellini and other stuffed pasta. If you can find *zampone* (a sausage made from stuffed pig's trotter), don't miss it—it's an adventurous Modena specialty. **Hosteria Giusti** (Vicolo Squallore 46, 059/222533, www.giusti1605.com) is a particularly good place to try local specialties; the adjacent **Salumeria Giusti** is reputedly the world's oldest deli, founded in 1605.

OTHER TASTES OF EMILIA

❏ **Cotechino**: a sausage made from pork and lard, a specialty of Modena

❏ **Culatello de Zibello**: raw cured ham produced along the banks of the Po River, and cured and aged for more than 11 months

❏ **Mortadella**: soft, smoked sausage made with beef, pork, cubes of pork fat, and seasonings, a specialty of Bologna

❏ **Ragù**: a sauce made from minced pork and beef, simmered in milk, onions, carrots, and tomatoes

❏ **Salama da sugo**: salty, oily sausage aged and then cooked, a specialty of Ferrara

❏ **Tortelli and cappellacci**: pasta pillows with the same basic form as tortellini, but stuffed with cheese and vegetables

TASTE 4 | TORTELLINI

The venerable city of **Bologna** is called "the Fat" for a reason: this is the birthplace of tortellini, not to mention other specialties such as mortadella and ragù. Despite the city's new reputation for chic nightclubs and flashy boutiques, much of the food remains as it ever was.

Making the dough

You'll find the many Emilian variations on stuffed pasta all over the region, but they're perhaps at their best in Bologna, especially the native tortellini.

INSPIRED BY THE GODS

According to one legend, tortellini was inspired by the bellybutton of Venus, goddess of love. As the story goes, Venus and some other gods stopped at a local inn for the night. A nosy chef went to their room to catch a glimpse of Venus. Peering through the keyhole, he saw her lying only partially covered on the bed. He was so inspired after seeing her perfect navel that he created a stuffed pasta, tortellini, in its image.

Stretching the dough

ON THE MENU

Tortellini is usually filled with beef (sometimes cheese), and is served two ways: *asciutta* is "dry," meaning it is served with a sauce such as ragù, or perhaps just with butter and Parmigiano. *Tortellini in brodo* is immersed in a lovely, savory beef broth.

Adding the filling

BEST SPOT TO BUY

Don't miss **Tamburini** (Via Drapperie 1, 051/234726), Bologna's best specialty food shop, where smells of Emilia-Romagna's famous spoils waft out through the room and into the streets.

Shaping each piece

WHERE TO EAT

The classic art deco restaurant **Rosteria Luciano** (Via Nazario Sauro 19, 051/231249, www.rosterialuciano.it) is a great place to try tortellini in brodo, one of the best choices on their fixed menu. A changing list of daily specials augments the menu. For a meat course it's usually best to order whatever special the kitchen has that day. The selection of local cheeses is also good. Please note that the restaurant is closed on Wednesday, the whole month of August, and Sunday from June through September.

Tortellini di Bologna

★ The **Galleria Ferrari,** in the suburb of Maranello 17 km (11 mi) south of Modena, has become a pilgrimage site for auto enthusiasts. The museum takes you through the illustrious history of Ferrari, from the early 1951 models to the present, such as the legendary F50, to the cars driven by Michael Schumacher in Formula One victories. You can also take a look at the glamorous life of Enzo Ferrari, including a re-creation of his office and a glance into the production process. ⊠ *Via Dino Ferrari, Maranello* ☎ *0536/943204* ⊕ *www.galleria.ferrari.com* ⊡ *€12* ⊙ *Oct.–Apr., daily 9:30–6; May–Nov., daily 9:30–7.*

You can do a tasting at the **Consorzio Produttori Aceto Balsamico Tradizionale di Modena,** have a tour of the small facility with its friendly staff, and, of course, buy their famous balsamic vinegar. ⊠ *Strada Vaciglio Sud 1085/1* ☎ *059/395633* ⊕ *www.balsamico.it* ⊡ *Free* ⊙ *By appointment.*

WHERE TO STAY & EAT

$$$$ ✕ **Hosteria Giusti.** The ancient stone walls here are shared with what is reputedly the world's oldest deli, the Salumeria Giusti, founded in 1605. There are only four tables and a host of antique furnishings in the tiny room, where the kitchen turns out dishes like your Italian grandmother might have cooked—handmade tagliolini, *gnocco fritto* (fried dough) with salumi from next door, and items using Modena's famous balsamic vinegar. Reserve well ahead; prices are high, but it's an unforgettable Modena experience. ⊠ *Vicolo Squallore 46* ☎ *059/222533* ⊕ *www.giusti1605.com* ⚭ *Reservations essential* ⊟ *AE, DC, MC, V* ⊙ *Closed Sun. and Mon. and Dec.–Jan. 10. No dinner.*

$ ✕ **Aldina.** On the second floor of a building across from the covered
★ market, steps from the Piazza Grande, this simple, typical trattoria is in the very nerve center of the city. Here you'll find exemplary preparations of the region's crown jewels: tortellini *in brodo* (in broth), *tagliatelle al ragù,* and roast meats. Wash it down with a local Lambrusco, as locals have for ages, and save room for the *zuppa inglese* (layered sponge cake with custard), which is terrific here. ⊠ *Via Albinelli 40* ☎ *059/236106* ⊟ *No credit cards* ⊙ *Closed Sun., and July and Aug. No dinner.*

$ ✕ **Da Enzo.** This big, cheerful, crowded trattoria is in the old town's pedestrian zone a few steps from Piazza Mazzini. All the classic Modenese specialties are represented, including *zampone* (stuffed pig's foot) and *cotechino* (a rich, deliciously fatty pork sausage). For your *primo piatto (first course),* try the *tortelloni* stuffed with ricotta and spinach. Reserve ahead for Friday- and Saturday-night dining. ⊠ *Via Coltellini 17* ☎ *059/225177* ⊟ *AE, DC, MC, V* ⊙ *Closed Mon. and Aug. No dinner Sun.*

$ ✕ **Ermes.** Ebullient host Ermes greets you as you walk in, and seats you wherever he happens to have room—no matter that you might be seated with people you don't know. It's part of the fun, as this quasi-communal style of lunching encourages conviviality. The wine is local, simple, and cheap; in the kitchen, Bruna, Ermes's wife, turns out splendid versions of *cucina casalinga modenesi* (home cooking, Modena style). Ermes recites the short list of *primi* and *secondi,* which change daily, and they arrive promptly at the table. It's no wonder this place is favored by everyone from suits to construction workers to students. ⊠ *Via Ganaceto 89–91* ☏ *No phone* ▭ *No credit cards* ⊘ *Closed Sun. No dinner.*

$$$ ▥ **Canalgrande.** Once a ducal palace, the Canalgrande today has a lobby so gilded as to be over-the-top, as well as large, airy rooms appointed with ornate dark-wood and upholstered pieces. The garden has a fountain and a pretty terrace where breakfast is served in summer. **Pro:** Significant discounts for lone travelers. **Cons:** Caters to business travelers, feels somewhat impersonal. ⊠ *Corso Canalgrande 6, 41100* ☏ *059/217160* ⊟ *059/221674* ⊕ *www.canalgrandehotel.it* ⟿ *75 rooms, 3 suites* ⚙ *In-room: safe. In-hotel: restaurant, bar, parking (fee), some pets allowed* ▭ *AE, DC, MC, V* ⍾ *BP.*</SI>

BOLOGNA

Bologna, a city rich with cultural jewels, has long been one of the best-kept secrets in northern Italy. Tourists in the know can bask in the shadow of its leaning medieval towers, devour the city's wonderful food, and spend a little less than elsewhere.

The charm of the centro storico, with its red-arcaded sidewalks and passageways, can be attributed to wise city counselors who, at the beginning of the 13th century, decreed that roads could not be built without *portici* (porticoes). Were these counselors to return to town eight centuries later, they would marvel at how little has changed.

The feeling of a university town permeates the air in Bologna. Its population is about 373,000, and it feels young and lively in a way that many other Italian cities do not. It also feels full of Italians in a way that many other towns, thronged with tourists, do not. Known as "Bologna the Fat" from as early as the Middle Ages, the town's agricultural prosperity led to a well-fed population, one that survives into the 21st century. Bolognesi food is, arguably, the best in Italy. With its sublime food, lively spirit, and largely undiscovered art, Bologna is well worth a visit.

9

GETTING HERE

Frequent train service from Florence to Bologna makes getting here easy. Eurostar and Intercity trains run several times an hour, and take about an hour. Trains from Milan run as frequently, and take about an hour and 45 minutes on the Eurostar, two hours on the Intercity. The historic center is an easy and interesting walk from the station. If you're driving from Florence, take the A1, exiting onto the A14 and then catching the RA1 to Uscita 7–Bologna Centrale. The trip takes about an hour. From Milan, take the A1, exiting to the A14 as you near the city; from there, take the A13 and exit at Bologna, then follow the RA1 to Uscita 7–Bologna Centrale. The trip is just under three hours.

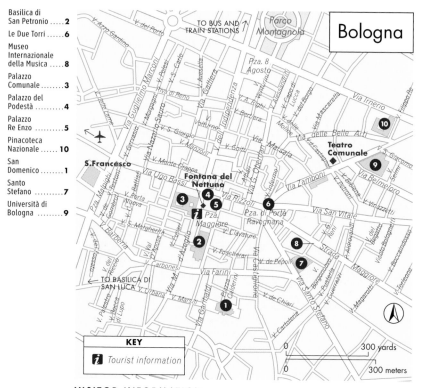

VISITOR INFORMATION

Bologna tourism offices (✉*Aeroporto Guglielmo Marconi, Via Tri-umvirato 84* ✚*10 km [6 mi] northwest of Bologna* ☎*051/239660* ✉*Stazione Centrale, 40121* ☎*051/239660* ✉*Piazza Maggiore 1, 40124* ☎*051/239660* ⊕*www.bolognaturismo.info*).

EXPLORING BOLOGNA

Piazza Maggiore and the adjacent Piazza del Nettuno are the historic centers of the city. Arranged around these two squares are the imposing Basilica di San Petronio, the massive Palazzo Comunale, the Palazzo del Podestà, the Palazzo di Re Enzo, and the Fontana del Nettuno—one of the most visually harmonious groupings of public buildings in the country. From here, sights that aren't one one of the piazzas are but a short walk away, along delightful narrow cobbled streets or under the ubiquitous arcades that double as municipal umbrellas. Take at least a full day to explore Bologna; it's compact and lends itself to easy exploration, but there is plenty to see.

THE MAIN ATTRACTIONS

 Basilica di San Petronio. Construction on this cathedral began in 1390, and work was still in progress on this vast building some 300 years later. It's not finished yet, as you can see: the wings of the transept are missing and the facade is only partially decorated, lacking most of the marble facade the architects had intended. The main doorway was carved in 1425 by the great Sienese master, Jacopo della Quercia. Above the center of the door is a Madonna and Child flanked by Saints Ambrose and Petronius, the city's patrons. Michelangelo, Giulio Romano, and Andrea Palladio (among others) submitted designs for the facade, which were all eventually rejected.

The interior of the basilica is huge: the Bolognesi had planned an even bigger church—you can still see the columns erected to support the larger church outside the east end—but had to tone down construction when the university seat was established next door in 1561. The **Museo di San Petronio** contains models showing how the church was originally intended to look. The most important art in the church is in the fourth chapel on the left; these frescoes by Giovanni di Modena date from 1410–15. ⊠ *Piazza Maggiore* ☎ *051/225442* ✉ *Free* ☉ *Church: Apr.–Sept., daily 7:45–12:30 and 3:30–6; Oct.– Mar., daily 7:30–1 and 2:30–6. Museum: Mon.–Sat. 9:30–12:30 and 2:30–5:30, Sun. 2:30–5:30.*

Fontana del Nettuno. Sculptor Giambologna's elaborate 1563–66 baroque fountain and monument to Neptune occupying Piazza Nettuno has been aptly nicknamed *Il Gigante* (The Giant). Its exuberantly sensual mermaids and undraped God of the sea drew fire when it was constructed, but not enough, apparently, to dissuade the populace from using the fountain as a public washing stall for centuries. ⊠ *Piazza Nettuno, next to Palazzo Re Enzo, Piazza Maggiore area.*

★ ❻ **Le Due Torri.** Two landmark towers, mentioned by Dante in *The Inferno*, stand side by side in the compact Piazza di Porta Ravegnana. Every family of importance had a tower as a symbol of prestige and power, and as a potential fortress; only 60 remain out of more than 200 that once presided over the city. **Torre Garisenda** (from the late 11th century), which tilts 10 feet off perpendicular, was shortened to 165 feet in the 1300s and is now closed to visitors. **Torre degli Asinelli** (circa 1109) is 320 feet tall and leans 7½ feet. If you're up to a serious physical challenge—and you're not claustrophobic—you may want to climb the 500 narrow, wooden steps to get to the view over Bologna. ⊠ *Piazza di Porta Ravegnana, east of Piazza Maggiore* ✉ *€3* ☉ *Torre degli Asinelli: daily 9–5.*

☺ ❼ **Santo Stefano.** This splendid and unusual basilica actually contains Fodor's Choice between four and seven connected churches (authorities differ). Origi- ★ nally on this site there was a 4th-century pagan temple to Isis, though much of what you see dates from the 10th through the 12th centuries. The oldest existing building is **Santi Vitale e Agricola,** parts of which date from the fifth century. It contains a 14th-century Nativity scene much loved by Bologna's children, who come at Christmastime to pay their respects to the Christ Child. Within the church of **San Sepolcro** (probably dating from the fifth century, but remodeled in the late 11th and early 12th centuries) is the **Cortile di Pilato** (Pilate's Courtyard), named for the basin in its center that's said to be where Pontius

Pilate washed his hands after condemning Christ—despite the fact that the basin was probably crafted around the eighth century. Also in the building is a **museum** displaying various medieval religious works and with a shop where you can buy honey, shampoos, and jams made by the monks. ⊠ *Via Santo Stefano 24, Piazza Santo Stefano, University area* ☎ *051/223256* 🎫 *Free* ⊗ *Daily 9–noon and 3:30–6.*

❾ Università di Bologna. Take a stroll through the streets of the university area, a jumble of buildings, some dating as far back as the 15th century and most to the 17th and 18th. The neighborhood, as befits a college town, is full of bookshops, coffee bars, and inexpensive restaurants. None of them are particularly distinguished, but they're all characteristic of student life in the city. Try eating at the *mensa universitaria* (cafeteria) if you want to strike up a conversation with local students (most speak English). Political slogans and sentiments are scrawled on walls all around the university and tend to be ferociously leftist, sometimes juvenile, often entertaining. Among the university museums, the most interesting are the **Musei di Palazzo Poggi,** which display scientific instruments and paleontological, botanical, and university-related artifacts. ⊠ *Via Zamboni 33, University area* ☎ *051/2099610* ⊕ *www. museopalazzopoggi.unibo.it* 🎫 *Free* ⊗ *Tues.–Fri. 10–1 and 2–4, weekends 10:30–1:30 and 2:30–5:30.*

ALSO WORTH SEEING

❽ Museo Internazionale della Musica. The music museum in the spectacular Palazzo Aldini Sanguinetti, with its 17th- and 18th-century frescoes, offers among its exhibits a 1606 harpsichord and a collection of beautiful musical manuscripts dating from the 1500s. ⊠ *Strada Maggiore 34, University area* ☎ *051/2757711* ⊕ *www.museomusicabologna.it* 🎫 *Free* ⊗ *Oct.–July, Tues.–Fri. 10–1, weekends 10–5.; closed Aug. and Sept.*

❸ Palazzo Comunale. A mélange of building styles and constant modifications characterize this huge palace dating from the 13th to 15th centuries. When Bologna was an independent city-state, this was the seat of government, a function it still serves today. Over the door is a statue of Bologna-born Pope Gregory XIII (reigned 1572–85), most famous for reorganizing the calendar. There are good views from the upper stories of the palace. The first-floor **Sala Rossa** (Red Room) is open on advance request and during some exhibitions, while the **Sala del Consiglio Comunale** (City Council Hall) is open to the public for a few hours in the late morning. The old stock exchange, part of the Palazzo Comunale which you enter from Piazza Nettuno, has been turned into a library, the **Sala Borsa** (⊕ *www.bibliotecasalaborsa.it*), which has an impressive interior courtyard. Within the palazzo there are also two museums. The **Collezioni Comunali d'Arte** exhibits paintings from the Middle Ages as well as some Renaissance works by Luca Signorelli (circa 1445–1523) and Tintoretto (1518–94). The **Museo Giorgio Morandi** (⊕ *www.museomorandi.it*) is dedicated to the 20th-century still-life artist Giorgio Morandi; in addition to his paintings, there's a re-creation of his studio and living space. Underground caves and the foundations of the old cathedral can be visited by appointment made through the tourist office. ⊠*Piazza Maggiore 6* ☎*051/203111 Palazzo, 051/203526 Collezioni, 051/203332Museo* ✆*Free, except during special art exhibitions* ⊙*Sala del Consiglio Comunale: Tues.–Sat. 10–1. Sala Borsa: Mon. 2:30–8, Tues.–Fri. 10–8, Sat. 10–7. Collezioni and Museo: Tues.–Fri. 9–3, weekends 10–6:30.*

4 Palazzo del Podestà. This classic Renaissance palace facing the Basilica di San Petronio was erected in 1484, and attached to it is the soaring **Torre dell'Arengo.** The bells in the tower have rung whenever the city has celebrated, mourned, or called its citizens to arms. ⊠*Piazza Nettuno, Piazza Maggiore area* ☎*051/224500* ⊙*During exhibitions only.*

5 Palazzo Re Enzo. Built in 1244, this palace became home to King Enzo of Sardinia, who was imprisoned here in 1249 after he was captured during the fierce battle of Fossalta. He died here 23 years later in 1272. The palace has other macabre associations: common criminals received last rites in the tiny courtyard chapel before being executed in Piazza Maggiore. The courtyard is worth peeking into, but the palace merely houses government offices. ⊠*Piazza Re Enzo, Piazza Maggiore area* ☎*051/224500* ⊙*During exhibitions only.*

10 Pinacoteca Nazionale. Bologna's principal art gallery contains many works by the immortals of Italian painting spanning the 13th to the 19th centuries. Its prize possession is the famous *Ecstasy of St. Cecilia* by Raphael (1483–1520). There's also a beautiful multipanel painting by Giotto (1267–1337), as well as *Madonna and Saints* by Parmigianino. ⊠*Via delle Belle Arti 56, University area* ☎*051/4209411* ⊕*www.pinacotecabologna.it* ✆*€4* ⊙*Tues.–Sun. 9–7.*

1 San Domenico. The tomb of St. Dominic, who died here in 1221, is called the **Arca di San Domenico** and is found in this church in the sixth chapel on the right. Many artists participated in its decoration, notably Niccolò di Bari, who was so proud of his contribution that he changed his name to Niccolò dell'Arca to recall this famous work. The young Michelangelo (1475–1564) carved the angel on the right. In the right transept of the church is a tablet marking the last resting place of the hapless King Enzo, the Sardinian ruler imprisoned in the Palazzo Re Enzo. The attached **museum** displays religious relics and art. ⊠*Piazza San Domenico 13, off Via Garibaldi, south of Piazza Maggiore* ☎*051/6400411* ⊙*Church: daily 8–12:30 and 3:30–6:30. Museum: weekdays 10–noon and 3:30–6, Sat. 9:30–noon and 3:30–5:30, Sun. 3:30–5:30.*

OFF THE BEATEN PATH

Museo del Patrimonio Industriale. Offering a refreshing change from all the art museums, this museum's displays document the development of Bologna's industries and industrial technologies from the 16th to 21st centuries, including fascinating examples of antique machinery, scientific devices, and cars. ⊠*Via della Beverara 123, northwest of city center* ☎*051/6356611* ⊕*www.comune.bologna.it/patrimonioindustriale* ✆*Free* ⊙*Oct.–May, Tues.–Fri. 9–1, Sat. 9–1 and 3–6, Sun. 3–6; Jun.–Sept. weekdays 9–1.*

9

WHERE TO EAT

$$$$ ✕ **Bitone.** It's hard to get good value for your money on the top end in Bologna, but if you are committed to the idea of sitting down at one of the city's most prestigious tables, this restaurant, which dates to 1834, is a good way to go. An airy atrium, ringed by greenery, provides a good foil for the white-tablecloth setting. You might try the *fagottino croccante di formaggio caprino con fonduta di formaggi ed erba cipollina* (a crunchy pasta stuffed with goat cheese, topped with melted cheese and chives) or the legendary tortelli *all'erbette* (with ricotta, herbs, and hazelnut butter). If you're undecided, the eight-course tasting menu (€70) provides a taste of just about everything. ⊠ *Via Emilia Levante 111, San Lazzaro* ☎ *051/546110* ⊕ *www.ristorantebitone.it* ⊟ *AE, MC, V* ⊗ *Closed Mon. and Tues., and Aug.*

$$$
Fodor's Choice
★
✕ **Drogheria della Rosa.** Chef Emanuele Addone, who presides over his intimate little restaurant, hits the food markets every day and buys what looks good. This brings a seasonality to his exceptional menu; he sauces his tortelli stuffed with squacquerone and stracchino (two creamy, fresh cow's-milk cheeses) with artichokes, zucchini flowers, or mushrooms depending on the time of year. In order to do this place justice, you need to come with an appetite—you won't want to skip a course. Kick off the proceedings with a glass of prosecco and a plate of affettati misti (mixed cured meats, a local specialty). Among the secondi, the tender filetto al balsamico (filet mignon with marvelous balsamic vinegar sauce on top) is exquisite. So is the wine list. ⊠ *Via Cartoleria 10, University area* ☎ *051/222529* ⊕ *www.drogheriadellarosa.it* ⊟ *AE, DC, MC, V* ⊗ *Closed Sun.*

$$$ ✕ **Godot Wine Bar.** It's beloved by locals and visitors alike, perhaps because the kitchen stays open until 2 am. The wine list is long and full of temptations, as is the menu. The chef offers four menus—meat, fish, vegetarian, and the intriguing *tradizione un po' rivisitata* (loosely, "slightly updated tradition"). They're also masters of Bolognese classics, including a mean tagliatelle *al ragù.* ⊠ *Via Cartoleria 12, University area* ☎ *051/226315* ⊟ *AE, MC, V* ⊗ *Closed Sun. and 3 wks in Aug.*

★ **$$–$$$** ✕ **Da Cesari.** It's the creative menu options—delicate squash gnocchi, a slowly braised veal cheek—that make Da Cesari truly memorable. Local standards such as veal cutlet Bolognese (with ham and melted cheese) are also reasonably priced and well executed. Accompany your meal with wine made by the owner's brother: the Liano is excellent. The gentle romantic buzz in the dining room is warm and welcoming; the restaurant is in the very heart of the *centro storico.* ⊠ *Via de' Carbonesi 8, south of Piazza Maggiore* ☎ *051/237710* ⚏ *Reservations essential* ⊟ *AE, DC, MC, V* ⊗ *Closed Sun., Aug., and 1 wk in Jan.*

$$–$$$ ✕ **È Cucina.** Stark white walls, paintings with oversize sculpted spoons, and an (empty) clawfoot bathtub greet you as you enter this intimate restaurant. Such setting provides a dramatically simple and whimsical backdrop for chef Cesare Marretti's short menu of artfully presented dishes that changes daily; a typical offering might be the creative *insalatina di astice con radicchini di campo* (lobster-and–wild radicchio salad). A four-course tasting menu for a reasonable €40 (meat, fish, or

CLOSE UP

Cooking alla Bolognese

A hot travel trend in Italy is spending a day at a cooking school to learn local recipes and techniques—and where better to do it than in Bologna? Barbara Bertuzzi, the author of cookbook *Bolognese Cooking Heritage,* teaches classes at **La Vecchia Scuola Bolognese** *(the Old Bolognese Cooking School).* Her four-hour sessions focus on pasta making and are offered daily; they begin at 9:30 AM and continue to lunchtime, when you can eat the fruits of your labor. Evening courses are available, and Bertuzzi also offers lunches and dinners without the lessons. These tastings of traditional Bolognese recipes cost €30; Tuesday night is a traditional deep-fried meat, vegetable, and fruit dinner. The school is near the Ospedale Maggiore—take Bus 19 from Via Rizzoli near Piazza Maggiore, or a €15 taxi from the *centro storico.* If you're the only aspiring chef in your party, the rest can join after the lesson for dinner at €20 each. ⊠ *Via Malvasia 49* ☏ *051/6491576* ⊕ *www.lavecchi-ascuola.com* ✉ *€70 per person, €90 with meal.*

If you prefer your cooking classes in a truly regal setting, you might want to try **La Tavola della Signoria**, held in the spectacular 17th-century rooms of the **Palazzo Albergati** (⊕ *www. palazzoalbergati.it*). These classes are offered only four or five times per month and are more expensive than some others, but they're also longer and more serious. Class starts at 8:30 AM and runs until 5:30 PM; you can choose between different modules, such as bread making, pasta making, desserts, and so on. For the true aficionados, two- and three-day fruit-and-vegetable courses are offered periodically. It's 10 km (6 mi) west of the city center; to get here take SS569, get off at the last Zona Predosa exit, and follow signs for the Palazzo Albergati. You can sign up via the Web site. ⊠ *Via Masini 46* ☏ *051/750247* ⊕ *www.tavoladellasignoria.it* ✉ *€170–€200 per person for 1 day; up to €480 for 3 days.*

9

vegetarian) is a great gustatory and financial deal; prices are even better at lunch. ⊠*Piazza Aldrovandi, Via San Vitale 21/c, University area* ☏*051/2750069* ⊟*MC, V* ✲*Closed Mon.*

$$ ✕ **Da Gianni a la Vecia Bulagna.** Locals simply call it "da Gianni," and they fill these two unadorned rooms at lunch and at dinner. Though the decor is plain and unremarkable, it doesn't much matter—this place is all about food. The usual starters such as a tasty tortellini in brodo are on hand, as are daily specials such as gnocchi made with pumpkin, then sauced with melted cheese. *Bollito misto* (mixed meats boiled in a rich broth) is a fine option here, and the *cotechino con purè di patate* (a deliciously oily sausage with mashed potatoes) elevated to sublimity by the accompanying *salsa verde* (green sauce). ⊠*Via Clavature 18, Piazza Maggiore area* ☏*051/229434* ⚑*Reservations essential* ⊟*AE, DC, MC, V.*

$$ ✕ **Victoria.** It's not unusual for this unpretentious and charming trattoria-pizzeria off Via dell'Indipendenza to have lines, so reserve ahead. Locals come for the cheap pizzas, which are indisputably the highlight—*mozzarella di bufala* (buffalo mozzarella) is an excellent topping

choice—and much less expensive than the primi and secondi on the menu. The back room has a lovely 17th-century painted wooden ceiling. ⊠ *Via Augusto Righi 9/c, north of Piazza Maggiore* ☎*051/233548* ⊟*AE, DC, MC, V* ⊘*Closed Thurs.*

$ ✕ **Trattoria del Rosso.** Though the decor's nothing to write home about
★ (slightly glaring yellow walls with the oddly placed ceramic plate), the place teems with locals, mostly young folks, chowing down on delicious basic Bolognese fare at rock-bottom prices. The nimble staff bearing multiple plates sashays neatly between the closely spaced tables delivering such standards as *crescentine con salumi e squacquerone* (deep-fried flour puffs with cured meats and soft cheese) and tortellini in brodo. This is the kind of place where they don't glare at you if you only order a plate of pasta and little more, perhaps another reason why it's a favorite of university students. ⊠ *Via Augusto Righi 30, University area* ☎*051/236730* ⊟*AE, DC, MC, V* ⊘*Closed Thurs.*

¢ ✕ **Tamburini.** Two small rooms inside, and kegs and bar stools outside comprise the seating arrangements at this lively, packed little wine bar. At lunchtime, office workers swarm at the "bistrot self service" with remarkably tasty primi and secondi. After lunch, it becomes a wine bar with a vast array of selections by the glass and the bottle. The overwhelming plate of affettati misti is crammed with top-quality cured local ham products and succulent cheeses (including, sometimes, a goat Brie). ⊠ *Via Drapperie 1, Piazza Maggiore area* ☎*051/234726* ⊟*AE, MC, V* ⊘*No dinner.*

WHERE TO STAY

$$$$ ⚄ **Art Hotel Novecento.** A 2003 overhaul has given a great lift to this
★ swank place inspired by the 1930s Viennese Secession movement. It's in a remarkably serene cul-de-sac just minutes from Piazza Maggiore. Clean lines and elegant restraint are the hallmarks of the rooms, the lobby, and even the elevators, and equally svelte, well-dressed people like to stay here. It's well worth the extra €20 or so to upgrade from a basic double, as the rooms are that much bigger. The copious breakfast includes eggs, and happy hour comes with free wine and snacks. **Pros:** Spacious single rooms ideal for solo travelers; friendly, capable concierge service. **Con:** Some standard doubles are small. ⊠*Piazza Galileo 4/3i, Piazza Maggiore area, 40126* ☎*051/7457311* 🖷*051/7457322* ⊕*www.bolognarthotels.it/novecento* ⇱ *24 rooms, 1 suite* ⚅*In-room: safe, ethernet. In-hotel: bar, bicycles, concierge, laundry service, public Internet, parking (fee), some pets allowed* ⊟*AE, DC, MC, V* ⍟*BP.*

$$$$ ⚄ **Art Hotel Orologio.** The location can't be beat: it's right around the corner from Piazza Maggiore, tucked in a quiet little side street. Reception is on the ground floor, and a flight of stairs takes you up to the second floor to the elevator and the charming breakfast room. The rooms are mostly painted yellow, with hardwood floors, and some have tremendous views of 14th-century Palazzo Comunale just across the way. A couple of rooms are ideally suited to families, as they're spacious and have extra beds. **Pros:** Central location, great views. **Con:** Short flight of steps to elevator. ⊠*Via IV Novembre 10, Piazza Mag-*

giore area, 40123 ☎*051/7457411* 🖶*051/7457422* ⊕*www.bolognar-thotels.it/orologio* 🛏*29 rooms, 5 suites, 1 apartment* ♿*In-room: safe, ethernet, Wi-Fi. In-hotel: restaurant, bicycles, public Internet, public Wi-Fi, parking (fee), some pets allowed* ▤*AE, DC, MC, V* ⊘*BP.*

$$$$ ★ 🏨 **Corona d'Oro 1890.** The Azzaguidi family lived here in the 15th century, and though little traces of their palace remain, the place still has an aristocratic glow. The interior's been redone in art nouveau, and the airy, light-filled white atrium provides a perfect place to read a newspaper or enjoy a glass of wine. Rooms have floral lithographs on the walls; cool, muted earth-tone colors; and bathrooms with heated towel racks. Some have their own private balcony. The English-speaking staff are courteous and helpful, and are delighted when children are their guests. **Pros:** Stuffed animals for kids, great location. **Con:** Street-facing rooms can get a bit noisy. ✉*Via Oberdan 12, north of Piazza Maggiore 40126* ☎*051/7457611* 🖶*051/7457622* ⊕*www. bolognarthotels.it/corona* 🛏*37 rooms, 3 suites* ♿*In-room: safe, ethernet, Wi-Fi. In-hotel: bar, bicycles, public Internet, public Wi-Fi, parking (fee), some pets allowed* ▤*AE, DC, MC, V* ⊘*Closed 1st 3 wks in Aug.* ⊘*BP.*

$$$ 🏨 **Accademia.** A mid-range, comfortable base for exploring the area, this small hotel is right in the center of the university quarter. The rooms are adequate, the staff friendly. Look for discounted prices on the Web site. A few of the less-expensive rooms have a shared bath. **Pros:** Rates are very low in off-season, children under 5 sleep for free, good group rates. **Cons:** Rooms are mostly utilitarian, popular with groups. ✉*Via delle Belle Arti 6, at Via delle Moline, University area, 40126* ☎*051/232318* 🖶*051/263590* ⊕*www.hotelaccademia.com* 🛏*28 rooms, 24 with bath* ♿*In-room: safe, refrigerator. In-hotel: bar, public Internet, public Wi-Fi, parking (fee), some pets allowed* ▤*MC, V* ⊘*BP.*

$ 🏨 **San Vitale.** Modern furnishings and a garden distinguish this modest hostelry, about 1 km (½ mi) east of the center of town. The service is courteous, and rooms are clean and bright. There are private bathrooms, but facilities are very basic. **Pro:** A good budget option. **Con:** Location removed from the sights. ✉*Via San Vitale 94, University area, 40125* ☎*051/225966* 🖶*051/239396* 🛏*17 rooms* ♿*In-hotel: no elevator, public Internet, parking (fee)* ▤*No credit cards* ⊘*BP.*

NIGHTLIFE & THE ARTS

THE ARTS

Bologna's arts scene is one of the liveliest in Italy. Opera, ballet, rock concerts, and theatrical extravaganzas happen year-round, as do food festivals. The **Bologna tourism office** (☎*051/239660* ⊕*www.bolognaturismo.info*) has information on performances and events.

MUSIC & OPERA

The 18th-century **Teatro Comunale** (✉*Largo Respighi 1, University area* ☎*199/107070* ⊕*www.comunalebologna.it*) presents concerts by Italian and international orchestras throughout the year, but is dominated by the highly acclaimed opera performances November–May, so reserve seats well in advance. The ticket office is open Tuesday–Saturday 11–6:30.

NIGHTLIFE

As a university town, Bologna has long been known for its busy nightlife. As early as 1300 it was said to have had 150 taverns. Most of the city's current 200-plus pubs and bars are frequented by Italian students, young adults, and international students, with the university district forming the hub. In addition to the university area, the pedestrians-only zone on Via del Pratello, lined with plenty of bars, is also a hopping night scene, as is Via delle Moline, with cutting-edge cafés and bars. A more upmarket, low-key evening experience can be had at one of Bologna's many wine bars that are also restaurants. And then there are the hypertrendy bar-lounges that represent the newest of Bologna's many faces.

BARS

If you want a night out at a trendy spot, Bologna offers a lot to choose from.

Elegant **Bar Calice** (✉ *Via Clavature 13/a, at Via Marchesana, Piazza Maggiore area* ☎ *051/264508*) runs an indoor-outdoor operation year-round (with heat lamps). It's extremely popular with thirtysomethings. At **Le Stanze** (✉ *Via del Borgo di San Pietro 1, University area* ☎ *051/228767* ⊕ *www.lestanzecafe.com* ⊘ *Closed Mon., and July and Aug.*) you can sip an *aperitivo* or a late-night drink at a modern bar. The decor includes seventh-century frescoes in what was once the private chapel of Palazzo Bentivoglio. The adjoining avant-garde restaurant serves modern Italian fusion cooking. Buca San Petronio, an arcaded tunnel street tucked near the Piazza Maggiore, has become quite the evening scene. The loud **Nu Bar Lounge** (✉ *Off Buca San Petronio, Via de' Musei 6, Piazza Maggiore area* ☎ *051/222532* ⊕ *www.nu-lounge.com*) draws a cocktail-loving crowd, who enjoy the free snacks that show up around 8 PM.

MUSIC VENUES

It's not hard to find drinks accompanied by live music in the city. **Balmoral** (✉ *Via de' Pignattari 1, Piazza Maggiore area* ☎ *051/228694*), a restaurant right near Piazza Maggiore, has good live music most nights, and a vaguely Middle Eastern theme. With live jazz staged every night (€4 cover), **Cantina Bentivoglio** (✉ *Via Mascarella 4/b, University area* ☎ *051/265416*) is one of Bologna's most appealing nightspots. You can enjoy light meals and nibbles as well. **Osteria Buca delle Campane** (✉ *Via Benedetto XVI 4/a, University area* ☎ *051/220918*), an underground tavern in a 13th-century building, has good, inexpensive food and a lively after-dinner scene popular with locals, including students who come to listen to live music.

WINE BARS

Bologna has one of Italy's highest concentrations of wine bars. A wine bar with romantic ambient lighting and a good draft beer selection, **Contavalli** (✉ *Via Belle Arti 2, University area* ☎ *051/268395*) is a relaxing choice. The casually hip **Divinis** (⊠ *Via Battibecco 4/c, University area* ☎*051/2961502*) wine bar has a remarkable, if pricey, selection by the glass (as well as high-end food) served in chichi surroundings until 1:30 AM. *Don't overlook* **Godot Wine Bar** *(⇨ Where to Eat, above), whose wine list is even more exciting than its food menu.*

SHOPPING

WINE & FOOD

Bologna is a good place to buy wine. Several shops have a bewilderingly large selection—to go straight to the top, ask the managers which wines have won the prestigious *Tre Bicchieri* (Three Glasses) award from Gambero Rosso's wine bible, *Vini d'Italia.*

Repeatedly recognized as one of the best wine stores in Italy, **Enoteca Italiana** (⊠ *Via Marsala 2/b, north of Piazza Maggiore* ☎*051/235989*) lives up to its reputation with shelves lined with excellent selections from all over Italy at reasonable prices. Their delicious sandwiches with wine by the glass also make a great stand-up light lunch. Friendly owners run the midsize, down-to-earth **Scaramagli** (⊠*Strada Maggiore 31/d, University area* ☎*051/227132*) wine store. **La Boutique del Formaggio** (⊠*Viale Oriani 16/a, Piazza Maggiore area* ☎*051/347813*) is a cheese shop from another era, a place where time stands still and where all revolves around the nuances of esoteric cheeses. To shop here is to remember that there are still pockets of Italy where food is life. **La Baita** (⊠*Via Pescherie Vecchia 3/a, Piazza Maggiore area* ☎*051/223940*) sells fresh tagliolini, tortellini, and other Bolognese pasta delicacies, as well as sublime food to take away. Their cheese counter teems with local cheeses of superlative quality.

If you favor sweets, head to **Le Dolcezze** (⊠*Via Murr 21i, Piazza Maggiore area* ☎*051/444582*), a top local *pasticceria* (pastry shop) whose cakes are excellent, and whose *panettone,* the sweet bread produced only around the holiday season, is considered by some to be the best in town. **Roccati** (⊠ *Via Clavature 17/a, Piazza Maggiore area* ☎*051/261964* ⊕*www.roccaticioccolato.com*) has been crafting sculptural works of chocolate, as well as basic bonbons and simpler stuff since 1909. For fresh produce, meats, and other foods, head to **Via Oberdan** (⊠*Piazza Maggiore area*), the street just off Via dell'Indipendenza downtown. The **Mercato delle Erbe** (⊠ *Via Ugo Bassi, Piazza Maggiore area* ☎*051/230186*) is an equally bustling food market, open Monday through Wednesday, and Friday 7–1:15 and 5–7:30 (4:30–7:30 October–March), Thursday and Saturday 7–1:15. The **Mercato di Mezzo** (⊠*Via Peschiere Vecchie, Piazza Maggiore area*), which sells specialty foods, fruits, and vegetables, is an intense barrage of sights and smells. It's open Monday through Saturday 7–1 and 4:15–7:30, with the exception of Thursday afternoon, when it's closed.

9

FERRARA

47 km (29 mi) northeast of Bologna, 74 km (46 mi) northwest of Ravenna.

When the legendary Ferrarese filmmaker Michelangelo Antonioni called his beloved hometown "a city that you can see only partly, while the rest disappears to be imagined," perhaps he was referring to the low-lying mist that rolls in off the Adriatic each winter and shrouds Ferrara's winding knot of medieval alleyways, turreted palaces, and ancient wine bars—once inhabited by the likes of Copernicus—in a ghostly fog. But perhaps Antonioni was also suggesting that Ferrara's striking beauty often conceals a dark and tortured past.

Though it was settled as early as the sixth century ad, Ferrara's history really begins with the arrival of the Este, who first made their appearance in the city in 1196. For more than three centuries the dynasty ruled with an iron fist; brother killed brother, son fought father, husband murdered wife. The majestic moated castle, now the architectural gem of the historic center, was originally built as a fortress to protect the ruthless Este dukes from their own citizens; deep within the castle the Este kept generations of political dissidents in dank cells. The greatest of the dukes, Ercole I (1433–1505), attempted to poison a nephew who challenged his power, and when that didn't work he beheaded him. Though the Jews were already well established in Ferrara as early at the 1380s, it is Ercole I who invited Sephardic Jews exiled from Spain to settle in Ferrara, thus giving form to one of the liveliest Jewish communities in western Europe. The maze of twisting cobblestone streets in the ghetto witnessed the persecution of its Jews once Fascist Italy was officially at war with Nazi Germany in October 1943. This tragedy was documented in Giorgio Bassani's semi-autobiographical book and Vittorio De Sica's film, *The Garden of the Finzi-Continis.*

Today you are likely to be charmed by Ferrara's prosperous air and meticulous cleanliness, its excellent restaurants and coffeehouses, and its lively wine bar scene. You'll find aficionados gathering outside any of the wine bars near the Duomo even on the foggiest of weekend evenings. Though Ferrara is a UNESCO World Heritage site, the city still draws amazingly few tourists—which only adds to its appeal.

GETTING HERE
Train service is frequent from Bologna (usually three trains per hour) and takes either a half hour or 45 minutes, depending upon which train type you take. It's a two-hour ride from Florence, and trains go just about every hour. The walk from the train station is easy but not particularly interesting. If you're driving from Bologna, take the RA1 out of town, take the A13 in the direction of Padova, and exit at Ferrara Nord. Follow the SP19 directly into the center of town. The trip should take about 45 minutes.

VISITOR INFORMATION
Ferrara tourism office (✉ *Castello Estense, 44100* ☎ *0532/299303* ✉ *Piazza Municipale 11, 44100* ☎ *0532/419474* ⊕ *www.ferrarainfo.com).*

EXPLORING FERRARA

If you plan to explore the city fully, consider buying a Card Musei ("museum card"; €14) at the Palazzo dei Diamanti or at any of the museums around town; it grants admission to every museum, palace, and castle in Ferrara. The first Monday of the month is free at many museums.

THE MAIN ATTRACTIONS

★ Massive **Castello Estense**, the former seat of Este power, dominates the center of town. The building was a suitable symbol for the ruling family: cold and menacing on the outside, lavishly decorated within. The public rooms are grand, but deep in the bowels of the castle are chilling dungeons where enemies of the state were held in wretched conditions—a function these quarters served as recently as 1943, when antifascist prisoners were detained there. In particular, the **Prisons of Don Giulio, Ugo, and Parisina** have some fascinating features, like 15th-century graffiti protesting the imprisonment of lovers Ugo and Parisina, who were beheaded in 1425 because Ugo's father, Niccolò III, didn't like the fact that his son was cavorting with Niccolò's wife.

The castle was established as a fortress in 1385, but work on its luxurious ducal quarters continued into the 16th century. Representative of Este grandeur are the **Sala dei Giochi,** extravagantly painted with athletic scenes, and the **Sala dell'Aurora,** decorated to show the times of the day. The tower, the terraces of the castle, and the hanging garden—once reserved for the private use of the duchesses—have fine views of the town and the surrounding countryside. You can cross the castle's moat, traverse its drawbridge, and wander through many of its arcaded passages at any time. Do note that the entrance price is substantially higher if there is a special exhibition on. ⊠*Piazza Castello* ☎*0532/299233* ⊕*www.castelloestense.it* ⊠*Castle €7, tower €1 extra* ⊗*Castle: Tues.–Sun. 9:30–5:30. Tower: Tues.–Sun. 10–4:45. Ticket office closes at 4:45.*

9

NEED A BREAK? **Caffetteria Castello** (⊠*Largo Castello 1* ☎*0532/299337* ⊗*Tues.–Sun. 9:30–5:30*) is spectacularly situated amid centuries of history. The second floor provides a great place to break for coffee while touring the castle, or to mingle with locals enjoying the lunchtime buffet. Right next door is a small book and gift shop.

★ The magnificent Gothic **Duomo,** a few steps from the Castello Estense, has a three-tier facade of slender arches and beautiful carvings over the central door. Work began in 1135 and took more than 100 years to complete. The interior was completely remodeled in the 17th century. ⊠*Piazza Cattedrale* ☎*0532/207449* ⊗*Mon.–Sat. 7:30–noon and 3–6:30, Sun. 7:30–12:30 and 3:30–7:30.*

The collection of ornate religious objects in the **Museo Ebraico** *(Jewish Museum)* bears witness to the long history of the city's Jewish community. This history had its high points—1492, for example, when Ercole I invited the Jews to come over from Spain—and its lows, notably 1627, when Jews were enclosed within the **ghetto,** where they were forced to live until the advent of a united Italy in 1859. The triangular warren of narrow, cobbled streets that made up the ghetto originally extended as far as Corso Giovecca (originally Corso Giudecca, or Ghetto Street); when it was enclosed, the neighborhood was restricted to the area between Via Scienze, Via Contrari, and Via di San Romano. The museum, in the center of the ghetto, was once Ferrara's synagogue. All visits are led by a museum guide. ⊠ *Via Mazzini 95* ☎*0532/210228* ⊕*www.comune. fe.it/museoebraico* ⊠*€4* ⊙*Sept.–July, guided tours Sun.–Thurs. at 10, 11, and noon.*

WORD OF MOUTH

"Check out what special exhibits are at Ferrara's Palace of Diamonds at the time of your visit. We were lucky enough to hit a John Singer Sargent exhibit, exclusively his work in Italy."
–Ralstonlan

The **Palazzo dei Diamanti** *(Palace of Diamonds)* is so called because of the 12,600 small, pink-and-white marble pyramids ("diamonds") that stud the facade. The building was designed to be viewed in perspective—both faces at once—from diagonally across the street. Work began in the 1490s, and finished around 1504. Today the palazzo contains the **Pinacoteca Nazionale,** which has an extensive art gallery and rotating exhibits. ⊠ *Corso Ercole I d'Este 19–21* ☎*0532/205844* ⊕*www.artecultura.fe.it* ⊠*€4* ⊙*Tues.–Sun. 9–7.*

The oldest and most characteristic area of Ferrara is south of the Duomo, stretching between the Corso Giovecca and the city's ramparts. Here various members of the Este family built pleasure palaces, the most famous of which is the **Palazzo Schifanoia** (*schifanoia* means "carefree" or, literally, "fleeing boredom"). Begun in the late 14th century, the palace was remodeled between 1464 and 1469. The lavishly decorated interior, particularly the **Salone dei Mesi,** with an extravagant series of frescoes showing the months of the year and their mythological attributes, is well worth visiting. ⊠ *Via Scandiana 23* ☎*0532/244949* ⊕*www.artecultura.fe.it* ⊠*€10* ⊙*Tues.–Sun. 10–8.*

One of the streets most characteristic of Ferrara's past, the 2-km-long (1-mi-long) **Via delle Volte** is also one of the best preserved medieval streets in Europe. The series of ancient *volte* (arches) along the narrow cobblestone alley once joined the merchants' houses on the south side of the street to their warehouses on the north side. The street ran parallel to the banks of the Po River, which was home to Ferrara's busy port.

ALSO WORTH SEEING
One of the loveliest of the Renaissance palaces along Ferrara's old streets is the charming **Casa Romei.** Mid-15th-century frescoes decorate rooms on the ground floor; the *piano nobile* (main floor) contains detached frescoes from local churches as well as lesser-known Renaissance sculptures. ⊠ *Via Savonarola 30* ☎*0532/240341* ⊕*www.artecultura.fe.it* ⊠*€3* ⊙*Tues.–Sun. 8:30–7:30.*

On the busy Corso Giovecca is the **Palazzina di Marfisa d'Este,** a grandiose 16th-century palace that belonged to a great patron of the arts. It has painted ceilings, fine 16th-century furniture, and a garden containing a grotto and an outdoor theater. ⊠*Corso Giovecca 170* ☎*0532/207450* ⊕*www.artecultura.fe.it* ⊠*€3* ⊘*Tues.–Sun. 9–1 and 3–6.*

WHERE TO EAT

$$$$ ✗ **Il Don Giovanni.** Just down the street from Castello Estense, and
★ inside a lovely 17th-century palace, this warm and inviting restaurant has a handful of tables and top-notch service. Chef Pier Luigi Di Diego and partner Marco Merighi pay strict attention to what's seasonal, and the menu reflects this. Complex mozzarella di bufala is paired with raw shrimp so fruity it's like a dab of marmalade. Melt-in-your-mouth-tender raw scallops reveal just a whisper of sweetness. Cooked fish is equally impressive: juicy, well-seasoned *branzino* (striped sea bass) sits daringly atop chili peppers. Next door, the same proprietors run the less-expensive **La Borsa** wine bar, which has excellent cured meats, cheeses, and a fantastic wine-by-the-glass list. It's open for lunch. ⊠*Corso Ercole I d'Este 1* ☎*0532/243363* ⊕*www.ildongiovanni.com* ⌖*Reservations essential* ▤*AE, DC, MC, V* ⊘*Closed Mon. No lunch.*

$$ ✗ **L'Oca Giuliva.** Food, service, and ambience unite in blissful harmony
Fodor'sChoice at this casual yet elegant restaurant minutes from Piazza Repubblica.
★ Two small rooms in a 12th-century building provide the backdrop for exquisitely prepared local foods. The chef has a deft hand with local specialties, and executes them either in *tradizionale* (traditional) or *rivisitata* (updated) style. Particularly impressive are the primi, especially the cappellacci di zucca al ragù. It might be the best version in town. Meat-and-potatoes folk can opt for the salama da sugo with mashed potatoes, and adventuring sorts might try the *trancio di anguilla* (roast eel) with polenta on the side. The amazing wine list is complemented by a terrific cheese plate. ⊠*via Boccanale di Santo Stefano 38* ☎*0532/207628* ▤*AE, DC, MC, V* ⊘*Closed Mon. No lunch Tues.*

$$ ✗ **Osteria Al Brindisi.** Ferrara is a city of wine bars, beginning with this,
Fodor'sChoice Europe's oldest, which opened in 1435. Copernicus drank here while
★ a student in the late 1400s, and the place still has a somewhat undergraduate aura. Perfectly dusty wine bottles line the walls, and there are wooden booths in another small room for those who want to eat while they drink. A young staff pours terrific wines by the glass, and offers three different sauces (butter and sage, tomato, or ragù) with its cappellacci di zucca. Those in search of lighter fare might enjoy any of the salads or the grilled vegetable plate with melted pecorino. ⊠*Via degli Adelardi 11* ☎*0532/209142* ▤*AE, DC, MC, V* ⊘*Closed Mon.*

$$ ✗ **Trattoria La Romantica.** The former stables of a 17th-century merchant's house have been transformed into this welcoming restaurant, which is a great favorite among local cognoscenti. Although the decor—warm light and wood-beam ceilings, incongruous prints, and a piano—seems to be in perpetual transition, the rustic food is fully real-

9

ized. Ferrarese specialties like cappellacci di zucca are served side by side with French oysters. ⊠ *Via Ripagrande 36* ☎*0532/765975* ⊟*AE, DC, MC, V* ⊗*Closed Wed., Jan. 7–17, and Aug. 1–15.*

WHERE TO STAY

The city-run **Prenotel hotel reservation hot line** (☎*0532/462046*) helps you make reservations at any place in town.

$$$ 🏨 **Annunziata.** The flower-covered mini-balconies of this hotel could hardly be any closer to the castle and Ferrara's old town—this might just be the best location in the city. The building feels like an old private home, the lobby is inviting, and the pleasantly understated rooms have ceilings with old wooden beams. **Pro:** American-style breakfast (with eggs). **Con:** Noise can be a problem. ⊠*Piazza Repubblica 5, 44100* ☎*0532/201111* 🖷*0532/203233* ⊕*www.annunziata.it* ⬅*26 rooms* ♿*In-room: safe, Wi-Fi. In-hotel: room service, bar, bicycles, parking (fee)* ⊟*AE, DC, MC, V* ⦿*BP.*

$$$ 🏨 **Hotel Ripagrande.** The courtyards, vaulted brick lobby, and break-
Fodor'sChoice fast room of this 15th-century noble's palazzo retain much of their
★ lordly Renaissance flair. Rooms are decidedly more down-to-earth, but standard doubles and some of the enormous bi- and tri-level suites have faux-Persian rugs, tapestries, and cozy antique furniture; top-floor rooms and suites resemble a Colorado ski lodge, with terraces, and are roomy—especially good for families. Everything here, including the room service, is impeccable. The location is quiet but fairly convenient. **Pros:** Beyond-helpful staff, good choice for families. **Con:** Staff goes home at midnight. ⊠ *Via Ripagrande 21, 44100* ☎*0532/765250* 🖷*0532/764377* ⊕*www.ripagrandehotel.it* ⬅*20 rooms, 20 suites* ♿*In-room: safe, Wi-Fi. In-hotel: restaurant, room service, bar, laundry service, public Wi-Fi, parking (no fee), some pets allowed* ⊟*AE, DC, MC, V* ⦿*BP.*

$ 🏨 **Locanda Borgonuovo.** This old-fashioned but lovely bed-and-breakfast is in a 17th-century monastery on a quiet but central pedestrians-only street. It books up months in advance, partly because it's very small and because musicians and actors from the local theater make this their home away from home. Rooms are furnished with antiques, and one has its own kitchen for longer stays. Summer breakfasts are served in the leafy courtyard. **Pro:** Kindly staff. **Con:** Steep stairs to reception and rooms. ⊠*Via Cairoli 29, 44100* ☎*0532/211100* 🖷*0532/246328* ⊕*www.borgonuovo.com* ⬅*4 rooms, 2 apartments* ♿*In-room: safe, kitchen (some), Wi-Fi. In-hotel: restaurant, bicycles, no elevator, public Internet, public Wi-Fi, parking (no fee)* ⊟*AE, MC, V* ⦿*BP.*

ROMAGNA

Anywhere in Emilia-Romagna, the story goes, a weary, lost traveler will be invited into a family's home and offered a drink. But the Romagnesi claim that he'll be served water in Emilia and wine in Romagna. The hilly, mostly rural, and largely undiscovered Romagna region has crum-

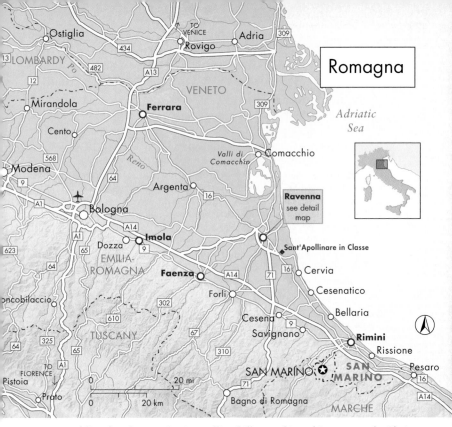

bling farmhouses dotting rolling hills, smoking chimneys, early Christian churches, and rowdy local bars dishing out rounds and rounds of *piadine* (a pita-thin bread filled with meat, cheese, vegetables, or any combination thereof, and then quickly grilled). Ravenna, the site of shimmering Byzantine mosaics, dominates the region, as does Rimini, a crowded, Coney Island–like seaside resort.

Heading southeast out of Bologna, Via Emilia (SS9) and the parallel A14 autostrada lead to the towns of Dozza and Faenza. From here, go north to the Adriatic Coast on the SS71 to reach Ravenna, or continue southeast on the A14 to reach Rimini. Alternatively, the slower SS16 cuts a northwest–southeast swath through Romagna, directly connecting Ravenna and Rimini.

IMOLA

42 km (26 mi) southeast of Bologna.

GETTING HERE

Imola is an easy train ride from Bologna; local trains run frequently and take a little under a half hour. If you're coming from Milan, you can take the Eurostar to Bologna, and then transfer to the local train. Travel time from Milan is about 2½ hours, and the walk from the station to the centro storico is easy. If you're driving from Bologna, take the SP253 to the RA1, and then the A11, following signs to Ancona. Then take the SP610, and follow signs for Imola.

VISITOR INFORMATION

Imola tourism office (⊠ *Arcade of the City Center 135* ☎ *0542/602207*).

EXPLORING

The affluent town of Imola, with its wide and stately avenues, lies on the border between Emilia and Romagna. It was populated as early as the Bronze Age, came under Roman rule, and was eventually annexed to the Papal States in 1504. Now it is best known for its Formula One auto-racing tradition; the San Marino Grand Prix has been held here in spring of every year since 1981. Auto-racing as a serious sport in Imola dates to 1953, when, with the support of Enzo Ferrari, the racetrack just outside the city center was inaugurated. However, unless you happen to pop into town in mid-April for the race, you'll more likely find yourself in Imola shopping for its well-known ceramics or sampling the cuisine at the town's world-famous restaurant, San Domenico.

WHERE TO EAT

$$$$ ✕ **San Domenico.** San Domenico has defended its position as one of
★ Italy's most refined dining destinations year after year, and heads of state, celebrities, and those with bottomless pocketbooks flock here to savor the fare. The majestic appointments complement chef Valentino Marcattilii's wondrous creations, like his memorable *uovo in raviolo San Domenico,* in which large ravioli are each stuffed with a whole eggthe yolk spills out and mixes with Parmesan cheese, *burro di malga* (butter from an Alpine dairy farm), and sensational white truffles. The impressive wine list has more than 3,000 choices. ⊠ *Via G. Sacchi 1* ☎ *0542/29000* ⊕ *www.sandomenico.it* ✍ *Reservations essential* ▤ *AE, DC, MC, V* ☺ *Closed Mon., Sun. June–Aug., 1 wk in Jan., and 1 wk in Aug. No lunch Sat. June–Aug. No dinner Sun. Sept.–May.*

FAENZA

23 km (14 mi) southeast of Dozza, 49 km (30 mi) southeast of Bologna.

GETTING HERE

Trains run frequently from Bologna to Faenza; the trip takes about a half hour. There's sporadic service from Florence; it's a beautiful ride and takes about two hours. The walk to the centro storico is easy but not particularly interesting. If you're going by car, it takes about an hour from Bologna. Take the SP253 to the RA1, at which point pick up on the A14/E45 heading in the direction of Ancona. Exit and take the SP8 into Faenza.

VISITOR INFORMATION

Faenza tourism office (⊠ *Voltore Molinella 21, 48018* ☎ *0546/2523*).

EXPLORING

In the Middle Ages, Faenza was the crossroad between Emilia-Romagna and Tuscany, and the 15th century saw many Florentine artists working in town. In 1509, the Papal States took control, and Faenza became something of a backwater. It did, however, continue its 12th-century tradition of making top-quality ceramic ware. In the 16th century, local artists created a color called *bianchi di Faenza* ("Faenza white") which was wildly imitated and wildly desired all over Europe; by the 16th century the Frenchified *faience* to refer to the color and technique entered the lexicon, where it remains to this day. In the central **Piazza del Popolo**, dozens of shops sell the native ceramic wares.

Faenza is home to the **Museo delle Ceramiche**, one of the largest ceramics museums in the world. It's a well-labeled, well-lighted museum with objects from the Renaissance among its highlights. Though the emphasis is decidedly on local stuff, the rest of Italy is represented as well. Do not miss the 20th- and 21st-century galleries, which illustrate that decorative arts often surpass their utile limitations and become, truly, magnificently sculptural. ⊠ *Viale Baccarini 19* ☎ *0546/697311* ⊕ *www.micfaenza.org* 💶 *€6* 🕙 *Apr.–Oct., Tues.–Sat. 9:30–7; Nov.– Mar., Tues.–Thurs. 9:30–1:30, Fri.–Sun. 9:30–5:30.*

WHERE TO EAT

$$ ✕ **Marianaza.** A large open-hearth fireplace dominates this simple trattoria; wonderful aromas of grilled meats and garlic greet you as you walk in. Marianaza, like the town of Faenza itself, successfully blends the best of Emilian-Romagnan and Tuscan cuisine: the extraordinary primi are mostly tortellini-based, and the secondi rely heavily on the grill. Grilled garlic toasts topped with prosciutto crudo delightfully whet the appetite; and the tortellini in brodo is tasty. The mixed grill is perfect for sharing. (Note that the person at the grill is a woman: a true rarity in Italy.) ⊠ *via Torricelli 21* ☎ *0546/681461* ▭ *AE, DC, MC, V.*

9

RIMINI

52 km (32 mi) southeast of Ravenna, 121 km (75 mi) southeast of Bologna.

GETTING HERE

Trains run hourly from Ravenna to Rimini and take about an hour. There's frequent train service (usually three trains per hour) from Bologna to Rimini. It takes between an hour and an hour and a half, depending upon what type of train you choose. By car from Ravenna, take the SS16/E55, then follow the SS3bis/E45/E55 in the direction of Roma/Ancona. Follow directions for Ancona Nord, then follow signs for Ancona. Take the A14/E55 to the Rimini Nord exit, then the SP136 to the SS16, and follow signs for the center of town. From Bologna, take the SP253 out of town, pick up the RA1, and then enter the A14 heading toward Ancona. Get off at the Rimini Nord exit, follow the SP136 to the SS16 to the center of town.

VISITOR INFORMATION

Rimini tourism office (⊠*Train station, Piazzale Cesare Battisti, 47037* ☎*0541/51331* ⊠*Piazzale Fellini 3, Marina Centro, 47037* ☎*0541/56902* ⊕*www.riminiturismo.it*).

EXPLORING

Rimini is the most popular summer resort on the Adriatic Coast and one of the most popular in Italy. July and August are the most crowded, packed with people who don't mind crammed beaches and not-all-that-blue water. In the off-season (October–March) Rimini is a cold, windy fishing port with few places open. Any time of year, one of Rimini's least touristy areas is the port; rambling down the **Via Sinistra del Porto** or **Via Destra del Porto** past all the fishing boats, you're far from the crush of sunbathers.

The town stands at the junction of two great Roman consular roads, the Via Emilia and the Via Flaminia. In Roman times it was an important port, making it a strategic and commercial center. From the 13th century onward, Rimini was controlled by the Malatesta family, an unpredictable group capable of grand gestures and savage deeds. The Malatesta constructed the **Tempio Malatestiano,** with a masterful facade by Leon Battista Alberti (1404–72). Inside, the second chapel to the right contains a wonderful (but faded) fresco by Piero della Francesca (1420–92). ⊠*Via IV Novembre 35* ☎*0541/51130* ⊕*www.diocesi. rimini.it/diocesi/tempio.htm* ⊠*Free* ⊗*Mon.–Sat. 8–12:30 and 3:30– 6:30, Sun. 9–1 and 3:30–7.*

Rimini's oldest monument is the **Arco d'Augusto,** now stranded in the middle of a square just inside the city ramparts. It was erected in 27 BC, making it the oldest surviving Roman arch. ⊠*Largo Giulio Cesare.*

WHERE TO STAY & EAT

$$–$$$ ✕ **La Locanda di San Martino.** Dishes such as the *spaghettoni ai frutti*
★ *di mare* (thick spaghetti with seafood sauce) and a grilled mixed seafood platter are uniformly fresh and superbly prepared; the mixed antipasto served with lunch is exquisite. An outdoor patio in the back is more romantic than the large main dining rooms. To get here take the road out of Rimini heading toward Bologna. ⊠*Via Emilia 226* ☎*0541/680127* ▤*AE, MC, V* ⊗*Closed Mon.*

$$$$ ▦ **Grand Hotel.** This 1908 extravaganza, made famous by filmmaker Federico Fellini in his *Amarcord,* is grander than ever. The hyperluxe stage is set by enormous crystal chandeliers in the lobby and inlaid wood in the rooms that seem playful rather than formal. A spotless private beach, with a restaurant open from June to September, completes the scene. This is also one of the few hotels in the region with kosher capabilities, and events are organized for Jewish holidays under rabbinical supervision. **Pros:** Grandiose style, beach across the street. **Con:** Not good if "grandiose" isn't your thing. ⊠*Parco Federico Fellini, 47900* ☎*0541/56000* ▤*0541/56866* ⊕*www.grandhotelrimini.com* ➥*108 rooms, 12 suites* ♿*In-room: safe. In-hotel: restaurant, bars, tennis court, pools, gym, beachfront* ▤*AE, DC, MC, V* ⊘❘*BP.*

CLOSE UP

San Marino, a Country on a Cliff

The world's smallest and oldest republic, as San Marino dubs itself, is landlocked entirely by Italy. It consists of three ancient castles perched high on cliffs of sheer rock rising implausibly out of the flatlands of Romagna, and a tangled knot of cobblestone streets below, lined with tourist boutiques, cheesy hotels and restaurants, and gun shops. The 45-minute drive from Rimini is easily justified, however, by the castle-top view of the countryside far below. The 3,300-foot-plus precipices will make jaws drop and acrophobes quiver.

San Marino was founded in the 4th century AD by a stonecutter named Marino who settled with a small community of Christians, escaping persecution by pagan emperor Diocletian. Over the millennia, largely because of the logistical nightmares associated with attacking a fortified rock, San Marino was more or less left alone by Italy's various conquerors, and continues to this day to be an independent country (population 26,000), supported almost entirely by its 3-million-visitors-per-year tourist industry.

San Marino's headline attractions are its **tre castelli** (three castles)—medieval architectural wonders that appear on every coat of arms in the city. Starting in the center of town, walk a few hundred yards past the trinket shops, along a paved cliff-top ridge, from the 10th-century **Rocca della Guaita** to the 13th-century **Rocca della Cesta** (which contains a museum of ancient weapons that's worthwhile mostly for the views from its terraces and turrets), and finally to the 14th-century **Rocca Montale** (closed to the public), the most remote of the castles. Every step of the way affords spectacular views of

Romagna and the Adriatic; it is said that on a clear day you can see Croatia. The walks make for a good day's exercise but are by no means arduous. Even if you arrive after visiting hours, they're supremely worthwhile. ☎ *0549/882670* ⊕ *www.museidistato. sm* ▦ *Rocca della Guaita and Rocca della Cesta €4.50* ⊙ *Sept. 21–Mar. 19, daily 8:50–5; Mar. 20–Sept. 20, daily 8–8.*

A must-see is the **Piazza della Libertà**, whose Palazzo Pubblico is guarded by soldiers in green uniforms. As you'll notice by peering into the shops along the old town's winding streets, the republic is famous for crossbows—and more: shopping for fireworks, firearms, and other items illegal for sale elsewhere is another popular tourist activity.

Visiting San Marino in winter—off-season—increases the appeal of the experience, as tourist establishments shut down and you more or less have the castles to yourself. In August, every inch of walkway on the rock is mobbed with sightseers. To get to San Marino by car, take highway SS72 west from Rimini. From Borgo Maggiore, at the base of the rock, a cable car will whisk you up to the castles and town. Alternatively, you can drive all the way up the winding road; public parking is available in the town itself. Don't worry about changing money, showing passports, and the like (although the tourist office at Contrada del Collegio will stamp your passport for €2.50); San Marino is, for all practical purposes, Italy—except, that is, for its majestic perch, its gun laws, and its reported 99% national voter turnout rate.

9

There are two auto routes between Ravenna and Rimini. The coastal road, SS16, hugs the shoreline much of the way, passing through Cervia. Although its length of 52 km (32 mi) is not great, this scenic route is naturally slower (beware of fog in winter). The coast north of Rimini is lined with dozens of small resort towns, only one having any charm—the seaport of Cesenatico; the others are mini-Riminis, and in summer the narrow road is hopelessly clogged with traffic. A faster route is to take the SS71 and the A14; the distance is 64 km (39 mi).

RAVENNA

76 km (47 mi) east of Bologna, 93 km (58 mi) southeast of Ferrara.

A small, quiet, well-heeled city, Ravenna has brick palaces, cobbled streets, magnificent monuments, and spectacular Byzantine mosaics to remind you of its storied past. The high point in Ravenna's history occurred in the fifth century, when Pope Honorious moved his court here from Rome. Gothic kings Odoacer and Theodoric ruled the city until it was conquered by the Byzantines in AD 540. Ravenna then fell under the sway of Venice, and then, inevitably, the Papal States.

Because Ravenna spent much of its past looking to the East, its greatest art treasures show that influence. Churches and tombs with the most unassuming exteriors contain within them walls covered with sumptuous mosaics. These beautifully preserved Byzantine mosaics put great emphasis on nature, which you can see in the delicate rendering of sky, earth, and animals. Outside Ravenna, the town of Classe hides even more mosaic gems.

GETTING HERE

By car from Bologna, take the SP253 to the RA1, and then follow signs for the A14/E45 in the direction of Ancona. From here, follow signs for Ravenna, taking the A14dir Ancona–Milano–Ravenna exit. Follow signs for the SS16/E55 to the center of Ravenna. It's a more convoluted, but more interesting, drive from Ferrara: take the SS16 to the RA8 in the direction of Porto Garibaldi taking the Roma/Ravenna exit. Follow the SS309/E55 to the SS309dir/E55, taking the SS253 Bologna/Ancona exit. Follow the SS16/E55 into the center of Ravenna.

VISITOR INFORMATION

Ravenna tourism office (⊠ *Via Salara 8, 48100* ☎ *0544/35404* ⊕ *www.turismo.ravenna.it*).

EXPLORING RAVENNA

A combination ticket (available at ticket offices of all included sights) admits you to six of Ravenna's important monuments: the Mausoleo di Galla Placidia, the Basilica di San Vitale, the Battistero Neoniano, Sant'Apollinare Nuovo, the church of Spirito Santo, and the Museo Arcivescovile e Cappella Sant'Andrea. Start out early in the morning to avoid lines (reservations are necessary for the Mausoleo and

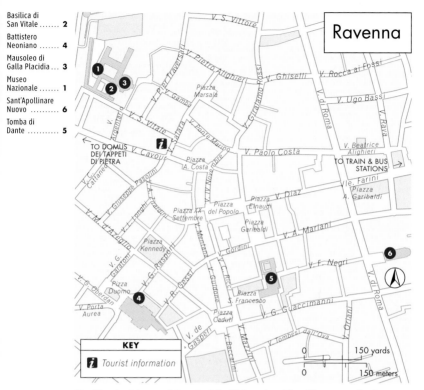

Basilica in May and June). A half day should suffice to walk the town alone; allow an hour each for the Mausoleo, the Basilica, and the Museo Nazionale. Ticket offices often close 15 to 30 minutes before the sights themselves.

THE MAIN ATTRACTIONS

❷ Basilica di San Vitale. The octagonal church of San Vitale was built in AD 547, after the Byzantines conquered the city, and its interior shows a strong Byzantine influence. In the area behind the altar are the most famous works in the church, depicting the emperor Justinian and his retinue on one wall, and his wife, Empress Theodora, with her retinue, on the opposite wall. Notice how the mosaics seamlessly wrap around the columns and curved arches on the upper sides of the altar area. Reservations are recommended from March through mid-June. ⊠ *Via San Vitale off Via Salara* ☎*0544/541688 reservations, 800/303999 toll-free information* ⊕*www.ravennamosaici.it* ✉*Combination ticket €8.50* ⊗*Nov.–Feb., daily 9:30–5; Mar. and Oct., daily 9–5:30; Apr.– Sept., daily 9–7.*

❹ Battistero Neoniano. The baptistry, next door to Ravenna's 18th-century cathedral, is one of the town's most important mosaic sights. It dates from the beginning of the fifth century ad, with work continuing through the century. In keeping with the building's role, the great mosaic in the dome shows the baptism of Christ, and beneath are the Apostles. The lowest register of mosaics contains Christian symbols, the Throne of God, and the Cross. Note the naked figure kneeling next to Christ—he is the personification of the River Jordan. ⊠ *Via Battistero* ☎ *0544/541688 reservations, 800/303999 toll-free information* ⊕ *www.ravennamosaici.it* ✉ *Combination ticket €8.50* ⊙ *Nov.–Feb., daily 10–5; Mar. and Oct., daily 9:30–5:30; Apr.–Sept., daily 9–7.*

> **WORD OF MOUTH**
>
> "Much of Ravenna is car-free, so we were on foot. Many local people rode bicycles; some of them smoked as they rode. Bikes for hire are parked in blue holders. One rents a key, and can take a bike from any holder and leave it at any holder, like luggage carts at an airport." –smalti

❸ Mausoleo di Galla Placidia. The little tomb and the great church stand

FodorśChoice
★

side by side, but the tomb predates the Basilica di San Vitale by at least a hundred years. These two adjacent sights are decorated with the best-known, and most elaborate, mosaics in Ravenna. Galla Placidia was the sister of Rome's emperor, Honorius, the man who moved the imperial capital to Ravenna in AD 402. She is said to have been beautiful and strong-willed, and to have taken an active part in the governing of the crumbling empire. This tomb, constructed in the mid-fifth century, is her memorial.

Viewed from the outside, the tomb is a small, unassuming redbrick building; the exterior's seeming poverty of charm only serves to enhance by contrast the richness of the interior mosaics, in deep midnight blue and glittering gold. The tiny, low central dome is decorated with symbols of Christ and the evangelists and striking gold stars. Over the door is a depiction of the Good Shepherd. Eight of the Apostles are represented in groups of two on the four inner walls of the dome; the other four appear singly on the walls of the two transepts. Notice the small doves at their feet, drinking from the water of faith. Also in the tiny transepts are some delightful pairs of deer (representing souls), drinking from the fountain of resurrection. There are three sarcophagi in the tomb, none of which are believed to contain the remains of Galla Placidia. She died in Rome in AD 450, and there is no record of her body having been transported back to the place where she wished to lie. Reservations are required for the Mausoleo from March through mid-June. ⊠ *Via San Vitale off Via Salara* ☎ *0544/541688 reservations, 800/303999 toll-free information* ⊕ *www.ravennamosaici.it* ✉ *€2 supplement in addition to obligatory €8.50 combination ticket Mar. 1–June 15* ⊙ *Nov.–Feb., Mon.–Sat. 9:30–5, Sun. 9:30–5:30; Mar. and Oct., Mon.–Sat. 9–5:30, Sun. 9–6; Apr.–Sept., daily 9–7.*

❻ Sant'Apollinare Nuovo. The mosaics displayed in this church date from the early sixth century, making them slightly older than those in San Vitale. Since the left side of the church was reserved for women, it's only fitting that the mosaics on that wall depict 22 virgins offering crowns to the Virgin Mary. On the right wall are 26 men carrying the crowns of martyrdom. They are approaching Christ, surrounded by angels.

⊠ *Via Roma at Via Guaccimanni* ☎*0544/219518, 0544/541688 reservations, 800/303999 toll-free information* ⊕*www.ravennamosaici.it* ✆*Combination ticket €8.50* ⊙*Nov.–Feb., daily 10–5; Mar. and Oct., daily 9:30–5:30; Apr.–Sept., daily 9–7.*

ALSO WORTH SEEING

Domus dei Tappeti di Pietra *(Ancient Home of the Stone Carpets).* This underground archaeological site was uncovered during the course of routine maintenance work by the city in 1993 and opened to the public in 2002. Below ground level (10 feet down) lie the remains of a sixth-century AD Byzantine palace, in which a beautiful and well-preserved network of floor mosaics display themes that are fascinatingly un-Christian. ⊠ *Via Barbiani, enter through Sant'Eufemia* ☎*0544/32512* ⊕*www.domusdeitappetidipietra.it* ✆*€3.50* ⊙*Sun.–Fri. 10–6:30, Sat. 10–4:30.*

❶ Museo Nazionale. The National Museum of Ravenna, next to the Church of San Vitale, contains artifacts from ancient Rome, Byzantine fabrics and carvings, and pieces of early Christian art. The collection is housed in a former monastery, but is well displayed and artfully lighted. ⊠ *Via Fiandrini* ☎*0544/34424* ✆*€4* ⊙*Tues.–Sun. 8:30–7:30.*

❺ Tomba di Dante. The tomb of Dante is in a small neoclassical building next door to the large church of St. Francis. Exiled from his native Florence, the author of *The Divine Comedy* died here in 1321. The Florentines have been trying to reclaim their famous son for hundreds of years, but the Ravennans refuse to give him up, arguing that since Florence did not welcome Dante in life it does not deserve him in death. ⊠*Via Dante Alighieri 4 and 9* ☎*0544/30252* ✆*Tomb free, museum €2* ⊙*Tomb: daily 9–noon and 2–5. Museum: Tues.–Sun. 9–noon.*

OFF THE BEATEN PATH

Sant'Apollinare in Classe. This church, about 5 km (3 mi) southeast of Ravenna, is landlocked now, but when it was built it stood in the center of the busy shipping port known to the ancient Romans as Classis. The arch above and the area around the high altar are rich with mosaics. Those on the arch, older than the ones behind it, are considered superior. They show Christ in Judgment and the 12 lambs of Christianity leaving the cities of Jerusalem and Bethlehem. In the apse is the figure of Sant'Apollinare himself, a bishop of Ravenna, and above him is a magnificent Transfiguration against blazing green grass, animals in skewed perspective, and flowers. ⊠ *Via Romea Sud, Classe* ☎*0544/473569* ✆*€3* ⊙*Mon.–Sat. 8:30–7:30, Sun. 1–7:30.*

9

WHERE TO EAT

$$ ✕ **Bella Venezia.** Graceful low archways lead into this attractive pink-and-white restaurant's two small, brightly lighted dining rooms. Try the beans with olive oil and *bottarga* (cured roe) or the owner's special risotto with butter, Parmesan, cured ham, mushrooms, and peas to start. For the second course, the *fegato alla Veneziana* (grilled liver with onions) is a good choice. The outdoor garden is quite pleasant in

season. ⊠ *Via IV Novembre 16* ☎ *0544/212746* ⊕ *www.bellavenezia.
it* ═ *AE, DC, MC, V* ⊘ *Closed Sun. and 3 wks in Dec. and Jan.*

$$ ✕ **Locanda del Melarancio.** This contemporary inn, in a palazzo in the
★ heart of the centro storico, has a pub on the ground floor, a restaurant on
the second, and rooms on the third. Decor is minimalist without being
stark, and modern artwork on the walls doesn't take away from the
warm, traditional feeling. So, too, for the menu, which makes brilliant
use of modern techniques to harness traditional Romagnan ingredients:
formaggio di fossa (cheese aged in a cave) is made into a *sformato* (like
a firm mousse) with julienned salami, honey, and balsamic vinegar,
while cappellacci are filled with mascarpone and truffle under a sauce
of porcini mushrooms. ⊠ *Via Mentana 33* ☎ *0544/215258* ⊕ *www.
locandadelmelarancio.it* ═ *AE, DC, MC, V.*

$ ✕ **Ca' de Ven.** A vaulted wine cellar in the heart of the old city, the Ca'
★ de Ven is great for a hearty meal. You sit at long tables with other din-
ers and feast on platters of delicious cold cuts, flat breads, and cold,
heady white wine. The tortelli *di radicchio e pecorino* (stuffed with
radicchio and goat cheese) makes the best first course. ⊠ *Via C. Ricci
24* ☎ *0544/30163* ═ *AE, DC, MC, V* ⊘ *Closed Mon., 3 wks in Jan.
and Feb., and 1st wk in June.*

$ ✕ **La Gardèla.** The kitchen seems to operate with an otherworldly effi-
ciency, making this bright, bustling downtown restaurant extremely
popular with the local business crowd—especially at lunch (always a
good sign). The place is best for classics like tagliatelle al ragù and Adri-
atic fish, such as *sardoncini* (tiny sardines, breaded and fried). ⊠ *Via
Ponte Marino 3* ☎ *0544/217147* ═ *AE, DC, MC, V* ⊘ *Closed Thurs.
and 10 days in Jan.*

WHERE TO STAY

$$–$$$ ⊡ **Hotel Bisanzio.** Steps from San Vitale and the Tomb of Galla Pla-
cidia, this Best Western hotel is the most convenient lodging for mosaic
enthusiasts. The exterior is drab, but rooms are comfortable and mod-
ern; the lobby's Florentine lamps add a touch of style. Ask to be on
the top floor and you may get a view of the basilica. **Pro:** No-smok-
ing rooms. **Cons:** Part of a chain, popular with groups. ⊠ *Via Salara
30, 48100* ☎ *0544/217111* ⊟ *0544/32539* ⊕ *www.bisanziohotel.com*
⇦ *38 rooms* ⟁ *In-room: safe, Wi-Fi. In-hotel: restaurant, bar, public
Wi-Fi, parking (fee), some pets allowed* ═ *AE, DC, MC, V* ⊡ *BP.*

$–$$ ⊡ **Sant'Andrea.** This simple B&B offers an absolutely prime location,
steps away from the Basilica di San Vitale. It's like staying in a well-
appointed house—rooms are big, bright, and clean, done up in primary
colors. The lobby is decked out with homey furniture, and breakfast
can be taken in the breakfast room, or in the garden in good weather.
Bathrooms are spotless and modern. A suite only costs €30 extra and
can accommodate a family of four or five. **Pros:** Children under 12
sleep free, breakfast outdoors when it's warm, discounts for stays of
three nights or more. **Cons:** Can get a little noisy, groups favor the
place. ⊠ *Via Carlo Cattaneo 33, 48100* ☎ *0544/215564* ⊕ *www.
santandreahotel.com* ⇦ *10 rooms, 2 suites* ⟁ *In-room: safe. In-hotel:
bar, parking (fee)* ═ *AE, DC, MC, V* ⊡ *BP.*

$ ☷   **Hotel Centrale Byron.** Tranquility is assured here in the center of Ravenna's old town, because it's in a pedestrian zone. The old-fashioned, well-managed hotel has spotless if uninspired rooms. You can drop off your luggage at the door, but you have to park your car in one of the nearby garages or lots. **Pro:** Plenty of triples and quads—great for families and friends. **Con:** Rooms are nothing special ⊠ *Via IV Novembre 14, 48100* ☎ *0544/212225* 🖶 *0544/34114* ⊕ *www.hotel-byron.com* ⬐ *54 rooms* ⚷ *In-room: safe. In-hotel: bar, parking (fee)* ⊟ *AE, DC, MC, V* ⦿ *BP.*

$ ☷   **Hotel Ravenna.** A functional stopover near the train station, the Ravenna is still only a few minutes' walk from the center. This modern hotel has smallish rooms. Service is friendly and helpful. **Pros:** Good budget option, near train station. **Con:** Rooms are short on character. ⊠ *Via Maroncelli 12, 48100* ☎ *0544/212204* 🖶 *0544/212077* ⊕ *www.hotelravenna.ra.it* ⬐ *26 rooms* ⚷ *In-hotel: bar, no elevator, parking (fee)* ⊟ *MC, V* ⦿ *BP.*

NIGHTLIFE & THE ARTS

Friday nights from June to August bring **Mosaics by Night,** when the Byzantine mosaic masterpieces in town are illuminated. The event is also held on certain Tuesdays; to check, call the tourist office, which also offers guided tours. The **Ravenna Festival** is a musical extravaganza held every year in June and July. Orchestras from all over the world come to perform in Ravenna's churches and theaters.

9

Part III: Central Italy

WHAT'S WHERE

1 Florence. It's hard to think of a place that's more closely linked to one specific historical period than Florence. In the 15th century the city was at the center of an artistic revolution, later labeled the Renaissance, that changed the way people see the world. Five hundred years later the Renaissance remains the reason people see Florence—the abundance of treasures is mind-boggling. Present-day Florentines have a somewhat uneasy relationship with their city's past; the never-ending stream of tourists is something they seem to tolerate more often than embrace. Still, they pride themselves on living well, and that means you'll find exceptional restaurants and first-rate shopping to go with all that amazing art.

2 Tuscany. Nature outdid herself in Tuscany, the central Italian region that has Florence as its principal city. Descriptions and photographs can't do the landscape justice—the hills, draped with woods, vineyards, and olive groves, may not have the drama of mountain peaks or waves crashing on the shore, yet there's an undeniable magic about them. Aside from Florence, Tuscany has several midsize cities that are well worth visiting, but the great-

est appeal lies in the smaller towns, often perched on hilltops and not significantly altered since the Middle Ages. Despite its popularity with fellow travelers, Tuscany remains a place you can escape to.

3 Umbria & the Marches. Umbria was the first region in Italy to be dubbed by travel writers "the next Tuscany," a term that's since been applied to locations all up and down the boot. There's some sense to the comparison—like Tuscany, Umbria has beautiful rolling hills with attractive old towns sitting on top of them. There's no city with the size or significance of Florence, but a number of the smaller cities, particularly Assisi, Perugia, Spoleto, and Orvieto, have lots to hold your interest. Umbria's Roman past is much in evidence—expect to see Roman villas, aqueducts, theaters, walls, and temples. To the east, in the region of the Marches, the main draw is the town of Urbino, where the Ducal Palace reveals more about the artistic energy of the Renaissance than a shelf of history books.

CENTRAL ITALY PLANNER

Biking & Hiking

In spring, summer, and fall, bicyclists pedaling up and down Tuscany's hills are as much a part of the landscape as the cypress trees. Many are on weeklong organized tours, but it's also possible to rent bikes for jaunts in the countryside or to join afternoon or daylong rides.

Hiking is a simpler matter: all you need is a pair of sturdy shoes. The tourist information offices in most towns can direct you on walks ranging from an hour to a full day in duration. You can also sign on for more elaborate guided tours.

Italy by Design (✉ Via delle Lame 52, Florence ☎ 055/6532381 ⊕ www.italy bydesign.com) provides you with bikes and hand-tailored itineraries, and will pick you up and drop you off at your hotel. The Massachusetts-based **Ciclismo Classico** (✉ 30 Marathon St, Arlington, MA 02474 ☎ 800/866-7314 ⊕ www. ciclismoclassico.com) offers guided bike tours throughout Italy. **Country Walkers** (✉ Box 180, Waterbury, VT 05676 ☎ 802/244-1387 or 800/464-9255 ⊕ www.countrywalkers. com) conducts weeklong (and longer) trips throughout Tuscany in spring and fall

Getting Here

Most flights to Tuscany originating in the United States stop either in Rome, London, Paris, or Frankfurt, and then connect to Florence's small **Aeroporto A. Vespucci** (commonly called **Peretola**), or to Pisa's **Aeroporto Galileo Galilei**. The only exception at this writing is Delta's New York/JFK flight going directly into Pisa.

There are several other alternatives for getting into the region. If you want to start your trip in Umbria, it works to fly into Rome's **Aeroporto Leonardo da Vinci** (commonly called Fiumincino); from Rome it's an hour by train or an hour and a half by car to reach the lovely town of Orvieto. You can also fly to Milan and pick up a connecting flight to Pisa, Florence, or Perugia. Finally, from May through September (as of this writing), the carrier Eurofly has nonstop flights between New York and Bologna, which is an hour by train or an hour and a half by car from Florence.

Typical Travel Times

	Hours by Car	Hours by Train
Florence–Rome	3:00	1:45
Florence –Venice	3:30	2:45
Florence–Siena	1:00	1:30
Florence–Pisa	1:30	1:20
Florence –Perugia	1:45	2:00
Siena–Perugia	1:30	3:00
Perugia–Assisi	0:30	0:20
Perugia–Orvieto	1:15	1:45
Assisi–Rome	2:15	2:00
Orvieto–Rome	1:30	1:00

On the Calendar: Events & Festivals

Several major events mark the calendar in Tuscany and Umbria, drawing attendees from around the world.

For the two weeks leading up to Lent, the town of **Viareggio along the coast of northwest Tuscany** is given over to the sometimes-bawdy revels of **Carnevale.** The festivities are second only to Venice's in size and lavishness.

Twice a year, on July 2 and August 16, Siena goes medieval with the **Palio,** a bareback horse race around its main square. It's more than a race—it's a celebration of tradition and culture dating back 1,000 years.

For two weeks in late June and early July, stars from the worlds of classical music and the performing arts make their way to the Umbria hill town of Spoleto to take part in the **Festival dei Due Mondi.**

While the big events are impressive, the calendar also overflows with smaller traditional *sagre* (festivals or fairs). You'll find them in towns of every size, January through December, with names like Sagra del Cinghiale (Wild Boar Festival), Sagra della Castagna (Chestnut Festival), and Festa del Fungo (Mushroom Festival). There's the Befanate (celebrating Italy's witch-like Santa equivalent) in Grossetto during Epiphany, the Teatro Povero (a folk theater production) in Monticchiello in July, and, throughout the southern Tuscany on the night of April 30, they perform the Canta il Maggio (Songs for Spring).

Sagre are fun, and there's often delicious traditionally prepared food to be had. You can check with the local or regional tourist information offices for the dates and times of any sagre that happen to coincide with your visit.

How's the Weather?

Throughout Tuscany and Umbria, the best times to visit are spring and fall. Days are warm, nights are cool, and though there are still tourists, the crowds are smaller. In the countryside, the scenery is gorgeous, with abundant greenery and flowers in spring, and burnished leaves in autumn.

July and August are the most popular times to visit. Note, though, that the heat is often oppressive and mosquitoes are prevalent. Try to start your days early and visit major sights first to beat the crowds and the midday sun. For relief from the heat, head to the mountains of the Garfagnana, where hiking is spectacular, or hit the beach at resort towns such as Forte dei Marmi and Viareggio, along the Maremma coast, or on the island of Elba.

November through March, you might wonder who invented the term "sunny Italy." The panoramas are still beautiful, even with overcast skies, frequent rain, and occasional snow. In winter, Florence benefits from shorter museum lines and less competition for restaurant tables. Outside the cities, though, many hotels and restaurants close for the season.

CENTRAL ITALY TOP ATTRACTIONS

Galleria degli Uffizi, Florence

(A) Florence has many museums, but the Uffizi is king. Walking its halls is like stepping into an art history textbook, except here you're looking at the genuine article—masterpieces by Leonardo, Michelangelo, Raphael, Botticelli, Caravaggio, and dozens of other luminaries. When planning your visit, make a point to reserve a ticket in advance. (⇨ Chapter 10.)

Duomo, Florence

(B) The Cathedral of Santa Maria del Fiore, commonly known as the Duomo, is Florence's most distinctive landmark, sitting at the very heart of the city and towering over the neighboring rooftops. Its massive dome is one of the world's great engineering masterpieces. For an up-close look, you can climb the 463 steps to the top—then gaze out at the city beneath you. (⇨ Chapter 10.)

Leaning Tower, Pisa

(C) This tower may be too famous for its own good (it's one of Italy's most popular tourist attractions), but there's something undeniably appealing about its perilous tilt, and climbing to the top is a kick. The square on which it sits, known as the Campo dei Miracoli, has a majestic beauty that no quantity of tourists can diminish. (⇨ Chapter 11.)

Piazza del Campo, Siena

(D) The sloping, fan-shaped square in the heart of Siena is one of the best places in Italy to engage in the distinctly Italian activity of hanging out and people-watching. The surrounding Palazzo Vecchio and Torre del Mangia are first-rate sights. (⇨ Chapter 11.)

San Gimignano, Central Tuscany

(E) This classic Tuscan hill town has been dubbed a "medieval Manhattan" because of its numerous towers, built by

noble families of the time, each striving to outdo its neighbors. The streets fill with tour groups during the day, but if you stick around till sunset the crowds diminish and you see the town at its most beautiful. (⇨ Chapter 11.)

Abbazia di Sant'Antimo, Southern Tuscany

In a peaceful valley, surrounded by gently rolling hills, olive trees, and thick oak woods, Sant'Antimo is one of Italy's most beautifully situated abbeys—and a great "off the beaten path" destination. Stick around for mass and you'll hear the halls resound with Gregorian chants. (⇨ Chapter 11.)

Palazzo Ducale, Urbino, the Marches

(F) East of Umbria in the Marches region, Urbino is a college town in the Italian style—meaning its small but prestigious university dates to the 15th century. The highlight here is the Palazzo Ducale, a palace that exemplifies the Renaissance ideals of grace and harmony. (⇨ Chapter 12.)

Basilica di San Francesco, Assisi

(G) The basilica, built to honor Saint Francis, consists of two great churches—one Romanesque, fittingly solemn with its low ceilings and guttering candles; the other Gothic, with soaring arches and stained-glass windows (the first in Italy). They're both filled with some of Europe's finest frescoes. (⇨ Chapter 12.)

Duomo, Orvieto

(H) The facade of Orvieto's monumental Duomo contains a bas-relief masterpiece depicting the stories of the Creation and the Last Judgment (with the horrors of hell shown in striking detail). Inside, there's more glorious gore in the right transept, frescoed with Lucca Signorelli's *Stories of the Antichrist and the Last Judgment.* (⇨ Chapter 12.)

CENTRAL ITALY TOP EXPERIENCES

The View from Florence's Piazzale Michelangelo

One of the best ways to introduce yourself to Florence is by walking up to this square on the hill south of the Arno. From here you can take in the whole city, and much of the surrounding countryside, in one spectacular vista. To extend the experience, linger at one of the outdoor cafés, and for the finest view of all, time your visit to correspond with sunset.

Strolling the Ramparts of Lucca

Lucca, 80 km (50 mi) west of Florence, isn't situated on a hilltop in the way commonly associated with Tuscan towns, and it doesn't have quite the abundance of art treasures that you find in Siena or Pisa (to say nothing of Florence). Yet for many visitors, Lucca is a favorite Tuscan destination, and the source of its appeal has everything to do with its ramparts. These hulking barricades have surrounded the city center since the 17th century; built as a source of security, they now act as an elevated, oval park, complete with walkways, picnic areas, grass, and trees. The citizens of Lucca spend much of their spare time here, strolling, biking, and lounging, oblivious to the novelty of their situation but clearly happy with it.

Taking the Waters at a Tuscan Spa

Tuscany is dotted throughout with small *terme* (thermal baths), where hot water flows from natural springs deep beneath the earth's surface. It's been believed for millennia that these waters have the power to cure whatever ails you; although their medicinal power may be questionable, that doesn't keep a dip from being an extremely pleasant way to spend an afternoon. In northwest Tuscany, you can take the waters at Montecatini Terme (made famous as a setting for Fellini's 8½ and seemingly little changed since then) or Bagni di Lucca (which had its heyday in the era of the 19th-century Romantic poets). To the south, Saturnia is the biggest draw, along with the more humble Chianiano Terme and Bagno Vignoni.

Wine-tasting in Chianti

The gorgeous hills of the Chianti region, between Florence and Siena, produce exceptional wines, and they never taste better than when sampled on their home turf. Many Chianti vineyards are visitor-friendly, but the logistics of a visit are different from what you may have experienced in other wine regions. If you just drop in, you're likely to get a tasting, but for a tour you usually need to make an appointment several days ahead of time. The upside is, your tour may end up being a half day of full emersion—including extended conversation with the wine-makers and even a meal.

Hiking in the Footsteps of Saint Francis

Umbria, which bills itself as "Italy's Green Heart," is fantastic hiking country. Among the many options are two with a Franciscan twist: from the town of Cannara, 16 km (10 mi) south of Assisi, an easy half-hour walk leads to the fields of Pian d'Arca, where Saint Francis delivered his sermon to the birds. For slightly more demanding walks, you can follow the saint's path from Assisi to the Ermeo delle Carceri (Hermitage of Prisons), where Francis and his followers went to "imprison" themselves in prayer, and from here continue along the trails that crisscross Monte Subasio.

CENTRAL ITALY TODAY

The People

"And what greater fortune, if in Italy there were more Tuscans and fewer Italians," writes Curzio Malaparte (Prato, 1898—Rome, 1957) in his celebrated novel *Maledetti Toscani* (*Those Cursed Tuscans*). He's being provocative and arrogant, qualities of which his fellow Tuscans, especially the Florentines, are often accused.

The Florentines, for their own part, acknowledge all this with evident pride, even using the term *toscanaccio* (nasty Tuscan) to describe themselves. Many attempts have been made to identify Italy's regional differences. In the "you are what you eat" category is Marcella Hazan's description (in the introduction to *The Classic Italian Cookbook*) of the "careful and calculating" Florentine, "a man who knows the measure of all things," whose "cooking is an austerely composed play upon essential and unadorned themes."

Culture & Tradition

In the 1950s, when Italy's largely agrarian population began to move to the city, large numbers of farmhouses in Tuscany and Umbria were abandoned. The essentially feudal system of land usage, called *mezzadria* (sharecropping), also disappeared, taking with it a long and rich tradition of *contadino* (peasant) culture. The abandoned farmhouses were restored as summer homes or permanent residences for the numerous English, Germans, and Americans who began to buy here. In the 1970s and '80s, a sort of "folk revival" began, with interest developing in the festivals, food, popular theater, songs, and local religious events that were once a vital part of local tradition.

Politics

Astonishingly frequent storms may rock Italy's national political boat, but the situation in Tuscany and Umbria, at the local and regional levels, is comparatively even-keeled. Along with the Marches and the Emilia-Romagna regions, Tuscany and Umbria form the so-called red quadrilateral of central Italy, each with strong left-wing political inclinations that date to World War II. The names of Italy's political parties change with a frequency that boggles the minds of Italians and foreigners alike, but one thing remains certain: Tuscans and Umbrians will always side with the left.

The Economy

With Italy's boom years of the 1960s long since over, the more recent adoption of the euro (which seemed to double the price of many commodities overnight), and the relative stability of the average wage, many Tuscans and Umbrians are finding it difficult, as the catch-phrase has it, "to make it to the end of the month." Some blame the euro, some the politicians, others the employers, or the "system" as a whole.

With large Italian industrial companies struggling to compete in a global market (here, everyone blames the politicians), the new trend is to encourage small and mid-size business ventures that emphasize the concept "Made in Italy." Tuscany and Umbria have also tried to support the production of what are essentially traditional local goods: leather and shoes in Florence; textiles and clothing in Prato and Perugia; jewelry in Arezzo; paper products in northern Umbria and the valleys between Florence and Pisa; furniture in both regions.

A GREAT ITINERARY

Day 1: Florence

If you're coming in on an international flight, you'll probably settle in Florence in time for an afternoon stroll or siesta (depending on your jet-lag strategy) before dinner.

Logistics: On your flight in, read through the restaurant listings in this guide and begin anticipating the first dinner of your trip. Look for a place near your hotel, and when you arrive, reserve a table (or have your concierge do it for you). Making a meal the focus of your first day is a great way to ease into Italian life.

Day 2: Florence

Begin your morning at the **Uffizi Gallery** (reserve your ticket in advance). The extensive collection will occupy much of your morning. Next, take in the neighboring **Piazza della Signoria**, Florence's most impressive square, then head a few blocks north to the **Duomo.** There, check out Ghiberti's famous bronze doors on the **Battistero,** and work up an appetite by climbing the 463 steps to the cupola of Brunelleschi's splendid cathedral dome, atop which you'll experience a memorable vista. Spend the afternoon relaxing, shopping, and wandering Florence's medieval streets; or, if you're up for a more involved journey, head out to **Fiesole** to experience the ancient amphitheater and beautiful views of the Tuscan countryside.

Day 3: Florence

Keep the energy level up for your second full day in Florence, sticking with art and architecture for the morning, trying to see most of the following: Michelangelo's *David* at the **Galleria dell'Accademia,** the **Palazzo Pitti** and **Boboli Gardens,** the **Medici Chapels,** and the churches of **Santa Maria Novella** and **Santa Croce.** If it's a clear day, spend the afternoon on a trip up to the **Piazzale Michelangelo,** high on a hill above Florence, for sweeping views of the idyllic Florentine countryside. Given all the walking you've been doing, tonight would be a good night to recharge by trying the famed *bistecca alla fiorentina* (a grilled T-bone steak with olive oil).

Logistics: You can get up to the Piazzale Michelangelo by taxi or by taking Bus 7 from Santa Maria Novella. Otherwise, do your best to get around on foot; Florence is a brilliant city for walking.

Day 4: San Gimignano

Now that you've been appropriately introduced to the bewildering splendor of Renaissance Italy, it's time for a change of pace—and time for a rental car, which will enable you to see the back roads of Tuscany and Umbria. After breakfast, pick up your car, stop back at your hotel for your luggage, and head on out. On a good day the lazy drive from Florence to **San Gimignano,** past vineyards and typical Tuscan landscapes, is truly spectacular. The first thing that will hit you when you arrive at the hill town of San Gimignano will be the towers everywhere. The medieval skyscrapers of Italy, they also once occupied the role now played by Ferrais or Hummers: they were public displays of wealth. After finding your way to a hotel in the old town, set out on foot and check out the city's turrets and alleyways, doing your best to get away from the trinket shops, and later enjoying a leisurely dinner with the light but delicious local white wine, Vernaccia di San Gimignano.

Logistics: Some hotels might be able to coordinate with some rental-car agencies so that your car can be brought to your hotel for you. Once you navigate your way

out of Florence (no easy task), San Gimi-gnano is only 57 km (35 mi) to the south-west, so it's an easy drive; you could even take a detour on the SS222 (Strada Chian-tigiana), stop at one of the Chianti wine towns, and visit a winery along the way.

Day 5: Siena

In the morning, set out for nearby **Siena**, which is known worldwide for its Palio, a festival that culminates in an elaborate horse race competition among the 17 *contrade* (medieval neighborhoods) of the city. Because of the enormous influx of tourists, especially in summer, Siena isn't everyone's cup of tea, but it's still one of Tuscany's most impressive sights; however many tourists you have to bump elbows with, it's hard not to be blown away by the city's precious medieval streets and memorable fan-shaped **Piazza del Campo**. Not to be missed while in town are the spectacular **Duomo**, the **Battistero**, and the **Spedale di Santa Maria della Scala**, an old hospital and hostel that now contains an underground archaeological museum.

Logistics: It's a short and pretty drive from San Gimignano to Siena, but once there, parking can be a challenge. Look for the *stadio* (soccer stadium), where there's a parking lot that often has space.

Day 6: Arezzo/Cortona

Get an early start, because there's a lot to see today. From Siena you'll first head to **Arezzo**, home to the **Basilica di San Fran-cesco**, which contains important fres-coes by Piero della Francesca. Check out the **Piazza Grande** along with its beauti-ful Romanesque church of **Pieve di Santa Maria**. Try to do all of this before lunch, after which you'll head straight to **Cor-tona**. If Arezzo didn't capture your imagi-nation, Cortona, which dates to the 5th century BC, will. Olive trees and vineyards give way to a medieval hill town with views over ridiculously idyllic Tuscan countryside and Lake Trasimeno. Cor-tona is a town for walking and relaxing, not sightseeing, so enjoy yourself, wan-dering through the **Piazza della Repubblica** and **Piazza Signorelli**, perhaps doing a bit of shopping.

Logistics: Siena to Arezzo is 63 km (39 mi) on the E78. From Arezzo to Cortona, it's just 30 km (18 mi)—take S71.

Day 7: Assisi

Today you'll cross over into Umbria, a region just as beautiful as Tuscany but still less trodden. Yet another impossibly beautiful hill town, **Assisi**, is the home of Saint Francis and host to the many reli-gious pilgrims that come to celebrate

A GREAT ITINERARY

his legacy. Going here is the most treasured memory of many a traveler's visit to Italy. Upon arriving and checking into your lodging, head straight for the **Basilica di San Francesco,** which displays the coffin of Saint Francis and a bevy of unbelievable frescoes. From here take Via San Francesco to **Piazza del Commune** and see the **Tempio di Minerva** before a break for lunch. After lunch, see **San Rufino,** the town cathedral, and then go back through the piazza to Corso Mazzini and see **Santa Chiara.** If you're a true Franciscan, you could instead devote the afternoon to heading out 16 km (10 mi) to **Cannara,** where Saint Francis delivered his sermon to the birds.

Logistics: From Cortona take the S71 to the A1 autostrada toward Perugia. After about 40 km (24 mi), take the Assisi exit (E45), and it's another 14 km (8 mi) to Assisi.

Day 8: Spoleto
This morning will take you from a small Umbrian hill town to a slightly bigger one: **Spoleto,** a walled city that's home to a world-renowned arts festival each summer. But Spoleto needs no festival to be celebrated. Its **Duomo** is wonderful. Its fortress, **La Rocca,** is impressive. And the **Ponte delle Torri,** a 14th-century bridge that separates Spoleto from Monteluco, is a marvelous sight, traversing a gorge 260 feet below and built upon the foundations of a Roman aqueduct. See all these during the day, stopping for a light lunch of a *panino* (sandwich) or salad, saving your appetite for a serious last dinner in Italy: Umbrian cuisine is excellent everywhere, but Spoleto is a memorable culinary destination. Do your best to sample black truffles, a proud product of the region; they're delicious on pasta or meat.

AN ITINERARY TIP

Because of spotty train service to Tuscan hill towns, this itinerary is extremely difficult to complete without a car. Driving is easy and relaxing in the region, whose roads can be windy but are generally wide, well kept, well marked, and not too crowded. If you absolutely don't want to drive, buses are the best way to go, but you'll often have to change buses in hubs like Florence, and it would be best to cut out some of the smaller Tuscan hill towns and spend extra time in Siena and Spoleto.

Logistics: One school of thought would be to time your visit to Spoleto's world-renowned arts festival that runs from mid-June through mid-July. Another would be to do anything you can to avoid it. It all depends on your taste for big festivals and big crowds. The trip from Assisi to Spoleto is a pretty 47-km (29-mi) drive (S75 to the S3) that should take you less than an hour.

Day 9: Spoleto/Departure
It's a fair distance from Spoleto to the Florence airport, your point of departure. Depending on your comfort level with Italian driving, allow at least 2½ hours to reach Florence's airport.

Logistics: An alternative possibility would be to try to get a flight out of Perugia's tiny airport, which is a lot closer to Spoleto than Florence. It offers connections to Milan and Rome (Ciampino)—but not many. Otherwise, just get an early start and drive to Florence along the A1 autostrada.

Florence

WORD OF MOUTH

"Michelangelo, Dante, Galileo. Gelato, red wine, amazing food. Some of the most wonderful art and architecture. Firenze is a magical city (and where my fiancé and I got engaged). It is an absolute gem."

–Kristin

WELCOME TO FLORENCE

TOP REASONS TO GO

★ **Galleria degli Uffizi:** Italian Renaissance art doesn't get much better than this vast collection bequeathed to the city by the last Medici, Anna Maria Luisa.

★ **The dome of the Duomo:** Brunelleschi's work of engineering genius is the city's undisputed centerpiece.

★ **Michelangelo's David:** One look and you'll know why this is the Western world's most famous sculpture.

★ **The view from Piazzale Michelangelo:** From this perch the city is laid out before you. The colors at sunset heighten the experience.

★ **Piazza Santa Croce:** After you've had your fill of Renaissance masterpieces, hang out here and watch the world go by.

1 **The Duomo to the Ponte Vecchio.** You're in the heart of Florence here. Among the numerous highlights are the city's greatest museum **(the Uffizi)** and its most impressive square **(Piazza della Signoria).**

2 **San Lorenzo to the Accademia.** The blocks from the church of **San Lorenzo** to the **Accademia** museum bear the imprints of the Medici and of Michelangelo, culminating in his masterful *David.* Just to the north, the former convent of **San Marco** is an oasis decorated with ethereal frescoes.

3 **Santa Maria Novella to the Arno.** This part of town includes the train station, 15th-century palaces, and the city's most chic shopping street, **Via Tornabuoni.**

4 **Santa Croce.** The district centers around its namesake basilica, which is filled with the tombs of Renaissance luminaries. The area is also known for its leather shops, some of which have been in operation since the 16th century.

5 **The Oltrarno.** Across the Arno you encounter the massive Palazzo Pitti and the narrow streets of the **Santo Spirito** district, which is filled with artisans' workshops and antique stores. A climb to **Piazzale Michelangelo** gives you a spectacular view of the city.

Piazza del Duomo

Santa Croce Church

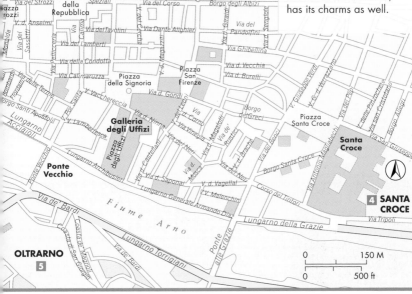

GETTING ORIENTED

The historic center of Florence is flat and compact—you could walk from one end to the other in half an hour. In the middle of everything is the Duomo, with its huge dome towering over the city's terra-cotta rooftops. Radiating out from the Duomo are Renaissance-era neighborhoods identified by their central churches and piazzas. Though the majority of sights are north of the Arno River, the area to the south, known as the Oltrarno, has its charms as well.

FLORENCE PLANNER

Avoiding an Art Hangover

Even for the most dedicated art enthusiast, trying to take in Florence's abundance of masterpieces can turn into a headache—there's just too much to see. Especially if you don't count yourself as an art lover, remember to pace yourself. Allow time to wander and follow your whims, and ignore any pangs of guilt if you'd rather relax in a café and watch the world go by than trudge on sore feet through another breathtaking palace or church.

Florence isn't a city that can be "done." It's a place you can return to again and again, confident there will always be more treasures to discover.

Piazza della Signoria

Making the Most of Your Time

With some planning, you can see Florence's most famous sights in a couple of days. Start off at the city's most awe-inspiring work of architecture, the **Duomo,** climbing to the top of the dome if you have the stamina. On the same piazza, check out Ghiberti's bronze doors at the **Battistero.** (They're actually high-quality copies; the Museo dell'Opera del Duomo has the originals.) Set aside the afternoon for the **Galleria degli Uffizi,** making sure to reserve tickets in advance.

On Day Two, visit Michelangelo's David in the **Galleria dell'Accademia**—reserve tickets here, too. Linger in the **Piazza della Signoria,** Florence's central square, where a copy of David stands in the spot the original occupied for centuries, then head east a couple of blocks to **Santa Croce,** the city's most artistically rich church. Double back and walk across Florence's landmark bridge, the **Ponte Vecchio.**

Do all that, and you'll have seen some great art, but you've just scratched the surface. If you have more time, put the **Bargello,** the **Museo di San Marco,** and the **Cappelle Medicee** at the top of your list. When you're ready for an art break, stroll through the **Boboli Gardens** or explore Florence's lively shopping scene, from the food stalls of the **Mercato Centrale** to the chic boutiques of the **Via Tornabuoni.**

Tourist Offices

The Florence tourist office, known as the APT (☎ 055/290832 ⊕ www.comune.firenze.it), has locations next to the Palazzo Medici-Riccardi, in the main train station, and around the corner from the Basilica di Santa Croce. The offices are generally open from 9 in the morning until 7 in the evening. The multilingual staff will give you directions (but usually not free maps) and the latest on happenings in the city. It's particularly worth a stop if you're interested in finding out about performing-arts events. The APT Web site is in Italian only.

Titian's *Venus of Urbino*

Florentine Hours

Florence's sights keep tricky hours. Some are closed on Wednesday, some on Monday, some on every other Monday. Quite a few shut their doors each day (or on most days) by 2 in the afternoon. Things get even more confusing on weekends. Make it a general rule to check the hours closely for any place you're planning to visit; if it's somewhere you have your heart set on seeing, it's worthwhile to call to confirm.

Here's a selection of major sights that might not be open when you'd expect—consult the sight listings within this chapter for the full details. And be aware that, as always, hours can and do change.

■ The **Uffizi** and the **Accademia** are both closed Monday. All but a few of the galleries at Palazzo Pitti are closed Monday as well.

■ The **Duomo** closes at 3:30 on Thursday (as opposed to 5:30 on other weekdays, 4:45 on weekends). The dome of the Duomo is closed on Sunday.

■ The **Battistero** is open from noon until 7, Monday through Saturday, and on Sunday from 8:30 to 2.

■ The **Bargello** closes at 1:50 PM, and is closed entirely on alternating Sundays and Mondays.

■ The **Cappelle Medicee** are closed on alternating Sundays and Mondays.

■ **Museo di San Marco** closes at 1:50 on weekdays but stays open until 7 on weekends—except for alternating Sundays and Mondays, when it's closed entirely.

■ **Palazzo Medici-Riccardi** is closed Wednesday.

With Reservations

At most times of day you'll see a line of people snaking around the Uffizi. They're waiting to buy tickets, and you don't want to be one of them.

Instead, call ahead for a reservation (☎055/294883; reservationists speak English). You'll be given a reservation number and a time of admission—the further in advance you call, the more time slots you'll have to choose from. Go to the museum's reservation door at the appointed hour, give the clerk your number, pick up your ticket, and go inside. You'll pay €4 for this privilege, but it's money well spent.

At this writing, an on-line reservation option has also been launched at ⊕*www.polo-museale.firenze.it; the booking process at this point is awkward, but it's likely to improve.*

Use the same reservation service to book tickets for the Galleria dell'Accademia, where lines rival those of the Uffizi. (Reservations can also be made for the Palazzo Pitti, the Bargello, and several other sights, but they aren't needed.) An alternative strategy is to check with your hotel—many will handle reservations.

GETTING HERE & AROUND

Getting Here by Car

Florence is connected to the north and south of Italy by the Autostrada del Sole (A1). It takes about 1½ hours of driving on scenic roads to get to Bologna (although heavy truck traffic over the Apennines often makes for slower going), about three hours to Rome, and 3 to 3½ hours to Milan. The Tyrrhenian Coast is an hour west on the A11.

Getting Here by Bus

Long-distance buses provide inexpensive if somewhat claustrophobic service between Florence and other cities in Italy and Europe. **Lazzi Eurolines** (⊠ *Via Mercadante 2, Santa Maria Novella* 🕾 *055/363041* ⊕ *www.lazzi.it*) and **SITA** (⊠ *Via Santa Caterina da Siena 17/r, Santa Maria Novella* 🕾 *055/214721* ⊕ *www.sita-on-line.it*) are the major lines; they have neatly divided up their routes, so there's little overlap.

Getting Here by Air

Florence's small **Aeroporto A. Vespucci** (✛ *10 km [6 mi] northwest of Florence* 🕾 *055/373498* ⊕ *www.aeroporto. firenze.it*), commonly called **Peretola**, is located just outside of town and receives flights from Milan, Rome, London, and Paris. To get into the city center from the airport by car, take the autostrada A11. Tickets for the local bus service into Florence are sold at the airport's second-floor bar—Bus 62 runs once an hour directly to the train station at Santa Maria Novella. The airport's bus shelter is beyond the parking lot.

Pisa's **Aeroporto Galileo Galilei** (✛ *12 km [7 mi] south of Pisa and 80 km [50 mi] west of Florence* 🕾 *050/849300* ⊕ *www.pisa-airport.com*) is the closest landing point with significant international service, including (at this writing) a few direct flights from the United States each week on Delta. It's a straight shot down SS67 to Florence. A train service connects Pisa's airport station with Santa Maria Novella, roughly a 1½-hour trip. Trains start running about 7 AM from the airport, 6 AM from Florence, and continue service every hour until about 7 PM from the airport, 4 PM from Florence.

For flight information, call the airport or **Florence Air Terminal** (⊠ *Stazione Centrale di Santa Maria Novella* 🕾 *055/216073*)—which, despite the misleading name, is simply an office at the Santa Maria Novella train station, around the corner from train tracks 1 and 2.

Getting Here by Train

Florence is on the principal Italian train route between most European capitals and Rome, and within Italy it is served frequently from Milan, Venice, and Rome by Intercity (IC) and nonstop Eurostar trains. **Stazione Centrale di Santa Maria Novella** (🕾 *892021* OK as is ⊕ *www.trenitalia.com*) is the main station and is in the center of town. Avoid trains that stop only at the Campo di Marte or Rifredi stations, which are not convenient to the city center.

Neptune Fountain,
Piazza della Signoria

Getting Around by Bus

Florence's flat, compact city center is made for walking, but when your feet get weary, you can use the efficient bus system, which includes small electric buses making the rounds in the center. Buses also climb to Piazzale Michelangelo and San Miniato south of the Arno.

Maps and timetables for local bus service are available for a small fee at the ATAF (Azienda Trasporti Area Fiorentina) booth next to the train station, or for free at visitor information offices. Tickets must be bought in advance from tobacco shops, newsstands, automatic ticket machines near main stops, or ATAF booths. The ticket must be canceled in the small validation machine immediately upon boarding.

You have several ticket options, all valid for one or more rides on all lines. A €1.20 ticket is good for one hour from the time it is first canceled. A multiple ticket—four tickets, each valid for 70 minutes—costs €4.50. A 24-hour tourist ticket costs €5. Two-, three-, and seven-day passes are also available.

Getting Around by Taxi

Taxis usually wait at stands throughout the city (in front of the train station and in Piazza della Repubblica, for example), or you can call for one (☎ *055/4390 or 055/4798OK as is*). The meter starts at €2.30, with a €3.60 minimum and extra charges at night, on Sunday, and for radio dispatch.

Getting Around by Bike & Moped

Brave souls (cycling in Florence is difficult at best) may rent bicycles at easy-to-spot locations at Fortezza da Basso, the Stazione Centrale di Santa Maria Novella, and Piazza Pitti. Otherwise, try **Alinari** (✉ *Via Guelfa 85/r, San Marco* ☎ *055/280500* ⊕ *www.alinarirental.com*). You'll be up against hordes of tourists and those pesky *motorini* (mopeds). (For a safer ride, try Le Cascine, a former Medici hunting ground turned into a large public park with paved pathways.) The historic center can be circumnavigated via bike paths lining the *viali*, the ring road surrounding the area. If you want to go native and rent a noisy Vespa (Italian for "wasp") or other make of motorcycle or *motorino*, you may do so at **Maxirent** (✉ *Borgo Ognissanti 155/r, Santa Maria Novella* ☎ *055/265420*) or **Massimo** (✉ *Via Campo d'Arrigo 16/r* ☎ *055/573689*). However unfashionable, helmets must be rented at either place, and by law are mandatory.

Getting Around by Car

An automobile in Florence is a major liability. If your itinerary includes parts of Italy where you'll want a car (such as Tuscany), pick the vehicle up on your way out of town.

EATING & DRINKING WELL IN FLORENCE

Food in Florence is not about sauces, foams, or fusion. Simply prepared meats, grilled or roasted, are the stars, and pair well with seasonal vegetables like artichokes, porcini, and cannellini beans. Bistecca's big here, but there's plenty more that tastes great on the grill, too.

Traditionalists (and many Florentines are) go for their gustatory pleasures in trattorie and osterie, places where décor is unimportant, place mats are mere paper, and service is often perfunctory. Culinary innovation comes slowly in this town, though some cutting-edge restaurants have been appearing, usually with young chefs who've traveled and worked outside Italy. Some of these places lack charm (many have an international, you-could-be-anywhere feel), their menus offer exciting, updated versions of Tuscan standards

By American standards, Florentines eat late: 1:30 or 2 is typical for lunch, and 9 for dinner. Consuming a primo, secondo, and dolce is largely a thing of the past, and no one looks askance if you don't order the whole nine yards. For lunch, many Florentines simply grab a panino and a glass of wine at a bar. Those opting for a simple trattoria lunch often order a plate of pasta and dessert.

STALE AND STELLAR

Florence lacks signature pasta and rice dishes, perhaps because the town's content to have raised frugality with bread to culinary craft. Stale bread is the basis for three classic Florentine primi: pappa al pomodoro, ribollita, and panzanella. "Pappa" is made with either fresh or canned tomatoes and that stale bread. Ribollita is a vegetable soup fortified with cavolo nero (sometimes called Tuscan kale elsewhere), cannellini beans, and thickened with bread. Panzanella, a summertime dish, is reconstituted Tuscan bread combined with tomatoes, cucumber, and basil. They all are greatly enhanced with a generous application of fragrant Tuscan olive oil.

A CLASSIC ANTIPASTO: CROSTINI DI FEGATINI

This beloved dish consists of a chicken liver spread, served warm or at room temperature, on toasted, garlic-rubbed bread. It can be served smooth, like a pâté, or in a rougher spread. It's made by sautéeing chicken livers with finely diced carrot and onion, enlivened with the addition of wine, broth, or Marsala reductions, and mashed anchovies and capers.

A CLASSIC SECONDO: BISTECCA FIORENTINA

The town's culinary pride and joy is a thick slab of beef, resembling a T-bone steak, from large white oxen called Chianina. The meat's slapped on the grill and served rare, sometimes with a pinch of salt. It's always seared on both sides, and just barely cooked inside (experts say five minutes per side, and then fifteen minutes with the bone sitting perpendicularly on the grill). To ask for it more well done is to incur disdain; some restaurants simply won't serve it any other way than rare.

A CLASSIC CONTORNO: CANNELLINI BEANS

Simply boiled, they provide the perfect accompaniment to a bistecca. The small white beans are best when they go straight from the garden into the pot. They should be annointed with a gener-

ous outpouring of Tuscan olive oil; the combination is oddly felicitous, and it goes a long way toward explaining why Tuscans are referred to as *mangiafagioli* (bean eaters) by other Italians..

A CLASSIC DOLCE: BISCOTTI DI PRATO

These are sometimes the only dessert on offer, and are more or less an afterthought to the glories that have proceeded them. "Biscotti" means twice-cooked (or, in this case, twice baked) hard almond cookies which soften considerably when dipped languidly into *vin santo* ("holy wine"), a sweet dessert wine, or into a simple *caffè*.

A CLASSIC WINE: CHIANTI CLASSICO

This blend from the region just south of Florence relies mainly on the local, hardy sangiovese grape; it's aged for at least one year before hitting the market. (*Riserve*—reserves—are aged at least an additional six months.) Chianti is usually the libation of choice for Florentines, and it pairs magnificently with grilled foods and seasonal vegetables. Traditionalists opt for the younger, fruitier (and usually less expensive) versions often served in straw flasks. You can sample *Chianti classico* all over town, and buy it in local *salumerie, enoteche,* and supermarkets.

10

Updated
by Patricia
Rucidlo

FLORENCE, THE CITY OF THE LILY, gave birth to the Renaissance and changed the way we see the world. For centuries it has captured the imagination of travelers, who have come seeking rooms with views and phenomenal art. Florence's is a subtle beauty—its staid, unprepossessing palaces built in local stone are not showy. They take on a certain magnificence when day breaks and when the sun sets; their muted colors glow in this light. A walk along the Arno offers views that don't quit and haven't much changed in 700 years; navigating Piazza Signoria, almost always packed with tourists and locals alike, requires patience. There's a reason why everyone seems to be here, however. It's the heart of the city, and home to the Uffizi—arguably the world's finest repository of Renaissance art.

Florence was "discovered" in the 1700s by upper-class northerners making the grand tour. It became a mecca for travelers, particularly the Romantics, who were inspired by the elegance of its palazzi and its artistic wealth. Today millions of modern visitors follow in their footsteps. When the sun sets over the Arno and, as Mark Twain described it, "overwhelms Florence with tides of color that make all the sharp lines dim and faint and turn the solid city to a city of dreams," it's hard not to fall under the city's spell.

THE DUOMO TO THE PONTE VECCHIO

The heart of Florence, stretching from the Piazza del Duomo south to the Arno, is as dense with artistic treasures as anyplace in the world. The churches, medieval towers, Renaissance palaces, and world-class museums and galleries contain some of the most outstanding aesthetic achievements of Western history.

Much of the *centro storico* (historic center) is closed to automobile traffic, but you still must dodge mopeds, cyclists, and masses of fellow tourists as you walk the narrow streets, especially in the area bounded by the Duomo, Piazza della Signoria, Galleria degli Uffizi, and Ponte Vecchio.

THE MAIN ATTRACTIONS

❺ Bargello. During the Renaissance, this building was headquarters for the
★ chief of police. It also was used as a prison, and the exterior served as a "most wanted" billboard: effigies of notorious criminals and Medici enemies were painted on its walls. Today it houses the **Museo Nazionale,** home to what is probably the finest collection of Renaissance sculpture in Italy. The concentration of masterworks by Michelangelo (1475–1564), Donatello (circa 1386–1466), and Benvenuto Cellini (1500–71) is remarkable; the works are distributed among an eclectic collection of arms, ceramics, and miniature bronzes, among other things. For Renaissance-art lovers, the Bargello is to sculpture what the Uffizi is to painting.

In 1401 Filippo Brunelleschi (1377–1446) and Lorenzo Ghiberti (circa 1378–1455) competed to earn the most prestigious commission of the day: the decoration of the north doors of the Baptistery in Piazza

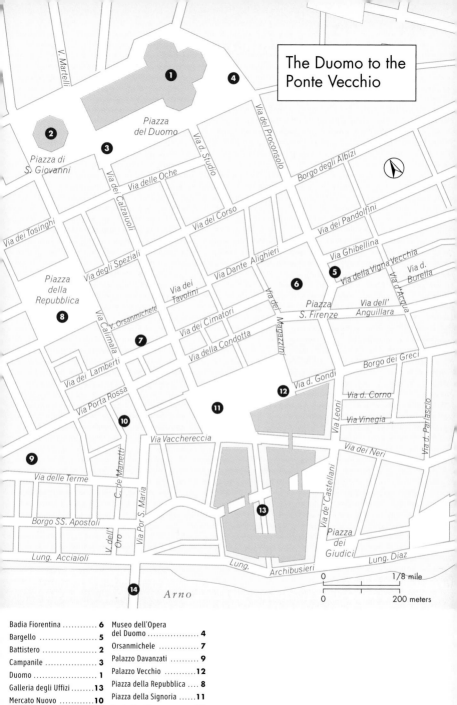

The Duomo to the Ponte Vecchio

V. Martelli

Piazza del Duomo

Via del Proconsolo

Via d. Studio

Piazza di S. Giovanni

Via delle Oche

Via dei Calzaiuoli

Borgo degli Albizi

Via dei Tosinghi

Via del Corso

Via dei Pandolfini

Via Ghibellina

Via degli Speziali

Via Dante Alighieri

Via della Vigna Vecchia

Via d. Burella

Piazza della Repubblica

Via dei Tavolini

V. Orsanmichele

Via dei Cimatori

Via dei Magazzini

Piazza S. Firenze

Via dell' Anguillara

Via d'Acqua

Via Calimala

Via della Condotta

Borgo dei Greci

Via dei Lamberti

Borgo dei Greci

Via d. Gondi

Via d. Corno

Via Porta Rossa

Via d. Pariascio

Via Leoni

Via Vinegia

Via Vacchereccia

Via dei Neri

C. de' Manetti

Via de' Castellani

Via delle Terme

Via Por S. Maria

Borgo SS. Apostoli

V. dell' Oro

Piazza dei Giudici

Lung. Acciaioli

Lung. Archibusieri

Lung. Diaz

Arno

0   1/8 mile

0   200 meters

FLORENCE THROUGH THE AGES

Guelph vs. Ghibelline. Though Florence can lay claim to a modest importance in the ancient world, it didn't come into its own until the Middle Ages. In the early 1200s, the city, like most of the rest of Italy, was rent by civic unrest. Two factions, the Guelphs and the Ghibellines, competed for power. The Guelphs supported the papacy, and the Ghibellines supported the Holy Roman Empire. Bloody battles—most notably one at Montaperti in 1260—tore Florence and other Italian cities apart. By the end of the 13th century the Guelphs ruled securely and the Ghibellines had been vanquished. This didn't end civic strife, however: the Guelphs split into the Whites and the Blacks for reasons still debated by historians. Dante, author of The *Divine Comedy*, was banished from Florence in 1301 because he was a White.

The Guilded Age. Local merchants had organized themselves into guilds by 1250. In that year they proclaimed themselves the "*primo popolo*" (literally, "first people"), making a landmark attempt at elective, republican rule. Though the episode lasted only 10 years, it constituted a breakthrough in Western history. Such a daring stance by the merchant class was a by-product of Florence's emergence as an economic powerhouse. Florentines were papal bankers; they instituted the system of international letters of credit; and the gold florin became the international standard of currency. With this economic strength came a building boom. Palaces and basilicas were erected, enlarged, or restructured. Sculptors such as Donatello and Ghiberti decorated them; painters such as Giotto and Botticelli frescoed their walls.

Mighty Medici. Though ostensibly a republic, Florence was blessed (or cursed) with one very powerful family, the Medici, who came to prominence in the 1430s and were the de facto rulers of Florence for several hundred years. It was under patriarch Cosimo il Vecchio (1389–1464) that the Medici's position in Florence was securely established. Florence's golden age occurred during the reign of his grandson Lorenzo de' Medici (1449–92). Lorenzo was not only an astute politician but also a highly educated man and a great patron of the arts. Called "Il Magnifico" (the Magnificent), he gathered around him poets, artists, philosophers, architects, and musicians.

Lorenzo's son, Piero (1471–1503), proved inept at handling the city's affairs. He was run out of town in 1494, and Florence briefly enjoyed its status as a republic while dominated by the Dominican friar Girolamo Savonarola (1452–98). After a decade of internal unrest, the republic fell and the Medici were recalled to power, but Florence never regained its former prestige. By the 1530s most of the major artistic talent had left the city—Michelangelo, for one, had settled in Rome. The now-ineffectual Medici, eventually attaining the title of grand dukes, remained nominally in power until the line died out in 1737, after which time Florence passed from the Austrians to the French and back again until the unification of Italy (1865–70), when it briefly became the capital under King Vittorio Emanuele II.

del Duomo. For the contest, each designed a bronze bas-relief panel depicting the sacrifice of Isaac; the panels are displayed together in the room devoted to the sculpture of Donatello, on the upper floor. The judges chose Ghiberti for the commission; see if you agree with their choice. ⊠ *Via del Proconsolo 4, Bargello* ☎ *055/294883* ⊕ *www.polomuseale.firenze.it* ⌨ *€4* ⊙ *Daily 8:15–1:50; closed 2nd and 4th Mon. of month and 1st, 3rd, and 5th Sun. of month.*

WORD OF MOUTH

"I think the Bargello might be the most underrated museum in Florence, if not Italy." –Jess

❷ Battistero *(Baptistery)*. The octagonal Baptistery is one of the supreme monuments of the Italian Romanesque style and one of Florence's oldest structures. Local legend has it that it was once a Roman temple dedicated to Mars; modern excavations, however, suggest that its foundations date from the fourth to fifth and the eighth to ninth centuries AD, well after the collapse of the Roman Empire. The round Romanesque arches on the exterior probably date from the 11th century. The interior dome mosaics from the beginning of the 14th century are justly renowned, but—glittering beauties though they are—they could never outshine the building's famed bronze Renaissance doors decorated with panels crafted by Lorenzo Ghiberti. The doors—or at least copies of them—on which Ghiberti worked most of his adult life (1403–52) are on the north and east sides of the Baptistery, and the Gothic panels on the south door were designed by Andrea Pisano (circa 1290–1348) in 1330. The original Ghiberti doors were removed to protect them from the effects of pollution and acid rain and have been beautifully restored; they are now on display in the Museo dell'Opera del Duomo.

Ghiberti's north doors depict scenes from the life of Christ; his later, east doors (dating from 1425–52), facing the Duomo facade, render scenes from the Old Testament. Both merit close examination, for they are very different in style and illustrate the artistic changes that marked the beginning of the Renaissance. Look at the far right panel of the middle row on the earlier (1403–24) north doors (*Jesus Calming the Waters*). Ghiberti here captured the chaos of a storm at sea with great skill and economy, but the artistic conventions he used are basically pre-Renaissance: Jesus is the most important figure, so he is the largest; the disciples are next in size, being next in importance; the ship on which they founder looks like a mere toy.

The exquisitely rendered panels on the east doors are larger, more expansive, more sweeping—and more convincing. The middle panel on the left-hand door tells the story of Jacob and Esau, and the various episodes of the story—the selling of the birthright, Isaac ordering Esau to go hunting, the blessing of Jacob, and so forth—have been merged into a single beautifully realized street scene. Ghiberti's use of perspective suggests depth: the background architecture looks far more credible than on the north-door panels, the figures in the foreground are grouped realistically, and the naturalism and grace of the poses (look at Esau's left leg and the dog next to him) have nothing to do

10

with the sacred message being conveyed. Although the religious content remains, the figures and their place in the natural world are given new prominence and are portrayed with a realism not seen in art since the fall of the Roman Empire nearly a thousand years before.

As a footnote to Ghiberti's panels, one small detail of the east doors is worth a special look. To the lower left of the Jacob and Esau panel, Ghiberti placed a tiny self-portrait bust. From either side, the portrait is extremely appealing—Ghiberti looks like everyone's favorite uncle—but the bust is carefully placed so that you can make direct eye contact with the tiny head from a single spot. When that contact is made, the impression of intelligent life—of *modern* intelligent life—is astonishing. It's no wonder that these doors received one of the most famous compliments in the history of art from an artist known to be notoriously stingy with praise: Michelangelo declared them so beautiful that they could serve as the Gates of Paradise. ⊠ *Piazza del Duomo* ☎ *055/2302885* ⊕ *www.operaduomo.firenze.it* ⊠ *€3* ☉ *Mon.–Sat. noon–7, Sun. 8:30–2;* 1st Sat. of month 8:30–2.

🔟 **Galleria degli Uffizi.** The venerable Uffizi Gallery occupies the top floor
Fodor'sChoice of the U-shaped **Palazzo degli Uffizi** fronting on the Arno, designed
★ by Giorgio Vasari (1511–74) in 1560 to hold the *uffizi* (administrative offices) of the Medici grand duke Cosimo I (1519–74). Later, the Medici installed their art collections here, creating what was Europe's first modern museum, open to the public (at first only by request) since 1591. Hard-core museum aficionados can pick up a complete guide to the collections at bookshops and newsstands.

Among the highlights are Paolo Uccello's *Battle of San Romano,* its brutal chaos of lances one of the finest visual metaphors for warfare ever captured in paint; the *Madonna and Child with Two Angels,* by Fra Filippo Lippi (1406–69), in which the impudent eye contact established by the angel would have been unthinkable prior to the Renaissance; the *Birth of Venus* and *Primavera* by Sandro Botticelli (1445–1510), the goddess of the former seeming to float on air and the fairy-tale charm of the latter exhibiting the painter's idiosyncratic genius at its zenith; the portraits of the Renaissance duke Federico da Montefeltro and his wife, Battista Sforza, by Piero della Francesca (circa 1420–92); the *Madonna of the Goldfinch* by Raphael (1483–1520), which, though darkened by time, captures an aching tenderness between mother and child; Michelangelo's *Doni Tondo*; a *Self-Portrait as an Old Man* by Rembrandt (1606–69); the *Venus of Urbino* by Titian (circa 1488/90–1576); and the splendid *Bacchus* by Caravaggio (circa 1571/72–1610). In the last two works, the approaches to myth and sexuality are diametrically opposed, to put it mildly. Six additional exhibition rooms opened in 2004, convoluting the way you exit the museum. Many of the more than 400 works now displayed would have been better left in storage, though a couple of Caravaggios at the very end of your hike out are well worth a look.

Late in the afternoon is the least crowded time to visit. For a €3 fee, advance tickets can be reserved by phone or, once in Florence, at the

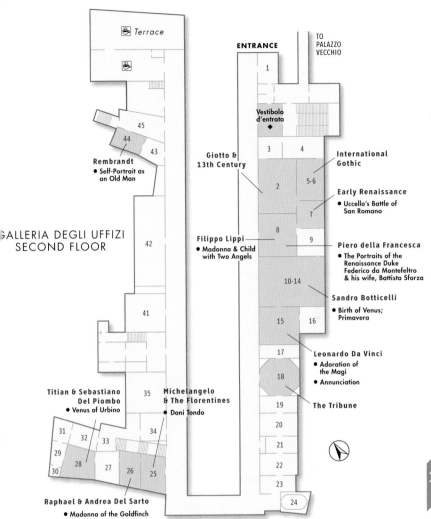

🧑‍🦽 Terrace

ENTRANCE

TO PALAZZO VECCHIO

1

Vestibolo d'entrata ◆

3   4

**Giotto &
13th Century**

2

5-6

**International
Gothic**

Early Renaissance
• Uccello's Battle of
San Romano

7

8

Filippo Lippi
• Madonna & Child
with Two Angels

9

Piero della Francesca
• The Portraits of the
Renaissance Duke
Federico da Montefeltro
& his wife, Battista Sforza

10-14

Sandro Botticelli
• Birth of Venus;
Primavera

15   16

17

Leonardo Da Vinci
• Adoration of
the Magi
• Annunciation

18

The Tribune

19

20

21

22

23

24

45

44   43

Rembrandt
• Self-Portrait as
an Old Man

GALLERIA DEGLI UFFIZI
SECOND FLOOR

42

41

35

**Michelangelo
& The Florentines**
• Doni Tondo

**Titian & Sebastiano
Del Piombo**
• Venus of Urbino

31
32   33
29
30   28   27   26   25

34

Raphael & Andrea Del Sarto
• Madonna of the Goldfinch

10

Uffizi reservation booth at least one day in advance of your visit. At this writing, an on-line reservation option has also been launched at ⊕*www.polomuseale.firenze.it; the booking process at this point is awkward, but it's likely to improve.* If you book by phone, remember to keep the confirmation number and take it with you to the door at the museum marked "Reserva-

tions." Usually you're ushered in almost immediately. Come with cash, because credit cards are not accepted (though you can use a credit card when booking on-line). When there's a special exhibit on, which is often, the base ticket price goes up to €10. ⊠*Piazzale degli Uffizi 6, Piazza della Signoria* ☎*055/23885 advance tickets* ⊠*Consorzio ITA, Piazza Pitti 1, 50121* ☎*055/294883* ⊕*www.uffizi.firenze.it; reservations www.polomuseale.firenze.it* 🖭*€6.50, reservation fee €4* ☉*Tues.–Sun. 8:15–6:50.*

⓫ ★ **Piazza della Signoria.** This is by far the most striking square in Florence. It was here, in 1497, that the famous "bonfire of the vanities" took place, when the fanatical friar Savonarola induced his followers to hurl their worldly goods into the flames; it was also here, a year later, that he was hanged as a heretic and, ironically, burned. A bronze plaque in the piazza pavement marks the exact spot of his execution.

The statues in the square and in the 14th-century **Loggia dei Lanzi** on the south side vary in quality. Cellini's famous bronze *Perseus* holding the severed head of Medusa is certainly the most important sculpture in the loggia. Other works here include *The Rape of the Sabine* and *Hercules and the Centaur,* both late-16th-century works by Giambologna (1529–1608), and in the back, a row of sober matrons dating from Roman times.

In the square, the Neptune Fountain, created between 1550 and 1575, takes something of a booby prize. It was created by Bartolomeo Ammannati, who considered it a failure himself. The Florentines call it Il Biancone, which may be translated as "the big white man" or "the big white lump." Giambologna's equestrian statue, to the left of the fountain, pays tribute to Grand Duke Cosimo I. Occupying the steps of the Palazzo Vecchio are a copy of Donatello's proud heraldic lion of Florence, the *Marzocco* (the original is now in the Bargello); a copy of Donatello's *Judith and Holofernes* (the original is in the Palazzo Vecchio); a copy of Michelangelo's *David* (the original is in the Galleria dell'Accademia); and Baccio Bandinelli's *Hercules* (1534). The Marzocco, the Judith, and the David were symbols of Florentine civic pride—the latter two subjects had stood up to their oppressors. They provided apt metaphors for the republic-loving Florentines, who often chafed at Medici hegemony.

⓮ **Ponte Vecchio** *(Old Bridge)*. This charmingly simple bridge is to Florence
★ what the Tower Bridge is to London. It was built in 1345 to replace an
earlier bridge that was swept away by flood, and its shops housed first
butchers, then grocers, blacksmiths, and other merchants. But in 1593
the Medici grand duke Ferdinand I (1549–1609), whose private corridor linking the Medici palace (Palazzo Pitti) with the Medici offices (the
Uffizi) crossed the bridge atop the shops, decided that all this plebeian
commerce under his feet was unseemly. So he threw out the butchers
and blacksmiths and installed 41 goldsmiths and eight jewelers. The
bridge has been devoted solely to these two trades ever since.

The **Corridoio Vasariano** (⊠ *Piazzale degli Uffizi 6, Piazza della Signoria*
☎ *055/23885 or 055/294883*), the private Medici corridor, was built
by Vasari in 1565. Though the ostensible reason for its construction
was one of security, it was more likely designed so that the Medici family wouldn't have to walk amid the commoners. The corridor is notoriously fickle with its operating hours; at this writing it was temporarily
closed, but it can often be visited by prior special arrangement. Call for
the most up-to-date details. Take a moment to study the Ponte Santa
Trinita, the next bridge downriver, from either the bridge or the corridor. It was designed by Bartolomeo Ammannati in 1567 (possibly from
sketches by Michelangelo), blown up by the retreating Germans during
World War II, and painstakingly reconstructed after the war. The view
from the Ponte Santa Trinita is beautiful, which might explain why so
many young lovers seem to hang out there.

ALSO WORTH SEEING

➏ **Badia Fiorentina.** Originally endowed by Willa, Marquess of Tuscany,
in 978, this ancient church is an interesting mélange of 13th-century,
Renaissance, baroque, and 18th-century architectural refurbishing. Its
graceful bell tower, best seen from the interior courtyard, is beautiful
for its unusual construction—a hexagonal tower built on a quadrangu-
lar base. The interior of the church (open Monday afternoon only) was
halfheartedly remodeled in the baroque style during the 17th century.
Three tombs by Mino da Fiesole (circa 1430–84) line the walls, including the *monumento funebre di Conte Ugo* (tomb sculpture of Count
Ugo), widely regarded as Mino's masterpiece. Executed in 1469–81, it
shows Mino at his most lyrical: the faces seem to be lit from within—no
small feat in marble. The best-known work of art here is the delicate
Vision of St. Bernard, by Filippino Lippi (circa 1457–1504), on the
left as you enter. The painting—one of Filippino's finest—is in superb
condition; note the Virgin Mary's hands, perhaps the most beautifully
rendered in the city. On the right side of the church, above the **cappella
di San Mauro,** is a monumental organ dating from 1558. Constructed
by Onofrio Zeffirini da Cortona (1510–86), it's largely intact but is
missing its 16th-century keyboard. ⊠ *Via Dante Alighieri 1, Bargello*
☎ *055/264402* 🖼 *Free* 🕙 *Mon. 3–6.*

10

Continued on page 571

THE DUOMO
FLORENCE'S BIGGEST MASTERPIECE

For all its monumental art and architecture, Florence has one undisputed centerpiece: the Cathedral of Santa Maria del Fiore, better known as the Duomo. Its cupola dominates the skyline, presiding over the city's rooftops like a red hen over her brood. Little wonder that when Florentines feel homesick, they say they have *"nostalgia del cupolone."*

The Duomo's construction began in 1296, following the design of Arnolfo da Cambio, Florence's greatest architect of the time. By modern standards, construction was slow and haphazard—it continued through the 14th and into the 15th century, with some dozen architects having a hand in the project.

In 1366 Neri di Fioravanti created a model for the hugely ambitious cupola: it was to be the largest dome in the world, surpassing Rome's Pantheon. But when the time finally came to build the dome in 1418, no one was sure how—or even if—it could be done. Florence was faced with a 143-ft hole in the roof of its cathedral, and one of the greatest challenges in the history of architecture.

Fortunately, local genius Filippo Brunelleschi was just the man for the job. Brunelleschi won the 1418 competition to design the dome, and for the next 18 years he oversaw its construction. The enormity of his achievement can hardly be overstated. Working on such a large scale (the dome weighs 37,000 tons and uses 4 million bricks) required him to invent hoists and cranes that were engineering marvels. A "dome within a dome" design and a novel herringbone bricklaying pattern were just two of the innovations used to establish structural integrity. Perhaps most remarkably, he executed the construction without a supporting wooden framework, which had previously been thought indispensable.

Brunelleschi designed the lantern atop the dome, but he died soon after its first stone was laid in 1446; it wouldn't be completed until 1461. Another 400 years passed before the Duomo received its façade, a 19th-century neo-Gothic creation.

DUOMO TIMELINE

1296 Work begins, following design by Arnolfo di Cambio.

1302 Arnolfo dies; work continues, with sporadic interruptions.

1331 Management of construction taken over by the Wool Merchants guild.

1334 Giotto appointed project overseer, designs campanile.

1337 Giotto dies; Andrea Pisano takes leadership role.

1348 The Black Plague; all work ceases.

1366 Vaulting on nave completed; Neri di Fioravanti makes model for dome.

1417 Drum for dome completed.

1418 Competition is held to design dome.

1420 Brunelleschi begins work on the dome.

1436 Dome completed.

1446 Construction of lantern begins; Brunelleschi dies.

1461 Michelozzo completes lantern.

1469 Gilt copper ball and cross added by Verrocchio.

1588 Original façade is torn down by Medici court.

1871 Emilio de Fabris wins competition to design new façade.

1887 Façade completed.

WHAT TO LOOK FOR INSIDE THE DUOMO

The interior of the Duomo is a fine example of Florentine Gothic with a beautiful marble floor, but the space feels strangely barren—a result of its great size and the fact that some of the best art has been moved to the nearby **Museo dell'Opera del Duomo.**

Notable among the works that remain are two towering equestrian frescoes of famous soldiers: *Niccolò da Tolentino* (1456), by Andrea del Castagno, and *Sir John Hawkwood* (1436), by Paolo Uccello. There's also fine terra-cotta work by Luca della Robbia. Ghiberti,

Brunelleschi's great rival, is responsible for much of the stained glass, as well as a reliquary urn with gorgeous reliefs. A vast fresco of the Last Judgment, painted by Vasari and Zuccari, covers the dome's interior. Brunelleschi had wanted mosaics to go there; it's a shame he didn't get his wish.

In the crypt beneath the cathedral, you can explore excavations of a Roman wall and an 11th-century cemetery; entry is near the first pier on the right. On the way down you pass Brunelleschi's modest tomb.

1. Entrance; stained glass by Ghiberti
2. Fresco of Niccolò da Tolentino by Andrea del Castagno
3. Fresco of John Hawkwood by Paolo Uccello
4. *Dante and the Divine Comedy* by Domenico di Michelino
5. Lunette: *Ascension* by Luca della Robbia
6. Above altar: two angels by Luca della Robbia. Below the altar: reliquary of St. Zenobius by Ghiberti.
7. Lunette: *Resurrection* by Luca della Robbia
8. Entrance to dome
9. Bust of Brunelleschi by Buggiano
10. Stairs to crypt
11. Campanile

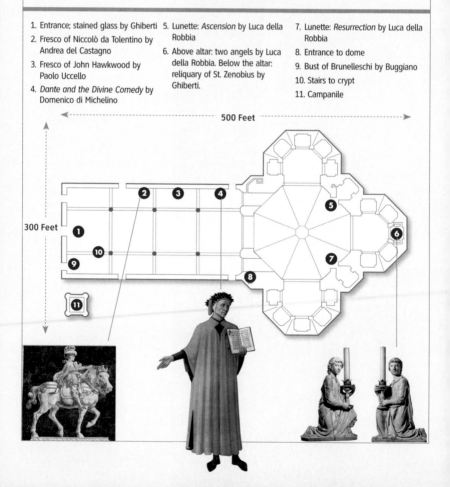

MAKING THE CLIMB

Climbing the 463 steps to the top of the dome is not for the faint of heart—or for the claustrophobic—but those who do it will be awarded a smashing view of Florence ❶. Keep in mind that the way up is also the way down, which means that while you're huffing and puffing in the ascent, people very close to you in a narrow staircase are making their way down ❷.

10

300 Feet

75 Feet

DUOMO GOOD TO KNOW

• Even first thing in the morning during high season (May through September), a line is likely to have formed to climb the dome. Expect an hour wait.

• For an alternative to the dome, consider climbing the less trafficked campanile, which gives you a view from on high of the dome itself.

• Dress code essentials: covered shoulders, no short shorts, and hats off upon entering.

✉ Piazza del Duomo
☎ 055/2302885
⊕ www.operaduomo.firenze.it
🎟 Free, crypt €3, cupola €6
🕐 Crypt: Mon.–Wed., Fri., Sun. 10–5; Thurs. 10–4:30; Sat. 10–5:45; first Sat. of month 10–3:30. Cupola: Weekdays 8:30–7, Sat. 8:30–5:40, 1st Sat. of month 8:30–4. Duomo: Mon.–Wed. and Fri. 10–5, Thurs. 10–4:30, Sat., 10–4:45, Sun 1:30–4:45, 1st Sat. of month 10–3:30.

BRUNELLESCHI vs. GHIBERTI
The Rivalry of Two Renaissance Geniuses

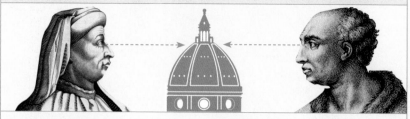

In Renaissance Florence, painters, sculptors, and architects competed for major commissions, with the winner earning the right to undertake a project that might occupy him (and keep him paid) for a decade or more. Stakes were high, and the resulting rivalries fierce—none more so than that between Filippo Brunelleschi and Lorenzo Ghiberti.

The two first clashed in 1401, for the commission to create the bronze doors of the Baptistery. When Ghiberti won, Brunelleschi took it hard, fleeing to Rome, where he would remain for 15 years. Their rematch came in 1418, over the design of the Duomo's cupola, with Brunelleschi triumphant. For the remainder of their lives, the two would miss no opportunity to belittle each other's work.

FILIPPO BRUNELLESCHI (1377–1446)

MASTERPIECE: The dome of Santa Maria del Fiore.

BEST FRIENDS: Donatello, whom he stayed with in Rome after losing the Baptistery doors competition; the Medici family, who rescued him from bankruptcy.

SIGNATURE TRAITS: Paranoid, secretive, bad tempered, practical joker, inept businessman.

SAVVIEST POLITICAL MOVE: Feigned sickness and left for Rome after his dome plans were publicly criticized by Ghiberti, who was second-in-command. The project proved too much for Ghiberti to manage on his own, and Brunelleschi returned triumphant.

MOST EMBARRASSING MOMENT: In 1434 he was imprisoned for two weeks for failure to pay a small guild fee. The humiliation might have been orchestrated by Ghiberti.

OTHER CAREER: Shipbuilder. He built a huge vessel, *Il Badalone*, to transport marble for the dome up the Arno. It sank on its first voyage.

INSPIRED: The dome of St. Peter's in Rome.

LORENZO GHIBERTI (1378–1455)

MASTERPIECE: *The Gates of Paradise,* the ten-paneled east doors of the Baptistery.

BEST FRIEND: Giovanni da Prato, an underling who wrote diatribes attacking the dome's design and Brunelleschi's character.

SIGNATURE TRAITS: Instigator, egoist, know-it-all, shrewd businessman.

SAVVIEST POLITICAL MOVE: During the Baptistery doors competition, he had an open studio and welcomed opinions on his work, while Brunelleschi labored behind closed doors.

OTHER CAREER: Collector of classical artifacts, historian.

INSPIRED: *The Gates of Hell* by Auguste Rodin.

The Gates of Paradise detail

❸ **Campanile.** The Gothic bell tower designed by Giotto (circa 1266–1337) is a soaring structure of multicolor marble originally decorated with reliefs that are now in the Museo dell'Opera del Duomo. A climb of 414 steps rewards you with a close-up of Brunelleschi's cupola on the Duomo next door and a sweeping view of the city. ✉ *Piazza del Duomo* ☎ *055/2302885* ⊕ *www.operaduomo.firenze.it* 💶 *€6* ⊗ *Daily 8:30–7:30.*

NEED A BREAK? Calling itself a "zupperia," La Canova di GustaVino (✉ *Via della Condotta 29/r, Piazza della Signoria* ☎ *055/2399806*) keeps several hearty, restorative soups on hand. Solid fare includes mixed cheese plates (both French and Italian), as well as *tomino con prosciutto* (mild cow's cheese, topped with thin slices of prosciutto) run under the broiler.

❿ **Mercato Nuovo** *(New Market).* The open-air loggia, built in 1551, teems with souvenir stands, but the real attraction is a copy of Pietro Tacca's bronze *Porcellino* (which translates as "little pig" despite the fact the animal is, in fact, a wild boar). The Porcellino is Florence's equivalent of the Trevi Fountain: put a coin in his mouth, and if it falls through the grate below (according to one interpretation), it means you'll return to Florence someday. The statue dates from around 1612, but the original version, in Palazzo Pitti, is an ancient Greek work. ✉ *Corner of Via Por Santa Maria and Via Porta Rossa, Piazza della Repubblica* ⊗ *Market: Tues.–Sat. 8–7, Mon. 1–7.*

❹ **Museo dell'Opera del Duomo** *(Cathedral Museum).* Ghiberti's original Baptistery door panels and the *cantorie* (choir loft) reliefs by Donatello and Luca della Robbia (1400–82) keep company with Donatello's *Mary Magdalene* and Michelangelo's *Pietà* (not to be confused with his more famous *Pietà* in St. Peter's in Rome). Renaissance sculpture is in part defined by its revolutionary realism, but in its palpable suffering Donatello's *Magdalene* goes beyond realism. Michelangelo's heart-wrenching *Pietà* was unfinished at his death; the female figure supporting the body of Christ on the left was added by Tiberio Calcagni (1532–65), and never has the difference between competence and genius been manifested so clearly. ✉ *Piazza del Duomo 9* ☎ *055/2302885* ⊕ *www.operaduomo.firenze.it* 💶 *€6* ⊗ *Mon.–Sat. 9–7:30, Sun. 9–1:40.*

10

❼ **Orsanmichele.** This multipurpose structure, which is closed indefinitely for restoration at this writing, began as an 8th-century oratory and then in 1290 was turned into an open-air loggia for selling grain. Destroyed by fire in 1304, it was rebuilt as a loggia-market. Between 1367 and 1380 the arcades were closed and two stories were added above; finally, at century's end it was turned into a church. Inside is a beautifully detailed 14th-century Gothic tabernacle by Andrea Orcagna (1308–68). The exterior niches contain sculptures dating from the early 1400s to the early 1600s by Donatello and Verrocchio (1435–88), among others, that were paid for by the guilds. Although it is a copy, Verrocchio's *Doubting Thomas* (circa 1470) is particularly deserving of attention. Here you see Christ, like the building's other figures, entirely framed within the niche, and St. Thomas standing on its bottom ledge, with his right foot outside the niche frame. This one detail, the positioning of a single foot, brings the whole composition to life. Most of the sculptures have since been replaced by copies; however, it's possible to see nearly all of them at the **Museo di Orsanmichele** (also closed at this writing for restoration). ⊠ *Via dei Calzaiuoli, Piazza della Repubblica* ☎*055/284944* ⌨*Free* ⊙*Closed for restoration.*

❾ Palazzo Davanzati. The prestigious Davanzati family owned this 14th-century palace in one of Florence's swankiest medieval neighborhoods. It reopened in May 2005 after a lengthy, 10-year restoration. The place is a delight, as you can wander through the surprisingly light-filled courtyard, and climb the steep stairs to the *piano nobile*, where the family did most of its living. The beautiful *Sala dei Pappagalli* (Parrot Room) is adorned with trompe l'oeil tapestries and gaily painted birds. Though some claim that these date from the 14th century, many art historians are much less sure. ⊠*Piazza Davanzati 13, Piazza della Repubblica* ☎*055/2388610* ⌨*Free* ⊙*Daily 8:15–1:50. Closed 1st, 3rd, and 5th Sun. of month; closed 2nd and 4th Mon. of month.*

⓬ Palazzo Vecchio *(Old Palace).* Florence's forbidding, fortresslike city hall was begun in 1299, presumably designed by Arnolfo di Cambio, and its massive bulk and towering campanile dominate Piazza della Signoria. It was built as a meeting place for the heads of the seven major guilds governing the city at the time; over the centuries it has served lesser purposes, but today it is once again City Hall. The interior courtyard is a good deal less severe, having been remodeled by Michelozzo (1396–1472) in 1453; a copy of Verrocchio's bronze *puttino* cherub), topping the central fountain, softens the space.

The main attraction is on the second floor: two adjoining rooms that supply one of the most startling contrasts in Florence. The first is the vast **Sala dei Cinquecento** (Room of the Five Hundred), named for the 500-member Great Council, the people's assembly established after the death of Lorenzo the Magnificent, that met here. The sala was decorated by Giorgio Vasari, around 1563–65, with huge—almost grotesquely huge—frescoes celebrating Florentine history; depictions of battles with nearby cities predominate. Continuing the martial theme, the sala also contains Michelangelo's *Victory*, intended for the never-completed tomb of Pope Julius II (1443–1513), plus other sculptures of decidedly lesser quality.

The second room is the little **Studiolo,** to the right of the sala's entrance. It was the study of Cosimo I's son, the melancholy Francesco I (1541–87). It was designed by Vasari and decorated by Vasari and Bronzino (1503–72) and is intimate, civilized, and filled with complex, questioning, allegorical art. ✉*Piazza della Signoria* ☎*055/2768465* 💶*€6* 🕙*Mon.–Wed. and Fri.–Sun. 9–7, Thurs. 9–2.*

❽ Piazza della Repubblica. The square marks the site of the ancient forum that was the core of the original Roman settlement. The street plan around the piazza still reflects the carefully plotted Roman military encampment. The Mercato Vecchio (Old Market), which had been here since the Middle Ages, was demolished and the current piazza was constructed between 1885 and 1895 as a neoclassical showpiece. The piazza is lined with outdoor cafés, affording an excellent opportunity for people-watching.

SAN LORENZO TO THE ACCADEMIA

A sculptor, painter, architect, and even a poet, Florentine native son Michelangelo was a consummate genius, and some of his finest creations remain in his hometown. The Biblioteca Medicea Laurenziana is perhaps his most fanciful work of architecture. A key to understanding Michelangelo's genius can be found in the magnificent Cappelle Medicee, where both his sculptural and architectural prowess can be clearly seen. Planned frescoes were never completed, sadly, for they would have shown in one space the artistic triple threat that he certainly was. The towering yet graceful *David,* his most famous work, resides in the Galleria dell'Accademia.

After visiting San Lorenzo, resist the temptation to explore the market that surrounds the church. You can always come back later, after the churches and museums have closed; the market is open until 7 PM. Note that the Museo di San Marco closes at 1:50 on weekdays.

THE MAIN ATTRACTIONS

❷ ★ Cappelle Medicee *(Medici Chapels).* This magnificent complex includes the **Cappella dei Principi,** the Medici chapel and mausoleum that was begun in 1605 and kept marble workers busy for several hundred years, and the **Sagrestia Nuova** (New Sacristy), designed by Michelangelo and so called to distinguish it from Brunelleschi's Sagrestia Vecchia (Old Sacristy) in San Lorenzo.

10

Michelangelo received the commission for the New Sacristy in 1520 from Cardinal Giulio de' Medici (1478–1534), who later became Pope Clement VII and who wanted a new burial chapel for his cousins Giuliano (1478–1534) and Lorenzo (1492–1519). The result was a tour de force of architecture and sculpture. Architecturally, Michelangelo was as original and inventive here as ever, but it is, quite properly, the powerful sculptural compositions of the sidewall tombs that dominate the room. The scheme is allegorical: on the tomb on the right are figures representing Day and Night, and on the tomb to the left are figures representing Dawn and Dusk; above them are idealized sculptures of the two men, usually interpreted to represent the active life and the contemplative life. But the allegorical meanings are secondary; what is most important is the intense presence of the sculptural figures and the force with which they hit the viewer. ✉*Piazza di Madonna degli Aldobrandini, San Lorenzo*

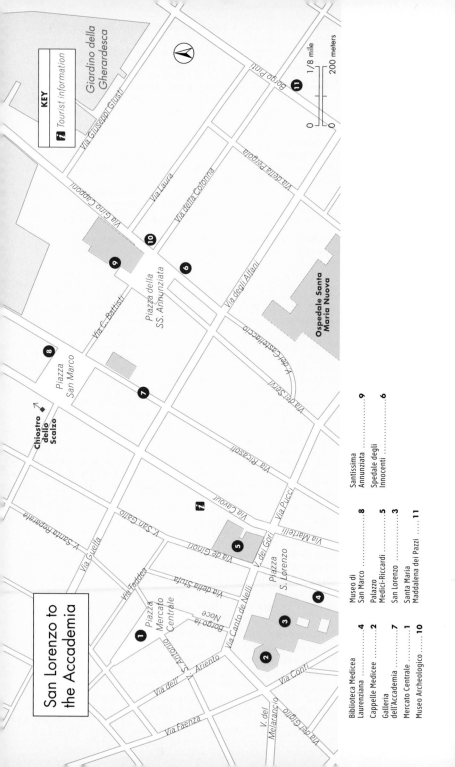

San Lorenzo to the Accademia

KEY

🛈 Tourist information

Giardino della Gherardesca

Ospedale Santa Maria Nuova

Chiostro dello Scalzo

Piazza San Marco

Piazza della SS. Annunziata

Piazza Mercato Centrale

Piazza S. Lorenzo

0   1/8 mile

0   200 meters

☎055/294883 reservations ☞€6 ⏰Daily 8:15–4:50. Closed 1st, 3rd, and 5th Mon. and 2nd and 4th Sun. of month.

7 Galleria dell'Accademia (Accademia Gallery). The collection of Florentine paintings, dating from the 13th to the 18th centuries, is largely unremarkable, but the sculptures by Michelangelo are worth the price of admission. The unfinished *Slaves*, fighting their way out of their marble prisons, were meant for the tomb of Michelangelo's overly demanding patron Pope Julius II (1443–1513). But the focal point is the original *David*, moved here from Piazza della Signoria in 1873. *David* was commissioned in 1501 by the Opera del Duomo (Cathedral Works Committee), which gave the 26-year-old sculptor a leftover block of marble that had been ruined by another artist. Michelangelo's success with the block was so dramatic that the city showered him with honors, and the Opera del Duomo voted to build him a house and a studio in which to live and work.

Today *David* is beset not by Goliath but by tourists, and seeing the statue at all—much less really studying it—can be a trial. Save yourself a long and tiresome wait in line by reserving tickets in advance. A Plexiglas barrier surrounds it, following a 1991 attack upon the sculpture by a hammer-wielding artist who, luckily, inflicted only a few minor nicks on the toes. A 2004 restoration in honor of his 500th birthday has, at the very least, cleaned up the sculpture. The statue is not quite what it seems. It is so poised and graceful and alert—so miraculously alive—that it is often considered the definitive embodiment of the ideals of the High Renaissance in sculpture. But its true place in the history of art is a bit more complicated.

As Michelangelo well knew, the Renaissance painting and sculpture that preceded his work were deeply concerned with ideal form. Perfection of proportion was the ever-sought Holy Grail; during the Renaissance, ideal proportion was equated with ideal beauty, and ideal beauty was equated with spiritual perfection. But *David*, despite its supremely calm and dignified pose, departs from these ideals. Michelangelo didn't give the statue perfect proportions. The head is slightly too large for the body, the arms are too large for the torso, and the hands are dramatically large for the arms. The work was originally commissioned to adorn the exterior of the Duomo and was intended to be seen from a distance and on high. Michelangelo knew exactly what he was doing, calculating that the perspective of the viewer would be such that, in order for the statue to appear proportioned, the upper body, head, and arms would have to be bigger as they are farther away from the viewer's line of vision. But he also did it to express and embody, as powerfully as possible in a single figure, an entire biblical story. David's hands *are* big, but so was Goliath, and these are the hands that slew him. ✉ *Via Ricasoli 60, San Marco* ☎*055/294883 reservations, 055/2388609 gallery* ☞€6.50, *reservation fee €3* ⏰*Tues.–Sun. 8:15–6:50.*

10

Florence's Trial by Fire

One of the most striking figures of Renaissance Florence was Girolamo Savonarola, a Dominican friar who, for a moment, captured the conscience of the city. In 1491 he became prior of the convent of San Marco, where he adopted a life of austerity and delivered sermons condemning Florence's excesses and the immorality of his fellow clergy. Following the death of Lorenzo de' Medici, Savonarola was instrumental in the formation of the republic of Florence, ruled by a representative council with Christ enthroned as monarch. In one of his most memorable acts, he urged Florentines to toss worldly possessions—from frilly dresses to Botticelli paintings—onto a "bonfire of the vanities" in Piazza della Signoria. Savonarola's antagonism toward church hierarchy led to his undoing: he was excommunicated in 1497, and the following year was hanged and burned on charges of heresy. Today, at the Museo di San Marco, you can visit Savonarola's cell and see his arresting portrait.

8 Museo di San Marco. A former Dominican convent adjacent to the church of San Marco now houses this museum, which contains many stunning works by Fra Angelico (circa 1400–55), the Dominican friar famous for his piety as well as for his painting. When the friars' cells were restructured between 1439 and 1444, he decorated many of them with frescoes meant to spur religious contemplation. His unostentatious and direct paintings exalt the simple beauties of the contemplative life. Fra Angelico's works are everywhere, from the friars' cells to the superb panel paintings on view in the museum. Don't miss the famous *Annunciation*, on the upper floor, and the works in the gallery off the cloister as you enter. Here you can see his beautiful *Last Judgment*; as usual, the tortures of the damned are far more inventive and interesting than the pleasures of the redeemed. ⊠ *Piazza San Marco 1* ☎ *055/2388608* ☎ *€4* ⊙ *Weekdays 8:15–1:50, weekends 8:15–6:50. Closed 1st, 3rd, and 5th Sun., and 2nd and 4th Mon. of month.*

3 San Lorenzo. Filippo Brunelleschi designed this basilica, as well as that of Santo Spirito in the Oltrarno, in the early 15th century. He never lived to see either finished. The two interiors are similar in design and effect and proclaim with ringing clarity the beginning of the Renaissance in architecture. San Lorenzo, however, has a grid of dark, inlaid marble lines on the floor, which considerably heightens the dramatic effect. The grid makes the rigorous geometry of the interior immediately visible and is an illuminating lesson on the laws of perspective. If you stand in the middle of the nave at the church entrance, on the line that stretches to the high altar, every element in the church—the grid, the nave columns, the side aisles, the coffered nave ceiling—seems to march inexorably toward a hypothetical vanishing point beyond the high altar, exactly as in a single-point-perspective painting. Brunelleschi's **Sagrestia Vecchia** (Old Sacristy) has stucco decorations by Donatello; it's at the end of the left transept. ⊠ *Piazza San Lorenzo* ☎ *055/2645144* ☎ *€2.50* ⊙ *Mon.–Sat. 10–5; Mar.–Oct., Sun. 1:30–5. Closed Sun. Nov.–Feb.*

ALSO WORTH SEEING

 Biblioteca Medicea Laurenziana *(Laurentian Library).* Michelangelo the architect was every bit as original as Michelangelo the sculptor. Unlike Brunelleschi (the architect of the Spedale degli Innocenti), however, he wasn't obsessed with proportion and perfect geometry. He was interested in experimentation and invention and in the expression of a personal vision at times highly idiosyncratic.

It was never more idiosyncratic than in the Laurentian Library, begun in 1524 and finished in 1568, and its famous **vestibolo.** This strangely shaped anteroom has had scholars scratching their heads for centuries. In a space more than two stories high, why did Michelangelo limit his use of columns and pilasters to the upper two-thirds of the wall? Why didn't he rest them on strong pedestals instead of on huge, decorative curlicue scrolls, which rob them of all visual support? Why did he recess them into the wall, which makes them look weaker still? The architectural elements here do not stand firm and strong and tall, as inside San Lorenzo, next door; instead, they seem to be pressed into the wall as if into putty, giving the room a soft, rubbery look that is one of the strangest effects ever achieved by classical architecture. It's almost as if Michelangelo intentionally flouted the conventions of the High Renaissance to see what kind of bizarre, mannered effect might result. His innovations were tremendously influential and produced a period of architectural experimentation. As his contemporary Giorgio Vasari put it, "Artisans have been infinitely and perpetually indebted to him because he broke the bonds and chains of a way of working that had become habitual by common usage."

The anteroom's staircase (best viewed straight-on), which emerges from the library with the visual force of an unstoppable lava flow, has been exempted from the criticism, however. In its highly sculptural conception and execution, it is quite simply one of the most original and fluid staircases in the world. ✉*Piazza San Lorenzo 9, entrance to the left of San Lorenzo* ☎*055/210760* ⊕*www.bml.firenze.sbn.it* ✍*Special exhibitions €5,* museum €3 ⊙*Sun.–Fri. 9–1.*

10

❶ **Mercato Centrale.** Some of the food at this huge, two-story market hall is remarkably exotic. The ground floor contains meat and cheese stalls, as well as some very good bars that have *panini* (sandwiches), and the second floor teems with vegetable stands. ✉*Piazza del Mercato Centrale, San Lorenzo* ☎*No phone* ⊙*Mon.–Sat. 7–2.*

❿ **Museo Archeologico** *(Archaeological Museum).* Of the Etruscan, Egyptian, and Greco-Roman antiquities here, the Etruscan collection is particularly notable—one of the largest in Italy. The famous bronze *Chimera* was discovered (without the tail, a reconstruction) in the 16th century. ✉*Via della Colonna 38, Santissima Annunziata* ☎*055/23575* ⊕*www. comune.firenze.it/soggetti/sat/didattica/museo.html* ✍*€4* ⊙*Mon. 2–7, Tues. and Thurs. 8:30–7, Wed. and Fri.–Sun. 8:30–2.*

❺ **Palazzo Medici-Riccardi.** The main attraction of this palace, begun in 1444 by Michelozzo for Cosimo de' Medici, is the interior chapel, the so-called **Cappella dei Magi** on the upper floor. Painted on its walls is

Benozzo Gozzoli's famous *Procession of the Magi,* finished in 1460 and celebrating both the birth of Christ and the greatness of the Medici family. Gozzoli wasn't a revolutionary painter and today is considered by some not quite first rate because of his technique, which was old-fashioned even for his day. Gozzoli's gift, however, was for entrancing the eye, not challenging the mind, and on those terms his success here is beyond question. The paintings are full of activity yet somehow frozen in time in a way that fails utterly as realism but succeeds triumphantly as soon as the demand for realism is set aside. Entering the chapel is like walking into the middle of a magnificently illustrated children's storybook, and this beauty makes it one of the most enjoyable rooms in the city. ⊠ *Via Cavour 1, San Lorenzo* ☎ *055/2760340* ▣ *€5* ⊗ *Thurs.–Tues. 9–7.*

⑪ Santa Maria Maddalena dei Pazzi. One of Florence's hidden treasures, a cool and composed *Crucifixion* by Perugino (circa 1445/50–1523), is in the chapter house of the monastery below this church. Here you can see the Virgin Mary and St. John the Evangelist with Mary Magdalene and Sts. Benedict and Bernard of Clairvaux posed against a simple but haunting landscape. The figure of Christ crucified occupies the center of this brilliantly hued fresco. Perugino's colors radiate—note the juxtaposition of the yellow-green cuff against the orange tones of the Magdalene's robe. ⊠ *Borgo Pinti 58, Santa Croce* ☎ *055/2478420* ▣ *Suggested €1* ⊗ *Mon.–Sat. 9–noon, 5–5:20, and 6–7; Sun. 9–noon and 5–6:20.*

⑨ Santissima Annunziata. Dating from the mid-13th century, this church was restructured in 1447 by Michelozzo, who gave it an uncommon (and lovely) entrance cloister with frescoes by Andrea del Sarto (1486–1530), Pontormo (1494–1556), and Rosso Fiorentino (1494–1540). The interior is a rarity for Florence: an overwhelming example of the baroque. But it's not really a fair example, because it's merely 17th-century baroque decoration applied willy-nilly to an earlier structure—exactly the sort of violent remodeling exercise that has given the baroque a bad name. The **Cappella dell'Annunziata,** immediately inside the entrance to the left, illustrates the point. The lower half, with its stately Corinthian columns and carved frieze bearing the Medici arms, was commissioned by Piero de' Medici in 1447; the upper half, with its erupting curves and impish sculpted cherubs, was added 200 years later. Each is effective in its own way, but together they serve only to prove that dignity is rarely comfortable wearing a party hat. Fifteenth-century-fresco enthusiasts should also note the very fine Holy Trinity with St. Jerome in the second chapel on the left. Done by Andrea del Castagno (circa 1421–57), it shows a wiry and emaciated St. Jerome with Paula and Eustochium, two of his closest followers. ⊠ *Piazza di Santissima Annunziata* ☎ *055/266186* ⊗ *Daily 7–12:30 and 4–6:30.*

⑥ Spedale degli Innocenti. Built by Brunelleschi in 1419 to serve as an orphanage, it takes the historical prize as the very first Renaissance building. Brunelleschi designed its portico with his usual rigor, building it out of the two shapes he considered mathematically (and therefore philosophically and aesthetically) perfect: the square and the circle.

Below the level of the arches, the portico encloses a row of perfect cubes; above the level of the arches, the portico encloses a row of intersecting hemispheres. The entire geometric scheme is articulated with Corinthian columns, capitals, and arches borrowed directly from antiquity. At the time he designed the portico, Brunelleschi was also designing the interior of San Lorenzo, using the same basic ideas. But because the portico was finished before San Lorenzo, the Spedale degli Innocenti can claim the honor of ushering in Renaissance architecture. The 10 ceramic medallions depicting swaddled infants that decorate the portico are by Andrea della Robbia (1435–1525/28), done in about 1487.

Within the Spedale degli Innocenti is a small museum, or **Pinacoteca** (€4 ۞ *Thurs.–Tues. 8:30–2*). Most of the objects are minor works by major artists, but well worth a look is Domenico Ghirlandaio's (1449–94) *Adorazione dei Magi (Adoration of the Magi)*, executed in 1488. His use of color, and his eye for flora and fauna, shows that art from north of the Alps made a great impression on him. ⊠ *Piazza di Santissima Annunziata 12* ☎ *055/20371* €4 ۞ *Mon.–Sat. 8:30–7, Sun. 8:30–2.*

SANTA MARIA NOVELLA TO THE ARNO

Piazza Santa Maria Novella, near the train station, suffers a degree of squalor, especially at night. Nevertheless, the streets in and around the piazza have their share of architectural treasures, including some of Florence's most tasteful palaces. Between Santa Maria Novella and the Arno is Via Tornabuoni, Florence's finest shopping street.

THE MAIN ATTRACTIONS

❶ Santa Maria Novella. The facade of this church looks distinctly clumsy by later Renaissance standards, and with good reason: it is an architectural hybrid. The lower half was completed mostly in the 14th century; its pointed-arch niches and decorative marble patterns reflect the Gothic style of the day. About 100 years later (around 1456), architect Leon Battista Alberti was called in to complete the job. The marble decoration of his upper story clearly defers to the already existing work below, but the architectural motifs he added evince an entirely different style. The central doorway, the four ground-floor half-columns with Corinthian capitals, the triangular pediment atop the second story, the inscribed frieze immediately below the pediment—these are borrowings from antiquity, and they reflect the new Renaissance style in architecture, born some 35 years earlier at the Spedale degli Innocenti. Alberti's most important addition, however, the S-curve scrolls that surmount the decorative circles on either side of the upper story, had no precedent whatever in antiquity. The problem was to soften the abrupt transition between wide ground floor and narrow upper story. Alberti's solution turned out to be definitive. Once you start to look for them, you will find scrolls such as these (or sculptural variations of them) on churches all over Italy, and every one of them derives from Alberti's example here.

10

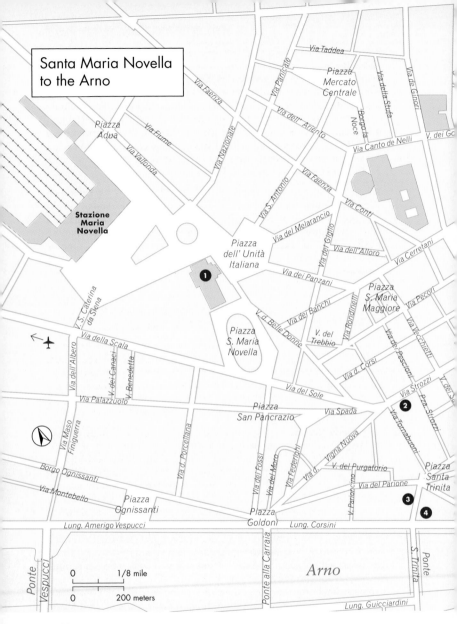

Santa Maria Novella
to the Arno

Via Taddea

Piazza
Mercato
Centrale

Via de' Ginori

V. dei Go

Via della Stufa

Via Panicale

Via dell'Ariento

Borgo la
Noce

Via Canto de Nelli

Via Faenza

Piazza
Adua

Via Fiume

Via Nazionale

Via Vallonda

Via S. Antonio

Via Faenza

Via Conti

Stazione
Maria
Novella

Piazza
dell' Unità
Italiana

Via del Melarancio

Via dei Panzani

Via dei Banchi

Via dell'Alloro

Via dei Gigilo

Piazza
S. Maria
Maggiore

Via Cerretani

Via Pecori

Via Rondinelli

V. S. Caterina
da Siena

Via della Scala

V. d. Belle Donne

V. del
Trebbio

Via de' Pescioni

Via Vecchietti

Piazza
S. Maria
Novella

Via d. Corsi

Via dei Canacci

V. dell'Albero

V. Benedetta

Via del Sole

Via Strozzi

V. dei Se

Via Palazzuolo

Pza. Strozzi

Piazza
San Pancrazio

Via Spada

2

Via Tornabuoni

Via Maso
Finiguerra

Via d. Porcellana

Vigna Nuova

V. del Purgatorio

Piazza
Santa
Trinita

Borgo Ognissanti

Via dei Fossi

Via del Moro

Via Federighi

Via d.

Via del Parione

3

Via Montebello

Piazza
Ognissanti

V. Parioncino

4

Lung. Amerigo Vespucci

Piazza
Goldoni

Lung. Corsini

S. Trinita

Ponte
Vespucci

Ponte
S. Trinita

Ponte
alla Carraia

Arno

0   1/8 mile

0   200 meters

Lung. Guicciardini

The architecture of the interior is, like that of the Duomo, a dignified but somber example of Florentine Gothic. Exploration is essential, however, because the church's store of art treasures is remarkable. Highlights include the 14th-century stained-glass rose window depicting the *Coronation of the Virgin* (above the central entrance); the Cappella Filippo Strozzi (to the right of the altar), containing late-15th-century frescoes and stained glass by Filippino Lippi; the *cappella maggiore* (the area around the high altar), displaying frescoes by Ghirlandaio; and the Cappella Gondi (to the left of the altar), containing Filippo Brunelleschi's famous wood crucifix, carved around 1410 and said to have so stunned the great Donatello when he first saw it that he dropped a basket of eggs.

Of special interest for its great historical importance and beauty is Masaccio's *Trinity*, on the left-hand wall, almost halfway down the nave. Painted around 1426–27 (at the same time he was working on his frescoes in Santa Maria del Carmine), it unequivocally announced the arrival of the Renaissance. The realism of the figure of Christ was revolutionary in itself, but what was probably even more startling to contemporary Florentines was the barrel vault in the background. The mathematical rules for employing perspective in painting had just been discovered (probably by Brunelleschi), and this was one of the first works of art to employ them with utterly convincing success.

In the cloisters of the **Museo di Santa Maria Novella** (⊠*Piazza Santa Maria Novella 19* 🕾*055/282187* 🎫*€2.70* 🕐*Mon.–Thurs. and Sat. 9–5, Sun. 9–2*), to the left of Santa Maria Novella, is a faded fresco cycle by Paolo Uccello depicting tales from Genesis, with a dramatic vision of the Deluge. Earlier and better-preserved frescoes painted in 1348–55 by Andrea da Firenze are in the chapter house, or the **Cappellone degli Spagnoli** (Spanish Chapel), off the cloister. 🕾*055/210113* 🎫*€2.50 for both museum and chapel* 🕐*Mon.–Thurs. and Sat. 9–5, Sun. 9–2.*

③ Santa Trinita. Started in the 11th century by Vallambrosian monks and originally Romanesque in style, the church underwent a Gothic remodeling during the 14th century. (Remains of the Romanesque construction are visible on the interior front wall.) Its major works are the fresco cycle and altarpiece in the Cappella Sassetti, the second to the high altar's right, painted by Ghirlandaio from around 1480 to 1485. His work here possesses such graceful decorative appeal as well as a proud depiction of his native city (most of the cityscapes show 15th-century Florence in all her glory). The wall frescoes illustrate scenes from the life of St. Francis, and the altarpiece, depicting the *Adoration of the Shepherds,* veritably glows. ⊠*Piazza Santa Trinita, Santa Maria Novella* 🕾*055/216912* 🕐*Mon.–Sat. 8–noon and 4–6.*

ALSO WORTH SEEING

④ Museo Salvatore Ferragamo. If there's such a thing as a temple for footwear, this is it. The shoes in this dramatically displayed collection were designed by Salvatore Ferragamo (1898–1960) beginning in the early 20th century. Born in southern Italy, the late master jump-started his career in Hollywood by creating shoes for the likes of Mary Pick-

Meet the Medici

CLOSE UP

The Medici were the dominant family of Renaissance Florence, wielding political power and financing some of the world's greatest art. You'll see their names at every turn around the city. These are some of the clan's more notable members:

Cosimo il Vecchio (1389–1464), incredibly wealthy banker to the popes, was the first in the family line to act as de facto ruler of Florence. He was a great patron of the arts and architecture; he was the moving force behind the family palace and the Dominican complex of San Marco.

Lorenzo il Magnifico (1449–92), grandson of Cosimo il Vecchio, presided over a Florence largely at peace with her neighbors. A collector of cameos, a writer of sonnets, and lover of ancient texts, he was the preeminent Renaissance man.

Leo X (1475–1521), also known as Giovanni de' Medici, became the first Medici pope, helping extend the family power base to include Rome and the Papal States. His reign was characterized by a host of problems, the biggest one being a former friar named Martin Luther.

Catherine de' Medici (1519–89) was married by her cousin Pope Clement VII to Henry of Valois, who later became Henry II of France. Wife of one king and mother of three, she was the first Medici to marry into European royalty. Lorenzo il Magnifico, her great-grandfather, would have been thrilled.

Cosimo I (1537–74), the first grand duke of Tuscany, should not be confused with his ancestor Cosimo il Vecchio.

---

ford and Rudolph Valentino. He then returned to Florence and set up shop in the basement of the 13th-century Palazzo Spini Ferroni. The collection includes about 16,000 shoes, and those on exhibition are frequently rotated. ⊠ *Via dei Tornabuoni 2, Santa Maria Novella* ☏ *055/3360846* 🎫 *€5* ⊘ *Mon. and Wed.–Sun. 10–6.*

❷ **Palazzo Strozzi.** The Strozzi family built this imposing palazzo in an attempt to outshine the nearby Palazzo Medici. Based on a model by Giuliano da Sangallo (circa 1452–1516) dating from around 1489 and executed between 1489 and 1504 under il Cronaca (1457–1508) and Benedetto da Maiaino (1442–97), it was inspired by Michelozzo's earlier Palazzo Medici-Riccardi. The palazzo's exterior is simple, severe, and massive: it's a testament to the wealth of a patrician, 15th-century Florentine family. The interior courtyard, entered from the rear of the palazzo, is another matter altogether. It is here that the classical vocabulary—columns, capitals, pilasters, arches, and cornices—is given uninhibited and powerful expression. Blockbuster art shows frequently occur here. ⊠ *Via Tornabuoni, Piazza della Repubblica* ☏ *055/2776461* ⊕ www.palazzostrozzi.org and www.contromodafirenze.it 🎫 *Free, except during exhibitions* ⊘ *Daily 10–7.*

SANTA CROCE

The Santa Croce quarter, on the southeast fringe of the historic center, was built up in the Middle Ages outside the second set of medieval city walls. The centerpiece of the neighborhood was the basilica of Santa Croce, which could hold great numbers of worshippers; the vast piazza could accommodate any overflow and also served as a fairground and, allegedly since the middle of the 16th century, as a playing field for no-holds-barred soccer games. A center of leatherworking since the Middle Ages, the neighborhood is still packed with leatherworkers and leather shops.

THE MAIN ATTRACTIONS

❷ Piazza Santa Croce. Originally outside the city's 12th-century walls, this piazza grew with the Franciscans, who used the large square for public preaching. During the Renaissance it was used for *giostre* (jousts), including one sponsored by Lorenzo de' Medici. "Bonfires of the vanities" occurred here, as well as soccer matches in the 16th century. Lined with many palazzi dating from the 15th century, it remains one of Florence's loveliest piazze and is a great place to people-watch.

❶ Santa Croce. Like the Duomo, this church is Gothic, but, also like the Duomo, its facade dates from the 19th century. As a burial place, the church probably contains more skeletons of Renaissance celebrities than any other in Italy. The tomb of Michelangelo is on the right at the front of the basilica; he is said to have chosen this spot so that the first thing he would see on Judgment Day, when the graves of the dead fly open, would be Brunelleschi's dome through Santa Croce's open doors. The tomb of Galileo Galilei (1564–1642) is on the left wall; he was not granted a Christian burial until 100 years after his death because of his controversial contention that Earth is not the center of the universe. The tomb of Niccolò Machiavelli (1469–1527), the political theoretician whose brutally pragmatic philosophy so influenced the Medici, is halfway down the nave on the right. The grave of Lorenzo Ghiberti, creator of the Baptistery doors, is halfway down the nave on the left. Composer Gioacchino Rossini (1792–1868) is buried at the end of the nave on the right. The monument to Dante Alighieri (1265–1321), the greatest Italian poet, is a memorial rather than a tomb (he is buried in Ravenna); it's on the right wall near the tomb of Michelangelo.

Fodor's Choice
★

10

The collection of art within the complex is by far the most important of any church in Florence. The most famous works are probably the Giotto frescoes in the two chapels immediately to the right of the high altar. They illustrate scenes from the lives of St. John the Evangelist and St. John the Baptist (in the right-hand chapel) and scenes from the life of St. Francis (in the left-hand chapel). Time has not been kind to these frescoes; through the centuries, wall tombs were placed in the middle of them, they were whitewashed and plastered over, and in the 19th century they suffered a clumsy restoration. But the reality that Giotto introduced into painting can still be seen. He did not paint beautifully stylized religious icons, as the Byzantine style that preceded him prescribed; he instead painted drama—St. Francis surrounded by griev-

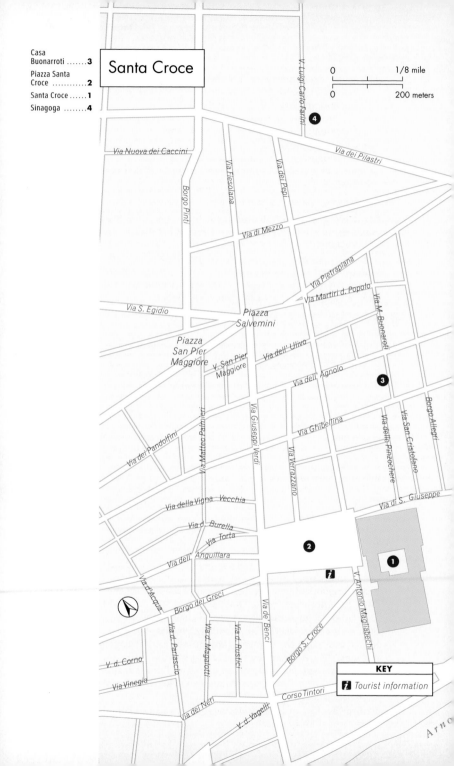

Santa Croce

| 0 | | 1/8 mile |
| 0 | | 200 meters |

4

Via Nuova dei Caccini

V. Luigi Carlo Farini

Via dei Pilastri

Borgo Pinti

Via Fiesolana

Via dei Pepi

Via di Mezzo

Via Pietrapiana

Via Martiri d. Popolo

Via M. Buonaroti

Via S. Egidio

Piazza
Salvemini

Piazza
San Pier
Maggiore

V. San Pier
Maggiore

Via dell' Ulivo

Via dell' Agnolo

3

Borgo Allegri

Via Ghibellina

Via San Cristofano

Via delle Pinzochere

Via dei Pandolfini

Via Matteo Palmieri

Via Giuseppi Verdi

Via Verrazzano

Via della Vigna Vecchia

Via di S. Giuseppe

Via d. Burella

Via Torta

Via dell' Anguillara

2

i

1

Via d'Acqua

Borgo dei Greci

Via d. Parlascio

Via d. Magalotti

Via d. Rustici

Via de' Benci

Borgo S. Croce

V. Antonio Magliabechi

V. d. Corno

Via Vinegia

Via dei Neri

V. d. Vagelli

Corso Tintori

Arno

KEY

i *Tourist information*

ing friars at the very moment of his death. This was a radical shift in emphasis: before Giotto, painting's role was to symbolize the attributes of God; after him, it was to imitate life. His work is indeed primitive compared with later painting, but in the early 14th century it caused a sensation that was not equaled for another 100 years. He was, for his time, the equal of both Masaccio and Michelangelo.

Among the church's other highlights are Donatello's *Annunciation,* a moving expression of surprise (on the right wall two-thirds of the way down the nave); 14th-century frescoes by Taddeo Gaddi (circa 1300–66) illustrating scenes from the life of the Virgin Mary, clearly showing the influence of Giotto (in the chapel at the end of the right transept); and Donatello's *Crucifix,* criticized by Brunelleschi for making Christ look like a peasant (in the chapel at the end of the left transept). Outside the church proper, in the **Museo dell'Opera di Santa Croce** off the cloister, is the 13th-century *Triumphal Cross* by Cimabue (circa 1240–1302), badly damaged by the flood of 1966. A model of architectural geometry, the Cappella Pazzi, at the end of the cloister, is the work of Brunelleschi. ⊠*Piazza Santa Croce 16* ☎*055/2466105* 🎟*€5 combined admission to church and museum* ⊗*Mon.–Sat. 9:30–5:30, Sun. 1–5.*

4 Sinagoga. Jews were well settled in Florence by 1396, when the first money-lending operations became officially sanctioned. Medici patronage helped Jewish banking houses to flourish, but by 1570 Jews were required to live within the large "ghetto," near today's Piazza della Repubblica, by the decree of Cosimo I, who had cut a deal with Pope Pius V (1504–72): in exchange for ghettoizing the Jews, he would receive the title of Grand Duke of Tuscany.

Construction of the modern Moorish-style synagogue began in 1874 as a bequest of David Levi, who wished to endow a synagogue "worthy of the city." Falcini, Micheli, and Treves designed the building on a domed Greek cross plan with galleries in the transept and a roofline bearing three distinctive copper cupolas visible from all over Florence. The exterior has alternating bands of tan travertine and pink granite, reflecting an Islamic style repeated in Giovanni Panti's ornate interior. Of particular interest are the cast-iron gates by Pasquale Franci, the eternal light by Francesco Morini, and the Murano glass mosaics by Giacomo dal Medico. The gilded doors of the Moorish ark, which fronts the pulpit and is flanked by extravagant candelabra, are decorated with symbols of the ancient Temple of Jerusalem and bear bayonet marks from vandals. The synagogue was used as a garage by the Nazis, who failed to inflict much damage in spite of an attempt to blow up the place with dynamite. Only the columns on the left side were destroyed, and even then, the Women's Balcony above did not collapse. Note the Star of David in black and yellow marble inlaid in the floor. The original capitals can be seen in the garden.

10

Some of the oldest and most beautiful Jewish ritual artifacts in all of Europe are displayed upstairs in the small **Museo Ebraico.** Exhibits document the Florentine Jewish community and the building of the synagogue. The donated objects all belonged to local families and date from as early as the late 16th century. Take special note of the exquisite needlework and silver pieces. A small but well-stocked gift shop is downstairs. ⊠ *Via Farini 4, Santa Croce* ☎*055/2346654* ⌨*Synagogue and museum €5* ⊗*Apr., May, Sept., and Oct., Sun.–Thurs. 10–5, Fri. 10–2; June–Aug., Sun.–Thurs. 10–6, Fri. 10–2; Nov.–Mar., Sun.–Thurs. 10–3, Fri. 10–2. English guided tours: 10:10, 11, noon, 1, 2 (no tour at 2 on Fri.).*

NEED A BREAK?

The only kosher–vegetarian restaurant in Tuscany is Ruth's (⊠ *Via Farini 2/ a, Santa Croce* ☎ *055/2480888*), adjacent to Florence's synagogue. On the menu: inexpensive vegetarian and Mediterranean dishes and a large selection of kosher wines. It's closed for Friday dinner and Saturday lunch.

ALSO WORTH SEEING

❸ **Casa Buonarroti.** If you are really enjoying walking in the footsteps of the great genius, you may want to complete the picture by visiting the Buonarroti family home, even though Michelangelo never actually lived there. It was given to his nephew, and it was the nephew's son, also called Michelangelo, who turned it into a gallery dedicated to his great-uncle. The artist's descendents filled it with art treasures, some by Michelangelo himself—a marble bas-relief; the *Madonna of the Steps*, carved when Michelangelo was only a teenager; and his wooden model for the facade of San Lorenzo—and some by other artists that pay homage to him. ⊠ *Via Ghibellina 70, Santa Croce* ☎*055/241752* ⊕*www. casabuonarroti.it* ⌨*€6.50* ⊗*Fri.–Wed. 9:30–2.*

THE OLTRARNO

A walk through the Oltrarno (literally "the other side of the Arno") takes in two very different aspects of Florence: the splendor of the Medici, manifest in the riches of the mammoth Palazzo Pitti and the gracious Giardino di Boboli; and the charm of the Oltrarno, a slightly gentrified but still fiercely proud working-class neighborhood with artisans' and antiques shops.

Farther east across the Arno, a series of ramps and stairs climbs to Piazzale Michelangelo, where the city lies before you in all its glory (skip this trip if it's a hazy day). More stairs (behind La Loggia restaurant) lead to the church of San Miniato al Monte. You can avoid the long walk by taking Bus 12 or 13 at the west end of Ponte alle Grazie and getting off at Piazzale Michelangelo; you still have to climb the monumental stairs to and from San Miniato, but you can then take the bus from Piazzale Michelangelo back to the center of town. If you decide to take a bus, remember to buy your ticket before you board.

Continued on page 593

WHO'S WHO IN RENAISSANCE ART

Michelangelo. Leonardo da Vinci. Raphael. This heady triumvirate of the Italian Renaissance is synonymous with artistic genius. Yet they are only three of the remarkable cast of characters whose work defines the Renaissance, that extraordinary flourishing of art and culture in Italy, especially in Florence, as the Middle Ages drew to a close. The artists were visionaries, who redefined painting, sculpture, architecture, and even what it means to be an artist.

THE PIONEER. In the mid-14th century, a few artists began to move away the flat, two-dimensional painting of the Middle Ages. **Giotto**, who painted seemingly three-dimensional figures who show emotion, had a major impact on the artists of the next century.

THE GROUNDBREAKERS. The generations of **Brunelleschi** and **Botticelli** took center stage in the 15th century. **Ghiberti**, **Masaccio**, **Donatello**, **Uccello**, **Fra Angelico**, and **Filippo Lippi** were other major players. Part of the Renaissance (or "re-birth") was a renewed interest in classical sources—the texts, monuments, and sculpture of Ancient Greece and Rome. Perspective and the illusion of three-dimensional space in painting was another discovery of this era, known as the Early Renaissance. Suddenly the art appearing on the walls looked real, or more realistic than it used to.

Roman ruins were not the only thing to inspire these artists. There was an incredible exchange of ideas going on. In Santa Maria del Carmine, Filippo Lippi was inspired by the work of Masaccio, who in turn was a friend of Brunelleschi. Young artists also learned from the masters via the apprentice system. Ghiberti's workshop (*bottega* in Italian) included, at one time or another, Donatello, Masaccio, and Uccello. Botticelli was apprenticed to Filippo Lippi.

THE BIG THREE. The mathematical rationality and precision of 15th-century art gave way to what is known as the High Renaissance. **Leonardo, Michelangelo**, and **Raphael** were much more concerned with portraying the body in all its glory and with achieving harmony and grandeur in their work. Oil paint, used infrequently up until this time, became more widely employed: as a result, Leonardo's colors are deeper, more sensual, more alive. For one brief period, all three were in Florence at the same time. Michelangelo and Leonardo surely knew one another, as they were simultaneously working on frescoes (never completed) inside Palazzo Vecchio.

When Michelangelo left Florence for Rome in 1508, he began the slow drain of artistic exodus from Florence, which never really recovered her previous glory.

A RENAISSANCE TIMELINE

IN THE WORLD

Black Death in Europe kills one third of the population, 1347-50.

Joan of Arc burned at the stake, 1431.

IN FLORENCE

Dante, a native of Florence, writes *The Divine Comedy*, 1302-21.

Founding of the Medici bank, 1397.

Medici family made official papal bankers.

1434, Cosimo il Vecchio becomes de facto ruler of Florence. The Medici family will dominate the city until 1494.

1300

1400

IN ART

EARLY RENAISSANCE

Masaccio and Masolino fresco Sant Maria del Carmine, 1424-28.

GIOTTO (ca. 1267-1337)

Giotto fresoes in Santa Croce, 1320-25.

BRUNELLESCHI (1377-1446)

LORENZO GHIBERTI (ca. 1381-1455)

DONATELLO (ca. 1386-1466)

PAOLO UCCELLO (1397-1475)

FRA ANGELICO (ca. 1400-1455)

MASACCIO (1401-1428)

FILIPPO LIPPI (ca. 1406-1469)

1334, 67-year-old Giotto is appointed chief architect of Santa Maria del Fiore, Florence's Duomo (below). He begins to work on the Campanile, which will be completed in 1359, after his death.

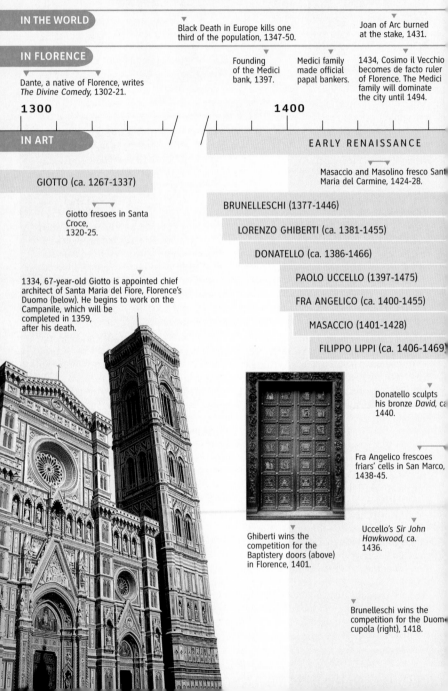

Donatello sculpts his bronze *David*, ca 1440.

Fra Angelico frescoes friars' cells in San Marco, 1438-45.

Ghiberti wins the competition for the Baptistery doors (above) in Florence, 1401.

Uccello's *Sir John Hawkwood*, ca. 1436.

Brunelleschi wins the competition for the Duom cupola (right), 1418.

Gutenberg Bible
is printed, 1455.

Columbus discovers
America, 1492.

Martin Luther posts his 95 theses on
the door at Wittenberg, kicking off the
Protestant Reformation, 1517.

Constantinople falls
to the Turks, 1453.

Machiavelli's *Prince*
appears, 1513.

Copernicus proves that
the earth is not the center
of the universe, 1530-43.

Lorenzo "il Magnifico"
(right), the Medici
patron of the arts, rules
in Florence, 1449-92.

Two Medici popes Leo X
(1513-21) and Clement
VII (1523-34) in Rome.

Catherine de'Medici
becomes Queen of Fran
1547.

1450   **1500**   **1550**

HIGH RENAISSANCE   MANNERISM

Fra Filippo Lippi's
*Madonna and
Child*, ca. 1452.

1508, Raphael begins
work on the chambers
in the Vatican, Rome.

Giorgio Vasari
publishes his first
edition of *Lives
of the Artists,*
1550.

1504, Michelangelo's
David is put on
display in Piazza
della Signoria,
where it remains
until 1873.

Michelangelo
begins to fresco
the Sistine Chapel
ceiling, 1508.

Botticelli paints the
Birth of Venus, ca.
1482.

BOTTICELLI (ca. 1444-1510)

LEONARDO DA VINCI (1452-1519)

RAPHAEL (1483-1520)

MICHELANGELO (1475-1564)

Leonardo paints *The Last Supper* in Milan,
1495-98.

10

Giotto's *Nativity* Donatello's *St. John the Baptist* Ghiberti's *Gates of Paradise*

GIOTTO (CA. 1267-1337)
Painter/architect from a small town north of Florence.

He unequivocally set Italian painting on the course that led to the triumphs of the Renaissance masters. Unlike the rather flat, two-dimensional forms found in then prevailing Byzantine art, Giotto's figures have a fresh, life-like quality. The people in his paintings have bulk, and they show emotion, which you can see on their faces and in their gestures. This was something new in the late Middle Ages. Without Giotto, there wouldn't have been a Raphael.

In Florence: **Santa Croce; Uffizi; Campanile; Santa Maria Novella**
Elsewhere in Italy: **Scrovegni Chapel, Padua; Vatican Museums, Rome**

FILIPPO BRUNELLESCHI (1377-1446)
Architect/engineer from Florence.

If Brunelleschi had beaten Ghiberti in the Baptistery doors competition in Florence, the city's Duomo most likely would not have the striking appearance and authority that it has today. After his loss, he sulked off to Rome, where he studied the ancient Roman structures first-hand. Brunelleschi figured out how to vault the Duomo's dome, a structure unprecedented in its colossal size and great height. His Ospedale degli Innocenti employs classical elements in the creation of a stunning, new architectural statement; it is the first truly Renaissance structure.

In Florence: **Duomo; Ospedale degli Innocenti; San Lorenzo; Santo Spirito; Baptistery Doors Competition Entry, Bargello; Santa Croce**

LORENZO GHIBERTI (CA. 1381-1455)
Sculptor from Florence.

Ghiberti won a competition—besting his chief rival, Brunelleschi—to cast the gilded bronze North Doors of the Baptistery in Florence. These doors, and the East Doors that he subsequently executed, took up the next 50 years of his life. He created intricately worked figures that are more true-to-life than any since antiquity, and he was one of the first Renaissance sculptors to work in bronze. Ghiberti taught the next generation of artists; Donatello, Uccello, and Masaccio all passed through his studio.

In Florence: **Door Copies, Baptistery; Original Doors, Museo dell'Opera del Duomo; Baptistry Door Competition Entry, Bargello; Orsanmichele**

DONATELLO (CA. 1386-1466)
Sculptor from Florence.

Donatello was an innovator who, like his good friend Brunelleschi, spent most of his long life in Florence. Consumed with the science of optics, he used light and shadow to create the effects of nearness and distance. He made an essentially flat slab look like a three-dimensional scene. His bronze *David* is probably the first free-standing male nude since antiquity. Not only technically brilliant, his work is also emotionally resonant; few sculptors are as expressive.

In Florence: ***David*, Bargello; *St. Mark*, Orsanmichele; Palazzo Vecchio; Museo dell'Opera del Duomo; San Lorenzo; Santa Croce**
Elsewhere in Italy: **Padua; Prato; Venice**

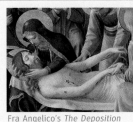

Fra Angelico's *The Deposition*

Masaccio's *Trinity*

Filippo Lippi's *Madonna and Child*

PAOLO UCCELLO (1397-1475)

Painter from Florence.

Renaissance chronicler Vasari once observed that had Uccello not been so obsessed with the mathematical problems posed by perspective, he would have been a very good painter. The struggle to master single-point perspective and to render motion in two dimensions is nowhere more apparent than in his battle scenes. His first major commission in Florence was the gargantuan fresco of the English mercenary Sir John Hawkwood (the Italians called him Giovanni Acuto) in Florence's Duomo.

In Florence: **Sir John Hawkwood, Duomo; *Battle of San Romano*, Uffizi; Santa Maria Novella**

Elsewhere in Italy: **Urbino**

FRA ANGELICO (CA. 1400-1455)

Painter from a small town north of Florence.

A Dominican friar, who eventually made his way to the convent of San Marco, Fra Angelico and his assistants painted frescoes for aid in prayer and meditation. He was known for his piety; Vasari wrote that Fra Angelico could never paint a crucifix without a tear running down his face. Perhaps no other painter so successfully translated the mysteries of faith and the sacred into painting. And yet his figures emote, his command of perspective is superb, and his use of color startles even today.

In Florence: **Museo di San Marco; Uffizi**

Elsewhere in Italy: **Vatican Museums, Rome; Fiesole; Cortona; Perugia; Orvieto**

MASACCIO (1401-1428)

Painter from San Giovanni Valdarno, southeast of Florence.

Masaccio and Masolino, a frequent collaborator, worked most famously together at Santa Maria del Carmine. Their frescoes of the life of St. Peter use light to mold figures in the painting by imitating the way light falls on figures in real life. Masaccio also pioneered the use of single-point perspective, masterfully rendered in his *Trinity*. His friend Brunelleschi probably introduced him to the technique, yet another step forward in rendering things the way the eye sees them. Masaccio died young and under mysterious circumstances.

In Florence: **Santa Maria del Carmine; *Trinity*, Santa Maria Novella**

FILIPPO LIPPI (CA. 1406-1469)

Painter from Prato.

At a young age, Filippo Lippi entered the friary of Santa Maria del Carmine, where he was highly influenced by Masaccio and Masolino's frescoes. His religious vows appear to have made less of an impact; his affair with a young nun produced a son, Filippino (Little Philip, who later apprenticed with Botticelli), and a daughter. His religious paintings often have a playful, humorous note; some of his angels are downright impish and look directly out at the viewer. Lippi links the earlier painters of the 15th century with those who follow; Botticelli apprenticed with him.

In Florence: **Uffizi; Palazzo Medici Riccardi; San Lorenzo; Palazzo Pitti**

Elsewhere in Italy: **Prato**

Botticelli's *Primavera*

Leonardo's *Portrait of a Young Woman*

Raphael's *Madonna on the Meadow*

BOTTICELLI (CA. 1444-1510)

Painter from Florence.
Botticelli's work is characterized by stunning, elongated blondes, cherubic angels (something he undoubtedly learned from his time with Filippo Lippi), and tender Christs. Though he did many religious paintings, he also painted monumental, nonreligious panels—his *Birth of Venus* and *Primavera* being the two most famous of these. A brief sojourn took him to Rome, where he and a number of other artists frescoed the Sistine Chapel walls.

In Florence: **Birth of Venus, Primavera, Uffizi; Palazzo Pitti**
Elsewhere in Italy: **Vatican Museums, Rome**

LEONARDO DA VINCI (1452-1519)

Painter/sculptor/engineer from Anchiano, a small town outside Vinci.
Leonardo never lingered long in any place; his restless nature and his international reputation led to commissions throughout Italy, and took him to Milan, Vigevano, Pavia, Rome, and, ultimately, France. Though he is most famous for his mysterious *Mona Lisa* (at the Louvre in Paris), he painted other penetrating, psychological portraits in addition to his scientific experiments: his design for a flying machine (never built) predates Kitty Hawk by nearly 500 years. The greatest collection of Leonardo's work in Italy can be seen on one wall in the Uffizi.

In Florence: **Adoration of the Magi, Uffizi**
Elsewhere in Italy: **Last Supper, Santa Maria delle Grazie, Milan**

RAPHAEL (1483-1520)

Painter/architect from Urbino.
Raphael spent only four highly productive years of his short life in Florence, where he turned out made-to-order panel paintings of the Madonna and Child for a hungry public; he also executed a number of portraits of Florentine aristocrats. Perhaps no other artist had such a fine command of line and color, and could render it, seemingly effortlessly, in paint. His painting acquired new authority after he came up against Michelangelo toiling away on the Sistine ceiling. Raphael worked nearly next door in the Vatican, where his figures take on an epic, Michelangelesque scale.

In Florence: **Uffizi; Palazzo Pitti**
Elsewhere in Italy: **Vatican Museums, Rome**

MICHELANGELO (1475-1564)

Painter/sculptor/architect from Caprese.
Although Florentine and proud of it (he famously signed his St. Peter's *Pietà* to avoid confusion about where he was from), he spent most of his 90 years outside his native city. He painted and sculpted the male body on an epic scale and glorified it while doing so. Though he complained throughout the proceedings that he was really a sculptor, Michelangelo's Sistine Chapel ceiling is arguably the greatest fresco cycle ever painted (and the massive figures owe no small debt to Giotto).

In Florence: **David, Galleria dell'Accademia; Uffizi; Casa Buonarroti; Bargello**
Elsewhere in Italy: **St. Peter's Basilica, Vatican Museums, and Piazza del Campidoglio in Rome**

THE MAIN ATTRACTIONS

5 **Giardino di Boboli** *(Boboli Gardens).* The main entrance to these landscaped gardens is from the right wing of ⇨ **Palazzo Pitti.** The gardens began to take shape in 1549, when the Pitti family sold the palazzo to Eleanor of Toledo, wife of the Medici grand duke Cosimo I.

The initial landscaping plans were laid out by Niccolò Tribolo (1500–50). After his death, work was continued by Vasari, Ammannati, Giambologna, Bernardo Buontalenti (circa 1536–1608), and Giulio (1571–1635) and Alfonso Parigi (1606–56), among others. Italian landscaping is less formal than French but still full of sweeping drama. A copy of the famous *Morgante,* Cosimo I's favorite dwarf astride a particularly unhappy tortoise, is near the exit. Sculpted by Valerio Cioli (circa 1529–99), the work seems to illustrate the perils of culinary overindulgence. A visit here can be disappointing because the gardens are somewhat underplanted and under-cared for, but it's still a great walk with some fabulous views. ⊠ *Enter through Palazzo Pitti* ☎ *055/294883* ⊕ *www.polomuseale.firenze.it* 🎟 *€6, combined ticket with Galleria del Costume and Giardino Bardini* ⊗ *Jan., Feb., Nov., and Dec., daily 8:15–4:30; Mar., daily 8:15–5:30; Apr., May, Sept., and Oct., daily 8:15–6:30; June–Aug., daily 8:15–7:30. Closed 1st and last Mon. of month.*

6 **Piazzale Michelangelo.** From this lookout you have a marvelous view of Florence and the hills around it, rivaling the vista from the Forte di Belvedere. It has a copy of Michelangelo's *David* and outdoor cafés packed with tourists during the day and with Florentines in the evening. In May, the **Giardino dell'Iris** (Iris Garden) off the piazza is abloom with more than 2,500 varieties of the flower. The **Giardino delle Rose** (Rose Garden) on the terraces below the piazza is also in full bloom in May and June.

4 **Palazzo Pitti.** This enormous palace is one of Florence's largest architectural set pieces. The original palazzo, built for the Pitti family around 1460, comprised only the main entrance and the three windows on either side. In 1549 the property was sold to the Medici, and Bartolomeo Ammannati was called in to make substantial additions. Although he apparently operated on the principle that more is better, he succeeded only in producing proof that more is just that: more.

Today the palace houses several museums: The **Museo degli Argenti** displays a vast collection of Medici household treasures. The **Galleria del Costume** showcases fashions from the past 300 years. The **Galleria d'Arte Moderna** holds a collection of 19th- and 20th-century paintings, mostly Tuscan. Most famous of the Pitti galleries is the **Galleria Palatina,** which contains a broad collection of paintings from the 15th to 17th centuries. The rooms of the Galleria Palatina remain much as the Medici left them. Their floor-to-ceiling paintings are considered by some to be Italy's most egregious exercise in conspicuous

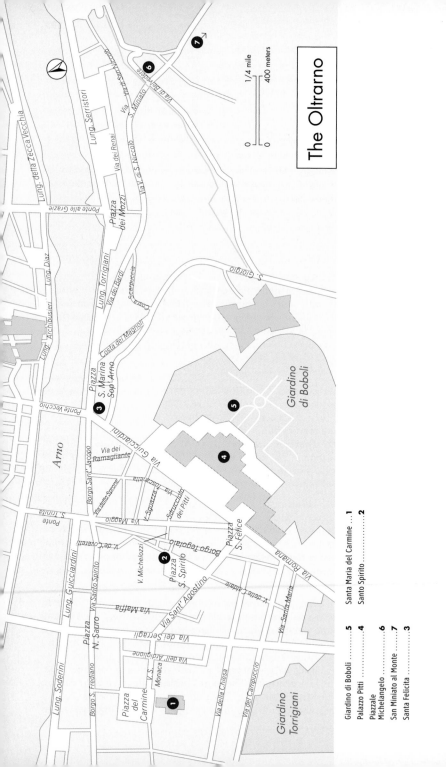

The Oltrarno

0   1/4 mile

0   400 meters

consumption, aesthetic overkill, and trumpery. Still, the collection possesses high points, including a number of portraits by Titian and an unparalleled collection of paintings by Raphael, notably the double portraits of Angelo Doni and his wife, the sullen Maddalena Strozzi. The price of admission to the Galleria Palatina also allows you to explore the former **Appartamenti Reali** containing furnishings from a remodeling done in the 19th century. ⊠ *Piazza Pitti* ☎ *055/210323* ✉ *Galleria Palatina and Galleria d'Arte Moderna, combined ticket* €*8.50; Galleria del Costume, Giardino Bardini, Giardino di Boboli, Museo degli Argenti, and Museo Porcelleane, combined ticket* €*6* ⊙ *Tues.–Sun. 8:15–6:50.*

❼ San Miniato al Monte. This church, like the Baptistery, is a fine example of Romanesque architecture and is one of the oldest churches in Florence, dating from the 11th century. A 12th-century mosaic topped by a gilt bronze eagle, emblem of San Miniato's sponsors, the Calimala (cloth merchants' guild) crowns the white and green marble facade. Inside are a 13th-century inlaid-marble floor and apse mosaic. Artist Spinello Aretino (1350–1410) covered the walls of the **Sagrestia** with frescoes depicting scenes from the life of St. Benedict. The nearby **Cappella del Cardinale del Portogallo** (Chapel of the Portuguese Cardinal) is one of the richest 15th-century Renaissance works in Florence. It contains the tomb of a young Portuguese cardinal, Prince James of Lusitania, who died in Florence in 1459. Its glorious ceiling is by Luca della Robbia, and the sculpted tomb by Antonio Rossellino (1427–79). ⊠ *Viale Galileo Galilei, Piazzale Michelangelo, Lungarno Sud* ☎ *055/2342731* ⊙ *Apr.–Oct., daily 8–7; Nov.–Mar., Mon.–Sat. 8–1 and 2:30–6, Sun. 3–5.*

❶ Santa Maria del Carmine. The **Cappella Brancacci,** at the end of the right transept of this church, houses a masterpiece of Renaissance painting: a fresco cycle that changed the course of Western art. Fire almost destroyed the church in the 18th century; miraculously, the Brancacci Chapel survived almost intact. The cycle is the work of three artists: Masaccio and Masolino (1383–circa 1447), who began it around 1424, and Filippino Lippi, who finished it some 50 years later after a long interruption during which the sponsoring Brancacci family was exiled. It was Masaccio's work that opened a new frontier for painting, as he was among the first artists to employ single-point perspective; tragically, he died in 1428 at the age of 27, so he didn't live to experience the revolution his innovations caused.

10

Masaccio collaborated with Masolino on several of the frescoes, but he alone painted the *Tribute Money,* on the upper-left wall; *St. Peter Baptizing,* on the upper altar wall; the *Distribution of Goods,* on the lower altar wall; and the *Expulsion of Adam and Eve,* on the chapel's upper-left entrance pier. If you look closely at the last painting and compare it with some of the chapel's other works, you should see a pronounced difference. The figures of Adam and Eve possess a startling presence primarily thanks to the dramatic way in which their bodies seem to reflect light. Masaccio here shaded his figures consistently, so as to suggest a single, strong source of light within the world of the painting but outside its frame. In so doing, he succeeded in imitating with paint the real-world effect of light on mass, and he thereby imparted to his figures a sculptural reality unprecedented in his day.

These matters have to do with technique, but with the *Expulsion of Adam and Eve* his skill went beyond mere technical innovation. In the faces of Adam and Eve, you see more than finely modeled figures; you see terrible shame and suffering depicted with a humanity rarely achieved in art. Reservations to see the chapel are mandatory, but can be booked on the same day. Your time inside is limited to 15 minutes—a frustration that's only partly mitigated by the 40-minute DVD about the history of the chapel you can watch either before or after your visit. ⊠ *Piazza del Carmine, Santo Spirito* ☎ *055/2768224 reservations* ✆ *€4* ⊘ *Mon. and Wed.–Sat. 10–5, Sun. 1–5.*

WORD OF MOUTH

"A good idea for Oltrarno: get lost between Borgo San Jacopo and Santo Spirito for wonderful antiques and restoration workshops. Extremely charming." –lcquinn2

ALSO WORTH SEEING

❸ **Santa Felicita.** This late-baroque church (its facade was remodeled between 1736 and 1739) contains the Mannerist Jacopo Pontormo's *Deposition,* the centerpiece of the Cappella Capponi (executed 1525–28) and a masterpiece of 16th-century Florentine art. The remote figures, which transcend the realm of Renaissance classical form, are portrayed in tangled shapes and intense pastel colors (well preserved because of the low lights in the church), in a space and depth that defy reality. Note, too, the exquisitely frescoed *Annunciation,* also by Pontormo, at a right angle to the *Deposition.* The granite column in the piazza was erected in 1381 and marks a Christian cemetery. ⊠ *Piazza Santa Felicita, Via Guicciardini, Palazzo Pitti* ⊘ *Mon.–Sat. 9–noon and 3–6, Sun. 9–1.*

❷ **Santo Spirito.** The plain, unfinished facade gives nothing away, but the interior, although it appears chilly compared with later churches, is one of the most important examples of Renaissance architecture in Italy. Unfortunately, it's closed to the public except durring mass (Mon.–Sat. 9, Sun. 9, 10:30, and 6). You're welcome to attend the service, but if you go, be prepared to sit through the whole thing.

The interior is one of a pair designed in Florence by Filippo Brunelleschi in the early 15th century (the other is San Lorenzo). It was here that Brunelleschi supplied definitive solutions to the two major problems of interior Renaissance church design: how to build a cross-shaped interior using classical architectural elements borrowed from antiquity and how to reflect in that interior the order and regularity that Renaissance scientists (among them Brunelleschi himself) were at the time discovering in the natural world around them.

Brunelleschi's solution to the first problem was brilliantly simple: turn a Greek temple inside out. While ancient Greek temples were walled buildings surrounded by classical colonnades, Brunelleschi's churches were classical arcades surrounded by walled buildings. This brilliant architectural idea overthrew the previous era's religious taboo against pagan architecture once and for all, triumphantly claiming that architecture for Christian use.

Brunelleschi's solution to the second problem—making the entire interior orderly and regular—was mathematically precise: he designed the ground plan of the church so that all its parts were proportionally related. The transepts and nave have exactly the same width; the side aisles are precisely half as wide as the nave; the little chapels off the side aisles are exactly half as deep as the side aisles; the chancel and transepts are exactly one-eighth the depth of the nave; and so on, with dizzying exactitude. For Brunelleschi, such a design technique was a matter of passionate conviction. Like most theoreticians of his day, he believed that mathematical regularity and aesthetic beauty were flip sides of the same coin, that one was not possible without the other. In the **Santo Spirito refectory** (⊠ *Piazza Santo Spirito 29* ☎ *055/287043*), adjacent to the church, you can see Andrea Orcagna's painting of the Crucifixion. ⊠ *Piazza Santo Spirito* ☎ *055/210030* ☜ *Church free, refectory €2.20* ⊙ *Church: open only during mass.. Refectory: Apr.– Sept., Tues.–Sat. 9–2; Oct.–Mar., Tues.–Sat. 9–1:30.*

NEED A BREAK?

Cabiria (⊠ *Piazza Santo Spirito 4/r* ☎ *055/215732*), across the piazza from the church of Santo Spirito, draws funky locals and visitors in search of a cappuccino, a quenching ade, or an expertly mixed drink. When it's warm, sit outside on the terrace.

WHERE TO EAT

Florence's popularity with tourists means that, unfortunately, there's a higher percentage of mediocre restaurants here than you'll find in most Italian towns. Some restaurant owners cut corners and let standards slip, knowing that a customer today is unlikely to return tomorrow, regardless of the quality of the meal. So, if you're looking to eat well, it pays to do some research, starting with the recommendations here—we promise there's not a tourist trap in the bunch.

Dining hours start at around 1 for lunch and 8 for dinner. Many of Florence's restaurants are small, so reservations are a must. You can sample such specialties as creamy *fegatini* (a chicken-liver spread) and *ribollita* (minestrone thickened with bread and beans and swirled with extra-virgin olive oil) in a bustling, convivial trattoria, where you share long wooden tables set with paper place mats, or in an upscale *ristorante* with linen tablecloths and napkins.

Those with a sense of culinary adventure should not miss the tripe sandwich, served from stands throughout town. This Florentine favorite comes with a fragrant *salsa verde* (green sauce) or a piquant red hot sauce—or both. Follow the Florentines' lead and take a break at an *enoteca* (wine bar) during the day and discover some excellent Chiantis and Super Tuscans from small producers who rarely export.

10

WHAT IT COSTS IN EUROS				
¢	$	$$	$$$	$$$$
AT DINNER	under €15	€15–€25	€25–€35	€35–€45	over €45

Prices are for a first course *(primo)*, second course *(secondo)*, and dessert *(dolce)*.

THE DUOMO TO THE PONTE VECCHIO

$–$$ ✕**Frescobaldi Wine Bar.** This swanky establishment serves both lunch and dinner. The food is typically Tuscan with some flights of fancy, including *acciughe marinate* (marinated anchovies) and *affettati misti* (a selection of sliced, cured meats). There's a separate wine bar within the restaurant called Frescobaldino. ⊠ *Via de' Magazzini 2–4/r, Piazza della Signoria* ☎ *055/284724* ▤ *MC, V* ✆ *Closed Sun. No lunch Mon.*

SAN LORENZO & BEYOND

$$$–$$$$ ✕**Taverna del Bronzino.** Want to have a sophisticated meal in a 16th-
Fodor'sChoice century Renaissance artist's studio? The former studio of Santi di Tito,
★ a student of Bronzino's, has a simple, formal decor, with white table-cloths and place settings. The classic, dramatically presented Tuscan food is superb, and the solid, afforable wine list rounds out the menu. The service is outstanding. Reservations are advised, especially for eating at the wine cellar's only table. ⊠ *Via delle Ruote 25/r, San Marco* ☎ *055/495220* ▤ *AE, DC, MC, V* ✆ *Closed Sun. and 3 wks in Aug.*

$ ✕**Mario.** Florentines flock to this narrow family-run trattoria near San
★ Lorenzo to feast on Tuscan favorites served at simple tables under a wooden ceiling dating from 1536. A distinct cafeteria feel and genuine Florentine hospitality prevail: you'll be seated wherever there's room, which often means with strangers. Yes, there's a bit of extra oil in most dishes, which imparts calories as well as taste, but aren't you on vacation in Italy? Worth the splurge is *riso al ragù* (rice with ground beef and tomatoes). ⊠ *Via Rosina 2/r, corner of Piazza del Mercato Centrale, San Lorenzo* ☎ *055/218550* ⊜ *Reservations not accepted* ▤ *No credit cards* ✆ *Closed Sun. and Aug. No dinner.*

¢ ✕**da Nerbone.** The place has been around since 1872, and it's easy to see why: this tiny stall in the middle of the covered Mercato Centrale has been serving up Florentine food to Florentines who like their tripe. Tasty primi and secondi are available every day, but cognoscenti come for the *panino con il lampredotto* (a type of tripe sandwich). Less adventurous sorts might want to sample the panino con il bollito (a boiled beef sandwich). Ask that the bread be "bagnato" (dipped, briefly, in the tripe cooking liquid), and have both the *salsa verde* (green sauce) and *salsa piccante* (a spicy, cayenne-laced sauce) slathered on top. ⊠ *Mercato San Lorenzo* ☎ *055/219949* ▤ *No credit cards* ✆ *Closed Sun. No dinner.*

BEST BETS, FLORENCE DINING

With hundreds of restaurants to choose from, how will you decide where to eat? Fodor's writers and editors have selected their favorite restaurants by price, cuisine, and experience in the Best Bets lists below. In the first column, Fodor's Choice properties represent the "best of the best."

FODOR'S CHOICE

Cibrèo, $$$$, Santa Croce

Ora d'Aria, $$$$, Santa Croce

Taverna del Bronzino, $$$, San Lorenzo & Beyond

Osteria de'Benci, $$–$$$, Santa Croce

Best by Price

BEST ¢

All'Antico Vinaio, Santa Croce

da Nerbone, San Lorenzo & Beyond

da Rocco, Santa Croce

BEST $

Cibrèo Trattoria, Santa Croce

La Casalinga, Oltrarno

Mario, San Lorenzo & Beyond

Osteria Antica Mescita San Niccolo, Oltrarno

BEST $$

Baldovino, Santa Croce

Frescobaldi Wine Bar, Centro Storico

La Mucca sul Tetto, Santa Croce

Quattro Leoni, Oltrarno

BEST $$$

Beccofino, Oltrarno

Il Latini, Centro Storico

La Giostra, Centro Storico

Osteria de'Benci, Centro Storico

BEST $$$$

Cibrèo, Centro Storico

L'Ora d'Aria, Centro Storico

Simon Boccanegra, Centro Storico

Taverna del Bronzino, San Lorenzo & Beyond

Best Experiences

FOR KIDS

Baldovino, $$, Santa Croce

Danny Rock, ¢, Santa Croce

Il Latini, $$$, Centro Storico

ROMANTIC

Enoteca Pinchiorri, $$$$, Santa Croce

Ora d'Aria, $$$, Santa Croce

BISTECCA FIORENTINA (TUSCAN STEAK)

Il Latini, $$$, Centro Storico

La Giostra, $$$, Santa Croce

Osteria de'Benci, $$$, Santa Croce

OUTDOOR DINING

Fuori Porta, ¢, Oltrarno

Osteria de'Benci, $$$, Santa Croce

Quattro Leoni, $$, Oltrarno

ALTA CUCINA (SOPHISTICATED CUISINE)

Enoteca Pinchiorri, $$$, Santa Croce

Ora d'Aria , $$$, Santa Croce

Taverna del Bronzino, $$–$$$, Santa Croce

CASALINGA (HOME COOKING)

La Casalinga, $, Oltrarno

Mario, $, San Lorenzo & Beyond

LUNCH SPOTS

Antico Noe, $$–$$$, Santa Croce

Cantinetta Antinori, $$$, Santa Maria Novella to the Arno

Benvenuto, $, Santa Croce

Frescobaldi Wine Bar, $$, Centro Storico

WINE LIST

Cantinetta Antinori, $$$, Santa Maria Novella to the Arno

Enoteca Pinchiorri, $, Santa Croce

Taverna del Bronzino, $, San Lorenzo & Beyond

10

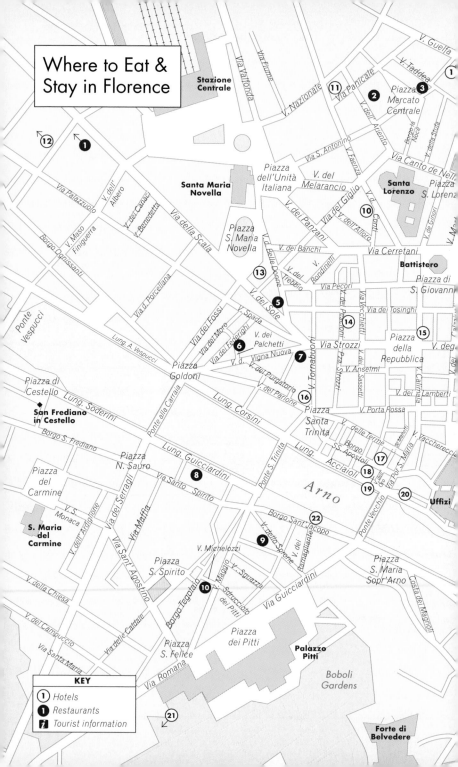

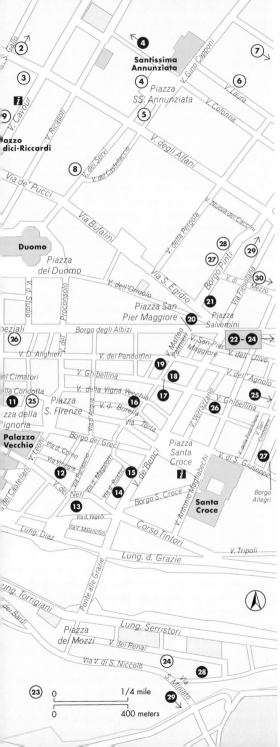

10

SANTA MARIA NOVELLA TO THE ARNO

$$$ ✕**Cantinetta Antinori.** After a rough morning of shopping on Via Tornabuoni, stop for lunch in this 15th-century palazzo in the company of Florentine ladies (and men) who lunch and come to see and be seen. The panache of the food matches its clientele: expect treats such as *tramezzino con pane di campagna al tartufo* (country pâté with truffles served on bread) and the *insalata di gamberoni e gamberetti con carciofi freschi* (crayfish and prawn salad with shaved raw artichokes). ⊠*Piazza Antinori 3, Santa Maria Novella* ☎*055/292234* ▭*AE, DC, MC, V* ⊘*Closed weekends, 20 days in Aug., and Dec. 25–Jan. 6.*

$$$ ✕**Il Latini.** It may be the noisiest, most crowded trattoria in Florence, but it's also one of the most fun. The genial host, Torello ("little bull") Latini, presides over his four big dining rooms, and somehow it feels as if you're dining in his home. Ample portions of *ribollita* prepare the palate for the hearty meat dishes that follow. Both Florentines and tourists alike tuck into the *agnello fritto* (fried lamb) with aplomb. Though reservations are advised, there's always a wait anyway. ⊠*Via dei Palchetti 6/r, Santa Maria Novella* ☎*055/210916* ▭*AE, DC, MC, V* ⊘*Closed Mon. and 15 days at Christmas.*

$–$$ ✕**Osteria delle Belle Donne.** Down the street from the church of Santa Maria Novella, this gaily decorated spot, festooned with ropes of garlic and other vegetables, has an ever-changing menu and stellar service led by the irrepressible Giacinto. The kitchen has Tuscan standards, but shakes up the menu with alternatives such as *sedani con bacon, verza, e uova* (thick noodles sauced with bacon, cabbage, and egg). If you want to eat alfresco, request a table outside when booking. ⊠*Via delle Belle Donne 16/r, Santa Maria Novella* ☎*055/2382609* ▭*AE, DC, MC, V.*

SANTA CROCE

$$$$ ✕**Cibrèo.** The food at this upscale trattoria is fantastic, from the creamy
Fodor's Choice crostini *di fegatini* (a savory chicken-liver spread) to the melt-in-your-
★ mouth desserts. Many Florentines hail this as the city's best restaurant, and Fodor's readers tend to agree—though some take issue with the prices and complain of long waits for a table (even with a reservation). If you thought you'd never try tripe—let alone like it—this is the place to lay any doubts to rest: the *trippa in insalata* (cold tripe salad) with parsley and garlic is an epiphany. The food is traditionally Tuscan, impeccably served by a staff that's multilingual—which is a good thing, because there are no written menus. Around the corner is Cibreino, Cibrèo's budget version, with a shorter menu and a no-reservations policy. ⊠*Via A. del Verrocchio 8/r, Santa Croce* ☎*055/2341100* ⟳*Reservations essential* ▭*AE, DC, MC, V* ⊘*Closed Sun. and Mon. and July 25–Sept. 5.*

$$$$ ✕**Enoteca Pinchiorri.** A sumptuous Renaissance palace with high, frescoed ceilings and bouquets in silver vases provides the backdrop for this restaurant, one of the most expensive in Italy. Some consider it one of the best, and others consider it a non-Italian rip-off, as the kitchen is presided over by a Frenchwoman with sophisticated, yet internationalist, leanings. Prices are high and portions are small; the vast holdings of the wine cellar, as well as stellar service, dull the pain, however, when the bill is presented. Interesting pasta combinations such as the *ignudi*—ricotta-and-spinach dumplings with a lobster-and-coxcomb fricassee—are always on the menu. ⊠ *Via Ghibellina 87, Santa Croce* ☎ *055/242777* ⌂ *Reservations essential* ⊟ *AE, MC, V* ⊗ *Closed Sun., Mon., and Aug. No lunch Tues. or Wed.*

$$$$

Fodor's Choice

★

✕ **Ora d'Aria.** The name means "Hour of Air" and refers to the time of day when prisoners were let outside for fresh air—alluding to the fact that this gem is across the street from what was once the old prison. In the kitchen, gifted young chef Marco Stabile turns out exquisite Tuscan classics as well as more-fanciful dishes, which are as beautiful as they are delicious; intrepid diners will be vastly rewarded for ordering the tortellini *farciti con piccione* (stuffed with pigeon) if it's on the day's menu. Two tasting menus give Stabile even greater opportunity to shine, and the carefully culled wine list has something to please every palate. Do not miss his tiramisu espresso—something halfway between a dessert and a coffee. ⊠ *Via Ghibellina 3/c, near Santa Croce* ☎ *055/2001699* ⊟ *AE, DC, MC, V* ⊗ *Closed Sun. No lunch.*

$$$$

✕ **Simon Boccanegra.** Florentine food cognoscenti flock to this place named for a condottiere (mercenary) hero in a Verdi opera. Under high ceilings, candles on every table cast a rosy glow; the fine wine list and superb service make a meal here a true pleasure. The chef has a deft hand with fish dishes, as well as an inventiveness when it comes to reinterpreting such classics as risotto with chicken liver—he adds leek and saffron to give it a lift. Remember to save room for dessert. A less-expensive, less-formal wine bar serving a basic Tuscan menu is also on the premises. ⊠ *Via Ghibellina 124/r, Santa Croce* ☎ *055/2001098* ⌂ *Reservations essential* ⊟ *AE, DC, MC, V* ⊗ *Closed Sun. No lunch.*

$$$

★

✕ **La Giostra.** This clubby spot, whose name means "carousel" in Italian, is owned and run by Prince Dimitri Kunz d'Asburgo Lorena, and his way with mushrooms is as remarkable as his charm. The unusually good pastas may require explanation from Soldano, one of the prince's good-looking twin sons. In perfect English he'll describe a favorite dish, *taglierini con tartufo bianco*, a decadently rich pasta with white truffles. Leave room for dessert: this might be the only show in town with a sublime tiramisu *and* a wonderfully gooey Sacher torte. ⊠ *Borgo Pinti 12/r, Santa Croce* ☎ *055/241341* ⊟ *AE, DC, MC, V.*

$$–$$$

✕ **Antico Noe.** If Florence had diners (it doesn't), this would be the best diner in town. The short menu at the one-room eatery relies heavily on seasonal ingredients picked up daily at the market. The menu comes alive particularly during truffle and artichoke season (don't miss the grilled artichokes if they're on the menu). Locals rave about the tagliatelle *ai porcini* (with mushrooms); the fried eggs liberally laced with truffle might be the greatest truffle bargain in town. Ask for the menu in Italian, as the English version is much more limited. The short wine list has some great bargains. ⊠ *Volta di San Piero 6/r, Santa Croce* ☎ *055/2340838* ⊟ *AE, DC, MC, V* ⊗ *Closed Sun. and 2 wks in Aug.*

10

$$–$$$ ✕**Osteria de'Benci.** A few minutes from Santa Croce, this charming oste-
Fodor'sChoice   ria serves some of the most eclectic food in Florence. Try the spaghetti
★   *degli eretici* (in tomato sauce with fresh herbs). The grilled meats are justifiably famous; the *carbonata* is a succulent piece of grilled beef served
rare. When it's warm, you can dine outside with a view of the 13th-cen-
tury tower belonging to the prestigious Alberti family. Right next door
is Osteria de'Benci Caffè (¢–$), serving selections from the menu from 8
AM to midnight. ✉ *Via de'Benci 11–13/r, Santa Croce* ☎ *055/2344923*
🖃 *AE, DC, MC, V* ✆ *Closed Sun. and 2 wks in Aug.*

$$ ✕**Baldovino.** David and Catherine Gardner, expat Scots, have created
this lively, brightly colored restaurant down the street from the church
of Santa Croce. From its humble beginnings as a pizzeria, it has evolved
into something more. It's a happy thing that pizza is still on the menu,
but now it shares billing with sophisticated primi and secondi. The
menu changes monthly and has such treats as *filetto di manzo alla Ber-
naise* (filet mignon with light béarnaise sauce). Baldovino also serves
pasta dishes and grilled meat until the wee hours. ✉ *Via San Giuseppe
22/r, Santa Croce* ☎ *055/241773* 🖃 *MC, V.*

$$ ✕**La Mucca sul Tetto.** The strangely named "Cow on the Roof" has an
equally odd, but pleasing, interior: anthracite-sponged walls adorned
with Moorish-style stencil work are bounded by 15th-century vaulting. The menu, which changes every few weeks, features Tuscan seasonal classics, as well as some unusual, tasty variations. Start with their
light-as-a-feather *coccoli* (fried, coin-size discs of dough) served with
stracchino (a soft, mild cheese) and prosciutto on the side. Meat lovers
should not miss the fried lamb chops, whose batter is laden with pistachios. The bilingual staff is happy to guide you through the well-culled
wine list, which caters to all budgets and all tastes. ✉ *Via Ghibellina
134/r, near Santa Croce* ☎ *055/2344810* 🖃 *AE, DC, MC, V* ✆ *No
lunch. Closed Sun.*

$–$$ ✕**Koime.** If you're looking for a break from the ubiquitous ribollita,
stop in at this eatery, which may be the only Japanese restaurant in
the world to be housed in a 15th-century Renaissance palazzo. High,
vaulted arches frame the Kaiten sushi conveyor belt. It's Japanese food,
cafeteria style: selections, priced according to the color of the plate,
make their way around a bar, where diners pick whatever they find
appealing. Those seeking a more substantial meal head to the second
floor, where Japanese barbecue is prepared at your table. The minimalist basement provides a subtle but dramatic backdrop for a well-
prepared cocktail. ✉ *Via dei Benci 41/r, Santa Croce* ☎ *055/2008009*
🖃 *AE, DC, MC, V*

$ ✕**Benvenuto.** At this Florentine institution, beloved for decades by locals
and Anglophone Renaissance scholars alike, the service is ebullient, the
menu long (with often unwittingly humorous English typographical
errors), and the food simple, Tuscan, and tasty. The list of primi and
secondi is extensive, and there are daily specials as well. Don't miss
the *scaloppine all Benvenuto* (veal cutlets with porcini). ✉ *Via della
Mosca 16/r, at Via de' Neri, Santa Croce* ☎ *055/214833* 🖃 *AE, DC,
MC, V* ✆ *Closed Sun.*

What Tripe!

While in Florence, those with a sense of culinary adventure should seek out a tripe sandwich, which is just about as revered by local gourmands as the bistecca alla fiorentina. In this case, however, the treasure comes on the cheap—sandwiches are sold from small stands found in the city center, topped with a fragrant green sauce or a piquant red hot sauce, or both. *Bagnato* means that the hard, crusty roll is first dipped in the tripe's cooking liquid; it's advisable to say *"sì"* when asked if that's how you like it. Sandwiches are usually taken with a glass of red wine poured from the tripe seller's *fiasco* (flask). If you find the tripe to your liking, you might also enjoy *lampredotto*, another, some say better, cut of stomach. For an exalted,

high-end tripe treat, try Fabio Picchi's cold tripe salad, served gratis as an *amuse-bouche* at the restaurant Cibrèo. It could make a convert of even the staunchest "I'd never try *that*" kind of eater.

Tripe carts are lunchtime favorites of Florentine working men—it's uncommon, but not unheard of, to see a woman at a tripe stand. Aficionados will argue which sandwich purveyor is best; here are three that frequently get mentioned: **La Trippaia** (⊠ *Via dell'Ariento, Santa Maria Novella* ☎ *No phone* ⊗ *Closed Sun.*). **Il Trippaio** (⊠ *Via de' Macci at Borgo La Croce, Santa Croce* ☎ *No phone* ⊗ *Closed Sun.*). **Nerbone** (⊠ *Inside the Mercato Centrale, Santa Maria Novella* ☎ *No phone* ⊗ *Closed Sun.*).

$ ✕ **Cibrèo Trattoria.** This intimate little trattoria, known to locals as Cibreino, shares its kitchen with the famed Florentine culinary institution that also shares its name. They share the same menu, too, though Cibreino's is much shorter. Start with *il gelatina di pomodoro* (tomato gelatin) liberally laced with basil, garlic, and a pinch of hot pepper, and then sample the justifiably renowned *passato in zucca gialla* (pureed yellow-pepper soup) before moving on to any of the succulent second courses. Save room for dessert, as the pastry chef has a dangerous hand with chocolate tarts. To avoid sometimes agonizingly long waits, come early (7 PM) or late (after 9:30). ⊠ *Via dei Macci 118, Santa Croce* ☎ *055/2341100* ⌔ *Reservations not accepted* ▭ *No credit cards* ⊗ *Closed Sun. and Mon. and July 25–Sept. 5.*

$ ✕ **Pallottino.** With its tile floor, photograph-filled walls, and wooden tables, Pallottino is the quintessential Tuscan trattoria, with hearty, heartwarming classics such as *pappa al pomodoro* (bread and tomato soup) and *peposa alla toscana* (beef stew laced with black pepper). The menu changes frequently to reflect what's seasonal; the staff is friendly, as are the diners who often share a table and, eventually, conversation. They also do pizza here, as well as great lunch specials. ⊠ *Via Isola delle Stinche 1/r, Santa Croce* ☎ *055/289573* ▭ *AE, DC, MC, V* ⊗ *Closed Mon. and 2–3 wks in Aug.*

¢ ✕ **All'Antico Vinaio.** Florentines like to grab a quick bite to eat at this narrow little sandwich shop near the Uffizi. A handful of stools offer a place to perch while chowing down on one of their very fine sandwiches; most folks, however, simply grab a sandwich, pour themselves a glass of inexpensive wine in a paper cup (more serious wines can be

10

poured into glasses) and mingle on the pedestrians-only street in front. If *porchetta* (a very rich, deliciously fatty roasted pork) is on offer, don't miss it. They also offer first-rate primi, which change daily. ✉ *Via de' Neri 65, Santa Croce* ☎ *No phone* ▭ *No credit cards* ⊘ *Closed Sun.*

¢ ✕ **Danny Rock.** There's a bit of everything at this restaurant, which is ☻ always hopping with Italians eager to eat well-made cheeseburgers and fries or one of the many tasty crepes (served both sweet and savory). You can also find a basic plate of spaghetti as well as a respectable pizza here. Interior decor isn't high on the list: you dine at a green metal table with matching chairs. The young-at-heart feel might explain why the main dining room has a big screen showing *Looney Tunes.* ✉ *Via Pandolfini 13/r, Santa Croce* ☎ *055/2340307* ▭ *AE, DC, MC, V.*

¢ ✕ **da Rocco.** At one of Florence's biggest markets you can grab lunch to go, or you could cram yourself into one of the booths and pour from the straw-cloaked flask (wine here is *da consumo,* which means they charge you for how much you drink). Food is abundant, Tuscan, and fast; locals pack in. The menu changes daily, and the prices are great. ✉ *In Mercato Sant'Ambrogio, Piazza Ghiberti, Santa Croce* ☎ *No phone* ⌕ *Reservations not accepted* ▭ *No credit cards* ⊘ *Closed Sun. No dinner.*

THE OLTRARNO

$$$ ✕ **Beccofino.** Forget that the noise level here often reaches the pitch of the Tower of Babel, and ignore the generic urban decor. Come here for the food: chef Robbie Pepin, who's worked with such heavy hitters as Gordon Ramsey and Alain Ducasse, has breathed life into this very cool place. His cooking, while wholly Italian, has a crisp simplicity reminiscent of Japanese food. He can do just about everything, but shines with fish and shellfish. He takes the Florentine classic gnudi and tops it with prawns, calamari, and fresh tomatoes; it creates a beautiful blend in your mouth. The menu changes frequently, the wine list is divine, and service is exceptional. ✉ *Piazza Scarlatti 1/r, Lungarno South* ☎ *055/2790076* ⌕ *Reservations essential* ▭ *MC, V* ⊘ *No lunch.*

$$ ✕ **Quattro Leoni.** The eclectic staff at this trattoria in a small piazza is an appropriate match for the diverse menu. In winter you can eat in one of two rooms with high ceilings, and in summer you can sit outside and admire the scenery. Traditional Tuscan favorites, such as *taglierini con porcini* (long, thin, flat pasta with porcini mushrooms), are on the menu, but so, too, are less typical dishes such as the earthy cabbage salad with avocado, pine nuts, and drops of *olio di tartufo* (truffle oil). Reservations are a good idea. ✉ *Piazza della Passera, Via dei Vellutini 1/r, Palazzo Pitti* ☎ *055/218562* ▭ *AE, DC, MC, V* ⊘ *No lunch Wed.*

$ ✕ **La Casalinga.** *Casalinga* means "housewife," and this place has the nostalgic charm of a 1950s kitchen with Tuscan comfort food to match. If you eat *ribollita* anywhere in Florence, eat it here—it couldn't be more authentic. Mediocre paintings clutter the semipaneled walls, tables are set close together, and the place is usually jammed. The menu is long, portions are plentiful, and service is prompt and friendly. Save room for dessert: the lemon sorbet perfectly caps off the meal. ✉ *Via Michelozzi*

9/r, Santo Spirito ☎*055/218624* ▭*AE, DC, MC, V* ☼*Closed Sun., 1 wk at Christmas, and 3 wks in Aug.*

$ ✕**Osteria Antica Mescita San Niccolò.** It's always crowded, always good, and always cheap. The osteria is next to the church of San Niccolò, and if you sit in the lower part you'll find yourself in what was once a chapel dating from the 11th century. The subtle but dramatic background is a nice complement to the food, which is simple Tuscan at its best. The *pollo con limone* is tasty pieces of chicken in a lemon-scented broth. In winter try the *spezzatino di cinghiale con aromi* (wild boar stew with herbs). Reservations are advised. ✉ *Via San Niccolò 60/r, San Niccolò* ☎*055/2342836* ▭*AE, MC, V* ☼*Closed Sun. and Aug.*

¢ ✕**Fuori Porta.** One of the oldest and best wine bars in Florence, this place serves cured meats and cheeses, as well as daily specials such as the sublime spaghetti *al curry. Crostini* and *crostoni*—grilled breads topped with a mélange of cheeses and meats—are the house specialty; the *verdure sott'olio* (vegetables with oil) are divine. All this can be enjoyed at rustic wooden tables, and outdoors when weather allows. One shortcoming is the staff; the members of which are sometimes disinclined to explain the absolutely wonderful wine list. ✉ *Via Monte alle Croci 10/r, San Niccolò* ☎*055/2342483* ▭*AE, MC, V.*

BEYOND THE CITY CENTER

$$$ ✕**Zibibbo.** Benedetta Vitali, formerly of Florence's famed Cibrèo, has a restaurant of her very own. It's a welcome addition to the sometimes claustrophobic Florentine dining scene—particularly as you have to drive a few minutes out of town to get here. Off a quiet piazza, it has two intimate rooms with rustic, maroon-painted wood floors and a sloped ceiling. The *tagliatelle al sugo d'anatra* (wide pasta ribbons with duck sauce) are aromatic and flavorful, and *crocchette di fave con salsa di yogurt* (fava bean croquettes with a lively yogurt sauce) are innovative and tasty. ✉ *Via di Terzollina 3/r, northwest of city center* ☎*055/433383* ▭*AE, DC, MC, V* ☼*Closed Sun.*

WHERE TO STAY

10

No stranger to visitors, Florence is equipped with hotels for all budgets; for instance, you can find both budget and luxury hotels in the *centro storico* (historic center) and along the Arno. Florence has so many famous landmarks that it's not hard to find lodging with a panoramic vista. The equivalent of the genteel *pensioni* of yesteryear still exist, though they are now officially classified as hotels. Generally small and intimate, they often have a quaint appeal that usually doesn't preclude modern plumbing.

Florence's importance not only as a tourist city but as a convention center and the site of the Pitti fashion collections guarantees a variety of accommodations. The high demand also means that, except in winter, reservations are a must. If you find yourself in Florence with no reservations, go to **Consorzio ITA** (✉ *Stazione Centrale, Santa Maria Novella* ☎*055/282893*). You must go there in person to make a booking.

WHAT IT COSTS IN EUROS				
¢	$	$$	$$$	$$$$
FOR TWO PEOPLE	under €80	€80–€140	€140–€210	€210–€290	over €290

Prices are for a standard double room in high season, including tax and service.

THE DUOMO TO THE ARNO

$$$$ **Hotel Helvetia and Bristol.** Painstaking care has gone into making this
★ hotel one of the prettiest and most intimate in town. It has the extra
plus of being in the center of the centro storico, making it a luxurious
base from which to explore the city. From the cozy yet sophisticated
lobby with its stone columns to the guest rooms decorated with prints,
you might feel as if you're a guest in a sophisticated manor house. The
restaurant serves sumptuous fare in a romantic setting. **Pros:** Central
location, superb staff. **Cons:** Rooms facing the street get some noise.
⊠ *Via dei Pescioni 2, Piazza della Repubblica, 50123* ☎ *055/26651*
🖷 *055/288353* ⊕ *www.hbf.royaldemeure.com* ➘ *54 rooms, 13 suites*
⚒ *In-room: safe, refrigerator, VCR, Wi-Fi. In-hotel: restaurant, room
service, bar, concierge, laundry service, parking (fee), some pets allowed*
🟰 *AE, DC, MC, V* ⧄ *EP.*

$$$$ **Hotel Savoy.** From the outside, it looks very much like the turn-
of-the-19th-century building that it is. Inside, sleek minimalism and
up-to-the-minute amenities prevail. Sitting rooms have a funky edge,
their cream-color walls dotted with contemporary prints. Muted colors dress the rooms, which have streamlined furniture and soaring
ceilings; many have views of the Duomo's cupola or the Piazza della
Repubblica. The deep marble tubs might be reason enough to stay
here—but you'll also appreciate the efficient and courteous staff.
Pros: Location, trendy clientele (if that's your thing). **Cons:** Smallish rooms, trendy clientele (if that's not your thing). ⊠ *Piazza della
Repubblica 7, 50123* ☎ *055/27351* 🖷 *055/2735888* ⊕ *www.rocco-
fortehotels.com* ➘ *88 rooms, 12 suites* ⚒ *In-room: safe, refrigerator,
VCR, dial-up, Wi-Fi. In-hotel: restaurant, room service, bar, concierge, children's programs (ages infant–12), laundry service, parking
(fee)* 🟰 *AE, DC, MC, V* ⧄ *EP.*

$$–$$$ **Hermitage.** A stone's throw from the Ponte Vecchio, this is a fine little
hotel with an enviable location. All rooms are decorated differently
with lively wallpaper; some have views of Palazzo Vecchio and others
of the Arno. The rooftop terrace, where you can have breakfast or an
aperitivo, is decked with flowers. The lobby suggests a friend's living
room—its warm yellow walls are welcoming. Double glazing and air-
conditioning help keep street noise at bay. **Pros:** Views; friendly, English-
speaking staff. **Cons:** Short flight of stairs to reach elevator. ⊠ *Vicolo
Marzio 1, Piazza della Signoria, 50122* ☎ *055/287216* 🖷 *055/212208*
⊕ *www.hermitagehotel.com* ➘ *27 rooms, 1 suite* ⚒ *In-room: safe. In-
hotel: laundry service, public Wi-Fi, parking (fee), some pets allowed*
🟰 *MC, V* ⧄ *BP.*

$$–$$$ **In Piazza della Signoria.** Proprietors Alessandro and Sonia Pini want
Fodor'sChoice you to use their house—in this case, part of a 15th-century palazzo—as
★ if it were your own. Such warm sentiments extend to the cozy feeling
created in the rooms, all of which are uniquely decorated and lovingly furnished; some have sweeping damask curtains, others fanciful
frescoes in the bathroom. **Pros:** Marvelous staff, tasty breakfast with
a view of Piazza della Signoria. **Cons:** Short flight of stairs to reach
elevator. ⊠ *Via dei Magazzini 2, near Piazza della Signoria, 50122*
☎ *055/2399546* ⊕ *www.inpiazzadellasignoria.com* ⊅ *10 rooms, 3*
apartments ⌂ *In-room: safe, kitchen (some), refrigerator (some), Wi-*
Fi. In hotel: laundry service, public Internet, parking (fee) ⊟ *AE, DC,*
MC, V |⊙|*BP.*

$$–$$$ **Palazzo Niccolini al Duomo.** This 16th-century family palace has been
lovingly restored by Ginevra and Filippo Niccolini di Camugliano—the
building has been in Filippo's family for more than 100 years. The
sumptuous rooms have high ceilings, spacious marble-floored bathrooms (a rarity in restored Renaissance palazzi); some are decorated
with sweeping frescoes. A few rooms have views of the Duomo (just
down the street); others retain their original Empire furnishings. The
Blue Suite accommodates up to four, and comes with its own kitchenette. **Pros:** Steps away from the Duomo. **Cons:** Street noise sometimes
a problem. ⊠ *Via dei Servi 2, 50122* ☎ *055/282412* 🖷 *055/290979*
⊕ *www.niccolinidomepalace.com* ⊅ *5 rooms, 5 suites* ⌂ *In-room:*
safe, refrigerator, Wi-Fi. In-hotel: public Internet, Wi-Fi, parking (fee)
⊟ *AE, DC, MC, V.*

$ **Albergo Firenze.** A block from the Duomo, this hotel is on one of the
oldest piazzas in Florence. Though the reception area and hallways
have all the charm of a college dormitory, the similarity ends upon
entering the spotlessly clean rooms. A good number of triple and quadruple rooms make this a good choice for families. **Pros:** For the location, a great bargain. **Cons:** No-frills public areas. ⊠ *Piazza Donati 4,*
Duomo, 50122 ☎ *055/214203* 🖷 *055/212370* ⊕ *www.hotelfirenze-*
fi.it ⊅ *58 rooms* ⌂ *In-hotel: public Internet (fee), parking (fee)* ⊟
MC, V |⊙|*BP.*

SAN LORENZO & BEYOND

$$–$$$ **Il Guelfo Bianco.** The 15th-century building has all modern conve-
niences, but its Renaissance charm still shines. Rooms have high ceilings (some are coffered) and windows are triple-glazed. Contemporary
prints and paintings on the walls contrast nicely with classic furnishings. Larger-than-usual single rooms have French-style beds and are a
good choice for those traveling alone. Breakfast can be enjoyed in a
small outdoor garden when weather permits. Though the hotel is in the
centro storico, it still feels somewhat off the beaten path. **Pros:** Stellar
multilingual staff. **Cons:** Rooms facing the street can be a little noisy.
⊠ *Via Cavour 29, San Marco, 50129* ☎ *055/288330* 🖷 *055/295203*
⊕ *www.ilguelfobianco.it* ⊅ *40 rooms* ⌂ *In-room: safe, refrigerator.*
In-hotel: concierge, laundry service, public Internet, parking (fee),
some pets allowed ⊟ *AE, DC, MC, V* |⊙|*BP.*

10

\$\$–\$\$\$ 🖫 **Loggiato dei Serviti.** Though this hotel was not designed by Brunelleschi, Florence's architectural genius, it might as well have been. The Loggiato is tucked away on one of the city's loveliest squares; a mirror image of the architect's famous Spedale degli Innocenti across the way. Occupying a 16th-century former convent, the building was once an inn for traveling priests. Vaulted ceilings, tasteful furnishings (some antique), canopy beds, and rich fabrics make this spare Renaissance building with modern comforts a find. An annex named The Dependance has five rooms of comparable quality. **Pros:** Prime location; helpful, English-speaking staff. **Cons:** Some furnishings show ware; some noise in rooms facing piazza ⊠ *Piazza Santissima Annunziata 3, 50122* ☎ *055/289592* 📠 *055/289595* ⊕ *www.loggiatodeiservitihotel.it* 🖙 *43 rooms* △ *In-room: safe, refrigerator, Wi-Fi (some). In-hotel: bar, laundry service, parking (fee), some pets allowed* ⊟ *AE, DC, MC, V* †⊙†*BP.*

\$\$ 🖫 **Bellettini.** You're in good hands at this small hotel on three floors run by Gina Naldini and Claudio, her husband. The top floor has two rooms with a view, and all the good-size guest rooms have Venetian or Tuscan provincial furnishings; bathrooms are bright and modern. Public rooms are simple but comfortable. A handful of triples and quadruples are available. An ample buffet breakfast includes tasty homemade cakes. **Pros:** Excellent staff. **Cons:** Two rooms have shared bath (but at significantly lower rates). ⊠ *Via dei Conti 7, Santa Maria Novella, 50123* ☎ *055/213561* 📠 *055/283551* ⊕ *www.hotelbellettini.com* 🖙 *28 rooms, 26 with private bath* △ *In-room: safe, refrigerator, ethernet. In-hotel: bar, parking (fee), some pets allowed* ⊟ *AE, DC, MC, V* †⊙†*BP.*

\$\$ 🖫 **Hotel Casci.** In this refurbished 14th-century palace, the home of Giacchino Rossini in 1851–55, the friendly Lombardi family runs a hotel with spotless rooms. Guest rooms are functional, and many of them open out onto various terraces (a view doesn't necessarily follow, however). It's on a very busy thoroughfare, but triple-glazed windows allow for a sound night's sleep. Many rooms easily accommodate an extra bed or two, and there are a number of triples and quads available. **Pros:** Helpful staff, good option for families. **Cons:** Bit of a college-dorm atmosphere; small elevator ⊠ *Via Cavour 13, San Marco, 50129* ☎ *055/211686* 📠 *055/2396461* ⊕ *www.hotelcasci.com* 🖙 *25 rooms* △ *In-room: safe, refrigerator, Wi-Fi. In-hotel: laundry service, public Internet, parking (fee), some pets allowed* ⊟ *AE, DC, MC, V* †⊙†*BP.*

\$\$ 🖫 **Hotel delle Arti.** If Florence had town houses, this would be one: the entrance to the public room downstairs feels as if you're in someone's living room. Pale, pastel walls, polished hardwood floors, and muted fabrics give rooms a simple, elegant look. Breakfast is taken on the top floor, and a small terrace provides city views. The highly capable staff is completely fluent in English. **Pros:** Down the street from the Duomo. **Cons:** Staff goes home at 11. ⊠ *Via dei Servi 38/a, Santissima Annunziata, 50122* ☎ *055/2645307* 📠 *055/290140* ⊕ *www.hoteldellearti.it* 🖙 *9 rooms* △ *In-room: refrigerator. In-hotel: laundry service, some pets allowed (fee)* ⊟ *AE, DC, MC, V* †⊙†*BP.*

$–$$ ⊡ **Firenze.** Each room in the intimate *residenza* is painted a different pastel color—peach, rose, powder blue. Simple furnishings and double-glazedwindows ensure a peaceful night's sleep. You might ask for one of the rooms that has a small private terrace; if you contemplate a longer stay, one of their well-located apartments might suit. Coffee, tea, and fresh fruit, available all day in the sitting room, are on the house. **Pros:** Ample DVD library, honor bar with Antinori wines. **Cons:** Staff goes home at 8, no credit cards accepted. ⊠ *Via San Gallo 72, San Marco, 50129* ☎*055/4627296* 🖷*055/4634450* ⊕*www.anticadimorafirenze.it* ⤙*6 rooms* ♺*In-room: safe, refrigerator, dial-up, Wi-Fi* ▭*No credit cards* ⏣*BP.*

$ ⊡ **Residenza Johanna I.** Savvy travelers and those on a budget should
★ look no farther, as this *residenza* is a tremendous value for quality and location. Though it's very much in the centro storico, the place is rather homey. You're given a large set of keys to let yourself into the building after 7 PM, when the staff goes home. Simple rooms have high ceilings and pale pastel floral prints. Morning tea and coffee (but no breakfast) are served in your room. **Pros:** Great value. **Cons:** Staff goes home at 7, no credit cards. ⊠ *Via Bonifacio Lupi 14, San Marco, 50129* ☎*055/481896* 🖷*055/482721* ⊕*www.johanna.it* ⤙*11 rooms* ♺*In-room: no a/c, no phone, no TV. In-hotel: parking (fee)* ▭*No credit cards* ⏣*EP.*

SANTA MARIA NOVELLA TO THE ARNO

$$$$ ⊡ **Gallery Hotel Art.** High design resides at this art showcase near the Ponte Vecchio. The coolly understated public rooms have a revolving collection of photographs by artists like Helmut Newton adorning the walls; the reception area is subtlely but dramatically lit. Rooms are sleek and uncluttered and dressed mostly in neutrals. Luxe touches, such as leather headboards and kimono robes, abound. Both the bar and restaurant attract sophisticated, fashionable locals; brunch happens on the weekends. **Pros:** Cookies in the room, comfortable beds. **Cons:** Sometimes elevator is slow. ⊠ *Vicolo dell'Oro 5, Santa Maria Novella, 50123* ☎*055/27263* 🖷*055/268557* ⊕*www.lungarnohotels. com* ⤙*65 rooms, 9 suites* ♺*In-room: safe, refrigerator, dial-up, Wi-Fi. In-hotel: restaurant, room service, bar, concierge, laundry service, parking (fee)* ▭*AE, DC, MC, V* ⏣*BP.*

$$$$ ⊡ **JK Place.** Ori Kafri, the manager of this boutique hotel, refers to it
Fodor's Choice as a house, and indeed it is a sumptuously appointed home away from
★ home. A library serves as the reception room; buffet breakfast is laid out on a gleaming chestnut table in an interior atrium. Soothing earth tones prevail in the rooms, some of which have chandeliers, others canopied beds. A secluded rooftop terrace makes a perfect setting for an aperitivo, as do the ground-floor sitting rooms with large, pillow-piled couches. The place is favored by young fashionistas, their entourages, and other beautiful people. **Pros:** Intimate feel, stellar staff. **Cons:** Breakfast at a shared table. ⊠ *Piazza Santa Maria Novella 7, 50123* ☎*055/2645181* 🖷*055/2658387* ⊕*www.jkplace.com* ⤙*14 doubles, 6 suites* ♺*In-room: safe, refrigerator, VCR, dial-up, Wi-Fi. In-hotel:*

10

bar, concierge, laundry service, parking (fee), some pets allowed ☰*AE, DC, MC, V* ⦿*BP.*

$$$ 🏨 **Beacci Tornabuoni.** Florentine pensioni don't get any classier than this.
★   It has old-fashioned style and enough modern comfort to keep you happy, and it's in a 14th-century palazzo. The sitting room has a large fireplace, the terrace has a tremendous view of some major Florentine monuments, and the wallpapered rooms are inviting. On Monday, Wednesday, and Friday nights from May through October, the dining room opens, serving Tuscan specialties. **Pros:** Multilingual staff, flower-filled terrace. **Cons:** Fodor's readers advise to request rooms away from reception area, which can be noisy. ✉ *Via Tornabuoni 3, Santa Maria Novella, 50123* ☎*055/212645* 🖷*055/283594* ⊕*www.tornabuonihotels.com* ↪*28 rooms* ⚘*In-room: refrigerator. In- hotel: restaurant, bar, laundry service, public Internet, parking (fee), some pets allowed* ☰*AE, DC, MC, V* ⦿*BP.*

$$ 🏨 **Torre Guelfa.** If you want to get a taste of medieval Florence, try this hotel hidden within a former 13th-century tower. The Torre Guelfa once protected the obscenely wealthy Acciaiuoli family; now it's one of the best small hotels in the center of Florence. Each guest room is different, some with canopied beds, some with balconies. Those on a budget might consider one of the six less expensive rooms on the second floor, which are comparable to the rest of the rooms but have no TV. **Pros:** Wonderful staff, some family-friendly triple rooms. **Cons:** Stairs to elevator. ✉*Borgo Santi Apostoli 8, Santa Maria Novella, 50123* ☎*055/2396338* 🖷*055/2398577* ⊕*www.hoteltorreguelfa.com* ↪*24 rooms, 2 suites* ⚘*In-room: safe (some), no TV (some). In-hotel: laundry service, public Wi-Fi, parking (fee), some pets allowed* ☰*AE, MC, V* ⦿*BP.*

$$ 🏨 **Villa Azalee.** The 19th-century villa deftly recalls its previous incarnation as a private residence. It's been in the hands of the Brizzi family for more than 100 years, and they understandably take pride in the prettiness of the place. Quilted, floral-print slipcovers dress the furniture; throw rugs pepper the floors. Many rooms have views of the hotel's garden, and some have private terraces. The hotel is five minutes on foot from the train station and steps from the Fortezza da Basso (site of the Pitti fashion shows). **Pros:** Proximity to train station, two garden apartments are wheelchair accessible. **Cons:** Feels a bit out of the way, despite being in city center. ✉ *Viale Fratelli Rosselli 44, Santa Maria Novella, 50123* ☎*055/214242* 🖷*055/268264* ⊕*www.villa-azalee.it* ↪*25 rooms* ⚘ *In-hotel: bar, bicycles, laundry service, public Internet, parking (fee), some pets allowed* ☰*AE, DC, MC, V* ⦿*BP.*

$–$$ 🏨 **Alessandra.** The location, a block from the Ponte Vecchio, and the clean, ample rooms make this a good choice. The building, known as the Palazzo Roselli del Turco, was designed in 1507 by Baccio d'Agnolo, a contemporary of Michelangelo. Though little remains of the original design save for the high wood ceilings, there's still an aura of grandeur. Friendly hosts Anna and Andrea Gennarini speak fluent English. **Pros:** Several rooms have views of the Arno, the spacious suite is a bargain. **Cons:** Stairs to elevator, some rooms share bath. ✉*Borgo Santi Apostoli 17, Santa Maria Novella, 50123* ☎*055/283438* 🖷*055/210619*

⊕*www.hotelalessandra.com* ⇆*26 rooms, 19 with bath; 1 suite; 1 apartment* ♻*In-room: safe, refrigerator, dial-up, Wi-Fi. In-hotel: laundry service, parking (fee)* ▭*AE, MC, V* ☽*Closed Dec. 10–26* ⦿*BP.*

¢–$　🏠**Nuova Italia.** The genial English-speaking Viti family runs this hotel near the train station and within walking distance of the sights. Its rooms are clean and simply furnished. Air-conditioning and triple-glazed windows ensure restful nights. Some rooms can accommodate extra beds. **Pros:** Reasonable rates. **Cons:** No elevator. ⊠ *Via Faenza 26, Santa Maria Novella, 50123* ☎*055/268430* ⎙*055/210941* ⊕*www. hotelnuovaitalia.it* ⇆*20 rooms* ♻*In-room: Wi-Fi (some). In-hotel: no elevator, laundry service, public Wi-Fi, parking (fee), some pets allowed* ▭*AE, MC, V* ☽*Closed Dec. 8–Dec. 26* ⦿*BP.*

THE OLTRARNO & BEYOND

$$$$　🏠**Lungarno.** Many rooms and suites here have private terraces that jut out right over the Arno, granting stunning views of the Palazzo Vecchio and the Lungarno. Four suites in a 13th-century tower preserve details like exposed stone walls and old archways and look over a little square with a medieval tower covered in jasmine. The very chic interiors approximate breezily elegant homes, with lots of crisp white fabrics with blue trim. A wall of windows and a sea of white couches make the lobby bar one of the most relaxing places in the city to stop for a drink. Inquire about the Lungarno Suites, across the river; they include kitchens, making them attractive if you're planning a longer stay. **Pros:** Upscale without being stuffy. **Cons:** Rooms without Arno views feel less special. ⊠*Borgo San Jacopo 14, Lungarno Sud, 50125* ☎*055/27261* ⎙*055/268437* ⊕*www.lungarnohotels.com* ⇆*60 rooms, 13 suites* ♻*In-room: dial-up, Wi-Fi. In-hotel: restaurant, bar, concierge, laundry service, parking (fee)* ▭*AE, DC, MC, V* ⦿*BP.*

$$　🏠**Hotel Silla.** The entrance to this slightly off-the-beaten-path hotel is through a 15th-century courtyard lined with potted plants and sculpture-filled niches. The hotel, formerly a palazzo dating from the 15th century, is up a flight of stairs and has two floors. Rooms are simply furnished and walls are papered; some have views of Via de' Renai and the Arno, while others overlook a less-traveled road. Breakfast may be taken in a room that preserves an Empire feel (including two chandeliers from the early 19th century); when it's warm, a large, sunny terrace is the perfect place to read or to write that postcard. **Pros:** A Fodor's reader raves, "It's in the middle of everything except the crowds." **Cons:** Some readers complain of street noise and too-small rooms. ⊠*Via de' Renai 5, San Niccolò, 50125* ☎*055/2342888* ⎙*055/2341437* ⊕*www.hotelsilla.it* ⇆*35 rooms* ♻*In-room: safe, refrigerator, Wi-Fi. In-hotel: bar, concierge, laundry service, parking (fee), some pets allowed* ▭*AE, DC, MC, V* ⦿*BP.*

10

SANTA CROCE

$$$$ ⚇**Hotel Regency.** The noise and crowds of Florence seem far from this stylish hotel in a residential district near the Sinagoga, though you're not more than 10 minutes from the Accademia and Michelangelo's *David.* Across the street is Piazza d'Azeglio, a small public park that somehow evokes 19th-century middle Europe. Rooms dressed in richly colored fabrics and antique-style furniture remain faithful to the hotel's 19th-century origins as a private mansion. The restaurant here is equally sophisticated. **Pros:** Faces one of the few green parks in the center of Florence. **Cons:** A small flight of stairs takes you to reception. ⊠ *Piazza d'Azeglio 3, Santa Croce, 50121* ☎ *055/245247* 🖷 *055/2346735* ⊕ *www.regency-hotel.com* ⇶ *30 rooms, 4 suites* ⟁ *In-room: safe, refrigerator, Wi-Fi. In-hotel: restaurant, room service, bar, concierge, laundry service, parking (fee), some pets allowed, no-smoking rooms,* ⊟ *AE, DC, MC, V* ⦿|*BP.*

$$$$ ⚇**Monna Lisa.** Housed in a 15th-century palazzo, with parts of the
★ building dating from the 13th century, this hotel retains some of its original wood-coffered ceilings from the 1500s, as well as its original marble staircase. Though some rooms are small, they are tasteful, and each is done in different floral wallpaper. The public rooms retain a 19th-century aura, and the intimate bar, with its red velveteen wallpaper, is a good place to unwind. **Pros:** Annex is wheelchair accessible. **Cons:** Rooms in annex are much less charming than those in palazzo. ⊠ *Borgo Pinti 27, Santa Croce, 50121* ☎ *055/2479751* 🖷 *055/2479755* ⊕ *www.monnalisa.it* ⇶ *45 rooms* ⟁ *In-room: safe, refrigerator. In-hotel: bar, concierge, laundry service, parking (fee), some pets allowed* ⊟ *AE, DC, MC, V* ⦿|*BP.*

$$$–$$$$ ⚇**J&J.** On a quiet street within walking distance of the sights sits this unusual hotel, a converted 16th-century convent. The large, suite-like rooms are ideal for honeymooners, families, and small groups of friends; some are on two levels, and many are arranged around a central courtyard. Pale travertine tiles used to refit some bathrooms provide a pleasing, ultramodern contrast to more traditional furnishings. Smaller rooms are more intimate, and some open onto a little shared courtyard. The gracious owners enjoy chatting in the light and airy lounge; breakfast is served in a glassed-in Renaissance loggia or in the central courtyard. **Pros:** Large rooms. **Cons:** One flight of steep stairs to get to rooms. ⊠ *Via di Mezzo 20, Santa Croce, 50121* ☎ *055/26312* 🖷 *055/240282* ⊕ *www.cavalierehotels.com* ⇶ *19 rooms, 7 suites* ⟁ *In-room: dial-up. In-hotel: bar, no elevator, laundry service, public Wi-Fi, parking (fee)* ⊟ *AE, DC, MC, V* ⦿|*BP.*

$$–$$$ ⚇**Morandi alla Crocetta.** You're made to feel like privileged friends of
★ the family at this charming and distinguished residence near Piazza Santissima Annunziata. The former convent is close to the sights but very quiet, and it's furnished comfortably in the classic style of a gracious Florentine home. One room retains original 17th-century fresco fragments, and two others have small private terraces. The Morandi is not only an exceptional hotel but also a good value. It's very small, so book well in advance. **Pros:** Interesting, offbeat location; terrific staff. **Cons:** Extra charge for breakfast, two flights of stairs to reach

reception and rooms. ⊠ *Via Laura 50, Santissima Annunziata, 50121* ☎*055/2344747* ☐*055/2480954* ⊕*www.hotelmorandi.it* 📞*10 rooms* ⚷*In-room: safe, refrigerator, dial-up, Wi-Fi. In-hotel: no elevator, concierge, laundry service, parking (fee), some pets allowed, minibar* ⊟*AE, DC, MC, V* ❛❍❜*EP.*

¢ 🖼**Albergo Losanna.** Most major sights are within walking distance of this tiny pensione steps away from the *viali*, the edge of the city center. Though dated and a little worn around the edges, the property is impeccably clean and the rooms have high ceilings; the mother and son who run the place are enthusiastic and cordial. Try to get a room facing away from the street; though there aren't any views, you won't hear as much street noise. **Pros:** Bargain price. **Cons:** On a noisy street. ⊠ *Via V. Alfieri 9, Santa Croce, 50121* ☎☐*055/245840* ⊕*www.albergolosanna.com* 📞*8 rooms, 3 with bath* ⚷*In-room: no a/c (some), no TV. In-hotel: parking (fee)* ⊟*AE, MC, V* ❛❍❜*BP.*

¢ 🖼**Istituto Oblate dell'Assunzione.** Twelve nuns run this convent, which is minutes from the Duomo. Rooms are spotlessly clean and simple; some of them have views of the cupola, and others look out onto a carefully tended garden where you are welcome to relax. Several rooms have three and four beds, making them well suited for families. Curfew is at 11:30 PM. You can join mass every morning at 7:30. For an additional three euros, you can get a simple Continental breakfast, and the nuns provide half or full pension for groups of 10 or more. None of the nuns speak English, and they don't have a Web presence, so unless you speak Italian, the best way to book is by fax. **Pros:** Bargain price. **Cons:** Curfew, no credit cards. ⊠*Borgo Pinti 15, Santa Croce, 50121* ☎*055/2480582* ☐*055/2346291* 📞*28 rooms, 22 with bath* ⚷*In-room: no a/c (some), no phone, no TV. In-hotel: parking (fee)* ⊟*No credit cards* ❛❍❜*EP.*

OUTSIDE THE CITY

$$$ 🖼**Torre di Bellosguardo.** *Bellosguardo* means "beautiful view"; given the view of Florence you get here, the name is fitting. The hotel, perched atop a hill minutes from the *viale*, is reached via a narrow road dotted with olive trees. Dante's friend Guido Calvacanti supposedly chose this serene spot for his country villa, but little remains from the early 14th century. The reception area, a former ballroom, has soaring ceilings with frescoes by Francavilla (1553–1615). Guest rooms, all with high ceilings, are simple and have heavy wooden furniture. **Pros:** Great for escaping heat of the city in summer. **Cons:** A car is a necessity. ⊠ *Via Roti Michelozzi 2, 50124* ☎*055/2298145* ☐*055/229008* ⊕*www.torrebellosguardo.com* 📞*9 rooms, 7 suites* ⚷*In-room: no a/c (some), refrigerator, no TV, dial-up. In-hotel: bar, pool, concierge, laundry service, parking (no fee), some pets allowed* ⊟*AE, MC, V.*

$$–$$$ 🖼**Villa Poggio San Felice.** Livia Puccinelli Sannini, the descendant of a
★ famed 19th-century Florentine hotelier, and her husband have turned her family's former country villa (documented in the 15th century) into a serene hotel outside the city limits. It retains the intimate feel of a single-family home with only five high-ceilinged rooms; some

10

have divine views of Brunelleschi's cupola down below, and others have working fireplaces. Simple landscaped gardens are peaceful. Though a daily shuttle service runs to the center of town, a car is vital. **Pros:** Affordable villa experience, pool is a great advantage in summer. **Cons:** You need a car. ⊠ *Via San Matteo in Arcetri 24, 50125* ☎*055/220016* 🖷*055/2335388* ⊕*www.villapoggiosanfelice. com* ⇆*4 rooms, 1 suite* ⌂*In-hotel: pool, no elevator, laundry service, public Internet, parking (no fee), some pets allowed* ▭*AE, MC, V* ⊗*Closed Jan. 10–Feb. 28* ❍*BP.*

NIGHTLIFE & THE ARTS

THE ARTS

Florence has a lively classical music scene. The internationally famous, annual Maggio Musicale lights up the musical calendar in early summer. Fans of rock, pop, and hip-hop might be somewhat surprised by the lack of live acts that make it to town (for such offerings, travel to Rome or Milan is often a necessity). What it lacks in contemporary music, however, is more than made up for with its many theatrical offerings.

MUSIC

The **Accademia Bartolomeo Cristofori** (⊠ *Via di Camaldoli 7/r, Santo Spirito/San Frediano* ☎*055/221646* ⊕*www.accademiacristofori.it*), also known as the Amici del Fortepiano (Friends of the Fortepiano), sponsors fortepiano concerts throughout the year. **Amici della Musica** (⊕*www.amicimusica.fi.it*) organizes concerts at the **Teatro della Pergola** (*Box office* ⊠ *Via Alamanni 39, Santissima Annunziata* ☎*055/210804* ⊕*www.pergola.firenze.it*).

The **Maggio Musicale Fiorentino** (⊠ *Via Alamanni 39* ☎*055/210804*), a series of internationally acclaimed concerts and recitals, is held in the **Teatro Comunale** (⊠*Corso Italia 16, Lungarno North* ☎*055/211158* ⊕*www.maggiofiorentino.com*). Within Italy, you can purchase tickets from late April through July directly at the box office or by phone at ☎*800/112211*. You can also buy them online. Other events—opera, ballet, and additional concerts—occur regularly throughout the year at different venues in town.

The **Orchestra da Camera Fiorentina** (⊠ *Via E. Poggi 6, Piazza della Signoria* ☎*055/783374*) performs various concerts of classical music throughout the year at Orsanmichele, the grain market–turned–church.

The concert season of the **Orchestra della Toscana** (⊠ *Via Ghibellina 101, Santa Croce* ☎*055/2340710*) runs from November to June. You can hear organ music in the baroque church of **Santa Margherita in Maria de' Ricci** (⊠*Via il Corso, Piazza della Signoria* ☎*055/215044*). Free concerts begin every night at 9:15, except Monday.

Visiting rock stars, trendy bands from Germany, and some American groups play at **Tenax** (⊠*Via Pratese 46* ⊕*www.tenax.org*).

NIGHTLIFE

Florentines are rather proud of their nightlife options. Most bars now have some sort of happy hour, which usually lasts for many hours and often has snacks that can substitute for a light dinner. (Check, though, that the buffet is free or comes with the price of a drink.) Clubs typically don't open until very late in the evening and don't get crowded until 1 or 2 in the morning. Though the cover charges can be steep, finding free passes around town is fairly easy.

BARS

Capocaccia (✉ *Lungarno Corsini 12/14r, Lungarno Sud* ☎ *055/210751*) makes great Bloody Marys, and it's the place to be at cocktail time. At night young Florentines crowd the doors and spill out into the street. **Colle Bereto** (✉ *Piazza Strozzi 4–6/r, Piazza della Repubblica* ☎ *055/283156*) draws in young Florentines and savvy tourists who like well-made cocktails and the huge spread that accompanies them. One of the hottest spots in town is the bar at the Gallery Art Hotel, **Fusion Bar** (✉ *Vicolo dell'Oro 5, Santa Maria Novella* ☎ *055/27263*). For a swanky experience, lubricated with trademark Bellinis and the best martinis in Florence, head to **Harry's Bar** (✉ *Lungarno Vespucci 22/r, Lungarno North* ☎ *055/2396700*). The oh-so-cool vibe at **La Dolce Vita** (✉ *Piazza del Carmine 6/r, Santo Spirito* ☎ *055/284595* ⊕ *www.dolcevitaflorence.com*) attracts Florentines and the occasional visiting American movie star. **Negroni** (✉ *Via de' Renai 17/r, San Niccolò* ☎ *055/243647* ⊕ *www.negronibar.com*) teems with well-dressed young Florentines at happy hour. **Rex** (✉ *Via Fiesolana 23–25/r, Santa Croce* ☎ *055/2480331*) attracts a trendy, artsy clientele. **Zoe** (✉ *Via de' Renai13/r, San Niccolò* ☎ *055/243111*) calls itself a "caffetteria," and while coffee may indeed be served, elegant youngish Florentines flock here for the fine cocktails. Here's people-watching at its very best, done while listening to the latest CDs imported from England. **Zona 15** (✉ *Via del Castellaccia 53–55/r [Piazza Brunelleschi], Duomo* ☎ *055/211678*) is coolly chic with its pale interior, blond woodwork, and metallic surfaces. Lunch, dinner, cocktails, and live music draw Florentine cognoscenti and others.

NIGHTCLUBS

BeBop (✉ *Via dei Servi 76/r, Santissima Annunziata* ☎ *No phone*) has loud, live music, Beatles nights, and teems with American kids enjoying their junior year abroad programs. **Central Park** (✉ *Via Fosso Macinante 2* ☎ *055/353505*) is a great spot for those who want to put on their dancing shoes for some house and hip-hop music. **Jazz Club** (✉ *Via Nuova de' Caccini 3, corner of Borgo Pinti, Santa Croce* ☎ *055/2479700*) puts on live music in a small basement. When last call's come and gone, go where the bartenders unwind after their shift: **Loch Ness** (✉ *Via de' Benci 19/r, Santa Croce* ☎ *No phone*) keeps the drinks flowing until 5 AM.

Maracaná (✉ *Via Faenza 4, Santa Maria Novella* ☎ *055/210298*) is a restaurant and pizzeria featuring Brazilian specialties; at 11 PM it transforms itself into a cabaret floor show, and then into a disco until

10

4 AM. Book a table if you want to eat. **Meccanò** (⌖*Le Cascine, Viale degli Olmi 1* ☎*055/331371*) is a multimedia experience in a high-tech disco with a late-night restaurant. People sip cocktails against a backdrop of exotic flowers, leopard-print chairs and chintz, and red walls and floors on the two crowded floors at **Montecarla** (⌖*Via de' Bardi 2, San Niccolò* ☎*055/2340259*). **Space Electronic** (⌖*Via Palazzuolo 37, Santa Maria Novella* ☎*055/293082*) has two floors, with karaoke downstairs and an enormous disco upstairs. **Yab** (⌖*Via Sassetti 5/r, Piazza della Repubblica* ☎*055/215160*) celebrated its 25th anniversary in 2004; it never seems to go out of style, though it increasingly becomes the haunt of Florentine high schoolers and university students intent on dancing and doing vodka shots.

SHOPPING

Window-shopping in Florence is like visiting an enormous contemporary-art gallery. Many of today's greatest Italian artists are fashion designers, and most keep shops in Florence. Discerning shoppers may find bargains in the street markets. ■ **TIP→Do not buy any knockoff goods from any of the hawkers plying their fake Prada (or any other high-end designer) on the streets.** It's illegal, and fines are astronomical if the police happen to catch you. (You pay the fine, not the vendor.)

Shops are generally open 9 to 1 and 3:30 to 7:30 and are closed Sunday and Monday mornings most of the year. Summer (June to September) hours are usually 9 to 1 and 4 to 8, and some shops close Saturday afternoon instead of Monday morning. When looking for addresses, you'll see two color-coded numbering systems on each street. The red numbers are commercial addresses and are indicated, for example, as 31/r. The blue or black numbers are residential addresses. Most shops take major credit cards and ship purchases, but because of possible delays it's wise to take your purchases with you.

MARKETS

Le Cascine's open-air market is held every Tuesday morning. Food, bargain clothing, and gadgets are sold. The **Mercato Centrale** (⌖*Piazza del Mercato Centrale, San Lorenzo*) is a huge indoor food market with a staggering selection of things edible. The clothing and leather-goods stalls of the **Mercato di San Lorenzo** in the streets next to the church of San Lorenzo have bargains for shoppers on a budget. It's possible to strike gold at the **Mercato di Sant'Ambrogio** (⌖*Piazza Ghiberti, off Via dei Macci, Santa Croce*), where clothing stalls abut the fruit and vegetables. Every Thursday morning from September through June, the covered loggia in Piazza della Repubblica hosts a **Mercato dei Fiori** (*flower market* ⌖*Piazza della Repubblica*); it's awash in a lively riot of plants and flowers. If you're looking for cheery, inexpensive trinkets to take home, you might want to stop and roam through the stalls under the loggia of the **Mercato del Porcellino** (⌖*Via Por Santa Maria at Via Porta Rossa, Piazza della Repubblica*). You can find bargains at the **Piazza dei**

Ciompi flea market (⊠ *Sant'Ambrogio, Santa Croce*) Monday through Saturday and on the last Sunday of the month. The second Sunday of every month brings the **Spirito flea market.** On the third Sunday of the month, vendors at the Fierucola organic fest sell such delectables as honeys, jams, spice mixes, and fresh vegetables.

SHOPPING DISTRICTS

Florence's most fashionable shops are concentrated in the center of town. The fanciest designer shops are mainly on **Via Tornabuoni** and **Via della Vigna Nuova.** The city's largest concentrations of antiques shops are on **Borgo Ognissanti** and the Oltrarno's **Via Maggio.** The **Ponte Vecchio** houses reputable but very expensive jewelry shops, as it has since the 16th century. The area near **Santa Croce** is the heart of the leather merchants' district.

SPECIALTY STORES

BOOKS & PAPER

Alberto Cozzi (⊠ *Via del Parione 35/r, Santa Maria Novella* ☎*055/294968*) keeps an extensive line of Florentine papers and paper products. The artisans in the shop rebind and restore books and works on paper. **Alice's Masks Art Studio** (⊠ *Via Faenza 72/r, Santa Maria Novella* ☎*055/287370*) preserves the centuries-old technique of papier-mâché masks. On hand are masks typical of 18th-century Venice, as well as some more whimsical ones: a mask of Vincent van Gogh is painted with brushstrokes reminiscent of his own inimitable style. One of Florence's oldest paper-goods stores, **Giulio Giannini e Figlio** (⊠*Piazza Pitti 37/r* ☎*055/212621*) is *the* place to buy the marbleized stock, which comes in many shapes and sizes, from flat sheets to boxes and even pencils. Photograph albums, frames, diaries, and other objects dressed in handmade paper can be purchased at **Il Torchio** (⊠ *Via dei Bardi 17, San Niccolò* ☎*055/2342862*). The stuff is high-quality, and the prices lower than usual. **La Tartaruga** (⊠*Borgo Albizzi 60/r, Santa Croce* ☎*055/2340845*) sells brightly colored, recycled paper in lots of guises (such as calendars and stationery), as well as toys for children. **Libreria d'Arte Galleria Uffizi** (⊠*Piazzale degli Uffizi 6, near Palazzo Vecchio* ☎ *055/284508*) carries monographs on famous artists, some of whose work can be found in the Uffizi; it also carries scholarly works in both Italian and English.

Long one of Florence's best art-book shops, **Libreria Salimbeni** (⊠ *Via Matteo Palmieri 14–16/r, Santa Croce* ☎*055/2340905*) has an outstanding selection. **Pineider** (⊠*Piazza della Signoria 13/r, Piazza della Signoria* ☎*055/284655*) has shops throughout the world, but the business began in Florence and still does all its printing here. Stationery and business cards are the mainstay, but the stores also sell fine leather desk accessories as well as a less stuffy, more lighthearted line of products.

10

CLOTHING

The usual fashion suspects—Prada, Gucci, Versace, to name but a few—all have shops in Florence.

The sleek, classic boutique **Giorgio Armani** (⊠ *Via Tornabuoni 48/ r, Santa Maria Novella* ☎*055/219041*) is a centerpiece of the dazzling high-end shops clustered in this part of town. **Bernardo** (⊠ *Via Porta Rossa 87/r, Piazza della Repubblica* ☎*055/283333*) specializes in men's trousers, cashmere sweaters, and shirts with details like mother-of-pearl buttons. **Cabó** (⊠ *Via Porta Rossa 77–79/r, Piazza della Repubblica* ☎*055/215774*) carries that sinuous Missoni knitwear. Trendy **Diesel** (⊠ *Via dei Lamberti 13/r, Piazza della Signoria* ☎*055/2399963*) started in Vicenza; its gear is on the "must-have" list of many self-respecting Italian teens. The outlandish designs of native son **Roberto Cavalli** (⊠ *Via Tornabuoni 83/r, Santa Maria Novella* ☎*055/2396226*) appeal to Hollywood celebrities and to those who want a little bit of rock star in their wardrobe. **Emporio Armani** (⊠*Piazza Strozzi 16/r, Santa Maria Novella* ☎*055/284315*), sister store of the Giorgio Armani boutique, has slightly more affordable, funky, nightclub- and office-friendly garb. **Prada** (⊠ *Via Tornabuoni 67/r, Santa Maria Novella* ☎*055/267471*), known to mix schoolmarmish sensibility with sexy cuts and funky fabrics, appeals to an exclusive clientele. The aristocratic Marchese di Barsento, **Emilio Pucci** (⊠ *Via Tornabuoni 20–22/r, Santa Maria Novella* ☎*055/2658082*), became an international name in the late 1950s when the stretch ski clothes he designed for himself caught on with the dolce vita crowd—his pseudo-psychedelic prints and "palazzo pajamas" became all the rage. You can take home a custom-made suit or dress from **Giorgio Vannini** (⊠ *Borgo Santi Apostoli 43/r, Santa Maria Novella* ☎*055/293037*), who has a showroom for his prêt-à-porter designs. The signature couture collection of **Gianni Versace** (⊠ *Via Tornabuoni 13–15/r, Santa Maria Novella* ☎*055/2396167*) revolutionized the catwalk with rubber dresses and purple leather pants; sister Donatella continues the line of high-priced, over-the-top couture for rock stars and movie celebs. **Versus** (⊠ *Via Vigna Nuova 36–38/r, Santa Maria Novella* ☎*055/217619*) is the more playful—and more affordable—Versace line.

The intrepid shopper might want to check out some other, lesser-known shops. Young Florentines have a soft spot in their hearts for the clingy, one-of-a-kind frocks designed by Angela Baldi at her tiny shop, **Babele** (⊠*Borgo Pinti 34/r, Santa Croce* ☎*055/244729*). **Blunauta** (⊠ *Via del Proconsolo 69/r, Duomo* ☎*055/212460*) sells casual, well-made clothes for men and women. At **L'essentiel** (⊠ *Via del Corso 10/r, Piazza della Signoria* ☎*055/294713*) Lara Caldieron has spun her club-going years into fashion that also works well on the street and in the office. **Geraldine Tayar** (⊠*Sdrucciolo de' Pitti 6/r, Palazzo Pitti* ☎*055/290405*) makes clothing and accessories of her own design in eclectic fabric combinations. **Il Guardaroba/Stock House** (⊠ *Via Verdi, Santa Croce* ☎*055/2340271*) is where savvy Florentines shop for one-off designer clothes at affordable prices. If you're looking for something hot to wear to the clubs, check out **Liu-Jo** (⊠ *Via Calimala 14/r, Piazza della Repub-*

blica ☎*055/216164*). The surreal window displays at **Luisa Via Roma** (✉*Via Roma 19–21/r, Duomo* ☎*055/217826*) hint at the trendy yet tasteful clothing inside this fascinating, *alta moda* (high-style) boutique, which stocks the world's top designers as well as Luisa's own

line. **Lo Stock di Max** (✉*Via Pietrapiana 15/r* ☎*055/241084*) sells last year's Max Mara stuff at a fraction of the original price.

Maçel (✉*Via Guicciardini 128/r, Palazzo Pitti* ☎*055/287355*) has collections by lesser-known Italian designers, many of whom use the same factories as the A-list. Florentine designer **Patrizia Pepe** (✉*Piazza San Giovanni 12/r, Duomo* ☎*055/2645056*) has body-conscious clothes perfect for all ages, especially for women with a tiny streak of rebelliousness. Members of the junior set desiring to look well clad, Florentine style, should consider stopping at **Piccolo Slam** (✉*Via dei Lamberti 13/r, Piazza della Signoria* ☎*055/214504*). **Principe** (✉*Via del Sole 2, Santa Maria Novella* ☎*055/292764*) is a Florentine institution with casual clothes for men, women, and children at far-from-casual prices. It also has a great housewares department. For cutting-edge fashion, the fun and funky window displays at **Spazio A** (✉*Via Porta Rossa 109–115/r, Piazza della Repubblica* ☎*055/212995*) merit a stop. The shop carries such well-known designers as Alberta Ferretti and Narciso Rodriguez, as well as lesser-known Italian, English, and French designers.

FRAGRANCES

Aromatherapy has been elevated to an art form at **Antica Officina del Farmacista Dr. Vranjes** (✉*Borgo La Croce 44/r, Santa Croce* ☎*055/241748* ✉*Via San Gallo 63/r* ☎*055/494537*). Dr. Vranjes makes scents for the body and for the house.

The essence of a Florentine holiday is captured in the sachets of the **Officina Profumo Farmaceutica di Santa Maria Novella** (✉*Via della Scala 16, Santa Maria Novella* ☎*055/216276*), an art-nouveau emporium of herbal cosmetics and soaps that are made following centuries-old recipes created by friars.

10

JEWELRY

Angela Caputi (✉*Borgo Santi Apostoli 44/46* ☎*055/292993*) wows Florentine cognoscenti with her highly creative, often outsized plastic jewelry. A small, but equally creative, collection of women's clothing made of fine fabrics is also on offer. **Carlo Piccini** (✉*Ponte Vecchio 31/r, Piazza della Signoria* ☎*055/292030*) has been around for several generations, selling antique jewelry as well as making pieces to order; you can also get old jewelry reset here. **Cassetti** (✉*Ponte Vecchio 54/r, Piazza della Signoria* ☎*055/2396028*) combines precious and semiprecious stones and metals in contemporary settings. **Gatto Bianco** (✉*Borgo Santi Apostoli 12/r, Santa Maria Novella* ☎*055/282989*) has breathtakingly beautiful jewelry worked in semiprecious and precious stones; the feel is completely contemporary. **Gherardi** (✉*Ponte*

Vecchio 5/r, Piazza della Signoria ☎*055/211809*), Florence's king of coral, has the city's largest selection of finely crafted pieces, as well as cultured pearls, jade, and turquoise. **Oro Due** (✉ *Via Lambertesca 12/r, Piazza della Signoria* ☎*055/292143*) sells gold jewelry the old-fashioned way: beauteous objects are priced according to the level of craftsmanship and the price of gold bullion that day. The two women who run **Oreria** (✉*Borgo Pinti 87/a, Santa Croce* ☎*055/244708*) create divine designs using silver and semiprecious stones. Send suitors to purchase significant gifts here. **Studio Ballerino** (✉*Borgo Allegri 25/r, Santa Croce* ☎*055/2344658*) has one-of-a-kind pieces crafted in semiprecious stone, gold, and silver. One of Florence's oldest jewelers, **Tiffany** (✉ *Via Tornabuoni 25/r, Santa Maria Novella* ☎*055/215506*) has supplied Italian (and other) royalty with finely crafted gems for centuries. Its selection of antique-looking classics has been updated with a selection of contemporary silver.

LINENS & FABRICS

Antico Setificio Fiorentina (✉ *Via L. Bartolini 4, Santo Spirito/San Frediano* ☎*055/213861*) has been providing damasks and other fine fabrics for royalty and those who aspire to it since 1786. Visits by appointment are preferred. **Blue Home** (✉*Borgo Santi Apostoli 58/r, Santa Maria Novella* ☎*055/2658262*) sells sumptuous fabrics which can be rendered into sofas, rugs, and other home furnishings to create divinely inspired interiors. Antique and contemporary rugs are also on hand. **Loretta Caponi** (✉*Piazza Antinori 4/r, Santa Maria Novella* ☎*055/213668*) is synonymous with Florentine embroidery, and the luxury lace, linens, and lingerie have earned the eponymous signora worldwide renown. Luxurious silks, beaded fabrics, lace, wool, and tweeds can be purchased at **Valli** (✉ *Via Strozzi 4/r, Piazza della Repubblica* ☎*055/282485*). It carries fabrics created by Armani, Valentino, and other high-end designers.

OUTLETS

For bargains on Italian designer clothing, you need to leave the city and hit the outlet stores. At**Barberino Designer Outlet** (✉ *Via Meucci snc,* ☎*055/842161*) you'll find Prada, Pollini, Missoni, and Bruno Magli, among others. To get here, take the A1 to the Barberino di Mugello exit, and follow signs to the mall.

One-stop bargain shopping awaits at **The Mall** (✉ *Via Europa 8* ☎*055/8657775*), where the stores sell goods by such names as Bottega Veneta, Giorgio Armani, Loro Piana, Sergio Rossi, and the decidedly non-Italian Yves St. Laurent. Cognoscenti drive 45 minutes or take the train to Montevarchi, and then taxi out of town to the **Prada Outlet** (✉*Levanella Spacceo, Estrada Statale 69, Montevarchi* ☎*055/91911*).

SHOES & LEATHER ACCESSORIES

Florentine women with a sense of whimsical style adore the purses at **Bracciolini** (✉ *Via delle Vigna Nuova 30/r*); if you're a fan of frogs, you'll adore the frog baguette bag with matching frog wallet.

The colorful, foot-friendly shoes at **Camper** (⊠ *Via Por Santa Maria 47/r, Piazza della Signoria* ☎*055/2670342*) are made in Spain, but they cost less here than they do in the United States. The ultimate fine leathers are crafted into classic shapes at **Casadei** (⊠ *Via Tornabuoni 33/r, Santa Maria Novella* ☎*055/287240*), winding up as women's shoes and bags. The late Salvatore Ferragamo earned his fortune custom-making shoes for famous feet, especially Hollywood stars. The classy **Ferragamo** (⊠ *Via Tornabuoni 2/r, Santa Maria Novella* ☎*055/292123*), in a 13th-century Renaissance palazzo, displays designer clothing and accessories, but elegant footwear still underlies the Ferragamo success. **Pollini** (⊠ *Via Calimala 12/r, Piazza della Repubblica* ☎*055/214738*) has beautifully crafted shoes and leather accessories for those willing to pay that little bit extra.

Beltrami (⊠ *Via della Vigna Nuova 70/r, Santa Maria Novella* ☎*055/287779*), which sells shoes and some apparel, has long been synonymous with style; classic looks are beautifully updated. **Cellerini** (⊠ *Via del Sole 37/r, Santa Maria Novella* ☎*055/282533*) is an institution in a city where it seems that just about everybody wears an expensive leather jacket. **Coccinelle** (⊠ *Via Por Santa Maria 49/r, Piazza della Signoria* ☎*055/2398782*) sells leather accessories in bold colors and funky designs. **Furla** (⊠ *Via Calzaiuoli 47/r, Piazza della Repubblica* ☎*055/2382883*) makes beautiful leather bags and wallets in up-to-the-minute designs. **Giotti** (⊠*Piazza Ognissanti 3–4/r, Lungarno North* ☎*055/294265*) has a full line of leather goods, including clothing. Florentine perennial **Gucci** (⊠ *Via Tornabuoni 73/r, Santa Maria Novella* ☎*055/264011*) puts its famous initials on just about everything it sells. Beware, however, of shop assistants with severe attitude problems. **Il Bisonte** (⊠ *Via del Parione 31/r, off Via della Vigna Nuova, Santa Maria Novella* ☎*055/215722*) is known for its natural-looking leather goods, all stamped with the store's bison symbol. **Madova** (⊠ *Via Guicciardini 1/r, Palazzo Pitti* ☎*055/2396526*) has high-quality leather gloves in a rainbow of colors and a choice of linings (silk, cashmere, and unlined). **Paolo Carandini** (⊠ *Via de' Macci 73/r, Santa Croce* ☎*055/245397*) works exclusively in leather, producing exquisite objects such as picture frames, jewelry boxes, and desk accessories.

Shoe styles at **Romano** (⊠ *Via Speziali 10/r, Piazza della Repubblica* ☎*055/216535*) span the staid to the offbeat at appealing prices. A consortium of leatherworkers plies its trade at **Scuola del Cuoio** (⊠*Piazza Santa Croce 16* ☎*055/244533* ⊕*www.leatherschool.com*), in the former dormitory of the convent of Santa Croce; high-quality, fairly priced jackets, belts, and purses are sold here.

10

A SIDE TRIP FROM FLORENCE: FIESOLE

GETTING HERE

The easiest way to get to Fiesole from Florence is by public bus: Take the number 7, marked "Fiesole," which you can pick up at Santa Maria Novella station or Piazza San Marco. If you decide to drive (the bus is so much easier), go to Piazza Liberta and cross the Ponte Rosso heading in the direction of the SS65/SR65. Turn right on to Via Salviati and continue on to Via Roccettini. Make a left turn to Via Vecchia Fiesolana, which will take you directly in the center of town. Visitor Information

VISITOR INFORMATION
Fiesole tourism office (✉ *Via Portigiani 3, 50014* ☎*055/598720* ⊕*www. comune.fiesole.fi.it*).

EXPLORING

A half-day excursion to Fiesole, in the hills 8 km (5 mi) above Florence, gives you a pleasant respite from museums and a wonderful view of the city. From here the view of the Duomo, with Brunelleschi's powerful cupola, gives you a new appreciation for what the Renaissance accomplished. Fiesole began life as an ancient Etruscan and later Roman village that held some power until it succumbed to barbarian invasions. Eventually it gave up its independence in exchange for Florence's protection. The medieval cathedral, ancient Roman amphitheater, and lovely old villas behind garden walls are clustered on a series of hilltops. A walk around Fiesole can take from one to two or three hours, depending on how far you stroll from the main piazza.

The trip from Florence by car or bus takes 20–30 minutes. Take Bus 7 from the Stazione Centrale di Santa Maria Novella, Piazza San Marco, or the Duomo. (You can also get on and off the bus at San Domenico.) A word of caution: pickpockets have been known to frequent this bus, so keep an eye out for reaching hands. There are several possible routes for the two-hour walk from central Florence to Fiesole. One route begins in a residential area of Florence called Salviatino (Via Barbacane, near Piazza Edison, on the Bus 7 route), and after a short time, offers peeks over garden walls of beautiful villas, as well as the view over your shoulder at the panorama of Florence in the valley.

The **Duomo** reveals a stark medieval interior. In the raised presbytery, the **Cappella Salutati** was frescoed by 15th-century artist Cosimo Rosselli, but it was his contemporary, sculptor Mino da Fiesole (1430–84), who put the town on the artistic map. The Madonna on the altarpiece and the tomb of Bishop Salutati are fine examples of the artist's work. ✉*Piazza Mino da Fiesole* ☎*055/59400* ◷*Nov.–Mar., daily 7:30– noon and 2–5; Apr.–Oct., daily 7:30–noon and 3–6.*

The beautifully preserved 2,000-seat **Anfiteatro Romano** *(Roman Amphitheater)*, near the Duomo, dates from the 1st century BC and is still used for summer concerts. To the right of the amphitheater are the remains of the **Terme Romani** (Roman Baths), where you can see the gymnasium, hot and cold baths, and rectangular chamber where the water was heated. A beautifully designed **Museo Archeologico,** an intricate series of levels connected by elevators, is built amid the ruins and contains objects dating from as early as 2000 BC. The nearby **Museo Bandini** is a small collection of interesting paintings. It's filled with the private collection of Canon Angelo Maria Bandini (1726–1803); he fancied 13th- to 15th-century Florentine paintings, terra-cotta pieces, and wood sculpture, which he later bequeathed to the Diocese of Fiesole. ⊠ *Via Portigiani 1* ☎ *055/59477* 💶 *€10, includes access to the archaeological park and museums* 🕙 *Apr.–Sept., daily 9:30–7; Oct.–Mar., Wed.–Mon. 10–4:30.*

The hilltop church of **San Francesco** has a good view of Florence and the plain below from its terrace and benches. Halfway up the hill you'll see sloping steps to the right; they lead to a lovely wooded park with trails that loop out and back to the church.

If you really want to stretch your legs, walk 4 km (2½ mi) toward the center of Florence along Via Vecchia Fiesolana, a narrow lane in use since Etruscan times, to the church of **San Domenico**. Sheltered in the church is the *Madonna and Child with Saints* by Fra Angelico, who was a Dominican friar here. ⊠ *Piazza San Domenico, off Via Giuseppe Mantellini* ☎ *055/59230* 💶 *Free* 🕙 *Daily 9–noon.*

From the church of San Domenico, it's a five-minute walk northwest to the **Badia Fiesolana**, which was the original cathedral of Fiesole. Dating to the 11th century, it was first the home of Camaldolese monks; later, Benedictines and Augustinians lived here. Thanks to Cosimo il Vecchio, the complex was substantially restructured. The facade, never completed due to the death of Cosimo, contains elements of its original Romanesque decoration. The attached convent once housed Cosimo's valued manuscripts; today it's the site of the European Institute, for pre- and postdoctoral studies. Its mid-15th-century cloister is well worth a look. ⊠ *Via della Badia dei Roccettini 11* ☎ *055/59155* 🕙 *Weekdays 9–6, Sat. 9:30–12:30.*

WHERE TO STAY & EAT

$$–$$$ ✕**Le Cave di Maiano.** If you're looking to get out of town, hop in your car (or take a taxi) to this simple trattoria in the hills just outside Florence. Italians flock here for Sunday lunch, probably because they enjoy the *buon rapporto fra qualità e prezzo* (the good rapport between quality and price). Tuscan staples are on hand, as is a fine plate of spaghetti with truffled asparagus. They grill well here, so consider something from the grill to follow. By all means leave room for dessert. Though the food is typical, they do it exceedingly well: the *zuppa cotta* should not be missed. ⊠ *Via Cave di Maiano 16* ☎ *055/59133* ▭ *AE, DC, MC, V.*

$ ✕**San Domenico.** Three-quarters of the way up the hill to Fiesole, this rather industrial-looking spot has tasty *pizze* as well as pastas. If you're hiking in the nearby hills, or going to see the Fra Angelico at the church of San Domenico, this is a perfect place to break for lunch. Outdoor seating in the summer looks directly onto a somewhat busy two-lane road. No matter: the air's still better here than in town and that makes the pizza taste so much better. ⊠ *Piazza San Domenico* ☎ *055/59182* ▭ *AE, DC, MC, V* 🕙 *Closed Mon.*

$$$$ 🏠**Villa San Michele.** The cypress-lined driveway provides an elegant preamble to this incredibly gorgeous (and very expensive) hotel nestled in the hills of Fiesole. The 16th-century building was originally a

10

Franciscan convent designed by Santi di Tito. Not a single false note is struck in the reception area (formerly the chapel), the dining rooms (a covered cloister and former refectory), or the tasteful antiques and art that decorate the rooms. The open-air loggia, where lunch and dinner are served, provides one of the most stunning views of Florence—a good thing, too, as the food is overpriced and bland. **Pros:** Exceptional convent conversion. **Cons:** Money must be no object. ⊠ *Via Doccia 4, 50014* ☎*055/59451* 🖷*055/5678250* ⊕*www.villasanmichele.com* ⟿*21 rooms, 24 suites* ⌂*In-room: safe, refrigerator, VCR, dial-up, Wi-Fi. In-hotel: restaurant, room service, bar, pool, gym, bicycles, concierge, laundry service, public Internet, parking (no fee), some pets allowed* ▭*AE, DC, MC, V* ⊗*Closed Dec.–Easter.*

$$$ 🏨 **Villa Aurora.** The attractive hotel on the main piazza takes advantage of its hilltop spot, with beautiful views in many of the rooms, some of which are on two levels with beamed ceilings and balconies. The building, constructed as a theater in 1860, was transformed into a hotel in the late 19th century. It's fit for queens, and quite a few of them—Queen Victoria and Margherita di Savoia among others—have stayed here. Rooms are sophisticated but understated, as is the hotel. **Pros:** Some rooms have pretty views, air quality better than in Florence. **Cons:** A little worn at the edges. ⊠*Piazza Mino da Fiesole 39, 50014* ☎*055/59363* 🖷*055/59587* ⊕*www.villaaurora.net* ⟿*23 rooms, 2 suites* ⌂*In-hotel: restaurant, bar, public Internet, some pets allowed* ▭*AE, DC, MC, V* ⦿*BP.*

Tuscany

WORD OF MOUTH

"The food in Tuscany, while simple and even rustic, can be some of the most satisfying in all of Italy. Wild boar ragù over pappardelle pasta, tagliatelle with sautéed porcini mushrooms, and savory grilled sausages are just some of the dishes we lust after stateside."

—mlt

WELCOME TO TUSCANY

TOP REASONS TO GO

★ **Piazza del Campo, Siena:** Sip a cappuccino, lick some gelato, and take in this spectacular shell-shaped piazza.

★ **Piero della Francesca's True Cross frescoes, Arezzo:** If your holy grail is great Renaissance art, seek out these 12 enigmatic scenes.

★ **San Gimignano:** Grab a spot at sunset on the steps of the Collegiata church as swallows swoop in and out of the famous medieval towers.

★ **Wine-tasting in Chianti:** Sample the fruits of the region's gorgeous vineyards, at either the wineries themselves or the wine bars found in the towns.

★ **Leaning Tower of Pisa:** It may be touristy, but now that you can once again climb to the top, it's touristy fun.

San Gimignano

1 Lucca. Relaxed yet elegant is a little world of its own, Lucca is surrounded by tree-bedecked 16th-century ramparts now used as delightful promenades.

2 Pisa. Thanks to an engineering mistake, the name Pisa is instantly recognized the world over. The Leaning Tower, the cathedral, and the baptistery (above) form one of Italy's prettiest religious complexes.

3 Chianti. The hillsides of Chianti present a rolling pageant of ageless vineyards and villas. Greve is the area's hub.

4 Hill Towns Southwest of Florence. The search for the best tiny hill town always leads to **San Gimignano**, known as the "medieval Manhattan" for its 15th-century stone towers. Farther west, Etruscan artifacts and Roman ruins are highlights of **Volterra**, set in a rugged moonscape of a valley.

5 Siena. The privileged hilltop site that helped Siena flourish in the Middle Ages keeps it one of Italy's most enchanting medieval towns today. At its heart is il Campo, where the frenzied 700-year-old horse race the Palio is held every July 2nd and August 16th.

6 Arezzo & Cortona. These two towns south of Chianti are rewarding side trips. Arezzo is best known for its sublime frescoes by Piero della Francesca. Cortona sits high above the perfectly flat Valdichiana valley, offering great views of beautiful countryside.

7 Southern Tuscany. Among the highlights of Tuscany's southern reaches are the wine-producing centers of **Montalcino** and **Montepulciano**, and, farther south, the thermal waters of **Saturnia**.

Lucca

GETTING ORIENTED

Hillsides blanketed with vineyards, silver-green olive groves, and enchanting towns are the essence of Tuscany, one of Italy's most beautiful landscapes. Little seems changed since the Renaissance: to the west of Florence, Pisa's tower still leans; to the south, Chianti's roads wind through cypress groves, taking you to Siena, with its captivating piazza.

Pistoia

Prato · Florence

A1

Greve

CHIANTI

71

San Gimignano

222

Castellina

68

Volterra

Arezzo

THE MARCHES

6

Cortona

Siena

326

Montalcino

7

Montepulciano

223

2

Grosseto

1

74

Porto Santo Stefano

Orbetello

GIGLIO

TUSCANY PLANNER

Making the Most of Your Time

Tuscany isn't the place for a jam-packed itinerary. One of the greatest pleasures here is indulging in rustic hedonism, marked by long lunches and show-stopping sunsets. Whether by car, bike, or foot, you'll want to get out into the glorious landscape, but it's smart to keep your plans modest. Set a church or a hill town or an out-of-the-way restaurant as your destination, knowing that half the pleasure is in getting there—admiring as you go the stately palaces, the tidy geometry of row upon row of grape vines, the fields vibrant with red poppies, sunflowers, and yellow broom.

You'll need to devise a Siena strategy. The place shouldn't be missed; it's compact enough that you can see the major sights on a day trip, and that's exactly what most people do. Spend the night, and you'll get to see the town breathe a sigh and relax upon the day-trippers' departure. The flip side is, your favorite Tuscan hotel isn't likely to be in Siena.

You face similar issues with Pisa and Lucca in the northwest. Pisa's famous tower is worth seeing, but ultimately Lucca has greater charms, making it a better choice for an overnight.

The Tourist Offices

The tourist information office in Greve is an excellent source for general information about the Chianti wine region and its hilltop towns. In Siena the centrally located tourist office, in Piazza del Campo, has information about Siena and its province. Both offices book hotel rooms for a nominal fee. Offices in smaller towns can also be a good place to check if you need last-minute accommodations.

Tourist bureaus in larger towns are typically open from 8:30 to 1 and 3:30 to 6 or 7; bureaus in villages are generally open from Easter until early November, but usually remain closed on Saturday afternoon and Sunday.

Finding a Place to Stay

A visit to Tuscany is a trip into the country. There are plenty of good hotels in the larger towns, but the classic experience is to stay in one of the rural accommodations—often converted private homes, sometimes working farms or vineyards (known as *agriturismi*). Though it's tempting to think you can stumble upon a little out-of-the-way hotel at the end of the day, you're better off not testing your luck. Make reservations before you go.

DINING & LODGING PRICE CATEGORIES (IN EUROS)				
¢	$	$$	$$$	$$$$
Restaurants				
under €15	€15–€25	€25–€35	€35–€45	over €45
Hotels				
under €70	€70–€110	€110–€160	€160–€220	over €220

Restaurant prices are for a first course (primo), second course (secondo), and dessert (dolce). Hotel prices are for two people in a standard double room in high season, including tax and service.

GETTING AROUND

By Car

Driving is the only way (other than hiking or biking) to get to many of Tuscany's small towns and vineyards. The cities west of Florence are easily reached by the A11, which leads to Lucca and then to the sea. The A1 takes you south from Florence to Arezzo and Chiusi (where you turn off for Montepulciano). Florence and Siena are connected by a superstrada and also the panoramic SS222, which threads through Chianti. The hill towns north and west of Siena lie along superstrade and winding local roads—all are well marked, but still arm yourself with a good map.

The Florence–Siena Superstrada (no number) is a four-lane, divided road with exits onto smaller country roads. The Via Cassia (SR2) winds its way south from Florence to Siena, along the western edge of the Chianti region. The superstrada is more direct, but much less scenic, than the SR2, and it can have a lot of traffic, especially on Sunday evenings. The Strada Chiantigiana (SR222) cuts through the center of Chianti, to the east of the superstrada, in a curvaceous path past vineyards and countryside.

By Train

Trains on Italy's main north–south rail line stop in Florence as well as Prato, Arezzo, and Chiusi. Another major line connects Florence with Pisa, and the coastal line between Rome and Genoa passes through Pisa as well. There's regular, nearly hourly service from Florence to Lucca, and several trips a day between Florence and Siena. Siena's train station is 2 km (1 mi) north of the centro storico, but cabs and city buses are readily available.

For other parts of Tuscany—Chianti, Montalcino, and Montepulciano, for example—you are better off going by bus or by car. Stations, when they exist, are far from the historic centers, and service is infrequent.

You can check the Web site of the state railway, the **Ferrovie dello Stato** (☎ *892021 toll-free within Italy* ⊕ *www.trenitalia.com*), for information. You can also get information and tickets at most travel agencies.

By Bus

Buses are a reliable but time-consuming means of getting around the region because they tend to stop in every town. Trains are a better option in virtually every respect when you're taking public transit to cities with good rail service, such as Pisa, Lucca, and Arezzo. But for most smaller towns, buses are the only option. Be aware that making arrangements for bus travel, particularly for a non-Italian speaker, can be a test of patience.

There are two primary bus services: **Tra-In** (☎ *0577/204111* ⊕ *www.trainspa.it*) covers much of the territory south of Siena, including Montalcino and Montepulciano. It also has several runs a day between Rome and Siena (2½ hours). **SITA** (☎ *0577/204270* ⊕ *www.sita-on-line.it*) has regular service between Florence and Siena (1 hour) as well as to numerous towns in Chianti. A third line, **CPT** (☎ *050/502564* ⊕ *www.cpt.pisa.it*), has infrequent buses between Volterra and Colle di Val d'Elsa, and also connects Volterra with nearest train station and Cecina.

EATING & DRINKING WELL IN TUSCANY

The influence of the ancient Etruscans—who favored the use of fresh herbs—is still felt in Tuscan cuisine three millennia later. Simple and earthy, Tuscan food celebrates the seasons with fresh vegetable dishes, wonderful bread-based soups, and meats perfumed with sage, rosemary, and thyme.

Throughout Tuscany there are excellent upscale restaurants that serve elaborate dishes, but to get a real taste of the flavors of the region, head for the family-run trattorias found in every town. The service and setting are often basic, but the food can be great.

Few places serve lighter fare at midday, so expect substantial meals at lunch and dinner, especially in out-of-the-way towns. Dining hours are fairly standard: lunch between 12:30 and 2, dinner between 7:30 and 10.

HOLD THE SALT

Tuscan bread is famous for what it's missing: it's made without salt. That's because it's intended to pick up seasoning from the food it accompanies; it's not to be eaten alone or dipped in a bowl of oil (which is a custom in American restaurants, but not Italian ones). Tuscans like their bread grilled and drizzled with olive oil (*crostino or fettunta*), covered with chicken-liver spread (*crostino di fegatini*), or rubbed with garlic and topped with tomatoes (*bruschetta*).

AFFETTATI MISTI

The name, roughly translated, means "mixed cold cuts," pictured left, and it's something Tuscans do exceptionally well. A platter of cured meats, served as an antipasto, is sure to include *prosciutto crudo* (ham, cut paper thin) and *salame* (dry sausage, prepared in dozens of ways—some spicy, some sweet). The most distinctly Tuscan affettati are made from *cinta senese* (a once nearly extinct pig found only in the heart of the region) and *cinghiale* (wild boar, which roam all of central Italy). You can eat these delicious slices unadorned or layered on a piece bread.

PASTA

Restaurants throughout Tuscany serve dishes similar to those in Florence, but they also have their own local specialties. Many recipes are from the *nonna* (grandmother) of the restaurant's owner, handed down through time but never written down. Look in particular for pasta creations made with *pici* (a long, thick, hand-rolled spaghetti), pictured below. *Pappardelle* (a long, flat pasta noodle), pictured upper right, is frequently paired with sauces made with game, such as *lepre* (hare) or cinghiale. In the northwest, a specialty of Lucca is *tordelli di carne al ragù* (meat-stuffed pasta with a meat sauce).

MEAT

Bistecca all fiorentina (a thick T-bone steak, grilled rare) is the classic meat dish of Tuscany, but there are other specialties as well. Many menus will include *tagliata di manzo* (thinly sliced, roasted beef, drizzled with olive oil), *arista di maiale* (roast pork with sage and rosemary), and *salsiccia e fagioli* (pork sausage and beans). In the southern part of the region, don't be surprised to find *piccione* (pigeon), which can be roasted, stuffed, or baked.

WINE

Grape cultivation here also dates from Etruscan times, and, particularly in Chianti, vineyards are abundant. The resulting medium-body red wine is a staple on most tables; however, you can select from a multitude of other varieties, including such reds as Brunello di Montalcino and Vino Nobile di Montepulciano and such whites as Vermentino and Vernaccia. Super Tuscans, a fanciful name given to a group of wines by American journalists, now command attention as some of the best produced in Italy; they have great depth and complexity. The dessert wine *vin santo* is made throughout the region and is often sipped with *biscotti* (twice-baked cookies), perfect for dunking.

Updated
by Peter
Blackman
& Patricia
Rucidlo

MIDWAY DOWN THE ITALIAN PENINSULA, Tuscany (Toscana in Italian) is distinguished by rolling hills, snowcapped mountains, dramatic cypress trees, and miles of coastline on the Tyrrhenian Sea—which all adds up to gorgeous views at practically every turn. The beauty of the landscape proves a perfect foil for the region's abundance of superlative art and architecture. It also produces some of Italy's finest wines and olive oils. The combination of unforgettable art, sumptuous views, and eminently drinkable wines that pair beautifully with its simple food makes a trip to Tuscany something beyond special.

Many of Tuscany's cities and towns have retained the same fundamental character over the past 500 years. Civic rivalries that led to bloody battles centuries ago have given way to soccer rivalries. Renaissance pomp lives on in the celebration of local feast days and centuries-old traditions such as the Palio in Siena and the Giostra del Saracino (Joust of the Saracen) in Arezzo. Often, present-day Tuscans look as though they might have served as models for paintings produced hundreds of years ago. In many ways, the Renaissance still lives on in Tuscany.

LUCCA

Ramparts built in the 16th and 17th centuries enclose a charming town filled with churches (99 of them), terra-cotta-roof buildings, and narrow cobblestone streets, along which local ladies maneuver bikes to do their daily shopping. Here Caesar, Pompey, and Crassus agreed to rule Rome as a triumvirate in 56 BC. Lucca was later the first Tuscan town to accept Christianity, and it still has a mind of its own: when most of Tuscany was voting communist as a matter of course, Lucca's citizens rarely followed suit. The famous composer Giacomo Puccini (1858–1924) was born here; his work forms the nucleus of the summer Opera Theater and Music Festival of Lucca. The ramparts circling the center city are the perfect place to take a stroll, ride a bicycle, kick a ball, or just stand and look down upon Lucca.

GETTING HERE
You can reach Lucca easily by train from Florence; the historic center is a short walk from the station. If you're driving, take the A11/E76.

VISITOR INFORMATION
Lucca tourism office (⊠ *Piazza Santa Maria 35* ☎ *0583/91991* ⊕ *www. lucca.turismo.toscana.it*).

EXPLORING LUCCA

The historic center of Lucca, 51 km (31 mi) west of Florence, is walled, and motorized traffic is restricted. Walking and biking are the most efficient and most enjoyable ways to get around. You can rent bicycles, and the flat center makes biking easy. A combination ticket costing €6.50 gains you admission to both the Museo Nazionale di Villa Guinigi and the Pinacoteca Nazionale di Palazzo Mansi.

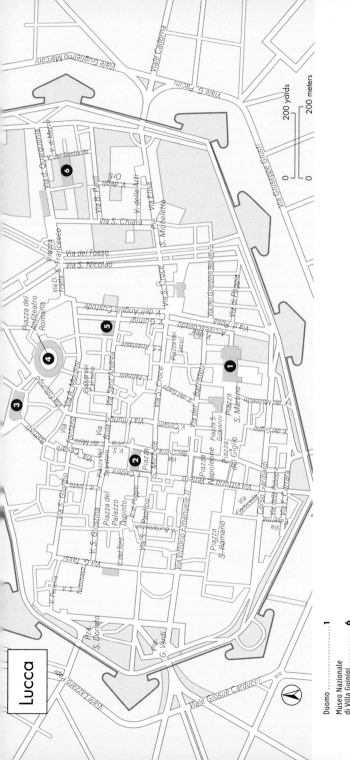

Lucca

THE MAIN ATTRACTIONS

❶ Duomo. The round-arch facade of the cathedral is a fine example of the rigorously ordered Pisan Romanesque style, in this case happily enlivened by an extremely varied collection of small carved columns. Take a closer look at the decoration of the facade and that of the portico below; they make this one of the most entertaining

church exteriors in Tuscany. The Gothic interior contains a moving Byzantine crucifix—called the Volto Santo, or Holy Face—brought here, according to legend, in the eighth century (though it probably dates from between the 11th and early 13th centuries). The masterpiece of the Sienese sculptor Jacopo della Quercia (circa 1371–1438) is the marble *Tomb of Ilaria del Carretto* (1407–1408). ⊠ *Piazza del Duomo* ☎ *0583/490530* 🎟 *€2* ⊙ *Duomo: weekdays 7–5:30, Sat. 9:30–6:45, Sun. 11:30–11:50 and 1–5:30. Tomb: Nov.–Mar., weekdays 9:30–4:45, Sat. 9:30–6:45, Sun. 11:30–11:50 and 1–5; Apr.–Oct., weekdays 9:30–5:45, Sat. 9–6:45, Sun. 9–10 and 1–5:45.*

★ **Passeggiata delle Mura.** Any time of day when the weather is clement, you can find the citizens of Lucca cycling, jogging, strolling, or kicking a soccer ball in this green, beautiful, and very large park—neither inside nor outside the city but rather right on the ring of ramparts that defines Lucca. Sunlight streams through two rows of tall plane trees to dapple the *passeggiata delle mura* (walk on the walls), which is 4.2 km (2½ mi) in length. Ten bulwarks are topped with lawns, many with picnic tables, and some with play equipment for children. Be aware at all times of where the edge is—there are no railings and the drop to the ground outside the city is a precipitous 40 feet.

NEED A BREAK?

Gelateria Veneta (⊠ *Via V. Veneto 74* ☎ *0583/467037*) makes outstanding gelato, sorbet, and ices (some sugar-free). They prepare their confections three times a day using the same recipes with which the Brothers Arnoldo opened the place in 1927. The pièces de résistance are frozen fruits stuffed with creamy filling: don't miss the apricot-sorbet-filled apricot. Note that they close shop in October and reopen around Easter.

❹ Piazza dell'Anfiteatro Romano. Here's where the ancient Roman amphitheater once stood; some of the medieval buildings built over the amphitheater retain its original oval shape and brick arches. ⊠ *Off Via Fillungo, near north side of old town.*

❸ San Frediano. The church of San Frediano, just steps from the Anfiteatro, has a 14th-century mosaic decorating its facade and contains works by Jacopo della Quercia (circa 1371–1438) and Matteo Civitali (1436–1501), as well as the lace-clad mummy of Saint Zita (circa 1218–78), the patron saint of household servants. ⊠ *Piazza San Frediano* ☎ *No phone* 🎟 *Free* ⊙ *Mon.–Sat. 8:30–noon and 3–5, Sun. 10:30–5.*

❷ San Michele in Foro. In the middle of the centro storico is this church with a facade even more fanciful than that of the Duomo. The upper levels of the facade have nothing but air behind them (after the front of the church was built, there were no funds to raise the nave), and the winged Archangel Michael, who stands at the very top, seems precariously poised for flight. The facade, heavily restored in the 19th century, displays busts of 19th-century Italian patriots such as Garibaldi and Cavour. Check out the superb Filippino Lippi (1457/58–1504) panel painting of Saints Girolamo, Sebastian, Rocco, and Helen in the right transept. ⊠ *Piazza San Michele* 🕾 *No phone* 🎫 *Free* 🕙 *Daily 9–noon and 3–6.*

❺ Torre Guinigi. The tower of the medieval Palazzo Guinigi contains one of the city's most curious sights: a grove of ilex trees has grown at the top of the tower and their roots have pushed their way into the room below. From the top you have a magnificent view of the city and the surrounding countryside. (Only the tower is open to the public, not the palazzo.) ⊠ *Palazzo Guinigi, Via Sant'Andrea* 🕾 *No phone* 🎫 *€3.50* 🕙 *Mar. and Apr., daily 9:30–6; May–Sept., daily 9–midnight; Oct.–Feb., daily 9–5.*

ALSO WORTH SEEING

❻ Museo Nazionale di Villa Guinigi. On the eastern end of the historic center, this museum has an extensive collection of local Romanesque and Renaissance art. The museum represents an overview of Lucca's artistic traditions from Etruscan times until the 17th century, housed in the former 15th-century villa of the Guinigi family. ⊠ *Villa Guinigi, Via della Quarquonia* 🕾 *0583/496033* 🎫 *€4, combination ticket €6.50 (includes Museo Nazionale di Palazzo Mansi)* 🕙 *Tues.–Sat. 8:30–7, Sun. 8:30–1:30.*

WHERE TO EAT

$$ ✕ **Buca di Sant'Antonio.** The staying power of Buca di Sant'Antonio—
★ it's been around since 1782—is the result of superlative Tuscan food brought to the table by waitstaff that doesn't miss a beat. The menu includes the simple-but-blissful, like *tortelli lucchesi al sugo* (meat-stuffed pasta with a tomato-and-meat sauce), and more daring dishes such as roast *capretto* (kid) with herbs. A white-wall interior hung with copper pots and brass musical instruments creates a classy but comfortable dining space. ⊠ *Via della Cervia 3* 🕾 *0583/55881* 🖃 *AE, DC, MC, V* 🕙 *Closed Mon., 1 wk in Jan., and 1 wk in July. No dinner Sun.*

$$ ✕ **Il Giglio.** Just off Piazza Napoleone, this restaurant has quiet, late-19th-century charm and classic cuisine. It's a place for all seasons, with a big fireplace for chilly weather and an outdoor patio in summer. If mushrooms are in season, try the *tacchonni con funghi*, a homemade pasta with mushrooms and a local herb called *niepitela*. A local favorite during winter is the *coniglio con olive* (rabbit stew with olives). ⊠ *Piazza del Giglio 2* 🕾 *0583/494508* 🖃 *AE, DC, MC, V* 🕙 *Closed Wed. and 15 days in Nov. No dinner Tues.*

$ ✕**Trattoria da Leo.** A few short turns away from the facade of San Michele, this noisy, informal, traditional trattoria delivers *cucina alla casalinga* (home cooking) in the best sense. Try the typical minestra di farro to start or just go straight to *secondi piatti* (entrées); in addition to the usual roast meats, there's excellent chicken with olives and a good cold dish of boiled meats served with a sauce of parsley and pine nuts. Save some room for a dessert, such as the rich, sweet, fig-and-walnut torte or the lemon sorbet brilliantly dotted with bits of sage, which tastes almost like mint. ⊠ *Via Tegrimi 1, at corner of Via degli Asili* ☎ *0583/492236* ⊟ *No credit cards* ☺ *No lunch Sun. Closed Sun. Nov.–Mar.*

WHERE TO STAY

$$$–$$$$ ⛋**Hotel Ilaria.** The former stables of the Villa Bottini have been transformed into a modern hotel within the historic center. A second-floor terrace, overlooking the villa, makes a comfortable place to relax, and there's a hot tub for the adventurous. Rooms are done in a warm wood veneer with blue and white fittings. The availability of free bicycles is a nice bonus in this bike-friendly city, and the sumptuous buffet breakfast could see you through dinner. Residenza dell'Alba, the hotel's annex across the street, was originally part of a 14th-century church; now it's a luxe accommodation with in-room hot tubs. **Pros:** A Fodor's reader sums it up as a "nice modern small hotel," free bicycles. **Cons:** Though in city center, it's a little removed from main attractions. ⊠ *Via del Fosso 26, 55100* ☎ *0583/47615* 🖷 *0583/991961* ⊕ *www.hotelilaria.com* ⟿ *36 rooms, 5 suites* ♿ *In-room: safe, refrigerator. In-hotel: bar, bicycles, concierge, laundry service, public Internet, parking (no fee), some pets allowed (fee)* ⊟ *AE, DC, MC, V* ⟊*BP.*

$$$ ⛋**Palazzo Alexander.** This small, elegant boutique hotel is on a quiet side street a short walk from San Michele in Foro. The building, dating from the 12th century, has been restructured to create the ease common to Lucchesi nobility: timbered ceilings, warm yellow walls, and brocaded chairs adorn the public rooms, and the motif continues into the guest rooms, all of which have high ceilings and that same glorious damask. Top-floor suites have sweeping views of the town. One suite is on the mezzanine floor, but also has city views. **Pros:** Intimate feel, gracious staff. **Cons:** Some Fodor's readers complain of too-thin walls. ⊠ *Via S. Giustina 48, 55100* ☎ *0583/583571* 🖷 *0583/583610* ⊕ *www.palazzo-alexander.com* ⟿ *9 rooms, 3 suites, 1 apartment* ♿ *In-room: safe, refrigerator, dial-up. In-hotel: bar, bicycles, concierge, laundry service, public Internet, parking (fee)* ⊟ *AE, DC, MC, V* ⟊*BP.*

$$ ⛋**Albergo San Martino.** Down a narrow street facing a quiet, sun-sprinkled *piazzale* (small square) stands this small hotel. The brocade bedspreads are fresh and crisp, the proprietor friendly. Although around the corner from the Duomo, the busy Corso Garibaldi, and the great walls of Lucca, the inn, tucked away as it is, feels private—a place to retreat to when you have seen all the church facades you can stand. Two of the eight rooms are wheelchair accessible. In the cheerful apricot breakfast room, filled with framed prints, you can get a more-than-solid breakfast. A little terrace with wicker chairs provides a

11

lovely place to unwind. **Pros:** Comfortable bed, great breakfast. **Cons:** Breakfast costs €20. ⊠ *Via della Dogana 9, 55100* ☎*0583/469181* 🖷*0583/991940* ⊕*www.albergosanmartino.it* ⇆*6 rooms, 2 suites* ⌂*In-room: refrigerator. In-hotel: bar, bicycles (fee), no elevator, laundry service*═*AE, DC, MC, V* ⊠❘*EP.*

$ 🖭**Piccolo Hotel Puccini.** Steps away from the busy square and church of San Michele, this little hotel is quiet and calm—and a great deal. Wallpaper, hardwood floors, and throw rugs are among the handsome decorations. Paolo, the genial manager, speaks fluent English and dispenses great touring advice. **Pros:** Cheery, English-speaking staff. **Cons:** Breakfast costs extra, some rooms are on the dark side. ⊠ *Via di Poggio 9, 55100* ☎*0583/55421* 🖷*0583/53487* ⊕*www.hotelpuccini.com* ⇆*14 rooms* ⌂*In-room: no a/c, safe. In-hotel: bar, laundry service, some pets allowed, no-smoking rooms* ═*AE, MC, V* ⊠❘*EP.*

SPORTS & THE OUTDOORS

A splendid bike ride (rental about €12.50 for the day) may be had by circling the entire historic center along the top of the bastions—affording something of a bird's-eye view. **Poli Antonio Biciclette** (⊠*Piazza Santa Maria 42, Lucca East* ☎*0583/493787*) is an option for bicycle rental on the east side.

SHOPPING

Lucca's justly famed olive oils are available throughout the city (and exported around the world). Look for those made by Fattoria di Fubbiano and Fattoria Fabbri—two of the best.

Antica Bottega di Prospero (⊠ *Via San Lucia 13* ☎*No phone)* sells top-quality local products, including farro, dried porcini mushrooms, olive oil, and wine.

★ Chocoholics can get their fix at **Caniparoli** (⊠ *Via S. Paolino 96, San Donato* ☎*0583/53456*). They are so serious about their sweets here that they do not make them from June through August because of the heat. Bargain hunters won't want to miss **Benetton Stock Outlet** (⊠ *Via Mordini 17/19, Anfiteatro* ☎*0583/464533*), with its brightly colored garments at reduced prices.

PISA

When you think Pisa, you think Leaning Tower. Its position as one of Italy's most famous landmarks is a heavy reputation to bear, and it comes accompanied by abundant crowds and kitschy souvenirs. But the building *is* interesting and novel, and even if it doesn't captivate you, Pisa has other treasures that make a visit worthwhile. Taken as a whole, the Campo dei Miracoli (Field of Miracles), where the Leaning Tower, Duomo, and Baptistery are located, is among the most dramatic architectural complexes in Italy.

Pisa may have been inhabited as early as the Bronze Age. It was certainly populated by the Etruscans and, in turn, became part of the Roman Empire. In the early Middle Ages it flourished as an economic powerhouse—along with Amalfi, Genoa, and Venice, it was one of the maritime republics. The city's economic and political power ebbed in the early 15th century as it fell under the domination of Florence, though it enjoyed a brief resurgence under Cosimo I in the mid-16th century. Pisa endured heavy Allied bombing—miraculously, the Duomo and Leaning Tower, along with some other grand Romanesque structures, were spared, though the Camposanto sustained heavy damage.

GETTING HERE

Pisa is an easy hour train ride from Florence. By car it's a straight shot on the Fi-Pi-Li autostrada. The Pisa–Lucca train runs frequently and takes about 30 minutes.

VISITOR INFORMATION

Pisa tourism office (⊠ *Piazza Vittorio Emanuele II* ☎ *050/42291*).

EXPLORING PISA

Pisa is 84 km (52 mi) west of Florence. Like many other Italian cities, the town is best seen on foot. The views along the Arno are particularly grand and shouldn't be missed—there's a sense of spaciousness here that the Arno in Florence lacks. You should weigh the different options for combination tickets to sights on the Piazza del Duomo when you begin your visit. Combination tickets are sold at the ticket office behind the Duomo opposite the Leaning Tower; one monument costs €5, two monuments €6, up to €8 for all the main sights, excluding the Leaning Tower.

THE MAIN ATTRACTIONS

❷ **Battistero.** This lovely Gothic baptistery, which stands across from the Duomo's facade, is best known for the pulpit carved by Nicola Pisano (circa 1220–84; father of Giovanni Pisano) in 1260. Ask one of the ticket takers if he'll sing for you inside; the acoustics are remarkable. ⊠ *Piazza del Duomo* ☎ *050/3872210* ⊕ *www.opapisa.it* ☜ *€5, discounts available if bought in combination with tickets for other monuments* ⊗ *Mar. 1–13, daily 9–6; Mar. 14–20, daily 9–7; Mar. 21–Sept., daily 8–8; Oct., daily 9–7; Nov.–Feb., daily 10–5.*

❸ **Duomo.** Pisa's cathedral brilliantly utilizes the horizontal marble stripe motif (borrowed from Moorish architecture) that became common to Tuscan cathedrals. It is famous for the Romanesque panels on the transept door facing the tower that depict scenes from the life of Christ. The beautifully carved 14th-century pulpit is by Giovanni Pisano (son of Nicola). ⊠ *Piazza del Duomo* ☎ *050/3872210* ⊕ *www.opapisa.it* ☜ *€2, discounts available if bought in combination with tickets for other monuments* ⊗ *Mar. 1–13, daily 9–6; Mar. 14–20, daily 10–7; Mar. 21–Sept., daily 10–8; Oct., daily 10–7; Nov.–Feb., daily 10–1 and 2–5.*

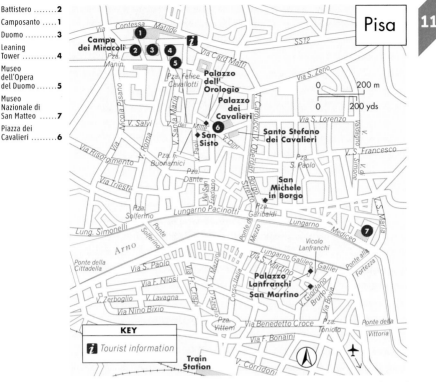

KEY

🛈 Tourist information

❹ **Leaning Tower** *(Torre Pendente)*. Legend holds that Galileo conducted
Fodor's Choice   an experiment on the nature of gravity by dropping metal balls from
★   the top of the 187-foot-high Leaning Tower of Pisa. Historians, however, say this legend has no basis in fact—which isn't quite to say that
it's false. Work on this tower, built as a campanile (bell tower) for the
Duomo, started in 1173: the lopsided settling began when construction
reached the third story. The tower's architects attempted to compensate
through such methods as making the remaining floors slightly taller on
the leaning side, but the extra weight only made the problem worse.
The settling continued, and by the late 20th century it had acceler-
ated to such a point that many feared the tower would simply topple
over, despite all efforts to prop it up. The structure has since been
firmly anchored to the earth. The final phase to restore the tower to its
original tilt of 300 years ago was launched in early 2000 and finished
two years later. The last phase removed some 100 tons of earth from
beneath the foundation. Reservations, which are essential, can be made
online or by calling the Museo dell'Opera del Duomo; it's also possible
to arrive at the ticket office and book for the same day. Note that children under eight years of age are not allowed to climb. ⊠ *Piazza del
Duomo* 🕾 *050/3872210* ⊕ *www.opapisa.it* 🎫 *€17* ☉ *Mar. 21–Sept.,
daily 8:30–8:30; Oct., daily 9–7; Nov.–Feb., daily 10–5; Mar. 1–Mar.
13, daily 9–6; Mar. 14–Mar. 20, daily 9–7.*

ALSO WORTH SEEING

1 Camposanto. According to legend, the cemetery—a walled structure on the western side of the Campo dei Miracoli—is filled with earth that returning Crusaders brought back from the Holy Land. Contained within are numerous frescoes, notably *The Drunkenness of Noah*, by Renaissance artist Benozzo Gozzoli (1422–97), presently under restoration; and the disturbing *Triumph of Death* (14th century; artist uncertain), whose subject matter shows what was on people's minds in a century that saw the ravages of the Black Death. ✉*Piazza del Duomo* ☎*050/3872210* ⊕*www.opapisa. it* 🎫*€5, discounts available if bought in combination with tickets for other monuments* ☉*Mar. 1–13, daily 9–6; Mar. 14–20, daily 9–7; Mar. 21–Sept., daily 8–8; Oct., daily 10–7; Nov.–Feb., daily 10–5.*

5 Museo dell'Opera del Duomo. At the southeast corner of the sprawling Campo dei Miracoli, this museum holds a wealth of medieval sculptures and the ancient Roman sarcophagi that inspired Nicola Pisano's figures. ✉*Piazza del Duomo* ☎*050/3872210* ⊕*www.opapisa.it* 🎫*€5, discounts available if bought in combination with tickets for other monuments* ☉ *Mar. 1–13, daily 9–6; Mar. 14–20, daily 9–7; Mar. 21–Sept., daily 8–8; Oct., daily 10–7; Nov.–Feb., daily 10–5.*

7 Museo Nazionale di San Matteo. On the north bank of the Arno, this museum contains some incisive examples of local Romanesque and Gothic art. ✉*Lungarno Mediceo* ☎*050/541865* 🎫*€5* ☉*Tues.–Sat. 9–7, holidays 9–2.*

6 Piazza dei Cavalieri. The piazza, with its fine Renaissance **Palazzo dei Cavalieri, Palazzo dell'Orologio,** and **Santo Stefano dei Cavalieri,** was laid out by Giorgio Vasari in about 1560. The square was the seat of the Ordine dei Cavalieri di San Stefano (Order of the Knights of St. Stephen), a military and religious institution meant to defend the coast from possible invasion by the Turks. Also in this square is the prestigious **Scuola Normale Superiore,** founded by Napoléon in 1810 on the French model. Here graduate students pursue doctorates in literature, philosophy, mathematics, and science. In front of the school is a large statue of Ferdinando I de' Medici dating from 1596. On the extreme left is the tower where the hapless Ugolino della Gherardesca (died 1289) was imprisoned with his two sons and two grandsons; legend holds that he ate them. Dante immortalized him in Canto XXXIII of *his Inferno.* Duck into the **Church of Santo Stefano** and check out Bronzino's *Nativity of Christ* (1564–65).

WHERE TO STAY & EAT

11

$$–$$$ ✕**Beny.** Apricot walls hung with etchings of Pisa make this small, single-room restaurant warmly romantic. Husband and wife Damiano and Sandra Lazzerini have been running the place for two decades, and it shows in their obvious enthusiasm while talking about the menu and daily specials. Beny specializes in fish: its *ripieno di polpa di pesce a pan grattato con salsa di seppie e pomodoro* (fish-stuffed ravioli with tomato-octopus sauce) is a delight. Another flavorful dish is the *sformato di verdura* (a flan with Jerusalem artichokes), which comes embellished with sweet *gamberoni* (shrimp). ⊠*Piazza Gambacorti 22* ☎*050/25067* ▤*AE, DC, MC, V* ⊙*Closed Sun. and 2 wks in mid-Aug. No lunch Sat.*

$$ ✕**Osteria dei Cavalieri.** This charming white-wall restaurant, a few steps
★ from Piazza dei Cavalieri, is reason enough to come to Pisa. They can do it all here—serve up exquisitely grilled fish dishes, please vegetarians, and prepare *tagliata* (thin slivers of rare beef) for meat lovers. Three set menus, from the sea, garden, and earth, are available, or you can order à la carte. For dinner there's an early seating (around 7:30) and a later one (around 9); opt for the later if you want time to linger over your meal. ⊠*Via San Frediano 16* ☎*050/580858* ⚭*Reservations essential* ▤*AE, DC, MC, V* ⊙*Closed Sun., 2 wks in Aug., and Dec. 29–Jan. 7. No lunch Sat.*

$$$$ ⌂**Hotel Relais dell'Orologio.** What used to be a private family palace opened as an intimate hotel in spring of 2003. Eighteenth-century antiques fill the rooms and public spaces; some rooms have stenciled walls and wood-beam ceilings. On the third floor, sloped ceilings add romance. A large shared sitting room, complete with fireplace, provides a relaxing spot to read or sip a glass of wine. **Pros:** Location—in the center of town, but on a quiet side street. **Cons:** Breakfast costs extra. ⊠*Via della Faggiola 12/14, off Campo dei Miracoli, Santa Maria, 56126* ☎*050/830361* ⊠*050/551869* ⊕*www.hotelrelaisorologio.com* ⇆*16 rooms, 5 suites* ⊘*In-room: safe, refrigerator, dial-up. In-hotel: restaurant, room service, bar, concierge, laundry service, parking (fee), some pets allowed, no-smoking rooms, minibar* ▤*AE, DC, MC, V* ⑩*EP.*

$$ ⌂**Royal Victoria.** In a pleasant palazzo facing the Arno, a 10-minute walk from the Campo dei Miracoli, this comfortably furnished hotel has been in the Piegaja family since 1837. That continuity may help explain why such notables as Charles Dickens and Charles Lindbergh enjoyed staying here. Antiques and reproductions are in the lobby and in some rooms, whose style ranges from the 1800s, complete with frescoes, to the 1920s. Ask for a room in the charming old tower. There's also a pretty rooftop garden where you can order cocktails. **Pros:** Friendly staff, free use of a Lancia that seats five—a great vehicle for tooling around Pisa. **Cons:** Rooms vary significantly in size; all are a little worn. ⊠*Lungarno Pacinotti 12, 56126* ☎*050/940111* ⊠*050/940180* ⊕*www.royalvictoria.it* ⇆*48 rooms, 40 with bath* ⊘*In-room: no a/c (some), dial-up. In-hotel: room service, bicycles, concierge, laundry service, parking (fee), some pets allowed* ▤*AE, DC, MC, V* ⑩*BP.*

CHIANTI

Chianti, directly south of Florence, is one of Italy's most famous wine-producing areas; its hill towns, olive groves, and vineyards are quintessential Tuscany. Many British and northern Europeans have relocated here, drawn by the unhurried life, balmy climate, and charming villages; there are so many Britons, in fact, that the area has been nicknamed Chiantishire. Still, it remains strongly Tuscan in character, with drop-dead views of vine-quilted hills and elegantly elongated cypress trees.

The sinuous SS222 highway, known as the Strada Chiantigiana, runs from Florence through the heart of Chianti. Its most scenic section connects Strada in Chianti, 16 km (10 mi) south of Florence, and Greve in Chianti, whose triangular central piazza is surrounded by restaurants and vintners offering *degustazioni* (wine tastings), 11 km (7 mi) farther south.

GREVE IN CHIANTI

40 km (25 mi) northeast of Colle Val d'Elsa, 27 km (17 mi) south of Florence.

GETTING HERE
Driving from Florence or Siena, Greve is easily reached via the Strada Chiantigiana (SR222). SITA buses travel frequently between Florence and Greve. Tra-In and SITA buses connect Siena and Greve, but a direct trip is virtually impossible. There is no train service to Greve.

VISITOR INFORMATION
Greve in Chianti tourism offices (⊠ *Via Giovanni da Verrazzano 59* ☎ *055/8546287* ⊠ *Via Giovanni da Verrazzano 33* ☎ *055/8546299*).

EXPLORING
If there's a capital of Chianti, it's Greve, a friendly market town with no shortage of cafés, *enoteche* (wine bars), and craft shops lining its main square.

The gently sloping, asymmetrical **Piazza Matteotti** is an attractive arcade whose center holds a statue of the discoverer of New York harbor, Giovanni da Verrazano (circa 1480–1527). Check out the lively market held here on Saturday morning.

The church of **Santa Croce** has a triptych by Bicci di Lorenzo (1373–1452) and an *Annunciation* painted by an anonymous Florentine master that dates from the 14th century. ⊠ *Small end of Piazza Matteotti* ☎ *No phone* 🎟 *Free* ⊙ *Daily 9–1 and 3–7.*

About 2 km (1 mi) west of Greve in Chianti is the tiny hilltop hamlet of **Montefioralle.** This is the ancestral home of Amerigo Vespucci (1454–1512), the mapmaker, navigator, and explorer who named America. (His niece Simonetta may have been the inspiration for Sandro Botticelli's *Birth of Venus,* painted sometime in the 1480s.)

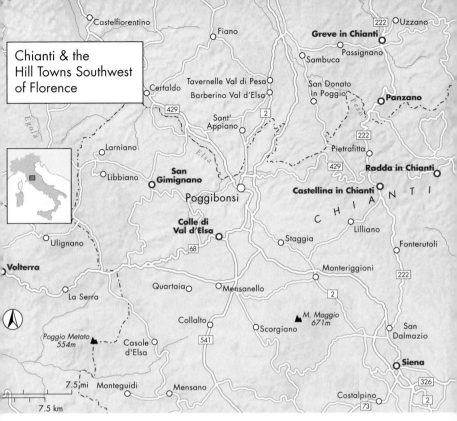

Chianti & the
Hill Towns Southwest
of Florence

WHERE TO STAY & EAT

★ **$$$$** ✕ **Osteria di Passignano.** Sophisticated country dining may not get better than at this deceptively simple restaurant next to a Vallombrosan abbey. A tiny sampling (maybe *sformatino di pecorino di fosso*, a flan made with aged pecorino) whets the appetite for what's to come. The young chefs in the kitchen can do traditional as well as whimsical Tuscan—and then divine things such as the *maccheroni del Martelli al ragù bianco di agnelli e carciofi morellini* (tubular pasta with a lamb and artichoke sauce), which really isn't Tuscan at all. The wine list is unbeatable, as is the service. ⊠ *Via Passignano 33, Località Badia a Passignano* ✛ *15 km (9 mi) east of Greve in Chianti* ☏ *055/8071278* ▤ *AE, DC, MC, V* ⊘ *Closed Sun., Jan. 7–Feb. 1, and 15 days in Aug.*

★ **$$–$$$** ✕ **Ristoro di Lamole.** Although off the beaten path (in this case, the SS222), this place is worth the effort to find—up a winding hill road lined with olive trees and vineyards. The view from the outdoor terrace is divine, as is the simple, exquisitely prepared Tuscan cuisine. Start with the bruschetta drizzled with olive oil or the sublime *verdure sott'olio* (vegetables marinated in oil) before moving on to any of the fine *secondi*. The kitchen has a way with *coniglio* (rabbit); don't pass it up if it's on the menu. ⊠ *Off SS222, Lamole in Chianti* ☏ *055/8547050* ▤ *AE, DC, MC, V* ⊘ *Closed Jan. 6–Feb. 28.*

★ $ ✕**Enoteca Fuoripiazza.** Detour off Greve's flower-strewn main square for food that relies heavily on local ingredients (especially those produced by nearby makers of cheese and salami). The lengthy wine list provides a bewildering array of choices to pair with *affettati misti* (a plate of cured meats) or one of their primi—the *pici* (a thick, short noodle) is deftly prepared here. All the dishes are made with great care. ⊠ *Via I Maggio 2, Piazza Trenta* ☎ *055/8546313* ▭ *AE, DC, MC, V* ⊗ *Closed Mon.*

$$$$ ⊞**Villa Bordoni.** David and Catherine Gardner, Scottish expats, have
Fodor's Choice transformed a ramshackle 16th-century villa into a stunning little hotel
★ nestled in the hills above Greve. Much care has been taken in decorating the rooms, no two of which are alike. All have stenciled walls; some have four-poster beds, others small mezzanines. Bathrooms are a riot of color, with tiles from Vietri. A sitting room on the second floor, with a cozy fireplace, is the perfect place for a cup of tea or a glass of wine. The hotel's restaurant has a talented young chef who gives cooking lessons in the modern kitchen. **Pros:** Splendidly isolated, beautiful decor, wonderful hosts. **Cons:** On a long and bumpy dirt road, need a car to get around. ⊠ *Via San Cresci 31/32, Località Mezzuola, 50022* ☎ *055/8547453* ⊕ *www.villabordoni.com* ⤶ *8 rooms, 3 suites* ⌂ *In-room: safe, dial-up, Wi-Fi. In-hotel: restaurant, pool, bicycles, laundry service, public Wi-Fi, parking (no fee)* ▭ *AE, DC, MC, V* ⊗ *Closed 3 wks in Jan. and Feb.* ⅋◎⅋*BP.*

$$ ⊞**Villa Vignamaggio.** Reputed to be the birthplace of the woman made famous by Leonardo da Vinci's *Mona Lisa,* the Villa Vignamaggio has origins in the 14th century. This historic estate, which includes the main building and two small cottages, is surrounded by manicured classical Italian gardens. Some rooms have exposed beams, whereas others have the genuine ancient plaster walls that faux-paint treatments attempt to replicate. The villa also produces some very fine wines; ask about tastings at the reception desk. Fodors.com users report that the villa is in a "good location for day trips in northern Tuscany." A minimum stay of two nights is required. **Pros:** Unbeatable views, informative wine tastings. **Cons:** No elevator to third floor, the staff seems less than attentive. ⊠ *Via Petriolo 5, Località Vicchiomaggio 50022* ☎ *055/854661* ⊕ *www.vignamaggio.com* ⤶ *3 rooms, 4 suites, 13 apartments, 2 cottages* ⌂ *In-room: kitchen (some). In-hotel: tennis court, pools, no elevator, laundry service, public Internet, some pets allowed* ▭ *AE, DC, MC, V* ⊗ *Closed mid-Nov.–mid-Mar.* ⅋◎⅋*BP.*

$ ⊞**Albergo del Chianti.** At a corner of the Piazza Matteotti, the Albergo del Chianti has rooms with views of the square or out over the tile rooftops toward the surrounding hills. Plain modern cabinets and wardrobes stand near wrought-iron beds. The swimming pool, sunny terrace, and grassy lawn behind the hotel are a nice surprise. **Pros:** Central location, best value in Greve. **Cons:** Rooms facing the piazza can be noisy, lobby is run-down, small bathrooms. ⊠ *Piazza Matteotti 86, 50022* ☎ *055/853763* ⊕ *www.albergodelchianti.it* ⤶ *16 rooms* ⌂ *In-room: refrigerator. In-hotel: restaurant, bar, pool, public Wi-Fi* ▭ *MC, V* ⊗ *Closed Jan.* ⅋◎⅋*BP.*

PANZANO

7 km (4½ mi) south of Greve, 29 km (18 mi) south of Florence.

GETTING HERE

From Florence or Siena, Panzano is easily reached by car along the Strada Chiantigiana (SR222). SITA buses travel frequently between Florence and Panzano. From Siena, the journey by bus is extremely difficult because SITA and Tra-In do not coordinate their schedules. There is no train service to Panzano.

EXPLORING

The little town of Panzano, between Greve in Chianti and Castellina in Chianti, has inviting shops, and enoteche offering tastes of the local wine.

An ancient church even by Chianti standards, the hilltop **San Leolino** probably dates from the 10th century, but it was completely rebuilt in the Romanesque style sometime in the 13th century. It has a 14th-century cloister worth seeing. The 16th-century terra-cotta tabernacles are attributed to Giovanni della Robbia, and there's also a remarkable triptych (attributed to the Master of Panzano) that was executed sometime in the mid-14th century. Open days and hours are unpredictable; check with the tourist office in Greve in Chianti for the latest. *3 km (2 mi) south of Panzano, Località San Leolino* *No phone* *Free.*

WHERE TO STAY & EAT

$$ **Solociccia.** "Abandon all hope, ye who enter here," announces the menu, "you're in the hands of a butcher." Indeed you are, for this restaurant is the creation of Dario Cecchini, Panzano's local merchant of meat. Served at communal tables, the set meal consists of no less than six meat courses, chosen at Dario's discretion. They are accompanied by seasonal vegetables, white beans with olive oil, and focaccia bread. Though Cecchini emphasizes that steak is never on the menu, this lively, crowded place is definitely not for vegetarians. The *entrance is on Via XX Luglio* *Via Chiantigiana 550022* *055/852727* *Reservations essential* *AE, DC, MC, V* *Closed Mon.–Wed. No dinner Sun.*

$$$$ Fodor's Choice ★ **Villa Le Barone.** Once the home of the Viviani della Robbia family, this 16th-century villa in a grove of ancient cypress trees retains many aspects of a private country dwelling. It feels like a "second home," according to some fodors.com users. The honor bar allows you to enjoy an *aperitivo* on the terrace while admiring the views of the pool to the rose gardens, across the hills to the town. Guest rooms have white-plaster walls, timber ceilings, and some tile floors. The restaurant uses fresh produce from the owner's farm in western Tuscany. Though the hotel staff may recommend it, the full, three-meal plan is not mandatory. **Pros:** Beautiful location, wonderful restaurant, great base for exploring the region. **Cons:** Noisy a/c, 20-minute walk to nearest town. *Via San Leolino 19, 50022* *055/852621* *www.villalebarone.it* *30 rooms* *In-room: no a/c (some), no TV. In-hotel: restaurant, bar, tennis court, pool, no elevator, concierge, laundry service, public Internet* *AE, MC, V* *Closed Nov.–Easter* *BP.*

RADDA IN CHIANTI

26 km (15 mi) south of Panzano, 52 km (32 mi) south of Florence.

GETTING HERE

Radda can be reached by car from either Siena or Florence along the SR222 (Strada Chiantigiana), and from the A1 highway. Three Tra-In buses make their way from Siena to Radda. One morning SITA bus travels from Florence to Radda. There is no train service convenient to Radda.

VISITOR INFORMATION

Radda in Chianti tourism office (⊠ *Piazza Ferrucci 1* ☎ *0577/738494*).

EXPLORING

Radda in Chianti sits on a hill separating two valleys, Val di Pesa and Val d'Arbia. It's one of many tiny Chianti villages that invite you to stroll their steep streets; follow the signs pointing you toward the *camminamento*, a covered medieval passageway circling part of the city inside the walls.

★ If you only have time for one castle, visit the stunning **Castello di Brolio.** At the end of the 12th century, when Florence conquered southern Chianti, Brolio became Florence's southernmost outpost, and it was often said, "When Brolio growls, all Siena trembles." Brolio was built about AD 1000 and owned by the monks of the Badia Fiorentina; the "new" owners, the Ricasoli family, have been in possession since 1141. Bettino Ricasoli (1809–80), the so-called Iron Baron, was one of the founders of modern Italy and is said to have invented the original formula for Chianti wine. Brolio, one of Chianti's best-known labels, is still justifiably famous. Its cellars may be toured by appointment. There's a sign at the Brolio gate that translates as RING BELL AND BE PATIENT. You pull a rope and the bell above the ramparts peals, and in a short time, the caretaker arrives to let you in. The grounds are worth visiting, even though the 19th-century manor house is not open to the public. (The current baron is very much in residence.) There are two apartments here available for rent by the week. ⊠ *Località Brolio ⊹ 2 km (1 mi) southeast of Gaiole* ☎ *0577/730227* 🎫 *€5* ☉ *June–Sept., daily 9–noon and 2–6:30; Oct.–May, Sat.–Thurs. 9–noon and 2–6:30.*

East of Radda a turnoff leads to the **Badia a Coltibuono** *(Abbey of the Good Harvest)*, which has been owned by Lorenza de' Medici's family for more than a century and a half (the family isn't closely related to the Renaissance-era Medici). Wine has been produced here since the abbey was founded by Vallombrosan monks in the 11th century. Today the family continues the tradition, making Chianti Classico and other wines, along with cold-pressed olive oil and various flavored vinegars and floral honeys. A small Romanesque church with campanile is surrounded by 2,000 acres of oak, fir, and chestnut woods threaded with walking paths—open to all—that pass two small lakes. Though the abbey itself, built between the 11th and 18th centuries, serves as the family's home, parts are open for tours (in English, German, or Italian). Visit the jasmine-draped main courtyard, the inner cloister with

Continued on page 655

GRAPE ESCAPES
THE PLEASURES OF TUSCAN WINE

The vineyards stretching across the landscape
of Tuscany may look like cinematic backdrops,
but in fact they're working farms, and they
produce some of Italy's best wines. No matter
whether you're a wine novice or a connoisseur,
there's great pleasure to be had from exploring this
lush terrain, visiting the vineyards, and uncorking a bottle
for yourself.

GETTING TO KNOW TUSCAN WINE

Most of the wine produced in Tuscany is red (though there are some notable whites as well), and most Tuscan reds are made primarily from one type of grape, sangiovese. That doesn't mean, however, that all wines here are the same. God (in this case Bacchus) is in the details: differences in climate, soil, and methods of production result in wines with several distinct personalities.

Chianti

Chianti is the most famous name in Tuscan wine, but what exactly the name means is a little tricky. It once identified wines produced in the region extending from just south of Florence to just north of Siena. In the mid-20th century, the official Chianti zone was expanded to include a large portion of central Tuscany. That area is divided into eight subregions. **Chianti Classico** is the name given to the original zone, which makes up 17,000 of the 42,000 acres of Chianti-producing vineyards.

WINE REGIONS OF CENTRAL TUSCANY

Classico wines, which bear the *gallo nero* (black rooster) logo on their labels, are the most highly regarded Chiantis (with **Rùfina** running second), but that doesn't mean Classicos are always superior. All Chiantis are strictly regulated (they must be a minimum 75% to 80% sangiovese, with other varieties blended in to add nuance), and they share a strong, woodsy character that's well suited to Tuscan food. It's a good strategy to drink the local product—**Colli Senesi Chianti** when in Siena, for example. The most noticeable, and costly, difference comes when a Chianti is from *riserva* (reserve) stock, meaning it's been aged for at least two years.

DOC & DOCG The designations "DOC" and "DOCG"—Denominazione di Origine Controllata (e Garantita)—mean a wine comes from an established region and adheres to rigorous standards of production. Ironically, the esteemed Super Tuscans are labeled *vini da tavola* (table wines), the least prestigious designation, because they don't use traditional grape blends.

Brunello di Montalcino

The area surrounding the hill town of Montalcino, to the south of Siena, is drier and warmer than the Chianti regions, and it produces the most powerful of the sangiovese-based wines. Regulations stipulate that Brunello di Montalcino be made entirely from sangiovese grapes (no blending) and aged at least four years. **Rosso di Montalcino** is a younger, less complex, less expensive Brunello.

The Super Tuscans

Beginning in the 1970s, some winemakers, chafing at the regulations imposed on established Tuscan wine varieties, began blending and aging wines in innovative ways. Thus were born the so-called Super Tuscans. These pricey, French oak–aged wines are admired for their high quality, led by such star performers as **Sassicaia**, from the Maremma region, and **Tignanello**, produced at the Tenuta Marchesi Antinori near Badia a Passignano. Purists, however, lament the loss of local identity resulting from the Super Tuscans' use of nonnative grape varieties such as cabernet sauvignon and merlot.

Vino Nobile di Montepulciano

East of Montalcino is Montepulciano, the town at the heart of the third, and smallest, of Tuscany's top wine districts.

Blending regulations aren't as strict for Vino Nobile as for Chianti and Brunello, and as a result it has a wider range of characteristics. Broadly speaking, though, Vino Nobile is a cross between Chianti and Brunello—less acidic than the former and softer than the latter. It also has a less pricey sibling, **Rosso di Montepulciano.**

The Whites

Most whites from Tuscany are made from **trebbiano** grapes, which produce a wine that's light and refreshing but not particularly aromatic or flavorful—it may hit the spot on a hot afternoon, but it doesn't excite connoisseurs.

Golden-hewed **Vernaccia di San Gimignano** is a local variety with more limited production but greater personality—it's the star of Tuscan whites. Winemakers have also brought chardonnay and sauvignon grapes to the region, resulting in wines that, like some Super Tuscans, are pleasant to drink but short on local character.

TOURING & TASTING IN TUSCAN WINE COUNTRY

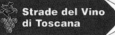

Strade del Vino di Toscana

Tuscany has visitor-friendly wineries, but the way you go about visiting is a bit different here from what it is in California or France. Many wineries welcome drop-ins for a tasting, but for a tour you usually need to make an appointment a few days in advance. There are several approaches you can take, depending on how much time you have and how serious you are about wine:

PLAN 1: FULL IMMERSION. Make an appointment to tour one of the top wineries (see our recommendations on the next page), and you'll get the complete experience: half a day of strolling through vineyards, talking grape varieties, and tasting wine, often accompanied by food. Groups are small; in spring and fall, it may be just you and the winemaker. The cost is usually €10 to €15 per person, but can go up to €40 if a meal is included. Remember to specify a tour in English.

PLAN 2: SEMI-ORGANIZED. If you want to spend a few hours going from vineyard to vineyard, make your first stop one of the local tourist information offices—they're great resources for maps, tasting itineraries, and personalized advice about where to visit. The offices in **Greve**, **Montalcino**, and **Montepulciano** are the best equipped. **Enoteche** (for more about them, turn the page) can also be good places to pick up tips about where to go for tastings.

PLAN 3: SPONTANEOUS. Along Tuscany's country roads you'll see signs for wineries offering **vendita diretta** (direct sales) and **degustazioni** (tastings). For a taste of the local product with some atmosphere thrown in, a spontaneous visit is a perfectly viable approach. You may wind up in a simple shop or an elaborate tasting room; either way, there's a fair chance you'll sample something good. Expect a small fee for a three-glass tasting.

THE PICK OF THE VINEYARDS

Within the Chianti Classico region, these wineries should be at the top of your to-visit list, whether you're dropping in for a taste or making a full tour. (Tours require reservations unless otherwise indicated.)

CHIANTI CLASSICO

Badia a Coltibuono

(✉ Gaiole in Chianti ☎0577/749498 ⊕ www.coltibuono. com). Along with an extensive prelunch tour and tasting, there are shorter afternoon tours, no reservation required, starting on the hour from 2 to 5. (See "Gaiole in Chianti" in this chapter.)

Castello di Fonterutoli

(✉ Castellina in Chianti ☎0577/73571 ⊕ www. fonterutoli.it). Hour-long tours include a walk through the neighboring village.

Castello di Volpaia

(✉ Radda in Chianti ☎0577/738066 ⊕ www. volpaia.com). The castle is part of the tiny town of Volpaia, perched above Radda.

Castello di Verrazzano

(✉ Via S. Martino in Valle 12, Greve in Chianti ☎055/854243 ⊕ www. verrazzano.com). Tours here take you down to the cellars, through the gardens, and into the woods in search of wild boar.

Villa Vignamaggio (✉ Via Petriolo 5, Greve in Chianti ☎055/854661 ⊕ www. vignamaggio.com). Along with a wine tour, you can spend the night at this villa where Mona Lisa is believed to have been born. (See "Where to Stay" under "Greve in Chianti" in this chapter.)

Rocca delle Màcie

(✉ Località Le Macìe 45, Castellina in Chianti ☎0577/732236 ⊕ www.rocca dellemacie.com). A full lunch or dinner can be incorporated into your tasting here.

Castello di Brolio

(✉ Gaiole in Chianti ☎0577/730220 ⊕ www.ricasoli.it). One of Tuscany's most impressive castles also has a centuries-old winemaking tradition. (See "Gaiole in Chianti" in this chapter.)

REMEMBER

Always have a designated driver when you're touring and tasting. Vineyards are usually located off narrow, curving roads. Full sobriety is a must behind the wheel.

MORE TUSCAN WINE RESOURCES

Enoteche: Wine Shops

The word *enoteca* in Italian can mean "wine store," "wine bar," or both. In any event, *enoteche* (the plural, pronounced "ay-no-*tek*-ay") are excellent places to sample and buy Tuscan wines, and they're also good sources of information about local wineries. There are scores to choose from. These are a few of the best:

Enoteca Italiana, Siena (Fortezza Medicea, Viale Maccari ☎ 0577/288497 ⊕ www. enoteca-italiana.it). The only one of its kind, this *enoteca* represents all the producers of DOC and DOCG wines in Italy and stocks over 400 labels. Wine by the glass and snacks are available.

Enoteca Osticcio, Montalcino (⊠ Via Matteotti 23 ☎ 0577/848271 ⊕ www. osticcio.com). There are more than one thousand labels in stock. With one of the best views in Montalcino, it is also a very pleasant place to sit and meditate over a glass of Brunello.

Enoteca del Gallo Nero, Greve in Chianti (⊠ Piazzetta S. Croce 8 ☎ 055/853297). This is one of the best stocked *enoteche* in the Chianti region.

Palazzo Avignonesi, Montepulciano (Via di Gracciano nel Corso 91 ☎ 0578/757872). The streets of Montepulciano are lined with *enoteche,* but these 12th-century cellars of the Avignonesi winery merit special mention.

Wine on the Web

Tuscan wine country is well represented on the Internet. A good place for an overview is ⊕ www.terreditoscana.regione.-toscana.it. (Click on "Le Strade del Vino"; the page that opens next will give you the option of choosing an English-language version.) This site shows 14 *strade del vino* (wine roads) that have been mapped out by consortiums representing major wine districts (unfortunately, Chianti Classico isn't included), along with recommended itineraries. You'll also find links to the consortium Web sites, where you can dig up more detailed information on touring. The Chianti Classico consortium's site is ⊕ www.chianticlassico.com. The Vino Nobile di Montepulciano site is ⊕ www.vinonobiledimontepulciano.it, and Brunello di Montalcino is ⊕ www. consorziobrunellodimontalcino.it. All have English versions.

its antique well, the musty old aging cellars, and the Renaissance-style garden redolent of lavender, lemons, and roses. In the shop, **L'Osteria,** you can taste wine and honey, as well as pick up other items like homemade beeswax hand lotion in little ceramic dishes. The Badia is closed on public holidays. ✉ *Località Badia a Coltibuono* ✥ *4 km (2½ mi) north of Gaiole* ☎ *0577/749498 for tours, 0577/749479 for shop* 🖷 *0577/749235* 🌐 *www.coltibuono.com* 🎫 *Abbey €3* ⏲ *Tours: May–July and Sept. and Oct., weekdays 2:30, 3, 3:30, 4; shop: Mar.–mid-Jan., daily 9–1 and 2–7.*

OFF THE BEATEN PATH

Volpaia. Perched atop a hill 10 km (6 mi) north of Radda is Volpaia, a fairy-tale hamlet that was a military outpost from the 10th to the 16th century and once a shelter for religious pilgrims. Every August, for the Festa di San Lorenzo, people come to Volpaia to watch for falling stars and a traditional fireworks display put on by the family that owns the adjacent wine estate and agriturismo lodging, **Castello di Volpaia** (✉ *Piazza della Cisterna 1, 53017* ☎ *0577/738066*).

WHERE TO STAY & EAT

$–$$ Fodor'sChoice ★ ✕ **Osteria Le Panzanelle.** Silvia Bonechi's experience in the kitchen—and a few precious recipes handed down from her grandmother—is one of the reasons for the success of this small restaurant. The other is the front-room hospitality of Nada Michelassi. These two *panzanelle* (women from Panzano) serve a short menu of tasty and authentic dishes at what the locals refer to as *prezzi giusti* (the right prices). Both the *pappa al pomodoro* (tomato soup) and the *peposo* (peppery beef stew) are exceptional. Whether you are eating inside or under large umbrellas on the terrace near a tiny stream, the experience is always congenial. "The best food we had in Tuscany," writes one user of fodors.com. Reservations are essential in July and August. ✉ *Località Lucarelli 29 j 8 km (5 mi) northwest of Radda on road to Panzano, 53017* ☎ *0577/733511* 💳 *MC, V* ⏲ *Closed Mon. and Jan. and Feb.*

$$$–$$$$ Fodor'sChoice ★ ✕🏨 **Relais Fattoria Vignale.** On the outside it's a rather plain manor house with an annex across the street. Inside it's a refined and comfortable country house with numerous sitting rooms that have terra-cotta floors and nice stonework. Guest rooms have exposed-brick walls and wood beams and are filled with simple wooden furnishings and handwoven rugs. The grounds, flanked by vineyards and olive trees, are equally inviting, with lawns, terraces, and a pool. The sophisticated Ristorante Vignale ($–$$$) serves excellent wines and local specialties like *cinghiale in umido con nepitella e vin cotto* (wild boar stew flavored with catmint and wine). **Pros:** Intimate public spaces, excellent restaurant, helpful and friendly staff. **Cons:** North-facing rooms blocked by tall cypress trees, single rooms are small, annex across a busy road. ✉ *Via Pianigiani 9, 53017* ☎ *0577/738300 hotel, 0577/738094 restaurant, 0577/738012 enoteca* 🌐 *www.vignale.it* 🛏 *37 rooms, 5 suites* 👍 *In-room: safe, refrigerator. In-hotel: restaurant, bar, pool, concierge, laundry service, public Internet* 💳 *AE, DC, MC, V* ⏲ *Closed Nov.–Mar. 15.* 🍽 *BP.*

¢ 🏨 **La Bottega di Giovannino.** The name is actually that of the wine bar run by Giovannino Bernardoni and his daughter Monica, who also rent rooms in the house next door. This is a fantastic place for the budget-conscious traveler, as rooms are immaculate. Most have a stunning view of the surrounding hills. All have their own bath, though most of them necessitate taking a short trip outside one's room. **Pros:** Great location in the center of town, close to restaurants and shops, super value. **Cons:** Some rooms are small, some bathrooms are down the hall, basic decor. ⊠ *Via Roma 6–8, 53017* ☎ *0577/738056* ⊕ *www.labottegadigiovannino.it* ⤴ *10 rooms, 2 apartments* ⟁ *In-room: no a/c, no phone. In-hotel: bar, no elevator* ⊟ *AE, MC, V* ❶ *EP.*

CASTELLINA IN CHIANTI

14 km (8 mi) west of Radda, 59 km (35 mi) south of Florence.

GETTING HERE

As with all the towns along the Strada Chiantigiana (SR222), Castellina is an easy drive from either Siena or Florence. From Siena, Castellina is well served by the local Tra-In bus company. However, only one bus a day travels here from Florence. The closest train station is at Castellina Scalo, some 15 km (9 mi) away.

VISITOR INFORMATION

Castellina in Chianti tourism office (⊠ *Piazza del Comune 1* ☎ *0577/741392*).

EXPLORING

Castellina in Chianti, or simply Castellina, is on a ridge above the Val di Pesa, Val d'Arbia, and Val d'Elsa, with beautiful panoramas in every direction. The imposing 15th-century tower in the central piazza hints at the history of this village, which was an outpost during the continuing wars between Florence and Siena.

WHERE TO STAY & EAT

$$$$ ✕ **Albergaccio.** The fact that the dining room can seat only 35 guests makes a meal here an intimate experience. The ever-changing menu mixes traditional and creative dishes. In late September and October *zuppa di funghi e castagne* (mushroom and chestnut soup) is a treat; grilled meats and seafood are on the list throughout the year. There's also an excellent wine list. When the weather is warm make sure you dine on the terrace. ⊠ *Via Fiorentina 2553011* ☎ *0577/741042* ⟁ *Reservations essential* ⊟ *No credit cards* ⊘ *Closed Sun. No lunch Wed. and Thurs.*

$–$$ ✕ **Ristorante Le Tre Porte.** The specialty of the house, a thick slab of beef called *bistecca alla fiorentina,* is usually served very rare. Paired with grilled fresh porcini mushrooms when in season (in spring and fall), it's a heady dish. The main floor of the restaurant has a small dining room serving full-course meals. In the evening, a second room is opened downstairs where you can order pizzas from the wood-burning oven. Reservations are essential in July and August. ⊠ *Via Trento e Trieste 453011* ☎ *0577/741163* ⊟ *AE, DC, MC, V* ⊘ *Closed Tues.*

11

$–$$$
Fodor'sChoice
★

☺ **Palazzo Squarcialupi.** In the center of Castellina, this 15th-century palace is a tranquil place to stay. Rooms are spacious, with high ceilings, tile floors, and 18th-century furnishings; bathrooms are tiled in local stone. Many of the rooms have views of the valley below, some look toward the town's main pedestrian street. Common areas are elegant, with deep, plush couches that invite you to recline. There's an ample breakfast buffet throughout the year, and you can arrange for a light lunch in the warmer months. The multilingual staff goes out of its way to be helpful. Users of fodors.com praised the "lovely room, fantastic views," and "friendly staff." **Pros:** Great location, elegant public spaces. **Cons:** On a street with no car access, across from a noisy restaurant. ✉ *Via Ferruccio 22, 53011* ☎*0577/741186* 🖷*0577/740386* ⊕*www.palazzosquarcialupi.com* 🖝*17 rooms* ⚐*In room: refrigerator. In-hotel: bar, pool, laundry service, public Wi-Fi, some pets allowed* ▤*AE, DC, MC, V* ⊗*Closed Nov.–Mar.* ⛶*BP.*

HILL TOWNS SOUTHWEST OF FLORENCE

Submit to the draw of Tuscany's enchanting fortified cities that crown the hills west of Siena, many dating to the Etruscan period. San Gimignano, known as the "medieval Manhattan" because of its forest of stout medieval towers built by rival families, is the most heavily visited. This onetime Roman outpost, with its tilted cobbled streets and ancient buildings, can make the days of Guelph-Ghibelline conflicts palpable. Rising from a series of bleak gullied hills and valleys, Volterra has always been popular for its minerals and stones, particularly alabaster, which was used by the Etruscans for many implements. Examples are now displayed in the exceptional and unwieldy Museo Etrusco Guarnacci.

VOLTERRA

48 km (30 mi) south of San Miniato, 75 km (47 mi) southwest of Florence.

GETTING HERE

By car, the best route from San Gimignano follows the SP1 south to Castel San Gimignano and then the SS68 all the way to Volterra. Coming from the west, take the SS1, a coastal road to Cecina, then follow the SS68 to Volterra. Either way, there's a long, winding climb at the end of your trip. Traveling to Volterra by bus or train is complicated; avoid it if possible, especially if you have lots of luggage. From Florence or Siena, the journey is best made by bus and involves a change in Colle di Val d'Elsa. From Rome or Pisa, it is best to take the train to Cecina and then take a bus to Volterra or a train to the Volterra-Saline station. The latter is 10 km (6 mi) from town.

VISITOR INFORMATION

Volterra tourism office (✉*Piazza dei Priori 20* ☎*0588/87257* ⊕*www. volterratur.it*).

EXPLORING

Unlike other Tuscan hill towns rising above sprawling vineyards and rolling fields of green, Volterra is surrounded by desolate terrain marred with industry and mining equipment. D. H. Lawrence described it as "somber and chilly alone on her rock" in his *Etruscan Places*. The fortress, walls, and gates still stand mightily over Le Balze, a distinctive series of gullied hills and valleys to the west that were formed by irregular erosion. The town has long been known for its alabaster, which has been mined since Etruscan times; today the Volterrans use it to make ornaments and souvenirs sold all over town. An €8 combined ticket is your only option for visiting the Museo Etrusco Guarnacci and the Pinacoteca e Museo Civico.

Volterra has some of Italy's best small museums. The extraordinarily large and unique collection of Etruscan artifacts at the **Museo Etrusco Guarnacci** is a treasure in the region. (Many of the other Etruscan finds from the area have been shipped off to state museums or the Vatican.) If only a curator had thought to cull the best of the 700 funerary urns rather than to display every last one of them. ✉ *Via Don Minzoni 15* ☎ *0588/86347* ⊕ *www.comune.volterra.pi.it* 🎫 *€8, includes admission to Museo Diocesano di Arte Sacra and Pinoteca* ⊗ *Mid-Mar.–early Nov., daily 9–6:45; early Nov.–mid-Mar., daily 9–1:15.*

The **Pinacoteca e Museo Civico** houses a highly acclaimed collection of religious art, including a *Madonna and Child with Saints* by Luca Signorelli (1445/50–1523) and a *Deposition* by Rosso Fiorentino (1494–1541) that is reason enough to visit Volterra. ✉ *Via dei Sarti 1* ☎ *0588/87580* ⊕ *www.comune.volterra.pi.it* 🎫 *€8, includes admission to Museo Etrusco Guarnacci and Museo Diocesano di Arte Sacra* ⊗ *Mid-Mar.–early Nov., daily 9–7; early Nov.–mid-Mar., daily 9–1:45.*

Next to the altar in the town's unfinished **Duomo** is a magnificent 13th-century carved-wood *Deposition*. Note the fresco by Benozzo Gozzoli in the Cappella della Addolorata. Along the left wall of the nave you can see the arrival of the Magi. ✉ *Piazza San Giovanni* ☎ *0588/86192* 🎫 *Free* ⊗ *Daily 7–7.*

Among Volterra's best-preserved ancient remains is the Etruscan **Porta all'Arco,** an arch dating from the 4th century BC now incorporated into the city walls.

The ruins of the 1st-century BC **Teatro Romano,** a beautifully preserved Roman theater, are worth a visit. Adjacent to the theater are the remains of the **terme** (baths). The complex is outside the town walls past Porta Fiorentina. ✉ *Viale Francesco Ferrucci* ☎ *0586/260837* 🎫 *€2* ⊗ *Mar.–May and Sept.–Nov., daily 10–1 and 2–4; June–Aug., daily 10–6:45; Dec.–Feb., weekends 10–1 and 2–4.*

WHERE TO STAY & EAT

$–$$$ ✕**Il Sacco Fiorentino.** Start with the *antipasti del Sacco Fiorentino*—a
★   medley of sautéed chicken liver, porcini mushrooms, and polenta drizzled with balsamic vinegar. The meal just gets better when you move on

to the *tagliatelle del Sacco Fiorentino,* a riot of curried spaghetti with chicken and roasted red peppers. The wine list is a marvel, as it's long and very well priced. White walls, tile floors, and red tablecloths create an understated tone that is unremarkable, but once the food starts arriving, it's easy to forgive the lack of decoration. ✉ *Piazza XX Settembre 1856048* ☎ *0588/88537* ⊟ *AE, DC, MC, V* ⊘ *Closed Wed.*

$ 🏨 **San Lino.** Within the town's medieval walls, this convent-turned-hotel has wood-beam ceilings, graceful archways, and terra-cotta floors in public spaces. The furnishings are contemporary wood laminate and straight-line ironwork. Sip a beverage or write a postcard on the small terrace filled with potted geraniums; the pool area is framed on one side by a church with a stained-glass window of the Last Supper. The restaurant ($–$$) serves Tuscan classics and local specialties such as *zuppa alla volterrana,* a thick vegetable soup. Half board is available. **Pros:** Steps away from center of town, friendly and helpful staff, convenient parking. **Cons:** A little run-down; elevators are noisy; breakfast is adequate, but nothing to write home about. ✉ *Via San Lino 26, 56048* ☎ *0588/85250* 🖶 *0588/80620* ⊕ *www.hotelsanlino.com* 📞 *43 rooms* ♿ *In-room: refrigerator, dial-up. In-hotel: restaurant, bar, pool, concierge, laundry service, public Internet, parking (fee), some pets allowed* ⊟ *AE, DC, MC, V* ⊘ *Closed Nov.–Jan.* 🍴 *BP.*

SAN GIMIGNANO

27 km (17 mi) east of Volterra, 57 km (35 mi) southwest of Florence.

GETTING HERE

You can reach San Gimignano by car from the Florence–Siena Superstrada. Exit at Poggibonsi Nord and follow signs for San Gimignano. Although it involves changing buses in Poggibonsi, getting to San Gimignano by bus is a relatively straightforward affair. SITA operates the service between Siena or Florence and Poggibonsi, while Tra-In takes care of the Poggibonsi to San Gimignano route. You cannot reach San Gimignano by train.

VISITOR INFORMATION

San Gimignano tourism office (✉ *Piazza Duomo 1* ☎ *0577/940008* ⊕ *www.sangimignano.com*).

EXPLORING

When you're on a hilltop surrounded by soaring medieval towers silhouetted against the sky, it's difficult not to fall under the spell of San Gimignano. Its tall walls and narrow streets are typical of Tuscan hill towns, but it's the medieval "skyscrapers" that set the town apart from its neighbors. Today 14 towers remain, but at the height of the Guelph–Ghibelline conflict there was a forest of more than 70, and it was possible to cross the town by rooftop rather than by road. The towers were built partly for defensive purposes—they were a safe refuge and useful for pouring boiling oil on attacking enemies—and partly for bolstering the egos of their owners, who competed with deadly seriousness to build the highest tower in town.

Today San Gimignano isn't much more than a gentrified walled city, touristy but still very much worth exploring because, despite the profusion of cheesy souvenir shops lining the main drag, there's some serious Renaissance art to be seen here. Tour groups arrive early and clog the wine-tasting rooms—San Gimignano is famous for its light white Vernaccia—and art galleries for much of the day, but most

sights stay open through late afternoon, when all the tour groups have long since departed.

The town's main church is not officially a *duomo* (cathedral) because San Gimignano has no bishop. Behind the simple facade of the Romanesque **Collegiata** lies a treasure trove of fine frescoes, covering nearly every part of the interior. Bartolo di Fredi's 14th-century fresco cycle of Old Testament scenes extends along one wall. Their distinctly medieval feel, with misshapen bodies, buckets of spurting blood, and lack of perspective, contrasts with the much more reserved scenes from the *Life of Christ* (attributed to 14th-century artist Lippo Memmi), painted on the opposite wall just 14 years later. Taddeo di Bartolo's otherworldly *Last Judgment* (late 14th century), with its distorted and suffering nudes, reveals the great influence of Dante's horrifying imagery in *The Inferno* and was surely an inspiration for later painters. Proof that the town had more than one protector, Benozzo Gozzoli's arrow-riddled *St. Sebastian* was commissioned in gratitude after the locals prayed to the saint for relief from plague. The Renaissance **Cappella di Santa Fina** is decorated with a fresco cycle by Domenico Ghirlandaio illustrating the life of Saint Fina. A small girl who suffered from a terminal disease, Fina repented for her sins—among them having accepted an orange from a boy—and in penance lived out the rest of her short life on a wooden board, tormented by rats. The scenes depict the arrival of Saint Gregory, who appeared to assure her that death was near; the flowers that miraculously grew from the wooden plank; and the miracles that accompanied her funeral, including the healing of her nurse's paralyzed hand and the restoration of a blind choirboy's vision. ✉*Piazza Duomo* ☎*0577/940316* 💶*€3.50; €5.50 includes the Museo d'Arte Sacra* ⊗*Apr.–Oct., weekdays 9:30–7:10, Sat. 9:30–5:10, Sun. 12:30–5:10; Nov. 1–15, Dec. 1–Jan. 15, and Feb. 1–Mar., Mon.–Sat. 9:30–4:40, Sun. 12:30–5:10. Closed Nov. 16–30 and Jan. 16–31.*

★ The impressive **Museo Civico** occupies what was the "new" Palazzo del Popolo; the Torre Grossa is adjacent. Dante visited San Gimignano for only one day as a Guelph ambassador from Florence to ask the locals to join the Florentines in supporting the pope—just long enough to get the main council chamber, which now holds a 14th-century *Maestà* by Lippo Memmi, named after him. Off the stairway is a small room containing the racy frescoes by Memmo di Filippuccio (active 1288–1324) depicting the courtship, shared bath, and wedding of a young, androgynous-looking couple. That the space could have been a private room for the commune's chief magistrate may have something to do with the work's highly charged eroticism.

Upstairs, paintings by famous Renaissance artists Pinturicchio (*Madonna Enthroned*), Benozzo Gozzoli (*Madonna and Child*), and two large *tondi* (circular paintings) by Filippino Lippi (circa 1457–1504) attest to the importance and wealth of San Gimignano. Also worth seeing are Taddeo di Bartolo's *Life of San Gimignano*, with the saint holding a model of the town as it once appeared; Lorenzo di Niccolò's gruesome martyrdom scene in the *Life of St. Bartholomew* (1401); and scenes from the *Life of St. Fina* on a tabernacle that was designed to hold her head. Admission includes the steep climb to the top of the Torre Grossa, which on a clear day has spectacular views. ⊠*Piazza Duomo* 🕾*0577/990312* 💶*€5* ⊙*Mar.–Oct., daily 9:30–7; Nov.–Feb., daily 10–5:30.*

There's no shortage of places to try Vernaccia di San Gimignano, the justifiably famous white wine with which San Gimignano would be singularly associated—if it weren't for all those towers. At **Enoteca Gustavo** (⊠*Via San Matteo 29* 🕾*0577/940057*) you can buy a glass of Vernaccia di San Gimignano and sit down with a cheese plate or with one of the fine crostini served up in this tiny wine bar.

★   Make a beeline for Benozzo Gozzoli's superlative frescoes inside the church of **Sant'Agostino.** This Romanesque–Gothic church contains Benozzo's stunning 15th-century fresco cycle depicting scenes from the life of Saint Augustine. The saint's work was essential to the early development of church doctrine. As thoroughly discussed in his autobiographical *Confessions* (an acute dialogue with God), Augustine, like many saints, sinned considerably in his youth before finding God. But unlike the lives of other saints, where the story continues through a litany of deprivations, penitence, and often martyrdom, Augustine's life and work focused on philosophy and the reconciliation of faith and thought. Benozzo's 17 scenes on the choir wall depict Augustine as a man who traveled and taught extensively in the fourth and fifth centuries. The 15th-century altarpiece by Piero del Pollaiolo (1443–96) depicts *The Coronation of the Virgin* and the various protectors of the city. On your way out of Sant'Agostino, stop in at the **Cappella di San Bartolo,** with a sumptuously elaborate tomb by Benedetto da Maiano (1442–97). ⊠*Piazza Sant'Agostino, off Via San Matteo* 🕾*0577/907012* 💶*Free* ⊙*Apr.–Oct., daily 7–noon and 3–7; Nov. and Dec. and Mar., daily 7–noon and 3–6; Jan. and Feb., Mon. 3–6, Tues. –Sun. 10–noon and 3–6.*

WHERE TO STAY & EAT

The **Cooperativa Hotels Promotion** (⊠*Via di San Giovanni 125* 🕾*0577/940809* ⊕*www.hotelsiena.com*) provides commission-free booking for local hotels and farmhouses.

$–$$ ✕**La Mangiatoia.** Multicolored gingham tablecloths provide an interesting juxtaposition with rib-vaulted ceilings dating from the 13th century. The lighthearted touch might be explained by the influence of chef Susi Cuomo, who has been presiding over the kitchen for more than 20 years. The menu is seasonal—in autumn, don't miss her *sacottino di pecorino al tartufo* (little packages of pasta stuffed with pecorino and seasoned with truffles). In summer eat lighter fare on the intimate, flower-bedecked terrace in the back. ⊠ *Via Mainardi 5, off Via San Matteo, 53037* ☎*0577/941528* ⊟*MC, V* ⊘*Closed Tues., 3 wks in Nov., and 1 wk in Jan.*

$–$$ ☷**Pescille.** A rambling farmhouse has been transformed into a handsome hotel with understated contemporary furniture in the bedrooms and country-classic motifs such as farm implements hanging on the walls in the bar. From this charming spot you get a splendid view of San Gimignano's towers. **Pros:** Splendid views, quiet atmosphere, 10-minute walk to town. **Cons:** Furnishings a bit austere, there's an elevator for luggage but not for guests. ⊠ *Strada Provinciale Castel San Gimignano, Località Pescille* ✢*4 km (2½ mi) south of San Gimignano town center, 53037* ☎*0577/940186* ⊕*www.pescille.it* ⟿*38 rooms, 12 suites* ⚷*In-room: refrigerator, Wi-Fi. In-hotel: bar, tennis court, pool, gym, no elevator, public Internet, public Wi-Fi, parking (no fee)* ⊟*AE, DC, MC, V* ⊘*Closed Nov.–Mar.* ⦿*BP.*

COLLE DI VAL D'ELSA

15 km (9 mi) southeast of San Gimignano, 50 km (31 mi) southwest of Florence.

GETTING HERE
You can reach Colle di Val d'Elsa by car on either the SR2 from Siena or the Florence–Siena Superstrada. Bus service to and from Siena and Florence is frequent.

VISITOR INFORMATION
Colle di Val d'Elsa (⊠ *Via Campana 43* ☎*0577/922791*).

EXPLORING
Most people pass through on their way to and from popular tourist destinations Volterra and San Gimignano—a shame, since Colle di Val d'Elsa has a lot to offer. It's another town on the Via Francigena that benefited from trade along the pilgrimage route to Rome. Colle got an extra boost in the late 16th century when it was given a bishopric, probably related to an increase in trade when nearby San Gimignano was cut off from the well-traveled road. The town is arranged on two levels, and from the 12th century onward the flat lower portion was given over to a flourishing paper-making industry; today the area is mostly modern, and efforts have shifted toward the production of fine glass and crystal.

WHERE TO STAY & EAT

$$$$ ✕**Ristorante Arnolfo.** Food lovers should not miss Arnolfo, one of Tusca-
Fodor'sChoice ny's most highly regarded restaurants. Chef Gaetano Trovato sets high
★ standards of creativity; his dishes daringly ride the line between innovation and tradition, almost always with spectacular results. The menu

changes frequently and has a fixed-price option, but you are always sure to find fish and lots of fresh vegetables in the summer. You're in for a special treat if the specials include *carrè di agnello al vino rosso e sella alle olive* (rack of lamb in a red wine sauce and lamb saddle with olives). ✉*Piazza XX Settembre 52, 53034* ☎*0577/920549* ▭*AE, DC, MC, V* ⊗*Closed Tues. and Wed., last wk in Jan.–Feb., and last wk in Aug.*

$$$$ ★ **La Suvera.** Pope Julius II once owned this luxurious estate in the valley of the River Elsa. The papal villa and an adjacent building have magnificently furnished guest rooms and suites appointed with antiques. A wall-size tapestry depicting the Roman army hangs beside a red canopy bed in the Angels Room. La Suvera's first-rate facilities include drawing rooms, a library, an Italian garden, a park, and the Oliviera restaurant (serving organic estate wines). **Pros:** Luxurious accommodations, historic setting, far from the madding crowd. **Cons:** Out-of-the-way location, showing its age, some bristle at the extremely formal service. ✉*Off SS541* ✣ *15 km (9 mi) south of Colle di Val d'Elsa, Pievescola 53030* ☎*0577/960300* 🌐*www.lasuvera.it* *36 rooms, 12 suites* *In-room: safe, refrigerator. In-hotel: restaurant, room service, bar, tennis court, pool, bicycles, concierge, laundry service, public Internet, no kids under 12* ▭*AE, DC, MC, V* ⊗*Closed Nov.–Easter* *BP.*

SIENA

With its narrow streets and steep alleys, a stunning Gothic Duomo, a bounty of early Renaissance art, and the glorious Palazzo Pubblico overlooking its magnificent Campo, Siena is often described as Italy's best-preserved medieval city. Victory over Florence in 1260 at Montaperti marked the beginning of Siena's golden age. During the following decades Siena erected its greatest buildings (including the Duomo); established a model city government presided over by the Council of Nine; and became a great art, textile, and trade center. Siena succumbed to Florentine rule in the mid-16th century, when a yearlong siege virtually eliminated the native population. Ironically, it was precisely this decline that, along with the steadfast pride of the Sienese, prevented further development, to which we owe the city's marvelous medieval condition today.

Although much looks as it did in the early 14th century, Siena is no museum. Walk through the streets and you can see that the medieval *contrade,* 17 neighborhoods into which the city has been historically divided, are a vibrant part of modern life. You may see symbols of the *contrada*—Tartuca (turtle), Oca (goose), Istrice (porcupine), Torre (tower)—emblazoned on banners and engraved on building walls. The Sienese still strongly identify themselves by the contrada where they were born and raised; loyalty and rivalry run deep. At no time is this more visible than during the centuries-old Palio, a twice-yearly horse race held in the Piazza del Campo, but you need not visit during the wild festival to come to know the rich culture and enchanting pleasures of Siena; those are evident at every step.

GETTING HERE

From Florence, the quickest way to Siena is via the Florence–Siena Superstrada. Otherwise, take the Via Cassia (SR2), for a scenic route. Coming from Rome, leave the A1 at Valdichiana, and follow the Siena–Bettole Superstrada. SITA provides excellent bus service between Florence and Siena. Because buses are direct and speedy, they are preferable over the train, which sometimes involves a change in Empoli.

VISITOR INFORMATION

Siena tourism office (⊠ *Piazza del Campo 56* ☎ *0577/280551* ⊕ *www. comune.siena.it*).

EXPLORING SIENA

If you come by car, you're better off leaving it in one of the parking lots around the perimeter of town. Driving is difficult or impossible in most parts of the city center. Practically unchanged since medieval times, Siena is laid out in a "Y" over the slopes of several hills, dividing the city into *terzi* (thirds). Although the most interesting sites are in a fairly compact area around the Campo at the center of town in the neighborhoods of Città, Camollìa, and San Martino, be sure to leave some time to wander into the narrow streets that rise and fall steeply from the main thoroughfares, giving yourself at least two days to really explore the town. At the top on the list of things to see is the Piazza del Campo, considered by many to be the finest public square in Italy. The Palazzo Pubblico sits at the lower end of the square and is well worth a visit. The Duomo is a must-see, as is the nearby Cripta.

Tra-In (☎ *0577/204111* ⊕ *www.trainspa.it*) buses also run frequently within and around Siena, including through the centro storico. Tickets cost €.90 and should be bought in advance at tobacconists or newsstands. Routes are marked with signposts.

The **Association of Official Tour Guides** (⊠ *Piazza del Campo 56* ☎ *0577/288084* ⊕ *www.terredisiena.it*) offers a two-hour walking tour that takes in most of the major sights such as the Duomo, the Campo, and the exterior of Palazzo Pubblico. You can arrange for English-speaking guides.

TIMING It's a joy to walk in Siena—hills notwithstanding—as it's a rare opportunity to stroll through a medieval city rather than just a town. (There is quite a lot to explore, in contrast to tiny hill towns that can be crossed in minutes.) The walk can be done in as little as a day, with minimal stops at the sights. But stay longer and take time to tour the church building and museums, and to enjoy the streetscapes themselves. Several of the sites have reduced hours on Sunday afternoon and Monday.

THE MAIN ATTRACTIONS

❸ **Cripta.** After it had lain unseen for possibly 700 years, a crypt was rediscovered under the grand *pavimento* (floor) of the Duomo during routine excavation work and was opened to the public in 2003. An unknown master executed the breathtaking frescoes here some-

Fodor's Choice
★

11

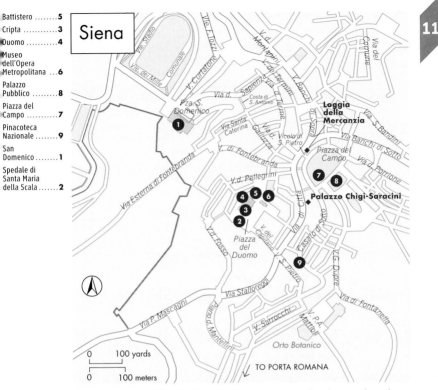

Siena

time between 1270–80; they retain their original colors and pack an emotional punch even with sporadic damage. The *Deposition/Lamentation* gives strong evidence that the Sienese school could paint emotion just as well as the Florentine school—and did it some 20 years before Giotto. Guided tours in English take place more or less every half hour and are limited to no more than 35 persons. ⊠*Piazza del Duomo, Città* ☎*0577/283048* ☎*€6; €10 combined ticket includes the Duomo, Battistero, and Museo dell'Opera Metropolitana* ☺*June–Aug., daily 9:30–8; Sept.–May, daily 9:30–7.*

❹ Duomo. Siena's Duomo is beyond question one of the finest Gothic cathedrals in Italy. The multicolored marbles and painted decoration are typical of the Italian approach to Gothic architecture—lighter and much less austere than the French. The amazingly detailed facade has few rivals in the region, although it's quite similar to the Duomo in Orvieto. It was completed in two brief phases at the end of the 13th and 14th centuries. The statues and decorative work were designed by Niccolo and Giovanni Pisano, although most of what we see today are copies, the originals having been removed to the nearby Museo dell'Opera Metropolitana. The gold mosaics are 18th-century restorations. The Campanile (no entry) is among central Italy's finest, with the number of windows increasing with each level.

FodorśChoice
★

The Duomo's interior, with its black-and-white striping throughout and finely coffered and gilded dome, is simply striking. Step in and look back up at Duccio's (circa 1255–1319) panels of stained glass that fill the circular window. Finished in 1288, it's the oldest example of stained glass in Italy. The Duomo is most famous for its unique and magnificent inlaid-marble floors, which took almost 200 years to complete; more than 40 artists contributed to the work, made up of 56 separate compositions depicting biblical scenes, allegories, religious symbols, and civic emblems. The floors are covered for most of the year for conservation purposes, but are unveiled during September and October. The Duomo's carousel pulpit, also much appreciated, was carved by Nicola Pisano (circa 1220–84) around 1265; the *Life of Christ* is depicted on the rostrum frieze. In striking contrast to all the Gothic decoration in the nave are the magnificent Renaissance frescoes in the **Biblioteca Piccolomini,** off the left aisle. Painted by Pinturicchio (circa 1454–1513) and completed in 1509, they depict events from the life of native son Aeneas Sylvius Piccolomini (1405–64), who became Pope Pius II in 1458. The frescoes are in excellent condition and have a freshness rarely seen in work so old.

The Duomo is grand, but the medieval Sienese people had even bigger plans. They wanted to enlarge the building by using the existing church as a transept for a new church, with a new nave running toward the southeast, to make what would be the largest church in the world. But only the sidewall and part of the new facade were completed when the Black Death struck in 1348, decimating Siena's population. The city fell into decline, funds dried up, and the plans were never carried out. (The dream of building the biggest church was actually doomed to failure from the start—subsequent attempts to get the project going revealed that the foundation was insufficient to bear the weight of the proposed structure.) The beginnings of the new nave, extending from the right side of the Duomo, were left unfinished, perhaps as a testament to unfulfilled dreams, and ultimately enclosed to house the adjacent ⇨**Museo dell'Opera Metropolitana.** The ⇨**Cripta** was discovered during routine preservation work on the church and has been opened to the public. ⊠*Piazza del Duomo, Città* ☏*0577/283048* ⊡*€3 Nov.–Aug.; €5 Sept. and Oct.; €10 combined ticket includes the Cripta, Battistero, and Museo dell'Opera Metropolitana* ☉*Mar.–Oct., Mon.–Sat. 10:30–7:30, Sun. 1:30–6:30; Nov.–Feb., Mon.–Sat. 10:30–6:30, Sun. 1:30–5:30.*

ALSO WORTH SEEING

❺ **Battistero.** The Duomo's 14th-century Gothic Baptistery was built to prop up one side of the Duomo. There are frescoes throughout, but the highlight is a large bronze 15th-century baptismal font designed by Jacopo della Quercia (1374–1438). It's adorned with bas-reliefs by various artists, including two by Renaissance masters: the *Baptism of Christ* by Lorenzo Ghiberti (1378–1455) and the *Feast of Herod* by Donatello. ⊠*Entrance on Piazza San Giovanni* ☏*No phone* ⊡*€3; €10 combined ticket includes the Duomo, Cripta, and Museo dell'Opera del Duomo* ☉*June–Aug., daily 9:30–8; Sept.–May, daily 9:30–7.*

11

6 Museo dell'Opera Metropolitana. Part of the unfinished nave of what was to have been a new cathedral, the museum contains the Duomo's treasury and some of the original decoration from its facade and interior. The first room on the ground floor displays weather-beaten 13th-century sculptures by Giovanni Pisano (circa 1245–1318) that were brought inside for protection and replaced by copies, as was a tondo of the *Madonna and Child* (now attributed to Donatello) that once hung on the door to the south transept. The masterpiece is unquestionably Duccio's *Maestà*, one side with 26 panels depicting episodes from the Passion, the other side with a *Madonna and Child Enthroned.* Painted between 1308 and 1311 as the altarpiece for the Duomo (where it remained until 1505), its realistic elements, such as the lively depiction of the Christ child and the treatment of interior space, proved an enormous influence on later painters. The second floor is divided between the treasury, with a crucifix by Giovanni Pisano and several statues and busts of biblical characters and classical philosophers, and La Sala della Madonna degli Occhi Grossi (the Room of the Madonna with the Big Eyes), named after the namesake painting it displays by the Maestro di Tressa, who painted in the early 13th century. The work originally decorated the Duomo's high altar, before being displaced by Duccio's *Maestà*. There is a fine view from the tower inside the museum. ⊠ *Piazza del Duomo, Città* ☎ *0577/283048* ✆ *€6; €10 combined ticket includes the Duomo, Cripta, and Battistero* ☉ *Mar.–May and Sept. and Oct., daily 9:30–7; June–Aug., daily 9:30 AM–10 PM; Nov.–Feb., daily 10–5.*

9 Pinacoteca Nazionale. The superb collection of five centuries of local painting in Siena's national picture gallery can easily convince you that the Renaissance was by no means just a Florentine thing—Siena was arguably just as important a center of art and innovation as its rival to the north, especially in the mid-13th century. Accordingly, the most interesting section of the collection, chronologically arranged, has several important "firsts." Room 1 contains a painting of the *Stories of the True Cross* (1215) by the so-called Master of Tressa, the earliest identified work by a painter of the Sienese school, and is followed in Room 2 by late-13th-century artist Guido da Siena's *Stories from the Life of Christ,* one of the first paintings ever made on canvas (earlier painters used wood panels). Rooms 3 and 4 are dedicated to Duccio, a student of Cimabue (circa 1240–1302) and considered to be the last of the proto-Renaissance painters. Ambrogio Lorenzetti's landscapes in Room 8 are the first truly secular paintings in Western art. Among later works in the rooms on the floor above, keep an eye out for the preparatory sketches used by Domenico Beccafumi (1486–1551) for the 35 etched marble panels he made for the floor of the Duomo. ⊠ *Via San Pietro 29, Città* ☎ *0577/281161* ✆ *€4* ☉ *Tues.–Sat. 8:15–7:15; Sun. 8:15–1:15; Mon. 8:30–1:30; last entrance ½ hr before closing.*

1 San Domenico. Although the Duomo is celebrated as a triumph of 13th-century Gothic architecture, this church, built at about the same time, turned out as an oversize, hulking brick box that never merited a finishing coat in marble, let alone a graceful facade. Named for the founder

Continued on page 672

Climbing the 400 narrow steps of the **Torre del Mangia** rewards you with unparalleled views of Siena's rooftops and the countryside beyond.

The **Palazzo Pubblico**, Siena's town hall since the 14th century.

Something about the fan-shaped, sloping design of **Il Campo** encourages people to s[it] and relax (except durin[g] the Palio, when they stand and scream). The communal atmosphere here is unlike that of a[ny] other Italian piazza.

PIAZZA DEL CAMPO

7 The fan-shaped **Piazza del Campo,** known simply as il Campo (The Field), is one of the finest squares in Italy. Constructed toward the end of the 12th century on a market area unclaimed by any contrada, it's still the heart of town. The bricks of the Campo are patterned in nine different sections—representing each member of the medieval Government of Nine. At the top of the Campo is a copy of the **Fonte Gaia,** decorated in the early 15th century by Siena's greatest sculptor, Jacopo della Quercia, with 13 sculpted reliefs of biblical events and virtues. Those lining the rectangular fountain are 19th-century copies; the originals are in the Spedale di Santa Maria della Scala. On Palio horse race days (July 2 and August 16), the Campo and all its surrounding buildings are packed with cheering, frenzied locals and tourists craning their necks to take it all in.

dor'sChoice ★

8 The Gothic **Palazzo Pubblico,** the focal point of the Piazza del Campo, has served as Siena's town hall since the 1300s. It now also contains the **Museo Civico,** with walls covered in early Renaissance frescoes. The nine governors of Siena once met in the Sala della Pace, famous for Ambrogio Lorenzetti's frescoes called *Allegories of Good and Bad Government,* painted in the late 1330s to demonstrate the dangers of tyranny. The good government side depicts utopia, showing first the virtuous ruling council surrounded by angels and then scenes of a perfectly running city and countryside. Conversely, the bad government fresco tells a tale straight out of Dante. The evil ruler and his advisers have horns and fondle strange animals, and the town scene depicts the seven mortal sins in action. Interestingly, the bad government fresco is severely damaged, and the good government fresco is in terrific condition. The **Torre del Mangia,** the palazzo's famous bell tower, is named after one of its first bell ringers, Giovanni di Duccio (called Mangiaguadagni, or earnings eater). The climb up to the top is long and steep, but the view makes it worth every step. ⊠ *Piazza del Campo 1, Città* ☎ *0577/41169* 🎫 *Museo €7, Torre €6, combined ticket €10* ☉ *Museo Nov.–Mar. 15, daily 10–6:30; Mar. 16–Oct., daily 10–7. Torre Nov.–Mar. 15, daily 10–4; Mar. 16–Oct., daily 10–7.*

THE PALIO

The three laps around a makeshift racetrack in Piazza del Campo are over in less than two minutes, but the spirit of Siena's Palio—a horse race held every July 2 and August 16—lives all year long.

The Palio is contested between Siena's contrade, the 17 neighborhoods that have divided the city since the Middle Ages. Loyalties are fiercely felt. At any time of year you'll see on the streets contrada symbols—Tartuca (turtle), Oca (goose), Istrice (porcupine), Torre (tower)—emblazoned on banners and engraved on building walls. At Palio time, simmering rivalries come to a boil.

It's been that way since at least August 16, 1310, the date of the first recorded running of the Palio. At that time, and for centuries to follow, the race went through the streets of the city. The additional July 2 running was instituted in 1649; soon thereafter the location was moved to the Campo and the current system for selecting the race entrants established. Ten of the contrade are chosen at random to run in the July Palio. The August race is then contested between the 7 contrade left out in July, plus 3 of the 10 July participants, again chosen at random. Although the races are in theory of equal importance, Sienese will tell you that it's better to win the second and have bragging rights for the rest of the year.

The race itself has a raw and arbitrary character—it's no Kentucky Derby. There's barely room for the 10 horses on the makeshift Campo course, so falls and collisions are inevitable. Horses are chosen at random three days before the race, and jockeys (who ride bareback) are mercenaries hired from surrounding towns. Almost no tactic is considered too underhanded. Bribery, secret plots, and betrayal are commonplace—so much so that the word for "jockey," *fantino*, has come to mean "untrustworthy" in Siena. There have been incidents of drugging (the horses) and kidnapping (the jockeys); only sabotaging a horse's reins remains taboo.

Above: The tension of the starting line. Top left: The frenzy of the race. Bottom left: A solemn flag bearer follows in the footsteps of his ancestors.

AQUILA	BRUCO	CHIOCCIOLA

17 MEDIEVAL CONTRADE

Festivities kick off three days prior to the Palio, with the selection and blessing of the horses, trial runs, ceremonial banquets, betting, and late-night celebrations. Residents don their contrada's colors and march through the streets in medieval costumes. The Campo is transformed into a racetrack lined with a thick layer of sand. On race day, each horse is brought to the church of the contrada for which it will run, where it's blessed and told, "Go little horse and return a winner." The Campo fills through the afternoon, with spectators crowding into every available space until bells ring and the piazza is sealed off. Processions of flag wavers in traditional dress march to the beat of tambourines and drums and the roar of the crowds. The *palio* itself—a banner for which the race is named, dedicated to the Virgin Mary—makes an appearance, followed by the horses and their jockeys.

The race begins when one horse, chosen to ride up from behind the rest of the field, crosses the starting line. There are always false starts, adding to the frenzied mood. Once underway, the race is over in a matter of minutes. The victorious rider is carried off through the streets of the winning contrada (where in the past tradition dictated he was entitled to the local girl of his choice), while winning and losing sides use television replay to analyze the race from every possible angle. The winning contrada will celebrate into the night, at long tables piled high with food and drink. The champion horse is guest of honor.

Reserved seating in the stands is sold out months in advance of the races; contact the Siena Tourist Office (✉ Piazza del Campo 56 ☎ 0577/280551) to find out about availability, and ask your hotel if it can procure you a seat. The entire area in the center is free and unreserved, but you need to show up early in order to get a prime spot against the barriers.

CIVETTA	DRAGO
GIRAFFA	ISTRICE
LEOCORNO	LUPA
NICCHIO	OCA
ONDA	PANTERA
SELVA	TARTUCA
TORRE	VALDIMONTONE

of the Dominican order, the church is now more closely associated with Saint Catherine of Siena. Just to the right of the entrance is the chapel in which she received the stigmata. On the wall is the only known contemporary portrait of the saint, made in the late 14th century by Andrea Vanni (circa 1332–1414). Farther down is the famous **Cappella di Santa Caterina,** the church's official shrine. Catherine, or bits and pieces of her, was literally spread all over the country—a foot is in Venice, most of her body is in Rome, and only her head and finger are here (kept in a reliquary on the altar). She was revered throughout the country long before she was officially named a patron saint of Italy in 1939. On either side of the chapel are well-known frescoes by Sodoma (aka Giovanni Antonio Bazzi, 1477–1549) of *St. Catherine in Ecstasy.* Don't miss the view of the Duomo and town center from the apse-side terrace. ⊠ *Costa di Sant'Antonio, Camollìa* ☎ *0577/280893* ✉ *Free* ☉ *Mid-Mar.–Oct., daily 7–1 and 2:30–6:30; Nov.–mid-Mar., daily 9–1 and 3–6.*

2 Spedale di Santa Maria della Scala. For more than a thousand years, this complex across from the Duomo was home to Siena's hospital, but now it serves as a museum to display some terrific frescoes and other Sienese Renaissance treasures. Restored 15th-century frescoes in the Sala del Pellegrinaio (once the emergency room) tell the history of the hospital, which was created to give refuge to passing pilgrims and to those in need, and to distribute charity to the poor. Incorporated into the complex is the church of the Santissima Annunziata, with a celebrated *Risen Christ* by Vecchietta (also known as Lorenzo di Pietro, circa 1412–80). Down in the dark Cappella di Santa Caterina della Notte is where Saint Catherine went to pray at night. The subterranean archaeological museum contained within the *ospedale* (hospital) is worth seeing even if you're not particularly taken with Etruscan objects: the interior design is sheer brilliance—it's beautifully lighted, eerily quiet, and an oasis of cool on hot summer days. The displays—including the *bucchero* (dark, reddish clay) ceramics, Roman coins, and tomb furnishings—are clearly marked and can serve as a good introduction to the history of regional excavations. Don't miss della Quercia's original sculpted reliefs from the Fonte Gaia. Although the fountain has been faithfully copied for the Campo, there's something incomparably beautiful about the real thing. ⊠ *Piazza del Duomo, Città* ☎ *0577/224811* ✉ *€6* ☉ *Mar. 16–Jan. 9, daily 10:30–6:30; Jan. 10–Mar. 15, daily 10:30–4:30.*

WHERE TO STAY & EAT

$$$–$$$$ ✕ **Antica Trattoria Botteganova.** Along the road that leads to Chianti is
★ arguably the best restaurant in Siena. Chef Michele Sorrentino's cooking is all about clean flavors, balanced combinations, and inviting pre-

11

sentation. Look for inspiring dishes such as spaghetti *alla chitarra in salsa di astice piccante* (with a spicy lobster sauce), or ravioli *di ricotta con ragù d'agnello* (with sheep's-milk cheese and lamb sauce). The interior, with high vaulting, is relaxed yet elegant, and the service is first rate. ⊠ *Strada per Montevarchi 29 j 2 km (1 mi) northeast of Siena, <zip>53100</zip>* ☎ *0577/284230* ⚠ *Reservations essential* ⊟ *AE, DC, MC, V* ☉ *Closed Sun.*

$$$–$$$$ ✕ **Le Logge.** Bright flowers provide a dash of color at this classic Tuscan dining room, and stenciled designs on the ceilings add some whimsy. The wooden cupboards (now filled with wine bottles) lining the walls recall its past as a turn-of-the-19th-century grocery store. The menu, with four or five *primi* (first courses) and *secondi* (second courses) changes regularly, but almost always includes their classic *malfatti all'osteria* (ricotta and spinach dumplings in a cream sauce). Desserts such as *coni con mousse al cioccolato e gelato allo zafferano* (two diminutive ice-cream cones with chocolate mousse and saffron ice cream) provide an inventive ending to the meal. When not vying for one of the outdoor tables, make sure to ask for one in the main downstairs room. ⊠ *Via del Porrione 33, San Martino, <zip>53100</zip>* ☎ *0577/48013* ⚠ *Reservations essential* ⊟ *AE, DC, MC, V* ☉ *Closed Sun. and 3 wks in Jan.*

$–$$ ✕ **Osteria del Coro.** Chef-owner Stefano Azzi promotes local produce,
Fodor's Choice uses age-old Sienese recipes, and backs it all up with a stellar wine
★ list. His *pici con le briciole al modo mio* (thick spaghetti with breadcrumbs), liberally dressed with fried *cinta senese* (a bacon made from a long-snouted pig), dazzles. The place was once a pizzeria, and it retains its unadorned, unpretentious air—you certainly wouldn't come because of the decor. ⊠ *Via Pantaneto 85/87 Città, 53100* ☎ *0577/222482* ⊟ *DC, MC, V* ☉ *Closed Mon.*

$–$$ ✕ **Trattoria Papei.** The menu hasn't changed for years, and why should
★ it? The *pici al cardinale* (handmade spaghetti with a duck and bacon sauce) is wonderful, and all the other typically Sienese dishes are equally delicious. Tucked away behind the Palazzo Pubblico in a square that serves as a parking lot for most of the day, the restaurant's location isn't great, but the food is. ⊠ *Piazza del Mercato 6, Città, 53100* ☎ *0577/280894* ⊟ *MC, V* ☉ *Closed Mon.*

$$$ 🏨 **Hotel Santa Caterina.** Manager Lorenza Capannelli and her fine staff
★ are welcoming, hospitable, enthusiastic, and go out of their way to ensure a fine stay. Dark, straight-lined wood furniture stands next to beds with floral spreads; some have upholstered headboards. Rooms in the back look out onto the garden or the countryside in the distance. When it's warm, breakfast is served on the flower-filled garden with a view of the Siena countryside, providing a gorgeous start to the day. The well-run hotel is outside Porta Romana—a 15-minute walk south of Piazza del Campo. **Pros:** Friendly staff, a short walk to center of town, breakfast in the garden. **Cons:** On a busy intersection, outside city walls. ⊠ *Via Piccolomini 7, San Martino, 53100* ☎ *0577/221105* ⊕ *www.hscsiena.it* ⇙ *22 rooms* ⚠ *In-room: refrigerator, dial-up. In-hotel: concierge, laundry service, public Internet, parking (fee), some pets allowed* ⊟ *AE, DC, MC, V* ☉❘ *BP.*

$$$
★
Palazzo Ravizza. This romantic palazzo exudes a sense of gentile shabbiness. Rooms have high ceilings, antique furnishings, and bathrooms decorated with hand-painted tiles. The location is key: from here it's just a 10-minute walk to the Duomo. Il Capriccio ($$–$$$), ably run by chef Fabio Tozzi, specializies in traditional Tuscan fare. In warm weather, enjoy your meal in the garden with a trickling fountain. "We have only positive things to say about Palazzo Ravizza ... from the amazing Tuscan view, to the proximity to Il Campo this hotel was by far the best one we stayed at throughout our Italy vacation," says one traveler on Fodors.com. **Pros:** 10-minute walk to the center of town, pleasant garden with a view beyond the city walls, professional staff. **Cons:** Not all rooms have views, some of the rooms are a little cramped. ⊠*Pian dei Mantellini 34, Città, 53100* ☎*0577/280462* ⊕*www.palazzoravizza.it* ↳*38 rooms, 4 suites* &*In-room: safe, refrigerator, Wi-Fi (some). In-hotel: restaurant, bar, concierge, laundry service, public Internet, public Wi-Fi, parking (no fee), some pets allowed* ▤*AE, DC, MC, V* ⦿|*BP.*

$$
Antica Torre. The cordial Landolfo family has carefully evoked a private home with their eight guest rooms inside a restored 16th-century tower. Simple but tastefully furnished rooms have ornate wrought-iron headboards, usually atop twin beds. The old stone staircase, large wooden beams, wood shutters, and original brick vaults here and there are reminders of the building's great age. Antica Torre is in a southeast corner of Siena, a 10-minute walk from Piazza del Campo. **Pros:** Near the town center, charming atmosphere. **Cons:** Narrow stairway up to the rooms, low ceilings, cramped bathrooms. ⊠*Via Fieravecchia 7, San Martino, 53100* ☎*0577/222255* ⊕*www.anticatorresiena.it* ↳*8 rooms* &*In-hotel: no elevator* ▤*AE, DC, MC, V* ⦿|*BP.*

AREZZO & CORTONA

The hill towns of Arezzo and Cortona carry on age-old local traditions—in June and September, for example, Arezzo's Romanesque and Gothic churches are enlivened by the Giostra del Saracino, a costumed medieval joust. Arezzo has been home to important artists since ancient times, when Etruscan potters produced their fiery-red vessels here. Fine examples of the work of Luca Signorelli are preserved in Cortona, his hometown.

AREZZO

63 km (39 mi) northeast of Siena, 81 km (50 mi) southeast of Florence.

GETTING HERE
Arezzo is easily reached by car from the A1 (Autostrada del Sole), the main highway running between Florence and Rome. Direct trains connect Arezzo with Rome (2½ hours) and Florence (1 hour). Direct bus service is available from Florence, but not from Rome.

VISITOR INFORMATION

Arezzo tourism office (✉*Piazza della Repubblica 28* ☎*0575/377678* ⊕*www.apt.arezzo.it*).

EXPLORING

The birthplace of the poet Petrarch (1304–74) and the Renaissance artist and art historian Giorgio Vasari, Arezzo is today best known for the magnificent Piero della Francesca frescoes in the church of

11

WORD OF MOUTH

"Arezzo holds a huge antiques fair the first weekend of each month that takes over the streets in the historical center of town. You may want to check your dates, either to avoid or take advantage of it."

–shellio

San Francesco. The city dates from pre-Etruscan times and thrived as an Etruscan capital from the 7th to the 4th century BC. During the Middle Ages it was fully embroiled in the conflict between the Ghibellines (pro–Holy Roman Emperor) and the Guelphs (pro-pope), losing its independence to Florence at the end of the 14th century after many decades of doing battle.

Urban sprawl testifies to the fact that Arezzo (population 90,000) is the third-largest city in Tuscany (after Florence and Pisa). But the old town, set on a low hill, is relatively small, and almost completely closed to traffic. Look for parking along the roads that circle the lower part of town, near the train station, and walk into town from there. You can explore the most interesting sights in a few hours, adding time to linger for some window-shopping at Arezzo's many antiques shops.

Fodor'sChoice ★ The remarkable frescoes by Piero della Francesca (circa 1420–92) in the **Basilica di San Francesco** were painted between 1452 and 1466. They depict scenes from the *Legend of the True Cross* on three walls of the *cappella maggiore,* or high altar choir. What Sir Kenneth Clark called "the most perfect morning light in all Renaissance painting" may be seen in the lowest section of the right wall, where the troops of the emperor Maxentius flee before the sign of the cross. A 15-year project restored the works to their original brilliance. Reservations are required to see the choir area with the frescoes. ✉*Piazza San Francesco 6* ☎*0575/20630 church, 0575/352757 Capella Bacci reservations* ⊕*www.pierodellafrancesca.it* ✍*Church free, Capella Bacci €6* ⊗*Church: daily 8:30–6:30. Capella Bacci: Apr.–Oct., weekdays 9–6:30, Sat. 9–5:30, Sun. 1–5:30; Nov.–Mar., weekdays 9–5:30, Sat. 9–5, Sun. 1–5.*

Some historians maintain that Arezzo's oddly shaped, sloping **Piazza Grande** was once the site of an ancient Roman forum. Now it hosts a first-Sunday-of-the-month antiques fair as well as the **Giostra del Saracino** (Joust of the Saracen), featuring medieval costumes and competition, held here in the middle of June and on the first Sunday of September. Check out the 16th-century loggia designed by native son Giorgio Vasari on the northeast side of the piazza.

The curving, tiered apse on Piazza Grande belongs to **Pieve di Santa Maria,** one of Tuscany's finest Romanesque churches, built in the 12th century. Don't miss the Portale Maggiore (great door) with its poly-

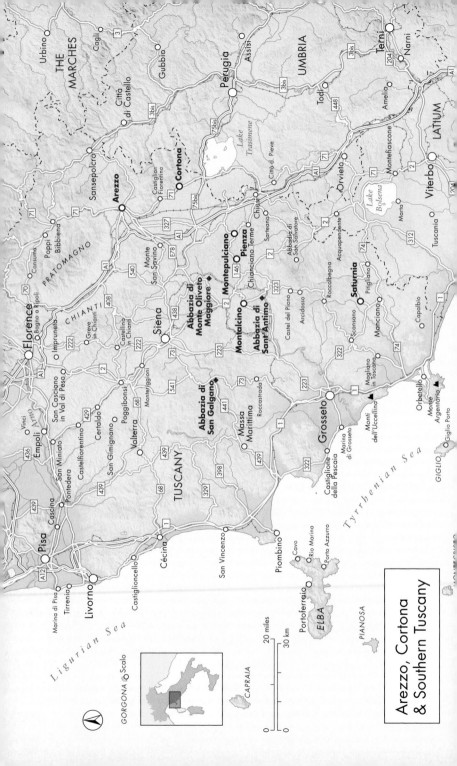

Arezzo, Cortona & Southern Tuscany

chrome figures representing the months; restored in 2002, they are remarkably vibrant. ⊠*Corso Italia* ☎*0575/22629* ⊙*May–Sept., daily 8–1 and 3–7; Oct.–Apr., daily 8–noon and 3–6.*

Arezzo's medieval **Duomo** (at the top of the hill) contains a fresco of a somber *Magdalen* by Piero della Francesca; look for it next to the large marble tomb near the organ. ⊠*Piazza del Duomo 1* ☎*0575/23991* ⊙*Daily 6:30–12:30 and 3–6:30.*

WHERE TO STAY & EAT

$$–$$$ ✕**Antica Trattoria da Guido.** Owned by a southern Italian, this small trattoria serves tasty adaptations of Calabrian dishes, such as homemade pasta served with *salsa ai pomodori secchi* (a spicy sauce of sun-dried tomatoes, capers, and red peppers). The display of homemade pastries makes decisions difficult at the end of the meal. The dining room is a pleasant mix of rustic and modern, and the service is friendly. ⊠*Via di San Francesco 1* ☎*0575/23271* ▭*MC, V* ⊙*Closed Sun. and 2 wks in mid-Aug.*

$–$$ ✕**La Torre di Gnicche.** Wine lovers shouldn't miss this wine bar/eatery with more than 700 labels on the list, located just off Piazza Grande. Seasonal dishes of traditional fare, such as *acquacotta del casentino* (porcini mushroom soup) and *baccalà in umido* (salt-cod stew), are served in the simply decorated, vaulted dining room. You can accompany your meal with one, or more, of the almost 30 wines that are available by the glass. Limited outdoor seating is available in warm weather. ⊠*Piaggia San Martino 8* ☎*0575/352035* ▭*AE, MC, V* ⊙*Closed Wed., Jan., and 2 wks in July.*

$$ 🏨**Cavaliere Palace Hotel.** On a quiet backstreet in the old town, the Cavaliere is moments away from the main sights. The carpeted rooms in the restored 19th-century town house are small but comfy, with contemporary furnishings. **Pros:** Location, location, location. **Cons:** Some complain of noise from nearby disco, very plain decor. ⊠*Via Madonna del Prato 83, Arezzo, 52100* ☎*0575/26836* 🖷*0575/21925* ⊕*www.cavalierehotels.com* ⬩*27 rooms* ⌂*In-room: refrigerator, Wi-Fi. In-hotel: public Wi-Fi, parking (fee)* ▭*AE, D, MC, V* ⫸*CP.*

$ 🏨**Calcione Country and Castle.** The elegant Marchesa Olivella Lotteringhi della Stufa has turned her six-centuries-old family estate (circa 1483) into a top-notch agriturismo. Think sophisticated rustic: many of the apartments have open fireplaces, and the stone houses have a private pool (the rest share the estate pool). Explore the grounds, which include olive groves, vineyards, and private lakes for fishing and windsurfing. "We hated leaving," says one user of fodors.com. To make up for the absence of room phones, mobile phones are made available to guests. From June to mid-September, a minimum one-week stay is mandatory. **Pros:** Houses can sleep up to 17; large swimming pools; quiet, beautiful, remote setting. **Cons:** Private transportation is a must: nearest village is 8 km (5 mi) away, some complain about insects in summer, no a/c. ⊠*Calcione, 26 km (15 mi) southwest of Arezzo, Lucignano 52046* ☎*0575/837100* 🖷*0575/837153* ⊕*www.calcione.com* ⬩*2 houses, 1 cottage, 6 apartments* ⌂*In-room: no a/c, no phone, kitchen,*

Fodor'sChoice
★

no TV (some). In-hotel: tennis court, pools, laundry facilities, some pets allowed ⊟*No credit cards* ⊘*Closed Nov.–Mar.* †⊙|*EP.*

SHOPPING

Ever since Etruscan goldsmiths set up their shops here more than 2,000 years ago, Arezzo has been famous for its jewelry. Today the town lays claim to being one of the world's capitals of jewelry design and manufacture, and you can find an impressive display of big-time baubles in the town center's shops. Arezzo is also famous, at least in Italy, for its antiques dealers.

CORTONA

29 km (18 mi) south of Arezzo, 79 km (44 mi) east of Siena, 117 km (73 mi) southeast of Florence.

GETTING HERE

Cortona is easily reached by car from the A1 (Autostrada del Sole): take the Valdichiana exit toward Perugia, then follow signs for Cortona. Regular bus service, provided by Etruria Mobilità, is available between Arezzo and Cortona (1 hour). Train service to Cortona is made inconvenient by the location of the train station, in the valley 3 km (1½ mi) steeply below the town itself. From there, you have to rely on bus or taxi service to get up to Cortona.

VISITOR INFORMATION

Cortona tourism office (⊠ *Via Nazionale 42* ☎*0575/630352* ⊕*www. apt.arezzo.it*).

With olive trees and vineyards creeping up to its walls, pretty Cortona—popularized by Frances Mayes's *Under the Tuscan Sun*—commands sweeping views over Lake Trasimeno and the plain of the Valdichiana. Its two galleries and churches are rarely visited; its delightful medieval streets are a pleasure to wander for their own sake. The heart of town is formed by Piazza della Repubblica and the adjacent Piazza Signorelli; both contain pleasant shops to browse in.

The **Museo Diocesano** *(Diocesan Museum)* houses an impressive number of large and splendid paintings by native son Luca Signorelli, as well as a stunning *Annunciation* by Fra Angelico, a delightful surprise in this small town. ⊠*Piazza Duomo* ☎*0575/62830* ▢*€5* ⊙*Tues.–Sun. 10–5.*

★ Legend has it that **Santa Maria del Calcinaio** was built between 1485 and 1513 after the image of the Madonna appeared on a wall of the medieval *calcinaio* (lime pit used for curing leather) that had occupied the site. The linear gray-and-white interior recalls Florence's Duomo. Sienese architect Francesco di Giorgio (1439–1502) most likely designed the sanctuary: the church is a terrific example of Renaissance architectural principles. ⊠*Località Il Calcinaio 227 j 3 km (2 mi) southeast of Cortona's center on Via Guelph* ☎*0575/604830* ▢*Free* ⊙*Mon.–Sat. 3:30–6, Sun. 10–12:30.*

WHERE TO STAY & EAT

$$-$$$ ✕**Osteria del Teatro.** Photographs from theatrical productions spanning many years line the walls of this tavern off Cortona's large Piazza del Teatro. The food is simply delicious—try the *filetto al lardo di colonnata e prugne* (beef cooked with bacon and prunes); service is warm and friendly. ⊠*Via Maffei 2* ☎*0575/630556* ▭*AE, DC, MC, V* ⊘*Closed Wed. and 2 wks in Nov. and in Feb.*

WORD OF MOUTH

"If you stay overnight, you can watch the mist rising from the valley below Cortona, and watch the churches emerge from the mist." –cmt

$$$$ ✕🖼 **Il Falconiere.** Choose here from rooms in an 18th-century villa, ★ suites in the *chiesetta* (chapel, or little church), or for more seclusion, Le Vigne del Falco suites at the far end of the property. Husband and wife team Riccardo and Silvia Baracchi run the show, serving an almost exclusively American and British clientele. Their restaurant's ($$$$) inventive seasonal menu includes *pici alla carbonara con lo zafferano di Centoia e pancetta croccante* (homemade thick spaghetti with carbonara sauce), over which, if your heart desires, you can add shaved white truffles. Cooking classes and guided wine tastings are available, and a small shop sells estate-produced olive oil and wine. **Pros:** Attractive setting, in the valley beneath Cortona; excellent service; elegant, but relaxed. **Cons:** A car is a must, some find rooms in main villa a little noisy, lacks full 24-hour service. ⊠*Località San Martino 370 j 3 km (1½ mi) north of Cortona, 52044* ☎*0575/612679* 🖷*0575/612927* ⊕*www.ilfalconiere.com* ⬎*13 rooms, 7 suites* ⌂*In-room: safe, refrigerator, dial-up. In-hotel: restaurant, room service, bar, pools, concierge, laundry service, public Internet, parking (no fee), some pets allowed (fee)* ▭*AE, MC, V* ⊘ *No lunch in restaurant Tues. Nov.–Mar. Hotel closed last 3 wks in Jan.–mid-Feb.* †O†*BP.*

SOUTHERN TUSCANY

Along the roads leading south from Siena, soft green olive groves give way to a blanket of oak, cypress, and reddish-brown earth. Towns are small and as old as the hills. The scruffy mountain landscapes of Monte Amiata make up some of the wildest parts of Tuscany, and once you're across the mountains the terrain is still full of cliffs. Southern Tuscany has good wine (try Brunello di Montalcino or the fruity, lesser-known Morellino di Scansano for a true treat), thermal baths at Saturnia, and Etruscan ruins.

MONTEPULCIANO

36 km (22 mi) southeast of Monte Oliveto Maggiore, 64 km (40 mi) southeast of Siena.

GETTING HERE

From Rome or Florence, take the Chiusi–Chianciano exit from the A1 highway (Autostrada del Sole). From Siena, take the SR2 south to San

Quirico and then the SP146 to Montepulciano. Tra-In offers bus service from Siena to Montepulciano several times a day. Montepulciano's train station is in Montepulciano Stazione, 10 km (6 mi) away.

VISITOR INFORMATION

Montepulciano tourism office (⊠ *Via di Gracciano nel Corso 59r* ☎ *0578/757341* ⊕ *www.prolocomontepulciano.it*).

EXPLORING

Perched high on a hilltop, Montepulciano is made up of a cluster of Renaissance buildings set within a circle of cypress trees. At an altitude of almost 2,000 feet, it's cool in summer and chilled in winter by biting winds that sweep the spiraling streets. Vino Nobile di Montepulciano, a robust red wine, is justifiably the town's greatest claim to fame. You can sample it in various wineshops and bars lining the twisting roads, as well as in most restaurants. The town is 13 km (8 mi) west of the A1 highway.

★ Montepulciano's pièce de résistance is the beautiful **Piazza Grande,** filled with handsome buildings. On the Piazza Grande is the **Duomo,** which has an unfinished facade that doesn't measure up to the beauty of the neighboring palaces. On the inside, however, its Renaissance roots shine through. You can see fragments of the tomb of Bartolomeo Aragazzi, secretary to Pope Martin V (who reigned from 1417 to 1431); it was created by Michelozzo between 1427 and 1436, and pieces of it have been dispersed to museums in other parts of the world. ⊠ *Piazza Grande* ☎ *0578/757761* ⊠ *Free* ⊗ *Daily 9–12:30.*

★ On the hillside below the town walls is the church of **San Biagio,** designed by Antonio Sangallo il Vecchio. A paragon of Renaissance architectural perfection, it's considered his masterpiece. Inside the church is a painting of a Madonna. According to legend, the painting was the only thing remaining in an abandoned church that two young girls entered on April 23, 1518. The two girls saw the eyes of the Madonna moving, and that same afternoon so did a farmer and a cow, who knelt down in front of the painting. In 1963 the image was proclaimed the *Madonna del Buon Viaggio (Madonna of the Good Journey)*, the protector of tourists in Italy. ⊠ *Via di San Biagio* ☎ *0578/7577761* ⊗ *Daily 9– 12:30 and 3:30–7:30.*

WHERE TO STAY & EAT

$$$–$$$$ ✕**La Grotta.** You might be tempted to pass right by the innocuous
★   entrance across the street from San Biagio, but you'd miss some fantastic food. Try the *tagliolini con carciofi e rigatino* (thin noodles with artichokes and bacon) or *tagliatelle di grano saraceno con asparagi e zucchine* (flat, buckwheat-flour noodles with asparagus and zucchini). Wash it down with the local wine, which just happens to be one of Italy's finest—Vino Nobile di Montepulciano. The desserts, such as an extravagantly rich triple-chocolate flan, are prepared with particular flair. ⊠ *Via di San Biagio 16, 53045* ☎ *0578/757479* ⊟ *AE, MC, V* ⊗ *Closed Wed. and Jan. and Feb.*

$$$ ★ ⚏ **Relais San Bruno.** Alberto Pavoncelli converted his family's summer home, just minutes from the town center, into a splendid inn. Set in extensive gardens with hammocks hidden here and there, the hotel's emphasis is on tranquillity and relaxation. The well-appointed rooms are located in four separate cottages; breakfast is served in a fifth. Reproductions of Columbian artist Fernando Botero's paintings add a touch of whimsy. A fodors.com user wrote: "the view of San Biagio and Montepulciano is stunning." **Pros:** King-size beds in most rooms, functioning fireplaces, relaxed but attentive service. **Cons:** Cottages can be chilly, need a car to get around. ⊠ *Via di Pescaia 5/7, 53045* ☎*0578/716222* ⊕*www.sanbrunorelais.com* ⇆*7 rooms, 1 suite* ⚙ *In-hotel: bar, pool, no elevator, public Internet* ▱*AE, DC, MC, V* ⎮⚬⎮*BP.*

$$ ★ ⚏ **San Biagio.** A five-minute walk from the church of the same name, the San Biagio makes a great base for exploring the surrounding countryside. All the rooms are simply decorated, but the lack of luxurious appointments is more than made up for by the friendly and professional service. A buffet breakfast prepares you for your day's explorations, and a dip in the indoor pool, no matter what the weather, provides a welcome finish. Several pleasant walking trails pass in front of the hotel: ask your hosts for details. **Pros:** Heated indoor pool, family-friendly atmosphere. **Cons:** Some rooms face a busy road, lots of tour groups. ⊠ *Via San Bartolomeo 2, 53045* ☎*0578/717233* ⊕*www.albergosanbiagio.it* ⇆*27 rooms* ⚙*In-hotel: restaurant, pool* ▱*AE, DC, MC, V* ⎮⚬⎮*BP.*

PIENZA

★ *15 km (9 mi) east of Montepulciano, 52 km (32 mi) southeast of Siena.*

GETTING HERE
From Siena, drive south along the SR2 to San Quirico d'Orcia and then the SP146. The trip should take just over an hour. Tra-In shuttles passengers between Siena and Pienza. There is no train service to Pienza.

VISITOR INFORMATION
Pienza tourism office (⊠*Piazza Pio II* ☎*0578/749071* ⊕*www.portalepienza.it*).

EXPLORING
Pienza owes its urban design to Pope Pius II, who had grand plans to transform his home village of Corsignano—the town's former name—into a model Renaissance town. The man entrusted with the project was Bernardo Rossellino (1409–64), a protégé of the great Renaissance architectural theorist Leon Battista Alberti (1404–74). His mandate was to create a cathedral, a papal palace, and a town hall (plus miscellaneous other buildings) that adhered to the humanist pope's principles. The result was a project that expressed Renaissance ideals of art, architecture, and civilized good living in a single scheme: it stands as a fine example of the architectural canon that Alberti formulated in the 15th century and emulated in many of Italy's finest buildings and piaz-

zas. Today the cool nobility of Pienza's center seems almost surreal in this otherwise unpretentious village, though at times it can seem overwhelmed by the tourists it attracts. Pienza's pecorino, a sheep's-milk cheese, is a superior gastronomic experience.

In 1459, Pius II commissioned Rossellino to design the perfect palazzo for his papal court. The architect took Florence's Palazzo Rucellai by Alberti as a model and designed the 100-room **Palazzo Piccolomini.** Three sides of the building fit perfectly into the urban plan around it, while the fourth, looking over the valley, has a lovely loggia uniting it with the gardens in back. Guided tours departing every 30 minutes take you to visit the papal apartments, including a beautiful library, the Sala delle Armi—with an impressive weapons collection—and the music room, with its extravagant wooden ceiling forming four letter P's, for Pope, Pius, Piccolomini, and Pienza. The last tour departs 30 minutes before closing. ⊠ *Piazza Pio II 1* ☎ *0578/286300* ⊕ *www.palazzopiccolominipienza.it* ✸€7 ⊗ *Mid-Mar.–mid-Oct., Tues.–Sun. 10–6:30; mid-Oct.–mid-Mar., Tues.–Sun. 10–4:30.*

The 15th-century **Duomo** was also built by the architect Rossellino under the influence of Alberti. The facade is divided in three parts with Renaissance arches under the pope's coat of arms encircled by a wreath of fruit. Inside, the cathedral is simple but richly decorated with Sienese paintings. The Duomo's perfection didn't last long—the first cracks appeared immediately after the building was completed, and its foundations have shifted slightly ever since as rain erodes the hillside behind. You can see this effect if you look closely at the base of the first column as you enter the church and compare it with the last. ⊠ *Piazza Pio II* ☎ *No phone* ✉ *Free* ⊗ *Tues.–Sun. 10–1 and 3–7.*

WHERE TO STAY & EAT

$–$$ ✕ **La Chiocciola.** Take the few minutes to walk from the old town for typical Pienza fare, including homemade *pici* (thick, short spaghetti) with hare or wild-boar sauce. The restaurant's version of *formaggio in forno* (baked cheese) with assorted accompaniments such as fresh porcini mushrooms is reason enough to venture here. ⊠ *Via dell'Acero 2* ☎ *0578/748683* ═ *MC, V* ⊗ *Closed Wed. and 10 days in Feb.*

$–$$ ▦ **Hotel Corsignano.** Just outside the old city walls, Hotel Corsignano is modern and comfortable. Two light-beige buildings, the older one right on the road, are connected by a hallway. Guest rooms are decorated with simple wooden furniture: those in the newer wing are quieter and larger than those in the front. The staff is exceptionally friendly and helpful. **Pros:** Steps away from center of town, helpful staff. **Cons:** Modern building lacks charm, some rooms face a busy street. ⊠ *Via della Madonnina 11, 53026* ☎ *0578/748501* ⊕ *www.corsignano.it* ⇄ *40 rooms* ⌂ *In-room: safe, refrigerator. In-hotel: restaurant, laundry service, public Internet, parking (no fee), some pets allowed* ═ *AE, DC, MC, V* ❙⊙❙*BP.*

¢ ▦ **Camere di Pienza.** A Renaissance building on the main street houses this tiny hotel. The four rooms have pretty, if simple, decoration and particularly nice ceilings—three with wood beams and one with a fresco. **Pros:** Charming rooms, convenient location in center of

11

town. **Cons:** No a/c, steps to climb. ⊠*Corso Il Rossellino 23, 53026* ☎*0578/748500* ➹*4 rooms* &*In-room: no a/c. In-hotel: no elevator* ⊟*No credit cards* ❍|*EP.*

MONTALCINO

24 km (15 mi) west of Pienza, 41 km (25 mi) south of Siena.

GETTING HERE

By car, follow the SR2 south from Siena, then follow the SP45 to Montalcino. Several Tra-In buses travel between Siena and Montalcino daily, making a tightly scheduled day trip possible. There is no train service available.

VISITOR INFORMATION

Montalcino tourism office (⊠*Costa del Municipio 8* ☎*0577/849331* ⊕*www.prolocomontalcino.it*).

EXPLORING

Another medieval hill town with a special claim to fame, Montalcino is the source for Brunello di Montalcino, one of Italy's most esteemed red wines. You can sample it in wine cellars in town or visit one of the nearby wineries for a guided tour and tasting; you must call ahead for reservations—your hotel or the local tourist office can help with arrangements.

La Fortezza, a 14th-century Sienese fortress, has well-preserved battlements. Climb up the narrow, spiral steps for the 360-degree view of most of southern Tuscany. There's also an enoteca for tasting wines on-site. ⊠*Via Panfilo dell'Oca* ☎*0577/849211* ✎*€3* ❍*Nov.–Mar., Tues.–Sun. 9–6; Apr.–Oct., daily 9–8.*

The **Museo Civico e Diocesano d'Arte Sacra** is in a building that belonged in the 13th century to the Augustinian monastic order. The ticket booth is in the glorious refurbished cloister, and the sacred art collection, gathered from churches throughout the region, is displayed on two floors in former monastic quarters. Though the art here might be called "B-list," a fine altarpiece by Bartolo di Fredi (circa 1330–1410), the *Coronation of the Virgin*, makes dazzling use of gold. In addition, there's a striking 12th-century crucifix that originally adorned the high altar of the church of Sant'Antimo. Also on hand are many wood sculptures, a typical medium in these parts during the Renaissance. ⊠*Via Ricasoli 21* ☎*0577/846014* ✎*€4.50* ❍*Apr.–Oct., Tues.–Sun. 10–1 and 4–5:50; Nov.–Mar., Tues.–Sun. 10–1 and 2–5:40.*

> **WORD OF MOUTH**
>
> "We rented an apartment in the Pienza area—arguably the most scenic area of Tuscany. From our apartment, we were able to explore the surrounding hill villages, the St. Antimo Abby, and also do a little hiking and biking. Just realize that maps can be deceiving—getting from one village to another can take a lot more time than it appears due to the narrow, twisting roads." –zootsi

WHERE TO STAY & EAT

$$-$$$ ✕ **Fattoria dei Barbi.** Set among the vineyards that produce excellent Brunello—as well as its younger cousin, Rosso di Montalcino—is this rustic taverna with a large stone fireplace. The estate farm produces many of the ingredients used in such traditional specialties as *stracotto nel brunello* (braised beef cooked with beans in Brunello wine). This eatery is a few minutes south of Montalcino, in the direction of Sant'Antimo. ✉ *Località Podernuovi* ☎ *0577/847117* ⚠ *Reservations essential* ☰ *AE, DC, MC, V* ✆ *Closed Wed. and mid-Jan.–mid-Feb.*

¢–$ ✕ **Enoteca Osteria Osticcio.** Tullio and Francesca Scrivano have beautifully remodeled this restaurant and wineshop. Upon entering, you descend a curving staircase to a tasting room filled with rustic wooden tables. Adjacent is a small dining area with a splendid view of the hills far below, and outside is a lovely little terrace perfect for sampling Brunello di Montalcino when the weather is warm. The menu is light and pairs nicely with the wines, which are the main draw. The *acciughe sotto pesto* (anchovies with pesto) is a particularly fine treat. ✉ *Via Matteotti 23* ☎ *0577/848271* ☰ *AE, DC, MC, V* ✆ *Closed Sun. No dinner.*

$ 🏠 **La Crociona.** A quiet and serene family-owned farm, La Crociona is in the middle of a small vineyard with glorious views. The apartments, which can sleep up to six people, have antique iron beds and 17th-century wardrobes. There's a big terrace and a pool where guests tend to congregate. You are invited to use the family's barbecue grill, as well as sample the owner's own wine supply. **Pros:** Peaceful location, great for families. **Cons:** No a/c, need a car to get around. ✉ *Località La Croce, 53024* ☎ *0577/848007* ⊕ *www.lacrociona.com* ➽ *7 apartments* ⚹ *In-room: no a/c, no phone, kitchen. In-hotel: pool, bicycles, no elevator, laundry facilities, laundry service, public Internet* ☰ *MC, V* ⦿ *EP.*

ABBAZIA DI SANT'ANTIMO

Fodor'sChoice
★

10 km (6 mi) south of Montalcino, 51 km (32 mi) south of Siena.

GETTING HERE

Abbazia di Sant'Antimo is a 15-minute drive from Montalcino. Tra-In bus service is extremely limited. The abbey cannot be reached by train.

It's well worth your while to visit this 12th-century Romanesque abbey, as it's a gem of pale stone in the silvery green of an olive grove. The exterior and interior sculpture is outstanding, particularly the nave capitals, a combination of French, Lombard, and even Spanish influences. The sacristy (seldom open) forms part of the primitive Carolingian church (founded in AD 781), its entrance flanked by 9th-century pilasters. The small vaulted crypt dates from the same period. Above the nave runs a *matroneum* (women's gallery), an unusual feature once used to separate the congregation. Equally unusual is the ambulatory, for which the three radiating chapels were almost certainly copied from a French model. Stay to hear the canonical hours celebrated in Gregorian chant. On the drive that leads up toward Castelnuovo dell'Abate is a small shop that sells souvenirs and has washrooms. A 2½-hour hiking trail (signed as #2) leads to the abbey from Montalcino. Starting near Montalcino's small cemetery, the trail heads south through woods, along a ridge road to the tiny hamlet of Villa a Tolli, and then downhill to Sant'Antimo. ✉ *Località Sant'Antimo, Castelnuovo dell'Abate* ☎ *0577/835659* ⊕ *www.antimo.it* 🎟 *Free* ⊗ *Daily 6 AM–9 PM.*

> ### WORD OF MOUTH
>
> "We stopped in at Sant'Antimo when the monks were conducting their Gregorian chants and it was one of the loveliest moments to experience." –caroltis

SATURNIA

75 km (45 mi) south of Montalcino, 129 km (77 mi) south of Siena.

GETTING HERE

Saturnia is a 30-minute drive from Pitigliano. Follow the SS74 to Manciano, then the SS322 to Montemerano, and then turn right onto the Strada Saturnia–La Croce. The RAMA bus company travels from Grosseto to Saturnia, but three changes make the journey particularly arduous. There is no train service to Saturnia.

EXPLORING

Etruscan and pre-Etruscan tombs cut into the local rock can be seen in this town, a lively center in pre-Etruscan times. Today it is known for its hot sulfur thermal waters.

Outside Saturnia, the hot, sulfurous waters cascade over natural limestone shelves at the **Cascate del Gorello** *(Gorello Falls)*, affording bathers a sweeping view of the open countryside. The falls are on public land and can be enjoyed 24 hours a day. They get extremely crowded—day and night—during August. ⊹ *2 km (1 mi) south of Saturnia, on road to Montemerano* ☎ *No phone* 🎟 *Free.*

WHERE TO STAY & EAT

$$$–$$$$ ✕**I Due Cippi–Da Michele.** Owner Michele Aniello captivates with a creative menu that emphasizes local ingredients like wild boar and duck. Try the *tortelli di castagne al seme di finocchio* (chestnut-stuffed pasta pillows with butter sauce and fennel seeds). In good weather you can enjoy your meal on a terrace overlooking the town's main square. ✉ *Piazza Veneto 26a* ☎ *0564/601074* ⚖ *Reservations essential* ▭ *AE, DC, MC, V* ⊗ *Closed Dec. 20–26, Jan. 10–25, and Tues. Oct.–June.*

$$$$ ⊡**Terme di Saturnia.** Spa living might not get any more top-notch than this: roam the spa resort in a plush white bathrobe (waiting in your room) before dipping into the 37.5°C (100°F) sulfurous thermal pools. Seemingly every possible health and beauty treatment is available. Sleek elegance pervades public and private rooms: tall windows have floor-to-ceiling draperies in rich colors like steel blue and gray or burnt umber and sage; floors are polished wood. Eclectic furniture includes some sleigh-shaped benches and oval night tables. You can opt for half or full board to complete the experience. **Pros:** Luxurious setting, excellent service, wide range of treaments. **Cons:** On the pricey side, aseptic

atmosphere. ⚓*3 km (2 mi) east of Saturnia on road to Montemerano, past Gorello Falls, 58050* ☎*0564/601061* ⊕*www.termedisaturnia.it* ⟳*130 rooms, 10 suites* ⚿*In-room: safe, refrigerator, VCR. In-hotel: 3 restaurants, room service, bar, tennis courts, pools, gym, spa, concierge, laundry facilities, laundry service, public Internet, some pets allowed* ⊟*AE, DC, MC, V* ⑩*BP.*

$ ▢**Villa Clodia.** The villa in the oldest part of town has splendid views
★ over the nearby hills and the steamy clouds coming from the hot springs. Inside it's just as nice, with hand-painted decoration in the rooms and a cozy library with a marble fireplace. Breakfast is served in a country-style room with gingham tablecloths, but early risers may be able to stake a claim on one of the terrace tables overlooking the valley. **Pros:** Excellent location on edge of town, great views, cozy environment. **Cons:** Some rooms are small, need a car to get around. ⊠*Via Italia 43, 58050* ☎*0564/601212* 🖷*0564/601305* ⊕*www.hotelvillaclodia. com* ⟳*8 rooms, 2 suites* ⚿*In-room: safe. In-hotel: pool, parking (no fee)* ⊟*MC, V* ⊗*Closed Dec.* ⑩*BP.*

Umbria & the Marches

WORD OF MOUTH

"I would suggest the Marches as a great, off-the-beaten-path region to visit. It has a very beautiful landscape and is just as central as Tuscany and Umbria (although, unlike Umbria, it has a coastline, and a nice one at that)."

—Jackie in Italy

WELCOME TO UMBRIA & THE MARCHES

TOP REASONS TO GO

★ **Palazzo Ducale, Urbino:** A visit here reveals more about the ideals of the Renaissance than a shelfful of history books.

★ **Assisi, shrine to St. Francis:** Recharge your soul in this rose-color hill town with a visit to the gentle saint's majestic Basilica, adorned with great frescoes.

★ **Spoleto, Umbria's musical Mecca:** Crowds may descend and prices ascend here during summer's Festival dei Due Mondi, but Spoleto's hushed charm enchants year-round.

★ **Tantalizing truffles:** Are Umbria's celebrated "black diamonds" coveted for their pungent flavor, their rarity, or their power in the realm of romance?

★ **Orvieto's Duomo:** Arresting visions of heaven and hell on the facade and brilliant frescoes within make this Gothic cathedral a dazzler.

1 Perugia. Umbria's largest town is easily reached from Rome, Siena, or Florence. Home to some of Perugino's great frescoes and a hilltop *centro storico* (historic center), it's also favored by chocolate lovers, who celebrate at October's Eurochocolate Festival.

2 Assisi. The city of Saint Francis is a major pilgrimage site, crowned by one of Italy's greatest churches. Despite the throngs of visitors, it still maintains its medieval hill-town character.

3 Northern Umbria. The quiet towns lying around Perugia include **Deruta**, which produces exceptional ceramics, and **Torgiano**, where you can tour the Wine Museum and taste local wines. A trip through the rugged terrain of northeast Umbria takes you to **Gubbio**, where from the Piazza della Signoria you can admire magnificent views of the countryside below.

4 Spoleto. Though it's known to the world for its annual performing-arts festival, Spoleto offers much more than Puccini in its Piazza del Duomo. There are Filippo Lippi frescoes in the cathedral, a massive castle towering over the town, and a bridge across the neighboring valley that's an engineering marvel.

Assisi

SAN MARINO

E78

Sansepolcro

Città Di Castello

3

E45

2

Perugia

Lago Di Trasimeno

71

Torgiano

Città della Pieve

Deruta

E45

Todi

A1

Orvieto

448

74

5

71

LAZIO

E

A1

5 Southern Umbria. Of central Italy's many hill towns, none has a more impressive setting than **Orvieto**, perched on a plateau 1,000 feet above the surrounding valley. Its cathedral ranks with Assisi's as the most spectacular in Umbria. Between Spoleto and Orvieto there's a collection of quiet, laid-back towns, including the jewel of the area, **Todi**.

GETTING ORIENTED

Central Italy doesn't begin and end with Tuscany; the pastoral, hilly provinces of Umbria and the Marches pick up where the more famous neighbor leaves off. Divided by the Apennine range, both regions are studded with Renaissance-era villages and fortresses—a landscape hallowed by St. Francis and immortalized in the works of native son Raphael.

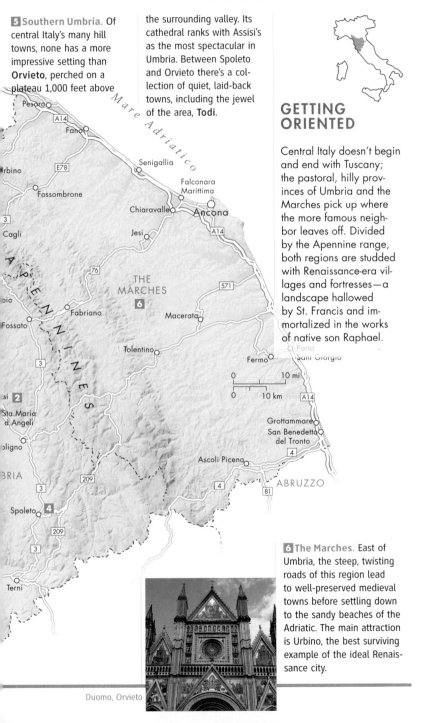

6 The Marches. East of Umbria, the steep, twisting roads of this region lead to well-preserved medieval towns before settling down to the sandy beaches of the Adriatic. The main attraction is Urbino, the best surviving example of the ideal Renaissance city.

Duomo, Orvieto

UMBRIA & THE MARCHES PLANNER

Festivals to Plan a Trip Around

Each summer Umbria hosts two of Italy's biggest music festivals. Spoleto's **Festival dei Due Mondi** (⊕ www.spoletofestival.it), from mid-June through mid-July, features classical music and also ventures into theater and the visual arts. Perugia is hopping for 10 days in July, when famous names in contemporary music perform at the **Umbria Jazz Festival** (⊕ www.umbriajazz.com).

If you want to attend either event, you should make arrangements in advance…and if you don't want to attend, you should plan to avoid the cities during festival time, when hotel rooms and restaurant tables are at a premium. A similar caveat applies for Assisi during religious festivals at Christmas, Easter, the feast of St. Francis (October 4), and Calendimaggio (May 1), when pilgrims arrive en masse.

If you've got a sweet tooth and you're visiting during the fall, head to Perugia for the **Eurochocolate Festival** (⊕ www.eurochocolate.perugia.it) in the third week of October.

Making the Most of Your Time

Umbria is a nicely compact collection of character-rich hill towns; you can settle in one, then explore the others, as well as the countryside and forest in between, on day trips.

Perugia, Umbria's largest and most lively city, is a logical choice for your base, particularly if you're arriving from the north. If you want something a little quieter, virtually any other town in the region will suit your purposes; even Assisi, which overflows with bus tours during the day, is delightfully quiet in the evening and early morning. Spoleto and Orvieto are the most developed town to the south, but they're still of modest proportions.

If you have the time to venture farther afield, consider trips to Gubbio, northeast of Perugia, and Urbino, in the Marches. Both are worth the time it takes to reach them, and both make for pleasant overnight stays. In southern Umbria, Valnerina and the Piano Grande are out-of-the-way spots with the region's best hiking.

Finding a Place to Stay

Virtually every older town, no matter how small, has some kind of hotel. A trend, particularly around Gubbio, Orvieto, and Todi, is to convert old villas, farms, and monasteries into first-class hotels. The natural splendor of the countryside more than compensates for the distance from town—provided you have a car. Hotels in town tend to be simpler than their country cousins, with a few notable exceptions in Spoleto, Gubbio, and Perugia.

DINING & LODGING PRICE CATEGORIES (IN EUROS)				
¢	$	$$	$$$	$$$$
Restaurants				
under €15	€15–€25	€25–€35	€35–€45	over €45
Hotels				
under €70	€70–€110	€110–€160	€160–€220	over €220
Restaurant prices are for a first course (primo), second course (secondo), and dessert (dolce). Hotel prices are for two people in a standard double room in high season, including tax and service.				

GETTING AROUND

By Car

On the western edge of the region is the Umbrian section of the Autostrada del Sole (A1), Italy's principal north–south highway. It links Florence and Rome with Orvieto and passes near Todi and Terni. The S3 intersects with A1 and leads on to Assisi and Urbino. The Adriatica superhighway (A14) runs north–south along the coast, linking the Marches to Bologna and Venice.

The steep hills and deep valleys that make Umbria and the Marches so idyllic also make for challenging driving. Fortunately, the area has an excellent, modern road network, but be prepared for tortuous mountain roads if your explorations take you off the beaten track. Central Umbria is served by a major highway, the S75bis, which passes along the shore of Lake Trasimeno and ends in Perugia. Assisi is served by the modern highway S75; S75 connects to S3 and S3bis, which cover the heart of the region. Major inland routes connect coastal A14 to large towns in the Marches, but inland secondary roads in mountain areas can be winding and narrow. Always carry a good road map, a flashlight, and, if possible, a cell phone in case of a breakdown.

By Bus

Perugia's bus station is in Piazza Partigiani, which you can reach by taking the escalators from the town center. Perugia is served by the **Sulga Line** (☎075/5009641 ⊕www.sulga.it), which has daily departures to Rome's Stazione Tiburtina and to Florence's Piazza Adua. Connections between Rome, Spoleto, and the Marches are provided by the bus companies **Bucci** (☎0721/32401 ⊕www.autolineebucci.com) and **Soget** (☎0721/371318).

Local bus services between all the major and minor towns of Umbria are good. Some of the routes in rural areas are designed to serve as many places as possible and are, therefore, quite roundabout and slow. Schedules change often, so consult with local tourist offices before setting out.

By Train

Several direct daily trains run by the Italian state railway, **Ferrovia dello Stato** (☎*892021 toll free in Italy* ⊕ *www.trenitalia.com*), link link Florence and Rome with Perugia and Assisi, and local service to the same area is available from Terontola (on the Rome–Florence line) and from Foligno (on the Rome–Ancona line). Intercity trains between Rome and Florence make stops in Orvieto, and the main Rome–Ancona line passes through Narni, Terni, Spoleto, and Foligno.

Within Umbria, a small, privately owned railway operated by **Ferrovia Centrale Umbra** (☎075/5729121) runs from Città di Castello in the north to Terni in the south via Perugia. Note: train service is not available to either Gubbio or Urbino.

Gubbio

EATING & DRINKING WELL IN UMBRIA

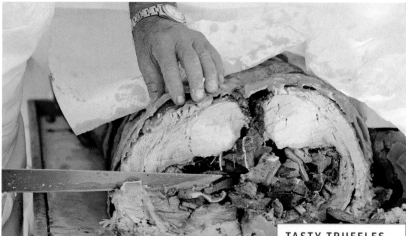

Central Italy is mountainous, and its food is hearty and straightforward, with a stick-to-the-ribs quality that sees hardworking farmers and artisans through a long day's work and helps them make the steep climb home at night.

In restaurants here, as in much of Italy, you're rewarded for seeking out the local cuisines, and you'll often find better, and cheaper, food if you're willing to stray a few hundred yards from the main sights. Spoleto is noted for its good food and service, probably a result of high expectations from the international arts crowd. For gourmets, however, it's hard to beat Spello, which has both excellent restaurants and first-rate wineshops.

A rule of thumb for eating well throughout Umbria is to order what's in season; the trick is to stroll through local markets to see what's for sale. A number of restaurants in the region offer *degustazione* (tasting) menus, which give you a chance to try different local specialties without breaking the bank.

TASTY TRUFFLES

More truffles are found in Umbria than anywhere else in Italy. Spoleto and Norcia are prime territory for the *tartufo nero* (reddish-black interior and fine white veins), pictured below right, prized for its extravagant flavor and intense aroma. The mild summer truffle, *scorzone estivo* (black outside and beige inside), is in season from May through December. The *scorzone autunnale* (burnt brown color and visible veins inside) is found from October through December. Truffles can be shaved into omelets or over pasta, pounded into sauces, or chopped and mixed with oil.

OLIVE OIL

Nearly everywhere you look in Umbria, olive trees grace the hillsides. The soil of the Apennines allows the olives to ripen slowly, guaranteeing low acidity, a cardinal virtue of fine oil. Look for restaurants that proudly display their own oil, often a sign that they care about their food.

Umbria's finest oil is found in Trevi, where the local product is intensely green and fruity. You can sample it in the town's wine bars, which often do double duty, offering olive-oil tastings.

PORK PRODUCTS

Much of traditional Umbrian cuisine revolves around pork. It can be cooked in wood-fire stoves, sometimes basted with a rich sauce made from innards and red wine. The roasted pork known as *porchetta*, pictured at left, is grilled on a spit and flavored with fennel and herbs, leaving a crisp outer sheen. The art of pork processing has been handed down through generations in Norcia, so much so that charcuterie producers throughout Italy are often known as *norcini*. Don't miss *prosciutto di Norcia*, which is aged for two years.

LENTILS AND SOUPS

The town of Castelluccio di Norcia is particularly known for its lentils and its *farro* (an ancient grain used by the

Romans, similar to wheat), and a variety of beans used in soups. Throughout Umbria, look for *imbrecciata*, a soup of beans and grain, delicately flavored with local herbs. Other ingredients that find their way into thick Umbrian soups are wild beet, sorrel, mushrooms, spelt, chickpeas, and the elusive, fragrant saffron, grown in nearby Cascia.

WINE

Sagrantino grapes are the star in Umbria's most notable red wines. For centuries they've been used in Sagrantino *passito*, a semisweet wine made by leaving the grapes to dry for a period after picking in order to intensify their sugar content. In recent decades, the *secco* (dry) Sagrantino has occupied the front stage. Both *passito* and *secco* have a deep red-ruby color, with a full body and rich flavor.

In the past few years the phenomenon of the *enoteca* (wineshop and wine bar) has taken off, making it easier to arrange wine tastings. Many also let you sample different olive oils on toasted bread, known as *bruschetta*. Some wine information centers, like La Strada del Sagrantino in Montefalco, will help set up appointments for wine tastings.

Updated
by Jonathan
Willcocks

BIRTHPLACE OF SAINTS AND HOME to some of the country's greatest artistic treasures, central Italy is a collection of misty green valleys and picture-perfect hill towns laden with centuries of history. Umbria and the Marches are the Italian countryside as you've imagined it: verdant farmland, steep hillsides topped with fairy-tale fortresses, winding country roads traveled by horses and FIAT 500s carrying crates of fresh olives. No single town here has the extravagant wealth of art and architecture of Florence, Rome, or Venice, but this works in your favor: small jewels of towns feel knowable, not overwhelming. And the cultural cupboard is far from bare. Orvieto's cathedral and Assisi's basilica are two of the most important sights in Italy, while Perugia, Todi, Gubbio, and Spoleto are rich in art and architecture.

East of Umbria, the Marches (Le Marche to Italians) stretch between the Apennines and the Adriatic Sea. It's a region of great turreted castles on high peaks defending passes and roads—a testament to the centuries of battle that have taken place here. Rising majestically in Urbino is a splendid palace, built by Federico da Montefeltro, where the humanistic ideals of the Renaissance came to their fullest flower, while the town of Ascoli Piceno can lay claim to one of the most beautiful squares in Italy. Virtually every small town in the region has a castle, church, or museum worth a visit—but even without them, you'd still be compelled to stop for the interesting streets, panoramic views, and natural beauty.

PERUGIA

Perugia is a majestic, handsome, wealthy city, and with its trendy boutiques, refined cafés, and grandiose architecture, it doesn't try to hide its affluence. A student population of more than 30,000 means that the city is abuzz with activity throughout the year. Umbria Jazz, one of the region's most important music festivals, attracts music lovers from around the world, and Eurochocolate, the international chocolate festival, is an irresistible draw for anyone with a sweet tooth.

GETTING HERE

The best approach to the city is by train. The area around the station doesn't attest to the rest of Perugia's elegance, but buses running from the station to Piazza d'Italia, the heart of the old town, are frequent. If you are driving to Perugia and your hotel doesn't have parking facilities, leave your car in one of the lots close to the center. Electronic signs indicate the location of lots and the number of spaces free. If you park in the Piazza Partigiani, take the escalators that pass through the fascinating subterranean excavations of the Roman foundations of the city and lead to the town center.

VISITOR INFORMATION

Umbria's regional tourism office (✉ *Piazza Matteotti 18* ☎ *075/5736458* 📠 *075/5720988* ⊕ *www.perugia.umbria2000.it*)is in Perugia. The staff is well informed about the area, and can give you a wide selection of

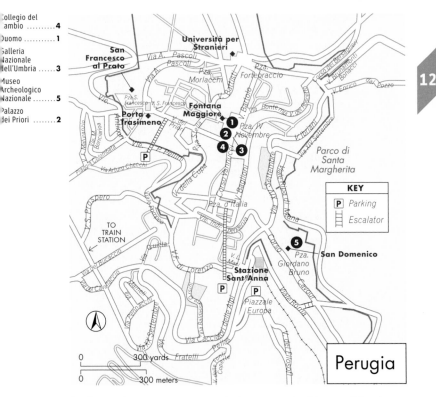

12

Perugia

leaflets and maps to assist you during your trip. It's open Monday to Saturday 8:30 to 1:30 and 3 to 6:30, and Sunday 8:30 to 1.

EXPLORING PERUGIA

Thanks to Perugia's hilltop position, the medieval city remains almost completely intact. It is the best-preserved hill town of its size, and few other places in Italy better illustrate the model of the self-contained city-state that so shaped the course of Italian history.

MAIN ATTRACTIONS

Collegio del Cambio *(Bankers' Guild Hall).* These elaborate rooms, on the ground floor of the **Palazzo dei Priori,** served as the meeting hall and chapel of the guild of bankers and money changers. Most of the frescoes were done by the most important Perugian painter of the Renaissance, Pietro Vannucci, better known as Perugino. He included a remarkably honest self-portrait on one of the pilasters. The iconography includes common religious themes, such as the Nativity and the Transfiguration seen on the end walls. On the left wall are female figures representing the virtues, beneath them the heroes and sages of antiquity. On the right wall are figures presumed to have been painted in part by Perugino's most famous pupil, Raphael. (His hand, experts say, is most apparent in the figure of Fortitude.) The *cappella* (chapel) of San Giovanni Battista has frescoes painted by Giannicola di Paolo, another student of Perugino. ⊠*Corso Vannucci 25* ☎*075/5728599* 📠*€4.50, €5.50 with Collegio della Mercanzia* ⊙*Mon.–Sat. 9–12:30 and 2:30–5:30, Sun. 9–1.*

Corso Vannucci. A string of elegantly connected *palazzi* (palaces) expresses the artistic nature of this city center, the heart of which is concentrated along Corso Vannucci. Stately and broad, this pedestrians-only street runs from Piazza d'Italia to Piazza IV Novembre. Along the way, the entrances to many of Perugia's side streets might tempt you to wander off and explore. But don't stray too far as evening falls, when Corso Vannucci fills with Perugians out for their evening *passeggiata,* a pleasant pre-dinner stroll that may include a pause for an aperitif at one of the many bars that line the street.

❸ Galleria Nazionale dell'Umbria. The region's most comprehensive art gallery is housed on the fourth floor of the **Palazzo dei Priori.** Enhanced by skillfully lit displays and computers that allow you to focus on the works' details and background information, the collection includes work by native artists—most notably Pintoricchio (1454–1513) and Perugino (circa 1450–1523)—and others of the Umbrian and Tuscan schools, among them Gentile da Fabriano (1370–1427), Duccio (circa 1255–1318), Fra Angelico (1387–1455), Fiorenzo di Lorenzo (1445–1525), and Piero della Francesca (1420–92). In addition to paintings, the gallery has frescoes, sculptures, and some superb examples of crucifixes from the 13th and 14th centuries. Some rooms are dedicated to Perugia itself, showing how the medieval city evolved. ⊠*Corso Vannucci 19, Piazza IV Novembre* ☎*075/5721009* ⊕*www.galleria nazionaleumbria.it* 📠*€6.50* ⊙*Tues.–Sun. 8:30–7:30; last admission ½ hr before closing.*

Fodor's Choice
★

❷ Palazzo dei Priori *(Palace of Priors).* A series of elegant connected buildings, the palazzo serves as Perugia's city hall and houses three of the city's museums. The buildings string along Corso Vannucci and wrap around the Piazza IV Novembre, where the original entrance is located. The steps here lead to the **Sala dei Notari** (Notaries' Hall). Other entrances lead to the **Galleria Nazionale dell'Umbria, the Collegio del Cambio,** and the **Collegio della Mercanzia.** The Sala dei Notari, which dates back to the 13th century and was the original meeting place of the town merchants, had become the seat of the notaries by the second half of the 15th century. Wood beams and an interesting array of frescoes attributed to Maestro di Farneto embellish the room. Coats of arms and crests line the back and right lateral walls; you can spot some famous figures from *Aesop's Fables* on the left wall. The palazzo facade is adorned with symbols of Perugia's pride and past power: the griffin is the city symbol, and the lion denotes Perugia's allegiance to the Guelph (or papal) cause. ⊠*Piazza IV Novembre* 📠 *Free* ⊙*June–Sept., Tues.–Sun. 9–1 and 3–7.*

Rocca Paolina. A labyrinth of little streets, alleys, and arches, this underground city was originally part of a fortress. It was built at the behest

UMBRIA THROUGH THE AGES

The earliest inhabitants of Umbria, the Umbri, were thought by the Romans to be the most ancient inhabitants of Italy. Little is known about them; with the coming of Etruscan culture the tribe fled into the mountains in the eastern portion of the region. The Etruscans, who founded some of the great cities of Umbria, were in turn supplanted by the Romans. Unlike Tuscany and other regions of central Italy, Umbria had few powerful medieval families to exert control over the cities in the Middle Ages—its proximity to Rome ensured that it would always be more or less under papal domination.

In the center of the country, Umbria has for much of its history been a battlefield where armies from north and south clashed. Hannibal destroyed a Roman army on the shores of Lake Trasimeno, and the bloody course of the interminable

Guelph-Ghibelline conflict of the Middle Ages was played out here. Dante considered Umbria the most violent place in Italy. Trophies of war still decorate the Palazzo dei Priori in Perugia, and the little town of Gubbio continues a warlike rivalry begun in the Middle Ages—every year it challenges the Tuscan town of Sansepolcro to a crossbow tournament. Today the bowmen shoot at targets, but neither side has forgotten that 500 years ago its ancestors shot at each other. In spite of—or perhaps because of—this bloodshed, Umbria has produced more than its share of Christian saints. The most famous is St. Francis, the decidedly pacifist saint whose life shaped the Church of his time. His great shrine at Assisi is visited by hundreds of thousands of pilgrims each year. St. Clare, his devoted follower, was Umbria-born, as were St. Benedict, St. Rita of Cascia, and the patron saint of lovers, St. Valentine.

of Pope Paul III between 1540 and 1543 to confirm papal dominion over the city. When the papacy fell parts of it were destroyed, but much still remains. Begin your visit by taking the escalators from Piazza Italia and Via Masi. In the summer this is the coolest place in the city. ⏱ *Daily 8–7.*

ALSO WORTH SEEING

① Duomo. Severe yet mystical, the Duomo, also called the Cathedral of San Lorenzo, is most famous for being the home of the wedding ring of the Virgin Mary, stolen by the Perugians in 1488 from the nearby town of Chiusi. The ring, kept high up in a red-curtained vault in the chapel immediately to the left of the entrance, is kept under lock—15 locks, to be precise—and key most of the year. It's shown to the public on July 30 (the day it was brought to Perugia) and the second-to-last Sunday in January (Mary's wedding anniversary). The cathedral itself dates from the Middle Ages and has many additions from the 15th and 16th centuries. The most visually interesting element is the altar to the Madonna of Grace; an elegant fresco on a column at the right of the entrance of the altar depicts *La Madonna delle Grazie* and is surrounded by prayer benches decorated with handwritten notes to the Holy Mother. Around the column are small amulets—symbols of gratitude from those whose prayers were answered. There are also elaborately carved choir stalls, executed by Giovanni Battista Bastone in 1520. The altarpiece (1484), an early masterpiece by Luca Signorelli (circa 1441–1523), shows the Madonna with Saint John the Baptist, Saint Onophrius, and Saint Lawrence. Sections of the church may be closed to visitors during religious services. ⊠ *Piazza IV Novembre* ☎ *075/5724853* ⌨ *Free* ⊘ *Mon.–Sat. 7–12:30 and 4–6:45, Sun. 8–12:30 and 4–6:45*

> ### WORD OF MOUTH
>
> "Two things you must not fail to do in Perugia are to (a) join the evening walk on the Corso Vannucci beginning at about 5 pm and (b) take the escalators that go up and down and through the historic city walls. Also: Hang out as often as you dare at Sandri's, one of Italy's most marvelous cafe/pastry shops, on the Corso Vanucci." –nessundorma

⑤ Museo Archeologico Nazionale. The museum, next to the imposing church of San Domenico, contains an excellent collection of Etruscan artifacts from throughout the region. Perugia was a flourishing Etruscan city long before it fell under Roman domination in 310 BC. Little else remains of Perugia's mysterious ancestors, although the Arco di Augusto, in Piazza Fortebraccio, the northern entrance to the city, is of Etruscan origin. ⊠ *Piazza G. Bruno 10* ☎ *075/5727141* ⊕ *www.archeopg.arti.beniculturali.it* ⌨ *€4* ⊘ *Mon. 2:30–7:30, Tues.–Sun. 8:30–7:30.*

WHERE TO EAT

$$–$$$ ✕ **Antica Trattoria San Lorenzo.** Brick vaults are not the only distinguishing feature of this small restaurant next to the Duomo, as both the food and the service are outstanding. Particular attention is paid to adapting traditional Umbrian cuisine to the modern palate. There is also a nice variety of seafood dishes on the menu. The *trenette alla farina di noce con pesce di mare* (flat noodles made with walnut flour topped with fresh fish) is a real treat. ⊠ *Piazza Danti 19-A* ☎ *075/5721956* ⊟ *AE, D, MC, V* ⊘ *Closed Sun.*

$–$$$ ✕ **La Rosetta.** The restaurant, in the hotel of the same name, is a peaceful, elegant spot. In winter you dine inside under medieval vaults; in summer, in the cool courtyard. The food is simple but reliable and flawlessly served. ⊠ *Piazza d'Italia 19* ☎ *075/5720841* ⌨ *Reservations essential* ⊟ *AE, DC, MC, V.*

$$ ✕ **La Taverna.** Medieval steps lead to a rustic two-story restaurant where wine bottles and artful clutter decorate the walls. Good choices from the regional menu include *caramelle al gorgonzola* (pasta rolls filled with red cabbage and mozzarella and topped with a Gorgonzola sauce) and grilled meat dishes, such as the *medaglioni di vitello al tartuffo* (grilled veal with truffles). ⊠ *Via delle Streghe 8, off Corso Vannucci* ☎ *075/5724128* ⊟ *AE, DC, MC, V* ⊘ *Closed Mon.*

$–$$ ✕ **Il Falchetto.** Exceptional food at reasonable prices makes this Perugia's best bargain. Service is smart but relaxed in the two medieval dining rooms that put the chef on view. The house specialty is *falchetti* (homemade gnocchi with spinach and ricotta cheese). ⊠ *Via Bartolo 20* ☎ *075/5731775* ⊟ *AE, DC, MC, V* ⊘ *Closed Mon. and last 2 wks in Jan.*

$ ✕ **Dal Mi' Cocco.** A great favorite with Perugia's university students, this
★ place is fun, crowded, and inexpensive. You may find yourself seated at a long table with other diners, but some language help from your neighbors could come in handy—the menu is in pure Perugian dialect. The fixed-price meals change with the season, and each day of the week brings some new creation *dal cocco* (from the "coconut," or head) of the chef. ⊠ *Corso Garibaldi 12* ☎ *075/5732511* ⚠ *Reservations essential* ⊟ *No credit cards* ⊘ *Closed Mon. and July 25–Aug. 15*

WHERE TO STAY

$$$ ⬚ **Castello dell'Oscano.** A splendid neo-Gothic castle, a late-19th-century villa, and a converted farmhouse hidden in the tranquil hills north of Perugia offer a wide range of accommodations. Step back in time in the castle, where spacious suites and junior suites, all with high oak-beam ceilings, and some with panoramic views of the surrounding country, are decorated with 18th- and 19th-century antiques. The sweeping wooden staircase of the main lounge, and the wood-paneled reading rooms and restaurant are particularly elegant. Rooms in the villa are smaller and more modern, and the apartments of the farmhouse, in the valley below the castle, have their own kitchens. The complex is in Cenerente, 5 km (3 mi) north of Perugia. **Pros:** Quiet elegance, fine gardens, Umbrian wine list. **Cons:** Distance from Perugia, not easy to find. ⊠ *Strada della Forcella 32, Cenerente, 06070* ☎ *075/584371* ⊟ *075/690666* ⊕ *www.oscano.it* ⤳ *24 rooms, 8 suites, 13 apartments* ⌂ *In-room: no a/c (some), ethernet. In-hotel: restaurant, bar, pool, gym, bicycles, no-smoking rooms* ⊟ *AE, D, V* ⦿ *BP*

$$ ⬚ **Hotel Fortuna.** The elegant decor in the large rooms of this friendly hotel complements the frescoes, which date from the 1700s. Some rooms have balconies. The building itself, just out of sight of Corso Vannucci, dates to the 1300s. **Pros:** Central but quiet, homely atmosphere. **Cons:** Some small rooms, no restaurant. ⊠ *Via Bonazzi 19, 06123* ☎ *075/5722845* ⊟ *075/5735040* ⊕ *www.umbriahotels.com* ⤳ *51 rooms* ⌂ *In-hotel: restaurant, bar, parking (fee)* ⊟ *AE, DC, MC, V* ⦿ *BP*

$$ ⬚ **Il Cantico della Natura.** Don't let the rustic appearance of the buildings fool you, this is one of the plushest agriturismi in Umbria. The rooms are furnished in varying ethnic styles, with nice little extras thrown in such as bedside kettles and an array of teas and herbal infusions. The owners also organize a series of outdoor activities. **Pros:** Views of Lake Trasimeno and the surrounding countryside. **Cons:** Not easy to find, road poor in winter. ⊠ *Vocabolo Penna, Montesperello di Magione* ☎ *075/841699* ⊕ *www.ilcanticodellanatura.it* ⤳ *12 rooms* ⌂ *In-hotel: restaurant, gym, bicycles* ⊟ *AE, DC, MC, V* ⦿ *BP*

$$ ⬚ **Locanda della Posta.** In the city's old district, this lodging is in an 18th-century palazzo. Renovations have left the lobby and other public areas rather bland, but the rooms are soothingly decorated in muted colors. Although facing busy Corso Vannucci and suppos-

edly soundproof, they're still a bit noisy. Those on the upper floors at the back of the building are quieter and have great views. **Pros:** Some fine views, central position. **Cons:** Uninspiring lobby, some small rooms, no restaurant. ⊠ *Corso Vannucci 97, 06121* ☎ *075/5728925* 🖷 *075/5732562* 🛏 *38 rooms, 1 suite* ♿ *In-hotel: bar, parking (fee)* ☰ *AE, DC, MC, V* ⊺◎⊺ *BP.*

NIGHTLIFE & THE ARTS

With its large student population, the city has plenty to offer in the way of bars and clubs. The best ones are around the city center, off Corso Vanucci. *Viva Perugia* is a good source of information about nightlife. The monthly, sold at newsstands, has a section in English.

MUSIC FESTIVALS

Summer sees two music festivals in Perugia. **Umbria Jazz** (☎ *075/5732432* ⊕ *www.umbriajazz.com*) is held for 10 days in July. Tickets are available starting at the end of April. The **Sagra Musicale Umbra** (☎ *075/5721374* ⊕ *www.perugiamusicaclassica.com*), held from mid-August to mid-September, celebrates sacred music.

SHOPPING

Take a stroll down any of Perugia's main streets, including Corso Vannucci, Via dei Priori, Via Oberdan, and Via S. Ercolano, and you'll see many well-known designer boutiques and specialty shops.

The most typical thing to buy in Perugia is some Perugina chocolate, which you can find almost anywhere. The best-known chocolates made by Perugina are the chocolate-and-hazelnut-filled nibbles called Baci (literally, "kisses"). They're wrapped in silver paper that includes a sliver of paper, like the fortune in a fortune cookie, with multilingual romantic sentiments or sayings.

ASSISI

The small town of Assisi is one of the Christian world's most important pilgrimage sites and home of the Basilica di San Francesco—built to honor Saint Francis (1182–1226) and erected in swift order after his death. The peace and serenity of the town is a welcome respite after the hustle and bustle of some of Italy's major cities.

Like most other towns in the region, Assisi began as an Umbri settlement in the 7th century BC and was conquered by the Romans 400 years later. The town was Christianized by Saint Rufino, its patron saint, in the third century, but it is the spirit of Saint Francis, a patron saint of Italy and founder of the Franciscan monastic order, that is felt throughout its narrow medieval streets. The famous 13th-century basilica was decorated by the greatest artists of the period.

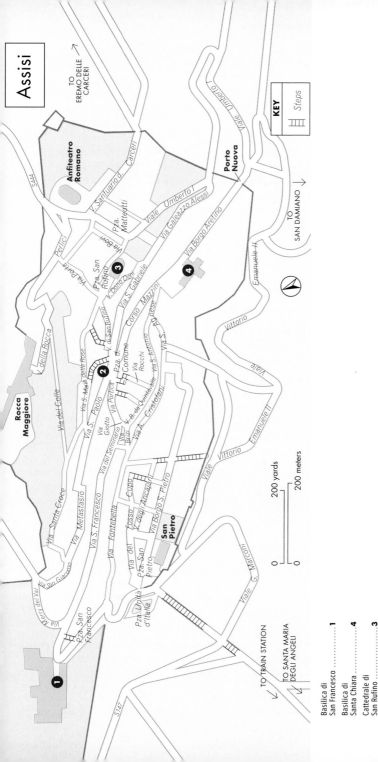

Assisi

TO EREMO DELLE CARCERI →

Anfiteatro Romano

Rocca Maggiore

Porto Nuova

TO SAN DAMIANO →

San Pietro

TO TRAIN STATION ↗

TO SANTA MARIA DEGLI ANGELI ↘

0 200 yards

0 200 meters

KEY

⊞ Steps

12

GETTING HERE

Assisi lies on the Terontola–Foligno rail line, with almost hourly connections to Perugia and direct trains to Rome and Florence several times a day. The Stazione Centrale is 4 km (2½ mi) from town, with a bus service about every half hour. Assisi is easily reached from the A1 Motorway (Rome–Florence) and the S75b highway. The walled town is closed to traffic, so cars must be left in the parking lots at Porta San Pietro, near Porta Nuova, or beneath Piazza Matteotti. (Pay your parking fee at the *cassa* [ticket booth] before you return to your car to get a ticket to insert in the machine that will allow you to exit.) It's a short but sometimes steep walk into the center of town; frequent minibuses (buy tickets from a newsstand or tobacco shop near where you park your car) make the rounds for weary pilgrims.

VISITOR INFORMATION

Assisi tourism office (✉ *Piazza del Commune 22* ☎ *075/812534* ⊕ *www. assisi.umbria2000.it*).

EXPLORING ASSISI

Assisi is pristinely medieval in architecture and appearance, owing in large part to relative neglect from the 16th century until 1926, when the celebration of the 700th anniversary of Saint Francis's death brought more than 2 million visitors. Since then, pilgrims have flocked here in droves, and today several million arrive each year to pay homage. But not even the constant flood of visitors to this town of just 3,000 residents can spoil the singular beauty of this significant religious center, the home of some of the Western tradition's most important works of art. The hill on which Assisi sits rises dramatically from the flat plain, and the town is dominated by a medieval castle at the very top.

Even though Assisi can become besieged with sightseers disgorged by tour buses, who clamor to visit the famous basilica, it's difficult not to be charmed by the tranquility of the town and its medieval architecture. Once you've seen the basilica, stroll through the town's narrow winding streets to see beautiful vistas of the nearby hills and valleys peeking through openings between the buildings.

MAIN ATTRACTIONS

❹ **Basilica di Santa Chiara.** The lovely, wide piazza in front of this church is reason enough to visit. The red-and-white-striped facade of the church frames the piazza's panoramic view over the Umbrian plains. Santa Chiara is dedicated to Saint Clare, one of the earliest and most fervent of Saint Francis's followers and the founder of the order of the Poor Ladies—or Poor Clares—which was based on the Franciscan monastic order. The church contains Clare's body, and in the **Cappella del Crocifisso** (on the right) is the cross that spoke to Saint Francis. A heavily veiled nun of the Poor Clares order is usually stationed before the cross in adoration of the image. ✉*Piazza Santa Chiara* ☎*075/812282* ☙*Nov.–mid-Mar., daily 6:30–noon and 2–6; mid-Mar.–Oct., daily 6:30–noon and 2–7.*

12

❸ **Cattedrale di San Rufino.** Saint Francis and Saint Clare were among those baptized in Assisi's Cattedrale, which was the principal church in town until the 12th century. The baptismal font has since been redecorated, but it is possible to see the crypt of Saint Rufino, the bishop who brought Christianity to Assisi and was martyred on August 11, 238 (or 236 by some accounts). Admission to the crypt includes the small **Museo Capitolare,** with its detached frescoes and artifacts. ✉*Piazza San Rufino* ☎*075/812283* ⊕*www.sistemamuseo.it* ✆*Crypt and Museo Capitolare €2.50* ☙*Cattedrale: daily 7–noon and 2–6; crypt and Museo Capitolare: mid-Mar.–mid-Oct., daily 10–1 and 3–6; mid-Oct.–mid-Mar., daily 10–1 and 2:30–5:30.*

ALSO WORTH SEEING

❷ **Santa Maria Sopra Minerva.** Dating from the time of the Emperor Augustus (27 BC–AD 14), this structure was originally dedicated to the Roman goddess of wisdom, in later times used as a monastery and prison before being converted into a church in the 16th century. The expectations raised by the perfect classical facade are not met by the interior, which was subjected to a thorough baroque transformation in the 17th century. ✉*Piazza del Comune* ☎*075/812268* ☙*Weekdays 7:15 AM–7:30 PM, weekends 8–7:30.*

OFF THE BEATEN PATH

Eremo delle Carceri. About 4 km (2½ mi) east of Assisi is a monastery set in a dense wood against Monte Subasio. The "Hermitage of Prisons" was the place where Saint Francis and his followers went to "imprison" themselves in prayer. The only site in Assisi that remains essentially unchanged since Saint Francis's times, the church and monastery are the kinds of tranquil places that Saint Francis would have appreciated. The walk out from town is very pleasant, and many trails lead from here across the wooded hillside of Monte Subasio (now a protected forest), with beautiful vistas across the Umbrian countryside. True to their Franciscan heritage, the friars here are entirely dependent on alms from visitors. ✉*Via Santuario delle Carcer* ✛*4 km (2½ mi) east of Assisi* ☎*075/812301* ⊕*www.eremocarceri.it* ✉*Donations accepted* ☙*Nov.–Mar., daily 6:30–6; Apr.–Oct., daily 6:30 AM–7:15 PM.*

WHERE TO EAT

Assisi is not a late-night town, so don't plan on any midnight snacks. What you can count on is the ubiquitous stringozzi pasta, as well as the local specialty *piccione all'assisana* (roasted pigeon with olives and liver). The locals eat *torta al testo* (a dense flat bread, often stuffed with vegetables or cheese) with their meals.

$$$–$$$$ ✕ **San Francesco.** An excellent view of the Basilica di San Francesco is the primary reason to come here. Locals consider this the best restaurant in

town, where creative Umbrian dishes are made with aromatic locally grown herbs. The seasonal menu might include gnocchi topped with a sauce of wild herbs and *oca stufata di finocchio selvaggio* (goose stuffed with wild fennel). Appetizers and desserts are especially good. ⊠ *Via di San Francesco 52* ☎*075/812329* ▭*AE, DC, MC, V* ⊘*Closed Wed. and July 15–30.*

$$–$$$ ✕**Osteria Piazzetta dell'Erba.** Hip service and sophisticated presenta-
★   tions attract locals to this trattoria. The owners carefully select wine at local vineyards, buy it in bulk, and then bottle it themselves, resulting in high quality and reasonable prices. Choose from the wide selection of appetizers, including smoked goose breast, and from four or five types of pasta, plus various salads and a good selection of torta al testo fillings. For dessert, try the homemade biscuits, which you dunk in sweet wine. Outdoor seating is available. ⊠ *Via San Gabriele dell'Addolorata 15b* ☎*075/815352* ▭*AE, V* ⊘ *Closed Mon. and a few wks in Jan. or Feb.*

$–$$$ ✕**Buca di San Francesco.** In summer, dine in a cool green garden; in winter, under the low brick arches of the restaurant's cozy cellars. The unique settings and the first-rate fare make this central restaurant Assisi's busiest. Try homemade spaghetti *alla buca,* served with a roasted mushroom sauce. ⊠ *Via Brizi 1* ☎*075/812204* ▭*AE, DC, MC, V* ⊘*Closed Mon. and July 20–30.*

$–$$$ ✕**La Fortezza.** Partially enclosed by Roman walls, this family-run restaurant has excellent service and reliably good food. A particular standout is *anatra al finocchio selvatico* (duck with wild fennel). ⊠ *Vicolo della Fortezza 2b* ☎*075/812993* ⌕*Reservations essential* ▭*AE, DC, MC, V* ⊘*Closed Thurs. and Feb.*

$–$$$ ✕**La Pallotta.** At this homey, family-run trattoria with a crackling fire-
Fodor'sChoice   place and stone walls, the women do the cooking and the men serve the
★   food. Try the stringozzi *alla pallotta* (with a pesto of olives and mushrooms). Connected to the restaurant is an inn whose eight rooms have firm beds and some views across the rooftops of town. Hotel guests get a discount if they dine here. ⊠ *Vicolo della Volta Pinta, 06081* ☎*075/812649 or 075/812307* ▭*AE, DC, MC, V* ⊘*Closed Tues. and 2 wks in Jan. or Feb.*

WHERE TO STAY

Advance reservations are essential at Assisi's hotels between Easter and October and over Christmas. Latecomers are often forced to stay in the modern town of Santa Maria degli Angeli, 8 km (5 mi) away. As a last-minute option, you can also inquire at restaurants to see if they are renting out rooms.

Until the early 1980s, pilgrim hostels outnumbered ordinary hotels in Assisi, and they present an intriguing and economical alternative to conventional lodgings. They are usually called *conventi* or *ostelli* ("convents" or "hostels") because they're run by convents, churches, or Catholic organizations. Rooms are spartan but peaceful. Check with the tourist office for a list.

Continued on page 709

ASSISI'S BASILICA DI SAN FRANCESCO

The legacy of St. Francis, founder of the Franciscan monastic order, pervades Assisi. Each year the town hosts several million pilgrims, but the steady flow of visitors does nothing to diminish the singular beauty of one of Italy's most important religious centers. The pilgrims' ultimate destination is the massive Basilica di San Francesco, which sits halfway up Assisi's hill, supported by graceful arches.

The basilica is not one church but two. The Romanesque **Lower Church** came first; construction began in 1228, just two years after St. Francis's death, and was completed within a few years. The low ceilings and candlelit interior make an appropriately solemn setting for St. Francis's tomb, found in the crypt below the main altar. The Gothic **Upper Church**, built only half a century later, sits on top of the lower one, and is strikingly different, with soaring arches and tall stained-glass windows (the first in Italy). Inside, both churches are covered floor to ceiling with some of Europe's finest frescoes: the Lower Church is dim and full of candlelit shadows, and the Upper Church is bright and airy.

VISITING THE BASILICA

THE LOWER CHURCH

The most evocative way to experience the basilica is to begin with the dark Lower Church. As you enter, give your eyes a moment to adjust. Keep in mind that the artists at work here were conscious of the shadowy environment—they knew this was how their frescoes would be seen.

In the first chapel to the left, a superb fresco cycle by Simone Martini depicts scenes from the life of St. Martin. As you approach the main altar, the vaulting above you is decorated with the *Three Virtues of St. Francis* (poverty, chastity, and obedience) and *St. Francis's Triumph*, frescoes attributed to Giotto's followers. In the transept to your left, Pietro Lorenzetti's *Madonna and Child with St. Francis and St. John* sparkles when the sun hits it. Notice Mary's thumb; legend has it Jesus is asking which saint to bless, and Mary is pointing to Francis. Across the way in the right transept, Cimabue's *Madonna Enthroned Among Angels and St. Francis* is a famous portrait of the saint. Surrounding the portrait are painted scenes from the childhood of Christ, done by the assistants of Giotto. Nearby is a painting of the crucifixion attributed to Giotto himself.

You reach the crypt via stairs midway along the nave—on the crypt's altar, a stone coffin holds the saint's body. Steps up from the transepts lead to the cloister, where there's a gift shop, and the treasury, which contains holy objects.

THE UPPER CHURCH

The St. Francis fresco cycle is the highlight of the Upper Church. (See facing page.) Also worth special note is the 16th-century choir, with its remarkably delicate inlaid wood. When a 1997 earthquake rocked the basilica, the St. Francis cycle sustained little damage, but portions of the ceiling above the entrance and altar collapsed, reducing their frescoes (attributed to Cimabue and Giotto) to rubble. The painstaking restoration is ongoing. ⚠ The dress code is strictly enforced—no bare shoulders or bare knees. Piazza di San Francesco, 075/819001, Lower Church Easter–Oct., Mon.–Sat. 6 AM–6:45 PM, Sun. 6:30 AM–7:15 PM; Nov.–Easter, daily 6:30–6. Upper Church Easter–Oct., Mon.–Sat. 8:30–6:45, Sun. 8:30–7:15; Nov.–Easter, daily 8:30–6.

FRANCIS, ITALY'S PATRON SAINT

PREGANDO ASPETTERO' CHE TORNI

St. Francis was born in Assisi in 1181, the son of a noblewoman and a well-to-do merchant. His troubled youth included a year in prison. He planned a military career, but after a long illness Francis heard the voice of God, renounced his father's wealth, and began a life of austerity. His mystical embrace of poverty, asceticism, and the beauty of man and nature struck a responsive chord in the medieval mind; he quickly attracted a vast number of followers. Francis was the first saint to receive the stigmata (wounds in his hands, feet, and side corresponding to those of Christ on the cross). He died on October 4, 1226, in the Porziuncola, the secluded chapel in the woods where he had first preached the virtue of poverty to his disciples. St. Francis was declared patron saint of Italy in 1939, and today the Franciscans make up the largest of the Catholic orders.

THE UPPER CHURCH'S ST. FRANCIS FRESCO CYCLE

The 28 frescoes in the Upper Church depicting the life of St. Francis are the most admired works in the entire basilica. They're also the subject of one of art history's biggest controversies. For centuries they thought to be by Giotto (1267-1337), the great early Renaissance innovator, but inconsistencies in style, both within this series and in comparison to later Giotto works, have thrown their origin into question. Some scholars now say Giotto was the brains behind the cycle, but that assistants helped with the execution; others claim he couldn't have been involved at all.

Two things are certain. First, the style is revolutionary—which argues for Giotto's in-

volvement. The tangible weight of the figures, the emotion they show, and the use of perspective all look familiar to modern eyes, but in the art of the time there was nothing like it. Second, these images have played a major part in shaping how the world sees St. Francis. In that respect, who painted them hardly matters.

Starting in the transept, the frescoes circle the church, showing events in the saint's life (and afterlife). Some of the best are grouped near the church's entrance—look for the nativity at Greccio, the miracle of the spring, the death of the knight at Celano, and, most famously, the sermon to the birds.

12

IN FOCUS ASSISI'S BASILICA DI SAN FRANCISCO

The St. Francis fresco cycle
1. Homage of a simple man
2. Giving cloak to a poor man
3. Dream of the palace
4. Hearing the voice of God
5. Rejection of worldly goods
6. Dream of Innocent III
7. Confirmation of the rules
8. Vision of flaming chariot
9. Vision of celestial thrones
10. Chasing devils from Arezzo
11. Before the sultan
12. Ecstasy of St. Francis
13. Nativity at Greccio
14. Miracle of the spring
15. Sermon to the birds
16. Death of knight at Celano
17. Preaching to Honorius III
18. Apparition at Arles
19. Receiving the stigmata
20. Death of St. Francis
21. Apparition before Bishop Guido and Fra Agostino
22. Verification of the stigmata
23. Mourning of St. Clare
24. Canonization
25. Apparition before Gregory IX
26. Healing of a devotee
27. Confession of a woman
28. Repentant heretic freed

FODOR'S FIRST PERSON

Sister Marcellina,
Order of St. Bridget

Sister Marcellina of the Order of St. Bridget talks about her life in Assisi, where she and 11 other sisters live in a convent and guesthouse on the outskirts of the town:

"Before coming to Assisi, I lived in various countries. I've lived in India, and in England, and been to Holland, to Sweden, and to Finland, as well as lived in Rome. But Assisi is the place that I would never want to change for any other. I don't know, I think there is something very special about this place. I've been here 13 years now, and each year I pray that I won't be sent somewhere else. I'm very happy here.

"I like the atmosphere of Assisi, it's very friendly, and of course with St. Francis and St. Claire, but especially St. Francis, there is a simplicity to life that I like very much. Even though I'm in the Order of St. Bridget, living here I feel very much a part of Franciscan spirituality. There is also a very strong ecumenical feeling to Assisi and this is very nice. There are over 60 different religious communities, with people from all over the world. And even though they come from different religious backgrounds they still feel a part of Assisi. Living here, you don't see the people of Assisi, you see people who have come from all over the world.

"There is something you feel when you come to Assisi, something you feel in your heart that makes you want to come back. And people do return! They feel the peacefulness and tranquility. Not that there aren't other aspects, like the commercialism—but these things happen. People return for the simplicity of this place. People feel attracted to Assisi. There's always something that people feel when they come here—even the hard-hearted ones!"

Asked if she thinks Assisi is changing, Sister Marcellina answers, with laughter in her voice, "When they wanted to make all the changes in the year 2000, the Jubilee Year, our Lord said, 'I must stop everything.' They had lots of projects to build new accommodations to house the people coming for the Jubilee Year, but the Lord said, 'No!'"

12

$$$ 🏨 **Hotel Subasio.** The converted monastery close to the Basilica di San Francesco is well past its prime, when guests included celebrities like Marlene Dietrich and Charlie Chaplin. If you can get past the kitschy hangings on the walls, you'll notice such vestiges of glamour as Venetian chandeliers. The hotel does have splendid views, comfortable sitting rooms, and flower-decked terraces, and it's a stone's throw from all those Giotto frescoes. Some rooms are grand in size and overlook the valley, whereas others are small and rough around the edges. The restaurant has a nice view, but the food could be better. **Pros:** Perfect location, views of the Assisi plain. **Cons:** Lobby a bit drab, some small rooms, service can be spotty. ⊠ *Via Frate Elia 2, 06082* ☎*075/812206* 🖷*075/816691* 🛏*54 rooms, 8 suites* ♿*In-room: no a/c. In-hotel: restaurant, bar, parking (fee)* ▤*AE, DC, MC, V* ⓘⓞⓘ*BP.*

$-$$$ 🏨 **San Francesco.** You can't beat the location—the roof terrace and some of the rooms look out onto the Basilica di San Francesco, which is opposite the hotel. Rooms and facilities range from simple to dreary, but you may be reminded that looks aren't everything by the nice touches like slippers, a good-night piece of chocolate, and soundproofing. Fruit, homemade tarts, and fresh ricotta make for a first-rate breakfast. **Pros:** Excellent location, great views. **Cons:** Simple rooms, sometimes noisy in peak season. ⊠ *Via San Francesco 48, 06082* ☎*075/812281* 🖷*075/816237* ⊕*www.hotelsanfrancescoassisi.it* 🛏*44 rooms* ♿*In-room: refrigerator, ethernet. In-hotel: restaurant, bar, public Internet, some pets allowed* ▤*AE, DC, MC, V* ⓘⓞⓘ*BP.*

$$ 🏨 **Castello di Petrata.** Built as a fortress in the 14th century, the Castello di Petrata rightfully dominates the area, with Monte Subasio, Assisi, and the distant hills and valleys of Perugia all in view. Every room is different from the last: wood beams and sections of exposed medieval stonework add character, and comfortable couches turn each room into a delightful retreat. **Pros:** Great views of Assisi hills, gardens, and walks. **Cons:** Slightly isolated, far from Assisi town center. ⊠ *Via Petrata 25, Località Petrata, 06081* ☎*075/815451* 🖷*075/8043026* ⊕*www.castellopetrata.com* 🛏*22 rooms, 1 suite* ♿*In-room: no a/c, ethernet. In-hotel: restaurant, bar, pool, some pets allowed* ▤*AE, DC, MC, V* ☽*Closed Jan.–Mar.* ⓘⓞⓘ*BP.*

Fodor'sChoice

★

$ 🏨 **Hotel Umbra.** A 16th-century town house is the setting for this charming hotel near Piazza del Comune. Ask for an upper room with a view over the Assisi rooftops to the valley below. The restaurant, closed for lunch on Tuesday and Wednesday, has a charming vine-covered terrace leading to a secluded garden. **Pros:** Friendly welcome, pleasant small garden. **Cons:** Difficult parking, some small rooms. ⊠ *Via degli Archi 6, 06081* ☎*075/812240* 🖷*075/813653* ⊕*www.hotelumbra.it* 🛏*6 suites, 19 rooms* ♿*In-hotel: restaurant, bar* ▤*AE, DC, MC, V* ☽*Closed mid-Jan.–mid-Mar.* ⓘⓞⓘ*BP.*

NORTHERN UMBRIA

To the north of Perugia, placid, walled Gubbio watches over green countryside, true to its nickname, City of Silence—except for its fast and furious festivals in May, as lively today as when they began more

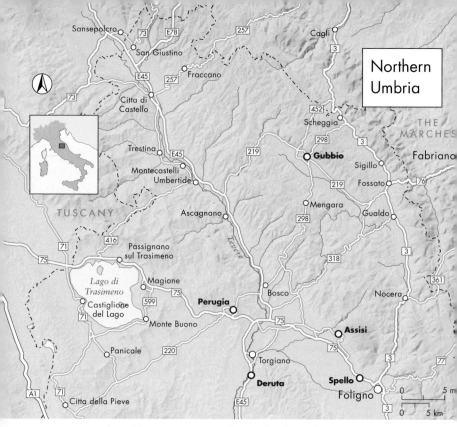

than 800 years ago. To the south, along the Tiber River valley, are the towns of Deruta and Torgiano, best known for their hand-painted ceramics and wine—as locals say, go to Deruta to buy a pitcher and to Torgiano to fill it.

GUBBIO

35 km (22 mi) southeast of Città di Castello, 39 km (24 mi) northeast of Perugia, 92 km (57 mi) east of Arezzo.

GETTING HERE
The closest train station is Fossato di Vico, about 12 mi from Gubbio. Ten daily buses connect the train station with the city, a 30-minute trip. If you are driving from Perugia take the SS298 which rises steeply up toward the Gubbio hills. The trip will take you one hour. There are also 10 buses a day that leave Perugia's Piazza Partigiani, the main Perugia bus terminal.

VISITOR INFORMATION
Gubbio tourism office (✉ *Piazza Oderisi 6* ☎ *075/9220693*).

EXPLORING

There is something otherworldly about this jewel of a medieval town tucked away in a mountainous corner of Umbria. Even at the height of summer, the cool serenity and quiet of Gubbio's streets remain intact. The town is perched on the slopes of Monte Ingino, meaning the streets are dramatically steep. Gubbio's relatively isolated position has kept it free of hordes of high-season visitors, and most of the year the city lives up to its Italian nickname, *La Città del Silenzio* (City of Silence). Parking in the central Piazza dei Quaranta Martiri—named for 40 hostages murdered by the Nazis in 1944—is easy and secure, and it is wise to leave your car in the piazza and explore the narrow streets on foot.

At Christmas, kitsch is king. From December 7 to January 10, colored lights are strung down the mountainside in a shape resembling an evergreen. Why? The town is proud to be the home of the world's largest Christmas tree.

The **Duomo,** on a narrow street on the highest tier of the town, dates from the 13th century, with some baroque additions—in particular, a lavishly decorated bishop's chapel. ✉ *Via Ducale* ⊙ *Daily 8–12:45 and 3–7:30.*

★ The striking Piazza Grande is dominated by the medieval **Palazzo dei Consoli,** attributed to a local architect known as Gattapone, who is still much admired by today's residents. Studies have suggested that the palazzo was in fact the work of another architect, Angelo da Orvieto. In the Middle Ages the Parliament of Gubbio assembled in this palace, which has become a symbol of the town.

The Palazzo dei Consoli houses a museum, famous chiefly for the Tavole Eugubine, seven bronze tablets written in the ancient Umbrian language, employing Etruscan and Latin characters and providing the best key to understanding this obscure tongue. Also in the museum is a fascinating miscellany of rare coins and earthenware pots. The museum has exhilarating views over Gubbio's roofscape and beyond from the lofty loggia. For a few days at the beginning of May, the palace also displays the famous *ceri,* the ceremonial wooden pillars at the center of Gubbio's annual festivities. ✉ *Piazza Grande* ☎ *075/9274298* ⊕ *www.comune.gubbio.pg.it* 🎟 *€5* ⊙ *Apr.–Oct., daily 10–1 and 3–6; Nov.–Mar., daily 10–1 and 2–5.*

The **Palazzo Ducale** is a scaled-down copy of the Palazzo Ducale in Urbino. (Gubbio was once the possession of that city's ruling family, the Montefeltro.) Gubbio's palazzo contains a small museum and a courtyard. Some of the public rooms offer magnificent views. ✉ *Via Ducale* ☎ *075/9275872* 🎟 *€2* ⊙ *Tues.–Sun. 8:30–7.*

Just outside the city walls at the eastern end of town is a **funicular** that provides a bracing ride to the top of Monte Ingino. (It's definitely not for those who suffer from vertigo.) ⊠ *Follow Corso Garibaldi or Via XX Settembre to the end* 🖾 *€4, €5 round-trip* ⏱ *Sept.–June, daily 10– 1:15 and 2:30–6; July and Aug., daily 8:30–7:30*

At the top of Monte Ingino is the **Basilica di Sant'Ubaldo**, repository of Gubbio's famous *ceri*—three 16-foot-tall pillars crowned with statues of Saints Ubaldo, George, and Anthony. The pillars are transported to the Palazzo dei Consoli on the first Sunday of May, in preparation for the Festa dei Ceri. ⊠ *Monte Ingino* 🕾 *075/9273872* 🖾 *Free* ⏱ *Daily 8:30–noon and 4–7.*

WHERE TO STAY & EAT

$$$–$$$$
Fodor'sChoice
★

✕ **Taverna del Lupo.** One of the city's most famous taverns, this popular place gets hectic on weekends and during the high season. Lasagne made in the Gubbian fashion, with ham and truffles, is an unusual indulgence, and the *suprema di faraono* (guinea fowl in a delicately spiced sauce) is a specialty. The restaurant has two fine wine cellars and an extensive wine list. Save room for the excellent desserts. ⊠ *Via Ansidei 21, 06024* 🕾 *075/9274368* 🖃 *AE, DC, MC, V* ⏱ *Closed Mon.*

$$–$$$$
✕ **Fornace di Mastro Giorgio.** The building dates to the 1300s, and its original stone-and-wood structure has been kept intact. (In the 1400s the space housed an important ceramics factory.) The menu, with seasonal changes, includes traditional but creative fare: *tagliatelle al tartuffo* (tagliatelle in a truffle sauce), *gnochetti al finocchio selvatico* (potato dumplings with wild fennel), *raviolini di faro con asparagi* (small ravioli with spelt and asparagus), and *filetto alle prugne* (filet mignon with prune sauce). ⊠ *Via Mastro Giorgio 2* 🕾 *075/9221836* 🖃 *AE, DC, MC, V* ⏱ *Closed Tues. No lunch Wed.*

$$$
✕ **Bosone Garden.** As the stone arches inside indicate, this space once served as the stables of the palace that now houses the Hotel Bosone. The menu includes a two-mushroom salad with truffles; risotto with porcini mushrooms, sausage, and truffles; and leg of pork. The garden, open in summer, seats 200. ⊠ *Via Mastro Giorgio 1* 🕾 *075/9220246* 🖃 *AE, MC, V* ⏱ *Closed Wed. Oct.–May and 2 wks in Jan.*

$–$$
✕ **Grotta dell'Angelo.** The rustic trattoria sits in the lower part of the old town near the main square. The menu features simple local specialties, including *capocollo* (a type of salami), *stringozzi* (very thick spaghetti), and lasagne *tartufata* (with truffles). The few outdoor tables are in high demand in the summer. The restaurant also offers a few small, basically furnished guest rooms, which should be booked in advance. ⊠ *Via Gioia 47* 🕾 *075/9273438* ⌨ *Reservations essential* 🖃 *AE, DC, MC, V* ⏱ *Closed Tues. and Jan. 10–31.*

$–$$
🔛 **Hotel Bosone Palace.** A former palace is now home to this elegant hotel. Elaborate frescoes grace the ceilings of the two enormous suites, which are furnished with painted antiques, and the hotel's small and delightful breakfast room. Standard rooms are comfortably, though more soberly, decorated with heavy wooden furniture. Ask for a room facing away from the sometimes-noisy street. **Pros:** Friendly welcome, excellent location. **Cons:** Some noise in tourist sea-

son, simple lobby. ⊠ *Via XX Settembre 22, 06024* ☎*075/9220688* 🖷*075/9220552* ⊕*www.mencarelligroup.com* ⟳*28 rooms, 2 suites* ♿*In-room: no a/c. In-hotel: restaurant, bar* ⊟*AE, DC, MC, V* ⊘*Closed 3 wks in Jan.* ⦿|*BP.*

DERUTA

12

7 km (4½ mi) south of Torgiano, 19 km (11 mi) southeast of Perugia.

GETTING HERE

From Perugia follow the directions for Rome and the E45 highway; Deruta has its own exits. There are also trains from the smaller St. Anna train station in Perugia. Take the train in the direction of Terni, and get off at Deruta.

> **WORD OF MOUTH**
>
> "Best purchase *and* encounter with local people was going to a ceramic studio in Deruta. There are lots of places to buy ceramics, and a couple of places where there are true artists." –marcy

VISITOR INFORMATION

Deruta tourism office (⊠*Piazza dei Consoli 4* ☎*075/9711559*).

EXPLORING

This 14th-century medieval hill town is most famous for its ceramics. A drive through the countryside to visit the ceramics workshops is a good way to spend a morning, but be sure to stop in the town itself.

The notable sights in Deruta include the **Museo Regionale della Ceramica** *(Regional Ceramics Museum)*, part of which extends into the adjacent 14th-century former convent of San Francesco. Half the museum tells the history of ceramics, with panels in Italian and English explaining artistic techniques and production processes. The museum also holds the country's largest collection of modern Italian ceramics—nearly 8,000 pieces are on display. The most notable are the Renaissance vessels using the lustro technique, which originated in Arab and Middle Eastern cultures some 500 years before coming into use in Italy in the late 1400s. Lustro, as the name sounds, gives the ceramics a rich finish, which is accomplished with the use of crushed precious materials, such as gold, and silver. ⊠*Largo San Francesco* ☎*075/9711000* ⊕*www. museoceramicaderuta.it* 💶*€5, includes admission to Pinoteca Comunale* ⊘*Apr.–June, daily 10:30–1 and 3–6; July–Sept., daily 10–1 and 3:30–7; Oct.–Mar., Wed.–Mon. 10:30–1 and 2:30–5.*

SHOPPING

Deruta is home to more than 70 ceramics shops. They offer a range of ceramics, including extra pieces from commissions for well-known British and North American tableware manufacturers. If you ask, most owners will take you to see where they actually throw, bake, and paint their wares. A drive along Via Tiberina Nord takes you past one shop after another.

SPELLO

12 km (7 mi) southeast of Assisi, 33 km (21 mi) north of Spoleto.

GETTING HERE

Spello is an easy half-hour drive from Perugia. From the E45 highway, take the exit toward Assisi and Foligno. Merge onto the SS75 and take the Spello exit. There are also regular trains on the Perugia–Assisi. line.

VISITOR INFORMATION

Spello tourism office (⊠ *Piazza Matteotti 3* ☎ *0742/301009* ⊕ *www.foligno.umbria2000.it*).

EXPLORING

Spello is a gastronomic paradise, especially compared to Assisi. Only a few minutes from Assisi by car or train, this hilltop town at the edge of Mt. Subasio makes an excellent strategic and culinary base for exploring nearby towns. Its hotels are well appointed and its restaurants serve some of the best cuisine and wines in the region—sophisticated in variety, and of excellent quality. Spello's art scene includes first-rate frescoes by Pinturicchio and Perugino and contemporary artists who can be observed at work in studios around town. If antiquity is your passion, the town also has some intriguing Roman ruins. And the warm, rosy-beige tones of the local *pietra rossa* stone on the buildings brighten even cloudy days.

Spello is 1 km (½ mi) from the train station, and buses run every 30 minutes for Porta Consolare, the Roman gate at the south end of town—the best place to enter. From Porta Consolare continue up the steep main street that begins as Via Consolare and changes names several times as it crosses the little town, following the original Roman road. As it curves around, notice the winding medieval alleyways to the right and the more uniform Roman-era blocks to the left.

The basilica of **Santa Maria Maggiore** has vivid frescoes by Pinturicchio in the Cappella Baglioni (1501). Striking in their rich colors, finely dressed figures, and complex symbolism, the *Nativity, Dispute at the Temple* (on the far left side is a portrait of Troilo Baglioni, the prior who commissioned the work), and *Annunciation* (look for Pinturicchio's self-portrait in the Virgin's room) are among Pinturicchio's finest works. They were painted after the artist had already won great acclaim for his work on the Palazzi Vaticani in Rome for Borgia Pope Alexander VI. Two pillars on either side of the apse are decorated with frescoes by Perugino (circa 1450–1523), the other great Umbrian artist of the 16th century. ⊠ *Piazza Matteotti 18* ☎ *0742/301792* ☷ *Free* ⊙ *May–Sept., daily 8:30–12:30 and 3–7; Oct.–Apr., daily 8:30–12:30 and 3–6.*

WHERE TO STAY & EAT

$$–$$$ ✕ **Il Molino.** Almost a destination in itself, this former mill is one of the
Fodor'sChoice region's best restaurants. The sophisticated food showcases the bounty
★ of Umbria. The types of olive oil used in the dishes and the names of

12

the local farmers who grew the produce are noted on the menu. Appetizers are varied, and often highlight foods found only here, like the *risina,* a tiny white bean. Pasta sauces can vary from exquisitely rich to extremely delicate. The meat is first-rate, either elaborately prepared or grilled and topped with a signature sauce. The service is attentive, and the wine list has plenty of local and Italian options, including the pungent Sagrantino di Montefalco and fresh Orvieto whites. If you want something with a bit more depth, go for one of the Montepulciano wines, or even a Brunello di Montalcino, one of Italy's greatest reds. Outside seating lets you soak up the passing street scene; inside are a series of impressive 14th-century arches. ✉ *Piazza Matteotti 6/7* ☎ *0742/651305* 📠 *0742/302235* 💳 *AE, DC, MC, V* ⏲ *Closed Tues.*

$$ ★ **La Bastiglia.** This cozy hotel is in a former grain mill, but polished wood planks and handwoven rugs have replaced the rustic flooring. The comfortable sitting rooms and bedrooms are filled with a mix of antique and modern pieces. Rooms on the top floor—some with terraces—have views of the valley below, silvery green with olive trees. A separate building with additional rooms is surrounded by a garden. Pack light, as there are plenty of steps and you carry your bags. The hotel's wood-beamed restaurant ($$–$$$) serves refined international cuisine and unusual adaptations of traditional recipes. The menu changes with the seasons, so look for roasted pigeon or a sorbetto of wild berries in the summer; toward winter, truffles will appear. The regionally known sommelier dispenses advice about wines. **Pros:** Lovely terrace restaurant, cozy rooms, fine views. **Cons:** Some shared balconies, breakfast is underwhelming. ✉ *Via Salnitraria 15, 06038* ☎ *0742/651277* 🌐 *www.labastiglia.com* *31 rooms, 2 suites* *In-hotel: restaurant, bar, pool* 💳 *AE, DC, MC, V* ⏲ *Closed early Jan.–early Feb.* *BP.*

$$–$$$ ★ **Hotel Palazzo Bocci.** Quiet and elegant, this hotel is centrally located on Spello's main street. The original building dates to the 14th century, but extensive restorations in the 18th and 19th centuries added bucolic ceiling and wall frescoes. You could settle in for a week and take a cooking course, or have the staff book you bicycle or horseback excursions through the countryside. The hotel has lovely sitting areas, a reading room, and a garden terrace off the bar. Several rooms have valley views. Consider splurging on the suite with the fireplace or reserving the room with the small terrace. **Pros:** Central location, splendid views of the valley. **Cons:** Noisy in summer months, not all rooms have views. ✉ *Via Cavour 17, 06038* ☎ *0742/301021* 🌐 *www.palazzobocci.com* *23 rooms* *In-room: safe, ethernet. In-hotel: restaurant, bar* 💳 *AE, DC, MC, V.*

SPOLETO

GETTING HERE

Spoleto is an hour's drive from Perugia. From the E45 highway, take the exit toward Assisi and Foligno, then merge onto the SS75 until you reach the Foligno Est exit. Merge onto the SS3, which leads to Spoleto. There are regular trains on the Perugia-Foligno line. From the train

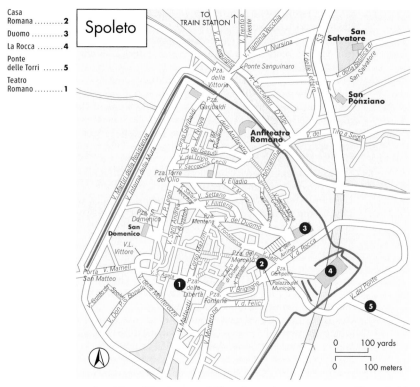

station it's a 15-minute uphill walk to the center, so you'll probably want to take a taxi.

VISITOR INFORMATION

Spoleto tourism office (✉ *Piazza della Libertà 7* ☎*0743/238921* ⊕*www. spoleto.umbria2000.it*).

EXPLORING SPOLETO

The walled city is set on a slanting hillside, with the most interesting sections clustered toward the upper portion. Parking options inside the walls include Piazza Campello (just below the Rocca) on the southeast end, Via del Trivio to the north, and Piazza San Domenico on the west end. You can also park at Piazza della Vittoria farther north, just outside the walls. There are also several well-marked lots near the train station. If you arrive by train, you can walk 1 km (½ mi) from the station to the entrance to the lower town. Regular bus connections are every 15 to 30 minutes. You can also use the "trenino," as locals call the shuttle service added in 2004, from the train station to Piazza della Libertà, near the upper part of the old town, where you'll find the tourist office.

Like most other towns with narrow, winding streets, Spoleto is best explored on foot. Bear in mind that much of the city is on a steep slope, so there are lots of stairs and steep inclines. The well-worn stones can be slippery even when dry; wear rubber-sole shoes for good traction. Several pedestrian walkways cut across Corso Mazzini, which zigzags up the hill. A €2.60 combination ticket purchased at the tourist office allows you entry to the Pinacoteca Comunale, Casa Romana, and Galleria d'Arte Moderna. It's an excellent deal, since a combination ticket purchased directly from any one of these sights is €6.

MAIN ATTRACTIONS

③ ★ Duomo. The cathedral's 12th-century Romanesque facade received a Renaissance face-lift with the addition of a loggia in a rosy pink stone. A stunning contrast in styles, the Duomo is one of the finest cathedrals in the region. The eight rose windows are especially dazzling in the late afternoon sun. Look under the largest rose window and you see two figures that appear to be holding up the structure; in the corners of the square surrounding the window, the four Evangelists are sculpted. Inside, the original tile floor dates from an earlier church that was destroyed by Frederick I (circa 1123–90).

Above the church's entrance is Bernini's bust of Pope Urban VIII (1568–1644), who had the rest of the church redecorated in 17th-century baroque; fortunately he didn't touch the 15th-century frescoes painted in the apse by Fra Filippo Lippi (circa 1406–69) between 1466–69. These immaculately restored masterpieces—the *Annunciation, Nativity,* and *Death of Mary*—tell the story of the life of the Virgin. The *Coronation of the Virgin,* adorning the half dome, is the literal and figurative high point. Portraits of Lippi and his assistants are on the right side of the central panel. The Florentine artist priest WHOSE COLORS EXPRESSED GOD'S VOICE (the words inscribed on his tomb) died shortly after completing the work. His tomb, which you can see in the right transept (note the artist's brushes and tools), was designed by his son, Filippino Lippi (circa 1457–1504).

Another fresco cycle, including work by Pinturicchio, is in the Cappella Eroli, off the right aisle. Note the grotesques in the ornamentation, then very much in vogue with the rediscovery of ancient Roman paintings. The bounty of Umbria is displayed in vivid colors in the abundance of leaves, fruits, and vegetables that adorn the center seams of the cross vault. In the left nave, not far from the entrance, is the well-restored 12th-century crucifix by Alberto Sozio, the earliest known example of this kind of work, with a painting on parchment attached to a wood cross. To the right of the presbytery is the Cappella della Santissima Icona (Chapel of the Most Holy Icon), which contains a small Byzantine painting of a Madonna given to the town by Frederick Barbarossa as a peace offering in 1185, following his destruction of the cathedral and town three decades earlier. ✉*Piazza Duomo* ☎*0743/44307* ⊙*Mar.–Oct., daily 8:30–12:30 and 3:30–6; Nov.–Feb., daily 8:30–12:20 and 3:30–6.*

⑤ **Ponte delle Torri** *(Bridge of the Tow-*
★ *ers).* Standing massive and graceful
through the deep gorge that separates Spoleto from Monteluco,
this 14th-century bridge is one of
Umbria's most photographed monuments, and justifiably so. Built
over the foundations of a Roman-
era aqueduct, it soars 262 feet
above the forested gorge—higher
than the dome of St. Peter's in

Rome. Sweeping views over the valley and a pleasant sense of vertigo
make a walk across the bridge a must, particularly on a starry night.
✉ *Via del Ponte.*

ALSO WORTH SEEING

② **Casa Romana.** Spoleto became a Roman colony in the 3rd century BC,
but the best excavated remains date from the 1st century AD. Excavated
in the late 9th century, the Casa Romana was not a typical Roman residence. According to an inscription, it belonged to Vespasia Polla, the
mother of Emperor Vespasian (one of the builders of the Coliseum and
perhaps better known by the Romans for taxing them to install public
toilets, later called "Vespasians"). The rooms, arranged around a large
central atrium built over an *impluvium* (rain cistern), are decorated
with black-and-white geometric mosaics. ✉ *Palazzo del Municipio, Via
Visiale 9* ☎ *0743/224656* 🎫 *€2.50, €6 combination ticket (includes
Pinacoteca Comunale and Galleria d'Arte Moderna)* ◔ *Oct. 15–Mar.
15, daily 10–6; Mar. 16–Oct. 14, daily 10–8.*

④ **La Rocca.** Built in the mid-14th century for Cardinal Egidio Albornoz,
this massive fortress served as a seat for the local pontifical governors,
a tangible sign of the restoration of the Church's power in the area
when the pope was ruling from Avignon. Several popes spent time
here, and one of them, Alexander VI, in 1499 sent his capable teenage
daughter Lucrezia Borgia (1480–1519) to serve as governor for three
months. The Gubbio-born architect Gattapone (14th century) used the
ruins of a Roman acropolis as a foundation and took materials from
many Roman-era sites, including the Teatro Romano. La Rocca's plan
is long and rectangular, with six towers and two grand courtyards, an
upper loggia, and inside some grand reception rooms. In the largest
tower, Torre Maesta, you can visit an apartment with some interesting frescoes. A small shuttle bus gives you that last boost up the hill
from the ticket booth to the entrance of the fortress. If you phone in
advance, you may be able to secure an English-speaking guide. ✉ *Via
del Ponte* ☎ *0743/223055* 🎫 *€6.50* ◔ *Mid-Mar.–early June and mid-
Sept.–Oct., weekdays 10–noon and 3–6:45, weekends 10–7; early
June–mid-Sept., daily 10–7; Nov.–mid-Mar., weekdays 10–noon and
3–5, weekends 10–5.*

① **Teatro Romano.** The Romans who had colonized the city in 241 BC, constructed this small theater in the first century AD; for centuries afterward
it was used as a quarry for building materials. The most intact portion

is the hallway that passes under the *cavea* (stands). The rest was heavily restored in the early 1950s and serves as a venue for Spoleto's Festival dei Due Mondi. The theater was the site of a gruesome episode in Spoleto's history: during the medieval struggle between Guelph (papal) and Ghibelline (imperial) forces, Spoleto took the side of the Holy Roman Emperor. Afterward, 400 Guelph supporters were massacred in the theater, their bodies burned in an enormous pyre. In the end, the Guelphs were triumphant, and Spoleto was incorporated into the states of the Church in 1354. Through a door in the west portico of the adjoining building is the **Museo Archeologico,** with assorted artifacts found in excavations primarily around Spoleto and Norcia. The collection contains Bronze Age and Iron Age artifacts from Umbrian and pre-Roman eras. Another section contains black-glaze vases from the Hellenistic period excavated from the necropolis of Saint Scolastica in Norcia. The highlight is the stone tablet inscribed on both sides with the Lex Spoletina (Spoleto Law). Dating from 315 BC, this legal document prohibited the desecration of the woods on the slopes of nearby Monteluco. ⊠ *Via Sant'Agata 18* ☎ *0743/223277* ⊒ *€4* ⊙ *Daily 8:30–7:30.*

WHERE TO EAT

$$–$$$ ✕ **Apollinare.** Low wooden ceilings and flickering candlelight make this monastery from the 10th and 11th centuries Spoleto's most romantic spot. The kitchen serves sophisticated, innovative variations on local dishes. Sauces of cherry tomatoes, mint, and a touch of red pepper, or of porcini mushrooms, top the long, slender strangozzi. The *caramella* (light puff pastry cylinders filled with local cheese and served with a creamy Parmesan sauce) is popular. In warm weather you can dine under a canopy on the piazza across from the archaeological museum. ⊠ *Via Sant'Agata 14* ☎ *0743/223256* ▱ *AE, D, MC, V* ⊙ *Closed Tues.*

$$–$$$ ✕ **Il Pentagramma.** This stable-turned-restaurant has terra-cotta floors, stone walls, and a wood-burning oven. Its fresh local dishes change seasonally. The farro soup has a new twist here: it is pureed and served inside a bread "bowl." Pastas might include *tortelli ai carciofi e noci* (artichoke-filled pasta with a hazelnut sauce) or, in summer, homemade fettucini served with sauce made from fresh vegetables and saffron. For your main course, you might try lamb in a truffle sauce. The stuffed zucchini flowers are lighter than usual, because they are baked (not fried) and filled with ricotta. The restaurant is off the Piazza della Libertà. ⊠ *Via Martani 4* ☎ *0743/223141* ▱ *DC, MC, V* ⊙ *Closed Mon. No dinner Sun., and for about 2 wks after Christmas.*

$$–$$$ ✕ **Il Tartufo.** As the name indicates, dishes prepared with truffles are the specialty here—don't miss the risotto al tartufo. But there are also dishes not perfumed with this expensive delicacy. Incorporating the ruins of a Roman villa, the restaurant's decor is rustic on the ground floor and more modern upstairs. In summer, tables appear outdoors and the traditional fare is spiced up to appeal to the cosmopolitan crowd attending (or performing in) the Festival dei Due Mondi. ⊠ *Pi-*

A Taste of Truffles

Umbria is rich with truffles—more are found here than anywhere else in Italy—and those not consumed fresh are processed into pastes or flavored oils. The primary truffle areas are around the tiny town of Norcia, which holds a truffle festival every February, and near Spoleto, where signs warn against unlicensed truffle hunting at the base of the Ponte delle Torri.

Although grown locally, the rare delicacy can cost a small fortune, up to $200 for a quarter pound—fortunately, a little goes a long way. At such a price there's great competition among

the nearly 10,000 registered truffle hunters in the province, who use specially trained dogs to sniff them out among the roots of several types of trees, including oak and ilex. Despite one or two incidences of poisoning truffle-hunting dogs and importing inferior tubers from China, you can be reasonably assured that the truffle shaved onto your pasta has been unearthed locally. Don't pass up the opportunity to try this delectable treat. The intense aroma of a dish perfumed with truffles is unmistakable and the flavor memorable.

azza Garibaldi 24 ☎*0743/40236* ⚓*Reservations essential* ▤*AE, DC, MC, V* ◷*Closed Mon. and last 2 wks in July. No dinner Sun.*

$$–$$$ ✕**Ristorante Panciolle.** In the heart of Spoleto's medieval quarter, this
★ restaurant has one of the most appealing settings you could wish for: a small garden filled with lemon trees. Dishes change throughout the year, and may include pastas served with asparagus or mushrooms, as well as grilled meats. More expensive dishes prepared with fresh truffles are also available in season. ⊠*Via Duomo 3/5* ☎*0743/221241* ⚓*Reservations essential* ▤*DC, MC, V* ◷*Closed Wed.*

$–$$ ✕**Osteria del Trivio.** At this friendly trattoria, everything is made on the premises. The menu changes daily, depending on what's in season. Dishes might include stuffed artichokes, pasta with local mushrooms, or chicken with artichokes. For dessert, try the homemade biscotti, made for dunking in sweet wine. There is a printed menu, but the owner can explain the dishes in a number of languages. A complete meal from appetizer to dessert with house wine is likely to cost no more than €25. ⊠*Via del Trivio 16* ☎*0743/44349* ▤*AE, DC, MC, V* ◷*Closed Tues.*

WHERE TO STAY

$$–$$$ ▦**Cavaliere Palace Hotel.** An arched passageway off one of the city's
★ busy shopping streets leads to an elegant world through a quiet courtyard. Built in the 17th century for an influential cardinal, the rooms, particularly those on the second floor, retain their sumptuous frescoed ceilings; care has been taken to retain a sense of old-world comfort throughout. In warm weather enjoy breakfast on the terrace or in the peaceful garden at the back of the hotel. **Pros:** Quiet elegance, central position. **Cons:** Finding parking can be a problem, crowded in summer. ⊠*Corso Garibaldi 49, 06049* ☎*0743/220350* ⊕*www.cavalierehotels.*

com 🛏29 *rooms, 2 suites* ♿*In-room: safe, refrigerator. In-hotel: restaurant, bar* ▭*AE, DC, MC, V* ⦿*BP.*

$$ 🏨**Hotel dei Duchi.** This well-run hotel is a favorite among performers in the festival. It's in the center of town, near the Roman amphitheater. The spacious rooms, some looking out onto the gardens, have simple modern furniture. **Pros:** Central location, friendly staff. **Cons:** Unattractive building, parking can be difficult in summer months. ✉*Viale Matteotti 4, 06049* ☎*0743/44541* ⊕*www.hoteldeiduchi.com* 🛏*47 rooms, 2 suites* ♿ *In-hotel: restaurant, bar, parking (no fee), some pets allowed* ▭*AE, DC, MC, V* ⦿*BP.*

$$
Fodor'sChoice
★

🏨**Hotel San Luca.** The elegant San Luca is one of Spoleto's finest hotels, thanks to its commendable attention to detail, such as the hand-painted friezes that decorate the walls of the spacious guest rooms and the generous selection of up-to-date magazines for your reading pleasure. The service is very gracious, and the prices are surprisingly modest. Enjoy an ample breakfast buffet, including homemade cakes, served in a cheerful room facing the central courtyard. You can sip afternoon tea in oversize armchairs by the fireplace, or take a walk in the hotel's sweet-smelling rose garden. The staff will give you route maps or help you book a guided bicycle tour. **Pros:** Very helpful staff, peaceful location. **Cons:** Outside the town center, a long walk to the main sites. ✉*Via Interna delle Mura 19, 06049* ☎*0743/223399* ⊕*www.hotelsanluca.com* 🛏*33 rooms, 2 suites* ♿*In-room: safe, refrigerator, ethernet. In-hotel: restaurant, laundry service, public Internet, parking (fee)* ▭*AE, DC, MC, V* ⦿*BP.*

$–$$ 🏨**Hotel Clitunno.** A renovated 18th-century building in the center of town houses this pleasant hotel. Cozy guest rooms and intimate public rooms, some with timbered ceilings, have the sense of a traditional Umbrian home—albeit one with a good restaurant. The staff is glad to light the fireplace in Room 212 in advance of winter arrivals. Upper-floor rooms look over Spoleto's rooftops. The "older style" rooms, which have wood ceilings, iron beds, and nicer textiles, are more attractive. **Pros:** Friendly staff, good restaurant. **Cons:** Difficult to find a parking space, some small rooms. ✉*Piazza Sordini 6, 06049* ☎*0743/223340* ⊕*www.hotelclitunno.com* 🛏*45 rooms* ♿*In-hotel: restaurant, bar* ▭*AE, DC, MC, V* ⦿*BP.*

THE ARTS

Fodor'sChoice
★

In 1958, composer Gian Carlo Menotti chose Spoleto for the first **Festival dei Due Mondi** (*Festival of Two Worlds* ✉*Piazza Duomo 8* ☎*0743/220320 or 800/565600* ⊕*www.spoletofestival.it*), a gathering of artists, performers, and musicians intended to bring together the "new" and "old" worlds of America and Europe. (A corresponding festival in South Carolina is no longer connected to this festival.) The annual event, held in late June to early July, is one of the most important cultural happenings in Europe, attracting big names in all branches of the arts, particularly music, opera, and theater.

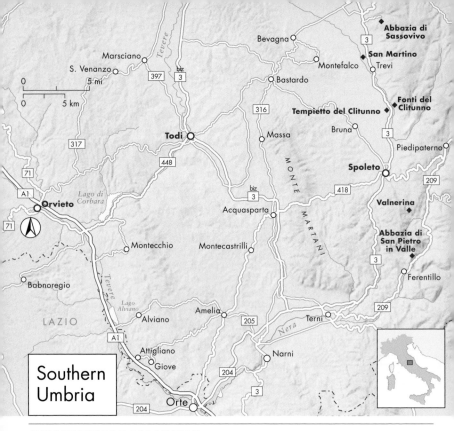

SOUTHERN UMBRIA

Orvieto, built on a tufa mount, produces one of Italy's favorite white wines and has one of the country's greatest cathedrals and most compelling fresco cycles. Nearby Narni and Todi are pleasant medieval hill towns. The former stands over a steep gorge, its Roman pedigree evident in dark alleyways and winding streets; the latter is a fairy-tale village with incomparable views and one of Italy's most perfect piazzas.

TODI

34 km (22 mi) south of Perugia, 34 km (22 mi) east of Orvieto.

GETTING HERE
Todi is best reached by car, as the town's two train stations are way down the hill and connected to the center by infrequent bus service. From Perugia, follow the E45 toward Rome. Take the Todi/Orvieto exit, then follow the SS79bis into Todi. The drive takes around 40 minutes.

12

VISITOR INFORMATION

Todi tourism office (✉ *Piazza del Popolo 38* ☎ *075/8945416* ⊕ *www. todi.umbria2000.it*).

EXPLORING

As you stand on Piazza del Popolo, looking out onto the Tiber Valley below, it's easy to see how Todi is often described as Umbria's prettiest hill town. Legend has it that the town was founded by the Umbri, who followed an eagle who had stolen a tablecloth to this lofty perch. They liked it so much that they settled here for good. The eagle is now perched on the insignia of the medieval palaces in the main piazza.

Built above the Roman Forum, **Piazza del Popolo** is Todi's high point, a model of spatial harmony with stunning views onto the surrounding countryside. In the best medieval tradition, the square was conceived to house both the temporal and the spiritual centers of power.

On one end of the Piazza del Popolo is the 12th-century Romanesque–Gothic **Duomo**, which was built over the site of a Roman temple. The simple facade is enlivened by a finely carved rose window. Look up at that window as you step inside and you will notice its peculiarity: each "petal" of the rose has a cherub's face in the stained glass. You can see the rich brown tones of the wooden choir near the altar, but unless you have binoculars or request special permission in advance, you cannot get close enough to see all the exquisite detail in this Renaissance masterpiece of woodworking (1521–30). The severe, solid mass of the Duomo is mirrored by the Palazzo dei Priori (1595–97) across the way. ✉ *Piazza del Popolo* ☎ *075/8943041* 🎫 *Free* 🕐 *May–Sept., daily 9–12:30 and 2:30–6:30; Oct.–Apr., daily 9–4:30.*

WHERE TO STAY & EAT

$$–$$$ ✕ **Ristorante Umbria.** Todi's most popular restaurant for more than four decades, the Umbria is reliable for its sturdy country food and its wonderful view from the terrace. With just 16 tables outside, make sure you reserve ahead. In winter try legume soup, homemade pasta with truffles, or *palombaccio alla ghiotta* (roasted squab). Steaks, accompanied by a rich dark-brown wine sauce, are good as well. ✉ *Via San Bonaventura 13* ☎ *075/8942737* ⊟ *AE, DC, MC, V* 🕐 *Closed Tues.*

$–$$ 🏨 **San Lorenzo 3.** Surrounded by antique furniture, paintings, and period knickknacks, you get a sense of a place more in tune with the 19th than the 21st century. This hotel doesn't pamper you with modern comforts; only three of the six rooms have private bathrooms, but all share a magnificent view over the valleys and hills to the north of the town. Don't be put off by the rather dark entrance to the building: climb the long flight of stairs that lead up to this intriguing guesthouse. **Pros:** Delightful old-world atmosphere, excellent central location. **Cons:** Few modern amenities, basic furnishings. ✉ *Via San Lorenzo 3, 06059* ☎ *075/8944555* ⊕ *www.todi.net/lorenzo* 🛏 *6 rooms, 3 with bath* ⚐ *In-room: no a/c, no phone, no TV. In-hotel: no elevator* ⊟ *No credit cards* 🕐 *Closed Jan. and Feb.* 🍴 *BP.*

ORVIETO

30 km (19 mi) west of Todi, 81 km (51 mi) west of Spoleto.

GETTING HERE

Orvieto is well connected by train to Rome, Florence, and Perugia. It's also adjacent to the A1 super-strada that runs between Florence and Rome. Parking areas in the upper town tend to be crowded. A better idea is to follow the signs for the Porta Orvietana parking lot, then take the funicular up the hill. It runs every 20 minutes, daily 7:15 AM–8:30 PM, and costs €1.

VISITOR INFORMATION

A *Carta Orvieto Unica* (single ticket) is expensive but a great deal if you want to visit everything; for €18 you get admission to the four major sights in town—Cappella di San Brizio (at the Duomo), Museo Claudio Faina, Torre del Moro, and Orvieto Underground—plus a bus-funicular pass or five hours of free parking.

Orvieto tourism office (✉*Piazza del Duomo 24* ☏*0763/341772* ⊕*www. orvieto.umbria2000.it*).

EXPLORING

Carved out of an enormous plateau of volcanic rock high above a green valley, Orvieto has natural defenses that made the high walls seen in many Umbrian towns unnecessary. The Etruscans were the first to settle here, digging a honeycombed network of more than 1,200 wells and storage caves out of the soft stone. The Romans attacked, sacked, and destroyed the city in 283 BC; since then, it has grown up out of the rock into an enchanting maze of alleys and squares. Orvieto was solidly Guelph in the Middle Ages, and for several hundred years popes sought refuge in the city, at times needing protection from their enemies, at times from the summer heat of Rome.

When painting his frescoes inside the Duomo, Luca Signorelli asked that part of his contract be paid in Orvietan wine, and he was neither the first nor the last to appreciate the region's popular white. In past times the caves carved underneath the town were used to ferment the Trebbiano grapes used in making Orvieto Classico; now local wine production has moved out to more traditional vineyards, but you can still while away the afternoon in tastings at any number of shops in town.

Fodor'sChoice ★ Orvieto's **Duomo** is, quite simply, stunning. The church was built to commemorate the Miracle at Bolsena. In 1263, a young priest who questioned the miracle of transubstantiation (in which the Communion bread and wine become the flesh and blood of Christ) was saying mass at nearby Lago di Bolsena. His doubts were put to rest, however, when a wafer he had just blessed suddenly started to drip blood, staining the linen covering the altar. The cloth and the host were taken to the pope, who proclaimed a miracle and a year later provided for a new religious holiday—the Feast of Corpus Domini. Thirty years later, construction began on a *duomo* to celebrate the miracle and house the stained altar cloth.

It is thought that Arnolfo di Cambio (circa 1245–1302), the famous builder of the Duomo in Florence, was given the initial commission for the Duomo, but the project was soon taken over by Lorenzo Maitani (circa 1275–1330), who consolidated the structure and designed the monumental facade. Maitani also made the bas-relief panels between the doorways, which graphically tell the story of the Creation (on the left) and the Last Judgment (on the right). The lower registers, now protected by Plexiglas, succeed in conveying the horrors of hell as few other works of art manage to do, an effect made all the more powerful by the worn gray marble. Above, gold mosaics are framed by finely detailed Gothic decoration.

Inside, the cathedral is rather vast and empty; the major works are in the transepts. To the left is the **Cappella del Corporale,** where the square linen cloth (corporale) is kept in a golden reliquary that's modeled on the cathedral and inlaid with enamel scenes of the miracle. The cloth is removed for public viewing on Easter and on Corpus Domini (the ninth Sunday after Easter). In the right transept is the **Cappella di San Brizio,** or Cappella Nuova. In this chapel is one of Italy's greatest fresco cycles, notable for its influence on Michelangelo's *Last Judgment,* as well as for the extraordinary beauty of the figuration. In these works, the damned fall to hell, demons breathe fire and blood, and Christians are martyred. Some scenes are heavily influenced by the imagery in Dante's (1265–1321) *The Divine Comedy.* ✉*Piazza del Duomo* ☎*0763/342477* ⛪*Church free, Cappella Nuova €5* ⊙*Nov.– Feb., daily 7:30–12:45 and 2:30–5:15; Mar. and Oct., daily 7:30–12:45 and 2:30–6:15; Apr.–Sept., daily 7:30–12:45 and 2:30–7:15.*

★ The superb private collection of the **Museo Archeologico Claudio Faina** is beautifully arranged and presented. It's particularly rich in Greek- and Etruscan-era pottery, from large Attic amphorae (6th–4th century BC) to Attic black- and red-figure pieces to Etruscan *bucchero* (dark, reddish clay) vases. Other interesting pieces in the collection include a 6th-century sarcophagus and a substantial display of Roman-era coins. ✉*Piazza del Duomo 29* ☎*0763/341511* ⊕*www.museofaina.it* ⛪*€4.50* ⊙*Oct.–Mar., Tues.–Sun. 11–3; Apr.–Sept., daily 9:30–6.*

There is no better way to get a sense of Orvieto's multilayered history than to take a tour of the maze of tunnels and chambers that make up **Orvieto Underground.** Members of an Umbrian speleological club lead small groups down below street level to explain the origins of the tufa plateau on which Orvieto sits and to reveal the fascinating purposes to which these hidden caverns were put. The most thorough **Orvieto Underground tour** (✉*Orvieto tourism office, Piazza del Duomo 24* ☎*0763/341772*) is run daily at 11, 12:15, 4, and 5:15. The price of the hour-long English tour is €5.50. If you are short on time but still want a look at what it was like down there, head for the **Pozzo della Cava** (✉ *Via della Cava 28* ☎*0763/342373*), an Etruscan well for spring water. It's open Tuesday through Friday from 8 to 8, and costs €3.

WHERE TO STAY & EAT

$$–$$$ ✕**Il Giglio D'Oro.** A great view of the Duomo is coupled with superb
Fodor'sChoice food. Eggplant is transformed into an elegant custard with black truf-
★ fles in the *sformatino di melenzane con vellutata al tartuffo nero*. Pastas, like *ombrichelli al pesto umbro*, are traditional, but perhaps with
a new twist like fresh coriander leaves instead of the usual basil. Lamb
roasted in a crust of bread is delicately seasoned with a tomato cream
sauce. The wine cellar includes some rare vintages. ✉*Piazza Duomo 8*
☎*0763/341903* ▤*AE, MC, V* ☉*Closed Wed.*

$$–$$$ ✕**Le Grotte del Funaro.** If you can't do the official hour tour of Under-
ground Orvieto, dine here instead, inside tufa caves under central
Orvieto, where the two windows have splendid views of the hilly
countryside during the day. The traditional Umbrian food is average, but with good, simple grilled meats and vegetables and pizzas.
Oddly, the food is outclassed by an extensive wine list with top local
and Italian labels and quite a few rare vintages. ✉*Via Ripa Seran-
cia 41* ☎*0763/343276* ⌂*Reservations essential* ▤*AE, DC, MC, V*
☉*Closed Mon. and 1 wk in July.*

$–$$$ ✕**Trattoria La Grotta.** The owner has been in this location for more than
★ 20 years, and locals are still fond of him. He has attracted a steady
American clientele without losing his touch with homemade pasta,
perhaps with a duck or wild-boar sauce. Roast lamb, veal, or pork
are all good, and the desserts are homemade. Franco knows the local
wines well and has a carefully selected list, including some from smaller
but excellent wineries, so ask about them. ✉*Via Luca Signorelli 5*
☎*0763/341348* ▤*AE, DC, MC, V* ☉*Closed Tues.*

$$$ ⌂**Hotel La Badia.** One of the region's best-known country hotels occu-
★ pies a 12th-century monastery. Vaulted ceilings and exposed stone
walls establish the rustic elegance in the guest rooms, which have
beamed ceilings and polished terra-cotta floors covered with rugs. The
rolling park around the hotel provides wonderful views of the valley.
It's 4 km (2½ mi) south of Orvieto. **Pros:** Elegant atmosphere, fine
views. **Cons:** Slightly overpriced, need a car to get around. ✉*Località
La Badia, Orvieto Scalo, 05018* ☎*0763/301959* ⊕*www.labadiahotel.
it* ↝*18 rooms, 9 suites* ⌂*In-room: refrigerator. In-hotel: restaurant,
bar, tennis courts, pool, parking (no fee)* ▤*AE, MC, V* ☉*Closed Jan.
and Feb.* ⍥*BP.*

$$ ⌂**Hotel Palazzo Piccolomini.** This hotel is often preferred by local wine-
makers and other professionals for its updated look with inviting lobby
areas and a convenient location near the church of San Giovanni.
From here, it's a lovely short walk past Piazza della Repubblica to
the Duomo. **Pros:** Peaceful atmosphere, efficient staff, good location.
Cons: Unattractive building, slightly overpriced. ✉*Piazza Ranieri 36,
05018* ☎*0763/341743* ⊕*www.hotelpiccolomini.it* ↝*28 rooms, 3
suites* ⌂*In-room: refrigerator, ethernet. In-hotel: bar, laundry service,
parking (fee), no-smoking rooms* ▤*AE, MC* ⍥*BP.*

NARNI

13 km (8 mi) southwest of Terni, 46 km (29 mi) southeast of Orvieto.

GETTING HERE
From Perugia, take the E45 highway toward Rome. Merge onto the SS675, then take the exit to San Gemini and follow signs for Narni Scalo. The drive takes around 1½ hours. There are also regular trains from Perugia.

VISITOR INFORMATION
Narni tourism office (✉*Piazza del Popolo 18* ☎*0744/715362* ⊕*www.terni.umbria2000.it).*

EXPLORING
Once a bustling and important town at a major crossroads on the Via Flaminia, Narni is now a quiet backwater with only the occasional tourist invading its hilltop streets. Modern development is kept out of sight in the new town of Narni Scalo, below. This means that you will find the older neighborhood safely preserved behind, and in the case of Narni's subterranean Roman ruins, beneath, the town's sturdy walls.

You can take a unique tour of Narni's underground **Roman aqueduct**—the only one open to the public in all of Italy—but it's not for the claustrophobic. Contact Narni Sotterranea at least one week ahead to book a visit. ✉*Narni Sotterranea, Via San Bernardo 12*☎*0744/722292* ⊕*www.narnisotterranea.it* ✉*€15* ⊙*Nov.–Mar., Sun. 11–1 and 3–5; Apr.–Oct., Sat. at 3 and at 6, Sun. 10–1 and 3–6; by appointment weekdays for groups.*

WHERE TO EAT
$$-$$$ ✕**Il Cavallino.** Run by the third generation of the Bussetti family, this trattoria is south of Narni on the Via Flaminia. The most dependable menu selections are the grilled meats. Rabbit roasted with rosemary and sage and juicy grilled T-bone steaks are house favorites; in the winter, phone ahead to request the wild pigeon. The wine has a limited selection of dependable local varieties. ✉*Via Flaminia Romana 220 j 3 km (2 mi) south of center* ☎*0744/761020* ▭*AE, DC, MC, V* ⊙*Closed Tues. and Dec. 20–26.*

VALNERINA

Terni is 13 km (8 mi) northeast of Narni, 27 km (17 mi) southwest of Spoleto.

The Valnerina (the valley of the River Nera, to the east of Spoleto) is the most beautiful of central Italy's many well-kept secrets. The twisting roads that serve the rugged landscape are poor, but the drive is well worth the effort for its forgotten medieval villages and dramatic

> ### WORD OF MOUTH
>
> "I highly recommend a drive up the Valnerina. The highlight is the miraculous Piano Grande, which is an enormous and strange flat plain surrounded by mountains."
> –pfeldman

Hiking the Umbrian Hills

Magnificent scenery makes the heart of Italy excellent walking, hiking, and mountaineering country. In Umbria, the area around Spoleto is particularly good; several pleasant, easy, and well-signed trails begin at the far end of the Ponte alle Torri bridge over Monteluco. From Cannara an easy half-hour walk leads to the fields of Pian d'Arca, the site of St. Francis's sermon to the birds. For slightly more-arduous walks, you can follow the saint's path, uphill from Assisi to the Eremo delle Carceri, and then continue along the trails that crisscross Monte Subasio. At 4,250 feet, the Subasio's treeless summit affords views of Assisi, Perugia, far-off Gubbio, and the distant mountain ranges of Abruzzo.

For even more challenging hiking, the northern reaches of the Valnerina are exceptional; the mountains around Norcia should not to be missed. Throughout Umbria and the Marches, you'll find that most recognized walking and hiking trails are marked with the distinctive red-and-white blazes of the Club Alpino Italiano (CAI). Tourist offices are a good source for walking and climbing itineraries to suit all ages and levels of ability, while bookstores, *tabacchi* (tobacconists), and *edicole* (newsstands) often have maps and hiking guides that detail the best routes in their area. Depending on the length and location of your walk, it can be important that you have comfortable walking shoes or boots, appropriate attire, and plenty of water to drink.

mountain scenery. You can head into the area from Terni on the S209, or on the SP395bis north of Spoleto, which links the Via Flaminia (S3) with the middle reaches of the Nera valley through a tunnel.

The **Cascata delle Marmore** are waterfalls engineered by the Romans in the 3rd century BC. To find them, drive east from Terni on the road to Lake Piediluco and Rieti. The waters are diverted on weekdays to provide hydroelectric power. On summer evenings, when the falls are in full spate, the cascading water is floodlit to striking effect. ⊠*SP79* ✛ *3 km (2 mi) east of Terni* ☎*0744/62982* ⊠*€4* ⊘*May, weekends noon–1 and 4–5; June–Aug., daily 11* AM*–10* PM*; mid-Mar.–Apr. and Sept., weekends noon–9; Jan.–mid-Mar., weekends noon–4.*

The Terni **tourist office** can provide information on the operating schedule of the Cascata delle Marmore, and on the region in general. ⊠*Viale C. Battisti 7a* ☎*0744/423047* ⊕*www.terni.umbria2000.it*

Close to the town of Ferentillo is the outstanding 8th-century abbey of **San Pietro in Valle**, with fine frescoes in the church nave and a peaceful cloister. One of the abbey outbuildings houses an excellent restaurant with moderate prices. ⊠*Strada di Monteluco* ✛ *1 km (½ mi) south of Spoleto* ☎*0743/44882* ⊠*Free* ⊘*Daily 9–6:30.*

Norcia, the birthplace of St. Benedict, is better known for its Umbrian pork and truffles. Norcia exports truffles to France and hosts a truffle

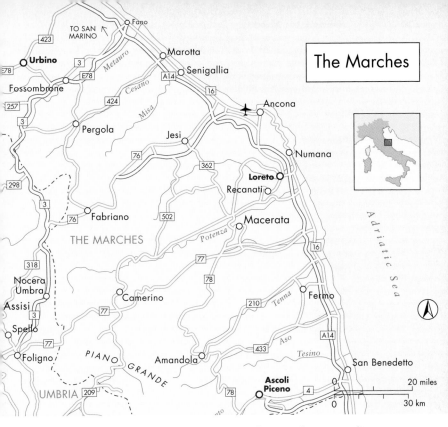

festival, the Sagra del Tartufo, every February. The surrounding mountains provide spectacular hiking. ⊠*67 km (42 mi) northeast of Terni.*

Piano Grande, a mountain plain 25 km (15 mi) to the northeast of the valley, is a hang glider's paradise, a wonderful place for a picnic or to fly a kite. It is also nationally famous for the quality of the lentils grown here, which are a traditional part of every Italian New Year feast.

THE MARCHES

An excursion from Umbria into the Marches region allows you to see a part of Italy rarely visited by foreigners. Not as wealthy as Tuscany or Umbria, the Marches has a diverse landscape of mountains and beaches, and marvelous views. Like that of neighbors to the west, the patchwork of rolling hills of Le Marche (as it is known in Italian) is stitched with grapevines and olive trees, bearing luscious wine and olive oil.

Traveling here isn't as easy as in Umbria or Tuscany. Beyond the narrow coastal plain and away from major towns, the roads are steep and twisting. An efficient bus service connects the coastal town of Pesaro to Urbino. Train travel in the region is slow, however, and stops are limited—although you can reach Ascoli Piceno by rail.

San Marino, perched high on the upper slopes of Monte Titano, is best reached from Rimini, on the southern coast of Emilia-Romagna. A main highway connects the two; a regular bus service to San Marino is available from Rimini's train station, airport, and city center.

URBINO

75 km (47 mi) north of Gubbio, 116 km (72 mi) northeast of Perugia, 230 km (143 mi) east of Florence.

GETTING HERE
Take the SS3bis from Perugia, and follow the directions for Gubbio and Cesena. Exit at Umbertide and take the SS219, then the SS452, and at Calmazzo the SS73bis to Urbino.

VISITOR INFORMATION
Urbino tourism office (⊠ *Piazza Duca Federico 35* ☎ *0722/2613* ⊕ *www. comune.orvieto.tr.it*).

EXPLORING
Majestic Urbino, atop a steep hill with a skyline of towers and domes, is something of a surprise to come upon. Although quite remote, it was once a center of learning and culture almost without rival in western Europe. The town looks much as it did in the glory days of the 15th century, a cluster of warm brick and pale stone buildings, all topped with russet-color tile roofs. The focal point is the immense and beautiful Palazzo Ducale.

The city is home to the small but prestigious Università di Urbino—one of the oldest in the world—and the streets are usually filled with students. Urbino is very much a college town, with the usual array of bookshops, bars, and coffeehouses. In summer the Italian student population is replaced by foreigners who come to study Italian language and arts at several prestigious private fine-arts academies.

Urbino's fame rests on the reputation of three of its native sons: Duke Federico da Montefeltro (1422–82), the enlightened warrior-patron who built the Palazzo Ducale; Raffaello Sanzio (1483–1520), or Raphael, one of the most influential painters in history and an embodiment of the spirit of the Renaissance; and the architect Donato Bramante (1444–1514), who translated the philosophy of the Renaissance into buildings of grace and beauty. Unfortunately there is little work by either Bramante or Raphael in the city, but the duke's influence can still be felt strongly.

The **Casa Natale di Raffaello** *(House of Raphael)* is the house in which the painter was born and where he took his first steps in painting, under the direction of his artist father. There is some debate about the fresco of the Madonna here; some say it's by Raphael, whereas others attribute it to the father—with Raphael's mother and the young painter himself standing in as models for the Madonna and Child. ⊠ *Via Raffaello 57* ☎ *0722/320105* 💶 *€3* ⊙ *Mon.–Sat. 9–1 and 3–7, Sun. 10–1.*

Fodor'sChoice
★

The **Palazzo Ducale** *(Ducal Palace)* holds a place of honor in the city. If the Renaissance was, ideally, a celebration of the nobility of man and his works, of the light and purity of the soul, then there is no place in Italy, the birthplace of the Renaissance, where these tenets are better illustrated. From the moment you enter the peaceful courtyard, you know you're in a place of grace and beauty, the harmony of the building reflecting the high ideals of the time. Today the palace houses the **Galleria Nazionale delle Marche** (National Museum of the Marches), with a superb collection of paintings, sculpture, and other objets d'art. Some works were originally the possessions of the Montefeltro family; others were brought here from churches and palaces throughout the region. Masterworks in the collection include Paolo Uccello's *Profanation of the Host,* Titian's *Resurrection* and *Last Supper,* and Piero della Francesca's *Madonna of Senigallia.* But the gallery's highlight is Piero's enigmatic work long known as *The Flagellation of Christ.* Much has been written about this painting, and few experts agree on its meaning. Legend had it that the figures in the foreground represent a murdered member of the Montefeltro family (the barefoot young man) and his two killers. However, Sir John Pope-Hennessy—the preeminent scholar of Italian Renaissance art—argues that they represent the arcane subject of the vision of Saint Lawrence. Academic debates notwithstanding, the experts agree that the work is one of the painter's masterpieces. Piero himself thought so: it is one of the few works he signed (on the lowest step supporting the throne). ⊠*Piazza Duca Federico* ☎*0722/322625* ⊕*www.comune. urbino.ps.it* ☑*€8* ☉ *Mon. 8:30–2, Tues.–Sun. 8:30–7:15.*

WHERE TO STAY & EAT

$–$$ ✗**La Vecchia Fornarina.** Locals often crowd the small, two-room trattoria near the Piazza della Repubblica. The specialty is meaty country fare, such as *coniglio* (rabbit) and *vitello alle noci* (veal cooked with walnuts) or *ai porcini* (with mushrooms). There's also a good selection of pasta dishes. ⊠*Via Mazzini 14* ☎*0722/320007* ⌲*Reservations essential* ⊟*AE, DC, MC, V.*

¢–$ ✗**Angolo Divino.** At this *osteria* (informal restaurant) in the center of Urbino, tradition reigns supreme: the menu is written in local dialect, flanked by Italian and English translations. Dishes range from the deliciously simple *spaghetti col pane grattugiato* (spaghetti with bread crumbs) to the temptingly rich *filetto al tartuffo* (beef fillet with truffles). ⊠*Via S. Andrea 14* ☎*0722/327559* ⊟*AE, D, MC, V* ☉*Closed Mon. and mid-Oct.–mid-Nov. No dinner Sun.*

$$–$$$ ⊞**Hotel Bonconte.** This classic hotel, dating from the beginning of the 20th century, is just inside the city walls and close to the Palazzo Ducale. Rooms are pleasant and include some antiques; those at the front of the hotel have views of the valley below Urbino, although they also face the street. A terrace in the tranquil garden to the rear of the hotel adjoins the cozy breakfast room and bar. **Pros:** Some nice views, away from the bustle. **Cons:** Slightly overpriced, service is sleepy. ⊠*Via delle Mura 28, 61029* ☎*0722/2463* 🖷*0722/4782* ⊕*www.viphotels. it* 🛌*23 rooms, 2 suites* ♿*In-room: ethernet. In-hotel: bar* ⊟*AE, DC, MC, V* ⒣*EP.*

LORETO

31 km (19 mi) south of Ancona, 118 km (73 mi) southeast of Urbino.

GETTING HERE

If you're driving from Perugia, take the SS318 and then the SS76 highway to Fabriano and then on to Chiaravalle, where it merges with the A14 autostrada. The drive takes around 2½ hours. Trains also go to Loreto, but the station is about a mile outside the town center. Regular buses leave from the station to the center.

VISITOR INFORMATION

Loreto tourism office (⊠ *Via Solari 3* ☎*071/970276* ⊕*www.turismo. marche.it*).

EXPLORING

★ Loreto is famous for one of the best-loved shrines in the world, that of the **Santuario della Santa Casa** (House of the Virgin Mary), within the **Basilica della Santa Casa.** Legend has it that angels moved the house from Nazareth, where the Virgin Mary was living at the time of the Annunciation, to this hilltop in 1295. The reason for this sudden and divinely inspired move was that Nazareth had fallen into the hands of Muslim invaders, whom the angelic hosts viewed as unsuitable keepers of this important shrine. Excavations made at the behest of the Catholic Church have shown that the house did once stand elsewhere and was brought to the hilltop—by either crusaders or a family named Angeli—around the time the angels (*angeli*) are said to have done the job.

The house itself consists of three rough stone walls contained within an elaborate marble tabernacle. Built around this centerpiece is the giant basilica of the Holy House, which dominates the town. Millions of visitors come to the site every year (particularly at Easter and on the December 10 Feast of the Holy House), and the little town of Loreto can become uncomfortably crowded with pilgrims. Many great Italian architects, including Bramante, Antonio da Sangallo the Younger (1483–1546), Giuliano da Sangallo (circa 1445–1516), and Sansovino (1467–1529), contributed to the design of the basilica. It was begun in the Gothic style in 1468 and continued in Renaissance style through the late Renaissance. The bell tower is by Luigi Vanvitelli (1700–73). Inside the church are a great many mediocre 19th- and 20th-century paintings but also some fine works by Renaissance masters such as Luca Signorelli and Melozzo da Forlì (1438–94).

If you're a nervous air traveler, you can take comfort in the fact that the Holy Virgin of Loreto is the patron saint of air travelers and that Pope John Paul II has composed a prayer for a safe flight—available in the church in a half-dozen languages. ⊠*Piazza della Madonna* ☎*071/970104* ⊕*www.santuarioloreto.it* ☉*June–Sept., daily 6:45 AM–8 PM; Oct.–May, daily 6:45 AM–7 PM. Santuario della Santa Casa closed daily 12:30–2:30.*

ASCOLI PICENO

88 km (55 mi) south of Loreto, 105 km (65 mi) south of Ancona.

GETTING HERE

From Perugia take the SS75 to Foligno, then merge onto the SS3 to Norcia. From here take the SS4 to Ascoli Piceno. There are also trains, but the journey would be quite long, taking you from Perugia to Ancona before changing for Ascoli Piceno.

12

VISITOR INFORMATION

Ascoli Piceno tourism office (✉*Piazza del Popolo 1* ☎*0736/257288* ⊕*www.comune.ascolipiceno.it*).

EXPLORING

Ascoli Piceno isn't a hill town but sits in a valley ringed by steep hills and cut by the fast-racing Tronto River. In Roman times it was one of central Italy's most important market towns and today, with almost 60,000 residents, it's a major fruit and olive producer, making it one of the most important towns in the region. Despite the growth Ascoli Piceno saw during the Middle Ages and at other times, the streets in the town center continue to reflect the grid pattern of the ancient Roman city. You'll even find the word *rua*, from the Latin *ruga*, used for "street" instead of the Italian *via*. Now largely closed to traffic, the city center is a great place to explore on foot.

★ The heart of the town is the majestic **Piazza del Popolo,** dominated by the Gothic church of **San Francesco** and the **Palazzo del Popolo,** a 13th-century town hall that contains a graceful Renaissance courtyard. The square itself functions as the living room of the entire city. At dusk each evening the piazza is packed with people strolling and exchanging news and gossip—the sweetly antiquated ritual called the *passeggiata,* performed all over the country.

WHERE TO STAY & EAT

$-$$ ✕**Ristorante Tornasacco.** You won't find nouvelle cuisine at this, one
★ of Ascoli Piceno's oldest restaurants. The owners pride themselves on meaty local specialties such as *olive ascolane* (olives stuffed with minced meat, breaded and deep-fried), *maccheroncini alla contadina* (homemade short pasta in a lamb, pork, and veal sauce), and *bistecca di toro* (bull steak). ✉*Piazza del Popolo 36* ☎*0736/254151* ▭*AE, DC, MC, V* ⊘*Closed Fri., and July 15–31 and Dec. 23–28.*

$ ☷**Il Pennile.** Look for this modern, family-run hotel in a quiet residential area outside the old city center, amid a grove of olive trees. Some rooms have views of the city. **Pros:** Peaceful, a good budget option. **Cons:** Distance from town center, basic rooms. ✉*Via G. Spalvieri, 63100* ☎*0736/41645* ☐*0736/342755* ⬗*33 rooms* ◔*In-room: ethernet. In-hotel: bar, gym, public Internet* ▭*DC, MC, V* ℉*BP.*

Part IV:
Southern Italy

WHAT'S WHERE

1 Naples & Campania.
Campania is the gateway to southern Italy—and as far south as many travelers get. The region's happy combination of spectacular geology and rich cultural heritage makes it a popular place both to unwind—on the pint-size island of Capri or the resorts of the Amalfi Coast—and to explore the past—at the archaeological ruins of Pompeii, Herculaneum, and Paestum. In the middle of everything is Naples, a chaotic metropolis that people love and hate in nearly equal measure, though after a decade of urban renewal the lovers now appear to be in the majority. On a good day it's Italy's most fun and friendly large city. On a bad one it's a giant traffic jam, filled with crooked cabbies and purse-snatching kids on scooters.

2 The Mezzogiorno. The southernmost regions of the peninsula—Puglia, Basilicata, and Calabria—are known informally as the *mezzogiorno.* The name translates literally as "midday," and it's meant to evoke the blazing sun that presides over the medieval villages, shimmering seas, and varied landscapes. The coastline of Puglia, along the heel of Italy's boot, is popular with beachgoers, but for the most part you're off the

beaten path here, with all the pleasures and challenges that entails. You'll find fewer English-speakers but more genuine warmth from the people you encounter. The most distinctive attractions are the *sassi* (cave dwellings in the Basilicata village of Matera) and *trulli* (mysterious conical-roof dwellings found in abundance in the Puglia town of Alberobello). Both are UNESCO World Heritage sites.

3 Sicily. The architecture of Sicily reflects the island's centuries of successive dominion by the Greeks, Byzantines, Arabs, Normans, and Spaniards. Baroque church–hopping could be a sport in the cacophonous streets of Palermo and seafaring Siracusa. The breezes are sultry, and everyday life is without pretense, as witnessed in the workaday stalls of the fish markets all along the ports of the Tyrrhenian and Ionian coasts, bursting with tuna, swordfish, and sardines. Greek ruins stand sentinel in Agrigento's Valley of the Temples, blanketed in almond, oleander, and juniper blossoms. All over the island the ins and outs of life are celebrated each day as they have been for centuries—over a morning coffee, at the family lunch table, and in the evening *passeggiata*.

SOUTHERN ITALY PLANNER

Speaking the Language

Even if you speak fluent Italian, you may not be able to make sense of conversations you hear in the south. When locals talk among themselves, their discussions often revert to dialect that's unintelligible to the student of textbook Italian. Each region has a dialect of its own; Sicilian is distinctive enough to be considered a separate language.

Thanks to the education system and the unifying influence of radio and television, everyone speaks standard Italian as well, so you'll still benefit from whatever knowledge you have of the language. English-speakers aren't as prevalent as in points north, but this is the land of creative gesticulation and other forms of improvised nonverbal communication. Chances are, you'll be able to get your message across.

Getting Here

Located just 8 km (5 mi) outside Naples, **Aeroporto Capodichino** (NAP) serves the Campania region. It handles domestic and international flights, including several flights daily between Naples and Rome (flight time 45 minutes).

The three main airports of the deep south are Bari and Brindisi, in Puglia, and Lamezia Terme, in Calabria. All three have regular flights to and from Rome and Milan. In addition, Reggio di Calabria's airport has flights to and from Rome.

Sicily can be reached from all major international cities on flights connecting through Rome, Milan, or Naples. Planes to Palermo land at **Aeroporto Falcone-Borsellino** (named in memory of two anti-Mafia judges famously assassinated in 1992) in Punta Raisi, 32 km (19 mi) west of town. Catania's Aeroporto Fontanarossa, 5 km (3 mi) south of the city center, is the main airport on Sicily's eastern side.

There are direct express trains from Milan and Rome to Palermo, Catania, and Siracusa. The Rome–Palermo and Rome–Siracusa trips take at least 10 hours. After Naples, the run is mostly along the coast, so try to book a window seat on the right if you're not on an overnight train. At Villa San Giovanni, in Calabria, the train is separated and loaded onto a ferryboat to cross the strait to Messina.

Typical Travel Times

	Hours by Car	Hours by Train
Naples–Rome	2:30	1:30
Naples–Bari	3:00	4:00
Bari–Lecce	2:00	1:45
Naples–Matera	3:15	6:00
Naples–Cosenza	4:00	3:45
Naples–Messina	7:00	5:30
Messina–Palermo	2:30	3:15
Messina–Siracusa	2:00	3:00
Siracusa–Palermo	3:00	5:30
Palermo–Agrigento	2:00	2:00

On the Calendar

These are some of the top seasonal events in southern Italy:

From December through June, the **stagione operistica** (opera season) is underway at Teatro San Carlo in Naples.

In early February Agrigento's Valley of the Temples, **Festa dei Fiori di Mandorlo** (Almond Blossom Festival) is a week of folk music and dancing, with participants from many countries.

The **Settimana Santa** (Holy Week), culminating with Easter, features parades and outdoor events in every city and most small towns. Naples has particularly noteworthy festivities.

Twice a year, on Sundays in early May and mid-September, Naples celebrates the **Feast of San Gennaro.** In the Duomo, at 9 am a remnant of the saint's blood miraculously liquefies, after which there's ceremonial parade.

Every fourth year on the first Sunday in June, the **Regatta Storica dell'Antiche Repubbliche Marinare** (Regatta of the Great Maritime Republics) see keen boating competition between Amalfi, Genoa, Pisa, and Venice. In the 2009 Amalfi is the site for the event.

Estate a Napoli (Summer in Naples) is a season-long festival of concerts and performances—a reward for those enduring the Neapolitan heat.

How's the Weather?

Spring: In April, May, and early June, southern Italy is at its best. The weather is generally pleasant and the fields are in full bloom. Easter is a busy time for most tourist destinations—if you're traveling then, you should have lodging reserved well ahead of time. By May the ocean water is warm enough for swimming, and you'll often have the beach to yourself.

Summer: Temperatures can be torrid in the summer months, making them a less-than-ideal time for a visit to the south. In Campania, Naples can feel like a sweltering inferno, the archaeological sites swarm with visitors, and the islands and Amalfi Coast resorts are similarly overrun. Even the otherwise perfect villages of the mezzogiorno's interior are too dazzlingly white for easy comfort from July to early September. If you seek a beach, whether on the mainland or Sicily, keep in mind that during August all of Italy flocks to the shores. Even relatively isolated resorts can be overrun by weeklong package tourists.

Fall: Visit the south from late September through early November and you'll find gentle, warm weather and acres of beach space; swimming temperatures last through October. Watch the clock, however, as the days get shorter. In Campania, excursions to Vesuvius, Pompeii, Herculaneum, and the islands all require some traveling, and it's easy to get caught with little daylight left. At most archaeological sites, you're rounded up two hours before sunset—but by then most crowds have departed, so late afternoon is still an optimum time to see Pompeii, Herculaneum, or Agrigento in peace and quiet.

Winter: Early winter is relatively mild (bougainvillea and other floral displays can bloom through Christmas), but particularly later in the season, cold fronts can arrive and stay for days. In resort destinations, many hotels, restaurants, and other tourist facilities close down from November until around Easter. Elsewhere, you need to reserve rooms well in advance for Christmas, Agrigento's almond festival in February, and the Carnevale in Acireale.

SOUTHERN ITALY TOP ATTRACTIONS

Underground Naples

(C) In Naples the locals point to the ground and say there's another city underneath. This is *Napoli Sotterranea*, a netherworld of ancient Greek quarries, Roman streets, medieval aqueducts, and World War II bomb shelters. Parts have been cleaned up and made accessible to the public. (⇨ Chapter 13.)

The Ruins around Vesuvius

(B) This may be the closest you'll ever get to time travel. Thanks to Vesuvius blowing its top in AD 79, the towns round its base were carpeted in fallout and preserved for posterity. Allow a good half day to look round bustling Pompeii or the more compact, less busy Herculaneum. For the best Roman frescoes, head to the Villa of Oplontis between the two ancient cities. (⇨ Chapter 13.)

The Amalfi Coast

(D) One moment you're gazing out at a luxury sailcraft, the next you're dodging mules on precipitous footpaths. "Comforts of the 21st century in a medieval setting" just about sums up the remarkable Amalfi Coast. (⇨ Chapter 13.)

Matera's Sassi

You can see why Matera is a favorite with filmmakers shooting biblical scenes. You get that time-warp feeling especially in early morning or at night among the *sassi*—buildings seemingly gouged out of the limestone cliffs. (⇨ Chapter 14.)

Lecce

(A) With its much-feted baroque facades and extensive Roman remains in the city center, Lecce has a legitimate claim to being Puglia's fairest city. As an added bonus, nearby are a largely undeveloped coastline and the magical walled town of Otranto. (⇨ Chapter 14.)

Bronzi di Riace, Reggio Calabria

(G) Few bronze statues have survived intact from the ancient Greek world. The presence of not one but two larger-than-life bronzes, restored to almost perfect condition, is reason enough to trek to Reggio Calabria, on the eastern side of the Strait of Messina. (⇨ Chapter 14.)

Mount Etna

(H) You can take the single-gauge railway round its foothills, splurge on a SUV-experience near the summit, or just stroll across old lavafields on its northern flank. Alternatively, go down into the gorge of Alcantara and see what happens when lava flow meets mountain spring water. (⇨ Chapter 15.)

Castelmola

When it comes to medieval hill towns and Norman castles, Sicilians definitely "do it better," and Castelmola is a prime example. Though difficult to believe, the town has even more dramatic views of Etna and the coastline than its neighbor Taormina. (⇨ Chapter 15.)

Imperial Roman Villa, Piazza Armerina

(F) "Villa" doesn't begin to describe this opulent palace from the latter years of the Roman empire. The stunning mosaics that fill every room are perhaps the best preserved and certainly the most extensive of the ancient Roman empire. (⇨ Chapter 15.)

Duomo, Siracusa

(E) Few buildings encapsulate history better than the Duomo of Siracusa. The cathedral started life as the temple dedicated to the goddess Athena sometime in the early 5th century BC, as one glance at the majestic fluted columns inside confirms. (⇨ Chapter 15.)

SOUTHERN ITALY TOP EXPERIENCES

Colori, Colori

Though still rather bracing for a dip in the Mediterranean, April and May guarantee a visual feast as you travel around southern Italy: a dazzling array of natural colors. Wherever you look—roadsides, archaeological sites, public gardens, even on wasteland and beside railroad tracks—you'll see seemingly barren land carpeted in flowers. Fields of scarlet poppies on the plains of Puglia, hillsides in Calabria covered with yellow Spanish broom, the purple of bugloss on the Hyblean plateau near Noto in Sicily, pink orchids on the limestone outcrops around Matera, and the yellow umbels of giant fennel on Capri: this is the Mediterranean at its most explosive. Come back in June, and much of the tapestry will have faded, with plants dispersing their seeds for next year's show. Too early for the spring splendor? Try to work in a trip to Agrigento's Almond Blossom Festival in February.

Pasticceria Siciliana

Cannolo, iris, sfinge, cartoccio, cassata, and daughter cassatina: it sounds like the list of characters from an opera, but these ricotta-filled delights can be found in any self-respecting pasticceria on the island of Sicily. The top performers cluster around Palermo and Catania: the Antico Chiosco in Mondello, a resort northwest of Palermo, has been delighting palates for almost 90 years, while Savia's pedigree in Catania stretches even farther back. The secret lies in the basic ingredient and simplicity: ricotta is best made from the whey of ultrafresh sheep or goat's milk, preferably untainted by chocolate, liqueur, or candied fruit.

Fiery Landscapes

Volcanoes have long fascinated people on the move. The ancient Greeks—among the first sailors around the central Mediterranean—explained away Etna as the place where the god Hephaestus had his workshop. Millennia later, northern European visitors to Naples in the 18th and 19th centuries would climb the erupting Vesuvius or cross the steaming craters of the Campi Flegrei west of the city. Farther south, in the Lipari islands of the northeast of Sicily, Stromboli performs a lightshow about every 20 minutes, ejecting incandescent cinder, lapilli, and lava bombs high into the air. To add to the fascination, several of the Lipari islands rise sheer out of the Mediterranean, and beaches are black with volcanic fall-out. Though stripped of their mythology by generations of geologists and deprived by local authorities of even a frisson of risk, Italy's volcanoes are still a terrific crowd-puller.

The Great Summer Performances

Exploiting both its Mediterranean climate and atmospheric venues, the south of Italy lays on an impressive range of cultural events during those hot summer months. The ancient theaters of Segesta, Siracusa, and Taormina in Sicily are used for anything from Greek plays to pop concerts, while in Campania the Greek temples at Paestum serve as a scenic backdrop for opera and symphonic music. The 18th-century villas near Herculaneum at the foot of Vesuvius have also joined the musical act in recent years. With time (and money) head across the bay to Capri for a sunset concert at Villa San Michele, high over the Mediterranean. But then, where do you go from there?

SOUTHERN ITALY TODAY

Southern Italy is slap bang in the middle of the Mediterranean, so it's no wonder that it has experienced invasions and migrations for millennia, many of which have left their mark culturally, linguistically, and architecturally.

The southerners really *are* different from Italians farther north. Under an ostensibly sociable and more expressive exterior, they are more guarded when dealing with strangers, less at home with foreign languages, and more oriented toward the family than the community. The trappings of affluence, like cars and scooters, become essential status symbols here, which is why cities like Naples and Palermo are strikingly congested and noisy.

Politics

Politics tends to be clientelistic in large swaths of the south. In this climate of mutual back-scratching and with unemployment rates (13.6%) twice the national average, the main preoccupation for many voters is *il posto fisso* (a steady job). Votes are all too often cast for the politician who promises opportunities for career advancement—or lucrative contracts—preferably in the public sector. Over the years this has insured inefficiencies, if not outright corruption.

The Economy

While the north has developed rapidly in the past 50 years, the Italian entrepreneurial spirit in the south struggles to make good. Despite a pool of relatively cheap, willing labor, foreign investment across the south is merely one-tenth of that going to Lombardy alone. This is primarily due to the stifling presence of organized crime. Each major region has its own criminal association: the *Camorra* in Naples, *Sacra Corona Unita* in Puglia,

'Ndrangheta in Calabria, and the *Mafia* in Sicily. The system creates add-on costs at many levels, especially in retail.

It is not all bad news though. Southern Italy has woken up to its major asset, its remarkable cultural and natural heritage. UNESCO lists 14 World Heritage Sites in southern Italy alone, while the last decade has seen the creation of several national parks, marine parks, and regional nature preserves. Environmental and cultural associations have mushroomed as locals increasingly perceive the importance of preserving across the generations.

In general, small average farm size in the south (5.8 hectares, under 15 acres) has helped preserve a pleasing mosaic of habitats in the interior. Landscape and product diversity has been aided by the promotion of traditionally grown products by the European Union and its PDO (Protected Designation of Origin) project.

Tourism

Hitching a ride with nature's cornucopia are some 1,600 *agriturismo* lodgings (farmhouse stays) throughout the *Mezzogiorno*. Conventional beach holidays are still popular in July and August, when Italy sees a massive southward migration along the Naples–Reggio Calabria motorway, and across the strait of Messina into Sicily. Religious tourism accounts for large visitor flows throughout the year—as many visitors pay their respects to the Madonna di Pompei sanctuary as they do to the archaeological site up the road. In almost every village and town in southern Italy you're likely to see the bearded statue of Capuchin priest Padre Pio.

A GREAT ITINERARY

Day 1: Naples

Fly into Naples's Aeroporto Capodichino, a scant 8 km (5 mi) from the city. Naples is rough around the edges and may be a bit jarring if you're a first-time visitor, but it's classic Italy, and most visitors end up falling in love with the city's alluring waterfront palazzi and spectacular pizza. First things first, though: recharge with a nap and, after that, a good caffè—Naples has some of Italy's best. Revive in time for an evening stroll down Naples's wonderful shopping street, Via Toledo—it's quintessential Italy—before dinner and bed.

Logistics: Under no circumstances should you rent a car for Naples. Take a taxi from the airport—it's not far, or overly expensive—and you should face few logistical obstacles on your first day in Italy.

Day 2: Naples

Start the day in Piazza Gesù, and head east along Spaccanapoli through the very heart of old Naples, stopping at the churches of Gesù Nuovo and Santa Chiara. Farther up Spaccanapoli, try to check out Cappella Sansevero and the Duomo, before heading left on Via Foria to the Museo Archeologico Nazionale. From there take a taxi to Da Michele, and begin your afternoon with the best pizza in the world. Post pizza, check out the harbor and the Castel Nuovo; then head past the Teatro San Carlo to the enormous Palazzo Reale. Walk 15 minutes south to the Castel dell'Ovo in the Santa Lucia waterfront area, one of Naples's most charming neighborhoods. Then it's back up to Via Caracciolo and the Villa Comunale, before heading back to your hotel for a short rest before dinner and perhaps a night out at one of Naples's lively bars or clubs.

Logistics: This entire day is easily done on foot, with the exception of the taxi for your midday pizza. Naples is one of the best walking cities in Italy.

Day 3: Pompeii/Sorrento

After breakfast, pick up your rental car, pack in your luggage, and drive from Naples to Pompeii, one of the true archaeological gems of Europe. If it's summer, be prepared for an onslaught of sweltering heat as you make your way through the incredibly preserved ruins of a city that was devastated by the whims of Mt. Vesuvius nearly 2,000 years ago. You'll see the houses of noblemen and merchants, brothels, political graffiti, and more. From Pompeii, get back in your car and it's on to Sorrento, your first taste of the wonderful peninsula that marks the beginning of the fabled Amalfi Coast. Sorrento is touristy, but it may well be the Italian city of your imagination: cliff-hanging, cobblestone-paved, and graced with an infinite variety of fishing-port and coastal views. There, have a relaxing dinner of fish and white wine before calling it a day.

Logistics: Naples to Pompeii is all about the A3: a short 24 km (15 mi) brings you to this archaeological gem. From Pompeii it's a short ride back on the A3 until the exit for Sorrento; from the exit, you'll take the S145 to reach Sorrento.

Day 4: Positano/Ravello

Your stay in Sorrento will be short, as there's much of the Amalfi Coast still to see: Positano, your next stop, is a must. It's one of the most visited towns in Italy for good reason: its blue-green seas, stairs "as steep as ladders," and white Moorish-style houses make for a truly memorable setting. Walk, gaze, and eat (lunch),

before heading on to the less-traveled, even-higher-up town of Ravello, your Amalfi Coast dream come true, an aerie that is "closer to the sky than the sea." Don't miss the Duomo, Villa Rufolo, or Villa Cimbrone before settling in for a dinner in the sky.

Logistics: Sorrento to Positano is just a 34-km (21-mi) jaunt, but the winding roads will draw it out for the better part of an hour—a scenic hour. From Positano, Ravello is another slow 40 km (24 mi) to the east, perched high above the rest of the world. Be prepared to use low gears if you're driving a stick shift (as you almost surely will be).

Day 5: Matera

It will take a bit of a drive to get to Basilicata from the Amalfi Coast; leaving Campania and entering Basilicata is generally a lonely experience. Little-traveled roads, wild hills, and distant farms are the hallmarks of this province, which produces deep, dark aglianico wines and has perfected the art of peasant food. You'll spend a while in your car to make it to Matera, a beautiful, ancient city full of Paleolithic *sassi* (cavelike dwellings hewn out of rock)—but it's worth it. Traversing the city is like taking a voyage through time. Spend the afternoon exploring the

sassi, but take care not to miss the new part of the city, too. Then enjoy a relaxing dinner at one of Matera's excellent restaurants—just decide whether you want flavorful local beef (Le Botteghe) or a flurry of Basilicatan tapas (Lucanerie). Basilicata, you'll soon discover, is full of unrivaled values at restaurants, and with such options you'll be guaranteed to sleep well in the sassi.

Logistics: It's a long haul from your starting point, Ravello, to Matera. It's a good thing Basilicata's landscape is so pretty. Once in Matera, if you're staying in the sassi, get extra-detailed driving and parking instructions from your hotel beforehand—navigating through thousand-year-old alleyways can be challenging.

Day 6: Lecce

This drive will take a good three hours, so get an early start. The baroque city of Lecce will mark your introduction to Puglia, the heel of Italy's boot. It's one of Italy's best-kept secrets, as you'll soon find out upon checking out the spectacular church of Santa Croce, the ornate Duomo, and the harmonious Piazza Sant'Oronzo. The shopping is great, the food is great, and the evening passeggiata is great. Don't miss the opportunity, if you wind up at a bar or café in the evening, to chat with

A GREAT ITINERARY

Lecce's friendly residents—unfazed by tourism, the welcoming Leccesi represent southern Italians at their best.

Logistics: It's not far from Matera to Lecce as the crow flies, but the trip is more involved than you might think; patience is required. The best route is via Taranto—don't make the mistake of going up through Bari.

Day 7: Bari

The trip from Lecce to Bari is a short one. Check into the pleasant Hotel Palace and spend the morning and afternoon wandering through Bari's centro storico. The wide-open doors of the town's humble houses and apartments, with bickering families and grandmothers drying their pasta in the afternoon sun, will give you a taste of the true flavor of the mezzogiorno, Italy's deep south. Don't miss Bari's castle and the walk around the ridge of the ancient city walls, with views of wide-open sea at every turn. Finish the day with a good fish dinner, and celebrate your last night in Italy by checking out one of the city's multitude of lively bars—Bari boasts one of southern Italy's most hopping bar scenes.

Logistics: This is one of your most straightforward, if not quickest, drives: just take the coastal S16 for 154 km (95 mi) until you hit Bari. They're two-lane highways, though, so don't be surprised if the trip takes two hours or more. If you get tired, beautiful Ostuni (the "città bianca," the white city) is a perfect hilltop pit stop halfway there.

Day 8: Bari/Departure

Bad news: this is your wake-up-and-leave day. Bari's Aeroporto Palese is small but quite serviceable. Exploit its absence of crowds and easy access and use it as your

TIPS

1 Alitalia usually doesn't mark up openjaw trips. However, VolareWeb (⊕ www.volareweb.com) has inexpensive domestic air service, and is now operating Milan (Linate)–Naples and Bari–Milan (Linate) routes. Alpi Eagles (⊕ www.alpieagles.com) also has service along those routes. If you're able to find a deep-discount round-trip fare from your home to Milan plus those two flights on low-cost carriers, you might save some money. (The Malpensa–Linate connection can be done on regularly scheduled buses.)

2 Also look at low-cost carriers that shuttle passengers between London and southern Italy; you can often save the most money of all by combining two such one-way fares with a round-trip discount fare to London; however, beware of inconvenient airport connections in London (Luton, for example).

way out of Italy. Connections through Rome or Milan are more frequent than you might think. Plan on leaving with southern Italy firmly established in your heart as the best way to see the Italy that once was—and be thankful that you were able to see it while it is still like this.

Logistics: Bari hotels offer easy airport transfers; take advantage of them. Return your rental car at the Bari airport; you won't have to arrive at the airport more than an hour or so before your flight.

Naples & Campania

WORD OF MOUTH

"Pompeii was everything I expected and more. I swear I could feel the spirits of the people going about their daily tasks, visiting the bar, the bakery, the spa, whisking down the street, being mindful to stay on the sidewalk and not step in the 'gutter.'"

—artstuff

WELCOME TO
NAPLES & CAMPANIA

TOP REASONS
TO GO

★ **Walking the streets of Naples:** Its energy, chaos, and bursts of beauty make Naples the most operatic of Italian cities.

★ **Exploring Pompeii:** The excavated ruins of Pompeii are a unique and occasionally spooky glimpse into every-day life—and sudden death—in Roman times.

★ **"The Living Room of the World":** Pose oh-so-casually with the beauti-ful people sipping their Camparis on La Piazzetta, the central crossroads of Capri: a stage-set square that always seems ready for a gala performance.

★ **Ravishing Ravello:** High above the Amalfi Coast, two spectacular villas compete for the title of most beautiful spot in southern Italy.

★ **A World Made of Stairs:** Built like a vertical amphite-ater piggybacked with houses, Positano may very well be the best triathalon training ground imagin-able. The town's only job is to look enchanting—and it does that very well.

1 Naples. Italy's third-largest city is densely packed with people, cafés, pizzerias, and an amazing number of Norman and baroque churches.

2 Herculaneum, Vesuvius & Pompeii. Two towns show you how ancient Romans defined the good life—until, one day in AD 79, Mt. Vesuvius buried them in volcanic ash and lava.

3 Capri. The rocky island mixes natural beauty and *dolce vita* glamour.

4 Procida & Ischia. Though they lack Capri's glitz, these two sister islands in the Bay of Naples share a laidback charm.

5 Sorrento & the Amalfi Coast. A trip around Sorrento Peninsula takes you to the resort towns of **Sorrento**, **Positano**, **Ravello**, and **Amalfi**. The road between them is one of Italy's most gorgeous (and demanding) drives. Farther south, **Paestum** contains remarkably well-preserved temples from the days of ancient Greek colonies in Italy.

Sorrento

GETTING ORIENTED

The Golfo di Napoli (Bay of Naples) holds many of Campania's attractions, including Italy's greatest archaeological sites—Pompeii and Herculaneum—and the city of Naples itself. Geological stepping-stones anchored in the bay, the islands of Capri, Ischia, and Procida tip the two points of the bay's watery crescent. Just to the south stands the Sorrentine Peninsula, home to 19th-century Sorrento. Then over the Lattari mountains lies the Amalfi Coast, famed for beauty spots like Positano, Amalfi, and Ravello.

PUGLIA

Mirabella

A16

A16

BASILICATA

attipaglia Eboli

Polla

18

Paestum

Teggiano

Agropoli

A3

stellabate

18

Pompeii

NAPLES & CAMPANIA PLANNER

Testing the Waters

Despite its miles of beautiful coast, Campania's beaches can be disappointing—most are small stretches of coarse sand. That doesn't mean you shouldn't pack your swimsuit, but leave any Caribbean-inspired expectations behind. The area around Positano has the best beach options: Spiaggia Grande (the main beach) is pleasant; a little farther west, Spiaggia di Fornillo gets better; and you can go by boat to the remote Spiaggia di Laurito for a leisurely day of swimming and lunching on seafood. On Ischia, the best sandy beach is at Citara, south of Forio, and on Capri you can take a dip in the waters around the famous Faraglioni rock formation. You may not be won over by the sand, but the water itself is spectacular, with infinite varieties of blue shimmering in the sun, turning transparent in the coves.

Making the Most of Your Time

In Campania, there are three primary travel experiences: Naples, with its restless exuberance; the resorts (Capri, Sorrento, the Amalfi Coast), dedicated to leisure and indulgence; and the archaeological sights (Pompeii, Herculaneum, Paestum), where the ancient world is frozen in time. Each is wonderful in its own way. If you have a week, you can get a good taste of all three, but with less time, you're better off choosing between them rather than stretching yourself thin.

Pompeii is the simplest to plan for: it's a day trip. To get a feel for Naples, you should give it a couple of days at a minimum. The train station makes a harsh first impression, but the city grows on you as you take in the sights and interact with the locals.

That said, many people bypass Naples and head right for the resorts. These places are all about relaxing—you'll miss the point if you're in a rush. Sorrento isn't as spectacular as Positano or Capri, but it's a good base because of its central location.

Finding a Place to Stay

Most parts of Campania have accommodations in all price categories, but they tend to fill up in high season, so reserve well in advance. In summer, hotels on the coast that serve meals almost always require you to take half board.

DINING & LODGING PRICE CATEGORIES (IN EUROS)				
¢	$	$$	$$$	$$$$
Restaurants				
under €15	€15–€25	€25–€35	€35–€45	over €45
Hotels				
under €70	€70–€110	€110–€160	€160–€220	over €220

Restaurant prices are for a first course (primo), second course (secondo), and dessert (dolce). Hotel prices are for two people in a standard double room in high season, including tax and service.

GETTING AROUND

By Train

There are trains every hour between Rome and Naples. Alta Velocità, Eurostar, and Intercity, the fastest types of train service, make the trip in less than two hours. Almost all trains to Naples stop at **Stazione Centrale** (✉ *Piazza Garibaldi* ☎ *892021* ⊕ *www.trenitalia.it*).

The efficient (though rundown) suburban **Circumvesuviana** (☎ *081/7722444* ⊕ *www.vesuviana.it*), which runs from Corso Garibaldi station and stops at Stazione Centrale before continuing to Herculaneum, Pompeii, and Sorrento. Travel time between Naples and Sorrento on the Circumvesuviana line is about 75 minutes.

As far as public transportation goes, the region is divided into travel zones depending on distance from Naples. A Fascia 2 ticket (€1.70 for 120 minutes) takes in Herculaneum; Fascia 3 (€2.30 for 140 minutes) includes Pompeii; and Fascia 5 (€3.20 for 180 minutes) covers trips to Sorrento. If you're traveling from Naples to anywhere else in Campania, there's no need to buy a separate ticket for your subway, tram, or bus ride to the train station. Your train ticket covers the whole journey. Buy the ticket the day before, as some of the ticket types are hard to find.

By Bus

Within Campania there's an extensive network of local buses, although finding information about it can be trying. Buses run by **CTP** (☎ *081/7005111* ⊕ *www.ctp.na.it*) connect Naples with Caserta in one hour, leaving every 20 minutes from Piazza Garibaldi (every 40 minutes on Sunday). **SITA** (☎ *081/5522176* ⊕ *www.sitabus.it*) buses bound for Salerno leave every 30 minutes Monday to Saturday and every two hours on Sunday from its terminal in the port *near the Stazione Marittima*. SITA buses also serve the Amalfi Coast, connecting Sorrento with Salerno. **Curreri** (☎ *081/8015420* ⊕ *www.bus.it/curreri/autolineee.htm*) operates a service (six runs daily) between Sorrento and Aeroporto Capodichino.

By Car

You can get along fine without a car in Campania, and there are plenty of reasons not to have one: traffic in Naples is even worse than in Rome; you can't bring a car to Capri or Ischia (except in winter, when everything's closed); and parking in the towns of the Amalfi Coast is hard to come by and expensive. Italy's main north–south route, the A1 (also known as the Autostrada del Sole), connects Rome with Naples and Campania. In good traffic the drive to Naples takes less than three hours. Autostrada A3, a continuation of the A1, runs south from Naples through Campania and into Calabria. Herculaneum (Ercolano), and Pompeii (Pompei); all have marked exits off the A3. For Vesuvius, take the Ercolano exit. For the Sorrento peninsula and the Amalfi Coast, exit at Castellammare di Stabia. To get to Paestum, take the A3 to the Battipaglia exit and take the road to Capaccio Scalo–Paestum. The roads on the Sorrento peninsula and Amalfi Coast are narrow and twisting, but they have outstanding views.

EATING & DRINKING WELL IN NAPLES & CAMPANIA

Think of Neapolitan food and you conjure up pasta, pizza, and tomatoes. The stereotype barely scratches the surface of what's available in Naples, and much less in the rest of Campania, whose cuisine reflects an enormously diverse landscape.

Campania is known for its enclaves of gastronomy, notable among them the tip of the Sorrento peninsula and the Campi Flegrei, west of Naples. You usually get better value outside Naples, and you may well come across *cucina povera*, a cuisine inspired by Campania's *contadino* roots, where all the ingredients are sourced from a nearby kitchen garden. Expect to see roadside stalls selling stellar local produce, including *annurca* apples (near Benevento), giant lemons (Amalfi Coast), roasted chestnuts (especially near Avellino), and watermelons (the plains around Salerno). Try to get to one of the local *sagre*, village feasts celebrating a *prodotto tipico* (local specialty), which could be anything from snails to wild boar to cherries, and, more commonly, wine.

A TIPPING TIP

Neapolitans are easily recognized in bars elsewhere in Italy by the tip they leave on the counter when ordering. This habit does not necessarily ensure better service in bars in Naples, notorious for their fairly offhand staff, but you do blend in better with the locals. In restaurants, service is usually included unless stated otherwise (in which case 5%—10% is reasonable). In pizzerias, tips are rarely given unless you have splurged on side dishes or sweets, or have had particularly good service.

13

PIZZA

Naples is the undisputed homeland of pizza, and you'll usually encounter it here in two classic forms: *margherita* and *marinara*. Given the size of standard pizzas—they virtually flop off the rim of the plate onto the tabletop—it is legitimate to ask for a *mignon* (kids' portion), or even share, divided on two plates. If pressed for time and stomach space, you'll find plenty of take-away outlets in most town centers selling pizza by the slice, along with the usual range of fried *arancini* (rice balls) and *crocchè di patate* (potato fritters).

COFFEE

Given the same basic ingredients—coffee grounds, water, a machine—what makes *caffè* taste so much better in Naples than elsewhere remains a mystery. If you find the end product too strong, ask to have it with a dash of milk (*caffè macchiato*) or a little diluted (*caffè lungo*).

BUFFALO

Long feted for the melt-in-your-mouth mozzarella cheese made from its milk, pictured at right, the river buffalo—related to the Asian water buffalo—is now the source of other culinary delights. In the province of Caserta look for more mature *nero di bufala* (aged like sheep's cheese), while around Salerno you'll find smoked *caciocavallo* cheese and also

carne di bufala (buffalo meat), which can be braised to perfection.

THE ORAL TRADITION

Locals in Campania like to bypass the restaurant menu and ask directly what the staff recommends. Take this approach and you'll often wind up with a daily special or house specialty that's the best the restaurant has to offer. Though you're unlikely to get multilingual staff outside the larger hotels and main tourist areas, the person you talk to will spare no effort to get the message across.

WINE

Wine in Campania has an ancient pedigree: some say fancifully that Campania's undisputed king of reds, the Aglianico varietal, got its name from the word "Hellenic," and Fiano, the primary white grape, closely resembles the Roman variety Apianus. Horace, the Latin poet, extolled the virtues of drinking wine from Campania. A century later, Pliny the Elder was harsher in his judgment: wine from Pompeii would give you a hangover until noon the next day, and Surrentum (Sorrento) wine tasted of vinegar. In recent decades though, Campania has gained respect for its boutique reds.

Updated by
Mark Walters

A KINETIC GUST OF 3-D garlic-and-basil aromatherapy for the soul, Campania is a destination that no one ever forgets. More travelers visit this region than any other in the south, and it's no wonder. A region of evocative names—Capri, Sorrento, Pompeii, Positano, Amalfi— Campania conjures up visions of cliff-shaded, sapphire-hued coves, sun-dappled waters, and mighty ruins. Home to Vesuvius, the area's unique geology is responsible for Campania's photogenic landscape. A languid coastline stretches out along a deep blue sea, punctuated by rocky islands. Through the ages, the area's temperate climate, warm sea, fertile soil, and natural beauty have attracted Greek colonists, then Roman emperors—who called the region Campania Felix ("the happy land")—and later Saracen raiders and Spanish invaders. The result has been a rich and varied history, reflected in everything from architecture to mythology. The highlights span millennia: the near-intact Roman towns of Pompeii and Herculaneum, the Greek temples in Paestum, the Norman and baroque churches in Naples, the white-dome fisherman's houses of Positano, the dolce vita resorts of Capri. Campania packs them all into one mammoth must-see sandwich.

The region's complex identity is most intensely felt in its major metropolis, Naples. It sprawls around its bay as though attempting to embrace the island of Capri, while behind it Mt. Vesuvius glowers. The most operatic city in Italy, Napoli exasperates both its critics and its defenders. Naples is lush, chaotic, scary, funny, confounding, intoxicating, and very beautiful. Few who visit remain ambivalent. You needn't participate in the mad whirl of the city, however. The best pastime in Campania is simply finding a spot with a stunning view and indulging in *"il dolce far niente"* ("the sweetness of doing nothing").

NAPLES

In the period before the Italian unification of 1860, Naples rivaled Paris as a brilliant and refined cultural capital, the ultimate destination for northern European travelers on their Grand Tour. Although a decade of farsighted city administration and a massive injection of European Union funds have put the city back on course, signs of urban malaise are still evident. Naples is a difficult place for the casual visitor to take a quick liking to: noise and air pollution levels are uncomfortably high, graffiti on urban trains and monuments are unsightly, unemployment protest marches and industrial disputes frequently disrupt public transportation and may even result in the temporary closure of major tourist attractions. Armed with the right attitude—"be prepared for the worst but hope for the best"—you will find that Napoli does not disappoint. Among other things, it's one of Italy's top *città d'arte,* with world-class museums and a staggering number of fine churches. The most important finds from Pompeii and Herculaneum are on display at the Museo Archeologico Nazionale—a cornucopia of sculpture, frescoes, and mosaics—and seeing them will add to the pleasure of trips to the ancient ruins. And Naples has a wonderful location: thanks to the backdrop of Vesuvius and the islands in the bay, it's one of those few

CAMPANIA THROUGH THE AGES

Ancient History. Lying on Mediterranean trade routes plied by several pre-Hellenic civilizations, Campania was settled by the ancient Greeks from approximately 800 BC onward. Here myth and legend blend with historical fact: the town of Herculaneum is said—rather improbably—to have been established by Hercules himself, and Naples in ancient times was called Parthenope, the name attributed to one of the sirens who preyed on hapless sailors in antiquity.

Thanks, to archaeological research, some of the layers of myth have been stripped away to reveal a pattern of occupation and settlement well before Rome became established. Greek civilization flourished for hundreds of years all along this coastline, but there was nothing in the way of centralized government until centuries later when the Roman Republic, uniting all Italy for the first time, absorbed the Greek colonies with little opposition. Generally, the peace of Campania was undisturbed during these centuries of Roman rule.

Foreign Influences. Naples and Campania, with the rest of Italy, decayed with the Roman Empire and collapsed into the abyss of the Middle Ages. Naples itself regained some importance under the rule of the Angevins in the latter part of the 13th century and continued its progress in the 1440s under Aragonese rule. The nobles who served under the Spanish viceroys in the 16th and 17th centuries enjoyed their pleasures, even as Spain milked the area for taxes.

After a short Austrian occupation, Naples became the capital of the Kingdom of the Two Sicilies, which the Bourbon kings established in 1738. Their rule was generally benevolent as far as Campania was concerned, and their support of papal authority in Rome was important in the development of the rest of Italy. Their rule was important artistically, too, contributing to the architecture of the region, and attracting great musicians, artists, and writers drawn by the easy life at court. Finally, Giuseppe Garibaldi launched his famous expedition, and in 1860 Naples was united with the rest of Italy.

Modern Times. Things were relatively tranquil through the years that followed—with visitors thronging to Capri, to Sorrento, to Amalfi, and, of course, to Naples—until World War II. Allied bombings did considerable damage in and around Naples. At the fall of the fascist government, the sorely tried Neapolitans rose up against Nazi occupation troops and in four days of street fighting drove them out of the city. A monument was raised to the *scugnizzo* (the typical Neapolitan street urchin), celebrating the youngsters who participated in the battle. The war ended. Artists, tourists, writers, and other lovers of beauty returned to the Campania region.

As the years have gone by, some parts gained increased attention from knowing visitors, while others lost the cachet they once had. Though years of misgovernment have left their mark, the tide appears to be turning: the region's cultural and natural heritage is finally being revalued as local authorities and inhabitants recognize the importance the area's largest industry—tourism.

13

cities in the world that is instantly recognizable.

In Naples you need a good sense of humor and a firm grip on your pocketbook and camera. Expect to do a lot of walking (take care crossing the chaotic streets); buses are crowded, and taxis often get held up in traffic. Use the funiculars or the new metro Line 1 to get up and down the hills, and take the quick—but erratic—metro Line 2 (the city's older subway system) when crossing the city between Piazza Garibaldi and Pozzuoli. For Pompeii, Herculaneum, and Sorrento, take the Circumvesuviana train line, while the Cumana line from Piazza Montesanto is best for the port of Pozzuoli, Baia, and Cumae.

> **WORD OF MOUTH**
>
> "We spent three days in Naples and had a wonderful time. We visited the Archaeology Museum, the Palace, and wandered through Spaccanapoli and other neighborhoods. Also hired a cab to take us up to Lago d'Averno. No bad experiences to report. Very glad I got over my Fear-of-Naples syndrome." –Pausanias

The *artecard* (⊕*www.artecard.it*) is a great way to save on public transportation and museums. A three-day card (€25) includes free admission to two museums or archaeological sites, half-price admission to other attractions, and free public transportation—including return trips on fast craft across the bay. A seven-day card (€28) gives free admission to museums and archaeological sites, but doesn't include a travel pass. You can purchase these cards at the airport or at the train station at Piazza Garibaldi. The Naples and Campi Flegrei card (€13) gives access to two museums, half-price admission to other museums, and transport throughout the area. It's available at the airport, train station, tourist information offices, and many hotels.

ROYAL NAPLES

Naples hasn't been a capital for 150 years, but it still prides itself on its royal heritage. Most of the modern center of the town owes its look and feel to various members of the Bourbon family, who built their palaces and castles in this area. Allow plenty of time for museum visits, especially the Palazzo Reale. The views of the bay from the Castel dell'Ovo are good at any time, but are especially fine at sunset.

THE MAIN ATTRACTIONS

❹ **Castel dell'Ovo.** Dangling over the Porto Santa Lucia on a thin promontory, this 12th-century fortress built over the ruins of an ancient Roman villa overlooks the whole harbor—proof, if you need it, that the Romans knew a premium location when they saw one. For the same reason, some of the city's top hotels share the site. It's a peaceful spot for strolling and enjoying the views. ⊠*Santa Lucia waterfront, Via Partenope, Santa Lucia* ☎*081/2400055* ☞*Free* ⊙*Oct.–May, Mon.–Sat. 8–5, Sun. 8:30–1:30; June–Sept., Mon.–Sat. 8–7, Sun. 8–1:30.*

❶ **Castel Nuovo.** Also known as the Maschio Angioino, this massive fortress was built by the Angevins (related to the French monarchy) in the 13th century and completely rebuilt by the Aragonese rulers (descendants of an illegitimate branch of Spain's ruling line) who succeeded them. The decorative marble triumphal arch that forms the entrance was erected during the Renaissance in honor of King Alfonso V of Aragon (1396–1458), and its rich bas-reliefs are credited to Francesco Laurana (circa 1430–1502). Set incongruously into the castle's heavy stone walls, the arch is one of the finest of its kind. Within the castle is the **Museo Civico,** comprising mainly local artwork from the 15th to 19th centuries. It's hard to avoid the impression that these last were rejects from the much finer collection at the Museo di Capodimonte. You can also visit the **Palatine Chapel** and the octagonal **Sala dei Baroni,** where Ferrante I disposed of a group of rebellious barons in 1485 by inviting them to a mock wedding party and then pouring boiling oil on their heads from the ceiling. In the left corner of the courtyard is the **Sala dell'Armeria,** the Armory, where part of the flooring has been conveniently glassed over to reveal the remains of a Roman villa and a medieval necropolis. ⊠ *Piazza Municipio* ☎ *081/7952003* 🎫 *€5* 🕙 *Mon.–Sat. 9–6.*

③ Palazzo Reale. Dominating Piazza del Plebiscito, the huge palace—best described as overblown imperial—dates from the early 1600s. It was renovated and redecorated by successive rulers, including Napoléon's sister Caroline and her ill-fated husband, Joachim Murat (1767–1815), who reigned briefly in Naples after the French emperor sent the Bourbons packing and before they returned to reclaim their kingdom. Don't miss seeing the **royal apartments,** sumptuously furnished and full of precious paintings, tapestries, porcelains, and other objets d'art. The monumental marble staircase gives you an idea of the scale on which Neapolitan rulers lived. ⊠ *Piazza del Plebiscito* ☎ *081/400547* 🎫 *€4* 🕙 *Thurs.–Tues. 9–7.*

NEED A BREAK? Kitty-corner to the Palazzo Reale is the most famous coffeehouse in town, the Caffè Gambrinus (⊠ *Piazza Trieste e Trento, near Piazza Plebiscito* ☎ *081/417582*). Founded in 1850, this 19th-century jewel functioned as a brilliant intellectual salon in its heyday but has fallen into a Sunset Boulevard–type existence, relying on past glamour and offering often-indifferent service. But the inside rooms, with amazing mirrored walls and gilded ceilings, makes this an essential stop for any visitor to the city.

Piazza del Plebiscito. The vast square next to the Palazzo Reale was laid out by order of Murat, whose architect was clearly inspired by the colonnades of St. Peter's in Rome. The large church of **San Francesco di Paola** in the middle of the colonnades was added as an offering of thanks for the Bourbon restoration by Ferdinand I, whose titles reflect the somewhat garbled history of the Kingdom of the Two Sicilies, which was made up of Naples (which included most of the southern Italian mainland) and Sicily. They were united in the Middle Ages, then separated, then unofficially reunited under Spanish domination during the 16th and 17th centuries. In 1816, with Napoléon out of the way on St. Helena, Ferdinand IV (1751–1825) of Naples, who also happened to be Ferdinand III of Sicily, officially merged the two kingdoms, proclaiming himself Ferdinand I of the Kingdom of Two Sicilies. His

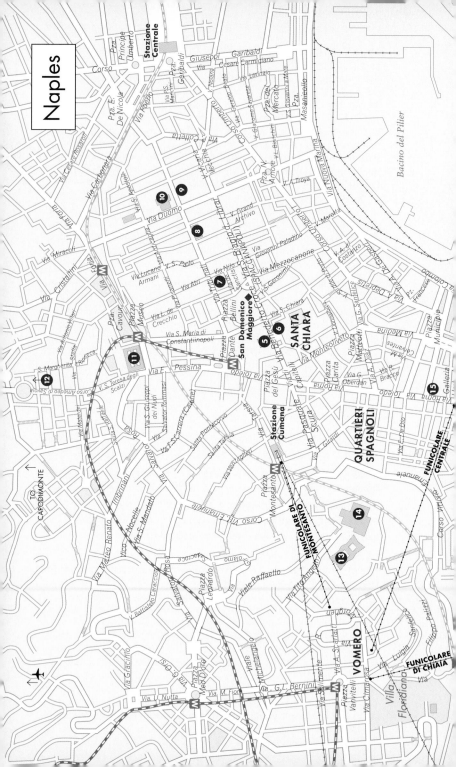

Golfo di Napoli

CHIAIA

SANTA
LUCIA

Piazza
del
Plebiscito

Bacino Angioino

Beverello

Porto
S. Lucia

KEY

Funicular
M Metro stop

0   300 yards
0   300 meters

13

reactionary and repressive rule earned him a few more-colorful titles among his rebellious subjects.

Via Toledo. Sooner or later you'll wind up at one of the busiest commercial arteries, also known as Via Roma, which has thankfully been closed to through traffic—at least along the stretch leading from the Palazzo Reale. Don't avoid dipping into this parade of shops and coffee bars where plump pastries are temptingly arranged.

★ ⓯ **Palazzo Zevallos.** A radical face-lift in 2007 revealed this palazzo in all its 17th-century opulence. The tone is set by Cosimo Fanzago's portal (1637–39) leading into the galleried halls of the Banca Intesa San Paolo, one of Italy's major high-street banks. An added treat is the small art gallery on the second floor housing Caravaggio's last painting, *Il Martirio di Sant'Orsola, and some landscapes by Gaspar Van Wittel and* Anton Sminck *Pitloo. A good audio guide covers the beautifully restored rooms and the artwork hanging in them.* ⊠ *Via Toledo 185, Piazza Plebiscito* ☎081/400547 ⬚€3 ⊗ *Mon.–Sat. 10–6.*

❷ **Teatro San Carlo.** This large theater was built in 1737, 40 years earlier than Milan's La Scala—though it was destroyed by fire and had to be rebuilt in 1816. You can visit the impressive interior, decorated in the white-and-gilt stucco of the neoclassical era, as part of a prearranged tour. ⊠ *Via San Carlo between Piazza Municipio and Piazza Plebiscito, Piazza Plebiscito* ☎081/7972331 or 081/7972412 ⊕*www.teatrosancarlo.it* ⬚€5 ⊗ *Daily 9–6.*

NEED A BREAK? **Across from the Teatro San Carlo towers the imposing entrance to the glass-roof neoclassical Galleria Umberto (** ⊠ *Via San Carlo, near Piazza Plebiscito***), a late-19th-century shopping arcade where you can sit at one of several cafés and watch the vivacious Neapolitans as they go about their business. Some people are put off by the throng of street vendors, however.**

VOMERO

Heart-stopping views of the Bay of Naples are framed by this gentrified neighborhood on a hill served by the Montesanto, Centrale, and Chiaia funiculars. The upper stations for all three are an easy walk from Piazza Vanvitelli, a good starting point for exploring this thriving district with no shortage of smart bars and trattorias.

THE MAIN ATTRACTIONS

⓭ **Castel Sant'Elmo.** Perched on the Vomero, this castle was built by the Angevins in the 14th century to dominate the port and the old city and remodeled by the Spanish in 1537. The stout fortifications are still in use today by the military, and occasionally there are performances, exhibitions, and fairs. You get in free if you have a ticket to the adjoining Certosa di San Martino. ⊠*Largo San Martino, Vomero* ☎*081/5784030* ⬚€3 ⊗*Thurs.–Tues. 8:30–7:30.*

★ ⓮ **Certosa di San Martino.** A Carthusian monastery restored in the 17th century in exuberant Neapolitan baroque style, this structure has now been

GETTING AROUND NAPLES

PUBLIC TRANSIT

Naples's rather old Metropolitana (subway system), also called Linea 2, provides fairly frequent service and can be the fastest way to get across the traffic-clogged city.

The other urban subway system, Metropolitana Collinare (or Linea 1), links the hill area of the Vomero and beyond with the National Archaeological Museum and Piazza Dante. Trains on both lines run from 5 AM until 10:30 PM.

For standard public transportation, including the subways, buses, and funiculars, a Giranapoli pass costs €1 and is valid for 90 minutes as far as Pozzuoli to the west and Portici to the east; €3 buys a *biglietto giornaliero*, good for the whole day.

Bus service has become viable over the last few years, especially with the introduction of larger buses on the regular R1, R2, and R3 routes. Electronic signs display wait times at many stops.

PARKING

If you come to Naples by car, find a garage, agree on the cost, and leave it there for the duration of your stay. (If you park on the street, you run the risk of theft.) **Garage Cava** (✉ *Via Mergellina 6 near Mergellina* ☎ *081/660023*), **Grilli** (✉ *Via Ferraris 40 near Stazione Centrale* ☎ *081/264344*), and **Turistico** (✉ *Via de Gasperi 14 near the port* ☎ *081/5525442*) are all centrally located, safe, and open 24 hours a day.

TAXIS

When taking a taxi in Naples, make sure that the meter is switched on at the start of your trip. Trips around the city are unlikely to cost less than €10 or more than €20. Set fares for various destinations within the city should be displayed in the taxi, as should extra charges for things like baggage and night service. For trips outside the city, negotiate your fare before getting in. Watch out for overcharging at three locations: the airport, the railway station, and the hydrofoil marina. And in peak summer weeks, don't forget that most cabs in Naples have no air-conditioning—which the city's buses and metro do have—and you can literally fry if caught in one during a half-hour traffic jam.

TOURS

Handily close to the port is the terminal for double-decker buses belonging to **City Sightseeing** (✉ *Piazza Castello* ⊕ *www.napoli. city-sightseeing.it*). For €20 you can take two or three different excursions, giving you reasonable coverage of the downtown sights and outlying attractions like the Museo di Capodimonte.

For in-depth tours of Naples, the **Comune di Napoli** (✉ *Piazza Municipio, Naples* ☎ *081/5422090* ⊕ *www.comune.napoli.it*) occasionally offers English-language guided tours. These tours are a great way to see monuments that are otherwise off limits. A welcome center in the old town, the **Centro di Accoglienza Turistica Museo Aperto Napoli** (✉ *Via Pietro Colletta 89* ☎ *081/5636062* ⊕ *www.museo-apertonapoli.com*), offers €6 audio guides you can listen to as you wander around. **Tourcar** (✉ *Piazza Matteotti 1* ☎ *081/5520429* ⊕ *www. tourcar.it*) offers tailor-made tours of the attractions in and around Naples.

13

transformed into a diverse museum. The gorgeous Chiostro Grande (great cloister) and the panoramic garden terraces—strangely quiet, with a view of the city sprawling below—are among the most impressive spots in the city. Popular exhibits include the *presepi* (Christmas crèches) and an anonymous painting that depicts the Naples waterfront in the 15th century and the return of the Aragonese fleet from the Battle of Ischia. Take the funicular from Piazza Montesanto to Vomero. ⊠ *Museo Nazionale di San Martino, Vomero* ☎ *081/5585942* ⚏ *€6 includes admission to Castel Sant'Elmo* ☉ *Thurs.–Tues. 8:30–7:30.*

SPACCANAPOLI & CAPODIMONTE

Nowhere embodies the spirit of Naples better than the arrow-straight street informally known as Spaccanapoli (literally, "split Naples"). Gazing down it, you can sense where the name comes from—the street resembles a trench, running from the central station (near where the old city walls stood) up to the San Martino hill, retracing one of the main arteries of the ancient Greek, and later Roman, settlements. Along its western section, Spaccanapoli is officially named Via Benedetto Croce, in honor of the illustrious philosopher born here in 1866, in the building at No. 12. As it runs its course, the street name changes to Via San Biagio dei Librai and then Via San Gregorio Armeno. No matter the name, it's a place of vibrant street culture.

Capodimonte, to the north, was open countryside until the Bourbon kings built a hunting lodge there, after which it rapidly became part of the city proper. Between the two neighborhoods is the Museo Archeologico, Naples's finest museum. It's best to visit shortly after lunchtime, when the crowds have thinned out. Two hours will be just enough to get your bearings and cover the more-important collections. The museum in Capodimonte—unlike many of the churches and the archaeological museum—is well lighted and can be viewed in fading daylight, so it's best left until last.

THE MAIN ATTRACTIONS

❼ Cappella Sansevero. Off Spaccanapoli, the Cappella di Santa Maria della Pietà dei Sangro, better known as the Cappella Sansevero, holds the tombs of the noble Sangro di San Severo family. Much of it was designed in the 18th century by Giuseppe Sammartino, including the centerpiece, a striking *Veiled Christ* carved from a single block of alabaster. If you can stomach it, take a peek in the crypt, where some of the anatomical experiments conducted by Prince Raimondo, a scion of the family and noted 18th-century alchemist, are gruesomely displayed. ⊠ *Via de Sanctis 19, Spaccanapoli* ☎ *081/5518470* ⊕ *www.museosansevero.it* ⚏ *€6* ☉ *Mon. and Wed.–Sat. 10–6, Sun. 10–1:30.*

❿ Duomo. Though the Duomo was established in the 1200s, the building you see was erected a century later and has since undergone radical changes, especially during the baroque period. Inside the cathedral, 110 ancient columns salvaged from pagan buildings are set into the piers that support the 350-year-old wooden ceiling. Off the left aisle you step down into the fourth-century church of **Santa Restituta,** which was incorporated into the cathedral; though Santa Restituta was redecorated in the late 1600s in the prevalent baroque style, a few very old mosaics remain in the **Battistero** (Baptistery). The chapel also gives access to an archaeological zone, a series of Paleo-Christian rooms dating from the Roman era.

> **WORD OF MOUTH**
>
> "The Naples Archaeological Museum has an incredible collection of real treasures, but the displays keep changing, and they close wings without notice or seeming reason." –mowmow

13

On the right aisle of the cathedral, in the **Cappella di San Gennaro,** are multicolor marbles and frescoes honoring St. Januarius, miracle-working patron saint of Naples, whose altar and relics are encased in silver. Three times a year—on September 19 (his feast day); on the Saturday preceding the first Sunday in May, which commemorates the transference of his relics to Naples; and on December 16—his dried blood, contained in two sealed vials, is believed to liquefy during rites in his honor. On these days large numbers of devout Neapolitans offer up prayers in his memory. The **Museo del Tesoro di San Gennaro** houses a rich collection of treasures associated with the saint. Paintings by Solimena and Luca Giordano hang alongside statues, busts, candelabras, and tabernacles in gold, silver, and marble by Cosimo Fanzago and other 18th-century baroque masters. An audio tour is included in the ticket price. ⊠ *Via Duomo 147, Spaccanapoli* ☎ *081/449097 Duomo, 081/294764 museum* ⊕ *www.museosangennaro.com* ✆ *€7* ⊙ *Daily 8:30–12:30 and 4:30–7.*

⑤ Gesù Nuovo. The oddly faceted stone facade of the church was designed as part of a palace dating from between 1584 and 1601, but plans were changed as construction progressed, and it became the front of an elaborately decorated baroque church. Be sure not to miss the votive chapel dedicated to San Ciro (St. Cyrus) in the far left corner of the church. Here hundreds of tiny silver ex-voto images have been hung on the walls to give thanks to the saint for his assistance in medical matters. ⊠ *Piazza Gesù Nuovo, Spaccanapoli* ☎ *081/5518613* ⊙ *Mon.–Sat. 7–12:45 and 4:15–7:30, Sun. 7–1:30.*

⑪ ★ Museo Archeologico Nazionale. The National Archaeological Museum's huge red building, a cavalry barracks in the 16th century, is undergoing a seemingly permanent restoration program, which means that at any given time, rooms are likely to be closed to the public with little prior warning. The museum holds one of the world's great collections of Greek and Roman antiquities, including such extraordinary sculptures as the *Hercules Farnese,* an exquisite Aphrodite attributed to the fourth-century BC Greek sculptor Praxiteles, and an equestrian statue of Roman emperor Nerva. Vividly colored mosaics and countless artistic and household objects from Pompeii and Herculaneum provide insight into the life and art of ancient Rome. The Gabinetto Segreto and its collection of occasionally shocking erotic art is now permanently open, after being kept under lock and key for many years. Invest in an up-to-date printed museum guide or audio guide, because exhibits tend to be poorly labeled. ⊠ *Piazza Museo 19, Spaccanapoli* ☎ *081/440166*

⊕*www.archeona.arti.beniculturali.it* ✉*€6.50, €10 for special exhibits* ⊙*Wed.–Mon. 9–7.*

NEED A BREAK?

Timpani e Tempura (✉ *Vico della Quercia 17, Spaccanapoli* ☎ *081/5512280*) is a tiny shrine to local culinary culture. There are no tables; instead, you perch yourself at the counter, but it's worth squeezing in for the *timballi di maccheroni* (baked pasta cakes) and the unique *mangiamaccheroni* (spaghetti in broth with *caciocavallo* cheese, butter, basil, and pepper). Wonderful wines by the glass make this a place for a quick, delicious lunch. You can also buy cheese and salami to take home with you.

★ ⑫ **Museo di Capodimonte.** The grandiose 18th-century neoclassical Bourbon royal palace houses an impressive collection of fine and decorative art. Capodimonte's greatest treasure is the excellent collection of paintings well displayed in the **Galleria Nazionale,** on the palace's first and second floors. Besides the art collection, part of the **royal apartments** still has a complement of beautiful antique furniture, most of it on the splashy scale so dear to the Bourbons, and a staggering collection of porcelain and majolica from the various royal residences. The walls of the apartments are hung with numerous portraits, providing a close-up of the unmistakable Bourbon features, a challenge to any court painter. Most rooms have fairly comprehensive information cards in English, whereas the audio guide is overly selective and somewhat quirky. The main galleries on the first floor are devoted to work from the 13th to 18th centuries, including many pieces by Dutch and Spanish masters. On the second floor look out for stunning paintings by Simone Martini (circa 1284–1344), Titian (1488/90–1576), and Caravaggio (1573–1610). The palace is situated in the vast Bosco di Capodimonte (Capodimonte Park), which served as the royal hunting preserve and later as the site of the Capodimonte porcelain works. ✉ *Via Miano 2, Porta Piccola, Via Capodimonte, Capodimonte* ☎ *848/800288* ✉ *€7.50, €6.50 after 2* PM ⊙ *Daily 8:30–7:30; ticket office closes at 6:30.*

★ ⑨ **Pio Monte della Misericordia.** One of the defining landmarks of Spaccanapoli, this octagonal church was built around the corner from the Duomo for a charitable institution founded in 1601 by seven noblemen. The institution's aim was to carry out acts of Christian charity: feeding the hungry, clothing the poor, nursing the sick, sheltering pilgrims, visiting prisoners, ransoming Christian slaves, and burying the indigent dead—acts immortalized in the history of art by the famous altarpiece painted by Caravaggio depicting the *Sette Opere della Misericordia* (*Seven Acts of Mercy*). In this haunting work the artist has brought the Virgin, borne atop the shoulders of two angels, down into the streets of Spaccanapoli (scholars have suggested a couple of plausible locations) populated by figures in whose spontaneous and passionate movements the people could see themselves. The original church was considered too small and destroyed in 1655 to make way for a new church, designed by Antonio Picchiatti and built between 1658 and 1678. Pride of place is given to the great Caravaggio above the altar, but there are other important baroque-era paintings on view here; some hang in the church while others are in the adjoining *pinacoteca* (picture gallery). ⊠ *Via Tribunali 253, Spaccanapoli* ☎081/446944 ⊕*www. piomontedellamisericordia.it* 🎟€5 ⊘*Thurs.–Tues. 9–2:30.*

⑥ Santa Chiara. This monastery church is a Neapolitan landmark and the subject of a famous old song. It was built in the 1300s in Provençal Gothic style, and it's best known for the quiet charm of its cloister garden, with columns and benches sheathed in 18th-century ceramic tiles painted with delicate floral motifs and vivid landscapes. An adjoining museum traces the history of the convent; the entrance is off the courtyard at the left of the church. ⊠*Piazza Gesù Nuovo, Spaccanapoli* ☎081/5526209 ⊕*www.santachiara.info* 🎟*Museum and cloister €4* ⊘*Church: daily 7–noon and 4:30–6:30. Museum and cloister: Mon.– Sat. 9:30–7, Sun. 9:30–1.*

NEED A BREAK? While you're exploring the old part of town, take a break at what the Neapolitans call "the best pastry shop in Italy"—Scaturchio (⊠*Piazza San Domenico Maggiore 19, Spaccanapoli* ☎081/5516944). The café was founded in 1918 by two brothers, one of whom, Francesco, invented the cakes called *ministeriali* to attract Anna Fouché, a famous actress of the time. You can still buy these cakes today, along with other Neapolitan baked goods such as *babà, rafioli,* and *pastiera,* which you can eat here with a coffee or have gift-wrapped.

ALSO WORTH SEEING

Quadreria dei Girolamini. Off an improbably quiet cloister enclosing a prolific forest of citrus, fig, and loquat trees, the Girolamini art museum is attached to the restored Girolamini church. Its intimate, high-quality collection of 16th- and 17th-century paintings is one of the city's best-kept secrets, well worth a half-hour visit. ⊠*Via Duomo 142, Spaccanapoli* ☎081/294444 ⊕*www.girolamini.it* 🎟*Free* ⊘*Daily 9–12:50.*

⑧ San Lorenzo Maggiore. It's unusual to find French Gothic style in Naples, but it has survived to great effect in this church, which was built in the Middle Ages and decorated with 14th-century frescoes. Outside the 17th-century cloister is the entrance to **excavations** revealing what was once part of the Roman forum, and before that the Greek agora. You can walk among the streets, shops, and workshops of the ancient city and see a model of how the Greek Neapolis might have looked. Next door to the church is the four-story **museum,** housed in a 16th-century palazzo, displaying a wealth of archaeological finds and religious art (panels regrettably are only in Italian). ⊠*Via Tribunali 316, Spaccanapoli* ☎081/2110860 ⊕*www.sanlorenzomaggiorenapoli.it* 🎟€5 ⊘*Mon.–Sat. 9–5:30, Sun. 9:30–1:30.*

WHERE TO EAT

$$$$ ✕ **Da Dora.** Despite its location up an unpromising-looking *vicolo* (alley) off the Riviera di Chiaia, this small restaurant has achieved cult status for its seafood platters. It's remarkable what owner-chef Giovanni can produce in his tiny kitchen. Start with the pasta dish linguine *alla Dora,* laden with local seafood and fresh tomatoes, and per-

Continued on page 768

PIZZA: IT WASN'T LIKE THIS BACK HOME...

Locally grown San Marzano tomatoes are a must.

The best pizza should come out with cheese bubbling and be ever-so-slightly charred around its edges.

Only buffalo-milk mozzarella or *fior di latte* cheese should be used.

The dough has to use the right kind of durum wheat flour and be left to rise for at least six hours.

OTHER FAVORITES ARE . . .

■ **CAPRICCIOSA** (the "capricious"), made with whatever the chef has on hand.

■ **SICILIANA** with mozzarella and eggplant.

■ **DIAVOLA** with spicy salami.

■ **QUATTRO STAGIONE** ("four seasons"), made with produce from each one.

■ **SALSICCIA E FRIARIELLI** with sausage and a broccoli-like vegetable.

Be prepared: ranging from the size of a 12-inch record to that of a Hummer wheel, Neapolitan pizza is pretty different from anything you might find elsewhere in Italy—or anything calling itself "pizza" served up around the world these days. Purists insist on the marinara, a simple base with a topping of tomatoes marinated in garlic and oregano.

A PIZZA FIT FOR A QUEEN

Legend has it that during the patriotic fervor following Italian unification in the late 19th century, a Neapolitan chef decided to celebrate the arrival in the city of the new Italian queen Margherita by designing a pizza in her—and the country's—honor. He took red tomatoes, white mozzarella cheese, and a few leaves of fresh green basil—reflecting the three colors of the Italian flag—and hey ho! gave birth to the modern pizza industry.

Margherita of Savoy

ONLY THE BEST

An association of Neapolitan pizza chefs have recently standardized the ingredients and methods that have to be used to make pizza certified doc (denominazione d'origine controllata) or stg (specialità tradizionale garantita). See the illustration on the opposite page to find out what makes the cut.

Buffalo-milk mozzarella

FIRED UP!

The Neapolitan pizza must be made in a traditional wood-burning oven. Chunks of beech or maple are stacked up against the sides of the huge, tiled ovens, then shoved onto the slate base of the oven where they burn quickly at high temperatures. If you visit Pompeii, you will see how similar the old Roman bread-baking ovens are to the modern pizza oven. The pizzaiolo (pizza chef) then uses a long wooden shovel to put the pizza into the oven where it cooks quickly.

A pizzaiolo at work

PIZZERIE

There are hundreds of restaurants that specialize in pizza in Naples, and the best of these make pizza and nothing else. As befits the original fast food, pizzerie tend to be simple, fairly basic places, with limited menu choices, and quick, occasionally brusque service: the less complicated your order, the happier the waiters.

Typical pizzeria in Naples

THE REAL THING

Naples takes its contribution to world cuisine seriously. The Associazione Verace Pizza Napoletana (www.pizzanapoletana. org) was founded in 1984 in order to share expertise, maintain quality levels, and provide courses for aspirant pizza chefs and pizza lovers. They also organize the annual Pizzafest—three days in September, dedicated to the consumption of pizza, when maestri from all over the region get together and cook off.

Simple, fresh toppings

haps follow up with grilled *pezzogna* (blue-spotted bream). Like many restaurants on the seafront, Da Dora has its own guitarist, who is often robustly accompanied by the kitchen staff. ☒ *Via Fernando Palasciano 30, Mergellina* ☎ *081/680519* ☖ *Reservations essential* ▤ *AE, DC, MC, V* ☺ *Closed Sun., 2 wks in Dec., and 2 wks in mid-Aug.*

★ **$$$–$$$$** ✕ **Coco Loco.** This place has taken the Naples dining scene by storm, thanks to the innovative cuisine of master chef Diego Nuzzo, a stylish ambience, and a quiet location off Via Filangieri, a 10-minute walk from the Palazzo Reale. If possible, take a table in the more-spacious outdoor section in the square, and then be pampered with subtle dishes like *insalata di aragosta e gamberi alla catalana* (lobster and prawn salad garnished with citrus). ☒ *Piazzetta Rodinò 31, Chiaia* ☎ *081/415482* ▤ *AE, DC, MC, V* ☺ *Closed Sun. and 3 wks in Aug. No lunch July–Sept.*

★ **$$$–$$$$** ✕ **La Stanza del Gusto.** The name means "Room of Taste," and this restaurant lives up to the billing. A minute's walk from some of the city's busiest streets, up a flight of stairs opposite the Teatro Sannazzaro on Via Chiaia, it feels removed from the hectic world outside. Chef Mario Avallone mixes traditional, but often nearly forgotten, southern Italian recipes with modern trends—hence the presence of the *tempura di verdura* (Japanese-style fried vegetables) alongside the *bomba savoia* (a savory cake of rice and potatoes). Save room for the delicious sweets. ☒ *Vicoletto Sant'Arpino 21, Piazza Plebiscito* ☎ *081/401578* ☖ *Reservations essential* ▤ *AE, DC, MC, V* ☺ *Closed Sun. and Mon., and Aug. Lunch by appointment only.*

Fodor's Choice ✕ **Palazzo Petrucci.** Nestled in a 17th-century mansion facing *Piazza*
★ *San Domenico Maggiore*, Palazzo Petrucci doesn't lack for dramatic
$$$ dining options. Choose between tables under the vaulted ceiling of the former stables, in the the gallery where a glass partition lets you keep an eye on the kitchen, or in the cozy room overlooking the piazza. Fortify yourself with a complimentary glass of prosecco before making the the agonizing choice between the à la carte offerings and the *menu degustazione* (€40). A popular starter is *lasagnette baccalà con scarole e pinoli tostati* (layered cod with escarole and roasted pine nuts). The *paccheri all'impiedi* (tube-shaped pasta served standing up) in a rich ricotta and meat sauce is an interesting twist on an old regional favorite. ☒ *Piazza San Domenico Maggiore 4, Spaccanapoli* ☎ *081/5524068* ☖ *Reservations essential* ▤ *AE, DC, MC, V* ☺ *Closed most of Aug. No dinner Sun., no lunch Mon.*

$$–$$$ ✕ **La Bersagliera.** You'll inevitably be drawn to eating at the Santa Lucia waterfront, in the shadow of the looming medieval Castel dell'Ovo. This spot is a little touristy but fun, with an irresistible combination of spaghetti and mandolins. The menu suggests uncomplicated, time-worn classics, such as spaghetti *alla pescatora* (with seafood sauce) and tagliatelle *alla bersagliera* (handmade pasta with cherry tomatoes, tiny octopuses, and clams). ☒ *Borgo Marinaro 10, Santa Lucia* ☎ *081/7646016* ▤ *AE, DC, MC, V* ☺ *Closed Tues.*

$$ ✕ **Umberto.** Run by the Di Porzio family since 1916, Umberto is one of the city's classic restaurants. It combines the classiness of the Chiaia neighborhood and the friendliness of other parts of the city. Try the

CLOSE UP

Folk Songs à la Carte

If you want to hear *canzoni napo-letane*—the fabled Neapolitan folk songs—performed live, you can try to catch the city's top troupes, such as the Cantori di Posillipo and I Virtuosi di San Martino, in performances at venues like the Teatro Trianon. But an easier alternative is to head for one of the city's more-traditional restaurants, such as La Bersagliera or Mimì alla Ferrovia, where most every night you can expect your meal to be interrupted by a *posteggiatore*. These singers aren't employed by the restaurants, but they're encouraged to come in, swan around the tables with a battered old guitar, and belt out classics such as "Santa Lucia," "O' Surdato Innamurate," "Torna a Surriento," and, inevitably, "Funiculi Funiculà."

These songs are the most famous of a vast repertoire that found international fame with the mass exodus of

southern Italians to the United States in the early 20th century. "Funiculi Funiculà" was written by Peppino Turco and Luigi Denza in 1880 to herald the new funicular railway up Vesuvius. "O Sole Mio," by Giovanni Capurro and Eduardo di Capua, has often been mistakenly taken for the Italian national anthem. "Torna a Surriento" was composed by Ernesto di Curtis in 1903 to help remind the current Italian prime minister how wonderful he thought Sorrento was (and how many government subsidies he had promised the township).

The singers are more than happy to do requests, even inserting the name of your *innamorato* or *innamorata* into the song. When they've finished they'll stand discreetly by your table. Give them a few euros and you'll have friends for life (or at least for the night).

13

---

tubettini 'do tre dita ("three-finger" pasta with a mixture of seafood), which bears the nickname of the original Umberto. Owner Massimo and sister Lorella (Umberto's grandchildren) are both wine experts and oversee a fantastic cellar. ⊠ *Via Alabardieri 30–31, Chiaia* ☎ *081/418555* ▭ *AE, DC, MC, V* ⊘ *Closed Mon. and 3 wks in Aug.*

$$ ✕ **Vadinchenia.** Though it identifies itself as a cultural and gastronomic association, Vadinchenia has all the trimmings of a high-class restaurant. You will be steered through an innovative menu against a backdrop of refreshingly minimalist decor. Adventurous palates will enjoy such bold combinations as *paccheri alle alici e pecorino* (pasta with sardines and sheep's-milk cheese), and meat eaters will delight in the *brasato di carne al vino rosso* (braised beef in red wine). ⊠ *Via Pontano 21, Chiaia* ☎ *081/660265* ⚲ *Reservations essential* ▭ *AE, DC, MC, V* ⊘ *Closed Sun. and Aug. No lunch.*

★ $ ✕ **L'Ebbrezza di Noè.** A small bar leads into a larger dining area decorated in the style of a very elegant farmhouse. Owner Luca has an enthusiasm for what he does that is quite moving—as you sip a recommended wine you can sense that he hopes you like it as much as he does. The attention paid to the quality of the wine carries over to the food—here you can taste delicate *carpaccio di chianina* (thinly sliced Tuscan steak), rare cheeses such as the Sicilian *ragusano di razza modicana* and the local *caciocavallo podolico*, and a daily selection of hot dishes. ⊠ *Vico Vetriera a Chiaia 8b/9, Chiaia* ☎ *081/400104* ⊟ *AE, DC, MC, V* ⊘ *Closed Mon. No lunch.*

$ ✕ **Osteria da Carmela.** Conveniently close to the archaeological museum, yet surprisingly off the tourist beat, this small eatery is patronized by *professori* from the nearby Academy of Fine Arts and theatergoers from the Teatro Bellini next door. A specialty here is the blend of seafood with vegetables—try the *tubettoni con cozze e zucchini* (tube-shaped pasta with mussels and zucchini) or a *risotto mare e monti (*garnished with prawns and mushrooms). The service is both swift and obliging. ⊠ *Via Conte di Ruvo 11–12, Spaccanapoli* ☎ *081/5499738* ⊟ *AE, DC, MC, V* ⊘ *Closed Sun.*

$ ✕ **Vecchia Cantina.** The location is on a rather dark side street in the tattier section of the Spaccanapoli, but this place is well worth seeking out for its combination of old-style Neapolitan hospitality, high-quality food and wine, and excellent prices. It's a family affair, with Gianni out front and his mother, Nunzia, and wife, Maria, busy in the kitchen—much like in a typical Neapolitan household. The decorations are an accumulation of kitsch, and everyone who comes here seems to know everyone else. The pasta *e ceci* (with chickpeas) shouldn't be missed, and neither should the *baccalà fritto* (fried salt cod). The wine list includes selections from all over Italy. ⊠ *Via San Nicola alla Carità 13–14, Spaccanapoli* ☎ *081/5520226* ⌑ *Reservations essential* ⊟ *AE, DC, MC, V* ⊘ *Closed Sun. June–Aug. and 2 wks in Aug. No dinner Tues. and Sun.*

¢   ✕ **Da Michele.** You have to love a place that has, for more than 130
FodorśChoice   years, offered only two types of pizza—marinara (with tomato, garlic,
★   and oregano) and *margherita* (with tomato, mozzarella, and basil)—and a small selection of drinks, and still manages to attract long lines. The prices have something to do with it, but the pizza itself suffers no rivals, and even those waiting in line are good-humored; the boisterous, joyous atmosphere wafts out with the smell of yeast and wood smoke onto the street. It's near the train station at Piazza Garibaldi. ⊠ *Via Sersale 1/3* ☎ *081/5539204* ⊟ *No credit cards* ⊘ *Closed Sun. and last 2 wks in Aug.*

★ ¢   ✕ **Gino Sorbillo.** There are three restaurants called Sorbillo along Via dei Tribunali, but this is the one with the crowds waiting outside. Take our advice and order a basic Neapolitan pizza (try the unique pizza al pesto or the stunningly simple marinara—just tomatoes and oregano). They're cooked to perfection by the third generation of pizza makers who run the place. The pizzas are enormous, flopping over the edge of the plate onto the white marble tabletops. ⊠ *Via dei Tribunali 32, Spaccanapoli* ☎ *081/446643* ⊟ *AE, DC, MC, V* ⊘ *Closed Sun. (except Dec.) and 2 wks in Aug.*

WHERE TO STAY

$$$$ ▥ **Grand Hotel Parker's.** This elegant hotel has been a local landmark since 1870. The gilt-trim Empire bureaus, 19th-century paintings, shimmering chandeliers, fluted pilasters, and ornate ceilings all create a splendidly luxurious feel. From the hotel's perch midway up Vomero

Hill (and convenient to funicular lines), you get fine views of the bay and Capri. If your room doesn't have one of these prized vistas, drink it all in from the excellent rooftop restaurant. There's also a day spa providing a full complement of health and beauty treatments. **Pros:** Panoramic views, old-world charm. **Cons:** On a busy road, expensive rates. ⊠ *Corso Vittorio Emanuele 135, Chiaia, 80121* ☎*081/7612474* ⊕*www.grandhotelparkers.it* ⬅*72 rooms, 9 suites* ⚷*In-room: safe, refrigerator, ethernet. In-hotel: restaurant, bar, gym, spa, parking (fee)* ▭*AE, DC, MC, V* ¶⊙*BP.*

13

★$$$–$$$$ ▦ **Grand Hotel Vesuvio.** You'd never guess from the modern exterior that this is the oldest of Naples's great seafront hotels—the place where Enrico Caruso died, Oscar Wilde escaped with lover Lord Alfred Douglas, and Bill Clinton charmed the waitresses. Fortunately, the spacious, soothing interior compensates for what's lacking on the outside. Guest rooms are done in luxurious, traditional style with antique accents, vibrantly colored walls, and gleaming bathrooms. The best ones overlook the bay. You can pamper yourself at the spa, where there are myriad special services. The famous Caruso restaurant sits atop the hotel, affording wonderful views. **Pros:** Oceanfront location, fine restaurant. **Cons:** Not all rooms have views, on a busy road. ⊠ *Via Partenope 45, Santa Lucia, 80121* ☎*081/7640044* ⊕*www.vesuvio.it* ⬅*163 rooms, 17 suites* ⚷*In-room: safe, refrigerator, dial-up. In-hotel: restaurant, bar, gym, some pets allowed* ▭*AE, DC, MC, V* ¶⊙*BP.*

★$$$ ▦ **Art Resort Galleria Umberto.** Inside the Galleria Umberto is this charming boutique hotel, one of the most recent additions to the lodging scene. Each room is named for an artist, and reproductions of that artist's work adorn the walls inside. Rooms are immaculately kept and comfortably plush. Book early, as this hotel has become a popular retreat for musicians and performers from the nearby opera house. **Pros:** Central location, appetizers served every evening. **Cons:** Hard to find, rooms with balconies reserved for smokers. ⊠*Galleria Umberto 83, Piazza Plebiscito 80132* ☎*081/4976224* ⊕*www.artresortgalleria. it* ⬅*10 rooms* ⚷*In-room: safe, dial-up* ▭*AE, DC, MC, V.*

$$$ ▦ **Costantinopoli 104.** An oasis of what Italians call *stile liberty* (art-nouveau style), this calm and elegant hotel sits in the bustling *centro storico* (historic center) near the Museo Archeologico Nazionale. Each room is individually decorated. Ask for a room with a balcony in the warmer months and enjoy your breakfast alfresco, or opt for one of the garden rooms that open out onto the small swimming pool. **Pros:** Peaceful atmosphere, close to good cafés in Piazza Bellini. **Cons:** In a seedy part of town, not all rooms have baconies. ⊠ *Via Costantinopoli 104, Spaccanapoli, 80139* ☎*081/5571035* ⊕*www.costantinopoli104. com* ⬅*8 rooms* ⚷*In-room: safe, refrigerator, dial-up. In-hotel: bar, pool, laundry service, parking (fee)* ▭*AE, DC, MC, V* ¶⊙*BP.*

★ $$$ ▦ **Palazzo Alabardieri.** One of the newest of the city's rapidly expanding list of luxury hotels, Palazzo Alabardieri is just off the chic Piazza dei Martiri. A spacious marble-floor lobby makes the place feel bigger than it actually is, yet maintains a feeling of discretion and intimacy. The hotel prides itself on its comfortable accommodations, especially its marble bathrooms. **Pros:** Impressive common areas; good location near restaurants, cafés, and wine bars. **Cons:** No sea view, difficult to reach by car. ✉ *Via Alabardieri 38, Chiaia, 80121* ☎*081/415278* ⊕*www. palazzoalabardieri.it* ⟳*29 rooms* ⟳*In-room: safe, dial-up, Wi-Fi. In-hotel: bar, parking (fee), some pets allowed* ▭*AE, DC, MC, V* ❍|*BP.*

★ 🏨 **Chiaja Hotel De Charme.** A two-minute walk from Piazza Plebiscito
$$–$$$ takes you to this hotel in a spruced-up 18th-century palazzo. It has a very colorful history, as part of the building was once a brothel. Above the fireplace in the homely entrance hall is a portrait of the marchese Nicola Le Caldano Sasso III, original owner of the building; his grandson Mimì now runs the place. Rooms are small but filled with opulent period furnishings. Savor the *momento napoletano* in the late afternoon when regional cakes are offered. **Pros:** Central location, friendly staff. **Cons:** Some rooms are small, noise from traffic. ✉ *Via Chiaia 216, Chiaia, 80121* ☎*081/415555* ⊕*www.hotelchiaia. it* ⟳*27 rooms* ⟳*In-room: safe, refrigerator, dial-up. In-hotel: bar* ▭*AE, DC, MC, V* ❍|*EP.*

$$–$$$ 🏨 **San Francesco al Monte.** This high-end hotel retains hints of its former life as a Franciscan monastery: the small lobby leads to narrow corridors lined with doors that look dauntingly cell-like, until you enter and find surprisingly spacious, simply decorated rooms, many with their own hot tubs, antique furnishings, majolica-tile floors, and stunning views of the city below and the bay beyond. The hotel's restaurant serves regional specialties, and the wine bar has a selection of smaller dishes. **Pros:** Rooftop pool, several dining options. **Cons:** Isolated location, need a taxi if you're going out at night. ✉ *Corso Vittorio Emanuele 328, Vomero 80135* ☎*081/4239111* ⊕*www.hotelsanfrancesco.it* ⟳*44 rooms* ⟳*In-room: safe, refrigerator, dial-up. In-hotel: restaurant, bar, pool* ▭*AE, DC, MC, V* ❍|*BP.*

$$ 🏨 **Hotel Toledo.** A centuries-old palazzo has been tastefully transformed into this boutique hotel two minutes from Via Toledo. Rooms are furnished in a pleasing rustic style, and the leafy rooftop terrace provides a quintessentially Neapolitan backdrop for your breakfast. **Pros:** Good value, free Internet access. **Cons:** Run-down neighborhood, noise from passing motorbikes. ✉ *Via Montecalvario 15, Piazza Municipio, 80134* ☎*081/406800* ⊕*www.hoteltoledo.com* ⟳*18 rooms* ⟳*In-room: refrigerator. In-hotel: bar* ▭*AE, DC, MC, V* ❍|*BP.*

$$ 🏨 **Il Convento.** In a 17th-century palazzo tucked away in the Quartieri Spagnoli, Il Convento is conveniently close to Via Toledo. Rooms are small but elegant, with original architectural features such as arched or beamed ceilings. They are decorated in simple, modern Mediterranean style. Two junior suites have private roof gardens. **Pros:** Close to cafés and shops, free Internet access. **Cons:** Church bells may wake you in the morning, on a busy street. ✉ *Via Speranzella 137/A, Piazza Municipio, 80132* ☎*081/403977* ⊕*www.hotelilconvento.com* ⟳*12 rooms, 2 suites* ⟳*In-room: refrigerator. In-hotel: bar* ▭*AE, DC, MC, V* ❍|*BP.*

$$ 🏨 **Neapolis.** Situated on a narrow alley just off the humming Via Tribunali and close to Piazza Bellini, this small hotel looks out over the 13th-century Pietrasanta bell tower. The mix of modern and traditional furnishings, the lovely terra-cotta floors, and data ports in every room make this a good base for exploring Napoli's medieval center. **Pros:** Central location, pretty city views. **Cons:** Small elevator, neighborhood sketchy at night. ⊠ *Via Francesco Del Giudice 13, Spaccanapoli, 80138* ☎*081/4420815* ⊕*www.hotelneapolis.com* ⤶*19 rooms* ♿*In-room: safe, refrigerator, dial-up. In-hotel: restaurant, bar* ⊟*AE, DC, MC, V* ⎮○⎮*BP.*

$$ 🏨 **Pinto Storey.** This fascinating hotel overflows with warmth and
★ charm. The simple and airy guest rooms are on the fourth and fifth floors of an elegant late-19th-century building off the chic Piazza Amedeo. Rooms here are always in demand, so book far in advance. **Pros:** Safe neighborhood, near public transportation. **Cons:** Not close to major city sights, gets booked early. ⊠ *Via G. Martucci 72, Chiaia, 80121* ☎*081/681260* ⊕*www.pintostorey.it* ⤶*16 rooms* ♿*In-room: safe, refrigerator, dial-up* ⊟*AE, MC, V* ⎮○⎮*EP.*

★ $$ 🏨 **Weekend a Napoli.** From their tastefully restored family villa in the fairly genteel quarter of the Vomero—only a short funicular ride from the action downtown—owners Paolo and Patrizia lavish southern Italian hospitality on guests at this upscale bed-and-breakfast. For longer stays, try the self-catering flats. Hedonists will prefer the luxuriant Pompeii suite with its own indoor pool. **Pros:** On quiet side street, great attention to detail. **Cons:** Far from major sites, few good dining options nearby. ⊠ *Via Alvino 157, Vomero, 80129* ☎*081/5781010* ⊕*www.weekendanapoli.com* ⤶*10 rooms, 3 suites* ♿*In-room: safe, refrigerator* ⊟*AE, MC, V* ⎮○⎮*BP.*

NIGHTLIFE & THE ARTS

OPERA

Opera is a serious business in Naples—not in terms of the music so much as the costumes, the stage design, the players, and the politics. What's happening on stage can be secondary to the news of who's there, who they're with, and what they're wearing. Given the circumstances, it's hardly surprising that the city's famous San Carlo Company doesn't offer a particularly innovative repertoire. Nonetheless, the company is usually of very high quality—and if they're not in form the audience lets them know it. Performances take place in the luxury liner of southern Italian opera houses, the historic **Teatro San Carlo** (⊠ *Via San Carlo, Piazza Plebiscito* ☎*081/7972331 or 081/7972412* ⊕*www. teatrosancarlo.it*). The hall still gleams with its mid-19th-century gilded furnishings and thick red-velvet drapes. For the opera and ballet seasons (generally December through June), many seats are pre-sold by subscription, but there are often some available at the box office in the months before the performance. You can also book ahead by calling **Concerteria** (⊠ *Via Schipa 23, Chiaia* ☎*081/7611221*). For an additional fee you can order tickets on the theater Web site.

NIGHTLIFE

Bars and clubs are found in many areas around Naples. The sophisticated crowd heads to Posillipo and the Vomero, Via Partenope along the seafront, and the Chiaia area (between Piazza dei Martiri and Via dei Mille). A more-bohemian crowd makes for the centro storico and the area around Piazza Bellini. The scene is relatively relaxed—you might even be able to sit down at a proper table. Keep in mind that clubs, and their clientele, can change rapidly, so do some investigating before you hit the town.

Caffè Intramoenia (⊠ *Piazza Bellini 70, Spaccanapoli* ☎ *081/290720*) is the granddaddy of all the bars in Piazza Bellini; it was set up as a bookshop in the late 1980s and still has its own small publishing house with a variety of attractive titles. Seats in the heated veranda are at a premium in winter, though many sit outside all year round. **Bere Vino** (⊠ *62 Via San Sebastiano, Spaccanapoli* ☎ *081/29313*) looks like a shop from the outside, but inside you'll find long wooden tables and shelves of wine from all over Italy that are consumed on the premises. Peppery *taralli* biscuits, olives, and selections of cheeses and smoked meats can be used to *apoggiare* ("prop up") whatever you're drinking. Look for recommended wines by the glass on the chalkboard or spend ages perusing the encyclopedic list. **Aret' a' Palm** (⊠ *Piazza Santa Maria la Nova, Spaccanapoli*) is Neapolitan for "behind the palm tree," and that's exactly where you'll find this agreeably dark bar on Piazza Santa Maria La Nova. Its long marble bar and mirrored walls suggest Paris more than Naples. The **Enoteca Belledonne** (⊠ *Vico Belledonne a Chiaia 18, Chiaia* ☎ *081/403162*) is something of an institution among inhabitants of the more-upscale Chiaia area. Between 8 and 9 in the evening it seems like the whole neighborhood has descended into the tiny space for an *aperitivo* (cocktail). The small tables and low stools are notably uncomfortable, but the cozy atmosphere and the pleasure of being surrounded by glass-front cabinets full of wine bottles with beautiful labels more than makes up for it. Excellent local wines are available by the glass at great prices. **66** (⊠ *Via Bisignano 66, Chiaia* ☎ *081/5720269*) is a good place to meet for an aperitivo; the range of snacks on the bar (several types of olives, fresh capers, spinach-and-ricotta pies, and even small helpings of spaghetti—virtually a meal in itself) makes the crowds of young professionals and steep drink prices worth it. **Spacafé Culti** (⊠ *Via Carlo Poerio 47, Chiaia* ☎ *081/7644619*), in the swish Chiaia district, is an unusual combination of day spa, furniture shop, and classy bar/restaurant. It's refreshingly quiet and beautifully designed, with long low chairs and lots of black-lacquer wood.

SHOPPING

Leather goods, jewelry, and cameos are some of the best items to buy in Campania. In Naples you'll generally find good deals on handbags, shoes, and clothing. If you want the real thing, make your purchases in shops, but if you don't mind imitations, rummage around at the various street-vendor *bancherelle* (stalls). Most boutiques and department stores are open Monday 4:30–8 and Tuesday–Saturday 9:15–1 and 4:30–8. The larger chains now open on Sunday.

SHOPPING DISTRICTS

The immediate area around **Piazza dei Martiri,** in the center of Chiaia, has the densest concentration of luxury shopping, with perfume shops, fashion outlets, and antiques on display. **Via dei Mille** and **Via Filangieri,** which lead off Piazza dei Martiri, are home to Bulgari, Mont Blanc, and Hermès stores. The small, pedestrian-only **Via Calabritto,** which leads from Piazza dei Martiri toward the sea, is where you'll find high-end retailers such as Prada, Gucci, Versace, Vuitton, Cacharel, Damiani, and Cartier. **Via Chiaia** and **Via Toledo** are the two busiest shopping streets for most Neapolitans; there you'll find reasonably priced clothes and shoes, with a sprinkling of cafés and food shops. The **Vomero** district yields more shops, especially along Via Scarlatti and Via Luca Giordano. **Via Santa Maria di Costantinopoli,** which runs from Piazza Bellini to the Archaeological Museum, is the street for antiques shops. You'll also find an antiques market on the third weekend of each month in the gardens of Villa Comunale and a flower market early every morning in the Castel Nuovo moat.

SPECIALTY STORES

CHIAIA

Gay Odin (⊠ *Via Toledo 214, Piazza Plebiscito* ☎*081/400063*) produces handmade chocolates that you can find only in its Naples shops. Buy a delicious chocolate Mt. Vesuvius, or try the famous *foresta* (flaked chocolate). **Lo Stock** (⊠ *Via Fiorelli 7, Piazza dei Martiri* ☎*081/2405253*) is a large basement in which designer-label remainders can be found at hugely reduced prices. Be prepared to rummage and hope they have your size. **Marinella** (⊠ *Via Riviera di Chiaia 287/a, Chiaia* ☎*081/2451182*) sells old-fashioned made-to-measure ties that are favorites of the British royal family.

SPACCANAPOLI

Colonnese (⊠ *Via San Pietro a Maiella 32/33, Spaccanapoli* ☎*081/459858*) is an old-fashioned bookstore with antique wooden cabinets and tables laden with volumes on art, local history, and esoterica. **Mario Raffone** (⊠ *Via Santa Maria di Costantinopoli 102, Spaccanapoli* ☎*081/459667*) is a family printing business where they still use old presses. They sell prints of Nativity figures and Vesuvius and have a catalog of antique prints. **Melinoi** (⊠ *Via Benedetto Croce 34, Spaccanapoli* ☎*081/5521204*) stands out from the many small boutiques in Naples for its originality; it stocks clothes and accessories by Romeo Gigli as well as a number of French designers. **Nel Regno di Pulcinella** (⊠*Piazza San Domenico Maggiore, Spaccanapoli* ☎*081/5514171*) is the workshop of Lello Esposito, renowned Neapolitan artist, famous for his renderings of a famous puppet named Pulcinella.

The **Ospedale delle Bambole** (⊠ *Via San Biagio dei Librai 81, Spaccanapoli* ☎*081/203067*), a tiny storefront operation, is a world-famous "hospital" for dolls. It's a wonderful place to take kids.

HERCULANEUM, VESUVIUS & POMPEII

Volcanic ash and mud preserved the Roman towns of Herculaneum and Pompeii almost exactly as they were on the day Mt. Vesuvius erupted in AD 79, leaving them not just archaeological ruins but museums of daily life in the ancient world. The two cities and the volcano that buried them can be visited from either Naples or Sorrento, thanks to the Circumvesuviana, the suburban railway that provides fast, frequent, and economical service.

HERCULANEUM

★ *10 km (6 mi) southeast of Naples.*

GETTING HERE
Take a train on the Circumvesu-viana to Ercolano. From the station, walk across at the nearest roundabout and head down Via 4 Novembre for five minutes. If driv-ing from Naples, take the Ercolano exit from the Napoli–Salerno auto-strada. Follow signs for Scavi di Ercolano.

> **WORD OF MOUTH**
>
> "Herculaneum is definitely not to be missed. The buildings look as if you could move in with just a little restoration." –Juneisy

Lying more than 60 feet below the present-day town of Ercolano, the ruins of Herculaneum are set among the acres of greenhouses that make this area one of Europe's principal flower-growing centers. About 5,000 people lived here when it was destroyed; many of them were fishermen, craftsmen, and artists. In AD 79 the gigantic eruption of Vesuvius (which also destroyed Pompeii) buried the town under a tide of volcanic mud. The semiliquid mass seeped into the crevices and niches of every building, covering household objects and enveloping textiles and wood—sealing all in a compact, airtight tomb.

Casual excavation—and haphazard looting—began in the 18th century, but systematic digs were not initiated until the 1920s. Today less than half of Herculaneum has been excavated; with present-day Ercolano and the unlovely Resina Quarter (famous among bargain hunters for its secondhand-clothing market) sitting on top of the site, progress is limited. From the ramp leading down to Herculaneum's well-preserved edifices, you get a good overall view of the site, as well as an idea of the amount of volcanic debris that had to be removed to bring it to light.

Though Herculaneum had only one-fourth the population of Pompeii and has been only partially excavated, what has been found is generally better preserved. In some cases you can even see the original wooden beams, staircases, and furniture. Much excitement is presently focused on one excavation in a corner of the site, the Villa dei Papiri, built by Julius Caesar's father-in-law. The building is named for the 1,800 carbonized papyrus scrolls dug up here in the 18th century, leading scholars to believe that this may have been a study center or library. Given the right funds and political support, it is hoped that the villa can be properly excavated and ultimately opened to the public.

Bay of Naples

Pompeii Prep

Pompeii is impressive under any circumstances, but it comes alive if you do some preparation before your visit.

First, read up—there are piles of good books on the subject, including these engaging, jargon-free histories: *Pompeii: The Day a City Died* by Robert Etienne, *Pompeii: Public and Private Life* by Paul Zanker, and *The Lost World of Pompeii* by Colin Amery. For accurate historical information woven into the pages of a thriller, pick up *Pompeii: A Novel* by Robert Harris.

Second, be sure to visit the Museo Archeologico Nazionale in Naples. Most of the finest art from Pompeii has been moved to the museum. It's a rewarding place to visit even if Pompeii isn't in your plans.

Make sure to stock up on refreshments beforehand, as there is no food at the archaeological site. At the entrance, pick up a map showing the gridlike layout of the dig. Splurge on an audio guide (€6.50 for one, €10 for two) and head down the tunnel to start the tour at the old shoreline. Though many of the houses are closed and some are in dire need of restoration, a fair cross section of domestic, commercial, and civic buildings is still accessible. Decorations are especially delicate in the **Casa del Nettuno ed Anfitrite** (House of Neptune and Amphitrite), named for the subjects of a still-bright mosaic on the wall of the nymphaeum (a recessed grotto with a fountain), and in the **Terme Femminili** (Women's Baths), where several delicate black-and-white mosaics embellished the rooms. Annexed to the former house is a remarkably preserved wineshop, where amphorae still rest on carbonized wooden shelves. On the other side of the house is the **Casa del Bel Cortile** (House of the Beautiful Courtyard). In one of its inner rooms is the temporary display of a cast taken of two skeletons found in the storerooms down at the old seafront, where almost 300 inhabitants sought refuge from the eruption and were ultimately encapsulated for posterity. The **Casa dei Cervi** (House of the Stags), with an elegant garden open to the sea breezes, is evocative of a lively and luxurious way of life. The sumptuously decorated **Terme Suburbane** (Suburban Baths) was closed at the time of this writing, but is well worth a visit if it is open. ⊠ *Corso Ercolano, a 5-min walk downhill from Ercolano Circumvesuviana station* ☎ *081/8575347* ⊕ *www.pompeiisites.org* ☞ *€11; €20 includes 3-day ticket for Oplontis, Pompeii, and Boscoreale* ⊙ *Apr.–Oct., daily 8:30–7:30 (ticket office closes at 6); Nov.–Mar., daily 8:30–5 (ticket office closes at 3:30).*

Continued on page 787

ANCIENT POMPEII
TOMB OF A CIVILIZATION

The site of Pompeii, petrified memorial to Vesuvius's eruption on the morning of August 23, AD 79, is the largest, most accessible, and probably most famous of excavations anywhere.

A busy commercial center with a population of 10,000–20,000, ancient Pompeii covered about 160 acres on the seaward end of the fertile Sarno Plain. Today Pompeii is choked with both the dust of 25 centuries and more than 2 million visitors every year; only by escaping the hordes and lingering along its silent streets can you truly fall under the site's spell. On a quiet backstreet, all you need is a little imagination to sense the shadows palpably filling the dark corners, to hear the ancient pipe's falsetto and the tinny clash of cymbals, to envision a rain of rose petals gently covering a Roman senator's dinner guests. Come in the late afternoon when the site is nearly deserted and you will understand that the true pleasure of Pompeii is not in the seeing but in the feeling.

A FUNNY THING HAPPENS ON THE WAY TO THE FORUM

as you walk through Pompeii. Covered with dust and decay as it is, the city seems to come alive. Perhaps it's the familiar signs of life observed along the ancient streets: bakeries with large ovens just like those for making pizzas, tracks of cart wheels cut into the road surface, graffiti etched onto the plastered surfaces of street walls. Coming upon a *thermopolium* (snack bar), you imagine natives calling out, "Let's move on to the am-phitheater." But a glance up at Vesuvius, still brooding over the scene like an enormous headstone, reminds you that these folks—whether

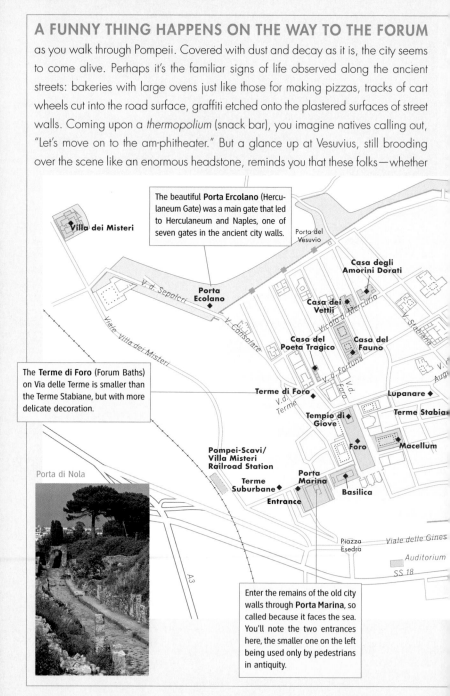

The beautiful **Porta Ercolano** (Herculaneum Gate) was a main gate that led to Herculaneum and Naples, one of seven gates in the ancient city walls.

The **Terme di Foro** (Forum Baths) on Via delle Terme is smaller than the Terme Stabiane, but with more delicate decoration.

Enter the remains of the old city walls through **Porta Marina**, so called because it faces the sea. You'll note the two entrances here, the smaller one on the left being used only by pedestrians in antiquity.

Via dell'Abbondanza

imagined in your head or actually wearing a mantle of lava dust—have not taken a breath for centuries. The town was laid out in a grid pattern, with two main intersecting streets. The wealthiest took a whole block for themselves; those less fortunate built a house and rented out the front rooms, facing the street, as shops. There were good numbers of *tabernae* (taverns) and *thermopolia* on almost every corner, and frequent shows at the amphitheater.

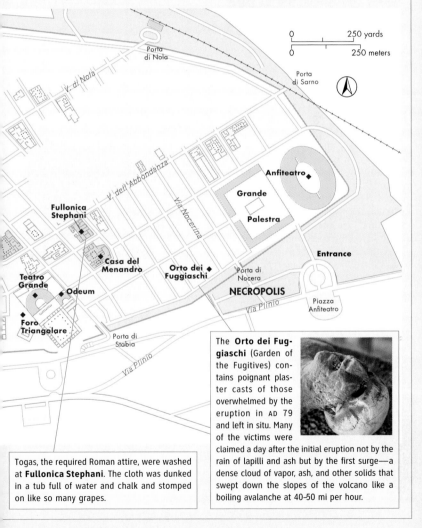

Togas, the required Roman attire, were washed at **Fullonica Stephani**. The cloth was dunked in a tub full of water and chalk and stomped on like so many grapes.

The **Orto dei Fuggiaschi** (Garden of the Fugitives) contains poignant plaster casts of those overwhelmed by the eruption in AD 79 and left in situ. Many of the victims were claimed a day after the initial eruption not by the rain of lapilli and ash but by the first surge—a dense cloud of vapor, ash, and other solids that swept down the slopes of the volcano like a boiling avalanche at 40–50 mi per hour.

PUBLIC LIFE IN ANCIENT POMPEII

Forum

THE CITY CENTER

As you enter the ruins at Porta Marina, make your way to the **Foro** (Forum), which served as Pompeii's cultural, political, and religious center. You can still see some of the two stories of colonnades that used to line the square. Like the ancient Greek *agora* in Athens, the Forum was a busy shopping area, complete with public officials to apply proper standards of weights and measures. Fronted by an elegant three-column portico on the eastern side of the forum is the **Macellum,** the covered meat and fish market dating to Augustan times; here vendors sold goods from their reserved spots in the central market. It was also in the Forum that elections were held, politicians let rhetoric fly, speeches and official announcements were made, and worshippers crowded the **Tempio di Giove** (Temple of Jupiter), at the northern end of the forum.

Basilica

On the southwestern corner is the **Basilica,** the city's law court and the economic center. These oblong buildings ending in a semicircular projection were the model for early Christian churches, which had a nave (central aisle) and two side aisles separated by rows of columns. Standing in the Basilica, you can recognize the continuity between Roman and Christian architecture.

THE GAMES

The **Anfiteatro** (Amphitheater) was the ultimate in entertainment for local Pompeians and offered a gamut of experiences, but essentially this was for gladiators rather than wild animals. By Roman standards, Pompeii's amphithe-

Amphitheater

ater was quite small (seating 20,000). Built in about 80 BC, it was oval and divided into three seating areas like a theater. There were two main entrances—at the north and south ends—and a narrow passage on the west called the Porta Libitinensis, through which the dead were most probably dragged out. A wall painting found in a house near the theater (now in the Naples Museum) depicts the riot in the amphitheater in AD 59 when several citizens from the nearby town of Nucera were killed. After Nucerian appeals to Nero, shows in the amphitheater were suspended for 10 years.

Fresco of Pyramus & Thisbe in the House of Loreius Tiburtinus

BATHS & BROTHELS

In its day, Pompeii was celebrated as the Côte d'Azur, the seaside Brighton, the Fire Island of the ancient Roman empire. Evidence of a Sybaritic bent is everywhere—in the town's grandest villas, in its baths, and especially in its rowdiest *lupanaria* (brothels), murals still reveal a worship of hedonism. Satyrs, bacchantes, hermaphrodites, and acrobatic couples are pictured indulging in hanky-panky.

The first buildings to the left after you've gone through the ticket turnstiles are the **Terme Suburbane** (Suburban Baths), built—by all accounts without planning permission—right up against the city walls. The baths have eyebrow-raising frescoes in the *apody-terium* (changing room) that strongly suggest that more than just bathing and massaging went on here.

On the walls of **Lupanare** (brothel) are scenes of erotic games in which clients could engage. The **Terme Stabiane** (Stabian Baths) had underground furnaces, the heat from which circulated beneath the floor, rose through flues in the walls, and escaped through chimneys. The water temperature could be set for cold, lukewarm, or hot. Bathers took a lukewarm bath to prepare themselves for the hot room. A tepid bath came next, and then a plunge into cold water to tone up the skin. A vigorous massage with oil was followed by rest, reading, horseplay, and conversation.

GRAFFITI

Thanks to those deep layers of pyroclastic deposits from Vesuvius that protected the site from natural wear and tear over the centuries, graffiti found in Pompeii provide unique insights into the sort of things that the locals found important 2,000 years ago. A good many were personal and lend a human dimension to the disaster that not even the sights can equal.

At the baths: "What is the use of having a Venus if she's made of marble?"

At the entrance to the front lavatory at a private house: "May I always and everywhere be as potent with women as I was here."

On the Viale ai Teatri: "A copper pot went missing from my shop. Anyone who returns it to me will be given 65 bronze coins."

In the Basilica: "A small problem gets larger if you ignore it."

PRIVATE LIFE IN ANCIENT POMPEII

The facades of houses in Pompeii were relatively plain and seldom hinted at the care and attention lavished on the private rooms within. When visitors arrived they passed the shops and entered an open atrium, from which the occupants received air, sunlight, and rainwater, the latter caught by the *impluvium*, a rectangular-shaped receptacle under the sloped roof. In the back was a receiving room, the *tablinum*, and behind was another open area, the *peristyle*. Life revolved around this uncovered inner courtyard, with rows of columns and perhaps a garden with a fountain. Only good friends ever saw this part of the house, which was surrounded by *cubicula* (bedrooms) and the *triclinium* (dining area). Interior floors and walls usually were covered with colorful marble tiles, mosaics, and frescoes.

Several homes were captured in various states by the eruption of Vesuvius, each representing a different slice of Pompeiian life.

House of Paquius Proculus

The **Casa del Fauno** (House of the Faun) displayed wonderful mosaics, now at the Museo Archeologico Nazionale in Naples. The **Casa del Poeta Tragico** (House of the Tragic Poet) is a typical middle-class house. On the floor is a mosaic of a chained dog and the inscription *cave canem* ("Beware of the dog"). The **Casa degli Amorini Dorati** (House of the Gilded Cupids) is an elegant, well-preserved home with original marble decorations in the garden. Many paintings and mosaics were executed at **Casa del Menandro** (House of Menander), a patrician's villa named for a fresco of the Greek playwright. Two blocks beyond the Stabian Baths you'll notice on the left the current digs at the **Casa dei Casti Amanti** (House of the Chaste Lovers). A team of plasterers and painters were at work here when Vesuvius erupted, redecorating one of the rooms and patching up the cracks in the bread oven near the entrance—caused by earth tremors a matter of days before.

Small Garden
Triclinium
Owner's Quarters
Kitchen
Servant's Quarters
Secondary Atrium
Entrance
Garden
Main Atrium
Impluvium
Peristyle

CASA DEI VETTII

The **House of the Vettii** is the best example of a house owned by wealthy *mercatores* (merchants). It contains vivid murals—a magnificent *pinacoteca* (picture gallery) within the very heart of Pompeii. The scenes here—except for those in the two wings off the atrium—were all painted after the earthquake of AD 62. Once inside, cast an admiring glance at the delicate frieze around the wall of the *triclinium* (on the right of the peristyle garden as you enter from the atrium), depicting cupids engaged in various activities, such as selling oils and perfumes, working as goldsmiths and metalworkers, acting as wine merchants, or performing in chariot races. Another of the main attractions in the Casa dei Vettii is the small cubicle beyond the kitchen area (to the right of the atrium) with its faded erotic frescoes now protected by Perspex screens.

UNLOCKING THE VILLA DEI MISTERI

Villa dei Misteri

There is no more astounding, magnificently memorable evidence of Pompeii's devotion to the pleasures of the flesh than the frescoes on view at the **Villa dei Misteri** (Villa of the Mysteries), a palatial abode built at the far northwestern fringe of Pompeii. Unearthed in 1909, this villa had more than 60 rooms painted with frescoes; the finest are in the *triclinium*. Painted in the most glowing Pompeiian reds and oranges, the panels relate the saga of a young bride (Ariadne) and her initiation into the mysteries of the cult of Dionysus, who was a god imported to Italy from Greece and then given the Latin name of Bacchus. The god of wine and debauchery also represented the triumph of the irrational—of all those mysterious forces that no official state religion could fully suppress.

Pompeii's best frescoes, painted in glowing reds and oranges, retain an amazing vibrancy.

The Villa of the Mysteries frescoes were painted circa 50 BC, most art historians believe, and represent the peak of the Second Style of Pompeiian wall painting. The triclinium frescoes are thought to have been painted by a local artist, although the theme may well have been copied from an earlier cycle of paintings from the Hellenistic period. In all there are 10 scenes, depicting children and matrons, musicians and satyrs, phalluses and gods. There are no inscriptions (such as are found on Greek vases), and after 2,000 years historians remain puzzled by many aspects of the triclinium cycle. Scholars endlessly debate the meaning of these frescoes, but anyone can tell they are the most beautiful paintings left to us by antiquity. In several ways, the eruption of Vesuvius was a blessing in disguise, for without it, these masterworks of art would have perished long ago.

PLANNING FOR YOUR DAY IN POMPEII

GETTING THERE

The archaeological site of Pompeii has its own stop (Pompei–Villa dei Misteri) on the Circumvesuviana line to Sorrento, close to the main entrance at the Porta Marina, which is the best place from which to start a tour. If, like many potential visitors every year, you get the wrong train from Naples (stopping at the other station "Pompei"), all is not lost. There's another entrance to the excavations at the far end of the site, just a seven-minute walk to the Amphitheater.

ADMISSION

Single tickets cost €11 and are valid for one full day. The site is open Apr.–Oct., daily 8:30–7:30 (last admission at 6), and Nov.–Mar., daily 8:30–5 (last admission at 3:30). For more information, call 081/8575347 or visit www.pompeiisites.org.

WHAT TO BRING

The only restaurant inside the site is both overpriced and busy, so it makes sense to bring along water and snacks. If you come so equipped, there are some shady, underused picnic tables outside the Porta di Nola, to the northeast of the site.

MAKING THE MOST OF YOUR TIME

Visiting Pompeii does have its frustrating aspects: many buildings are blocked off by locked gates, and enormous group tours tend to clog up more popular attractions. But the site is so big that it's easy to lose yourself amid the quiet side streets. To really see the site, you'll need four or five hours.

Three buildings within Pompeii—Terme Suburbane, Casa del Menandro, and Casa degli Amorini Dorati—are open for restricted viewing. Reservations must be made on-line at www.arethusa.net, where you can find information on opening times.

TOURS

To get the most out of Pompeii, rent an audio guide (€6.50 for one, €10 for two; you'll need to leave an ID card) and opt for one of the three itineraries (2 hours, 4 hours, or 6 hours). If hiring a guide, make sure the guide is registered for an English tour and standing inside the gate; agree beforehand on the length of the tour and the price, and prepare yourself for soundbites of English mixed with dollops of hearsay.

MODERN POMPEI

Caught between the hammer and anvil of cultural and religious tourism, the modern town of Pompei (to use the modern-day Italian spelling, not the ancient Latin) is now endeavoring to polish up its act. In attempts to ease congestion and improve air quality at street level, parts of the town have been pedestrianized and parking restrictions tightened. Several hotels have filled the sizable niche in the market for excellent deals at affordable prices. As for recommendable restaurants, if you deviate from the archaeological site and make for the center of town, you will be spoiled for choice.

IF YOU LIKE POMPEII

If you intend to visit other archaeological sites nearby during your trip, you should buy the *biglietto cumulativo* pass, a combination ticket with access to four area sites (Herculaneum, Pompeii, Oplontis, Boscoreale). It costs €20 and is valid for three days. Unlike many archaeological sites in the Mediterranean region, those around Naples are almost all well served by public transport; ask about transportation options at the helpful Porta Marina information kiosk.

VESUVIUS

8 km (5 mi) northeast of Herculaneum, 16 km (10 mi) east of Naples.

GETTING HERE

Take a train on the Circumvesuviana to Ercolano, then hop on the Vesuvio Express shuttle service. By car, take the Ercolano exit off the A3 autostrada and follow the brown signs to Vesuvio.

As you tour the cities that it destroyed, you may be overwhelmed by the urge to explore Vesuvius. In summer especially, the prospect of rising above the sticky heat of Naples is a heady one. The view when the air is clear is magnificent, with the curve of the coast and the tiny white houses among the orange and lemon blossoms. If the summit is lost in mist you'll be lucky to see your hand in front of your face. When you see the summit clearing—it tends to be clearer in the afternoon—head for it. If possible, see Vesuvius after you've toured the ruins of buried Herculaneum to appreciate the magnitude of the volcano's power.

The 10-seat minibuses run by Vesuvio Express are a quick, painless, and relatively cheap way of getting to the top (€10 round-trip from Ercolano train station). The vehicles thread their way rapidly up on back roads, reaching the top in 20 minutes. Allow at least 2½ hours for the journey, including a 30-minute walk to the crater on a soft cinder track. Admission includes a compulsory guide service, usually young geologists with a smattering of English. At the bottom you'll be offered a stout walking stick (a small tip is appreciated on return). The climb can be tiring if you're not used to steep hikes. Because of the volcanis stone you should wear athletic shoes, not sandals. ☎*081/7775720* 🎟*€6.50* 🕑*Daily 9* AM*–2 hrs before sunset.*

You can visit **Osservatorio Vesuviano** *(Vesuvius Observatory)*—2,000 feet up—and view instruments used to study the volcano, some dating to the mid-19th century. ☎*081/6108483* ⊕*www.ov.ingv.it* 🎟*Free* 🕑*Weekends 10–2.*

ISCHIA & PROCIDA

Though Capri gets star billing among the islands that line the bay of Naples, Ischia and Procida also have their own, lower-key appeal. Ischia is a popular destination on account of its spas, beaches, and hot springs. Procida, long the poor relation of the three, and the closest to Naples, is starting to capitalize on its chief natural asset, the unspoiled isle of Vivara. The pastel colors of Procida will be familiar to anyone who has seen the widely acclaimed film *Il Postino.*

PROCIDA

35 mins by hydrofoil, 1 hr by car ferry from Naples.

GETTING HERE

Take a ferry from Pozzuoli or a hydrofoil from Naples.

VISITOR INFORMATION

Procida tourism office (⊠ *Via Vittorio Emanuele 167, 80079* ☎ *081/8101968* ⊕ *www.procida.net*).

EXPLORING

Lying barely 3 km (2 mi) from the mainland and 10 km (6 mi) from the nearest port of Pozzuoli, Procida is an island of enormous contrasts. It is the most densely populated island in Europe—almost 11,000 people crammed into less than 3½ square km (less than 1½ square mi)—and yet there are oases such as Marina Corricella and Vivara that seem to have been bypassed by modern civilization. It's no surprise that picturesque Procida has strong artistic traditions and is widely considered a painters' paradise.

The sleepy fishing village of **Corricella,** used as the setting for the waterfront scenes in the Oscar-winning film *Il Postino,* has been relatively immune to life in the limelight. Apart from the opening of an extra restaurant and bar, there have been few changes. This is the type of place where even those with failing grades in art class feel like reaching for a paintbrush to record the delicate pink and yellow facades. The **Graziella** bar at the far end of the seafront offers the island's famous lemons squeezed over crushed ice to make an excellent granita.

WHERE TO EAT

$ ✕ **La Gorgonia.** This restaurant sits right on the waterfront, which draws in the crowds. The specialties here are combinations of seafood and locally grown vegetables, such as pasta *con fagioli e cozze* (with beans and mussels). ⊠ *Marina Corricella 50* ☎ *081/8101060* ⊟ *AE, DC, MC, V* ☉ *Closed Mon. and Nov.–Feb.*

ISCHIA

45 mins by hydrofoil, 90 mins by car ferry from Naples, 60 mins by ferry from Pozzuoli.

GETTING HERE

Ischia can be reached by car ferry and fast craft from Molo Beverello in central Naples, by fast craft from Mergellina, and by ferry from Pozzuoli.

VISITOR INFORMATION

Ischia Porto tourism office (⊠ *Via A. Sogliuzzo, 80077* ☎ *081/5074211* ⊕ *www.ischia.com*).

EXPLORING

Whereas Capri wows you with its charm and beauty, Ischia takes time to cast its spell. In fact, an overnight stay is probably not long enough for the island to get into your blood. It does have its share of vine-growing villages beneath the lush volcanic slopes of Monte Epomeo, and unlike Capri it enjoys a life of its own that survives when the tourists head home. But there are few signs of antiquity here, the architecture is unremarkable, the traffic can be overwhelming, and hoteliers have yet to achieve a balanced mix of clientele—most are either German (off-

GETTING TO CAPRI, ISCHIA & PROCIDA

Several companies offer a variety of fast craft and passenger and car ferries connecting the islands of Capri, Ischia, and Procida with Naples and Pozzuoli year-round. Boats leave from Naples's Molo Beverello, southeast of Piazza Municipio. Hydrofoils also leave from Mergellina, about 1½ km (1 mi) west of Piazza Municipio. Information on departures is published every day in the local paper, *Il Mattino,* and in local editions of national dailies *Corriere della Sera* and *La Repubblica.* Alternatively, ask at the tourist office or at the port, or contact the companies—**Alilauro** (☎ 081/7614909 ⊕ *www.alilauro.it*), **Caremar** (☎ 081/5513882 ⊕ *www. caremar.it*), **Coop Sant'Andrea** (☎ 089/873190 ⊕ *www.coop-santandrea.it*). **Navigazione Libera del Golfo** (*NLG* ☎ 081/5527209 ⊕ *www.navlib.it*)., and **SNAV** (☎ 081/7612348 ⊕ *www.snavali. com*)—directly. Always double-check schedules in stormy weather.

13

season) or Italian (in-season). But should you want to plunk down in the sun for a few days and tune out the world, this is an ideal spot; just don't expect an unspoiled, undiscovered Capri. When Augustus gave the Neapolitans Ischia for Capri, he knew what he was doing.

Ischia is volcanic in origin. From its hidden reservoir of seething molten matter come the thermal springs said to cure whatever ails you. As early as 1580 a doctor named Lasolino published a book about the mineral wells at Ischia. "If your eyebrows fall off," he wrote, "go and try the baths at Piaggia Romano. If you know anyone who is getting bald, anyone who suffers from elephantiasis, or another whose wife yearns for a child, take the three of them immediately to the Bagno di Vitara; they will bless you." Today the island is covered with thermal baths, often surrounded by tropical gardens.

A good 35-km (22-mi) road makes a circuit of the island; the ride takes most of a day if you stop along the way to enjoy the views and perhaps have lunch. You can book a boat tour around the island at the booths in various ports along the coast; there's a one-hour stop at Sant'Angelo. The information office is at the harbor. You may drive on Ischia year-round. There's also fairly good bus service, and you'll find plenty of taxis.

Ischia Porto is the largest town on the island and the usual point of debarkation. It's no workaday port, however, but a lively resort with plenty of hotels, the island's best shopping area, and low, flat-roof houses on terraced hillsides overlooking the water. Its narrow streets often become flights of steps that scale the hill, and its villas and gardens are framed by pines.

Most of the hotels are along the beach in the part of town called **Ischia Ponte,** which gets its name from the *ponte* (bridge) built by Alfonso of Aragon in 1438 to link the picturesque castle on a small islet offshore with the town and port. For a while the castle was the home of Vittoria Colonna, poetess, granddaughter of Renaissance Duke Federico da

Montefeltro (1422–82), and platonic soul mate of Michelangelo, with whom she carried on a lengthy correspondence. You'll find a typical resort atmosphere: countless cafés, shops, and restaurants, and a 1-km (½-mi) stretch of fine-sand beach.

Casamicciola, a popular beach resort, is 5 km (3 mi) west of Ischia Porto.

Chic and upscale **Lacco Ameno,** next to Casamicciola, is distinguished by a mushroom-shapes rock offshore and some of the island's best hotels. Here, too, you can enjoy the benefits of Ischia's therapeutic waters.

The far western and southern coasts of Ischia are more rugged and attractive. **Forio,** at the extreme west, has a waterfront church and is a good spot for lunch or dinner.

The sybaritic hot pools of the **Giardini Poseidon Terme** *(Poseidon Gardens Spa)* are on Citara Beach, south of Forio. You can sit like a Roman senator on a stone chair recessed in the rock and let the hot water cascade over you—all very campy, and fun.

Sant'Angelo, on the southern coast, is a charming village; the road doesn't reach all the way into town, so it's free of traffic. It's a five-minute boat ride from the beach of Maronti, at the foot of cliffs.

The inland town of Fontana is the base for excursions to the top of **Monte Epomeo,** the long-dormant volcano that dominates the island landscape. You can reach its 2,585-foot peak in less than 1½ hours of relatively easy walking.

WHERE TO STAY & EAT

★ $$$$ ✕ **Il Melograno.** A 10-minute walk south from the center of Forio takes you to the tranquil setting of one of Campania's finest restaurants. With antipasti such as *calamaretti crudi con pera* (fresh raw squid with pears) and many tempting pasta dishes, you could be forgiven for skipping the main course. Try the very reasonably priced local wines (both white and red) from the Pietratorcia winery up the road. Dessert, appropriately called *dulcis in fundo* (the best for last), also merits attention. ⊠ *Via G. Mazzella 110, Forio* ☎*081/998450* ⊕*www.ilmelogranoischia.it* ⌲*Reservations essential* ▭*AE, DC, MC, V* ♥*Closed Mon. in Oct., Mon. and Tues. in Nov. and Dec., and Jan. 7–Mar. 15.*

$–$$ ✕ **Gennaro.** This small family restaurant on the seafront in Ischia Porto serves excellent fish in a convivial atmosphere. Specialties include spaghetti *alle vongole* (with clam sauce, either white or red) and linguine *all'aragosta* (with lobster). ⊠ *Via Porto 66, Ischia Porto* ☎*081/992917* ▭*AE, DC, MC, V* ♥*Closed Nov.–mid-Mar.*

$$$$ ☷ **Grand Hotel Punta Molino.** Set in its own pine forest on the island's northeastern coastline, this hotel is still within walking distance of the best shopping. This pleasingly modern establishment provides privacy, relaxation, and low-key evening entertainment. Rooms are decorated in gentle Mediterranean hues—some of the best are in the villa annex. A crescent-shaped swimming pool wraps around part of the main building, and the gardens have walkways leading to shady pergolas. Rates include a buffet lunch or candlelight dinner. **Pros:** Delicious

food, soothing thermal pool, helpful staff. **Cons:** Narrow, crowded beach. ⊠*Lungomare C. Colombo 23, 80077* ☎*081/991544* ⊕*www. puntamolino.it* ➟*90 rooms* ⌂*In-room: safe, dial-up. In-hotel: 2 restaurants, bars, pools, gym, spa, beachfront* ☰*AE, DC, MC, V* ⊗*Closed late Oct.–Apr 15.* ⍭❙*MAP.*

$$$ ⊡ **Villarosa.** A highlight at this gracious family-run hotel—a villa with bright and airy rooms—is the thermal pool in the garden. In high season, make sure to book months ahead. It's in the heart of Ischia Porto and only a short walk from the beach. Rates include lunch or dinner. **Pros:** Very close to shopping, surrounded by greenery. **Cons:** Books up quickly in high season. ⊠*Via Giacinto Gigante 5, 80077 Ischia Porto* ☎*081/991316* ⊕*www.lavillarosa.it* ➟*37 rooms* ⌂*In-hotel: restaurant, pool* ☰*AE, DC, MC, V* ⊗*Closed Nov.–Mar.* ⍭❙*MAP.*

Fodor'sChoice   ⊡ **Albergo Il Monastero.** Within the Castello Aragonese at Ischia Ponte,

★ **$$**   this hotel has rustic rooms that peer down at the Mediterranean hundreds of feet below. This lodging is the ultimate in ambience combined with the peace and quiet of a traffic-free area. It's a highly popular getaway, so book far in advance. **Pros:** Reasonably priced restaurant, terrific sunset views. **Cons:** Spartan rooms, some steps to climb. ⊠*Castello Aragonese 3, Ischia Ponte 80077* ☎*081/994033* ⊕*www.albergoilmonastero.it* ➟*21 rooms* ⌂*In-hotel: restaurant, laundry service* ☰*MC, V* ⊗*Closed Oct. 20–Mar.* ⍭❙*BP.*

$ ⊡ **La Pergola.** The chance to stay on a working farm is the draw at La Pergola, a whitewashed villa perched on the slopes of Monte Epomeo. Surrounded by vineyards and olive and fruit trees, the villa has sweeping views westward over Citara Beach. The dynamic owner, Giosuè, also operates a thriving restaurant serving local specialties including the fabled *coniglio all'ischitana* (rabbit simmered with tomatoes). **Pros:** Quiet setting, homegrown produce served at meals. **Cons:** Skimpy furnishings, far from town. ⊠*Via San Giuseppe 8, 80075 Forio* ☎*081/909483* ⊕*www.agriturismolapergola.it* ➟*7 rooms* ⌂*In-room: no phone, no TV. In-hotel: restaurant, pool* ☰*No credit cards* ⍭❙*MAP.*

CAPRI

GETTING HERE
Capri can be reached by ferry and hydrofoil from Naples and Sorrento throughout the year. Additional departures from Salerno, Amalfi, Positano, and Castellammare are available in the summer months.

VISITOR INFORMATION
Capri tourism offices (⊠*Marina Grande, 80073* ☎*081/8370634* ⊠*Piazza Umberto I, 80073Capri Town* ☎*081/8370686* ⊕*www.capritourism.com*).

EXPLORING
Once a pleasure dome to Roman emperors and now Italy's most glamorous seaside getaway, Capri (pronounced with an accent on the first syllable) is a craggy island at the southern end to the bay, 75 minutes

by boat, 40 minutes by hydrofoil from Naples. The boom in cruises to the Naples area (almost 1 million passengers in 2006) means that Capri is inundated with day-trippers, making seemingly simple trips (like the funicular ride up from Marina Grande) a nerve-fraying experience. Yet even the crowds are not enough to destroy Capri's special charm. The town is a Moorish opera set of shiny white houses, tiny squares, and narrow medieval alleyways hung with flowers. It rests on top of rugged limestone cliffs hundreds of feet above the sea, and on which herds of *capre* (goats) once used to roam (giving the name to the island). Unlike the other islands in the Bay of Naples, Capri is not of volcanic origin; it may be a continuation of the limestone Sorrentine peninsula.

Limestone caves on Capri have yielded rich prehistoric and Neolithic finds. The island is thought to have been settled by Greeks from Cumae in the sixth century BC and later by other Greeks from Neapolis, but it was the Romans in the early imperial period who really left their mark. Emperor Augustus vacationed here; Tiberius built a dozen villas around the island, and, in later years, he refused to return to Rome, even when he was near death. Capri was one of the strongholds of the 16th-century pirate Barbarossa, who first sacked it and then made it a fortress. In 1806 the British wanted to turn the island into another Gibraltar and were beginning to build fortifications until the French took it away from them in 1808. Over the next century, from the opening of its first hotel in 1826, Capri saw an influx of visitors that reads like a Who's Who of literature and politics, especially in the early decades of the 20th century.

Like much else about Capri, the island's rare and delicious white wine is sensuous and intoxicating. Note that most of the wine passed off as "local" on Capri comes from the much-more-extensive vineyards of Ischia.

On arrival at the port, pick up the excellent map of the island at the tourist office (€1). You may have to wait in line for the funicular railway (€2.60 round-trip) to **Capri Town,** perched some 450 feet above the harbor. This might be the time to splurge on an open-top taxi—it could save you an hour in line for the funicular. From the upper station, walk out into Piazza Umberto I, much better known as the Piazzetta, the island's social hub.

You can window-shop in expensive boutiques and browse in souvenir shops along Via Vittorio Emanuele, which leads south toward the many-domed **Certosa di San Giacomo.** You will be able to visit the church and cloister of this much-restored monastery and also pause long enough to enjoy the breathtaking view of Punta Tragara and the Faraglioni, three towering crags, from the viewing point at the edge of the cliff. ⊠ *Via Certosa* ☎*081/8376218* ☼*Tues.–Sun. 9–2.*

OFF THE BEATEN PATH

Villa Jovis. From Capri Town, the 45-minute hike east to Villa Jovis, the grandest of those built by Tiberius, is strenuous but rewarding. Follow the signs for Villa Jovis, taking Via Le Botteghe from the Piazzetta, then continuing along Via Croce and Via Tiberio. At the end of a lane that climbs the steep hill, with pretty views all the way, you come to the precipice over which the emperor reputedly disposed of the victims of his perverse attentions. From a natural terrace above, near a chapel, are spectacular views of the entire Bay of Naples and, on clear days, part of the Gulf of Salerno. Here starts the footpath around the somewhat neglected ruins of Tiberius's palace. Allow 45 minutes each way for the walk alone. ✉ *Via Tiberio* ☎ *081/8370381* 💶 *€2* ⏱ *Daily 9–1 hr before sunset.*

From the terraces of **Giardini di Augusto** *(Gardens of Augustus)*, a beautifully planted public garden with excellent views, you can see the village of Marina Piccola below—restaurants, cabanas, and swimming platforms huddle among the shoals—and admire the steep and winding Via Krupp, actually a staircase cut into the rock. Friedrich Krupp, the German arms manufacturer, loved Capri and became one of the island's most generous benefactors. The staircase has been closed for years, but you can reach the beach by taking a bus from the Via Roma terminus down to Marina Piccola. ✉ *Via Matteotti beyond monastery of San Giacomo* ⏱ *Daily dawn–dusk.*

A tortuous road leads up to **Anacapri,** the island's "second city," about 3 km (2 mi) from Capri Town. To get here you can take a bus either from Via Roma in Capri Town or from Marina Grande (both €1.30), or a taxi (about €25 one-way; agree on the fare before starting out). Crowds are thick down Via Capodimonte leading to Villa San Michele and around the square, Piazza Vittoria, which is the starting point of the chairlift to the top of Monte Solaro. Elsewhere, Anacapri is quietly appealing. It's a good starting point for walks, such as the 80-minute round-trip journey to the **Migliara Belvedere,** on the island's southern coast.

An impressive limestone formation and the highest point on Capri (1,932 feet), **Monte Solaro** affords gasp-inducing views toward the bays of both Naples and Salerno. A 12-minute chairlift ride will take you right to the top (refreshments available at the bar), which is a starting point for a number of scenic trails on the western side of the island. Picnickers should note that even in summer it can get windy at this height, and there are few trees to provide shade or refuge. ✉ *Piazza Vittoria, Anacapri* ☎ *081/8371428* 💶 *€6 one-way, €8 round-trip* ⏱ *Mar.–Oct., daily 9:30–6; Nov.–Feb., daily 10:30–3.*

In the heart of Anacapri, the octagonal baroque church of **San Michele,** finished in 1719, is best known for its exquisite majolica pavement designed by Solimena and executed by the *mastro-riggiolaro* (master tiler) Chiaiese from Abruzzo. A walkway skirts the depiction of Adam and a duly contrite Eve being expelled from the Garden of Eden, but you can get a fine overview from the organ loft, reached by a winding staircase near the ticket booth (a privileged perch you have to pay for). Outside the church is the Via Finestrale, which leads to Anacapri's noted **Le Boffe quarter.** This section of town, centered on the Piazza Ficacciate, owes its name to the distinctive domestic architecture prevalent here, which uses vaults and sculpted groins instead of crossbeams. ✉ *Piazza Nicola, Anacapri* ☎ *081/8372396*

⊠ €3 ⊙ *Nov.–Mar., daily 9:30–3; Apr.–Oct., daily 9–7.*

★ From Anacapri's Piazza Vittoria, picturesque Via Capodimonte leads to **Villa San Michele**, the charming former home of Swedish doctor and philanthropist Axel Munthe (1857–1949) that Henry James called "the most fantastic beauty, poetry, and inutility that one had ever seen clustered together." At the ancient entranceway to Anacapri at the top of the Scala Fenicia,

WORD OF MOUTH

"The Blue Grotto (Grotta Azzurra) really is worth it; the color is not to be believed. But…you have to sit in the little motorboat outside the grotto with all the other boats until it is your turn. Bad fumes, queasiness in everyone….But I loved loved loved Capri. Not the main streets, but all the small byways." –humanone

the villa is set around Roman-style courtyards, marble walkways, and atria. Rooms display the doctor's varied collections, which range from bric-a-brac to antiquities. Medieval choir stalls, Renaissance lecterns, and gilded statues of saints are all part of the setting, with some rooms preserving the doctor's personal memorabilia. A spectacular pergola path overlooking the entire Bay of Naples leads from the villa to the famous Sphinx Parapet, where an ancient Egyptian sphinx looks out toward Sorrento; you cannot see its face—on purpose. It is said that if you touch the sphinx's hindquarters with your left hand while making a wish, it will come true. The parapet is connected to the little Chapel of San Michele, on the grounds of one of Tiberius's villas.

Besides hosting summer concerts, the Axel Munthe Foundation has an ecomuseum that fittingly reflects Munthe's fondness for animals. There you can learn about various bird species—accompanied by their songs—found on Capri. Munthe bought up the hillside and made it a sanctuary for birds. ⊠ *Viale Axel Munthe 34* ☎ *081/8371401* ⊕ *www. villasanmichele.eu* ⊠ €5 ⊙ *May–Sept., daily 9–6; Mar., daily 9:30– 4:30; Apr. and Oct., daily 9:30–5; Nov.–Feb., daily 10:30–3:30.*

★ Only when the **Grotta Azzurra** was "discovered" in 1826 by the Polish poet August Kopisch and Swiss artist Ernest Fries, did Capri become a tourist haven. The watery cave's blue beauty became a symbol of the return to nature and revolt from reason that marked the Romantic era, and it soon became a required stop on the Grand Tour. In fact, the grotto had long been a local landmark. During the Roman era—as testified by the extensive remains, primarily below sea level, and several large statues now at the Certosa di San Giacomo—it had been the elegant, mosaic-decorated nymphaeum of the adjoining villa of Gradola. Historians can't quite agree if it was simply a lovely little pavilion where rich patricians would cool themselves or truly a religious site where sacred mysteries were practiced. The water's extraordinary sapphire color is caused by a hidden opening in the rock that refracts the light. At highest illumination the very air inside seems tinted blue.

The Grotta Azzurra can be reached from Marina Grande or from the small embarkation point below Anacapri on the northwest side of the

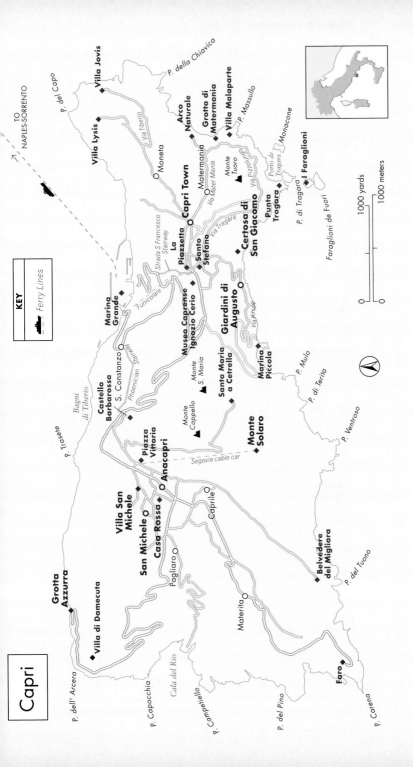

island, accessible by bus from Anacapri. If you're pressed for time, however, skip this sometimes frustrating and disappointing excursion. You board one boat to get to the grotto, then transfer to a smaller boat that takes you inside. If there's a backup of boats waiting to get in, you'll be given precious little time to enjoy the gorgeous color of the water and its silvery reflections. ⊠*Marina Grande* ☎€16–€19, *depending on boat company, including admission to grotto* ☉*Apr.– Sept., daily 9:30–2 hrs before sunset; Oct.–Mar., daily 10–noon.*

WHERE TO EAT

$$$$ ✕ **La Capannina.** One of Capri's finest restaurants, La Capannina is only a few steps from the busy social hub of the Piazzetta. It has a discreet covered veranda—open in summer—for dining by candlelight; most of the regulars avoid the stuffy dining rooms. The specialties are home-made ravioli and linguine *con lo scorfano* (with scorpion fish). Look for the authentic Capri wine with the house label. ⊠*Via Le Botteghe 12bis and 14, Capri Town* ☎*081/8370732* ⚐*Reservations essential* ▭*AE, DC, MC, V* ☉*Closed mid-Jan.–mid-Mar. and Wed. in Mar. and Nov.*

$$$ ✕ **I Faraglioni.** With shade provided by a 100-year-old wisteria plant, this popular restaurant is immersed in Mediterranean greenery. Meals in the fairly stylish dining room usually kick off with *uovo alla Mona-china,* an egg-shaped dish stuffed with mystery ingredients. For the first course, try the *straccetti con gamberi e pomodorini* (fresh green pasta with shrimp and cherry tomatoes). ⊠*Via Camerelle 75, Capri Town* ☎*081/8370320* ⚐*Reservations essential* ▭*AE, DC, MC, V* ☉*Closed Nov.–Mar.*

$$$ ✕ **La Canzone del Mare.** This is the legendary spot at the Marina Piccola, erstwhile haunt of Grace Fields, Emilio Pucci, Noël Coward, and any number of '50s and '60s glitterati. The VIPs may have departed for the beach at the Bagni di Tiberio, but the setting is as magical as ever. Enjoy lunch (no dinner is served) in the thatch-roof pavilion looking out over the sea and I Faraglioni in the distance—this is Capri as picture-perfect as it comes. ⊠*Via Marina Piccola 93, Capri Town* ☎*081/8370104* ▭*AE, DC, MC, V* ☉*Closed Nov.–Mar. No dinner.*

$$–$$$ ✕ **Le Grottelle.** Enjoying one of Capri's most unique settings, this infor-mal trattoria is built up against the limestone rocks not far from the Arco Naturale—a cave at the back doubles as the kitchen and wine cellar. The menu—as elsewhere—is chiefly seafood, with linguine *con gamberetti e rucola* (with shrimp and arugula) one of the more-inter-esting specialties. ⊠*Via Arco Naturale 13* ☎*081/8375719* ▭*MC, V* ☉*Closed mid-Nov.–Mar.*

★ **$$** ✕ **Buco di Bacco.** Just off the impossibly narrow Via Longano, this small restaurant—only two minutes from the Piazzetta—is a haven from Capri's madding crowds. The dining room is made even cozier by its vaulted ceilings. The versatile menu ranges from an ample vegetable buffet to a fine *filletto di tonno* (tuna steak). A good wine list and excel-lent service make this a popular venue, so book early—especially eve-nings—to avoid disappointment. ⊠*Via Longano 35* ☎*081/8370723* ▭*AE, DC, MC, V* ☉*Closed Wed. and Nov.*

$$ ✕ **Ristorante Pizzeria Aurora.** Though often frequented by celebrities—their photographs adorn the walls—this restaurant offers *simpatia* to all its patrons. Sit outside for maximum visibility or opt for extra privacy within. The cognoscenti start off by sharing a pizza *all'acqua*, a thin pizza with mozzarella and a sprinkling of *peperoncino* (dried chili peppers). If you're tiring of pasta, try the *sformatino alla Franco* (rice pie in a prawn sauce). Reservations are essential for dinner. ⊠ *Via Fuorlovado 18–20, Capri Town* ☎*081/8370181* ⊟*AE, DC, MC, V* ⊘ *Closed Jan. and Feb.*

$–$$ ✕ **La Giara.** A two-minute walk from Anacapri's bustling Piazza Vittoria, this casual eatery has a variety of delicious dishes served briskly and courteously. For a change from seafood, try the *pennette aum aum*, pasta pleasingly garnished with eggplant, mozzarella, cherry tomatoes, and basil. ⊠ *Via Orlandi 67, Anacapri* ☎*081/8373860* ⊟*AE, DC, MC, V* ⊘ *Closed Wed., and Dec. and Jan.*

WHERE TO STAY

$$$$ 🏠 **Punta Tragara.** Clinging to the Punta Tragara, this gorgeous hotel has
Fodor'sChoice a hold-your-breath perch directly over the rocks of I Faraglioni. Origi-
★ nally a villa visited by Churchill and Eisenhower, its exterior was renovated by Le Corbusier in traditional Capri style. Baronial fireplaces, gilded antiques, and travertine marble set the style in the main salons, while guest rooms—no two are alike—are sumptuous. The garden area has two beautiful saltwater pools and an arbor-covered restaurant, La Bussola, which might be the prettiest spot on the island. To top it off, the staff seems to have been sent to the finest finishing schools. **Pros:** Unbelievable views, good location for coastal walks. **Cons:** Room rates have skyrocketed, a 15-minute walk to town. ⊠ *Via Tragara 57, 80073 Capri Town* ☎*081/8370844* ⊕*www.hoteltragara.com* ⤳*48 rooms* △*In-room: safe, dial-up. In-hotel: restaurant, bar, pool, laundry service* ⊟*AE, DC, MC, V* ⊘*Closed Nov.–Apr.* ❏*BP.*

$$$$ 🏠 **Quisisana.** This grand hotel, one of the island's most luxurious, sits in the center of Capri Town. The bright and spacious rooms have some antique accents. Many have arcaded balconies with views of the sea or the charming enclosed garden surrounding a swimming pool. The Quisisana is particularly popular with Americans. **Pros:** Terrace good for people-watching, close to shopping. **Cons:** Extra charges can really add up, building lacks warmth. ⊠ *Via Camerelle 2, Capri Town 80073* ☎*081/8370788* ⊕*www.quisi.com* ⤳*149 rooms* △*In-room: safe, dial-up. In-hotel: 2 restaurants, bar, tennis court, pool, gym, spa* ⊟*AE, DC, MC, V* ⊘*Closed Nov.–mid-Mar.* ❏*MAP.*

★ $$$$ 🏠 **Scalinatella.** The name means "little stairway," and that's how this charming but modern small hotel is built, on terraces following the slope of the hill, overlooking the gardens, pool, and sea. The Scalinatella is the more-private neighbor of the nearby Quisisana, with intimate bedrooms in fresh, bright colors; the bathrooms have whirlpool baths. **Pros:** Attentive staff; discreet, quiet atmosphere. **Cons:** Pricey transfers from the port. ⊠ *Via Tragara 8, CapriTown 80073* ☎*081/8370633* 🖷*081/8378291* ⊕*www.scalinatella.com* ⤳*30 rooms* △*In-room: safe, dial-up. In-hotel: restaurant, bar, tennis court, pool, gym, laundry service* ⊟*AE, DC, MC, V* ⊘*Closed Nov.–mid-Mar.* ❏*BP.*

$$$$ 🏠 **Villa Brunella.** This gem sits in a garden just below the lane leading to the Faraglioni. Comfortable and tastefully furnished, the family-run

13

hotel has spectacular views and a swimming pool overlooking the sea. The terrace restaurant also benefits from the superb panorama and is renowned for its seafood and other local dishes. **Pros:** Rooms resemble villas, Internet access. **Cons:** Drinks are pricy, lots of steps to rooms. ✉ *Via Tragara 24, 80073 Capri Town* ☎ *081/8370122* 🌐 *www.villa-brunella.it* *20 rooms* *In-hotel: restaurant, bar, pool, public Internet* ▭ *AE, DC, MC, V* ⊙ *Closed Nov.–Mar.* *BP.*

★ $$–$$$ **Villa Sarah.** This family-run whitewashed Mediterranean building has a homey look and bright, simply furnished rooms. It's close enough to the Piazzetta (a 10-minute walk) to give easy access to the goings-on there, yet far enough away to ensure restful nights. There's a luxuriant garden and an enticing mosaic-tile pool. **Pros:** Secluded setting, friendly staff. **Cons:** No good restaurants nearby, basic rooms. ✉ *Via Tiberio 3/a, Capri Town 80073* ☎ *081/8377817* 🌐 *www.villasarah.it* *20 rooms* *In-hotel: bar, pool* ▭ *AE, DC, MC, V* ⊙ *Closed Nov.–Mar.* *BP.*

$$ **Il Girasole.** A popular option for those on a budget, Il Girasole is set in a grove of olive trees. It has small but bright rooms that look out onto a flower-filled terrace. **Pros:** Relaxing pool, obliging owner. **Cons:** Not in central Anacapri, poorly lighted paths. ✉ *Via Linciano 47, Anacapri 80071* ☎ *081/8372351* 🌐 *www.ilgirasole.com* *23 rooms* *In-hotel: pool* ▭ *AE, DC, MC, V* ⊙ *Closed Nov.–Mar.* *BP.*

★ $$ **La Tosca.** Although it's hard to find in the warren of side streets in Capri Town, La Tosca is worth all the trouble. Its quiet location, unassuming vibe, terrace views, and reasonable rates means it gets booked up ages in advance. As an added bonus, the owner is generous with island advice and restaurant recommendations. **Pros:** Recently renovated, great location, free wireless connection. **Cons:** Skimpy facilities, not all rooms have good views. ✉ *Via Birago 5, Capri Town 80073* ☎ *081/8370989* 🌐 *www.latoscahotel.com* *11* rooms *In-room: Wi-Fi* ▭ *AE, DC, MC, V* ⊙ *Closed Nov. –Feb.*

$ **Villa Eva.** Named for its dynamic owner, this is a popular international stopover for younger travelers chilling out from the island's hustle and bustle (often by the pool). Accommodations are in villas set in luxuriant gardens on the hillside above the Grotta Azzurra. ✉ *Via La Fabbrica 8, Anacapri 80073* ☎ *081/8371549* 🌐 *www.villaeva.com* *24 rooms* *In-room: no a/c (some), no phone, no TV. In-hotel: bar, pool* ▭ *AE, DC, MC, V* ⊙ *Closed Nov.–mid-Mar.* *BP.*

SORRENTO & THE AMALFI COAST

As you journey down the fabled Amalfi Coast, your route takes you past rocky cliffs plunging into the sea and small boats lying in sandy coves like brightly colored fish. Erosion has contorted the rocks into shapes resembling figures from mythology and hollowed out fairy grottoes where the air is turquoise and the water an icy blue. In winter, Nativity scenes of moss and stone are created in the rocks. White villages dripping with flowers nestle in coves or climb like vines up the steep, terraced hills. Lemon trees abound, loaded with blossoms (and

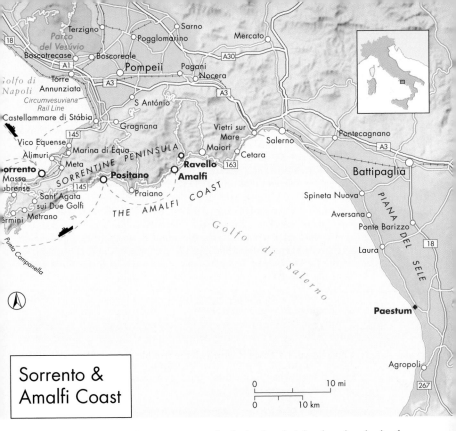

Sorrento &
Amalfi Coast

0   10 mi
0   10 km

netting in winter to protect the fruit—locals joke that they look after their lemons better than their children). The road must have a thousand turns, each with a different view, on its dizzying 69-km (43-mi) journey from Sorrento to Salerno.

SORRENTO

50 km (31 mi) south of Naples, 50 km (31 mi) west of Salerno.

GETTING HERE
You have many options for getting to Sorrento. From downtown Naples, take a Circumvesuviana train from Stazione Centrale or a ferry from Molo Beverello. If you're coming directly from the airport in Naples, grab a direct bus to Sorrento. By car, take the Naples–Salerno autostrada, exiting at Castellammare, and then following signs to Sorrento.

VISITOR INFORMATION
Sorrento tourism office (✉ *Via de Maio 35, 80067* ☎ *081/8074033* ⊕ *www.sorrentotourism.com*).

EXPLORING

Sorrento is across the Bay of Naples from Naples itself, on autostrada A3 and SS145. The Circumvesuviana railway, which stops at Herculaneum and Pompeii, provides another connection. The coast between Naples and Castellammare, where road and railway turn off onto the Sorrento peninsula, seems at times depressingly overbuilt and industrialized. Yet Vesuvius looms to the left, you can make out the 3,000-foot-high mass of Monte Faito ahead, and on a clear day you can see Capri off the tip of the peninsula. The scenery improves considerably as you near Sorrento, where the coastal plain is carved into russet cliffs of compacted volcanic ash rising perpendicularly from the sea. This is the Sorrento (north) side of the peninsula; on the other side is the more-dramatically scenic Amalfi Coast. But Sorrento has at least two advantages over Amalfi: the Circumvesuviana railway terminal and a fairly flat terrain. A stroll around town is a pleasure—you'll encounter narrow alleyways and interesting churches, and the views of the Bay of Naples from the Villa Comunale and the Museo Correale are priceless.

Until the mid-20th century Sorrento was a small, genteel resort favored by central European princes, English aristocrats, and American literati. During World War I American soldiers came to recuperate at the Hotel Vittoria. Now the town has grown and spread out along the crest of its famous cliffs, and apartments stand where citrus groves once bloomed. Like most resorts, Sorrento is best off-season, in spring, autumn, or even winter, when Campania's mild climate can make a stay pleasant anywhere along the coast.

A highlight of Sorrento is **Museo Correale di Terranova,** an 18th-century villa with a lovely garden on land given to the patrician Correale family by Queen Joan of Aragon in 1428. It has an excellent private collection amassed by the count of Terranova and his brother. The building itself is fairly charmless, with few period rooms, but the garden offers an allée of palm trees, citrus groves, floral nurseries, and an esplanade with a panoramic view of the Sorrento coast. The collection itself is one of the finest devoted to Neapolitan paintings, decorative arts, and porcelains, so for connoisseurs of the *seicento* (Italian 17th century), this museum is a must. Magnificent 18th-century inlaid tables by Giuseppe Gargiulo, Capodimonte porcelains, and rococo portrait miniatures are reminders of the age when pleasure and delight were all. Also on view are regional Greek and Roman archaeological finds, medieval marble work, glasswork, old master paintings, 17th-century majolicas—even Tasso's death mask. ⊠ *Via Correale* ☏ *081/8781846* ⊕ *www.sorrento-online.com/museocorreale* ☑ *€6* ☾ *Oct.–June, Wed.–Mon. 9–2; July–Sept., Wed.–Mon. 9–2 and 8:15–10:45.*

Worth checking out is the **Museo Bottega della Tarsialignea,** set up by local architects to ensure the continuity of the intarsia (wood inlay) tradition. It houses historical collections as well as exhibitions of modern work. Guided tours, the only way to see the displays, depart every half hour. Hours are a bit erratic in the low season, so call ahead. ⊠ *Via San Nicola 28* ☏ *081/8771942* ⊕ *www.alessandrofiorentinocollec-*

tion.it ✉ €8 ⊗ *Apr.–Oct., Tues.–Sun. 9:30–noon and 5–7; Nov.–Mar., Tues.–Sun. 9:30–noon and 3–5.*

Via Marina Grande turns into a pedestrian lane, then a stairway leading to Sorrento's only real beach at **Marina Grande,** where fishermen pull up their boats and there are some good seafood restaurants. A frequent bus also plies this route; tickets are sold at the *tabacchi* (tobacconist).

WHERE TO STAY & EAT

Fodor's Choice × **Antico Francischiello da Peppino.** Overlooking rows of olive trees that
★ $$$ seem to run into the sea, this eatery is away from the throng, halfway between Sorrento and Massa Lubrense. Two huge, beamed dining rooms with brick archways, old chandeliers, antique mirrored sideboards, hundreds of mounted plates, and tangerine tablecloths make for quite a sight. Specialties at this fourth-generation establishment include ravioli filled with sea bass and baked bream in a potato crust with lemon. The towering dessert trolley is full of goodies, and you can taste as many as you like. ✉ *Via Partenope 27, Massa Lubrense* ☎ *081/5339780* ⊟ *AE, DC, MC, V* ⊗ *Closed Wed. Nov.–Mar.*

$$–$$$ × **Aurora–'O Canonico 1898.** This 110-year-old institution actually consists of two side-by-side eateries differing in tone, price, and menu. To make up your mind, just look at the two menus outside: while Aurora serves wood-oven pizzas with a choice of 50 toppings, 'O Canonico specializes in homemade pasta and fresh fish, accompanied by a 1,750-label wine cellar. Wherever you sit, you can order the local specialty called *delizia al limone,* a rich spongy dessert with creamy lemon sauce. Both sets of outdoor tables look discreetly onto Sorrento's Piazza Tasso. ✉ *Via Piazza Tasso 7/10* ☎ *081/8783277* ⊟ *AE, DC, MC, V* ⊗ *Closed Mon. Nov.–Apr. and 2 weeks in Jan.*

★ $$–$$$ × **Don Alfonso 1890.** The most heralded restaurant in Campania is the domain of Alfonso Iaccarino; *haute*-hungry pilgrims come here to feast on culinary rarities, often centuries-old recipes given a unique spin. The braciola of lamb with pine nuts and raisins is a recipe that dates to the Renaissance, and the cannoli stuffed with foie gras pays homage to the Neapolitan Bourbon court. Nearly everything is homegrown, and the wine cellar is one of the finest in Europe. Those who want to make a night of it can stay in one of five apartments above the restaurant. ✉ *Corso Sant'Agata 13, Sant'Agata sui due Golfi* ⊹ *7 km (4 mi) south of Sorrento* ☎ *081/8780026* ⊟ *AE, DC, MC, V* ⊗ *Closed Mon. and Nov.–Mar. No dinner Tues.*

$$ × **La Favorita—O' Parrucchiano.** Set in a greenhouse with soaring ceilings, this sprawling eatery has enough tables and chairs amid enough tropical greenery to fill a Victorian conservatory. Opened in 1890 by a former priest (the name means "the priest's place" in the local dialect), La Favorita continues to serve Sorrentine classics. Though the prawns baked in lemon leaves, the long *candele* pasta with traditional meat and tomato *ragu* sauce, and the lemon tart are all excellent, it's the unique decor that sets La Favorita apart. ✉ *Corso Italia 71* ☎ *081/8781321* ⊟ *MC, V* ⊗ *Closed Wed. mid-Nov.–mid-Mar.*

$$ × **La Fenice.** In case you wonder where the locals go to escape from the crowds, this is it. Near the western end of Corso Italia, La Fenice

has a leafy veranda shielded from the passing traffic. The varied menu includes everything from pizzas to seafood, and the service is professional and efficient. ⊠ *Via degli Aranci 11* ☏ *081/8781652* ☰ *AE, DC, MC, V* ⊘ *Closed Mon. and Feb.*

$–$$ ✕ **Trattoria da Emilia.** You can sit outside at this trattoria on the Marina Grande and watch the life of the port go by. This simple, rustic restaurant with wooden tables has been run by Donna Emilia and her offspring since 1947 and provides typical Sorrento home cooking and a family atmosphere. Fried seafood is the specialty. Sofia Loren ate here while filming *Pane, amore....* ⊠ *Via Marina Grande 62* ☏ *081/8072720* ☰ *No credit cards* ⊘ *Closed Nov.–Mar. No lunch Tues.*

★ $$$$ ⊡ **Bellevue Syrene.** Set in a cliff-top garden close to the center of Sorrento, this exclusive hotel retains its old-fashioned comfort and sumptuous charm with Victorian nooks and alcoves, antique paintings, and exuberant frescoes. You can find interior-facing rooms at lower prices if you're willing to forgo the splendid views over the sea. Try breakfast on the sunny terrace in summer. **Pros:** Atmospheric bar, close to shopping, recently renovated. **Cons:** Rooms vary greatly in size, no pool. ⊠ *Piazza della Vittoria 5, 80067* ☏ *081/8781024* ⊕ *www.bellevuesyrene.it* ☞ *65 rooms* ⬡ *In-room: safe, Wi-Fi. In-hotel: 2 restaurants, bar, gym, beachfront, some pets allowed* ☰ *AE, DC, MC, V* ⦿ *BP.*

★ $$$$ ⊡ **Excelsior Vittoria.** Magnificently situated overlooking the Bay of Naples, this is a belle-epoque dream come true. Gilded salons, stunning gardens, and an impossibly romantic terrace where orchestras lull you twice a week with Neapolitan and modern music: in all, it's a truly intoxicating experience. Enrico Caruso stayed here and, more recently, Luciano Pavarotti. An outdoor swimming pool and gym add more-modern comforts. **Pros:** Secluded setting, great breakfast, good deals during low season. **Cons:** Pricey restaurant, some rooms are better than others. ⊠ *Piazza Tasso 34, 80067* ☏ *081/8071044* ⊕ *www.exvitt.it* ☞ *98 rooms, 20 suites* ⬡ *In-room: safe, dial-up. In-hotel: 2 restaurants, bars, pool, gym, some pets allowed* ☰ *AE, DC, MC, V* ⦿ *BP.*

$$ ⊡ **Settimo Cielo.** Even if your wallet won't allow a stay at one of Sorrento's grand hotels, you can still find lodgings overlooking the water. This hotel, an excellent choice for budget travelers, is on the road to Capo Sorrento. The grounds have pretty gardens and a swimming pool. The rooms, which all face the sea, are simple and modern. **Pros:** Plenty of parking, excellent views. **Cons:** No-frills decor, long walk along busy road into Sorrento. ⊠ *Via Capo 27, 80067* ☏ *081/8781012* ⊕ *www.hotelsettimocielo.com* ☞ *20 rooms* ⬡ *In-room: safe. In-hotel: bar, pool* ☰ *AE, DC, MC, V* ⊘ *Closed Nov.–mid-Dec. and Jan.–Mar.* ⦿ *BP.*

$ ⊡ **Mignon Meublé.** Spacious and simple yet stylish accommodations, a central location, friendly service, and bargain rates—with this winning combination, it's understandable why you should book well in advance. **Pros:** Pleasant rooms, near restaurants. **Cons:** Stairs to climb, no sea views. ⊠ *Via Sersale 9, 80067* ☏ *081/8073824* ⊕ *www.sorrentohotelmignon.com* ☞ *24 rooms* ⬡ *In-room: safe, no phone. In-hotel: no elevator, public Internet* ☰ *AE, DC, MC, V* ⦿ *BP.*

POSITANO

14 km (9 mi) east of Sorrento, 57 km (34 mi) south of Naples.

GETTING HERE

Local buses leave from the Circumvesuviana train station in Sorrento. In summer, buses also run from Rome and Naples. From June to September, your best option is the ferry from Sorrento, Salerno, or Naples.

WORD OF MOUTH

"For our honeymoon we went to Positano (and did day trips to Capri, Ravello, Sorrento, Amalfi, and Pompeii). It was the most romantic place—so beautiful. Wonderful shops and restaurants were everywhere! The drive along the cliffs was scary, but exhilarating, too!" –Gemini MBA

13

VISITOR INFORMATION

Positano tourism office (⊠ *Via del Saracino 4, 84017* ☏ *089/875067* ⊕ *www.aziendaturismopositano.it*).

EXPLORING

When John Steinbeck lived here in 1953, he wrote that it was difficult to consider tourism an industry because "there are not enough *tourists.*" It's safe to say that Positano, a village of white Moorish-style houses clinging to slopes around a small sheltered bay, has since been discovered. Another Steinbeck observation still applies, however: "Positano bites deep. It is a dream place that isn't quite real when you are there and becomes beckoningly real after you have gone.... The small curving bay of unbelievably blue and green water laps gently on a beach of small pebbles. There is only one narrow street and it does not come down to the water. Everything else is stairs, some of them as steep as ladders. You do not walk to visit a friend, you either climb or slide."

In the 10th century Positano was part of Amalfi's maritime republic, which rivaled Venice as an important mercantile power. Its heyday was in the 16th and 17th centuries, when its ships traded in the Near and Middle East carrying spices, silks, and precious woods. The coming of the steamship in the mid-19th century led to the town's decline; some three-fourths of its 8,000 citizens emigrated to America.

What had been reduced to a forgotten fishing village is now the number one attraction on the coast. From here you can take hydrofoils to Capri in summer, escorted bus rides to Ravello, and tours of the Grotta dello Smeraldo. If you're staying in Positano, check whether your hotel has a parking area. If not, you will have to pay for space in a parking lot, which is almost impossible to find during the high season, from Easter to September. The best bet for day-trippers is to arrive by bus—there is a regular, if crowded, service from Sorrento—or else get to Positano early enough to find an overpriced parking space.

No matter how much time you spend in Positano, make sure you have some comfortable walking shoes (no heels) and that your back and legs are strong enough to negotiate those daunting *scalinatelle* (little stairways). Alternatively, you can ride the municipal bus, which frequently plies along the one-and-only-one-way Via Pasitea, a hairpin road running from Positano's central Piazza dei Mulini to the mountains and back, making a loop through the town every half hour. Heading down from the Sponda bus stop toward the beach, you pass Le Sirenuse, the hotel where John Steinbeck stayed in 1953. Its stepped terraces offer vistas over the town, so you might splurge on lunch or a drink here on the pool terrace, a favorite gathering place for Modigliani-sleek jet-setters.

NEED A BREAK?   If you want to catch your breath after a bus ride to Positano, take a quick time-out for an espresso, a slice of Positanese (a delectable chocolate cake), or a fresh-fruit iced granita in the lemon-tree garden at Bar-Pasticceria La Zagara (✉ *Via dei Mulini 8* ☎ *089/875964*).

Past a bevy of resort boutiques, head to Via dei Mulini 23 to view the prettiest garden in Positano—the 18th-century courtyard of the **Palazzo Murat,** named for Joachim Murat, who sensibly chose the palazzo as his summer residence. This was where Murat, designated by his brother-in-law Napoléon as King of Naples in 1808, came to forget the demands of power and lead the simple life. Since Murat was one of Europe's leading style setters, it couldn't be *too* simple; he built this grand abode (now a hotel) just steps from the main beach.

Beyond the Palazzo Murat is the Chiesa Madre, or parish church of **Santa Maria Assunta,** its green-and-yellow majolica dome topped by a perky cupola visible from just about anywhere in town. Built on the site of the former Benedictine abbey of St. Vito, the 13th-century Romanesque structure was almost completely rebuilt in 1700. The last piece of the ancient mosaic floor can be seen under glass near the apse. Note the carved wooden Christ, a masterpiece of devotional religious art, with its bathetic face and bloodied knees, on view before the altar. At the altar is a Byzantine 13th-century painting on wood of Madonna with Child, known as the Black Virgin, carried to the beach every August 15 to celebrate the Feast of the Assumption. Legend claims that the painting was once stolen by Saracen pirates, who, fleeing in a raging storm, heard from a voice on high saying, "*Posa, posa*"—"Put it down, put it down." When they placed the image on the beach near the church, the storm calmed, as did the Saracens. Embedded over the doorway of the church's bell tower, set across the tiny piazza, is a medieval bas-relief of fishes, a fox, and a pistrice, the mythical half-dragon, half-dog sea monster. This is one of the few relics of the medieval abbey of St. Vito. ✉ *Piazza Flavio Gioia above main beach* ☎ *089/875067* ⊗ *Daily 8:30–noon and 4–7.*

The walkway from the Piazza Flavio Gioia leads down to the **Spiaggia Grande,** or main beach, bordered by an esplanade and some of Positano's best—and priciest—restaurants. Head over to the stone pier to the far right of the beach as you face the water.

A staircase leads to the **Via Positanesi d'America,** a lovely seaside walkway. Halfway up the path you'll find the Torre Trasìta, the most distinctive of Positano's three coastline defense towers, which, in various states of repair, define the edges of Positano. The Trasìta—now a residence available for summer rental—was one of the defense towers used to warn of pirate raids. Continuing along the Via Positanesi d'America you pass tiny inlets and emerald coves until the large beach, Spiaggia di Fornillo, comes into view.

If the Spiaggia Grande is too orderly for you, take the small boat to the **Spiaggia di Laurito.** (Look for the boat on the right side of the harbor as you approach the beach—it has a sign with a big red smiling fish on it.) You can spend an entire day in this little cove, taking the two steps up to the restaurant **Da Adolfo** when the exertion of swimming has worked up your appetite.

WHERE TO STAY & EAT

$$$–$$$$ ✕ **Buca di Bacco.** After an aperitif at the town's most famous and fashionable café downstairs, you dine on a veranda overlooking the beach. The specialties include *zuppa di cozze* (mussel soup), fresh *spigola* (sea bass), and figs and oranges in caramel. ⊠ *Via Rampa Teglia 8* ☎ *089/875699* ▤ *AE, DC, MC, V* ⊘ *Closed Nov.–Mar.*

$$$ ✕ **Donna Rosa.** This minimalist little hideaway in one-street Montepertuso, the hamlet high over Positano, gives a new twist to time-honored local dishes. Try the *tagliatella ai profumi di mare* (short pasta garnished with seafood) or the *ravioli ai carciofi* (stuffed with artichokes). Desserts are delectable: the *soufflé al cioccolato caldo* will have chocoholics swooning. Don't think of showing up without a reservation. ⊠ *Via Montepertuso 97/99* ☎ *089/811806* ⚭ *Reservations essential* ▤ *AE, DC, MC, V* ⊘ *No lunch Aug., and Mon. and Tues, July–Sept. Closed early Jan.–2 wks before Easter, and Tues. Oct.–June.*

$$–$$$ ✕ **'O Capurale.** Even though *'o capurale* ("the corporal") himself no longer runs the place, his eponymous restaurant is still a great find in the crowded center of Positano. There's one large dining room with simple wooden tables, a marble floor, and a high coved ceiling with Fauvist-style frescoes. The space remains cool even in the height of summer when filled with diners digging into fresh pasta with mussels and pumpkin or rockfish *all'acqua pazza,* with a few tomatoes and garlic. ⊠ *Via Regina Giovanna 12* ☎ *089/875374* ▤ *AE, DC, MC, V* ⊘ *Closed Nov.–mid-Feb.*

$$ ✕ **Da Adolfo.** At this completely informal spot on Spiaggia di Laurito, most diners sit for hours in their swimsuits, whiling away the time reading or chatting over a jug of the light local wine (with peaches in summer) or a hefty plate of *totani con patate* (squid and potatoes with garlic and oil). The brusque but amusing waiters are part of the scene. ⊠ *Spiaggia di Laurito* ☎ *089/875022* ⚭ *Reservations not accepted* ▤ *No credit cards* ⊘ *Closed Oct.–Apr.*

★$$ ✕ **La Tagliata.** If your enthusiasm for overpriced seafood dishes is waning, La Tagliata has the answer: great antipasti, homemade pastas with rich tomato sauce, and meats grilled before your eyes in the dining room. (Ask for a *porzioni piccole* unless you are ravenous.) All this comes with endless views of the Amalfi Coast. The prices are reasonable, and include a jug of red wine. Aficionados will do better choosing their own bottle, however. Though it lies between Montepertuso and Nocelle, the restaurant will arrange a shuttle to pick you up from your

13

hotel in Positano. ✉ *Via Tagliata 22* ☎ *089/875872* ⌕ *Reservations essential* ▤ *DC, MC, V* ⊘ *Closed weekdays, Dec.–Feb.*

$$$$ ⊞ **Il San Pietro.** An oasis for its affluent international clientele, the San Pietro lies a few bends outside the town and is set amid gardens high above the sea. The hotel has sumptuous Neapolitan baroque decor and masses of flowers in the lounges, elegantly understated rooms (most with terraces), and marvelous views. There's a pool on an upper level, and an elevator whisks you down to the private beach and beach bar. The proprietors organize boating excursions and provide car and minibus service into town. **Pros:** Secluded and quiet, all rooms have sea views, includes complimentary boat tour. **Cons:** Outside Positano, three-night minimum in high season. ✉ *Via Laurito 2, 84017* ☎ *089/875455* ⊕ *www.ilsanpietro.it* ⇖ *60 rooms* ⌕ *In-room: safe, dial-up. In-hotel: restaurant, bars, tennis court, pool, gym, spa, beachfront* ▤ *AE, DC, MC, V* ⊘ *Closed Nov.–Mar.* ⓞ|*BP.*

★ **$$$$**   ⊞ **Le Sirenuse.** A handsome 18th-century palazzo in the center of town has been transformed into this luxury hotel with bright tile floors, precious antiques, and tasteful furnishings. The bedrooms are spacious and comfortable; most have splendid views from balconies or terraces. The top-floor suites have huge bathrooms and whirlpool baths. One side of a large terrace has an inviting swimming pool; on the other is an excellent restaurant. **Pros:** Personalized service, impressive gym, amazing breakfasts. **Cons:** Sea-view rooms cost much more, meals are pricey. ✉ *Via Cristoforo Colombo 30, 84017* ☎ *089/875066* ⊕ *www.sirenuse.it* ⇖ *51 rooms, 9 suites* ⌕ *In-hotel: restaurant, bar, pool, gym, spa* ▤ *AE, DC, MC, V* ⓞ|*BP.*

$$$$ ⊞ **Palazzo Murat.** The location is perfect—in the heart of town, near the beachside promenade, but set inside a quiet, walled garden. The older wing is a historic palazzo with tall windows and wrought-iron balconies; the modern wing is a whitewashed Mediterranean building with arches and terraces. You can relax in antiques-accented lounges or in the charming vine-draped patio and enjoy gorgeous views from the comfortable bedrooms. **Pros:** Central location, secluded feel, beautiful leafy courtyard. **Cons:** No pool, expensive parking. ✉ *Via dei Mulini 23, 84017* ☎ *089/875177* ⊕ *www.palazzomurat.it* ⇖ *31 rooms* ⌕ *In-room: safe, refrigerator, dial-up. In-hotel: restaurant, bar* ▤ *AE, DC, MC, V* ⊘ *Closed Nov.–Mar.* ⓞ|*BP.*

$$$ ⊞ **Casa Albertina.** Clinging to the cliff, this little house is well loved for its Italian charm, its homey atmosphere, and its owners, the Cinque family. Rooms have high ceilings, bright fabrics, tile flooring, and sunny terraces or balconies overlooking the sea and coastline. Cars can't drive to the doorway, but porters will ferry your luggage. Note: it's 300 steps down to the main beach. Half or full board is required in summer. **Pros:** Wonderful restaurant, excellent breakfast on terrace, attentive staff. **Cons:** Difficult to find, many steps to climb. ✉ *Via della Tavolozza 3, 84017* ☎ *089/875143* ⊕ *www.casalbertina.it* ⇖ *21 rooms* ⌕ *In-room: safe, dial-up. In-hotel: restaurant, parking (fee), some pets allowed* ▤ *AE, DC, MC, V* ⓞ|*MAP.*

$$$ ⊞ **Villa Rosa.** Sharing almost the same views as hotels that go for twice the price, this family-run lodging has long been a favorite with independent travelers. It's centrally located but slightly set back from the road up the inevitable steps. Ask for one of the rooms on the first floor, which are quieter and have better views. Breakfast is served in your room. **Pros:** Helpful advice from staff, large rooms. **Cons:** No common areas, lots of steps. ⊠ *Via Cristoforo Colombo 127, 84017* ☎*089/811955* ⊕*www.villarosapositano.it* ↘*18 rooms* ₺*In-room: refrigerator, dial-up. In-hotel: laundry service* ☰*AE, DC, MC, V* ☾*Closed Nov.–mid-Mar.* ◉*BP.*

★ **$$** ⛱ **La Fenice.** Paradise found. This tiny and unpretentious hotel on the outskirts of town beckons with bougainvillea-laden vistas, castaway cottages, and a turquoise sea water pool, all perched over a private beach, just across a cove from Franco Zefferelli's famous villa. Once past the gate, you climb a steep stairway to the main house—but tread slowly: the paths and stairways here enchantingly frame (sometimes literally with vines) vistas over land and sea. Thanks to the wonderful family of the owner, Constantino Mandara, you'll feel right at home in a few minutes—that's because this is his home. Guest rooms, accented with coved ceilings, whitewashed walls, and native folk art, are simple havens of tranquillity. Several accommodations are in a house perched above the road (a bit noisy if trucks rumble by, but this rarely happens at night), although others are adorable little cottages set close to the sea. All are linked by very steep walkways—covered with arbors and zigzagging across the hill, they tie together these little acres of heaven. **Pros:** Gorgeous hillside by the sea, happy guests. **Cons:** Not facing scenic Positano, lots of steps. ⊠*Via G. Marconi 4, 84017* ☎*089/875513* ⊕ *fenicepositano@virgilio.it* ↘ *15 rooms* ₺*In-room: no a/c, no TV. In-hotel: pool* ☰*No credit cards* ◉*BP.*

NIGHTLIFE

L'Africana (⊠*Vettica Maggiore, Praiano* ✛*10 km [6 mi] east of Positano on coast road* ☎*089/874042*) is the premier nightclub on the Amalfi Coast, built into a fantastic grotto above the sea.

GROTTA DELLO SMERALDO

13 km (8 mi) east of Positano, 27 km (17 mi) east of Sorrento.

GETTING HERE

Boat tours leave from the seafront at Amalfi. The charge is €6 per person.

A peculiar green light that casts an eerie emerald glow over impressive formations of stalagmites and stalactites, many of them underwater, inspired the name of the Grotta dello Smeraldo (Emerald Grotto). You can park at the signposts for the grotto along the coast road and take an elevator down, or you can drive on to Amalfi and return to the grotto by more-romantic means—via boat. ☎*089/871107* ⛵*Grotto €5.50* ☾*Apr.–Sept., daily 9–5; Oct.–Mar., daily 10–4.*

AMALFI

17 km (11 mi) east of Positano, 35 km (22 mi) east of Sorrento.

GETTING HERE

From April to October, the best way to get to Amalfi is by ferry from Salerno. From June to September, you can also get here from Naples by fast craft. For the rest of the year, buses from Sorrento and Salerno are the only option.

VISITOR INFORMATION

Amalfi tourism office (⊠ *Corso delle Repubbliche Marinare 27, 84011* ☎ *089/871107* ⊕ *www.amalfitouristoffice.it*).

EXPLORING

"The sun—the moon—the stars—and Amalfi," Amalfitans used to say. During the Middle Ages Amalfi was an independent maritime state with a population of 50,000. The republic also brought the art of papermaking to Europe from Arabia. Before World War II there were 13 mills making paper by hand in the Valle Molini, but now only two small ones remain. The town is romantically situated at the mouth of a deep gorge and has some good-quality hotels and restaurants. It's also a convenient base for excursions to Capri and the Grotta dello Smeraldo. The parking problem here is as bad as that in Positano. The small lot in the center of town fills quickly; if you're willing to pay the steep prices, make a lunch reservation at one of the hotel restaurants and have your car parked for you.

★ Amalfi's main historical sight is its **Duomo** (also known as Cattedrale di Sant'Andrea), which shows an interesting mix of Moorish and early Gothic influences. You're channeled first into the adjoining **Chiostro del Paradiso** (Paradise Cloister), built around 1266 as a burial ground for Amalfi's elite and one of the architectural treasures of southern Italy. Its flower-and-palm-filled quadrangle has a series of exceptionally delicate intertwining arches on slender double columns in a combination of Byzantine and Arabian styles. Next stop is the ninth-century basilica, a **museum** housing sarcophagi, sculpture, Neapolitan gold artifacts, and other treasures from the cathedral complex.

Steps from the basilica lead down into the **Cripta di Sant'Andrea** (Crypt of St. Andrew). The cathedral above was built in the 13th century to house the saint's bones, which came from Constantinople and supposedly exuded a miraculous liquid believers call the "manna of St. Andrew." Following the one-way traffic up to the cathedral itself, you finally get to admire the elaborate polychrome marbles and painted, coffered ceilings from its 18th-century restoration; art historians shake their heads over this renovation, as the original decoration of the apse must have been one of the wonders of the Middle Ages. ⊠ *Piazza del Duomo* ☎ *089/871059* 🎫 *€2.50* ⊙ *Mar.–June and Oct., daily 9–7; July–Sept., daily 9–8; Nov.–Feb., daily 10–1 and 2:30–5:30.*

The **Valle dei Mulini** *(Valley of the Mills)*, uphill from town, was for centuries Amalfi's center for papermaking, an ancient trade learned from the Arabs (who learned it from the Chinese). Beginning in the 12th century, former flour mills in the town were converted to produce paper made from cotton and linen, being among the first in Europe to do so. In 1211 Frederick II of Sicily prohibited this lighter, more-readable paper for use in the preparation of official documents, favoring traditional sheepskin parchment, but by 1811 more than a dozen mills here, with more along the coast, were humming. Natural waterpower ensured that the handmade paper was cost-effective, but catastrophic flooding in 1954 closed most of the mills for good, and many of them have now been converted into private housing. The **Museo della Carta** (Museum of Paper) opened in 1971 in a 15th-century mill; paper samples, tools of the trade, old machinery, and the audiovisual presentation are all enlightening. ⊠ *Via delle Cartiere 23* ☎ *089/8304561* ⊕ *www. museodellacarta.it* ☒ *€3.50* ⊙ *Nov.–Feb., Tues.–Sun. 10–3:30; Mar.– Oct., daily 10–6:30.*

13

WHERE TO STAY & EAT

★ **$$$$** ✕ **Da Gemma.** Since 1872 cognoscenti have sung the praises of this understated landmark, which has a terrace set above the main street. The menu, printed on local handmade paper, announces such favorites as oven-baked fish with lemon peel and the *tubettoni alla masaniello* (tiny pieces of pasta with capers, mussels, and prawns). Traces of Amalfi's Arabic roots can be found in the sweets made with almonds and citrus fruits that come from the glistening kitchen. ⊠ *Via Fratello Gerardo Sasso 9* ☎ *089/871345* ▤ *AE, DC, MC, V* ⊙ *Closed mid-Jan.–mid-Feb. and Wed. Sept.–June.*

$$ ✕ **A Paranza.** Located in the hamlet of Atrani, a 15-minute walk from the center of Amalfi along the road to Salerno, this seafood restaurant is worth the walk. With coved ceilings and immaculate linen tablecloths, the two dining rooms are at once homey and quite formal. Each day's menu depends on the catch; the tasting menu (antipasti ranging from marinated tuna to fried rice balls, pasta, and risotto, and a choice of dessert) is a good option. If that sounds like too much, go for the scialatielli ai frutti di mare. Finish your meal with one of the divine cakes. ⊠ *Via Dragone 1/2* ☎ *089/871840* ▤ *AE, DC, MC, V* ⊙ *Closed Dec. 8–26 and Tues. Oct.–May.*

$$ ✕ **Trattoria di Maria.** At this friendly establishment presided over by the convivial Enzo (son of Maria) you can dine with the locals on delicious pizza baked in a wood oven, local fish dishes, and lemon profiteroles. Ask for a glass of the limoncello or one of the other home-made liqueurs made from bay leaves, fennel, or bilberries (similar to blueberries). ⊠ *Piazza ad Amalfi* ☎ *089/871880* ▤ *AE, DC, MC, V* ⊙ *Closed Mon. and Nov.*

★ **$$$$** ▦ **Santa Caterina.** A large mansion perched above a terraced and flowered hillside just outside Amalfi proper, the Santa Caterina is one of the top hotels on the coast. The rooms are tastefully decorated; most have small terraces or balconies with spectacular views. There are lovely lounges, gardens, and terraces for relaxing, and an elevator delivers you to the seaside saltwater pool, bar, and swimming area. On grounds lush with lemon and orange groves, there are two romantic villa annexes. **Pros:** Romantic atmosphere, airy rooms. **Cons:** Need a car to get around, a long walk from Amalfi's sights. ⊠*Strada Amalfitana 9, 84011* ☎*089/871012* ⊕*www.hotelsantacaterina.it* ↘*57 rooms, 9 suites* ⑆*In-room: safe, dial-up. In-hotel: 2 restaurants, bars, pool, gym, beachfront, parking (no fee)* ▤*AE, DC, MC, V* ᵀᴼᴵ*BP.*

★$$ ☷ **L'Antico Convitto.** Up an impossibly narrow alley two blocks from the Duomo, this compact hotel is in the heart of Amalfi. The rooms, all renovated in 2006, are elegantly but sparsely furnished. Opt for lodging on the upper floor where the views are slightly better. **Pros:** Charming staff, quiet location. **Cons:** No sea views, basic furnishings. ⊠*Via Salita dei Curiali 4, 84011* ☎*089/871849* ⊕*www.lanticoconvitto.com* ↘*16 rooms* ⑆*In-room: safe, refrigerator, dial-up* ▤*AE, DC, MC, V* ⊘*Closed Nov.–mid-Dec. and early Jan.–Feb.*

RAVELLO

5 km (3 mi) northeast of Amalfi, 40 km (25 mi) east of Sorrento.

GETTING HERE

Buses from Amalfi make the 20-minute trip along white-knuckle roads. From Naples, take the Naples–Salerno motorway, then exit at Angri and follow signs for Ravello. The journey takes about 75 minutes. Save yourself the trouble of driving by hiring a car and driver.

VISITOR INFORMATION

Ravello tourism office (⊠*Via Roma 18b, 84010* ☎*089/857096* ⊕*www. ravellotime.it*).

EXPLORING

Perched on a ridge high above Amalfi and the neighboring town of Atrani, the enchanting village of Ravello has stupendous views, quiet lanes, two important Romanesque churches, and several irresistibly romantic gardens. Set "closer to the sky than the sea," according to André Gide, the town has been the ultimate aerie ever since it was founded as a smart suburb for the richest families of Amalfi's 12th-century maritime republic. Rediscovered by English aristocrats a century ago, the town now hosts one of Italy's most famous music festivals.

The **Duomo,** dedicated to patron saint Pantaleone, was founded in 1086 by Orso Papiro, the town's first bishop. Rebuilt in the 12th and 17th centuries, it retains traces of medieval frescoes in the transept, an original mullioned window, a marble portal, and a three-story 13th-century bell tower playfully interwoven with mullioned windows and arches. The 12th-century bronze door has 54 embossed panels depicting Christ's life, and saints, prophets, plants, and animals, all narrating biblical lore. It was crafted by Barisano da Trani, who also fashioned the doors of the cathedrals of Trani and Monreale. The nave's three aisles are divided by ancient columns, and treasures include sarcophagi from Roman times and paintings by southern Renaissance artist Andrea da Salerno. Most impressive are the two medieval pulpits: the earlier one (on your left as you face the altar), used for reading the Epistles, is inset with a mosaic scene of Jonah and the whale, symbolizing death and redemption. The more-famous one opposite, used for reading the Gospels, was commissioned by Nicola Rufolo in 1272 and created by Niccolò di Bartolomeo da Foggia. It seems almost Tuscan in style, with exquisite mosaic work and bas-reliefs and six twisting columns sitting on lion pedestals. An eagle grandly tops the inlaid marble lectern.

13

A chapel to the left of the apse is dedicated to St. Pantaleone, a physician who was beheaded in the third century in Nicomedia. Every July 27 devout believers gather in hope of witnessing a miracle (similar to that of San Gennaro in Naples), in which the saint's blood, collected in a vial and set out on an inlaid marble altar, appears to liquefy and come to a boil; it hasn't happened in recent years. In the crypt is the **Museo del Duomo,** which displays treasures from about the 13th century, during the reign of Frederick II of Sicily. Enter through the side door when the church is closed. ⊠ *Piazza del Duomo* ☎ *089/857212* ✉ *€2.50* ⊙ *Church: daily 9–1 and 3–7; museum: daily 9:30–7.*

Directly off Ravello's main piazza is the **Villa Rufolo,** which—if the master storyteller Boccaccio is to be believed—was built in the 13th century by Landolfo Rufolo, whose immense fortune stemmed from trade with Moors and Saracens. Within is a scene from the earliest days of the Crusades. Norman and Arab architecture mingle in profusion in a welter of color-filled gardens so lush that composer Richard Wagner used them as his inspiration for the home of the Flower Maidens in his opera *Parsifal*. Beyond the Arab-Sicilian cloister and the Norman tower are two flower-bedded terraces that offer a splendid vista of the Bay of Salerno; the lower "Wagner Terrace" is the major site for the yearlong **Festival Musicale di Ravello** (☎ *089/858149* ⊕ *www.ravelloarts.org*). ⊠ *Piazza del Duomo, 84010* ✉ *€5* ⊙ *Apr.–Oct., daily 9–8; Nov.–Mar., daily 9–6.*

From Ravello's main piazza, head west along Via San Francesco and Via Santa Chiara to the **Villa Cimbrone,** a medieval-style fantasy that sits 1,500 feet above the sea. Created in 1905 by England's Lord Grimthorpe and made world famous when Greta Garbo stayed here in 1937, the Gothic castle is set in fragrant rose gardens that lead to the **Belvedere dell'Infinità** (Belvedere of Infinity), a grand stone parapet that overlooks the impossibly blue Gulf of Salerno and frames a panorama that former Ravello resident Gore Vidal has called "the most beautiful in the world." The villa itself is now a hotel. ⊠ *Via Santa Chiara 26* ☎ *089/857459* ✉ *€5* ⊙ *Daily 9–sunset.*

WHERE TO STAY & EAT

$$ ✕ **Cumpà Cosimo.** This family-run restaurant a few steps from the Piazza del Duomo offers a cordial welcome in two simple but attractive dining rooms. There's no view, but the pasta dishes are excellent, with many ingredients from owner Donna Netta's garden or her butcher

shop next door. Among the specialties are cheese crepes, roast lamb, and a dish including seven types of homemade pasta. ⊠ *Via Roma 44* ☎ *089/857156* ⊟ *AE, DC, MC, V* ☉ *Closed Mon. Nov.–Feb.*

$–$$ ✕ **Vittoria.** Down the bustling arcade of pottery shops adjacent to the Villa Rufolo, this is a good place to escape the crowds. Vittoria's thin-crust pizza with loads of fresh toppings is the star attraction, but also consider the pasta, maybe fusilli with tomatoes, zucchini, and mozzarella. The decor is extremely simple, with white walls and a few etchings of Ravello. ⊠ *Via dei Rufolo 3* ☎ *089/857947* ⊟ *AE, DC, MC, V* ☉ *Closed Tues. Nov.–Mar.*

★ $$$$ ⬚ **Hotel Palumbo.** Occupying a 12th-century patrician palace outfitted with antiques and modern comforts, this elegant hotel has the feel of a private home as well as its own annexed winery. Everyone from Richard Wagner to a young Jack and Jackie have stayed here (and Brad and Angelina were recent guests). It has beautiful garden terraces, breathtaking views, and a sumptuous, 18th-century dining room, ashimmer with chandeliers and Old Master paintings. In summer you can descend to a villa and be pampered in the hotel's seaside retreat. Half board is compulsory except in winter, when the restaurant is closed. **Pros:** Romantic atmosphere, majestic dining room. **Cons:** Some rooms are small, needs some renovations. ⊠ *Palazzo Confalone, Via San Giovanni del Toro 16, 84010* ☎ *089/857244* ⊕ *www.hotelpalumbo.it* ⇄ *20 rooms* ⚲ *In-room: safe, dial-up. In-hotel: restaurant, bar, pool, beachfront, laundry facilities, parking (fee)* ⊟ *AE, DC, MC, V* ⵔ *MAP.*

$$$$ ⬚ **Palazzo Sasso.** Glitzy with gold trim and offering the latest word in comfortable amenities, this 12th-century palace was renovated by Richard Branson almost a decade ago and dazzles some with its marble atrium and lofty coastal views. But in genteel Ravello, the naked nymph fountain and hot tubs on the roof strike a wrong, Donald Trump note. Happily, the Rossellini restaurant, open to the public only in the evenings, is highly recommended, with a top chef and very elegant decor. Most rooms have ocean views, with high arched ceilings and tile floors that lend a Mediterranean feel—some are accented with antiques. The "infinite suite" has to be seen to be believed, though its price also approaches infinity. **Pros:** Great attention to detail, tasty breakfasts. **Cons:** Silly glass elevators, overly restored historic mansion. ⊠ *Via San Giovanni del Toro 28, 84010* ☎ *089/818181* ⊕ *www.palazzosasso.com* ⇄ *32 rooms, 8 suites* ⚲ *In-room: dial-up. In-hotel: 2 restaurants, bar, pool, spa, some pets allowed* ⊟ *AE, DC, MC, V* ☉ *Closed Nov.–Mar* ⵔ *BP.*

★ $$$$ ⬚ **Villa Cimbrone.** Suspended over the azure sea and set amid rose-laden gardens, this magical place was once the home of Lord Grimthorpe and the holiday hideaway of Greta Garbo. Now the Gothic-style *castello* (castle) has guest rooms ranging from cozy to palatial. (Opt for the Peony Room, which has its own terrace.) Tapestried armchairs, framed prints, vintage art books, and other antiques that belonged to Viscountess Frost, the lord's daughter, still grace the enchantingly elegant sitting room. Best of all, guests have the villa's world-famous gardens all to themselves once the gates are closed at sunset. The villa is a strenuous hike from the town center, but porters will carry your luggage and the distance helps keep this the most peaceful place on the Amalfi Coast. **Pros:** Good restaurant, access to gardens after crowds have left. **Cons:** Parking lot not at the hotel, a 10-minute walk from town center. ✉ *Via Santa Chiara 26, 84010* ☎ *089/857459* ⊕ *www.villacimbrone. com/en* ⇆ *13 rooms* ♿ *In-room: ethernet. In-hotel: restaurant, bar, pool* ☰ *AE, DC, MC, V* ☾ *Closed Nov.–Easter* ⦿ *BP.*

$$ 🏨 **Parsifal.** Offering a viable alternative to its deluxe neighbors up the road, this diminutive property originally housed an order of Augustinian friars. Ancient ivy-covered stone arches and a tiled walkway lead to a cozy interior. Sunny terraces, a lush garden, and an alfresco dining area (better food at lunch) all overlook the sea. As rooms are small (they were monks' cells, after all), ask for one with a balcony. **Pros:** Friendly staff, old-world atmosphere. **Cons:** Some rooms are small, no pool. ✉ *Viale Gioacchino d'Anna 5, 84010* ☎ *089/857144* ⊕ *www. hotelparsifal.com* ⇆ *19 rooms* ♿ *In-hotel: restaurant, bar, public Internet* ☰ *AE, DC, MC, V* ⦿ *BP.*

$ 🏨 **Villa Amore.** A 10-minute walk from the Piazza Duomo, this family-run hotel has a pretty garden and an exhilarating view of the sea from most of its bedrooms. If you're looking for tranquillity, you've found it, especially at dusk, when the valley is tinged with a glorious purple light. Rooms are small, with modest modern furnishings. Full board is available, and at least half board is required from July through September. Let the staff know in advance if you need luggage transported from the parking lot or bus stop. **Pros:** Good value, quiet location. **Cons:** Books up long in advance, far from parking lot, €4 charge for each bag transported to hotel. ✉ *Via del Fusco 5, 84010* ☎ *089/857135* ⇆ *12 rooms* ♿ *In-room: no a/c, no TV. In-hotel: restaurant, bar, some pets allowed* ☰ *DC, MC, V* ⦿ *MAP.*

PAESTUM

★ *99 km (62 mi) southeast of Naples.*

GETTING HERE
Trains to Paestum depart from Stazione Centrale in Naples every hour. The archaeological site is a 10-minute walk from the station.

VISITOR INFORMATION
Paestum tourism office (✉ *Via Magna Grecia 887* ☎ *0828/811016* ⊕ *www.infopaestum.it*).

EXPLORING
One of Italy's most majestic sights lies on the edge of a flat coastal plain: the remarkably well-preserved **Greek temples** of Paestum. This is the site of the ancient city of Poseidonia, founded by Greek colonists probably in the sixth century BC. When the Romans took over the colony in 273 BC and the name was latinized to Paestum, they changed the layout of the settlement, adding an amphitheater and a forum. Much of the archaeological material found on the site is displayed in the well-labeled **Museo Nazionale,** and several rooms are devoted to the

unique tomb paintings discovered in the area, rare examples of Greek and pre-Roman pictorial art.

At the northern end of the site opposite the ticket barrier is the **Tempio di Cerere** (Temple of Ceres). Built in about 500 BC, it's now thought to have been originally dedicated to the goddess Athena. Follow the road south past the **Foro Romano** (Roman Forum) to the **Tempio di Nettuno** (Temple of Poseidon), a magnificent Doric edifice with 36 fluted columns and an extraordinarily well-preserved entablature (area above the capitals) that rivals those of the finest temples in Greece. Beyond is the so-called **Basilica,** the earliest of Paestum's standing edifices; it dates from early in the sixth century BC. The name is an 18th-century misnomer, for the structure was in fact a temple to Hera, the wife of Zeus. Try to see the temples in the late afternoon, when the light enhances the deep gold of the limestone and tourists have left temples almost deserted. ☎*0828/722654* ✉*Excavations €4, museum €4, excavations and museum €6.50* ☯*Excavations: July–Sept., daily 9 AM–10 PM; Oct.–June, daily 9–1 hr before sunset. Museum: July–Sept., daily 9 AM–10 PM; Oct.–June, daily 9–6:30. Closed 1st and 3rd Mon. of month.*

WHERE TO STAY & EAT

$ ✕⌂   **Helios.** A few steps from the temples, the Helios has cottage-type rooms in a garden setting surrounded by olive trees. Seven rooms have their own whirlpool baths. A pleasant restaurant ($) serves local specialties. The ricotta and mozzarella made on the premises are especially good. The hotel also organizes visits to a local mozzarella producer and excursions on horseback. **Pros:** Cottages surrounded by pretty gardens, very close to archaeological site, good value. **Cons:** Skimpy facilities in rooms. ✉*Via Principe di Piemonte 1, 84063* ☎*0828/811020* ⇄*30 rooms* ⌂*In-room: no a/c (some), no TV (some). In-hotel: restaurant, pool* ☰*AE, DC, MC, V* ⎰*MAP.*

GETTING AROUND

By Car

The mezzogiorno is a fairly easy place to get around by car. Roads are generally good, and major cities are linked by fast autostrade. From Puglia's Bari, take the SS96 south for 44 km (28 mi) to Altamura, then the SS99 south 19 km (12 mi) to Matera. The A3 Autostrada del Sole runs between Salerno and Reggio di Calabria, with exits for Crotone (the Sila Massif), Pizzo, Rosarno (for Tropea), Palmi, and Scilla; it takes an inland route as far as Falerna, then tracks the Tyrrhenian Coast south (except for the bulge of the Tropea Promontory). The A3 is free south of Salerno, but it's under seemingly eternal construction, so factor in plenty of time for delays. Take the SS18 for coastal destinations—or for a better view—on the Tyrrhenian side, and likewise the SS106 (which is uncongested and fast) for the Ionian.

Entering the centers of many towns requires a very small car, folding side-view mirrors, and a bit of nerve; tentative drivers should park outside the center and venture in by foot. If you're squeamish about getting lost, don't plan on night driving in the countryside—roads can be confusing without the aid of landmarks or large towns. Bari, Brindisi, and Reggio di Calabria are notorious for car thefts and break-ins. In these cities, do not leave valuables in the car, and find a guarded parking space if possible.

By Bus

Direct, if not always frequent, connections operate between most destinations within Calabria, Puglia, and Basilicata. In many cases bus service is the backup when problems with train service arise. Matera is linked with Bari by frequent **Ferrovie Appulo-Lucane** (☎ 080/5725229 ⊕ www.fal-srl.it) buses and with Taranto by **SITA** (☎ 080/5562446 ⊕ www.sitabus.it). In Calabria various companies make the north–south run with stops along both coasts; **Ferrovie della Calabria** (☎ 0961/896111 ⊕ www.ferroviedellacalabria.com) operates many of the local routes. From Reggio di Calabria, Salzone runs to Scilla. **Italy Bus** (⊕ www.italybus.it) gives listings of buses throughout the peninsula.

By Train

Within Puglia, the Italian national railway **FS** (☎ 892021 ⊕ www.trenitalia.com) links Bari to Brindisi, Lecce, and Taranto, but smaller destinations can often be reached only by completing the trip by bus. The private **Ferrovie Sud-Est** (☎ 080/5462111 in Bari, 0832/668111 in Lecce ⊕ www.fseonline.it) connects Martina Franca with Bari and Taranto, and the fishing port of Gallipoli with Lecce. **Ferrovie Appulo-Lucane** (☎ 080/5725229 ⊕ www.fal-srl.it) links Matera to Altamura in Puglia (for connections to Bari) and to Ferrandina (for connections to Potenza). FS trains run to Calabria, either following the Ionian Coast as far as Reggio di Calabria or swerving inland to Cosenza and the Tyrrhenian Coast.

Piazza del Duomo, Lecce

EATING & DRINKING WELL IN THE MEZZOGIORNO

Southern cuisine is hearty and healthful, based around homemade pastas and cheeses, fresh vegetables, seafood, and olive oil. A defining principle of Italian cooking is to take exceptional ingredients and prepare them simply. That philosophy reaches its purest—and most delicious—form in the Mezzogiorno.

The best—and cheapest—meals are often found at a rustic family-run trattoria (sometimes referred to as a *casalinga*), commonly located in the countryside or city outskirts. These bare-bones places often dispense with printed menus, but they manage to create flavors rivaling those of any highbrow restaurant. Assent to the waiter's suggestions with a simple *va bene* (that's fine) and leave yourself in the chef's hands.

More upscale establishments turn authentic local ingredients into deliciously inventive dishes. Fish, unsurprisingly, is the star attraction on the coast. Many such restaurants are set in breathtaking locations, yet prices remain relative bargains compared to similar places farther north.

FABULOUS FAVA

Fava puré cicorielle, a puree of dried fava beans and chicory, is unique to Puglia and Basilicata. The simple recipe has been prepared here for centuries and continues to be a staple of the local diet. The beans are soaked overnight, then mashed and blended with pureed potato, seasoned with salt and olive oil, and served warm with wild green chicory, often presented in a hollowed loaf of bread. Mix it together before eating and wash it down with a glass of *primitivo* or *aglianico*.

14

PASTA

Puglia is the home of *orecchiette* (ear-shaped pasta), pictured at right, with *cime di rape* (bitter greens) and olive oil, a melodious preparation that's wondrous in its simplicity. Try also *strascenate*—rectangles of pasta with one rough side and one smooth side.

MEAT

With cattle grazing on the plains and pigs fed only natural foods, the Mezzogiorno is a meat eater's paradise. As well as its excellent beef, Basilicata is known for its *salsicee lucani* (sausages), seasoned with salt, peperoncino, and fennel seeds. Enormous grills are a feature of many the region's restaurants, infusing the dining area with the aroma of freshly cooked meat. Adventurous eaters in Puglia should look for *gnomarelli* (a blend of lamb's innards) and horsemeat.

PEPPERS

Calabria is known for hot peppers—try peperonata, a stew of peppers and local capers. They also pop up in *salame piccante* (spicy salami) and *salsiccia piccante* (hot sausage), pictured at left, often sold by street vendors on a roll with peppers, onions, french fries, and mayonnaise. Pasta dishes are often seasoned with dried *peperoncini* (hot peppers) or *olio piccante* (spicy olive oil). The delicious *peperoni cruschi* or *senesi*

are grown in Basilicata—these can be eaten fresh or dried, and are often powdered for seasoning local cheeses and cured meats.

SEAFOOD

With so much coastline, seafood is an essential element of the Mezzogiorno cuisine. Fish can be grilled (*alla griglia*), baked (*al forno*), roasted (*arrosto*), or steamed (*al umido*). Among the highlights are delicate *orata* (sea bream), pictured below, *branzino* (sea bass), *pesce spada* (swordfish), and calamari, while Puglia is the home of the *cozze pelose* (an indigenous clam). The *frutti di mare* (shellfish) can be enjoyed as an antipasto, in a *zuppa* (soup) or with homemade linguine.

WINES

Puglia produces 17% of Italy's wine. For years, most of it was *vino sfuso* (jug wine), but since the mid-1990s quality has risen. The ancient primitivo grape (which purportedly was brought to California and renamed zinfandel), yields strong, heady wines. Look for primitivo di Manduria, as well as the robust Salice Salentino and sweet red aleatico di Puglia. Top winemakers include Conti Zecca, Leone di Castris, Rubino, and Tormaresca.

Updated
by Fergal
Kavanagh

MAKING UP THE HEEL AND toe of Italy's boot, the Puglia, Basilicata, and Calabria regions are the largest part of what is known informally as the *mezzogiorno,* a name that translates literally as "midday." It's a curiously telling nickname, because midday is when it's quietest here. While the blazing sun bears down, cities, fishing ports, and sleepy hillside villages turn into ghost towns, as residents retreat to their homes for four or more hours. This is Italy's deep south, where whitewashed buildings stand silently over the turquoise Mediterranean, castles guard medieval alleyways, and grandmothers dry their handmade *orecchiette* (ear-shaped pasta), the most Puglian of pastas, in the mid-afternoon heat. The city-states of Magna Graecia (Greek colonies) once ruled here, and ancient names, such as Lucania and Salento, are still commonly used.

At every turn, these three regions boast unspoiled scenery, a wonderful country food tradition, and an openness to outsiders that's unequaled elsewhere on the boot. It's here that the Italian language is at its lilting, hand-gesturing best, and it's here that a local you've met only minutes before is most likely to whisk you away to show you the delights of the region.

Some of Italy's finest beaches grace the rugged Gargano peninsula, the south of Puglia, and the coastline of Calabria, and there are cultural gems everywhere, from Alberobello's fairy-tale *trulli* (curious conical structures dating from the Middle Ages) to Matera's *sassi* (a network of ancient dwellings carved out of rock) to the baroque churches in vibrant Lecce, the town that's the jewel of the south. Beyond the cities, seaside resorts, and the few major sights, there's a sparsely populated, sunbaked countryside where road signs are rare and expanses of silvery olive trees, vineyards of primitivo and aglianico grapes, and giant prickly pear cacti fight their way through the rocky soil in defiance of the relentless summer heat. Farmhouses, country trattorias, and weary low-lying factories sit among eternally half-built structures that tell a hard-luck story of economic stagnation. Year after year, even as tourism grows in the region—especially in Salento—economic woes persist. In any case, the mezzogiorno still doesn't make it onto the itineraries of most visitors to Italy. This translates into an unusual opportunity to engage with a rich culture and landscape virtually untouched by international tourism.

BARI & THE ADRIATIC COAST

The coast of Puglia has a strong flavor of the Norman presence in the south, embodied in the distinctive Puglian-Romanesque churches, the most atmospheric being in Trani. The busy commercial port of Bari offers architectural nuggets in its compact, labyrinthine Old Quarter abutting the sea, while Polignano a Mare combines accessibility to the major centers with the charm of a medieval town. For a unique excursion, drive inland to the imposing Castel del Monte, an enigmatic 13th-century octagonal fortification.

260 km (162 mi) southeast of Naples, 450 km (281 mi) southeast of Rome.

GETTING HERE

By car, take the Bari exit from the A14 motorway. Bari's train station is a hub for Puglia-bound trains. Alitalia and Air One fly to Bari Airport from Rome and Milan.

VISITOR INFORMATION

Bari tourism office (✉ *Piazza Moro 33/a, 70122* ☎ *080/5242361* ⊕ *www.viaggiareinpuglia.it/apt-bari*).

EXPLORING

The biggest city in the region, Bari is a major port and a transit point for travelers catching ferries across the Adriatic to Greece, but it's also a cosmopolitan city with one of the most interesting historic centers in the region. Most of Bari is set out in a logical 19th-century grid, following the designs of Joachim Murat (1767–1815), Napoléon's brother-in-law and King of the Two Sicilies. The heart of the modern town is **Piazza della Libertà**, but just beyond it, across Corso Vittorio Emanuele, is the *città vecchia* (old town), a maze of narrow streets on the promontory that juts out between Bari's old and new ports, circumscribed by Via Venezia, offering elevated views of the Adriatic in every direction.

NEED A BREAK? When you're exploring around Via Venezia, stop for a drink at Greta (✉ *Via Venezia 21*). The outdoor seating provides a commanding view of the port and sea.

By day, explore the old town's winding alleyways, where Bari's open-door policy offers a glimpse into the daily routine of southern Italy—matrons hand-rolling pasta with their grandchildren home from school for the midday meal, and handymen perched on rickety ladders, patching up centuries-old arches and doorways. Back in the new town, join the evening *passeggiata* (stroll) on pedestrians-only **Via Sparano,** then, when night falls, saunter among the exploding scene of outdoor bars and restaurants in Piazza Mercantile, past Piazza Ferrarese at the end of Corso Vittorio Emanuele.

In the città vecchia, overlooking the sea and just off Via Venezia, is the **Basilica di San Nicola,** built in the 11th century to house the bones of St. Nicholas, also known as St. Nick, or Santa Claus. His remains, buried in the crypt, are said to have been stolen by Bari sailors from Myra, where St. Nicholas was bishop, in what is now Turkey. The basilica, of solid and powerful construction, was the only building to survive the otherwise wholesale destruction of Bari by the Normans in 1152. ✉ *Piazza San Nicola* ☎ *080/5737111* 🎫 *Free* 🕐 *Daily 7–1 and 4–7.*

Bari's 12th-century **Cattedrale** is the seat of the local bishop and was the scene of many significant political marriages between important families in the Middle Ages. The cathedral's solid architecture reflects

14

Puglia

50 miles
75 km

Adriatic Sea

Golfo di Taranto

KEY

Ferry lines

ISOLE TREMITI
I Cameroni
ISOLE S. DOMINO

TO TERMOLI

Vieste
Peschici
Rodi Garganico
Foresta Umbra
Mattinata
Monte Sant'Angelo
Manfredonia
L'Annunziata
GARGANO PROMONTORY
San Giovanni Rotondo
Lago di Varano
Golfo di Manfredonia
Zapponeta
San Severo
Lucera
Foggia
Cerignola
S. Angelo dei Lombardi
Melfi
Spinazzola
Gravina in Puglia
Potenza
Auletta
Eboli
Battipaglia
Salerno
TO NAPLES

CAMPANIA
BASILICATA
LUCAN

Trani
Barletta
Andria
Corato
Molfetta
Bari
Castel del Monte
Santeramo in Colle
Gioia del Colle
Altamura
Matera
Castellaneta Marina
Lido di Metaponto
Scanzano

Polignano a Mare
Grotte di Castellana
Fasano
TRULLI DISTRICT
Locorotondo
Alberobello
Martina Franca
Ostuni
Ceglie Messapica
Grottaglie
Massafra
Taranto
Mare Piccolo
Mare Grande

Brindisi
Mesagne
Campi
Lecce
Francavilla Fontana
Manduria
Nardò
Gallipoli
SALENTO
Maglie
Otranto
Santa Cesarea Terme
Castro
Leuca
Capo Santa Maria di Leuca

Via Appia

16 · 611 · 16 · 275 · 274 · 611 · 101 · 7 · 174 · 16 · 7 · 100 · 106 · 653 · 598 · 92 · 407 · 96 · 7 · 97 · 170 · 96 · 271 · A14 · 168 · 91 · 407 · 91 · 166 · A3 · 91 · 164 · 655 · 90 · 16 · A14 · A16 · 16 · 89 · 272 · 89 · A14 · 160 · 17 · 159 · 528 · 89

the Romanesque style favored by the Normans of that period. ☒*Piazza dell'Odegitria* ☎*080/5210605* ☒*Free* ☉*Daily 8–12:30 and 4–7:30.*

Looming over Bari's cathedral is the huge **Castello Svevo.** The current building dates from the time of Holy Roman Emperor Frederick II (1194–1250), who rebuilt an existing Norman-Byzantine castle to his own exacting specifications. Designed more for power than beauty, it looks out beyond the cathedral to the small Porto Vecchio (Old Port). Inside a haphazard collection of medieval Puglian art is frequently enlivened by changing exhibitions featuring local, national, and international artists. ☒*Piazza Federico II di Svevia* ☎*080/5286218* ⊕*www. sbap-ba.beniculturali.it* ☒*€2* ☉*Daily 8:30–7:30. Last entrance at 6:30. Closed Wed.*

WHERE TO STAY & EAT

$$$ ✗ **Ristorante al Pescatore.** This is one of Bari's best seafood restaurants, in the old town opposite the castle and just around the corner from the cathedral. In the summer the fish is grilled outdoors, so you can enjoy the delicious aroma as you sit amid a cheerful clamor of quaffing and dining. Try a whole fish accompanied by crisp salad and a carafe of invigorating local wine. Reservations are essential in July and August. ☒*Piazza Federico II di Svevia 6* ☎*080/5237039* ☰*AE, DC, MC, V.*

★ $$ ⌂ **Hotel Palace.** This downtown landmark is steps away from Corso Vittorio Emanuele in the new city, but is also extremely convenient to the medieval center. The large, comfortable rooms are furnished lightly and tastefully. There are several special rooms set aside for those traveling with children and a room for music lovers that comes complete with stereo and collection of classical CDs. Other amenities include Smart Car rental service (€50 per day). The rooftop restaurant has great views outdoors in summer. **Pro:** Convenient location. **Con:** Can be very busy. ☒*Via Lombardi 13, 70122* ☎*080/5216551* ☒*080/5211499* ⊕*www. palacehotelbari.it* ☜*196 rooms* ♿*In-room: safe, refrigerator. In-hotel: restaurant, bar, bicycles, parking (fee)* ☰*AE, DC, MC, V* ☉*MAP.*

TRANI

43 km (27 mi) northwest of Bari.

GETTING HERE

By car, take the Trani exit from the A14 motorway. Frequent trains run from Bari.

VISITOR INFORMATION

Trani tourism office (☒*Piazza Trieste 10, 70059* ☎*0883/588830*).

EXPLORING

Smaller than the other ports along this coast, Trani has a harbor filled with fishing boats and a quaint old town with polished stone streets and medieval churches. Trani is also justly famous for its sweet dessert wine, Moscato di Trani.

14

The stunning, pinkish-white-hue 11th-century **Duomo** ($\boxtimes$ *Piazza Duomo* $\odot$ *Daily 8–noon and 3:30–6*), considered one of the finest in Puglia, is built on a spit of land jutting into the sea.

The boxy, well-preserved **Castello** ($\boxtimes$ *0883/506603* $\boxed{\cdot}\,€2$ $\odot$ *Daily 8:30–7*) was built by Frederick II in 1233.

The Jewish community flourished here in medieval times, and on **Via Sinagoga** *(Synagogue Street)* two of the four synagogues still exist: **Santa Maria Scolanova** and **Santa Anna**, both built in the 13th century; the latter still bears a Hebrew inscription.

WHERE TO STAY & EAT

★ $$ ✕⊡ **La Regia.** This small hotel-restaurant occupies a 17th-century palazzo superbly positioned in front of the Duomo, on a swath of land jutting out into the sea. Don't expect grand or spacious rooms, though they are perfectly adequate. The restaurant ($$) has attractive stonework and vaulted ceilings. Regional specialties are imaginatively presented in dishes like grilled fish and baked crepes (similar to cannelloni). Reservations are essential for Sunday lunch and for dinner on summer weekends. **Pros:** Great restaurant, hospitable staff. **Cons:** Very little parking, is a crowded area. $\boxtimes$ *Piazza Mons. Addazi 2, 70059* $\boxtimes$ *0883/584444* $\oplus$ *www.hotelregia.it* $\rightleftharpoons$ *10 rooms* $\diamond$ *In-room: safe, refrigerator. In-hotel: restaurant, bar, public Internet* $\boxminus$ *MC, V* $\odot$ *Restaurant closed Mon.* $\lceil$O$\rceil$*BP.*

POLIGNANO A MARE

35 km (22 mi) southeast of Bari, 14 km (9 mi) north of Castellana.

GETTING HERE

From Bari, take the Polignano exit from the SS16. Frequent trains run from Bari.

EXPLORING

With a well-preserved whitewashed old town perched on limestone cliffs overlooking the Adriatic, Polignano a Mare makes an atmospheric base for exploring the surrounding area. The town is virtually lifeless all winter, but becomes something of a weekend hot spot for city dwellers in summer.

WHERE TO STAY & EAT

★ $$$–$$$$ ✕⊡ **Grotta Palazzese.** Carved out of a cliff opening onto the Adriatic, the Grotta Palazzese inhabits a stunning group of rocks and grottoes that have wowed onlookers from time immemorial. Though most rooms have sea views, ask for one of the seven cave-apartments across the road rather than the more-boxlike rooms in the main block. Grotta Palazzese's true tour de force is its summer restaurant ($$$$), serving impeccably prepared fish (try the assortment of raw Adriatic shellfish called *frutti di mare crudi*). The dramatic setting incorporates rock formations, with tables actually standing on an implausible bridge inside a jagged cave, while waves cast blue-green shadows on the grotto walls. It's one of the most romantic settings in all Italy.

Pro: Fantastic restaurant. **Con:** A long climb down to the sea. ✉ *Via Narciso 59, 70059* ☎*080/4240677* ⊕*www.grottapalazzese.it* ↘*25 rooms* ♿*In-room: refrigerator, dial-up. In-hotel: 2 restaurants, bar, beachfront, parking (fee)* ▭*AE, DC, MC, V* ⊗*Outdoor restaurant closed Oct.–Apr.* ♸*BP.*

CASTEL DEL MONTE

★ *30 km (19 mi) south of Barletta, 56 km (35 mi) southwest of Bari.*

GETTING HERE

Take the Andria-Barletta exit from the A14 motorway, then follow the SS170d to Castel del Monte.

Built by Frederick II in the first half of the 13th century on an isolated hill, Castel del Monte is an imposing octagonal castle with eight austere towers. Very little is known about the structure, since virtually no records exist: the gift shop has many books that explore its mysterious past and posit fascinating theories based on its dimensions and Federico II's love of mathematics. It has none of the usual defense features associated with medieval castles, so it probably had little military significance. Some theories suggest it might have been built as a hunting lodge or may have served as an astronomical observatory, or even a stop for pilgrims on their quest for the Holy Grail. *Guided tours in English and Italian are available daily at 10:30, 11:30, 3:30, and 4:30; call ahead to reserve.* ✉*On signposted minor road 18 km (11 mi) south of Andria* ☎*0883/569997, 339/1146908 tour reservations* ⊕*www.casteldelmonte.beniculturali.it* ☒*€3* ⊗*Mar. –Sept., daily 10:15 –7:45, Oct. –Feb., daily 9 –6:30.*

GARGANO PROMONTORY

Forming the spur of Italy's boot, the Gargano Promontory (Promontorio del Gargano) is a striking contrast to the Adriatic's generally flat, unenthralling coastline. This is a land of whitewashed coastal towns, wide sandy beaches interspersed with secluded coves, and craggy limestone cliffs topped by deep-green pine and lush Mediterranean maquis. Not surprisingly, it pulls in the crowds in July and August, driving up the prices considerably. Camping is almost always an option, as plentiful and pretty campgrounds dot the Gargano's curvy, cliff-hugging roads. For the kids, the beaches and the Foresta Umbra national park are great places to let off steam.

MATTINATA

138 km (86 mi) northwest of Bari.

GETTING HERE

From Foggia, take the winding SS89. Regular buses leave from Foggia's train station.

VISITOR INFORMATION

Mattinata tourism office (✉ *Corso Mattino 68, 71030* ☎ *0884/55911169*).

EXPLORING

Just inland from a fine sandy beach, where you'll find most of the campsites and hotels, this is a generally quiet village that comes into its own in the summer season.

Pilgrims have flocked to the nearby town of Monte Sant'Angelo for nearly 1,500 years—among them, St. Francis of Assisi and crusaders setting off for the Holy Land from the then-flourishing port of Manfredonia. Monte Sant'Angelo is centered on the **Santuario di San Michele** (☎ *0884/561150* ⊕ *www.santuariosanmichele.it* ⊗ *May–Oct., daily 9–1 and 3–7; Nov.–Apr., daily 9–1 and 2:30–5:30*), built over the grotto where the archangel Michael is believed to have appeared before shepherds in the year 490. Walk down a long series of steps to get to the grotto itself; on its walls you can see the hand tracings left by pilgrims.

WHERE TO STAY & EAT

$$–$$$ ✕ **Trattoria dalla Nonna.** The waves lap at the shore just inches from your table at this elegant but unpretentious coastal restaurant. The memorable assorted raw seafood antipasto includes some shellfish you might not find anywhere else. *Cozze pelose* (an indigenous Puglian clam), hiding inside spiked-hair shells, are briny and buttery; tiny *noci* shellfish have a wonderful sweetness; and big, rich local oysters are all about texture. Try sweet grilled scampi with oil and lemon, and wash it all down with one of the great white wines on the extensive list. If you find it hard to leave, there are also some inexpensive rooms. ✉ *Contrada Funi, Mattinata Mare* ☎ *0884/559205* ⊕ *www.dallanonna.it* ▭ *AE, DC, MC, V* ⊗ *Closed Tues. Oct.–Apr., 15 days in Nov., and 15 days in Jan.*

$$ ▥ **Baia delle Zagare.** This secluded cluster of modern cottages is on the shore road around the Gargano Promontory, overlooking an inlet and stands of 500-year-old olive trees. A pair of elevators built into the cliff takes you down to a long private beach. The hotel's restaurant is good enough to warrant staying on the premises all day. (In mid-August you're expected to stay a minimum of seven nights and to take half board.) Be careful when approaching on the road, as the gated entrance is easy to miss. **Pro:** Incredible location. **Con:** Impossible to get to without a car. ✉ *Litoranea Mattinata-Vieste* ✛ *17 km (10 mi) northeast of Mattinata, 71030* ☎ *0884/550155* ⊕ *www.hotelbaiadellezagare.it* ⇥ *150 rooms* ♿ *In-room: safe, refrigerator. In-hotel: restaurant, tennis court, pool, beachfront, children's programs (ages 11 and under)* ▭ *MC, V* ⊗ *Closed mid-Sept.–May* ⊚ *MAP.*

VIESTE

93 km (58 mi) northeast of Foggia, 179 km (111 mi) northwest of Bari.

GETTING HERE

If you're driving from Foggia, take the winding SS89. Regular buses leave from Foggia's train station.

VISITOR INFORMATION

Vieste tourism office (✉*Piazza Kennedy, 71019* ☎*0884/708806*).

EXPLORING

This large, whitewashed town jutting off the tip of the spur of Italy's boot is the Gargano's main commercial center and an attractive place to wander around. Though curvy mountain roads render it slightly less accessible from the autostrada and mainline rail stations than, say, Peschici and Mattinata, the range of accommodations (including camping) makes it a useful base for exploring Gargano. The resort attracts legions of tourists in summer, some bound for the Isole Tremiti, a tiny archipelago connected to Vieste by regular ferries.

While in Vieste, make for the **castello**. Its interior has reopened to the public. There are good views from its high position overlooking the beaches and town. ✉*Via Duomo* ☎*0884/712232* 🎟*Free* ⊙*Daily 7–10 PM.*

WHERE TO STAY & EAT

★ $$–$$$ ✕ **San Michele.** Dine on exquisite Gargano fare at this charmingly intimate eatery on the town's main street. Their legendary antipasti include grilled eggplant and marinated anchovies. The porcini mushrooms picked from the region's Foresta Umbra are worth the visit alone. ✉*Viale XXIV Maggio 72* ☎*0884/708143* ▬*AE, DC, MC, V* ⊙*Closed Mon. and Jan.–mid-Mar.*

$$ 🏨 **Punta San Francesco.** After starting its life as an olive-oil factory, this hotel was tastefully refurbished in the mid-1990s. Thanks to its location near the waterfront in the heart of old Vieste, it is both quiet and close to the action. The owner is a warm, welcoming friend (and ardent promoter of local culture) to all who arrive, and the view from the rooftop is beautiful, especially at dawn. **Pros:** Quiet location, hospitable staff. **Con:** Parking can be difficult. ✉*Via San Francesco 2, 71019* ☎*0884/701422* ⊕*www.hotelpuntasanfrancesco.it* 🛏*14 rooms* ⌂*In-room: refrigerator. In-hotel: bar, no elevator* ▬*MC, V* ⦿*EP.*

PESCHICI

22 km (14 mi) northwest of Vieste, 199 km (124 mi) northwest of Bari.

GETTING HERE

From Foggia, take the winding S89 road. Regular buses leave from Foggia's train station.

VISITOR INFORMATION

Peschici tourism office (✉*Via Magenta 3, 71010* ☎*0884/915362*).

Peschici is a pleasant resort on Gargano's north shore, a cascade of whitewashed houses and streets with a beautiful view over a sweeping cove. Some surrounding areas are particularly popular with campers from northern Europe. Development has not wreaked too much havoc on the town: the mazelike center retains its characteristic low houses topped with little Byzantine cupolas.

★ In the middle of the Gargano Promontory is the majestic **Foresta Umbra** (Shady Forest), a dense growth of beech, maple, sycamore, and oak generally found in more-northerly climates, thriving here because of the altitude, 3,200 feet above sea level. Between the trees in this national park are occasional dramatic vistas opening out over the Golfo di Manfredonia.

OFF THE BEATEN PATH

Isole Tremiti. A ferry service from Termoli, west of the Gargano (1¾ hours), and hydrofoil service from Vieste, Peschici, and Rodi Garganico (40 minutes to 1 hour) connect the mainland with these three small islands north of the Gargano. Although somewhat crowded with Italian tourists in summer, they are famed for their sea caves, pine forests, and craggy limestone formations. Interesting medieval churches and fortifications dot the islands. ☎ 041/781611 ⊕ www.adriatica.it/it/tremiti-orari.htm.

THE TRULLI DISTRICT

The inland area to the southeast of Bari is one of Italy's oddest enclaves, mostly flat terrain given over to olive cultivation and interspersed with the idiosyncratic habitations that have lent their names to the district. The origins of the beehive-shaped trulli go back to the 13th century and maybe further. The trulli, found nowhere else in the world, are built of local limestone, without mortar, and with a hole in the top for escaping smoke. Some are painted with mystical or religious symbols, some are isolated, and others are joined together with roofs on various levels. Legends of varying credibility surround the trulli (for example, that they were originally built so that residents could quickly take apart their homes when the tax collectors came by). The center of trulli country is Alberobello in the enchanting Valle d'Itria: it has the greatest concentration of the buildings. You will spot them all over this region, some in the middle of desolate fields, and many in disrepair, but always adding a quirky charm to the landscape.

ALBEROBELLO

59 km (37 mi) southeast of Bari, 45 km (28 mi) north of Taranto.

GETTING HERE
By car, take the Monopoli exit from the SS16, and follow the smaller road to Alberobello. Trains run hourly from Bari.

VISITOR INFORMATION
Alberobello tourism office (✉ *Piazza Ferdinando IV, 70011* ☎ *080/4325171*).

EXPLORING

Although Alberobello is something of a tourist trap, the amalgamation of more than 1,000 trulli huddled together along steep, narrow streets is nonetheless an unusual sight (as well as a national monument and a UNESCO World Heritage Site). As one of the most popular destinations in Puglia, Alberobello has spawned some excellent restaurants (and some not-so-excellent trinket shops).

Alberobello's largest trullo, the **Trullo Sovrano**, is up the hill through the trulli zone (head up Corso Vittorio Emanuele past the obelisk and the basilica). Though you can go inside, where you'll find a fairly conventional domestic dwelling, the real interest is the structure itself.

The trulli in Alberobello itself are impressive, but the most beautiful concentration of trulli are along **Via Alberobello–Martina Franca.** Numerous conical homes and buildings stand along a stretch of about 15 km (9 mi) between those two towns. Amid expanses of vineyards, you'll see delightfully amusing examples of trulli put to use in every which way—as wineries, for instance.

14

WHERE TO STAY & EAT

$$$$
Fodor'sChoice
★
✕ **Il Poeta Contadino.** Proprietor Marco Leonardo serves creative regional cooking in this upscale country restaurant in the heart of the attractive trulli zone. The refined, understated dining room features candles casting shadows on the ancient stone walls. Dishes might include *triglie vinaigrette alla menta* (red mullet with a mint vinaigrette) or *coda di rospo incrostita di patate* (monkfish in a potato crust). In season, try anything with white truffle. ⊠ *Via Indipendenza 21* ☎ *080/4321917* ⌖ *Reservations essential* ▭ *AE, DC, MC, V* ☉ *Closed Mon. and 3 wks in Jan. No dinner Sun. Sept.–June.*

★ **$$–$$$$**
✕ **Trullo d'Oro.** This welcoming rustic restaurant set in five trulli houses has dark-wood beams, whitewashed walls, and an open hearth. Local country cooking includes dishes using lamb and veal, vegetable and cheese antipasti, pasta dishes with crisp raw vegetables on the side, and almond pastries. Among the seasonal specialties are roast lamb with *lampasciuni* (a type of wild onion) and spaghetti *al trullo*, made with tomatoes, *rughetta* (arugula), and four cheeses. ⊠ *Via F. Cavallotti 27* ☎ *080/4323909* ⌖ *Reservations essential* ▭ *AE, DC, MC, V* ☉ *Closed Mon. Sept.–May and 3 wks mid-Jan.– early Feb. No dinner Sun.*

$$$
⌂ **Dei Trulli.** Trulli-style cottages in a pine forest make this a magical place to stay. It's decorated with rustic furnishings and folk-art rugs. The modestly priced restaurant serves local specialties. You're required to take half or full board in high season. **Pros:** Distinctive location, unusual lodgings. **Con:** In a crowded area. ⊠ *Via Cadore 32, 70011* ☎ *080/4323555* ⊕ *www.hoteldeitrulli.it* ⇥ *19 apartments* ⌖ *In-room: safe, refrigerator. In-hotel: restaurant, pool* ▭ *AE, DC, MC, V* ☉ *Closed Nov.–Apr.* ⏺*MAP.*

OSTUNI

50 km (30 mi) west of Brindisi, 40 km (25 mi) northeast of Locorotondo.

GETTING HERE
By car, take the Ostuni exit from the SS16. The Ferrovie dello Stato runs frequent trains from Bari.

VISITOR INFORMATION
Ostuni tourism office (⊠ *Corso Mazzini 6, 72017* ☎ *0831/301268*).

EXPLORING

This sun-bleached, medieval town lies on three hills not far from the coast. From a distance, Ostuni is a jumble of blazingly white houses and churches spilling over a hilltop and overlooking the sea—thus earning it the nickname *la città bianca* (the White City).

The **old town,** on the highest of the hills, has steep cobbled lanes, wrought-iron lanterns, some good local restaurants, and stupendous views out over the coast and the surrounding plain.

Piazza Libertà, the city's main square, divides the new town to the west and the old town to the east.

WHERE TO EAT

★ $$$$ ✕ **Al Fornello Da Ricci.** Any respectable culinary tour of Puglia must pass through this high-priced, elegant dining room run in the white-washed town of Ceglie Messapica, *11 km (7 mi) southwest of Ostuni.* The distinguished kitchen sends out *antipasti* in a long succession, all inspired by ancient Pugliese traditions—meats, cheeses, perhaps fried zucchini flowers stuffed with fresh goat's ricotta. Then come delicate pasta dishes and ambitious meat preparations. It's an haute Pugliese experience not to be missed. ⊠ *Contrada Montevicoli* ☎ *0831/377104* ♨ *Reservations essential* ⊟ *AE, DC, MC, V* ⊗ *Closed Tues., Feb. 1–10, and Sept. 10–30. No dinner Mon.*

$$–$$$ ✕ **Osteria del Tempo Perso.** Buried in the side streets of the old town, this laid-back restaurant has rough-hewn stone interiors, with intriguing objects adorning the walls. Service is friendly and preparations focus on local cuisine such as delectable stuffed hot peppers and orecchiette with bitter greens and olive oil. ⊠ *Via G. Tanzarella Vitale 47* ☎ *0831/303320* ⊕ *www.osteriadeltempoperso.com* ⊟ *AE, DC, MC, V* ⊗ *Closed Mon. and 2 wks in Jan.*

MARTINA FRANCA

6 km (4 mi) south of Locorotondo, 36 km (22 mi) north of Taranto.

GETTING HERE
By car, take the Fasano exit from the SS16, then follow the SS172. The Ferrovie dello Stato runs frequent trains from Bari.

VISITOR INFORMATION
Martina Franca tourism office (✉ *Piazza Roma 37, 74015* ☎ *080/4805702* ⊕ *www.martinafrancatour.it*).

EXPLORING

Martina Franca is a beguiling town with a dazzling mixture of medieval and baroque architecture in the light-color local stone. Ornate balconies hang above the twisting, narrow streets, with little alleys leading off into the hills. Martina Franca was developed as a military stronghold in the 14th century, when a surrounding wall with 24 towers was built, but now all that remains of the wall are the four gates that had once been the only entrances to the town. Each July and August, the town holds a music festival.

14

WHERE TO STAY & EAT

$$ ✕ **La Cantina del Toscano.** This restaurant has a convenient location under the *portici* (archways) of one of the city's main piazzas, but it's not a tourist joint. Locals love the pizzas, grilled meats (lamb chops and sausage are first-rate), and whole fish that are prepared with skill and love in the kitchen. The atmosphere is warm and cozy. ✉ *Piazza Maria Immacolata* ☎ *080/4302827* ▭ *AE, DC, MC, V.*

$$ 🏠 **Park Hotel San Michele.** This garden hotel makes a pleasant base in the warm months, thanks to its pool. There are two types of rooms: those with shower and a view of Martina Franca, and larger ones with a bathtub overlooking the garden. All are spacious and include nice touches like complimentary bowls of fruit. **Pro:** Pretty pool area. **Con:** Old-fashioned handheld showers. ✉ *Viale Carella 9, 74015* ☎ *080/4807053* ⊕ *www.parkhotelsm.it* 🛏 *81 rooms* 🔑 *In-room: refrigerator, Wi-Fi. In-hotel: restaurant, bar, pool* ▭ *AE, DC, MC, V* 🍴 *BP.*

SALENTO & PORTS OF THE HEEL

This far south, the mountains run out of steam and the land is uniformly flat. The monotonous landscape, besides being agriculturally important, is redeemed by some of the region's best sandy coastline and a handful of small, alluring fishing towns, such as Otranto and Gallipoli. Taranto and Brindisi don't quite fit this description: both are big ports where historical importance is obscured by unsightly heavy industry. Nonetheless, Taranto has its archaeological museum, and Brindisi, an important ferry jumping-off point, marks the end of the Via Appia (the Imperial Roman Road). Farther south, Salento (the Salentine Peninsula) is the local name for the part of Puglia that forms the end of the heel. Lecce is an unexpected oasis of grace and sophistication, and its swirling architecture will melt even the most uncompromising critic of the baroque.

TARANTO

100 km (62 mi) southeast of Bari, 40 km (25 mi) south of Martina Franca.

GETTING HERE
By car, the A16 motorway takes you directly to Taranto. The Ferrovie dello Stato runs frequent trains from Bari and Brindisi.

VISITOR INFORMATION
Taranto tourism office (⊠ *Corso Umberto 113, 74100* ☎*099/4532392* ⊕ *www.viaggiareinpuglia.it/hp/en*).

Taranto (the stress is on the first syllable) was an important port even in Roman times. It lies toward the back of the instep of the boot on the broad Mare Grande bay, which is connected to a small internal Mare Piccolo basin by two narrow channels, one artificial and one natural. The old town is a series of old palazzi in varying states of decay and narrow cobblestone streets on an island between the larger and smaller bodies of water, linked by causeways; the modern city stretches inward along the mainland. Circumnavigate the old town and take in a dramatic panorama to the north, revealing Italy's shipping industry at its busiest: steelworks, dockyards, a bay dotted with fishing boats, and a fish market teeming with pungent activity along the old town's western edge.

Little remains of Taranto's past except the 14th-century church of **San Domenico** (⊠ *Via Duomo 33* ☎*099/4713511* ⊘ *Daily 8:30–7*) jutting into the sea at one end of the island, and its famous naval academy.

★ A compendium on the millennia of local history, Taranto's **Museo Nazionale** has a large collection of prehistoric, Greek, and Roman artifacts discovered mainly in the immediate vicinity, including Puglian tombs dating from before 1000 BC. Just over the bridge from the old town, the museum is a testament to the importance of this ancient port, which has always taken full advantage of its unique trading position at the end of the Italian peninsula. ⊠ *Via Cavour 10* ☎*099/4532112* ☜*€2* ⊘ *Daily 8:30–7:30*.

LECCE

Fodor's Choice ★ *40 km (25 mi) southeast of Brindisi, 87 km (54 mi) east of Taranto.*

GETTING HERE
By car, take the SS16 to Brindisi and continue along the SS613 to Lecce. Frequent trains run along the coast from Bari and beyond.

VISITOR INFORMATION
Lecce tourism office (⊠ *Via Libertini 76, 73100* ☎*0832/245497* ⊕*www. salento4you.it*).

EXPLORING
Lecce is the crown jewel of the mezzogiorno. The city is affectionately referred to as "the Florence of the south," but that sobriquet doesn't do justice to Lecce's uniqueness in the Italian landscape. Though its great shopping, lively bars, and the impossibly intricate baroque architecture draw comparisons to the Renaissance cities of the north, Lecce's lively streets, laid-back student cafés, magical evening passeggiata, and open-

ness to visitors are distinctively southern. The city is a cosmopolitan oasis two steps from the idyllic Otranto–Brindisi coastline and a hop from the olive-grove countryside of Puglia. Relatively undiscovered by tourists, Lecce exudes an optimism and youthful joie de vivre unparalleled in any other baroque showcase. There is no Lecce of the north.

Summer is a great time to visit. In July, courtyards and piazzas throughout the city are the settings for **dramatic productions**. Autumn has its charms as well. A **baroque music festival** is held in churches throughout the city in September.

Although Lecce was founded before the time of the ancient Greeks, it's often associated with the term *Lecce baroque,* the result of a citywide impulse in the 17th century to redo the town in the baroque fashion. But this was baroque with a difference. Such architecture is often heavy and monumental, but here it took on a lighter, more-fanciful air. Just look at the church of **Santa Croce** and the adjoining **Palazzo della Prefettura.** Although every column, window, pediment, and balcony is given a curling baroque touch—and then an extra one for good measure—the overall effect is lighthearted. The buildings' proportions are unintimidating, and the local stone is a glowing honey color: it couldn't look menacing if it tried. ☒ *Via Umberto I* ☎ *0832/241957* ☉ *Daily 9–noon and 5–7:30.*

Lecce's ornate **Duomo**, first built in 1114 but reconstructed in baroque style from 1659 to 1670, is uncharacteristically set in a solitary lateral square off a main street, rather than at a crossroads of pedestrian traffic. To the left of the Duomo, the more-austere **bell tower,** reconstructed by master baroque architect Giuseppe Zimbalo in the 17th century, takes on a surreal golden hue at dusk. The facades of the adjoining 18th-century **Palazzo Vescovile** (Bishops' Palace), farther past the right side of the Duomo, and the **Seminario** on the piazza's right edge complement the rich ornamentation of the Duomo to create an effect almost as splendid as that of Santa Croce. The Seminario's tranquil **cloister** is also worth a visit. ☒ *Piazza Duomo off Corso Vittorio Emanuele* ☎ *0832/308884* ☉ *Daily 9–noon and 5–7:30.*

In the middle of **Piazza Sant'Oronzo,** the city's putative center, surrounded by cafés, pastry shops, and newsstands, is a **Roman column** of the same era and style as the one in Brindisi, but imaginatively surmounted by an 18th-century statue of the city's patron saint, Orontius. Next to the column, the shallow rows of seats in the **Anfiteatro Romano** suggest Verona's arena or a small-scale Roman Colosseum.

WHERE TO STAY & EAT

$$ ✕ **Alle Due Corti.** Rosalba de Carlo, a local character, runs this traditional trattoria. The menu is printed in the ancient *Leccese* language; the adventurous can try country dishes like *pezzetti te cavallu* (spicy horse meat in tomato sauce) or *turcineddhi* (roasted baby goat entrails)—a crisp, gamy, fully flavored delight. The white-wall decor is stark, but character comes from the red-and-white checked tablecloths and the gregarious local families and groups of friends that inevitably

fill the place. ⊠ *Via Leonardo Prato 42* ☎*0832/242223* ⊟*AE, MC, V* ☺*Closed Sun.*

★ **$$** ✕ **Trattoria Cucina Casareccia.** This is an excellent place to try traditional Pugliese cooking in a warm, casual setting of white walls and loud chatter. Don't expect a menu; choose from the daily specials, which might include homemade whole-wheat pasta served with a delicate sauce of tomato and sharp, aged ricotta *forte*. The rustic *purè di fave e cicoria* (puree of fava bean with chicory) is topped with local olive oil and hot peppers; mix it together before eating. Service is informal and welcoming. ⊠ *Via Costadura 19* ☎*0832/245178* ⊟*AE, DC, MC, V* ☺*Closed Mon., Aug. 27–Sept. 11, 1 wk at Easter, and Dec. 23–Jan. 2. No dinner Sun.*

★ **$** ✕ **Corte dei Pandolfi.** Here you can choose from a vast list of Salento's best wines and feast on an unparalleled spread of artisanal *salumi* (cured meats) and local cheeses, accompanied by delicious local honey and *mostarda* (preserved fruit). Traditional *primi* and *seconds courses are also served, as well as vegetarian specialties*. The location is on a little piazza just off Via degli Ammirati, which starts on the back side of the Duomo. ⊠ *Piazzetta Orsini* ☎*0832/332309* ⊟*AE, MC, V* ☺*No lunch Mon.–Wed. Oct.–Apr.*

$$$$

Fodor's Choice

★ **Patria Palace.** It's a nice coincidence that the best hotel in Lecce happens to be in one of the best possible locations, a few steps from all the action. This hotel is impeccable from top to bottom, from the warm and elegant lobby with its recessed bar to the sumptuously designed rooms. For 70 more, you can reserve a room with a stunning private terrace overlooking Santa Croce, the crown jewel of Lecce baroque. If not, there's a beautiful rooftop gazebo for all. **Pros:** Luxurious rooms, ideal location. **Con:** Not all rooms have great views. ⊠ *Piazzetta Riccardi 13, 73100* ☎*0832/245111* ⊕*www.patriapalacelecce.com* ⇥*67 rooms* ⚖*In-room: safe, refrigerator, Wl-Fi. In-hotel: restaurant, bar, public Internet, parking (fee)* ⊟*AE, DC, MC, V* ❘⊙❘*BP.*

$$ **President.** Rub elbows with visiting dignitaries at this business hotel near Piazza Mazzini. The reception is expansive and furnishings are 1980s tasteful, with an emphasis on primary colors and modernist fixtures. **Pros:** Comfortable rooms, convenient location. **Cons:** More for business than pleasure, a bit dated. ⊠ *Via Salandra 6, 73100* ☎*0832/456111* ⊕*www.hotelpresidentlecce.it* ⇥*148 rooms, 4 suites* ⚖*In-room: safe, refrigerator, Wi-Fi. In-hotel: restaurant, bar, parking (fee)* ⊟*AE, DC, MC, V* ❘⊙❘*BP.*

OTRANTO

36 km (22 mi) southeast of Lecce, 188 km (117 mi) southeast of Bari.

GETTING HERE
By car from Lecce, take the southbound SS16 and exit at Maglie. To follow the coast, take the SS53 from Lecce, then follow SS611 south. There is regular train service from Maglie.

VISITOR INFORMATION
Otranto tourism office (⊠ *Piazza Castello, 73028* ☎ *0834/801436).*

EXPLORING

14

In one of the first great Gothic novels, Horace Walpole's 1764 *The Castle of Otranto,* the English writer immortalized this city and its mysterious medieval fortress. Otranto (the stress is on the first syllable) has likewise had more than its share of dark thrills. As the easternmost point in Italy—and therefore closest to the Balkan peninsula—it has often borne the brunt of foreign invasions during its checkered history. A flourishing port from ancient Greek times, Otranto (Hydruntum to the Romans) has a history like most of southern Italy: after the fall of the western Roman Empire, centuries of Byzantine rule interspersed with Saracen incursions, followed by the arrival of the Normans. Modern Otranto's dank cobblestone alleyways alternatively reveal dusty, forgotten doorways and modern Italian fashion chains, and the spooky castle still looms above, between city and sea. On a clear day you can see across to Albania.

The historic city center nestles within impressive city walls and bastions, dominated by the famous **Castello,** which is attributed to the Spanish of the 16th century. ⊠ *Piazza Castello* ☎*€2* ⊙*May–Oct., daily 9–1 and 4–9; Nov.–Apr., daily 10–1 and 3:30–6:30.*

The real jewel in Otranto is the **Cattedrale,** originally begun by the Normans and conserving an extraordinary 12th-century mosaic pavement in the nave and aisles. ⊠ *Piazza Basilica* ☎ *0836/802720* ☎*Free* ⊙ *Daily 7–noon and 3–5.*

OFF THE BEATEN PATH

Coastline South to Leuca. The coastal road between Otranto and Leuca is one of the most beautiful in southern Italy. Sandy beaches are replaced by rocky outcrops and sheer cliffs watched over by scattered castles and seaside pleasure palaces. Along the way, Santa Cesarea Terme, with a pleasant shoreline and famous fanciful Moorish resort, and Castro, with another attractive marina, are worthwhile stops; this is land that few foreign tourists traverse. At the end of the journey, Capo Santa Maria di Leuca has a lighthouse at the most southeastern point in Italy, the end of the Puglian Aqueduct, and the quiet, sparse basilica of Santa Maria Finibus Terrae ("land's end"). From here, you are only 70 km (44 mi) from Albania. The Marina di Leuca, below, is a little fishing village with excursion boats and a few summertime hotels and bars. If, after the drive, you're heading back to Lecce or points east, the inland highway is a faster route.

WHERE TO STAY

$$$$ 🏠 **Masseria Montelauro.** This masseria—a working farmhouse for communal living, quite common in these parts—has had many incarnations since it was built in 1878: monastery, herbal pharmacy, discotheque, and restaurant. Now, the owners have refurbished the place in whitewashed Mediterranean minimalist chic. Wrought-iron beds, arched ceilings, gorgeous stone and marble bathrooms, and flowing white curtains all contribute to beautiful rooms, and the lobby looks like something out of a magazine. Friendly, helpful service and delicious food (much of which is plucked from the hotel's own garden) at breakfast, lunch (poolside), and dinner make this an oasis of comfort a short drive from lovely Otranto. **Pros:** Interesting building, lovely decor, great food. **Con:** No on-site parking. ⊠ *S.P. Otranto–Uggiano, Località Montelauro, Otranto-Lecce, 73028* ☎ *0836/806203* ⊕ *www.masseriamontelauro.it* ⇆ *29 rooms, 3 suites* ⚒ *In-room: safe, refrigerator. In-hotel: restaurant, pool* ▭ *AE, MC, V* ⊗ *Closed Nov.–Mar.* ⊙ *BP.*

GALLIPOLI

37 km (23 mi) south of Lecce, 190 km (118 mi) southeast of Bari.

GETTING HERE

From Lecce, take the SS101. From Taranto, follow the coastal SS174. Frequent trains run from Lecce.

VISITOR INFORMATION

Gallipoli tourism office (⊠ *Piazza Imbriani 10, 73014* ☎ *0833/262529*).

EXPLORING

The fishing port of Gallipoli, on the Golfo di Taranto, is divided between a new town, on the mainland, and a beautiful fortified town, across a 17th-century bridge, crowded onto its own small island in the gulf. The Greeks called it Kallipolis, the Romans Anxa. Like the infamous Turkish town of the same name on the Dardanelles, the Italian Gallipoli occupies a strategic location and thus was repeatedly attacked through the centuries—by the Normans in 1071, the Venetians in 1484, the British in 1809. Today, life in Gallipoli revolves around its fishing trade. Bright fishing boats in primary colors breeze in and out of the bay during the day, and Gallipoli's fish market, below the bridge, throbs with activity all morning.

Gallipoli's historic quarter, a mix of narrow alleys and squares, is guarded by **Castello Aragonese,** a massive fortification that grew out of an earlier Byzantine fortress you can still see at the southeast corner.

Gallipoli's **Duomo** (⊠ *Via Antonietta de Pace* ☎ *0833/261987*), open daily 8:30–noon and 5–8:30, is a notable baroque church.

The church of **La Purità** (✉ *Riviera Nazaro Sauro* ☎ *0833/261699*) has a stuccoed interior as elaborate as a wedding cake, with an especially noteworthy tile floor. You can visit daily 10–noon and 5–8.

WHERE TO STAY & EAT

$$$ ✗ **Marechiaro.** Unless you arrive by boat—as many do—you have to cross a little bridge to reach this simple waterfront restaurant, not far from the town's historic center. It's built out onto the sea, replete with wood paneling, flowers, and terraces, with panoramic coastal views. Try the renowned *zuppa di pesce alla gallipolina* (a stew of fish, shrimp, clams, and mussels) and linguine with seafood. ✉ *Lungomare Marconi* ☎ *0833/266143* ▭ *AE, DC, MC, V.*

★ $$$$ ⊡ **Costa Brada.** The rooms all have terraces with sea views at this modern white beach hotel of classic Mediterranean design. The interiors are uncluttered and tasteful; the suites (rooms 110 through 114) are particularly spacious and overlook the private beach. The hotel, just outside Gallipoli, accepts only half- or full-board guests in summer. Room rates go down significantly at other times of year. **Pros:** Lovely views, stunning location. **Con:** Meal plans required in summer. ✉ *Baia Verde, Litoranea Santa Maria di Leuca, 73014* ☎ *0833/202551* ⊕ *www.grandhotelcostabrada.it* ⇌ *80 rooms* ⌂ *In-room: safe, refrigerator, Wi-Fi. In-hotel: 3 restaurants, pools, gym, beachfront* ▭ *AE, DC, MC, V* ⏍ *MAP.*

BEACHES

☉ Ample swimming, water sports, and clean, fine sand make Gallipoli's **beaches** a good choice for families. The 5-km (3-mi) expanse of sand sweeping south from town has both public and private beaches, the latter equipped with changing rooms, sun beds, and umbrellas. Water-sports equipment can be bought or rented at the waterfront shops in town.

BASILICATA

Occupying the instep of Italy's boot, Basilicata has long been one of Italy's poorest regions, memorably described by Carlo Levi (1902–75) in his *Christ Stopped at Eboli,* a book that brought home to the majority of the Italians the depths of deprivation to which this forgotten region was subject. (The tale of Levi's internment was poignantly filmed by Francesco Rosi in 1981.) Basilicata was not always so desolate, however. For the ancient Greeks, the area formed part of Magna Graecia, the loose collection of colonies founded along the coasts of southern Italy whose wealth and military prowess rivaled those of the city-states of Greece itself. The city of Matera, the region's true highlight, is built on the side of an impressive ravine that is honeycombed with sassi, some of them still occupied, forming a separate enclave that contrasts vividly with the attractive baroque town above.

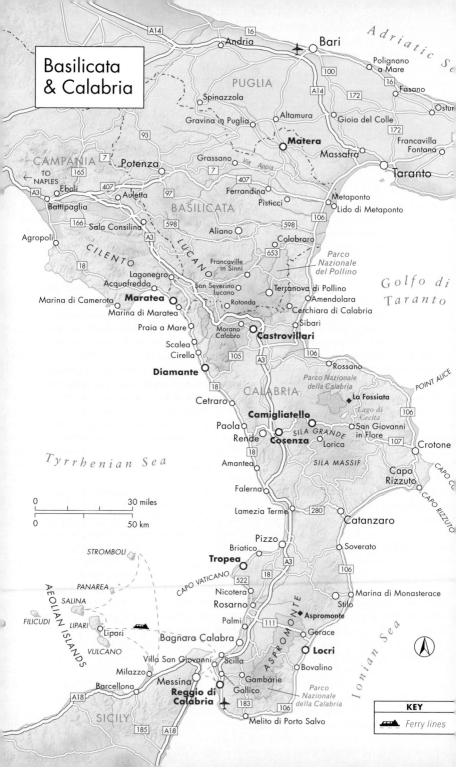

MATERA

62 km (39 mi) south of Bari.

GETTING HERE
From Bari, take the SS96 to Altamura, then the SS99 to Matera.

VISITOR INFORMATION
Matera tourism office (⊠ *Via Spine Bianche 22, 75100* ☎*0835/331817* ⊕*www.aptbasilicata.it*). **La Rubrica Sassi** (⊠ *Via O. Tataranni 32, 75100* ☎*0835/337374* ⊕*www.rubricasassi.com*) arranges tours of the sassi areas, charging around €40.

EXPLORING
Matera is one of southern Italy's most unusual towns. On their own, the elegant baroque churches, palazzi, and broad piazzas—filled to bursting during the evening passeggiata, when the locals turn out to stroll the streets—would make Matera stand out in Basilicata's impoverished landscape. But what really sets this town apart are its sassi.

Fodor'sChoice
★
Matera's **sassi** are rock-hewn dwellings piled chaotically atop one another, strewn across the sides of a steep ravine. They date from Paleolithic times, when they were truly cave homes. In the years that followed, the grottoes were slowly adapted as houses only slightly more modern, with their exterior walls closed off and canals regulating rainwater and sewage. Until relatively recently, these troglodytic abodes presented a Dante-esque vision of squalor and poverty, graphically described in Carlo Levi's *Christ Stopped at Eboli,* but in the 1960s most of them were emptied of their inhabitants, who were largely consigned to the ugly block structures seen on the way into town. Today, having been designated a World Heritage Site, the area has been cleaned up and is gradually being populated once again—and even gentrified, as evidenced by the bars and restaurants that have moved in. (The filming here of Mel Gibson's controversial film *The Passion of the Christ* also raised the area's profile.) The wide Strada Panoramica leads you safely through this desolate region, which still retains its eerie atmosphere and panoramic views.

There are two areas of sassi, the **Sasso Caveoso** and the **Sasso Barisano,** and both can be seen from vantage points in the upper town. Follow the Strada Panoramica down into the sassi and feel free to ramble among the strange structures, which, in the words of H. V. Morton in his *A Traveller in Southern Italy,* "resemble the work of termites rather than of man." Among them you will find several *chiese rupestri,* or rock-hewn churches, some of which have medieval frescoes, notably **Santa Maria de Idris,** right on the edge of the Sasso Caveoso, near the ravine. ⊠*Sasso Caveoso* ☎*0835/319458* 🎟*€5* ⏰*Daily 9:30–1:30 and 2:30–4:30.*

The **Duomo** in Matera was built in the late 13th century and occupies a prominent position between the two areas of sassi. It has a pungent Apulian-Romanesque flavor; inside, there's a recovered fresco, probably painted in the 14th century, showing scenes from the *Last Judgment.* On the Duomo's facade the figures of Sts. Peter and Paul stand

14

on either side of a sculpture of Matera's patron, Madonna della Bruna. At the time of writing, the church was closed for restorations until mid-2009. ✉ *Via Duomo* ☎*0835/332908*

In town you'll find the 13th-century Romanesque church of **San Giovanni Battista,** restored to its pre-baroque simplicity in 1926. As you go in through a side door—the original end door and facade were incorporated into later buildings—note the interesting sculpted decorations in the porch. The interior still maintains its original cross vaulting, ogival arches, and curious capitals. ✉ *Via San Biagio* ☎*0835/334182* ☉*Daily 7:30–12:30 and 3:30–9.*

NEED A BREAK?

The distinguished, timeworn patina of downtown's elegant little Caffè Tripoli (✉*Piazza Vittorio Veneto 17* ☎*0835/333991*) only hints at the treasures that lie within: some of southern Italy's best coffee and gelato. It's also renowned for their unbelievably rich hot chocolate and other decadent drinks that blend coffees, creams, and gelatos. You can't go wrong.

Matera's archaeological **Museo Ridola** is housed in the former monastery of Santa Chiara. Illustrating the history of the area, the museum includes an extensive selection of prehistoric and classical finds, notably Bronze Age weaponry and beautifully decorated Greek ceramics. ✉ *Via Ridola 24* ☎*0835/310058* 🎟*€2.50* ☉*Tues.–Sun. 9–8, Mon. 2–8.*

WHERE TO STAY & EAT

$$$–$$$$
Fodor's Choice
★

✕ **Le Botteghe.** This stylish restaurant occupies a pleasingly restored building in the sassi. Carnivores will delight in the charcoal-grilled steak, especially selected by a local butcher. Cooked wonderfully rare, this is one of the finest pieces of meat in the region. It's best washed down with local Aglianico del Vulture red wine. Solid renditions of local pasta dishes are also available. ✉*Piazza San Pietro Barisano 22* ☎*0835/344072* ▭*DC, MC, V* ☉*Closed Wed. Oct.–Mar.*

$$–$$$

✕ **Nadì.** In the heart of the sassi, this restaurant was once a cave dwelling. It still has a cavelike atmosphere, calling to mind the town's interesting history. The *peperoni cruschi* (dried peppers) hanging from the ceiling and the aroma of meat on the main room's central grill let you know you're in for a treat. Try the local specialty of *purè di fave con cicorielle campestri* (puree of dried fava beans and chicory) for a taste of simpler times. Top off your meal with a slice of homemade ricotta cake. ✉*Via Fiorentini 1/3* ☎*0835/332892* ▭*AE, MC, V* ☉*Closed 1 wk in July.*

$$–$$$
Fodor's Choice
★

🛏 **Locanda di San Martino.** Combining good taste, an agreeable ambience, and excellent value, the Locanda is a prime place to stay among Matera's sassi. In fact, you can drive right up to the front door. The historic rooms—formerly cave dwellings—have been impeccably restored under the guidance of owner Antonio Panetto and Dorothy Zinn. An elevator whisks you to your floor, and a short walk outdoors takes you to your room. Stepping out onto your terrace overlooking the old town is like being on a film set. In 2008, the couple transformed one of the old town wells into an indoor swimming pool. **Pros:** Convenient location, comfortable rooms. **Con:** Rooms are reached via outdoor walkway. ✉*Via Fiorentini 71, 75100* ☎*0835/256600* ⊕*www.locandadisan*

martino.it ⟿*19 rooms, 9 suites* ⟳*In-room: safe, refrigerator, dial-up. In-hotel: bar, public Wi-Fi, parking (fee)* ⊟*AE, DC, MC, V* ⊠*BP.*

$$ ⬚ **Hotel Sant'Angelo.** Just above the church of San Pietro Caveoso, this unusual hotel has an ideal view of the Sasso Caveoso. Each of the 16 rooms was once a cave dwelling, so they have authentic touches like rough-hewn walls. Don't worry, there are also modern touches like air-conditioning. Because of the number of steps, this hotel is not ideal for people with limited mobility. **Pros:** Unrivalled views, atmospheric rooms. **Con:** Many steps to climb. ⊠*Piazza San Pietro Caveoso, 75100* ☎*0835/314010* ⊕*www.hotelsantangelosassi.it* ⟿*16 rooms, 5 suites* ⟳*In-room: safe, refrigerator, dial-up. In-hotel: no elevator* ⊟*AE, DC, MC, V* ⊠*BP.*

14

MARATEA

103 km (64 mi) southwest of Aliano, 217 km (135 mi) south of Naples.

GETTING HERE

By car, take the Lagonegro exit from the A3 motorway and continue along the SS18. Most trains stop at Maratea. In the summer months there is a bus linking the bus station and town 4 km (2½ mi) away.

VISITOR INFORMATION

Maratea tourism office (⊠*Piazza del Gesù 32, 85046* ☎*0973/876908* ⊕*www.aptbasilicata.it*).

EXPLORING

When encountering Maratea for the first time, you can be forgiven for thinking you've somehow arrived at the French Riviera. The high, twisty road resembles nothing so much as a corniche, complete with glimpses of a turquoise sea below. Divided by the craggy rocks into various separate localities—Maratea, Maratea Porto, Marina di Maratea, Fiumicello—the sequence ends above the main inland village, a tumble of cobblestone streets where the ruins of a much older settlement (Maratea Antica) can be seen. At the summit of the hill stands a dramatic, gigantic Christ, donated by an industrialist from Piemonte. This massive statue is reminiscent of the one in Rio de Janeiro. There's no shortage of secluded sandy strips in between the rocky headlands, which can get crowded in August. A summer minibus service connects all the different points once or twice an hour.

WHERE TO STAY & EAT

$$–$$$ ✕ **Taverna Rovita.** Housed in a former convent with exposed beams and other authentic touches, this restaurant sits in the heart of the old town. The menu is based on traditional recipes, but the food is in a different league from that of Maratea's other eateries. The antipasti, for a start, are varied and abundant, and the homemade pasta comes with a selection of rich sauces that changes according to the season. Choose a locally caught fish for your second course. ⊠*Via Rovita 13* ☎*0973/876588* ⊟*AE, DC, MC, V* ⊘*Closed Tues.*

$$$$ ✕▦ **Villa Cheta Elite.** Immersed in Mediterranean greenery, this historic villa is in the seaside village of Acquafredda, just north of Maratea. Although not on the beach, the Villa is just across the street. Rooms are spruce and stylish without being overfurnished, while dining out on the restaurant's garden terrace ($$$$) is simply fabulous. **Pros:** Surrounded by lush vegetation, beautiful views of the coast. **Con:** On a busy road. ✉ *Via Nazionale 46, Località Acquafredda Maratea 85041* ☎*0973/878134* ⊕*www.villacheta.it* ↝*23 rooms* &*In-room: safe, refrigerator. In-hotel: restaurant, bar, no elevator* ⊟*AE, DC, MC, V* ☯*Closed Nov.–Mar.* †⊚|*MAP.*

CALABRIA

Italy's southernmost mainland region has seen more than its fair share of oppression, poverty, and natural disaster, but this land of Magna Graecia, mountains, and *mare* (sea) also claims more than its share of fantastic scenery and great beaches. The accent here is on the landscape, the sea, and the constantly changing dialogue between the two. Don't expect much in the way of sophistication in this least trodden of regions, but do remain open to the simple pleasures to be found—the country food, the friendliness, the disarming hospitality of the people. Aside from coast and culture, there are also some sights worth going out of your way for, from the vividly colored murals of Diamante to the ruins of Magna Graecia at Locri. Inland, the Parco Nazionale Pollino and mountainous Sila Massif, which includes a nature reserve, are draws for hikers.

The drive on the southbound A3 highway alone is a breathtaking experience, the more so as you approach Sicily, whose image grows tantalizingly nearer as the road wraps around the coastline once challenged by Odysseus. The road has been under reconstruction since his time, with little sign of completion.

DIAMANTE

51 km (32 mi) south of Maratea, 225 km (140 mi) south of Naples.

GETTING HERE
Driving from Maratea, take the SS18; from Cosenza, take the SS107 to Paola, then the SS18. Regional trains leave from Paola five times a day.

VISITOR INFORMATION
Diamante tourism office (✉*Discesa Corvino Superiore, 87023* ☎*0985/876046*).

EXPLORING
One of the most fashionable of the string of small resorts lining Calabria's north Tyrrhenian coast, Diamante makes a good stop for its whitewashed maze of narrow alleys, brightly adorned with a startling variety of large-scale murals. The work of local and international artists, the murals—which range from cartoons to poems to serious por-

traits, and from tasteful to downright ugly—give a sense of wandering through a huge open-air art gallery. Flanking the broad, palm-lined seaside promenade are sparkling beaches to the north and south.

WHERE TO STAY

$$$ ⊞ **Grand Hotel San Michele.** A survivor from a vanishing age, the San Michele, operated by the illustrious Claudia Sinisalchi and her marine biologist son Andrea, occupies a belle epoque–style villa. It sits on the top of a cliff near the village of Cetraro, 20 km (12 mi) south of Diamante on SS18. Mingling Mediterranean charm with old-style elegance, the hotel is set within extensive gardens, and an elevator takes you down to three private beaches at the base of the cliff, as well as a summer bar and restaurant. As with most hotels on Calabria's coast, substantial bargains are available on room rates outside July and August. **Pros:** Lovely views, nice gardens, comfortable accommodations. **Con:** A bit pricey. ✉*Località Bosco 8/9, 87022 Cetraro* ☎*0982/91012* ⊕*www.sanmichele.it* ↩*82 rooms, 6 suites, 40 apartments* ♿*In-room: refrigerator, dial-up. In-hotel: restaurant, bar, golf course, tennis court, beachfront* ⊟*AE, DC, MC, V* ⊘*Closed Nov.* ⦾*BP.*

CASTROVILLARI

㉔ *68 km (43 mi) east of Diamante, 75 km (48 mi) north of Cosenza.*

GETTING HERE

By car, take the A3 motorway and exit at Frascineto-Castrovillari. Ferrovie della Calabria runs buses from Sapri, but service is irregular.

VISITOR INFORMATION

Castrovillari tourism office (✉*Corso Garibaldi 60, 87012* ☎*0981/27750).*

EXPLORING

Accent the first "i" when you pronounce the name of this provincial Calabrian city, notable for its Aragonese castle, Jewish synagogue, and 16th-century San Giuliano church. It's also a great jumping-off point for the Parco Nazionale Pollino. Castrovillari's world-class restaurant-inn, La Locanda di Alia, has made the city something of an out-of-the-way gastronomical destination in Calabria.

OFF THE BEATEN PATH

Cerchiara di Calabria. There may be no more characteristically Calabrian, time-frozen village than this community of 2,800 people, which can be reached by a winding 32-km (20-mi) climb from Castrovillari via SS105 and SS92. Like so many rural towns in southern Italy, this one is aging and shrinking: the death rate is about double the birthrate. You may get some curious stares as you ramble through the ancient sloping cobblestone streets and take in the memorable views straight across to the Ionian Sea—but the experience will transport you back a century.

WHERE TO STAY & EAT

$$ ✕🖼 **La Locanda di Alia.** It's hard to say what's more surprising about this inn and gastronomical temple: its improbable location in Castrovillari, or the fact that it's been here since 1952. At the restaurant ($$$–$$$$), Chef Gaetano Alia's menu swerves from the comforting (beef with a delicious strawberry and onion sauce) to the dangerously spicy (*candele,* like rigatoni without the ridges, in a tomato, pork, and hot pepper sauce). Pleasant guest rooms ($$) are on one floor, surrounded by plenty of greenery. They are decorated in bright colors with frescoes from local artists; some have separate living areas. **Pro:** The best food in Calabria. **Con:** Difficult to reach without a car. ⊠ *Via Letticelle 55* ☎ *0981/46370* ⊕ *www.alia.it* 📡 *14 rooms, 1 suite* ♿ *In-room: refrigerator, dial-up. In-hotel: restaurant, bar, beachfront* ⊟ *AE, DC, MC, V* ⊗ *Closed Nov.* ⊚ *BP.* ⚮ *Restaurant reservations essential*

COSENZA

75 km (48 mi) south of Diamante, 185 km (115 mi) north of Reggio di Calabria.

GETTING HERE

By car, take the Cosenza exit from the A3 motorway. By train, change at Paola on the main Rome–Reggio di Calabria line. Ferrovie della Calabria runs infrequent buses.

VISITOR INFORMATION

Cosenza tourism office (⊠ *Via Galliano 6, 87100* ☎ *0984/814527* ⊕ *www.aptcosenza.it*).

EXPLORING

Cosenza has a steep, stair-filled centro storico that truly hails from another age. Wrought-iron balconies overlook narrow alleyways with old-fashioned storefronts and bars that have barely been touched by centuries of development. Flung haphazardly—and beautifully—across the top and side of a steep hill ringed by mountains, and watched over by a great, crumbling medieval castle, Cosenza also provides the best gateway for the Sila, whose steep walls rear up to the town's eastern side. Though Cosenza's outskirts are largely modern and ugly, culinary and photographic gems await in the rolling farmland nearby and the mountains to the east.

Crowning the Pancrazio hill above the old city, with views across to the Sila mountains, **Castello Svevo** is largely in ruins, having suffered successive earthquakes and a lightning strike that ignited gunpowder stored within. The castle takes its name from the great Swabian emperor Frederick II (1194–1250), who added two octagonal towers, though it dates originally to the Normans, who fortified the hill against their Saracen foes. Occasional exhibitions and concerts are staged here in summer, and any time of year it's fun to check out the old ramparts and take in the views of the old and new cities—a shocking study in contrast. ⊠ *Colle Pancrazio* ☎ *0984/813336* 🎫 *Free* ⊗ *Daily 8–8.*

Cosenza's noblest square, **Piazza XV Marzo** (commonly called Piazza della Prefettura), houses government buildings as well as the elegant **Teatro Rendano**. From the square, the **Villa Comunale** (public garden) provides plenty of shaded benches for a rest.

NEED A BREAK? In the heart of the centro storico since 1803, the charming and historic Gran Caffè Renzelli (✉ *Corso Telesio 46* ☎ *0984/26814*) makes a fine spot for a pause. At tables inside or out you can enjoy *varchiglia* (a dry almond cake) along with a host of sweet and wonderful coffee-liqueur combinations, each served with lightly whipped cream in a tall glass. Join in the *chiacchiere al caffè* (talks over coffee), echoing the discussions of the literary salon that once met here.

14

Cosenza's original **Duomo** was probably built in the middle of the 11th century but was destroyed by the earthquake of 1184. A new cathedral was consecrated in the presence of Emperor Frederick II in 1222. After many baroque additions, later alterations have restored some of the Provençal Gothic style. Inside, look for the lovely monument to Isabella of Aragon, who died after falling from her horse en route to France in 1271. ✉ *Piazza del Duomo* ☎ *0984/77864* ◷ *Daily 8–noon and 3:30–7.*

WHERE TO STAY & EAT

★ **$$$** ✕ **Pantagruel.** You are completely in the hands of the chef at this prix fixe–only temple to seafood, located in the tiny town of Rende, 13 km (8 mi) northwest of Cosenza. They are good hands indeed, which is why Pantagruel is one of the most respected restaurants in Calabria. The set menu depends on the day's catch, but you'll surely encounter something memorable: for instance, a salad of octopus so thinly sliced and delicate that it's reminiscent of carpaccio, or a tender fillet of *spigola* (Mediterranean bass) with a sweet sauce of brandy, cream of licorice, and lemon rind. It's set in an elegant old house with sweeping views of hills dotted with little towns. ✉ *Via Santanna Pittor 2* ☎ *0984/443847* ▭ *AE, DC, MC, V* ◷ *Closed Sun., 1 wk in late Dec., and 1 wk in mid-Aug.*

$$ ✕ **Osteria dell'Arenella.** Right on the banks of the river, this grilled-meat specialist caters to the local bourgeoisie with a comfortable, friendly set of rooms under old archways. The place is for carnivores only; go for the *grigliata mista* and enjoy the wonderful meatiness of local grass-fed beef—but be sure to ask for it all *al sangue* (rare). The wine list, too, is excellent. ✉ *Via Arenella 12* ☎ *0984/76573* ▭ *MC, V* ◷ *Closed Mon. Oct.–Mar. No lunch Tues.–Sat.*

$$ ✕ **Taverna L'Arco Vecchio.** This tavern-restaurant, right in the middle of the old town along the path up to the castle, sits under the famous Arch of Ciaccio. It serves traditional Calabrian dishes in a warm, elegant vaulted room. Try the excellent *lagane e ceci* (homemade pasta with chickpeas, garlic, and oil). ✉ *Via Archi di Ciaccio 21* ☎ *0984/72564* ⊕ *www.arcovecchio.it* ▭ *AE, DC, MC, V* ◷ *Closed Sun. July–Sept., Tues. Oct.–June, and 2 wks in Aug.*

$ 🛏   **Royal Hotel.** Decent accommodations are hard to come by in Cosenza, which makes this hotel in the new center quite a find. The location is a 15-minute walk from the town's centro storico. The lobby is regal, the rooms not so much; still, they're simple and clean, with sober furnishings. **Pro:** One of the town's best lodgings. **Con:** Not in the best part of the city. ⊠ *Via Molinella 24/e, 87100* 🕾*0984/412165* ⊕*www.hotelroyalsas.it* ⬐*44 rooms* ☖*In-room: refrigerator. In-hotel: restaurant, bar, public Internet* ⊟*AE, DC, MC, V* ❧❙*BP.*

CAMIGLIATELLO

30 km (19 mi) east of Cosenza.

GETTING HERE
By car, take the Cosenza Nord exit from the A3, then follow the SS107.

VISITOR INFORMATION
Camigliatello tourism office (⊠ *Via Roma, 87052* 🕾*0984/578159*).

EXPLORING
Lined with chalets, Camigliatello is one of the Sila Massif's major resort towns. Most of the Sila is not mountainous at all; it is, rather, an extensive, sparsely populated plateau with areas of thick forest. Unfortunately, the region has been exploited by construction and fuel industries, resulting in considerable deforestation. However, since 1968, when the area was designated a national park (Parco Nazionale della Calabria), strict rules have limited the felling of timber, and forests are now regenerating. There are well-marked trails through pine and beech woods, and ample opportunities for horseback riding. Fall and winter see droves of locals hunting mushrooms and gathering chestnuts, while ski slopes near Camigliatello draw crowds.

A couple of miles east of town, Lago Cecita makes a good starting point for exploring **La Fossiata,** a lovely wooded conservation area within the park.

WHERE TO STAY
$ 🛏   **Tasso.** On the edge of Camigliatello, less than 1 km (½ mi) from the ski slopes, this hotel is in a peaceful, picturesque location. Don't be put off by its oddly futuristic 1970s look—it's well equipped, with plenty of space for evening entertainment, including live music, and relaxation after a day of hiking or skiing. The restaurant has a terrace shaded by a walnut tree, and all rooms have balconies. There are sometimes good full-board deals for seniors in summer. **Pros:** Beautiful surroundings, nice views, lively atmosphere. **Con:** Dated architecture. ⊠ *Via degli Impianti Sportivi, Spezzano della Sila, 87058* 🕾🕾*0984/578113* ⊕*www.hoteltasso.it* ⬐*82 rooms* ☖*In-room: no a/c. In-hotel: restaurant, bar, parking (no fee)* ⊟*AE, DC, MC, V* ☉*Closed Mar.–May and Nov.* ❧❙*BP.*

TROPEA

28 km (17 mi) southwest of Pizzo, 107 km (66 mi) north of Reggio di Calabria.

GETTING HERE

By car, exit the A3 motorway at Pizzo and follow the southbound SS18. Five trains depart daily from Lamezia.

VISITOR INFORMATION

Tropea tourism office (⊠*Piazza Ercole, 88038* ☎*0963/61475* ⊕*www.prolocotropea.eu*).

14

EXPLORING

Ringed by cliffs and wonderful sandy beaches, the Tropea promontory is still mostly undiscovered. The main town of Tropea, its old palazzi built in simple golden stone, easily wins the contest for prettiest town on the Tyrrhenian Coast. On a clear day the seaward views from the waterfront promenade take in Stromboli's cone and at least four of the other Aeolians. If you hear them calling, the islands can be visited by motorboats that depart daily in the summer. Accommodations are good, and beach addicts will not be disappointed by the choice of magnificent sandy bays within easy reach of here. Some of the best are south at Capo Vaticano and north at Briatico.

In Tropea's harmonious warren of lanes, seek out the old Norman **Cattedrale**, whose interior displays a couple of unexploded U.S. bombs from World War II, with a grateful prayer to the Madonna attached to each. ⊠*Piazza Sedile* ☎*0963/761388* ⊙*Daily 7:30–noon and 4–7.*

From the belvedere at the bottom of the main square, Piazza Ercole, the church and Benedictine monastery of **Santa Maria dell'Isola** glisten on a rocky promontory above an aquamarine sea. Stroll out to visit the church on a path lined with fishermen's caves. Dating to medieval times, the church was remodeled in the Gothic style, then given another face-lift after an earthquake in 1905. The interior has an 18th-century Nativity and some fragments of medieval tombs. At this writing, the monastery was closed for reconstruction. Call ahead if you'd like to visit. ⊠*Santa Maria dell'Isola* ☎*0963/61388*

WHERE TO STAY & EAT

$$$–$$$$ ✕ **Pimm's.** Since its glory days in the 1960s, this underground restaurant in Tropea's historic center has offered the town's top dining experience. Seafood is the best choice, with such specialties as pasta with sea urchins, smoked swordfish, and stuffed squid. The splendid sea views are an extra enticement. ⊠*Corso Vittorio Emanuele 2* ☎☎*0963/666105* ▭*AE, DC, MC, V* ⊙*Closed Mon. Sept.–June.*

$$ ⟳ ▦ **Rocca Nettuno.** Perched on the cliffs south of the town center, this large complex has reasonably spacious rooms, almost all with balco-

nies. A favorite with families, it has plenty of activities for children and a babysitting service. Some of the best—and quietest—rooms are immersed in greenery near the cliff top. **Pros:** Family-friendly environment, nice location. **Con:** Not the place for a quiet getaway. ⊠ *Via Annunziata* ☎*0963/998111* 🖷*0963/603513* ⊕*www.roccanettuno.com* ☞*276 rooms* ⌂*In-room: safe, refrigerator. In-hotel: 3 restaurants, bars, pool, tennis court, beachfront* ▭*AE, DC, MC, V* ⊗*Closed Nov.–Apr.* ⫟*FAP.*

REGGIO DI CALABRIA

26 km (16 mi) south of Scilla, 499 km (311 mi) south of Naples.

GETTING HERE
The A3 motorway runs directly to Reggio di Calabria. Trains depart from Naples every hour. There are daily flights from Rome.

VISITOR INFORMATION
Reggio di Calabria tourism office (⊠*Corso Garibaldi 329, 89100* ☎*0965/27120*).

EXPLORING
Reggio di Calabria, the city on Italy's toe tip, is the jumping-off point for Messina- and Sicily-bound ferries, and was laid low by the same catastrophic earthquake that struck Messina in 1908. This raw city is one of Italy's most active ports, where you'll find every category of container ship and smokestack.

FodorśChoice Reggio has one of southern Italy's most important archaeological muse-
★ ums, the **Museo Nazionale della Magna Grecia.**Prize exhibits here are two statues, known as the **Bronzi di Riace,** that were discovered by an amateur deep-sea diver off Calabria's Ionian coast in 1972. Flaunting physiques that gym enthusiasts would die for, the pair are thought to date from the fifth century BC and have been attributed to both Pheidias and Polykleitos. It's possible that they were taken by the Romans as trophies from the site of Delphi and then shipwrecked on their return to Italy. Coins and votive tablets are among the numerous other treasures from Magna Graecia contained in the museum. ⊠*Piazza de Nava 26, Corso Garibaldi* ☎*0965/812255* ⊕*www.museonazionalerc.it* 🖾*€4* ⊗*Tues.–Sun. 9–7.*

WHERE TO STAY
$$$ ⊡ **Grande Albergo Miramare.** On the seafront midway between the port and the station, Miramare has one of the best locations in Reggio. It has been restored to evoke the charm of the early 20th century, yet has modern facilities. ⊠*Via Fata Morgana 1, 89127* ☎*0965/812444* ⊕*www.montesanohotels.it* ☞*96 rooms* ⌂*In-hotel: restaurant, bar, parking (fee)* ▭*AE, DC, MC, V* ⫟*BP.*

Sicily

WORD OF MOUTH

"Palermo/Monreale was our first stop. Come here for the monuments and churches...an endless array. If I had to pick a favorite place, it would be the Palatine Chapel in Palazzo Reale. It managed to be dazzlingly beautiful, while retaining a remarkable sense of warmth."

–Elizabeth S

WELCOME TO SICILY

TOP REASONS TO GO

★ **A walk on Siracusa's Ortygia Island:** Classical ruins rub elbows with faded seaside palaces and fish markets in Sicily's most beautiful port city, whose Duomo is literally built upon the columns of an ancient Greek temple.

★ **The palaces, churches, and crypts of Palermo:** Virtually every great European empire once ruled Sicily's strategically positioned capital, and it shows most of all in the diverse architecture, from Roman to Byzantine to Arab-Norman.

★ **The Valley of the Temples, Agrigento:** This stunning set of ruins is proudly perched above the sea in a grove full of almond trees; not even in Athens will you find Greek temples this finely preserved.

★ **Taormina's Teatro Greco:** Watch a Greek tragedy in the very amphitheater where it was performed two millennia ago—in the shadow of smoking Mt. Etna.

1 **The Ionian Coast.** For many, the Ionian Coast is all about touristy **Taormina**, spectacularly perched on a cliff near Mount Etna; but don't overlook lively **Catania**, Sicily's modern nerve center.

2 **Palermo.** Sicily's capital and one of Italy's most hectic cities, Palermo conceals notes of extraordinary beauty amid the uncontained chaos of fish markets and impossible traffic.

3 **Western Sicily.** Following the island's northern edge west of Palermo, the Western Coast meanders past **Monreale** and its mosaics, **Segesta** with its temple, and the fairy-tale town of **Erice**. Greek ruins stand sentinel in **Agrigento** at the Valley of the Temples, blanketed in almond and juniper blossoms. Scarcely less impressive is **Selinunte**, rising above rubble and overlooking the sea.

4 **Tyrrhenian Coast.** Filled with summer beachgoers, the Tyrrhenian Coast also boasts the quaint town of **Cefalù**, with its famous cathedral.

5 **The Interior.** In hill towns such as **Enna**, the interior of Sicily reveals a slower pace of life than in the frenetic coastal cities. **Piazza Armerina** features the Villa Casale and its ancient Roman mosaics.

A29 • **2** Palermo
Monreale • Bagheria
Trapani • Erice
Segesta • Alcamo
Termini Imerese
624
115
Marsala A29
Castelvetrano
3
189
Mazara del Vallo
Sciacca
115 Canica
3 Western Sicily.
115
Mare Mediterráneo
Agrige
Lipari

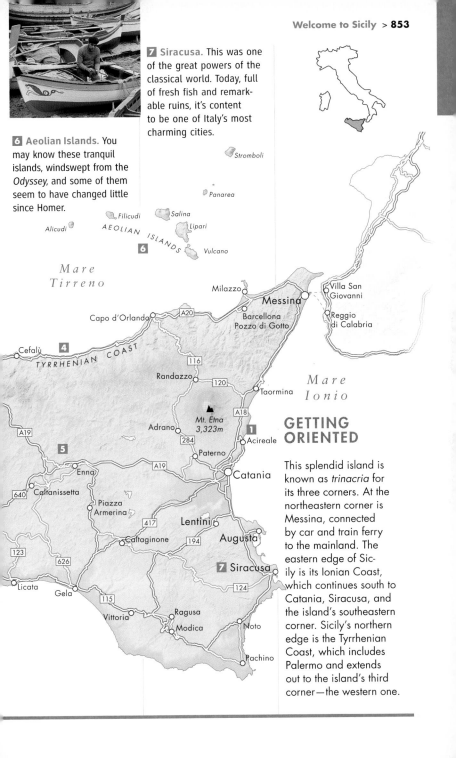

7 **Siracusa.** This was one of the great powers of the classical world. Today, full of fresh fish and remarkable ruins, it's content to be one of Italy's most charming cities.

6 **Aeolian Islands.** You may know these tranquil islands, windswept from the *Odyssey*, and some of them seem to have changed little since Homer.

Stromboli

Panarea

Filicudi   *Salina*

Alicudi   *A E O L I A N*   *Lipari*

6   *ISLANDS*   *Vulcano*

M a r e
T i r r e n o

Milazzo
Messina
Capo d'Orlando   A20
   Barcellona   Villa San
   Pozzo di Gotto   Giovanni
Cefalù   **4**   Reggio
TYRRHENIAN COAST   di Calabria

   116
Randazzo   *M a r e*
   120   *I o n i o*
   Taormina
   ▲   A18
   Mt. Etna
Adrano   *3,323m*   **1**   **GETTING**
   284   Acireale   **ORIENTED**
   Paterno
A19   This splendid island is
   Catania   known as *trinacria* for
Enna   its three corners. At the
5   northeastern corner is
640   Caltanissetta   Messina, connected
   Piazza   by car and train ferry
   Armerina   to the mainland. The
   417   Lentini   eastern edge of Sic-
Caltaginone   Augusta   ily is its Ionian Coast,
123   194   which continues south to
626   **7** Siracusa   Catania, Siracusa, and
Licata   124   the island's southeastern
Gela   corner. Sicily's northern
115   edge is the Tyrrhenian
Vittoria   Ragusa   Coast, which includes
   Modica   Noto   Palermo and extends
   out to the island's third
   Pachino   corner—the western one.

SICILY PLANNER

Making the Most of Your Time

You should plan a visit to Sicily around Palermo, Taormina, Siracusa, and Agrigento, four don't-miss destinations. The best way to see them all is to travel in a circle. Start your circuit in the northeast in Taormina, worth at least a night or two. If you have time, stay also in Catania, a lively, fascinating city that's often overlooked. From there, connect to the regional, two-lane SS114 toward the spectacular ancient Greek port of Siracusa, which merits at least two nights.

Next, backtrack north on the SS114, and take the A19 toward Palermo. Piazza Armerina's impressive mosaics and Enna, a sleepy mountaintop city, are worthwhile stops in the interior. Take the SS640 to the Greek temples of Agrigento. Stay here for a night before driving west along the coastal SS115, checking out Selinunte's ruins before reaching magical Erice, a good base for one night. You're now near some of Sicily's best beaches at San Vito Lo Capo. Take the A19 to Palermo, the chaotic and wonderful capital city, to wrap up your Sicilian experience. Give yourself at least two days here—or, ideally, four or five.

The Mob Mentality

Though Sicily may conjure up images of Don Corleone and his Hollywood progeny, you won't come in contact with the Mafia during your time in Sicily other than in the newspapers. The "Cosa Nostra," as the Italians sometimes refer to it (don't use the term yourself) is focused on its own business and poses virtually no risk to tourists.

Wandering through sleepy interior Sicilian hill towns like Corleone (yes, it's a real place) and Prizzi, you might be subject to some curious and guarded stares by the locals and feel the haze of a silent old-boy network, but nothing more than that.

Finding a Place to Stay

The good-quality hotels tend to be limited to the major cities and resorts of Palermo, Taormina, Siracusa, and Agrigento, along with the odd beach resort, but there has also recently been an explosion in the development of *agriturismo* lodgings (rural bed-and-breakfasts), many of them quite basic, but others providing the same facilities found in hotels. These country houses also offer all-inclusive, inexpensive full-board plans that can make for some of Sicily's most memorable meals.

DINING & LODGING PRICE CATEGORIES (IN EUROS)

¢	$	$$	$$$	$$$$
Restaurants				
under €15	€15–€25	€25–€35	€35–€45	over €45
Hotels				
under €70	€70–€110	€110–€160	€160–€220	over €220

Restaurant prices are for a first course (primo), second course (secondo), and dessert (dolce). Hotel prices are for two people in a standard double room in high season, including tax and service.

GETTING AROUND

By Car

This is the ideal way to explore Sicily. Modern highways circle and bisect the island, making all main cities easily reachable. A20 connects Messina and Palermo; Messina and Catania are linked by A18; running through the interior, from Catania to west of Cefalù, is A19; threading west from Palermo, A29 runs to Trapani and the airport, with a leg stretching down to Mazara del Vallo. The *superstrada* (highway) SS115 runs along the southern coast, and connecting superstrade lace the island.

You will likely hear stories about the dangers of driving in Sicily. Some are true, and others less so. In the big cities—especially Palermo, Catania, and Messina—streets are a honking mess, with lane markings and traffic lights taken as mere suggestions; you can avoid the chaos by leaving your car in a garage. However, once outside the urban areas and resort towns, the highways and regional state roads are a driving enthusiast's dream—they're winding, sparsely populated, and well maintained, and around most bends there's a striking new view.

By Bus

Air-conditioned coaches connect major and minor cities and are often faster and more convenient than local trains, but are also slightly more expensive. Various companies serve the different routes. SAIS runs frequently between Palermo and Catania, Messina, and Siracusa, in each case arriving at and departing from near the train stations. **Cuffaro** (☎ *091/6161510* ⊕ *www.cuffaro.info*) runs between Palermo and Agrigento. On the south and east coasts and in the interior, **SAIS** (☎ *800/211020 toll-free* ⊕ *www.sais-autolinee.it*) connects the main centers, including Catania, Agrigento, Enna, Taormina, and Siracusa. **Interbus/Etna Trasporti** (☎ *0935/565111* ⊕ *www.interbus.it*) operates between Catania, Caltagirone, Piazza Armerina, Taormina, Messina, and Siracusa.

By Train

There are direct express trains from Milan and Rome to Palermo, Catania, and Siracusa. The Rome–Palermo and Rome–Siracusa trips take at least 10 hours. After Naples, the run is mostly along the coast, so try to book a window seat on the right if you're not on an overnight train. At Villa San Giovanni, in Calabria, the train is separated and loaded onto a ferryboat to cross the strait to Messina.

Within Sicily, main lines connect Messina, Taormina, Siracusa, and Palermo. Secondary lines are generally very slow and unreliable. The Messina–Palermo run, along the northern coast, is especially scenic. For schedules, check the Web site of the Italian state railway, **FS** (☎ *892021* ⊕ *www.trenitalia.com*).

EATING & DRINKING WELL IN SICILY

Sicilian cuisine is one of the oldest in existence, with records of cooking competitions dating to 600 BC. Food in Sicily today reflects the island's unique cultural mix, imaginatively combining fish, fruits, vegetables, and nuts with Italian pastas and Arab and North African elements.

It is hard to eat badly in Sicily. From the lowliest of trattorias to the most highfalutin' *ristorante*, you'll find the classic dishes that have been the staples of the family dinner table for years—basically pasta and seafood. A more sophisticated place may introduce a few adventurous items onto the menu, but the main difference between the cheapest and the most expensive restaurants will be the level of service and the accoutrements: in more formal places you'll find greater attention to detail and a more respectful atmosphere, while less pretentious trattorias tend to be family-run affairs, often without even a menu to guide you. However, in this most gregarious of regions in the most convivial of countries, you can expect a lively dining experience wherever you choose to eat.

SICILIAN MARKETS

Sicily's natural fecundity is evident wherever you look, from the prickly pears sprouting on roadsides to the slopes of vine and citrus groves covering the inland to the ranks of fishing boats moored in every harbor. You can come face-to-face with this bounty in the clamorous street markets of Palermo (pictured above) and Catania. Here, you'll encounter teetering piles of olives and oranges, enticing displays of cheeses and meats, and pastries and sweets of every description. The effect is heady and sensuous. Immerse yourself in the hustle and bustle of the Sicilian souk, and you'll emerge enriched.

DELICIOUS FISH

In Sicily, naturally, you'll find some of the freshest seafood in all of Italy. Pasta *con le sarde* (an emblematic dish that goes back to the Saracen conquerors, with fresh sardines (pictured at right), olive oil, raisins, pine nuts, and wild fennel) gets a different treatment at every restaurant. Grilled *tonno* (tuna) and *orata* (daurade) are coastal staples, while delicate *ricci* (sea urchins) are a specialty. King, however, is *pesce spada* (swordfish), best enjoyed *marinato* (marinated), *affumicato* (smoked), or as the traditional *involtini di pesce spada* (swordfish roulades).

SNACKS

Sicily offers a profusion of toothsome snacks, two prime examples being *arancini* ("little oranges"—rice croquettes with a cheese or meat filling) pictured below, and *panelle* (seasoned chickpea flour boiled to a paste, cooled, sliced, and fried), normally bought from a street vendor. Other tidbits to look out for include special foods associated with festivals, often pastries and sweets, such as the ominously named *ossa dei morti* ("dead men's bones"). But the most eye-catching of all are the *frutta martorana,* also known as *pasta reale*—intensely sweet marzipan confections shaped to resemble fruits, temptingly arrayed in bars and *pasticcerie* (pastry shops).

LOCAL SPECIALITIES

Though there are Sicilian dishes you'll find on menus throughout the island, there is also a range of ingredients and recipes that are unique to particular towns and regions. In Catania, for example, you'll be offered spaghetti *alla Norma* (with a sauce of tomato, fried eggplant, ricotta, and basil), named after an opera by Bellini (a Catania native). Meanwhile, the *mandorla* (bitter almond), the pride of Agrigento, plays into everything from *risotto alle mandorle* (almond risotto) to sweet almond liqueur to incomparable almond granita—an absolute must in summer. Pistachios produced on the lower slopes of Etna go into pasta sauces as well as ice cream, while capers grown on the outlying islands add zest to salads and fish sauces.

WINES

Long neglected, Sicilian wines are some of the most up-and-coming in the world, but they're still the bargains of Italy. The earthy Nero d'Avola grape bolsters many of Sicily's traditionally sunny, expansive reds, but lately it's often cut with cabernet or merlot. The islands of Lipari and Pantelleria produce sweet, golden Malvasia and Passito, but Marsala remains Sicily's most famous dessert wine. Look for anything from the world-renowned winemaker Planeta.

15

Updated
by Robert
Andrews

SICILY HAS BECKONED SEAFARING WANDERERS since the trials of Odysseus were first sung in Homer's *Odyssey*—perhaps the world's first travel guide. Strategically poised between Europe and Africa, this mystical land of three corners and a fiery volcano once hosted two of the most enlightened capitals of the West—one Greek, in Siracusa, and one Arab-Norman, in Palermo. The island has been a melting pot of every great civilization on the Mediterranean: Greek and Roman; then Arab and Norman; and finally French, Spanish, and Italian. Today, the ancient ports of call peacefully fuse the remains of sackings past: graceful Byzantine mosaics rubbing elbows with Greek temples, Roman amphitheaters, Romanesque cathedrals, and baroque flights of fancy.

The invaders through the ages weren't just attracted by the strategic location; they recognized a paradise in Sicily's deep blue skies and temperate climate, its lush vegetation and rich marine life—all of which prevail to this day. Factor in Sicily's unique cuisine—another harmony of elements, mingling Arab and Greek spices, Spanish and French techniques, and some of the world's finest seafood, all accompanied by big, fruity wines—and you can understand why visitors continue to be drawn here, and often find it hard to leave.

In modern times, the traditional graciousness and nobility of the Sicilian people have survived side by side with the destructive influences of the Mafia under Sicily's semiautonomous government. Alongside some of the most exquisite architecture in the world lie the shabby, half-built results of some of the worst speculation imaginable. In recent years coastal Sicily, like much of the Mediterranean coast, has experienced a surge in condominium development and tourism. The island has emerged as something of an international travel hot spot, drawing increasing numbers of visitors. Astronomical prices in northern Italy have contributed to the boom in Sicily, where tourism doesn't seem to be leveling off as it has elsewhere in the country. Brits and Germans flock in ever-growing numbers to Agrigento and Siracusa, and in high season, Japanese tour groups seem to outnumber the locals in Taormina. And yet, in Sicily's windswept heartland, a region that tourists have barely begun to explore, vineyards, olive groves, and lovingly kept dirt roads leading to family farmhouses still tie Sicilians to the land and to tradition, forming a happy connectedness that can't be defined by economic measures.

THE IONIAN COAST

On the northern stretch of Sicily's eastern coast, Messina commands an unparalleled position across the Ionian Sea from Calabria, the mountainous tip of mainland Italy's boot. Halfway down the coast, Catania has the vivacity of Palermo, if not the artistic wealth; the city makes a good base for exploring lofty Mt. Etna, as does Taormina.

MESSINA

8 km (5 mi) by ferry from Villa San Giovanni, 94 km (59 mi) northeast of Catania, 237 km (149 mi) east of Palermo.

GETTING HERE

Frequent hydrofoils and ferries carry passengers across the Straits of Messina. There are many more daily departures from Villa San Giovanni than from Reggio di Calabria. Trains are ferried here from Villa San Giovanni.

VISITOR INFORMATION

Messina tourism office (⊠ *Via Calabria 301bis, 98123* ☎*090/674236* ⊕*www.aptmessina.it*).

EXPLORING

Messina's ancient history lists a series of disasters, but the city nevertheless managed to develop a fine university and a thriving cultural environment. At 5:20 AM on December 28, 1908, Messina changed from a flourishing metropolis of 120,000 to a heap of rubble, shaken to pieces by an earthquake that turned into a tidal wave and left 80,000 dead and the city almost completely leveled. As you approach the city by ferry, you won't notice any outward indication of the disaster, except for the modern countenance of a 3,000-year-old city. The somewhat flat look is a precaution of seismic planning: tall buildings are not permitted.

The reconstruction of Messina's Norman and Romanesque **Duomo**, originally built by the Norman king Roger II in 1197, has retained much of the original plan, including a handsome crown of Norman battlements, an enormous apse, and a splendid wood-beam ceiling. The adjoining **bell tower** contains one of the largest and most complex mechanical clocks in the world, constructed in 1933 with a host of gilded automatons, including a roaring lion, that spring into action every day at the stroke of noon. ⊠*Piazza del Duomo* ☎*090/774895* ☯ *Weekdays 7:20–7, weekends 7:20–12:30 and 4–7.*

WHERE TO STAY & EAT

$ ✕ **Al Padrino.** The jovial owner of this stripped-down trattoria keeps everything running smoothly. Meat and fish dishes are served with equal verve in the white-wall dining room. Start with antipasti like eggplant stuffed with ricotta, then move on to supremely Sicilian dishes such as pasta with chickpeas or *polpette di alalunga* (albacore croquettes). ⊠*Via Santa Cecilia 54* ☎*090/2921000* ▭*AE, MC, V* ☯*Closed Sun. and Aug. No dinner Sat.*

$$ ▦ **Grand Hotel Liberty.** Across from the train station, this hotel is a haven from the hustle and bustle of the surrounding streets. There's meticulous attention to detail in the public rooms, which are sumptuously fitted out in a black-and-white neoclassical style. Marble adds a touch of elegance. The bedrooms are plainer, but comfortably equipped. **Pros:** Close to bus and train stations, plush public rooms. **Cons:** Carpets a bit threadbare, no views. ⊠*Via I Settembre 15, 98123* ☎*090/6409436* ☐*090/6409340* ⊕*www.nh-hotels.com* ⊅*49 rooms,*

Eastern Sicily &
the Aeolian Islands

TO NAPLES

TO NAPLES

TO TROPEA

Stromboli

A E O L I A N   I S L A N D S

Panarea

Alicudi **Filicudi**

Salina

Lipari

Vulcano

T y r r h e n i a n   S e a

Golfo di Gioia

Mortelle

Milazzo

Villa San Giovanni

Messina

CAPO D'ORLANDO

St Agata di Militello

[113] [A20]

Patti

[113]

Reggio di Calabria

Cefalù

Caldura

[113]

[106]

[A20]

T Y R R H E N I A N   C O A S T

[116]

[185]

[114]

[A18]

Pizzo Carbonara

[117]

Randazzo

Castelmola

Taormina

[120]

[120]

Bronte

Giardini-Naxos

Riposto

Giarre

Nicosia

Mt. Etna

[A19]

[121]

Adrano

Nicolosi

Acireale

Biancavilla

Enna

[192]

Paternò

Aci Castello

Aci Trezza

Caltanissetta

[A19]

Catania

Golfo di Catania

[288]

Piazza Armerina

[417]

[191]

Casale

[117b]

Agnone

Mazzarino

[626]

Palagonia

[385]

[114]

Caltagirone

[124]

[194]

Augusta

Vizzini

Euryalus

Gela

Palazzolo Acreide

[194]

[124]

[A18]

Golfo di Gela

Vittoria

Comiso

Ragusa

Siracusa
see detail map

I o n i a n   S e a

Noto

[115]

Avola

Modica

[19]

Golfo di Noto

TO MALTA

[115]

Pachino

CAPO PASSERO

0   20 mi

0   20 km

KEY

🚢 *Ferry lines*

⛷ *Ski Area*

2 junior suites ♿ *In-room: safe, refrigerator, DVD (some). In-hotel: restaurant, bar, public Internet* ═AE, DC, MC, V ⫧BP.

TAORMINA

43 km (27 mi) southwest of Messina.

GETTING HERE
Buses from Messina or Catania arrive near the center of Taormina, while trains from these towns pull in at the station at the bottom of the hill. Local buses bring you the rest of the way. A cable car takes passengers up the hill from a parking lot about 2 km (1 mi) north of the train station.

VISITOR INFORMATION
Taormina tourism office (⊠ *Palazzo Corvaja, Piazza Santa Caterina, 98039* ☎ *0942/23243* ⊕ *www.gate2taormina.com*).

EXPLORING
The medieval cliff-hanging town of Taormina is overrun with tourists, but its natural beauty is still hard to dispute. The view of the sea and Mt. Etna from its jagged cactus-covered cliffs is as close to perfection as a panorama can get, especially on clear days, when the snowcapped volcano's white puffs of smoke rise against the blue sky. Writers have extolled Taormina's beauty almost since its founding in the sixth century BC by Greeks from Naples; Goethe and D.H. Lawrence were among its well-known enthusiasts. The town's boutique-lined main streets get old pretty quickly, but don't overlook the many hiking paths that wind through the beautiful hills surrounding Taormina. Nor should you miss the trip up to stunning Castelmola—whether by foot or by car.

Below the main city of Taormina is **Taormina Mare,** where beachgoers jostle for space on the minuscule pebble beach in summer. It's accessible by a **funivia** *(gondola)* that glides past incredible views on its way down. It departs every 15 minutes. In June, July, and August, the normal hours are extended until midnight or later. ☒€2 ⊙ *Daily 8 AM–8 PM.*

The Greeks put a premium on finding impressive locations to stage their dramas, such as Taormina's hillside **Teatro Greco.** Beyond the columns you can see the town's rooftops spilling down the hillside, the arc of the coastline, and Mt. Etna in the distance. The theater was built during the third century BC and rebuilt by the Romans during the second century AD. Its acoustics are exceptional: even today a stage whisper can be heard in the last rows. In summer Taormina hosts an arts festival of music and dance events and a film festival; many performances are held in the Teatro Greco. ⊠ *Via Teatro Greco* ☎ *0942/620666* ☒€6 ⊙ *Daily 9–1 hr before sunset.*

Many of Taormina's 14th- and 15th-century palaces have been carefully preserved. Especially beautiful is the **Palazzo Corvaja,** with characteristic black-lava and white-limestone inlays. Today it houses the tourist office and the **Museo di Arte e Storia Popolare,** which has a collection of puppets and folk art, carts and cribs. ⊠*Largo Santa Caterina* ☎*0942/610274* ☒*Museum €2.60* ☉*Museum Tues.–Sun. 9–1 and 4–8.*

NEED A BREAK?

A marzipan devotee should not leave Taormina without trying one of the almond sweets—maybe in the guise of the ubiquitous *fico d'India* (prickly pear), or in more-unusual *frutta martorana* (fruit-shaped) varieties—at Pasticceria Etna (⊠*Corso Umberto 112* ☎*0942/24735*). A block of almond paste makes a good souvenir—you can bring it home to make an almond latte or granita. It's closed on Monday.

★ Stroll down Via Bagnoli Croce from the main Corso Umberto to the **Villa Comunale.** Also known as the Parco Duca di Cesarò, the lovely public gardens were designed by Florence Trevelyan Cacciola, a Scottish lady "invited" to leave England following a romantic liaison with the future Edward VII (1841–1910). Arriving in Taormina in 1889, she married a local professor and devoted herself to the gardens, filling them with Mediterranean plants, ornamental pavilions (known as the beehives), and fountains. Stop by the panoramic bar, which has stunning views. ☉*Daily 9* AM–*sunset.*

A 20-minute walk along the Via Crucis footpath takes you to the medieval **Castello Saraceno,** perched on an adjoining cliff above town. (You can also drive, of course.) The gate is often locked, but it's worth the climb just for the panoramic views. (⊠*Monte Tauro* ☎*No phone*)

WHERE TO STAY & EAT

$$$$ ✕ **La Giara.** This restaurant, named after a giant vase unearthed under the bar, is famous for being one of Taormina's oldest restaurants. The food's not bad, either. The kitchen blends upscale modern techniques with the simple flavors of traditional specialties. One spectacular dish is the fish *cartoccio* (wrapped in paper and baked in the oven). You can extend your evening by enjoying an after-dinner drink at the popular, if touristy, piano bar. There's also a terrace with stunning views. ⊠*Vico La Floresta 1* ☎*0942/23360* ⊕*www.lagiara-taormina.com* ⊟*AE, DC, MC, V* ☉*Closed Sun. Apr.–Oct., Sun.–Fri. Nov.–Mar. No lunch.*

$$–$$$ ✕ **La Piazzetta.** Sheltered from the city's hustle and bustle, this elegant little eatery exudes a mood of relaxed sophistication. Classic dishes such as *risotto alla marinara* (with seafood) are competently prepared, the grilled fish is extremely fresh, and the service is informal and friendly. The modest room has simple white walls—you're not paying for a view. ⊠*Vico Paladino 5/7, off Corso Umberto* ☎*0942/626317* ⊟*AE, DC, MC, V* ☉*Closed Mon. and Nov.*

$$ ✕ **L'Arco dei Cappuccini.** Just off *Via Costantino Patricio* lies this diminutive restaurant. Outdoor seating and an upstairs kitchen help make room for a few extra tables—a necessity, as locals are well aware that neither the price nor the quality is equaled elsewhere in town. Indulge in *sopressa di polipo* (steamed octopus carpaccio), linguine *alle vongole veraci* (with clam sauce), or the fresh catch of the day. ⊠*Via Cappuccini 5a, off Via Costantino Patricio* ☎*0942/24893* ⌥*Reservations essential* ⊟*AE, DC, MC, V* ☉*Closed Wed., 1 wk in Nov., and 1 wk in Feb.*

$$ ✕ **Taverna al Paladino.** On a little side street you'll find this dimly lighted haunt, where you can enjoy ancient dishes in what feels like an old wine bar. The traditional Sicilian *sarde a beccaficu* is a sweet-and-sour dish of sardines marinated in lemon juice, split open, and stuffed with bread crumbs, pine nuts, and sugar. Also on the menu is risotto with wild fennel. ⊠ *Via Naumachia 21* ☎*0942/24614* ▭*AE, DC, MC, V* ⊘ *Closed Jan.*

★ $ ✕ **Vecchia Taormina.** Warm, inviting, and unassuming, Taormina's best pizzeria produces deliciously seared crusts topped with fresh, well-balanced ingredients. Try the pizza *alla Norma*, featuring the classic Sicilian combination of eggplant and ricotta—here, in the province of Messina, it's made with ricotta *al forno* (cooked ricotta), while in the province of Catania, it's made with ricotta *forte* (strong, uncooked ricotta). There's a good list of Sicilian wines. Choose between small tables on two levels or on a terrace. ⊠ *Vico Ebrei 3* ☎*0942/625589* ▭*AE, DC, MC, V.*

¢–$ ✕ **Bella Blu.** If you fancy a meal with a view but don't want to spend a lot, it would be hard to do much better than to come here for the decent €18 three-course prix-fixe meal. Seafood is the specialty; try the spaghetti with fresh clams and mussels. Through giant picture windows you can watch the gondola fly up and down from the beach, with the coastline in the distance. A pianist performs Saturday night in winter. ⊠ *Via Pirandello 28* ☎*0942/24239* ▭*AE, DC, MC, V.*

$$$$ ⌂ **Grand Hotel Timeo and Villa Flora.** The deluxe Timeo—on a princely perch overlooking the town—wears a graceful patina that suggests la dolce vita. A splash of baroque mixes with the Mediterranean in the lobby, which has tile- and brickwork and vaulted ceilings. Wrought-iron and wicker chairs surround marble tables in the original bar from 1873 (made of gesso) and on the adjoining palatial patio. Exquisite moldings hang on walls the color of butter. Fine linens and drapes, Oriental rugs, and prints in gilt frames decorate the rooms, 32 of which are in the neighboring Villa Flora. Ask for a room with a terrace—given the extraordinary prices you're already paying, it's worth a few more euros to be able to gaze over one of Italy's most memorable vistas. **Pros:** Feeling of indulgence, central location, quiet setting. **Cons:** Very expensive, some rooms are small, staff can be scarce. ⊠ *Via Teatro Greco 59, 98039* ☎*0942/23801* ⊕*www.framonhotels.com* ⇆*84 rooms* ♿*In-room: safe, refrigerator, Wi-Fi. In-hotel: restaurant, room service, bar, pool, gym* ▭*AE, DC, MC, V* ⦿*MAP.*

Fodor's Choice ★

$$$$ ⌂ **San Domenico Palace.** Sweeping views from this converted 15th-century Dominican monastery linger in your mind: the sensuous gardens—full of red trumpet flowers, bougainvillea, and lemon trees—afford a dramatic vista of the castle, the sea, and Mt. Etna. Expect luxury and ease at this hotel, considered to be among the best in Europe. Rooms have hand-painted or hand-carved furnishings, exquisite linens, and ultramodern amenities. Not all have sea views, but at this price you should make sure to ask for one. The San Domenico's Renaissance flavor is preserved by two exquisite cloisters, convent rooms, and the chapel, now a conference facility. **Pros:** Overflowing with character, attentive service, quiet and restful. **Cons:** Very expensive, dull corridors, some small rooms. ⊠*Piazza San Domenico 5, 98039* ☎*0942/613111*

Fodor's Choice ★

15

⊕www.lhw.com ↩87 rooms, 15 suites △In-room: refrigerator, ethernet. In-hotel: 3 restaurants, room service, bar, pool, gym, concierge, public Internet ▤AE, DC, MC, V ⍩BP.

$$$–$$$$　▦ **Villa Ducale.** The former summer residence of a local aristocrat has been converted into a luxurious hotel. Individually styled rooms, furnished with antiques, each have their own balconies. An intimate wood-paneled library is at once homelike and romantic, and the vast roof terrace, where a fantastic breakfast is served, takes full advantage of the wide panorama embracing Etna and the bay below. It's a 10- to 15-minute walk to the center of Taormina, and in summer a free shuttle bus whisks you to the area's best beaches. **Pros:** Away from the hubbub, fantastic views. **Cons:** Long walk to the center. ⊠Via L. da Vinci 60, 98039 ☏0942/28153 ⊕www.villaducale.com ↩10 rooms, 6 suites △In-room: ethernet. In-hotel: room service, bar, gym, public Internet, parking (fee) ▤AE, DC, MC, V ⊗Closed last 3 wks of Jan. ⍩BP.

$$$　▦ **Hotel Villa Paradiso.** On the edge of the old quarter, overlooking the lovely public gardens and facing the sea, this smaller hotel is not as well known as some of its neighbors. But with views of Etna from many rooms, delightful service, and a good rooftop restaurant, it's only a matter of time. Proprietor Salvatore Martorana will gladly share stories of Taormina in Goethe's day over an *aperitivo*. A regular hotel bus service runs to the beach between June and October. **Pros:** Friendly service, good value, great rooftop views. **Cons:** Only three free parking spaces, not all rooms have views, disappointing food. ⊠Via Roma 2, 98039 ☏0942/23921 ⊕www.hotelvillaparadisotaormina.com ↩20 rooms, 17 junior suites △In-hotel: restaurant, room service, bar, beachfront, public Internet, ▤AE, DC, MC, V ⍩BP.

$$　▦ **Villa Fiorita.** This converted private home near the cable car station has excellent north-coast views from nearly every room. Rooms vary in size and furnishings, but most are bright, breezy, and colorful, with large windows and balconies (do ask). Prices are reasonable considering amenities like the compact swimming pool and the garden. You have to climb 65 steps to get to the elevator. **Pros:** Good rates, pretty rooms. **Cons:** Service can be slack, lots of stairs to climb. ⊠Via Pirandello 39, 98039 ☏0942/24122 ☏0942/625967 ⊕www.villafioritahotel.com ↩24 rooms, 2 suites △In-room: safe, refrigerator. In-hotel: bar, pool ▤AE, MC, V ⍩BP.

NIGHTLIFE & THE ARTS

The Teatro Greco and the Palazzo dei Congressi, near the entrance to the theater, are the main venues for the summer festival dubbed **Taoarte** (☏0942/21142 ⊕www.taormina-arte.com), held each year between June and August. Performances encompass classical music, ballet, and theater. The famous **film festival** (⊕www.taorminafilmfest.it) takes place in June. The **Teatro dei Due Mari** (⊠Via Teatro Greco ☏0941/243176 ⊕www.teatrodeiduemari.net) stages Greek tragedy at the Teatro Greco, usually in May.

The 50-km (30-mi) stretch of road between Taormina and Messina is flanked by lush vegetation and seascapes. Inlets are punctuated by gigantic, oddly shaped rocks.

CASTELMOLA

5 km (3 mi) west of Taormina.

GETTING HERE
Regular buses bound for Castelmola leave from two locations in Taormina: the bus station on Via Pirandello and Piazza San Pancrazio.

EXPLORING
Although many believe that Taormina has the most spectacular views, tiny Castelmola, floating 1,800 feet above sea level, takes the word "scenic" to a whole new level. Along the cobblestone streets within the ancient walls, the 360-degree panoramas of mountain, sea, and sky are so ubiquitous that you almost get used to them (but not quite). Collect yourself with a sip of the sweet almond wine (best served cold) made in the local bars, or with lunch at one of the humble pizzerias or *panino* shops.

Fodor's Choice ★ The best place to take in Castelmola's views is from the ruins of **Castello Normanno**, reached by a set of steep staircases rising out of the town center. In all Sicily, there may be no spot more scenic than atop the castle ruins, where you can gaze upon two coastlines, smoking Mt. Etna, and the town spilling down the mountainside. You can visit any time, but come during daylight hours for the view. A 10-minute drive on a winding but well-paved road leads from Taormina to Castelmola; you must park in one of the public lots on the hillside below and climb a series of staircases to reach the center. On a nice day, hikers are in for a treat if they walk instead of drive. It's a serious uphill climb, but the 1½-km (¾-mi) path is extremely well maintained and not too challenging. You'll begin at Porta Catania in Taormina, with a walk along Via Apollo Arcageta past the Chiesa di San Francesco di Paolo on the left. The Strada Comunale della Chiusa then leads past Piazza Andromaco, revealing good views of the jagged promontory of Cocolanazzo di Mola to the north. Allow around an hour on the way up, a half hour down. There's another, slightly longer—2-km (1-mi)—path that heads up from Porta Messina past the Roman aqueduct, Convento dei Cappuccini, and the northeastern side of Monte Tauro. You could take one path up and the other down. In any case, avoid the midday sun, wear comfortable shoes, and carry plenty of water with you.

WHERE TO STAY & EAT
$ ✕ **Il Vicolo.** This is one of the simpler dining choices in town, and also one of the better ones. It might not boast the views you'll find elsewhere, but a pleasant rustic ambience and a great selection of pastas and, in the evening, *forno a legna* (wood-fired oven) pizzas make up for that shortcoming (in winter, pizzas are served at weekends only). Friendly staff

serves the food in a pleasant little room along a side street. ⊠ *Via Pio IX 26* ☎ *0942/28481* ⊟ *MC, V* ⊘ *Closed Tues. Oct.–June.*

$ ✕ **Ristorante Pizzichella.** On the road heading down to Taormina stands this three-level terrace restaurant. The food—seafood dishes like mixed shellfish risotto, grilled prawns or swordfish, and pizzas from a wood-burning oven—is

eclipsed by the memorable views from almost every table on the terraces. ⊠ *Via Madonna della Scala 1* ☎ *0942/28831* ⊕ *www.pizzichella. it* ⊟ *AE, MC, V* ⊘ *Closed Wed. Oct.–Apr.*

$$$ 🏨 **Villa Sonia.** All of the rooms at Castelmola's best hotel have private terraces with spectacular views. Along with a refreshing swimming pool, public spaces include a lobby, bar, and lounge that take advantage of the vistas, plus a restaurant with a wine bar and wine store called Enoteca Divino. The rates are a good value when you bear in mind the price gouging in nearby Taormina. **Pros:** Far from the madding crowds, stupendous views. **Cons:** Not much to do in the evening, a bit old-fashioned. ⊠ *Via Porta Mola 9, 98030* ☎ *0942/28082* 🖷 *0942/28083* ⊕ *www.hotelvillasonia.com* 🛏 *42 rooms, 2 suites* ⚒ *In-room: safe, refrigerator. In-hotel: restaurant, bar, pool, parking (fee)* ⊟ *AE, DC, MC, V* ⊘ *Closed Dec.–Feb.* ⊪ *BP.*

NIGHTLIFE

The famous **Bar Turrisi** (⊠ *Piazza del Duomo* ☎ *0942/28181*) is truly one of the most unusual places to have a drink in all of Italy. The cozy nooks and crannies of its three levels are decked out with phallus images of every size, shape, and color imaginable, from bathroom wall murals inspired by the brothels of ancient Greece to giant wooden carvings honoring Dionysus. The roof terrace has extraordinary views of Taormina and the coast.

★ The **Bar San Giorgio** (⊠ *Piazza San Antonino* ☎ *0942/28228*) has lorded over Castelmola's town square since 1907. The interior of the bar is filled with knickknacks that tell a fascinating history of the tiny town.

MT. ETNA

Fodor'sChoice
★ *64 km (40 mi) southwest of Taormina, 30 km (19 mi) north of Catania.*

GETTING HERE

Reaching the lower slopes of Mt. Etna is easy, either by driving yourself or taking a bus from Catania. Getting to the more interesting higher levels requires taking one of the stout four-wheel-drive minibuses that leave from Piano Provenzana on the north side and Rifugio Sapienza on the south side. A cable car from Rifugio Sapienza takes you part of the way.

VISITOR INFORMATION

Nicolosi tourism office (⊠Piazza Vittorio Emanuele ☎*095/914488* ⊕*www. aast-nicolosi.it*) has plenty of information about nearby Mt. Etna.

EXPLORING

Mt. Etna is one of the world's major active volcanoes and is the largest and highest in Europe—the cone of the crater rises to 10,902 feet above sea level. Plato sailed in just to catch a glimpse in 387 BC; in the ninth century AD, the oldest gelato of all was shaved off its snowy slopes; and in the 21st century the volcano still claims annual headlines. Etna has erupted 12 times in the past 30 or so years, most spectacularly in 1971, 1983, 2001, and 2002. The most recent was a medium-size eruption in 2006. Travel in the proximity of the crater depends on Mt. Etna's temperament, but you can walk up and down the enormous lava dunes and wander over its moonlike surface of dead craters. The rings of vegetation change markedly as you rise, with vineyards and pine trees gradually giving way to growths of broom and lichen.

Club Alpino Italiano in Catania is a great resource for Mt. Etna climbing and hiking guides. If you have some experience and don't like a lot of hand-holding, these are the guides for you. ⊠*Piazza Scammacca* ☎*095/7153515* ⊕*www.caicatania.it.*

If you're a beginning climber, call the **Gruppo Guide Etna Nord** to arrange for a guide. Their service is a little more personalized—and expensive—than others. Reserve ahead. ⊠*Via Roma 93, Linguaglossa* ☎*095/7774502* ⊕*www.guidetnanord.com.*

Instead of climbing up Mt. Etna, you can circle it on the **Circumetnea,** which runs near the volcano's base. The private railway almost circles the volcano, running 114 km (71 mi) between Catania and Riposto—the towns are 30 km (19 mi) apart by the coast road. The line is small, slow, and only single-track, but has some dramatic vistas of the volcano and goes through lava fields. The round-trip takes about four hours; there are about 10 departures a day. ⊠*Via Caronda 352, Catania* ☎*095/541250* ⊕*www.circumetnea.it* ☐*€11.50 round-trip* ⊙*Mon.–Sat. 6 AM–9 PM.*

WHERE TO STAY

$$$$ ☒ **Hotel Villa Paradiso dell'Etna.** This 1920s hotel 10 km (6 mi) northeast of Catania was a haunt for artists before General Rommel took over during World War II. When the tide turned in the war, it became a military hospital. Today, after a painstaking renovation, Paradiso dell'Etna resembles an elegant private villa housing mementos of a memorable past. The hotel has four exceptional suites and 30 sumptuous rooms, each filled with tasteful 19th-century Sicilian antiques and all the modern accessories befitting a four-star hotel—the pool is even heated. **Pros:** Beautiful furnishings, delightful gardens, excellent food. **Cons:** Difficult to find, not much to do in the area. ⊠*Via per Viagrande 37, exit A18 toward San Gregorio, San Giovanni La Punta 95036* ☎*095/7512409* ⊕*www.paradisoetna.it* ↻*30 rooms, 4 suites* ⚑*In-room: safe, refrigerator, Wi-Fi. In-hotel: restaurant, room service, bar, pool, gym, public Internet, parking (no fee)* ☐*AE, DC, MC, V* ⦿*BP.*

ACIREALE

40 km (25 mi) south of Taormina, 16 km (10 mi) north of Catania.

GETTING HERE

Buses arrive frequently from Taormina and Catania. Acireale is on the main coastal train route, though the station is a long walk south of the center. Local buses pass every 20 minutes or so.

VISITOR INFORMATION

Acireale tourism office (✉ *Via Oreste Scionti 15, 95024* ☎ *095/892129* ⊕ *www.acirealeturismo.it*).

EXPLORING

Acireale sits amid a clutter of rocky pinnacles and lush lemon groves. The craggy coast is known as the Riviera dei Ciclopi, after the legend narrated in the *Odyssey* in which the blinded Cyclops Polyphemus hurled boulders at the retreating Ulysses, thus creating spires of rock, or *faraglioni* (pillars of rock rising dramatically out of the sea). Tourism has barely taken off here, so it's a good destination if you feel the need to put some distance between yourself and the busloads of tourists in Taormina. And, though the beaches are rocky, there's good swimming here, too.

The Carnival celebrations, held the two weeks before Lent, are considered the best in Sicily. The streets are jammed with thousands of revelers. Acireale is an easy day trip from Catania.

Begin your visit to Acireale with a stroll down to the public gardens, **Villa Belvedere,** at the end of the main Corso Umberto, for superb coastal views.

With its cupola and twin turrets, Acireale's **Duomo** is an extravagant baroque construction dating to the 17th century. In the chapel to the right of the altar, look for the 17th-century silver statue of Santa Venera, patron saint of Acireale, made by Mario D'Angelo, and the early-18th-century frescoes by Antonio Filocamo. ✉ *Piazza del Duomo* ☎ *095/601797* ☉ *Daily 8–noon and 4–7:30.*

NEED A BREAK?

El Dorado (✉ *Corso Umberto 5* ☎ *095/601464*) serves delicious ice creams, and the granita *di mandorla* (almond granita), available in summer, invites a firsthand acquaintance.

The sulfur-rich volcanic waters from Mt. Etna found at **Terme di Acireale** were first enjoyed by the Greeks. Book in advance to use the baths and enjoy spa treatments, or just show up and wander around the gardens for free. ✉ *Via delle Terme 47* ☎ *800/378560 toll-free* ⊕ *www.terme-acireale.com* ✉ *Gardens free* ☉ *Daily 9–8.*

Lord Byron (1788–1824) visited the **Belvedere di Santa Caterina** to look out over the Ionian Sea during his Italian wanderings. The Santa Caterina viewing point is south of the old town, near the Terme di Acireale, off SS114.

Sweet Sicily

Sicily is famous for its desserts, none more than the wonderful cannoli (*cannolo* is the singular), whose delicate pastry shell and just-sweet-enough ricotta barely resemble their foreign impostors. They come in all sizes, from pinkie-size bites to holiday cannoli the size of a coffee table. Even your everyday bar will display a window piled high with dozens of varieties of ricotta-based desserts, including delicious fried balls of dough. The traditional cake of Sicily is the *cassata siciliana,* a rich chilled sponge cake with sheep's-milk ricotta and candied fruit. Often brightly colored, it's the most popular dessert at many Sicilian restaurants, and you shouldn't miss it. From behind bakery windows and glass cases beam tiny marzipan sweets fashioned into brightly colored apples, cherries, and even hamburgers and prosciutto.

If it's summer, do as the locals do and dip your morning brioche—the best in Italy—into a cup of brilliantly refreshing coffee or almond granita. The world's first ice cream is said to have been made by the Romans from the snow on the slopes of Mt. Etna, and the practice of producing top-quality gelato, and eating it in great quantities, is still prevalent throughout the island.

15

WHERE TO EAT

$$ ✕ **La Grotta.** This rustic trattoria above the harbor of Santa Maria La Scala hides a dining room within a cave, part of whose wall is exposed. Try the *insalata di mare* (a selection of delicately boiled fish served with lemon and olive oil), pasta with clams or cuttlefish ink, or fish grilled over charcoal. Chef Rosario Strano's menu is small, but there isn't a dud among the selections. ✉ *Via Scalo Grande 46* 🕾 *095/7648153* ✍ *Reservations essential* ▭ *AE, DC, MC, V* ☉ *Closed Tues. and Oct. 15–Nov. 5.*

NIGHTLIFE & THE ARTS

☾ Although it has died out in most other parts of the island, the puppet-theater tradition carries on in Acireale. The **Teatro dell'Opera dei Pupi** (✉ *Via Alessi 11* 🕾 *095/606272* ⊕ *www.teatropupimacri.it*) has puppet shows and a puppet exhibit.

SHOPPING

Acireale is renowned in Sicily for its marzipan, made into fruit shapes and delicious biscuits available at many *pasticcerie* (pastry shops) around town. Open since 1963, **Castorina** (✉ *Piazza del Duomo 20* 🕾 *095/601546*) sells marzipan candies (and cute gift boxes for them). A unique creation at **Belvedere** (✉ *Corso Umberto 230* 🕾 *095/894164*) is the *nucatole,* a large cookie made with heaping quantities of chocolate, Nutella, nuts, and other wholesome ingredients.

OFF THE BEATEN PATH

Aci Castello and Aci Trezza. These two gems of the coastline between Acireale and Catania—the Riviera dei Ciclopi (Cyclops Riviera)—fill with city dwellers in the summer months, but even in colder weather their beauty is hard to fault. Heading south from Acireale on the coast-hugging *litoranea* road, you'll first reach Aci Trezza, said to be the land of the blind Cyclops in Homer's *Odyssey*. Legend has it that when the Cyclops threw boulders at Odysseus they became the faraglioni offshore. It should be easy to satisfy your literal rather than literary hunger at **Da Federico** (⊠ *Via Magrì 4, Aci Trezza* ☎ *095/276364* ⊙ *Closed Mon.*), which lays out a sprawling antipasto buffet featuring delectable marinated anchovies and eggplant parmigiana. Less developed than Aci Trezza, Aci Castello has its own fish houses plus the imposing Castello Normanno (Norman Castle), which sits right on the water. The castle was built in the 11th century with volcanic rock from Mt. Etna—the same rock that forms the coastal cliffs.

CATANIA

16 km (10 mi) south of Acireale, 94 km (59 mi) south of Messina, 60 km (37 mi) north of Siracusa.

GETTING HERE

Catania is well connected by bus and train with Messina, Taormina, Siracusa, Enna, and Palermo.

VISITOR INFORMATION

Catania tourism office (⊠ *Via Cimarosa 10, 95124* ☎ *095/7306222* ⊠ *Via Etnea 6395100* ☎ *095/7306233* ⊠ *Stazione Centrale, 95129* ☎ *095/7306255* ⊠ *Aeroporto Fontanarossa, 95121* ☎ *095/7306266* ⊕ *www.apt.catania.it*).

EXPLORING

The chief wonder of Catania, Sicily's second city, is that it is there at all. Its successive populations were deported by one Greek tyrant, sold into slavery by another, and driven out by the Carthaginians. Every time the city got back on its feet it was struck by a new calamity: plague decimated the population in the Middle Ages, a mile-wide stream of lava from Mt. Etna swallowed part of the city in 1669, and 25 years later a disastrous earthquake forced the Catanese to begin again.

Today Catania is completing yet another resurrection—this time from crime, filth, and urban decay. Although the city remains loud and full of traffic, signs of gentrification are everywhere. The elimination of vehicles from the Piazza del Duomo and the main artery of Via Etnea, and scrubbing of many of the historic buildings has added to Catania's newfound charm. Home to what is arguably Sicily's best university, Catania is full of exuberant youth, and it shows in the chic *osterie* (taverns) that serve wine, designer bistros, and trendy ethnic boutiques that have popped up all over town. Even more impressive is the vibrant cultural life.

Each February 3–5, the **Festa di Sant'Agata** (☎ *095/7306222*) honors Catania's patron saint with one of Italy's biggest religious festivals. A staggering number of people crowd the streets and piazzas for several processions and music, dancing, art, theater, and all-out street partying. Many of the town's buildings are constructed from three-centuries-old lava; the black buildings combine with baroque architecture to give the city a singular appearance. Nowhere is this clearer than in the *centro storico* (historic center). Don't miss the stunning **Piazza Universitaria,** a nerve center made interesting by the facade of a majestic old university building, and the nearby Castello Ursino.

At the heart of **Piazza del Duomo,** which is closed to traffic, stands an elephant carved out of lava, balancing an Egyptian obelisk—the city's informal mascot. The piazza shines from a 21st-century renovation. From here you can look way down the long, straight Via Garibaldi to see a black-and-white-striped fortress and entrance to the city, the Porta Garibaldi.

The Giovanni Vaccarini–designed facade of the **Cattedrale di Sant'Agata (Duomo)** dominates the Piazza del Duomo. Inside the church, composer Vincenzo Bellini is buried. Also of note are the three apses of lava that survive from the original Norman structure and a fresco from 1675 in the sacristy that portrays Catania's submission to Etna's attack. ⊠ *Piazza del Duomo, bottom end of Via Etnea* ☎ *095/320044* ⊗ *Mon.– Sat. 8–noon and 4–7, Sun. 4–7.*

Via Etnea is host to one of Sicily's most enthusiastic *passeggiate* (early-evening strolls), in which Catanese of all ages take part. Closed to automobile traffic until 10 PM during the week and all day on weekends, the street is lined with cafés and jewelry, clothing, and shoe stores.

15

NEED A BREAK? The lively Savia (⊠ *Via Etnea and Via Umberto near Villa Bellini*) makes superlative *arancini* (fried risotto balls) with *ragù* (a slow-cooked, tomato-based meat or seafood sauce). Or you could choose cannoli or other snacks to munch on while you rest. It's closed Monday.

Catania's greatest native son was the composer Vincenzo Bellini (1801–35), whose operas have thrilled audiences since their premieres in Naples and Milan. His home, now the **Museo Belliniano,** preserves memorabilia of the man and his work. ⊠ *Piazza San Francesco 3* ☎ *095/7150535* ⊡ *Free* ⊗ *Mon.– Sat. 9–1.*

An underground river, the Amenano, flows through much of Catania. You can glimpse it at the Fontana dell'Amenano, but the best place to experience the river is at the bar-restaurant of the **Agorà Youth Hostel.** Here you can sit at an underground table as swirls of water rush by. If you're not there when the bar is open, someone at the reception desk can let you in. ⊠ *Piazza Currò 6* ☎ *095/7233010* ⊕ *www.agorahostel.com.*

WHERE TO STAY & EAT

★ $$$ ✕ **La Siciliana.** Salvo La Rosa and sons serve memorable seafood and meat dishes, exquisite homemade desserts, and a choice of more than 220 wines. The restaurant specializes in the ancient dish *ripiddu nivicatu* (risotto with cuttlefish ink and fresh ricotta cheese), as well as *sarde a beccafico* (stuffed sardines) and *calamari ripieni alla griglia* (stuffed and grilled squid). A meal at this fine eatery more than justifies the short taxi ride 3 km (2 mi) north of the city center. ⊠ *Viale*

Marco Polo 52 ☏*095/376400* ⊕*www.lasiciliana.it* ☰*AE, DC, MC, V* ⊘*Closed Mon. No dinner Sun.*

$$–$$$ ✕ **Ambasciata del Mare.** When a seafood restaurant sits next door to a fish market, it bodes well for the food's freshness. Choose swordfish or *gamberoni* (large shrimp) from a display case in the front of the restaurant, then enjoy it simply grilled with oil and lemon. This simple, bright, and cozy place could not be friendlier or more easily accessed—it's right on the corner of Piazza del Duomo by the fountain. Book early. ✉*Piazza del Duomo 6* ☏*095/341003* ⊕*www.ambasciatadelmare.it* ☰*AE, DC, MC, V* ⊘*Closed Mon.*

★ ¢–$ ✕ **Pizzeria Vico Santa Filomena.** This typical *forno a legna* (wood-burning oven) pizzeria, on a narrow side street off Via Umberto, is one of the most respected in the city for its outstanding "apizza," as the locals call it. Enjoy it as Catanians do: only at night, and with a beer or soda—never wine. The pizzas are named after saints, for example Santa Lucia, with cream, Parmesan slivers, and Parma ham. The antipasti spreads are delicious, as are the meat and seafood dishes. The setting is simple, with brick arches and a few agricultural tools displayed on the exposed stone walls. Expect a long wait on weekend evenings. ✉*Vico Santa Filomena 35* ☏*095/316761* ☰*MC, V* ⊘*Closed Mon.*

$$$$ 🏨 **Excelsior Grand Hotel.** This large, modern hotel sits in a quiet part of downtown Catania. Ask for a room facing Piazza Verga, a neat tree-lined square. The atmosphere is restrained, with a spacious, marbled lobby. Impeccably designed rooms have a careful balance of neoclassical and new furnishings, and double-pane windows add to the peace. The service can be erratic, as the hotel tends to fill up with groups. The American Bar should provide solace if you're craving a Manhattan. **Pros:** Efficient staff, modern facilities, clean rooms. **Cons:** Chain hotel lacking personality, a longish walk from the main sights. ✉*Piazza Verga 39, 95129* ☏*095/7476111* ⊕*www.excelsiorcatania.thi.it* ⤳*158 rooms, 18 suites* ♿*In-room: safe, refrigerator. In-hotel: restaurant, room service, bar, gym, spa* ☰*AE, DC, MC, V* ⦿*BP.*

$$–$$$ 🏨 **Residence Angiolucci.** This renovated 19th-century *palazzo* is stunning—not just for the impressive detail of the restoration work, but **Fodor's**Choice even more for the elegance of the modern apartments inside. The **★** gleaming units, unique in eastern Sicily, almost all have two floors (even the studios) and all have basic kitchen fittings, including a microwave. Some also have large living rooms. There are discounts for weeklong stays. **Pros:** Friendly service, elegant building, nice kitchens. **Cons:** Rooms a little sterile, limited parking. ✉*Via E. Pantano 1, 95129* ☏*095/3529420* ⊕*www.angiolucciresidence.com* ⤳*30 apartments* ♿*In-room: safe, kitchen, ethernet. In-hotel: room service, laundry service, parking (fee)* ☰*AE, DC, MC, V* ⦿*EP.*

SHOPPING

Catania is justly famous for its sweets and bar snacks. Of the numerous pastry shops along Via Etnea, **Al Caprice** (✉*Via Etnea 32, near Piazza Universitaria* ☏*095/320840*) has the largest variety of homemade goodies and edible gifts, plus hot and cold snacks. The selection of almond-based delights from **I Dolci di Nonna Vincenza** (✉*Palazzo Biscari, Piazza San Placido 7* ☏*095/7151844* ⊕*www.dolcinon-*

navincenza.it ✉*Aeroporto Fontanarossa* ☎*095/7234522*) may be small, but everything is fresh and phenomenally good. It will ship internationally, too. The **outdoor fish and food market**, which begins on Via Zappala Gemelli and emanates in every direction from Piazza di Benedetto, is one of Italy's most memorable. It's a feast for the senses: thousands of impeccably fresh fish, some still wriggling, plus endless varieties of meats, ricotta, and fresh produce, and a symphony of vendor shouts to fill the ears. Open Monday–Saturday, the market is at its best in the morning.

SIRACUSA

15

Siracusa, known to English speakers as Syracuse, is a wonder to behold. One of the great ancient capitals of Western civilization, the city was founded in 734 BC by Greek colonists from Corinth and soon grew to rival, and even surpass, Athens in splendor and power; Siracusa became the largest, wealthiest city-state in the West and a bulwark of Greek civilization. Although the city lived under tyranny, rulers such as Dionysus filled their courts with Greeks of the highest artistic stature—among them Pindar, Aeschylus, and Archimedes. The Athenians did not welcome the rise of Siracusa and set out to conquer Sicily, but the natives outsmarted them in what was one of the greatest naval battles of ancient history (413 BC). Siracusa continued to prosper until it was conquered two centuries later by the Romans.

Siracusa still has some of the finest examples of baroque art and architecture; dramatic Greek and Roman ruins; and a Duomo that is the stuff of legend, a microcosm of the city's entire history in one building. The modern city also has a wonderful lively baroque old town worthy of extensive exploration, pleasant piazzas, outdoor cafés and bars, and a wide assortment of excellent seafood. There are essentially two areas to explore in Siracusa: the Parco Archeologico, on the mainland; and the island of Ortygia, the ancient city first inhabited by the Greeks, which juts out into the Ionian Sea and is connected to the mainland by two small bridges. Ortygia is becoming increasingly popular with tourists, and is starting to lose its old-fashioned charm in favor of modern boutiques.

Siracusa's old nucleus of Ortygia is a compact area, a pleasure to amble around without getting unduly tired. In contrast, mainland Siracusa is a grid of wider avenues. At the northern end of Corso Gelone, above Viale Paolo Orsi, the orderly grid gives way to the ancient quarter of Neapolis, where the sprawling Parco Archeologico is accessible from Viale Teracati (an extension of Corso Gelone). East of Viale Teracati, about a 10-minute walk from the Parco Archeologico, the district of Tyche holds the archaeological museum and the church and catacombs of San Giovanni, both off Viale Teocrito (drive or take a taxi or city bus from Ortygia). Coming from the train station, it's a 15-minute trudge to Ortygia along Via Francesco Crispi and Corso Umberto. If you're not up for that, take one of the free electric buses leaving every 10 minutes from the bus station around the corner.

GETTING HERE

On the main train line from Messina and Catania, Siracusa is also linked to Catania by frequent buses.

VISITOR INFORMATION

Siracusa tourism office (✉ *Via San Sebastiano 45, 96100* ☎ *0931/67710* ⊕ *www.apt-siracusa.it* ✉ *Via Maestranza 33, Ortygia, 96100* ☎ *0931/65201* ⊕ *www.aatsr.it*).

ARCHAEOLOGICAL ZONE

THE MAIN ATTRACTIONS

Parco Archeologico. Siracusa is most famous for its dramatic set of Greek and Roman ruins. Though the various ruins can be visited separately, see them all, along with the Museo Archeologico. If the park is closed, go up Viale G. Rizzo from Viale Teracati to the belvedere overlooking the ruins, which are floodlighted at night. The last tickets are sold one hour before closing.

Before the park's ticket booth is the gigantic **Ara di Ierone** (Altar of Hieron), which was once used by the Greeks for spectacular sacrifices involving hundreds of animals. The first attraction in the park is the **Latomia del Paradiso** (Quarry of Paradise), a lush tropical garden full of palm and citrus trees. This series of quarries served as prisons for the defeated Athenians, who were enslaved; the quarries once rang with the sound of their chisels and hammers. At one end is the famous **Orecchio di Dionisio** (Ear of Dionysus), with an ear-shaped entrance and unusual acoustics inside, as you will hear if you clap your hands. The legend is that Dionysus used to listen in at the top of the quarry to hear what the slaves were plotting below.

★ The **Teatro Greco** *(Greek Theater)* is the chief monument in the Archaeological Park—and indeed one of Sicily's greatest classical sites and the most complete Greek theater surviving from antiquity. Climb to the top of the seating area (which could accommodate 15,000) for a fine view: all the seats converge upon a single point—the stage—which has the natural scenery and the sky as its background. Hewn out of the hillside rock in the fifth century BC, the theater saw the premieres of the plays of Aeschylus. Greek tragedies are still performed here every year in May and June. Above and behind the theater runs the Via dei Sepulcri, in which streams of running water flow through a series of Greek sepulchres. The well-preserved and striking **Anfiteatro Romano** (Roman Amphitheater) reveals much about the differences between the Greek and Roman personalities. Where drama in the Greek theater was a kind of religious ritual, the Roman amphitheater emphasized the spectacle of combative sports and the circus. This arena is one of the largest of its kind and was built around the second century AD. The corridor where gladiators and beasts entered the ring is still intact, and the seats, some of which still bear the occupants' names, were hauled in and constructed on the site from huge slabs of limestone. ✉ *Viale Teocrito (entrance on Via Agnello), Archaeological Zone* ☎ *0931/65068* ✐ *€6*

⊙ *Apr.–mid-Sept., daily 9–7; mid-Sept.–mid-Oct., daily 9–5; mid-Oct.–Feb., Mon.–Sat. 9–4, Sun. 9–1; Mar., daily 9–6.*

NEED A BREAK?

For some great Sicilian cakes and ice cream on your way to the Archaeological Park, visit Leonardi (⊠ *Viale Teocrito 123, Archaeological Zone* ☏ *0931/61411*), a bar-cum-pasticceria. It's popular with the locals, so you may have to line up for your cakes during holiday times. It's closed Wednesday.

ALSO WORTH SEEING

Catacomba di San Giovanni. Not far from the Archaeological Park, off Viale Teocrito, the catacombs below the church of San Giovanni are one of the earliest-known Christian sites in the city. Inside the crypt of San Marciano is an altar where St. Paul preached on his way through Sicily to Rome. The frescoes in this small chapel are mostly bright and fresh, though some dating from the fourth century AD show their age. Open hours may be extended in summer. ⊠ *Piazza San Giovanni, Tyche* ☏ *0931/66751* ☑ *€5* ⊙ *Daily 9:30–12:30 and 2:30–5:30; last entrance at 4:30.*

Museo Archeologico. The impressive collection of Siracusa's splendid archaeological museum is organized by region around a central atrium and ranges from Neolithic pottery to fine Greek statues and vases. Compare the *Landolina Venus*—a headless goddess of love who rises out of the sea in measured modesty (a first-century AD Roman copy of the Greek original)—with the much earlier (300 BC) elegant Greek statue of Hercules in Section C. Of a completely different style is a marvelous fanged Gorgon, its tongue sticking out, that once adorned the cornice of the Temple of Athena to ward off evildoers. The last tickets are sold an hour before closing. ⊠ *Viale Teocrito 66, Tyche* ☏ *0931/464022* ☑ *€6* ⊙ *Tues.–Sat. 9–7, Sun. 9–2.*

Museo del Papiro. Close to Siracusa's Museo Archeologico, the Papyrus Museum demonstrates how papyri are prepared from reeds and then painted—an ancient tradition in the city. Siracusa, it seems, has the only climate outside the Nile Valley in which the papyrus plant—from which the word "paper" comes—thrives. ⊠ *Viale Teocrito 66, Tyche* ☏ *0931/61616* ☑ *Free* ⊙ *Tues.–Sun. 9–1.*

ORTYGIA ISLAND

THE MAIN ATTRACTIONS

④ Duomo. Siracusa's Duomo is an archive of island history: the bottommost excavations have unearthed remnants of Sicily's distant past, when the Siculi inhabitants worshipped their deities here. During the fifth century BC (the same time as Agrigento's Temple of Concord was built), the Greeks built a temple to Athena over it, and in the seventh century Siracusa's first Christian cathedral was built on top of the Greek structure. The massive columns of the original Greek temple were incorporated into the present structure and are clearly visible, embedded in the exterior wall along Via Minerva. The Greek columns

Fodor'sChoice
★

15

were also used to dramatic advantage inside, where on one side they form chapels connected by elegant wrought-iron gates. The baroque facade, added in 1700, displays a harmonious rhythm of concaves and convexes. In front, the piazza is encircled by pink and white oleanders and elegant buildings ornamented with filigree grillwork. ⊠*Piazza del Duomo, Ortygia* ☎*0931/65328* ⊘*Daily 8–7.*

6 Fonte Aretusa. A freshwater spring, the Fountain of Arethus, sits next to the sea, studded with Egyptian papyrus that is reportedly natural. This anomaly is explained by a Greek legend that tells how the nymph Arethusa was changed into a fountain by the goddess Artemis (Diana) when she tried to escape the advances of the river god Alpheus. She fled from Greece, into the sea, with Alpheus in close pursuit, and emerged in Sicily at this spring. It's said if you throw a cup into the Alpheus River in Greece it will emerge here at this fountain, which is home to a few tired ducks and some faded carp—but no cups. If you want to stand right by the fountain, you need to gain admission through the aquarium; otherwise look down on it from Largo Aretusa. ⊠*Off promenade along harbor, Ortygia.*

2 Piazza Archimede. The center of this piazza has a baroque fountain, the *Fontana di Diana,* festooned with fainting sea nymphs and dancing jets of water. Look for the Chiaramonte-style **Palazzo Montalto,** an arched-window gem just off the piazza on Via Montalto.

5 Piazza del Duomo. In the heart of Ortygia, this ranks as one of Italy's most beautiful piazzas, its elongated space lined with Sicilian baroque treasures and outdoor cafés.

1 Tempio di Apollo. Scattered through the piazza just across the bridge to Ortygia are the ruins of a temple dedicated to Apollo, a model of which is in the Museo Archeologico. In fact, little of this noble Doric temple remains except for some crumbled walls and shattered columns; the window in the south wall belongs to a Norman church that was built much later on the same spot. ⊠*Piazza Pancali, Ortygia.*

ALSO WORTH SEEING

7 Castello Maniace. The southern tip of Ortygia island is occupied by a castle built by Frederick II (1194–1250), now an army barracks, from which there are fine views of the sea.

3 Palazzo Beneventano del Bosco. At one end of Piazza del Duomo, this elegant palazzo is a private residence, but you can take a peek at the impressive interior courtyard with its central staircase. ⊠*Piazza del Duomo, Ortygia.*

WHERE TO EAT

$$$–$$$$
Fodor'sChoice
★

✕ **Don Camillo.** A gracious series of delicately arched rooms, lined with wine bottles and sepia-tone images of Old Siracusa, overflows with locals in the know. Preparations bring together fresh seafood and inspired creativity: taste, for instance, the sublime spaghetti *delle Sirene* (with sea urchin and shrimp in butter); a delicate *zuppa di*

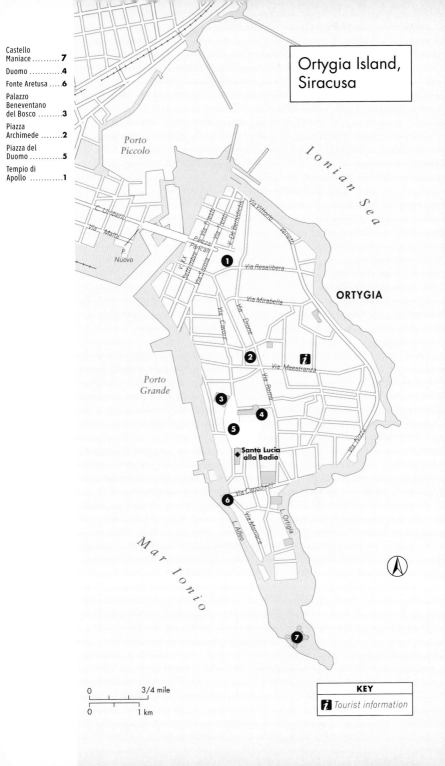

Ortygia Island,
Siracusa

*Porto
Piccolo*

I o n i a n   S e a

Via Vittorio   Veneto

C. Umberto

Via Matta

*P.
Nuovo*

Via Trieste

*Piazza
Pancali*

V. Del Benedittini

Via Tersi

❶

Via Resalibera

Via Mirabella

ORTYGIA

*Vi XX
Settembre*

Via Savoia

Via Cavour

Via Dione

❷

Via Maestranza

🛈

*Porto
Grande*

❸

Via Roma

❹

❺

◆ **Santa Lucia
alla Badia**

Via Nizza

Via Capodieci

❻

L. Alfeo

Via Maniace

L. Ortigia

M a r   I o n i o

🧭

❼

0 ——————— 3/4 mile

0 ——————— 1 km

mucco (tiny fish floating in a broth with cherry tomatoes, olive oil, and egg); or *gamberoni* (sweet, large prawns) prepared, unexpectedly (and wonderfully), in pork fat. The wine list is, in a word, extraordinary. ⊠ *Via Maestranza 96, Ortygia* ☎ *0931/67133* ⊟ *AE, DC, MC, V* ⊘ *Closed Sun.*

$$$ ⤬ **Il Fermento.** "Hip" and "family-run" aren't normally terms you'll find in close proximity, but they accurately describe this Ortygia eatery. It's a lovely place, graced with a wonderful vaulted ceiling in the dining area. The menu revolves around seafood, including some of the freshest fish around. Leave room for the luscious homemade desserts. Two-course set-price menus (€15 and €20) provide a good sampler of the delights on offer. ⊠ *Via Crocifisso 44/46, Ortygia* ☎ *0931/64422* ⊟ *AE, MC, V* ⊘ *Closed Tues.*

$$-$$$ ⤬ **Oinos.** This wine bar and restaurant's ambitious food represents the most modern face of Siracusa. The dining rooms are stark but inviting, carefully balancing style consciousness with restrained refinement. Surrender to the sensational antipasto *sformatino di patate, cavolo capuccio, scamorza e braduro,* a molded potato tart with cabbage and rich, creamy cheeses. In season, special dishes spotlight white truffles from Alba priced by the gram (as is customary) and worth every penny. ⊠ *Via della Giudecca 69/75, Ortygia* ☎ *0931/464900* ⊟ *AE, DC, MC, V* ⊘ *No dinner Sun. No lunch Mon.*

★ $$-$$$ ⤬ **Vite e Vitello.** Sooner or later, you'll need a break from the nonstop seafood of the Sicilian coast, and you'll find just that in these yellow dining rooms surrounding an open kitchen. A menu of some of the best beef and veal in Sicily includes an antipasto sampler with cubes of veal gelatin and homemade ricotta. Your primo might be *cavatelli* (small pasta twists) with *guanciale* (pig's jowl bacon) and delicious pistachios, and your secondo an incredible Angus steak shipped in from Ireland. For dessert, try the *cannollata,* a cake that resembles a deconstructed *cannolo* (singular of cannoli). The restaurant faces Via Maestranza, but the entrance is just round the corner. ⊠ *Piazza Francesco Corpaci 1, Ortygia* ☎ *0931/464269* ⊟ *AE, DC, MC, V* ⊘ *Closed Sun.*

$-$$ ⤬ **Ionico.** Enjoy seaside dining in the coastal Santa Lucia district. The Ionico has a terrace and veranda for alfresco meals, and the interior is plastered with diverse historical relics and has a cheerful open hearth for winter. Chef-proprietor Roberto Giudice cooks meals to order or will suggest a specialty from a selection of market-fresh ingredients. Try the *farfalle ricotta e gamberi* (pasta with ricotta and prawns). ⊠ *Riviera Dionisio il Grande 194, Santa Lucia* ☎ *0931/65540* ⊟ *AE, DC, MC, V* ⊘ *Closed Tues. Sept.–May.*

¢-$ ⤬ **Archimede.** Considered the best pizzeria in Ortygia, this place offers pizzas with classical names: for example, the Medea has tomato, ham, and mayonnaise, while the Teocrite is topped with fresh tomato, mozzarella, garlic, onion, and basil. If you can't face the full-size offerings, mini pizzas are also available. The calzone del ciclope (literally "of the Cyclops") is stuffed with tomato, mozzarella, ham, and egg. Wash it all down with a good selection of beers. ⊠ *Via Gemmellaro 8, Ortygia* ☎ *0931/69701* ⊟ *MC, V.*

WHERE TO STAY

$$$$ 🏨 **Grand Hotel Ortigia.** An elegant, fantasy-inspired design prevails at this venerable institution, which has enjoyed a prime position, the Porto Grande, at the base of Ortygia, since 1898. A surreal seascape painting and a whimsical chandelier set a dreamy tone in the lobby. Guest rooms have fine wood floors, inlaid wood furniture, and stained-glass windows. Spacious bi-level suites with staircases cost about €60 more. While you indulge in excellent food, look out from the rooftop restaurant at superb views over the harbor and seafront. A shuttle service is provided to the hotel's private beach between Juneand September. **Pros:** Wonderful views from the rooftop restaurant, attentive service. **Cons:** Back rooms have no view, bathrooms are small. ⊠ *Viale Mazzini 12, Ortygia, 96100* ☎*0931/464600* ⊕*www.grandhotelsr.it* ⬅*41 rooms, 17 suites* ⚖*In-room: safe, refrigerator, Wi-Fi. In-hotel: restaurant, bar, beachfront, parking (no fee)* ▤*AE, DC, MC, V* ⎮◎⎮*BP.*

★ $$$$ 🏨 **Hotel des Étrangers et Miramare.** This stylish hotel is one of the city's top addresses for visiting dignitaries and luxury tourists. Rooms are refreshingly simple for a hotel of this caliber, but at the same time elegant. Some have balconies overlooking the sea. The hotel, which stands beside the Fonte Aretusa in Ortygia, has a rooftop restaurant with nice views of the city—a great place to meet for a cocktail. **Pros:** Well-maintained facility, attentive service, central location. **Cons:** Some bathrooms are poorly designed, no parking. ⊠*Passeggio Adorno 10/12, Ortygia, 96100* ☎*0931/319100* ⊕*www.hotel-desetrangers.it* ⬅*65 rooms, 11 suites* ⚖*In-room: safe. In-hotel: restaurant, room service, bars, pool, gym, spa, concierge, public Internet* ▤*AE, DC, MC, V* ⎮◎⎮*BP.*

$$ 🏨 **Domus Mariae.** You can see the sea at the end of the corridor as you enter this hotel on Ortygia's eastern shore. In an unusual twist, it's owned by nuns of the Ursuline order, who help to make the mood placid and peaceful. There's a chapel and library for guests. Don't expect monastic conditions, however: refined furnishings distinguish the public rooms. Guest rooms—six with sea views (an extra €15) and six others with balconies overlooking the street—are bright, modern, and comfortable. A pretty roof terrace takes advantage of the hotel's superb position. **Pros:** Nice breakfast room, gorgeous sea views, enthusiastic staff. **Cons:** Stairs to climb. ⊠ *Via Vittorio Veneto 76, Ortygia, 96100* ☎*0931/24854 or 0931/24858* ⊕*www.sistemia.it/domusmariae* ⬅*12 rooms* ⚖*In-room: refrigerator. In-hotel: bar, gym, no elevator, parking (no fee)* ▤*AE, DC, MC, V* ⎮◎⎮*BP.*

¢–$ 🏨 **Airone.** In a pretty old palazzo, this bare-bones B&B (liberally interpreted—breakfast may be served at a separate establishment) caters mostly to backpackers and those who have the stamina to brave the four-story climb. Service is friendly and hassle-free (you get your own key to the building), and the price and location can't be beat. Rooms are aging but clean enough; some are spacious, and some overlook the coastline. **Pros:** Good value, full of character. **Cons:** Breakfast is not always served on the premises, some rooms are poorly furnished, stairs to climb. ⊠*Via Maestranza 111, Ortygia, 96100* ☎*0931/69005* ⎘*0931/449863* ⊕*www.bedandbreakfastsicily.com* ⬅*9 rooms, 5 with bath* ⚖*In-hotel: no elevator* ▤*No credit cards* ⎮◎⎮*BP.*

15

NIGHTLIFE & THE ARTS

From mid-May to late June, Siracusa's **Teatro Greco** (⊠ *Parco Archeologico, Archaeological Zone* ☎ *800/542644 toll-free* ⊕ *www.indafondazione.org*) stages performances of classical drama and comedy. Tickets run €30 to €60.

★ The folks at **Eunoè** (⊠ *Via Castello Maniace, Ortygia* ☎ *0335/6496803*) are passionate about Sicilian wines. The place serves almost every local wine by the glass. It's open for lunch, but is at its best in the evening when it draws in jazz aficionados and arty types.

Popular and filled with locals, **Il Bagatto** (⊠ *Piazza San Giuseppe 1, Ortygia* ☎ *0931/464076*) is a bar in the heart of Ortygia, with tables in the piazza.

THE INTERIOR

Sicily's interior is for the most part untrammeled, though the Imperial Roman Villa at Casale, outside Piazza Armerina, gives precious evidence from an epoch gone by. Don't miss windy mountaintop Enna, called the Navel of Sicily, or Caltagirone, a ceramics center of renown.

RAGUSA

90 km (56 mi) southwest of Siracusa.

GETTING HERE

Trains and buses leave from Siracusa four or five times daily.

VISITOR INFORMATION

Ragusa tourism office (⊠ *Via Capitano Bocchieri 33, 97100* ☎ *0932/221511* ⊕ *www.ragusaturismo.it).*

Ragusa and Modica are the two chief cities in Sicily's smallest and sleepiest province, and the centers of a region known as Iblea. The dry, rocky, gentle countryside filled with canyons and grassy knolls is a unique landscape in Sicily. Iblea's trademark squat walls divide swaths of land in a manner reminiscent of the high English countryside—but summers are decidedly Sicilian, with dry heat so intense that life grinds to a standstill for several hours each day. This remote province hums along to its own tune, clinging to local customs, cuisines, and traditions in aloof disregard even for the rest of Sicily.

★ Ragusa is known for some great local red wines and its wonderful cheese, a creamy, doughy, flavorful version of caciocavallo, made by hand every step of the way. It's a modern city with a beautiful old town called **Ibla,** which was completely rebuilt after the devastating earthquake of 1693. A tumble of buildings perched on a hilltop and suspended between a deep ravine and a sloping valley, Ibla's tiny squares and narrow lanes make for pleasant meandering.

The **Basilica di San Giorgio,** designed by Rosario Gagliardi in 1738, is a fine example of Sicilian baroque.

CALTAGIRONE

66 km (41 mi) northwest of Ragusa.

GETTING HERE

Buses and trains from Catania stop in the lower town, connected by local buses and taxis to the center. Connections with Ragusa, Enna, and Piazza Armerina are less frequent.

VISITOR INFORMATION

Caltagirone tourism office (⊠ *Via Volta Libertini 3, 95041* ☎*0933/53809*).

15

Built over three hills, this charming baroque town is a center of Sicily's ceramics industry. Here you can find majolica balustrades, tile-decorated windowsills, and a monumental tile staircase of 142 steps—each decorated with a different pattern—leading up to the neglected **Santa Maria del Monte**. On the feast of San Giacomo (July 24), the staircase of the church is illuminated with candles that form a tapestry design over the steps. It's the result of months of work preparing the 4,000 *coppi,* or cylinders of colored paper that hold oil lamps. At 9:30 PM on the nights of July 24, July 25, August 14, and August 15 a squad of hundreds of boys springs into action to light the lamps, so that the staircase flares up all at once. ◷ *Daily 7–12:30 and 4–7.*

PIAZZA ARMERINA

30 km (18 mi) northwest of Caltagirone.

GETTING HERE

Piazza Armerina is linked to Caltagirone, Catania, Enna, and Palermo by regular buses. There is no train station.

VISITOR INFORMATION

Piazza Armerina tourism office (⊠*Piazza Santa Rosalia, 94015* ☎*0935/683049* ⊕ *www.comune.piazzaarmerina.en.it*).

EXPLORING

A quick look around the fanciful town of Piazza Armerina is rewarding—it has a provincial warmth, and the crumbling yellow stone architecture with Sicily's trademark bulbous balconies creates quite an effect. The greatest draw, however, lies just down the road.

Fodor'sChoice
★
The exceptionally well-preserved **Imperial Roman Villa** is thought to have been a hunting lodge of the emperor Maximianus Heraclius (fourth century AD). The excavations were not begun until 1950, and the wall decorations and vaulting have been lost. However, some of the best mosaics of the Roman world cover more than 12,000 square feet under a shelter that hints at the layout of the original buildings. The mosa-

ics were probably made by North African artisans; they are similar to those in the Tunis Bardo Museum. The entrance was through a triumphal arch that led into an atrium surrounded by a portico of columns, after which the *thermae*, or bathhouse, is reached. It's colorfully decorated with mosaic nymphs, a Neptune, and slaves massaging bathers. The peristyle leads to the main villa, where in the Salone del Circo you look down on mosaics illustrating Roman circus sports. Room 38 even reveals a touch of eroticism—surely only scratching the surface of the bacchanalian festivities that Maximianus conjured up. As this book went to press, renovations meant the villa was only open a few hours each day. They were scheduled to be complete in 2008, but call ahead to make sure. ⊠*SP15*, 4 km (2½ mi) southwest of Piazza Armerina ☎*0935/680036* ⊕*www.villaromanadelcasale.it* ⊠*€6* ☉*Daily 8–1 hr before sunset.*

WHERE TO EAT

$$$ ✕   **Al Fogher.** A beacon of culinary light shines in Sicily's interior, a region generally filled with good, but simple, places to eat. Ambitious—and successful—dishes include tuna tartare with orange essence and fillet of baby pig that's served with a sauce made from *bottarga* (cured tuna roe) and green olives. The dining room decor is simple and elegant, but the terrace is the place to be in summer. From town, follow Viale Ciancio and Viale Gaeta about 1 km (½ mi) north of Piazza Cascino. ⊠*Contrada Bellia near SS117bis, Aidone exit* ☎*0935/684123* ⊟*AE, DC, MC, V* ☉*Closed Mon. No dinner Sun.*

ENNA

33 km (20 mi) northwest of Piazza Armerina, 136 km (85 mi) southeast of Palermo.

GETTING HERE

Just off the A19 autostrada, Enna is easily accessible by car. With the train station 5 km (3 mi) below the upper town, the most practical public transport is by bus from Palermo or Catania.

VISITOR INFORMATION

Enna tourism office (⊠*Via Roma 413, 94100* ☎*0935/528228* ⊕*www. apt-enna.com*).

EXPLORING

Deep in Sicily's interior, the fortress city of Enna (altitude 2,844 feet) commands exceptional views of the surrounding rolling plains, and, in the distance, Mt. Etna. It is the highest provincial capital in Italy and, thanks to its central location, it is known as the Navel of Sicily. Virtually unknown by tourists and relatively untouched by industrialization, this sleepy town charms and prospers in a distinctly old-fashioned, provincial, and Sicilian way. Enna makes a good stopover for the night or just for lunch, as it's right along the autostrada between Palermo and Catania (and thus Siracusa).

The narrow, winding streets are dominated at one end by the impressive cliff-hanging **Castello di Lombardia,** built by Frederick II, easily visible as you approach town. Inside the castle, you can climb up the tower for great views from the dead center of the island; on a very clear day, you can see to all three coasts. ⚑*Free* ☉*Daily 9–1 hr before sunset.*

★ The Greek cult of Demeter, goddess of the harvest, was said to have centered around Enna. It's not hard to see why its adherents would have worshipped at the **Rocca di Cerere** *(Rock of Demeter)*, protruding out on one end of town next to the Castello di Lombardia. The spot enjoys spectacular views of the expansive countryside and windswept Sicilian interior. From here you can see Lake Pergusa, where mythology asserts that Persephone was abducted by Hades. While a prisoner in his underworld realm she ate six pomegranate seeds, and therefore was doomed to spend half of each year there. Because of its sulfur content, Lake Pergusa turns red once a year, a phenomenon that some say represents the blood of Persephone, and others believe represents the pomegranate seeds.

In town, head straight for Via Roma, which leads to **Piazza Vittorio Emanuele,** the center of Enna's shopping scene and evening passeggiata. The attached **Piazza Crispi,** dominated by the shell of the grand old Hotel Belvedere, affords breathtaking panoramas of the hillside and smoking Etna looming in the distance. The bronze fountain at the center of the piazza is a reproduction of Gian Lorenzo Bernini's famous 17th-century sculpture *The Rape of Persephone,* a depiction of Hades abducting Persephone.

The mysterious **Torre di Federico II** stands above the lower part of town. This octagonal tower, of unknown purpose, has been celebrated for millennia as marking the exact geometric center of the island—thus the tower's, and city's, nickname, Umbilicus Siciliae (Navel of Sicily). The interior is not open to the public, but the surrounding park is.

WHERE TO STAY & EAT

$ ✕ **Centrale.** Housed in an old palazzo, this casual place has served meals since 1889. One entire wall is covered with a vast mirror, the others are adorned with Sicilian pottery. An outdoor terrace soothes diners in summer. The seasonal menu includes local preparations such as *coppole di cacchio* (peppers stuffed with spaghetti, potato, and basil) and grilled pork chops. Choose from a decent selection of Sicilian wines to accompany your meal. ✉*Piazza VI Dicembre 9* ☎*0935/500963* ▤*AE, DC, MC, V* ☉*Closed Sat. Oct.–Mar.*

$$ 🛏 **Hotel Sicilia.** Sicily's interior has few decent accommodations, and of Enna's two hotels, this one has most character. Behind the unprepossessing exterior you'll find an art-deco lobby and sunny rooms dotted with antiques. Reserve ahead for one of the back-facing rooms, which have views of the hillside rather than the piazza. Low-season discounts can be as much as 50%. **Pros:** Central location, friendly staff, a good breakfast. **Cons:** Needs some renovations, rooms can be noisy. ✉*Piazza Napoleone Colajanni 7, 94100* ☎*0935/500850* ☎*0935/500488* ⊕*www.hotelsiciliaenna.it* ↪*65 rooms* ⌂*In-room: safe, refrigerator. In-hotel: room service, bar, parking (no fee)* ▤*AE, DC, MC, V* ⍾*BP.*

AGRIGENTO & WESTERN SICILY

The crowning glory of western Sicily is the concentration of Greek temples at Agrigento, on a height between the modern city and the sea. The mark of ancient Greek culture also lingers in the cluster of ruined cliff-side temples at Selinunte and at the splendidly isolated site of Segesta. Traces of the North African culture that for centuries exerted a strong influence on this end of the island are most tangible in the coastal towns of Trapani and Marsala, and on the outlying island of Pantelleria, nearer to the Tunisian coast than the Sicilian. In contrast, the cobbled streets of hilltop Erice, outside Trapani, retain a strong medieval complexion, giving the quiet town the air of a last outpost on the edge of the Mediterranean. On the northern coast, not far outside Palermo, Monreale's cathedral glitters with mosaics that are among the finest in Italy.

AGRIGENTO

60 km (37 mi) southwest of Caltanissetta.

GETTING HERE

You can reach Agrigento by bus from Palermo, Caltanissetta, and Catania, and by train from Palermo, Caltanissetta, and occasionally from Enna. Both bus and train stations are centrally located. By car, the town is easily accessed by the coastal SS115, by the SS189 from Palermo, and by the SS640 from Caltanissetta.

VISITOR INFORMATION

Agrigento tourism office (⊠*Piazzale Aldo Moro, 92100* ☎*0922/20454*).

EXPLORING

Agrigento owes its fame almost exclusively to its ancient Greek temples—though it was also the birthplace of playwright Luigi Pirandello (1867–1936).

Among the reasons to go up the hill from Valle dei Templi to the modern city is the opportunity to eat a more-local, less-overpriced meal or to stay at an inexpensive hotel; another is to ring the doorbell at the **Convento di Santo Spirito** and try the *kus-kus* (sweet cake), made of pistachio nuts and chocolate, that the nuns prepare. ⊠*Salita di Santo Spirito off Via Porcello* ☎*No phone.*

WHERE TO STAY & EAT

$$–$$$ ✕ **Kókalos.** On a hillside opposite the temple ridge, 6 km (4 mi) to the southeast, this restaurant in an old ranch-style house has beautiful views over the temples. As well as serving local specialties, Kókalos serves pizza in the evening. In summer, there's a well-stocked enoteca. This place hops on weekend nights all through the year. ⊠*Via Cavaleri Magazzeni 3, Villagio Mosè* ☎*0922/606427* ▭*AE, MC, V.*

$$–$$$ ✕ **Trattoria dei Templi.** Along a road on the way up to Agrigento proper from the temple area, this simple vaulted restaurant can get very busy after it becomes too dark for temple exploring. The menu includes satisfying homemade *maccheroni* (tubular pasta) and plenty of grilled fish. The antipasti, such as the carpaccio of *cernia* (grouper), are exceptional. Fodors.com readers said this place has "great food and service." ✉ *Via Panoramica dei Templi 15* ☎*0922/403110* ⊟*AE, DC, MC, V* ☯*Closed June 15–July 7, Sun. last 3 wks in July and Aug., and Fri. Sept.–June.*

$$$–$$$$ ☷ **Domus Aurea.** The newest hotel in the area, Domus Aurea still manages to feel old-fashioned. The sofa-filled lounge is comfortable, if evocative of a cruise ship with its tacky decor. Superior rooms overlook the temple, while junior suites in a small tower have terraces with even better panoramas. Domus Aurea is 3 km (2 mi) southeast of old town—next to Foresteria Baglio della Luna and equally hard to find. **Pros:** Friendly staff, relaxing terrace and garden, great temple views from some rooms. **Cons:** Rooms and bathrooms are small, decor is sometimes unattractive, hard to find. ✉*Contrada Maddalusa, SS640 Km 4150, 92100* ☎*0922/511500* ⊕*www.hoteldomusaurea.it* ☞*18 rooms, 2 suites* ♿*In-room: refrigerator, safe. In-hotel: restaurant, bar, spa, public Internet* ⊟*AE, DC, MC, V* ⦿*BP.*

$$$–$$$$ ☷ **Foresteria Baglio della Luna.** Fiery sunsets and moonlight cast a glow over a tower dating from the eighth century, which is central to the farmhouse-hotel complex. Stone buildings surround a peaceful geranium- and ivy-filled courtyard and a garden beyond. Standard rooms, some with views of the temples, are nothing fancy, with mellow walls and wooden furniture. The rustic restaurant, Il Dehors, serves extremely expensive foodie fare that is ambitious but only sometimes successful. The wine list is seemingly unrelated to what's in the cellar. The hotel, in the valley below the temples, is on an unmarked dirt road about 3 km (2 mi) southeast of the old town. **Pros:** Good location, serene environment. **Cons:** Service can be slipshod, restaurant is unreliable, generally overpriced. ✉*Contrada Maddalusa, SS640 Km 4150, 92100* ☎*0922/511061* ⊕*www.bagliodellaluna.com* ☞*23 rooms, 4 suites* ♿*In-room: refrigerator. In-hotel: restaurant, bar, no elevator, some pets allowed* ⊟*AE, DC, MC, V* ⦿*BP.*

$$ ☷ **Tre Torri.** Stay here if you are sports-minded and bent on exploring the countryside around Agrigento. Bicycle tours and nature walks can be arranged or a boat booked for fishing trips and water sports. The heated pool is pleasant, the public areas spacious, and rooms modern. The hotel's location is in Villagio Mosè, 5 km (3 mi) southeast of town. **Pros:** Good facilities, sociable atmosphere, multilingual staff. **Cons:** A bit run-down, some rooms are small, busy with tour groups. ✉*Villagio Mosè, 92100* ☎*0922/606733* ⊕*www.htretorri. com* ☞*118 rooms* ♿*In-hotel: restaurant, bars, pool, gym, spa, bicycles* ⊟*AE, DC, MC, V* ⦿*BP.*

15

Continued on page 890

VALLE DEI TEMPLI

Built on a broad open field that slopes gently to the sun-simmered Mediterranean, Akragas (ancient Agrigento's Greek name) was a showpiece of temples erected to flaunt a victory over Carthage. Despite a later sack by the Carthaginians, mishandling by the Romans, and neglect by the Christians and Muslims, the eight or so monuments in the Valle dei Templi are considered to be, along with the Acropolis in Athens, the finest Greek ruins in all the world.

TIMING TIP

The temples are at their very best in February, when the valley is awash in the fragrant blossoms of thousands of almond trees.

Whether you first come upon the Valle dei Templi in the early morning light, or bathed by golden floodlights at night, it's easy to see why Akragas was celebrated by the Greek poet Pindar as "the most beautiful city built by mortal men."

MAKING THE MOST OF YOUR VISIT

GETTING AROUND

Though getting to, from, and around the dusty ruins of the Valle dei Templi is no great hassle, this important archaeological zone deserves several hours. The site, which opens at 8:30 AM, is divided into western and eastern sections. For instant aesthetic gratification, walk through the eastern zone; for a more comprehensive tour, start way out at the western end and work your way back uphill.

The temples are a bit spread out, but the valley is all completely walkable and generally toured on foot. However, note that there is only one hotel (Villa Athena) that is close enough to walk to the ruins, so you will most likely have to drive to reach the site; parking is at the entrance to the temple area.

WHAT TO BRING

It's a good idea to pack your own snacks and drinks, as there are hardly any restaurants in the temple area, and the handful of high-priced bars around the site cater to tourists.

In summer the site can get extremely hot, so wear light clothing, a hat, and sun protection if possible.

A BRIEF HISTORY OF AGRIGENTO

Cornice
Frieze
Architrave
Capital
Shaft
Stylobate
Stereobate

KEY DATES	
750 BC	Greek city-states begin to colonize Sicily and southern Italy.
734 BC	Neighboring Siracusa founded.
582 BC	Akragas settled. The city grows wealthy through trade with Carthage, just across the Mediterranean.
ca. 450 BC– 350 BC	Temples at Akragas erected over a period of about 100 years to celebrate the city's propserity.
413 BC	Battle of Siracusa vs. Athens.
406 BC	Fire from Carthaginian attack destroys much of Akragas. Despite this and future attacks, the city and its temples survive through the Roman era, the Middle Ages, and into the modern age.

The natural defenses of ancient Akragas depended on its secure and quite lovely position between two rivers on a floodplain a short distance from the sea. In Agrigento you will be treated to what many experts consider the world's best-preserved remains of classical Greece. All of the temples in the Valle dei Templi are examples of Doric architecture, the earliest and simplest of the Greek architectural orders (the others are Ionic and Corinthian). Some retain capitals in addition to their columns, while others are reduced to nothing more than fragments of stylobate.

THE TEMPLES

TEMPIO DI ERCOLE

The eight pillars of the **Temple of Hercules**, down the hill from the Temple of Concord, make up Agrigento's oldest temple complex (dating from the 6th century BC), dedicated to the favorite god of the often-warring citizens of Akragas. Partially reconstructed in 1922, it reveals the remains of a large Doric temple that originally had 38 columns. Like all the area temples, it faces east. The nearby Museo Archeologico Regionale contains some of the marble warrior figures that once decorated the temple's pediment.

Tempio di Ercole

TEMPIO DELLA CONCORDIA

The beautiful **Temple of Concord** is perhaps *the* best-preserved Greek temple in existence. The structure dates from about 430 BC, and owes its exceptional state of preservation to the fact that it was converted into a Christian church in the 6th century and was extensively restored in the 18th century. Thirty-two Doric columns surround its large interior, and everything but the roof and treasury are still standing. For preservation, this temple is blocked off to the public, but you can still get close enough to appreciate how well it's withstood the past 2,400 years.

TEMPIO DI GIUNONE

The **Temple of Juno**, east on the Via Sacra from the Temple of Concord, commands an exquisite view of the valley, especially at sunset. It's similar to but smaller than the Concordia and dates from about 450 BC. Traces of a fire that probably occurred during the Carthaginian attack in 406 BC,

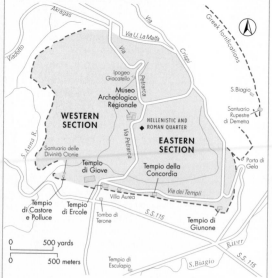

Valle dei Templi
Phone: 0922/621611
Web site: www.valledeitempli.net
Admission: Site €6, with museum €10. One ticket covers all temples.
Open daily 8:30–7; Nov.–Mar., western section closes at 5.

Museo Archeologico Regionale
Contrada San Nicola, 12
Phone: 0922/401565
Admission: €6, with temples site €10
Open Tues.–Sat. 9–7, Sun.–Mon. 9–1

Agrigento tourist information
Via Cesare Battisti 15, 92100
Phone: 0922/20454

which destroyed the ancient town, can be seen on the walls of the cellar. Thirty of the original 34 columns still stand, of which 16 have retained their capitals.

TEMPIO DI GIOVE

Though never completed, the **Temple of Jupiter** was considered the eighth wonder of the world. With a length of more than 330 feet, it was once the biggest of the Akragas temples and one of the largest temples in the Greek world. The temple was probably built in gratitude for victory over Carthage and was constructed by prisoners captured in that war. Basically Doric in style, it did not have the usual colonnade of freestanding columns but rather a series of half columns attached to a solid wall. This design is unique among known Doric temples—alas, only the stereobate was left behind. Inside the excavation you can see a cast (not the original) of one of the 38 colossal Atlas-like figures, or telamones, that supported the temple's massive roof.

Tempio di Giove

TEMPIO DI CASTORE E POLLUCE

The **Temple of Castor and Pollux** is a troublesome reconstruction of a 5th-century BC temple. It was pieced together by some enthusiastic if misguided 19th-century romantics who, in 1836, haphazardly put together elements from diverse buildings. Ironically, the four gently crumbling columns supporting part of an entablature of the temple have become emblematic of Agrigento.

15

IN FOCUS VALLE DEI TEMPLI

OTHER SITES OF INTEREST

To the left of the Temple of Concord is a Paleochristian **necropolis**. Early Christian tombs were both cut into the rock and dug into underground catacombs.

Right opposite the Temple of Castor and Pollux, facing north, the **Santuario delle Divinità Ctonie** (Sanctuary of the Chthonic Divinities) has cultic altars and eight small temples dedicated to Demeter, Persephone, and other Underworld deities. In the vicinity are two columns of a temple dedicated to Hephaestus (Vulcan).

At the end of Via dei Templi, where it turns left and becomes Via Petrarca, stands the **Museo Archeologico Regionale**. An impressive collection of antiquities from the site includes vases, votives, everyday objects, weapons, statues (including one of the surviving original telamones from the Temple of Jupiter), and models of the temples.

The **Hellenistic and Roman Quarter**, across the road from the archaeological museum, consists of four parallel streets, running north–south, that have been uncovered, along with the foundations of some houses from the Roman settlement (2nd century BC). Some of these streets still have their original mosaic pavements, and the complex system of sidewalks and gutters is easy to make out—reminding you that the ancient world wasn't all temples and togas.

SELINUNTE

100 km (60 mi) northwest of Agrigento, 114 km (71 mi) south of Palermo.

GETTING HERE

You can get here by bus or car via the town of Castelvetrano, 11 km (7 mi) north, which is itself accessible from Palermo by car on the A29 autostrada, as well as by bus and train.

VISITOR INFORMATION

Selinunte tourism office (⌧ *Parco Archeologico, 91022* ☎ *0924/46251* ⊕ *www.apt.trapani.it/Selinunte.htm*).

EXPLORING

★ Near the town of Castelvetrano, numerous **Greek temple ruins** perch on a plateau overlooking an expanse of the Mediterranean at Selinunte (or Selinus). The city was one of the most superb colonies of ancient Greece. Founded in the seventh century BC, Selinunte became the rich and prosperous rival of Segesta, which in 409 BC turned to the Carthaginians for help. The Carthaginians sent an army commanded by Hannibal to destroy the city. The temples were demolished, the city was razed, and 16,000 of Selinunte's inhabitants were slaughtered. The remains of Selinunte are in many ways unchanged from the day of its sacking—burn marks still scar the Greek columns, and much of the site still lies in rubble at its exact position of collapse at the hands of the Carthaginian attack. The original complex held seven temples scattered over two sites separated by a harbor. Of the seven, only one—reconstructed in 1958—is whole. This is a large archeological site, so you might make use of the *navetta* (shuttle) to save a bit of walking.

Selinunte is named after a local variety of wild parsley (*Apium graveolens* or *petroselinum*) that in spring grows in profusion among the ruined columns and overturned capitals. Although there are a few places to stay right around Selinunte, many people see it as an easy stop along the road to or from Agrigento. It only takes an hour or two to see—a richly rewarding stopover. ⌧ *SS115, 13 km (8 mi) southeast of Castevetrano* ☎ *0924/46277* ⌧ *€6* ⊙ *Apr.–Oct., Mon.–Sat. 9–5; Nov.–Mar., daily 9–4.*

ERICE

15 km (9 mi) northeast of Trapani.

GETTING HERE

A funivia (cable car) runs from the outskirts of Trapani to Erice Monday 2 PM to 8:30 PM, Tuesday to Friday 7:30 AM to 8:30 PM, and weekends 9:45 AM to midnight. Going by car or bus from Trapani takes around 40 minutes.

VISITOR INFORMATION

Erice tourism office (⌧ *Via Tommaso Guarrasi, 91016* ☎ *0923/869388*).

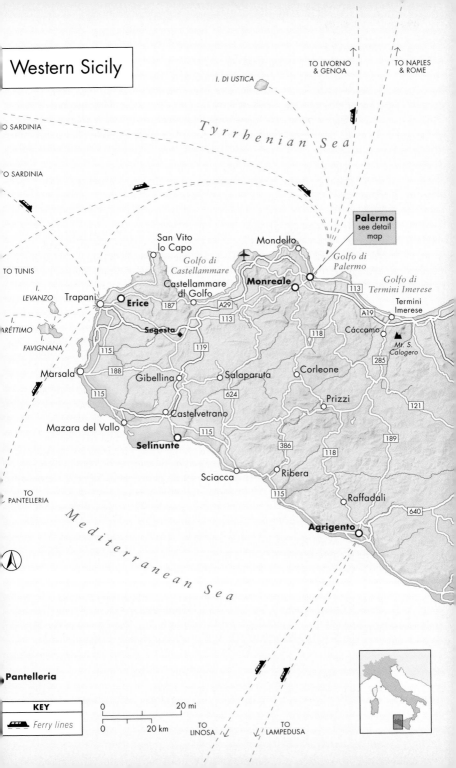

EXPLORING

Perched 2,450 feet above sea level, Erice is an enchanting medieval mountaintop aerie of palaces, fountains, and cobblestone streets. Shaped like an equilateral triangle, the town was the ancient landmark Eryx, dedicated to Aphrodite (Venus). When the Normans arrived they built a castle on Monte San Giuliano, where today there's a lovely public park with benches and belvederes from which there are striking views of Trapani, the Egadi Islands offshore, and, on a *very* clear day, Cape Bon and the Tunisian coast. Because of Erice's elevation, clouds conceal much of the view for most of winter. Sturdy shoes (for the cobbles) and something warm to wear are recommended.

Fans of Sicilian sweets make a beeline for **Pasticceria Grammatico** (⊠ *Via Vittorio Emanuele 14* ☎*0923/869390*). The place is run by Maria Grammatico, a former nun who gained international fame with *Bitter Almonds,* her life story cowritten with Mary Taylor Simeti. Her almond-paste creations are works of art, molded into striking shapes, including dolls and animals. There are a few tables and a tiny balcony with wonderful views.

At **Pasticceria del Convento** (⊠ *Via Guarnotti 1* ☎*0923/869777*), Maria Grammatico's sister sells similar delectable treats.

Capo San Vito, 40 km (25 mi) north of Erice, is a cape with a long sandy beach on a promontory overlooking a bay in the Gulf of Castellammare. The town here, San Vito Lo Capo, is famous for its North African couscous, made with fish instead of meat. In late September it hosts the five-day **Cous Cous Fest,** a serious international couscous competition and festival with live music and plenty of free tastings.

WHERE TO STAY & EAT

$–$$ ✕ **Elimo.** On Erice's main cobblestone street, Carmelo Tilotta's restaurant offers superb views of passersby through large picture windows. But your eyes will be on the food, made with fresh local ingredients. The pasta all'ericina (pasta with basil, garlic, tomatoes, and almonds) is worth the trip. Tables spread onto the terrace in summer. There are also spacious and sometimes quirky rooms if you want to stay over ($$–$$$). ⊠ *Via Vittorio Emanuele 75* ☎*0923/869377* ☰*AE, DC, MC, V* ⊘*Closed Jan. and 2 wks in Feb.*

$–$$ ✕ **Monte San Giuliano.** At this traditional restaurant, you'll sit out on the tree-lined patio or in the white-wall room and munch on the free *panelle* (chickpea fritters), which are delicate, judiciously seasoned, and addictive. Next come the citrusy *sarde a beccafico* (sardines rolled with bread crumbs) and exemplary ravioli in cuttlefish ink. Or try the seafood couscous, served with a bowl of fish broth on the side so you can add as much as you wish. The restaurant, near the main piazza, is hidden within the labyrinth of lanes that makes up Erice. ⊠ *Vicolo San Rocco 7* ☎*0923/869595* ☰*AE, DC, MC, V* ⊘*Closed Mon., 2 wks in mid-Jan., and 1st 2 wks in Nov.*

$$ ⌂ **Moderno.** This delightful hotel has a creaky old feel to it, but that's part of the charm. The lobby area, scattered with books, magazines, and knickknacks, feels like your aunt's living room. There's a lovely

15

Prizzi's Honor

Buried in the heart of Mafia country (22 km [14 mi] west of Lercara Friddi, which gave the world the mobster Lucky Luciano), Prizzi, population 6,000, is a fairy-tale aerie, a floating apparition of twisting stone alleyways and brown rooftops gently dusting the peak of a 3,267-foot mountain. Its medieval layout and architecture—surreally frozen in another age—and dreamy views of the surrounding countryside, perhaps best seen at sunset, make it well worth a stop along the way between Palermo and Agrigento. Prizzi was founded by the Greeks in about 480 BC, and was alternately conquered by the Byzantines (eighth century AD) and Saracens (ninth century AD), the latter of whom built three lofty castles and created a "cult of water" with an elaborate network of drinking troughs. Christian conquest came in the 11th century.

The name "Prizzi" became known to the outside world through 1985's wryly comic mobster movie *Prizzi's Honor,* but the town feels as far removed as imaginable from Hollywood glamour and glitz. There's little in the way of significant art or monuments, and the secrets of the Mafia presence lie out of reach to visitors, buried in inaccessible crevices of local culture. But you can spend hours wandering in and out of the maze of steeply sloped alleyways, with tiny, still-inhabited houses built into the rock, eventually giving way to the remains of the three castles and the mountain's dazzling peak, from which, on a clear day, you can view the sea of Sciacca to one side and the cone of Mt. Etna to the other.

Coming from Palermo, follow the signs to Sciacca; both Prizzi and Corleone—another name familiar to moviegoers—are on the way.

---

terrace where you can enjoy breakfast, and a well-known restaurant serving seafood pasta and homemade desserts. **Pros:** Central location, great rooftop terrace. **Cons:** Rooms are overpriced, can feel deserted in winter. ⊠ *Via Vittorio Emanuele 67, 91016* ☎*0923/869300* ⊕*www. hotelmodernoerice.it* ⌁*40 rooms* ⌂*In-hotel: restaurant, bar* ☐*AE, DC, MC, V* ⑩*BP.*

SEGESTA

35 km (22 mi) east of Erice, 85 km (53 mi) southwest of Palermo.

GETTING HERE

Three or four daily buses travel from Trapani to Segesta. About as many trains from Palermo and Trapani stop at Segesta-Tempio station, a 20-minute uphill walk from Segesta. The site is easily reached via the A29dir autostrada.

★ Segesta is the site of the **Tempio Dorico** *(Doric Temple),* one of Sicily's most impressive, constructed on the side of a windswept barren hill overlooking a valley of wild fennel. Virtually intact today, the temple is considered by some to be finer in its proportions and setting than any other Doric temple left standing. The temple was actually started in the fifth century BC by the Elymian people, who some believe were refugees from Troy. At the very least, evidence indicates that they were non-Greeks; for example, they often sided with the Carthaginians. However, the style is in many ways Greek. The temple was never finished; the walls and roof never materialized, and the columns were never fluted. A little more than 1 km (½ mi) away, near the top of the hill, are the remains of a fine **amphitheater,** with impressive views, especially at sunset, of the sea and the nearby town of Monte Erice. Concerts and plays are staged here in summer. ⊠ *Calatafimi-Segesta* ☎ *0924/952356* 🎫 *€6* 🕙 *May–Sept., daily 9–7; Oct.–Apr., daily 9–5. Last entry 1 hr before closing.*

MONREALE

59 km (37 mi) northeast of Segesta, 10 km (6 mi) southwest of Palermo.

GETTING HERE

You can reach Monreale on the frequent buses that depart from Palermo's Piazza dell'Indipendenza. From Palermo, drivers can follow Corso Calatafimi west, though the going is slow.

> ### WORD OF MOUTH
>
> "The Cathedral of Monreale dwarfs everything in Palermo, and I mean everything. It's the grandest and most spectacular church in all of southern Italy." –GAC

EXPLORING

★ Monreale's splendid **Duomo** is lavishly executed with mosaics depicting events from the Old and New Testaments. After the Norman conquest of Sicily the new princes showcased their ambitions through monumental building projects. William II (1154–89) built the church complex with a cloister and palace between 1174 and 1185, employing Byzantine craftsmen. The result was a glorious fusion of Eastern and Western influences, widely regarded as the finest example of Norman architecture in Sicily.

The major attraction is the 68,220 square feet of glittering gold mosaics decorating the cathedral interior. *Christ Pantocrator* dominates the apse area; the nave contains narratives of the Creation; and scenes from the life of Christ adorn the walls of the aisles and the transept. The painted wooden ceiling dates from 1816–37. The roof commands a great view (a reward for climbing 172 stairs).

Bonnano Pisano's **bronze doors,** completed in 1186, depict 42 biblical scenes and are considered among the most important of medieval artifacts. Barisano da Trani's 42 panels on the north door, dating from 1179, present saints and evangelists. ⊠ *Piazza del Duomo* ☎ *091/6404413* 🕙 *Mid-Apr.–mid-Oct., Mon.–Sat. 8–6:30, Sun. 8–12:30 and 3:30–7; mid-Oct.–mid-Apr., Mon.–Sat. 8–12:30 and 3:30–6:30, Sun. 8–12:30 and 3:30–7.*

The lovely **cloister** of the abbey adjacent to the Duomo was built at the same time as the church but enlarged in the 14th century. The beautiful enclosure is surrounded by 216 intricately carved double columns, every other one decorated in a unique glass mosaic pattern. Afterward, don't forget to walk behind the cloister to the **belvedere,** with stunning panoramic views over the Conca d'Oro (Golden Conch) valley toward Palermo. The last tickets are sold a half hour before closing. ⊠ *Piazza del Duomo* 🕿 *091/6404403* 💶 *€6* ⊘ *Daily 9–6:30.*

WHERE TO EAT

$$ ✕ **La Botte 1962.** It's worth the short drive or inexpensive taxi fare from Monreale to reach this restaurant, which is famous for well-prepared local specialties. Dine alfresco on seafood dishes such as *bavette don Carmelo,* a narrow version of tagliatelle with a sauce of swordfish, squid, shrimp, and pine nuts. Other regular favorites include *involtini alla siciliana,* meat roulades stuffed with salami and cheese. Local wines are a good accompaniment. The restaurant is only open on Sunday afternoon, except by reservation. ⊠ *Contrada Lenzitti 20, SS186 Km 10* 🕿 *091/414051* ⊕ *www.mauriziocascino. it* 🍴 *Reservations essential* 🖃 *AE, DC, MC, V* ⊘ *Closed Mon.–Sat., and July–mid-Sept. No dinner Sun.*

15

PALERMO

Once the intellectual capital of southern Europe, Palermo has always been at the crossroads of civilization. Favorably situated on a crescent bay at the foot of Monte Pellegrino, it has attracted almost every culture touching the Mediterranean world. To Palermo's credit, it has absorbed these diverse cultures into a unique personality that is at once Arab and Christian, Byzantine and Roman, Norman and Italian. The city's heritage encompasses all of Sicily's varied ages, but its distinctive aspect is its Arab-Norman identity, an improbable marriage that, mixed in with Byzantine and Jewish elements, created some resplendent works of art. These are most notable in the churches, from small jewels such as San Giovanni degli Eremiti to larger-scale works such as the cathedral. No less noteworthy than the architecture is Palermo's chaotic vitality, on display at some of Italy's most vibrant outdoor markets, public squares, street bazaars, and food vendors, and above all in its grand, discordant symphony of motorists, motor bikers, and pedestrians that triumphantly climaxes in the new town center each evening with Italy's most spectacular passeggiata (the leisurely social stroll along the principal thoroughfare).

GETTING HERE

Palermo is well connected by road and rail; its airport links it to other cities in Italy, as well as around Europe.

VISITOR INFORMATION

Palermo tourism office (⊠ *Piazza Castelnuovo 34, 90141* 🕿 *091/6058351* ⊠ *Stazione Centrale, Piazza Giulio Cesare, 90127* 🕿 *091/6165914* ⊠ *Aeroporto Falcone-Borsellino, 90045* 🕿 *091/591698* ⊕ *www.palermotourism.com).*

Palermo

KEY

🅸 *Tourist Information*

Catacombe dei Cappuccini	**1**
Cattedrale	**4**
La Martorana	**11**
Museo Archeologico Regionale Salinas	**6**
Museo delle Marionette	**13**

Palazzo Abatellis	**12**
Palazzo Reale	**3**
Piazza Pretoria	**8**
Quattro Canti	**7**
San Cataldo	**10**
San Giovanni degli Eremiti	**2**

Santa Caterina	**9**
Teatro Massimo	**5**

EXPLORING PALERMO

Sicily's capital is a multilayered, vigorous metropolis; approach with an open mind when exploring the enriching city with a strong historical profile. You're likely to encounter some frustrating instances of inefficiency and, depending on the season, stifling heat. If you have a car, park it in a garage as soon as you can, and don't take it out until you are ready to depart.

Palermo is easily explored on foot, though you may choose to spend a morning taking a bus tour to help you get oriented. The Quattro Canti, or Four Corners, is the hub that separates the four sections of the old city: La Kalsa (the old Arab section) to the southeast, Albergheria to the southwest, Capo to the northwest, and Vucciria to the northeast. Each of these is a tumult of activity during the day, though at night the narrow alleys empty out and are best avoided in favor of the more-animated avenues of the new city north of Teatro Massimo. Sights to see by day are scattered along three major streets: Corso Vittorio Emanuele, Via Maqueda, and Via Roma. The tourist information office in Piazza Castelnuovo will give you a map and a valuable handout that lists opening and closing times, which sometimes change with the seasons.

15

THE MAIN ATTRACTIONS

★ **4** **Cattedrale.** This church is a lesson in Palermitan eclecticism—originally Norman (1182), then Catalan Gothic (14th to 15th century), then fitted out with a baroque and neoclassical interior (18th century). Its turrets, towers, dome, and arches come together in the kind of meeting of diverse elements that King Roger II (1095–1154), whose tomb is inside along with that of Frederick II, fostered during his reign. The back of the apse is gracefully decorated with interlacing Arab arches inlaid with limestone and black volcanic tufa. ⊠ *Corso Vittorio Emanuele, Capo* ☎ *091/334373* ⊕ *www.cattedrale.palermo.it* ⊞ *Church free, crypt €2.50* ⊗ *Mon.–Sat. 9:30–1:30 and 2:30–5:30, Sun. 7:30–1:30 and 4–7.*

11 **La Martorana.** Distinguished by an elegant Norman campanile, this church was erected in 1143 but had its interior altered considerably during the baroque period. High along the western wall, however, is some of the oldest and best-preserved mosaic artwork of the Norman period. Near the entrance is an interesting mosaic of King Roger II being crowned by Christ. In it Roger is dressed in a bejeweled Byzantine stole, reflecting the Norman court's penchant for all things Byzantine. Archangels along the ceiling wear the same stole wrapped around their shoulders and arms. The much plainer San Cataldo is next door. ⊠ *Piazza Bellini 3, Quattro Canti* ☎ *091/6161692* ⊗ *Mon.–Sat. 9:15–1 and 3:30–7, Sun. 8:30–1.*

6 **Museo Archeologico Regionale Salinas** (*Salinas Regional Museum of Archaeology*). Especially interesting pieces in this small but excellent collection are the examples of prehistoric cave drawings and a marvelously reconstructed Doric frieze from the Greek temple at Selinunte. The frieze reveals the high level of artistic culture attained by the Greek colonists in Sicily some 2,500 years ago. ⊠*Piazza Olivella 24, Via Roma, Olivella* ☎*091/6116805* 🎫*€6* ⏱*Tues.–Fri. 8:30–1:15 and 3–6:15, Sat.–Mon. 8:30–1:15.*

❸ Palazzo Reale *(Royal Palace).* This historic palace, also called Palazzo dei Normanni (Norman Palace), was for centuries the seat of Sicily's semiautonomous rulers. The building is an interesting mesh of abutting 10th-century Norman and 17th-century Spanish structures. Because it now houses the Sicilian Parliament, little is accessible to the public. The **Cappella Palatina** (Palatine Chapel) remains open. Built by Roger II in 1132, it's a dazzling example of the harmony of artistic elements produced under the Normans. Here the skill of French and Sicilian masons was brought to bear on the decorative purity of Arab ornamentation and the splendor of 11th-century Greek Byzantine mosaics. The interior is covered with glittering mosaics and capped by a splendid 10th-century Arab honeycomb stalactite wooden ceiling. Biblical stories blend happily with scenes of Arab life—look for one showing a picnic in a harem—and Norman court pageantry.

Upstairs are the royal apartments, including the **Sala di Re Ruggero** (King Roger's Hall), decorated with medieval murals of hunting scenes—an earlier (1120) secular counterpoint to the religious themes seen elsewhere. To see this area of the palace, ask one of the tour guides (free) to escort you around the halls once used by one of the most splendid courts in Europe (call in advance if you want to be sure a guide is available). French, Latin, and Arabic were spoken here, and Arab astronomers and poets exchanged ideas with Latin and Greek scholars in one of the most interesting marriages of culture in the Western world. The last tickets are sold a half hour before closing. ⊠*Piazza Indipendenza, Albergheria* ☎*091/7051111* 🎫*€6* ⏱*Palazzo Reale: Mon., Fri., and Sat. 8:30–noon and 2–4:30, Sun. 8:30–12:30. Cappella Palatina: Mon.–Sat. 8:30–noon and 2–4:30, Sun. 8:30–12:30.*

★ ❿ San Cataldo. Three striking Saracenic scarlet domes mark this church, built in 1154 during the Norman occupation of Palermo. The church now belongs to the Knights of the Holy Sepulchre, and has a spare but intense stone interior. If closed, inquire next door at La Martorana. ⊠*Piazza Bellini 3, Kalsa* ☎*091/6375622* 🎫*€1* ⏱*Apr.–Nov., Mon.–Sat. 9:30–1 and 3:30–7, Sun. 9:30–1; Dec.–Mar., Mon.–Sat. 9:30–1.*

❷ San Giovanni degli Eremiti. Distinguished by its five reddish-orange domes and stripped-clean interior, this 12th-century church was built by the Normans on the site of an earlier mosque—one of 200 that once stood in Palermo. The emirs ruled Palermo for nearly two centuries and brought to it their passion for lush gardens and fountains. One is reminded of this while sitting in San Giovanni's delightful cloister of twin half columns, surrounded by palm trees, jasmine, oleander, and citrus trees. The last tickets are sold half an hour before closing. At press time, construction meant half the church was not viewable. ⊠*Via dei Benedettini, Albergheria* ☎*091/6515019* 🎫*€4.50* ⏱*Mon.–Sat. 9–7, Sun. 9–1.*

PALERMO'S MULTICULTURAL PEDIGREE

Palermo was first colonized by Phoenician traders in the sixth century BC, but it was their descendants, the Carthaginians, who built the important fortress here that caught the covetous eye of the Romans. After the First Punic War the Romans took control of the city in the third century BC. Following several invasions by the Vandals, Sicily was settled by Arabs, who made the country an emirate and established Palermo as a showpiece capital that rivaled both Córdoba and Cairo in the splendor of its architecture. Nestled in the fertile Conca d'Oro (Golden Conch) plain, full of orange, lemon, and carob groves and enclosed by limestone hills, Palermo became a magical world of palaces and mosques, minarets and palm trees.

It was so attractive and sophisticated a city that the Norman ruler Roger de Hauteville (1031–1101) decided to conquer it and make it his capital (1072). The Norman occupation of Sicily resulted in Palermo's golden age (1072–1194), a remarkable period of enlightenment and learning in which the arts flourished. The city of Palermo, which in the 11th century counted more than 300,000 inhabitants, became the European center for the Norman court and one of the most important ports for trade between East and West. Eventually the Normans were replaced by the Swabian ruler Frederick II (1194–1250), the Holy Roman Emperor, and incorporated into the Kingdom of the Two Sicilies. You will also see plenty of evidence in Palermo of the baroque art and architecture of the long Spanish rule. The Aragonese viceroys also brought the Spanish Inquisition to Palermo, which some historians believe helped foster the protective secret societies that evolved into today's Mafia.

❺ Teatro Massimo. Construction of this formidable neoclassical theater was started in 1875 by Giovanni Battista Basile and completed by his son Ernesto in 1897. A fire in 1974 rendered the theater inoperable but it reopened with great fanfare in 1997, its interior as glorious as ever. *The Godfather: Part III* ended with a famous shooting scene on the theater's steps. Visits are by 25-minute guided tour only. English-speaking guides are available. ✉ *Piazza Verdi 9, at top of Via Maqueda, Olivella* ☎ *091/6090831* ⊕ *www.teatromassimo.it* 💶 *€5* ⊙ *Tues.–Sun. 10–3.*

ALSO WORTH SEEING

❶ Catacombe dei Cappuccini. The spookiest sight in all of Sicily, this 16th-century catacomb houses more than 8,000 corpses of men, women, and young children, some in tombs but many mummified and preserved, hanging in rows on the walls. Many of the fully clothed corpses wear priests' smocks (most of the dead were Capuchin monks). The Capuchins were founders and proprietors of the bizarre establishment from 1559 to 1880. It's memorable, but not for the faint of heart; children might be frightened or disturbed. ✉ *Piazza Cappuccini off Via Cappuccini, near Palazzo Reale* ☎ *091/212117* 💶 *€1.50* ⊙ *Oct.–May, daily 9–noon and 3–5; June–Sept., daily 9–noon and 4–6*

🤚 ⓭ **Museo delle Marionette.** The traditional Sicilian *pupi* (puppets), with their glittering armor and fierce expressions, have become a symbol of Norman Sicily. Plots of the weekly performances center on the chivalric legends of the troubadours, who, before the puppet theater, kept alive tales of Norman heroes in Sicily such as William the Bad (1120–66). ⊠ *Piazzetta Niscemi 1, at Via Butera, Kalsa* ☎ *091/328060* ⊕ *www.museomarionettepalermo.it* 🎫 *€5* ☉ *Weekdays 9–1 and 3:30–6:30, Sun. 9–1.*

⓬ **Palazzo Abatellis.** Housed in this late-15th-century Catalan Gothic palace with Renaissance elements is the **Galleria Regionale.** Among its treasures are an *Annunciation* (1474) by Sicily's prominent Renaissance master Antonello da Messina (1430–79) and an arresting fresco by an unknown painter, titled *The Triumph of Death,* a macabre depiction of the plague years. ⊠ *Via Alloro 4, Kalsa* ☎ *091/6230011* 🎫 *€6* ☉ *Tues.–Fri. 9–1 and 2:30–7, Sat.–Mon. 9–1.*

❽ **Piazza Pretoria.** The square's centerpiece, a lavishly decorated fountain with 500 separate pieces of sculpture and an abundance of nude figures, so shocked some Palermitans when it was unveiled in 1575 that it got the nickname "Fountain of Shame." It's even more of a sight when illuminated at night.

❼ **Quattro Canti.** The Four Corners is the intersection of Corso Vittorio Emanuele and Via Maqueda. Four rather exhaust-blackened baroque palaces from Spanish rule meet at concave corners, each with its own fountain and representations of a Spanish ruler, patron saint, and one of the four seasons.

❾ **Santa Caterina.** The walls of this splendid baroque church (1596) in Piazza Bellini are covered with decorative 17th-century inlays of precious marble. ⊠ *Piazza Bellini, Quattro Canti* ☎ *091/6162488* ☉ *Apr.–Sept., daily 9:30–1 and 3:30–7; Oct.–Mar., daily 9:30–1.*

WHERE TO EAT

★ $$$–$$$$ ✕ **Osteria dei Vespri.** A foodie paradise occupies a cozy-but-elegant space on an unheralded piazza in the historic city center. Try the superb antipasto *sei variazioni di crudo dal mare* (six variations of raw delicacies from the sea). Sheep's-milk cheese ravioli with basil, fresh tomato, eggplant, and crispy onions adds creative depth to traditional preparation. Local fish is presented in dishes like *cordon bleu di pesce spada* (swordfish stuffed with almonds). The wine list is one of the best in Palermo. ⊠ *Piazza Croce dei Vespri 6, Kalsa* ☎ *091/6171631* ⊕ *www.osteriadeivespri.it* ▭ *AE, DC, MC, V* ☉ *Closed Sun.*

$$$–$$$$ ✕ **Il Ristorantino.** Pippo Anastasio, one of the true personalities of Sicilian cooking, has created one of the most modern restaurants on the island. Here *pesce spada* (swordfish) reaches its loftiest heights, served simply marinated with olive oil, lemon, herb butter, and toast; meanwhile, Pippo's flights of fancy include *astice* (lobster) tortellini with cherry tomatoes, *bottarga* (cured tuna roe), and hot pepper. Dark wood contrasts with recessed lighting and stylized wall panels to create a

design fusion that echoes the creativity of the menu. The suburban restaurant is an easy taxi ride from the center. ✉*Piazzale Alcide De Gasperi 19, Resuttana* ☎*091/512861* 🟰*AE, MC, V* ⊘*Closed Mon. and 2 wks in Aug.*

$$$ ✕ **Piccolo Napoli.** Founded in 1951, Piccolo Napoli is one of Old Pal-
Fodor's Choice   ermo's most esteemed seafood restaurants. Locals come at midday to
★   feast on the freshest of fish. You'll begin with a memorable buffet featuring baby octopus, raw *neonata* (tiny fish resembling sardines, but with a milder flavor), and chickpea fritters. Continue with spaghetti with *ricci* (sea urchin) or casarecce (partially rolled pasta) with swordfish and mint, and finally, the glorious fresh fish or shellfish, roasted or grilled. Depending on the fish you select, the bill can creep up on you, but it's worth every cent. Dinner is only served Friday and Saturday nights between October and June. ✉*Piazzetta Mulino a Vento 4, Borgo Vecchio* ☎*091/320431* 🟰*AE, DC, MC, V* ⊘*Closed Sun. and last 2 wks in Aug. No dinner July–Sept. and Mon.–Thurs. Oct.–June.*

$$$ ✕ **Trattoria Biondo.** It would be hard to argue that the *lasagne al forno* at this traditional local restaurant, located on a convenient block near Politeama, is anything less than the best in Sicily. The baked lasagna is made with perfectly al dente noodles, a wonderfully seasoned ragù, and a silky béchamel, then throws in ham for good measure. The other traditional pasta specialties are also excellent, as are fish dishes. None of the dining rooms is bigger than an oversize pantry, making for a cozy atmosphere. ✉*Via Carducci 15, Libertà* ☎*091/583662* 🟰*AE, MC, V* ⊘*Closed Wed. and Aug.*

$$ ✕ **Casa del Brodo.** On the edge of the Vucciria is a restaurant that dates to 1890, one of Palermo's oldest. In winter, tortellini *in brodo* (in beef broth), the restaurant's namesake, is the specialty of the house. There's an extensive antipasto buffet, and you can't go wrong with the *fritella di fave, piselli, carciofi, e ricotta* (fried fava beans, peas, artichokes, and ricotta). A mix of tourists and locals crowd the two small rooms. ✉*Corso Vittorio Emanuele 175, Vucciria* ☎*091/321655* ⊕*www.casadelbrodo.it* 🟰*AE, DC, MC, V* ⊘*Closed Tues. Nov.–Apr., Sun. May–Oct.*

$$ ✕ **Trattoria Gagini.** In the 15th-century wine cellar of sculptor Antonio Gagini, this restaurant is a great place to escape the chaos of Via Cala and the nearby Vucciria Market. Given the historic location, you might not expect an exciting menu, but the kitchen takes traditional ingredients in interesting modern directions. Highlights include spaghetti *verdi alla chitarra con ragù di triglie e finocchietto* (green spaghetti with a sauce of tomato, red mullet, and wild fennel) and flat tagliatelle noodles in a lamb sauce with shaved Ragusano cheese. ✉*Via dei Cassari 35/37, off Via Cala, Kalsa* ☎*091/321518* ⊕*www.gaginitrattoria.com* 🟰*AE, DC, MC, V* ⊘*Closed Sun. June–Sept. and Mon. Oct.–May. No lunch Mon.–Sat., no dinner Sun. Oct.–May.*

★ **$**   ✕ **Trattoria Altri Tempi.** This "olden days" restaurant is a favorite among locals searching for the rustic dishes served by their ancestors. Knickknacks fill the walls of the small, friendly dining room. A meal begins when the server plunks down a carafe of the house red and a superb spread of traditional antipasti on your table. Dishes have old-fash-

15

ioned names: *fave a cunigghiu* is fava beans prepared with olive oil, garlic, and remarkably flavorful oregano, and *vampaciucia c'anciova* is a lasagne-like dish with a concentrated sauce of tomatoes, anchovies, and grapes. The meal ends well, too, with free house-made herb or fruit liquors and excellent cannoli. ⊠*Via Sammartino 65/67, Libertà* ☎*091/323480* ⊟*AE, DC, MC, V* ☼*Closed mid-Aug.–mid-Sept. and Sun. June–Aug. No dinner Sun.*

★ ¢–$ ✕ **Antica Focacceria San Francesco.** Turn-of-the-20th-century wooden cabinets, marble-top tables, and cast-iron ovens characterize this neighborhood bakery. Come here for the locally beloved snacks that can be combined to make an inexpensive meal. The big pot on the counter holds the delicious regional specialty *pani ca meusa* (boiled calf's spleen with caciocavallo cheese and salt). The squeamish can opt for some chickpea fritters, an enormous *arancino* (deep-fried ball of rice filled with meat), or the outstanding cannoli. ⊠*Via Paternostro 58, Kalsa* ☎*091/320264* ⊟*AE, DC, MC, V* ☼*Closed Tues. Oct.– May and 2 wks mid-Jan.*

¢ ✕ **Pani Ca Meusa.** This supremely local institution facing Palermo's old fishing port has had only one item on the menu—and one legendary manager–cum–sandwich maker—for more than 50 years. Calf's spleen sandwich, the joint's namesake, is sprinkled with a bit of salt and some lemon and served with or without cheese to a buzzing crowd of Palermo's battle-wearied elders. In our book, their sandwich beats the Antica Focacceria San Francesco's for the title of best in town. There's no seating, though—only counters—and the overall menu is better at San Francesco. ⊠*Porta Carbone, Via Cala 62, Kalsa* ☎*No phone* ⌨*Reservations not accepted* ⊟*No credit cards* ☼*Closed Sun. and Mon., and unpredictable other days.*

¢ ✕ **Pizzeria Ai Comparucci.** One of Palermo's best pizzerias doubles as a modern art gallery. The colorful paintings give the place a fun, casual vibe. Better yet are the delicious Neapolitan pizzas coming out of the big oven in the open kitchen. The genius is in the crust, which is seared in the oven in a matter of seconds (so don't expect a long, leisurely meal). The place often serves until midnight—later than almost any other restaurant in the neighborhood. ⊠*Messina 36, between Via Yarzili and Via Libertà, Libertà* ☎*091/6090467* ⊟*AE, MC, V* ☼*Closed Mon.*

WHERE TO STAY

$$$$ 🏠 **Hilton Villa Igiea.** This grand dame, a local landmark for a century, hasn't changed much since becoming a Hilton. You'll have to take a €12 taxi ride over some rough-looking roads to reach this oasis of luxury and comfort, set in a private tropical garden at the edge of the bay. A stroll around the grounds reveals such relics as an ancient Greek temple at the water's edge. Large rooms are individually furnished, the nicest with an art-nouveau flavor. Spacious public rooms unfold onto a terrace and restaurant. **Pros:** Secluded setting, historic building, lots of style. **Cons:** Noise and fumes from nearby marina, service is hit or miss. ⊠*Salita Belmonte 43, 90142 Acquasanta* ⊹*3 km (2 mi) north of Palermo* ☎*091/6312111* ⊕*www.hilton.com* ⤴*110 rooms, 6 suites*

♿ *In-room: safe, ethernet. In-hotel: restaurant, room service, bar, tennis court, pool, gym, parking (no fee)* ☐ *AE, DC, MC, V* ⦿*BP.*

$$$$ 🏨 **Hotel Principe di Villafranca.** Fine Sicilian antiques, imperial striped silks, creamy marble floors, and vaulted ceilings evoke a luxurious private home in the heart of Palermo's glitzy shopping district. It's easy to get comfortable in the understated surroundings: relax in the library with an aperitif or savor an authentic meal in the rustic Hippopotamus, which drizzles some of its dishes with a sublime, homemade balsamic vinegar. Rooms are elegant, with fine linens and more antiques. Ask for a room facing the quieter street side. **Pros:** Helpful staff, well-maintained building, safe neighborhood. **Cons:** Breakable knickknacks make it not suitable for small children, bathrooms are on the small side. ✉ *Via G. Turrisi Colonna 4, Libertà, 90141* 🕿 *091/6118523* ⊕ *www.principedivillafranca.it* ⇆ *32 rooms, 2 suites* ♿ *In-room: safe. In-hotel: restaurant, bar, gym, public Wi-Fi, parking (no fee)* ☐ *AE, DC, MC, V* ⦿*BP.*

★ $$$–$$$$ 🏨 **Centrale Palace Hotel.** A stone's throw from Palermo's main historic sites, the Centrale Palace is the only hotel in the heart of the centro storico that was once a stately private palace. Built in 1717, the hotel weaves old-world charm with modern comfort like few establishments on the island. The "classic" rooms have antiques and well-chosen reproductions, while the slightly pricier "neoclassic" rooms are done in a more-modern style. The young, welcoming staff provides professional service. The rooftop restaurant serves creative Sicilian cuisine. **Pros:** Sparkling clean, good bathrooms, convenient garage parking. **Cons:** Traffic noise, some rooms have no view. ✉ *Corso Vittorio Emanuele 327, Vucciria, 90134* 🕿 *091/336666* ⊕ *www.centralepalacehotel. it* ⇆ *88 rooms, 16 suites* ♿ *In-room: safe (some), refrigerator, ethernet. In-hotel: restaurant, bar, parking (fee)* ☐ *AE, DC, MC, V* ⦿*BP.*

★ $$$ 🏨 **Grande Albergo Sole.** Here's an unusual and exciting concept: reopen a faded century-old hotel building in the gritty old center as a gleaming, ultramodern hotel. The result is an ideal base for exploring Palermo. The expansive rooftop balcony boasts a hot tub and encircles the restaurant and bar in a sleek wood frame that feels almost Scandinavian. Minimalist (for Italy, anyway) rooms have all the modern amenities. The service is friendly. **Pros:** Great rooftop bar and restaurant, very central location. **Cons:** No views from many rooms, charmless decor. ✉ *Corso Vittorio Emanuele 291, Kalsa, 90133* 🕿 *091/6041111* ⊕ *www.angalahotels.it* ⇆ *113 rooms* ♿ *In-room: safe, refrigerator. In-hotel: 2 restaurants, bar, parking (fee)* ☐ *AE, DC, MC, V* ⦿*BP.*

$$$ 🏨 **Massimo Plaza Hotel.** This hotel has one of Palermo's best locations— opposite the renovated Teatro Massimo, on the border of the old and new towns. It is small and select; the rooms are spacious, comfortably furnished, and well insulated from the noise on Via Maqueda. The service is personal and polite, with continental breakfast served in your room with the newspaper of your choice. Book in advance for one of the seven rooms that have theater views. **Pros:** Central location, modern bathrooms. **Cons:** Plain decor, some noisy rooms, breakfast choices are limited. ✉ *Via Maqueda 437, Vucciria, 90133* 🕿 *091/325657* ⊕ *www.*

15

massimoplazahotel.com ⟳*15 rooms* ⛆*In-room: safe, ethernet. In-hotel: bar, parking (fee)* ☰*AE, DC, MC, V* ⦵|*BP.*

$ ⊞ **Le Terrazze.** Though just steps from the bustling streets around the Cattedrale, complete calm envelops this small, beautifully restored B&B. The name refers to its five roof terraces, all of which have sublime views of Palermo's skyline, and where breakfast is served in summer. When you're not on the roof, you can pore over the collection of books about Sicily in the sitting area. The rooms are a major draw, furnished in period style. **Pros:** Convenient location, glorious views from terraces. **Cons:** Parking can be difficult, books up quickly. ⊠*Via Pietro Novelli 14, Capo 90134* ☎*091/6520866* ⊕*www.leterrazzebb. it* ⟳*2 rooms* ⛆*In-room: no phone, refrigerator. In-hotel: no elevator* ☰*No credit cards* ⊗*Closed Nov.* ⦵|*BP.*

NIGHTLIFE & THE ARTS

THE ARTS

CONCERTS & OPERA

Teatro Massimo (⊠*Piazza Verdi at the top of Via Maqueda, Capo* ☎*091/6053111* ⊕*www.teatromassimo.it*), modeled after the Pantheon in Rome, is truly larger than life—it's the biggest theater in Italy. Concerts and operas are presented throughout the year. Live out your *Godfather* fantasies; an opera at the Massimo is an unforgettable Sicilian experience. The box office is open Tuesday to Sunday 10 to 3. The shamelessly grandiose neoclassical **Teatro Politeama Garibaldi** (⊠*Piazza Ruggero Settimo, Libertà* ☎*091/6053315*) stages a season of opera and orchestral works from November through May.

PUPPET SHOWS

☾ Palermo's tradition of puppet theater holds an appeal for children and adults alike. Street artists often perform outside the Teatro Massimo in summer. The **Figli d'Arte Cuticchio Association** (⊠*Via Bara all'Olivella 95, Kalsa* ☎*091/323400* ⊕*www.figlidartecuticchio.com* ☒€8) hosts performances September to July on most weekends at 6:30 PM.

NIGHTLIFE

Each night between 6 and 9, Palermo's youth gather to shop, socialize, flirt, and plan the evening's affairs in an epic passeggiata along Via Ruggero Settimo (a northern extension of Via Maqueda) and filling Piazza Ruggero Settimo in front of Teatro Politeama. Some trendy bars also line Via Principe del Belmonte, intersecting with Via Roma and Via Ruggero Settimo.

BARS & CAFÉS

Kursaal Kalhesa (⊠*Foro Umberto I 21, Kalsa* ☎*091/6162111* ⊕*www. kursaalkalhesa.it*) is one of the most fascinating places to drink or socialize down by the port and the Porta Felice. An energetic, eclectic crowd of Palermitan youth takes in lively jazz, coffee, and drinks inside an ancient city wall with spectacular 100-foot ceilings and an idyllic courtyard—it's truly representative of the New Palermo. Interesting, if pricey, Sicilian food with an Arab touch is served in the adjacent restaurant. Kursaal

Kalhesa is closed Sunday night and Monday. **Mikalsa** (⊠ *Via Torremuzza 27, Kalsa* ☎*339/3146466*) is a hip nightspot boasting Sicily's best selection of Belgian beers. Try the interesting Wild Spirit beer, a painstaking product of one of Sicily's first microbreweries (also available elsewhere around town). **Parco Letterario Giuseppe Tomasi di Lampedusa** (⊠ *Vicolo della Neve all'Alloro 2/5, near Piazza Marina, Kalsa* ☎*091/6160796* ⊕*www.parcotomasi.it*) is a bar, café, language school, and tour operator. The center sponsors concerts, readings, and art shows. The little library (and just about everything else) focuses not just on Palermitan history but on the life and times of the center's namesake, Lampedusa, author of the canonical *Il Gattopardo* (*The Leopard*).

Tinto (⊠ *Via XX Settembre 56/A, at Via Messina, Libertà* ☎*091/582137*) is a sleek establishment serving double duty as a Sicily-centric wine bar and restaurant. The room achieves a sense of effortless grace, with dark furniture and greenery. Come around *aperitivo* time and you'll be treated to free snacks. **Santa Monica** (⊠ *Via E. Parisi 7, Libertà* ☎*091/324735*) is a pub that's immensely popular with the twenty- and thirtysomething crowd, who belly up to the bar for pizza, bruschetta, and, of course, excellent German-style draft beer. It's also a good place to watch soccer.

SHOPPING

North of Piazza Castelnuovo, Via della Libertà and the surrounding streets represent the luxury end of the shopping scale. A second nerve center for shoppers is the pair of parallel streets connecting modern Palermo with the train station, Via Roma, and Via Maqueda, where boutiques and shoe shops become increasingly upmarket as you move from the Quattro Canti past Teatro Massimo to Via Ruggero Settimo.

Most shops are open 9–1 and 4 or 4:30–7:30 or 8 and closed Sunday; in addition, most food shops close Wednesday afternoon, and other shops normally close Monday morning.

FOOD & WINE

Enoteca Picone (⊠ *Via Marconi 36, Libertà* ☎*091/331300* ⊠ *Viale Strasburgo 235, Resuttana* ☎*091/6880357* ⊕*www.enotecapicone.it*) is the best wine shop in town, with a fantastic selection of Sicilian and national wines. Though the service can be curt, you can taste a selection of wines by the glass in the front of the store. There are tables in the back, where meats and cheeses are also served. The branch on Viale Strasburgo offers full meals. Both branches are closed on Sunday. **Pasticceria Alba** (⊠ *Piazza Don Bosco 7/c, off Via della Libertà near La Favorita Park, Libertà* ☎*091/309016* ⊕*www.baralba.it*), one of the most famous sweets shops in Italy, is the place to find favorite pastries such as cannoli and *cassata siciliana* (a rich chilled sponge cake with sheep's-milk ricotta and candied fruit). With a name that means "Mamma Andrea's Small Sins," the charming **I Peccatucci di Mamma Andrea** (⊠ *Via Principe di Scordia 67, near Piazza Florio, Vucciria* ☎*091/334835*) sells a plethora of mouthwatering original creations,

15

including jams, preserves, and Sicilian treats like the superb marzipan *frutta di Martorana.*

MARKETS

If you're interested in truly connecting with local life while searching for souvenirs, a visit to one of Palermo's many bustling markets is essential. Between Via Roma and Via Maqueda the many **bancherelle** *(market stalls)* on Via Bandiera sell everything from socks to imitation designer handbags.

★ It's easy to see how the **Vucciria Market** got its name, which translates in dialect as "voices" or "hubbub." Palermo's most established outdoor market in the heart of the centro storico is a maze of side streets around Piazza San Domenico, where hawkers deliver incessant chants from behind stands brimming with mounds of olives, blood oranges, wild fennel, and long-stem artichokes. One hawker will be going at the trunk of a swordfish with a cleaver while across the way another holds up a giant squid or dangles an octopus. Morning is the best time to see the market in full swing. Wind your way through the Albergheria district and the historic **Ballarò Market,** where the Saracens did their shopping in the 11th century—joined by the Normans in the 12th. The market remains faithful to seasonal change as well as the original Arab commerce of fruit, vegetables, and grain. Go early; the action dies out by 4 PM most days.

THE TYRRHENIAN COAST

Sicily's northern shore, the Tyrrhenian Coast, is mostly a succession of small holiday towns interspersed with stretches of sand. It's often difficult to find a calm spot among the thousands of tourists and locals in high summer, though the scene quiets down considerably after August. The biggest attraction is the old town of Cefalù, with one of Sicily's most remarkable medieval cathedrals, encrusted with mosaics. The coast on either side is dotted with ancient archaeological remains and Arab-Norman buildings. A couple of miles south of Cefalù, Pizzo Carbonara (6,500 feet) is the highest peak in Sicily after Mt. Etna. Piano della Battaglia has a fully equipped ski resort with lifts. The area has a very un-Sicilian aspect, with Swiss-type chalets, hiking paths, and even Alpine churches.

CEFALÙ

★ *70 km (42 mi) east of Palermo, 161 km (80 mi) west of Messina.*

GETTING HERE

Trains and buses run between Palermo and Messina. Drivers can take the A20 autostrada.

VISITOR INFORMATION

Cefalù tourism office (⊠*Corso Ruggero 77, 90015* ☎*0921/421050*).

EXPLORING

Cefalù is a classically appealing Sicilian old town built on a spur jutting out into the sea. It's dominated by a massive rock—*la rocca*—and a 12th-century Romanesque **Duomo,** one of the finest Norman cathedrals in Italy. Ruggero II began the church in 1131 as an offering of thanks for having been saved here from a shipwreck. Its mosaics rival those of Monreale; whereas Monreale's Byzantine Pantocratic Christ figure is an austere and powerful image, emphasizing Christ's divinity, the Cefalù Christ is softer, more compassionate, and more human. The traffic going in and out of Cefalù town can be heavy in summer; you may want to take the 50-minute train ride from Palermo instead of driving. At the Duomo you must be suitably attired—no shorts or beachwear are permitted. ⊠*Piazza Duomo* ☎*0921/922021* ☉*Oct.–Apr., daily 8–noon and 3:30–5; May–Sept., daily 8–7:30.*

15

WHERE TO STAY & EAT

$$–$$$ ✕ **Al Gabbiano.** Its name, which translates "seagull," is an appropriate name for a beachside seafood restaurant with a nautical theme. House specialties are *involtini di pesce spada* (swordfish roulades) and spaghetti *alla marinara* (with mixed shellfish). ⊠*Via Lungomare Giardina 17* ☎*0921/421495* ▭*AE, DC, MC, V* ☉*Closed Nov.–Jan. and Wed. Sept.–June.*

$$–$$$ ✕ **Al Porticciolo.** Nicola Mendolia's restaurant is comfortable, casual, and faithfully focused on the food. You might start with the *calamaretti piccoli fritti* (fried baby squid and octopus) and then follow with one of the chef's specials, which change weekly. Regardless, a refreshing *sgroppino* (whipped lemon sorbet with spumante) should end the meal. Dark, heavy, wooden tables create a comfortable environment filled with a mix of jovial locals and businesspeople. ⊠*Via C. Ortolani di Bordonaro 66* ☎*0921/921981* ▭*AE, DC, MC, V* ☉*Closed Feb. and Wed. Nov.–Apr.*

$$–$$$ ▦ **Kalura.** Caldura, 2 km (1 mi) east along the coast, is where you'll find this modern hotel on a small promontory. You can get here in a few minutes by taxi from Cefalù. Sports facilities keep you from getting too sedentary, and the private beach is ideal for swimming. Rooms are bright and cheerful. **Pros:** Beautiful sea views, good swimming, family-friendly environment. **Cons:** Far from town center, best rooms often reserved, occasionally indifferent service. ⊠*Via V. Cavallaro 13, 90015 Località Caldura* ☎*0921/421354* ⊕*www.hotel-kalura.com* ⬑*72 rooms* ⌂*In-hotel: restaurant, bar, tennis court, pool, beachfront, public Wi-Fi* ▭*AE, DC, MC, V* ☉*Closed Nov.–early Mar.* ❙⊙❙*MAP.*

THE AEOLIAN ISLANDS

Off Sicily's northeast coast lies an archipelago of seven spectacular islands of volcanic origin. The Isole Eolie (Aeolian Islands), also known as the Isole Lipari (Lipari Islands), were named after Aeolus, the Greek god of the winds, who is said to keep all the Earth's winds stuffed in a bag in his cave here. The Aeolians are a world of grottoes and clear-water caves carved by waves through the centuries. Superb snorkeling and scuba diving abound in the clearest and cleanest of Italy's waters. The beautiful people of high society discovered the archipelago years ago—here Roberto Rossellini courted his future wife, the star Ingrid Bergman, in 1950—and you should not expect complete isolation, at least on the main islands. August, in particular, can get unpleasantly overcrowded, and lodging and travel should always be booked as early as possible.

Lipari provides the widest range of accommodations and is a good jumping-off point for day trips to the other islands. Most exclusive are Vulcano and Panarea, the former noted for its black sands and stupendous sunsets (and prices), as well as the acrid smell of its sulfur emissions, whereas the latter is, according to some, the prettiest. Most remarkable is Stromboli (pronounced with the accent on the first syllable) with its constant eruptions, and remotest are Filicudi and Alicudi, where electricity was introduced only in the 1980s. Access to the islands is via ferry and hydrofoil from Milazzo (on Sicily) or from Naples. The bars in the Aeolian Islands, and especially those on Lipari, are known for their granitas of fresh strawberries, melon, peaches, and other fruits. Many Sicilians on the Aeolians (and in Messina, Taormina, and Catania) begin the hot summer days with a granita *di caffè* (a coffee ice topped with whipped cream), into which they dunk their breakfast rolls. You can get one any time of day.

VULCANO

18 km (11 mi) south of Lipari, 25 mins by ferry, 10 mins by hydrofoil; 55 km (34 mi) northwest of Milazzo, 90 mins by ferry.

GETTING HERE

Frequent ferries and hydrofoils arrive here from Milazzo and Lipari.

EXPLORING

True to its name—and the origin of the term—Vulcano has a profusion of fumaroles sending up jets of hot vapor, but the volcano here has long been dormant. Many come to soak in the strong-smelling sulfur springs: when the wind is right, the odors greet you long before you disembark. The island has some of the archipelago's best beaches, though the volcanic black sand can be off-putting at first. You can ascend to the crater (1,266 feet above sea level) on muleback for a wonderful view or take boat rides into the grottoes around the base. From Capo Grillo there is a view of all the Aeolians.

WHERE TO STAY

★ **$$$–$$$$** ⊡ **Les Sables Noirs.** Named for the black sands of the beach in front, this luxury hotel is superbly sited on the beautiful Porto di Ponente. The cool modern furnishings and inviting pool induce a sybaritic mood, and the white-wall guest rooms are tasteful and spacious. The restaurant, naturally, looks out over the bay: sunsets are framed by the towering faraglioni. **Pros:** Stunning beachfront location, nice restaurant. **Cons:** Not as clean as it should be, pesky mosquitoes. ⊠*Porto di Ponente, 98050* ☎*090/9850* ⊕*www.framon-hotels.com* ⟿*45 rooms, 3 suites* ⟨*In-room: safe. In-hotel: restaurant, bar, pool, beachfront* ⊟*AE, MC, V* ⊘*Closed mid-Oct.–Apr.* ⊡*BP.*

LIPARI

37 km (23 mi) north of Milazzo; 2 hrs, 10 mins by ferry; 1 hr by hydro-foil. Milazzo: 41 km (25 mi) west of Messina.

15

GETTING HERE

Ferries and hydrofoils from Milazzo stop here. There's also service from Reggio Calabria and Messina.

VISITOR INFORMATION

Lipari tourism office (⊠*Corso Vittorio Emanuele 202, 98055* ☎*090/9880095* ⊕*www.comunelipari.it*).

EXPLORING

The largest and most developed of the Aeolians, Lipari welcomes you with distinctive pastel-color houses. Fields of spiky agaves dot the northernmost tip of the island, Acquacalda, indented with pumice and obsidian quarries. In the west is San Calogero, where you can explore hot springs and mud baths. From the red-lava base of the island rises a plateau crowned with a 16th-century castle and a 17th-century cathedral.

★ The vast, multibuilding **Museo Archeologico Eoliano** is a terrific museum, with an intelligently arranged collection of prehistoric finds—some dating as far back as 4000 BC—from various sites in the archipelago. ⊠*Via Castello* ☎*090/9880174* ⊡*€6* ⊘*Daily 9–1:30 and 3–7.*

WHERE TO STAY & EAT

★ **$$$** ✕ **Il Filippino.** The views from the flower-strewn outdoor terrace of this restaurant in the upper town are a fitting complement to the superb fare. Founded in 1910, the restaurant is rightly rated one of the archipelago's best. Top choice is seafood: the *zuppa di pesce* (fish soup) and the antipasto platter of smoked and marinated fish are absolute musts. Leave some room for the local version of cassata siciliana, accompanied by sweet Malvasia wine from Salina. ⊠*Piazza Mazzini Lipari* ☎*090/9811002* ⊟*AE, DC, MC, V* ⊘*Closed mid-Nov–late Dec. and Mon. Oct.–Mar.*

$$$$ ⊡ **Gattopardo Park Hotel.** Bright bougainvillea and fiery hibiscus set the tone at this grand villa, and its restaurant has sweeping views of the sea. Guest quarters are in the 19th-century main villa or in whitewashed bungalows in the surrounding tranquil parkland. Public rooms have wood-beam ceilings and rustic-style furnishings. A minibus shuttles between the hotel and Spiagge Bianche, one of Lipari's better beaches. There are also trips around the island, boat excursions to Vulcano and Stromboli, and folklore evenings. Weekly discounts are available. **Pros:** Friendly staff, good recreational facilities, large pool. **Cons:** A bit removed from the port, staff doesn't speak English. ⊠ *Via Diana, 98055* ☏*090/9811035* ⊕*www.gattopardoparkhotel.it* ⤭*53 rooms* ⌂*In-hotel: restaurant, bar, pool* ▤*MC, V* ⊗*Closed Nov.–Mar.* ⦿*MAP.*

PANAREA

18 km (11 mi) north of Lipari, 2 hrs by ferry, 25–50 mins by hydrofoil; 55 km (33 mi) north of Milazzo.

GETTING HERE
Ferries and hydrofoils arrive here from Lipari and Naples.

Panarea has some of the most dramatic scenery of the islands: wild caves carved out of the rock and dazzling flora. The exceptionally clear water and the richness of life on the sea floor make Panarea especially suitable for underwater exploration, though there is little in the way of beaches. The outlying rocks and islets make a gorgeous sight, and you can enjoy the panorama on an easy excursion to the small Bronze Age village at Capo Milazzese.

WHERE TO STAY
$$$$ **La Raya.** This discreet, expensive hotel is perfectly in keeping with the elite style of Panarea, most exclusive of the Aeolian Islands. Public areas, including a broad terrace and an open-air restaurant, are built into a hillside right on the port; the residential area is a 10-minute walk inland, though the rooms still enjoy the serene prospect of the sea and Stromboli from their balconies. The decor is elegant and understated, with Moorish-type hangings and low divans helping to create a tone of serene luxury. Families with young children are asked to book elsewhere. **Pros:** Great views of Stromboli, fashionable ambience. **Cons:** Snooty staff, uphill trudge to rooms, mediocre food. ⊠*San Pietro, 98050* ☏*090/983103* ⊕*www.hotelraya.it* ⤭*30 rooms* ⌂*In-room: safe. In-hotel: restaurant, bar* ▤*AE, DC, MC, V* ⊗*Closed mid-Oct.–mid-Apr.* ⦿*BP.*

STROMBOLI

40 km (25 mi) north of Lipari; 3 hrs, 45 mins by ferry; 65–90 mins by hydrofoil. 63 km (40 mi) north of Milazzo.

GETTING HERE
Ferries and hydrofoils arrive here from Lipari and Naples.

This northernmost of the Aeolians consists entirely of the cone of an active volcano. The view from the sea—especially at night, as an endless stream of glowing red-hot lava flows into the water—is unforgettable. Stromboli is in a constant state of mild dissatisfaction, and every now and then its anger flares up, so authorities insist that you climb to the top (about 3,031 feet above sea level) only with a guide. The round-trip—climb, pause, and descent—usually starting around 6 PM, takes about six hours; the lava is much more impressive after dark. Some choose to camp overnight atop the volcano—again, a guide is essential. The main town has a small selection of reasonably priced hotels and restaurants and a choice of lively clubs and cafés for the younger set. In addition to the island tour, excursions might include boat trips around the naturally battlemented isle of Strombolicchio.

Numerous tour operators have guides that can lead you up Stromboli, among them **Pippo Navigazione** (☎ *090/986135 or 338/9857883*). Rates are around €28 per person for six hours.

FILICUDI

15

30 km (16 mi) west of Salina, 30–60 mins by hydrofoil; 82 km (54 mi) northwest of Milazzo.

GETTING HERE
Ferries and hydrofoils arrive throughout the year from Lipari, and also in summer from Palermo and Cefalù.

Just a dot in the sea, Filicudi is famous for its unusual volcanic rock formations and the enchanting *Grotta del Bue Marino* (Grotto of the Sea Ox). The crumbled remains of a prehistoric village are at Capo Graziano. The island, which is spectacular for walking and hiking and is still a truly undiscovered, restful haven, has a handful of hotels and pensions, and some families put up guests. Car ferries are available only in summer.

WHERE TO STAY

★ $$ **La Canna**. Set on a height above the tiny port, this hotel commands fabulous views of sky and sea from its flower-filled terrace. It's wonderful to wake up to the utter tranquillity that characterizes any stay on this island. Rooms are small but adequate, kept clean and tidy by the friendly family staff. The cooking is quite good, usually centered around the day's catch (half or full board required in peak season). Arrange ahead of time to be collected at the port. **Pros:** Relaxed setting, family-friendly atmosphere, great views. **Con:** An uphill climb from the port. ✉ *Via Rosa 43, 98050* ☎ *090/9889956* ⊕ *www.lacannahotel.it* ⤶ *14 rooms* ♿ *In-room: safe. In-hotel: restaurant, bar, pool, no elevator* ⊟ *MC, V* ⟟⊚*MAP.*

ITALIAN VOCABULARY

	ENGLISH	ITALIAN	PRONOUNCIATION
BASICS			
	Yes/no	Sí/No	see/no
	Please	Per favore	pear fa-**vo**-ray
	Yes, please	Sí grazie	see **grah**-tsee-ay
	Thank you	Grazie	**grah**-tsee-ay
	You're welcome	Prego	**pray**-go
	Excuse me, sorry	Scusi	**skoo**-zee
	Sorry!	Mi dispiace!	mee dis-spee-**ah**-chay
	Good morning/ afternoon	Buongiorno	bwohn-**jor**-no
	Good evening	Buona sera	**bwoh**-na **say**-ra
	Good-bye	Arrivederci	a-ree-vah-**dare**-chee
	Mr. (Sir)	Signore	see-**nyo**-ray
	Mrs. (Ma'am)	Signora	see-**nyo**-ra
	Miss	Signorina	see-nyo-**ree**-na
	Pleased to meet you	Piacere	pee-ah-**chair**-ray
	How are you?	Come sta?	**ko**-may **stah**
	Very well, thanks	Bene, grazie	**ben**-ay **grah**-tsee-ay
	Hello (phone)	Pronto?	**proan**-to
NUMBERS			
	one	uno	**oo**-no
	two	due	**doo**-ay
	three	tre	tray
	four	quattro	**kwah**-tro
	five	cinque	**cheen**-kway
	six	sei	say
	seven	sette	**set**-ay
	eight	otto	**oh**-to
	nine	nove	**no**-vay
	ten	dieci	dee-**eh**-chee
	eleven	undici	**oon**-dee-chee

twelve	dodici	**doe**-dee-cee
thirteen	tredici	**tray**-dee-chee
fourteen	quattordici	kwa-**tore**-dee-chee
fifteen	quindici	**kwin**-dee-chee
sixteen	sedici	**say**-dee-chee
seventeen	diciassete	dee-cha-**set**-ay
eighteen	diciotto	dee-**cho**-to
nineteen	diciannove	dee-cha-**no**-vay
twenty	venti	**vain**-tee
twenty-one	ventuno	vain-**too**-no
twenty-two	ventidue	vain-tee-**doo**-ay
thirty	trenta	**train**-ta
forty	quaranta	kwa-**rahn**-ta
fifty	cinquanta	cheen-**kwahn**-ta
sixty	sessanta	seh-**sahn**-ta
seventy	settanta	seh-**tahn**-ta
eighty	ottanta	o-**tahn**-ta
ninety	novanta	no-**vahn**-ta
one hundred	cento	**chen**-to
one thousand	mille	**mee**-lay
ten thousand	diecimila	dee-eh-chee-**mee**-la

USEFUL PHRASES

Do you speak English?	Parla inglese?	**par**-la een-**glay**-zay
I don't speak Italian	Non parlo italiano	non **par**-lo ee-tal-**yah**-no
I don't understand	Non capisco	non ka-**peess**-ko
Can you please repeat?	Può ripetere?	pwo ree-**pet**-ay-ray
Slowly!	Lentamente!	**len**-ta-men-tay
I don't know	Non lo so	non lo **so**
I'm American	Sono americano(a)	**so**-no a-may-ree-**kah**-no(a)
I'm British	Sono inglese	so-no een-**glay**-zay
What's your name?	Come si chiama?	**ko**-may see kee-**ah**-ma
My name is . . .	Mi chiamo . . .	mee kee-**ah**-mo

What time is it?	Che ore sono?	kay **o**-ray **so**-no
How?	Come?	**ko**-may
When?	Quando?	**kwan**-doe
Yesterday/today/ tomorrow	Ieri/oggi/domani	**yer**-ee/**o**-jee/do-**mah**-nee
This morning/	Stamattina/Oggi	sta-ma-**tee**-na/**o**-jee
afternoon	pomeriggio	po-mer-**ee**-jo
Tonight	Stasera	sta-**ser**-a
What?	Che cosa?	kay **ko**-za
What is it?	Chee cos'é?	kay ko-**zay**
Why?	Perché?	pear-**kay**
Who?	Chi?	kee
Where is . . .	Dov'è . . .	doe-**veh**
the bus stop?	la fermata dell'autobus?	la fer-**mah**-tadel ow-toe-**booss**
the train station?	la stazione?	la sta-tsee-**oh**-nay
the subway?	la metropolitana?	la may-tro-po-lee-**tah**-na
the terminal?	il terminale?	eel ter-mee-**nah**-lay
the post office?	l'ufficio postale?	loo-**fee**-cho po-**stah**-lay
the bank?	la banca?	la **bahn**-ka
the . . . hotel?	l'hotel . . .?	lo-**tel**
the store?	il negozio?	eel nay-**go**-tsee-o
the cashier?	la cassa?	la **kah**-sa
the . . . museum?	il museo . . .?	eel moo-**zay**-o
the hospital?	l'ospedale?	lo-spay-**dah**-lay
the first-aid station?	il pronto soccorso?	Eel **pron**-to so-**kor**-so
the elevator?	l'ascensore?	la-shen-**so**-ray
a telephone?	un telefono?	oon tay-**lay**-fo-no
the restrooms?	Dov'è il bagno?	do-**vay** eel **bahn**-yo
Here/there	Qui/là	kwee/la
Left/right	A sinistra/a destra	a see-**neess**-tra/a **des**-tra
Straight ahead	Avanti dritto	a-**vahn**-tee **dree**-to
Is it near/far?	È vicino/lontano?	ay vee-**chee**-no/lon-**tah**-no
I'd like . . .	Vorrei . . .	vo-**ray**
a room	una camera	**oo**-na **kah**-may-ra
the key	la chiave	la kee-**ah**-vay
a newspaper	un giornale	oon jor-**nah**-lay
a stamp	un francobollo	oon frahn-ko-**bo**-lo
I'd like to buy . . .	Vorrei comprare . . .	vo-**ray** kom-**prah**-ray

How much is it?	Quanto costa?	**kwahn**-toe **coast**-a
It's expensive/ cheap	È caro/economico	ay **car**-o/ ay-ko-**no**-mee-ko
A little/a lot	Poco/tanto	**po**-ko/**tahn**-to
More/less	Più/meno	pee-**oo**/**may**-no
Enough/too (much)	Abbastanza/troppo	a-bas-**tahn**-sa/**tro**-po
I am sick	Sto male	sto **mah**-lay
Call a doctor	Chiama un dottore	kee-**ah**-mah oon doe-**toe**-ray
Help!	Aiuto!	a-**yoo**-toe
Stop!	Alt!	ahlt
Fire!	Al fuoco!	ahl **fwo**-ko
Caution/Look out!	Attenzione!	a-ten-**syon**-ay

DINING OUT

A bottle of . . .	Una bottiglia di . . .	**oo**-na bo-**tee**-lee-ahdee
A cup of . . .	Una tazza di . . .	**oo**-na **tah**-tsa dee
A glass of . . .	Un bicchiere di . . .	oon bee-key-**air**-ay dee
Bill/check	Il conto	eel **cone**-toe
Bread	Il pane	eel **pah**-nay
Breakfast	La prima colazione	la **pree**-ma ko-la-**tsee**-oh-nay
Cocktail/aperitif	L'aperitivo	la-pay-ree-**tee**-vo
Dinner	La cena	la **chen**-a
Fixed-price menu	Menù a prezzo fisso	may-**noo** a **pret**-so **fee**-so
Fork	La forchetta	la for-**ket**-a
I am diabetic	Ho il diabete	o eel dee-a-**bay**-tay
I am vegetarian	Sono vegetariano/a	**so**-no vay-jay-ta-ree-**ah**-no/a
I'd like . . .	Vorrei . . .	vo-**ray**
I'd like to order	Vorrei ordinare	vo-**ray** or-dee-**nah**-ray
Is service included?	Il servizio è incluso?	eel ser-**vee**-tzee-o ay een-**kloo**-zo
It's good/bad	È buono/cattivo	ay **bwo**-no/ka-**tee**-vo

It's hot/cold	È caldo/freddo	ay **kahl**-doe/**fred**-o
Knife	Il coltello	eel kol-**tel**-o
Lunch	Il pranzo	eel **prahnt**-so
Menu	Il menù	eel may-**noo**
Napkin	Il tovagliolo	eel toe-va-lee-**oh**-lo
Please give me . . .	Mi dia . . .	mee **dee**-a
Salt	Il sale	eel **sah**-lay
Spoon	Il cucchiaio	eel koo-kee-**ah**-yo
Sugar	Lo zucchero	lo **tsoo**-ker-o
Waiter/Waitress	Cameriere/ cameriera	ka-mare-**yer**-ay/ ka-mare-**yer**-a
Wine list	La lista dei vini	la **lee**-sta **day**-ee **vee**-nee

Italy
Essentials

There are planners and there are those who, excuse the pun, fly by the seat of their pants. We happily place ourselves among the planners. Our writers and editors try to anticipate all the issues you may face before and during any journey, and then they do their research. This section is the product of their efforts. Use it to get excited about your trip to Italy, to inform your travel planning, or to guide you on the road should the seat of your pants start to feel threadbare.

GETTING STARTED

We're really proud of our Web site: Fodors.com is a great place to begin any journey. Scan Travel Wire for suggested itineraries, travel deals, restaurant and hotel openings, and other up-to-the-minute info. Check out Booking to research prices and book plane tickets, hotel rooms, rental cars, and vacation packages. Head to Talk for on-the-ground pointers from travelers who frequent our message boards. You can also link to loads of other travel-related resources.

■ RESOURCES

ONLINE TRAVEL TOOLS

Currency Conversion Google (⊕www.google.com) does currency conversion. Just type in the amount you want to convert and an explanation of how you want it converted (e.g., "14 Swiss francs in dollars"), and then voilà. **Oanda.com** (⊕www.oanda.com) also allows you to print out a handy table with the current day's conversion rates. **XE.com** (⊕www.xe.com) is a good currency conversion Web site.

Maps Google (⊕www.google.com) can give you a road map, a satellite view of the terrain, or a hybrid of both. The site can also provide you with directions for getting from place to place. **ViaMichelin** (⊕www.viamichelin.com) is easy to use to find a small town or a small street in a large city on a printable map, to get directions for both driving and walking routes, as well as to discover the distances, travel time, and estimated cost to drive from one location to another.

Safety Transportation Security Administration (TSA ⊕www.tsa.gov)

Time Zones Timeanddate.com (⊕www.timeanddate.com/worldclock) can help you figure out the correct time anywhere in the world.

Weather Accuweather.com (⊕www.accuweather.com) is an independent weather-forecasting service with especially good coverage of hurricanes. **Weather.com** (⊕www.weather.com) is the Web site for the Weather Channel.

Other Resources CIA World Factbook (⊕www.odci.gov/cia/publications/factbook/index.html) has profiles of every country in the world. It's a good source if you need some quick facts and figures.

VISITOR INFORMATION

Contacts at Home Italian Government Tourist Board (ENIT ⊠New York ☎212/245–4822 🖨212/586–9249 ⊠Chicago ☎312/644–0990 🖨312/644–3019 ⊠Los

Angeles ☎310/820–0098 🖨310/820–6357).

Tourist Offices in Italy Each city or town has a tourist information office (usually operated by the national Agenzia Per il Turismo (APT) and most of them have Web sites. See contact information at the beginning of town listings throughout this guide.

■ THINGS TO CONSIDER

PASSPORTS & VISAS

U.S. citizens need only a valid passport to enter Italy for stays of up to 90 days.

PASSPORTS

We're always surprised at how few Americans have passports—only 25% at this writing. This number is expected to grow in coming years, when it becomes impossible to reenter the United States from trips to neighboring Canada or Mexico without one. Remember this: a passport verifies both your identity and nationality—a great reason to have one.

U.S. passports are valid for 10 years. You must apply in person if you're getting a passport for the first time; if your previous passport was lost, stolen, or damaged; or if your previous passport has expired and was issued more than 15 years ago or when you were under 16. All children under 18 must appear in person to apply for or renew a passport. Both parents must accompany any child under 14 (or send a notarized statement with their permission) and provide proof of their relationship to the child.

There are 13 regional passport offices, as well as 7,000 passport acceptance facilities in post offices, public libraries, and other governmental offices. If you're renewing a passport, you can do so by mail. Forms are available at passport acceptance facilities and online.

The cost to apply for a new passport is $97 for adults, $82 for children under 16; renewals are $67. Allow six weeks for processing, both for first-time passports and renewals. For an expediting fee of $60 you can reduce this time to about two weeks. If your trip is less than two weeks away, you can get a passport even more rapidly by going to a passport office with the necessary documentation. Private expediters can get things done in as little as 48 hours, but charge hefty fees for their services.

■**TIP**→Before your trip, make two copies of your passport's data page (one for someone at home and another for you to carry separately). Or scan the page and e-mail it to someone at home and/or yourself.

VISAS

When staying for 90 days or less, U.S. citizens are not required to obtain a visa prior to traveling to Italy. If you plan to travel or live in Italy or the European Union for longer than 90 days, you must acquire a valid visa from the Italian consulate serving your state before you leave the United States. Plan ahead because the process of obtaining a visa will take at least 30 days and the Italian government does not accept visa applications submitted by visa expediters.

U.S. Passport Information U.S. Department of State (☎877/487–2778 ⊕www.travel.state.gov/passport).

U.S. Passport Expediters A. Briggs Passport & Visa Expeditors (☎800/806–0581 or 202/338–0111 ⊕www.abriggs.com). **American Passport Express** (☎800/455–5166 or 603/559–9888 ⊕www.americanpassport.com). **Passport Express** (☎800/362–8196 or 401/272–4612 ⊕www.passportexpress.com). **Travel Document Systems** (☎800/874–5100 or 202/638–3800 ⊕www.traveldocs.com). **Travel the World Visas** (☎866/886–8472 ⊕www.world-visa.com).

SHOTS & MEDICATIONS

No immunizations, inoculations, or health certificates are needed to travel in Italy. Bring a supply of your personal medications—enough to cover your entire vacation plus any travel days. Bring a copy of each of your prescriptions in case you lose medications during your stay. *For more information see Health under On the Ground in Italy, below.*

■**TIP**→If you travel a lot internationally—particularly to developing nations—refer to the CDC's *Health Information for International Travel* (aka Traveler's Health Yellow Book). Info from it is posted on the CDC Web site (⊕www.cdc.gov/travel/yb), or you can buy a copy from your local bookstore for $24.95.

Health Warnings National Centers for Disease Control & Prevention (CDC ☎877/394–8747 international travelers' health line ⊕www.cdc.gov/travel). **World Health Organization** (WHO ⊕www.who.int).

BOOKING YOUR TRIP

Italy is an easy destination to plan for without the use of a travel agent. Booking flights, making hotel reservations, and reserving museum tickets are all things that can be done online or by telephone before you leave home.

In certain cases, however, a travel agent can provide specific assistance. Making train reservations online during peak times can be difficult to manage, and a travel agent can help. A travel agent who specializes in Italy may also have contacts with private tour guides for individual and small-group custom tours.

Agent Resources American Society of Travel Agents (☎703/739–2782 ⊕ www. travelsense.org).

Italy Travel Agents Century Travel (☎512/327–8760 ⊕ www.sallywatkins.com). **Ciao Bambino** (☎866/802–0300 ⊕ www. ciaobambino.com). **Select Italy** (☎800/877–1755 ⊕ www.selectitaly.com). **Zurer Travel** (☎202/210–6975 ⊕ www.zurer.com).

▌ ACCOMMODATIONS

Italy has a varied and abundant number of hotels, bed-and-breakfasts, *agriturismi (farm stays),* and rental properties. Throughout the cities and the countryside you can find very sophisticated, luxurious palaces and villas as well as rustic farmhouses and small hotels. Six-hundred-year-old palazzi and converted monasteries have been restored as luxurious hotels, while retaining the original atmosphere. At the other end of the spectrum, boutique hotels inhabit historic buildings using chic Italian design for the interiors. Increasingly, the famed Italian wineries are creating rooms and apartments for three-day to weeklong stays.

The lodgings we list are the cream of the crop in each price category. We always list the facilities that are available, but we don't specify whether they cost extra; when pricing accommodations, always ask what's included and what costs extra. Properties are assigned price categories based on the range between their least and most expensive standard double room at high season (excluding holidays).

Hotels with the designation BP (for Breakfast Plan) at the end of their listing include breakfast in their rate; offerings can vary from coffee and a roll to an elaborate buffet. Those designated EP (European Plan) have no meals included; MAP (Modified American Plan) means you get breakfast and dinner; FAP (Full American Plan) includes all meals.

APARTMENT & HOUSE RENTALS

More and more travelers are turning away from the three-countries-in-two-weeks style of touring and choosing to spend a week in one city or a month in the countryside. Renting an apartment, a farmhouse, or a villa can be economical depending on the number of people in your group and your budget. All are readily available throughout Italy. Most are owned by individuals and managed by rental agents who advertise available properties on the Internet. Many properties are represented by more than one rental agent, and thus the same property is frequently renamed ("Chianti Bella Vista," "Tuscan Sun Home," and "Casa Toscana Sole" are all names of the same farmhouse) on the various Internet rental sites. The rental agent may meet you at the property for the initial check-in or the owner may be present, while the rental agent only handles the online reservation and financial arrangements.

Issues to keep in mind when renting an apartment in a city or town are the neighborhood (street noise and ambience), the availability of an elevator or number of stairs, the furnishings (including pots and pans and linens), and the cost of utilities (are they included in the rental rate?). Inquires about countryside properties should also include how isolated the property is. (Do you have to drive 45 minutes to reach the nearest town?)

Contacts **At Home Abroad** (☎212/421–9165 ⊕www.athomeabroadinc.com). **Barclay International Group** (☎800/845–6636 or 516/364–0064 ⊕www.barclayweb.com). **Drawbridge to Europe** (☎888/268–1148 or 541/482–7778 ⊕www.drawbridgetoeurope. com). **Homes Away** (☎800/374–6637 or 416/920–1873 ⊕www.homesaway.com). **Rent A Villa** (☎800/964–1891 or 206/417–3444 ⊕www.rentavilla.com). **Suzanne B. Cohen & Associates** (☎207/622–0743 ⊕www.villaeurope.com). **Italy Rents** (☎800/844–6939 ⊕www.italyrents.com).**Tuscan House** (☎8 00/844-6939 ⊕www.tuscanhouse.com). **Villas & Apartmen ts Abroad** (☎800/433–3020 or 212/213–6435 ⊕www.vaanyc.com). **Villas International** (☎800/221–2260 or 415/499–9490 ⊕www.villasintl.com). **Villas of Distinction** (☎800/289–0900 or 707/778–1800 ⊕www.villasofdistinction.com). **Wimco** (☎800/449–1553 ⊕www.wimco.com).

CONVENTS & MONASTERIES

Throughout Italy, tourists can find reasonably priced lodging at convents, monasteries, and religious houses. Religious orders usually charge from 30 to 60 euros per person per night for rooms that are clean, comfortable, and convenient. Most have private bathrooms; spacious lounge areas and secluded gardens or terraces are standard features. A Continental breakfast ordinarily comes with the room. Sometimes, for an extra fee, family-style lunches and dinners are available.

Be aware of three issues when considering a convent or monastery stay: most have a curfew of 11 PM or midnight; you need to book in advance, because they fill up quickly; and your best means of booking is usually e-mail or fax—the person answering the phone may not speak English. For a list of convents throughout Italy, go to ⊕www.hospites.it.

FARM HOLIDAYS & AGRITOURISM

Rural accommodations in the *agriturismo* (agricultural tourism) category are increasingly popular with both Italians and visitors to Italy; you stay on a working farm or vineyard. Accommodations vary in size and range from luxury apartments, farmhouses, and villas to very basic facilities. Agriturist has compiled *Agriturism*, which is available only in Italian, but includes more than 1,600 farms in Italy; pictures and the use of international symbols to describe facilities make the guide a good tool. Local APT tourist offices also have information.

Information **Agriturist** (☎06/6852342 ⊕www.agriturist.it). **Agriturismo.net** (⊕www.agriturismo.net). **Italy Farm Holidays** (☎914/631–7880 ᐧ914/631–8831 ⊕www.italyfarmholidays.com). **Italy Tourist: Farm Holiday** (⊕www.italytourist.it).

HOME EXCHANGES

With a direct home exchange you stay in someone else's home while they stay in yours. Some outfits also deal with vacation homes, so you're not actually staying in someone's full-time residence, just their vacant weekend place.

Italians have historically not been as enthusiastic about home exchanges as others have been; however, there are many great villas and apartments in Italy owned by foreigners, such as Americans, who use the home exchange services.

Exchange Clubs **Home Exchange.com** (☎800/877-8723 ⊕www.homeexchange. com); $99 for a one-year online listing. **HomeLink International** (☎800/638-3841 ⊕www.homelink.org); $110 yearly for Web-only membership; $170 includes Web access and two catalogs. **Intervac U.S.** (☎800/756-4663 ⊕www.intervacus.com); $95 for Web-only international membership; $140 includes Web access and a catalog.

HOSTELS

Hostels offer bare-bones lodging at low, low prices—often in shared dorm rooms with shared baths—to people of all ages, though the primary market is young travelers, especially students. Most hostels serve breakfast; dinner and/or shared cooking facilities may also be available. In some hostels you aren't allowed to be in your room during the day, and there may be a curfew at night. Nevertheless, hostels provide a sense of community, with public rooms where travelers often gather to share stories. Many hostels are affiliated with Hostelling International (HI), an umbrella group of hostel associations with some 4,500 member properties in more than 70 countries. Other hostels are independent and may be nothing more than a really cheap hotel.

Membership in any HI association, open to travelers of all ages, allows you to stay in HI-affiliated hostels at member rates. One-year membership is about $28 for adults; hostels charge about $20–$40 per night. Members have priority if the hostel is full; they're also eligible for discounts around the world, even on rail and bus travel in some countries.

Hostels in Italy run the gamut from low-end hotels to beautiful villas. In Florence, the campground and hostel near Piazzale Michelangelo has a better view of the city than any luxury hotel in town.

Information Hostelling International—USA (☎ 301/495–1240 national office, check online for the phone number of the office in your state ⊕ www.hiusa.org). **Hostel World** (⊕ www.hostelworld.com). **Ostelli on Line** (☎ 06/48907740 ⊕ www.ostellionline.org).

▌ RENTAL CARS

When you reserve a car, ask about cancellation penalties, taxes, drop-off charges (if you're planning to pick up the car in one city and leave it in another), and surcharges (for being under or over a certain age, for additional drivers, or for driving across state or country borders or beyond a specific distance from your point of rental). All these things can add substantially to your costs. Request child car seats and extras, such as GPS, when you book.

Rates are sometimes—but not always—better if you book in advance or reserve through a rental agency's Web site. There are other reasons to book ahead, though: for popular destinations, during busy times of the year, or to ensure that you get certain types of cars (vans, SUVs, exotic sports cars).

▌TIP→Make sure that a confirmed reservation guarantees you a car. Agencies sometimes overbook, particularly for busy weekends and holiday periods.

Renting a car in Italy is helpful for exploring the countryside, but not if you plan to stick to the cities. The Italian countryside has an intricate network of *autostrade* routes (toll highways), good highways, and secondary roads, making renting a car a better but expensive alternative (because of high gas prices and freeway tolls) to public transportation. A rental car can be a good investment for carefree countryside rambles, offering time to explore more-remote towns. Signage on country roads is usually good, but be prepared for fast and impatient fellow drivers.

Having a car in major cities, however, often leads to parking and traffic headaches, plus the additional expense of garage and parking fees. In major cities, such as Rome, Milan, Florence, and Siena, there are restricted zones for cars. These areas are monitored by camera. If you have to drive to your hotel in the city center of these cities, inquire at the front desk of your hotel as to whether your rental car's license tag number must be submitted by the hotel to the police or traffic authority. Failure to do this may result in a large fine being levied on your car-rental company and passed on to you at a later date.

Fiats and Fords in a variety of sizes are the most typical rental cars. Remember that most Italian cars have standard transmission. If you want to rent an automatic, be specific when you reserve the car. Higher rates will apply.

Most American chains have affiliates in Italy, but the rates are usually lower if you book a car before you leave home. A company's rates are the same throughout the country: you will not save money, for example, if you pick up a vehicle in a city rather than at an airport.

In Italy a U.S. driver's license is acceptable to rent a car, but consider getting an International Driver's Permit (IDP). Italy, by law at least, requires non-Europeans to carry an IDP along with their domestic license because the IDP states in Italian (and a dozen other languages) that your license is valid. In practice, it depends on the police officer who pulls you over whether you will be penalized for not carrying the IDP. Check the AAA Web site for more info as well as for information on obtaining an IDP ($15).

In Italy you must be 18 years old to drive a car. Most rental companies will not rent to someone under age 21 and also refuse to rent any car larger than an economy or subcompact car to anyone under age 23, and, further, require customers under age 23 to pay by credit card. Additional drivers must be identified in the contract and must qualify with the age limits. There may be an additional daily fee for more than one driver. Upon rental, all companies require credit cards as a warranty; to rent bigger cars (2,000 cc or more), you must often show two credit cards. There are no special restrictions on senior citizen drivers. Book car seats, required for children under age three, in advance (the cost is generally about €36 for the duration of the rental).

Hiring a car with a driver can come in handy, particularly if you plan to do some wine tasting or drive along the Amalfi Coast. Ask at your hotel for recommended drivers, or inquire at the local tourist office. Drivers are paid by the day, and are usually rewarded with a tip of about 15% upon completion of the journey.

CAR-RENTAL INSURANCE

All rental agencies operating in Italy require that you buy CDW and a theft-protection policy, but those costs will already be included in the rates you are quoted. Be aware that coverage may be denied if the named driver on the rental contract is not the driver at the time of the incident. In Sicily there are some roads for which rental agencies deny coverage; ask in advance if you plan to travel in remote regions. Also ask your rental company about other included coverage when you reserve the car and/or pick it up.

▌ TRAIN PASSES

If you plan to travel by rail, know that there are many different train passes available to help you save money. Some require purchase before you leave home, while others can be bought when you arrive in Italy. Both Eurail Passes and the Eurail Italy Pass require advance purchase in the United States. If Italy is your only destination in Europe, **consider purchasing a Eurail Italy Pass** (aka Trenitalia Pass or Italian Flexi Rail Card), which allows a limited number of travel days within one month. Four days of travel cost $278 (first class) or $223 (second class); additional days cost $30 (first class) or $25 (second class). If you are traveling with others, you should consider the discounted **Italian Flexi Rail Card Saver** (aka Trenitalia Pass Saver), which allows a limited number of travel days within one month for groups of two to five people. Four days of travel, for instance, cost $238 (first class) or $190 (second class); additional days are $27 (first class) and $20 (second class).

Italy is one of 17 countries that accept Eurail Pass, which allows unlimited first-class travel. Order the passes online before you leave for Europe. If you plan to rack up the miles, get a standard Eurail Pass.

The Eurail Select Pass allows for travel in three to five contiguous countries. In addition to standard Eurail Passes, ask about special plans. Among these are the Eurail Youth Pass (for those under 26), the Eurail Flexipass (which allows a certain number of travel days within a set period), the Eurail Saver Flexipass (which gives a discount for two or more people traveling together), and the Eurail Drive Pass (which combines travel by train and rental car).

Remember that you need to reserve seats even if you are using a rail pass. *For more information on traveling by rail in Italy, see By Train in Transportation, below.*

Contacts **Europe on Rail** (☎866/858–6854 ⊕ www.europeonrail.com). **Rail Europe** (☎800/438–7245 or 877/257–2887 ⊕www. raileurope.com). **RailPass** (☎877/724–5727 ⊕www.railpass.com).

∎ GUIDED TOURS

Guided tours are a good option when you don't want to do it all yourself. You travel along with a group (sometimes large, sometimes small), stay in prebooked hotels, eat with your fellow travelers (the cost of meals sometimes included in the price of your tour, sometimes not), and follow a schedule. But not all guided tours are an if-it's-Tuesday-this-must-be-Belgium experience. A knowledgeable guide can take you places that you might never discover on your own, and you may be pushed to see more than you would have otherwise. Tours aren't for everyone, but they can be just the thing for trips to places where making travel arrangements is difficult or time consuming (particularly when you don't speak the language). Whenever you book a guided tour, find out what's included and what isn't. A "land-only" tour includes all your travel (by bus, in most cases) in the destination, but not necessarily your flights to and from or even within it. Also, in most cases prices in tour brochures don't include fees and taxes. And remember that you'll be expected to tip your guide (in cash) at the end of the tour.

Also keep in mind that every province and city in Italy has tour guides licensed by the government. Some are eminently qualified in relevant fields such as architecture and art history; others have simply managed to pass the test. Many local guides have Web sites: check online before you leave home. Tourist offices and hotel concierges, also, can provide the names of knowledgeable local guides and the rates for certain services. Before you hire a local guide, ask about their background and qualifications and make sure you can understand each other. Tipping is appreciated, but not obligatory, for local guides.

Recommended Generalists **Abercrombie & Kent** (☎800/554–7016 ⊕www.abercrombiekent.com). **CIE Tours International** (☎800/243–8687 ⊕www.cietours.com). **Maupin Tour** (☎800/255–4266 ⊕www.maupintour.com). **Perillo Tours** (☎800/431–1515 ⊕www.perillotours.com). **Travcoa** (☎866/591–0070 ⊕www.travcoa.com).

Biking & Hiking Tour Contacts **Backroads** (☎800/462–2848 ⊕www.backroads.com). **Butterfield & Robinson** (☎866/551–9090 ⊕www.butterfield.com). **Ciclismo Classico** (☎800/866–7314 ⊕www.ciclismoclassico.com).

Culinary Tour Contact **Epiculinary** (☎888/380–9010 ⊕www.epiculinary.com).

Golf Tour Contact **Rosso Soave** (*☎039/0552305210 ⊕www.rossosoave.com*). **Tuscany Golf & Tourism** (*☎039/0574600269 ⊕www.tuscanygolftourism.com*).

Volunteer Programs **Elderhostel** (☎800/454–5768 ⊕www.elderhostel.com).

Wine Tour Contacts **Cellar Tours** (☎034/915–213–939 ⊕www.cellartours.com). **Food & Wine Trails** (☎800/367–5348 ⊕www.foodandwinetrails.com).

TRANSPORTATION

It is not difficult to see two or three diverse parts of Italy in a one-week vacation because of the ease of travel by car on the fast freeway system, via the comprehensive railway with the speedy Eurostar trains, and lastly, by air from the two major airports in Milan and Rome to the smaller efficient airports serving Venice, Florence, Pisa, Naples, and Palermo. While you are planning your itinerary, remember that Italy is a long narrow country and that you don't want to spend your entire vacation in transit. When traveling by car along the smaller country roads or by train on local lines that stop at every station, it will probably take you longer than you think to get from place to place.

▮ BY AIR

Air travel to Italy is frequent and virtually problem-free, except for airport- or airline-related union strikes that may cause delays. Alitalia, Italy's national flag carrier, has the most nonstop flights to Rome and Milan. Many travelers to Florence and Tuscany find it much more convenient to bypass the Rome and Milan airports and fly to Florence or Pisa. The airport in Venice also caters to international carriers.

Flying time to Milan or Rome is approximately 8–8½ hours from New York, 10–11 hours from Chicago, and 11½ hours from Los Angeles.

Confirm flights within Italy the day before travel. Labor strikes are frequent and can affect not only air travel, but also the local trains that serve the airport. Your airline will have information about strikes directly affecting its flight schedule. If you are taking a train to get to the airport, check with the local tourist agency or rail station about upcoming strikes.

Airline Security Issues Transportation Security Administration (⊕ www.tsa.gov) has answers for almost every question that might come up.

Contact Italy Air Travel Resources A helpful Web site for information (location, phone numbers, local transportation, etc.) about all of the airports in Italy is ⊕ www.travel-library.com.

AIRPORTS

The major gateways to Italy include Rome's Aeroporto Leonardo da Vinci (FCO), better known as Fiumicino, and Milan's Aeroporto Malpensa (MIL). Most flights to Venice, Florence, and Pisa make connections at Fiumicino and Malpensa or another European airport. You can also take the FS airport train to Rome's Termini station or a bus to Milan's central train station (Centrale) and catch a train to any other location in Italy. It will take about one hour to get from either Fiumicino or Malpensa to the appropriate train station.

Alitalia and other European carriers fly into the smaller airports. Venice is served by Aeroporto Marco Polo (VCE), Naples by Aeroporto Capodichino (NAP), and Palermo by Aeroporto Punta Raisi (PMO). Florence is serviced by Aeroporto A. Vespucci (FLR), which is also called Peretola, and by Aeroporto Galileo Galilei (PSA), which is about a mile outside the center of Pisa and about one hour from Florence. The train to Florence stops within 100 feet of the entrance to the Pisa airport terminal.

Italy's major airports are not known for being new, fun, or efficient. Airports in Italy have been ramping up security measures, which include random baggage inspection and bomb-detection dogs. All of the airports have restaurants and snack bars, and there is Internet access. Each airport has at least one nearby hotel. In the case of Florence and Pisa, the city centers are only a 15-minute taxi ride

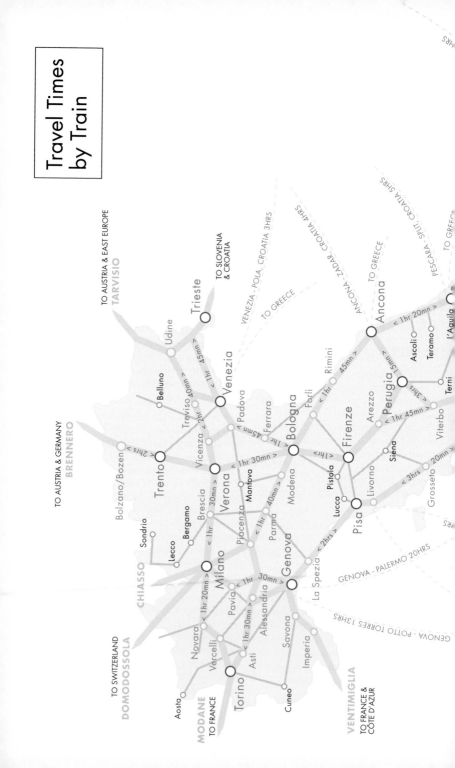

Travel Times by Train

TO AUSTRIA & GERMANY
BRENNERO

TO AUSTRIA & EAST EUROPE
TARVISIO

TO SLOVENIA & CROATIA

Trieste

Udine

< 1hr 45mn >

Belluno

< Treviso 40mn >

Venezia

Vicenza 2hr >

Padova

TO SWITZERLAND
DOMODOSSOLA

Bolzano/Bozen

< 2hrs >

Trento

Sondrio

Bergamo

Brescia

< 1hr 30mn >

Verona

Mantova

< 40mn >

Modena

Ferrara

< 1hr 45mn >

Bologna

Forlì

Rimini

< 1hr 45mn >

< 1hr >

Firenze

Arezzo

TO GREECE

Ancona

< 1hr 20mn >

Ascoli

Teramo

L'Aquila

PESCARA - SPLIT, CROATIA 5HRS

TO GREECE

Perugia

< 15mn >

< 3hrs >

Terni

< 1hr 45mn >

Viterbo

< 20mn >

Grosseto

ANCONA - ZADAR, CROATIA 4HRS

VENEZIA - POLA, CROATIA 3HRS

TO GREECE

Lecco

< 1hr 20mn >

Milano

< 1hr 30mn >

< 1hr 30mn >

Pavia

Piacenza

< 1hr >

Parma

Novara

Vercelli

Asti

Alessandria

< 1hr 30mn >

Genova

< 1hr 30mn >

La Spezia

< 2hrs >

Pisa

Lucca

Pistoia

Livorno

Siena

< 3hrs >

GENOVA - PALERMO 20HRS

GENOVA - PORTO TORRES 13HRS

Aosta

Savona

Imperia

Cuneo

Torino

CHIASSO

MODANE
TO FRANCE

VENTIMIGLIA
TO FRANCE & CÔTE D'AZUR

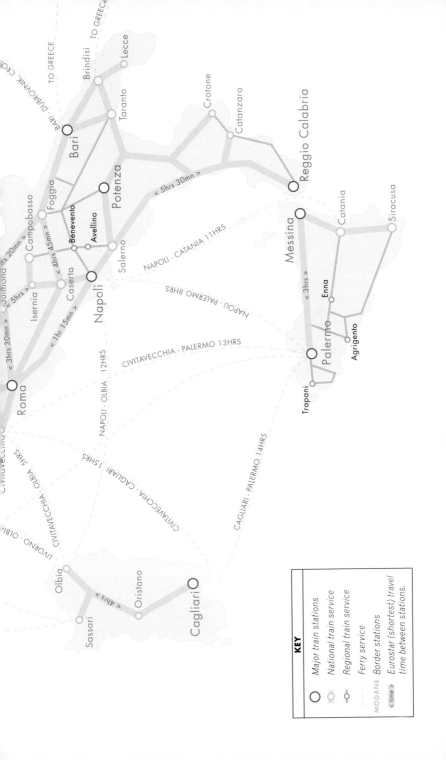

KEY

○ Major train stations

National train service

Regional train service

--- Ferry service

MODANE Border stations

< time > Eurostar (shortest) travel time between stations.

away—so if you encounter a long delay, spend it in town.

When you take a connecting flight from a European airline hub (Frankfurt or Paris, for example) to a local Italian airport (Florence or Venice), be aware that your luggage might not make it onto the second plane with you. The airlines' lost-luggage service is efficient, however, and your delayed luggage is usually delivered to your hotel or holiday rental within 12 to 24 hours.

Departure taxes from Italian destinations are included in the price of your airline ticket.

Airport Information **Aeroporto A. Vespucci** (FLR, also called Peterola ✈6 km [4 mi] north-west of Florence ☎055/3061300 ⊕www. aeroporto.firenze.it). **Aeroporto di Venezia** (VCE, also called Marco Polo ✈6 km [4 mi] from Venice ☎041/2609240 ⊕www.ven-iceairport.it). **Aeroporto Galileo Galilei** (PSA ✈2 km [1 mi] south of Pisa, 80 km [50 mi] west of Florence ☎050/849300 ⊕www.pisa-airport.com). **Aeroporto Leonardo da Vinci** (FCO, also called Fiumicino ✈35 km [20 mi] southwest of Rome ☎06/65951 ⊕www.adr. it). **Aeroporto Malpensa** (MIL ✈45 km [28 mi] north of Milan ☎02/74852200 ⊕www. sea-aeroportimilano.it). **Naples International Airport** (NAP, also called Capodichino ✈7 km [4 mi] northeast of Naples ☎081/7896272 ⊕www.naples-airport.com). **Palermo International Airport** (PMO, also called Punt Raisi ✈32 km [19 mi] northwest of Palermo ☎050/500707 ⊕www.gesap.it).

FLIGHTS

When flying internationally, you must usually choose between a domestic carrier, the national flag carrier of the country you are visiting (Alitalia for Italy), and a foreign carrier from a third country. National flag carriers have the greatest number of nonstops. Domestic carriers may have better connections to your hometown and serve a greater number of gateway cities. Third-party carriers may have a price advantage.

On flights from the United States, Alitalia and Delta Air Lines serve Rome, Milan, and Venice. The major international hubs in Italy, Milan and Rome are also served by Continental Airlines and American Airlines, and US Airways serves Rome. From April through October, the Italy-based EuroFly has nonstop flights from New York to Rome, Naples, Bologna, and Palermo.

Alitalia and British Airways have direct flights from London to Milan, Venice, Rome, and 10 other locations in Italy. Smaller, no-frills airlines also provide service between Great Britain and Italy. EasyJet connects Gatwick with Milan, Venice, Rome, and Bologna. British Midland connects Heathrow and Milan (Linate), Naples, and Venice. Ryanair, departing from London's Stansted airport, flies to Milan, Rome, Pisa, and Venice. Meridiana has flights between Gatwick and Olbia on Sardinia in summer, and flights to Rome and Florence throughout the year.

Tickets for flights within Italy, on Alitalia and small carriers, such as EuroFly, Meridiana, and Air One, cost less when purchased from agents within Italy. Tickets are frequently sold at discounted prices, so check the cost of flights, even one-way, as an alternative to train travel.

Airline Contacts **Alitalia** (☎800/223–5730 in U.S., 06/65641 in Rome, 848/865641 elsewhere in Italy ⊕www.alitalia.it). **American Airlines** (☎800/433–7300, 02/69682464 in Milan ⊕www.aa.com). **British Airways** (☎800/403–0882 in U.S., 06/52492800 in Italy ⊕www.britishairways.com). **British Midland** (☎0807/6070–222 for U.K. reservations, 1332/64–8181 callers outside U.K. ⊕www.flybmi.com). **Continental Airlines** (☎800/523–3273 for U.S. reservations, 800/231–0856 for international reservations, 02/69633256 in Milan, 800/296230 elsewhere in Italy ⊕www.continental.com). **Delta Air Lines** (☎800/221–1212 for U.S. reservations, 800/241–4141 for international reservations, 06/65954406 in Italy ⊕www.delta.com). **Easy-**

Jet (☎0870/607–6543 in U.K., 848/887766 in Italy ⊕www.easyjet.com). **EuroFly** (☎800/459–0581 in U.S., 199/509960 in Italy ⊕www.euroflyusa.com). **Northwest Airlines** (☎800/225–2525 ⊕www.nwa.com). **Ryanair** (☎08701/56–569 in U.K., 199/114114 in Italy ⊕www.ryanair.com). **United Airlines** (☎800/864–8331 for U.S. reservations, 800/538–2929 for international reservations ⊕www.united.com). **US Airways** (☎800/428–4322 for U.S. reservations, 800/622–1015 for international reservations, 848/813177 in Italy ⊕www.usairways.com).

National Carriers Air One (☎06/488800 in Rome, 800/900966 elsewhere in Italy ⊕www.flyairone.it). **Meridiana** (☎199/111333 in Italy ⊕www.meridiana.it).

▌ BY BUS

Italy's regional bus network, often operated by private companies, is extensive, although buses are not as attractive an option as in other European countries, partly because of cheap, convenient train travel. Schedules are often drawn up with commuters and students in mind and may be sketchy on weekends. Regional bus companies often provide the only means (not including car travel) of getting to out-of-the-way places. Even when this isn't the case, buses can be faster and more direct than local trains, so it's a good idea to compare bus and train schedules. SITA operates throughout Italy; Lazzi Eurolines operates in Tuscany and central Italy.

Most of the major cities in Italy have urban bus services. These buses are inexpensive, but they can become jammed, particularly at rush hours.

No buses permit smoking, and both public and private buses offer only one class of service. Cleanliness and comfort levels are high on private buses, which have plenty of legroom and comfortable seats, but no toilets. Private bus lines usually have a ticket office in town or allow you to pay when you board. When traveling on city buses, you must buy your ticket from a machine, newsstand, or tobacco shop and stamp it after you board.

Bus Information ATAC (⊠Rome ☎800/431784 or 06/46952027 ⊕www.atac.roma.it [info not in English]). **ATAF** (⊠Stazione Centrale di Santa Maria Novella, Florence ☎055/5650642 or 055/5650222 ⊕www.ataf.net). **Lazzi Eurolines** (⊠Via Mercadante 2, Florence ☎055/363041 ⊕www.lazzi.it). **SITA** (⊠Via Santa Caterina da Siena 17/r, Florence ☎055/214721 ⊕www.sitabus.it).

▌ BY CAR

Italy has an extensive network of autostrade, complemented by equally well-maintained but free *superstrade* (expressways). Save the ticket you are issued at an autostrada entrance, as you need it to exit; on some shorter autostrade, you pay the toll when you enter. Viacards, on sale for €25 at many autostrada locations, allow you to pay for tolls in advance. At special lanes you simply slip the card into a designated slot.

An *uscita* is an "exit." A *raccordo* is a ring road surrounding a city. *Strade regionale* and *strade provinciale* (regional and provincial highways, denoted by *S, SS, SR,* or *SP* numbers) may be two-lane roads, as are all secondary roads; directions and turnoffs aren't always clearly marked.

GASOLINE

Gas stations are located along the main highways. Those on autostrade are open 24 hours. Otherwise, gas stations generally are open Monday–Saturday 7–7, with a break at lunchtime. At self-service gas stations the pumps are operated by a central machine for payment, which doesn't take credit cards; accepts only bills in denominations of 5, 10, 20, and 50 euros; and does not give change. Those with attendants accept cash and credit cards. It's not customary to tip the attendant.

At this writing, gasoline (*benzina*) costs about €1.40 per liter and is available in unleaded (*verde*) and super-unleaded (*super*). Many rental cars in Italy use diesel (*gasolio*), which costs about €1.10 per liter (ask about the fuel type for your rental car before you leave the agency).

PARKING

Parking is at a premium in most towns, especially in the *centri storici* (historic centers). Fines for parking violations are high, and towing is common. Don't think about tearing up a ticket, as car-rental companies can use your credit card to be reimbursed for any fines you incur. It's a good idea to park in a designated (and preferably attended) lot. And don't leave valuables in your car, as thieves often target rental cars.

In congested cities, indoor parking costs €23–€30 for 12–24 hours; outdoor parking costs about €10–€20. Parking in an area signposted *zona disco* (disk zone) is allowed for short periods (from 30 minutes to 2 hours or more—the time is posted); if you don't have a cardboard disk (check in the glove box of your rental car) to show what time you parked, you can use a piece of paper. The *parcometro*, a central parking meter that, after coins are inserted, prints a ticket that you leave on your dashboard, has been introduced in most metropolitan areas.

ROAD CONDITIONS

Autostrade are well maintained, as are most interregional highways. Most autostrade have two lanes in both directions; the left lane is used only for passing. Italians drive fast and are impatient with those who don't, so tailgating (and flashing with bright beams to signal an intent to pass) is the norm here; the only way to avoid it is to get out of the way.

The condition of provincial (county) roads varies, but road maintenance at this level is generally good in Italy. In many small hill towns the streets are winding and extremely narrow; consider

parking at the edge of town and exploring on foot.

Driving on the back roads of Italy isn't difficult as long as you're on the alert for bicycles and passing cars. In addition, street and road signs are often missing or placed in awkward spots, so a good map and patience are essential.

Be aware that some maps may not use the *SR* or *SP* (*strade regionale* and *strade provinciale*) highway designations, which took the place of the old *SS* designations in 2004. They may use the old *SS* designation or no numbering at all.

ROADSIDE EMERGENCIES

Automobile Club Italiano offers 24-hour road service. English-speaking operators are available. Your rental-car company may also have an emergency tow service with a toll-free call. Be prepared to tell the operator which road you're on, the *verso* (direction) you're headed, and your *targa* (license plate number). Also, in an emergency, call the police (113).

When you're on the road, always carry a good road map, a flashlight, and, if possible, a cellular phone for emergencies. On the autostrade and superstrade, emergency phones are available. To find the nearest one, look on the pavement for painted arrows and the term "SOS."

Emergency Services Automobile Club Italiano (ACI ☎803/116 emergency service ⊕www.aci.it).

RULES OF THE ROAD

Driving is on the right. Speed limits are 110 kph (70 mph) on autostrade and 100 kph (60 mph) on state and provincial roads, unless otherwise marked. Right turns on red lights are forbidden. Headlights are required to be on while driving on all roads (large or small) outside of municipalities. You must wear seat belts and strap young children into car seats at all times. Using handheld mobile phones while driving is illegal; fines can exceed €100. In most Italian towns the use of the horn is forbidden in many areas; a large sign, *zona di silenzio*, indicates a no-honking zone.

The blood-alcohol content limit for driving is 0.5 gr (stricter than U.S. limits) with fines up to €5,000 for surpassing the limit and the possibility of six months' imprisonment. Although enforcement of laws varies depending on the region, fines for speeding are uniformly stiff: 10 kph over the speed limit can warrant a fine of up to €500; greater than 10 kph, and your license could be taken away from you. The police have the power to levy on-the-spot fines.

▌ BY TRAIN

In Italy, traveling by train is simple and efficient. Service between major cities is frequent, and trains usually arrive on schedule. *For information on train passes which must be purchased before you leave home, see Train Passes in Booking Your Trip, above.*

The fastest trains on the Ferrovie dello Stato (FS), the Italian State Railways, are the Eurostar trains that run between major cities. A high-speed Eurostar called Alta Velocità runs between Rome and Naples and is also planned for Florence, Bologna, Venice, and Milan in the future. Seat reservations are mandatory on the Eurostar trains. You will be assigned a specific seat in a specific coach. To avoid having to squeeze through narrow aisles, board only at your designated coach (the number on your ticket matches the one near the door of each coach).

The next-fastest trains are the *Intercity* (IC) trains. Reservations, required for some IC trains, are always advisable. *Diretto* and *Interregionale* trains make more stops and are a little slower. *Regionale* and *locale* trains are the slowest; many serve commuters. There are refreshments on all long-distance trains, purchased from a mobile cart or a dining car.

Most Italian trains have first and second classes. On local trains a first-class fare gets you little more than a clean doily on your headrest, but on long-distance trains you get wider seats, more legroom, and better ventilation and lighting. At peak travel times, a first-class fare is worth the price as the coaches are less crowded. In Italian, *prima classe* is first class; second is *seconda classe*.

Some cities—Milan, Turin, Genoa, Naples, Florence, and Rome included—have more than one train station, **so be sure you get off at the right place.** When buying train tickets be particularly aware that in Rome and Florence some trains do not stop at all of the cities' train stations and may not stop at the main central station. This is a common occurrence with regional and some Intercity trains. When scheduling train travel on the Internet or through a travel agent, be sure to request a train that goes to the train station closest to your destination in Rome and Florence.

Except for Pisa and Rome, none of the major cities have trains that go directly to the airports, but there are commuter bus lines connecting train stations and airports.

You can pay for your train tickets in cash or with a major credit card such as American Express, Diners Club, MasterCard, and Visa. Always purchase tickets before boarding the train, as you cannot purchase one from a conductor. Fines are steep for passengers without tickets. Trains can be very crowded, so it's always a good idea to make a reservation. You can reserve seats up to two months in advance at the train station or at an Italian travel agency displaying the FS emblem. Remember that you need to reserve seats even if you are using a rail pass. In summer it's fairly common to see people standing for part of the journey.

You must validate your ticket before boarding the train by punching it at a yellow box located in the waiting area of smaller train stations or at the end of the track in larger stations.

Train strikes of various kinds are also common, so it's a good idea to make sure your train is running.

Traveling by night is a good deal, as you do not pay extra for a hotel bed. More-comfortable trains run on the longer routes (Sicily–Rome, Sicily–Milan, Sicily–Venice, Rome–Turin, Lecce–Milan); ask for the good-value T3 (three single beds), Intercity Notte, and Carrozza Comfort.

The Vagone Letto Excelsior has private bathrooms and suites with a double bed or two single beds.

Information **Trenitalia** (☎892021 in Italy ⊕www.trenitalia.com).

Information & Passes *See Train Passes in Booking Your Trip, above.*

■TIP➔Ask the local tourist board about hotel and local transportation packages that include tickets to major museum exhibits or other special events.

ON THE GROUND

■ COMMUNICATIONS

INTERNET

Getting online in Italian cities isn't difficult: public Internet stations and Internet cafés, some open 24 hours, are becoming more and more common. Prices differ from place to place, so spend some time to find the best deal. This isn't always readily apparent: a place might appear to have higher rates, but if it belongs to a chain, it might not charge you an initial flat fee again when you visit a branch in another city.

Wi-Fi hot spots are often within high-end hotels, major airports and train stations, cafés, and shopping centers. Although there is no official map of Italian hot spots, you can check ⊕*www.hotspots.com* for locations in Tuscany and Umbria.

Some hotels have in-room modem lines, but, as with phones, using the hotel's line is relatively expensive. Always check modem rates before plugging in. You may need an adapter for your computer for the European-style plugs. If you are traveling with a laptop, carry a spare battery and an adapter. Never plug your computer into any socket before asking about surge protection. IBM sells a tiny modem tester that plugs into a telephone jack to check whether the line is safe to use.

Contact **Cybercafes** (⊕www.cybercafes.com) lists more than 4,000 Internet cafés worldwide.

PHONES

The good news is that you can now make a direct-dial telephone call from virtually any point on Earth. The bad news? You can't always do so cheaply. Calling from a hotel is almost always the most expensive option; hotels usually add huge surcharges to all calls, particularly international ones. Calling cards usually keep costs to a minimum, but only if you purchase them locally. And then there are mobile phones; as expensive as mobile phone calls can be, they are still usually a much cheaper option than calling from your hotel.

When calling Italy from abroad, begin by entering 011 (which gets you an international line), followed by Italy's country code, 39. Note that Italian telephone numbers do not have a standard number of digits (they can range anywhere from four to eight). The area code for Rome is 06, so a call from the United States to Rome would be dialed as 011 + 39 + 06 + phone number.

CALLING WITHIN ITALY

Public pay phones are scarce, although they can be found at train and subway stations, post offices, in hotel lobbies, and in some bars. In rural areas, town squares usually have a pay phone. Pay phones may take coins, but usually require a *carta telefonica* (phone card; ⇨*below*).

For all calls within Italy, whether local or long-distance, dial the area code followed by the number. Rates for long-distance calls vary according to the time of day; it's cheaper to call before 9 AM and after 7 or 8 PM. Italy adopted the prefix "800" for toll-free or "green" numbers.

CALLING OUTSIDE ITALY

Because of the high rates charged by most hotels for long-distance and international calls, you're better off making such calls from public phones with a national or international telephone card, or using a mobile phone (⇨*below*). If you want to use the hotel phone to make an international call, you'll save money by using an international calling card (⇨*below*).

To place international calls or collect calls through an operator, dial 170. Rates to the United States are lowest on Sunday around the clock and between 10 PM–8 AM (Italian time) on weekdays and Saturday. You can also place a direct call to the United States using your U.S. phone calling-card number. You automatically reach a U.S. operator and thereby avoid all language difficulties.

The country code for the United States is 1 (dial 00 + 1 + U.S. area code and number).

Access Codes **AT&T Direct** (☎800/172–444). **MCI WorldPhone** (☎800/905–825). **Sprint International Access** (☎800/172–405).

CALLING CARDS

Prepaid *carte telefoniche* (phone cards) are available throughout Italy. Cards in different denominations are sold at post offices, newsstands, tobacco shops, and bars. Cards for calls within Italy are for use with pay phones; tear off the corner of the card and insert it in the phone's slot. When you dial, the card's value appears in a display window. After you hang up, the card is returned.

International calling cards are different; you call a toll-free number and then enter a code found on the back of the card. The best card for calling North America and elsewhere in Europe is the Europa card, which comes in two denominations, €5 for 180 minutes and €10 for 360 minutes.

MOBILE PHONES

If you have a multiband phone (some countries use different frequencies than what's used in the United States) and your service provider uses the world-standard GSM network (as do T-Mobile, Cingular, and Verizon), you can probably use your phone abroad. Roaming fees can be steep, however: 99¢ a minute is considered reasonable. And overseas you normally pay the toll charges for incoming calls. It's almost always cheaper to send a text message than to make a call, since text messages have a very low set fee (often less than 5¢).

If you just want to make local calls, consider buying a new SIM card (note that your provider may have to unlock your phone for you to use a different SIM

card) and a prepaid service plan in the destination. You'll then have a local number and can make local calls at local rates. If your trip is extensive, you could also simply buy a new cell phone in your destination, as the initial cost will be offset over time.

■TIP→If you travel internationally frequently, save one of your old mobile phones or buy a cheap one on the Internet; ask your cell phone company to unlock it for you, and take it with you as a travel phone, buying a new SIM card with pay-as-you-go service in each destination.

The cost of cell phones is dropping; you can purchase a cell phone with a prepaid calling card (no monthly service plan) in Italy for less than €70. Inexpensive cell phones are dual band and will not allow you to call the United States, but using an international calling card and the cell phone solves that problem in a very inexpensive manner. Most medium to large towns have stores dedicated to selling cell phones. You will need to present your passport to purchase the SIM card that goes with the phone.

Rental cell phones are available in cities and large towns. Many Internet cafés offer them, but shop around for the best deal. Most rental contracts require a refundable deposit that covers the cost of the cell phone (€75–€125) and then set up a monthly service plan that is automatically charged to your credit card. Frequently, rental cell phones will be triple band and allow you to call the United States. Be sure to check the rate schedule before you rent a cell phone and commence calling to prevent a nasty surprise when you receive your credit-card bill two or three months later.

■TIP→ Beware of cell phone (and PDA) thieves. Keep your phone or PDA in a secure pocket or purse. Do not lay it on the bar when you stop for an espresso. Do not zip it into the outside pocket of your backpack in crowded cities. Do not leave it in your hotel room. If you are using a phone with a monthly service plan, notify your provider immediately if it is lost or stolen.

Contacts **Cellular Abroad** (☎800/287–5072 ⊕www.cellularabroad.com) rents and sells GMS phones and sells SIM cards that work in many countries. **Mobal** (☎888/888–9162 ⊕www.mobalrental.com) rents mobiles and sells GSM phones (starting at $49) that will operate in 140 countries. Per-call rates vary throughout the world. **Planet Fone** (☎888/988–4777 ⊕www.planetfone.com) rents cell phones, but the per-minute rates are expensive.

▌ CUSTOMS & DUTIES

You're always allowed to bring goods of a certain value back home without having to pay any duty or import tax. But there's a limit on the amount of tobacco and liquor you can bring back duty-free, and some countries have separate limits for perfumes; for exact figures, check with your customs department. The values of so-called duty-free goods are included in these amounts. When you shop abroad, save all your receipts, as customs inspectors may ask to see them as well as the items you purchased. If the total value of your goods is more than the duty-free limit, you'll have to pay a tax (most often a flat percentage) on the value of everything beyond that limit.

Travelers from the United States should experience little difficulty clearing customs at any airport in Italy.

Italy requires documentation of the background of all antiques and antiquities before the item is taken out of the country. Under Italian law, all antiquities found on Italian soil are considered state property and there are other restrictions on antique artwork. Even if purchased from a business in Italy, legal ownership of such artifacts may be in question if brought into the United States. Therefore, although they do not necessarily confer ownership, you must have documents such as export permits and receipts when importing such items into the United States.

For returning to the United States, clearing customs is sometimes more difficult. U.S. residents are normally entitled to a duty-free exemption of $800 on items accompanying them. You cannot bring back any of that delicious prosciutto or salami or any other meat product. Fresh mushrooms, truffles, or fresh fruits and vegetables are also forbidden. There are also restrictions on the amount of alcohol allowed in duty-free. Generally, you are allowed to bring in one liter of wine, beer, or other alcohol without paying a customs duty.

Information in Italy **Dogana Sezione Viaggiatori** (☎06/65954343 ⊕www.agenziadogane.it). **Ministero delle Finanze, Direzione Centrale dei Servizi Doganali, Divisione I** (☎06/50242117 ⊕www.finanze.it).

U.S. Information **U.S. Customs and Border Protection** (⊕www.cbp.gov).

▌ EATING OUT

Italian cuisine is still largely regional. Ask what the local specialties are: by all means, have spaghetti *alla carbonara* (with bacon and egg) in Rome, pizza in Rome or Naples, *bistecca alla fiorentina* (steak) in Florence, *chingale* (wild boar) in Tuscany, truffles in the Piedmont, and risotto *alla milanese* in Milan. Although most restaurants in Italy serve traditional local cuisine, you can find Asian and Middle Eastern alternatives in Rome, Venice, and other cities.

The restaurants we list are the cream of the crop in each price category. Properties indicated by a ✕⊞ are lodging establishments whose restaurant warrants a special trip.

MEALS & MEALTIMES
What's the difference between a ristorante and a trattoria? Can you order food at an enoteca? Can you go to a restaurant just for a snack, or order just a

LOCAL DO'S & TABOOS

GREETINGS

Upon meeting and leave-taking, both friends and strangers wish each other good day or good evening (*buon giorno, buona sera*); *ciao* isn't used between strangers. Italians who are friends greet each other with a kiss, usually first on the left cheek, then on the right. When you meet a new person, shake hands.

SIGHTSEEING

Italy is full of churches, and many of them contain significant works of art. They are also places of worship, however, so be sure to dress appropriately.

Shorts, tank tops, and sleeveless garments are taboo in most churches throughout the country. In summer carry a sweater or other item of clothing to wrap around your bare shoulders before entering a church.

You should never bring food into a church, and do not sip from your water bottle while inside. If you have a cell phone, turn it off before entering. And never enter a church when a service is in progress, especially if it is a private affair such as a wedding or baptism.

OUT ON THE TOWN

Table manners in Italy are formal; rarely do Italians share food from their plates. In a restaurant, be formal and polite with your waiter—no calling across the room for attention.

When you've finished your meal and are ready to go, ask for the check (*il conto*); unless it's well past closing time, no waiter will put a bill on your table until you've requested it.

Italians do not have a culture of sipping cocktails or chugging pitchers of beer. Wine, beer, and other alcoholic drinks are almost always consumed as part of a meal. Public drunkenness is abhorred.

Smoking has been banned in all public establishments, much like in the United States.

Flowers, chocolates, or a bottle of wine are appropriate hostess gifts when invited to dinner at the home of an Italian.

DOING BUSINESS

Showing up on time for business appointments is the norm and expected in Italy. There are more business lunches than business dinners, and even business lunches aren't common, as Italians view mealtimes as periods of pleasure and relaxation.

Business cards are used throughout Italy, and business suits are the norm for both men and women. To be on the safe side, it is best not to use first names or a familiar form of address until invited to do so.

Business gifts are not the norm, but if one is given it is usually small and symbolic of your home location or type of business.

LANGUAGE

One of the best ways to avoid being an Ugly American is to learn a little of the local language. You need not strive for fluency; even just mastering a few basic words and terms is bound to make chatting with the locals more rewarding.

"Please" is *per favore*, "thank you" is *grazie*, and "you're welcome" is *prego*.

In larger cities such as Venice, Rome, and Florence, language is not a big problem. Most hotels have English speakers at their reception desks, and if not, they can always find someone who speaks at least a little English.

You may have trouble communicating in the countryside, but a phrase book and expressive gestures will go a long way.

A phrase book and language-tape set can help get you started.

Fodor's Italian for Travelers (available at bookstores everywhere) is excellent.

salad at a pizzeria? The following definitions should help.

Not too long ago, *ristoranti* tended to be more elegant and expensive than *trattorie* and *osterie*, which serve traditional, home-style fare in an atmosphere to match. But the distinction has blurred considerably, and an osteria in the center of town might be far fancier (and pricier) than a ristorante across the street. In any sit-down establishment, be it a ristorante, osteria, or trattoria, you are generally expected to order at least a two-course meal, such as: a *primo* (first course) and a *secondo* (main course) or a *contorno* (vegetable side dish); an *antipasto* (starter) followed by either a primo or secondo; or a secondo and a *dolce* (dessert).

In an *enoteca* (wine bar) or pizzeria it's common to order just one dish. An enoteca menu is often limited to a selection of cheese, cured meats, salads, and desserts, but if there's a kitchen you'll also find soups, pastas, and main courses. The typical pizzeria fare includes *affettati misti* (a selection of cured pork), simple salads, various kinds of bruschetta, *crostini* (similar to bruschetta, with a variety of toppings) and, in Rome, *fritti* (deep-fried finger food) such as *olive ascolane* (green olives with a meat stuffing) and *supplì* (rice balls stuffed with mozzarella).

The handiest and least expensive places for a quick snack between sights are probably bars, cafés, and pizza *al taglio* (by the slice) spots. Pizza al taglio shops are easy to negotiate but very few have seats. They sell pizza by weight: just point out which kind you want and how much.

Bars in Italy are primarily places to get a coffee and a bite to eat, rather than drinking establishments. Most bars have a selection of *panini* (sandwiches) warmed up on the griddle (*piastra*) and *tramezzini* (sandwiches made of untoasted white bread triangles). In larger cities, bars also serve vegetable and fruit salads, cold pasta dishes, and gelato. Most bars offer beer

and a variety of alcohol as well as wines by the glass (sometimes good but more often mediocre). A café (*caffè* in Italian) is like a bar but usually with more tables. Pizza at a café should be avoided—it's usually heated in a microwave.

If you place your order at the counter, ask if you can sit down: some places charge for table service, others do not. In self-service bars and cafés it's good manners to clean your table before you leave. Note that in some places you have to pay a cashier, then place your order and show your *scontrino* (receipt) at the counter. Menus are posted outside most restaurants (in English in tourist areas); if not, you might step inside and ask to take a look at the menu (but don't ask for a table unless you intend to stay). Italians take their food as it is listed on the menu, seldom if ever making special requests such as "dressing on the side" or "hold the olive oil." If you have special dietary needs, however, make them known; they can usually be accommodated. Although mineral water makes its way to almost every table, you can order a carafe of tap water (*acqua di rubinetto* or *acqua semplice*) instead, but keep in mind that such water can be highly chlorinated.

Wiping your bowl clean with a (small) piece of bread is usually considered a sign of appreciation, not bad manners. Spaghetti should be eaten with a fork only, although a little help from a spoon won't horrify locals the way cutting spaghetti into little pieces might. Order your espresso (Italians don't usually drink cappuccino after breakfast time) after dessert, not with it. Don't ask for a doggy bag.

Breakfast (*la colazione*) is usually served from 7 to 10:30, lunch (*il pranzo*) from 12:30 to 2:30, dinner (*la cena*) from 7:30 to 10. Peak times are usually 1:30 for lunch and 9 for dinner. Enoteche and *bacari* (wine bars) are open also in the morning and late afternoon for a snack at the counter. Most pizzerias open at 8 PM and close around midnight—later in summer and on weekends. Most bars and cafés are open from 7 AM until 8 or 9 PM; a few stay open until midnight.

Unless otherwise noted, the restaurants listed in this guide are open daily for lunch and dinner.

PAYING

Most restaurants have a cover charge per person, usually listed at the top of the check as *coperto* or *pane e coperto*. It should be a modest charge (€1–€2.50 per person) except at the most expensive restaurants. Whenever in doubt, ask before you order to avoid unpleasant discussions later. It is customary to leave a small tip (around 10%) in appreciation of good service. If *servizio* is included at the bottom of the check, no tip is necessary. Tips are always given in cash.

The price of fish dishes is often given by weight (before cooking), so the price you see on the menu is for 100 grams of fish, not for the whole dish. (An average fish portion is about 350 grams.) In Tuscany, *bistecca alla fiorentina* (Florentine steak) is also often priced by weight (€4 for 100 grams or €40 for 1 kilogram [2.2 lbs]).

Major credit cards are widely accepted in Italy, though cash is usually preferred. More restaurants take Visa and Master-Card than American Express.

When you leave a dining establishment, take your meal bill or receipt with you; although not a common experience, the Italian finance (tax) police can approach you within 100 yards of the establishment at which you've eaten and ask for a receipt. If you don't have one, they can fine you and will fine the business owner for not providing the receipt. The measure is intended to prevent tax evasion; it's not necessary to show receipts when leaving Italy.

For guidelines on tipping see Tipping below.

▮ ELECTRICITY

The electrical current in Italy is 220 volts, 50 cycles alternating current (AC); wall outlets take Continental-type plugs, with two or three round prongs.

Consider making a small investment in a universal adapter, which has several types of plugs in one lightweight, compact unit. Most laptops and mobile phone chargers are dual voltage (i.e., they operate equally well on 110 and 220 volts), so require only an adapter. These days the same is true of small appliances such as hair dryers. Always check labels and manufacturer instructions to be sure. Don't use 110-volt outlets marked FOR SHAVERS ONLY for high-wattage appliances such as hair dryers.

Contacts Steve Kropla's Help for World Traveler's (⊕ www.kropla.com) has information on electrical and telephone plugs around the world. **Walkabout Travel Gear** (⊕ www.walkabouttravelgear.com) has a good coverage of electricity under "adapters."

▮ EMERGENCIES

No matter where you are in Italy, you can dial 113 in case of emergency. Not all 113 operators speak English, so you may want to ask a local person to place the call. Asking the operator for *"pronto soccorso"* (first aid and also the emergency room of a hospital) should get you an *ambulanza* (ambulance). If you just need a doctor, ask for *"un medico."*

Italy has the *carabinieri* (national police force) as well as the *polizia* (local police force). Both are armed and have the power to arrest and investigate crimes. Always report the loss of your passport to the police as well as to your embassy. When reporting a crime, you'll be asked to fill out *una denuncia* (official report); keep a copy for your insurance company.

Local traffic officers, known as *vigili,* are responsible for, among other things, giving out parking tickets. They wear white (in summer) or black uniforms. Should you find yourself involved in a minor car accident in town, contact the vigili.

Pharmacies are generally open weekdays 8:30–1 and 4–8, and Saturday 9–1. Local pharmacies cover the off-hours in shifts: on the door of every pharmacy is a list of which pharmacies in the vicinity will be open late.

Foreign Embassies U.S. Consulate Florence (✉ Via Lungarno Vespucci 38, Florence ☎ 055/2398276). U.S. Consulate Milan (✉ Via Principe Amedeo 2/10, Milan ☎ 02/290351). U.S. Consulate Naples (✉ Piazza della Repubblica, Naples ☎ 081/5838111). U.S. Embassy (✉ Via Veneto 121, 00187 Rome ☎ 06/46741 ⊕ www.usembassy.it).

General Emergency Contacts Emergencies (☎ 113). National police (☎ 112).

❚ HOURS OF OPERATION

Religious and civic holidays are frequent in Italy. Depending on the holiday's local importance, businesses may close for the day. Businesses do not close on a Friday or Monday when the holiday falls on the weekend.

Banks are open weekdays 8:30–1:30 and for an hour in the afternoon, depending on the bank. Most post offices are open Monday–Saturday 9–12:30; central post offices are open 9–6:30 weekdays, 9–12:30 on Saturday. On the last day of the month all post offices close at midday.

Most churches are open from early morning until noon or 12:30, when they close for three hours or more; they open again in the afternoon, closing at about 6 PM. A few major churches, such as St. Peter's in Rome and San Marco in Venice, remain open all day. Walking around during services is discouraged. Many museums are closed one day a week, often Monday. During low season, museums often close early; during high season, many stay open until late at night.

Pharmacies are generally open weekdays 8:30–1 and 4–8, and Saturday 9–1. Local pharmacies cover the off-hours in shifts: on the door of every pharmacy is a list of which pharmacies in the vicinity will be open late.

Most shops are open Monday–Saturday 9–1 and 3:30 or 4–7:30. Clothing shops are generally closed Monday mornings. Barbers and hairdressers, with some exceptions, are closed Sunday and Monday. Some bookstores and fashion and tourist-oriented shops in places such as Rome and Venice are open all day, as well as Sunday. Large chain supermarkets such as Standa, COOP, and Eselunga do not close for lunch and are usually open Sunday; smaller *alimentari* (delicatessens) and other food shops are usually closed one evening during the week (it varies according to the town) and are almost always closed Sunday.

HOLIDAYS

If you can avoid it, don't travel through Italy in August, when much of the population is on vacation. Most cities are deserted (except for foreign tourists) and many restaurants and shops are closed.

National holidays in 2009 include January 1 (New Year's Day); January 6 (Epiphany); April 12 and April 13 (Easter Sunday and Monday); April 25 (Liberation Day); May 1 (Labor Day or May Day); June 2 (Festival of the Republic); August 15 (Ferragosto); November 1 (All Saints' Day); December 8 (Immaculate Conception); and December 25 and 26 (Christmas Day and the feast of St. Stephen).

Feast days of patron saints are observed locally. Many businesses and shops may be closed in Florence, Genoa, and Turin on June 24 (St. John the Baptist); in Rome on June 29 (Sts. Peter and Paul); in Palermo on July 15 (Santa Rosalia); in Naples on September 19 (San Gennaro); in Bologna on October 4 (San Petronio); in Trieste on November 3 (San Giusto); and in Milan on December 7 (St. Ambrose). Venice's feast of St. Mark is April 25, the same as Liberation Day, so the Madonna della Salute on November 21 makes up for the lost holiday.

▌MAIL

The Italian mail system is notoriously slow, but it is improving with some privatization. Allow from 7 to 15 days for mail to get to the United States. Receiving mail in Italy, especially packages, can take weeks; so don't forget your medications or other unique necessary items at home.

Most post offices are open Monday–Saturday 9–12:30; central post offices are open weekdays 9–6:30, Saturday 9–12:30. On the last day of the month, post offices close at midday. You can buy stamps at tobacco shops as well as post offices.

Posta Prioritaria (for small letters and packages) is the name of the most commonly used postage. It supposedly guarantees delivery within Italy in three to five business days and abroad in five to six working days. The more-expensive express delivery, *Postacelere* (for larger letters and packages), guarantees one-day delivery to most places in Italy and three- to five-day delivery abroad.

Mail sent as Posta Prioritaria to the United States costs €0.85 for up to 20 grams, €1.50 for 21–50 grams, and €1.85 for 51–100 grams. Mail sent as Postacelere to the United States costs €43–€50 for up to 500 grams.

Other package services to check are Quick Pack Europe, for delivery within Europe; and EMS Express Mail Service, a global three- to five-day service for letters and packages that can be less expensive than Postacelere.

Two-day mail is generally available during the week in all major cities and at popular resorts via UPS and Federal Express. Service is reliable; a Federal Express letter to the United States costs about €35. If your hotel can't assist you, try an Internet café, many of which also offer two-day mail services using major carriers.

SHIPPING PACKAGES

You can ship parcels via air or surface. Air takes about two weeks, and surface anywhere up to three months to most countries. If you have purchased antiques, ceramics, or other objects, ask if the vendor will do the shipping for you; in most cases, this is a possibility. If so, ask if the article will be insured against breakage. When shipping a package out of Italy, it is virtually impossible to find an overnight delivery option—the fastest delivery time is 48 to 72 hours.

▌MONEY

Prices vary from region to region and are substantially lower in the country than in the cities. Of Italy's major cities, Venice and Milan are by far the most expensive. Resorts such as the Costa Smeralda, Portofino, and Cortina d'Ampezzo cater to wealthy people and charge top prices. Good values can be had in the scenic Trentino–Alto Adige region and the Dolomites and in Umbria and the Marches. With a few exceptions, southern Italy, Sicily, and Sardinia also offer bargains for those who do their homework before they leave home.

▌TIP➔Banks never have every foreign currency on hand, and it may take as long as a week to order. If you're planning to exchange funds before leaving home, don't wait till the last minute.

ATMS & BANKS

An ATM (bancomat in Italian) is the easiest way to get euros in Italy. There are numerous ATMs in large cities and small towns, as well as in airports and train stations. They are not common in places such as grocery stores. Be sure to memorize your PIN in numbers, as ATM keypads in Italy don't always display letters. Check with your bank to confirm that you have an international PIN (*codice segreto*), to find out your maximum daily withdrawal allowance, and to learn what the bank fee is for withdrawing money.

Your own bank may charge a fee for using ATMs abroad or charge for the cost of conversion from euros to dollars. Nevertheless, you'll usually get a better rate of exchange at an ATM than you will at a currency-exchange office or even when changing money inside a bank with a teller. Extracting funds as you need them is a safer option than carrying around a large amount of cash.

CREDIT CARDS

Throughout this guide, the following abbreviations are used: **AE**, American Express; **DC**, Diners Club; **MC**, Master-Card; and **V**, Visa.

It's a good idea to inform your credit-card company before you travel, especially if you're going abroad and don't travel internationally very often. Otherwise, the credit-card company might put a hold on your card owing to unusual activity—not a good thing halfway through your trip. Record all your credit-card numbers—as well as the phone numbers to call if your cards are lost or stolen—in a safe place, so you're prepared should something go wrong. Both MasterCard and Visa have general numbers you can call (collect if you're abroad) if your card is lost, but you're better off calling the number of your issuing bank, since MasterCard and Visa generally just transfer you to your bank; your bank's number is usually printed on your card.

If you plan to use your credit card for cash advances, you'll need to apply for a PIN at least two weeks before your trip. Although it's usually cheaper (and safer) to use a credit card abroad for large purchases (so you can cancel payments or be reimbursed if there's a problem), note that some credit-card companies *and* the banks that issue them add substantial percentages to all foreign transactions, whether they're in a foreign currency or not. Check on these fees before leaving home, so there won't be any surprises when you get the bill.

■ TIP → Before you charge something, ask the merchant whether or not he or she plans to do a dynamic currency conversion (DCC). In such a transaction the credit-card *processor* (shop, restaurant, or hotel, not Visa or MasterCard) converts the currency and charges you in dollars. In most cases you'll pay the merchant a 3% fee for this service in addition to any credit-card company and issuing-bank foreign-transaction surcharges.

Dynamic currency conversion programs are becoming increasingly widespread. Merchants who participate in them are supposed to ask whether you want to be charged in dollars or the local currency, but they don't always do so. And even if they do offer you a choice, they may well avoid mentioning the additional surcharges. The good news is that you *do* have a choice. And if this practice really gets your goat, you can avoid it entirely thanks to American Express; with its cards, DCC simply isn't an option.

MasterCard and Visa are preferred by Italian merchants, but American Express is usually accepted in Italian tourist spots. Credit cards aren't accepted everywhere; if you want to pay with a credit card in a small shop, hotel, or restaurant, it's a good idea to make your intentions known early on.

Reporting Lost Cards **American Express** (☎800/992–3404 in the U.S., 336/393–1111 collect from abroad ⊕www.american express.com). **Diners Club** (☎800/234–6377 in the U.S., 303/799–1504 collect from abroad ⊕www.dinersclub.com). **MasterCard** (☎800/622–7747 in the U.S., 636/722–7111 collect from abroad ⊕www.mastercard.com). **Visa** (☎800/847–2911 in the U.S., 410/581–9994 collect from abroad ⊕www.visa.com).

CURRENCY & EXCHANGE

The euro is the main unit of currency in Italy, as well as in 12 other European countries. Under the euro system there are 100 *centesimi* (cents) to the euro. There are coins valued at 1, 2, 5, 10, 20, and 50 centesimi as well as 1 and 2 euros. There are seven notes: 5, 10, 20, 50, 100, 200, and 500 euros.

At this writing, the exchange rate was about 0.68 euros to the U.S. dollar.

Post offices exchange currency at good rates, but you will rarely find an employee who speaks English, so be prepared.

■ TIP➔Even if a currency-exchange booth has a sign promising no commission, rest assured that there's some kind of huge, hidden fee. As for rates, you're almost always better off getting foreign currency at an ATM or exchanging money at a bank.

■ TAXES

A 9% V.A.T. (value-added tax) is included in the rate at all hotels except those at the upper end of the range. At luxury hotels a 12% tax is added to the bill.

No tax is added to the bill in restaurants. A service charge of approximately 10%–15% is often added to your check; in some cases a service charge is included in the prices.

The V.A.T. is 20% on clothing, wine, and luxury goods. On consumer goods it's already included in the amount shown on the price tag, whereas on services it may not be. If your purchases total more than €155 you may be entitled to a refund of the V.A.T.

When making a purchase, ask for a V.A.T. refund form and find out whether the merchant gives refunds—not all stores do, nor are they required to. Have the form stamped like any customs form by customs officials when you leave the country or, if you're visiting several European Union countries, when you leave the EU. After you're through passport control, take the form to a refund-service counter for an on-the-spot refund (which is usually the quickest and easiest option), or mail it to the address on the form (or on the envelope with it) after you arrive home. You receive the total refund stated on the form, but the processing time can be long, especially if you request a credit-card adjustment.

Global Refund is a Europe-wide service with 225,000 affiliated stores and more than 700 refund counters at major airports and border crossings. Its refund form, called a Tax Free Check, is the most common across the European continent. The service issues refunds in the form of cash, check, or credit-card adjustment.

V.A.T. Refunds **Global Refund** (☎800/566–9828 ⊕ www.globalrefund.com).

■ TIME

Italy is in the Central European Time Zone. From March to October it institutes Daylight Saving Time. Italy is 6 hours ahead of U.S. Eastern Standard Time, 1 hour ahead of Great Britain, 10 hours behind Sydney, and 12 hours behind Auckland. Like the rest of Europe, Italy uses the 24-hour (or "military") clock, which means that after noon you continue counting forward: 13:00 is 1 PM, 23:30 is 11:30 PM.

■ TIPPING

In restaurants a service charge of 10% to 15% may appear on your check. If so, it's not necessary to leave an additional tip. If service is not included, leave a tip of up to 10% in cash. Always leave your tip in cash. Usually there will not be a line item on your credit-card slip for a tip—but even if there is, tip in cash. Tip checkroom attendants €1 per person and restroom attendants €0.50 (more in expensive hotels and restaurants). In major cities tip €0.50 or more for table service in cafés. At a hotel bar tip €1 and up for a round or two of drinks.

Italians rarely tip taxi drivers, which is not to say that you shouldn't. A euro or two is appreciated, particularly if the driver helps with luggage. Service-station attendants are tipped only for special services; give them €1 for checking your tires. Railway and airport porters charge a fixed rate per bag. Tip an additional €0.25 per person, more if the porter is helpful. Give a barber €1–€1.50 and a hairdresser's assistant €1.50–€4 for a shampoo or cut, depending on the type of establishment.

On sightseeing tours, tip guides about €1.50 per person for a half-day group tour, more if they are especially knowledgeable. In monasteries and other sights where admission is free, a contribution (€0.50–€1) is expected.

In hotels give the *portiere* (concierge) about 10% of his bill for services, or €2.50–€5 for help with dinner reservations and such. Leave the chambermaid about €0.75 per day, or about €4.50–€5 a week in a moderately priced hotel; tip a minimum of €1 for valet or room service. Double these amounts in an expensive hotel. In expensive hotels tip doormen €0.50 for calling a cab and €1.50 for carrying bags to the check-in desk and bellhops €1.50–€2.50 for carrying your bags to the room.

INDEX

A

Abbazia di Novacella, *323*
Abbazia di San Fruttuoso, *464*
Abbazia di Sant'Antimo, *684–685*
Accademia ✕, *308*
Accademia Carrara, *378*
Accademia delle Belle Arti, *475*
Accommodations, *920–922*
Aci Castello, *869–870*
Aci Treza, *869–870*
Acireale, *868–870*
Acquario (Camogli), *466*
Acquario di Genova, *474*
Adler ✕, *330–331*
Adriatic Coast, *822–823, 825–827*
Aeolian Islands, *907–911*
Agata e Romeo ✕, *104*
Agorà Youth Hostel, *871*
Agritourism, *921*
Agrigento, *884–885*
Air travel, *178, 554, 925, 928–929*
Airports, *925, 928*
Al Bersagliere ✕, *376*
Al Donizetti ✕, *379*
Al Fico Vecchio ✕, *155*
Al Fornello Da Ricci ✕, *832*
Al Garamond ✕, *412*
Al Ritrovo Marittimo ✕, *294*
Al Sole ✕, *281–282*
Al Sole da Tiziano ✕, *278*
Alassio, *483*
Alba, *424, 428*
Albergo Il Monastero ✕, *791*
Albergo Santa Chiara ✕, *110–111*
Alberobello, *830–831*
Albisola Marina, *481–482*
Aldina ✕, *508*
Alla Vedova ✕, *219*
Alle Fratte di Trastevere ✕, *107*
Alle Testiere ✕, *219*
Alle Ore (wine bar), *280*
Alto Adige & Cortina, *318–327*
Amalfi, *808–810*
Amalfi Coast, *798–814*
Ambasciata ✕, *376*
Anacapri, *793*
Ancient City Gates, *271–272*
Ancient Rome, *20, 50–59*
Anfiteatro Romano (Fiesole), *624–625*
Anfiteatro Romano (Lecce), *835*
Anfiteatro Romano (Siracusa), *874*
Antica Focacceria San Francesco ✕, *902*
Antica Locanda dei Mercanti ✕, *359*

Antica Osteria al Duomo ✕, *273*
Antica Osteria del Ponte ✕, *354*
Antica Osteria del Teatro ✕, *497*
Antica Trattoria Botteganova ✕, *672–673*
Antico Cimitero Ebraico, *209*
Antico Francischiello da Peppino ✕, *801*
Antico Ristorante Pagnanelli ✕, *157*
Antico Ristorante Sibilla ✕, *152*
Antipastoteca di Mare ✕, *294*
Aosta, *433–435*
Apartment and house rentals, *122, 920–921*
Aquariums, *348, 466, 474*
Aquileia, *290–291*
Ara Pacis Augustae, *73*
Arche Scaligere, *270–271*
Archeological Zone, *874–875*
Arco d'Augusto, *528*
Arco di Augusto (Aosta), *433*
Arco di Costantino, *59*
Arena di Verona (opera), *268, 275*
Arezzo, *674–675, 677–678*
Ariccia, *157–158*
Armeria Reale, *410*
Arquade ✕, *272*
Arsenale, (Venice), *207*
Art Hotel Novecento ✕, *516*
Art Resort Galleria Umberto ✕, *771*
Ascoli Piceno, *733*
Asolo, *279–282*
Assisi, *700–709*
Asti, *423–424*
ATMs, *940–941*
Auditorium-Parco della Musica, *127*
Auto-racing, *526*
Avogaria ✕, *220*

B

Bacari, *180*
Badia a Coltibuono, *648, 655*
Badia a Fiesilana, *625*
Badia Fiorentina, *565*
Bagnaia, *148*
Bagni Vecchi, *312*
Bancogiro ✕, *224*
Bar San Giorgio, *866*
Bardolino, *381*
Bargello, *558, 561*
Bari, *822–823, 825*
Barolo wine, *425–427*
Basilica dei Santi Maria e Donato, *215*
Basilica della Santa Casa, *732*

Basilica di San Francesco (Arezzo), *675*
Basilica di San Francesco (Assisi), *21, 705–708*
Basilica di San Marco, *174, 189, 190–192*
Basilica di San Petronio, *510–511*
Basilica di San Pietro, *75–78*
Basilicas
 Aquileia, 290–291
 Paestum, 814
 San Giorgio, 880
 San Marco, 174, 189, 190–192
 San Nicola, 823
 San Petronio, 510–511
 San Pietro, 75–78
 San Vitale, 531
 Sant'Ambrogio, 351
 Sant'Antonio, 251
 Sant'Ubaldo, 712
 Santa Chiara, 702–702
 Superga, 412
Basilicata, *839–844*
Bassano del Grappa, *277–279*
Battistero
 Bergamo, 378
 Florence, 561–562
 Parma, 500
 Pisa, 640
 Siena, 666
Battistero Neoniano, *531–532*
Battistero Paleocristiano, *349*
Batzenhausl ✕, *317*
Bauer il Palazzo ✕, *234*
Beacci Tornabuoni ✕, *612*
Beaches, *790, 818, 839*
Beehive, The ✕, *121*
Bellagio, *386–389*
Bellevue Syrene ✕, *802*
Belvedere, *158*
Belvedere di Santa Caterina, *868*
Belvedere di Sardagna, *307*
Bergamo, *377–379*
Biblioteca Medicea Laurenziana, *577*
Bicycle travel, *555, 639*
Biennale, *176*
Black market, *19*
Boat and ferry travel, *380, 394–395, 443, 789, 807, 830, 908, 909, 910, 911*
Boating and sailing, *393*
Bobsledding, *326*
Bologna, *509–519*
Bolzano, *314–318*
Bomarzo, *149*
Bordighera, *485–486*
Borgo Medioevale, *410*
Bormio, *311–313*
Bormio Terme, *312*
Brenta Canal, *265*
Bressanone, *323–324*

Photo credits

NOTES

ABOUT OUR WRITERS

After six years in Calabria, Robert Andrews considers himself an honorary Italian. He has written guidebooks to Sicily and Sardinia, and now lives in Bristol, England, where he compiles anthologies when he's not travel writing.

Hailing from Washington, D.C., Lynda Albertson relocated to Italy in 2003 to write a monthly wine column, "In Vino Veritas," for The American magazine. Updater of our Rome shopping section, she has an uncanny knowledge of where to purchase absolute necessities from truffle oil to that perfect Piranesi print.

After her first Italian coffee and her first Italian bacio in 1999, Nicole Arriaga headed to the Eternal City to work on her Master's Degree at Rome's La Sapienza University, write for The American, and work for American Study Abroad. She is the author of our Experience Rome chapter.

After completing his master's degree in art history, Peter Blackman settled permanently in Italy in 1986. Since then he's worked as a biking and walking tour guide. When he's not leading a trip, you'll find Peter at home in Chianti.

Martin Wilmot Bennett's vast background in Italian art and civilization made him a natural to write our photo-feature on the Sistine Ceiling. A major contributor to Fodor's Rome and a graduate of Cambridge University, he teaches at Rome's University of Tor Vergata.

Shannon Essa and Ruth Edenbaum are authors of the food guide Chow! Venice— Savoring the Food and Wine of La Serenissima. When not in Venice, Ruth resides in Princeton Junction, New .Jersey. where she is the doting grandmother of two. Shannon is a moderator for the travel Web site www.slowtrav.com, and when not traveling lives in San Diego.

Updater of our Rome nightlife/arts pages, Erica Firpo writes for Luxe City Guide, Zing Magazine, Very Style Guide, National Geographic Traveler, authored the Rome Little Black Book, and tracks modern Rome in her blog, moscerina.com.

Madeleine Johnson is an unrepentant Midwesterner who has lived in Italy— with a two-year break in Paris—since 1988. Her writing has appeared in *Connoisseur, The Journal of Art,* and *The American*—where she has a monthly column about life in Milan.

Updater of our Rome restaurant reviews, Dana Klitzberg trained in top restaurant kitchens in New York and Rome and is owner of Blu Aubergine (www.bluaubergine.com) through which she caters, instructs, and writes about food.

Jen Laskey became smitten with Rome during a summer MFA program in 2000; she returned to become a resident five years later. She updated our Rome restaurant and hotel reviews.

Bruce Leimsidor studied Renaissance literature and art history at Swarthmore College and Princeton University, and in addition to his scholarly works, he has published articles on political and social issues in the International Herald Tribune and the Frankfurter Allgemeine Zeitung. He lives in Venice, where he teaches at the university, works for the municipality, collects 17th and 18th century drawings, and is rumored to make the best pasta e fagioli in town.

After a dozen trips to and two decade long love affair with Liguria, Megan McCaffrey-Guerrera move to the seaside village of Lerici in 2004. Soon after, she started a personal travel concierge service. When not organizing tailor-made vacations of the area, Megan can be found hiking the trails of the Cinque Terre, sailing the Gulf of Poets or searching for the freshest anchovies in the Mediterranean.

Specializing in the Neapolitan art of arrangiarsi (getting by), Fergal Kavanagh has dabbled in teacher training, DJ-ing, writing guidebooks, translating, and organizing cultural exchanges. He currently teaches at the university of Naples and through his Web site (www.tuneintoenglish.com) demonstrates how pop music can help students learn English.

Nan McElroy is the author of the highly acclaimed, purely practical travel guide *Italy: Instructions for Use*. She first set foot in Venice in 1995, relocated there in 2004, and now is part of the Your Friend in Venice travel service.

Florence resident Patricia Rucidlo holds master's degrees in Italian Renaissance history and art history. When she's not extolling the virtues of a Pontormo masterpiece or angrily defending the Medici, she's leading wine tours in Chianti and catering private dinner parties.

California native Pamela Santini came to study art history 15 years ago at Venice's Ca' Foscari University, where she currently teaches. She's also a writer and translator, and enjoys traveling with her husband and son.

During her four decades in Rome, Margaret Stenhouse was correspondent for Scotland's leading daily, *The Herald,* and a contributor to the *International Herald Triune* and the monthly *Italy Italy.* She now lives in the Castelli Romani hills south of Rome.

An editor, travel writer, and naturalist, Mark Walters first settled in Naples as a British Council lecturer in the 1980s. He spends several months a year leading tours around the Mediterranean.

Jonathan Willcocks, a Brit by birth with degrees in French and English literature from the Sorbonne, teaches language, literature, and translation at the university in Perugia.

Megan K. Williams is a Rome-based writer and correspondent, covering Italy and Africa in print for many newspapers and magazines, as well as on the radio for the CBC, Marketplace, and NPR. Her short-story collection *Saving Rome* was published in 2006 to rave reviews.